THE LEADING FACTS
OF
NEW MEXICAN HISTORY

Volume II

THE LEADING FACTS OF NEW MEXICAN HISTORY

Volume II
Facsimile of Original 1912 Edition

by
Ralph Emerson Twitchell

New Foreword
by
Richard Melzer, Ph.D.

SANTA FE

New Material © 2007 by Sunstone Press. All Rights Reserved.

No part of this book may be reproduced in any form or by any electronic or mechanical means including information storage and retrieval systems without permission in writing from the publisher, except by a reviewer who may quote brief passages in a review.

Sunstone books may be purchased for educational, business, or sales promotional use. For information please write: Special Markets Department, Sunstone Press, P.O. Box 2321, Santa Fe, New Mexico 87504-2321.

Library of Congress Cataloging-in-Publication Data

Twitchell, Ralph Emerson, 1859–1925.
 The leading facts of New Mexican history : facsimile of original 1912 ed. / by Ralph Emerson Twitchell ; new foreword by Richard Melzer.
   p. cm -- (Southwest heritage series)
 Originally published in 5 v.: Cedar Rapids, Iowa : Torch Press, 1911–17.
 Includes bibliographical references and index.
 ISBN 0-86534-565-1 (v. 1 : softcover : alk. paper) -- ISBN 0-86534-584-8 (v. 1 hardcover)
 ISBN 0-86534-566-X (v. 2 : softcover: alk. paper) -- ISBN 0-86534 -585-6 (v. 2 hardcover)
 1. New Mexico--History. I Title.

F796. T97 2007
978.9--dc22
                    2006052281

WWW.SUNSTONEPRESS.COM
SUNSTONE PRESS / POST OFFICE BOX 2321 / SANTA FE, NM 87504-2321 /USA
(505) 988-4418 / ORDERS ONLY (800) 243-5644 / FAX (505) 988-1025

The Southwest Heritage Series is dedicated to Jody Ellis and Marcia Muth Miller, the founders of Sunstone Press, whose original purpose and vision continues to inspire and motivate our publications.

CONTENTS

THE SOUTHWEST HERITAGE SERIES / I

FOREWORD TO THIS EDITION / II

FACSIMILE OF 1912 EDITION / III

I

THE SOUTHWEST HERITAGE SERIES

The history of the United States is written in hundreds of regional histories and literary works. Those letters, essays, memoirs, biographies and even collections of fiction are often first-hand accounts by people who wanted to memorialize an event, a person or simply record for posterity the concerns and issues of the times. Many of these accounts have been lost, destroyed or overlooked. Some are in private or public collections but deemed to be in too fragile condition to permit handling by contemporary readers and researchers.

However, now with the application of twenty-first century technology, nineteenth and twentieth century material can be reprinted and made accessible to the general public. These early writings are the DNA of our history and culture and are essential to understanding the present in terms of the past.

The Southwest Heritage Series is a form of literary preservation. Heritage by definition implies legacy and these early works are our legacy from those who have gone before us. To properly present and preserve that legacy, no changes in style or contents have been made. The material reprinted stands on its own as it first appeared. The point of view is that of the author and the era in which he or she lived. We would not expect photographs of people from the past to be re-imaged with modern clothes, hair styles and backgrounds. We should not, therefore, expect their ideas and personal philosophies to reflect our modern concepts.

Remember, reading their words and sharing their thoughts is a passport back into understanding how the past was shaped and how it influenced today's world.

Our hope is that new access to these older books will provide readers with a challenging and exciting experience.

II

FOREWORD TO THIS EDITION
by
Richard Melzer, Ph.D.

Historians have long admired Ralph Emerson Twitchell's *The Leading Facts of New Mexican History*, considered the first major history of the state. Put succinctly by former State Historian Robert J. Tórrez, Twitchell's five-volume work (of which this is one of the first two volumes Sunstone Press is reprinting in its Southwest Heritage Series) has "become the standard by which all subsequent books on New Mexico history are measured."[1]

As Twitchell wrote in the preface of his first volume, his goal in writing *The Leading Facts* was to respond to the "pressing need" for a history of New Mexico with a commitment to "accuracy of statement, simplicity of style, and impartiality of treatment." Twitchell added that he sought to make his work "available to the person of moderate means," a truly ironic goal as copies of the first edition of *The Leading Facts* sell for well over $500 on the current rare book market, if one can find them.[2]

Ralph Emerson Twitchell was born in Ann Arbor, Michigan, on November 29, 1859. According to a fifty-seven page genealogy he prepared and published privately, the Twitchells (or Twichels or Twichells) date back to the time of William the Conqueror in English history. The earliest Twitchell to emigrate to the American colonies arrived in Massachusetts in 1630, "imbued with the spirit of the Puritans," in Twitchell's words. Twitchell's great grandfather fought on the rebel side in the American Revolutionary battles of Lexington and Bunker Hill.[3]

Twitchell earned his LL.B. degree from the University of Michigan in 1882. By December of that year the twenty-three year old had arrived in Santa Fe to serve as a law clerk to Henry L. Waldo, solicitor of the Atchison, Topeka and Santa Fe Railroad in New Mexico.[4] Upon his arrival, the *Santa Fe New Mexican* described Twitchell as "a pleasant young gentleman of excellent social qualities and fine legal attainments."[5] Twitchell worked for the Santa Fe in increasingly important roles for the balance of his legal career.

Twitchell was involved in political and civic activities from his earliest days in New Mexico. In 1885 he helped organize a new territorial militia in Santa Fe and saw active duty in western New Mexico. Later appointed judge advocate of the Territorial Militia, he attained the rank of colonel, a title he was proud to use for the rest of his life. By 1893 he was elected the mayor of Santa Fe and, thereafter, district attorney of Santa Fe County. He was, in fact, one of the capital city's greatest boosters, supporting the use of traditional Southwest architecture, serving as the president of the local chamber of commerce, and acting as director of the Santa Fe Fiesta when it was rejuvenated shortly after World War I.

Twitchell probably promoted New Mexico as much as any single New Mexican of his generation. An avid supporter of New Mexico statehood, he argued the territory's case for elevated political status, celebrated its final victory in 1912, and even designed New Mexico's first state flag in 1915. He served on the management team of New Mexico's prize-winning state exhibit at the Panama-California Exposition in San Diego and was responsible for suggesting the exhibit's unique design, a replica of a Spanish colonial mission church, which later became the design of Santa Fe's new Museum of Fine Arts. Twitchell served on the board of regents at the Museum of New Mexico and, briefly, on the board of regents at New Mexico A&M (now New Mexico State University).

Active in seemingly countless organizations, from New Mexico's Good Roads Club to the National Irrigation Congress, Twitchell consistently rose to leadership roles in each group he joined. In the Republican Party, he chaired the party's central committee in New Mexico from 1902 to 1903. A life member of the Historical Society of New Mexico, he served as the society's vice president from 1910 to 1924 and its president in 1924.[6] Twitchell was even credited with rescuing the Spanish and Mexican archives when the territorial capitol burned in May 1892. Many of his contemporaries must have reiterated the question that former governor L. Bradford Prince posed in a personal letter to Twitchell in 1919: "How [do you] do it?"[7]

No person could have served so long and have done so much without controversy; Twitchell was no exception. As early as the 1890s he had joined other Republican leaders in the Knights of Liberty, a secret society often identified with the Santa Fe Ring.[8] Twitchell split with several key leaders of his own party, including Max Frost, the editor of the *Santa Fe New Mexican*, whom Twitchell described as "a lying scoundrel,"[9] and Thomas Catron, the most powerful Republican in the territory in the late nineteenth century. In 1892 Catron went so far as to accuse Twitchell of being "under the influence of whiskey and frequenting a very low dive," among other things, at the territorial fair in Albuquerque.[10] Such behavior would have been unusual for Twitchell, if it happened at all, but Catron's charges illustrate the degree of animosity that had developed between the two men within a decade of Twitchell's arrival on the scene.

Twitchell could more accurately be accused of being overly zealous and, as a result, sometimes offensive. In 1901, for example, he wrote to the editor of the *Albuquerque Evening Citizen* with the assertion that any businessman who did not publicly support New Mexico statehood should be "smoke[d] out," implying that those who opposed statehood should no longer be welcomed in the territory.[11] As a result of such statements and poor relations with top Republican leaders like Catron, Twitchell was not included as a delegate to the state constitutional convention of 1910, an affront that undoubtedly bruised his considerable ego.

Twitchell was also involved in two serious controversies regarding Native American rights. In the first of these confrontations, Twitchell had overseen the filming of the sacred Corn Dance, banned to the general public at Taos Pueblo. Without obtaining permission, Twitchell included images of the dance in a movie shown to thousands of visitors to the New Mexico exhibit at the Panama-California Exposition. Convinced that these public showings had caused illness among Indians employed at the exposition, someone broke into the New Mexico building and confiscated the ill-gotten film. Despite an investigation by Pinkerton detectives, the thief was never found. Far worse, Twitchell showed no remorse for betraying the Indians' trust. In fact, he wired Santa Fe for another copy of the film (stored at the Museum of New Mexico), showed the second copy, and blatantly exploited the incident to promote New Mexico and its exhibit at the exposition.[12]

Twitchell became embroiled in a far wider Indian controversy when he served as one of the principal authors of the infamous Bursum Bill in the early 1920s. Introduced by New Mexico's Senator H.O. Bursum, the bill gravely threatened pueblo water rights and considerable portions of Indian lands. Although Twitchell was appointed special assistant to the U.S. Attorney General and traveled to Washington, D.C., to testify before House and Senate committees, the legislation was defeated by the combined effort of pueblo leaders, organized as the All-Pueblo Council, and agitated artists and authors of the Taos and Santa Fe art colonies.[13]

Fortunately for Twitchell, he is less remembered for his involvement in such controversies than for his magnum opus, *The Leading Facts of New Mexican History*. Relying on his own extensive library, the libraries of many colleagues, and every document that might "throw light upon the occurrences of the past," Twitchell created a work in which he "tried to be accurate and fair."[14]

While many contemporaries praised Twitchell's accuracy and fairness, others wondered how fair he could be if one of his major goals, as stated on the first page of his first volume, was to "impress upon the reader's mind the fortitude, the courage, the suffering, and the martyrdom of those who first brought to New Mexico the banner of Christianity and civilization."[15]

Native Americans might well take exception to the idea that only those representing the Catholic faith and Spanish culture displayed fortitude, courage, suffering, and martyrdom in the Spanish colonial period. Spanish newspaper editors also took exception to Twitchell's devotion to English as the preferred language in schools and businesses, at the risk of losing *"el idioma de Cervantes"* and, hence, a major part of their Hispanic culture.[16] Others, like the Hispanic historian Benjamin M. Read, questioned how well Anglo authors like Twitchell could translate Spanish documents and how much accurate historical information was literally lost in their ethnocentric translations.[17] Finally, some questioned Twitchell's objectivity when it was rumored that "the amount of space allocated to contemporaries [in *The Leading Facts*] was weighed by the amount of their subscriptions to help pay for [publication costs]" of at least volumes three, four, and five.[18]

There is no indication that Twitchell heeded this criticism, especially given the near universal acclaim his books received among Anglo peers in New Mexico and across the country.[19] Inspired by this success and truly devoted to the study of history, Twitchell became the most prolific historian of his era, writing several additional histories of the Southwest, making frequent historical addresses, and founding, financing, and editing an ambitious, but short-lived, periodical called, *Old Santa Fe: A Magazine of History, Archaeology, Genealogy, and Biography*.[20]

But *The Leading Facts* remained Twitchell's major contribution to New Mexico history. Limited to fifteen hundred copies in its first edition, *The Leading Facts* had become a rare book by the 1960s when its first two volumes were reissued by Horn and Wallace in 1963. A rare book again by the late twentieth century, a new, affordable edition is long overdue and quite timely. Just as Twitchell's first edition in 1911 helped celebrate New Mexico's entry into statehood in 1912, the newest edition serves as a tribute to the state's centennial celebration of 2012.

Colonel Twitchell would have wanted it that way; boosting New Mexico, its resources and citizens was, after all, the central purpose of Twitchell's long life and productive career. In the apt words of an editorial in the *Santa Fe New Mexican* at the time of Twitchell's death in 1925: "As press agent for the best things of New Mexico, her traditions, history, beauty, glamour, scenery, archaeology, and material resources, he was indefatigable and efficient."[21]

NOTES

1   Robert J. Tórrez, *UFOs Over Galisteo and Other Stories of New Mexico's History* (Albuquerque: University of New Mexico Press, 2004): 131. Also see Howard Robert Lamar, *The Far Southwest* (Albuquerque: University of New Mexico Press, 2000): 457.

2   Ralph Emerson Twitchell, *The Leading Facts of New Mexican History* (Cedar Rapids, Iowa: The Torch Press, 1911): I:ix.

3   Ralph Emerson Twitchell, *Genealogy of the Twitchell Family* (n.c.: privately printed, 1929). A rare copy of Twitchell's genealogy can be found in the Ralph Emerson Twitchell Papers, Box 1, Folder 4, Fray Angélico Chávez Library, Museum of New Mexico, Santa Fe, New Mexico; hereafter cited as the Twitchell Papers. General biographical works on Twitchell include Myra Ellen Jenkins, "Ralph Emerson Twitchell," *Arizona and the West*, vol. 8 (Summer 1966): 102-06; J. Michael Pattison, "Four 'Gentlemen' Historians of New Mexico" (Unpublished M.A. thesis, New Mexico Highlands University, 1992): 43-9.

4   Twitchell so admired Waldo that he named his first and only son after his supervisor. The boy's mother, Twitchell's first wife Margaret, died on January 29, 1900. Twitchell dedicated *The Leading Facts* in Margaret's memory. He married his second wife, Estelle Bennett (1872-1952), in 1916. Twitchell, *Genealogy*, 446.

5   Quoted in the *Santa Fe New Mexican*, August 15, 1999.

6   Appropriately, the Historical Society of New Mexico's annual Ralph Emerson Twitchell Award is given "for significant contributions to the field of history by individuals, organizations, or institutions."

7   L. Bradford Prince to Ralph Emerson Twitchell, Flushing, New York, September 10, 1919, Ralph Emerson Twitchell Collection, New Mexico State Records Center and Archives, Santa Fe, New Mexico; hereafter cited as the NMSRCA.

8   Victor Westphall, *Thomas Benton Catron and His Era* (Tucson: University of Arizona Press, 1973): 208-09.

9   Quoted in ibid, 390n.

10 Quoted in ibid., 261. Twitchell and Catron also argued about a loan Catron had made to Twitchell near the turn of the century. Ibid., 390.

11 *Albuquerque Evening Citizen*, April 25, 1901, quoted in Robert W. Larson, *New Mexico's Quest for Statehood, 1846-1912* (Albuquerque: University of New Mexico Press, 1968): 200.

12 Matthew F. Bokovoy, *The San Diego World Fairs and Southwestern Memory, 1880-1940* (Albuquerque: University of New Mexico Press, 2005): 132-34.

13 The best description of Twitchell's role in drafting and defending the Bursum Bill is found in Lawrence C. Kelly, *The Assault on Assimilation: John Collier and the Origins of Indian Policy Reform* (Albuquerque: University of New Mexico Press, 1983): 203-54. According to Kelly, Twitchell's defense of the bill "crumbled and his composure wilted" under close examination before a Senate committee. "By the time [Twitchell] completed his presentation, there was little doubt that the original Bursum Bill was indeed a dead letter." Ibid., 239. On the *Santa Fe New Mexican*'s coverage of the bill and its fate, see Oliver LaFarge, *Santa Fe* (Norman: University of Oklahoma Press, 1959): 274-81.

14 Twitchell, *The Leading Facts*, I:viii.

15 Ibid.

16 Doris Meyer, *Speaking for Themselves: Neomexicano Cultural Identity and the Spanish Language Press, 1880-1920* (Albuquerque: University of New Mexico Press, 1996): 119-20.

17 Ibid., 200-01. For Twitchell's strong feelings regarding the teaching of English, see *The Leading Facts*, II:508-09, and his address, "The Public School," delivered at high school commencement in Raton, New Mexico, on May 24, 1899. Ralph Emerson Twitchell, Vertical File, Fray Angélico Chávez Library, Museum of New Mexico, Santa Fe, New Mexico.

18 Beatrice Chauvent, *Hewett and Friends: A Biography of Santa Fe's Vibrant Era* (Santa Fe: Museum of New Mexico Press, 1983): 104. For a sample prepublication subscription card for volumes one and two of *The Leading Facts*, see the Twitchell Papers, Box 2, Folder 7, Twitchell Papers.

19 For a sample of this praise for *The Leading Facts*, see a promotional brochure produced by its publisher, the Torch Press, found in the L. Bradford Prince Collection, NMSRCA.

20 Twitchell's other histories include *Spanish Archives of New Mexico*, 2 vols. (Cedar Rapids, Iowa: The Torch Press, 1914) and *Old Santa Fe: The Story of New Mexico's Ancient Capital* (Santa Fe: Santa Fe New Mexican, 1925). The periodical, *Old Santa Fe*, served as the Historical Society of New Mexico's official bulletin from its inception in 1913 till its demise three years later.

21 Editorial, *Santa Fe New Mexican*, August 26, 1925. Twitchell died at the Clara Barton Hospital in Los Angeles, California, of a paralytic stroke and heart failure on August 26, 1925. He was sixty-five. His last wish, to be buried below the Cross of the Martyrs in Santa Fe, was unanimously approved by the Santa Fe city council, but he was temporarily buried at Fairview Cemetery until a site below the cross could be identified. His funeral was one of the largest in Santa Fe history, with leading members of both major political parties present and a line of cars stretching half a mile. His temporary burial site at Fairview has become permanent and his last wish was never fulfilled. *Santa Fe New Mexican*, August 26-29 and 31, 1925; Paul A.F. Walter, "Obituary: Ralph Emerson Twitchell," *New Mexico Historical Review*, Vol. 1 (January 1926): 78-85; Richard Melzer, *Buried Treasures: Famous and Unusual Gravesites in New Mexico History* (Santa Fe: Sunstone Press).

III

FACSIMILE OF 1912 EDITION

THE LEADING FACTS OF NEW MEXICAN HISTORY

The Leading Facts of New Mexican History

BY

RALPH EMERSON TWITCHELL, Esq.
VICE-PRESIDENT NEW MEXICO HISTORICAL SOCIETY

"A PEOPLE THAT TAKE NO PRIDE IN THE NOBLE ACHIEVEMENTS OF REMOTE ANCESTORS WILL NEVER ACHIEVE ANYTHING WORTHY TO BE REMEMBERED WITH PRIDE BY REMOTE DESCENDANTS."
—*Macaulay*

VOL. II

THE TORCH PRESS
CEDAR RAPIDS, IOWA
1912

COPYRIGHT 1912
BY R. E. TWITCHELL

THE TORCH PRESS
CEDAR RAPIDS
IOWA

THE SUNSHINE STATE

Amid the galaxy of spheres,
Divinely sweet to mortal ears,
Rings out a symphony sublime,
A jubilant, victorious chime,
From yon bright place where, throned on high,
Columbia's daughters gild the sky.

Piercing the mists of sixty years,
Lo, in the West a gleam appears;
And, flashing through the purple night,
Fills all the firmament with light.
Another Star! The Planets cry:
Welcome, thrice welcome to the sky!

Star of our hopes, whose gladdening beams
Fulfill the promise of our dreams;
Late born among thy Sisters fair,
Yet peer of e'en the brightest there;
So long desired, so long delayed,
Shine forth exultant, unafraid!

Shine forth, O conqueror of fate,
Triumphant over scorn and hate;
Thou, in Columbia's diadem,
The newest, yet the fairest gem;
Send down upon us from above
The Light of Liberty and Love.

Past is the night, the dawning fair
Is flooding all the ambient air;
And, spurning with a high disdain
The clouds that barred his way in vain,
The Sun God in his golden car
Rides forth to greet the new born Star.

Ride on, victorious, elate,
Thou symbol of our Sunshine State;
And beam throughout thy pathway bright
Effulgent on our raptured sight;
O, glorious Sun! O Star divine,
New Mexico, forever shine!

—EDWARD McQUEEN GRAY

PREFATORY NOTE

THE object, primarily, in the publication of these volumes, has been the supplying of information to the people of New Mexico relative to the events occurring since the coming of the Spaniard and such information of the pre-Spanish period as has been made possible through the researches and investigations of archaeologists in that field. In accomplishing this purpose every available sourcebook and manuscript has been used, and the information therein contained appropriated wherever necessary to the concrete chronological arrangement of the leading facts of southwestern history. Necessarily, the result is a compilation, and the work has been that of an editor. No claim to authorship, in the strict sense of the word, has ever been asserted or maintained. Occasionally the reader will find a few reflections and conclusions differing from those who have heretofore written respecting the history of this portion of the United States, and these may be attributed solely to the writer.

The first acquaintance of the writer with the journey of Alvar Nuñez and his companions came from reading the *Spanish Conquest of New Mexico*, by W. W. H. Davis, at one time United States attorney for the territory. Later the writer read *Autores Españoles, Historiadores Primitivos de las Indias*, by Enrique de Vedia, Madrid, 1852. In this work are found the *Comentarios* and *Naufragios* of Alvar Nuñez. Dr. de Vedia, in his *Apuntes*, in the same volume, gives the biography of the distinguished Adelantado. It may safely be said that no writer in English, since the publication of *Historiadores Primitivos*, has contributed anything to the sum total of knowledge as to Alvar Nuñez as recited in the *Apuntes* of Dr. de Vedia. The story of Coronado's journey is taken from the *Relacion* of Castañeda and the monographs of General J. H. Simpson and George Parker Winship, both of which were published by the United States government. Much information, as has been stated, was compiled from the elaborate works of A. F. Bandelier and Hubert Howe Bancroft.

In all this work the writer believes that the principal duties of the historian have been faithfully performed. *Ne quid falsi dicere audeat, ne quid veri non audeat.* The reader will soon ascertain that few pretensions to what may be termed the philosophy of history have been advanced. The novelist and writer of later day fiction alone enjoy the privilege of an intimate acquaintance with the secret motives of those whose conduct or character is delineated. The historian, if he writes truthfully, knows no more than the authorities disclose or the facts suggest. He is not permitted to indulge in flights of the imagination. In so doing he is likely to impose even upon himself. Much research gives us the right to opinions, but the philosophical historian is quite often a perverter of truth. In his eagerness to establish a theory, or, perhaps, a reputation for some favorite, he often overlooks the weight of some troublesome authority or fact.

When the extent of this work is considered, comprising as it does the transactions in New Mexican history during nearly four centuries, the writer would indeed feel flattered if some critic found no error in the entire narrative or a failure to credit some translator or writer whose information came from sources identical with those used in this work. Only those who are familiar with historical composition are aware how difficult it is in all work of this nature to guard against mistakes of omission and commission. At times we are misled by the very prejudices of the authorities consulted.

The documentary history of New Mexico, prior to the American Occupation, is very limited. During the Mexican period no books of any consequence relative to events in New Mexico were published. The *Santa Fé Archives* are quite voluminous but fail to give much light on the events of the period. Subsequent to the American Occupation we find much material in the *Reports* of government officials in the War, Interior and Indian Departments. The reports of Governor Calhoun, while Indian agent, found in *California and New Mexico Ex. Doc. 17, 31st Congress, 1st Session*, are valuable. In the report of a congressional committee, which made a thorough investigation of the Indian question, *Indian Affairs Report, Joint Special Commission, 1867*, there is a great wealth of material. The reports of the governors of New Mexico, the military commanders and Indian agents, are filled with information of great interest to the student of conditions existing in the Southwest at that time.

It is unfortunate that so few books were written by those peculiarly qualified. The Spaniard, during his more than two centuries of control, wrote few books, but he preserved many records which are invaluable. This is peculiarly true of the records made by the Franciscans. Present day New Mexicans, cognizant of important events, should profit by the example of their Spanish predecessors.

Alvar Nuñez Cabeza de Vaca was no greater than any one of his companions. All would have passed into oblivion had it not been that he wrote his *Relacion*.

Francisco Vasquez Coronado was a great figure in the days following the Spanish Conquest of Mexico. Only his name would have come down to us had it not been that an humble soldier in his expedition preserved to us the narrative of those early explorations. Coronado lives because Castañeda wrote his *Relacion.*

More than two hundred Franciscans labored for the conversion of the Indian in New Mexico. Frayles Marcos de Niza and Alonzo de Benavides are remembered because they made reports in writing.

General Zebulon Montgomery Pike will live forever as the American officer whose publication of the account of his travels first attracted American attention to the Spanish Provinces.

Others have been leaders of great armies, have conquered great nations; the crimson glories of great battles have come to military men in every age. Xenophon and his Ten Thousand are among the immortals. Xenophon wrote the *Anabasis.*

Alexander W. Doniphan was as great as Xenophon, and yet the story of his exploits and the deeds of his One Thousand Missourians would scarce be known had it not been that John T. Hughes, a soldier in his regiment, wrote *Doniphan's Expedition.*

In the Nineteenth century New Mexico produced abler men than Don Pedro Bauptista Pino. He lives where greater men are forgotten. He wrote the *Exposicion.*

Pattie was only a trapper and mountaineer, no better qualified than hundreds of others who pursued the same calling. He will live while others are not mentioned. He wrote a *Personal Narrative.*

Captain William Becknell, William Bent, Ceran St. Vrain, Dr. David Waldo, and Dr. Josiah Gregg were early traders over the Santa Fé Trail. Gregg wrote the *Commerce of the Prairies* and achieved immortality.

General Christopher Carson was no more courageous than dozens of his type upon the frontier; and yet he lives when Bent, Bridger, and Wootton are only memories. He is the idol of the romance magazine writer.

General W. W. H. Davis was "one of them literary fellows" who will live when even the names of abler secretaries of New Mexico cannot be recalled. He wrote *El Gringo*, and the *Spanish Conquest of New Mexico*.

There have been many governors of New Mexico. General Lew Wallace, soldier, governor, would have been forgotten, but so long as the English language is spoken the *Fair God* and *Ben Hur* will be read by the children of men.

In the military history of the great southwest we find the names of soldiers whose exploits in the service of their country entitle them to everlasting fame. Only one or two have followed the example of General Xenophon. General Nelson A. Miles will live where countless capable captains who gave their lives to civilization are forgotten. General Miles has written several books.

New Mexico owes something to the memory of those who have contributed to the productive scholarship of the State. To the living, to Bandelier, Prince, Lummis, Hewett, and Read, a grateful people should render acknowledgment. Men who accomplish things the country always produces, but they have all been careless of what record has been made of their achievements. Our pioneers, soldiers, and state-builders owe something to their ancestors, to posterity, to history, to patriotism, and to themselves. There are many now living in New Mexico whose duty it is to make record of important events which have occurred during the past century. This can best be done by contributing papers to the Historical Society of New Mexico.

With some pleasure the writer makes mention of the fact that all of the illustrations in this book are by New Mexicans. He tenders his thanks to Messrs. Clarence Batchelor, of Las Vegas, K. M. Chapman, of Santa Fé, and W. R. Walton, of Alburquerque, for their assistance in reproducing so many old scenes and portraits. The maps were made by the writer's son, Waldo C. Twitchell.

RALPH EMERSON TWITCHELL

Las Vegas, New Mexico
    July 1, 1912

CONTENTS OF VOLUME II

CHAPTER I A TERRITORY OF THE REPUBLIC OF MEXICO — TERRITORY AND DEPARTMENT — POLITICAL CHIEFS AND GOVERNORS, CIVIL AND MILITARY — VISCARRA TO ARMIJO — INDIAN AFFAIRS 3

CHAPTER II THE CENTRAL SYSTEM OF GOVERNMENT — THE REVOLUTION OF 1837-8 — INTRIGUES AND CONSPIRACIES — THE KILLING OF GOVERNOR PEREZ — GONZALES REVOLUTIONARY GOVERNOR — BATTLES WITH REVOLUTIONISTS — MANUEL ARMIJO DECLARES HIMSELF GOVERNOR AND COMMANDING-GENERAL — DEFEAT OF REVOLUTIONARY FORCES — EXECUTION OF GONZALES AND CONFEDERATES . . 53

CHAPTER III. THE TEXAS-SANTA FÉ EXPEDITION — CAPTURE OF THE TEXANS WHO ARE SENT TO THE CITY OF MEXICO — MURDER OF DON ANTONIO JOSÉ CHAVEZ — SNIVELY'S RAID — COL. WARFIELD ATTACKS TOWN OF MORA — DEFEAT OF VANGUARD OF ARMIJO'S ARMY ON THE ARKANSAS — CAPTAIN COOKE DISARMS THE TEXANS — CLOSING OF PORTS OF ENTRY BY GENERAL SANTA ANA 69

CHAPTER IV THE OVERLAND TRADE — OLD SANTA FÉ TRAIL — COMMERCE OF THE PRAIRIES — STORIES AND INCIDENTS OF THE DAYS OF THE STAGE COACH, . 1804-1872 . . 91

CHAPTER V THE CITY OF SANTA FÉ — THE OLD PALACE — CHURCHES — MANNERS AND CUSTOMS OF THE PEOPLE — COSTUMES — AGRICULTURE AND STOCK RAISING — MINES AND MINING — THE MISSIONS, FRAYLES, AND PRIESTS — VISITS OF THE CHURCH DIGNITARIES — THE BISHOP OF DURANGO — LISTS OF FRAYLES AND PRIESTS, 1540 TO 1846 146

CHAPTER VI THE WAR WITH MEXICO — THE AMERICAN OCCUPATION — ARMY OF THE WEST — GENERAL MANUEL ARMIJO — BRIGADIER-GENERAL STEPHEN W. KEARNY OCcupies Santa Fé — A Civil Form of Government Proclaimed and Officials Named — Colonel Alexander W. Doniphan Makes Treaty with the Navajós — Colonel Sterling W. Price — Uprising of 1846-1847 — Murder of Governor Bent at Taos — Donaciano Vigil — Military Government, 1846-1851 194

Chapter VII Territory of New Mexico — The Organic Act — Civil and Military Authorities — Col. E. V. Sumner — Legislative Assemblies — Delegates to Congress — Indian Campaigns — Counties — Population — Agriculture and Stock-raising — Gadsden Purchase — Disputed Boundaries — The Mesilla Valley — Explorations 280

Chapter VIII The Catholic Church in New Mexico — Career of Most Rev. John B. Lamy and His Successors, 1851 to 1912 — The Protestant Churches — Their Work Since the American Occupation . . 328

Chapter IX New Mexico during the Civil War — Colonel W. W. Loring — General H. H. Sibley — Confederate Invasion — Colonel John R. Baylor — Fall of Fort Fillmore — Major E. Lynde — New Mexicans not Secessionists — Hatred of the Texans — Battle of Valverde — Confederate Occupation of Albuquerque and Santa Fé — Engagements at Apache Canyon and Glorieta — Fight at Peralta — Confederate Retreat — Colorado Volunteers — Arrival of the California Column — General J. H. Carleton — Governor Henry Connelly — Delegates in Congress — Governors Mitchell, Pile, Giddings, Arny, Axtell, and Wallace — Bench and Bar — Lincoln County War — Advent of Railroads — Population — Statistics — 1861-1880 357

Chapter X Indian Campaigns — Army Posts — Military Commanders — The Apache and Navajó Indians — Bosque Redondo — Comanches, Apaches, Utes, and Pueblos — The Reservations — Victorio's Raids — Geronimo — His Raids and Capture — General Nelson A. Miles — 1864-1887 428

CONTENTS OF VOLUME II

CHAPTER XI SPANISH AND MEXICAN LAND GRANTS — ACT OF CONGRESS CREATING OFFICE OF SURVEYOR GENERAL — PRIVATE LAND CLAIMS — GEORGE W. JULIAN — EFFORTS FOR CONGRESSIONAL ACTION — ESTABLISHMENT OF COURT OF PRIVATE LAND CLAIMS — THE COURT AND ITS WORK — THE BARONY OF ARIZONA — PERALTA-REAVIS . . . 451

CHAPTER XII ADVENT OF THE RAILWAYS — GOVERNORS AND THEIR ADMINISTRATIONS — LEGISLATIVE ENACTMENTS — DELEGATES IN CONGRESS — NATIONAL LEGISLATION — INDUSTRIAL PROGRESS — MINES AND MINING — CITIES AND TOWNS — EDUCATION — THE FERGUSSON ACT — RECLAMATION ACT — NATIONAL AID IN IRRIGATION — POLITICAL AFFAIRS — CRIMES AND CRIMINALS — LABOR STRIKES AND TROUBLES — EFFORTS FOR STATEHOOD — SPANISH-AMERICAN WAR — ROOSEVELT'S ROUGH RIDERS — CONGRESSIONAL INVESTIGATING COMMITTEES — SENATOR ALBERT J. BEVERIDGE — THE ENABLING ACT — CONSTITUTIONAL CONVENTION — STATE ELECTION — 1880-1912 . . . 482

LIST OF ILLUSTRATIONS

PORTRAIT OF THE AUTHOR	FRONTISPIECE
DON AGUSTIN DE ITURBIDE, EMPEROR OF MEXICO	3
FAC-SIMILE OF LETTER FROM EMPEROR ITURBIDE RELATIVE TO CHANGES IN THE TEXT OF THE PLAN DE IGUALA	8
GEN. DON ANTONIO LOPEZ DE SANTA ANNA	12
RT. REV. JOSÉ ANTONIO LAUREANO DE ZUBIRÍA, BISHOP OF DURANGO	16
FAC-SIMILE OF WILL OF DON JUAN ANTONIO CABEZA DE BACA	20
COSTUMES OF THE RICOS DURING THE FIRST QUARTER OF THE NINETEENTH CENTURY	24
EARLIEST METHOD OF TRANSPORTATION OVER THE SANTA FÉ TRAIL	28
EARLY TRAPPERS, TRADERS, PLAINSMEN, AND MOUNTAINEERS	32
F. X. AUBREY, PATHFINDER	34
RUINS OF OLD PECOS MISSION, 1846	36
A SANTA FÉ CARAVAN CROSSING THE GREAT PLAIN	40
DON JOSÉ CHAVES, GOVERNOR OF NEW MEXICO	44
PROMINENT OFFICERS, MILITARY AND CIVIL, OF THE AMERICAN OCCUPATION PERIOD	48
MEDALLIONS OF THE EMPEROR AGUSTIN ITURBIDE	51
GEN. MANUEL ARMIJO, GOVERNOR OF NEW MEXICO	56
BRIG.-GEN. PHILIP ST. GEORGE COOKE	64
PUEBLO INDIAN BOY	67
NEW MEXICAN BURRO	68
JUDGE JOAB HOUGHTON	72
COL. J. M. WASHINGTON	80
JAMES S. CALHOUN, FIRST CIVIL GOVERNOR OF NEW MEXICO UNDER THE ACT OF CONGRESS, MARCH 3, 1851	88
MEXICAN ARRASTRA	89
A SANTA FÉ TRADER	90

THE CARAVAN IN SIGHT OF SANTA FÉ	96
END OF THE SANTA FÉ TRAIL — THE OLD FONDA	104
OFFICERS IN THE ARMY OF THE WEST, 1846	112
REPRESENTATIVE NEW MEXICANS OF THE AMERICAN OCCUPATION PERIOD	120
REPRESENTATIVE NEW MEXICANS OF THE AMERICAN OCCUPATION PERIOD	124
FAC-SIMILES OF BALLOT CAST AT LAST ELECTION UNDER MEXICAN GOVERNMENT AND OF BALLOT CAST AT THE FIRST ELECTION UNDER AMERICAN GOVERNMENT	128
PROMINENT INDIAN CHIEFS	132
GEN. CHRISTOPHER CARSON ABOUT 1845	136
GOVERNORS OF NEW MEXICO UNDER ACT OF MARCH 3, 1851	140
HEADQUARTERS OF PRESIDENT HAYES AT SANTA FÉ	144
FREIGHTERS ON THE SANTA FÉ TRAIL, WITH KIOWA SCOUT	148
ATTORNEYS-GENERAL OF NEW MEXICO	152
ARCHBISHOPS OF THE ROMAN CATHOLIC CHURCH	160
EARLY PROTESTANT MISSIONARIES AND EDUCATORS	168
SECRETARIES OF NEW MEXICO	176
FAC-SIMILE OF ADVERTISEMENT OF STAGE COACH LINE TO SANTA FÉ, 1853	184
CHAPEL OF SAN MIGUEL	192
PUEBLO INDIAN POTTERY	193
KIOWA CHIEFS	200
GEN. CHRISTOPHER CARSON AND FRIENDS, 1865	208
MISSIONARY BISHOPS OF THE PROTESTANT EPISCOPAL CHURCH	216
REPRESENTATIVE NEW MEXICANS OF THE NINETEENTH CENTURY	224
REPRESENTATIVE NEW MEXICANS OF THE NINETEENTH CENTURY	232
DELEGATES IN CONGRESS	240
CHEYENNE INDIAN PRISONERS ON THE SANTA FÉ TRAIL CAPTURED BY GOVERNMENT TROOPS IN 1869	248
GOVERNORS OF INDIAN PUEBLOS WHO VISITED PRESIDENT LINCOLN IN 1862	256
PROMINENT OFFICERS DURING THE CIVIL WAR PERIOD	264
FAC-SIMILE OF OATH OF ALLEGIANCE ADMINISTERED TO CAPTAIN SOLOMON SPIEGELBERG BY CHIEF JUSTICE KIRBY BENEDICT	272

LIST OF ILLUSTRATIONS

FAC-SIMILE OF PASSPORT GIVEN TO LEHMAN SPIEGELBERG BY GEN. H. H. SIBLEY, C. S. A.	276
COLONEL DONIPHAN'S ARMY ON THE MARCH	278
UNION AND CONFEDERATE SOLDIERS IN NEW MEXICO, 1861-1866	280
CHIEF JUSTICE KIRBY BENEDICT	282
SPIEGELBERG BROTHERS, MERCHANTS AND FREIGHTERS OF THE SANTA FÉ TRAIL PERIOD	284
MERCHANTS AND FREIGHTERS OF THE SANTA FÉ TRAIL PERIOD	288
MAXWELL'S MANSION ON THE CIMARRON	296
THE GOVERNMENT DISTRIBUTING RATIONS TO THE INDIANS	304
UNION AND CONFEDERATE OFFICERS IN NEW MEXICO, 1862	320
PROMINENT OFFICERS AND SOLDIERS OF THE CIVIL WAR PERIOD	324
REV. DONATO M. GASPARRI, S. J.	328
CELEBRATED APACHE CHIEFS	336
PROMINENT NEW MEXICANS AND APACHE CHIEFS AT FORT. STANTON, MESCALERO APACHE RESERVATION, 1875	344
WILLIAM F. BONNEY, "BILLY THE KID"	352
PRE-SPANISH POTTERY SHARDS, GILA BASIN	355
PRE-SPANISH POTTERY SHARDS, GILA BASIN	356
PATRICK F. GARRETT	360
HENRY L. WALDO, CHIEF JUSTICE, 1876-1878; ATTORNEY-GENERAL, 1878-1880	364
JUSTICES OF THE SUPREME COURT OF NEW MEXICO	368
GROSS, BLACKWELL & COMPANY — MEMBERS AND EMPLOYEES, 1881	376
BUILDERS AND OPERATORS OF THE ATCHISON, TOPEKA & SANTA FÉ RAILROAD	384
PROMINENT MEN OF AFFAIRS IN NEW MEXICO DURING THE LAST HALF OF THE NINETEENTH CENTURY	392
GOVERNORS OF NEW MEXICO UNDER THE ACT OF MARCH 3, 1851	400
DELEGATES IN CONGRESS	408
CHIEF JUSTICE AND ASSOCIATE JUSTICES OF THE SUPREME COURT OF NEW MEXICO APPOINTED BY PRESIDENT CLEVELAND IN 1885	416
PROMINENT NEW MEXICANS OF THE NINETEENTH CENTURY	420
PRESIDENTS OF THE NEW MEXICO BAR ASSOCIATION	424
SANTA RITA COPPER MINE, 1850	426
NAVAJÓ CHIEF	427

FRANK SPRINGER, PRESIDENT NEW MEXICO BAR ASSOCIATION — PALEONTOLOGIST	432
JUSTICES OF THE SUPREME COURT OF NEW MEXICO	440
PRE-SPANISH POTTERY SHARDS	448
PROMINENT NEW MEXICANS OF THE NINETEENTH CENTURY	448
REPRESENTATIVE DELEGATES TO THE THIRTEENTH NATIONAL IRRIGATION CONGRESS, NOVEMBER, 1904	456
FAC-SIMILE OF RESOLUTION APPROVING THE CONSTRUCTION OF THE ELEPHANT-BUTTE RECLAMATION PROJECT	464
CHIEF JUSTICE AND ASSOCIATE JUSTICES OF THE COURT OF PRIVATE LAND CLAIMS	472
BENT'S FORT ON THE ARKANSAS RIVER	481
ATTORNEY FOR THE COURT OF PRIVATE LAND CLAIMS AND ASSISTANTS	482
EARLY BANKERS OF NEW MEXICO	484
CHIEF JUSTICE AND ASSOCIATE JUSTICES OF THE LAST SUPREME COURT OF THE TERRITORY OF NEW MEXICO	488
COL. THEODORE ROOSEVELT, 1ST U. S. VOLUNTEER CAVALRY	496
BATTLE OF LAS GUASIMAS	504
CAPT. MAXIMILIANO LUNA, 1ST U. S. VOLUNTEER CAVALRY	508
BATTLE OF SAN JUAN HILL	512
MAJ. W. H. H. LLEWELLYN, 1ST U. S. VOLUNTEER CAVALRY	516
PROMINENT NEW MEXICANS OF THE NINETEENTH CENTURY	520
FAC-SIMILE OF LETTER FROM COL. THEODORE ROOSEVELT RELATIVE TO THE PERSONNEL OF THE ROUGH RIDERS	528
OFFICERS OF ROOSEVELT'S ROUGH RIDERS	532
OFFICERS OF THE 1ST TERRITORIAL INFANTRY, U. S. A.	536
PROMINENT NEW MEXICAN EDUCATORS	540
THE PENS USED BY PRES. WILLIAM HOWARD TAFT IN SIGNING THE ENABLING ACT OF 1910	544
WILLIAM J. MILLS, LAST GOVERNOR OF THE TERRITORY OF NEW MEXICO	548
MEMBERS OF THE CONSTITUTIONAL CONVENTION OF 1910	552
OPENING SESSION OF THE CONSTITUTIONAL CONVENTION OF 1910	560
PROMINENT NEW MEXICANS OF THE NINETEENTH CENTURY	564
FAC-SIMILE OF SIGNATURES OF THE FRAMERS OF THE CONSTITUTION OF 1910	568

LIST OF ILLUSTRATIONS

Fac-simile of Signatures of the Framers of the Constitution of 1910	576
Members of the Constitutional Convention of 1910	584
Members of the Constitutional Convention of 1910	588
Prominent New Mexicans of the Nineteenth Century	592
Pres. William Howard Taft signing the Proclamation admitting New Mexico into the Union	596
William C. McDonald, First Governor of the State of New Mexico	600
Military Post near El Paso, 1851	606

NEW MEXICO

Don Agustin de Iturbide, Emperor of Mexico
Copy of Painting in the Sala of the National Palace, City of Mexico

CHAPTER I

A TERRITORY OF THE REPUBLIC OF MEXICO — TERRITORY AND DEPARTMENT — POLITICAL CHIEFS AND GOVERNORS, CIVIL AND MILITARY — VISCARRA TO ARMIJO — INDIAN AFFAIRS

IT WAS now ten years since the Grito de Dolores had been heard. Hidalgo's cry had not been in vain. The fires of revolution which this noble curate had lighted on the 15th of September, 1810, had burned fiercely and finally resulted in the independence of Mexico. The revolt against the Spanish yoke had been carried on, with varying success, until February 24, 1821. On that day, the plan of Iguala, asserting the independence of Mexico, was adopted and proclaimed. From this time the revolutionists were generally successful, and on the 24th day of August, what is known as the treaty of Cordoba was signed by General Agustin de Iturbide for Mexico, and by Viceroy Don Juan O'Donoju, for Spain, the latter, however, not acting under authority from his government. By the terms of this treaty the independence of Mexico was recognized, a constitutional monarchy established, and Ferdinand VII invited to the throne. Hostilities, however, did not cease until the City of Mexico was taken by Iturbide, September 27, 1821, whereby the independence of Mexico was consummated.

A junta or provisional council, consisting of thirty-six members, was immediately created under the plan of Iguala. This body appointed a regency of five persons, with General Iturbide as president and commander-in-chief of the army and navy. On the 13th day of February, the year following, the Spanish government disapproved the treaty of Cordoba.

Meanwhile, pursuant to the provisions of the plan of Iguala and the treaty of Cordoba, an election of deputies to a congress was held, and on the 24th of February, 1822, this congress assembled in the City of Mexico for the purpose of drafting a constitution. Immediately a struggle began between President Iturbide and the members of the congress, which finally culminated in the election of Iturbide as emperor on the 19th day of May, 1822. He was crowned on the 21st day of July following.[1]

AGUSTIN ITURBIDE ELECTED EMPEROR

On the 30th of October, 1822, Iturbide dissolved the constituent congress by force and created the national instituent council or junta. This body was installed three days later. Meanwhile the masses of the people and many officers of the army were much dissatisfied. General Santa Anna revolted, proclaiming, in the name of the nation, a republican government, and declaring that the three guaranties of the plan of Iguala must be inviolably observed. From

[1] Bancroft, H. H., *History of Arizona and New Mexico*, vol. iv, pp. 777-8: "Elaborate preparations were made for the coronation of the emperor and his consort. The commissioners appointed to draw up the regulations and formalities to be observed at the ceremony had handed into congress the result of their labors more than a month before. In the impecunious condition of the treasury, it was impossible to manufacture crowns and other insignia of royalty appropriately magnificent. But display must not be wanting, so jewels and gems were borrowed, and though the national pawn-shop refused to lend its diamonds and pearls, the regalia were bright and glittering with fictitious splendor. When the eventful day arrived the city was gay with many colors, as from balconies and windows fluttered banners and streamers and pennons; while the walls were decked with floral wreaths and devices in fresh evergreens, and flags waved from church towers and turrets. The congress met at eight o'clock, and two deputations, each composed of twenty-four members, proceeded to the provisional palace to escort the emperor and empress to the cathedral. Here on two raised daises, one lower than the other, thrones had been erected, to the right and left of which were seats for the 'venerable' sire and the princes and princesses of this mushroom monarchy. The procession which accompanied the royal presence along the carpeted streets was as imposing as inexperience, by the aid of imitation, could make it. There were masters-at-arms and ushers, pages and maids-of-honor in gorgeous attire, and a master of the ceremonies with his suite of attendants. On velvet cushions were borne the royal apparel with which the imperial couple were about to array themselves, and the signet ring and the sceptre, and the patch-work crowns. At the entrance to the cathedral two obsequious bishops received the emperor and empress and administered to them the holy water. Then they were conducted to the lower thrones and the ceremonies commenced. The regalia were placed on the altar and high mass celebrated, after which Iturbide and his spouse were consecrated with sacred oil, and assumed the royal robes. The regalia having been blessed, Mangino, the president of the congress, now placed the diadem on Iturbide's head, who then performed with his own hands the act of coronation of the empress. Thereupon they ascended the thrones on the higher dais. At the conclusion of the service the officiating bishop, in a loud voice, exclaimed, 'Vivat Imperator in aeternum!' and the people replied, 'Long live the emperor and empress.'"

December 5, 1822, until they were finally successful, Santa Anna and other generals remained in arms against the empire.

The only official act, during the reign of Iturbide, of moment or consequence to the people of New Mexico, so far as recorded, is what is known as the "Colonization Law of Iturbide," which was passed by the national council on January 3, 1823, and on the day following was signed by the emperor and promulgated. This act provided for two kinds of grants; the one to promoters called *empresarios*, who should bring in two hundred families under contract with the executive, and the other to individuals to be made by the common councils, called *ayuntamientos*. On March 7, 1823, the constituent congress, which had been dissolved by force of arms by the emperor, reconvened, and on the 19th of March, Iturbide presented his abdication to that body. The congress refused to allow him to abdicate, but on April 7, 1823, declared that his coronation had been an act of force and violence and void, as were also hereditary succession and all titles that had emanated from the crown.[2]

THE COLONIZATION LAW OF ITURBIDE

The colonization law of Iturbide seems to have been a matter of great concern to the people and their representatives in the constituent congress, for within a week after the promulgation of the decree of banishment for Iturbide, the congress passed an order suspending this colonization law until such a time as a new act or resolution on the subject might be enacted.

Under the plan of Iguala it was expressly proclaimed that all officials then in New Spain, or Mexico, whether political, ecclesiastical, civil, or military, should remain and exercise the same func-

[2] *Mex. Col. Ley. Fund.*, 115: The decree of banishment was as follows: "The coronation of D. Agustin de Iturbide being the work of violence and void of right, there is no occasion to discuss his abdication of the crown. 2. Consequently the hereditary succession and the titles emanating from the coronation are declared null; and all acts of the government from May 19th to March 29th are illegal, remaining subject to the revision of the existing government for approval or revocation. 3. The Executive power shall take measures for the speedy departure of D. Agustin de Iturbide from the territory of the nation. 4. This shall take place at one of the ports of the Mexican Gulf, a neutral vessel being chartered at the state's expense to convey him and his family to such place as he may designate. 5. During his life $25,000 annually are assigned to D. Augustin de Iturbide payable in this capital, on the condition that he establish his residence at some point in Italy. After his death his family shall enjoy a pension of $8,000 under the rules established for pensions of the *montepío militar*."

tions as were at the time being exercised by them. When the treaty of Cordoba was made the plan of Iguala was specifically adopted, and it will thus be seen that so far as Mexico and her provinces were concerned, all the then existing laws of the mother country were continued in force and all officials who had held under Spanish authority were continued in office with the same power and exercising the same duties and functions as had been previously exercised by them when subjects of the crown of Spain.

Two years prior to the act suspending the colonization law a decree of the government under Iturbide, passed before he was elected emperor, was promulgated, by the terms of which all officials were habilitated and confirmed in their offices and their official acts recognized, authorized, and confirmed. After the fall of Iturbide the constituent congress never saw fit to modify this act, and it thus appears that all the laws of Spain relative to the granting, disposition, or sale of the lands of the country were continued in force. In this respect these laws, the plan of Iguala, and the treaty of Cordoba have had some bearing upon the official acts of the executive and legislative authorities of New Mexico.

The empire had followed the revolution, and by revolution the empire fell. Iturbide, the soldier, thought to govern as he had ruled his regiments. The people had expected freedom; they had gained a despot; they demanded political independence; Iturbide was banished, and for violating the act of proscription by secretly returning to Mexico, was executed by order of the existing government.[3]

FALL OF EMPEROR ITURBIDE

The fires of revolution, however, had not burned in New Mexico,

---

[3] Notwithstanding the act of proscription against him, Iturbide, after his banishment, decided to return to Mexico. He landed at a place near Soto la Marina. He was subsequently arrested by General Garza, the commander of the government forces at Soto la Marina, who informed the congress of Tamaulipas of the fact. The congress assembled in extraordinary session, and notwithstanding Garza's appeals for Iturbide, his efforts were in vain. The congress confirmed its previous sentence and Garza was ordered forthwith to carry it into execution. Iturbide was informed that his hour had come and at six o'clock in the evening he was led forth to execution. A soldier to the last, he addressed the troops assembled, saying, "Mexicans, in this last moment of my life I recommend to you the love of your country, and the observance of our holy religion. I die for having come to aid you; and depart happy because I die among you. I die with honor, not as a traitor. That stain will not attach to my children and their descendants. Preserve order and be obedient to your commanders. From the bottom of my heart, I forgive all my enemies."

even though a major portion of the Spanish inhabitants was disloyal to the crown. The representative men of the province were undoubtedly favorably impressed with the form of government which was proving so advantageous and successful in the American republic. Hidalgo had appealed for independence but the cry of Dolores was only an echo in New Mexico. In the constitution of 1814 Morelos had declared for a republic of the extreme type. But liberty and equality were not the only elements necessary for convincing appeal to the Mexican in the south. The passions of the natives were aroused. Their hearts were filled with a desire for vengeance for years of Spanish cruelty and oppression. No such sentiment obtained among the people of New Mexico. The patriotism of Hidalgo and Morelos found no counterpart among their brethren in the priesthood north of the Rio Grande. The revolution, the empire, Iturbide, his fall, the republic, all these events happened and the people of New Mexico pursued the same paths that had been followed for two centuries before, with scarce a ripple of excitement — nothing but a celebration at Santa Fé, with addresses from prominent men, every one of whom had been an official under Spanish authority, the most prominent being Facundo Melgares, the last Spanish governor, an officer whom Pike had declared was one of the very few who was loyal to his king.

New Mexico was a province until the year 1824, being one of the Provincias Internas.[4] On January 31st of that year, by an act of the constituent congress, it was joined to

NEW MEXICO A TERRITORY the provinces of Chihuahua and Durango, forming the Estado Interno del Norte. The people of Durango were not satisfied with this, however, and,

---

[4] The name was used in official documents as early as 1712. — *N. Mexico, Cédulas*, Ms., 322-4. As a recognized division of Spanish territory, under this name, it became such by a royal order of August 22, 1776, by which the northern provinces of Nueva Viscaya, Coahuila, Texas, New Mexico, Sinaloa, and Sonora, and the Californias were formed into a new government. This government was under a governor and comandante-general, who was entirely independent of the viceroy of New Spain, responsible directly to the king, the audiencia of Guadalajara retaining its judicial authority. For all practical purposes, this governor was a viceroy. The first incumbent of this position was General Teodoro de Croix, who came from Spain in 1776. He occupied the position until 1782 when he was succeeded by Don Felipe de Neve, governor of the Californias. In 1783 he was made viceroy of Peru. He was a native of Flanders, a nephew of the viceroy, Marqués de Croix, and a senior lieutenant of the Flemish company of Royal Guards.

having made a strong protest to the congress, the principal ground of objection being that the capital was located at Chihuahua, New Mexico was made a territory of the Mexican republic, and Durango and Chihuahua erected into states.

The official title of the executive of the territory of New Mexico under the Mexican government was political chief, *jefe politico*, from 1823 until 1837, when he was known officially as governor, *gobernador*. Under the constitution of 1836, the territory became a department,[5] and was so called down to the occupation of the territory by General Kearny, in 1846.

In 1823, the constituent congress passed an election law, the terms of which provided that the day following that of the election of deputies to congress, the same electoral board should renew the provincial deputations in their totality, being at liberty to reëlect the persons of which they were at that time composed.

In the following year, the congress adopted what is known as the constitutive act, under which the general constituent congress was elected. In this act provision was made by GENERAL CONSTITUENT which the territories were directly subject CONGRESS to the supreme power, which was divided into legislative, executive, and judicial.[6] On the 18th day of August, the colonization law [7] of the republic was passed by the congress, and under section 16 of that act, the general government was commanded to proceed with the colonization of the territories of the republic. In October, 1824, the congress adopted the constitution which continued in force until the constitution of December 29, 1836,[8] was adopted.

The constitution of 1824 does not prescribe any form of government for the territories, but provides that congress shall pass laws for that purpose. Diligent search has failed to bring to light any law passed by the congress upon this subject, but numerous laws of a subsequent date recognize the existence in the territories of governors and territorial deputations. The territorial deputation was the successor of the provincial deputation created by the decree

---
[5] Arrillaga, *Recop.*, 1836, p. 379. N. Mexico será departmento.
[6] Reynolds, M. G., *Spanish and Mexican Land Laws*, p. 121.
[7] *Ibid.*, p. 121.
[8] *Ibid.*, p. 124.

inútil añadir q[ue] si V. juzga conducentes
otras proclamas, y pueden venir serán bien
recibidas.

Me atrevo á hacer á V. otra indi-
cación: si V. puede salir de ahí reservada-
mente hasta Cuernavaca, no tendria V. mo-
tivo de arrepentirse de ese paso, y se lo
agradeceria mucho su muy af[ec]t[isi]mo amo. q. b.
s. m.

Agustin de Yturbide

P. D.

De todos modos, verifique V. ó no el viage,
aunque el propio me traiga, como espero, los
papeles todos que deseo; tenga V. la bondad
de seguir ocupado todo de este importante
asunto. Proclamas p[ar]a el orden y unión, &[c].—
Y.

Fac-simile of Letter from Emperor Iturbide relative to Changes in
the Text of the Plan de Iguala

nifiestos sobre lo q.e requiera mayor extension. Planes q.e fluyen del actual Sistema p.a la Junta, p.a las Cortes, p.a el Exercito: &c. &c. &c. No falta campo y V. preferirá los asuntos mas dignos de su pluma en el concepto de que muy breve no se ocuparán las prensas de otra cosa; y que entretanto conducirán tambien obras q.e V. considere mas necesarias q.e las del publico, al acierto à que anelo.

Las cartas de V. siempre deberán venir por el conducto q.e entregue à V. las mias.

of the Spanish Córtes of March 18, 1812, the renewal of which was ordered by the law of June 17, 1823.

DEPUTATIONS AND AYUNTAMIENTOS

Under the Mexican republic there was little change in the form of government which had previously obtained in the territories, but it seems that the *jefe politico* or *gobernador* somewhat arbitrarily controlled all branches of the government. The territorial deputation was a sort of legislature, more like the common council of an American city government, composed of four or six members. After the adoption of the constitution of 1837, this body was known as the *junta departamental*, and later on was called the *asamblea*. According to Barreiro the territorial deputation was of little force and there is but slight record of any of its acts. Under the Spanish régime there were *alcaldes mayores*, but under the republic these were changed into *ayuntamientos* in the larger towns, while the smaller settlements had only ordinary *alcaldes*. According to Pino only Santa Fé, Santa Cruz de la Cañada, and Taos had *ayuntamientos*. The territory was entitled to representation in the congress of the republic but we know of only two men having filled that position, Don Jose Antonio Chavez and General Chavez, for many years a resident of Rio Arriba county, New Mexico. It has been said that General Diego Archuleta was also a deputy in the congress but there is no official record of his election to or participation in the deliberations of that body.

JUDICIAL TRIBUNALS

The only tribunals of justice were those of the *alcaldes* or justices of the peace. From the decision of this class of officials there was an appeal to the supreme court sitting at Chihuahua. The course of litigation was exceedingly simple, so far as the proceedings before the *alcaldes* was concerned. The plaintiff made a verbal complaint or demand to the *alcalde*, whereupon the latter would order the complainant to summon the defendant. The service of this summons was a very simple matter as all that was required was a verbal announcement by the complainant to the defendant that he appear forthwith before the *alcalde*.[9] If the defendant saw fit to refuse to obey this simple mandate, which was a very rare occurrence, the alcalde would send to him his *baston de justicia*, or

[9] Gregg, Josiah, *Commerce of the Prairies*, i, pp. 233-234; Bloom, Lansing B., *Investigations and Researches*:

judicial staff, an ordinary walking cane, distinguished only by a peculiar black silk tassel. The presentation of the *baston* never failed to enforce compliance, for a refusal to attend after being shown

DIPUTADOS of New Mexico,
1822-1846
I. — Diputacion Provincial.

March, 1822: —
 vocales
 FranCO X. Chabes (1st)
 Pedro Ignacio Gallegos
 Juan Bautista Vigil (Sec'y)
 Juan Estevan Pino
 —— —— Martin
 Agapito Albo (from El Paso)
 Manuel Rubi

 suplentes
 Juan Rafael Ortiz
 Capt. Bartolome Baca

Sept. 15, 1823: —
 AntO Ortiz
 Pedro García
 Je. FranCO Baca
 Mariaño de la Peña
 Je. FranCO Ortis
 Pedro Je. Perea
 Je. García de la Mora

 Je. AntO Chaves
 Pedro Bautista Pino
 Matias Ortiz
 Juan Tomas Terrazas
 Juan Estevan Pino
 Juan Rafael Ortiz

Through absence from the Province of 2 members of the Junta Electoral, the election ordered for Oct. 22, 1824, was not "verified" until May 15, 1825; sessions beginning July 16:

May 15, 1825: —
1. FranCO Ortiz
2. FranCO X. Chaves
3. Rafael Sarracino
4. Sr. Cura de Tomé D. FranCO YgO de Madariaga.
5. Severino Martinez
6. Juan Felipe Ortiz
7. AntO Sandoval

 Juan Rafael Ortiz
 Augustín Durán (1/4/26)

Some of the above were absent for long periods, others serving during this term being: —
 vocales
 Gregorio Ortiz
 FranCO Perez Serrano y Aguirre.
 Jose FranCO Ortiz

 suplente
 Pablo Lucero

Oct. 16, 1826: —
 FranCO Perez Serrano y Aguirre (suplentes)
 AntO Ortiz
 FranCO Baca y Ortiz
 Gregorio Ortiz
 Je. FranCO Ortiz
 Pedro IgO Gallego
 FranCO Sarracino

 Manuel Ruvín de Celis
 Je. Maria Ortiz

Dec. 3, 1828: —
 Juan Estevan Pino
 Juan Felipe Ortiz
 Je. FranCO Leyva
 Rafael Sarracino

 Mauricio de Arze

TERRITORY OF THE REPUBLIC OF MEXICO 11

the staff of justice, was construed into a contempt of court and punished with severity. As a rule the witnesses were never put under

(Dec. 3, 1828)
      vocales   suplentes
  (5) Santiago Abreu
      Je. FranCO Baca
      Juan AntO Cabeza de Baca

Nov. 7, 1830: — ("for the term of 1831 and 1832")
      "proprietarios"   "suplente" (only *1*)
      AntO Sandoval   Jose Maria Baca
      Santiago Abreu
      Juan Rafael Ortiz
      Pro. D. AntO Jose Martinez
      Jose Maria Salasar
      Teodocio Quintana
      Julian Tenorio

Mar. 3, 1833: — ("newly elected for 'el bienio Corriente' " — they should have been elected in October, 1832).
      "proprietarios"
      Gregorio Sanchez
      Jose Andres Sandoval
      Juan Andres Archuleta
      Manuel AntO Baca
      Ignacio Ortiz
      Je. FrO Leyba
      Jn. AntO Cabesa de Baca

Oct. 7, 1834: —
      Jn. Rafael Ortiz
      Mariano Chavez   (some of these signed minutes which
      FrCO IgO Madariaga   had been left *in draft* from Aug. of
      Fernando Ortiz   *previous year*).
      — — — — — — —
      Santiago Ulivarri
      Rafael Garcia   (last 3 took oath in Mar. of '35, but
      FrCO Sandoval   signed sessions of previous Oct.)

M. Chavez is included above only because Bancroft states he was "Governor, interino" during May-July of 1835. The others (except Madariaga, who was absent because of sickness) all signed the sessions of 1/4/36 and 3/24/35; as did also the new vocal, —
      Nereo AntO Montoya.

II. — Junta Departamental.

The Federal Law of Oct. 3, 1835, required State legislatures "to cease immediately, after naming a *junta departamental*, composed for the present of 5 individuals, that they might serve as 'council of the governor' ".

(?) Nov., 1835: —
      Jn. R. Ortiz.
      FernDO Ortiz.
      Rafael Garcia.
      Gregorio Ortiz.
      J. Maria Alarid, Sec'y.

The "Constitutional Law" of Dec. 29, 1836, by the Federal Congress prescribed that the junta departamental should consist of 7 members; their term to commence on January 1, and all to be renewed every 4 years.

oath, but when this formality was had, they were sworn upon a cross cut on the *baston*, or more frequently upon a cross formed

In the law of Mar. 20, 1837, it was decreed that 4 members were to constitute a quorum.

The only sessions of record for the Junta Departamental of New Mexico were Feb. 15 and 16, 1837. Governor Manuel Armijo, who came into power the following winter, "prorogued" the Junta early in 1838, and there was no legislative body until after Armijo had been suspended in 1844, — altho a decree of the Dictator, Santa Anna, Aug. 26, 1842, refers to the "junta departamental de Nuevo Mexico."

Oct. 10, 1841, the Central Government in Mexico ended, giving place to a Dictatorship.

Under the Constitution of June 13, 1843, the supreme government was changed back to the Central form. Also, each Department was to have an Asamblea of not less than 7 nor more than 11 vocales, with an equal number of suplentes, to be elected "for this occasion" by the Departmental Council. The vocales were to hold office 4 years, half the number being renewed every 2 years.

Under this Constitution, Santa Anna became the first President on June 4, 1844; and by the following spring the Asamblea of New Mexico was holding regular sessions.

The 2 seats created in the Junta Departamental by the law of Dec. 29, 1836, were probably never filled in N. Mex.

III. — Asamblea Departamental.

(?) January 1, 1844: — (perhaps elected in fall of 1843.)

	vocales	suplentes
	Jesus Maria Gallegos, President	(1) AntO Sena
These 3 were	Felipe Sena (was Pres. — 9/1/44)	(2) ....
"1st named".	Juan Bautista Vigil, Sec'y	(3) ....
	....	
"2nd named".	José Chavez	(4) ....
	Pro. Manuel Gallegos	(5) ....
	Mariano Chaves	(6) Je. Fransisco Leyva
	Augustín Durán	(7) ....

Some of the above dropped out during 1844-6 and others were very irregular in attendance, and we find later as vocales:

Santiago Martinez
Donaciano Vigil
Pedro Otero
——— Cabeza de Vaca

The minutes of the sessions of this Asamblea are all missing until May 9, 1845. The first four leaves of this journal were expunged — with a knife; as was also a leaf between those numbered "11" and "12." It is very possible that Manuel Armijo, when reinstated as governor in the summer of 1845, found minutes on record which did not meet his approval.

January 1, 1846: —

vocales	suplentes
Jose Chavez, Pres.	Pedro Otero
Pro. Manuel Gallegos	Je. Fr. Leyva
Tomás Ortiz, Sec'y	(Manuel?) Pino
Antonio Je. Martinez	Santiago Vigil
Juan Perea	Serafin Ramirez y Casanova

Gen. Don Antonio Lopez de Santa Anna
Twice President of the Republic of Mexico; Dictator in 1841 and 1853, with the title of Serene Highness in the last Epoch of his Rule

with the finger and thumb.[10] When no witnesses were subpœnaed, oftentimes the alcalde would render judgment solely upon the statements of the parties to the litigation. There was no record in writing of these proceedings preserved by the alcalde. There was also a sort of arbitration by which the issues in a given complaint were referred to what were denominated *hombres buenos*. This proceeding was approximately a trial by jury. In all of the judicial proceedings little attention was paid to any code of laws; in fact there was scarcely an alcalde who knew what the law was or who ever saw a law-book. The judgment of the alcalde was the law, and when not influenced by corrupt agencies, such judgment conformed to the prevailing customs of the country. There were no lawyers or *jueces de letras* in New Mexico at this time and the prosecution of appeals to the courts of Chihuahua, Durango, or Zacatecas was rare on account of the immense cost.[11]

In the administration of justice there were three distinct and privileged jurisdictions, known as *Fueros*: the *eclesiástico*, which provided that no member of the clergy, at least of the rank of curate and upwards, should ever be arraigned before a civil tribunal, but should be tried by his superiors in the order; the *militar*, which made a similar provision in favor not only of commissioned officers but of every common soldier of the ranks; and the *civíl* or ordinary courts, for all cases in which the defendants were laymen.

Under the laws of Spain these *Fueros* were charters or privileges granted to kingdoms, provinces, towns, or persons, and played a

vocales	suplentes
Santiago Armijo	(? Nicolas Quintana y Rosas)
Felipe Sena	

The first 2 vocales above were of "los antiguos," who at the former election were named for the four-year term.

The last session of the Asamblea Departamental of New Mexico was on August 10, 1846. It is of interest to note that the Supreme Government continued Central in form until August 5, 1846, when it became again a Federal Republic. By the law of Aug. 22, 1846, the Constitution of 1824 was provisionally reëstablished; the Departmental Assemblies being suspended, but the governors continuing as "governors of the States."

[10] It is noticeable today that when Spanish speaking citizens of New Mexico are sworn as witnesses in a given case, many of them use the sign of the cross with the fore-finger crossing the thumb of the uplifted hand.

[11] Barreiro, in his *Ojeada*, 38-9, says: "jamas se castigan los delitos, porque no hay en lo absoluto quien sepa formar una sumaria, evacuar una defensa, ni llevar la voz fiscal;" that few were able to carry their cases to Mexico; and that he despaired of being able to introduce order into the admin-

great part in the constitutional development of her colonies. The *Fueros* maintained the ecclesiastical and military authorities in complete independence of the courts; in fact the *civil* was for all practical purposes subordinate to the other two. It had no jurisdiction over them, and the lay plaintiff in the privileged tribunals was liable to have judgment entered up against him, a consequence that could never follow the suits of the ecclesiastical or military orders before the civil tribunals. The judgments of the latter, in such cases, were void.

According to Gregg, imprisonment was the only sort of punishment resorted to in New Mexico. For debt, petit larceny, highway robbery, and murder, the usual sentence was "*A la Cárcel*" (to jail) where persons were likely to remain about as long for inability to pay *dos reales* as for the worst of crimes; always provided he had not the means to pacify the offended majesty of the law.[12]

---

istration of justice in New Mexico. Barreiro was *asesor* or legal adviser in New Mexico for several years.

[12] Gregg, Josiah, *Commerce of the Prairies*, i, pp. 235-238: "I never heard of but one execution for murder in New Mexico, since the declaration of independence. The most desperate and blood-stained criminals escape with impunity, after a few weeks of incarceration, unless the prosecutor happens to be a person of great influence; in which case, the prisoner is detained in the *calabozo* at will, even when the offense committed has been of a trivial character. Notwithstanding this laxity in the execution of the laws, there are few murders of any kind committed.

"In case of debt, as before remarked, the delinquent is sent to jail — provided the creditor will not accept his services. If he will, however, the debtor becomes *nolens volens* the servant of the creditor till the debt is satisfied; and, serving as he does, at very reduced wages, his expenses for clothing and other necessaries but too often retain him in perpetual servitude. This system does not operate, however, upon the higher classes, yet it acts with terrible severity upon the unfortunate poor, whose condition is but little better, if not worse indeed than that of the slaves of the South. They labor for fixed wages, it is true; but all they can earn is hardly sufficient to keep them in the coarsest clothing and pay their contingent expenses. Men's wages range from two to five dollars per month, and those of women from fifty cents to two dollars; in payment of which, they rarely receive any money; but instead thereof, articles of apparel and other necessaries at the most exorbitant prices. The consequence is that the servant soon accumulates a debt which he is unable to pay, his wages being often engaged for a year or two in advance. Now, according to the usages, if not the laws of the country, he is bound to serve his master until all arrearages are liquidated; and is only enabled to effect an exchange of masters, by engaging another to pay his debt, to whom he becomes in like manner bound.

"Capital crimes and highway robberies are of comparatively rare occurrence in the North, but in smaller delinquencies, such as pilfering and petty rogueries of every shade and description, the common classes can very successfully compete with any other people. Nothing, indeed, can be left exposed or unguarded without great danger of its being immediately stolen. No hus-

TERRITORY OF THE REPUBLIC OF MEXICO

As has been stated, instead of the *alcaldes mayores* of Spanish times, under the Mexican rule there were *ayuntamientos* in the larger settlements, with alcaldes in the smaller. There were also prefects. The prefect was a very important officer and his duties, in many respects, combined those now within the jurisdiction of boards of county commissioners and probate judges. In 1844, by a decree of the *Asamblea*, and published by the governor, the department was divided into three districts and seven partidos.[13]

---

bandman would think of leaving his axe or his hoe, or anything else of the slightest value, lying out over night. Empty wagons are often pillaged of every movable piece of iron, and even the wheels have been carried away.

"The impunity with which delinquencies of this description are every day committed is perhaps in some degree the consequence of those severe enactments, such as the *Leyes de las Indias*, which rendered many thefts and robberies punishable with death. The magistracy contracted the habit of frequently winking at crime, rather than resort to the barbarous expedients prescribed by the letter of the law."

[13] Abert, *Report of the Secretary of War*, pp. 23-24. Lieutenant Abert, while at Santa Fé in 1846-1847, in endeavoring to ascertain the population of New Mexico, found among the archives the following, which gives the information as to population, districts, and counties, as follows:

"MARIANO MARTINEZ DE LEJANZA, brevet brigadier general and Constitutional Governor of the Department of New Mexico, to its inhabitants sends greeting, that the Assembly of the Department has agreed to decree the following:

"The Assembly of the Department of New Mexico, in discharging the powers which are conceded by the 134th article of the organic law of the republic, decrees the following:

"*Division of the Department.*

"ART. 1. The Department of New Mexico, conformably to the 4th article of the constitution, is hereby divided into three districts, which shall be called the Central, the North, and the Southeast. The whole shall be divided into seven counties, and these into three municipalities. The population, according to the statistics which are presented for this purpose, is 100,064. The capital of this Department is Santa Fé.

"*Central District.*

"ART. 2. This district is hereby divided into three counties, which shall be called Santa Fé, Santa Ana, and San Miguel del Bado. The capital of these three counties shall be the City of Santa Fé.

"ART. 3. The first county shall comprise all the inhabitants of Santa Fé, San Ildefonso, Pojoaque, Nambé, Cuyamungue, Tesuque, Rio Tesuque, Cienega, Cieneguilla, Agua Fria, Galisteo, El Real del Oro, and Tuerto. The county seat is Santa Fé. The number of inhabitants is 12,500.

"ART. 4. The second county shall comprise the inhabitants of Rayado, Cochiti, Peña Blanca, Chilili, Santo Domingo, Cubero, San Felipe, Jemez, Cia, Santa Ana, Angostura, and Algodones. The number of inhabitants is 10,500. The county seat is fixed at Algodones.

"ART. 5. The third county shall comprise the inhabitants of Pecos, Gusano, Rio de la Vaca, Mula, Estramosa, San José, San Miguel del Bado, Pueblo,

16 LEADING FACTS OF NEW MEXICAN HISTORY

The first executive of New Mexico under the Mexican republic, with the title of *jefe politico*, was Colonel Antonio Viscarra. The people of New Mexico, by petition, asked for his appointment. He was a native of the province of Chihuahua but had served a number of years in the Spanish army in New Mexico, with headquarters at the presidio of Valverde and also at Santa Fé. Like his predecessor, Don Facundo Melgares, he was a noted Indian fighter, having led many expeditions against the hostile tribes. After he served his first term as *jefe politico*, and about the time that he held the position a second time, probably immediately after the appointment of his successor, Colonel Viscarra commanded the bat-

<small>JEFES POLITICOS
ANTONIO VISCARRA</small>

Puertecito, Cuesta, Cerrito, Anton Chico, Tecolote, Vegas and Sapello. Inhabitants, 18,800. The county seat shall be San Miguel.

"Northern District.

"ART. 6. This district is divided into two counties, called Rio Arriba and Taos. The capital is Los Luceros.

"ART. 7. The county of Rio Arriba comprises the inhabitants of Santa Cruz de la Cañada, Chimayo, Cañada, Truchas, Santa Clara, Vegas, Chama, Cuchillo, Abiquíu, Rito Colorado, Ojo Caliente, Ranchitos, Chamita, San Juan, Rio Arriba, Joya, and Embudo. The county seat is Los Luceros. The number of inhabitants is 15,000.

"ART. 8. The county of Taos comprises the inhabitants of Don Fernandez, San Francisco, Arroyo Hondo, Arroyo Seco, Desmontes, Cienegeuilla, Picuries, Santa Barbara, Trampas, Chamizal, Llano, Peñasco, Mora, Huerfano, and Cimarron. The county seat is Don Fernandez. The number of inhabitants amounts to 14,200.

"Southeastern District.

"ART. 9. This district is divided into two counties, called Valencia and Bernalillo. The capital is Valencia.

"ART. 10. The county of Valencia comprises, Valencia, San Fernando, Tomé, Socorro, Limitar, Polvaderas, Sabinal, Elames, Casa Colorada, Cebolleta, Sabino, Parida, Luis Lopez, Belen, Lunas, Lentes, Zuñi, Acoma and Rito. County seat, Valencia. Number of inhabitants 20,000.

"ART. 11. The county of Bernalillo comprises, Isleta, Padilla, Pajarito, Ranchos de Atrisco, Atrisco, Polaceres, Alburquerque, Alameda, Corrales, Sandia, and Bernalillo. County seat, Bernalillo. Number of inhabitants 8,204. The whole number of inhabitants of the district, 28,204.

"This decree shall be made known to the governor, that he may carry it into execution.

"JESUS MARIA GALLEGOS, President.

"Juan Bautista Vigil y Alarid, Secretary.

"BY VIRTUE OF THE PREMISES, I command that this act be published, circulated, and made known, to all whom it may concern, for its most active observance and fulfillment.

"Palace of the Government, Santa Fé.

"MARIANO MARTINEZ.

"Jose Felix Rubio, Secretary.
"June 17, 1844."

Rt. Rev. José Antonio Laureano de Zubiría, Bishop of Durango
Collections of New Mexico Historical Society

talion of Mexican troops which was occupied in protecting the caravans on the Santa Fé Trail. Colonel Viscarra filled the position of *jefe politico* the first time until the month of June, 1823, and again served as acting *jefe politico* during a portion of the year 1828. In the last named year he was inspector-general of the Mexican forces in the territory.

In the year 1829, under an arrangement made between the government of the United States and the republic of Mexico, it was agreed that detachments of United States troops would guard the great caravans moving from western Missouri to Santa Fé, as far as the Arkansas river, the boundary between the possessions of the United States and those of Mexico under the treaty of 1819. Pursuant to this agreement four companies of the Sixth U. S. Infantry marched across the great plains to a point on the Arkansas near what was known as Chouteau island.[14] One of the officers with this detachment was Lieutenant Philip St. George Cooke,[15] afterward a general in the army of the United States and an officer under General Kearny in 1846. The battalion was under the command of Major Bennett Riley.[16] The republic of Mexico undertook

[14] Chouteau Island was at the upper ford of the Arkansas, just above the present town of Hartland, Kearny county, Kansas. The name of the island dates from the disastrous expedition of 1815-1817, when Chouteau, a trader from St. Louis, Missouri, retreated to the island and resisted an attack from the Indians, finally making his escape.

[15] General Philip St. George Cooke was born in Virginia in 1809, and graduated from the military academy at West Point in 1827. He was an officer in the United States army forty-six years. His first active service was in the Black Hawk War, wherein he served with the regulars at the battle of Bad Axe August 1, 1832; the next year he was appointed lieutenant in the dragoons, and captain two years later. During the war with Mexico, he was with General Kearny in New Mexico and California, returning in time to enter the City of Mexico with General Scott, in 1848. At the beginning of the Civil War, he decided for the Union, and commanded the cavalry in the peninsular campaign. At the close of the war he was successively commander of the departments of the Platte, and of the Great Lakes, retiring in 1873. He died March 20, 1895. He wrote two books, *Scenes and Adventures in the Army*, and *Conquest of New Mexico and California*.

[16] Major Bennett Riley was born in Virginia in 1787 and entered the army as an ensign, from Maryland, in 1813. He was commissioned a captain in 1818 and was breveted major in 1828 for long and efficient service. He was a great Indian fighter and was distinguished for his bravery in the Seminole War. In the Mexican War he was a trusted lieutenant of General Scott, who gave Major Riley great credit for his prowess at Monterey and Cerro Gordo. He was made a brigadier-general in 1848 and in 1849 was sent to California in command of the division of the west; in California he acted as the last territorial governor and aided in forming the constitution of the state. He died in Buffalo, N. Y., in 1853.

to protect the caravans from the Arkansas river to Santa Fé, and Colonel Viscarra was in command of the Mexican troops detailed for that purpose. Indian outrages on the trail from the Missouri river to Santa Fé at this time were particularly numerous and the government had been petitioned by the Santa Fé traders for military protection, which was granted; this escort, however, constituted the only government protection ever afforded to the Santa Fé trade, until 1843, when large escorts under Captain Cooke accompanied two different caravans as far as the Arkansas river.[17]

In the month of August, 1829, shortly after the arrival of the United States troops at the Mexican border, occurred the first invasion of New Mexican territory by American soldiers pursuing hostile Indians, who had attacked a caravan going to Santa Fé.

---

[17] Gregg, Josiah, *Commerce of the Prairies*, i, pp. 27-29: "The fall of 1828 proved still more fatal to the traders on their homeward trip, for by this time the Indians had learned to form a correct estimate of the stock with which return companies were generally provided. Two young men named McNees and Monroe, having carelessly lain down to sleep on the banks of the stream, since known as McNees' creek, were barbarously shot, with their own guns, as it was supposed in very sight of the caravan. When their comrades came up they found McNees lifeless, and the other almost expiring. In this state the latter was carried nearly forty miles to the Cimarron river where he died and was buried according to the custom of the prairies. Just as the funeral ceremonies were about to be concluded, six or seven Indians appeared on the opposite side of the Cimarron. Some of the party proposed inviting them to a parley, while the rest, burning for revenge, evinced a desire to fire upon them at once. It is more than probable, however, that the Indians were not only innocent but ignorant of the outrage that had been committed, or they would hardly have ventured to approach the caravan. Being of quick perception they very soon saw the belligerent attitude assumed by some of the company, and therefore wheeled around and attempted to escape. One shot was fired which wounded a horse and brought the Indian to the ground, when he was instantly riddled with balls! Almost simultaneously another discharge of several guns followed, by which all the rest were either killed or mortally wounded, except one, who escaped to bear his tribe the news of their dreadful catastrophe! These wanton cruelties had a most disastrous effect upon the prospects of the trade; for the exasperated children of the desert became more and more hostile to the pale-faces, against whom they continued to wage a cruel war for many successive years. In fact, this same party suffered very severely a few days afterward. They were pursued by the enraged comrades of the slain savages on the Arkansas river, where they were robbed of nearly a thousand head of mules and horses. But the Indians were not yet satisfied. Having beset a company of about twenty men, who followed shortly after, they killed one of their number, and subsequently took from them all the animals they had in their possession. The unfortunate band were now not only compelled to advance on foot, but were even constrained to carry nearly a thousand dollars each upon their backs to the Arkansas river, where it was *cached* (concealed in the ground) till a conveyance was procured to convey it to the United States."

Major Riley and his command of four companies of infantry crossed the Arkansas and pursued the Indians for two days, but, owing to the fact that the American troops were not mounted accomplished nothing, except the recovery of the body of one of the traders who had been killed and inducing the caravan to proceed on the journey to the capital of New Mexico.[18] The American troops remained in the vicinity of Chouteau island until the return of the caravan in the fall, meanwhile having several skirmishes with the hostile Kiowas,[19] in

AMERICAN AND MEXICAN TROOPS ON THE ARKANSAS

[18] Gregg, Josiah, *Commerce of the Prairies*, i, pp. 29-30: "Such repeated and daring outrages induced the traders to petition the federal government for an escort of United States troops. The request having been granted, Major Riley with three companies of infantry and one of riflemen, was ordered to accompany the caravan which left in the spring of 1829. The escort stopped at Chouteau's island, on the Arkansas river, and the traders thence pursued their journey through the sand-hills beyond. They had hardly advanced six or seven miles, when a startling incident occurred, which made them wish once more for the company of the gallant major and his well disciplined troops. A van-guard of three men, riding a few hundred yards ahead, had just dismounted for the purpose of satisfying their thirst, when a band of Kiowas, one of the most savage tribes that infest the western prairies, rushed upon them from the immense hillocks of sand which lay scattered in all directions. The three men sprang upon their animals but only two who had horses were enabled to make their escape to the wagons; the third, a Mr. Lamme, who was unfortunately mounted upon a mule, was overtaken, slain and scalped before anyone could come to his assistance. Somewhat alarmed at the boldness of the Indians, the traders despatched an express to Major Riley, who immediately ordered his tents struck; and such was the rapidity of his movements, that when he appeared before the anxious caravan everyone was lost in astonishment. The re-enforcement having arrived in the night, the enemy could have obtained no knowledge of the fact, and would no doubt have renewed the attack in the morning, when they would have received a wholesome lesson from the troops, had not the *reveille* been sounded through mistake, at which they precipitately retreated. The escort now continued as far as Sand Creek, when, perceiving no further signs of danger, they returned to the Arkansas, to await the return of the caravan in the ensuing fall."

General Philip St. George Cooke, who was an officer under Major Riley, in his *Scenes and Adventures in the Army*, pp. 47-48, says of this affair: "We reached the encampment at one o'clock at night. All was quiet, and remained so until dawn, when, at the sound of our bugles, the pickets reported they saw a number of Indians moving off. On looking around us, we perceived ourselves and the caravan in the most unfavorable defenseless situation possible — in the arena of a natural amphitheatre of sand-hills, about fifty feet high, and within gun-shot all around. There was the narrowest practicable entrance and outlet. We ascertained that some mounted traders, in spite of all remonstrance or command, had ridden on in advance, and when in the narrow pass beyond this spot had been suddenly beset by about fifty mounted Indians; all fled and escaped, save one, who, mounted on a mule, was *abandoned* by his companions, overtaken and slain."

[19] Mooney, James, in *Handbook of American Indians*, vol. i, pp. 699-700:

which several soldiers were killed and much stock run off by the Indians. Just why the American government sent infantry to the great plains for the purpose of protecting the Santa Fé traders from assaults by the hostile savages, all of whom were well mounted, is not apparent. As it was, the American commander could not send out a small hunting party of his own men, without subjecting them to almost certain attack from the hostiles. The position of Major

---

"A tribe at one time residing about the upper Yellowstone and Missouri, but better known as centering about the upper Arkansas and Canadian in Colorado and Oklahoma and constituting, so far as present knowledge goes, a distinct linguistic stock. They are noticed in Spanish records as early, at least, as 1732. Their oldest tradition, which agrees with the concurrent testimony of the Shoshoni and Arrapaho, locates them about the junction of Jefferson, Madison and Gallatin forks, at the extreme head of the Missouri river, in the neighborhood of the present Virginia City, Montana. They afterward moved down from the mountains and formed an alliance with the Crows, with whom they have since continued on friendly terms. From here they drifted southward along the base of the mountains, driven by the Cheyenne and Arrapaho, with whom they finally made peace about 1840, after which they commonly acted in concert with the latter tribes. The Sioux claim to have driven them out of the Black Hills, and in 1805, they were reported by Lewis and Clark as living on the North Platte. According to the Kiowa account, when they first reached the Arkansas river, they found their passage opposed by the Comanche, who claimed all the country to the south. A war followed, but peace was finally concluded, when the Kiowa crossed over to the south side of the Arkansas and formed a confederation with the Comanche, which continues to the present day. In connection with the Comanche they carried on a constant war upon the frontier settlements of Mexico and Texas, extending their incursions as far south at least as Durango. Among all the prairie tribes they were noted as the most predatory and blood-thirsty, and have probably killed more white men in proportion to their numbers than any of the others. They made their first treaty with the government in 1837, and were put on their present reservation jointly with the Comanche and Kiowa Apache in 1868. Their last outbreak was in 1874-75 in connection with the Comanche, Kiowa, Apache and Cheyenne. While probably never very numerous, they have been greatly reduced by war and disease. Their last terrible blow came in the spring of 1892, when measles and fever destroyed more than three hundred of the three confederated tribes. The Kiowa do not have the gentile system, and there is no restriction as to inter-marriage among the divisions, of which they have six, including the Kiowa Apache associated with them, who form a component part of the Kiowa camp circle. Although brave and warlike, the Kiowa are considered inferior in most respects to the Comanche. In person they are dark and heavily built, forming a marked contrast to the more slender and brighter complexioned prairie tribes farther north. Their language is full of nasal and choking sounds and is not well adapted to rhythmic composition. The present chief is Lone Wolf, but his title is disputed by another chief called Apiatan. They occupied the same reservation with the Comanche and Kiowa Apache, between Washita and Red rivers in southwestern Oklahoma, but in 1901, their lands were allotted in severalty and the remainder opened to settlement. Population, 1,165 in 1905." Consult Mooney, James, *Ghost Dance Religion*, 14th Rep. B. A. E., pt. i, 1896, and *Calendar History of the Kiowa*, 17th Rep. B. A. E., pt. i, 1898.

Fac-simile of Will of Don Juan Antonio Cabeza de Baca

Made in the Canyon de Chelly shortly after receiving a mortal wound in a campaign against the Navajó Indians. The witnesses, Don Francisco Sarracino and Don Santiago Abreu, were prominent men and Indian fighters of the period

Riley on the Arkansas was one of constant and serious danger. Hardly a day was passed without his being subjected to some annoyance from bands of hostile Indians who seemed resolved to check all further concourse of the whites upon the great plains, and fearful of the terrible extremes to which their excesses might be carried, the traders continued to unite in single caravans for mutual protection for many years afterward. Major Riley remained in this vicinity until October, when he met the returning caravan which was escorted as far as the Arkansas by Mexican troops under command of Colonel Viscarra.

Two or three days prior to the arrival, at the Arkansas, of the caravan escorted by Colonel Viscarra,[20] the latter had been visited by several hundreds of Arapahos [21] and Comanches, who were on

---

[20] Cooke, Gen. Philip St. George, *Scenes and Adventures in the Army*, pp. 84-88.

[21] Mooney, James, in *Handbook of American Indians*, vol. i, pp. 72-73: ''An important Plains tribe of the great Algonquian family closely associated with the Cheyennes for at least a century past. They call themselves Inuñaina, about the equivalent to 'our people.' The name by which they are commonly known is of uncertain derivation, but it may possibly be, as Dubar suggests, from the Pawnee *tirapahu* or *larapihu*, 'trader.' By the Sioux and Cheyenne they are called 'Blue-sky men' or 'Cloud men,' the reason for which is unknown. According to the tradition of the Arapaho they were once a sedentary, agricultural people, living far to the north-east of their more recent habitat, apparently about the Red river valley of north Minnesota. From this point they moved south-west across the Missouri, apparently about the time that the Cheyenne moved out of Minnesota, although the date of the formation of the permanent alliance between the two tribes is uncertain. The Atsina, afterward associated with the Siksika, appear to have separated from the parent tribe and moved off toward the north after their emergence into the plain. The division into northern and southern Arapaho is largely geographic, and made permanent by the placing of the two bands on different reservations. The northern Arapaho, in Wyoming, are considered the nucleus or mother tribe and retain the sacred tribal articles, namely, a tubular pipe, one ear of corn and a turtle figurine, all of stone. Since they crossed the Missouri the drift of the Arapaho, as of the Cheyenne and Sioux, has been west and south, the northern Arapaho making lodges on the edge of the mountains about the head of the North Platte, while the southern Arapaho continued down toward the Arkansas. About the year 1840 they made peace with the Sioux, Kiowa and Comanche, but were always at war with the Shoshoni, Ute and Pawnee until they were confined upon reservations, while generally maintaining a friendly attitude toward the whites. By the treaty of Medicine Lodge, in 1867, the southern Arapaho, together with the southern Cheyenne, were placed upon a reservation in Oklahoma, which was thrown open to white settlement in 1892, the Indians at the same time receiving allotments in severalty, with the rights of American citizenship. The northern Arapaho were assigned to their present reservation on Wind River in Wyoming in 1876, after having made peace with their hereditary enemies, the Shoshoni, living upon the same reservation. The Atsina division, usually regarded as a distinct tribe, is associated with the Assinboine on Fort Belknap reservation in

foot and seemed to be on a horse-stealing expedition. They pretended friendship, but, accustomed to the practices of these wily savages, only a guarded intercourse took place. The Indians, however, were bent on mischief and while Colonel Viscarra was holding conversation with one of the Comanche chiefs, the latter being a few steps off, presented his rifle and fired at Viscarra. One of the Pueblo Indians from New Mexico, belonging to the escorting party, who had been most suspicious of the Comanches and stood by closely watching, with heroic devotion, sprang between, just in time to receive the ball through his own heart. Near by stood a brother, who, as the Indian chief turned to fly, sprang upon him like a tiger, and buried his knife to the hilt in his back. Almost at the same instant another chief fell, shot by one of the traders, who had marked him in anticipation of the result. The Indians fled and many of the Mexican escort together with the traders pursued them on horseback. The ammunition of the Indians soon gave out, and their pursuers would overtake them in succession, dismount, fire, take the scalp — without being particular whether the man was dead or not — reload, and pursue again. In this manner many were slain by the Mexican Indians and the traders, and nothing but nightfall saved the entire band from utter annihilation. The Mexican regulars did not participate in this slaughter, but the cruelty and barbarity of the American traders disgusted the Mexicans and Spaniards. One Indian was shot down, unarmed, and, while yet alive and able to contend against it, was brutally scalped by the trader who had overtaken him.

On the evening of the arrival of the caravan Captain Wharton, one of the American officers, extended an invitation to Colonel Vis-

---

Montana. They numbered respectively 889, 859 and 535 in 1904, a total of two thousand two hundred and eighty-three, as against a total of two thousand six hundred and thirty-eight ten years earlier. As a people the Arapaho are brave, but kindly and accommodating, and much given to ceremonial observances. The annual sun-dance is their greatest tribal ceremony, and they were active propagators of the ghost-dance religion a few years ago. In arts and home-life, until within a few years past, they were a typical plains tribe. They bury their dead in the ground, unlike the Cheyenne and Sioux, who deposit them upon scaffolds or on the surface of the ground in boxes. They have the military organization common to most of the plains tribes and have no trace of the clan system.''

See Mooney, *Ghost Dance Religion*, in 14th B. A. E., ii, 1896; Dorsey and Kroeber, *Traditions of the Arapaho*, Field Columb. Mus. Pubs., Anthrop. ser. v, 1903; Dorsey, *Arapaho Sun-Dance*, ibid., iv, 1903.

carra and some of his officers, among them Captain Obrazo and Captain Lobato, to dine at his tent. This was in all probability the first time that Mexican officers, on duty, and in command of Mexican troops, ever partook, on American soil, of the hospitality of an American officer. The account of this dinner and the one given in return by Colonel Viscarra has been preserved to us by General Cooke. Seated cross-legged around a green blanket in the bottom of a tent, the assembled guests were treated to a feast of bread, buffalo meat, and, as an extraordinary rarity, some salt pork, and crowning all were several large raw onions, of the El Paso variety, for which the American captain was indebted to the arrival of the escort, as they were brought from Santa Fé and had doubtless been raised in the *Rio Abajo*. Accompanying this delicious repast and served in a tin-cup was a liberal allowance of whiskey, which like the pork had been reserved for an unusual occasion.

Colonel Viscarra was a man of commanding appearance, dignified, with perfect manners. His horsemanship, extraordinary for a Spaniard, was witnessed by the American officers. An immense drove of horses, the *caballada* with the escort, became suddenly frightened and disposed to run away. Colonel Viscarra, mounted upon a magnificent horse, rode at full speed to prevent it and seemed in many places at once; stopping his horse, with the aid of the unmerciful Spanish bit, in full career, more suddenly than if shot, and throwing him on his haunches, he would whirl him around and cause him to plant the fore foot, with equal speed, in an opposite direction. On the march from Santa Fé Viscarra pursued a noble wild horse, which had baffled all others, and both being at utmost speed, had thrown his *riata* for a fore-foot and caught it. Unfortunately the shock broke the poor animal's leg, when the colonel drew an arrow and shot him through the heart.

COLONEL VISCARRA, INDIAN FIGHTER

On this occasion there was gathered upon the frontier, in all probability the strangest collection of men and animals ever assembled. There were a few Creoles, polished gentlemen, magnificently clothed in Spanish costume; a larger number of grave Spaniards, exiled from Mexico, on their way to the United States, with much property in stock and coin, their entire equipage being Spanish; there was a company of Mexican Regulars, as they were called, in uniform, hardly up to the standard as soldiers; several tribes of Indians and Mexicans, much more formidable as warriors, who stood about in groups, along with their horses, each man armed with a lance and bow and arrows; there were many Frenchmen; added to these was the American command of about one hundred and eighty men, hardy veterans in rags, but well armed and equipped for any service; four or five languages were spoken, and to complete the picture was the *caballada* of more than two thousand horses, mules, and asses (burros), which kept up an incessant braying. The Spaniards and their attendants were in constant motion, throwing the *lazo*, catching wild mules, and dashing headlong after buffalo which seemed disposed to send representatives to this congress of men and animals of all nations.[22]

The American battalion was reviewed and drilled for the edification of the Mexican officers, who were highly pleased. After the review the American officers visited the Mexican camp, where their motley force was drawn up and paraded.

After the parade, the American officers, by invitation, dined with Colonel Viscarra and his officers; his tent was very large and comfortable, oval in shape and very roomy. There were sixteen at the table, all of the service being of silver. This the Americans did not notice particularly in view of the inviting contents, among which was fried ham; this course was followed by another of various kinds of cakes and delightful chocolate; there were several kinds of Mexican wines, all of which had been brought from Santa Fé purposely for this occasion.

In the dusk of the evening a large group of the Mexican Indians came into camp, bearing aloft on their lances the scalps which had been lately taken, and all singing Indian songs; dark figures, with matted hair streaming over their shoulders, uttering the wild notes of their deep-toned choruses, they resembled demons rather than men. Suddenly an Indian would enter the circle and indulge in an extravagant display of grief, beating his forehead and breast and howling like a famished wolf; and then, dashing the scalps to the ground, would stamp upon them and fire his gun at them. After this propitiatory lament to the manes of a departed friend, or relative, he would burst forth, along with the others, into the wildest and most

---

[22] Cooke, Gen. Philip St. George, *Scenes and Adventures in the Army*, p. 86.

Courtesy of Fred. Harvey
Costumes of the Ricos during the first quarter of the Nineteenth Century

unearthly song of triumph and exaltation. The Indian who had lost and avenged his brother had been in camp that day; he seemed a fine man but was inconsolable. He made speeches to the Americans, unintelligible of course, but expanding his bare chest and striking it with great force with his palm, he would end each sentence in his own tongue with "Me die for *los Americanos*." [23]

On the 14th of October the day of parting came and Colonel Viscarra and his entire force began the return march to Santa Fé, while Major Riley, guarding the immense caravan, returned to Fort Leavenworth on the Missouri river.

Colonel Viscarra held the office of *jefe politico* until the month of June, 1823, when he was succeeded by Don Francisco Javier Chavez, who served as acting *jefe politico* for two months and was in turn succeeded by Don Bartolomé Baca, who held the office until September, 1825.[24]

---

[23] Cooke, Gen. Philip St. George, *Scenes and Adventures in the Army*, p. 88.

[24] List of *jefes politicos* and *gobernadores* from 1823 to 1846: Colonel Antonio Viscarra to June, 1823; Don Francisco Javier Chavez, acting during the months of June and July, 1823; Don Bartolomé Baca from 1823 to September, 1825. Colonel Antonio Narbona, September, 1825, to May, 1827; General Manuel Armijo, 1827, 1828; Colonel Antonio Viscarra, acting in 1828; Don José Antonio Chavez, 1828 to 1831; Don Santiago Abreu, 1831-1833; Don Francisco Sarracino, 1833; Don Juan Rafael Ortiz, during a part of 1834; Don Francisco Sarracino, 1835; Don Mariano Chavez, acting from May to July, 1835; Colonel Albino Perez, 1835-1837; Don Pedro Muñoz, acting 1837-8; Colonel José Gonzales, revolutionist, 1837-1838; General Manuel Armijo from January, 1838, to 1846, during which last named period the following acted in that capacity: Antonio Sandoval, in 1841; Mariano Martinez de Lejanza, in 1844-45; José Chavez, 1845; J. B. Vigil y Alarid, 1846.

Francisco Javier Chavez was a native of Belen, Valencia county, New Mexico, where he was born in the year 1780. He married Ana Maria Castillo, a native of the same place. There were nine children of this marriage; Barbara, who married Juan Gutierrez of Pajarito; Mariano, who married Dolores Perea of Bernalillo; José, who married Manuela Armijo of Los Ranchos de Alburquerque; Manuela Antonia, who married José Maria Gutierrez of Bernalillo; Antonio José David, who married Barbara Armijo of Los Ranchos de Alburquerque; Francisca, who married Antonio José Otero of Peralta; Mercedes, who married Juan Perea of Bernalillo, the father of Col. Francisco Perea; Dolores, who married José Leandro Perea of Bernalillo; Tomas, who, when twelve years of age was sent to Durango, Mexico, to receive his education. He never returned to New Mexico and little is known of him, other than the fact that he became an eminent lawyer and judge, noted for his impartiality and fairness; he married a Miss Zubiria of Durango, a niece of the bishop of that diocese; José Maria Gutierrez, the husband of Manuela Antonia, was murdered by the Apaches between Tecolote and Bernal Springs in San Miguel county, in the fall of 1846, shortly after the American occupation. Antonio José David was murdered by a band of Texan outlaws near Chavez creek in the state of Kansas. Two of the sons of Francisco Javier Chavez served as governor of New Mexico, the first in 1835, Mariano

During his first incumbency of the office Colonel Viscarra waged war upon the Navajós who were constantly making raids upon the settlers in the Rio Grande and adjacent settlements. He led the forces of the territory in person in all of his campaigns, as did also each one of his successors in office. In the month of February, 1823, he made a treaty with the Navajós, by which captives were restored; the Indians, however, were unable to pay for the many robberies of sheep and cattle which had been committed by them, as they claimed that large numbers of their tribe were dying of hunger owing to a failure of crops in the Indian country. A limited time was given them within which to make settlement for their many robberies.

During the administration of Captain Bartolomé Baca more troubles were had with the Navajós and Apaches, but owing to the pronounced activity of the executive they were soon suppressed. The system of treaties and bribes was in vogue and the majority of the tribes found it to their interest to remain on peaceful relations with the Mexican people. In 1824, a Kentuckian by the name of Pattie, an Indian trader and trapper, happened to be in Santa Fé with a large company of frontiersmen when news came to the capital of a raid by the Comanches upon the people living upon the Pecos river, east of Santa Fé. It was claimed that a number of settlers had been killed by the Indians, including two Americans; that one American and four Spanish women, one of whom was the daughter of a former governor of New Mexico, had been taken prisoner and were being carried away by the Indians. The whole city was soon filled with great excitement. The narration of the facts in connection with this affair as given by Pattie is very interesting. He says [25] that early in the morning following the news of the raid by the Indians the governor came to their camp and asked if the Americans would not aid in the attempt to recapture the prisoners who had been taken. Pattie and

INDIAN FIGHTS — PATTIE'S EXPERIENCES

---

and José in 1845. Don Antonio José Chavez who served as governor from 1828 to 1831, succeeding Governor Manuel Armijo, was a near relative of the elder Chavez. Four grandsons of governor Chavez served as delegates in congress from the territory of New Mexico; Francisco Perea in the 38th congress, J. Francisco Chavez, in the 39th, 40th and 41st congresses, Mariano S. Otero, in the 46th congress, and Pedro Perea in the 56th congress. Governor Chavez had one sister, Ursula, who in middle life married Governor Antonio Sandoval.

[25] Pattie, *Personal Narrative*, pp. 78-80, vol. i.

his companions readily agreed to comply with the request of the governor as they were anxious to be on good terms with the authorities and the people, and very shortly the entire force of Americans set off with the Mexican command, the latter consisting of approximately four hundred men, all mounted. Within twenty-four hours the place where the murders had been committed was reached. From the trail left by the departing Indians it was apparent that they were in considerable force and were moving rapidly in the direction of the plains in eastern New Mexico. All night long the rescuing party pressed forward and as they proceeded found the Indian fires still smoking. At eight o'clock on the morning of the 15th of December, 1824, the trail being very fresh, the command proceeded with great rapidity and by noon came in sight of the Indians advancing toward a low gap in the mountains. The governor called a council of the officers and it was unanimously determined that Pattie be given command, the Mexicans promising obedience to him in every respect. Through the gap in the mountains flowed a small stream. The Indians were now entering this gap; immediately a plan was formed by Pattie, by which the Mexican force was commanded to keep in the rear of the Indians. The Americans took a circuitous route screened from the hostiles by a small table-land and endeavored to gain unobserved a small hollow in advance of the savages. The Mexicans were to close in on the Indians immediately upon hearing the discharge of the American rifles. The Americans succeeded in reaching the hollow, in which they formed themselves into half circle, the horses being tied in the rear. Every man was ordered to prime his gun; the right flank was ordered to fire first, the left reserving its fire, thus giving the right a time to re-load. The Indians surrounding the prisoners were to be killed if possible by the first discharge, thus preventing the immediate murder of their captives. An hour and a half the Americans waited in their ambush for the approaching savages. Finally they came in sight, the captive women, without any clothing, driving a large drove of sheep and horses. Immediately following were the Indians. When within about forty yards, the order to fire was given. The women immediately ran toward the Americans; three were pierced by the lances of the savages; the cry now raised was, "Save the women!" A son of Pattie and another young man sprang forward, rescuing the two remaining. Pattie's companion fell in the attempt. An Indian raised his lance to inflict death upon another unfortunate captive, when he was shot by one of the Americans. The captives, one of whom was very beautiful and the daughter of the governor referred to, were quickly wrapped in blankets for it was very cold.

The savages stood the second fire and then retreated. The Americans immediately gave pursuit, expecting every moment to hear the report of the Mexican guns in the rear, but the entrance to the plain was in sight before the Mexican muskets were heard. The Indians now began to yell and the Mexicans broke and fled. The Indians did not pursue, but satisfied as to the small force of Americans, now that they were out upon the plain, soon rallied and rushed upon them. Pattie ordered a retreat to the pine trees, which were soon reached. From this point a destructive fire was poured into the advancing Indians, who returned it bravely, still pressing forward. The battle waged fiercely for about ten minutes, when the Indians again began to retreat and were soon in full flight, pursued by the Mexicans, who still took good care not to come near enough to the fleeing Comanches to hurt them or receive any injury themselves. In this engagement the Americans lost ten men, Commander Pattie being severely wounded in the shoulder. A large number of the Indians were slain.[26]

---

[26] The younger Pattie in his *Personal Narrative* says: "We removed our horses and the rescued captives into the plain, and encamped. The Spaniards (the frontiersman at this time always designated the Mexican as a Spaniard) had killed an Indian already wounded, and were riding over the dead bodies of those on the ground, spearing them and killing any who still breathed. My father commanded them to desist, or he would fire upon them, and the Spanish officer added his order to the same effect. The latter then demanded of us the two women whom we had rescued, with as much assurance as though he himself had been the cause of their deliverance. My father replied, by asking what authority or right he had to make much a request, when his cowardice withheld him from aiding in their release? The officer became enraged and said that he was unable to rally his men, and that he did not consider the captives any safer in our hands than in those of the Indians, as we were not christians (meaning catholics). This insult coupled with such a lame apology only made my father laugh, and reply that if cowardice constituted a claim to christianity, himself and his men were prime and undoubted christians. He added further, that if the rescued women preferred to accompany him, rather than remain until he should have buried his brave comrades, who fell in their defense, and accept his protection, he had nothing to say. The subjects of our discussion, being present while it took place, decided the point before they were appealed to. The youngest said, that nothing would induce her to leave her deliverers, and that when they were ready to go, she would accompany them, adding, that she should pray hourly for the salvation of those, who had

Earliest Method of Transportation over the Santa Fé Trail

Having buried their dead the Americans saddled their horses and began the return trip to Santa Fé. Having traveled all day and night, at noon the day following they reached Pecos, where they were met by the father of the youngest of the two ladies, accompanied by a great crowd of Mexicans. The old man was transported almost to frenzy when he saw his daughter. Remaining here during

resigned their lives in the preservation of hers. The other expressed herself willing to remain with her, and manifested the same confidence and gratitude. The enraged officer and his men set off on their return to Santa Fé.''

Davis, W. W. H., in *El Gringo*, pp. 217-218, does not agree with young Pattie as to the courage of the times. Davis could see but very little commendable in the Mexican of the times. Davis could see but very little commendable in the Mexican and still says: ''I believe the Mexicans have been unjustly accused of cowardice as a race, and denied the attributes of personal courage that belong to every other people. In looking at the source whence they sprung, we see no reason why they should not possess all the physical virtues that belong to the human race. In former times the Spaniard was justly celebrated for his gallantry and courage, for proof of which we need only cite his conquest of a large portion of the two Americas, in which he encountered every hardship that falls to the lot of a soldier. In those days the Spanish infantry was among the best soldiery in the world. The history of the Moorish battlefields establishes the courage of that race beyond a doubt; and the manner in which the American Indians have ever resisted the approach of white settlers settles the question as to them. Hence we find the blood of three brave races uniting in their veins, and there is every reason why they should possess the ordinary amount of courage. In the late war between the United States and Mexico, the rank and file of the Mexican army, in many instances, exhibited a bravery that would have done honor to any troops in the world; and upon the frontiers of New Mexico, in their conflicts with the Indians, the peasantry have frequently behaved in the most gallant manner. That which has given appearance in the field of cowardice has been a lack of confidence in their officers, which begat a lack of reliance in themselves. The great body of the population have ever been an oppressed and down-trodden people, and have never received from their superiors that kind of treatment which fosters courage. At home, their manhood has been almost crushed out of them; and when led to the field, they had no interest in the contest, and nothing to fight for. They had been so long taught to believe themselves an inferior race, and destitute of manly attributes, that they came to believe this their condition, and ceased to have confidence in themselves. With American officers to lead them, they will make excellent troops; and they possess a power of endurance under fatigue which excels most other people.

''An evidence both of their patriotism and courage came under my observation. In the month of January, 1855, the governor of the Territory called for a battalion of mounted volunteers to assist the regulars in chastising the Indian tribes who were in hostile array, and in a very few days more companies offered their services than could be accepted. They served for a period of six months; and it is the unanimous testimony of the United States officers who were on duty with them, that in all the conflicts with the enemy they exhibited a courage equal to, and power of endurance greater than the troops of the line. They were ever among the foremost in the fight, and were noted for their good order and discipline; and I am justified in saying that a desire to serve the country sent them into the field, since the greater part of them had nothing to lose from Indian depredations.''

the remainder of the day and night the following morning they started for Santa Fé, the governor insisting that the two Patties must ride with him in his carriage, but this honor was declined, the two Americans riding alongside in company with the interpreter. The old governor was very lavish in his praises of the Americans, caressing and embracing them repeatedly, and saying a great many things, which the younger Pattie declares he did not believe he deserved. The day following they arrived at the capital where they were received with a salute from the garrison artillery.[27]

[27] "The governor came in the evening, and invited my father and the interpreter to sup with him. He ordered some fat beeves to be killed for the rest of us. The father of Jacoba, for that was the name of the young lady I had rescued, came and invited us all to go and drink coffee at his son-in-law's, who kept a coffee-house. We went, and when we had finished our coffee, the father came and took me by the hand, and led me up a flight of steps, and into a room, where were his two daughters. As soon as I had entered the room Jacoba and her sister both came and embraced me, this being the universal fashion of interchanging salutations between men and women among these people, even when there is nothing more than a simple introduction between strangers. After I had been seated an hour, looking at them, as they made signs, and listening to their conversation, of which I did not understand a syllable, I arose with the intention of returning to my companions for the night, but Jacoba, showing me a bed, prepared for me, placed herself between me and the door. I showed her that my clothes were not clean. She immediately brought me others belonging to her brother-in-law. I wished to be excused from making use of them, but she seemed so much hurt, that I finally took them, and re-seated myself. She then brought me my leather hunting shirt, which I had taken off to aid in protecting her from the cold, and begged the interpreter, who was now present, to tell me, that she intended to keep it as long as she lived. She then put it on, to prove to me that she was not ashamed of it. I went to bed early, and arose and returned to my companions before any of the family were visible. At eight the governor and my father came to our quarters, and invited us all to dine with him at two in the afternoon. Accordingly we all dressed in our best and went at the appointed time. A band of musicians played during dinner. After it was finished, and the table removed, a fandango was begun. The ladies flocked in, in great numbers. The instruments to which the dancers moved, were a guitar and a violin. Six men and six women also added their voices. Their mode of dancing was a curiosity to me. The women stood erect, moving their feet slowly, without any spring or motion of the body, and the men half-bent, moved their feet like drum sticks."

Inasmuch as Pattie refers to the costume of the frontiersman of the time, it has seemed desirable to give a description of the wearing apparel of the mountaineer. Prof. Sylvester Waterhouse, of Washington University, St. Louis, Mo., in an article appearing in the *Encyclopedia* of St. Louis, says: "Partly from inclination and partly from necessity the hunter in his dress adopted the customs of the Indians. The clothes which he brought from the States quickly fell to pieces under the wear and tear of the life in which he was engaged. The Indian costume was the most convenient substitute. There was moreover a manifest pride on the part of the hunter in imitating the garb of his red brethren, and it is doubtful if the fondness of the latter for the incongru-

The hardy frontiersmen of this day had but a poor opinion of the "Spaniards" — as they designated them — as fighters, and Pattie was no exception to the rule. It must be remembered, however, that the Mexicans engaged in the battle of which he gives an account were nearly all civilians from the capital, and it is more than likely that the Mexican officer was correct in his statement to the elder Pattie that it had been impossible for him to rally his men. Again, there was hardly a tribe of Indians upon the plains for whom the Mexicans had so much fear as the Comanche. This Indian was a very dangerous and courageous foe and the Spaniards and Mexicans held him in great respect as a warrior. Long after the occupation of the territory by the Americans the Comanche Indians were recognized as fearless and relentless foes. They were hunters of and lived off the buffalo, and in their expeditions after the great quadruped roamed as far north as the thirty-eighth parallel of latitude; and, passing the Rio Grande five hundred miles from their homes, they occasionally invaded the dominions of Mexico to within three hundred miles of her capital. In small parties and unsupported, they would penetrate to the densest settlements

CAMPAIGNS AGAINST COMANCHES, APACHES, AND NAVAJÓS

---

ous combinations of his own and the white man's clothing was more marked than that of the hunter for the wild attire of the savage. The head-dress in summer usually consisted of a light handkerchief, adjusted in the style of a turban so as to be attractive in appearance while serving as a protection against heat and insects. The upper part of the body was clad in a light blue shirt of coarse cotton or other cloth, and in some cases, breeches with long deerskin leggings were worn, leaving the thighs and hips bare. The cloth which was folded around the loins was held in place by the girdle, while a 'hunting-shirt with a large cape and loose sleeves reached nearly to the knees. . . It opened in front like a coat and was made so large as to lap at least a foot across the breast. The folds of the bosom served the purpose of a pocket. . . The moccasin was made of a single piece of heavy dressed buckskin. A plain seam ran from the heel to the ankle, but the upper part, from the toe to the instep, was gathered. The shoe thread was the sinews of deer or of buckskin.' In winter the clothing as just described was materially increased, both in quantity and quality. The hunting shirt was made of dressed deer-skin. A heavy hooded cloak, called a capote, was thrown over the shoulders. The tops of the moccasins were made with long folds which could be wrapped around the ankles and the interior was lined with wool or deer-hair. All portions of this picturesque attire, whether for summer or winter use, were ornamented with gay embroidery, fringes, bead-work, hair, feathers, and other gewgaws. A belt hung over the left shoulder and under the right arm in which the ammunition for his rifle was carried. In leather bags attached to his girdle were his knife and hatchet and material for mending his moccasins, while his few remaining equipments were bestowed upon other portions of his body.''

of the northern states of Mexico, and in broad daylight, and nearly unopposed, carry into captivity hundreds of human beings and thousands of horses and mules, oftentimes laying under contribution populous towns, and even large cities. To the Mexican, the Comanche was an object of great terror. The very sight of a half-naked Comanche, with his shaggy horse, his lance, and his quiver of arrows produced a perfect paralysis of fear. Shut up in their walled and closely barred villages, the Mexicans, as a rule, would look forth despairingly upon one-third of their number of armed Comanches, ravaging the fields and haciendas under their very eyes, and carrying off into hopeless captivity the miserable women and children who had not succeeded in making good their escape. Under the uncontrollable influence of this singular and despicable apprehension it does not seem strange that the Mexican people should have attached so much value to American protection from these Indians,[28] nor that they should have insisted with so much earnestness upon inserting, in the treaty of Guadalupe Hidalgo, the provision relative to guarding the frontier from the ravages of these desert marauders. Whenever the Comanche took Mexican women and children captives, they took the women as wives and made servants of the boys; the men, after a probation more or less lengthy, were adopted into the tribe, most generally in a dependent condition.[29]

---

[28] Pope, Brevet Captain John, *Report of Exploration of a Route for the Pacific Railroad*, p. 14: "It is related that a single Comanche, even at midday, dashed at speed into the public square of the City of Durango, and by his mere presence caused the hasty closing of the stores and public places of the city, and the rapid retreat of a population of thirty thousand souls to their barred houses. He remained an hour roaming through the deserted streets and was only captured by being lassoed from the window of a house as he was riding triumphantly but carelessly from the suburbs. Such an occurrence must appear amazing to the last degree to an American, who has been accustomed to deal with the Indian upon terms of advantage."

[29] *Ibid.*, p. 15: "Of the many I have seen thus held in captivity, I have never yet met one who was willing to return to his home or his country. In the women this feeling is not difficult to understand. They have all been subjected to the inhuman but invariable outrages which are perpetrated by Indians upon their female prisoners when captured; and they afterwards most probably form attachments to the warriors who have taken them to wife, and by whom they have borne children, who enjoy every privilege of the most favored of the tribe. In the men the feeling is more difficult to understand. Their cowed and sullen look, and shuffling, timid manner, sufficiently betray the position they occupy; and their avowed reluctance to return to their homes is probably due to a fear of the punishment which the expression of such a wish would be certain to bring upon them."

Early Trappers, Traders, Plainsmen, and Mountaineers
1. James Magoffin. 2. Dr. Josiah Gregg. 3. Lucien B. Maxwell. 4. Antoine Robidoux. 5. James P. Beckwourth. 6. Dick Wootton. 7. James Bridger. 8. William Bent. 9. Ceran St. Vrain

It is certain that whenever the Mexican was successful in the many campaigns conducted against these Indians, his treatment of Indian captives was not at all commendatory. Quarter was rarely shown and the life of no adult warrior was ever spared. The Mexican soldier, whether in the regular army or volunteer, rarely showed mercy or pity and scalped the Indian or cut off his ears with the same spirit of cruelty and revenge as characterized the deeds of the most demoniac savage of the plains.

In truth, whether waging campaigns against the Comanche, the Apache, the Ute, or the Navajó, the Mexican was as relentless as the Indian. In treating with the tribes of the plains the American officer seldom found the Indian willing to agree to maintain terms of friendship with the Mexican, whom he always regarded as a foe. The Indian and the Mexican both knew what to expect should the one fall into the hands of the other.[30] Many years after the achieve-

[30] Bartlett, *Personal Narrative*, p. 174. Mr. Bartlett describes an event in the Indian fighting of the southwest which shows how the Indian was treated when in the power of the Mexican. He says: ''In a deep cleft in the rock, on the south side of the road, which we followed for one hundred and fifty feet into the interior, were many bones of wild beasts. Near this the hills expand, forming an amphitheatre, which is celebrated from its being the place where the Apaches used formerly to hold councils, and the scene of a contest between them and the Mexicans. The Indians had been committing some depredations and murders in the settlements, and, being pursued, were traced to the Waco mountains. A party set off from El Paso, and surprised them in the narrow space or amphitheatre alluded to. The besieged retreated as far as possible; and finding no chance to escape, they built a wall across the entrance, which is about one hundred feet from one perpendicular mass of rock to the other. Here they were kept several days, when they were finally overcome, and all, to the number of one hundred and fifty, put to death.''

Ruxton, in his *Adventures in Mexico and the Rocky Mountains*, 1848, p. 157 et seq., relates an occurrence of particularly barbarous treatment of the Apaches by the Mexicans. In writing of conditions existing in northern portions of the state of Chihuahua and southern New Mexico, he says: ''It is infested with hostile Indians, who ravage the whole country. . . These Indians are the Apaches, who inhabit the ridges and plains of the Cordillera, the Sierra Madre on the west and the tracts between the Conchos and Del Norte on the east, while scattered tribes roam over all parts of the state, committing devastations on the ranchos and haciendas, and depopulating the remote villages. For the purpose of carrying on a war against the daring savages, a species of company was formed by the Chihuahueños, with a capital raised by subscription. The company, under the auspices of the government, offered a bounty of fifty dollars a scalp, as an inducement to people to undertake a war of extermination against the Apaches. One Don Santiago Kirker (James Kirker) an Irishman, long resident in Mexico, and for many years a trapper and Indian trader in the Far West, whose exploits in Indian-killing would fill a volume, was placed at the head of a band of some hundred and fifty men, including several Shawnee and Delaware Indians, and sent *en campaña* against the Apaches. . . In the month of August, the Apaches being then '*en paz*' with

ment of independence by the Mexicans, and up to the period of the occupation of New Mexico and Texas by the troops of the government of the United States, the Comanches were accustomed to equip large expeditions, which, traversing the state of Texas and portions of eastern New Mexico by various routes, and passing the Rio Grande at numerous points in its course, even as low down as Matamoras, laid waste the northern states of the republic. They sent raiding parties up the Pecos river as far as the settlements in the neighborhood of the present town of San Miguel, ravaging all the territory in the neighborhood of Las Vegas and adjoining settlements; their raids upon the towns situate upon the eastern bank of the Rio Grande were frequent, one upon the plaza of Tomé being particularly noteworthy; on one occasion they captured the town of Galisteo and compelled the inhabitants to perform all sorts of menial service. Under the policy of the United States government immediately subsequent to the acquisition of New Mexico under the treaty of Guadalupe Hidalgo, a chain of military posts was established enclosing the extreme settlements; this seriously interrupted the excursions of the Comanche and as a consequence their marauding parties to the frontiers of Mexico were conducted through routes lying largely in the eastern portions of New Mexico. Later on posts were established as far to the west as the valley of the Rio Grande.

In all probability the tribes with whom the Mexicans had the most trouble were the Apaches and the Navajós. The Apaches at

---

the state, entered, unarmed, the village of Galeana, for the purpose of trading. This band, which consisted of a hundred and seventy, including women and children, was under the command of a celebrated chief, and had, no doubt, committed many atrocities on the Mexicans; but at this time they had signified their desire for peace to the government and were now trading in good faith and under protection of the faith of the treaty. News of their arrival having been sent to Kirker, he immediately forwarded several kegs of spirits, with which they were to be regaled, and detained in the village until he could arrive with his band. On a certain day, about ten in the morning, the Indians being at the time drinking, dancing and amusing themselves, and unarmed, Kirker sent forward a messenger to say that at such an hour he would be there. The Mexicans, when they saw him approach with his party, suddenly seized their arms and set upon the unfortunate Indians, who, without even their knives, attempted no resistance, but, throwing themselves on the ground when they saw Kirker's men surrounding them, submitted to their fate. The infuriated Mexicans spared neither age nor sex; with fiendish shouts they massacred their unresisting victims, glutting their long pent-up revenge of many years of persecution. A hundred and sixty men, women, and children were slaughtered.''

F. X. Aubrey, Pathfinder

this time and for many years afterward were the most numerous of the Indians in New Mexico. They roamed along both sides of the Rio Grande from the Navajó country in the north to the extreme southern line of the territory and from thence over the states of Chihuahua, Sonora, and Durango, in Mexico. Their range to the east was as far as the Pecos valley and they roamed the deserts and mountainous regions of western New Mexico, now Arizona, as far as the Pima villages on the Gila river. They were divided into numerous bands, each of which took its name from the district of country in which it was most frequently found, and all of which were under the control of separate and independent chiefs. It was never possible to control these Indians during the Mexican sovereignty, as they not only infested the entire portion of New Mexico but carried their depredations and plundering forays as far south as the city of Durango itself. The valley of the Rio Grande below the parallel of 33° 30' was midway between the haunts of the Mescaleros or White Mountain Apaches and the Gila or Copper Mine and Mimbres river members of this tribe; as a consequence, along the valley of the Rio Grande and the highway known as the *Jornada del Muerto*, most of their depredations were committed, although they often raided the settlements in the vicinity of Socorro and other settlements much farther north. It was always a very difficult matter for the Mexicans to keep the route between El Paso and Valverde open so that travelers or trains would be approximately safe in making the journey from New Mexico to Chihuahua. The Apache would lie in wait along portions of the route remote from settlements, for small parties and unprotected trains, and having plundered both travelers and wagons, would rapidly retreat to the fastnesses of the mountains east and west of the river. The Apaches, except on a very limited scale, were not an agricultural people; their country did not abound in game, and no treaties or inducements could for any length of time restrain their plundering expeditions into the settlements of New Mexico. Prior to the advent of the Spaniard they had ravaged the towns and villages of the sedentary tribes. The Apache was entirely different in his characteristics from the majority of the tribes of the great plains; he was less intelligent, less bold, and had none of the war-like tastes or accomplishments of the Pawnee, the Kiowa, or the Sioux and other

Indians of the north. Their sole object was plunder and murder; they were entirely destitute of the ambition or courage to distinguish themselves by war-like achievements. Their war expeditions were directed to the plundering of small ranchos or settlements, the driving off of flocks of sheep and other live stock, and the murder of miserable and helpless shepherds and remote settlers. They were prone to carry off the children from these settlements and either adopt them into the tribe or reduce them to a miserable servitude. They were the relentless enemy of the Spaniard and Mexican.[31] Insofar as the taking of captives and reducing them to slaves was concerned the Apache acquired this custom from the Spaniard or Mexican, and it is safe to say that during the period of which I write there was not a settlement in the valley of the Rio Grande that did not number among the inhabitants a large number of Apache and Navajó Indian slaves. This custom continued down to the time of the American occupation in 1846, and later.[32]

As has been said these Indians, occupying the mountain fastnesses east and west, were in the habit of descending upon the valley of the Rio Grande as far north as the town of Socorro, and oftentimes upon settlements much farther to the north and east and as far to the south as San Elizario, in Texas. They could make their raids and drive off great herds of cattle and sheep before intelligence of their presence could be made known at the larger places where there would be a garrison of regulars or a company of *vecinos* or militia. The Apache would never stand and fight; he would rarely attack a force of Spaniards or Mexicans having as many as ten persons in the party. The great difficulty in controlling or chastising them consisted in the impossibility of overtaking or bringing them to an engagement. Upon the approach of a body of armed men, they would scatter like quail to all points of the compass over the mountains and trails, and only re-unite at some point far removed from danger. On their wiry and active ponies they were able to scale

---

[31] Pattie, *Personal Narrative*, p. 113.

[32] Pattie, *ibid.*, p. 113: "These poor creatures are bought and sold like horses or mules, and it seems rather too much to expect that the Indians shall deliver up the Mexican prisoners in their possession to the authorities which countenance openly the sale and slavery of numbers of their tribe. So far as three years' experience in the country has enabled me to judge, it has seemed to me that the amount of robbery is about equal between the lower classes of New Mexicans and the Indians, whose herds of stock are frequently together."

Reprint from Emory's Account, 1846

Ruins of Old Pecos Mission

heights apparently impracticable and rush at headlong speed through the most difficult and dangerous passes of the mountains. Against such a foe as this it is easy to understand how difficult it was for the Spaniard and Mexican with his limited force and numbers to cope, and it is still easier to realize that the Mexican had long concluded that the only warfare against the Apache was one of extermination, if not by fair means, then by any which circumstances might provide.

In the fall of 1825 the two Patties, who have been mentioned, were engaged in working at the copper mines at Santa Rita, in what is now Grant county, New Mexico. The experiences of these men with the Apaches and the treaty of peace which was made by them with some of the chiefs of the tribe in that district clearly demonstrates the mutual hatred existing at that time beween the Spaniard and Mexican and their ancient foes. One day young Pattie and two companions were out hunting deer, when they discovered the trail of six Indians approaching the mines. Following the trail for about a mile they came upon the Indians, who immediately fled. The Americans pursued and soon overtook them, when one of the Indians dodged into a ravine, where he was quickly surrounded. As soon as he saw that it was impossible for him to escape, the Indian threw away his bow and arrows and begged the Americans not to kill him. One of the men rode up to him, while the other two stood with guns cocked ready to shoot if he made the least sign or motion to secure his weapons. The Indian, however, remained perfectly quiet and was quickly tied by the hands and driven ahead toward the mines. The party had gone only about a hundred yards when the Indian pointed out a hollow tree, intimating that another Indian was concealed there. He was ordered to instruct his companion to make no resistance or he would be killed. The Indian immediately came out with his bow and his hands were tied in the same manner as the other's. They were taken to the mines and put in prison. The Mexicans who were working at the mines, exasperated with their recent cruelties and murders, were determined to kill them, but their lives were spared owing to the interference of the Americans. On the day following the Indians were questioned and one of them was told to leave the camp and tell his chief to come in, with all his warriors and make peace. One Indian was detained as a hostage, the other being assured that if the chief did not come in and make peace his companion would be put to death. After the Indian had left, the elder Pattie, by way of precaution, put in requisition all the arms that could be found in the neighborhood of the mines with which he armed thirty of the Mexicans working there. He then ordered a trench dug at a point one hundred yards distant from the place where the Indians were to meet with him for the consummation of the treaty. This trench was to be occupied during the consideration of the treaty, ready for any emergency should the Indians prove insolent or menacing in their conduct.

On the fifth of August, the Indians to the number of eighty appeared. A council fire, pipe and tobacco had been prepared and a blanket spread upon which the chief might be seated. As soon as the Indians appeared they threw down their arms; four chiefs came up and all, including the two Patties, sat down upon the blanket. The subject of the treaty was discussed; the Indians were asked whether they were ready to make peace, and if not, what were their objections? They replied that they had no objections to a peace with the Americans, but would never make one with the Spaniards. When asked their reasons they replied that they had been at war with the Spaniards for many years and that a great many murders had been committed by both sides. They admitted that they had stolen a great many horses, but indignantly alleged that a large party of their people, who had come in for the purpose of making peace with the Spaniards, when once within the walls of the town where the peace was to be negotiated, had been brutally butchered like a flock of sheep. The very few who had escaped had taken an unalterable resolution never to make peace with the Spaniards; further stating that pursuant to their determination for revenge, great numbers of the Apache nation had gone to the Spaniards and had been baptized; there they remained faithful spies, informing their kinsmen when and where there were favorable opportunities for plundering and killing their enemies.

TREATY WITH APACHES— CEREMONIES

The chiefs were told that if they really felt disposed to be at peace with the Americans, the copper mines were now being worked jointly by the latter and Spaniards; that the Indians were wrong in seeking revenge upon people who were not guilty of the crimes which they had mentioned; that the Spaniards at the mines had taken no part in the inhuman butchery which they had mentioned, and that if they would not be peaceable and permit the work at the mines to proceed without danger from them, the Americans would consider them at war and would raise a sufficient body of men to pursue them to the mountains and kill them. The chiefs answered that if the mines belonged to the Americans, they would promise never to disturb the people who worked them. They were of this opinion and the Americans did not undeceive them as to the real ownership. The pipe was then lit and all the Indians gathered in a circle around the fire. The four chiefs, in succession, made long speeches; the others nodding their heads at times, listened with profound attention. The Americans then commenced smoking and the pipe was passed around the circle. The Indians dug a hole in the center of the circle, and each one spat in it. The hole was then filled up with earth, they danced around it and stuck their arrows in the ground. A large pile of stones was next placed over the place and the Indians decorated their faces and bodies with red paint. This was the Apache ceremony of making peace. All of the forms of the ceremony were familiar, except the pile of stones and the spitting into the hole which they had excavated; among the Indians of the plains this part was not practised; they were asked why they had done this and they replied that they did it in token of spitting out all their spite and revenge, and burying their anger. These ceremonies consumed several hours and were finally concluded. The Americans then showed the Indians the reserve force in the trench. They evinced great alarm at the sight of the Mexicans so close and ready for action. It was explained to them that the Americans were in good faith if they were and that the Mexicans had been thus posted only to fire in the event the Indians showed any disposition for violence. Their fears vanished and tranquillity returned to the countenances of the Indians. The chiefs laughed and said to each other, these Americans know how to fight as well as make peace. The chief displayed utter contempt for the Mexicans, saying that if we ever had a fight, we would have to get Americans entirely, for the Mexicans would be sure to desert in time of action. The entire company then proceeded to the copper mines, where three fat beeves were killed for food for the Indians. After they had eaten and were in excellent humor, the head chief made a present to the elder Pattie of a tract of land ten miles square, lying on a river about three miles from the mines. The tract was one very favorable for cultivation and the Mexicans had attempted several times to grow crops of grain upon it, but the Indians had regularly killed the cultivators and destroyed the grain. The Indians were told that even though the land was Pattie's he would be compelled to employ Mexicans in order to cultivate it, and that those thus employed must be considered within the terms of the peace that had been made. With a look of great firmness the chief replied that he was a man of truth and had given his word and that no one employed on that land or belonging to the mines would be molested and that the terms of the treaty would never be violated. Continuing, he said that he wanted to be at peace with the Americans because he had ascertained that they never showed any disposition to kill except in battle; that they had proof of this because the two Indians who had been captured had not been executed, but one had been sent to invite him and his people to make peace, which he was glad to do.

The sentiment entertained by the Indians as evidenced in the story told by the Patties was almost universal among the tribes in New Mexico. The Navajó, the Ute, and the Apache had no respect for the Spaniard or the Mexican, nor had the sedentary tribes. Careful search does not reveal any documentary evidence which can in any manner sustain the feelings which were entertained by the Indians other than the massacre at Tiguex, in the time of Coronado, and the murder of the Navajós at the pueblo of Cochití after 1823. These feelings, however, were mutual. The Spaniard and the Mexican regarded the Indian, particularly the Apache, as a barbarian with whom treaties could not be made or kept, and very early in the history of the country arrived at the conclusion, later adopted by the American settler, that the only "good" Apache was a dead one. During two centuries of almost constant warfare between the Spanish settlers and the wild tribes, many treaties were made and broken, and finally during the

REASONS FOR APACHE HOSTILITY TO MEXICANS

A Santa Fé Caravan Crossing the Great Plains

nineteenth century the almost unanimous opinion of the inhabitants of Spanish descent that perfect peace would only come with the extermination of the Apache became a policy of the settlers and the government.

At no time after the independence of the country was achieved down to the date of the American occupation did the general government of the republic of Mexico provide military protection to the people of the territory of a kind worthy of the name. As matter of fact the inhabitants were compelled to protect themselves from the predatory incursions of the war-like Apaches as best they could. Poorly armed, many communities were practically helpless. Murders were committed, ranchos burned, and stock driven away, and days would elapse before any effort to overtake or punish the Indians could possibly be made by the feeble military establishment which was attempted to be maintained in the territory.

THE MEXICAN MILITARY ESTABLISHMENT

Until 1839 the territory was under the rule of a *comandante*, who was called *militar, principal*, or *de armas*. This officer reported to the *comandante-general* of Chihuahua. At times the military and the civil commander was the same individual. During the administration of Bartolomé Baca, *jefe politico*, the entire garrison at Santa Fé, including officers and men, numbered only one hundred and nineteen. Captain Baca, the *jefe politico*, was in command of this company. So far as protection from the hostile tribes was concerned the Spanish government, at least during the last days of Spanish rule, had done no better. The veteran company at Santa Fé mustered only one hundred and twenty-one men. This company had been ostensibly supported by the general government, but the pay of the men was very irregularly provided for. Under Spanish rule the settlers, at their own cost, maintained some militia, Pino, in his *Exposicion*, stating that the average number of this sort of troops was fifteen hundred men. This statement is undoubtedly exaggerated, but the same system was continued under the republic. The cost of the maintenance of the presidial company at Santa Fé when Bartolomé Baca was in command, for the year 1824, was $35,488. In the year 1826, the general government passed an act by which provision was made for three permanent troops of cavalry and troops of active mounted militia, in all a force of five hundred men, at an annual cost of $439,110, but as late as 1832, there was stationed in New Mexico only one company of regular troops. Barreiro, writing in that year on military matters, urged the necessity of an increased force for the purpose of holding the Americans as well as the Indians in check, and also recommended that the garrison at Santa Fé be transferred to Valverde, as it was of no practical use at the capital. He also urged the establishment of a military school and a complete reorganization of the militia.[33]

Mention has been made of the murder of some members of the Navajó tribe of Indians at the pueblo of Cochití. This event occurred shortly after the independence of Mexico was attained. The government of New Mexico, according to Gregg,[34] greatly embittered the disposition of the wild tribes, particularly the Navajós, by repeated acts of cruelty and ill-faith, all of which were well calculated to provoke hostilities. On one occasion, during the rule of Viscarra, a party of chiefs and warriors of this tribe assembled at Cochití, by invitation of the government, for the purpose of celebrating a treaty of peace. When the Indians had arrived, the New Mexicans, exasperated by the remembrance of many outrages committed by these Indians, fell upon them unawares and put them all to death. With these facts before us, there is need of little comment upon the attitude of the Apaches and Navajós toward the Mexican. The utter helplessness of the Mexican authorities from a military standpoint is illustrated by another incident which occurred during this period, showing that the government was powerless to protect not only its own citizens but those unfortunates who happened to be prisoners of war. It was at this time that three Indians, Comanches, one adult and two boys, had come into Fernandez de Taos for purposes of trade. They were peremptorily

[33] In 1834, Captain Blas Hinójos was captain of the company at Santa Fé. He also was the *comandante-principal* of New Mexico. Anastasio Bustamante had been president of Mexico, but prior to this time, in 1832, by means of a revolution, led by Santa Anna, he had been driven from power. Captain Hinójos, as *comandante-principal* of the territory of New Mexico, signed a proclamation in favor of General Santa Anna, the document also having the signatures of the sergeants and corporals of Santa Fé, Taos, and San Miguel del Bado. This would indicate either that the Santa Fé company had been divided or that under the law of 1826 three companies were in active service in New Mexico.

[34] Gregg, Josiah, *Commerce of the Prairies*, i, p. 287.

demanded by the Jicarilla Apaches, who were their bitter enemies. The Mexican authorities, dreading the resentment of this tribe, quietly complied with the barbarous request and suffered the adult Comanche to be butchered before their very eyes. The alcalde of Taos at this time was Juan Antonio Martinez, upon whom the Apaches made the demand; he became very much alarmed and determined to surrender the Comanches in order to appease the wrath of the savages, and to make his conduct more dastardly, he caused the gun of the Comanche to be discharged and loaded with dirt, thus depriving him of the means of self-defense. He was then turned over to his enemies, who fell upon him with great fury; he defended himself as well as he could with his bow and arrows, but was soon overpowered by numbers and killed and scalped. The boys were made slaves. "It is small wonder, then," says Gregg, who lived in New Mexico very shortly after these occurrences, "that the New Mexicans were so generally warred upon by the savages of the country."

The Spaniards first began having serious trouble with the Navajó tribe shortly after the Pueblo uprising of 1680. There were many campaigns against them and at one time, in 1744, they attempted to establish a mission among them, but as we have seen, it was abandoned. During a major portion of the eighteenth century there was not a great deal of trouble as they remained practically unmolested by the Spaniards, the Franciscans, who were the moving spirits in all governmental affairs, not caring to venture among them for purposes of conversion to the holy faith. During the last twenty years of Spanish rule, however, the Navajó became very troublesome, and many raids and murders were committed by marauding bands of this great and war-like tribe.

Of the Spanish and Mexican commanders in New Mexico at that time, Colonel Viscarra seems to have been the most successful in his efforts to punish and pacify them. After that officer's departure from New Mexico there does not appear to have been a single officer of sufficient capacity to inspire the Navajó with either respect or fear, until the coming of the Americans under General Kearny in 1846. During the rule of both Baca and Narbona, both of whom were Mexican officers, the latter a lieutenant sent to New Mexico from Chihuahua expressly for the purpose of repelling the Navajós,

44   LEADING FACTS OF NEW MEXICAN HISTORY

and down to the time of Governor Perez, these savages ravaged the country with impunity, murdering and destroying just as humor happened to prompt them. It was the custom of this tribe when the spring of the year approached to propose terms of peace to the government at Santa Fé, which the latter never failed to accept. This arrangement enabled the cunning savage to sow his crops at leisure and dispose of the property he had stolen from the Mexicans during the marauding excursions in the winter; when the crop season was over, upon some slight pretext, hostilities were invariably renewed and the game of rapine and destruction played over again.[35]

In 1835, it seems that Governor Perez, who was also *comandante-principal*, endeavored to reorganize the military forces of the territory, but with very poor results. Toward the close of this year, a corps of militia was organized by Perez, in which were enlisted almost all of the leading men of the territory, so acute had become the condition of affairs with the Navajós and Apaches, for the purpose of carrying the war into the very home of the Navajós. The Indians were well posted as to the purposes and route of the Mexican forces, and having selected a large band of their most valiant warriors, went forth to meet the Mexicans, and, if possible, intercept them in a mountain pass. In this the Indians were successful. The Mexicans, utterly unconscious of the reception that awaited them, soon came jogging along in scattered groups, indulging in every kind of boisterous mirth. Suddenly the Navajó war-whoop, loud and shrill, followed by a volley, threw the Mexicans into a state of speechless consternation. Some tumbled off their horses, so great was their fright; others fired their muskets at random; a terrific panic ensued, and some minutes elapsed before they could recover their senses sufficiently to betake themselves to their heels. Several Mexicans were slain in this engagement, if such it may be called, the most prominent of whom was Captain Hinójos, who was in command of the regular troops accompanying the volunteers. Don Donaciano Vigil, afterwards governor of New Mexico, was a sergeant with this expedition.[36]

BATTLE WITH NAVAJÓS — DEATH OF CAPTAIN HINÓJOS

---

[35] Gregg, Josiah, *Commerce of the Prairies*, i, p. 289.
[36] Gregg, *Commerce of the Prairies*, i, p. 290, says of Vigil: "A very curious but fully authentic anecdote may not be inappropriately inserted here, in which

Don José Chaves, Governor of New Mexico
Collections of New Mexico Historical Society

"The northern Mexicans have often been accused of cowardice," says Gregg, "but this stigma should not be permitted to rest upon the rancheros, or as they might still more appropriately be styled, the yeomanry of the country. Inured as the people of this period in the history of the country were to every kind of fatigue and danger, they possessed as a race a high grade of courage. Their want of firmness in the field was partially the result of their want of confidence in their commanders, while the inefficacy and worthlessness of their weapons was alone sufficient to fill a valiant heart with dismal forebodings. In the early days of Mexican independence the regular troops were provided with English muskets, but a great portion of the militia were obliged to use the clumsy, old-fashioned escopeta, or fire-lock of the sixteenth century; while others had nothing but the bow and arrow, and sometimes the lance, which was a weapon very much in use at that time. The people of the lower classes in this period were really possessed of a superlative degree of courage; they undertook journeys solitary and alone through desert wildernesses teeming with murderous savages, frequently undertaking these perilous trips wholly unarmed."

During the rule of Perez the Americans at that time in the country seem to have acquired the same opinion of the Apache as that entertained by the Mexican; at any rate one American named James Johnson, acting under a commission from the governor of the state of Sonora, began the work of exterminating the Indians and was not particular as to the means by which the end was accomplished. At this time there was a celebrated Apache chief called Juan José, whose extreme cunning and audacity caused his name to be dreaded throughout the entire country. What contributed more than anything else to render him a dangerous enemy was the fact of his having received a liberal education at Chihuahua, which enabled him, when he afterwards rejoined his tribe, to outwit his pursuers, and,

---

this individual (Hinójos) was concerned. On one occasion, being about to start on a belligerent expedition, he directed his orderly-sergeant to fill a powder-flask from an unbroached keg of twenty-five pounds. The sergeant, having bored a hole with a gimlet, and finding that the powder issued too slowly, began to look about for something to enlarge the aperture, when his eyes haply fell upon an iron poker which lay in a corner of the fire-place. To heat the poker and apply it to the hole in the keg was the work of but a few moments; when an explosion took place which blew the upper part of the building into the street, tearing and shattering everything else to atoms. Miraculous as their escape may appear, the sergeant, as well as the captain who witnessed the whole operation, remained more frightened than hurt, although they were both very severely scorched and bruised. This ingenious sergeant was afterwards secretary of state to Governor Gonzales, of revolutionary memory, and has nearly ever since held a clerkship in some of the offices of state, but is now a captain in the regular army."

by robbing the mails, to acquire timely information of every expedition that was set on foot against him. The government of Sonora, desirous to make some efforts to check the depredations of the Apaches, issued a proclamation, giving a sort of *carte blanche* patent of "marque and reprisal," and declaring that all the booty that might be taken from the savages should become the property of the captors. Accordingly, in the spring of 1837, a party of some twenty men, mostly Americans, spurred on by the love of gain, and never doubting that the Indians, after so many years of successful robberies, must be possessed of vast wealth, under the command of Johnson, set out to make war upon the murderous Apache. In a few days they reached a *rancheria* of about fifty warriors with their families, among whom was the celebrated chief, Juan José. Along with Juan José were three other principal chiefs of the Apaches. On seeing the Americans advance, Juan José at once gave them to understand that if they had come to fight they were ready to accommodate them, but on being assured by Johnson that they were merely on a trading expedition, a friendly interview was immediately established between the parties. The American captain having determined to put these obnoxious chiefs to death under any circumstances, soon caused a little field-piece which had been concealed from the Indians to be loaded with chain and cannister shot, and held in readiness for use. The warriors were then invited to the camp to receive presents of flour, which were placed within range of the cannon. While they were occupied in dividing the contents of the bags, they were fired upon and a considerable number of the party killed. The remainder were then attacked with small arms, and about twenty slain, including Juan José and the other chiefs. Thus was begun the fearful animosity which has always been entertained by the Apache for the American. Those who escaped this massacre became their own avengers in a manner which proved terribly disastrous to another party of Americans who happened to be trapping on the Gila river not far distant. The enraged savages took summary vengeance upon these unfortunate trappers, and falling upon them, massacred every one, about fifteen in number. This party was under the command of Charles Kemp.[37]

---

[37] Gregg, Josiah, *Commerce of the Prairies*, i, pp. 80-81. Benj. D. Wilson, *Observations*, Ms. 2-18, gives the most complete account of the massacre of Kemp's party, having been camped on the Gila at the time. His party was

The projector of this enterprise, says Gregg, had probably been under the impression that treachery was justifiable against a treacherous enemy. He also believed, no doubt, that the act would be highly commended by the Mexicans who had suffered so much from the depredations of these notorious chiefs. But in this he was mistaken, for the affair was received with general reprehension, although the Mexicans had been guilty of similar deeds themselves.

Previous to this date, the Apaches had committed but few depredations upon Americans, being restrained either by fear or respect. Small parties of Americans were permitted to pass the highways of the wilderness unmolested, while large caravans of Mexicans suffered frequent attacks. This apparent partiality produced unfounded jealousies, and the Americans were openly accused of holding secret treaties with the Indians, and even of supplying them with arms and ammunition. Although an occasional foreigner engaged in this clandestine and culpable traffic, yet the Mexicans themselves embarked in it very extensively. This unjust impression against Americans was partially effaced by the attacks upon them made about this time. The most dangerous place in New Mexico was on the trail from Santa Fé to Chihuahua, south of Socorro, and particularly along the *Jornada del Muerto*.[38]

On one occasion a band of Apache warriors boldly approached the town of Socorro, when a battle ensued between them and the Mexi-

---

also attacked and several men killed, Wilson being captured and barely escaping with his life. James Johnson never received the reward from the Mexicans that he had hoped for, and went to California, where he died in great poverty. His accomplice in this massacre of the Apaches was a man named Glisson.

[38] Gregg, Josiah, *Commerce of the Prairies*, ii, pp. 297-298: "In the summer of 1839, a few Apache prisoners, among whom was the wife of a distinguished chief, were confined in the *calabozo* at Paso del Norte. The bereaved chief, hearing of their captivity, collected a band of about sixty warriors, and, boldly entering the town, demanded the release of his consort and friends. The *comandante* of the place wishing to gain time, desired them to return the next morning, when their request would be granted. During the night the forces of the country were concentrated; notwithstanding, the Apaches reappeared, the troops did not show their faces, but remained concealed, while the Mexican *comandante* strove to beguile the Indians into the prison, under pretext of delivering to them their friends. The unsuspecting chief and twenty others were entrapped in this manner and treacherously murdered in cold blood; not, however, without some loss to the Mexicans, who had four or five men killed in the fracas. Among these was the commandant himself, who had no sooner given the word, 'Matan á los carajos!' than the chief retorted, 'Entónces moritás tu primero, carajo!' and immediately stabbed him to the heart!''

can force, composed of a small detachment of regulars and the local militia. The Mexicans were soon completely routed and chased into the streets of the town, suffering a loss of thirty-three killed and many wounded. The savages bore away their dead and wounded, of which there were only six or seven. Gregg, who happened to be in the vicinity on the day following the fight, says that the utmost consternation prevailed among the inhabitants, who were hourly in expectation of another raid from the savages.

Many schemes were devised from time to time to check these horrible outrages, but with poor success. A regular price was paid for the scalp or ears of the hostiles, and it was customary, during the time of Manuel Armijo, to decorate the walls of the executive office in the old palace with these barbarous trophies of battles with the Indians.[39]

One of the most extensive Indian tribes, living partly in New Mexico, was the Ute. Large numbers of these Indians were in the habit of spending their winters in the vicinity of Taos and in the summer time wandered to the east in search of buffalo upon the plains. These Indians were nominally at peace with the people of New Mexico, but it was their custom, whenever they had the advantage, to lay the hunters and traders who happened to fall in with their scouting parties under severe contributions, and on some occasions to subject them to violence. A prominent Mexican officer, Don Juan Andrés Archuleta, happened at one time to fall into the clutches of a party of Utes and was fearfully assaulted and whipped by the Indians, and so feeble was the Mexican government that it never dared to resent the outrage.

In the summer of 1837, a small party of Shawnees fell in with a large band of Ute Indians south of the Arkansas, on the northern confines of New Mexico. At first they were received with every demonstration of friendship, but the Utes, noting the small number of their visitors, very soon concluded to relieve them of their surplus property. The Shawnees, however, much to the surprise of the marauders, instead of quietly surrendering their goods and chattels, offered to defend them, upon which a skirmish ensued which cost the Utes several of their men, including their chief, while the Shawnees made good their escape to their eastern homes.

---

[39] Gregg, Josiah, *Commerce of the Prairies*, i, p. 299.

Prominent Officers, Military and Civil, of the American Occupation Period
1. Gov. Charles Bent. 2. Gov. Donaciano Vigil. 3. Gen. Stephen W. Kearny.
4. Gen. Edwin Vose Sumner. 5. Gen. Alexander W. Doniphan

Shortly after this occurrence, and while the Utes were still bewailing the loss of their chief and warriors, a small caravan, under the charge of Dr. Josiah Gregg, happened to pass their village. Gregg's entire force only mustered about thirty-five men. Camp had hardly been made by the Americans until the Utes began to flock around them in large numbers; the warriors were very sullen and morose, now and then muttering a curse upon the Americans because of the treatment they had received from the Shawnees, whom the Utes considered as half-castes and allies of the Americans. Suddenly a young warrior seized a fine horse belonging to the Americans, and, leaping upon his back, galloped off at full speed. The Americans at once resolved to make a peremptory demand for the return of the animal. The principal chief treated the request with contumely, when the Americans sent in a declaration of war and immediately began preparations for a descent upon the Indian village. The war-whoop resounded in every direction, and as the Utes bore a high reputation for bravery and skill, the readiness with which they accepted the American challenge created some alarm among the Americans who had defied them to mortal combat merely by way of bravado. It was too late, however, to withdraw. No sooner had the alarm been given than the Indians began exhibiting their preliminary feats of horsemanship, and the squaws and papooses scattered like partridges to the adjoining rocks and hills. One-third of the party with Gregg was composed of Mexicans, and the first step of the Indians was to proclaim a general *indulto* to them, in hopes of reducing the American force. A young warrior rode up and exclaimed in good Spanish, "My Mexican friends, we do not wish to hurt *you*; so leave those Americans, for we intend to kill every one of *them.*" The Mexicans, however, only answered, "*Al diablo*! We have not forgotten how you treat us when you catch us alone; now that we are with Americans, who will defend their rights, expect ample retaliation for past insults." In truth the Mexicans were anxious for a fight. The Indians now seemed less disposed to have trouble and sent in an old squaw for the purpose of opening up negotiations for peace. The stolen horse was returned, peace was proclaimed, and the *capitanes* exchanged ratifications by a social smoke.

The Jicarilla Apaches also harbored an enmity for the Americans.

In 1834, having met with a Missourian and some companions, they had stolen a number of their horses; having been pursued into the mountains near Taos, a fight occurred in which several Indians were killed and the horses regained. A few days later all of the Jicarilla warriors visited Santa Fé and demanded of the Mexican authorities that the Americans be given over to them for vengeance. All of the foreigners in the capital began preparations for a defense, and the savages shortly departed for their mountain homes.

Through experiences of this sort the frontiersman and trader came to have but a poor opinion of the Indian in the southwest and soon entertained the same regard for his usefulness as did the Mexican, who believed that the only manner in which these merciless freebooters could be made to fear and respect them was by killing them off as rapidly as circumstances would permit and by any means which good fortune presented for the purpose.

The opinion of a hardy frontiersman, given to Captain R. B. Marcy, in the days of the American occupation, relative to the Apache Indian, only too well voices the sentiment of the times among Americans as well as Mexicans. Captain Marcy says that he does not endorse all of the sentiments of this mountaineer, yet most of them were deduced from long and matured experience and critical observation. This "mountain-man" who had lived upon the plains and in the mountains, trapping and hunting during nearly all of the first half of the nineteenth century, said: "They are the most onsartainest varmints in all creation, and I reckon tha'r not mor'n half human; for you never seed a human, arter you'd fed and treated him to the best fixins in your lodge, jist turn round and steal all your horses, or ary other thing he could lay his hands on. No, not adzackly. He would kinder feel grateful, and ask you to spread a blanket in his lodge ef you passed that-a-way. But the Injun he don't care shucks for you, and is ready to do you a heap of mischief as soon as he quits your feed. No, Cap.; it's not the right way to give um presents to buy peace; but ef I war governor of these yeer United States, I'll tell you what I'd do. I'd invite um all to a big feast, and make b'lieve I wanted to have a big talk; and as soon as I got um all together, I'd pitch in and sculp about half of um, and then t'other half would be mighty glad to make a peace that would stick. That's the way I'd make a treaty with the dog'ond varmints;

and as sure as you're born, Cap., that's the only way. Tain't no use to talk about honor with them, Cap.; they hain't got no such thing in um. They won't show fair fight and they kill and sculp a white man when-ar they get the best on him, and ef you treat um decent, they think you are afeard. No, Cap., the only way is to whip um and then the balance will sorter take to you and behave themselves.''

The foe to civilization and progress in the southwest, the Indian, from the days of De Vargas, for two centuries, continued to be a menace to the peace and prosperity of the country, and only after the expenditure of millions of dollars by the government of the United States was he finally subdued.

MEDALLIONS OF THE EMPEROR AUGUSTIN ITURBIDE

BIBLIOGRAPHY

Abert, J. W.	Report to Secretary of War, *Gov. Doc.*, Wash., 1848.
Arrillaga, Basilio	*Recopilacion de las Leyes*, Mexico, 1838-50. 22 vols.
Bancroft, Hubert Howe,	*History of Mexico*, vol. iv, San Francisco, 1889.
Bartlett, J. R.	*Personal Narrative*, etc., New York, 1864.
Cooke, Philip St. George,	*Scenes and Adventures in the Army*, Phila., 1859.
Davis, W. W. H.	*El Gringo*, New York, 1856; *Spanish Conquest of New Mexico*, Doylestown, 1869.
Dorsey and Kroeber	*Traditions of the Arapaho*, Field Columb. Mus. Pubs., Anthrop., ser. v, 1903; *Arapaho Sun Dance*, ibid., iv, 1903
Gregg, Dr. Josiah	*Commerce of the Prairies*, New York, 1844.
Hall	Mexican Law.
Marcy, Capt. R. B.	*Thirty Years of Army Life*, New York, 1866.
Mooney, James	*Ghost Dance Religion*, 14 B. A. E., ii, 1896; *Hand Book of American Indians*, vol. i.
Pattie, James O.	*Personal Narrative*, Cincinnati, 1833.
Pope, Captain John	*Report of Exploration of a Route for the Pacific Railroad*, Gov. Doc., Washington.
Reynolds, Matthew G.	*Spanish and Mexican Land Laws*, St. Louis, Mo., 1895.
Ruxton, George F.	*Adventures in Mexico*, New York, 1848.
Santa Fé Archives	Smithsonian, Washington, D. C., and in office of the Surveyor General, Santa Fé, N. M.

CHAPTER II

THE CENTRAL SYSTEM OF GOVERNMENT — THE REVOLUTION OF 1837-8 — INTRIGUES AND CONSPIRACIES — THE KILLING OF GOVERNOR PEREZ — GONZALES REVOLUTIONARY GOVERNOR — BATTLES WITH REVOLUTIONISTS — MANUEL ARMIJO DECLARES HIMSELF GOVERNOR AND COMMANDING-GENERAL — DEFEAT OF REVOLUTIONARY FORCES — EXECUTION OF GONZALES AND CONFEDERATES

THE first epoch of the central system of government of the republic of Mexico was initiated in 1835, when, on the 3d day of October of that year, by act of congress, the state legislatures were abolished and departmental councils or juntas established. On the 23d of the same month, bases for a new constitution were adopted, declaring that the national territory should be divided into departments, the number, extent, and sub-divisions of which should be thereafter determined by congressional enactments. A little over a year later the new constitution was adopted by which it was provided that the national territory should be divided into departments, governors appointed, with an election of departmental councils and their powers defined. At the same session of congress the territory of New Mexico was made a department. Later on regulations were made for the government of the departments and the powers and duties of the governors and departmental councils were defined.

The creation of this central system of government and the adoption of the new constitution were in some degree responsible for the revolution which occurred in 1837. Under REVOLUTION OF 1837-8 this constitution a system for direct taxation was provided, a decided innovation, causing great dissatisfaction and disapproval among the people, and affording a pretext at least for the revolt which occurred. But there were other reasons for the revolution. A prominent Mexican historian [40] recites the fact that the trouble was in some degree at least instigated by the American traders, although this may not be true,[41] yet it is more than likely that Americans in the country and Texas sympathizers may have had something to do in arousing the people, believing that by fomenting the almost universal discontent, by means of a revolution, New Mexico might become independent of the republic.

There were a great many causes contributing to the revolutionary outbreak. The corruption and cupidity of the government officials were well known. For the purpose of
CAUSES OF THE REVOLUTION ridding the country of all native-born Spaniards, the Mexican congress, in the year 1828, had passed what was known as the expulsion law.

---

[40] Bustamante, Carlos M., says: "La causa de la revolucion la habia dado la entrada de una porcion de carros del Norte-América que trajeron muchas mercaderías, cuyos derechos no querian pagar los anglo-americanos, y tratando de estrecharlos á la exhibicion el gobernador, le suscitaron el alzamiento."

[41] Gregg, Josiah, *Commerce of the Prairies*, i, p. 134. Dr. Gregg was in Santa Fé at the time of this revolution. His statements as to the causes may be taken almost as conclusive, so far as the persons engaged in the Santa Fé-Chihuahua trade and their relation thereto are concerned. He says: "In the south, the Americans were everywhere accused of being the instigators of this insurrection, which was openly pronounced another Texas affair. Their goods were confiscated or sequestered, upon the slightest pretexts, or for some pretended irregularity in the accompanying documents; although it was evident that these and other indignities were heaped upon them, as a punishment for the occurrence of events which it had not been in their power to prevent. Indeed, these ill-used merchants were not only innocent of any participation in the insurrectionary movements, but had actually furnished means to the government for the purpose of quelling the disturbances.

"As I have observed before, the most active agents in this desperate affair were the Pueblo Indians, although the insurgent party was composed of all the heterogeneous ingredients that Mexican population teems with. The *rancheros* and others of the lowest class, however, were only the instruments of certain discontented *ricos*, who, it has been said, were in hope of elevating themselves upon the wreck of their enemies. Among these was the present Governor Armijo, an ambitious and turbulent demagogue, who, for some cause or other, seemed anxious for the downfall of the whole administration."

Davis, in *El Gringo*, p. 85, says that a combination of circumstances, among which was included the intrigue of a party in the territory who desired to ride into power regardless of the means, led to the outbreak.

The central system of government was a reactionary movement and was supported by the clergy and army in Mexico. General Santa Ana also did all he could to further it; under this system the Mexican states were deprived of their local self-government and reduced to departments. This was one of the causes which brought about the Texas revolution.

The enforcement of this act in New Mexico, or rather its lack of enforcement, was a source of great revenue to some of the officials. Under this act many Spaniards were expelled from the territory, the major portion of them leaving the country in company with the caravans which crossed the great plains to the Missouri river, preferring this route, with all its dangers of attack from the hostile Indians of the western prairies, to the southern route which took them through the republic to the port of Vera Cruz. At this time there were a number of Franciscan friars in the country, who were subject to this decree, but two of them, Fr. Alvino and Fr. Castro, were excepted and permitted to remain, in consequence of their great age, as it was said, but in reality because they paid five hundred dollars to two leading officials of the territory for the privilege. The motive was one of avarice and not of charity and in this way the laws of the country were notoriously violated by those charged with their administration. The arrangement by which these two friars were permitted to remain was perfected by a priest of San Miguel named Leiva, afterwards an important and prominent man in the uprising against the American authorities in 1846-47. Avarice and disregard of the law, at this time, had such a hold upon the officials that money would buy off almost any delinquent. It may be safely stated that very few Spanish-born residents of New Mexico would have left the territory had they been provided with sufficient funds to satisfy the demands of the officials. For this reason the law against them was carried out to the very letter.

The first cause of discontent was created in 1835 when General Santa Ana sent Colonel Albino Perez as governor of the territory. Perez was an excellent man but he was not a New Mexican and this fact caused a great deal of dissatisfaction among those who had been in power since the day of independence, accustomed as they had been for a number of years to have none but native governors or executives. The opposition to Governor Perez was not open, but the change of executives gave the designing demagogues, of whom there seem to have been a great many, a pretext in preparing the public mind for their designs. He was also a great believer in the education of the people and issued a proclamation in relation to the establishment of a public school system, which, so far as documentary proof is concerned, is the first ever issued by a governor of New

Mexico. His position on this subject and the pronounced opposition from certain quarters, together with a decree of the national government in the matter of public revenue, aided his enemies in bringing about the revolution which was soon to follow. In 1836 occurred an event which added fuel to the flames, giving an additional stimulant to the discontented leaders and *ricos* in the territory.

About a year subsequent to the advent of Governor Perez, charges were preferred against some of the disbursing officials of the territory, who were arrested and brought to trial. The court was composed of certain so-called judges, named Nafere, Santiago Abreu, and Juan Estevan Pino, the first two named not being permitted to sit at the hearing as they were charged with being accomplices. The men were tried before Pino alone and were found guilty, but before sentence could be passed upon them the cause was removed from the court by Governor Perez. This action on the part of the governor caused a great deal of dissatisfaction throughout the entire territory, and opposition to the administration became open and pronounced in its character. During the suspension of the principal disbursing officer, the duties of his office were discharged by General Manuel Armijo, and when Perez restored the official to his office, Armijo returned to Alburquerque, where he lived, in the vernacular — *mui discontento*. Armijo had been well pleased with the office and determined to regain it, if possible. His first efforts to secure it were by intrigue and bribery, and failing in these, he changed his plans, which resulted favorably, being aided by circumstances which produced terrible consequences. Armijo took into his confidence Juan Estevan Pino and Juan Rafael Ortiz, both declared enemies of Perez and his administration and men of great prominence, standing, and wealth in New Mexico. These men took advantage of a favorable event happening at the time and which was the real cause of the success of their efforts. On the 17th of April, 1837, a decree of the general government of Mexico relative to the national revenues became effective. Under this and a subsequent decree the governor of a department was charged with the duty of supervising the collection of the national revenues and of all matters in connection therewith.[42]

---

[42] *Decree* of April 17th, 1837: ''3. The management, administration and distribution of national funds, shall be made in the Departments, after the

Gen. Manuel Armijo

As soon as the provisions of this decree became known in New Mexico, Armijo and his powerful friends took strong ground against it and were open in their denouncement of the powers thus conferred upon the governor, who was charged with the collection of the revenues. The people had never been accustomed to the payment of

publication of this decree, under the responsibility of the officers therein designated."

By virtue of the provisions of another *decree* of the national government, it appears that "Until the decree issued by the government on the 17th of last April is revised, and a law enacted to prescribe the manner in which the governors of the Departments are to exercise the power of supervision given them by the Sixth Constitutional Law, in its Article 7, Part 12, it shall be the duty of these officials, in the exercise of said power:

"First: To witness or vise, in person in the capitals and by the civil authority in each one of the other places in the Department, the monthly and annual cash statements made by the several chiefs of the offices of the treasury and to report without delay to the Supreme Government the omissions and abuses they may observe.

"Second: To preside over the Boards of Sale of the treasury, with power to defer the resolutions of these latter until, in the first or second session thereafter, the matter under consideration is more thoroughly examined into.

"2. In the exercise of said faculty the Governor shall have power;

"First. To witness the examination of the drafts in the money chests.

"Second. To supply, in urgent cases, the approval of the Director General of Revenues, for the appointment of Inspectors and Inventors, but the Superior Chiefs, may nevertheless, give immediate notice to said office.

"Third. To suspend by executive order, after proceedings of investigation, with report of the superior chief, the subordinate employe or employes of the offices of the treasury and customs offices, who do not perform their duties or do not inspire confidence in the service, and report immediately to the Supreme Government."

In the *Santa Fé Archives* we find the proclamation and plan for public instruction made by Governor Perez. Owing to its being the very first plan for the education of the youth of the city of Santa Fé, it is reproduced in full, as follows:

"R. AYUNTAMIENTO

"Ignorance, and idleness, have always been the cause of infinite evil among men in society, and to diminish them, the only remedy and the most efficacious adopted in all countries of the world, is the education of Youth. In this valuable and interesting province securing the good of the people being the principal object, the true lovers of the public weal should attend to this, and it is also the most sacred obligation of the local authorities. This important branch is in a sad state throughout the territory, and more especially in this capital, which by its very nature and elements, does not think profoundly on the means to overcome these false difficulties, which seem by their continuation, to justify the neglect. Running the streets are children who ought to be receiving the education so necessary at the fitting and proper age; youths of evil disposition, abandoned to laziness and licentiousness, practicing vices; useless aims which only serve to corrupt, like the plague, the city that tolerates and feeds them; and above all, what are the results? Robbery, immorality, poverty, desertion, and the most humiliating shame of the city, which if it

taxes and these leaders went from place to place, representing the measure in the most objectionable manner possible, and among other obnoxious features, they declared that under this act, taxes would be collected upon poultry; that husbands would be taxed for the privileges generally attaching to connubial bliss; the people were

were cared for by its municipal authorities, should be the enviable example of others composing a most interesting part of the Mexican Nation.

"Moved by such salutary reflections, and the love I bear to the inhabitants of this soil, and by the obligation imposed upon me by my position, I issue for the relief of the Royal Municipality the following Plan of Regulation of Public Instruction.

"Art. 1. There shall be in this city two schools, particularly of primary instruction, in charge of Masters who may present themselves to conduct them, and who have the proper capacity in the judgment of a commission named by the corporation, which shall examine them in reading, writing, and counting.

"2. The schools of the same nature now existing, gone through by heads of families, shall be destroyed, provided always that the Masters who conduct them have not the capacity and the approval required by the preceding article, to which end they may present themselves for examination, in opposition.

"3. The Masters shall enjoy such salary or recompense as may be agreed upon with the heads of families, and shall receive pay from those known to be poor, in products of the soil, teaching gratis, orphan children, or those of the absolutely miserable, who have no livelihood or power to pay.

"4. All Fathers or Guardians who have children in their care from the age of five to twelve years, are obliged to send them to one of the schools whichever best suits them, and the youths of twelve years or more [must be] in houses of artisans in the different branches of industry, that they may earn a living by honest occupation.

"5. Those who fail to comply with the first part of the preceding article, by omission or neglect, shall be required by law, to pay a fine of from, one to five p. according to their means, in the first, double in the second, and triple in the third, and those who are still recalcitrant, and those who cannot pay the fine, shall be punished by law with three days arrest, doubling this punishment in the same way as the pecuniary one.

"6. The Youths spoken of in the second part of the fourth article who do not consent to learn a trade, or who have no honest occupation, shall be treated as vagrant or vicious, and be tried and sentenced by the established Court and the laws governing such cases.

"7. The Justices of the Wards, the wardens or deputies of the police, may arrest youths of twelve years or over, whom they find in the streets and public places engaged in betting games, at the end of eight days giving notice to one of the magistrates for the recognizance; and the children of twelve or under whom they find behaving ill, they shall take to the school that they may there suffer the same penalty of detention, advising the Master to punish them without fail.

"8. Every one or two wards shall form two blocks divided proportionately, and designated by known names and fixed numbers.

"9. To facilitate the better carrying out of this proclamation there shall be in each block a commissioner of Public Instruction, named by three justices unanimously whose duties shall be;

"First. To make exact lists of the inhabitants of their blocks, with a statement of ages and occupations by which they live.

"Second. To make another list of the children who shall attend the school,

urged not to submit to such a law and, never having been accustomed to the payment of direct taxes of any kind, being too ignorant to make proper inquiry as to the truth of the matter, they were soon aroused to the highest pitch of exasperation against the government. The leaders despatched secret agents into all portions of the department, exciting the populace and inducing them to resist the collection

and go to each of the two, in order to learn if they are there; an account of the youths who ought to apply themselves to a trade, in what shop and with what Masters, and of the day laborers and where, they work, so that they can certify to the correctness of all this.

"Third. To announce, courteously, one, two, or three times, to the fathers of families or guardians of children, what is set forth in the clauses of the preceding articles.

"Fourth. To give notice in writing, to the magistrate of the precinct of those who, having been admonished, still do not comply, so that through him, or by advising the judge, the law may inflict the penalty, to which they have made themselves liable.

"Fifth. To give notice, in the same manner, of all those living in idleness, who, having been admonished, do not find occupation, declaring all they can testify as to the proper or objectionable habits of the individuals.

"Sixth. To give notice also, of any suspicious persons that may be in their blocks, who are spending money without knowing whether they come by it honestly, with the grounds for the suspicion.

"Seventh. To visit every month, the schools to which the children go, to learn from the Masters whether they attend, and to get the information for their guidance. Similar visits shall be made to the workshops for the same purpose.

"Eighth. They shall make note, in their lists, of the inhabitants who leave their blocks, to what others they go, and of those who come to live in their own.

"Ninth. They shall be charged with the cleanliness of the streets and public places in their blocks, giving to the magistrate of the precinct of any neglect they notice.

"Art. 10. Any person interfering with the commissioner in the discharge of his duty, shall be punished by a fine of from five to twenty-five p. without prejudice that if the fault be serious, he may be punished according to the laws relating to ordinary transgressions.

"11. The duty of a commissioner of Public Instruction shall be a compulsory one, and no one can be excused from discharging it; it is obligatory for six months, without being required to continue, this term completed, until the end of the year, and the magistrates can remove him, for sufficient cause, as neglect or bad management, if proven.

"12. For any offense committed by the commissioner in the discharge of his duties, he shall be punished by a fine of from ten to thirty p. and deprivation of duty; and if the offence be the concealment of mischievous persons, or the toleration of them without giving notice to the Judges there shall be exacted fifty p. or two months forced labor.

"13. This ordinance may be amended in whole or in part when the R. Ayuntamiento may deem proper, being convinced of its advantages or invalidity.

"Santa Fé, July 16, 1836. ALBINO PEREZ."

of any taxes, while they, in secret, matured the plans for rebellion.[43] The people in the northern part of the department were the most active in their opposition, and the leaders had the promise of large assistance from the Pueblo Indians of Taos and the upper portion of the valley of the Rio Grande in the neighborhood of Santa Cruz de la Cañada.[44]

The conspiracy had thus been brewing for some time, but there were no indications of violence or demonstrations until, on account of some trifling misdemeanor, an alcalde of Taos was imprisoned by the *prefect* of the northern district, Don Ramon Abreu. It is said that this order was made by authority of the governor, Perez. This act brought matters to a crisis; the alcalde was released by a mob and the Pueblo Indians and other malcontents flew to arms.

The revolutionary movement began about the first of August, 1837, and extended through several of the northern pueblos, and differed from all previous outbreaks of these Indians in that it had the countenance and support of the disaffected portion of the Mexican population which had been secretly plotting under the leadership of Armijo, Ortiz, and Pino. The insurgents established headquarters at the village of Santa Cruz, twenty-five miles north of Santa Fé. Here an immense rabble soon gathered, among them the

---

[43] Gregg, Josiah, *Commerce of the Prairies*, i, p. 129: "A new governor, Col. Albino Perez, was then sent from the City of Mexico, to take charge of this isolated Department; which was not very agreeable to the 'sovereign' people as they had previously been ruled chiefly by native governors. Yet while the new form of government was a novelty and did not affect the pecuniary interests of the people, it was acquiesced in, but it was now found necessary for the support of the new organization, to introduce a system of direct taxation, with which the people were wholly unacquainted; and they would sooner have paid a *doblon* through a tariff than a *real* in this way."

[44] "The rancorous hatred of the Pueblo Indian for his conqueror," says Gregg, *ibid.*, p. 129, "has never entirely subsided, yet no further outbreak took place till 1837, when they joined the Mexican insurgents in another bloody conspiracy. Some time before these tragic events took place, it was prophesied among them that a new race was about to appear from the east, to redeem them from the Spanish yoke. I heard this spoken of several months before the subject of the insurrection had been seriously agitated. It is probable that the Pueblos built their hopes upon the Americans, as they seemed as yet to have no knowledge of the Texans. In fact, they have always appeared to look upon foreigners as a superior people, to whom they could speak freely of their discontent and grievances. The truth is, the Pueblos, in every part of Mexico, have always been ripe for insurrection. It is well known that the mass of the revolutionary chief Hidalgo's army was made up of this class of people. The immediate cause of the present outbreak in the north, however, had its origin among the Hispano-Mexican population."

principal warriors of all the northern pueblos, the most prominent being from Taos, San Juan, San Yldefonso, Santa Clara, Jacona, Pojoaque, Cuyamungué, and Nambé. On the 3d, at a meeting held for the purpose, a plan of government and a declaration of principles were adopted, which were published to the people. This plan was as follows:

"Viva, God and the nation, and the faith of Jesus Christ; for the principal points which we defend are the following:
"1st. To be with God and the nation, and the faith of Jesus Christ.
"2d. To defend our country until we spill every drop of blood in order to obtain the victory we have in view.
"3d. Not to admit the departmental 'plan.'
"4th. Not to admit any tax.
"5th. Not to admit the disorder desired by those who are attempting to procure it. God and the nation.
"ENCAMPMENT.
"Santa Cruz de la Cañada, August 3d, 1837."

When the authorities at Santa Fé were advised of these proceedings they were filled with great alarm and at once steps were taken to quell the insurrection. The governor called upon the alcaldes to assemble the militia, but few of them, however, showed any disposition to muster. Perez only succeeded in assembling a force of about one hundred and fifty men, including a number of warriors from the pueblo of Santo Domingo, at the head of which he marched from Santa Fé, on the 7th of August, to meet the enemy assembled at La Cañada. The government's forces encamped that night at Pojoaque, about eighteen miles from the capital, and on the day following met the enemy in ambush near La Cañada, when the governor's troops deserted him, and the governor and about twenty-five trusted friends made their escape toward Santa Fé as best they could, arriving there about three o'clock the same afternoon. Perez remained in the capital until about ten o'clock that night, when he left for the *Rio Abajo*, accompanied by a few trusted followers. When the Indians had put the troops to flight, and saw that the day was their own, they sent instructions to all the Indian villages to the south through which the fugitives would be compelled to pass, to apprehend and put them to death. On the night of his departure the governor and party slept at the Alamo, and on the following day his retreat to the south was prevented by some of the Indians of the pueblos in the valley of the Rio Grande. His party having been routed, they separated and fled in different directions, each bent upon saving himself. The governor returned toward Santa Fé on foot for greater security, having sent his saddle-horse forward by one of his followers. He reached the home of Don Salvador Martinez, about three miles from Santa Fé, on the road to Alburquerque, where he took refuge, and where the Indians who had followed his trail, overtook and killed him before sun-down.

While still alive the Indians cut off his head, which they carried in triumph to the camp of the *insurrectos*, which had been established near the chapel of Rosario,[45] about a quarter of a mile west of the plaza in Santa Fé. The same day they captured and killed Don Jesus Maria Alaria,[46] secretary of state, whom they took in his own house, stripped, and then lanced him to death. Don Ramon Abreu, Don Mariano Abreu, Lieutenant Hurtado, and two soldiers named Escoto and Ortega were also killed and their bodies horribly mutilated.

Don Santiago Abreu, former governor or *jefe politico* of the territory, was captured the same day near Los Cerrillos, carried to the pueblo of Santo Domingo, where he was kept in the stocks that night and was killed the following day in a most cruel manner. His hands and feet were cut off, one at a time, and shaken in his face, his tongue and eyes pulled out, while the brutes taunted him with the crimes of which he had been accused. Thus perished nearly a dozen of the most conspicuous men of the obnoxious party, whose bodies lay for several days exposed to the beasts and birds of prey, left until some christian hand gave them burial.

On the tenth of August the *insurrectos* entered and took posses-

---

[45] La Capilla de nuestra Señora del Rosario. This chapel was erected by Don Diego de Vargas Zapata Lujan Ponce de Leon pursuant to a vow made by that captain-general that he would do so provided he was successful in an engagement with the Pueblo Indians on that day occupying the city of Santa Fé and in rebellion against his authority as governor. See vol. i, pp. 392-393.

[46] Gregg, Josiah, *Commerce of the Prairies*, i, p. 131: "I had left the city the day before this sad catastrophe happened and beheld the Indians scouring the fields in pursuit of their victims, though I was yet ignorant of their barbarous designs. I saw them surround a house and drag from it the secretary of state, Jesus Maria Alaria, generally known by the sobriquet of Alarid. He and some other principal characters (including Prefect Abreu), who had also taken refuge among the ranches, were soon afterwards stripped, and finally dispatched *á lanzadas*, that is, pierced through and through with lances, a mode of assassination very common among those demi-civilized savages."

sion of Santa Fé, when they repaired to the parish church and offered up thanks for the victory they had achieved. On the same day they elected one of their boldest leaders, a Taos Indian named José Gonzales, governor, who was duly installed into office and began the administration of affairs. The property of the murdered officials was confiscated and distributed among the insurrectionists, and the major part of the effects of Governor Perez fell to the portion of Gonzales.[47] This distribution of the property of the victims of the revolution was made pursuant to a decree of a council summoned by Gonzales, composed of all the alcaldes and principal men of the revolutionary movement and was called the *Asamblea General*. The families of the unfortunate victims were thus left destitute of everything and the American merchants who had given the officers credit for very large amounts, upon the strength of their positions and salaries, remained without a single resource with which to cover their demands. As these losses were chiefly experienced in consequence of a want of protection from the general government, a memorial was drawn up setting forth their claims, which, together with a schedule of the accounts due, was sent to the American minister at Mexico.

At this stage of the proceedings General Armijo stepped forth upon the theatre of action, to play out the part he had commenced, and for which purpose he had to resort to more intrigue and bad faith. At the meeting of the *Asamblea General*, held on the 27th and 28th days of August, 1837, presided over by Gonzales, Armijo was present and took part in the consideration of the business of the convention. Others present were the very worthy Fr. Antonio José Martinez and Don Juan José Esquivel, who together with General Armijo were named as a committee to draft a statement of the grievances of the people and their loyalty. The committee named

[47] Gregg, Josiah, *Commerce of the Prairies*, i, p. 132: "On the 9th of August about two thousand of the insurgent mob, including the Pueblo Indians, pitched their camp in the suburbs of the capital. The horrors of a *saqueo* (or plundering of the city) were now anticipated by everyone. The American traders were particularly uneasy, expecting every instant that their lives and property would fall a sacrifice to the ferocity of the rabble. But to the great and most agreeable surprise of all, no outrage of any importance was committed upon either inhabitant or trader. A great portion of the insurgents remained in the city for about two days, during which one of their boldest leaders, José Gonzales, of Taos, a good honest hunter, but a very ignorant man, was elected for governor."

were instructed to present this statement to the supreme government of Mexico. General Armijo recognized the provisional government established by Gonzales and the report of the committee signed and authenticated by Gonzales, the acting governor, the commanding general, the inspector, José Maria Ronquillo, and the acting secretary, Sergeant Donaciano Vigil, was duly promulgated.

Having thus far contributed to the success of the rebellion, Armijo now changed his plans and with the view of securing for himself the supreme power of the country, which he had aimed at from the first, he therefore retired, Santa Ana-like, to his residence at Alburquerque, to plot, in imitation of his great prototype, some measures for counteracting the operation of his own base intrigues. In this he succeeded so well that towards September he was able to collect a considerable force in the *Rio Abajo*, where he proclaimed a *contra revolucion* in favor of the supreme government of Mexico. About the same time the disbanded troops of the capital under Captain Cavallero, made a similar *pronunciamento*, demanding their arms and offering their services gratis. Gonzales's government had gone so far as to deny allegiance to the supreme government and proposed sending to Texas for protection, although there had not been any previous understanding with that republic. The valiant Armijo now marched to Santa Fé with all his force. Before Armijo arrived, Gonzales heard of his approach and leaving the capital, retired to *Rio Arriba*, where there was still a considerable body of insurrectionists under arms in the vicinity of Santa Cruz and the adjacent pueblos. As soon as Armijo reached Santa Fé he took possession of the palace, assumed control of the government, and proclaimed himself governor and *comandante-general* of the department. He quickly despatched a courier to the supreme government in Mexico, with an account of affairs, not forgetting to mention his own services in the restoration of the power of the government of Santa Ana. For the part he played and the treachery he exhibited to his co-conspirators he was subsequently confirmed in the office he had seized upon, which he maintained for eight years, ruling the country with a rod of iron.

Meanwhile, the supreme government of Mexico took steps effectively to crush the rebellion. Troops to the number of four hundred were sent from Chihuahua and Zacatecas, reaching Santa Fé

Brig.-Gen. Philip St. George Cooke

THE REVOLUTION OF 1837-8

early in 1838. The *insurrectos*, meanwhile, had been kept in a state of comparative peace by Armijo, under the pretext of desiring to treat with them, but on the arrival of the dragoons from the south, open hostilities were proclaimed against them.

General Armijo, commanding the entire force of regulars and militia, now marched against the insurrectionary army at La Cañada, where they had again assembled in considerable force. A battle ensued which resulted in the complete defeat and route of the *insurrectos*. Gonzales, who was in command, fell into the hands of Armijo, as did other leading men connected with the rebellion. Armijo now demonstrated his true character of tyrant. Having the supreme power in his own hands, he concluded summarily to dispose of those confederates whom he could not reward, and therefore ordered a court-martial for the trial of many of the persons who had aided him with money and with arms, and through whose efforts together with his own base treachery he had come to his present commanding position. The court-martial, inspired by Armijo, promptly found a great many of the persons taken in rebellion against the supreme government guilty as charged, and sentenced Desiderio Montoya, Antonio Abad Montoya, Juan José Esquivel, who was alcalde, to death, and it was said that Armijo caused many others to be privately assassinated. He was highly censured for his cruelty toward the Montoyas and Gonzales. Many persons of influence exerted themselves to procure a remittance of the death sentence, but Armijo was deaf to every appeal on behalf of his former associates and confederates. The only answer he made to these intercessions was, that the court had found them guilty, and that he had no authority to pardon them. The two Montoyas, General "Chopon," and the alcalde, Esquivel, were shot within three hundred yards of the plaza at Santa Fé, at the *garita*. Juan Antonio Vigil was executed near Cuyamungué and Gonzales was shot by the immediate command of Armijo himself.[48]

BATTLE AT LA CAÑADA — DEATH OF GONZALES

When the army left Santa Fé to meet the insurgents, the greatest uneasiness and excitement prevailed, lest the rabble should again prove victorious, in which case they would not fail to come back and

---

[48] Prince, L. Bradford, *Historical Sketches*, etc., p. 289: "The story is that Gonzales, on being captured at Cañada, was brought before Armijo, who was then in the outskirts of the town, and, on seeing the General, Gonzales came

sack the city. The American merchants had as usual the greatest cause for fear, as vengeance had been openly vowed against them for having furnished the government party with supplies. These, therefore, kept up a continual watch, and had everything in readiness for precipitate flight to the United States. But in a short time their fears were completely dispelled by the news of the utter defeat of the insurgents. It appeared that when the army arrived within view of the insurgents, General Armijo evinced the greatest perturbation. In fact, he was upon the point of retiring without venturing an attack, when Captain Muños, of the Vera Cruz Dragoons, exclaimed, "What's to be done, General Armijo? If your Excellency will but permit me, I will oust that rabble in an instant with my little company alone." Armijo gave his consent, the gallant captain rushed upon the insurgents, who yielded at once, and fled precipitately, suffering a loss of about a dozen men, among whom was the insurgent chief, Gonzales, who, having been caught in the town after the battle, was instantly shot, without the least form of a trial.[49]

---

forward with hand extended, saying, 'How do you do, Compañero?' as was proper between two of equal rank as governors. Armijo replied, 'How do you do, Compañero? Confess yourself, Compañero.' Then turning to his soldiers, added, 'Now, shoot my compañero!' — which command was immediately executed."

[49] Kendall, George W., *Texas-Santa Fé Expedition*, vol. i, p. 350: "The unfortunate governor was immediately shot, and four of his chief officers met with the same fate by order of Armijo. The latter were put out of the way more, it is said, to prevent disclosures than for any crime they had committed; for they had been Armijo's confidential emissaries in the formation of his original plot. The ambitious tyrant, now that his enemies were either murdered or dispersed, reigned supreme in New Mexico."

Bancroft, H. H., *History of Arizona and New Mexico*, note, p. 318: "Those named as killed, all on or before August 9th, were Col. Albino Perez, gov.; Santiago Abreu, chief justice and ex-gov.; Jesus Maria Alarid, sec. state; Ramon Abreu, prefect of Rio Arriba; lieut. Miguel Serna, Joaquin Hurtado, and Madrigal; sergt. Diego Sais or Saenz; Marcelino Abreu, Loreto Romero, Escoto and Ortega."

Bancroft, H. H., *ibid.*, p. 318, says: "Now Manuel Armijo, formerly *jefe politico* and customs officer, either as a part of his original plot, or perhaps disappointed because Gonzalez was preferred to himself as rebel governor, or possibly moved by patriotic devotion to the legitimate government — for the exact truth eludes all research — 'pronounced' at Tomé, the 8th of September, raised a force with the aid of curate Madariaga, and marched to the capital to 'suffocate the rebellion.' Gonzales retired up the river, and Armijo had little difficulty in making himself recognized as acting governor and commandant-general. Possibly, also, he marched north and induced the rebels to submit to his authority and give up the leaders of the movement. At any

THE REVOLUTION OF 1837-8

rate he reported his patriotic achievements to the Mexican government, and asked for reënforcements.''

Bustamante follows the reports made by General Armijo in the *Diario del Gobierno,* and says that Armijo induced the rebels to give up their leaders. I think much more of the statements of Dr. Gregg, who was on the ground, was in position to know what was going on, and who is an entirely fair and unbiased witness.

David J. Miller, who had charge of the *Santa Fé Archives* for a long period, who was, however, anything but careful in his written statements, and who was personally acquainted with many of the men who took part in the revolution, stated to the writer that General Armijo marched on the 13th of September against Gonzales and his second in command, Antonio Domingo Lopez, at Pojoaque, where he induced them through the influence of a priest to negotiate for peace, but finally insisted on a surrender. This is more than likely true, but the fact of the battle at La Cañada, later, was never disputed by Mr. Miller, who also told the writer that it occurred about as stated by Gregg. Davis in his *El Gringo* says that the rebels were kept in a comparative peace by the authorities. Davis derived most of his information from Dr. Gregg's work, *Commerce of the Prairies,* and from personal interviews with Don Donaciano Vigil and other prominent men living at Santa Fé at the time Davis was United States attorney. Don Donaciano Vigil was one of the Mexican soldiers accompanying Governor Perez at the time of his defeat at La Cañada, and was captured by the revolutionary army and put in jail at La Cañada; after the assassination of Perez, Vigil was removed from his place of confinement to Santa Fé, by order of the rebel governor, Gonzales.

Bustamante gives the particulars of the two battles, one at Pojoaque, the other at La Cañada. The troops numbered 582. Four dragoons were killed and a number wounded. There were more than 1300 rebels in the engagement, their loss being twenty killed, many wounded and eight taken prisoner. Antonio Vigil, the commander, was among the slain in the battle at Pojoaque. Bustamante's statements are founded almost entirely upon the report made by Armijo and published in the *Diario del Gobierno,* November 30, 1837.

Colonel Manuel Chavez told the writer that he considered General Armijo a great coward; that he knew him only too well; that at one time he laid in wait for him to come out of the palace, intending to kill him with an arrow; he also repeated the story told by Kendall, viz: that it was a familiar statement of Armijo that he believed that it was better to be thought brave than really to be so — ''*Vale mas estár tomado por valiente que serlo.*''

PUEBLO INDIAN BOY

BIBLIOGRAPHY

Bancroft, Hubert Howe,	*History of Arizona and New Mexico*, San Francisco, 1889.
Bustamante, Carlos M.	*Apuntes para la Historia de Santa Ana*, Mexico, 1845; *Diario de Mexico*, 1841-43; *El Gabinete Mexicano*, Mexico, 1839-41, *Invasion de los Anglo-Americanos*.
Davis, W. W. H.	*El Gringo*, New York, 1856.
Gregg, Dr. Josiah	*Commerce of the Prairies*, New York, 1844.
Kendall, George W.	*Texas-Santa Fé Expedition*, New York, 1844. 2 vols.
Prince, L. Bradford	*Historical Sketches*, New York, 1883.
Read, Benj. M.	*Historia Illustrada*, etc., Santa Fé, N. M., 1911.
Santa Fé Archives	Smithsonian, Washington, D. C.

NEW MEXICAN BURRO

CHAPTER III

THE TEXAS-SANTA FÉ EXPEDITION — CAPTURE OF THE TEXANS WHO ARE SENT TO THE CITY OF MEXICO — MURDER OF DON ANTONIO JOSÉ CHAVEZ — SNIVELY'S RAID — COL. WARFIELD ATTACKS TOWN OF MORA — DEFEAT OF VANGUARD OF ARMIJO'S ARMY ON THE ARKANSAS — CAPTAIN COOKE DISARMS THE TEXANS — CLOSING OF PORTS OF ENTRY BY GENERAL SANTA ANA

IN 1841 General Mirabeau B. Lamar was holding the office of president of the republic of Texas. The Texans claimed, as the western boundary of the Lone Star Republic, the Rio Grande. Yet, so isolated were the settlements east of that stream, the new republic had never been able to exercise jurisdiction over a people really within her limits. The time had now arrived, so thought the rulers of Texas, when the republic should exercise its authority over the length and breadth of her domain, when the citizens of her farthest borders should be brought into the common fold, and as the Texans believed, and as is claimed by the historian of the Texas-Santa Fé expedition, with the full belief in the readiness and willingness of the inhabitants of New Mexico, the Texas-Santa Fé Expedition was organized. On its arrival at the destined point, should the inhabitants really manifest a disposition to declare their full allegiance to Texas, the flag of the single-star republic was to be raised over the old palace; but if not, the Texan commissioners were merely to make such arrangements with the authorities as would best tend to the opening of trade, and then retire. This approximately covers the Texan side of the story as related by the historian,[50] Kendall, an American citizen, who accom-

---
[50] Kendall, George W., *Narrative of the Texas-Santa Fé Expedition*, p. 16: "The idea, which has obtained credence to some extent in the United States,

panied the expedition and underwent all the hardships, sufferings, and privations of the invading Texans. General Lamar seems to have been very poorly informed as to the sentiments of the people of New Mexico. The reception accorded these so-called Texan pioneers was of an entirely different sort.

The position taken by the republic of Texas and successfully maintained by her people, at least in being paid the sum of ten million dollars by the government of the United States for that portion of the present territory of New Mexico lying east of the Rio Grande and west of the 103d parallel, after the treaty of Guadalupe Hidalgo, in the bill creating the territory of New Mexico, is well summed up in a letter written by General Sam Houston to General Santa Ana in 1842, at the time when the members of the Texas-Santa Fé Expedition were in the power of the Mexican government.

In that letter it is said: "Now the tribunal to which you have appealed, will have an opportunity of contrasting the treatment which you and the prisoners taken at San Jacinto, received, with that of those who have fallen within your power, and particularly those perfidiously betrayed on a recent trading expedition to Santa Fé. You have endeavoured to give that expedition the complexion of an invading movement upon the rights of Mexico. To believe you serious in the idle display of words made on this occasion, would be presenting an absurdity to the common sense of the age. Your fears may have given it a character different from that to which it was entitled. Examine the circumstances accompanying it. It was not an act of Texas. Congress had refused to sanction any enterprise of the kind. A number of individuals were anxious to open a lucrative trade (as they believed it would be) with Santa Fé. Such a commerce had been carried on for years by the citizens of the United States from Missouri; and the preparations, connected with the fact that the citizens took with them a considerable amount of merchandize, show that their enterprise was not one of conquest or invasion. You may allege that it had connection with the government from the fact that the president identified himself with it, by furnishing arms to those connected with the project. This may have induced you to characterize the expedition as you have, in your tirade against Texas. Whatever part the president bore in this

---

that the first Texan-Santa Fé pioneers were but a company of marauders, sent to burn, slay and destroy in a foreign and hostile country, is so absurd as not to require contradiction; the attempt to conquer a province, numbering some one hundred and fifty thousand inhabitants within its borders, was a shade too Quixotical to find favour in the eyes of the three hundred and twenty pioneers."

transaction was contrary to law, and in violation of his duty. A large portion of the people of Texas were apprized of the existence of such an enterprise. You doubtless would insist that it had means of offense against Mexico. So far as their preparations could give character to the undertaking, by carrying with them artillery and other munitions of war, it can be accounted for most readily. They had to pass through a wilderness six hundred miles from the frontier of Texas, before they could reach Santa Fé. It was reasonable to suppose that they would encounter many hostile tribes of Indians, and it was proper and necessary that they should be in a situation to repel any attacks made upon them, and, as their objects were pacific, they were justified in resisting aggression from any quarter. The instructions given to them by the president did not contemplate hostilities, but that the enterprise would terminate without bloodshed and violence. Scientific gentlemen from Europe and the United States accompanied them, not for warlike purposes, but for the purpose of adding rich stores to the treasury of science. It had likewise been communicated to the people of Texas, that all the inhabitants east of the Rio Grande were anxious to enjoy the benefits of our institutions. You cannot allege that you were not willing to admit the justice of our claims to the Rio Grande, or that you were not anxious to facilitate the object. Your communication to me on that subject is conclusive. Texans were apprized of it from your repeated declarations to that effect while in this country, and on your way to Washington City. At the time the expedition started, no hostilities were carried on between this country and Mexico. Commissioners from General Arista were at Austin at the time the party started for Santa Fé. They were kindly received, and made the most sincere profession of amity and reconciliation with this government. They were treated with kindness, and corresponding commissioners appointed to General Arista. To them every facility was extended, and they were permitted to return without molestation. This was the attitude of the two countries at the time. Will you allege that this was not sanctioned by your government, or will you insist that it was a trick of diplomacy? For myself, I would not have been deluded by any professions which might have been tendered to Texas by Mexico, when a departure from the most solemn pledges would result in injury to the former, and benefit to the latter. That the ministers of General Arista played their parts with fidelity to their instructions, I have no doubt, and that all the information that could be derived in relation to the trading company was faithfully transmitted to the government of Mexico. Nor do I doubt but that the population of the northern parts of your country, so soon as the intelligence was received, were thrown into the utmost consternation, and a nation numbering eight millions of people, inhabiting 'valleys, mountains, plains and large cities . . . by so many titles respectable,' was convulsed at the apprehended approach of three hundred Texan traders! But what has been the sequel of this expedition? On their approach to the settlements of the Rio Grande they obtained supplies from the inhabitants, not as a hostile marauding party, but they paid a valuable consideration for every supply they obtained. They were met by the Mexican authorities with overtures of peace, assurances of friendship, and pledges of security, provided they would give up their arms for the purpose of tranquilizing the Mexican population. Detached, as the company was, into parties remote from each other, and deluded by pledges, they acquiesced in the wishes of the authorities of the country, thereby evincing to them that they had no disposition to disturb the tranquillity of the inhabitants, and that their objects were pacific. But no sooner were they in the power of the authorities than they were stripped of their clothing, deprived of everything valuable, treated in the most barbarous manner, and marched like convicts to the capital of Mexico. On their route every act of inhumanity cruelty and hatred was evinced. When their sick and helpless condition required the assistance of Christian charity and humanity, it was denied them. They were barbarously shot, their bodies mangled, and their corpses left unburied. The butchery of McAllister, Galphin, Yates, and others, appeals to Heaven and this nation for retribution upon the heads of their inhuman murderers. You may allege that you did not authorize the perpetration of these outrages, committed upon men who had violated no rule of law known to this civilized age. This will be no excuse for you. Your sanction to these acts is as culpable as their perpetration was to their authors. Their detention as prisoners by you, may gratify the malignity of their little minds; but the just, the chivalric, the brave, and the generous of all nations, may pity, but must despise your conduct. Had it not been for the faithless professions tendered to them, and their too ready belief, they could have maintained their position against all the forces of northern Mexico, and, if necessary, could have made good their retreat to their homes, defying the 'generous effort of the people of New Mexico.' Your conduct on this occasion will present your humanity and sense of propriety in very awkward contrast with the treatment extended to you and your followers after the victory of San Jacinto, being not, as you suppose, one of the 'freaks of fortune' but one of the accompaniments of that destiny which will mark the course of Texas until the difficulties between the two countries shall be satisfactorily settled.''

General Houston outlines very well what probably was the belief of a great majority of the people of the single-star republic, but the

Chief Justice Joab Houghton

facts and circumstances, taken as an entirety, fail to uphold his contention, for in reality they were an armed, invading force, entering a country claimed by Mexico, whether justly or unjustly it makes no difference, for the purpose of hoisting the Texan flag by connivance with traitors and outsiders.[51] To be sure, it was not proposed to undertake the conquest of New Mexico with a force of three hundred Texans against the will of the inhabitants; but, if the people were willing, the Texans were on hand ready to make that sort of a conquest. It cannot be said that such an enterprise was not hostile to Mexico, and while no apology can be offered for the barbarous manner in which the Texans were treated by the infamous Salazar, still the Texans were in the wrong and they received what sometimes has come through the "fortunes of war." They were nothing more or less than armed invaders, who might be expected to meet with opposition, and if defeated to be treated as rebels, or at best, as Texas belligerency and independence had been recognized by several nations, as prisoners of war.

The expedition left Austin in the month of June, 1841. There were six companies, under the command of Hugh McLeod, brevet brigadier-general of the Texan army. Accompanying them came three commissioners, Colonel William G. Cooke, José Antonio Navarro, and Dr. Richard F. Brenham. The commissioners carried

---

[51] Bancroft, H. H., *History of Arizona and New Mexico*, pp. 319-320: "Hitherto there had been little or no direct intercourse between the New Mexicans and their neighbors of the adjoining but distant Texas; yet the comparative success of the eastern rebels was not unknown to the less fortunate agitators of the west. Texan influences, probably not inactive in the troubles of 1837-8, had certainly been potent in fomenting later discontent. Santa Fé traders from the United States seem as a class to have feared a revolution, which might for a time imperil their commercial interests; but among them, especially those who had become residents, there was an element fully in sympathy with the filibusters. These sympathizers reported that the New Mexicans awaited only an opportunity to rise and declare their independence, and that even the authorities were not disposed to offer much resistance. Besides crediting these exaggerated reports, the Texans had a theory, without foundation in fact or justice, that their territory extended to the Rio Grande, and it was therefore their duty to release from tyranny all inhabitants of that territory, including, of course, the New Mexicans living east of the river."

In *Niles' Register*, lxi., 61, 100, is a letter from Santa Fé, which represents all the Pueblo Indians and Americans, with two-thirds of the Mexicans, as anxious for the Texans to come. The governor tells the writer that he neither can nor will resist. That such reports were circulated and believed in Texas and the United States is shown by the general tenor of all the records and other documentary evidence of conditions as they then existed.

with them proclamations, printed in English and Spanish, explaining the advantages of the freedom which the Texans offered. "In the minds of the Texans," says Kendall, "not a doubt existed that the liberal terms offered would be at once acceded to by a population living within the limits of Texas, and who had long been groaning under a misrule the most tyrannical."

THE EXPEDITION LEAVES AUSTIN FOR NEW MEXICO

Governor Manuel Armijo and the other authorities had been advised that an invasion from Texas was not only possible but probable, and special warnings had come to him from the City of Mexico to be constantly on the *qui vive* for the McLeod party. Reënforcements were promised him. While it is more than likely that some dissatisfaction did exist among the native people owing to the official abuses of Armijo in his capacity as executive, still the great majority of New Mexicans were not ready to hail the Texans as deliverers, and naturally Armijo, well settled in power and influence, was opposed to any change in the form of government of which he was the head. As a consequence every precaution was taken and among the common classes the Texans were represented as being a choice assortment of reckless and desperate men, from whom nothing other than pillage, murder, and outrage could be expected. Many arrests were made by the authorities [52] of persons believed by them to be in collusion with the Texans. No foreign born residents of New Mexico were permitted to leave their places of residence and Captain Damasio Salazar was sent to reconnoitre the eastern frontier of the department. On the 4th day of September Salazar sent in three men by the name of Howland, Baker, and Rosenburg, whom he had captured, regarding them as

---

[52] Bustamante says: "En julio de 1839 los estrangeros del Norte en Sta Fé, se protestó de pedir justicia atentaron descaradamente contra el gobierno, de quien exigian por la fuerza de las armas que se fusilaron por el mismo gobernador, ó se les entregasen unos reos que en 1837 mataron á un estrangero, regentaban este atentado Guillermo Driden y Santiago Querque que comandaba una gavilla de indios sahuanos; mas se resistió á ello el gobernador. Desde aquella época hasta último de agosto de 1841 se suscitaron conspiraciones por diferentes puntos del departamento contra el gobierno, y si entodas no han sido los estrangeros los pricipales motores, á lo ménos han tenido parte. La de agosto la dirigia el Americano Julian Werkeman, á quien los Tejanos tenian apoderado en este departamento, con el solo objeto de que formara la revolucion, para lo que vino desde Taos á Sta Fé, acompañados de otros paisanos suyos decididos á asesinar al gobernador Armijo."

spies. Later these made their escape but were recaptured, Rosenburg being killed in resisting re-capture and the other two were executed.[53] The expedition, after a tedious march over bad routes in an unknown country, ragged, worn out, and half starved, had reached the Pecos country in the neighborhood of Anton Chico. On the 16th of September five men, Van Ness, Lewis, Howard, Fitzgerald, and Kendall, were captured by Captain Salazar on the Pecos, near La Cuesta, in the following manner, as described by Kendall. They were in the valley near La Cuesta, when suddenly they were surrounded by more than a hundred soldiers, armed with

---

[53] Kendall says: "The expedition was unfortunate, and, as a natural consequence, the censorious world has said that it was conceived in unwise policy. It will be seen that its failure arose from causes purely fortuitous; in a word, that the enterprise had failed and been broken up long before those engaged in it had reached the confines of New Mexico."

Kendall tells of the execution of Howland at San Miguel, the order for his execution coming direct from General Armijo. Says Kendall: "'Gentlemen,' commenced the governor, stopping in front of us, 'gentlemen, you told me the truth yesterday — Don Samuel has corroborated your statements — I save your lives. I have ordered Don Samuel to be shot — he will be shot in five minutes. He ran away from Santa Fé, and, in attempting to reach Colonel Cooke's party, has been retaken. You now see the penalty of trying to escape. His fate will be yours if you attempt it. Sergeant of the guard, conduct these gentlemen back to prison.' This was delivered in a loud, military voice. While congratulating ourselves upon this most unexpected termination of a trial of such harrowing interest, and wondering who the Don Samuel was whose testimony had thus evidently saved our lives, our old friend and guide, Howland, was led forth from the little room. The truth now flashed upon us — we knew that his name was Samuel, that he had been acquainted in former years with Armijo, and that the Mexicans seldom use other than the Christian appellative when addressing or speaking of a man. Howland's hands were tied closely behind him, and as he approached us we could plainly see that his left ear and cheek had been cut entirely off, and that his left arm was also much hacked, apparently by a sword. The guard conducted their doomed prisoner directly by us to the left, and when within three yards of us the appearance of his scarred cheek was ghastly; but as he turned his head to speak, a placid smile, as of heroic resignation to his fate, lit up the other side of his face, forming a contrast almost unearthly. . . With a firm, undaunted step he walked up to the place of execution, and there, by the side of his companion, was compelled to fall upon his knees with his face towards the wall. Six of the guard then stepped back a yard or two, took deliberate aim at his back, and before the report of their muskets died away poor Howland was in eternity. Thus fell as noble, as generous, and as brave a man as ever walked the earth. He was a native of New Bedford, Massachusetts, of a good family, and by his gentlemanly and affable deportment had endeared himself to every member of the expedition. In a daring attempt to escape, and reach Colonel Cooke's party, in order to give him important information, he had been retaken after a desperate struggle, and the life he could not lose in the heat of that struggle was taken from him in this base and cowardly manner."

lances, swords, bows and arrows, and old-fashioned carbines or escopetas. Captain Salazar rode up, addressing them as *amigos*, apparently with great cordiality, asked who they were and whether they were not from Texas. Lewis at once informed him that they were and that they were a detachment from the main body, then some thirty miles distant, for the purpose of consulting with the authorities, either at San Miguel or Santa Fé, and that they were anxious to see the governor. To this Salazar bowed, as much as saying "all right," his manner being so frank and plausible that his intentions were entirely concealed. The party was now conducted to a near-by house, and after his men had completely surrounded the Texans, Salazar announced that it must be apparent to the Texans that they could not enter the country with arms in their hands, that it was contrary to the laws and usages of nations and that he hoped there would be no objection to his taking possession of their rifles and pistols, until such a time as the business the Texans had with the authorities might be arranged. He declared that he had been ordered by his superiors to request the Texans to deliver up their arms and hoped that they would excuse him. Finding themselves surrounded by a force of at least twenty times their number, without the remotest chance to escape by flight, even if they felt so disposed, and completely imposed upon by the apparent fairness and openness of Salazar's conduct, the Texans gave up their arms. Kendall, who was an American citizen, accompanying the expedition, here showed Salazar his passport from the Mexican consul at New Orleans. Salazar, who was unable to read, handed it to a fellow officer, who returned it saying that he presumed it was all right, but demanded Kendall's arms, saying that they would be held until they met Governor Armijo. Salazar now distributed all the weapons among his principal men. Shortly coming from a house near-by he ordered the Texans to form in line, saying that he was compelled to make search for and take all papers which were in their possession. This was done. Up to this time, the conduct of Salazar was to a certain degree honorable and his deep treachery and atrocious designs were not detected by the Texans. Having taken all of the papers and other effects belonging to the Texans, suddenly Salazar ordered twelve of his men, all armed with old muskets or carbines, to march up in front of the

Texans. The movement seemed strange, more particularly when it was noticed that the soldiers, parading immediately in front of their captives, were pale and fairly trembling as with fright. Still the horrible designs of Salazar were not suspected. The suspense of the Texans was of short duration, for no sooner had he arranged the twelve men in their front than it became too evident that the Texans were to be executed on the spot. Fitzgerald was the first to speak. The brave but eccentric Irishman had seen service in Spain, understood the language and now fathomed the intentions of the Mexican captain. Prefacing his short speech with a strong oath, the excited man, with fists clenched said: "They're going to shoot us boys; let's pitch into 'em and die in hot blood; it's much easier!" At the same moment it was noticed that the crowd in the rear was falling back in two straight lines, as if to escape the balls in their passage, while the women and girls were wringing their hands and flying from point to point, apparently in deep despair. It was now terribly manifest that the Texans were to be shot. Descriptive of his own feelings at the time, Kendall says:

"We exchanged glances with each other, and those glances plainly told that each of my companions, in obedience to Fitzgerald's emphatic call, was prepared to rush upon the cowardly and faithless miscreants the moment they were in the act of leveling their guns, to wrest their weapons from them, and then to sell his life at as dear a rate as possible. I will give Lewis [54] the credit of acting, in that moment of extreme peril, as became a man. My station happened to be on the extreme left of my companions, the position bringing me within a yard of a young Mexican whom I afterward ascertained to be a son of the alcalde of San Miguel. Tied loosely around his waist was a coarse cotton handkerchief, in which he had stuck two of Colt's revolving pistols taken from one of my friends. These I instantly determined to seize upon in the melee, while each of my companions had singled out his man to spring upon at the signal. A man lives almost an age in a single moment of imminent danger — his thoughts crowd upon each other with such lightning rapidity, that his past life, its promises and hopes, are reviewed at a glance. I thought of home relations, friends, in the fleeting moment which passed after Salazar had manifested his inhuman intentions; but the thoughts that came uppermost with all of us were of deep regret that we had given up our arms to such cowardly assassins, mingled with the bitter consciousness that we were to

---

[54] It was afterwards discovered that Lewis was a traitor to the Texans.

be shot down like dogs without a possible chance that our friends could ever know the place or manner of our death. But our thoughts were suddenely checked by a motion from Salazar, as if to give the word of command for our execution. I cast hurried glances at Fitzgerald and my comrades for a signal to make a dash; but at this junction an altercation ensued between Damasio and a Mexican named Vigil. Not a word could I understand, but from my companions I learned that the latter was interfering for our lives. He contended that we had entered the settlements openly and peacefully, and that we had asked to see and hold converse with Governor Armijo. With him rested the power of life and death, and before him we must be taken. Vigil prevailed over the bloodthirsty captain, and thus were our lives spared; but in the few moments which had passed since we were first drawn up, we had lived a common lifetime of excitement.''

The man thus saving the lives of the captives was Don Gregorio Vigil. He was a man of great prominence in that locality and possessed of considerable wealth. He was of good heart and correct principles and had great influence in that portion of New Mexico.

On the 17th of September Colonel Cooke and Captain Sutton, with ninety-four men, surrendered to General Armijo at Anton Chico. Armijo established his headquarters at Las Vegas, the prefect, Antonio Sandoval, having been summoned to Santa Fé, where he was acting as governor. All of the property taken from the Texans was distributed among the soldiers, and in the plaza in Las Vegas, a great celebration was had, at which the printed copies of Lamar's proclamations were burned. Armijo sent out Colonel Juan Andrés Archuleta with a strong command to find the remainder of the Texans. On the 5th of October they were found at a place called Laguna Colorada where they surrendered without opposition to Colonel Archuleta. Armijo now left Las Vegas for his capital, where on the 16th of October he was given a public and most enthusiastic reception. On the day following the last of the prisoners were sent on their tedious march to the City of Mexico, where they arrived in several divisions at the beginning of 1842.[55]

---

[55] Captain Salazar was in command of the escort which took one division of the captives south from Santa Fé. Kendall, in his narrative, gives the details of Salazar's brutal conduct while on the journey from Santa Fé to El Paso. He says, in giving an account of the death of a Texan, named Ernest, who had died from exposure: ''Salazar immediately ordered one of his men to cut off and preserve the dead man's ears, as a token that he had not escaped,

After the arrival of the prisoners at the City of Mexico, some of them were released upon the intercession of foreign ministers, who claimed that they were not Texans, and had joined the expedition not knowing its real objects. The remainder were finally released by

and by the orders of the same brute, the body was thrown into a neighboring ditch. One of the prisoners, a man named McAllister, a native of Tennessee, became so foot-sore that he was unable to proceed, and was riding in a cart which had been procured by the alcalde of Valencia for the purpose of transporting some of the sick and lame prisoners, but before it had proceeded a mile upon the road, it either broke down or was found to be too heavily loaded. At all events, McAllister was ordered by Salazar to hobble along as best he might, and to overtake the main body of prisoners, now some quarter of a mile in advance. The wretch had frequently told those who, from inability or weakness, had fallen behind, that he would shoot them rather than have the march delayed; not that there was any necessity for the hot haste with which we were driven, but to gratify his brutal disposition did he make these threats. Although he had struck and in several cases severely beaten many of the sick and lame prisoners, we could not believe that he was so utterly destitute of feeling, so brutal, as to murder a man in cold blood whose only fault was that he was crippled and unable to walk. He could easily have procured transportation for us all if he had wished, and that he would do so rather than shoot down any of the more unfortunate we felt confident; how we mistook the man! On being driven from the cart, McAllister declared his inability to proceed on foot. Salazar drew his sword and peremptorily ordered him to hurry on, and this when he had half a dozen led mules, upon either of which he could have placed the unfortunate man. Again McAllister, pointing to his swollen and inflamed ankle, declared himself unable to walk. Some half a dozen of his comrades were standing around him, with feelings painfully wrought up, waiting the denouement of an affair which, from the angry appearance of Salazar, they now feared would be tragical. Once more the blood-thirsty savage, pointing to the main body of prisoners, ordered the cripple to hurry forward and overtake them — he could not. 'Forward!' said Salazar, now wrought up to a pitch of frenzy. 'Forward, or I'll shoot you on the spot!' 'Then shoot!' replied McAllister, throwing off his blanket and exposing his manly breast, 'and the quicker the better!' Salazar took him at his word, and a single ball sent as brave a man as ever trod the earth to eternity! His ears were then cut off, his shirt and pantaloons stripped from him, and his body thrown by the roadside as food for wolves!''

When this inhuman monster arrived at El Paso, he turned his prisoners over to the commanding general at that place, Don J. M. Elias Gonzales, or as he was generally termed, General Elias, a well bred, liberal, and gentlemanly officer. No sooner had he been acquainted with the conduct of Salazar than he expressed great indignation, and, as the Texans had suffered so much from want of food and excessive fatigue, he at once gave orders for three days' rest to recruit and give them strength for the march to the City of Mexico. On the afternoon of the day of the arrival of the Texans at El Paso, and while the prisoners were some of them being entertained at the residence of General Elias, Salazar entered the room, his object being to render an account of his stewardship in relation to the Texans whom he had brought from Santa Fé. He began by saying that Governor Armijo had intrusted him with the charge of guarding a certain number of men from San Miguel to El Paso; that he had turned over the whole number with the exception of five, who had unfortunately died upon the road; and to prove that they had really died, and had not escaped, he had brought their ears, at the same time throwing upon

General Santa Ana on the 13th of June, 1842. The only exception was the commissioner, Navarro, who was condemned to death, but who finally bought his way out of prison and escaped to Texas.[56] General Houston, president of the republic of Texas, left no resource untried in his efforts to effect the release of the prisoners.

---

the table five pairs of them which he had strung upon a strip of buckskin: General Elias at once told him that he had murdered, basely murdered, three of these men. The miscreant denied this charge, at the same time turning a black look in the direction where several of the Texan officers were smoking. He said that he was a brave man, and that when he was in advance his master, Armijo, could always sleep in quiet and security. The comandante coolly told him that the business before them had nothing to do with his personal prowess and bravery, or with the estimation in which Armijo held him; they were talking of the three men whom he had cruelly put to death for no crime. General Elias also charged Salazar with the larceny of some cattle and mules, and concluded the interview by ordering him under arrest.

[56] A complete narrative of the events happening in New Mexico in connection with the capture of the party under McLeod is to found in Bustamante, *Gabinete Mexicano*, ii, 216-25, entitled "*Una memoria que se me ha remitido de Santa Fé de Nuevo Mexico de la que he copiado lo siguiente.*" The writer concludes the narrative with an extract from an address of John Quincy Adams, in which he denounced this invasion of adventurers, or pirates, from the United States, rejoicing at their failure, and ridiculing their pretensions as traders and travelers.

A portion of the diary of Lieutenant-Colonel Archuleta's operations from September 30th to October 9th, including the details of the capture of General McLeod and his party, is to be found in the *Archives of Santa Fé*.

In *Mex. Mem. Guerra*, 1844, doc. i, xl, appears the diplomatic correspondence in Mexico on the case of Kendall and others, who claimed the protection of the United States.

In reading Kendall's account of the expedition, one must remember that he is exceedingly biased, and that his judgment is likely to be warped. I see no reason to doubt the truth of his statements relative to the treatment of the prisoners by Salazar. He was one of the editors of the New Orleans *Picayune*. Mr. Bancroft, in a note, p. 324, of his *History of Arizona and New Mexico*, says of his book: "His narrative is a most fascinating one, and is full of valuable information respecting the countries through which he passed. No effort is made to conceal his intensely bitter hatred of the New Mexicans, though he speaks well of the women and of a few men who were kind to the Texans in their misfortunes. Governor Armijo is described not only as a tyrant, but as an inhuman and bloodthirsty wretch, an unprincipled libertine, and a boastful coward, whose fortune was founded on early success as a sheep thief, and whose only good quality was a fine personal appearance. Captain Salazar and other officers are described as worthy followers of such a chief. The author's views of Armijo are supported to a considerable extent by Gregg and other Americans who knew the governor, and they have been adopted more or less fully by later writers. Kendall narrates minutely the capture and treatment of his own little party, and he gives particular attention to Captain Lewis, who had lived in Spanish-American provinces, knew the language, and was implicitly trusted by the Texans. Lewis is accused of having betrayed his comrades, revealed all their plans and induced Cooke and McLeod to surrender, by false assurances of kind treatment and false representations of the enemy's force. Of course, the subject of Lewis' treachery

Col. J. M. Washington

He appealed to all the friendly powers to mediate in their behalf. The congress of Texas had adjourned after the news of their capture had arrived, without doing anything to aid the president in restoring them to their liberty. They had been given up as doomed men; they had gone to Santa Fé in violation of the law of nations, and with no constitutional authority from their government. They had been thrown on Houston's hands; his only reliance was on the terms of their capitulation, for he insisted that, even if they had been outlaws before, this had brought them within the pale of civilized warfare. The details of the negotiations that were carried on for the release of these brave but misguided men belong to the history of Texas.

General Armijo was now a man of great prominence in the department. He had executed a great *coup de main*. His reputation as a soldier and executive necessarily was enhanced at the seat of government in Mexico. The Mexican authorities were justified in the course which had been pursued. In the eyes of the Mexicans the Texans were nothing short of desperadoes, entering a peaceful province under false pretenses for the purpose of stirring up trouble and in aid of the Texan republic. The fact of the capture of the printed proclamations and their contents is enough to justify the Mexicans in their estimate of the entire performance. Armijo really is deserving of some congratulation in having so easily taken the Texans into camp, for it was no simple undertaking, considering the character of Armijo's forces, to have accomplished this feat. Even if it be admitted that Armijo did break his promises, still, when he ascertained from an inspection of the Lamar proclamations, just what were the intentions of the invading party, he was justified in disregarding any promise which he

---

and that of Kendall's wrongs, real or pretended, as an innocent citizen of the United States, have very little importance as part of the annals of New Mexico.''

Thomas Falconer, an Englishman, who was with the party, and who was set at liberty immediately upon the arrival of the Texans at the City of Mexico, wrote *Notes of a Journey through Texas and New Mexico in the years 1841 and 1842*. Of the capture of McLeod, he says: ''A surrender was agreed upon, and the terms, securing to the party the treatment of prisoners of war, were signed by the officers of both sides.'' He confirms Kendall's statement that on the march several men were shot and their ears cut off.

Waddy Thompson, United States minister to Mexico at the time, mentions this affair in his *Recollections*, and states, what is practically admitted by all, that the prisoners were well enough treated while in Mexico.

had made. The Mexicans and Armijo have been the subjects of great abuse for their conduct and treatment of the Texans, but generally speaking, all fair-minded people must admit that the invaders were simply out of luck and received the same sort of treatment that would have been accorded by their own people had Texan territory been invaded by a hostile force or one acting and moving under pretenses acknowledged and proven to be false.

The people of Texas were loud in their threats of vengeance for what they called the treachery and barbarous conduct of Armijo. No sooner had the captive Texans returned from Mexico than retaliatory enterprises were openly discussed. The newspapers teemed with editorials denouncing the Mexicans and calling upon the people of the single-star republic to rise for purposes of invasion and revenge. Not content with invading New Mexico they proposed to plant their banners in the city of Chihuahua; all of northern Mexico must be revolutionized and above everything General Armijo, Captain Salazar, and the traitor, Captain Lewis, must be taken dead or alive. There was great popular enthusiasm. The project shortly became known at Santa Fé, and at the seat of government in Mexico there was considerable apprehension, because it was believed that the United States would in some way foster the Texan enterprise. The Texans, for the purpose of this invasion, contemplated the raising of a force of eight hundred men, under the command of Colonel Jacob Snively, and such enthusiasm prevailed that it was with difficulty that that number was kept down, so many applications were made for joining the enterprise. The Mexican government took immediate steps to meet the contemplated invasion and sent a large force into New Mexico, under General José M. Monterde, to support General Armijo, but, as results proved, the latter had small need for assistance.

RAIDS BY THE TEXANS IN 1843

The grand army of invasion and vengeance, the revolutionizing and capture of all of northern Mexico, finally resolved itself into nothing but the attempted plundering of caravans supplying the Santa Fé-Chihuahua trade, which, at this time, was to a very considerable extent in the hands of citizens of Mexico, Santa Fé, and Chihuahua particularly. The first attack occurred in the territory

THE TEXAS-SANTA FE EXPEDITION 83

of the United States and this fact had much to do with the undoing of all the great plans of the Texans.

It was currently reported in New Mexico, as early as November, 1842, that a party of Texans was out upon the plains, prepared to attack any Mexican traders who should attempt to cross to the Missouri river the succeeding spring. Some of the Americans living at Santa Fé and other portions of New Mexico were accused of being spies and in collusion with the Texans. This rumor caused a great deal of trouble for a number of innocent people who were ordered into Santa Fé by Armijo for examination and subjected to the strictest surveillance.[57]

MURDER OF DON ANTONIO JOSÉ CHAVEZ

So little apprehension, says Gregg, seemed to exist, however, that in February, 1843, Don Antonio José Chavez, of New Mexico, left Santa Fé for Independence, with but five servants, two wagons, and fifty-five mules. He had with him some ten or twelve thousand dollars in specie and gold bullion, besides a small lot of furs. As the month of March was extremely inclement, the party suffered inconceivably from cold and privations. Most of the party were frost-bitten and all of the animals, except five, perished from the extreme severity of the weather. On this account Chavez was compelled to leave one of the wagons on the plains. Continuing with his single wagon and his valuables, on the 10th of April he reached the Little Arkansas, about a hundred miles within the territory of the United States. Here he was met by fifteen men from the Missouri border, professing to be Texan troops, under the command of John McDaniel. This band of ruffians had been collected for the most part on the frontier, by McDaniel, who had come from Texas and from the government of which he claimed to have a captain's commission. They had started from the Missouri with the intention of joining Colonel Warfield, also said to be holding a Texan commission, who had been upon the plains near the mountains for several months, with a small party, avowedly intending to attack the Mexican traders.

---

[57] B. D. Wilson, in his *Observations*, Ms., says that two men, Rowland and Workman, and about twenty others left for California on account of Texan complications, as they did not think it safe to remain in New Mexico. Workman and Rowland were under suspicion of having been instrumental in sending information to the Texans prior to the Texas-Santa Fé expedition.

Upon meeting Chavez, the party of McDaniel at once determined to rob him, even though he was then within the limits of the United States. The unfortunate Mexican was therefore taken a few miles south of the road and his baggage rifled. Seven of the desperadoes then left for the settlements on the border, carrying with them their share of the booty, amounting to some four or five hundred dollars each. The journey was made on foot, as their horses had taken a stampede and escaped. The remaining eight, soon after the departure of their comrades, determined to put Chavez to death, for what cause does not appear as he had been their unresisting prisoner for two days. Lots were cast to determine which four of the party should be the cruel executioners; and their wretched victim was taken off a few rods and shot down in cold blood. After his murder a considerable amount of gold was found about his person and in his trunk. The body of the unfortunate man, together with his wagon and baggage, was thrown into a neighboring ravine; and a few of the lost animals of the marauders having been found, their booty was packed upon them and borne away to the frontier of Missouri.

Great exertions had been made to intercept this lawless band at the very beginning; but they escaped the vigilance of a detachment of United States dragoons that had followed them for over a hundred miles. The honest citizens of the border, however, were too much on the alert to permit them to return to the interior with impunity. However, five of the whole number, including three of the party that killed Chavez, made their escape, but the other ten were arrested and sent to St. Louis where they were tried, some for the murder of Chavez and others for robbery. In due course the sentence of the court which found them guilty was carried out and John McDaniel and his brother David were both hanged. The others were sentenced to a fine and imprisonment.[58]

Colonel Jacob Snively and his "gallant" band of Texan "avengers," to the number, not of eight hundred, but about one hundred and eighty, now appear upon the scene, engaged in an enterprise supposed at that time to be the particular occupation of hostile and murdering, marauding savages. Snively organized his force of "avengers" in the north of Texas, and in May, 1843, set out

---

[58] *Niles' Register*, lxiv, pp. 195, 280, gives names of the other participators.

from the settlements to attack the caravans on the Santa Fé Trail. It was at first reported that a descent upon Santa Fé was contemplated, but even this gallant Texan did not believe his force strong enough for such an attempt, so it appears that his prime object was an attack upon the Mexicans engaged in the trade who were expected to cross the plains during the months of May and June.

Upon the arrival of Snively and his command upon the Arkansas, they were joined by Warfield, with a few followers. Not long prior to this date Warfield, with about twenty men, had attacked the village of Mora, on the frontier, at that time killing five men and driving off a number of horses. They were afterward followed by a strong party of Mexicans, who succeeded in regaining not only their own live stock but all that belonged to the Texans as well. In consequence, the Texans burned their saddles and walked to Bent's Fort on the Arkansas, where the party was disbanded, Warfield and a few faithful followers passing over to Snively and his band.

Snively now marched down the Santa Fé Trail beyond the sandhills south of the Arkansas, when a party of Mexicans was discovered. The Texans soon came upon them, and in a skirmish, eighteen Mexicans were killed and a number wounded, the Texans suffering no loss. This fight occurred on the 19th of June, 1843, the Mexicans being an advance party from General Armijo's command, who, with five hundred men, had left Santa Fé on the 1st of May to meet the caravans at the Arkansas. The troops thus defeated by Snively consisted of one hundred militiamen under the command of Captain Ventura Lobato. The entire command, with the exception of one or two who escaped to Armijo, surrendered to Snively. General Armijo was encamped at Cold Springs, one hundred and forty miles beyond. As soon as Armijo received notice of the defeat of Lobato, he broke camp most precipitately and retreated to Santa Fé. A gentleman of the caravan which passed shortly afterward testifies that spurs, lariats, and other kinds of equipage, were found scattered in every direction about Armijo's camp, left by his troops in the hurly-burly of the retreat.[59]

---

[59] Bancroft, H. H., *History of Arizona and New Mexico*, in a note on page 328, says that Bustamante's statement that Snively ''á todos los pasó a cuchillas despues de rendidas las armas'' is probably unfounded. Some other

The defeat of the militia under Lobato was attended by consequences very disastrous to American interests in New Mexico. Lobato's command was made up almost entirely of citizens of Taos, most of them Pueblo Indians. These Indians had remained very much embittered against General Armijo owing to his treatment of the men captured at the battle of La Cañada and their subsequent execution by his orders. In truth, the revolutionists under Gonzales had declared in favor of Texas, and so loath were these Indians to enter the campaign against the Texans that the governor found it necessary to bind a number of them upon their horses, to prevent their escape, till he got them fairly upon the plains. And yet these, of all of Armijo's command, were the ones who had to bear the vengeance of Snively's "avengers."

When the news of the defeat of Lobato's command reached Taos,

---

authorities say that the prisoners were released. The Texans and Americans all state that Armijo, on learning of the disaster, retreated in great haste, without waiting for the caravan.

Yoakum, H., *History of Texas* (New York, 1856), ii, pp. 399-405, gives a detailed account of Snively's expedition and the fight with Lobato's command.

Gregg, Josiah, *Commerce of the Prairies*, ii, pp. 170-172, says: "Keeping beyond the territory of the United States, the right of the Texans to harass the commerce of the Mexicans will hardly be denied, as they were at open war; yet another consideration, it would seem, should have restrained them from aggressions in that quarter. They could not have been ignorant that but a portion of the traders were Mexicans — that many American citizens were connected in the same caravans. The Texans assert, it is true, that the lives and property of Americans were to be respected, provided they abandoned the Mexicans. But did they reflect upon the baseness of the terms they were imposing? What American, worthy of the name, to save his own interests, or even his life, could deliver up his trading companions to be sacrificed? Then, after having abandoned the Mexicans, or betrayed them to their enemy — for such an act would have been accounted treachery — where would they have gone? They could not then have continued on to Mexico; and to have returned to the United States with their merchandise, would have been the ruin of most of them.

"The unfortunate Chavez, whose murder, I suppose, was perpetrated under pretext of the cruelties suffered by the Texans, in the name of whom the party of McDaniel was organized, was of the most wealthy and influential family of New Mexico, and one that was anything but friendly to the ruling governor, Armijo. Don Mariano Chavez, a brother of the deceased, is a gentleman of very amiable character, such as is rarely met in that unfortunate land. It is asserted that he furnished a considerable quantity of provisions, blankets etc., to Col. Cooke's division of Texan prisoners. Señora Chavez, the wife of Don Mariano, as is told, crossed the river from the village of Padillas, the place of their residence, and administered comforts to the unfortunate band of Texans. Though the murder of young Chavez was evidently not sanctioned by the Texans generally, it will notwithstanding, have greatly embittered this powerful family against them — a family whose liberal principles could not otherwise have been very unfavorable to Texas."

the friends and relatives of the slain, the whole population, indeed, were incensed beyond measure; and two or three naturalized foreigners, who were supposed to favor the Texan cause, and who hitherto had been in good standing, were now compelled to flee for their lives, leaving their houses and property a prey to the rabble. Such appears to have been the reaction of public sentiment resulting from the catastrophe upon the prairies.[60]

---

[60] Gregg, J., *Commerce of the Prairies*, ii, p. 173: "Had the Texans proceeded differently — had they induced the Mexicans to surrender without battle, which they might no doubt easily have accomplished, they could have secured their services, without question, as guides to General Armijo's camp, and that unmitigated tyrant might himself have fallen into their hands. The difficulty of maintaining order among the Texans was perhaps the cause of many of their unfortunate proceedings."

In the *Santa Fé Archives*, Ms. *Libro de Ordenes*, is found an account of Armijo's operations from May 1st to July 1st, including the capture of five Texans on June 6th or 7th.

Niles' Register, lxiv, 195, 234-5, 406, contains a large amount of information on the details of the affair.

In July of this year Colonel John C. Fremont was on Fountain creek — *Fontaine que bouit*, or Boiling Spring river. In his report to Colonel J. J. Abert, chief of the corps of topographical engineers, U. S. A., Fremont says: "Continuing down the river we encamped at noon on the 14th [July] at its mouth on the Arkansas river. A short distance above our encampment, on the left bank of the Arkansas is a *pueblo* (as the Mexicans call their civilized Indian villages) where a number of mountaineers, who had married Spanish women in the valley of Taos, had collected together and occupied themselves in farming, carrying on at the same time a desultory Indian trade. They were principally Americans, and treated us with all the rude hospitality their situation admitted; but as all commercial intercourse with New Mexico was now interrupted, in consequence of Mexican decrees to that effect, there was nothing to be had in the way of provisions. They had, however, a fine stock of cattle, and furnished us an abundance of excellent milk. I learned here that Maxwell, in company with two other men had started for Taos on the morning of the 9th, but that he would probably fall into the hands of the Ute Indians, commonly called the *Spanish Utes*. As Maxwell had no knowledge of their being in the vicinity when he crossed the Arkansas, his chance of escape was very doubtful; but I did not entertain much apprehension for his life, having great confidence in his prudence and courage. I was further informed that there had been a popular tumult among the *Pueblos*, or civilized Indians, residing near Taos against the 'foreigners' of that place, in which they had plundered their houses and ill-treated their families. Among those whose property had been destroyed was Mr. Beaubien, father-in-law of Maxwell, from whom I had expected to obtain supplies, and who had been obliged to make his escape to Santa Fé.

"By this position of affairs, our expectation of obtaining supplies from Taos was cut off. I had here the satisfaction to meet our good buffalo hunter of 1842, Christopher Carson, whose services I considered myself fortunate to secure again; and as a re-enforcement of mules was absolutely necessary, I despatched him immediately with an account of our necessities to Mr. Charles Bent, whose principal post is on the Arkansas river about seventy-five miles below *Fontaine qui Bouit*; he was directed to proceed from that post by the

Shortly after the departure of Armijo from the Arkansas, the caravans, escorted by two hundred United States dragoons, under command of Captain Philip St. George Cooke, arrived. Snively with about a hundred men was at the time encamped on the right bank of the Arkansas, some ten or fifteen miles below the point called Caches. He crossed the river and met Captain Cooke who soon made known his intention of disarming the Texans, which he forthwith proceeded to do. A portion of the Texans, however, deceived Cooke by delivering over the worthless guns which had been captured from the Mexicans under Lobato, keeping their valuable Colt's repeating rifles.[61]

Captain Cooke with his command soon after returned to the United States accompanied by a number of the disarmed Texans. A large number of the latter now left for Texas, while about sixty or seventy men, under Warfield, organized and started in pursuit of the caravan, which had already passed on its way to Santa Fé. They pursued it a short distance but made no attack and shortly returned to Texas. As a consequence of this trouble with the avenging Texans, General Santa Ana, by decree, closed the north-

nearest route across the country and meet me with what animals he should be able to obtain at St. Vrain's Fort.''

Bustamante, *Apuntes Hist. Santa Ana*, 206-9, gives information of the *nueva invasion de Nuevo-Mexico por los Anglo-Americanos*. In **Mex. Mem. Guerra**, 1844, doc. lxiii, ix, is noted that on June 17, 1843, the Mexican government had been obliged to decree death to all foreigners entering the country as bandits, or fighting under a flag not recognized in Mexico.

[61] Gregg, J., *Commerce of the Prairies*, ii, p. 174: ''Captain Cooke has been much abused by the Texans and accused of having violated a friendly flag — of having taken Colonel Snively prisoner while on a friendly visit. This is denied by Captain Cooke, and by other persons who were with the party at the time. But apart from the means employed by the American commander (the propriety or impropriety of which I shall not attempt to discuss), the act was evidently the salvation of the Santa Fé caravan, of which a considerable portion were Americans. Had he left the Texans their arms, he would doubtless have been accused by the traders of escorting them to the threshold of danger, and then delivering them over to certain destruction, when he had it in his power to secure their safety.''

Although this expedition was composed wholly of Texans, or persons not claiming to be citizens of the United States, and organized entirely in Texas — and, notwithstanding the active measures adopted by the United States government to defend the caravans, as well of Mexicans as of Americans, against their enemy — Señor Bocanegra, Mexican minister of foreign relations, made a formal demand upon the United States for damages resulting from the invasion.

Bocanegra was at one time president ad interim of Mexico. He belonged to the liberal party which came into power under Guerrero in 1829.

James S. Calhoun, first Civil Governor of New Mexico under the
Act of Congress March 3, 1851

ern ports of Mexico to foreign commerce, which for the time being terminated the trade over the Santa Fé Trail. By decree of March 31, 1844, the ports were reopened and about ninety wagons, with perhaps $200,000 worth of merchandise, the caravan employing about two hundred men, crossed the plains to Santa Fé, during the summer and fall of that year.[62]

Mexican Arrastra

---

[62] Gregg, J., *Commerce of the Prairies*, ii, p. 177. The decree was of date August 7th, 1843, and closed the customs houses of Taos, Paso del Norte and Presidio del Norte. The only port in New Mexico was nominally at Taos, the custom house actually being at Santa Fé where all entrances were made.

Bancroft, H. H., *History of Arizona and New Mexico*, pp. 329, 338: "In July and August the Mexican Minister complained to Waddy Thompson that the United States government was responsible for the so-called Texan invasion; but the reply denied such responsibility, even if there had been any invasion, which was declared doubtful. Meanwhile, General Monterde marched northward to New Mexico with some 700 men; and he and Armijo flattered themselves that they had saved the country. Good luck and a broad desert frontier had done more to defeat Texan schemes than the zeal of Mexican patriots."

Waddy Thompson was born in South Carolina, in the year 1798. He served in the legislature of his state and was a member of congress 1835-1841. In 1842 he was made minister to Mexico, which position he filled for two years. He went to his post as an advocate of the annexation of Texas but returned opposed to it, convinced that slavery could not be maintained on soil acquired from Mexico. He died in Florida in 1868.

BIBLIOGRAPHY

Bancroft, Hubert Howe	*History of Arizona and New Mexico*, San Francisco, 1889.
Derby, J. C.	*Life of Sam Houston*, New York, 1855.
Fremont, John C.	Upham's *Life of*, Boston, 1856.
Gregg, Dr. Josiah	*Commerce of the Prairies*, New York, 1844.
Kendall, George W.	*Texas-Santa Fé Expedition*, New York, 1844.
Niles' Register	Baltimore, 1811-1849, 76 vols.
Thompson, Waddy	*Recollections of Mexico*, New York, 1846.
Santa Fé Archives	Smithsonian, Washington, D. C.
Wilson, Benj. D.	*Observations*, Ms.
Yoakum, Henry	*History of Texas*, New York, 1856.

A Santa Fé Trader
From a Print of 1835

CHAPTER IV

THE OVERLAND TRADE — OLD SANTA FÉ TRAIL — COMMERCE OF THE
PRAIRIES — STORIES AND INCIDENTS OF THE DAYS
OF THE STAGE COACH, 1804-1872

A SUBJECT of more enduring interest than the story of the old Santa Fé Trail, the great highway over which was carried the commerce of the prairies, is not to be found in the history of the great southwest.

In the early part of the nineteenth century the tide of western immigration had reached the valleys of the Mississippi and Missouri. Stories of the northern provinces of New Spain, the inhabitants, their condition, their commercial and industrial needs, were brought to the western merchants and traders by the trappers, plainsmen and mountaineers. The opening of commercial relations was believed worthy of investigation. Between the extreme western line of settlements and the capital of New Mexico, the most northern Spanish province, was an almost unknown stretch of treeless, trackless plains, infested with hordes of hostile savages. None but the hardy trapper, the plainsman, and the mountaineer had dared to penetrate the mysteries of the great American desert and the mighty mountain ranges far beyond. Coupled with the spirit of progress which always characterized the pioneer of the far west was the desire for gain. In that far-off land of boundless distances lay opportunity for fortune. Beyond the pathless prairies was a sleeping empire; there existed opportunities for trade unsurpassed in the history of the west. Spanish provinces! The very thought was an inspiration. On the American frontier were merchants, sturdy men, ready to force the way in the interest of advancing civilization and commercial interchange.

It was known from the trappers that the Spanish authorities in

New Mexico did not look with favor upon overland commercial relations with the people of the United States. The experience of Lieut. Zebulon M. Pike, when communicated to the American people, seems only to have served to whet the American appetite for trade and even conquest. In New Mexico, as in all the colonies, Spain was extremely jealous of the activities of her rival powers, France and the United States. Feeling was particularly bitter toward the American people, whose enterprise seemed to them a menace to their government and institutions. The official and commercial influence of Chihuahua in New Mexican affairs was supreme. Before the American people succeeded in opening the trade with Santa Fé foreign goods came into New Mexico from Vera Cruz by way of Chihuahua, over a road nearly two thousand miles in length. When these consignments reached New Mexico's capital they brought prices almost incredible when compared with those of today. As a consequence the people were compelled to do without many things which others living nearer the coast were able to procure. Indeed, it was a blessing to the New Mexican when the dreaded Anglo-American trader succeeded in opening the commercial gates of the province. The New Mexican himself soon grasped the opportunities thus presented. In 1826 the residents of New Mexico began to send caravans over the plains to the Missouri and by the year 1843 had monopolized more than half of the entire trade.

The official opposition which was encountered did not, however, deter the American trader from his purpose. He determined to open the trail to Santa Fé. Strangely enough the trail as established later was approximately the same route which had been pursued by the early Spanish explorers at various periods during the preceding two centuries. Traveling to the west and south, the Anglo-American trader trod the paths of the Spanish cavalier who, in 1842, had journeyed to the east, carrying the cross of christianity, searching for the famed Quivira and claiming the country for the Spanish crown, meeting descendants of those savage nomads the Spaniard had sought to pacify, the painted hordes who had given the Franciscan friar his coveted crown of martyrdom.

The facts surrounding the beginning of the Santa Fé trade are somewhat enveloped in mystery. The first expedition of which we have any account was that of Mallet brothers who, in 1739, with six companions, set out from the French settlements on the Mississippi for the Spanish settlements of New Mexico. They ascended the Missouri river, believing that their route lay by the headwaters of that stream. Having reached some villages of the Aricara Indians, they ascertained the correct route, and retracing their steps for a number of miles, they went across the country to the southwest, passing the Pawnee villages, and arrived at Santa Fé July 22, 1739. In the spring of the following year they started back, three of the party going by the Pawnee villages and the others down the Arkansas and the Mississippi to New Orleans.

BEGINNING OF THE SANTA FÉ TRADE

The first recorded expedition made for purposes of trade, strictly, was made prior to 1763, the exact date not being known.

Captain Amos Stoddard in his *Sketches of Louisiana* tells us that "While Louisiana was in the hands of France, some of the French traders from the upper Mississippi transported a quantity of merchandize by way of the Arkansas to the Mexican mountains where they erected a temporary store, and opened a trade with the Indians and likewise with the Spaniards of northern Mexico. The Spanish traders at or near Santa Fé, deeming this an infringement of their privileged rights, procured the imprisonment of the Mississippi adventurers, and the seizure of their effects; and demanded punishment and confiscation. The cause was ultimately decided at Havana. The prisoners were liberated and their property restored on the ground that the store in question (situated on the east side of the summit of the mountains, and below the source of the Arkansas) was within the boundaries of Louisiana."

This store was in all probability located in the immediate vicinity of the present city of Pueblo, Colorado, and was the first trading post known to have been established in that state by white men.

The second trading expedition to Santa Fé was that of William Morrison, of Kaskaskia, Illinois, who sent one Baptiste La Lande, a French Creole, to find his way thither and carry with him a small stock of goods with the view of ascertaining what sort of market existed in the provinces of northern Mexico. La Lande reached Santa Fé in the summer or fall of 1804.[63]

---

[63] *History of the American Fur Trade*, H. M. Chittenden: "La Lande traveled by way of the Pawnee villages, ascended the Platte river to the mountains, and then sent some Indians to Santa Fé to see if he would be

The year following the arrival of La Lande, an American trapper and hunter arrived in Santa Fé. His name was James Purcell, a native of Bardstown, Kentucky. In his narrative, Major Pike (who calls Purcell, Pursley) declares that Pursley was the first American who ever crossed the plains to New Mexico. As we have seen, Major Pike knew of La Lande being in Santa Fé, but in all probability he did not consider him an "American."[64]

permitted to visit the town. Some Spaniards came out to meet him and escorted him and his merchandize to the village. He probably reached Santa Fé in the summer or fall of 1804. He told Pike in March, 1807, that he had been there nearly three years. The goods found ready market and La Lande quickly accomplished the purpose of his mission. But he was a long way from home, between which and him intervened many hundreds of miles of desert country and many hundreds of dangerous savages. The dread of these perils was magnified by the Spaniards, who wanted La Lande to stay there. The government also lent its assistance by offering him land, doubtless preferring that he should stay rather than return with reports which would inevitably lead to a renewal of the enterprise. Last, and perhaps most effectual, the influence of female admirers turned the scale of the doubtful adventurer. He shuffled off without apparent compunction his obligation to his employer, appropriated the money to his own use, and decided to make Santa Fé his home."

La Lande was born in Illinois, his name appearing on the list of the militia of St. Clair county in 1790. One of Major Pike's supposed errands to Santa Fé was to recover for Morrison the money owed him by La Lande. The latter came to Pike, as the American officer thought, as a spy from the Spanish government. Pike did not collect the amount due. Escudero, in his *Noticias Historicas*, says La Lande was wealthy and left many descendants.

William Morrison was a native of Pennsylvania and came to Kaskaskia in 1790, where he began merchandising. He founded the firm of Bryant and Morrison, maintained a large fleet of boats on the Mississippi river, and was a very successful man. He died at Kaskaskia in 1837.

[64] Pike, Lieut. Z. M., *Narrative*: "In the historical anecdotes of New Mexico, it may not be improper to record the name of James Pursley, the first American who ever penetrated the immense wilds of Louisiana, and showed the Spaniards of New Mexico that neither the savages who surround the deserts which divide them from the habitable world, nor the jealous tyranny of their rulers, was sufficient to prevent the enterprising spirit of the Americans from penetrating the arcanum of their rich establishments in the New World. Pursley was from near Bairds Town, Kentucky, which he had left in 1799." Pike says: "While in the extreme northwest, on the Missouri, Pursley had been despatched by his employer on a hunting and trading tour, with some bands of the Paducas and Kiowas, with a small quantity of merchandize. In the ensuing spring they were driven by the pursuing Sioux from the plains into the mountains which give rise to the Platte, Arkansas, etc., and it was their sign which we saw in such amazing abundance on the headwaters of the Platte, their party consisting of nearly two thousand souls, with ten thousand beasts. The Indians knowing they were approximate to New Mexico, determined to send Pursley with his companions and two of their body into Santa Fé, to know of the Spaniards if they would receive them amicably, and enter into a trade with them. This being acceded to by the governor (Allencaster) the Indian deputies returned to their bands; but Pursley thought proper to remain with a civilized people, among whom a fortuitous event had thrown him, a

In 1802, Purcell with two companions left St. Louis for the purpose of trapping in the country of the Osages. After a successful season and when on the eve of his departure down the Arkansas river for New Orleans, he was robbed of his furs by the Kansas Indians. He recovered his property, however, later to lose it all in the Missouri river near the mouth of the Kansas. After the loss of his furs, Purcell met a trader on his way up the Missouri to the Mandan Indians and joined the expedition. Having arrived at their point of destination Purcell was sent to the valley of the Platte to trade with the Indians in that locality. The spring of 1805 found Purcell and his Indian companions near the source of the South Platte river, from which place the Indians, knowing that they were near the Spanish settlements, sent Purcell to Santa Fé to secure permission to come in and trade. He arrived in June, 1805, and did not return with his Indian companions. He remained in Santa Fé for many years, pursuing his trade of carpenter. He was held under very strict surveillance, was not permitted to write, and very narrowly escaped being shot for having broken the local law by manufacturing some gunpowder for his own use.[65]

circumstance which he assured me he had at one time entirely despaired of. He arrived at Santa Fé, June, 1805, and had been following his trade of carpenter ever since, at which he made a great deal of money, except when working for the officers, who paid him little or nothing. He was a man of strong natural sense, and of undaunted intrepidity and entertained me with numerous interesting anecdotes of his adventures with the Indians, and of the jealousy of the Spanish government. He was once nearly being hanged for making a few pounds of powder, which he innocently did, as he was accustomed to do in Kentucky, but which is a capital crime in these provinces. He still retained his gun, which he had with him during his whole tour, and spoke confidently that if he had two hours start, not all the province could take him. He was forbidden to write but was assured he should have a pass-port whenever demanded; he was obliged, however, to give security that he would not leave the country without the permission of the government. I brought letters out for him. He assured me that he had found gold on the head of the Platte and had carried some of the virgin mineral in his shot pouch for months, but that being in doubt whether he should ever again behold the civilized world, and closing his mind to all the ideal value which mankind has spent on that metal, he threw his sample away; that he had imprudently mentioned it to the Spaniards, who had frequently solicited him to go and show a detachment of cavalry the place, but conceiving it to be in our territory he had refused, and was fearful that the circumstance might create a great obstacle to his leaving the country.''

[65] The *Missouri Intelligencer* of April 10, 1824, contains an article relative to the Navajós, written by James Purcell, lately returned from Santa Fé and ''for nineteen years a citizen of New Mexico.''

Chittenden, H. M., *History of the American Fur Trade*, p. 493, says: ''In 1806 there was being organized at St. Louis by a prominent trader a project

After the return of Lieutenant Pike,[66] whose relation of events transpiring and conditions existing in the northern provinces of New Spain caused a great deal of excitement throughout the west, commercial possibilities with the Spaniards attracted a great deal of attention. Previous to this time New Mexico had no outside market for any of its products and the only source of supply was from Mexico by way of Chihuahua. The New Mexican exports were sheep, furs, buffalo robes, dressed deer-skins, salt, tobacco, and finely wrought copper vessels. In return for these came cotton, silk and velvet, arms, iron, steel, ammunition, and choice liquors. According to Major Pike, high grade imported cloth sold in Santa Fé as high as twenty to twenty-five dollars the yard, linen at four dollars the yard, and other dry goods in proportion.

Pike gave to the people of the United States the first information of a reliable character concerning the conditions existing in northern Mexico, and his expedition unquestionably was the means of inducing traders to come to New Mexico in quest of profitable

---

for trade with Santa Fé. The scheme was to form a large depot among the Osages, and then at the proper time to push on with an escort of friendly Indians to within 'three or four days' travel of the Spanish settlements.' Leaving the main party with the goods under guard of the friendly Indians, the leader was to go to Santa Fé with a few well selected articles and try to get permission to bring in his entire outfit. If not successful he was to induce as many Spaniards as possible to go back with him and trade at his camp. Nothing more was ever heard of the venture, and it is known to us only through a letter of instruction from General Wilkinson to Lieutenant Pike, dated August 6, 1806. In this letter Wilkinson takes strong ground against the enterprise and urges Pike to do all in his power to frustrate it. The name of this enterprising trader is not mentioned but it is thought to be Manuel Lisa.''

[66] Chittenden, H. M., *History of the American Fur Trade*, p. 494: ''Pike was ordered to visit certain tribes of Indians in the newly-acquired regions to the west and southwest of St. Louis, among them the Comanches, near the sources of the Arkansas and Red rivers, and also to determine the 'direction, extent and navigation' of those two streams. It was inevitable that these instructions should take him into Spanish territory and there is strong reason to suspect that he had other instructions, not in writing, that required him to push his explorations much nearer the Spanish capital of Santa Fé than his published orders or his skilful disclaimer in his journal would indicate. No one may ever know whether the trap into which Pike ran, when he built his redoubt on the west bank of the Rio Grande and hoisted the American flag in the very faces of the Spaniards, was a trap set by himself or not; but every circumstance of the expedition indicates that it was all a scheme to get into Santa Fé and learn what he could of the country without having his purpose suspected. Such at any rate was the outcome of the affair.'' See vol. i, pp. 461-468.

The Caravan in Sight of Santa Fé

returns in business ventures. It was not, however, for several years after his return that attempts were made to open the trade.

"It is an interesting coincidence," says Chittenden, "that almost simultaneously with the United States' exploring expedition into Spanish territory there took place a much more formidable one from Santa Fé far into United States territory. The Spanish expedition consisted of one hundred dragoons of the regular army and five hundred mounted militia, with two extra horses and a mule to each man and ammunition for six months. It was commanded by a distinguished Spanish officer, Don Facundo Melgares. It left Santa Fé probably about the middle of June, for that was the date of a commission carried by Melgares to the chief of the Pawnees. The route of the party at first lay down the Canadian, thence northeast to the Arkansas, and from that point to the Pawnee villages where a grand council was held. The expedition then returned to Santa Fé where it arrived in October. The Spaniards could scarcely have been a month ahead of the Americans at the Pawnee villages. Their expedition, according to Pike, was intended to forestall his own, and it is a remarkable instance of the energetic fashion in which a Spaniard could execute an enterprise when he once really set about it.

EXPEDITION UNDER MELGARES

"There is a profound significance in the almost simultaneous presence of these two expeditions upon the boundless prairies that separated the frontier settlements of their respective countries. One was looking into the future and paving a way for the irresistible expansion of his people. The other was clinging to the past and watching with distrustful eye the too rapid progress of a rival power. Both were visiting the wild inhabitants of the plains and seeking with presents and speeches and grandiloquent pictures of the greatness of their respective nations, to secure their attachment. In this preliminary skirmish between two powers, which were even then, did they but know it, preparing the way for inevitable conflict, the advantage was on the side of the Spaniards. Between the powerful and well-appointed expedition of Melgares and the small and poorly equipped handful of men with Pike the contrast was great, and to the untutored mind of the prairie inhabitant, there could be no doubt of the outcome of a trial of strength between their governments. He could not see the forces behind these outward manifestations — the expanding vigor of a young nation and the decadent energies of the old; but in due time he came to know." [67]

In November, 1809, three men by the names of Smith, McClan-

---

[67] Chittenden, H. M., *History of the American Fur Trade*, pp. 495-496.
See also vol. i, this work, pp. 480-1.

ahan, and Patterson, under the guidance of a Spaniard, Manuel Blanco, left St. Louis for Santa Fé. Nothing further was ever heard of them, and it is supposed that they were killed by Indians on the plains.

An expedition of twelve men, under the leadership of Robert McKnight, James Baird, and Samuel Chambers, crossed the plains in 1812 and reached Santa Fé. They were arrested by the Spanish authorities, their goods confiscated, and they were held as prisoners at Durango and Chihuahua until 1822, when they were released by order of Iturbide. Efforts had been made in 1817 in their behalf by Secretary of State Adams through the Spanish minister, Onís, but nothing was accomplished, although the latter wrote both to the viceroy and to the king of Spain.[68]

IMPRISONMENT OF MC KNIGHT, BAIRD, AND CHAMBERS

In 1815, Auguste P. Chouteau and Julius De Munn,[69] partners, led an expedition to the headwaters of the Arkansas, where they hunted and traded with the Indians. The following year they visited Taos and Santa Fé, securing permission from the Spanish governor, Alberto Maynez, to trap and trade east of the mountains and north of Red river. Early in 1817, however, under Governor Allande, came a change of policy. A force of two hundred men under Lieutenant Francisco Salazar marched from Santa Fé to the Rio de las Animas, where it was said the Americans had established a fort. No such fort existed, but in June, Sergeant Mariano Ber-

---

[68] They were induced to undertake the journey in the belief that Spanish authority in New Mexico was overthrown by the revolutionary chief, Hidalgo, and that they should find the baneful customs and regulations which were practically prohibitive of foreign trade, removed. Their hopes were doomed not only to disappointment, but to a reality exactly the reverse of what they expected. The Hidalgo movement had failed, the chief had been executed, and the Spanish authorities, intensely suspicious of foreigners and especially of Americans, seized the traders immediately upon their arrival, sent them to Chihuahua and put them in prison. Here they remained upward of nine years, or until the revolutionary movement under Iturbide finally succeeded, when they were set at liberty.

[69] *Message* from the president of the United States, transmitting information relative to the arrest and imprisonment of certain American citizens at Santa Fé, Washington, 1818. See also *Annals of Congress*, 1817-1818. Some of the party were Robert McKnight, Benjamin Shrive, James Baird, Alfred Allen, Michael McDonough, William Mines, Peter Baum, Samuel Chambers, Thomas Cook, and an interpreter, whose name was Miers. Two of these escaped down the Canadian, in 1821.

nal was sent out for the purpose of arresting Chouteau, De Munn, and their companions. This he succeeded in doing, bringing them to Santa Fé, where they were tried by court-martial, kept in jail forty-eight days, and finally released.

Auguste Chouteau was the head of the celebrated family of that name and was one of the founders of the city of St. Louis. He was born in New Orleans, August 14, 1750. The Chouteaus were the leaders in the fur trade in the early part of the nineteenth century. Pierre Chouteau was a brother, six years younger than Auguste. St. Louis was the seat of their business operations, and as owners of the Missouri Fur Company they controlled the fur traffic west of the Kansas river, reaching to the headwaters of the Platte, the Arkansas, and the Rio Grande. In the year 1813 the company controlled by the Chouteaus was merged with the American Fur Company, a corporation organized in New York in 1808 by John Jacob Astor.

It seems that Chouteau and De Munn left St. Louis on the 10th of September, 1815, in company with a trader named Phillebert, who had gone to the Rocky Mountain country the year previous and had returned for the purpose of buying supplies with which to trade for horses with the Indians so that he could bring in his supply of furs. On the way out Chouteau and De Munn purchased Phillebert's entire outfit. Phillebert had named Huerfano creek as the rendezvous for his hunters, but when Chouteau and his companions arrived in December, 1815, they were informed by Indians that Phillebert's men, thinking he would never return, and being without supplies of any kind, had gone to New Mexico. De Munn went to New Mexico in search of them and found them at Taos, where they had been well treated. De Munn now went to Santa Fé where he had a very favorable interview with Governor Maynez. He did not secure permission, however, to trap beaver in the streams in New Mexico, but the governor promised to recommend to the government at Chihuahua that such permission be given. De Munn now returned to Chouteau's camp on the Huerfano, and soon, in company with Phillebert and another trapper, returned to St. Louis, making the journey in forty-six days.

ARREST AND COURT-MARTIAL OF CHOUTEAU AND DE MUNN

De Munn and a new party left St. Louis July 15, 1816, and at the mouth of the Kansas river met Chouteau who had come in to the river with his furs. On the way in he had had a very severe fight with the Pawnees, in which one white man and several Indians were killed.

Chouteau and De Munn now returned to the mountains, having in the party forty-five trappers and hunters. The hunters went to the Sangre de Cristo Mountains and De Munn started for Santa Fé to see the governor. Before arriving at the New Mexican capital he learned that Allande was governor and that he was illy disposed toward the fur traders. Indeed Allande ordered Chouteau and De Munn to leave Spanish territory, which they did, Chouteau and De Munn and their hunters proceeding to the headwaters of the Arkansas where they trapped and hunted during the fall and winter.

In the following spring De Munn intended to leave for St. Louis, taking with him the furs which had been *cached*. Before it was possible for him to leave, however, he was arrested by Sergeant Bernal, along with Chouteau, and taken to Santa Fé. Their property was confiscated and they were even put in irons in the old jail, which stood in the plaza in front of the old palace. Finally, after a court-martial, sentencing them to leave the dominions of Spain, they returned to St. Louis, where they arrived in September, 1817.

In a letter to Governor William Clark, written from St. Louis, November 25, 1817, De Munn gives in detail the facts connected with the court-martial at Santa Fé. He says:

"After forty-eight days' imprisonment we were presented before a court martial composed of six members and a president who was the governor himself (Pedro Maria de Allande). Only one of the six members appeared to have any information, the others not even knowing how to sign their names. Many questions were asked, but particularly why we stayed so long in Spanish dominions. I answered that, being on the Arkansas river we did not consider ourselves in the domains of Spain, as we had a license to go as far as the headwaters of said river. The president denied that our government had a right to give such a license, and entered into such a rage that it prevented his speaking, contenting himself with striking his fist several times on the table, saying, 'Gentlemen, we must have this man shot.'

"At such conduct of the president I did not think much of my life, for all the members were terrified in his presence, and unwilling to resist him; on the contrary [were ready] to do anything to please him.

"He talked much of a big river that was the boundary line between the two countries, but did not know its name. When mention was made of the Mississippi he jumped up saying that was the big river he meant; that Spain had never ceded the west side of it. It may be easy to judge of our feelings to see our lives in the hands of such a man.

"That day the court did not come to any determination, because the president (as I heard him say to Lieutenant de Arce) had forgotten everything he had to say. Next day we were again presented to the court, but as I knew the kind of man we had to deal with, I never attempted to justify myself of any of his false assertions. We were dismissed and Mr. Chouteau and myself put in the same room.

"Half an hour afterward the Lieutenant came in with a written sentence; we were forced to kneel down to hear the citure of it, and forced, likewise, to kiss the unjust and iniquitous sentence that deprived harmless men of all they possessed — of the fruits of two years' labors and perils.

"What appears the more extraordinary is that the governor acknowledged to me afterward in the presence of Don Piedro Piero [Don Pedro Bautista Pino] the deputy of New Mexico to the Córtes, and several others, that we were very innocent men; yet notwithstanding this all our property was kept and we were permitted to come home, each with one of the worst horses we had."[70]

At the time of the imprisonment of Chouteau and De Munn,

---

[70] When Chouteau and De Munn returned to St. Louis, through the Missouri congressman, Scott, they put in a claim for damages. As late as 1836, this claim and the one preferred by McKnight was still being urged. I do not know whether it was ever finally liquidated by the Spanish government. See *U. S. Gov. Doc.*, 24th cong., 1st sess., *Sen. Docs.*, Nos. 400 and 424.

In a manuscript on file with the Missouri Historical Society, *Ms.*, No. 135, by William Waldo, the following anecdote appears: "Chouteau, having been brought up in the city of St. Louis, which in its early history had perhaps more Spanish inhabitants than those of any other nationality, spoke the Spanish language, which enabled him to communicate freely with the authorities and priests [of Santa Fé]. His superior powers of conversation and his courtly address so captivated the Spanish governor that he would frequently have the Colonel carried from the prison to his house to amuse him and entertain him. On one of these occasions, when the governor had favored his visitor with a long catalogue of his numerous benefactions in his behalf, he paused and with great earnestness demanded what more he would have. The Colonel quietly replied, '*Mi libertad, Señor Gobernador!*' This so incensed the boastful magistrate that the prisoner was quickly ordered back to his vile cell." The author of this anecdote was the uncle of Henry L. Waldo, of Las Vegas, New Mexico.

McKnight, James Baird, Samuel Chambers, and other Americans were in jail in Chihuahua, and the treatment thus accorded to the traders seems to have discouraged any further attempts to carry on commercial relations with the people of New Mexico until the overthrow of Spanish power in 1821. "There is some evidence, however," says Chittenden, "that parties must have gone to Santa Fé during these years, for otherwise it is difficult to see upon what the *St. Louis Enquirer* of September, 1822, could have based the remark that 'it is becoming a familiar operation for our citizens to visit this capital.' " [71]

In the year 1819, David Merriwether, an Indian trader, in company with a war-party of Pawnee Indians, came as far as the Spanish frontier on the Arkansas, where they were defeated in a pitched battle with the Spaniards under Colonel Viscarra. Merriwether was captured, taken to Santa Fé, and imprisoned. In 1853 Merriwether returned to Santa Fé, having been appointed governor of the territory of New Mexico by the president of the United States.

Owing to the pronounced opposition on the part of the Spanish authorities in New Mexico it is evident that trade with New Mexico was not really begun until the period of Spanish dominion had terminated. As soon as Mexican independence was achieved the Santa Fé trade was inaugurated. When the Americans who had been imprisoned in Chihuahua were released, James Baird and the two McKnights, one of whom had gone to Chihuahua to secure the release of his brother, returned by way of Santa Fé and Taos. When they arrived at Taos they met a party of Americans led by Hugh Glenn, a merchant from Ohio, and Jacob Fowler, who had come out from the states the year previous. They joined his party,

---

[71] James Conklin came to Santa Fé from Canada, via St. Louis, in 1821, and four years later was married to Juana Ortiz, of which marriage there were six children, all of whom are now dead, except Charles M. Conklin, now a resident of Santa Fé. Juana Ortiz was the daughter of Don Pedro Ortiz and Barbara Lopez, distinguished citizens of Santa Fé. She was the first cousin of Rt. Rev. Juan Felipe Ortiz, vicario, and Don Tomás Ortiz, chief alcalde and president of the Ayuntamiento of Santa Fé, both of whom were very prominent in the affairs of the territory after the independence of Mexico was achieved. They were both in Santa Fé at the time of the American occupation, in 1846, and were leaders in the revolution of 1846-7. They afterwards held office under the American government. James Conklin served as interpreter to Col. J. M. Washington at the time of his campaign against the Navajós in 1849. He died in Santa Fé, in the year 1882, at the age of ninety-one years.

who were about to return, and reached St. Louis in July, 1822. John McKnight subsequently built a post on the upper Arkansas, where he was killed by the Comanches in 1823.[72] Robert McKnight returned to New Mexico and made a fortune in working the copper mines at Santa Rita. Colonel Kit Carson was in his employ as a teamster in 1828.[73]

Captain William Becknell, of Missouri, was the father of the Santa Fé Trail and the real founder of the commerce of the prairies.

CAPTAIN WILLIAM BECKNELL, FATHER OF THE SANTA FÉ TRAIL

It was he who took the first successful trading expedition to Santa Fé. In 1821, with four companions, Captain Becknell crossed the plains. They started from the town of Franklin, Missouri, with the original purpose of trading with the Indians, but having fallen in with a party of Mexican rangers, they were prevailed upon to go to Santa Fé, where, notwithstanding the small amounts of merchandise which they carried, very handsome profits were realized.[74]

Upon his return to Missouri, Captain Becknell gave very glowing accounts of the possibilities of trade with Santa Fé, which stimulated others to begin in the business, and, in the spring following the return of Becknell, Colonel Benjamin Cooper and his two nephews, Braxton and Stephen, with others to the number of fifteen, carrying their merchandise upon pack-horses, set out upon the trail. They went directly to Taos, where they arrived in safety.[75] Captain Joseph Walker, with a party of trappers, joined Cooper's party on the way and accompanied them to Taos.

[72] *Missouri Intelligencer*, August 12, 1823.
[73] Peter's *Province Life and Frontier Adventures*, p. 33.
[74] Captain Becknell left Arrow Rock, Mo., near Franklin, September 1, 1821. On the 13th of November his party met a detachment of Mexican troops by whom they were escorted to San Miguel, where a Frenchman was found who acted as interpreter. From here they were taken to Santa Fé, where they met the governor. In December they returned to Missouri in a journey of forty-eight days duration.
[75] *Senate Ex. Docs.*, 18th cong. 2 sess., 79. Braxton Cooper was killed by the Comanche Indians. Major Stephen Cooper also led a party from Missouri to New Mexico in 1823. Later he went to California and, as late as 1886, was still living, according to Mr. Bancroft, who received from one of his companions, Joel P. Walker, a narrative of their adventures. Major Cooper also gives an account of his adventures and sufferings on the trail, in *History of Howard and Cooper Counties*, pp. 152-155, St. Louis, 1883.
Chittenden, H. M., *History of the American Fur Trade*, p. 501, says: ''In

The second expedition conducted by Captain Becknell had a very difficult and hazardous journey to Santa Fé. He left Arrow Rock, Missouri near Franklin, May 22, with twenty-one men and three wagons, carrying merchandise of the value approximately of five thousand dollars. Between the Missouri and the Arkansas he was stopped by the Osage Indians, who threatened to confiscate his property, but through the good offices of one of the Chouteaus, who was trading with these Indians at the time, he was allowed to proceed.

Upon his arrival at the Arkansas he was joined by the party of John Heath who is not elsewhere mentioned in the narratives of the times. This journey is of historic importance in that it was the first which led directly to San Miguel by way of the Cimarron river instead of following the Arkansas to the mountains.

Anxious to avoid the circuitous route through the upper Arkansas country he decided, after reaching that point on the Arkansas known as the Caches, to go directly to Santa Fé, entertaining little or no fear of the terrible trials which awaited him in crossing the pathless desert. With no other guide than the stars and possibly a pocket compass, the party started across the arid region lying between the Arkansas and Cimarron rivers.

They left the Arkansas carrying with them a scant supply of water in their canteens. This source of supply was soon exhausted and the sufferings of both men and animals became intense. They were at last reduced to the necessity of killing their dogs and cutting off the ears of their mules with the vain hope of assuaging their burning thrist by drinking the hot blood.

This only served to irritate their palates and madden the senses of the sufferers. Frantic with despair, in prospect of the horrible death which now stared them in the face, they scattered in every direction in search of water, but without success. The party had traveled almost to the banks of the Cimarron when they determined to return to the Arkansas, but they were unequal to the task and

---

the *Missouri Intelligencer*, of Franklin, Mo., June 10, 1822, Becknell had an advertisement calling for a company of seventy men 'to go westward for the purpose of trading for horses and mules and catching wild animals of every description.' Although Santa Fé is not mentioned, it is difficult to conceive of any other place 'westward' where mules could be traded for. Thither in fact the party was bound. They rendezvoused at the home of Ezekiel Williams (of *Lost Trappers* fame) on the fourth of August and crossed the Missouri at Arrow Rock, September 1st.''

The End of the Santa Fé Trail — The Old Fonda

would undoubtedly have perished had not a buffalo, fresh from the Cimarron, with stomach distended with water, been discovered by some of the party. The animal was quickly despatched and the water taken from his stomach served to revive the unfortunate men. Thus revived, some of the strongest men in the party now reached the Cimarron, where they filled their canteens, hurrying back to the assistance of their weaker comrades whom they found prostrate and incapable of further exertion.

It has been declared by some that Captain Becknell failed to cross the desert on this trip, but there is no doubt of his having experienced the privations mentioned, and that he finally succeeded in crossing to Santa Fé by way of San Miguel, and not by way of Taos, as Dr. Gregg has stated.[76]

It may be said that the Santa Fé trade became firmly established when Mexico achieved its independence. All opposition from the authorities of New Mexico ceased at this time and a profitable market was assured for all goods coming from the United States. The eastern rendezvous was Franklin down to 1831, and later, Independence, Missouri. From this point [77] in May of each year

---

[76] Chittenden, H. M., *History of the American Fur Trade*, p. 504 and note: "To William Becknell, therefore, belongs the credit of having made the first regular trading expedition from the Missouri to Santa Fé; of being the first to follow the route direct to San Miguel instead of by way of Taos; and the first to introduce the use of wagons in the trade. This last achievement was four years before Ashley took his wheeled cannon to the Salt Lake valley, eight years before Smith, Jackson and Sublette took wagons to Wind river, and ten years before Bonneville took them to Green river. The evidence on this point is conclusive. See *Journal of Jacob Fowler*, p. 167: 'We have to leave the wagon [road] we fell into two days back, which road was made by Becknell and his party on their way to the Spanish settlements.' This was July 1st, 1822. Becknell himself in a letter written in 1825 referred to this year as the time 'when I opened the road to Santa Fé.' The *Missouri Intelligencer*, February 18, 1823, says: 'But one wagon has ever gone from this state to Santa Fé and that was taken by Captain William Becknell . . . in the early part of last spring, and sold there for $700, which cost here $150.' This might mean that Becknell lost two wagons on the way, but Becknell's journal indicates that he took all the wagons through. *Niles' Register* mistakenly refers to Cooper as having taken the three wagons to Santa Fé, 'to the great astonishment of the people.' It was, of course, Becknell. Gregg, usually so accurate, evidently errs in saying that Becknell was defeated in his efforts to cross the Cimarron desert, and had to return to the Arkansas and go by way of Taos. Becknell's journal makes it plain that he crossed the desert.''

[77] J. S. Chick, who came to Westport, Mo., in 1836, and who lived there in 1843, in speaking of the eastern terminus of the Santa Fé Trail in his day, says that after the trail from Ft. Osage (Sibley, Mo.) was abandoned, Blue Mills Landing, or Owen's Landing (it was called by both names) was the starting point from the Missouri river. Very little, if any, of the goods

set out the caravans, pack animals down to 1823, and from that time on wagons, drawn at first by horses and mules, but later by mules or oxen, four pairs usually to each wagon, but sometimes five or six pairs, with a load of five thousand pounds.

In 1824, a company of traders, about eighty-one in number, made the trip across the plains to Santa Fé. A portion of the company used pack-mules. About the 1st of April, in a tavern in the town of Franklin, Missouri, this expedition was organized. It was pro-

---

destined for Santa Fé were landed at Wayne City. From Blue Mills landing the trains passed through Independence, thence southwesterly by the Barnes and Rice farms, crossing the Blue at Red bridge, south of Leeds, following the divide between the Blue and Indian creek, and crossing the state line at the town of Little Santa Fé, and continuing on the divide to the Lone Elm on the headwaters of Cedar creek, a tributary of the Kaw river, thence to Council Grove and the Arkansas.

"I do not think," says Mr. Chick, "there can be any controversy as to the location of the trail. There were several crossings of the Arkansas, some trains taking the Cimarron route, others the Aubrey crossing, others following up the Arkansas to Bent's Fort and thence south over the Raton mountains, all uniting not far east of Las Vegas, New Mexico. The earliest trail went by way of Taos. It is not my recollection that any trains leaving Independence crossed the Blue river on the old Westport and Independence road and passed through Westport."

The spot which was known to all travelers upon the plains as the Lone Elm was a very noted point. In the very early days, long before the settlements had come further west than along the lower Missouri, this tree was a great rendezvous or rallying point for the Indian tribes. Solitary and alone it stood upon the prairies and its top could be seen for many miles around. It served as a landmark for those seeking the frontiers, and the traders used the place as a camping ground. Travelers came to look upon it as an old friend and nothing could have induced them to cut it down. Some vandal felled the tree in the early days of the Mexican war and in 1853 it was all gone but a part of the stump.

The first road from the Missouri river to Westport started from Chouteau's Landing, at the east end of Chouteau's island, since called Mensing island, about where Cleveland avenue, in Kansas City, intercepts the river; thence up the river to the east side of Lydia avenue, east of Ransom's pond, crossing Independence avenue about Highland, thence southwesterly, crossing Ninth street at Charlotte, and thence southwesterly to the crossing of Main street and Eighteenth street. The road from Kansas City to Westport started at the foot of Main street, thence along the levee to Grand avenue, thence to Third street, thence southwesterly through the city hall square, crossing Main street at Fifth, thence southwesterly to Missouri avenue and Delaware and along Delaware to the Junction. At that time Main street was not graded from Fifth street to the Junction. Main street south of Missouri avenue was not practicable even for horseback travel. Before there was much fencing, roads were located upon the most practicable and direct route, regardless of land boundaries. From the Junction the road followed the present line of Main street to about Eighteenth street; at Eighteenth street it bore a little to the west, crossing O. K. creek near Main street, thence following the most practicable route to about where the Egelhoff residence is located, thence a little to the east, intersecting Main street at about the southwest corner of

posed to make it the largest yet undertaken. Here all the details were arranged and a rendezvous appointed at Mount Vernon, Missouri, on May 5th, each man to be equipped with a rifle, one pistol, four pounds of powder, eight pounds of lead and provisions sufficient for twenty days.

On May 15, 1824, the party started, crossed the Missouri six miles above Franklin, and on May 23d arrived at the place of organization, three miles from the settlements of the Missouri frontier. A. Le Grand, well known in the history of the frontier, was chosen captain. In this expedition were Mr. Augustus Storrs, who next year was named United States consul at Santa Fé, and Mr. Marmaduke. The expedition arrived in Santa Fé on July 28th and after a most successful trade most of the party returned to Missouri. Marmaduke remained in Santa Fé during the winter, kept a diary of his experiences and returned to Missouri May 31, 1825. It was in the following year that traders with abundant capital began to embark in the trade. The earlier traders were not often molested by the Indians, but later on, owing to the conduct of the traders themselves, the Indians became very hostile.

"Many seemed to forget the wholesome precept," says Gregg, "that they should not be savage themselves because they dealt with savages. Instead of cultivating friendly feelings with those few who remained peaceful and honest, there was an occasional one always disposed to kill, even in cold blood, every Indian that fell into his power, merely because some of the tribe had committed some outrage either against themselves or their friends."

Union cemetery, thence crossing Mt. Auburn hill, it bore a little east of Main street to avoid a ravine running west from Hunter's spring, again crossing Main street at Hunter avenue, as now located, and on Hunter avenue to Broadway, and on Broadway to Westport.

Leaving Independence, Missouri, as now shown upon maps, the old trail bore distinctly to the southwest and crossed the state boundary just east of the village of Glenn, Kansas; thence to the southwest, passing a little north of the towns of Olathe and Gardner, in Johnson county. Thence it followed the divide between the waters of the Kansas and Osage rivers and near Baldwin, Worden, and Baden in Douglas county; Overbrook, Scranton, and Burlingame in Osage county; Wilmington in Wabaunsee; Waushara and Agnes in Lyon, and thence to Council Grove, in Morris county.

The commencement of the Santa Fé trade began in Kansas City in 1849 and 1850, but owing to the cholera prevailing at that time, the insufficiency of warehouse facilities, this trade was largely lost to Kansas City for the next year or two, but when it came back it was retained until driven away in 1863 by the disturbance prevailing at that time, and went to Leavenworth for a year or two. As the railroads were extended west the trade followed them.

Owing to this desire for revenge alluded to by Gregg, whenever the Indians came across a small party of traders, who, through carelessness or recklessness, attempted to cross the plains poorly armed or equipped, they were more than likely to work some hardship or imposition upon the traders, indeed they were lucky if they escaped with their scalps. In 1826, a small party of twelve men camped on the Cimarron, armed with only four serviceable guns. They were visited by a party of Indians, believed to be Arapaho, who at first made strong representations of friendship and good will. Observing, however, the defenseless condition of the traders, they went away, but soon returned about thirty strong, each provided with a *lazo,* and all on foot. The chief then began by informing the Americans that his men were tired of walking, and must have horses. Thinking it folly to offer any resistance, the terrified traders told them that if one animal apiece would satisfy them, to go and catch them. This they soon did; but finding their request so easily complied with, the Indians held a little parley, which resulted in a demand for more — they must each have two. "Well, catch them" was the reply, upon which the savages mounted the horses they had already secured, and swinging their *lazos* over their heads, plunged among the stock with a furious yell and drove off the entire *caballada.*[78]

CONFLICTS WITH INDIANS

The town of Franklin, on the Missouri river, opposite Booneville, about one hundred and fifty miles westward from St. Louis, in conjunction with several of the neighboring settlements, furnished the majority of the early traders, who sent caravans over the old trail. Later, as has been stated, the point of starting was moved farther up the Missouri river, and for a long period Independence, now a residential suburb of Kansas City, Missouri, remained the eastern terminus of the trail.

---

[78] Gregg, J., *Commerce of the Prairies,* i, p. 26: "Since the commencement of the trade, returning, the parties have performed the homeward journey across the plains with the proceeds of their enterprise, partly in specie, and partly in furs, buffalo rugs and animals. Occasionally these straggling bands would be set upon by marauding Indians, but if well informed and of resolute spirit, they found very little difficulty in persuading the savages to let them pass unmolested; for, as Mr. Storrs very justly remarks, in his representation presented by Colonel Benton, in 1825, to the United States senate, the Indians are always willing to compromise when they find that they cannot rob 'without losing the lives of their warriors, which they hardly ever risk, unless for revenge or in open warfare.' "

Oxen were employed by the United States government in transporting the baggage accompanying the escort over the plains in 1829, commanded by Major Riley; these were found to almost equal mules, and subsequent to that period many oxen were used in the caravans. Oftentimes the traders were accustomed to shoe their animals with raw buffalo hide, which performed its purpose very well so long as the weather remained dry, but when wet, they soon wore through. Mules, oftentimes, were driven over the entire trip without being shod at all. The loading of the wagons of the caravans was quite an art; every precaution was taken to so stow away the packages that no jolting during the journey disturbed the order in which they were placed in the wagons. The latter, in the earliest times, were brought from Pittsburgh, but later on were manufactured at Independence in many instances.

ORGANIZATION OF THE CARAVANS

The experiences of the early traders, with large caravans, passing over the old trail, differed only slightly during every year. Fights with Indians, now and then, robberies of live stock by these Arabs of the plains, heavy rains, break-downs, good or poor grazing, the diaries, kept by some of the traders and preserved to this day, all show that each had a similar experience. Dr. Josiah Gregg, in his work, has preserved to us by far the best account of the experiences of the Santa Fé traders of the time. Starting with the caravan from Council Grove,[79] in the days of the trail one of its most important stations, having proceeded that far from Independence, Dr. Gregg says:

" 'Catch up! catch up!' the familiar note of preparation, was now sounded from the captain's camp, and re-echoed from every

---

[79] Gregg, J., *Commerce of the Prairies*, i, pp. 42-44: "Early on the 26th of May we reached the long-looked for rendezvous of Council Grove; here we joined the main body of the caravan. Lest this imposing title suggest to the reader a snug and thriving village, it should be observed, that, on the day of our departure from Independence, we passed the last human abode upon our route; thenceforth from the borders of Missouri to those of New Mexico not even an Indian settlement greeted our eyes. This point is nearly a hundred and fifty miles from Independence, and consisted of a continuous strip of timber nearly half a mile in width, comprising the richest varieties of trees; such as oak, walnut, ash, elm, hickory, etc., and extending all along the valleys of a small stream known as Council Grove creek, the principal branch of the Neosho river. . . Messrs. Reeves, Sibley and Mathers, having been commissioned by the United States, in the year 1825, to mark a road from the

division and scattered group along the valley. On such occasions, a scene of confusion ensues, which must be seen to be appreciated. The woods and dales resound with the gleeful yells of the light-hearted wagoners, who, weary of inaction and filled with joy at the prospect of getting under way, become clamorous in the extreme. Scarcely does the jockey on the race-course ply his whip more promptly at that magic word 'Go,' than do these emulous wagoners fly to harnessing their mules at the spirit-stirring sound of 'Catch up.' Each teamster vies with his fellows who shall be soonest ready; and it is a matter of boastful pride to be the first to cry out — 'All's set!'

"The uproarious bustle which follows — the halloing of those in pursuit of animals — the exclamations which the unruly brutes call forth from their wrathful drivers; together with the clatter of bells — the rattle of yokes and harness — the jingle of chains — all conspire to produce a clamorous confusion, which would be altogether incomprehensible without the assistance of the eyes; while these alone would hardly suffice to unravel the labyrinthian manoeuvres and hurly-burly of this precipitate breaking up.

" 'All's set!' is finally heard from some teamster — 'All's set,' is directly responded from every quarter. 'Stretch out!' immediately vociferates the captain. Then, the 'heps!' of drivers — the cracking of whips — the trampling of feet — the occasional creak of wheels — the rumbling of wagons —form a new scene of exquisite confusion, which I shall not attempt further to describe. 'Fall in' is heard from headquarters, and the wagons are forthwith strung out upon the long inclined plain, which stretches to the heights beyond Council Grove."

The make-up of a caravan was as well defined as a modern freight train. As has been said, both mules and cattle were used, the cattle being always designated as "bulls;" in later days more "bulls" than mules were used. The drivers were known by the choice ap-

---

confines of Missouri to Santa Fé, met on this spot with some bands of Osages, with whom they concluded a treaty, whereby the Indians agreed to allow all citizens of the United States and Mexico to pass unmolested, and even to lend their aid to those engaged in the Santa Fé trade; for which they were to receive a gratification of eight hundred dollars in merchandize. The commissioners, on this occasion, gave the place the name of 'Council Grove.'"

Council Grove, the name of the town on this site, is now the seat of Morris county, Kansas, with a population of about three thousand. There are some buildings still standing that were used in the days of the Trail. After crossing the Neosho, going west, the first building is the old blacksmith shop. This was at one time the last chance to have horses and mules shod. The next building is the hotel, built of native oak and walnut. For many years this was the most noted tavern along the route. Almost a block west of this is the pioneer store, the last place where neglected or forgotten supplies could be obtained.

pellation of "bull-whackers." The caravan, or train, consisted of twenty-six wagons, twenty-five for freight and one for a mess-wagon. There were twenty-six drivers, one wagon-master, one assistant wagon-master, one "extra hand," and two night herders. Each wagon had usually five yoke of cattle, with from six to ten teams of six yokes extra. These extra cattle were taken along to fill the places of those that had to be left on the way. It was easier to drive the extra ones in the team than to allow them to run loose. Each wagon's load was usually from five to seven thousand pounds. Ordinarily a train traveled about eighteen miles a day. The drivers always walked on the left side of the team, and each carried a whip from ten to sixteen feet long, with a stalk from sixteen to twenty inches in length. Camping places were selected in advance by scouts, with a view to securing plenty of water and good pasturage for the stock. It was the practice for a caravan to move in four divisions for the reason that, moving in this manner, it was the easier to arrange the wagons for defensive purposes in the event of attack.

Upon encamping the wagons were formed into a hollow square, each division to a side, constituting at once an enclosure or corral for the animals when needed and a fortification against the Indians. All camp fires were lighted outside of the wagons, where also the travelers spread their beds, which consisted for the most part of buffalo robes or rugs and blankets. At night the mules were tethered around the wagons, at proper intervals, with ropes twenty-five or thirty feet in length, tied to stakes fifteen or twenty inches long, driven into the ground, a supply of which, as well as mallets, the wagoners always carried with them.

To the west of Council Grove the country began to change from the pleasant and fertile prairie to the arid plains where the caravans were exposed not only to the attacks of the Indians but also to the action of the elements, dangers by no means insignificant. The tricks of the Indians were many and very ingenious. In some instances they would stampede the buffalo in the direction of a caravan, so that in the confusion, they would be able to commit depredations upon the caravan. Some of the tribes had their horses trained so they would run among the traders' animals and cause a stampede, after which the decoys would lead them to their camp.[80]

Some of the most famous camping stations west of Council Grove were Diamond Spring, Lost Spring, Cottonwood and Turkey creeks, and Cow creek, at the mouth of which now stands the city of Hutchinson, Kansas. Beyond Hutchinson the first place of real historic interest is Pawnee Rock. This locality was common ground for the Indians in buffalo hunting. The rock was of sandstone, about twenty feet high; for a long time it was considered one of the most dangerous points on the trail, as the Indians were in the habit of lying in wait here for the caravans. The rock has almost entirely disappeared, the railroad company and the earlier settlers in the vicinity having used it for foundations for water-tanks, in the case of the railroad company, and for houses and barns by the settlers. The rock was originally surmounted by a pyramidal pile of stones. It was a great place for inscriptions both by Americans and the Indians. "Here was a confused medley of cognomens," says Sage, "English, French, Spanish, German, Irish, Scotch — all entered upon the register of

IMPORTANT STATIONS ON TRAIL

---

[80] Early in the fifties, Alexander Majors, a trader over the old trail for many years, had arrived with his train at the point known as Hundred and Ten Mile Creek. One morning, at early dawn, having arisen, he rode around what he supposed to be his entire herd of cattle or "bulls," but in rounding them up he discovered that a number of them were missing. He then made a large circle, leaving the ones he had herded together. He had not traveled far when he struck the trail of the missing oxen, which was very plain. He rode his horse at a gallop, following it for about a mile when he discovered the tracks of Indian ponies. He was unarmed, having left his wagons not expecting to go far and not having reached the territory where it was likely he would meet with hostile Indians. Thinking that the tracks were of friendly ones that had driven his oxen away for the purpose of claiming a fee for finding and bringing them back, he took a course ahead of the trail, expecting to overtake them at any moment. Passing through a skirt of timber that divided one section of the open prairie from the other, he overtook thirty-four head of his oxen resting from their travel. About sixty yards to the east of the cattle were six painted Indian warriors, who had dismounted, each one leaning against his horse, his right hand upon the saddle, his gun in the left. Majors came upon the Indians very suddenly, the timber preventing the Indians from seeing him until he was within a very few rods. Throwing up his hand, Majors went in a gallop around his oxen, giving some hideous yells, all the while "speaking" to the cattle and telling them they could go back to the wagons. The cattle at once heeded him and started. Six meaner and more surprised looking "bucks" were never seen. Put off their guard by Majors' apparent fearlessness, and believing that he had an armed party immediately in his rear, the noble red man quickly mounted his fleet-footed pony and fled.

Officers in the Army of the West, 1846
1. Gov. William Gilpin. 2. Col. J. W. Reid. 3. General Sterling Price.
4. Dr. David Waldo. 5. Major H. L. Kendrick

fancied immortality." The name of this rock, according to Philip St. George Cooke, "came from a siege there, once upon a time, of a small party of Pawnees by the Comanche hordes; the rocky mound was impregnable; but, alas for valor! they were parched with thirst, and the shining river glided in their sight through green meadows! They drank their horses' blood, and vowed to Wah-Condah that their fates should be one. Death before slavery! Finally in a desperate effort to cut their way to liberty, they all met heroic death; ushering their spirits with defiant shouts to the very threshold of the happy hunting grounds! The Comanches, after their melancholy success, were full of admiration and erected on the summit a small pyramid which we see to this day."

Major Inman, in his *Santa Fé Trail*, in a story of Kit Carson, endeavors to connect that noted frontiersman with the christening of the rock. The story may be true, but it did not happen as Inman relates it: "It is singular," says Chittenden, "that so noted a character as Kit Carson should be so entirely unknown in the annals of the fur trade as he actually was. His name occurs only once in the correspondence or newspaper literature prior to 1843, so far as it has fallen under our observation." [81]

---

[81] Chittenden, H. M., *History of the Fur Trade*, p. 539. This reference is an interesting one and positively fixes the year in which he commenced his wild west career. It was in 1826 when he joined a Santa Fé caravan under Charles Bent. The *Missouri Intelligencer* of October 12, 1826, had the following notice relating to the event: "Notice: To whom it may concern: That Christopher Carson, a boy about sixteen years old, small of his age, but thick set, light hair, ran away from the subscriber, living in Franklin, Howard Co., Mo., to whom he had been bound to learn the saddler's trade, on or about the first day of September last. He is supposed to have made his way toward the upper part of the state. All persons are notified not to harbor, support or subsist said boy under penalty of the law. One cent reward will be given to any person who will bring back the said boy. (signed) David Workman, Franklin, Oct. 6, 1826."

Kit Carson's career — in the newspapers — began after his association with Fremont. Jim Bridger, in the last days of his life, when living at Westport, Mo., who knew Carson from the time the latter first came to the mountains, in telling of his companions and friends, and their characteristics, was very frank in saying that Carson was not a "trapper or mountaineer" in the proper acceptation of the term. Carson first became famous through the official reports of General Fremont and the friendship of Senator Benton. His exploits with General Kearny, in 1846, along with Lieutenant Beale, in California, gave him much newspaper and "story-book" notoriety.

Jim Bridger was the most conspicuous figure among the old mountaineers. He was a trail-maker in every sense of the word. The greatest fur-hunter and the greatest pathfinder of them all, and possessing the most intimate knowledge of the Indian nature ever vouchsafed a white man, Bridger will

Another point of interest beyond Pawnee Rock, on the Arkansas, about five miles west of Dodge City of today, was "*Caches*." "The history of the origin of these '*Caches*,'" says Gregg, "may be of sufficient interest to merit a brief recital. Baird, of the unfortunate party of 1812, having returned to the United States in 1822, together with Chambers, who had descended the Canadian river the year before, induced some small capitalists of St. Louis to join in an enterprise, and then undertook to return to Santa Fé the same fall, with a small party and an assortment of merchandise. Reaching the Arkansas late in the season, they were overtaken by a heavy snow-storm and driven to take shelter on a large island. A rigorous winter ensued, which forced them to remain pent-up in that place for three long months. During this time the greater portion of the animals perished; so that, when the spring began to open they were unable to continue their journey with their goods. In this emergency they made a *cache* some distance above, on the north side of the river, where they stowed away the most of their merchandise. From thence they proceeded to Taos, where they procured mules and returned to get their hidden property." The term "*cache*," meaning a place of concealment, was originally used by the Canadian-French trappers and voyageurs. It was made by digging a hole in the ground, somewhat in the shape of a jug, which was lined with dry sticks, grass, or anything else that would protect its contents from the dampness of the earth. In this place the goods to be concealed were carefully stowed away; and the aperture was then so effectually closed as to protect them from the rains. In caching a great deal of skill was often required so that no signs might be left whereby the cunning Indian might discover the place of deposit. To this end the excavated earth was carried to some distance and carefully concealed or thrown into a stream, if one

---

grow in stature as time goes on and accurate history is written. The Rocky Mountains had no secrets from him. He was the first white man, after John Colter, to view the wonders of the Yellowstone park, and the first to look upon the Great Salt Lake. Seemingly bearing a charmed life, he wandered through the Indians' country, sometimes fighting but more often living their life and finding a solace of true brotherhood at the lodge fire. Every mountain climbed by him, every stream he crossed, was written down in the most marvelous memory ever granted to a mountaineer. When the white man, with his wagons, came, Bridger showed them the best trails. Bridger was of great service to the engineers who built the Union Pacific Railway. General Grenville M. Dodge showed his gratitude by rescuing Bridger's body from a neglected grave and interring it at Kansas City under an appropriate shaft.

were at hand. The place selected for a *cache* was usually some rolling point sufficiently elevated to be secure from inundations. If it was well set with grass, a solid piece of turf was cut out large enough for the entrance. The turf was afterwards laid back, and, taking root, in a short time no signs remained of its ever having been molested. At times a camp-fire was built over the *cache* and again the animals were penned over it. This mode of concealing goods seems to have been in use from the time of the earliest French voyageurs in America. Father Hennepin, during his passage down the Mississippi river in 1680, describes an operation of this kind.[82]

Before reaching *Caches* the early trader, in his course across the plains, followed the Arkansas river for upwards of a hundred miles and beyond that point often fifty or a hundred more before crossing that river. Between the Arkansas and the Cimarron rivers, a distance of more than fifty miles, there was not even a trail. Prior to 1830 there was no regular ford across the first named stream.[83]

The upper ford of the Arkansas, which was used as late as 1829, was located at Chouteau island, just above where the town of Hartland, Kansas, now stands. This was the crossing recommended by surveyor J. C. Brown in 1825-7 and was the nearest point on the Arkansas to the lower spring of the Cimarron which lay directly south. Far beyond this point the earlier caravans pursued their course and crossed the river near Bent's Fort, the terminus of the upper Arkansas route being Taos and that of the lower, or Cimarron route, being San Miguel and Santa Fé.[84]

---

[82] Father Hennepin says: "We took up the green sodde and laid it by, and digg'd a hole in the earth where we put our goods, and covered them with pieces of timber and earth, and then put in again the green turf; so that 'twas impossible to suspect that any Hole had been digg'd under it, for we flung the Earth into the River."

[83] The ford of the Arkansas was 392 miles from Independence. This was the regular crossing after 1829 and was known as the Cimarron Crossing. Its location is twenty miles below Dodge City. There was another, or Lower Crossing, seventeen miles below Dodge City. It was near the mouth of Mulberry creek at the extreme point of the large southern bend of the river.

The principal trouble in crossing the Arkansas was that of quicksand. Unless the trader happened along during the June rise, he was never bothered by water in the river. The river bottom, however, was very treacherous, and it was customary to double and treble the teams and not stop while crossing over for fear the heavy loads would sink so deep that the teams could not pull them out.

[84] Storrs, A., *Santa Fé Trade in 1824*, gives the route as from Ft. Osage W. S. W. to the Arkansas; up the Arkansas N. of W. 240 miles; S. to the Cimarron; up the Cimarron W. 100 miles; and S. W. to Taos. Gregg, vol. i,

The success of the early traders attracted the attention of capitalists and shortly the government of the United States became interested. The prominent Missourians began sending memorials to congress, setting forth the opportunities of trade promotion and demanding government protection for the caravans. Treaties were made with the Indian tribes. In 1825, congress passed an act authorizing the survey or marking out of the road and appropriated thirty thousand dollars for the purpose and for securing the consent of the Indians.

In accordance with this law a commission consisting of Benjamin Reeves, George C. Sibley, and Thomas Mather, with a surveyor named J. C. Brown, began the execution of the work, leaving the settlements in June, 1825. The survey was made by chain and compass with sextant observations for latitude and longitude. The line as surveyed followed the trail pretty

UNITED STATES SURVEY OF 1825

---

pp. 24-25, *Commerce of the Prairies*, implies that the wagons reached Santa Fé, and his map shows no route to Taos. Storrs accompanied the caravan and his narrative, or statement, drawn out in government investigations, was published in *Niles' Register*, xxvii, 312-315, as also in *Government Document*, 18th congress, 2d session, *Senate Document*, 7, pp. 1-14 This was the best account before Gregg.

Chouteau island was a well-known point on the upper Arkansas. The name dates with the Chouteau-De Munn expedition of 1815-17. While on his way to the Missouri in the spring of 1816 with the furs collected during the previous winter, Chouteau was attacked by the Pawnees, losing one man and three wounded. He retreated to this island for purposes of defense and this fact gave the island its name. Chouteau had no trading post here. In the early days the Chouteaus had a trading post near the present Bonner Springs, Kansas. It was called the "Four Houses," because of the manner in which four log houses were arranged for purposes of defense. In 1826 a great flood in the Missouri washed away a warehouse belonging to the Chouteaus which stood about two and a half miles below the present foot of Main street, Kansas City, Mo. When the flood washed this post away the furs and other merchandise saved were taken to the post on the Kansas river. Some time after 1826 Chouteau (Francois) rebuilt his warehouse on the Missouri river, but on higher ground. This was the "Chouteau's warehouse" of the early traders. Francois Chouteau subsequently derived title from the government to the land upon which this warehouse stood and he lived there until 1840. The great flood of 1844 also destroyed this warehouse and thereafter the Chouteau family gave up trading and engaged in other pursuits.

The Fort Osage, mentioned by Augustus Storrs, was established in 1808 and was located on a tract of land ceded by the Osage Indians. The fortifications were located on the high bluff of the Missouri at the place known as Old Sibley. For several years this post was the first on the frontier. The post was commanded, in 1809, by Captain Clemson, 1st U. S. Inf. It was abandoned in 1825. The government itself bartered with the Indians at this point, trading powder, traps, and scalping knives for furs and pelts.

closely until after it left the Cimarron river, where it bore off to the westward and terminated at Taos. The memoir accompanying the maps of the survey states that the road was "surveyed and marked" from Osage to Taos, but this would seem to be wrong. As far as the Arkansas river it was plainly marked with raised mounds, but beyond this point, if marked at all, it must have been in so temporary a way that the evidence of it quickly disappeared.

The great mistake made in this survey was in attempting to force travelers to take any but the shortest practicable route. It is always a dangerous experiment to ignore the tendency of human nature, and of the American type in particular, to take the short cut. Knowing the perils of the Cimarron desert, Brown thought it better to ascend the Arkansas to Chouteau island and then go straight south to the Lower Spring of the Cimarron, which would be reached in one day. But it was traveling two sides of a triangle where it was possible to follow the third, and the traders preferred to take their chances by the shorter route. In like manner Brown thought it better for travelers to go first to Taos because that was the "nearest of the Mexican settlements, the most northern and the most abundant in provision for man and beast." He accordingly turned off to the right at a point some distance beyond the head of the Cimarron and made straight for Taos. But here again the traders refused to follow him.

From a practical point of view the survey was of little use; but it was a substantial contribution, or would have been if published, to the geographical knowledge of the west. The survey was carefully executed, was extremely accurate, and was mapped in conjunction with descriptive notes in a most convenient method. Had the government published these notes exactly in the form in which they were written, which could have been done at very slight expense, they would have made a succinct guide book of the trail sufficient for all requirements down to the day of railroads. It is an instance almost without parallel where the government, after doing a really useful piece of work, has pigeon-holed it in perpetuity and deprived the public of any benefit from it.[85]

---

[85] Chittenden, H. M., *History of the American Fur Trade*, p. 534: "On the 14th of December, 1824, Senator Thomas H. Benton, who took a great interest in the Far West, presented a petition to Congress reciting the nature, magnitude, and importance of the Santa Fé trade, and praying that the govern-

While it is true that the line of the old trail was as has been described, this was not the only route to Santa Fé, nor was this particular one strictly followed. It was the custom for many parties to go by way of Taos. Some of the more important and prominent merchants had regular establishments at Taos, among others, Dr. David Waldo, of Independence, Missouri. Many parties did not rendezvous at Council Grove nor did they go to Independence at all, but followed the Arkansas river from Fort Smith or Little Rock. In the year 1839 Gregg left Van Buren, Arkansas, and followed the Canadian river until he struck the old trail; returning he kept still more to the south.

The native people of New Mexico, after the trade began to be developed, were eager to assist in protecting the caravans. This interest in the trade extended also to the merchants of Chihuahua, and in 1825, Don Manuel Escudero, who was the first Mexican to take a caravan over the trail, was commissioned by the governor of New Mexico, Captain Bartolomé Baca, to visit the United States in the interest of the international commerce. He visited St. Louis and Washington, and also Franklin, Missouri. During the administration of Governor Baca, it was announced that New Mexico proposed marching to the Missouri river with 1,500 men in the interest of the trade and particularly for the pacification of the Indian tribes.

NEW MEXICANS ENGAGE IN THE OVERLAND TRADE

In the year that the trail was surveyed Dr. Willard went from St. Charles, Mo., with a caravan to Santa Fé and thence to Chihuahua, and during the years that followed, from 1827 to 1843, Mr. Collins, afterwards superintendent of Indian affairs in New Mexico, made many trips through to Chihuahua, as did also Dr. David Waldo and many others.

"Attempts to simplify the problem of transportation," says Chittenden, "led to numerous absurd schemes. One man secured a concession giving him the exclusive right to navigate the Rio

---

ment would endeavor to secure from the Indians the right of undisturbed passage through their lands, and that it would establish a military post on the Arkansas at the point where the Trail crossed it. The subject was energetically pressed during that session of congress and resulted in an appropriation of ten thousand dollars for marking the line of the road from the Missouri frontier to New Mexico, and one of twenty thousand dollars for securing concessions from the Indians."

Grande, and doubtless imagined that a vast fortune would fall to him when his boats should carry merchandise to Santa Fé along that dusty stream, and put to rout the antiquated caravans of the plains. Another party made an importunate appeal to Congress to remove the 'raft' in Red river, for if this obstruction could be removed, of the practicability of which he said there could be no doubt, the 'Red river will then become navigable for steamboats of moderate size to within sixty miles of Santa Fé, whence it will be easy to go in barges twenty-four leagues farther,' or twelve miles beyond Santa Fé!''

The revolution of 1837 did some injury to the trade, inasmuch as the property of some of the richest New Mexicans was confiscated. The results of the Texas-Santa Fé expedition and the Texas raids immediately following, as we have seen, closed the port of entry at Taos, but the decree of Santa Ana was repealed almost before it had gone into effect, so that the trade in 1844-1846 was as large as ever.[86]

From the year 1838, as has been stated, there was a great deal of interest in the trade among the people of Missouri. Efforts were made by the legislature of that state, the governor, by chambers of commerce, through their representatives in congress, to secure a custom house on the Missouri river. Nothing, however, was ever done, except the final passage of an act in 1845, one year before the breaking out of the war with Mexico. In 1839, an attempt was made by the Mexicans with the aid of Henry Connelly, afterward governor of New

BENT'S FORT

---

[86] Chittenden, H. M., *History of the American Fur Trade*, p. 513: ''The trade pursued the even tenor of its course during these years with little of incident or note except the never ending troubles at the custom house. But the situation of affairs, as regarded the provincial government, became less and less satisfactory. Mexico was falling into the same habit of suspicion and jealousy that had been so fatal to commercial intercourse during the Spanish régime. From their point of view there may have been some cause for this feeling. The onward march of American settlement they conceived to be fraught with great danger to their own authority in the northern provinces. Already Texas was as good as lost and the same might soon prove true of New Mexico. There was consequently a growing opposition among the Santa Fé authorities to a continuance of the trade, although it was always popular with the people.

''The ephemeral insurrection of 1837, which for a short time subverted Mexican authority, bore hard on the American traders, for they were suspected though apparently without foundation, of complicity in this movement. The various Texas-Santa Fé expeditions, so injudiciously managed, were another great annoyance to the trade; for here again the authorities believed that the traders were privy to the plans of the Texans. The lamentable tragedies to which they gave rise burned deeply into the public mind in the United

Mexico, to divert the trade from Santa Fé to Chihuahua direct. A caravan of one hundred men made the trip through Texas, and returned to Chihuahua in 1840, but the attempt was never repeated, although no serious difficulties were encountered in making the experiment. During this period Governor Armijo imposed a duty of five hundred dollars upon each wagon-load of goods, but the size of the wagons soon brought into use necessitated a return to ad valorem duties.

When expeditions were first made from the Missouri river to Santa Fé, the route was up the Arkansas river to the vicinity of the location of the present town of La Junta, Colorado, and then turning south, went first to Taos and thence to Santa Fé. Even after the Cimarron route was established, traders also used the upper Arkansas trail as there was always a great deal of business in that direction, particularly at Taos. Bent's Fort was the great stopping place on this branch of the trail.

Bent's Fort was about 530 miles from Independence, and in every respect was one of the most important trading posts in the Rocky Mountain country. It was the great cross-roads station of the southwest. The north and south route between the Platte river country and Santa Fé, and the east and west route up the Arkansas and into the mountains found this the most natural trading point.

This branch of the old trail crossed the Arkansas very near where La Junta now stands, and thence ran south, crossing the Raton Pass, and joined the main trail at Santa Clara Spring. This branch of the trail has been closely followed by the line of railway known as "The Santa Fé Route."

William Bent and Céran St. Vrain maintained this trading post and also one on the South Platte opposite the mouth of the St. Vrain Fork.[87]

States and went far to justify the sweeping conquest which followed so shortly after.

"This brief sketch of the Santa Fé trade prior to 1843 would be incomplete if we omitted to refer to its supreme importance in the war which was even then (1843) gathering like a storm on the prairies. The long intercourse of twenty years had made our people thoroughly familiar with the routes, distances, character of the country, and the people to be encountered in military operations in that quarter. The interchange of commerce had made the New Mexicans better acquainted with our people, had created a friendly feeling toward them, and had effectually paved the way for the change of allegiance that was soon to follow."

[87] The Bent family was well known in Missouri. Silas Bent was born in

Representative New Mexicans of the American Occupation Period
1. Gen. José Maria Chavez. 2. Don Ramon Luna. 3. Gen. Nicolas Pino.
4. Gen. Diego Archuleta and Don Manuel S. Salazar

The most dangerous division of the route between Independence and Santa Fé was that portion between the Arkansas and the Cimarron. This was a high plain, the ele-
THE CIMARRON DESERT vation of which is about three thousand feet above sea-level. The natural difficulties here were many and in addition the Indians were most dangerous and there was a greater loss of life in this section than upon any other portion of the trail. Within the distance of sixty-six miles from the Arkansas to the Lower Springs of the Cimarron, there was not a single watercourse or pool upon which dependence

---

the state of Massachusetts in 1744 and came to St. Louis in 1804, where he held several important offices and died in 1827. He had seven sons, the most distinguished of whom were William and Charles. They built the post on the Arkansas, known sometimes as Fort William but oftener as Bent's Fort. When the American army under Brigadier-General Kearny occupied New Mexico, Charles Bent, then living at Santa Fé, was named as governor by General Kearny. In 1852, William Bent destroyed Bent's Fort and built another farther down stream called Bent's New Fort. He had offered the post to the government of the United States for the sum of fifty thousand dollars, which the government would not pay. The action of the government was very displeasing to Bent and he destroyed the post.

Colonel Céran St. Vrain, whose name will appear often in a later chapter, was a very distinguished man in the west. His father came to America in 1770, moved to St. Louis where he married and passed the remainder of his life. He died in 1818, leaving five sons of whom the most celebrated was Céran, afterwards so closely identified with the social, official, military, and commercial life of New Mexico.

In the spring of 1837 the Pawnees were on the warpath, killing isolated persons whenever found and attacking the smaller caravans. On one occasion two men were killed very close to Bent's Fort. One day, shortly afterward, a party of hunters led by Dick Wootton, left the fort for the purpose of meeting a caravan coming from the east. At Pawnee Fork, where the year previous had occurred a bitter fight between the plainsmen and a large band of Comanches, Wootton's party met a band of sixteen Pawnees watching the trail and seeking an opportunity to rob some small party which could be taken at a disadvantage. There was a strip of country in that vicinity which the Indians always considered the best fighting ground, and it was a lucky wagon that got through without being attacked. The band of Pawnees were on foot and Wootton and his companions were mounted, so even though the Indians outnumbered the Americans two to one, still the advantage was with the latter. It was possible to keep almost entirely clear of the arrows of the Indians, while the Americans were able to approach within effective rifle range, and in the fight which ensued thirteen of the sixteen Indians were slain, the Americans losing none. The three remaining Indians escaped by throwing down their tomahawks, bows and arrows and running to the wagon train which just at this time hove in sight.

"It wasn't customary," says Wootton, "to take any prisoners in those days of Indian warfare, but when an Indian came into camp in that way we observed the same unwritten law that governed most of the Indian tribes under similar circumstances. It was a custom of the Indians never to harm the man who came into their camp voluntarily, so long as he remained there, although,

could be placed during the dry season. The soil was dry and hard; the vegetation poor, and little grew other than the short buffalo grass and some cacti. For miles not a shrub or tree upon which the eye could be fixed and no other game than an occasional antelope. On this sandy desert plain the traveler first became acquainted with the mirage. There in the plain before him emerged a beautiful lake; over its crystal surface the wind moved but slightly; to assuage his thirst, unacquainted with the deception, he hurried toward it, but the nearer his approach, the sooner he became disenchanted; in his very presence the lake would disappear.[88]

This route entered the present confines of New Mexico very close to what is known as the Upper Spring of the Cimarron. This

---

when he went away, they might follow and kill him before he had gone half a mile.

"Another custom of the Indians was to spare at least one of their conquered enemies when they were at war among themselves. Bloodthirsty and vindictive as they were, and as near as one band sometimes came to exterminating another, one or two of the defeated braves were always left to carry the news of the slaughter to their friends. We observed the same Indian rule in dealing with the three Pawnees who had made themselves our prisoners.

"First we gave them as much as they could eat when we went into camp for the night, and after breakfast in the morning supplied them with food enough to last until they could reach a Pawnee village. Then we told them to go back to their friends and tell them what had happened, giving them fair warning that we intended to kill all the Pawnees if they didn't behave better in the future."

[88] Wislizenus, Dr. A., *A Tour to Northern Mexico in 1846 and 1847*, p. 12: "Although it [the mirage] also appears in other parts of the prairie, it is nowhere so common, so deceptive and so well developed as here. In examining the causes which produce it at this high plain, I have arrived at the following conclusions: The phenomenon of mirage requires—

"1. A wide, high plain, with extensive horizon, and but slight undulations of ground.

"2. A dry hard ground, either quite barren, or coated with parched and isolated vegetation, like the short buffalo grass.

"3. Dry and warm weather, with clear sky. On such days, and less in the morning and evening, but rather when the sun has the most power, mirage is the most frequent and the plainest.

"4. A slight hollow in the undulating plain, however insignificant it may be, producing a background. Where this low background is interrupted by the horizon, on that place the mirage grows more dim and disappears entirely.

"5. The distance of several miles, from the stand of the observer. The nearer one approaches, the more distinct becomes the mirage, and it changes at last into a glimmering of the air such as can be seen on hot summer days upon dry, solid macadamized roads, from which the rays of the sun are powerfully reflected.

"6. The mirage is, therefore, the effect of a strong reflection of the rays of the sun from the ground seen out of a certain distance in certain localities."

spring was situate in a small ravine which emptied into the Cimarron some three or four miles further north. It was located just beyond the boundary line between New Mexico and Oklahoma. From this point to Santa Fé, the caravans passed Cold Spring, McNees' Creek, Rabbit Ear Creek, Round Mound, Rock Creek, Point of Rocks, Rio Colorado, Ocaté Creek, Santa Clara Spring (Wagon Mound), Rio Mora, Rio Gallinas (Las Vegas), Ojo de Bernal, San Miguel, Ruins of Pecos, Cottonwood Branch (near Glorieta), and finally Santa Fé, a total distance from Indepenedence of 775 miles.

Of the many tragedies of the Santa Fé Trail one of the most deplorable was the killing of Jedediah S. Smith, which occurred on the banks of the Cimarron in the spring of 1831. Mr. Smith was a member of the firm of Smith, Jackson and Sublette, one of the most celebrated engaged in the Rocky Mountain fur trade. In this year these men, having sold out their business to the Rocky Mountain Fur Company, entered the Santa Fé trade. "With a large and costly expedition of some twenty wagons," says Chittenden, "and eighty men said to have been the finest outfit ever yet sent to Santa Fé, these veteran traders set out, never doubting that their long experience would enable them to cope with the dangers of the route. Everything went well to the ford of the Arkansas, for there was a plain track all the way. But it was very different on the desert waste between the Arkansas and the Cimarron. There was not a person with them who had ever been over the route before, and they now found themselves in a featureless country with no track of any kind except buffalo trails which crossed each other in the most confusing directions. The alluring mirage deceived and exasperated the men, and after two days of fruitless wanderings, with animals dying and men frantic for water, the condition of things seemed well nigh desperate. In this emergency Smith declared that he would find water or perish in the attempt. He was a bold and fearless man and unhesitatingly sallied forth alone for the salvation of the caravan. Following a buffalo trail for several miles he came upon the valley of the Cimarron, but only to find it destitute of water. He knew enough of the character of these streams, however, to believe that there was

MURDER OF JEDEDIAH S. SMITH

water near the surface, and he accordingly scooped out a little hollow into which, indeed the water began to collect. Meanwhile some stealthy Comanches, whom Smith had not observed, were stealing upon him and while he was in the act of stooping down to drink, mortally wounded him with several arrows. He rose and displayed his undaunted spirit in resisting his savage foes to the last, and killed two of them before he expired. The spot where he fell was never precisely known and no grave protects the earthly remains of this Christian and knightly adventurer. A sadder fate or a more heroic victim the parched wastes of the desert never knew."[89]

Near the place known as Rock Creek, on the Dry Cimarron route, occurred shortly after the Mexican War, the massacre of the White party by Jicarilla Apaches. Dr. White was a merchant of Santa Fé and was on his return to New Mexico from the states with his family, in company with the train of F. X. Aubrey. All danger was considered at an end when they arrived at this place, and Dr. White and his family started on ahead. His party consisted of himself, wife and child, a German named Lawberger, an American whose name is not known, a Mexican, and a negro servant. There is a difference of opinion as to the manner of attack, but Major John Greiner, then Indian Agent at Santa Fé, stated that Chacow, a Jicarilla chief, had told him that while the

MASSACRE OF
DR. WHITE'S PARTY

---

[89] Jedediah S. Smith was one of the most remarkable men ever engaged in the commerce of the mountains and prairies. He was born in the state of New York, was well educated and went to St. Louis in 1823. He traveled all over the west from the British boundary to the Mexican provinces and from the Mississippi to the Pacific coast. On several occasions his escape from the Indians, grizzly bears, and from starvation bordered on the miraculous. In 1826 he became senior partner of the firm of Smith, Jackson and Sublette and in 1831 embarked in the Santa Fé trade, but lost his life in the first expedition.

Mr. William Waldo, *Ms*. No. 135, Missouri Historical Society, says of Smith: "He was a bold, outspoken, professing and consistent Christian, the first and only one known among the early Rocky Mountain trappers and hunters. No one who knew him well doubted the sincerity of his piety. He had become a communicant of the Methodist church before leaving his home in New York and in St. Louis he never failed to occupy a place in the church of his choice, while he gave generously to all objects connected with religion which he professed and loved. Besides being an adventurer and a hero, a trader and a Christian, he was himself inclined to literary pursuits and had prepared a geography and atlas of the Rocky Mountain region extending perhaps to the Pacific, but his death occurred before its publication."

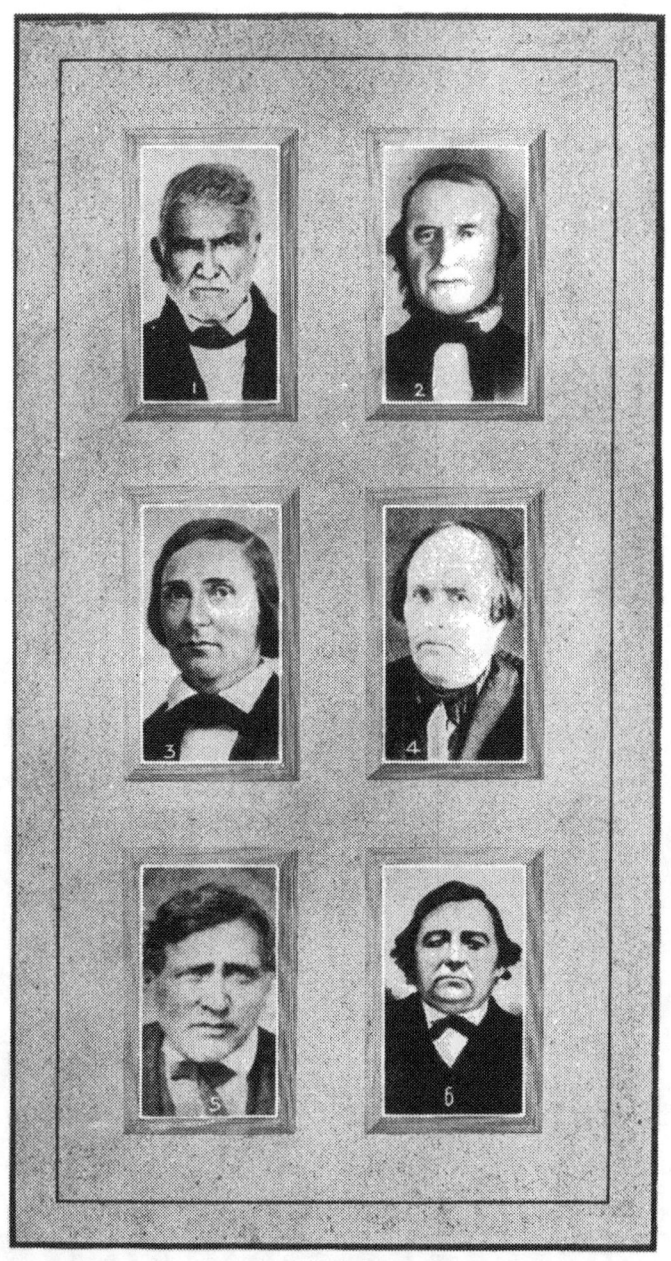

Representative New Mexicans of the American Occupation Period
1. Don Pedro José Perea. 2. Don Antonio José Luna. 3. Col. Manuel A. Chaves. 4. Rev. Antonio José Martinez. 5. Don Nazario Gallegos. 6. Don Hilario Gonzales

Americans were in camp, a small party of Indians rode up and demanded presents. These Dr. White refused to give them, and drove them out of the camp; they returned shortly and were again treated in the same manner. This time they did not go away, but commenced an attack upon the party by shooting the negro and Mexican, the latter falling upon the fire. The others made an attempt to escape, but were all killed except Mrs. White and child, who were made prisoners. The bodies of the dead were laid along side of the road, but were not scalped or stripped. A short time afterward a party of Mexicans came along and began to plunder the wagon, when the Indians, who had concealed themselves, fired upon them and wounded a boy, who was left for dead. He laid still until the Indians had left, when he got up and started toward the settlements, with an arrow sticking between the bones of his arm. He came up with a party of Americans the same day and came through in safety. The Indians who committed the outrage were a raiding party who had been in the southern part of New Mexico. When the facts of the outrage became known at Santa Fé, a company of dragoons, with Kit Carson as guide, was sent in pursuit. They struck the trail and followed it for three or four days, when they came up with and attacked the Indians. They succeeded in killing several of the savages, but during the fight the latter murdered both Mrs. White and the child. Several of the women and children of the Indians perished in a snow storm that came on, and the troops came near sharing the same fate. The barbarous character of these Indians may be understood when it is known that the principal chief of this band came into Santa Fé wearing a necklace made of the teeth of Dr. White, according to Colonel Carson.

Some conception of the dangers which beset the trader and traveler, even as late as the year 1850, may be had from reading portions of a report made by James L. Collins, a trader from Booneville, Missouri, to William Carr Lane, governor of New Mexico in 1852. Governor Lane asked for the information contained in the report for the purposes of making recommendations to Washington relative to the advisability of keeping the trail open in the winter time. Mr. Collins says:

"The first attempt was made by a small party from St. Louis

in the year 1824 or 1825, by Messrs. Faulkner and Anderson. They were caught by a heavy fall of snow at Chouteau's island, on the Arkansas river, and lost nearly all of their horses and mules. They wintered on an island that has been known since as 'Log Island' on account of the many trees they had to cut for the subsistence of their few remaining animals and for sheltering the men from the storm.

"Subsequently the road, being better known, was traveled frequently even in winter, but often the attempt resulted in loss of property, and not infrequently of human life.

"In December, 1841, Don Manuel Alvarez, with a small party, was caught in a storm on Cottonwood creek, near Council Grove. In a few hours two men and all the mules were frozen to death. Alvarez saved the remainder of his men by forcing them into motion until the storm abated; many of them, however, were badly frozen.

"About the same period another party, under the charge of Don Antonio Robidoux, had to stand a storm at the same place. They lost in one night one or two men and over four hundred horses and mules.

"In 1844 Dr. Henry Connelly and M. Speyer got into a storm near the Arkansas river, and on October 12th lost a number of mules and saved the remainder only by driving them into the timber of the river, where they could be protected. The same party encountered another rough storm on the Cimarron, in which they lost over three hundred mules and were compelled to remain until animals were sent from Santa Fé to their relief.

[sidenote: TRAGEDIES OF THE TRAIL]

"In 1848, Messrs. Waldo, McCoy & Company, government freighters, in returning to Missouri, lost nearly all their cattle, amounting to eight or nine hundred head. The wagons were left on the spot until spring.

"In 1849, Messrs. Brown, Russell & Company, in crossing the 'Jornada' from the Arkansas to the Cimarron, with some twenty wagons, were caught by a terrific wind- and snow-storm. The men took refuge in the wagons, leaving the cattle go where they pleased. The animals would not leave, but gathered in the enclosure formed by the wagons, where they perished in a few hours. Fortunately provisions were plenty, and the wagons were used for fuel. Thus the men subsisted until succor arrived in the spring.

"In 1850, the same company, with government freight, was caught by another snow-storm between Cimarron and San Miguel and lost over a thousand head of cattle.

"In 1851, Cottonwood creek was again the scene of an awful destruction of life. Colonel Sumner was overtaken by a storm at that place and lost nearly three hundred mules, one man was lost and several others badly frozen.''

Cold Spring was 535 miles from Independence and it was here the trail left the valley of the Cimarron. The water at this spring was very cold and delicious.

McNees' Creek was the site of one of the melancholy tragedies of the days of the old trail. Here McNees and Munroe, two traders from Franklin, Missouri, on their way home from Santa Fé, in 1828, were killed by the Indians. This creek is now known by the name of Currumpaw; it flows into Beaver creek, thence into the north fork of the Canadian.

Another fatality occurred at this point during the same year and also with a party returning from Santa Fé. The date is confirmed by the *Missouri Intelligencer* of October 24, 1828, which states that the company comprised about twenty-five persons. The party had about one hundred and fifty mules, five wagons, and a small amount of specie. At the Upper Cimarron Springs they were surrounded by a large band of Comanches who ordered the Americans to camp with them for the night. This the traders declined to do and they decided to make their way ahead in spite of the Indians. Captain John Means, a man named Ellison, and another by the name of Bryant brought up the rear with the wagons. When the Indians saw that the traders were bound to proceed, they immediately began the attack. Ellison and Bryant escaped, but Captain Means was instantly shot down and scalped before life had left his body. The party then continued their route by short stages, constantly beset by the Indians, but escaping with no more disastrous loss than the serious wounding of one of their number. At length they got to such desperate straits that it was resolved to abandon the wagons and a portion of the specie. Taking what other property they could with them and about ten thousand dollars, specie, they set out quietly at night, and by traveling all the next day and into the following night they reached the Arkansas. Here they *cached* the remainder of their specie to lighten their load. By the time they arrived at Walnut creek they were so exhausted that they despaired of reaching the settlements and despatched five of the most able-bodied of their number to Independence for help. A rescue party was immediately formed and sent off after the sufferers, who were picked up, scattered along the trail, sometimes one in a place, sometimes two, but all on the verge of starvation.

Rabbit Ear creek derived its name from the fancied resemblance of two hills near-by to rabbit ears. These mounds were a guide to travelers on that part of the journey.

IMPORTANT STATIONS IN NEW MEXICO

It was near the head of this creek that Major Stephen H. Long passed in 1820 in his futile search for the Red river. They are situated just north of the present town of Clayton, the county seat of Union county, New Mexico.

Round Mound was about eight miles from Rabbit Ear creek. Dr. Wislizenus found its elevation to be 6,655 feet above sea-level. On top of the mound were cedars. The view from the top is most beautiful. The Taos mountains to the west are distinctly visible and to the northwest can be seen the famous Wah-to-yah or Cumbres Españoles.

Point of Rocks is a mass of blocks of syenite, towering to the height of several hundred feet above the plain. A clear mountain spring comes out of the rock.

Rio Colorado is the principal headwaters of the Canadian. Previous to the year 1820 this stream was considered to be the source of Red river; but in the expedition of Major Long of that year, he discovered it to be the head branch of the Canadian. This discovery cost him dearly, for striking a branch of the Colorado, near the mountains, he followed down its course believing it to be the main Red river. He was not fully undeceived until arriving at its junction with the Arkansas; through this mistake he failed in the principal object of the expedition which was the exploration of the true sources of the "Red river of Natchitoches." The nearest headwaters of the Red river are about a hundred miles south of this point on the old trail.

It was near this point, in March, 1833, that a party of twelve traders, while en route from Santa Fé to Independence, was attacked by about two hundred Comanches. The attack occurred about January 1, 1833, and lasted thirty-two hours. A tinner by the name of Pratt was killed while trying to catch a mule at a distance from camp. The party tied their mules to a tree and entrenched themselves as quickly as possible. During this time a Mr.

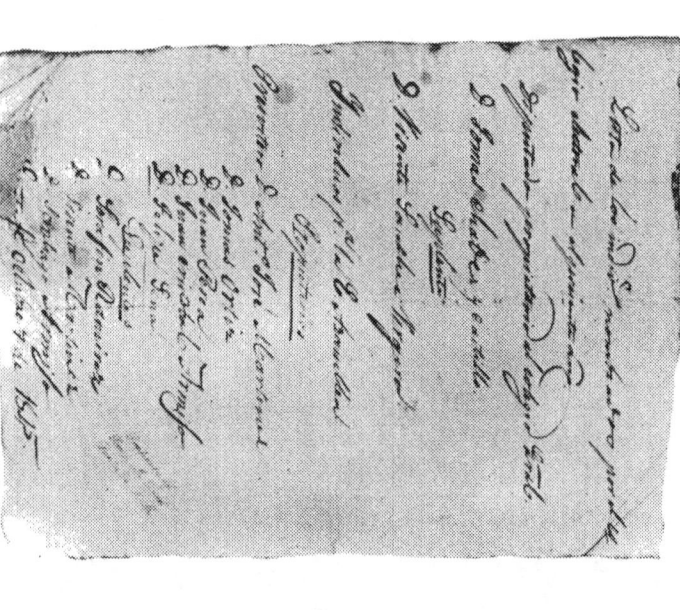

Courtesy Benj. M. Read
Ballot Cast at Last Election under the Mexican Government

Ballot Cast at the first Election under the American Government

Mitchell, of Boone county, Missouri, was killed. About midnight the party tried to get away, but was driven back. The fight continued all of the next day, by which time the traders had expended all of their ammunition and most of them were wounded. They had almost given up when they were most unexpectedly hailed by the Indians, who told them in Spanish that they might go. The traders had lost all of their horses and mules and they were compelled to abandon their property, including about twelve thousand dollars in specie. The next day after leaving the battle-ground they separated, one part taking the nearest cut to the settlements and the other going down the river. They suffered incredible hardships. It was winter and most of them were wounded. They were likewise nearly destitute of clothing, and being without ammunition, could not procure food. The fate of the division going down the river is not known but evidently no lives were lost.

Ocaté creek, at the point reached by the Cimarron trail, was a noted place; in the early days there were pines growing there, the first seen on the trail. The elevation is six thousand feet above sea-level at this point.

Wagon Mound was a well known place on the trail; near-by is the Santa Clara Spring. The rock composing the mound is a black and spotted basalt. In this vicinity the party transporting the mail from the United States was cut off by the Indians in 1850; they were en route from Fort Leavenworth to Santa Fé, ten in number, all of whom were killed, together with their mules, and the wagon rifled of its contents. From information afterwards obtained, it was ascertained to have been the work of Apache and Ute Indians. The first attack was made in the morning, the fight lasting all day, without much damage, only a man or two having been wounded. This was done by the Apaches alone. In the evening they were joined by a party of Utes, who told them they did not know how to fight Americans, but they would show them. The attack was renewed the next morning, when the combined force of the Indians rushed upon and overpowered them after a short resistance. The final struggle took place at a pass between the hills, where the savages had every advantage. When intelligence of the fight reached Santa Fé, a party of soldiers was sent out to bury the dead. Two men were found dead in the wagon, having been wounded probably early in the engagement, and placed there by their companions, where they were afterward killed. The mules and the remainder of the party were lying dead near-by. The men had been shot with arrows and the animals with balls. The former were partly stripped but none was scalped. A great quantity of arrows covered the ground, and the mail matter was scattered about. The details of this battle were given to the commander at Santa Fé shortly afterward by an Apache chief who came to visit the commanding general.

The Rio Mora, says the old trader, in his diary, was a fine mountain stream and a charming valley; soil, grass, and water are excellent. In the early part of the nineteenth century there were no settlements here, owing to depredations of the Utes, Apaches, and the Comanches.

Rio Gallinas, or Las Vegas, was a prominent point on the trail. The place was not known by the latter name until the thirties. Here the first waters of the Rio Grande watershed were reached. In 1832 Dr. Gregg found where the city of Las Vegas now stands only "a little hovel at the foot of a cliff." This was the first house built in Las Vegas. It was definitely colonized in 1835 and eleven years afterward, when Dr. Wislizenus crossed the plains with Speyer and Armijo's caravan, the place had over a hundred houses.

The first settlement of any consequence in New Mexico reached by the early Santa Fé traders coming over the Cimarron route was San Miguel.[90] In the time of Dr. Gregg it consisted of irregular clusters of adobe houses.

---

[90] The town of San Miguel was a very important place during the rule of Governor Armijo; it was the county seat of San Miguel county. In 1850 it was a place of near one thousand inhabitants. Davis, in *El Gringo*, says: "The spot was pointed out to me where Howland and two others were shot, at the southeast corner of the plaza. Three others of the prisoners, one of whom was Kendall, were also led out to the place of execution, and the file of men who were to settle their final account was already drawn up, when they were rescued by the kindness and intrepidity of a Mexican gentleman named Gregorio Vigil. He threw himself between the Americans and the soldiers, and forbade the latter to fire upon unarmed men. He was then a man of influence and his conduct prevented the execution and saved them from death. He still resides in San Miguel, in reduced circumstances. Such magnanimous conduct should be held in grateful remembrance by every American."

Don Gregorio Vigil did not prevent the execution of the Texans at San Miguel; he prevented the perpetration of this outrage at La Cuesta, further down the river Pecos.

After two days' journey from San Miguel the caravan, following the road which skirted the foot-hills of the Santa Fé range, came in sight of Santa Fé, the capital of New Mexico. To the trader "New Mexico was the Egypt of America and Santa Fé its Thebes." Beyond in the little valley was the Mecca of the Missourian. There were occasional groups of trees, skirted with corn and wheat fields, with here and there a cluster of adobe buildings. As the caravan ascended the ridge which overlooks the city the clamorings of the men, and the rejoicings of the bull-whackers could be heard on every side. "Even the animals," says Gregg, "seemed to participate in the humor of their riders, who grew more and more merry as they descended towards the city. I doubt, in short, whether the first sight of the walls of Jerusalem were beheld by the crusaders with much more tumultuous and soul-enrapturing joy."

ARRIVAL OF THE CARAVANS AT SANTA FÉ

The arrival of the caravan always was productive of great excitement among the inhabitants. "Los Americanos!"—Los carros!"—"La entrada de la caravana!" says the historian, "were to be heard in every direction. Crowds of women and boys flocked around to see the new-comers, while crowds of *leperos* hung about as usual to see what they could pilfer. The wagoners were by no means free from excitement on this occasion. Informed of the 'ordeal' they had to pass, they had spent the previous morning in 'rubbing up;' and now they were prepared, with clean faces, sleek-combed hair, and their choicest Sunday suit, to meet the 'fair eyes' of glistening black that were sure to stare at them as they passed. There was yet another preparation to be made in order to 'show off' to advantage. Each wagoner must tie a brand new 'cracker' to the lash of his whip; for, on driving through the streets and the *plaza publica*, everyone strives to outvie his comrades in the dexterity with which he flourishes this favorite badge of authority."

Immediately after the arrival of the caravan the wagons were unloaded, the contents being stored in the ware-rooms of the custom-house. Now the traders were busy in getting their cargoes through the custom-house, in order to begin trade with the country merchants and

THE CUSTOM-HOUSE—DUTIES AND REQUIREMENTS

store-keepers who flocked to the city at this time. There was an "inspection," but this was seldom carried on with rigid adherence to rules or regulations; for an "actuated sympathy" for the traders and merchants and a "specific desire" to promote business caused the government officials to open a few of such parcels only as would exhibit the least discrepancy with the manifest.

The *derechos de arancel* — impost duties — of Mexico were extremely oppressive, averaging about one hundred per cent upon the cost "back in the States." On cotton goods this was particularly the case. According to the *arancel* of 1837, and it was still heavier before that time, all plain-wove cottons, whether white or printed, paid twelve and a half cents duty per *vara* besides the *derecho de consumo* (consumption duty) which brought the total up to at least fifteen.[91] The selling price of goods was about double

---

[91] The receipts of the custom house, as reported to the Mexican government, according to Prieto, *Rentas*, 204, doc. 3, the sums in parentheses being from the government *memorias*, and differing somewhat, were: 1825, 8 months, $2,053 (12 months, $3,595); 1826, 10 months, $10,391; 1826-7, $8,607; 1827-8, $5,938; 1828-9, $27,008; ($27,907); 1829-30, $12,691; 1830-1, $10,581 ($31,882); 1831-2, $31,314; 1833-4, $29,297; 1836-7, $21,219; 1841, $1,195; 1842, $27,921; 1843 ($81,000).

Gregg says: "An 'arrangement' — a compromise — is expected, in which the officers are sure at least to provide for themselves. In some ports, a custom has been said to prevail of dividing the legal duties into three equal parts; one for the officers, a second for the merchants, the other for the government. For a few years, Governor Armijo of Santa Fé, established a tariff of his own, entirely arbitrary, exacting five hundred dollars for each wagon load, whether large or small, of fine or coarse goods! Of course this was very advantageous to such traders as had large wagons and costly assortments, while it was no less onerous to those with smaller vehicles or coarse, heavy goods. As might have been anticipated, the traders soon took to conveying their merchandize only in the largest wagons, drawn by ten or twelve mules, and omitting the coarser and more weighty articles of trade. This caused the governor to return to an ad valorem system, though still without regard to the *arancel general* of the nation. How much of these duties found their way into the public treasury, I will not venture to assert."

The custom-house was only nominally at Taos, the goods being actually entered at Santa Fé. The business of 1844 was estimated at $750,000, but during that year and the one following there was a big loss of animals and there were constant rumors of war with Mexico.

In 1841, the returning caravan from Santa Fé was accompanied by a large body of native New Mexicans who brought with them $80,000 with which to purchase goods, and returning in the spring of 1842 the caravan consisted of 62 wagons, 800 mules, and $150,000 in merchandise.

The measures, weights, and coins of the Santa Fé Trail period were as follows: 1 onza (gold) equals 16 dollars, 1 peso (silver) equals 1 dollar, 1 real (silver) equals 12 1-2 cents, 1-2 real (silver) equals 6 1-4 cents, 1 quartillo (copper) equals 3 1-8 cents, 1 tlaco (copper) equals 1-9-16 cents, 1 onza (8 ochavos) equals 1 ounce, 1 marco (8 onzas) equals 1-2 pound, 1 libra

Prominent Indian Chiefs
1. Narbona, Navajó. 2. Asa Havi, Comanche. 3. Scabby Bull, Arapaho.
4. Agustin Vigil, Jicarilla Apache

the cost and at this rate, was, for a time, sufficiently low to control the market as against foreign goods imported by way of Vera Cruz and Chihuahua. A large portion of the merchandise brought from the Missouri river was sent south for the Chihuahua trade. Merchandise was paid for mainly in gold and silver, though furs, robes, and blankets were also taken in exchange, and on return trips the wagons were sometimes partly laden with wool as there was no duty on exported products. Dr. David Waldo, who was engaged in the Santa Fé trade for over thirty years, at

MAGNITUDE OF THE TRADE that time, says of the magnitude of the trade for the year 1846, that the cost of the goods transported over the trail was $937,500; cost of outfits, insurance, wages, etc., $414,750; profit, $400,000. There were 375 wagons, 1,700 mules, 2,000 oxen, and 500 men employed during that year.

Subsequent to 1825 the expeditions were of frequent occurrence. In an elaborate note, Chittenden has given us a résumé of the business of the trail, which is given below.[92]

(2 marcos) equals 1 pound, 1 arroba (25 libras) equals 25 pounds, 1 quintal (4 arrobas) equals 100 pounds, 1 carga (3 quintals) equals 300 pounds, 1 fanega (140 pounds) about 2 bushels, 1 almuer (almuerza) equals 1-12 of a fanega, 1 frasco equals about 5 pints. 1 foot Mexican equals 0.920 foot English, 1 vara (3 feet Mexican) equals 2.759 feet, 1 legua (26.63 to 1 meridian) equals 5,000 varas equals 2.636 miles English; 209.01 chains. 1 cordel equals 137.95 feet equals 2.09 chains, 1 chain equals .478 cordel, 1 sitio de ganada mayor equals a square league of 4,428 acres, 1 sitio equals 4,338.464 acres, 1 caballeria equals 105.75 acres, 1 acre equals 5,762 square varas, 1 meter equals 39.37 miles, 1 fanega of corn equals 8.82 acres, 1 fanega of wheat equals 1.53 acres.

[92] Chittenden, H. M., *History of American Fur Trade*, p. 508, note 14: "1825. Becknell returned from Santa Fé June 1.— Marmaduke left Santa Fé May 31; date of arrival in Franklin not known. Another party left Santa Fé in June arriving in Franklin August 1 with 500 mules and horses; pursued usual route; went from San Miguel to the Canadian; down this stream 300 miles; thence N. E. to Arkansas at mouth of Little Arkansas; thence through Osage country home; were roughly handled by the Osages.— May 16, large party, 105 men, 34 wagons, 240 mules and horses, Augustus Storrs, newly appointed consul to Santa Fé, Captain, left Ft. Osage for Santa Fé; party returned by detachments at different times and by different routes during the fall; a number, among them Storrs, remained. — Another caravan left in May with 81 men, 200 horses and thirty thousand dollars worth of goods; no further record. — A party of Tennesseans left Jackson, Tennessee, for Santa Fé in April; returned as far as Arkansas river with some of the above parties and then continued down that stream.

"1826— Early in April a party arrived in Franklin from Santa Fé— About the same time a party of 100 left for Santa Fé — About June 1, another party of between eighty and one hundred persons, 'with wagons and car-

The following table, which is the only complete summary of the trade ever prepared, was compiled by Dr. Gregg, a most competent authority:

Year	Mdse.	Wagons	Men	Traders	To Chihuahua
1822	$ 15,000		70	60	
1823	12,000		50	30	
1824	35,000	26	100	80	$ 3,000
1825	65,000	37	130	90	5,000
1826	90,000	60	100	70	7,000
1827	85,000	55	90	50	8,000
1828	150,000	100	200	80	20,000
1829	60,000	30	50	20	5,000
1830	120,000	70	140	60	20,000
1831	250,000	130	320	80	80,000
1832	140,000	70	150	40	50,000
1833	180,000	105	185	60	80,000
1834	150,000	80	160	50	70,000
1835	140,000	75	140	40	70,000
1836	130,000	70	135	35	60,000
1837	150,000	80	160	35	80,000
1838	90,000	50	100	20	40,000
1839	250,000	130	250	40	100,000
1840	50,000	30	60	5	10,000
1841	150,000	60	100	12	80,000
1842	160,000	70	120	15	90,000
1843	450,000	230	350	30	300,000

In a business of so hazardous and uncertain a character the profits must necessarily have been large to justify a pursuit of it. The

---

riages of every description' left Franklin for Santa Fé — June 9, 'six or seven new and substantial wagons' laden with goods arrived in Franklin en route for Santa Fé; owned by Mexican, Mr. Escudero, who was in charge of them. This was about the beginning of Mexican proprietorship in trade which monopolized more than half the business in 1843.— It appears that in September of this year a party under Céran St. Vrain (if we may trust Inman) set out for Santa Fé arriving there in November; in this party was a run-away boy, Kit Carson, then 17 years old.

"1827.— Spring caravan from Franklin had 52 wagons and 105 men; Ezekiel Williams, captain; Augustus Storrs and David Workman along; the largest party yet; the only outgoing expedition mentioned, but of course there were others; about 60 of the party returned about September 30, with 800 head of stock, valued at $20,000; absent 4 months; cleared 40% — May 31, a party returned from Santa Fé with several hundred mules and $30,000 specie.

"1828. — About the 1st of May, caravan left Franklin for Santa Fé with $150,000 worth of merchandize and 150 persons. — May 18, a party was at Blue Springs en route to Santa Fé, with 37 wagons, and $41,000 worth of goods; September 12, 70 to 80 persons arrived in Franklin from Santa Fé; venture profitable but lost 2 men, Monroe and McNees. — October 28, party

goods were mostly bought in eastern markets, and were sold at a great advance, often more than one hundred per cent on the first cost. But by the time the sales were accomplished and the various expenses and losses in transporting them so far were de-

---

of 25 arrived in Franklin from Santa Fé; had been attacked by Indians who stole all their animals; killed John Means of Franklin, and compelled them to cache their specie. Bent's Fort erected this year; according to some authorities, the following year.

"1829. — Spring caravan consisted of about 70 persons and 35 wagons; Charles Bent, captain; military escort under Major Riley; Samuel C. Lamme killed en route; returned cargo valued at $34,000.00; reached Franklin early in November. — There seems to have been no other caravan this year.

"1830. — About May 22, party of 120 with 60 wagons left Franklin for Santa Fé, returning in October with fair profits.

"1831. — May 15, large party, of which Josiah Gregg was a member, numbering nearly 200, and including some ladies, 100 wagons, 2 small cannon, and $200,000 worth of goods, left Independence, Mo. and having organized at Council Grove, left that place May 27; crossed the Arkansas June 13, and arrived at San Miguel in due course. — May 21, there was preparing at Franklin, a large party for Santa Fé with about $200,000.00 worth of goods. — Some of the members had put their entire property in the venture. — One of the above parties returned in October, after a successful trip. — October 20, a party of 25 or 30 persons passed Columbia, Mo. for Santa Fé, mostly from eastern states. It is this year that Smith, Jackson and Sublette made their unfortunate journey across the plains in which Smith lost his life.

"1832. — Principal caravan under Charles Bent; date of departure not given; returned about November 1, with $100,000.00 specie and $90,000.00 other property. — A party returning in the fall and winter of this year, attacked by Indians on Canadian January 1 and lost all their property and one man.

"1833. — June 20, spring caravan at Diamond Grove, 184 men, 93 wagons, under Charles Bent; November 9, 100 of above party returned with $100,000.00 specie and large amount of other property. — Gregg returned this fall.

"1834. — May 24, caravan of about 125 wagons; Gregg probably with it; part of caravan under captain Kerr, left Santa Fé September 10, arrived home in October, 140 men and 40 wagons, with returns amounting to over $200,000.00.

"The record of the caravans during the following years is very obscure, although it is certain that they continued as heretofore. — Various causes contributed to the deficiency of record. Of all the authorities relied on in this note the *Missouri Intelligencer* is the most important, and next are the St. Louis papers and the *Niles Register*. The *Missouri Intelligencer* and Boone's Lick *Advertiser* began its career in Franklin, where the Santa Fé trade had its origin, and for a full decade its headquarters. As the trade was at that time peculiarly an industry of the country around Franklin the local paper kept a close account of its doings. June 29, 1826, the paper was transferred to Fayette, in the same county, but back from the river, and four years later, May 4, 1830, it was removed to Columbia, Mo. As its habitat was moved away from the river, it became less in touch with the Santa Fé trade. The trade itself gradually transferred its headquarters to Independence, Mo., which by 1830, had become the main starting point. This town had no paper, and reports of events at so great a distance often failed to be made. While, therefore, we should expect that the later records would be more complete they are in reality less so."

ducted, the net profit rarely exceeded forty per cent and was frequently as low as ten per cent. There were, of course, occasionally instances of actual loss.

"A striking characteristic," says Chittenden, "of the Santa Fé trade was its division among a great number of proprietors. The above table shows to what degree this was true and only in later years did the investments average as much as one thousand dollars per proprietor. It was a business of small dealers and no 'American Fur Company' followed the Santa Fé Trail. Not infrequently individuals took with them all they possessed and as the enterprises were generally profitable the trade was undoubtedly a great benefit. Often individuals would secure credits by mortgages upon their property until their return in the fall. If, as occasionally happened, the Santa Fé market proved dull and it required considerable time to get rid of one's cargo by retail these home obligations enforced a resort to the less profitable method by wholesale in order that the business might terminate in time for the trader to get back home and satisfy his creditors." [93]

Although the trade was thus divided among a large number of people, it was of great importance and after the Mexican War, in particular, when the newly acquired territories were occupied by American troops, the business of freighting over the plains became still more profitable.

Of the old traders very few continued in the business during this period although it was during the fifties, sixties and early seventies that the profits were the greatest.

---

[93] The following letter from Colonel Céran St. Vrain shows the custom at that time prevailing:

"San Fernando del Taos, September 14, 1830.
"Messrs. B. Pratte and Co.

"Gentlemen:—It is with pleasure that I inform you of my last arrival at Santa fe, which was the 4th of August. we were met at Red river by General Biscara the customhouse officer and a few soldiers, the object in coming out so far to meet us was to prevent smuggling and it had the desired effeck, there was a guard placed around our wagons until we entered Santafe, we had all to pay full dutys which amounts to 60 per cent on cost. I was the first that put goods in the Customhouse and I opened immediately, but goods sold very slow, so slow that it was discouraging. I found that it was impossible to meet my payments if I continued retailing. I there fore thought it was best to hole saile & I have done so. I send you by Mr. Andru Carson and Lavoise Ruel one wagon, eleven mules, one horse and 653 skins of Beaver; 961 lbs. nine hundred and sixty-one pounds, which you will have sold for my account. I do not wish the mules sold unless they sell for a good price.

"I am with much respect,
"Your obdt. servt.
"Céran St. Vrain."

Gen. Christopher Carson. Earliest Portrait, about 1845

Some conception of the growth and magnitude of the business over the Santa Fé Trail in later years may be had when we consider that with 230 wagons coming from the Missouri river in 1843, in 1865 there came into New Mexico from the States three thousand wagons belonging to traders alone, exclusive of the government transportation.

<small>ITS VOLUME IN LATER YEARS</small>

"In the year 1866," says Meline, in his *Two Thousand Miles on Horseback*, "there will be from five to six thousand wagons, two hundred and fifty of which are now between Fort Union and Santa Fé, coming in. Most of the large trains return empty. Some of them occasionally get a freight of copper or other mineral and a still greater number take in wool. The exports of both those articles should, and will be, indefinitely increased. The yield of wool could be made enormous, and in proportion to extent of territory, not even California is richer in mineral wealth. But one condition is needed for all of this, which stands for prosperity and civilization — it is a condition precedent: — Get rid of the Indian!"

One of the most charming features of the business was the long journey over the plains. In the early days, no permanent abode of civilized men greeted the trader's eye from the time he left the frontier settlements until he came to San Miguel. The very dangers made the trip attractive. The entire journey, with the exception of trifling distances at either end, was infested with some of the most treacherous Indians ever known upon the continent, and the perils of the trip made it extremely dangerous for small parties to undertake the journey alone. It was on this account that the large caravans were organized.

Manuel Alvarez, *Diary of*, when American consul at Santa Fé, New Mexico, gives the stations on the Old Santa Fé Trail, as follows:

From Independence to	M.	Total		M.	Total
Round Grove	35		Turkey Creek	25	212
Narrows	30	65	Little Arkansas	17	229
110-Mile Creek	30	95	Cow Creek	20	249
Bridge Creek	8	103	Arkansas River	16	265
Big John Spring (crossing several Crs)	40	143	Walnut Creek (Up. Ark. r.)	8	273
Council Grove	2	145	Ash Creek	19	292
Diamond Spring	15	160	Pawnee Fork	6	298
Lost Spring	15	175	Coon Creek	33	331
Cottonwood Creek	12	187	Caches	36	367

From Independence to	M.	Total		M.	Total
Ford of Arkansas	20	387	Round Mound	8	583
Sand Cr. (leave Ark. r.)	50	437	Rock Creek	8	591
Cimarron r. (Lower			Point of Rocks	19	610
Sp.)	8	445	Rio Colorado	20	630
Middle Spring (Up.			Ocaté	6	636
Cim. r.)	36	481	Santa Clara Springs	21	657
Willow Bar	26	507	Rio Mora	22	679
Upper Spring	18	525	Rio Gallinas (Vegas)	20	699
Cold Spring (leave			Ojó de Bernal (spr)	17	716
C. r.)	5	530	San Miguel	6	722
McNees Creek	25	555	Pecos Village	23	755
Rabbit Ear Creek	20	575	Santa Fé	25	770

The most notable landmark of the Santa Fé Trail was at its terminus, the old Fonda, the adobe hotel that still stands, in part, at the southwest corner of the plaza; from the very beginning to its close it was the end of the great highway of commerce. This one-story structure and its great corral, with adobe walls almost as high as those of the hostelry, was the destination of the great caravans of Conestoga wagons which crossed the plains annually for more than fifty years. It was the rendezvous of the scouts, pioneers, and plainsmen from the earliest days of the trail down to the building of the great transcontinental railways, when a new era was inaugurated. Its gaming tables were the attraction that lured the prospectors, soldiers, traders, trappers, and mountaineers for miles around, and its liquid cheer soon gave to the tenderfoot sojourner all the courage, dash, and dare-devil spirit of the true son of the desert. When the railway was built into Santa Fé the Fonda fell upon evil days. Its patronage began to decline with the construction of more modern accommodations and late in the last century it was abandoned for hotel purposes. The corner, which in its palmy days contained the entrance to the office of the hotel, was rented for a curio store, while the back rooms were rented for rooming purposes. Finally the walls began to show signs of weakening, no repairs to them having been made for many years, and they were propped up with heavy timbers. Soon the "roomers" sought other quarters and today the historic Fonda is almost deserted and with the present progress in the construction of modern buildings in the capital, this old landmark, that has

THE FONDA AT SANTA FÉ

withstood the vicissitudes of more than a hundred years and witnessed the mutations from Spanish to Mexican and from Mexican to American sovereignty, will soon be obliterated to make room for a modern business block.

As early as 1849 a stage line was established between Independence, Missouri,[94] and Santa Fé. The history of staging over the Santa Fé Trail in itself would fill a volume.
THE OVERLAND STAGES At times the Indians were very hostile and guards were furnished the coaches when passing through the Indian country. There were eight of these, in the early days, each armed with two revolvers and a rifle, giving fair protection to the travelers, who, as a rule, were also well armed.

[94] Independence and Westport, Mo., were very important trade centers in their day. When the pioneers first came to Jackson county, in the early part of the nineteenth century, they foresaw that somewhere near the mouth of the Kaw river, some day would be built a great city. Independence was founded in 1827, and until 1840 it gave promise of being the great city; then the preponderance of trade centered in Westport, which was established in 1833, and for fifteen years it seemed that this was destined to be the city. Kansas City was founded in 1839, at the river landing, and soon overshadowed both Independence and Westport.

The Santa Fé trade began in Independence in 1831 and a boat landing was established at Blue Mills on the Missouri river, six miles distant. A custom house was established here at one time. From the close of the Mexican War to 1857, Independence was an important outfitting point for the western caravans. The manufacture of wagons and other equipment needed by the overland traders was a very important industry. Men of that day engaged in the business were Hiram Young, Lewis Jones, Robert Stone, and John W. Modie.

John C. McCoy, an old settler of Jackson county, Missouri, in addressing a meeting of the old settlers' society of Jackson county, gives a most interesting account of the business at that terminus of the Santa Fé Trail. He says: "Independence in those early years was selected as a place of arrival and departure and as an outfitting place for trappers and hunters of the mountains and western plains. It was well worth while to witness the arrival of some of the pack-trains. Before entering they gave notice of their arrival by the shooting of guns, so that when they reached Owens and Aull's store a goodly number of people were there to welcome them. A greasy, dirty set of men they were. Water, surely, was a rare commodity with them. They little cared for it except to slack their thirst. Their animals were loaded down with heavy packs of buffalo robes and peltry. Occasionally, they had a small wagon, which, after long usage, had the felloes and spokes wrapped with rawhide to keep the vehicle from falling to pieces. So accustomed were they to their work that it took them little time to unload the burdens from the backs of the animals and store their goods in the warehouse. The trappers let the merchants attend to the shipping. The arrival in Independence was always a joyous ending of a hazardous trip, and when once safely over it, they were always ready for a jolly time, which they had 'to their hearts' content. They made the welkin ring and filled the town with high carnival for many days. The mountain trade at length gave way to the Mexican trade, this being on a much larger scale. Pack mules and donkeys were discarded and wagons

When the stage line was first established, stages were run once a month; later the service was increased to once a week, then to three times a week, and, after the travel demanded it, daily stages were run. The fare from the Missouri river to Santa Fé was two hundred and fifty dollars, the baggage being limited, at first to forty pounds. Anything in excess of that amount was paid for extra at the rate of fifty cents per pound.

After the Civil War, and during the war for that matter, a coachload from Kansas City to Santa Fé consisted of a driver, a messenger, and ten passengers with an allowance of one hundred and ten pounds of baggage to each passenger. This was the limit. All excess in baggage was then charged for at the rate of one dollar a pound. The fare from Kansas City to Santa Fé was two hundred dollars. It took thirteen days and six hours of constant traveling to make the trip. Relays of horses were kept at stations along the route so that changes of animals were made at intervals of fifteen to twenty-five miles, with the exception of one portion of the road, one hundred and ten miles across the "desert" from Zarah station to Fort Dodge. It was never possible to maintain a station on this portion of the road owing to the lack of water and because of the depredations of the Indians who destroyed any construction on this section of the plains. This stretch was known as "The Long Route." It was made with one relay of four horses, and a camp of one night upon the plains so that the animals might receive a needed rest. Water, feed and provisions were carried in the rear "boot" of the coach. The water often gave out upon this portion of the journey and the passengers suffered from thirst as did also the horses, particularly in the hot summer months. Zarah was a little east of the present city of Great Bend. The coach was always in charge of a conductor or messenger. He had the same authority over the coach, property, and passengers as the captain

---

drawn by mule and ox teams were substituted. Such men as David Waldo, Solomon Houke, William and Solomon Sublette, Josiah Gregg, St. Vrain, Chavez and others of like character were early adventurers, and as the governor gave permission to them to enter and trade with the people, they ventured across the plains regardless of the dangers. Samuel C. Owens, it is said, was the first trader in Independence. He came to Missouri from Kentucky when he was a young man. He was the first clerk of the circuit court of Jackson county. John Aull, his business partner, had owned a store in Lexington, Mo. Owens and James Aull lost their lives while with Doniphan's expedition in Mexico.''

Governors of New Mexico under the Act of March 3, 1851

1. David Merriwether. 2. Abraham Rencher. 3. Henry Connelly. 4. Robert B. Mitchell. 5. William Carr Lane. 6. William A. Pile. 7. Marsh Giddings. 8. Samuel B. Axtell. 9. Lewis Wallace

has over a ship and its crew. He had control of the treasure box and was responsible for its safe delivery at the termination of the route. Drivers were changed quite often between Kansas City and Santa Fé, but the messengers remained in charge over the entire distance. The company always chose the bravest and coolest men for this position, as there were many brushes with Indians and sometimes with outlaws who had designs on the treasure box. Sometimes great amounts of gold dust and silver coin would be transported. Only men of the greatest endurance could stand this long trip across the plains. The messenger had to sleep as best he could upon the seat beside the driver, and throughout the entire trip of thirteen days, he secured very little rest. He was armed with a Sharpe's repeating rifle and two Colt's revolvers. The greatest danger was from the hostile Indians; these were poorly armed in those days, using few guns and almost always bows, arrows, and the deadly lance.

In 1866, Barlow and Sanderson, the stage and express company running the line of stages across the plains, moved the offices of the company from Kansas City to Junction City, which became in that year the western terminus of the Kansas Pacific railway, and from that point the stages began their journey across the plains to Santa Fé. From Junction City the offices of the Overland Stage Company kept moving westward until the railway reached Denver, and shortly thereafter, with the exception of the business into New Mexico, which continued until the building of the Atchison, Topeka & Santa Fé Railway, the stage coach of the prairies was numbered with the institutions of the past. There were many dangers to be encountered on the route, and the stories of Indian attacks could be related almost ad infinitum.[95]

---

[95] A messenger in the stage coach days, named Peter Kelly, was one of the bravest men who ever crossed the plains; he never figured in the literature of the frontier; still he was a hero of the trail. Al Carpenter was his driver on many trips. Once while making the "long route" between Zarah and Ft. Dodge, they were camped upon the plain. The night was moon-lit. A fire having been made of buffalo chips, the party enjoyed a meal of broiled buffalo hump, "slap-jacks," and black coffee, sweetened with molasses, this being considered a "square meal" under the circumstances. Shortly the passengers were sound asleep, covered with their warm blankets and buffalo robes. Presently the messenger informed Carpenter that the "Indian sign" during the day, in the neighborhood of Pawnee Fork, had been anything but pleasing. "I think we'll have a brush with the Cheyennes before we get to Dodge," said he. "So you lie down and get what rest you can and I'll keep watch."

Communication with California began in 1827, when Richard Campbell, with a party [96] of thirty-five men and a number of pack

---

Kelly knew well enough that a band of Cheyennes had been following the coach all day, but had kept the information to himself so as not to frighten the passengers. Shortly before daybreak Kelly awakened Carpenter, telling him he thought it best to be moving, as he believed the Indians would commence the attack at daylight. The horses were quickly hitched up and soon the stage was on its way to Dodge. By nine o'clock no Indians had been seen, so a rest was taken and the remaining few gallons of water in the cask were given to the horses. They could not hope to reach Dodge before eight o'clock in the evening and until that time there was not a drop of water for the passengers, all had to be given to the horses. "No breakfast this morning, boys," cheerily said Kelly. "Time is too precious and we can't stop to cook." All forenoon Kelly sat upon the boot, his rifle across his knees, his eyes eagerly scanning the horizon. About noon he caught sight of Indians, bobbing up and down, in sight and out again as they rode single file over the sand-hills about two miles distant. Kelly began giving orders. Carpenter was told, in the event of an attack, to crouch low down into the boot and give his entire attention to the horses; under no circumstances to let go of the reins; handing a lot of mail sacks down from the boot, the passengers were told to barricade the sides of the coach. "Get your guns ready for action boys," said he, "and don't waste your ammunition. Keep your nerve and we'll beat 'em off; they are nine and we are five; we will whip them if you keep cool." Now the arrows began to shower upon the coach. In the midst of it all, Kelly changed his position from the boot to the top of the coach where he presented a fine target for the arrows of the savages, but he was in better position to use his rifle with effect. As he mounted to the top the savages began to yell, riding up close and showering arrows upon them; twice he was hit in the leg and thigh; swiftly the horses, guided by the brave Carpenter, galloped on; deliberate and cool Kelly kept firing upon the savages; the Indians retreated, leaving their leader and another dead upon the prairie. "That's it," shouted Kelly. Kelly, himself, had tumbled them over, but he gave the passengers inside to understand that they had accomplished this feat, which seemed to give them great encouragement. Quickly the Indians charged again; another savage rolled off his pony. Three of the Indian mounts were wounded and now only five Indians were following the coach, vicious looking "bucks" who seemed determined to succeed. At times they charged so close that they could almost be struck with the driver's whip. At this critical moment Kelly declared that his rifle was hot and wouldn't work and began telling Carpenter that they would have to round up and fight it out hand to hand. At the very moment, however, the Indians made a dash across the prairies. Looking around, the cause for their sudden departure became apparent, for far ahead, coming in their direction was a long wagon train. It was Don Miguel Otero's caravan on the way to Kansas City from New Mexico. The Indians had seen them first and made good their escape. Quickly the passengers crawled out of the coach; not one was wounded, although the coach fairly bristled with arrows. The arrows were extracted from Kelly's thigh and leg ·and his wounds dressed. Dinner was had with the Mexican "bull-whackers" and after a good rest the stage proceeded on its way to Dodge, where they arrived in safety late in the evening. Kelly was the hero; his courage and judgment had saved the lives of all. Kelly made many trips as messenger and had many conflicts with the savages, but in all was never seriously wounded. When the staging days were over, he retired to his farm near Westport, Mo., where he died several years since.

[96] Simpson, Gen. J. H., *Reconnoisances in New Mexico and Texas*, p. 64:

animals traveled from New Mexico to San Diego by way of Zuñi and the valley of the Rio de Zuñi, and TRAILS TO CALIFORNIA found no difficulty throughout the whole distance. Later, about 1830, Don José Antonio Baca visited that country with a small number of New Mexicans, and Ewing Young,[97] with a company of foreign trappers, made a fur-hunting tour in the western valleys. During the succeeding two years, three trading and trapping parties made the journey under Wolfskill, Jackson, and Young, the first named opening the long followed trail from Taos north of the Colorado river. From this time the trail was followed every year, often by parties of a few individuals only. Trade between the two territories or departments consisted in the exchange of New Mexican blankets for California mules and horses, and it must be confessed that the traders soon earned a most unenviable reputation. There were many honorable exceptions, but most of the trading parties were

"I think it proper to bring to the notice of the department the expediency of having the country examined west of the pueblo of Zuñi, for the ascertainment of a wagon route from the former point to the *Pueblo de Los Angeles*, or, failing in this, to San Diego. The route from Santa Fé to Zuñi — a distance of two hundred and four miles — is, with a very slight application of labor, practicable for wagons; and the guide, Carbajal, who has been down the Rio de Zuñi to its junction with the Colorado of the West, says it continues practicable all the way along its tributary to the point mentioned.

"Mr. Richard Campbell, of Santa Fé, since my return, has informed me that in 1827, with a party of thirty-five men, and a number of pack animals, he traveled from New Mexico to San Diego by the way of Zuñi and the valley of the Rio de Zuñi, and found no difficulty throughout the whole distance. He further states, there is no question of a good wagon route, furnishing the proper quantum of wood, water and grass, can be found in this direction, both to San Diego and the *Pueblo de Los Angeles*. He informs me, however, that in order to reach the Rio Colorado, the Rio de Zuñi would have to be diverged from at the falls, within a few miles of its confluence with the Colorado, and a valley running generally southwardly followed down to its junction with the valley of that river. He has further informed me that above the mouth of the Rio de Zuñi there is a ford, called *El Vado de los Padres* (The Ford of the Fathers) to which a route leads from Zuñi by the way of the pueblos of the Moquis. This route, which he represents as much shorter than the other, is, however, on account of the difficulty in crossing the canyon of the river at the ford, only practicable for pack animals."

[97] Ewing Young was born in Tennessee. He early became a hunter and trapper in the far west and had passports for Mexican territories signed at Washington in 1828-29. In these years he made his first overland trip to California, where he aided the *Padres* of San José in an expedition against revolted neophytes. In 1829 he returned to New Mexico, was married to a Mexican woman in Taos and again went to California. In 1834 he went to Oregon. He left a son called Joaquin, born in New Mexico, who inherited his property in Oregon.

composed of New Mexicans, foreigners, and Indian vagabonds, whose object was to obtain mules, without scruple as to method, often by simple theft, and oftener by connivance with hostile Californian tribes.

In 1833, especially, they caused a great excitement, and some of them, including Villapando, their leader, were arrested at Santa Fé. In 1835-37, John A. Sutter, afterwards famous in California, was engaged in trade at Santa Fé; in 1841, the Workman-Rowland party brought many foreigners and native New Mexicans to California, and in 1842, a large trading party under Vigil settled in the San Bernardino region, and down to the end of the Mexican rule, the movement of traders and emigrants continued. Among many native New Mexicans who went to California were members of the Chavez, Baca, Luna, and Armijo families.

HEADQUARTERS OF PRESIDENT HAYES AT SANTA FÉ, N. M.

BIBLIOGRAPHY

Bancroft, Hubert H.	*History of Arizona and New Mexico*, San Francisco, 1889.
Boone's Lick *Advertiser*	Custody of Irvin Switzler, Columbia, Mo.
Chittenden, H. M.	*American Fur Trade*, New York, 1902.
Cooper, Stephen	*History of Howard and Cooper Cos., Mo.*
Gregg, Dr. Josiah	*Commerce of the Prairies*, New York, 1844.
Hayes, A. A.	*New Colorado and The Santa Fé Trail*, New York, 1880.
Inman, Henry	*Santa Fé Trail.*
Kansas Historical Society	*Records*, Topeka, Kansas.
Larpenteur, Charles	*Forty Years a Fur Trader.*
Missouri Gazette	Files of St. Louis *Republic*, St. Louis, Mo.
Missouri Intelligencer	Custody of Irvin Switzler, Columbia, Mo.
Missouri Historical Society	*Ms.* No. 135 — William Waldo.
Messages and Papers of the Presidents	Richardson, Washington, D. C., 1897.
Meline, J. F.	*Two Thousand Miles on Horseback*, New York, 1867.
New Mexico	Acts of Legislative Assemblies.
Niles' Register	Baltimore, 1811-1849, 76 vols.
Pike, Z. M.	*Account of Travels*, Phila., 1810; *Explanatory Travels*, London, 1811.
Peter	*Province Life and Adventures.*
Pino, P. B.	*Noticias Historicas*, Mexico, 1849.
Prince, L. Bradford	*Historical Sketches*, New York, 1883.
Read, Benjamin M.	*Historia Illustrada de Nuevo Mexico*, Santa Fé, 1911.
Ruxton, George F.	*Adventures in Mexico*, New York, 1848.
Stoddard, Amos	*Sketches of Louisiana.*
Senate Executive Documents	18th Congress, 2d Session.
Simpson, Gen. J. H.	*Reconnoisances in New Mexico and Texas*, Phil., 1852.
Storrs, Augustus	Santa Fé Trade in 1824, *Niles' Register.*
Ritch, W. G.	*Aztlan*, Boston, 1885.
Santa Fé Archives	Smithsonian, Washington; Office of Surveyor General, Santa Fé, N. M.
Wislizenus, Dr. A.	*Tour of Northern Mexico in 1846-1847*, Gov. Doc., Washington, 1848.
Winsor, Justin	*Narrative and Critical History of America*, New York, 1889.

CHAPTER V

THE CITY OF SANTA FÉ — THE OLD PALACE — CHURCHES — MAN-
NERS AND CUSTOMS OF THE PEOPLE — COSTUMES — AGRICUL-
TURE AND STOCK RAISING — MINES AND MINING — THE
MISSIONS, FRAYLES, AND PRIESTS — VISITS OF CHURCH
DIGNITARIES — THE BISHOP OF DURANGO — LISTS
OF FRAYLES AND PRIESTS, 1540 TO 1846

THE city of Santa Fé, prior to the American occupation, was, in all probability, a place of at least five thousand inhabitants.[98] The census report of 1827 by Governor Narbona is the only official authority as to the number of inhabitants of New Mexico prior to the decree of the *Asamblea*, in 1844, published by Governor Martinez, with the exception THE CITY OF SANTA FÉ of the Armijo census of 1840, when the population is given at 55,403. Undoubtedly there is an error in the census of 1840, for the population four years later is given as 99,204. During this period in the history of New Mexico, the great majority of the people lived in towns or villages; there was practically no country population, a condition almost necessary for the protection of the settlers from the raids of the marauding savages, by whom they were surrounded on all sides. The principal settlements were those of the valley of the Rio Grande, those lying in the valley south of the capital being known as the *Rio Abajo* and those to the north as *Rio Arriba*. The

---

[98] According to the census report of 1827, found in Pino, *Not. Hist.*, pp. 56-57, the total population of New Mexico was 43,433, about evenly divided between the sexes. Married couples 7,677; farmers 6,588; artisans 1,237; laborers 2,475; traders 93; teachers 17; curates 17; surgeon 1. There is no separation of whites and Indians. The larger towns, most of them including one or more small pueblos, had: Santa Fé 5,757; San Miguel del Vado, 2,893; Alburquerque, 2,547; Tomé 2,043; Cañada 6,508; San Juan 2,915; Taos 3,606; and Abiquiú 3,557.

most important settlement, next to Santa Fé, was that of Taos. The city of Santa Fé, which was the most pretentious of all the towns, was very irregularly laid out; most of the streets were no better than highways traversing scattered settlements, interspersed here and there with corn and wheat fields. The only attempt at anything like architectural compactness was found in the buildings surrounding the plaza, all of which were shaded in front by *portales* of the rudest description. The buildings around the plaza comprised the *Palacio*, or governor's house, the custom-house, barracks, which was connected with the jail or *calabozo*, the *Casa Consistorial* of the *alcaldes*, the *Capilla de los Soldados* or military chapel, several private residences, and the stores occupied by the American traders.

The *Palacio* was a long, low adobe building, very much as it appears today, having a portal or portico extending along its entire front, and exhibited two great curiosities, windows of glass and festoons of Indian ears. Glass was a great luxury in New Mexico; the ordinary dwellings had closed shutters fastened on the inside with heavy bars, instead of windows; some of the houses had windows, very small ones, closed with crystalized gypsum in place of glass. The festoons of Indian ears were made up of several strings of dried ears of Indians killed by parties sent out by the government against the savages, who were paid a certain sum for each head. In Chihuahua, a great exhibition was made with the entire scalps of Indians which they had killed by proxy. At Santa Fé only the ears were exhibited or retained. This building has other claims to distinction.

THE OLD PALACE

"Without disparaging the importance of any of the cherished historical localities in the East," says Dr. Prince, "it may be truthfully said that this ancient palace surpasses in historic interest and value any other place or object in the United States. It antedates the settlement of Jamestown, New Amsterdam and Plymouth, and has stood during the three centuries since its erection, not as a cold rock or monument, with no claim upon the interest of humanity, except the bare fact of its continued existence, but as the living center of everything of historic importance in the Southwest. Through all that long period, whether under Spanish, Pueblo, Mexican or American control, it has been the seat of power and authority. Whether the ruler was called viceroy, captain-general, political chief, department commander, or governor, and whether he presided over a kingdom, a province, a department, or a territory, this has been his official residence.

"Here, within the walls fortified as for a siege, the bravest Spaniards were massed in the revolution of 1680; here on the 19th of August of that year, was given the order to execute forty-seven Pueblo prisoners in the Plaza which faces the building; here but a few days later, was the sad war council held which determined on the evacuation of the city; here was the scene of triumph of the Pueblo chieftains as they ordered the destruction of the Spanish archives and the church ornaments in one grand conflagration; here De Vargas gave thanks to the Virgin Mary, to whose aid he attributed his triumphant capture of the city; here, more than a century later, on March 3d, 1807, Lieutenant Pike was brought before Governor Alencaster as an invader of Spanish soil; here, in 1822, the Mexican standard, with the eagle and the cactus, was raised in token that New Mexico was no longer a dependency of Spain; from here, on the 6th day of August, 1837, Governor Perez started to subdue the insurrection in the north, only to return two days later and to meet his death on the ninth, near Agua Fria; here on the succeeding day, José Gonzales, a Pueblo Indian of Taos, was installed as governor of New Mexico, soon after to be executed by order of Armijo; here, in the principal reception room, in 1844, Governor Martinez killed the chief of the Utes by one blow with his chair; here on August 12, 1846, Captain Cooke, the American envoy, was received by Governor Armijo and sent back with a message of defiance; and it was here, six days later, General Kearny formally took possession of the city, and slept after his long and weary march on the carpeted earthen floor of the Palace. From every point of view, it is the most important historical building in the country, and its ultimate use should be as the home of the wonderfully varied collections of historical antiquaries which New Mexico will furnish.[99]

"Coming down to more modern times, it may be added that here General Lew Wallace wrote *Ben Hur*,[100] while governor, in 1879 and 1880."

---
[99] Historical Society of New Mexico, *Bulletin No. 14*.
Governor Prince, in his record of events transpiring in this old structure might have said also that here the Pueblo chieftan, Antonio Bolsas, who commanded the Indian forces at the time of the victory of De Vargas, committed suicide by hanging himself.

[100] That there may never be any doubt as to the truth of this statement, and inasmuch as the room in which *Ben Hur* was written is now known as the Rito de los Frijoles room, and owing to the widespread interest and circumstances connected with it, the following letter, written to the curator of the New Mexico Historical Society, by General Wallace, is worth preserving:

"Crawfordsville, Indiana, May 6th, 1890.
"Mr. A. J. Wissler,
"Dear Sir: Touching your inquiry whether *Ben Hur* was written in the Old Palace of Santa Fé, I beg to say it was finished there; that is, the Ms. was completed at the time of my appointment to the governorship of New Mexico down to the sixth book of the volume, and I carried it with me. When in the

Freighters on the Santa Fé Trail, with Kiowa Scouts
Bernard Seligman, Zadoc Staab, Lehman Spiegelberg

The old palace was not far from three hundred and fifty feet in length and was from twenty to seventy-five feet in width. The portal in front was about fifteen feet in width and ran the entire length of the building, the roof being supported by a row of unhewn pine logs, set at a distance of approximately twelve feet apart. At each end was a small adobe projection, extending a few feet in front of the main portion of the building. On the east end was located the post-office and on the west end was the *calabozo*.[101]

---

city my habit was to shut myself after night in the bed-room back of the executive office proper, and write there till after twelve o'clock. The sixth, seventh and eighth books were the result, and the room has ever since been associated in my mind with the Crucifixion. The retirement, impenetrable to incoming sound, was as profound as a cavern's.

"Very respectfully, LEW WALLACE."

[101] At the time of the American occupation and for a number of years thereafter the old palace furnished quarters to the officials of the territory. Davis in *El Gringo*, p. 169, says: "The first apartments we come to in going the rounds of the palace are the office of the secretary of the territory, which we enter through a quaint little old-fashioned door. The office is divided into two rooms; an inner one, in which the books and records are kept, and where the secretary transacts his official business, and an outer one, used as an ante-room and a store-room. The latter is divided by a cotton curtain, hanging down from the beams above, into two compartments, one of which is stored with the old manuscript records of the territory which have been accumulating for nearly three hundred years. The stranger will be struck with the primitive appearance of these ruins; the roof is supported by a layer of great pine beams, blackened and stained by age; the floors are earthen, and the wood-work is heavy and rough, and in the style of two centuries ago. We next visit the chamber of the Legislative Council. Passing along under the portal, we again enter the palace about midway of the front, and, turning from a small vestibule to the right, we find ourselves in the room where a portion of the wisdom of New Mexico annually assembles to make laws. The room is a comfortable one, with a good hard floor, and just large enough to accommodate the thirteen councilmen and the eight officers. The pine desks are ranged around the wall facing inward, and the president occupies a raised platform at one end, which is ornamented with a little red muslin drapery. Figured calico is tacked to the walls to prevent the members carrying away the whitewash on their coats — a thing they have no right to do in their capacity of law-makers. The executive chamber is on the opposite side of the passage-way, into which we step, and find his excellency hard at work. This room is in keeping with the republican simplicity that marks the appearance of the whole establishment. A few chairs, an old sofa and bureau, with a pine center table, make up the furniture. Within the last year the luxury of an American-made carpet has been indulged in, but before the advent of which the floor was covered by a domestic article called gerga, worth thirty cents per yard. Bleached muslin is tacked to the beams overhead for a ceiling, and a strip of flashy calico, about four feet wide, is nailed to the four walls.

"Next in order is the House of Representatives — *La Camara de Representantes* — the door of which opens upon the portal. This room differs in no essential particular from the council-chamber except being about one-half larger, and having a small gallery separated from the body of the room by an adobe

The military chapel was on the south side of the plaza. The building was in the form of a cross, about one hundred feet in length, and nearly as many in width. The front LA CASTRENZA door opened upon the plaza. It had two plain towers which rose a few feet above the roof. Upon the roof were suspended two bells, which were rung by boys ascending the roof and pulling the clappers from side to side. The style of construction differed from the true gothic cross in that the transept ran north and south, instead of east and west. The appearance of the building, inside and out, like all of the church edifices of the period was very primitive and exceedingly plain. The altar was in the south transept and was quite plain. The ornaments were few. The wall behind the altar was inlaid with brown-stone work, representing scriptural scenes; some old Spanish paintings hung upon the walls. The choir was over the north transept, and was reached by a ladder. A chandelier, lighted with tallow candles, was suspended over the center of the cross and

wall breast-high, where the 'unwashed' and 'unterrified' sit and behold the operation of making laws with wonder and astonishment, but fail to discover whence comes so much wisdom as they imagine presides over the deliberations of this august assembly. . . Leaving the Hall of the House we enter the territorial library, which opens into a small vestibule leading from the portal. We find ourselves in a room not more than fifteen feet square, filled with books from the floor to the beams over-head, ranged around the walls on shelves, and numbering some two thousand volumes. They embrace the standard text books on the various branches of common and civil law and equity, the reports of the United States and the state courts, and the codes of various states and territories, besides a number of congressional documents. The judge, other United States officers, and members of the bar have access to the library, and can take out books to keep, a limited time, after they shall have been registered by the librarian and being responsible for their safe return. Opening into the same vestibule is the office of Superintendent of Indian affairs, which, with another room adjoining, used for a store-room, occupies the west end of the Palace building. Near-by is a large vacant room appropriated to the use of the Indians when they come in to see the superintendent on business, at which times they are fed by the government.''

It will be noted that a room in the palace was used for post-office purposes. In passing it may be said that according to a notation in the diary of Manuel Alvarez, U. S. consul at Santa Fé, the postage on a letter from Washington, D. C., to him, via Vera Cruz and the City of Mexico, was one dollar and seventy-five cents. There was no mail service over the plains until 1849.

Gregg, *Commerce of the Prairies*, ii, p. 67, says: ''Speaking of mails, I beg leave to observe, that there are no conveniences of this kind in New Mexico, except on the route from Santa Fé to Chihuahua, and these are very irregular and uncertain. Before the Indians had obtained such complete possession of the highways through the wilderness, the mails between these two cities were carried semi-monthly; but now they are much less frequent, being mere expresses, in fact, despatched only when an occasion offers.''

THE CITY OF SANTA FE 151

engravings and small paintings of saints were to be seen in various parts of the building. The roof was supported by large unpainted pine beams, ornamented with a sort of bracket where the ends entered the adobe walls. In the facade, above the door, there was a large rectangular slab of freestone elaborately carved. It represented "Our Lady of Light" in the act of rescuing a human being from the jaws of Satan, while angels were placing a crown upon her head. The brown-stone tablet, referred to, which stood back of the altar, was a beautiful piece of art, and represented the principal saints. Above all was Santa Maria, then St. Iago, riding over the turbanned heads of his enemies; on the right was San Juan de Pomasan, the background ornamented with a representation of an aqueduct; under him was St. Francis Xavier, baptizing the Indians, and in the background conical huts, such as were built by the wild tribes. On the left was San José and below him San Francisco de Santa Fé, standing on two globes. At the bottom of the tablet were two elliptical spaces, containing the following inscriptions: [102]

+

A DEVOCIONDE	IDES VESPOSA
SENOR DN. FRANCO. ANT.	DA. MARIA IGNACIA
MARIN DLVALLEGOVE	MARTINEZ DE
NADORI CAPIN GENDES	VGARTE AÑO
TE REINO.	E 1761.

Every morning the bells of the parroquia or parish church of Santa Fé summoned the good citizens of the capital to early mass.

THE PARROQUIA
RELIGIOUS CUSTOMS

Attending the morning service, in the early days, one would witness the devout women of the parish, veiled in their *rebozos*, seated, after the Turkish fashion, on the bare ground to the right-hand side of the aisle. The men stood up, except when the ritual required them to kneel. They maintained their station on the left side of the church. The body of this building was long and narrow; the roof was lofty; the ground plan, that of a cross. Near the altar were two wax figures, life size, representing hooded

---

[102] Translation: *A devocion de Señor Dn. Fco. Ant. Maria del Valle, gobernador y capitan general deste reino. Y de Su. esposa Da. Maria Ignacia de Ugarte, Año Cristiano, 1761.*

This reredos is now in the cathedral at Santa Fé. It was presented to the *Capilla de los Soldados* by Don Francisco Marin del Valle, who was governor.

friars, with shaved heads, except a crown of short hair that encircled the head like a wreath. One was clad in a blue and the other in a white robe; their garments were long and flowing, with knotted girdles around the waist. The wall back of the altar was covered with innumerable mirrors, oil paintings, and bright colored tapestry. From a high window a flood of crimson light, tinged by a curtain it passed through, poured down upon the altar. The incense smoke curled about in the rays, and, in graceful curves ascending, lent much beauty to the group around the priests, who were all habited in rich garments. There were many wax tapers burning, and music, from unseen musicians, fell pleasantly upon the ear, and was frequently mingled with the sounds of the tinkling bell.[103]

Another historic spot in the ancient capital is the site upon which stands the Guadalupe church. From the best information obtainable this building was erected about the year 1640. According to tradition the date of its erection is carved upon one of the old beams which surmount the choir gallery, but now covered with the plaster cornice. In 1680, the church was sacked but not destroyed by the Pueblo Indians. The building was remodeled by Rev. James H. Defouri in 1880. Prior to this time it had a flat mud roof constructed in the same style as all other church edifices in New Mexico of the Spanish period. No priest was especially attached to this church, at least during the nineteenth century, until the coming of Fr. Defouri, who, without changing the walls of the structure, gave it a modern roof, and began the beautifying of the surrounding grounds. It is said that prior to his coming mass was only sung in the church once each

CHAPEL OF OUR LADY OF GUADALUPE

---

[103] The major portion of the parroquia was torn down in 1870 to give way for the present cathedral, built by Mt. Rev. John B. Lamy, archbishop of Santa Fé. A peculiar feature of the construction of the present cathedral is that of the roof, which is made of lava, transported to Santa Fé from an old crater about twelve miles west of the city.

When the parroquia was torn down and the floor of the present building was installed it became necessary to excavate a considerable portion of the interior, as well as portions of the grounds immediately adjoining. In doing this the bones of many wealthy individuals whose remains had been buried there were disinterred and along with the excavated earth in many instances were carried to a dumping place on the right side of the Santa Fé river, just beyond the archbishop's garden, where they were deposited and used in filling up an area now used as a highway.

Attorneys-General of New Mexico
1. Merrill Ashurst. 2. Thomas F. Conway. 3. Edward L. Bartlett. 4. John P. Victory. 5. William Breeden. 6. William C. Reid. 7. George W. Pritchard. 8. James M. Hervey. 9. Frank W. Clancy

year, on the 12th of December. The interior remains as for nearly three centuries, the flat ceiling resting upon heavy beams, with carved brackets at each end.

Behind the altar is a magnificent painting of the Virgin of Guadalupe [104] and her apparitions to the Indian, Juan Diego, the work of an artist of the city of Mexico, in 1683. Here also may be found another painting upon a copper plate, three or four feet square, upon which may be seen numbers of figures and views surrounding the image of the Virgin.

In the old days, as at present, the plaza was the place for daily

---

[104] Gregg, Josiah, *Commecre of the Prairies*, says of the story of Our Lady of Guadalupe that "on the 12th of December, 1531, an Indian called Juan Diego, while passing over the barren hill of Tepeyacac (about a league northward from the City of Mexico), in quest of medicinal herbs, had his attention suddenly arrested by the fragrance of flowers and the sound of delightful music; and, on looking up he saw an angelic sort of figure directly before him. Being terrified he attempted to flee; but the apparition calling to him by name, 'Juan Diego,' said she, 'go tell the bishop to have me a place of worship erected on this very spot.' The Indian replied that he could not return, as he was seeking *remedios* for a dying relative. But the figure bade him do as commanded, and to have no further care about his relative — that he was then well. Juan Diego went to the city, but being unable to procure an audience from the bishop, he concluded he had been acting under a delusion, and again set off for his *remedios*. Upon ascending the same hill, however, the apparition again accosted him, and hearing his excuse, upbraided him for his want of faith and energy; and said, 'Tell the bishop that it is Guadalupe, the Virgin Mary, come to dwell amongst and protect the Mexicans, who sends thee.' The Indian, returning again to the city, forced his way into the presence of the bishop, who received the messenger with jeers, and treated him as a maniac; telling him finally to bring some sign, which, if really the Mother of God, his directress could readily furnish. The perplexed Indian left the bishop's presence resolved to avoid further molestation from his spiritual acquaintance, by taking another route; yet, when near the place of his first meeting, he again encountered the apparition, who, hearing the result of his mission, ordered him to climb a naked rock hardby, and collect a bouquet of flowers which he would find growing there. Juan Diego, albeit without faith, obeyed, when, to his surprise he found the flowers referred to, and brought them to the Virgin, who, throwing them into his *tilma*, commanded him to carry them to the bishop; saying, 'When he sees these he will believe, as he well knows that flowers do not bloom at this season, much less upon the barren rock.' The humble messenger now with more courage sought the bishop's presence, and threw out the blooming credentials of his mission before him; when lo! to the astonishment of all, and to the entire conviction of his *Señoria ilustrisima*, the perfect image of the apparition appeared imprinted on the inside of the *tilma*. The reverend Prelate now fully acknowledged the divinity of the picture, and in a conclave of ecclesiastics, convened for the purpose, he pronounced it the image of *La Verdadera Virgen* and protectress of Mexico. A splendid chapel was soon after erected upon the spot designated in the mandate, in which the miraculous painting was deposited, where it is preserved to the present day."

A tilma is a loose sort of mantle made of the fibre of the maguey plant.

promenade, although then there were no trees, nor had any attempt been made to bring it to its present beauty. It was the market place. The principal stations for the public market were in that portion of the plaza near the western end of the palace. Here the country people sold the meats, fruits, and vegetables which were brought to town. The supply was very scanty, hardly sufficient to meet the demands of the city.

THE PLAZA
THE MARKET-PLACE

There were offered for sale, mutton, kid, pigs, chilli, beans, onions, milk, bread, cheese, and, during the season, grapes, wild plums, raspberries, and melons. In the winter the Indians and others brought in, almost daily, fine venison, wild turkeys, and occasionally the carcass of a large bear, all of which were shot in the neighboring mountains. All of these articles were transported upon burros or upon the backs of Indians; one of the latter would often come a long distance with not more than a dollar's worth of marketing. The meats were hung upon a line stretched to the pillars of the palace portal, while the vegetables were displayed on little mats or pieces of board, beside which the venders would sit for hours waiting for customers. Vegetables were a very scarce article, being confined almost entirely to the varieties mentioned. The hay market was located on San Francisco street where it enters the plaza at the southwest corner. During the summer and fall the *rancheros* were accustomed to come in from the country every morning with newly-cut grass or hay, each with a bundle of about twelve or fifteen pounds tied up in a blanket and carried upon a burro. The bundles were arranged side by side along the side of the street, and were sold at twelve and a half cents, a *real*, each, cash, without the blanket.

The houses of the earlier days, particularly those of the wealthier classes, were built of adobe, in the form of a square, surrounding a court-yard or *patio*. This style of architecture was adopted for protection purposes, because of the hostility of the Indians. The entrance to the residence was through a door opening, generally, into the *patio*. Having entered this court-yard, the house proper was entered by way of a reception hall or *sala*. In its arrangement every room in the building opened upon the *patio*, except some which communicated directly with the *sala* or with each other. The style was essentially Spanish, blended with which were many traces of the Moors. It was a very rare thing to see a board floor in the houses, the substitute being earth. A coating of soft mud was carefully spread over the earth, which, when dry, made a firm and comfortable floor. The common covering for the floors, when they were covered at all, was a coarse article of domestic manufacture, called *gerga*, which answered the purpose of a carpet. The inside walls were whitened with calcined *yezo* or gypsum, which was used instead of lime; this would not adhere to the walls and would come off upon every article that touched it. To prevent this, the rooms were lined with calico to the height of four feet. The coating of mud and *yezo* on the inside of the house was generally put on by the women, who made use of their hands and a piece of sheep-skin with the wool on for that purpose, instead of using brushes and plasterers' tools. The ceiling was never plastered, but in those of the wealthier classes the beams that supported the roof were planed and painted in various colors, and sometimes an artificial ceiling was made by tacking bleached muslin, called *manta*, to them. In some sections of the country, small round sticks were laid from beam to beam in herring-bone style; these beams were called *vigas*; sometimes the small round sticks were painted green, blue or yellow. The fireplace was always built in one corner of the room, and occupied a very small space. The mouth was something of the shape of a horseshoe, not more than eighteen inches or two feet in height, and the same in width at the bottom. The back was slightly concave instead of being a plane surface, and the small circular hearth in front was raised a half a foot above the floor. They knew nothing of the use of andirons, the wood being placed on end against the back of the fireplace. Whenever a room needed renovating, it was the custom to go carefully over it on the outside with a coating of soft mud, and on the inside with a fresh coat of *yezo*, followed by a fresh layer of mud for the floor.

The furniture, as well as the manner of arranging the same, was peculiar. Few chairs or wooden seats of any kind were used, but in their stead mattresses were folded up and placed around the room, next to the wall, all of which, carefully covered with bright colored Navajó blankets, gave a pleasing appearance to the apart-

NEW MEXICAN DWELLINGS
MODE OF CONSTRUCTION

ment and also served as sofas. This custom was also undoubtedly borrowed from the Moors. At night these *colchones* were spread out and used for beds. Bedsteads [105] were almost entirely unknown. The only one seen by Lieutenant Pike in 1806 was at La Cañada and was a great curiosity. Sometimes the mattresses were placed upon a small platform raised off the floor a few inches. Bureaus and chiffoniers were unknown; their places were supplied by chests and trunks. These chests and the locks thereon were marvelous affairs. Sometimes the trunks were made of rawhide and quite curiously ornamented. In the house of the wealthier classes chairs and settees were to be found, always made out of pine and homemade. This economy in furniture in early times was made necessary for the reason that there were no mechanics in the province. Even after the American occupation many years passed before American furniture came into use. The women in particular seemed to prefer the *colchon* to the ordinary chair. Of kitchen utensils they had very few. The cooking was almost entirely done in earthen vessels, and a stove was a great rarity. The *sala* was the largest room in the establishment, and in the colder portions of New Mexico, was only used during warm weather, when, for the time being, the family fairly lived there, lounging among the *colchones* during the day, receiving visitors, and using it as a sleeping apartment at night. The family room was adorned with a number of engravings of saints, among which that of the Virgin of Guadalupe was always conspicuous. These engravings or paintings were familiarly called "*Santos*."

A principal article of diet with the people was the *tortilla*, a thin cake made of corn. The making of these was always in the hands of the women, who prided themselves upon the skill and rapidity with which they were able to prepare them. The method was crude and simple. The corn was boiled in water containing a little lime, so that the skin would easily peel off, whereupon it was ground into a sort of paste upon an oblong hollowed stone, called a *metate*.

MEXICAN CUISINE

---

[105] It is said that Don Pedro Sanchez, a very prominent citizen of New Mexico, and a resident of Taos, once purchased a bedstead in St. Louis and had it shipped across the plains to his home in Taos. It was among the first ever seen in the community, and was of such dimensions that after its arrival, it became necessary to tear out one of the walls of his residence in order to get it properly installed in his bedroom.

The operator knelt down behind the *metate*, taking in both hands another round stone like an ordinary rolling-pin, between which and the *metate* the corn was carefully mashed. When ready for baking the substance thus prepared was spread upon a thin sheet of iron, tin, or copper, and in a few minutes was ready for eating. The *tortilla*, when hot, is quite palatable. Along with the *tortilla* came the other principal article of diet, the *frijole*, or Mexican bean. Prominent dishes of the Mexican cuisine were *chilli con huevos, chilli con carne*, and *tamales*. Chocolate was always served along with a delicious kind of sponge cake. The better classes were accustomed to use wine, made from grapes grown in the *Rio Abajo*. After the trade with New Mexico was fairly well established the Missourians brought in large quantities of the finest of wines and other liquors, all of which found a ready sale, at enormous profit, among the *ricos*, or very wealthy citizens of the department. They also used a domestic brandy, made at El Paso, which was commonly known as "pass whiskey."

MANNERS, HABITS AND CUSTOMS

The New Mexicans are an affectionate people; they have a genuine regard for their friends, and in the early days, prior to the advent of American customs, it was usual and customary for them to embrace each other whenever they met; this was particularly true when friendships were intimate and of long standing. In suavity of manners the Mexican was without a superior; this characteristic was not confined to the higher classes; the humblest beggars often exhibited an address and air of refinement that a prince of the blood might envy. In this their treatment of friends, acquaintances, or strangers was identical. In the privacy of their firesides, among members of the same family, brothers, sisters, relatives, *compadres*, and *primos*, there was always a courtesy equal to the demands of the most refined code of politeness, and further, there was nothing assumed; it was altogether natural.

Smoking was a habit of both sexes; drunkenness was very rare amongst high or low. The American cigar was rarely used; all indulged in the *cigarrito*; this was made with a cornhusk wrapper and finecut tobacco. These were rolled by each individual as required, as he always had on hand for that purpose his *guage*, filled with tobacco, and his package of *hojas*, also a flint and steel, with which in less time than is consumed in the relation, the *cigarrito* would be manufactured.[106] Obedience to their parents and respect for their elders were prominent features of Mexican character. A son, no matter what his age or position, would never smoke in the presence of his father, until permission, unsought by the son, had first been granted by the parent. A native New Mexican of the old school never lights his *cigarrito* in the presence of another without saying "*Con su licencia, Señor.*"

Gambling was, in the earlier days, a vice quite common to all classes of society. It was licensed and protected by the laws of the country, and, in most circles, the keeping of a gambling house was not considered a disreputable occupation. These resorts were frequented by rich and poor, high and low. In all the larger towns public gambling houses were to be found, where large sums were wagered and lost or won. The love of gambling was a distinguishing propensity of the people. The dignity of station was not proof against the fascinations of this exciting vice.[107]

THE VICE OF GAMBLING

In relating his experiences in New Mexico, as also his observations in the northern provinces of the republic a quarter of a century prior to the advent of American authority, the historian of the period, Dr. Gregg, says:

---

[106] Gregg, *Commerce of the Prairies*, i, 243-244, says: "Of all the petty vices practised by the New Mexicans, the *vicio inocente* of smoking among ladies, is the most intolerable; and yet it is a habit of which the loveliest and the most refined equally partake. The *puro* or *cigarro* is seen in the mouths of all; it is handed round in the parlor, and introduced at the dinner table, even in the ball-room it is presented to ladies as regularly as any other species of refreshment; and in the dance the señorita may often be seen whirling round with a lighted *cigarrito* in her mouth. The belles of the southern cities are very frequently furnished with *tenazitas de oro*, little golden tongs, to hold the cigar with, so as to prevent their delicate fingers from being polluted either with the scent or stain of tobacco."

[107] Gregg, *Commerce of the Prairies*, i, p. 239: "It prevails in the lowly hut, as well as in the glittering saloon; nor is the sanctity of the gown nor the dignity of station sufficient proof against the fascinations of this exciting vice. No one considers it a degradation to be seen frequenting a *monte* bank; the governor himself and his lady, the grave magistrate and the priestly dignity, the gay *caballero* and the titled *señora* may all be seen staking their doubloons upon the turn of a card; while the humbler *ranchero*, the hired domestic and the ragged pauper, all press with equal avidity to test their fortune at the same shrine. There are other games at cards practiced among these people, depending more upon skill; but that of *el monte*, being one exclusively of chance, seems to possess an all-absorbing attraction, difficult to be conceived by the uninitiated spectator."

"Among the multitude of games which seem to constitute the real business of life in New Mexico, that of *chuza* evidently presents the most attractions to ladies; and they generally lay very heavy wagers upon the result. It is played with three little balls, and bears some faint resemblance to what is called *roulette*.

"Bull-baiting and cock-fighting, about which so much has been said by every traveler in Mexico, are also very popular amusements in the North, and generally lead to the same excesses and the same results as gaming. The cock-pit rarely fails to be crowded on Sundays and other feast-days; on which occasion the church, the ball-room, the gambling house and the cock-pit look like so many opposition establishments; for nothing is more common than to see people going from one place to another by alternate fits, just as devotional feeling or love of pleasure happens to prompt them.

AMUSEMENTS AND GAMES

"One of the most attractive sports of the *rancheros* and the peasantry and that which, more than any other, calls for the exercise of skill and dexterity, is that called *correr el gallo*, practiced generally on St. John's day. A common cock or hen is tied by the feet to some swinging limb of a tree, so as to be barely within the reach of a man on horseback; or the fowl is buried alive in a small pit in the ground, leaving only the head above the surface. In either case, the racers, passing at full speed, grapple the head of the fowl, which being well greased, generally slips out of their fingers. As soon as some one, more dexterous than the rest, has succeeding in tearing it loose, he claps spurs to his steed, and endeavors to escape with the prize. He is hotly pursued, however, by the whole sporting crew, and the first who overtakes him tries to get possession of the fowl, when a strife ensues, during which the poor chicken is torn into atoms. Should the holder of the trophy be able to outstrip his pursuers, he carries it to a crowd of fair spectators and presents it to his mistress, who takes it to the *fandango*, which usually follows, as a testimony of the prowess of her lover.

"Among the *vaqueros*, and even among persons of distinction, *el coleo* (tailing) is a much nobler exercise than the preceding, and is also generally reserved for days of festivity. For this sport, the most untractable ox or bull is turned loose upon a level common, when all the parties who propose to join in the amusement, being already mounted, start off in pursuit of him. The most successful rider, as soon as he gets near enough to the bull, seizes him by the tail, and with a sudden manœuver, whirls him topsy-turvy upon the plain — to no little risk of breaking his own neck, should his horse stumble or be tripped by the legs of the falling bull."

Another very popular amusement was the game known as *pelota*, resembling very much the American game of hockey or shinny. Whole communities were accustomed, upon feast-days, to engage in this exhilarating sport, having chosen sides for the purpose.

"Respecting *fandangos*," says Gregg, "I will observe that this term, as it is used in New Mexico, is never applied to any particular dance, but is the usual designation for those BALLS AND BAILES ordinary assemblies where dancing and frolicking are carried on; *baile*, or ball, being generally applied to those of a higher grade. The former especially are very frequent; for nothing is more general throughout the country, and with all classes, than dancing. From the gravest to the buffoon — from the richest nabob to the beggar — from the governor to the *ranchero* — from the soberest matron to the flippant belle — from the grandest *señora* to the *cocinera* — all partake of this exhilarating amusement. To judge from the quantity of tuned instruments which salute the ear almost every night in the week, one would suppose that a perpetual carnival prevailed everywhere. The musical instruments used at the *bailes* and *fandangos* are usually the fiddle and the *bandolin*, or *guitarra*, accompanied in some villages by the *tombé*, or little Indian drum. The musicians occasionally acquire considerable proficiency in the use of these instruments."

The term "*fandango*," as used by Dr. Gregg, is essentially a misnomer. The "*fandango*" was a species of dance. The old Santa Fé traders, trappers, and backwoodsmen were responsible for this mistake in terms. One might as well call an American ball a "two-step." The proper term for this form of public amusement was and is "*baile*," pronounced—by-lay. All important personages visiting the capital were welcomed and all public enterprises were inaugurated and concluded with a *baile*. If there was any which could be called the national amusement of the New Mexicans the *baile* is entitled to the name. These were usually held in the *sala* of a private residence or in some building used for this purpose or for other public gatherings. In the principal towns of New Mexico, down to very recent years, public *bailes* were held almost nightly. The *sala* or room was usually wide enough for a single cotillion and long enough for half a dozen or more; at the end of the room, opposite the entrance, was a raised platform for the *musicos*, an orchestra composed of persons playing the violin, guitar, harp, and sometimes the cornet and clarinet, and again, at times,

Archbishops of the Roman Catholic Church
1. Mt. Rev. J. B. Salpointe. 2. Mt. Rev. Placidus L. Chapelle. 3. Mt. Rev. J. B. Lamy. 4. Mt. Rev. Peter Bourgade. 5. Mt. Rev. J. B. Pitaval

the Indian *tombé* was in evidence. The leader of the orchestra was called the *maestro*, and the master of the ceremonies of the *baile* was known as the *bastonero*, the latter carrying a small cane, his badge of authority. Sitting on the platform with the *musicos* was an individual with more or less ability at impromptu versification, and during the progress of the festivities of the evening this important personage would delight the assembled audience with more or less choice ebullitions of native wit, directed almost invariably to the persons of consequence or notoriety who happened to be present and whose personality suggested to this humble poet occasional brilliant sallies in verse, to the confusion of the person mentioned and to the infinite joy of the dancers and spectators, and always to the satisfaction of the versifier. No invitations were extended to these affairs, except in the evening after sun-down the *musicos* were accustomed to parade around the public plaza, all the while performing upon their instruments; this was the *gallo*, or notice of the *baile*.

Arriving at the place where the *baile* was to be held, the spectators would take seats on both sides of the *sala*. The young ladies were invariably accompanied by their mothers or some other lady relative or intimate friend of the family. It was never the custom, as in the "states," to have the sets called by a "caller," dancing in all its forms being too well known to every Mexican, young or old, although some of the Spanish cotillions were very complicated. The *bastonero* had full charge of everything connected with the dance, and when the spectators and dancers were very numerous it was his duty, always well performed, to select the men who would take part in any dance, they, of course, selecting their own partners.

The ordinary waltz was known as the *valse redondo*, but the dances par excellence were the *cuna* and the *valse despacio*. In the last named the music is slow and somewhat mournful, but the elegant movement is difficult to describe. In the one, the first figure might be called a sort of "waltz quadrille," ending with two lines, each señorita facing her partner. Thence she would advance toward him, with graceful gesture, bowing, sinking, rising, extending hands and again clasping them and retreating, waving scarf or handkerchief, all in perfect time and without faulty or ungraceful motion. Finally and apparently following the lead of the first couple, the dancers came rapidly together, and, as the *musicos* struck some lively air, would whirl to all portions of the ball-room. Shortly this subsides, and the dancers waltz back to a sort of square formation, from which in turn each lady made the circuit of the entire set in a slow waltz. The dance to the onlooker was beautiful and enchanting. In the small villages, the country towns, and settlements far removed from the effects of American civilization, these *bailes* are still given by the native people. Another custom at *bailes*, not witnessed in these later days, was one which was always calculated to provoke mirth and amusement from all present. Those attending would provide themselves with egg-shells filled with cologne water and other sweet-smelling articles which they would break over the heads of their friends as a matter of sport, all of which was looked upon as a capital joke.[108]

COURTING AND MARRIAGE CUSTOMS

The Spanish custom in the giving and taking in marriage was of course in vogue in New Mexico among the natives. All proposals of marriage were made to the father, or, if he was dead, to the mother, as the parents were supposed to be the rightful keepers of a daughter's affection. In brief, the mode of procedure was as follows, and to a degree, still continues as the custom of the country among the people of Mexican descent. If a young man became enamored of a young lady and desired to

---

[108] When Governor Merriwether and W. W. H. Davis, U. S. attorney, were once attending a *baile* given at the residence of Captain Martinez, a brother of Fr. Antonio José Martinez, the curate of Taos, these distinguished gentlemen were entertained not only by the versified bon mots of the village poet but also by attacks from several of the señoritas present armed with these cologne filled egg-shells. Mr. Davis says of his experience on this occasion: "I had not been long in the room and in the recess of dancing when I observed three pretty girls coming toward the place where the governor and myself were sitting, with countenances beaming with fun, as though they were bent upon some mischief. They approached within touching distance, and before we had time to stand on the defensive, or were even aware of their object, smash! dash! went the egg-shells over our heads in quick succession, and down our faces streamed the *eau de cologne*. Like the episode of the boys and the frogs, the current of fun seemed to run in one direction, and on this occasion there was no question about the young ladies having it. Satisfied with their gallant exploit, they marched composedly back whence they came, and quietly took their seats. This looked very much like storming the citadel. There is a twin custom upon such occasions, which is, that you may kiss the fair assailants, provided you can catch them and inflict the penalty before they regain their seats. But in this instance they were out of harm's way before I had time to

make her his wife, he made known his wishes to his father, who thereupon wrote a formal letter to the young lady's father, in which he asked for the hand of his daughter in marriage for his son. The matter was then carefully considered by the parents of the young lady, and, if the alliance was viewed as an advantageous one, in nine cases out of ten, the proposal was accepted without consulting the wishes of the daughter, who, as a dutiful child, usually did just as her parents desired. The length of time given to parents to consider a proposition of this kind was generally about thirty days, at the end of which the affair was concluded and an answer given in due form. It was very seldom that a young lady thought seriously of matrimony, unless the subject was broached by the parent. Of course there were exceptions and once in a while love affairs were carried on after the manner of the Anglo-American. Among the better classes the wedding ceremony was a very elaborate affair. Relatives and friends received invitations. Large sums were spent in decorations and refreshments, and, in many cases, where the high contracting parties, or their parents, were people of wealth and position, the wedding was a great event. A house wedding ceremony was always performed in the *sala* of the residence of the bride. Here would be assembled the invited guests, all arranged around the room, each holding a candle. At the head of the room an altar was erected, in front of which stood the officiating priest and attendants, duly robed and book in hand, ready for the service. At one side were musicians. Shortly the bridal couple came in, four or six others in the party, each carrying a candle, and advanced to a position in front of the priest. The service of the Catholic church was performed and the couple declared to be man and wife. Immediately after the performance of the ritual the musicians would strike up a march,[109] and after

---

take any steps towards so delicate a performance, or even the deluge of cologne permitted me to open my eyes. As there was no help for such misfortune, I submitted to my fate, with a most commendable resignation, wiped away the flowing cologne, and straightened up my drooping shirt-collar.''

[109] The writer once attended a wedding ceremony in Santa Fé which was a most elaborate function in the way of post-ceremonial entertainment. Champagne flowed like water and hundreds of people were served during a period lasting several hours. A very peculiar occurrence marked the ceremonial; after the happy couple had been pronounced man and wife, much to the astonishment of the American guests who were present, the musicians struck up that soul-inspiring tune — ''Marching Through Georgia.''

this was concluded the benediction would follow; the ladies then retired, and the men were invited to partake of refreshments. In later years the wedding was invariably celebrated with a *gran baile*, which always continued until a late hour.

The services attendant upon burials were the same as in all countries where performed by the clergy of the Catholic church.

BURIALS AND BURIAL FEES

The expense incident to the interment, particularly when the unfortunate deceased was a member of a prominent or wealthy family, was considerable.[110]

No people were more punctual in their attendance upon religious worship than the New Mexicans. In Santa Fé, in the olden days, each evening towards the close of twilight,

RELIGIOUS PROCESSIONS AND CEREMONIES

the large bell of the parroquia would peal for *la oracion*, or vespers. All conversation was instantly suspended — all labor ceased, people of all classes, whether on foot or on horseback, would stop suddenly, even the laden porter, groaning under the weight of an unsupportable burden, stopped in the midst of his career and stood still. An almost breathless silence reigned throughout

---

[110] Davis, W. W. H., *El Gringo*, p. 186, gives a fee bill of the church for religious services, in the case of a young Mexican gentleman whose remains were buried at Santa Fé, as follows:

"Dobles (tolling the bells).................................... $ 10.00
El Sepulcro (the grave)....................................... 30.00
La Cruz Alta (the grand cross)................................ 1.00
La capa (high mass vestments)................................. 3.00
La agua bendita (holy water).................................. 1.00
Los Ciriales (candlesticks)................................... 1.00
El incensario (vessel for incense)............................ 1.00
Las Mesas (resting places).................................... 3.00
El entierro (the interment)................................... 30.00
La misa (the mass).. 20.00
El organo (use of the organ).................................. 15.00
Los cantores (the chanters)................................... 6.00
El responso del oratorio (the response of the oratory)........ 10.00
Mas al diácono (the deacon's fee-additional).................. 10.00

$141.00"

In August, 1730, Bishop Benedict Crespi, to prevent any undue exaction of fees, fixed during his visitation by a public document, the amount to be given for baptism, marriages, burials, and requiem masses. Even as thus limited, they would now be regarded as high, sixteen dollars for a marriage, or a funeral, with requiem mass, and generally some incidental expenses. From this we can see that the bishop's order was not very faithfully carried out in New Mexico.

the city, disturbed only by the occasional sibilations of the devout multitude; all of which accompanied by the slow, heavy peals of the sonorous bell, afforded a scene most solemn and appropriate. After the expiration of about two minutes, the charm was suddenly broken by the clatter of livelier-toned bells; and a *buenas tardes* (good evening) to those present closed the ceremony; when *presto*, all was bustle and confusion again — the colloquial chit-chat was resumed — the smith plied upon his anvil with redoubled energy — the clink of the hammer resounded in every direction — the wayfarers resumed their journey, both pleasure and business, in short, resumed their respective sway.

Under the auspices of the church, a goodly number of religious processions were held during the year. The principal procession was held during Holy Week, on Good Friday, when religious feeling and sentiment were most pronounced. This procession was one of great pomp and splendor. An image of Christ upon the cross was carried along the principal thoroughfares, accompanied by an array of other images representing the Virgin Mary, Mary Magdalene, and others, while in the procession also would be found men dressed to represent the characters of the time of Christ, the centurion with the band of guards, armed with lances, and other persons representative of the period. This procession is no longer held. Other processions, however, are still maintained at the capital, the principal ones being those of Nuestra Señora de Guadalupe and Corpus Christi.[111]

There existed during the time of the Franciscan friars an order of that religious institution known as the Third Order of St. Francis. These friars had a chapel, adjoining the THE THIRD ORDER OF parochial church on the south side, in Santa SAINT FRANCIS Fé. As it was a Franciscan institution which, by its constitution, could be governed only by priests of the order, it ceased to have a canonical existence in New

---

[111] Gregg, Josiah, *Commerce of the Prairies*, i, p. 259.
A religious procession, commemorative of the vow of Don Diego de Vargas, is also annually held in Santa Fé, when an image of the Virgin Mary, said to be the same one which De Vargas carried into battle in his fight with the Pueblos, is carried from the cathedral to the chapel of Rosario. Over three thousand persons have been known to take part in this procession. Archbishop Salpointe, in his *Soldiers of the Cross*, p. 91, says: "The tradition has it in Santa Fé, that Vargas carried always with him a statue of the Blessed Virgin, which is yet preserved in the cathedral as our Lady of the Rosary."

Mexico when the Franciscans were superseded in the several missions by secular priests. This chapel, when visited by the vicar-general of the diocese in 1826, Don Agustin Fernandez de San Vicente, was found lacking everything required for the celebration of the mass, its document of concession was annulled, and orders given to the parish priest, Rev. Juan Tomas Terrazas, no longer to attempt to celebrate mass therein.

Subsequent to the fall of the Spanish government in Mexico the church suffered severely throughout the republic on account of the numerous revolutions which alienated many influential churchmen owing to their necessarily close association with others who were opposed to the church. To remedy this evil the ecclesiastical authority made strong efforts to extend civil and religious instruction among the clergy and the masses of the people. This movement reached New Mexico in the year 1826, when, on the 19th of May of that year a college was opened in Santa Fé, under the protection and direction of the vicar-general, for the instruction of the young men. At the same time the church authorities received permission from Durango to erect a chapel at San José del Bado. In this year the missions of Taos, San Juan, Abiquiú, Belen, and San Miguel del Bado were made parishes and provided with secular priests.[112]

---

[112] Salpointe, Most Rev. J. B., *Soldiers of the Cross*, pp. 160-161, says: "At the same epoch, by order of the Vicar Capitular of Durango, the See being vacant, the Vicar-general of the diocese, Don Agustin Fernandez, made the pastoral visitation of the missions of New Mexico. In his report, a copy of which has been kept in the church records, he describes the old St. Francis church, Santa Fé, thus: 'An adobe building 54 yards long by 9½ in width, with two small towers not provided with crosses, one containing two bells and the other empty; the church being covered with a flat clay terrace. Inside, communicating with the "crucero" (the place where a church takes the form of a cross by the side chapels), are two large separate chapels, the one on the north side dedicated to our Lady of the Rosary, called also "la Conquistadora," and on the south side the other dedicated to St. Joseph.' (1) The Chapel of Our Lady of Light, known also by the name of 'La Castrense,' military church, that of our Lady of Guadalupe were visited at the same time. After the visit of the parochial church and public chapels of the city, the Vicar-general visited the following private oratories: One in the house of Don Antonio Ortiz, that of the Holy Trinity in the house of Juan Bautista Vigil, and that of San José in the house of Pablo Montoya, which were found to be in all the conditions which had been required for their concession from the ecclesiastical authority.

"The last chapel visited was that of the Third Order of St. Francis, adjoining the parochial church on its southern side. . . The Vicar-general at the end of his report complains, as did visitor Guevara, in 1817, that the Regulars refused to give obedience to the decrees and dispositions of the

It was the custom, during the régime of the Franciscans, for this Third Order of St. Francis to give religious processions at the capital, in addition to the devotions practised by the members of the order. These were the feast of St. Louis, King of France, and of the Immaculate Conception, which were their paternal feasts. They also had a special high mass sung on every second Sunday of the month for their particular purposes, and this was followed by a procession in which the members of the order marched, wearing the habit of the Franciscan Order, which they were allowed to use also in the church during the exercises of Holy Week. This Third Order was known also by the name of "*La Tercera Orden de Penitencia*" and was established in Santa Fé and in Santa Cruz de la Cañada, between the dates of 1692 and 1695, under the administration of Captain-general Don Diego De Vargas, who was a highly religious personage.[113]

bishop, induced to it by the Father Custodio of Santa Fé, Fray Sebastian Alvarez, and by the Political Chief, Don Antonio Narbona."

Archbishop Salpointe, *ibid.*, pp. 164-165, also says that in 1831 "permission was given by the bishop of Durango for the construction of a chapel in the town of La Cuesta, on the Pecos river, and of another at Peña Blanca, at the request of Juan Antonio Cabeza de Vaca. In the year following, the Rev. Juan Felipe Ortiz, a native of Santa Fé, and descendant of the old Spanish family of that name, was appointed Vicar-general Forane of the territory. In 1833, the bishop of Durango, Don José Antonio Zubiria, visited the parishes of New Mexico. His lordship, while in the villa of Santa Fé, found that the parochial church, though the first established in the city, and the head of all the others in the territory, was entirely destitute of suitable vestments for the celebration of the holy sacrifice, and intimated his wish of a contribution from the faithful to provide for this want."

This finding of Bishop Zubiria most effectually disposes of the erroneous impressions which have gained credence in some quarters as to the great accumulations of wealth by the Franciscans during their administration of the religious affairs of the country. To the well-informed it is well known that nearly every mission altar in New Mexico, at that time, was equally devoid of the necessary accessories for the celebration of the mass.

[113] In the records of the Church of St. Francis, at Santa Fé, now preserved in the cathedral, the former having been partially demolished in 1870, is to be found the following document relative to the Third Order of St. Francis:

"*Informacion dada al Gobernador Fernando Chacon por el Rev. P. Custodio, F. Cayetano José Bernal. Santa Fé, 17 de Setiembre 1794.*"

"*En las dos referidas Villas (Santa Cruz de la Cañada & Santa Fé) está fundada en cada una de ellas la Venerable Orden Tercera de Penitencia, desde los principios de la Reconquista de esta provincia con licencia de los Prelados de Nuestra Serafica Religion como Superiores Legitimos inmediatos de ella.*

"*La Venerable Orden Tercera de Penitencia de N. S. P. San Francisco. Casi desde los principios de la Reconquista, (aunque no se sabe el año fijo) con previa la licencia de los Prelados de Nuestra Serafica Religion como Superiores*

168 LEADING FACTS OF NEW MEXICAN HISTORY

"LOS PENITENTES"

"There is now in New Mexico," says Archbishop Salpointe, "a society of men who call themselves 'Los Penitentes' or 'Los Miembros de la Hermandad,' which must have come from the Third Order of St. Francis, but so different from it that no relationship can be traced between the two. The first was a true religious order authorized by the Church, and one whose members were placed under the direction of the Franciscan Fathers, while the second, though an off-shoot of the same, has so degenerated that it is nothing to-day but an anomalous body of simple, credulous men, under the guidance of some unscrupulous politicians. Their leaders encourage them, despite the admonitions of the Church, in the practice of their unbecoming so-called devotions, in order to secure their votes for the times of political elections." [114]

legitimos é enmediatos de ella, y á quienes solo pertenece su conocimiento y gobierno como de las muchas Bulas, declaratorias y confirmatorias de muchos Romanos Pontifices, por lo que la pongo separada de las Cofradias por no tener nada de estas, y por ser verdadera Orden como la primera que profesamos los religiosos, aunque con distintas reglas y constituciones. Estos solo existen y han existido, y existen á esmero de la devocion de los hermanos 3os y asi su fondo es aquel que se paga en la de la Cañada la fiesta de San Louis Rey de Francia y la de la Purisima Concepcion como á sus patrones, y cantar cada mes una misa en uno de sus Domingos con procesion, pero siempre esta empeñada, ó es necesario que el ministro haga las mas de valde y de pura devocion por no alcanzo las limosnas por ser muy pecos los 3os. La de la Villa de Santa Fé invierte sus limosnas en pagar la Funcion de San Luis, las misas con procesion de los Domingos segundos de todos los meses y el sermon de tres caidas el Viernes Santo que lo paga por costumbre, y comprar ceras de dichas funciones y aunque en esta santa 3a Orden hay bastantes hermanos siempre esta empeñada como puede verse."

In 1695, April 18th, Don Diego de Vargas founded, with the seventy families brought from Mexico by Fr. Farfan, the Villa of Santa Cruz de la Cañada, which he called "*de los Españoles Mexicanos del Señor Carlos.*" It was called the "New City" because the valley of the Cañada had been settled by some of the families Juan de Oñate had brought in 1598. The same day, April 18th, the founders of the Villa were put in possession of a certain extent of land, and swore they would keep it by all possible means in their power under the domination of Spain.

These families made their residences in the houses the Tanos had built on the north bank of the river of La Cañada since the rebellion, when they left Galisteo. These Indians were ordered to go to the pueblo of San Juan, and those of San Cristobal left also their lands and houses to the Spaniards. The Villa of Santa Cruz was given the title of second in the province, Santa Fé keeping the priority of foundation. The first priest appointed by the custodio to administer the Villa de Santa Cruz was Fr. Antonio Moreno.

[114] Salpointe, J. B., *Soldiers of the Cross*, pp. 162-163: "As we had, a few years ago, the opportunity of traveling with an old resident of Santa Fé, who had been a member of the Third Order under the administration of the Franciscan Fathers, we asked him if the '*Penitentes*' we had now in New Mexico were the remnants of the Terciarios. '*Estos diablos* (those devils),' said the old gentleman, indignantly (his name we remember was N . . . de la Peña). 'I disown them as members of the Order to which I was affiliated as

Early Protestant Missionaries and Educators
1. Rev. Thomas Harwood. 2. Dr. John Menaul. 3. Mrs. Charity Ann Gaston Menaul. 4. Rev. George Smith. 5. Rt. Rev. J. M. Walden.

MANNERS AND CUSTOMS OF THE PEOPLE 169

The ordinary customs incident to home-life in Anglo American communities did not obtain in the early days in New Mexico; nor were there any of the customs ordinarily RELIGIOUS INSTRUCTION prevalent in European Latin countries, in AND HOME LIFE educational matters, other than those incident to religious instruction and formalities. There were no public schools, and the education of the people, except in some of the wealthiest families, was very limited, and in many instances entirely neglected. There was, however, a branch of learning which was most scrupulously maintained from

long as it lasted in this country, when I was a young man. The *Penitentes*, it is true, have framed a constitution somewhat resembling that of the Third Order, but entirely suited to their own political views. In fact, they have but self-constituted superiors; they do what they please and accomplish nothing good.'

"'The *Penitentes*, who were formerly distributed mostly over the whole territory of New Mexico, have, since 1850, retreated towards the north, especially in the counties of San Miguel, Mora, Rio Arriba, and Taos, where they have the darkness of the woods to add more mystery to their nocturnal performances. They were divided into two classes of members: Those of '*La Luz*,' The Light, consisting of the '*Hermano Mayor*,' Chief Brother, and other directors with particular titles, and the common brothers called '*De Las Tinieblas*,' or Of the Darkness. The men of the Light wore their dress, while those of the Darkness had their faces covered and no other clothing but light trousers. This arrangement was made in the '*morada*,' the private meeting hall of the Penitentes, the roles to be performed publicly were distributed; these were the flagellation, the carrying of the crosses, the singing, etc. Those who had to flagellate themselves were furnished with a scourge terminating sometimes in a prickly pear articulation (*cactus opuntia*), or some pad of heavy and coarse stuff. The cross-bearers were furnished with heavy and rude crosses. Another preparation, and the procession was ready to start. It consisted of the rubbing with a piece of flint of the skin of the flagellants at the place the lash would strike, in order to have some flowing of blood without too much injury to the body. This operation was performed by the '*Hermano Caritativo*,' Charitable Brother, of the association. At this time the procession emerged from the '*morada*' to go to a designated place where a cross had been planted for the occasion. The order of the procession was the following: First, the 'flagellantes,' next the cross-bearers and the directors chanting in low tone the psalm, 'Miserere,' with accompaniment of the rattling of iron chains dragged on the ground, and of a cracked flute, all of this producing a kind of infernal harmony. We have seen and heard it a couple of times, and the most astonishing feature of the ceremony was to see it followed by numerous good old women, devoutly saying their beads.

"We will overlook in this writing many strange accounts that the newspapers give from time to time of the ceremonies and performances of the Penitentes, like the crucifixion of one of the brothers, which on certain occasions have, they say, caused the death of the victim. From 1859 until 1866, when we lived in New Mexico, we never heard of such criminal extravagances.

"The processions of the *Penitentes* took place on every Friday in Lent, and on the three last days of Holy Week, and these were never countenanced by the Church; on the contrary, since there have been bishops in New Mexico, they

the time of Oñate — the teaching of the catechism and christian prayers. Of course the Franciscans, in their dealings with the people, impressed upon them the necessity for a christian education, but the actual carrying out of the orders of the friars and the teaching itself must be attributed to the christian character of the devout and pious women of those days. Communities there were where a priest was seen very seldom, and, in many places, not once in a year, and oftentimes, in certain isolated settlements no priest came for more than a decade.

Archbishop Salpointe, who was a very early-comer to New Mexico, says of the christian customs of the people, prior to the matter-of-fact influence of American manners upon the native people, that "prayers and catechism were taught orally to the young children by some member of the family or by some trusted person of the neighborhood, and repeated word for word, question after question, until some part of the lesson would remain in the memory of the hearers. This was a hard work but a meritorious one, and of great value to the missionary, who had only to explain the mysteries and the chief points of our religion to the children thus instructed at home, when he had to prepare them for their first communion. This teaching is now mostly left to the parochial schools, where they exist, but at the time we refer to there were no parochial schools except in the city of Santa Fé, and, in our opinion, these schools can accomplish very little in inculcating religion in the hearts of the young, if this work has not been commenced at home."

"Every evening," says the venerable archbishop of Tomi, "it was customary to make the children say some prayers which always terminated with the words: *Bendito y alabado sea el Santisimo*

---

have denounced the practice and made of it the subject of some very strong circulars. Little by little, heed has been given to the voice of the ecclesiastical authority, and at the present date, there are only a few interested men who are trying to keep alive yet the old association."

It is possible that the customs of the *Penitentes*, particularly their scourging themselves with whips made of cactus, come from the order of Flagellants which was a body of religious persons who believed by whipping and scourging themselves for religious discipline they could appease the divine wrath against their sins and the sins of the age. An association of Flagellants, founded A. D. 1260, spread throughout Europe, its members marching in processions, publicly scourging their own bodies till the blood ran. Having by these practices given rise to great disorder, they were suppressed, but the same scenes were repeated on a larger scale in 1348, and several subsequent years, in consequence of the desolating plague called the Black Death.

MANNERS AND CUSTOMS OF THE PEOPLE 171

Sacramento del Altar, 'Blessed and hallowed be the most holy Sacrament of the Altar.' After this, the innocent creatures, still kneeling, had to kiss the hand of their parents and receive their blessing before going to bed. The same blessing had also to be asked, even by the grown children of the house, when they were coming from their confession.''

The way to introduce oneself in a house was to say, on opening the door: *"Deo gratias"* (Thanks be to God), or *"Ave Maria Purissima"* (Hail Mary Immaculate), and the answer received was: *"Para siempre bendito sea Dios y la siempre Virgin Maria; pase adelante"* (Forever blessed be God and the holy Virgin Mary; come in).

The salutation "good morning" or "good evening" had to be given in the name of God and returned in the same manner. *"Buenos dias (buenas tardes), le dé Dios,"* which was responded to by: *"Que Dios se los dé buenos á Vd"* (May God give them good to you).

Another kind of pious and interesting salutation was used by persons at a distance from each other. The one who could first address the other by the words *"Ave Maria"* had the right to be answered by the recitation of the whole Hail Mary, for his intention. These and many other manifestations of a christian spirit were very common among the people of New Mexico before the coming of the "American." [115]

[115] In his message to the territorial legislative assembly, December 7, 1852, Governor William Carr Lane, said: "I also urge upon all to learn the English language and to adopt all the customs of the United States, that are suitable and proper for this country. But I do not advise them (the Mexican people) to change any of their beneficial or praiseworthy customs, nor do I advise them to forget their parent stock, and the proud recollections that cluster around Castilian history. I do not advise them to disuse their beautiful language, to lay aside their dignified manners and punctilious attention to the proprieties of social life, and I sincerely hope that the profound deference that is now paid to age by the young will undergo no change. . . True it is, that the Mexican people have been always noted for their distinguished manners and Christian customs, it is only to be regretted to see that some of their good usages are disappearing little by little before what is called progress in our days.''

W. W. H. Davis, in *El Gringo*, p. 183, says: "Among the elite of Spanish society, they are more exact in the observance of etiquette and formalities than the rather primitive people of New Mexico. In speaking of leave-taking, the Honorable Joel R. Poinsett makes the following remarks: 'Remember, when you take leave of a Spanish grandee, to bow as you leave the room, at the head of the stairs, where the host accompanies you; and, after descending the

172 LEADING FACTS OF NEW MEXICAN HISTORY

Contemporaneous with the coming of the American merchant and trader European and American styles of dress for the men began to displace the national costume of the Mexicans among the better and wealthier classes of society. It was not, however, until the coming of the American soldier during the occupation period, and the bringing to the country of American ladies, wives, and members of the families of American officers, that the Mexican women ever began to adopt European and American fashions in dress. Many years passed before the women of New Mexico could be induced to wear the bonnet or hat of modern fashion. Instead they wore the *rebozo*, which was a fixture in the dress of the New Mexican lady until, approximately, the coming of the railroads to the territory.[116] The *rebozo* was a long scarf, made of silk or cotton, according to the taste and purse of the wearer, which was worn over the head, with one end thrown across the left shoulder. A lady was never seen in the street without this article of feminine apparel, and even indoors it was seldom laid aside, when it was drawn loosely around the person. When walking or promenading in the plaza, the lady's face was so closely muffled that not more than one eye was visible, and it was next to

NATIVE DRESS AND COSTUMES

---

first flight, turn round, and you will see him expecting a third salutation, which he returns with great courtesy, and remains until you are out of sight; so that, as you wind down the stairs, if you catch a glimpse of him, kiss your hand, and he will think you a most accomplished cavalier.' This is not an overdrawn picture of Spanish politeness, and frequently have I made the same parade in leaving the house of Mexican gentlemen. At each stage of the above-described leave-taking, it is customary for the host to say *adios*, the last of which is waved to you from the window after you have entered the street.''

[116] In the year 1880, upon the completion of the Atchison, Topeka and Santa Fé Railroad into Santa Fé, the New Mexico legislature was in session. The officers of the railway company invited all the members of the legislature, with their wives and daughters, to visit Topeka where the Kansas state legislature was then in session. Everybody accepted the invitation, including quite a number of ladies. Among others in the party were Major José D. Sena and his wife, very prominent people in the political and social life of New Mexico at that time. Prior to their departure the gallant major, who had been in the ''states'' and knew the styles of dress of American women quite well, after much argument, persuaded his wife to discard her *rebozo* and purchase a magnificent specimen of millinery to wear on the trip east. This Mrs. Sena did, although at a great sacrifice of comfort and patience. Upon their return, and just after the train had passed the northern borders of New Mexico, lifting up the window of the Pullman in which they were riding, she threw the triumph of the milliner's art out of the window, exclaiming ''*Dios y Libertad*,'' a patriotic expression used by the Mexicans in all official documents.

impossible to recognize your most intimate friend in the street. The dress of the lower classes with the women consisted of little more than a chemise and *enaguas*, a petticoat of home-made flannel, generally of bright colors. They seldom wore shoes, and wore the *rebozo* upon the head. The men wore a *serape*, a sort of blanket, the head being thrust through a hole in the middle, and the whole person enveloped in its ample folds. With the coming of the American trader and merchant the *serape* rapidly disappeared and the people began the use of shirts, waistcoats, and coats. The vast majority of the country people wore garments of dressed deer-skin and moccasins. The women were very fond of jewelry and in dress were very partial to bright colors, a taste which was readily catered to by the merchant and trader of the early days, who seems to have made a specialty in devising, procuring, and supplying the most peculiar shades of the brightest sort.

The costume of the Spanish or Mexican *caballero* was a dress both striking and handsome. His head was covered with a *sombrero* with a very wide brim, with a high or a low crown, to suit the taste of the wearer. A band of silver or gold cord surrounded it, and on each side was an ornament woven in silver or gold. The hat was made of plaited grass, covered with oiled silk; some hats were made of felt, and these also were richly embroidered with silver or gold thread. The jacket was of blue or brown cloth, handsomely embroidered, and adorned with buttons of silver. The trousers, called *calzones*, were the most stylish article of his wardrobe; these also were made of cloth and foxed with the same material, of a different color. The legs were ornamented with silver buttons on the outer seams from the hips down, besides two or three silver clasps on each side near the waistband. They were unacquainted with suspenders and in their place wore a silk sash which was drawn tightly around the waist, with the ends hanging down on one side. A pair of embossed or carved leather leggins, called *botas*, were fastened to the leg below the knee, for the protection of the pantaloons. These were often richly embroidered and were both ornamental and useful. The personal costume was completed with a beautiful *serape* thrown over the shoulder or laid across the saddle-bow. The *serapes* were made of wool, woven in bright colors, and oftentimes were very expensive. They were always carried when mounted and afforded the wearer good protection from the elements.

The furniture of his mount was in perfect keeping with that of the rider. The style of saddle was peculiar; the pommel was high and the tree deep, which afforded a firm and easy seat. The stirrups were of wood, at least four inches in width, and were suspended from the tree by a broad strip of leather, carved and otherwise ornamented, sometimes with rosettes of silver; hanging down at the sides were two long leathern flaps with a piece of stiff leather in front which gave protection to the feet. A quilted cushion of leather, oftentimes wrought in silver, covered the seat of the tree, and attached to the rear tree was an ornamented housing of leather of deer or wild-cat skin, tanned with the hair on. This was called the *cola de pato*, and was made to correspond with the *coraza* or cushion. The saddles were richly trimmed with silver, the head of the pommel being entirely covered with it. The bridle was fairly loaded down with ornaments of silver and sometimes the bit was also made of this metal. The bit was of a barbarous sort and of such power that the rider could guide the most restive horse with ease, and could with small effort bring him to his knees. The spurs were made of steel inlaid with silver, with the rowels two or three inches long. The equipment of man and horse was completed with the *armas de palo*, which were made of goat-skins, tanned with the shaggy hair on. These were drawn over the legs in case of falling rain and buckled around the waist and afforded complete protection to the lower extremities.

The New Mexicans in the early days knew little of the mechanic arts. There were a few carpenters, blacksmiths, and some jewellers.

LACK OF KNOWLEDGE OF MECHANIC ARTS

The last named excelled all the other workmen, and some specimens of their workmanship, in point of ingenuity and skill, would compare with any in other parts of the world. Nearly all of the lumber used for cabinet-making and building was sawed by hand and carried to market on burros, two or three sticks or boards at a time, and sold by the piece. The heavier pieces of timber were dressed with axes and sold in the same manner. Saw-mills were unknown. All the implements used in husbandry were of the rudest description, and, until about the middle of the nineteenth century, the hoes and spades, like the plows, were made entirely of wood. There were no wagons, other than those brought to the country by the Santa Fé traders. The Mexicans used carts — *carretas*.[117] Among the *ricos* there were a few old-fashioned Spanish carriages, which were drawn by four or six mules, with outriders and postillions. When a Mexican traveled he carried with him both bed and board and camped upon mountain or plain wherever night overtook him. He and his attendants always went armed. There were no public houses, and the traveler, unless he reached a settlement where he had friends or relatives, was obliged to camp out.

The New Mexicans were not agriculturists. They were essentially a pastoral people. What little agriculture existed was of a very primitive sort. Their fields were small and irregular; cultivation was done with the hoe; the plow was used only in soft mellow ground. The plow was a wooden affair fashioned from the trunk of an oak tree; a section of the trunk of a tree, usually about two feet long, with a small branch projecting upward for a handle, served for this implement; with it was connected a beam to which oxen were yoked; the block, with its fore-end sloped downwards

MEXICANS NOT AGRICULTURISTS

---

[117] Davis, W. W. H., *El Gringo*, p. 212, says: "The vehicles in common use for farm purposes, and for hauling produce to market when burros and pack-mules are dispensed with, are called *carretas*, a rude cart, made in the style of two centuries ago among the first settlers. If exhibited in the states they would attract as much attention as the hairy horse or the sea-serpent. They are generally made without iron, being fastened together with strips of rawhide or wooden pegs. The wheels are frequently solid pieces of wood, being a section of a large cottonwood tree, with a hole through the center for the axle. Sometimes they consist of three parts, the middle one with a bolt in it, and the two sides, segments of a circle pegged on to the first. An undressed pole of proper length is fastened to the axle for a tongue. The body of the *carreta* consists of a frame-work of poles, much like a crockery-ware crate, which is made fast by being tied to the tongue and axle. The machine has no bottom, and, when necessary to prevent the load falling out, a bull-hide is spread down. These carts are universally drawn by oxen, and sometimes three or four yoke are hitched to one at the same time. The ox-yoke is in keeping with the vehicle, and consists of a straight piece of wood laid across the head of the oxen behind the horns, lashed fast with raw-hide, and is secured to the tongue in the same manner. For the peasantry of the country these primitive carts answer every purpose, and on feast and holy days you will often see the whole family pleasuring in them, or driving to the nearest town to attend mass. The wheels are never greased, and as they are driven along they make an unearthly sound, which echoes through the mountains far and near, being a respectable tenor for a double-bass horse-fiddle."

to a point, would run flat, and opened a furrow similar to the ordinary shovel-plow.

Their fields, called *labores* and *milpas*, were seldom fenced. Owners of cattle were required to keep herdsmen with them constantly or else graze the stock at a considerable distance from the cultivated fields, and if any damage happened to growing crops on account of trespassing stock, the owner of the stock, upon complaint to the alcalde, responded in damages. Nearly all crops were grown by irrigation, although at places at high elevations crops known as *temporal* (dry farming) were grown with some success. In irrigation the community ditch system was in vogue. The main ditch was known as the *acequia madre*, and this generally served for the conveyance of water to the cultivated fields owned by the people of any single town or settlement.[118]

The staple productions of the country were Indian corn and wheat. No cotton was grown in the country after the eighteenth century, although it was indigenous to the country and used by the Indians very extensively at the time of the Spanish *entradas*. The potato was not grown until late in the second quarter of the nineteenth century, although this was also an indigenous plant, being found in a state of nature in the mountain valleys, the tubers being of small size.

Tobacco was universally used, but very little of it was grown, this being of a light and very weak species, called *punche*. The reason for the neglect in growing this plant was owing to the monopoly of the federal government. The laws relative to the growing of tobacco were very strict, and although there was no public store-house in New Mexico, the people could not carry it elsewhere for purposes of sale, without risk of its being immediately confiscated by the government officials.

Fruits there were practically none; there were a few orchards of apples, peaches, apricots, and some pear trees. There were

---

[118] The ditch was made and kept in repair by the community, under the supervision of the alcaldes, and mayor-domos. The people worked upon the ditches in the same manner as road-taxes were worked out in the states. The size of the main ditch depended upon the amount of land served. More trouble arose in New Mexico over the distribution and use of water than from any other cause, and in all sessions of the legislative assembly in days of the American rule, the New Mexican always stood guard for the perpetuation of the ancient systems of irrigation practised in the country.

Secretaries of New Mexico

1. W. W. H. Davis. 2. William G. Ritch. 3. George W. Lane. 4. Lorion Miller. 5. W. F. M. Arny. 6. Benjamin M. Thomas. 7. J. Wallace Raynolds. 8. Nathan Jaffa. 9. George H. Wallace

vineyards in the *Rio Abajo*, mainly growing at the missions in the valley of the Rio Grande, and in the vicinity of Paso del Norte.

As has been said, the New Mexicans were distinctly a pastoral people. The high table lands afforded a most excellent pasturage, the grass growing thereon being of a most nutritious character and known as *grama*. For grazing purposes the *grama* reached its perfection from August to October, curing upon the ground and making most excellent hay. Although the winters in the northern portions were rigorous, stock-feeding was unknown, the great herds of cattle, sheep, goats, and other animals maintaining themselves in excellent condition upon the dry *grama* pasturage, until the rains of spring and summer brought forth the green grass upon the prairies.

Mining in New Mexico during the Spanish and Mexican rule was very limited. Prior to the revolt of 1680, it may be safely said that no mines were worked in New Mexico. An official report of 1725 declares that not a single mine of gold or silver had ever been worked in the territory and that all the plate required for the services of the missions was brought from the provinces south of New Mexico. All of the traditions concerning lost Spanish mines, buried treasures of the Franciscan friars, and kindred tales are only myths.[119]

The conclusion is justified that mining of any consequence was only commenced in the first years of the nineteenth century. True

---

[119] Dr. Gregg was undoubtedly imposed upon in the matter of "lost mines;" stories of the location or probable location of these mines were poured into the ears of the Americans and Gregg undoubtedly received his full share. He says: "Tradition speaks of numerous and productive mines having been in operation in New Mexico before the expulsion of the Spaniards in 1680; but that the Indians, seeing that the cupidity of the conquerors had been the cause of their former cruel oppressions, determined to conceal all the mines by filling them up, and obliterating as much as possible every trace of them. This was done so effectually, as is told, that after the second conquest (the Spaniards in the meantime not having turned their attention to mining pursuits for a series of years), succeeding generations were never able to discover them again. Indeed, it is now generally credited by the Spanish population, that the Pueblo Indians, up to the present day, are acquainted with the *locales* of a great number of these wonderful mines, of which they most sedulously preserve the secret. Rumor further asserts that the old men sages of the Pueblos periodically lecture the youths on this subject, warning them against discovering the mines to the Spaniards, lest the cruelties of the original conquest be renewed towards them, and they be forced to toil and suffer in those mines as in days of yore. To the more effectual preservation of secrecy, it is also

it is that some mining, at some time, prior to 1800, was done in the Sandias, in the mountains of Rio Arriba and Taos counties, and near Los Cerrillos in Santa Fé county, but the most extensive mining of which there is any documentary record was that done in the copper mines of Santa Rita,[120] in Grant county. No silver

---

stated that they have called in the aid of superstition, by promulgating the belief that the Indian who reveals the location of these hidden treasures, will surely perish by the wrath of their gods.

"Playing upon the credulity of the people, it sometimes happens that a roguish Indian will amuse himself at the expense of his reputed superiors in intelligence, by proffering to disclose some of these concealed treasures. I once knew a waggish savage of this kind to propose to show a valley where 'virgin gold could be scraped up by the basketful.' On a bright Sunday morning, the time appointed for the expedition, the chuckling Indian set out with a train of Mexicans at his heels, provided with mules and horses, and a large quantity of meal-bags to carry in the golden treasure; but, as the shades of evening were closing around the party, he discovered — that he could't find the place. It is not at all probable, however, that the aborigines possess a tenth part of the knowledge of these ancient fountains of wealth, that is generally attributed to them; but that many valuable mines *were* once wrought in this province, not only tradition but authenticated records and existing relics sufficiently prove."

[120] Wislizenus, Dr. A., *Tour through Northern Mexico*, etc., at page 26, says: "Of the copper mines in the state of Chihuahua, the most celebrated is the 'Santa Rita de Cobre,' in the western angle of the *Sierra de Mogoyon*, near the headwaters of the Gila. The mine, known for a long time to the Apaches, passed through the hands of several proprietors, till in 1828, it was effectually worked by Mr. Coursier, a French resident of Chihuahua, who is reported and generally believed to have cleared in seven years about half a million dollars from it. The ore looks extremely rich; it is a remarkably pure oxyde of copper, accompanied sometimes with the native metal and said to contain some gold. Mr. Coursier soon monopolized the whole copper trade in Chihuahua; and as the state at that time coined a great deal of this metal, he made a very profitable business of it; but at last the mine, which seems to be inexhaustible, had to be abandoned on account of the hostile Indians, who killed some of the workmen, and attacked the trains. These copper mines are claimed by the State of Chihuahua, as belonging to its territory; but as not even the latitude of the city of Chihuahua had been well determined by the Mexicans, more exact astronomical observations may perhaps prove that they fall within the territory of New Mexico. This question may become of importance, because this whole range of mountains is intersected with veins of copper and placers of gold. Also, says rumor, cinnabar was discovered there in 1824, but nothing positive is known in relation to it."

Pattie, *Narrative*, 71-81, 112, 115, 123, 129-32, says that the mine was worked by a Spanish superintendent, Juan Oñis, for the Spanish owner, Francisco Pablo Legara. Within the circumference of three miles there is a mine of copper, gold, and silver, and besides, a cliff of load-stone. The silver mine is not worked, as not being so profitable as either the copper or gold mines. The Indians were very troublesome, and the trappers did good service in keeping them in order by force and treaties. Finally, the Patties leased the mines for five years, at $1,000 per year, and the elder Pattie remained there, established a stock ranch on the Mimbres, and made money. But in 1827, when he thought of buying the property, a rascally Spanish agent, intrusted with thirty

mines were worked in the Mexican period. When Lieutenant Z. M. Pike was in New Mexico, in 1807, as stated by him, "there are no mines known in the Province except one of copper, situated in a mountain on the west side of the Rio del Norte, in latitude 34. It is worked, and produces 20,000 mule-loads of copper annually. It contains gold, but not quite sufficient to pay for its extraction." [121]

thousand dollars in gold, ran away with the money, and ruined Pattie. At the same time the owner was exiled as a Spaniard, and it is implied that the mines were abandoned.

Bancroft, H. H., p. 340, *History of Arizona and New Mexico*, seems to have some doubts as to the veracity of the statements of young Pattie. Bancroft undoubtedly did not possess the information given to us by Dr. Wislizenus above quoted.

[121] Prince, L. B., *Historical Sketches*, etc., p. 241, says of this mine and the locality named by Major Pike: "The locality . . . would be directly west of Socorro, in the Magdalenas; but it is very possible that the latitude given is wrong, and that the description refers to the Santa Rita mine, near Silver City. This was discovered in 1800 by Lieutenant Colonel Carrisco, through the aid of an Indian. In 1804 he sold it to Don Francisco Manuel Elguea, a wealthy merchant of Chihuahua, who at once commenced extensive developments, and found the metal of such fine quality that the whole product was contracted to the royal mint for coinage; and was transported to the City of Mexico by pack-mules and wagons, 100 mules, carrying 300 pounds each, being constantly employed."

It will be remembered that the Indians gave to Andrés Dorantes, one of the companions of Alvar Nuñez Cabeza de Vaca, a hawk-bell, made of copper. (See vol. i, p. 97, of this work). It has always been a question whether or not the Indians, prior to the advent of the Spaniards, knew anything of the use of metals. From recent explorations and research work done by archæologists, evidence is constantly accumulating that the Indians of New Mexico and Arizona did know of the use of this metal for some purposes. In a mound near Phoenix, Arizona, on the Lossing ranch, were found two copper bells. Reporting on these bells, Dr. J. Walter Fewkes, of the Bureau of Ethnology, says: "This mound situated two miles west of Phoenix, is prehistoric or at least antedates the advent of Europeans into the Gila valley. . . In my excavations in different parts of Arizona, I have repeatedly found copper bells, one or two of which closely resemble those referred to above. A specimen found at Four-Mile Ruin (see 22d Ann. Rep. B. A. E.) is approximately the same, although much corroded; and another from a ruin on the Little Colorado is even closer in size. The latter has a human face in relief on one side. The three copper bells found at Casa Grande are smaller than those here considered and more spherical in shape. None show as well as one of these the marks of coils. The copper bells I have found were generally buried, which implies, but does not prove age. Any suggestion I might make about their origin or original provenance from a microscopic examination would be speculative. I have always regarded the Arizona copper bells as made in Mexico, but aboriginal. Any chemist could by analysis determine whether the copper is native or alloyed. As related to this analysis, I may call attention to my finding a piece of float copper in Compound B of Casa Grande."

It might be well for Dr. Fewkes to remember that when the negro, Estevan, came to the pueblo of Hawaikúh, gaily bedecked in feathers, gourds and *bells*, the Indian chief said, "*Those bells are not of our fashion,*" a statement per-

The oldest gold mining district in the United States was discovered and worked by the Mexicans beginning in the year 1828.

OLD AND NEW PLACERS

It was incorporated as the *Real de Dolores*, but was familiarly known as *El Placer*.

The district was discovered by a citizen of Sonora, who was herding some cattle in that vicinity. He found, while in the mountains, some rock which resembled that in the gold regions of his native state. A careful examination revealed particles of gold and the news of the discovery occasioned great excitement. Great numbers flocked to the locality and washing was carried on with good success. The winter season was the favored time for operations, owing to the facilities afforded for obtaining water from snow, which was thrown into a sink and melted with hot stones. The washing was done in a round wooden bowl, called a *batea*, about eighteen inches in diameter, which was filled with earth and then immersed in a pool and constantly stirred until nothing was left but the heavy black sand and grains of gold.[122]

The quantity of gold extracted between the years 1832 and 1835 amounted to from $60,000 to $80,000 per annum. Up to the time of the American occupation the output was approximately three million dollars.

Not long subsequent to the discovery of the gold bearing sand and gravel district called *El Placer*, a vein of gold ore was found on the property of a Mexican by the name of Ortiz. "This mine," says Dr. Gregg, "different from the rest of the *Placer*, consisted of a vein of gold in a stratum of rock, which it was necessary to grind and separate with quicksilver; and as it belonged to a native named Ortiz, who knew nothing of this operation, the latter formed a partnership with Don Damasio Lopez, the *Gachupin* (a term used to designate European Spaniards in America) before alluded

---

suasive, at least, that the Cibolans had a knowledge of copper bells and used them for certain purposes.

The bells discovered near Phoenix are very similar in appearance to ordinary sleigh-bells, but are heavily corroded. They still have a musical quality, are made of copper, and have a tiny cobble-stone inside, instead of a metal ball.

[122] Gregg, J., *Commerce of the Prairies*, i, p. 167: "Although the amount procured from these mines, was, for the first two or three years, very insignificant, yet it answered for the purpose of testing the quality of the metal, which was found to be of uncommon purity. A market was therefore very soon opened with foreign merchants.

to, who had some experience and skill in mining operations and the extraction of metals. The partners went vigorously to work, and at the close of the first month found that their net profits amounted to several hundred dollars, consisting of a few balls of gold. At the sight of these Ortiz was so overjoyed that he must needs exhibit his valuable acquisitions to the governor and other officers and magnates of the capital, who, with characteristic cupidity, at once begrudged the *Gachupin* his prospective fortune. A compact was thereupon entered into between the *oficiales* and the acquiescent Ortiz, to work the mine on their joint account, and to exclude Lopez altogether. This they effected by reviving the old decree of expulsion (spoken of in another place), which had virtually become obsolete. The unfortunate victim of this outrageous conspiracy was accordingly ordered to the frontier, as the patriotic officers alleged that they 'could no longer connive at his residence so near the capital in contravention of the laws.'" A new company, including several officials, with Ortiz, then proceeded with the wealth-producing work; but from lack of knowledge did not obtain a grain of gold. Subsequently an order was made prohibiting any but natives from working at the mines; and thus foreign capital and energy were prevented from taking any part in the necessary developments. The greater part of the work was done by poor men working on their own account; these were known as *Gambusinos*; and satisfied if they could realize a few *reales* per day. Each miner was allowed ten paces in all directions from his pit, as his claim, and no new-comer could interfere with the right thus acquired, unless the place was abandoned for a specified period, when the ground again became open to location. The gold was mainly in dust, but occasionally large nuggets were found, the most valuable being worth $3,400, although it was sold by its finder for $1,400. In 1839, the "New Placers" were discovered a short distance to the southwest, and the miners speedily deserted their old diggings for the greater charms of the new. The little town of Tuerto rose into large importance as a business point. In 1845 this town contained twenty-two stores, transacting more business in the aggregate than the establishments of Santa Fé.[123]

[123] The first American possessing any scientific knowledge worth mentioning who visited this district was Dr. Wislizenus, who made a trip to the Placers in July, 1846, before the coming of the American troops. His description of his

The Mr. Watrous mentioned by Dr. Wislizenus was Samuel B. Watrous, a very prominent citizen of New Mexico in later days, and for whom the town of Watrous on the line of the Atchison, Topeka & Santa Fé Railway was named by the railway company's officials. At that time the property known as the "Big Copper Mine,"[124] was not being worked, although it was visited and ex-

visit and what he found at that time is peculiarly interesting. Dr. W. says, at pp. 26 and 27: "Several foreigners live here. The first one I saw was Mr. Watrous, a New Englander, but for many years a resident of this country. He received me very hospitably, and invited me to his dwelling. Some fresh skins of grizzly bears were spread out on scaffolds, the sure American rifle stood in the corner, and everything else bore the character of a back-woodsman; but by his intelligent conversation he showed himself a man of very good sense, and as an acute observer. Though Mr. Watrous had not himself been engaged in mining, he paid attention to his whole neighborhood, and showed me many specimens of gold ores, which in his rambles through the mountains he had collected. I took a walk with him to the nearest gold washes. The first instance of this operation I witnessed on the small creek that runs through Old Placer. From the bed of the creek, which was in most places dry, they took up some of the ground — gravel, sand and earth — put it in a spacious, rather flat wooden bowl (*batéa*), added water, removing first, by stirring with the hand, the coarse pieces of gravel, and then, by well-balanced shaking, all the earthy and sandy particles, till at last nothing is left at the bottom but the finest sand, from which all the visible portions of gold are picked out. The poorer class of Mexicans are generally occupied with these gold-washes in the creek; and they divide for that purpose the creek with the water amongst themselves, in lots, which often call forth as many claims and contests as the finest building lots in our cities. . . . On the next day I went to see a gold mine near the upper part of the town, belonging to Mr. Tournier, a French resident of the place. The mine lies between one and two miles west of the town, on the slope of some mountains. It was discovered several years ago by Mr. Robidoux, who commenced working it, but for some reason gave it up. Mr. Tournier had worked it for one year, and found it very profitable. The old vein runs from SSE to NNW with a very slight dip. It is generally from two to four feet wide. Mr. Tournier has sunk a shaft already in the entire depth of forty varas, and with the drift of about thirty varas, and the ore promises to hold out very fairly. The ores are carried in bags to the surface, and on mules to the amalgamation mill in town. After the ores have been ground, by hand (pounding them with rocks), they are put in the mill, a small circular basin formed with rocks, with one or two mill stones, which are constantly turned around in it by mule-power. These mill stones are placed on their face, revolving round a center pole, which is turned by the animals. To the coarsely powdered ore, water, and then quicksilver are added, and the amalgamation goes on in the usual way. Mr. Tournier told me he had worked in this way every day about two and a half cargas (750 pounds) of the ore, and that he draws, on the average three quarters of an ounce (about $12.00 worth of gold) out of it."

Dr. Wislizenus met here Mr. Nolan and a Mr. Trigg, both prominent citizens of New Mexico of that period. He also met Mr. Richard Campbell, for many years a resident of the territory.

[124] This is known as the San Pedro mine and belongs today to the Santa Fé Copper Company. In the month of October, 1846, Lieutenant J. W. Abert, U. S. A., visited this district. In his report he says: "In the evening we

amined by an officer of the United States army. This is the mine which, subsequent to the coming of the railroad, gave rise to so much litigation as to title and with which were identified many distinguished men of the United States, including General U. S. Grant. A number of prominent citizens of New Mexico were imprisoned in the county jail at Santa Fé by Chief Justice Axtell, for contempt of court, having been charged with the violation of a writ of injunction issuing from the court of the first judicial district of New Mexico.[125]

---

visited a town at the base of the principal mountain; here, mingled with the houses, were huge mounds of earth, thrown out of the wells so that the village looked like a village of gigantic prairie-dogs. Nearly all the people there were at their wells, and were drawing up bags of loose sand by means of windlasses. Around little pools, men, women, and children were grouped, intently poring over these bags of loose sand, washing the earth in wooden platters or goat horns. One can not but feel pity for these miserable wretches, and congratulate himself that he does not possess a gold mine. Even the life of the poor *pastores* is much preferable to that of these diggers of gold. Tuerto contains about 250 inhabitants. It is situated on a ravine, that just furnishes sufficient water for this place and the town at the base of the mountains, which is one and a half miles distant. Some of the people own large flocks of sheep, which they keep in the valley of the Pecos. In the evening we saw the 'Villanos' milking their goats. This business requires considerable dexterity and is not one of the least amusing scenes in New Mexico. We now started to examine the mines of the New Placer. Mr. Campbell kindly furnished us mules in order that ours might have an opportunity to rest and graze. We first visited a lead mine, situated near the road that runs to San Antonio; it is in a direction nearly south, situated at the foot of the mountains and overlaying a bed of fossiliferous limestone. We collected specimens of the lead ore, and the lime stone; then proceeding eastwardly, commenced ascending the mountain. Near the summit of the mountain we visited a large copper mine. Mr. Campbell proceeded to enter with great caution, and told us that he feared least some evil disposed Mexicans should be lurking in these caverns, for there were many discontented spirits about the country, trying to revolutionize the people, and some were said to dwell in these mines and caverns. We found beautiful specimens of ore of copper of various kinds. Mr. Campbell ground up some with the aid of a couple of stones, and after a little washing showed us a great many particles of gold and silver; indeed, the ore was quite rich with these metals.''

[125] The individuals imprisoned for contempt of court were: P. B. Otero and his brother, Miguel A. Otero, sons of Don Miguel A. Otero, at one time secretary and delegate in congress from New Mexico; R. W. Webb, a prominent citizen of Golden, N. M., afterward clerk of the district court at Santa Fé; their attorneys, Francis Downs and William A. Vincent, the last named afterward appointed chief justice of the supreme court of New Mexico by President Cleveland, and later removed by him on charges of too close intimacy with Hon. S. W. Dorsey, which charges were groundless. Miguel A. Otero was subsequently clerk of the district court of the fourth judicial district, and was appointed governor of New Mexico by President McKinley and re-appointed by President Roosevelt.

The imprisonment of these men was a farce, as, owing to close political

During the Mexican rule there were no educational institutions worthy of the name. There was a slight increase in interest owing to the endeavors of the clergy.

EDUCATIONAL INSTITUTIONS In 1826 the territorial deputation began the establishment of a sort of college at Santa Fé. The archives show that there were some primary schools at the principal towns from 1827 to 1832,[126] but two years later there was no school at Santa Fé, as the *diputacion* announced that there were no funds and asked the *ayuntamientos* to see that the schools were re-opened by private subscription, if possible.

About the year 1834 a printing press was brought to New Mexico. It was operated by Jesus Maria Baca, who came from the City of Mexico. Upon this press was printed a proclamation by Governor Perez, dated June 26, 1835, in which he announces that he has assumed the reins of government. Upon this press was done the first printing between the Missouri river and the Rio Grande.

Upon the same press was published a weekly paper called *La Verdad*. It had sixteen pages, ten by fourteen inches in size, which were chiefly filled with official announcements, decrees and literary essays. One number contains an elaborate essay in favor of matrimony. Padre Martinez issued for four weeks at Taos the *Crepusculo*. He also states that some primers and catechisms were printed on this press prior to 1844. In the newspapers of 1876 was

---

affiliations between all of them and the sheriff of Santa Fé county, Don Romulo Martinez and his chief deputy, Francisco Chavez, they were only constructively confined. The office of the county jail was turned into a reception room where nightly the "prisoners" received their friends and had every luxury that money could buy or friends procure. The company owning or claiming the property at that time was known as the San Pedro and Cañon del Agua Company.

[126] *Arch. Santa Fé*, Ms., including "*estatutos para el régimen de la escuela general.*" Schools opened at 6 A. M. in summer and 7 in winter. Thirty pupils at La Cañada in 1828. Marcelino was teacher of a Lancasterian school at Santa Fé in 1829-30. Pino, *Not. Hist.*, 56-7, indicates eighteen schools and seventeen teachers at Santa Fé, Vado, Cochití, San Juan, Cia, Sandía, Alameda, Alburquerque, Tomé, Belen, Laguna, La Cañada, Taos, and Abiquiú, but Barreiro, *Ojeada*, gives forty-three names for 1832 only. Santa Fé, with $500 assigned for teachers' salary, San Miguel, Cañada, Taos, Alburquerque, and Belen, with from $250 to $300 each. Ritch, in *Aztlan*, 249, speaks of private schools established at Taos by Padre Martinez and by Padre Leiva at San Miguel.

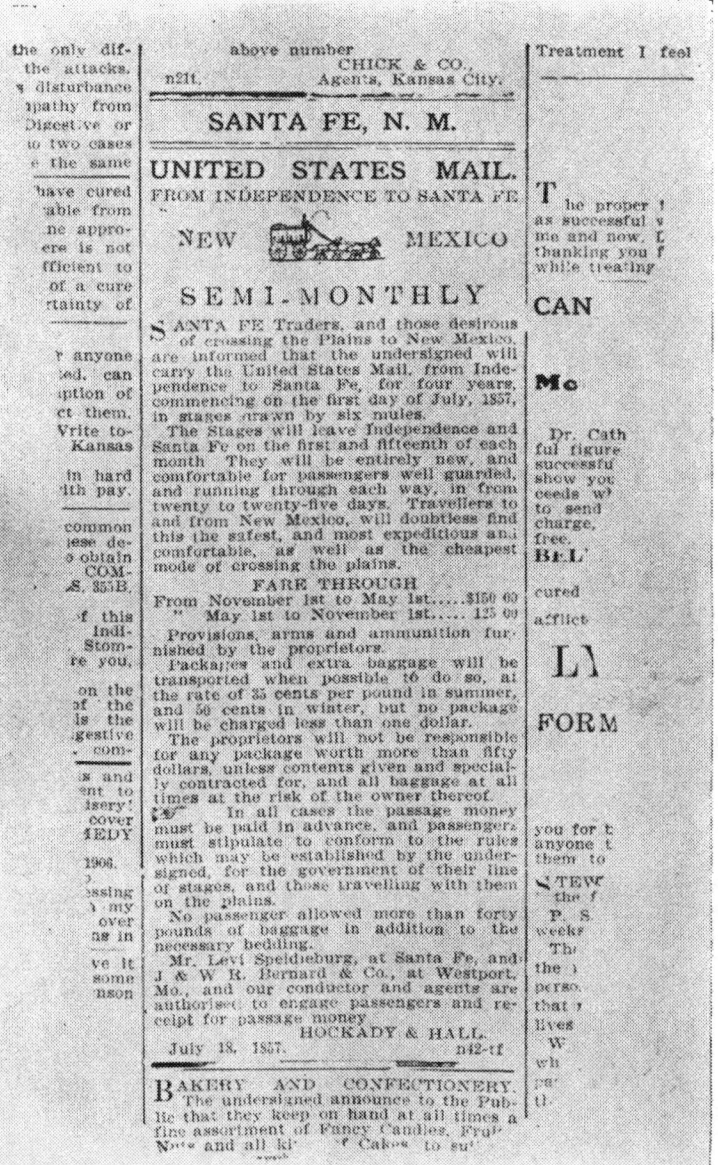

Fac-simile of Advertisement of Stage Coach Line to Santa Fé

noted the death of Jesus Maria Baca, who was a printer on the *Crepusculo*.

When Iturbide was made emperor, the Marquis de Castañiza was the bishop of Durango. He was holding this position in 1824, at which time he appointed Don Agustin Fernandez de San Vicente his vicar-general, visitor, and ecclesiastical governor of New Mexico, but this distinguished clergyman did not reach Santa Fé until after the death of the bishop. He entered upon the performance of his duties on the 10th of April, 1826.

THE MISSIONS UNDER MEXICAN RULE

"The missions of Taos, San Juan, Abiquiú, Belen and Bado," says Dr. Shea,[127] "had been secularized and were now passing into the hands of secular priests. The religious protested, but Fr. Sebastian Alvarez, custos or superior of the Franciscan fathers, co-operated with the visitor as far as he could, although the latter was very hostile to the friars, and a friend and adherent of Manuel Arispe. His rule was severe and inflexible. The Custos, Fr. Alvarez, drew up a plan of studies for a college which the government proposed to found at Santa Fé. The Rev. A. J. Martinez was appointed parish priest of Abiquiú, Rev. Leyva (Fr. José de Jesus Leiva) of Alburquerque, Rev. John T. Terrazas of Santa Fé, Rev. John F. Ortiz of San Juan de los Caballeros, Rev. Francis I. de Madariaga of Tomé. New Mexico received a new ecclesiastical ruler in the person of the Bachelor Don Juan Rafael Rascon, appointed in 1828, Ecclesiastical Governor, Vicar-General Forain, and Visitor, by the chapter of Durango. He reached Santa Fé on the 5th of March, 1829, and was received by the authorities political, military, and ecclesiastical, who conducted him to the parish church, where a *te Deum* was sung. The Franciscan Custodia was nearing its end. It was now subject to Father Manuel Garcia del Valle, as vice-custos. This clergyman died at Sandía in June, 1834. Dr. Rascon, as usual on visitations called for the production of faculties, renewing them where he found no obstacle. His rule was more kindly than that of San Vicente. Dr. Rascon was authorized by the Sovereign Pontiff to confer the sacrament of confirmation in New Mexico, and on the first of August, 1829, issued a circular to the parish priests directing them to prepare the children for its reception. The number of priests in New Mexico was now greatly reduced, so that two or three places were attended by the same clergyman, and for the first time in the history of the province,

---

[127] Shea, Dr. John Gilmary, *History of the Catholic Church in the United States*, pp. 302-303.

it became necessary to permit some priests to say two masses on Sunday. The old church of San Miguel in Santa Fé, used as a chapel of ease to the parish church, was in a tottering condition, and Dr. Rascon, in April, 1831, authorized the sale of a small piece of land in front of it, in order to effect the repairs. Dr. Rascon's report in 1830, on the condition of the Church in New Mexico, was a melancholy picture. Churches and parochial residences were in a deplorable, almost ruinous condition, some so utterly unfit that necessity alone justified their use for divine service; the vestments were old and the altar plate scanty, so that, unless they were restored, it would in a few years be impossible to maintain the services of religion. As in former times churches had been erected and missionaries maintained by the king; the people had never been accustomed to contribute and now, reduced in number, impoverished by revolution, they could not be induced to begin. In Santa Fé, Alburquerque, and in La Cañada the fees and voluntary contributions had for a long time supported the clergy; but elsewhere they amounted to nothing." [128]

At this time the parishes of Alburquerque, San Juan de los Caballeros, and Socorro were vacant, and the missions of Picuríes, Nambé, Pojoaque, Pecos, Santo Domingo, Sandía, Jemez, Cía, Santa Ana, Laguna, Acoma, and Zuñi as well. These missions were all served from the places where six secular priests and five Franciscans still resided. Barreiro, in his notes to Pino's history, says that many persons died without confession or extreme unction, and that nothing was more rare than to see the Holy Eucharist administered; that the churches were nearly all in ruins, and most of them unworthy of being called temples of God.[129]

---

[128] Shea, Dr. J. Gilmary, *History of the Catholic Church in the United States*, p. 303. Bancroft, H. H., *History of Arizona and New Mexico*, says: "The government still paid — or at least made appropriations for — the sinodos of from 23 to 27 Franciscan friars; but these were for the most part acting curates at the Mexican settlements, making occasional visits to the Indian pueblos under their spiritual charge."

[129] Pino, P. B., *Noticias Historicas del Nuevo Mexico*, p. 33: "*Libro primero de gobierno ecclesiástico, 1828-1832; Libro en que se asientan los autos de la santa visita ecca. qe en el año 1829, comen zo* L L L *el Dr. Don Juan Rafael Rascon.*"

Shea, Dr. J. Gilmary, *History of the Catholic Church in the United States*, p. 304 and note.

O'Gorman, Thomas, *History of the Roman Catholic Church in the United State*, pp. 112, 113, says of the work of the church from 1520 to 1840, a period of more than three hundred years: "In space it expanded from the Atlantic to the Pacific, south of the thirty-eighth degree of latitude, and covered our present states of Florida, Alabama, Texas, New Mexico, Arizona and California. Over a hundred thousand of the aborigines were brought to

In the year 1832, Rt. Rev. José Antonio Laureano de Zubiria was made bishop of Durango and the official announcement of the fact and instructions from him reached Santa Fé in February, 1832. He was at Abiquíu in July, and on the Feast of the Assumption at Santa Fé where he was received with great enthusiasm. Special preparations were made at all points for his reception when he made his visitation of the department; roads and bridges were repaired and the houses gaily decorated with flags and flowers.[130] At this time Rev. Juan Felipe Ortiz was the vicar-general, and in October, 1833, this prelate and the parish priests at

VISIT OF THE BISHOP OF DURANGO

the knowledge of Christianity, and introduced, if not into the palace, at least into the ante-chamber of civilization. It was a glorious work, and the recital of it impresses us by the vastness and success of the toil. Yet, as we look around to-day, we can find nothing of it that remains. Names of saints in melodious Spanish stand out from maps in all that section where the Spanish monk trod, toiled and died. A few thousand Christian Indians, descendants of those they converted and civilized, still survive in New Mexico and Arizona and that is all. It is well worth while to inquire what made the success, what the ruin, of the Spanish missions.

"What made their success? I answer; the blood of martyrs; the zeal of missionaries; the reduction of the roving tribes into fixed communities; the industrial training imparted to the Indians; the patriarchal and paternal character of the friars' government; the generosity of Spain in furnishing the temporal means of subsistence; the military protection given the missionaries; the separation of the Indians from the whites even to the difference of their spiritual guardians, the whites, as a rule, being under diocesan, the Indians under religious priests.

"What their ruin? I name as external causes the wild roving tribes that remained heathen; the revolution of Mexico, and the consequent confiscation of funds and secularization of missions in the southwestern mission field; the withdrawal of that military protection that had been so influential in building them up. I name as internal causes the want of gradual preparation in the passage of the Indian tribes from tutelage to independent manhood, and in the transfer of the missions from the religious orders to the diocesan clergy; the tardiness in appointing bishops, who alone could prepare for the transfer and create the diocesan clergy that would take place of the early missionaries.

"This one glorious truth stands prominent; the Spaniards in the United States did not drive the natives from their homes, much less destroy them. These accusations, if made at all, must fall on some other race."

[130] Gregg, Dr. Josiah, *Commerce of the Prairies*, i, p. 255, mentions this visit of the bishop of Durango. As an observer Dr. Gregg was a success, but it is very evident that he was very much prejudiced whenever he wrote of the church or any of its dignitaries or its ritual. Of this visit, he says: "On the occasion of the Bishop of Durango's visit to Santa Fé in 1833, an event which had not taken place for a great many years, the infatuated population hailed his arrival with as much devotional enthusiasm as if it had been the second advent of the Messiah. Magnificent preparations were made everywhere for his reception; the streets were swept, the roads and bridges on the route repaired and decorated; and from every window in the city there hung such a profusion of fancy curtains and rich cloths that the imagination was carried

188 LEADING FACTS OF NEW MEXICAN HISTORY

Taos and Tomé were empowered by the sovereign pontiff, Gregory XVI, to administer confirmation.

Bishop Zubiria found conditions in New Mexico as Dr. Rascon had pictured them. He did everything in his power to arouse the zeal of the faithful, seeing little to be hoped for from the Mexican government, which soon drove him into exile. During his visit he made regulations in regard to the repair of the churches and improvements in the service of the altar, as well as in regard to marriages with persons from the United States. He left New Mexico, however, with a heavy heart, seeing so much to be done, and without any resources or power to effect a remedy. He visited the territory again in 1845, and labored to revive a spirit of faith and sacrifice in the people. The year following the last visit of Bishop Zubiria, there was a strange riot at Tomé, caused by the attempt of the priest to take some statues from the church in the Holy Week procession at Valencia. When General Manuel Armijo, about the 8th of August, 1846, learned that General Kearny was on his way to New Mexico with the Army of the West, he compelled the vicar-general, Juan Felipe Ortiz, to give him all the money he had, also all plate and live stock, to enable him to resist the American army; but he did nothing to prevent the peaceful entry of the American general two weeks later, but fled ingloriously, deserting his people and abandoning his capital.

A list of all the friars and priests, who ever came to New Mexico during Spanish and Mexican rule, as prepared by Archbishop J. B. Salpointe, from records at his disposal, with his comments, is given below.[131]

---

back to those glowing descriptions of enchanted worlds which one reads of in the fables of necromancers. I must observe, however, that there is a custom in all the towns of Mexico (which it would not be safe to neglect), providing that whenever a religious procession takes place, all the doors and windows facing the street along which it is to pass, shall be decorated with shawls, carpets, or fancy cloths, according to the means and capabilities of the proprietor. During the bishop's sojourn in Santa Fé, which to the great joy of the inhabitants, lasted for several weeks, he never appeared in the streets but that all true catholics who were so fortunate as to obtain a glimpse of his *Señoria Ilustrísima* immediately dropped upon their knees and never moved from that position till the mitred priest had either vouchsafed his benediction or had disappeared. Even the principal personages of the city would not venture to address him till they had first knelt at his feet and kissed his pastoral ring.''

[131] Salpointe, Most Rev. J. B., *Soldiers of the Cross*, pp. 122-123: ''The list we give of the names of the venerable missionaries who preached the

MISSIONS, FRAYLES, AND PRIESTS 189

NOTE 131 — continued.

gospel in New Mexico, is far from being complete, as all the church documents, from the establishment of the missions to the year 1681 were destroyed in the general revolt of the Pueblos in 1680. As regards the remaining period of time, until the fall of Spanish rule in Mexico, we must say that we have not, thus far, been able to explore all the records yet in existence in the churches, and consequently many names of the missionaries of our country will remain unmentioned in the pages of these notes, until a more complete investigation. This list, however, gives us a pretty fair idea of how numerous must have been the phalanx of the brave soldiers of the cross, the zealous sons of St. Francis, who followed and many times out-stepped, in New Mexico and Arizona, the march of the valorous Spanish conquistadores. The soldier looked to the conquest of lands and peoples for his king, and the missionary to the conquest of souls for Heaven. Both advanced, now together and then apart from each other, but both always facing to the right point, though with different views and differently equipped. The soldier brilliantly clad, mounted on his steed, with spear in hand to fight the Indians if need be; and the missionary, dressed in the poor habit of his order, walking on foot and bearing the cross, to console the conquered native, and to show him that there was One who had suffered before him and for him, in order to win his heart and to make him happy in another world.''

1540: (1) Fray Marcos de Niza. (2) Fray Juan de Padilla and Brother Louis de Escalona (Expedition of Coronado).

1581: (3) Fray Francisco Lopez. (4) Fray Juan de Santa Maria, Brother Agustin Ruiz (Ruiz expedition).

1582: (5) Fray Bernardino Beltran (Espejo's expedition).

1596: (6) Fray Alonzo Martinez. (7) Fray Francisco de San Miguel. (8) Francisco de Zamorra. (9) Fray Juan de Rosas. (10) Fray Alonzo de Lugo. (11) Fray Andrés Corchado. (12) Fray Juan Claros. (13) Fray Cristobal Salazar, Brothers Pedro de Vergara and Juan de Buenaventura (Juan de Oñate expedition).

1608: (16) Fray Juan Ramirez.

1629: (17) Fray Zarate Salmeron.

1632: (18) Fray Juan Letrado, Fray Martin Arbide.

1678-80 (Otermin being governor of the province): (19) Fray Juan de Jesus Morador. (20) Fray Cristobal Figueroa. (21) Fray Albino Maldonado. (22) Fray Juan Mora. (23) Fray Juan Lorenzo Analiza. (24) Fray Juan de Jesus Espinosa. (25) Fray Sebastian Calzada.

1681: (26) Fray Francisco Gomez de la Cadena. (27) Fray Andrés Duran. (28) Fray Francisco Farfan. (29) Fray N. Ayeta. (30) Fray Juan de Vallada. (31) Fray Jesus de Lombardi. (32) Fray N. N. (his title) Procurador. (33) Fray Juan de Jesus.

1692 (Vargas being governor): (34) Fray Francisco Corvera. (35) Fray Miguel Muniz. (36) Fray Francisco Alonzo Barroso.

1698: (37) Fray Salvador de San Antonio. (38) Fray Juan de Zavaleta. (39) Fray Francisco Jesus Maria. (40) Fray Juan de Alpuente. (41) Fray Juan Muños de Castro. (42) Fray Juan Daza. (43) Fray José Dies. (44) Fray Antonio Carbonel. (45) Fray Geronimo Prieto. (46) Fray Juan Antonio de Corral. (47) Fray Antonio Vahomonde. (48) Fray Antonio Obregon. (49) Fray Domingo de Jesus Maria. (50) Fray Buenaventura Contreras. (51) Fray José Nevares Velarde. (52) Fray Diego Zeiños.

1694: (53) Fray Francisco Vargas. (54) Fray Antonio Moreno. (55) Fray José Garcia Marin. (56) Fray Miguel Tirso. (57) Fray Antonio Acevedo. (58) Fray José Arvizu. (59) Fray Juan de Peña.

NOTE 131 — continued.

From this date we give the names of the priests alphabetically, omitting the time of their arrival in this country:

60	Fray Alvares Cristobal		113	F. Gonzales Francisco
61	F. Aumatel Estevan		114	F. Gonzales Manuel
62	F. de Arros Antonio		115	F. Garcia Andrés
63	F. de Arros Domingo		116	F. Garcia Angel
64	F. de Arrenguas José		117	F. Garcia José
65	F. Aparicio Antonio		118	F. Guzman N.
66	F. Alvarez Juan		119	F. Gonzales Jacinto
67	F. Alvarez Francisco		120	F. Gravino Joseph
68	F. Arivala Lucas		121	F. Guerra Ambrosio
69	F. de Abadiano Manuel		122	F. Gonzales Ramon
70	F. Alvarez Sebastian		123	F. Garacochea N.
71	F. Aguilar Pedro		124	F. Gomez Caynola N.
72	F. Anton Sebastian		125	F. Hernandez José
73	F. Alcina Teodoro		126	F. Hossio Francisco
74	F. A. Francisco de Jesus		127	F. Hernandez Juan
75	F. B. Francisco Manuel		128	F. de Haro Joseph
76	F. Brisuela Antonio		129	F. Hernandez J. Bautista
77	F. Bermejo Juan		130	F. Hernandez Juan José
78	F. Benavides Rafael		131	F. Hermida Buenaventura
79	F. B. de la Parra Francisco		132	F. Irizabal Francisco
80	F. Brotone Francisco		133	F. de Ibares Antonio
81	F. Burgos Joseph		134	F. Irigoin J. Nepomuceno
82	F. Bercenilla Isidoro		135	F. Irigoin N.
83	F. Camargo Antonio		136	F. de Inojosa Juan
84	F. Corral José		137	F. Iniesta Agustin
85	C. Caballero Antonio		138	F. Junco y Juncoso
86	F. de la Cruz Murciano		139	F. La Borreria Pedro
87	F. Cellar Patricio		140	F. Llanos Juan José
88	F. de Castro José		141	F. Lopez Salvador
89	F. Correa Andrés		142	F. de Lesoun N.
90	F. Chavarria Francisco		143	F. Lerchundi Francisco
91	F. de Sta Cruz M. Antonio		144	F. de Lago Gabriel
92	F. de Colina Agustin		145	F. de Liñan Geronimo
93	F. Claramonte Andrés		146	F. Lerchundi Bravo N.
94	F. C. Redondo Francisco		147	F. Moreno Manuel
95	F. Chabarria Diego		148	F. Medrano José
96	F. Campos Miguel		149	F. Merno Bueno N.
97	F. Celis Juan Antonio		150	F. Muños Jurado Diego
98	F. Castro Juan Joseph		151	F. Minguez Juan
99	F. Diez de Aguilar Pedro		152	F. Miranda Antonio
100	F. Dominguez Antonio		153	F. Miraval José
101	F. D. Francisco Javier		154	F. de Matha Juan
102	F. Dronzozo Joseph		155	F. de M. Estanislado Mariano
103	F. Delgado Carlos		156	F. Martinez Diego
104	F. De Aguir Joseph		157	F. Montaño Pedro
105	F. E. Diego de los Monteros		158	F. Mestas Antonio
106	F. Esparagoza N.		159	F. Mignagori Manuel
107	F. F. de Sierra Santiago		160	F. Martinez de la Vega N.
108	F. Farfan Francisco		161	F. Miguel N.
109	F. Fernandez Sebastian		162	F. Mestas Agustin
110	F. Flores Manuel		163	F. Monchero Juan Miguel
111	F. Gavaldon Antonio		164	F. Moreno Antonio and Two More
112	F. Guerrera Antonio			

MISSIONS, FRAYLES, AND PRIESTS

NOTE 131 — continued.

165	F. Noriega José		203	F. Sanchez Juan Antonio
166	F. Orquera Pedro Antonio		204	F. Salvidar Mariano
167	F. Oliden Gregorio		205	F. Sospedra Pascual
168	F. de Ortega José Vivian		206	F. Sanchez Juan
169	F. Ortiz Rafael		207	F. S. Leraun Buenaventura
170	F. de Otero Cayetano		208	F. S. Vergara Mariano
171	F. Orongoroso Joseph		209	F. Trigo Nepomuceno
172	F. Obregon Antonio		210	F. Toledo Joseph
173	F. Padilla Diego		211	F. de Tagle Juan
174	F. Palacios José		212	F. Trevino Joseph
175	F. de la Prada José		213	F. Torres José Antonio
176	F. Patero Severo		214	F. Urquijo Joseph
177	F. de la Peña Francisco		215	F. Varo Andrés
178	F. del Pino Juan		216	F. Vermejo Juan
179	F. de la Peña Manuel		217	F. Villa Nueva Andrés
180	F. Padilla Juan José		218	F. Veles de Escalante
181	F. Pino Ignacio		219	F. Silvestre
182	F. P. Francisco Antonio		220	F. Vega Manuel
183	F. Perez Miraval Joseph		221	F. Velasco Carlos
184	F. Pereyro José		222	F. de Vera Joseph
185	F. de la Peña J. Francisco		223	F. Xardon Joseph
186	F. Oleata Joseph		224	F. Xeres Joaquin
187	F. del Pino George		225	F. Ximenes Francisco
188	F. Parral Joseph		226	F. Ximenes Alonzo
189	F. Pino Pedro Ignacio		227	F. Yrizabal Francisco
190	F. Polanco José Antonio		228	F. Zarte Francisco
191	F. de la Quintana Gabriel		229	F. Zepeda Miguel
192	F. Roybal Santiago		230	F. Zenallos Andrés
193	F. Roy Manuel		231	F. Zamora Antonio
194	F. Rodriguez Joseph		232	F. Zavaleta Juan
195	F. Rod. de la Torre Mariano		233	F. de Zando Juan
196	F. Rubi Joseph		234	F. Zambrano Manuel
197	F. Rosete Mariano		235	F. Zeprano Francisco
198	F. Rodriguez José		236	F. Zardo José
199	F. Rodriguez Ildefonso		237	F. Zeiños Diego
200	F. Rodriguez Joaquin			
201	F. Romero Francisco			Total of 239 priests, brothers not being counted.
202	F Ruiz Joaquin de Jesus			

Of these priests, thirty-two were killed by the Indians, viz: 1. Fray Juan de Padilla. 2. Brother Louis de Escalona. 3. Fray Francisco Lopez. 4. Fray Juan de Santa Maria. 5. Brother Agustin Ruiz. 6. Fray Juan Letrado. 7. Fray Martin de Arvide. 8. Fray Juan de Jesus Morador. 9. Fray Cristobal Figueroa. 10. Fray Albino Maldonado. 11. Fray Juan de Mora. 12. Fray Juan Lorenzo Analiza. 13. Fray Juan de Jesus Espinosa. 14. Fray Juan de Vallada. 15. Fray Sebastian Calzado. 16. Fray Juan de Lombardi. 17. (his title) Procurador. 18. Fray Juan de Jesus. 19. Fray Francisco Corvera. 20. Fray Juan de Alpuente. 21. Fray Antonio Carbonel. 22. Fray Antonio Morino. 23. Fray Juan Arvisu. 24. Fray Francisco de Jesus Abundo. 25. Fray Antonio Moreño. 26. Fray Juan del Val. 27. Fray José Trujillo. 28. Fray José Espeleta. 29. Fray Agustin de Santa Maria. 30. Fray Louis de Baesa and two whose names are not given.

The priests and frayles who administered the missions of New Mexico under Mexican rule, according to Archbishop Salpointe, were:

192 LEADING FACTS OF NEW MEXICAN HISTORY

NOTE 131 — concluded.

1	Fray Teodoro Alcina	18	Rev. Francisco Minguez
2	Rev. Manuel Bellido	19	Very Rev. Juan Felipe Ortiz
3	Fray José Castro	20	Rev. Fernando Ortiz
4	Rev. Juan Caballero	21	Rev. José Antonio Otero
5	Rev. Vicente Chavez	22	Fray Rafael Ortiz
6	Rev. José Manuel Gallegos	23	Rev. José de la Prada
7	Rev. Ramon Antonio Gonzales	24	Rev. Manuel de Jesus Prada
8	Rev. Francisco Hurtado	25	Rev. Geronimo Riega
9	Rev. Mariano de Jesus Lopez	26	Fray José Francisco Rodriguez
10	Rev. José de Jesus Leiva	27	Fray Joseph Rubi
11	Rev. José de Jesus Lujan	28	Rev. Ramon Salazar
12	Rev. Francisco Ignacio Madariaga	29	Rev. Antonio Jesus Salazar
		30	Fray Vergara José
13	Fray Diego Martinez	31	Rev. Mariano José Sanchez
14	Rev. José Vicente Montaño	32	Rev. Juan Tomas Terrazas
15	Rev. José Antonio Marin	33	Rev. Juan de Jesus Trujillo
16	Rev. Manuel Martinez	34	Rev. Manuel del Valle
17	Rev. Antonio José Martinez	35	Rev. Eulogio Valdez

CHAPEL OF SAN MIGUEL

BIBLIOGRAPHY

Bancroft, Hubert H.	*History of Arizona and New Mexico*, San Francisco, 1889.
Davis, W. W. H.	*El Gringo*, New York, 1856.
Gregg, Dr. Josiah	*Commerce of the Prairies*, New York 1844.
Historical Society of N. M.	Bulletin No. 14.
Lane, William Carr	*Message* to Assembly, Dec. 7, 1852, Santa Fé.
O'Gorman, Thomas	*History of the Roman Catholic Church in the United States*, New York, 1895.
Pattie, J. O.	*Personal Narrative*, Cincinnati, 1833.
Pino, Pedro B.	*Noticias Historicas*, Mexico, 1848.
Prince, L. B.	*Historical Sketches*, New York, 1883.
Ritch, W. G.	*Aztlan*, Boston, 1884.
Santa Fé Archives	Smithsonian, Washington, D. C.; Surveyor General's office, Santa Fé.
Salpointe, Mt. Rev. J. B.	*Soldiers of the Cross*, Banning, Calif., 1898.
Shea, John Gilmary	*History of the Catholic Church in the United States*, New York, 1892.
Wislizenus, Dr. A.	*Tour through Northern Mexico*, Washington, 1848.

PUEBLO INDIAN POTTERY

CHAPTER VI

THE WAR WITH MEXICO — THE AMERICAN OCCUPATION — ARMY OF THE WEST — GENERAL MANUEL ARMIJO — BRIGADIER-GENERAL STEPHEN W. KEARNY OCCUPIES SANTA FÉ — A CIVIL FORM OF GOVERNMENT PROCLAIMED AND OFFICIALS NAMED — COLONEL ALEXANDER W. DONIPHAN MAKES TREATY WITH THE NAVAJÓS — COLONEL STERLING W. PRICE — UPRISING OF 1846-1847 — MURDER OF GOVERNOR BENT AT TAOS — DONACIANO VIGIL — MILITARY GOVERNMENT, 1846-1851

SPANISH and Mexican diplomacy always surpassed the American. In the first years of the nineteenth century Spain and the representatives of that country in her American colonies and provinces, both civil and military, were seemingly much better advised as to the condition of public affairs in the United States than were the authorities at Washington.[132] Spain not only feared

---

[132] Meline, J. F., *Two Thousand Miles on Horseback*, pp. 240-241: "The relations between Spain and the United States had been in a disturbed condition ever since the cession of Louisiana by Napoleon in 1803 and the Spanish and the United States troops had almost come to actual hostilities on the Texas and Louisiana frontier. There was every appearance of a crisis in June, 1806, when Spanish emissaries at St. Louis reported the fitting out of Pike's expedition to their consul at New Orleans. The consul immediately advised the commanding officer at Nacogdoches by whom the despatch was transmitted through Colonel Cordero, at San Antonio (Texas), to the seat of government. Swiftly following on the heels of this report came intelligence of Burr's conspiracy; and as General Wilkinson, from whom Pike received his instructions, was more than suspected by the Spanish authorities of being deeply implicated with Burr, the conclusion that some design detrimental to Spanish authority in the New Mexican province lay hidden in Pike's movements was certainly not a violent one. Straightway the Spanish government fitted up an expedition consisting of one hundred regular dragoons, and five hundred mounted men, enlisted at Santa Fé, under the command of Lieutenant Don Facundo Melgares. . . . This expedition was fitted out on a very liberal

the loss of Mexico but believed that aid and comfort for the discontented portion of her colonists would be found in the sturdy young American republic. Spanish statesmen both abroad and in Mexico, subsequent to the sale to America of Louisiana by Napoleon, were in constant fear of American influence, aggression, and possible conquest. Her representatives in New Mexico were ever watchful and no American was permitted within the Spanish dominions without giving a strict account of his acts and purposes. The report of Governor Alencaster to his superior on the arrest of Lieutenant Zebulon M. Pike peculiarly demonstrates how well posted the New Mexican governor was and how apprehensive the Spaniards were on the subject of possible American aggression. The astuteness of Spanish character is fully revealed in this report.[133]

The independence of Mexico having been achieved, for a number of years commercial, social, and other relations between the two

---

scale and cost the Spanish government ten thousand dollars. Meantime the conspiracy of Burr, of which the Spanish government had, as we have seen, timely advice, became known in the United States, although Pike remained in entire ignorance of the event until he heard of it en route for Chihuahua, at Caracal, on the 27th of March.''

[133] *Santa Fé Archives*, Ms. Translation: ''Report of a Late Occurrence in this Province of New Mexico. On the 15th of February last two Indians of the Ute tribe arrived and brought into my presence an Anglo-American, a young man of genteel appearance whose statement I heard, and even invited him to dine with me, in order to satisfy myself that he was what I supposed him to be as to intelligence and good breeding.

''I did not believe him, and suspecting the truth of his statement as to the nature of his escort, I sent out a small regular detachment and some provincial troops to reconnoitre, who not only fell in with a first lieutenant with six soldiers in an excellent fort built on the Conejos not far from its junction with the Del Norte, two days' journey from the capital of this province towards the same direction, but overcoming the obstacles of deep snows, succeeded in finding the sergeant and corporal belonging to the detachment, making a total of thirteen soldiers, completing the full number, two of them with frozen feet and having lost nearly all their fingers.

''On the 2d of March last, the above-mentioned lieutenant, whose name is Mungo-Meri-Paike, came in with six men of his detachment, and on the 18th the remainder of his men. Without any resistance they acquiesced in the notification made them, that being in my territory it was absolutely necessary that they should appear before me.

''They did so, with their arms, and I assured them that in no respect should they be treated as prisoners, saving only, that in accordance with the orders of the general commanding, it was necessary they should appear before him and fully explain the objects of their mission.

''Paike showed me his instructions from General Wilkinson, his journal, and a rough sketch of a chart of all the rivers and countries he had explored.

''Placing all which papers in a trunk, of which I requested him to retain

republics were cordial. This state of affairs continued until the period covered by the troubles with the province, afterward republic, of Texas. To be sure there was always trouble at the custom-house. The manner in which Texas had achieved its independence and thereafter become one of the states of the American union was a demonstration to the New Mexicans that the onward march of American settlement was a pronounced menace to their own authority. They feared that American influence would finally predominate, and among the officials, civil and military, a strong opposition to the continuance of further commercial relations with the United States became apparent, although among the plain people of the territory the trade with the United States was very popular. The insurrection of 1837 added much to the distrust that was then becoming apparent, for all of the foreigners in Santa Fé and other portions of New Mexico were secretly accused of having been friendly to the movement. The Texas-Santa Fé expedition also served to bring about a wider breach for again it was believed that the traders were privy to the plans of the Texans. The raids by the Texans in 1843, the attack on the village of Mora, and the

---

the key, I delivered the same to the officer commanding the escort — not to be opened save in presence of the aforesaid general commanding.

"From all which circumstances, from what I gathered from Robinson and from the above named officer, I conclude distinctly that the expedition of July was specially designed to conciliate the Indian tribes in behalf of the government of the United States, to make them liberal presents, and drawing them into friendship, treaty, and commerce, to place them under the Anglo-American protection — all this referring specially to the Comanche tribe, the most powerful of our allies.

"Furthermore, that the Anglo-American government considers as included within the boundaries of Louisiana all the rivers that empty into the Mississippi and all of the territories that extend to the headwaters of the Rio Colorado which rise a few leagues from the Pueblo of Taos further to the north in this province; that it is their intention this year or the next to establish forts or settlements on all these rivers, in order to monopolize all the trade and commerce carried on by a large number of tribes in this province.

"The detachment of Anglo-American troops referred to went to Chihuahua to appear before the commanding general, guarded by an escort, being allowed to carry their arms and ammunition on account of the danger of hostile Apaches on the route.

"All of which is submitted to the general commanding, reminding him of the representation made in my communication of the fourth of January last year, concerning the necessity of placing this province on a respectable footing, and of having frontier posts and positions thrown out to oppose the ambitious views of the aforesaid Anglo-American government, exposing also the wretchedly defenseless condition at present existing and so found by whomsoever has been in command.

"Santa Fé, April 1, 1807."

defeat of Armijo's forces on the Arkansas by Colonel Snively, convinced the New Mexican officials that great political changes were within the realm of probability which might result in the acquisition of the territory by the United States. Being convinced that the American government had ulterior designs upon New Mexico, the authorities immediately began to do all in their power to maintain the Mexican position as far north as the Arkansas. A policy of making great concessions of lands to settlers, other than Americans or other foreigners, across the entire northern frontier of New Mexico was initiated. The grants of land later known as the Tierra Amarilla, the Maxwell, the Mora, the St. Vrain, the Nolan, and the Montoya and Anton Chico were made for the purpose of aiding and carrying out this policy. Petitions for lands lying within the districts covered by these immense concessions were made at times by persons of American birth who had become Mexican citizens which were denied by the governor and granting authorities at Santa Fé. A well organized system of espionage was maintained and the presence of strangers on the Arkansas, at Bent's Fort, and in other localities, was immediately reported to the governor at Santa Fé.

The tragedies growing out of the Texas-Santa Fé expedition, largely through the wide circulation of a book published by one of the men [134] who was captured, who was himself not a Texan, created a public opinion in the United States that was unfortunate in the extreme. It was readily foreseen that war with Mexico was likely to break out at any moment. No one understood this better than the authorities at Santa Fé, for it was believed that the American people would invade New Mexican territory at the first opportunity. Indeed, they were right in their apprehensions, as is disclosed by the preparations made at Washington in advance of the breaking out of hostilities on the Rio Grande.[135]

The knowledge gained by the traders of the conditions existing in New Mexico proved of great value to the government of the United States when it was determined to send an army over the

---
[134] Kendall, George W., *Texas-Santa Fé Expedition*, Harper and Brothers, 1844.

[135] Advice given to the president of the United States by Senator Thomas H. Benton in the organization of the Army of the West and Gen. Wool's division.

plains for the conquest of the Internal Provinces. The character and opinions of the people, the routes and distances were well known at Washington.

There also existed in New Mexico a sentiment favorable to a change of sovereignty, and the knowledge which the New Mexicans had acquired relative to the American people, in some quarters, had created a very friendly feeling toward them. The constant trouble with the marauding Indians and the almost total lack of assistance given to the people of New Mexico by the government in controlling these savages made many believe that American sovereignty might be preferable. Their allegiance to Mexico was not overly strong. They were daily witnesses of conditions indicating that the rulers of the country cared more for themselves than they did for the people. This feeling, there is small doubt, the intercourse with the American people arising and growing out of the Santa Fé trade did much to foster and encourage, and when the American army arrived in New Mexico there were many who regarded the coming of the American as best for the interests of the citizens of the territory. Insofar as the native races were concerned, with whom the settlers in New Mexico for over two hundred years had mingled to such an extent as to produce a mixed class in which the Spanish and native blood about equally prevailed, these, notwithstanding their consanguinity, had never become loyal supporters of either the Spanish or the Mexican rulers of the country. The power and influence of the clergy in temporal affairs was everywhere manifest. Together with the officers of the army and a few prominent men they were the ruling power. Although a feeble attempt was made in the days immediately succeeding the inauguration of the republican form of government, by the establishment of the ayuntamientos and the territorial and departmental deputations, and later the assembly, to establish a truly representative government, within a very few years the functions of these bodies practically were nil and the conduct of affairs was either placed in or usurped by the unrestricted will of the governors. Justice was administered on the basis of open and unblushing corruption and money was the most powerful passport to judicial and executive favors.[136]

---
[136] Chittenden, H. M., *History of the American Fur Trade*, vol. ii, p. 486.

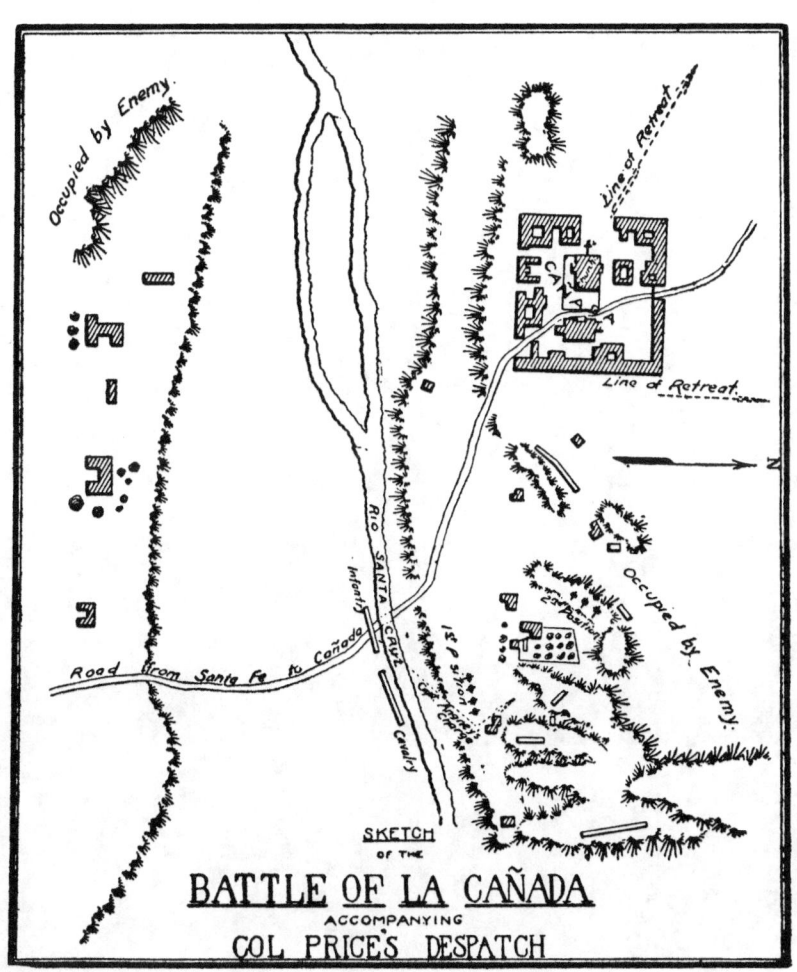

THE WAR WITH MEXICO

On the 24th day of April, 1846, the Mexican general, Arista, informed General Zachary Taylor, in command of American forces on the lower Rio Grande, in Texas, that "he considered hostilities commenced and should prosecute them." On the same day, a party of dragoons, sent out by General Taylor, became engaged with a superior force of the Mexican army in which sixteen Americans were killed and the others captured. On the 13th day of May following, President Polk, by proclamation, announced the existence of war with Mexico. Volunteers were called for by the governors of several of the states and the president asked congress for authority to call for troops and for means to carry on the war.[137]

THE MEXICAN WAR
THE ARMY OF THE WEST

The United States immediately began the formation of plans for the invasion of New Mexico, Chihuahua, and California. An ex-

---

[137] *Letter* of General Zachary Taylor to the adjutant general of the army, *Ex. Doc.* 60, p. 288. *Messages and Papers of the Presidents*, Richardson, vol. iv, p. 442: "As war exists, and, notwithstanding all our efforts to avoid it, exists by the act of Mexico herself, we are called upon by every consideration of duty and patriotism to vindicate with decision the honor, the rights, and the interests of our country." Twitchell, R. E., *The Military Occupation of New Mexico*, p. 36.

My views on the reasons leading up to the war with Mexico are fully given in *The Military Occupation of New Mexico, 1846-1851*. It may be well, however, to remember that there were many things not fully understood at the time nor since, in the matter of justification for the position taken by the United States. The British and Foreign Anti-Slavery Society, "having its seat in London . . . entered with strange eagerness into the cause of Mexico, at an early period, against Texas; they promoted the building and fitting out of Mexican war steamers designed to ravage the coasts of Texas. These war steamers were light-draught vessels built on models furnished by the admiralty; carried each two 68-pound Paixhan pivot guns besides lighter armament; and were commanded by two distinguished British officers — Captains Cleveland and Charlwood, of the Royal Navy — by permission of the admiralty, to serve in the Mexican navy; manned by British seamen, recruited mostly in London and Portsmouth." (*Texas Hist. Series* no. i, Galveston, 1876; *Reminiscences of Texas Republic*, Ashbel Smith, p. 39.)

"Should such an exhibition of British neutrality seem incredible to any one, let him read in McCarthy's *History of Our Own Times* of the building and equipment and manning of the *Alabama*. The stories are almost identical except for change of dates.

"There was plenty of reason for any citizen to believe that the danger of a European government or protectorate of Texas, or California, indeed of both, was so great as to make it necessary in self-defense to undertake the protection of Texas ourselves, and not leave it to another. At any rate the representatives of the people appear to have so believed; the people had pronounced for annexation by the election of Polk; and the nation which for nine years had refused to take Texas into the Union, whose senate, April 22, 1844, had voted by more than a two-thirds majority not to ratify a treaty to

pedition, called the Army of the West, was organized and its command given to Colonel, afterwards Brigadier-General, Stephen W. Kearny.[138] The command consisted of two batteries of artillery, Major Clark; three squadrons of dragoons, Major Sumner; 1st regiment of Missouri cavalry, Colonel Doniphan; and two companies of infantry, Captain Angney. The march across the plains from Fort Leavenworth to Santa Fé was commenced in the latter part of June, 1846. When concentrated upon the Arkansas, near Bent's Fort,[139] the entire command consisted of 1,558 men and sixteen pieces of ordnance. The exact point of concentration is not known, but it is said to have been at a point nearly nine miles below the fort. It was here that the expedition was joined by Francis P. Blair, Jr.,[140] afterwards named by Kearny as district attorney

annex Texas, by May 1, 1846, had learned so much of some new reason, Lord Aberdeen's 'diplomatic act' or something else, that congress passed a joint resolution to annex Texas, with the boundary of the Rio Grande still claimed by her; virtually joining war with Mexico, who had formally declared that such a resolution would be regarded equivalent to a declaration of war.

"There had been plenty of other provocations, motives, causes for war; and, with a patience almost unparalleled in the history of nations, the great republic had forborne to join issue of battle with a weaker neighbor; had refused to extend slave territory; had refused to punish insults to the flag, seizure of ships, murder and robbery of citizens; had refused to collect just and long-past-due claims for spoliations except in courts of arbitration; or to do battle for unsurveyed boundaries. But a French and Mexican empire or a British suzerainty on our immediate borders the United States would not allow. Texas was made a state of the Union, Fremont was ordered to the Pacific, and the war which had been held back for a decade, as too inglorious with a weaker nation, was at last offered unhesitatingly to three powerful nations."— Owen, Charles H., in *Journal of American History*, vol. ii, p. 615.

[138] Stephen Watts Kearny was a student of Columbia college, in the city of New York, in 1812, and would have graduated in the summer of that year. When it became certain that war must ensue between the United States and Great Britain he obtained a commission in the U. S. army; a first lieutenant 13th U. S. Infantry at the age of eighteen. He distinguished himself in the assault on Queenstown Heights, October 13, 1812; captain, April, 1813; brevet major, April, 1823, and major, May, 1829; March 4, 1833, lieutenant-colonel 1st U. S. dragoons, and three years later, 1836, was commissioned colonel of his regiment; June 30, 1846, commissioned brigadier-general and placed in command of the Army of the West; brevetted major general, December, 1846. Died at Vera Cruz, Mexico, October 31, 1848. See Twitchell, R. E., *The Military Occupation of New Mexico*, pp. 203-5.

[139] Four years were required in the construction of this noted frontier post. On the northwest and southwest corners were hexagonal bastions, in which cannon were mounted. The walls of the fort served as walls for the rooms, all of which faced inwardly on a court or patio. The walls were loopholed for musketry, and the entrance was through large wooden gates made of very heavy timbers. William Bent destroyed the fort in 1852.

[140] The ancestors of Francis P. Blair, Jr., came to America from Ireland in 1735. He was born in Lexington, Kentucky, February 19, 1821, and died at

Kiowa Chiefs
Red Moon Powder Face Whirl Wind

for New Mexico. On the 31st day of July, at Bent's Fort, General Kearny issued the following proclamation, which was distributed as the army proceeded: "The undersigned enters New Mexico with a large military force, for the purpose of seeking union with and ameliorating the condition of its inhabitants. This he does under instructions from his government, and with the assurance that he will be amply sustained in the accomplishment of this object. It is enjoined on the citizens of New Mexico to remain quietly at their homes, and pursue their peaceful avocations. So long as they continue in such pursuits, they will not be interfered with by the American army, but will be respected and protected in their rights, both civil and religious. All who take up arms or encourage resistance against the government of the United States will be regarded as enemies, and will be treated accordingly."

At this point Kearny despatched Lieutenant De Courcey, with twenty men, to the Taos valley, for the purpose of ascertaining the disposition of the inhabitants in that portion of New Mexico, with instructions to report to him en route. This officer joined the column August 11th, on the Poñil, a stream in Colfax county, bringing in a number of prisoners who gave exaggerated accounts of the Utes

KEARNY SENDS DETACHMENT TO TAOS VALLEY

St. Louis, Missouri, July 11, 1875. He graduated from Princeton in 1841. He was a law student in the office of Lewis Marshall and began the practice of his profession in St. Louis. He came to the Rocky Mountain region, a health-seeker, in 1845; he joined the Army of the West under Kearny and marched overland to Santa Fé, where he aided Colonel Doniphan, Willard P. Hall, and Dr. David Waldo in the preparation of the code of laws promulgated by Kearny. The latter appointed him United States attorney and in this capacity he drew the indictments for treason found against certain New Mexicans engaged in the revolution of 1846-1847. In 1847 he returned to Missouri, Colonel Sterling Price, then in command at Santa Fé, having abolished the office of United States attorney. During the Civil War, Blair was a strong Union man. Shortly after the battle of Wilson's Creek he was commissioned a major general by President Lincoln; he participated in the Vicksburg campaign in which he commanded the second division of Sherman's corps. He was twice elected to congress. He commanded the 17th army corps and marched with Sherman from Atlanta to the sea. In 1866 he was appointed a commissioner of the Union Pacific Railroad. In 1868 he received the democratic nomination for vice-president. From 1871 to 1873 he was a senator of the United States, having been appointed to the position by the governor of Missouri. He was a man of great courage. On the day of his funeral the city of St. Louis was black with mourning. General Sherman characterized him as "one of the truest of patriots, most honest and honorable of men, and one of the most courageous soldiers this country ever produced."

and other Indians joining the Mexicans in opposing the American advance.

On August 2d, Captain Philip St. George Cooke,[141] of the 1st dragoons, with twelve men, was sent to Santa Fé, nominally as an ambassador, but really for the purpose of escorting James Magoffin, who was the real emissary on the part of the American government, as he was entrusted with a secret mission and having full instructions from the president of the United States.[142]

CAPTAIN COOKE AND JAMES MAGOFFIN GO TO SANTA FÉ

Captain Cooke and his party arrived safely at Santa Fé on the 12th of August where he was hospitably received by General Armijo, the governor of the territory. Armijo had been advised by the alcalde at Las Vegas, Juan de Dios Maes, that Cooke was on his way to Santa Fé, having sent a messenger over the mountains by a short route to the capital. Although Armijo informed Captain Cooke that it was his opinion that "the approach of the

[141] Cooke, Philip St. George, *Conquest of New Mexico*, p. 7: "My mission was in fact a pacific one. The general had just issued a proclamation of annexation of all the territory east of the Rio Grande; the government thus adopting the old claim of Texas and thus manifestly, in a statesman's view, a bloodless process would lead to its confirmation in the treaty of peace; and the population would be saved from the bitterness of passing *sub jugum*. The difficulty of a half measure remains; it cuts the isolated province in two! There must be an influential Micawber in the cabinet. As a plaintiff compliment, that I went to plant the olive, which he would reap a laurel, the general endeavored to gloss the barren field of toil to which his subordinates, at least, were devoted."

[142] Bancroft, H. H., *History of Arizona and New Mexico*, p. 412 and note: "Magoffin or Don Santiago, was an Irish Kentuckian, long in the Santa Fé trade, a man of wealth, with unlimited capacity for drinking wine and making friends, speaking the Spanish language, and on friendly terms with most of the leading men in New Mexico and Chihuahua. At Washington he was introduced by Senator Benton to the president and to the secretary of war, and at the request of the three agreed to accompany the expedition, professing his ability to prevent any armed resistance on the part of Governor Armijo and his officers." In the *Cal. and N. Mex. Mess. and Doc.*, 1850, p. 240-1, are letters of June 18th from Secretary Marcy to General Kearny and to General Wool, introducing Magoffin as a man regarded by the president as one who could render important services. Magoffin was accompanied by a friend, Gonzales, a trader of Chihuahua; and after accomplishing his purpose at Santa Fé, he went south to prepare the way for General Wool as he had done for Kearny. Here, however, he was suspected and kept a prisoner for a long time. After the peace he returned to Washington, where Benton, in a secret session of the senate, obtained for him an appropriation of $50,000 for secret services, of which sum a new administration paid $30,000, a sum barely covering Magoffin's expenses and losses.

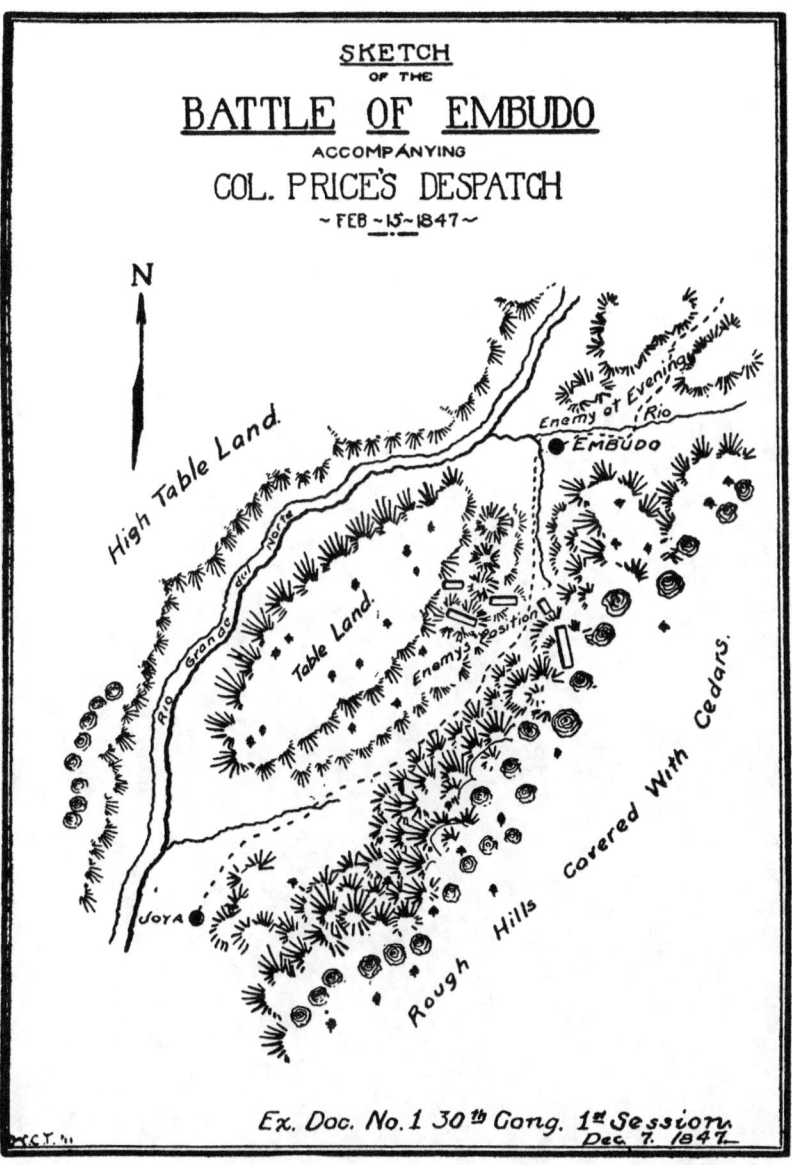

army was rather sudden" he concluded to send a commissioner to General Kearny in the person of Dr. Henry Connelly, with whom on the following day, Captain Cooke set out on his return to meet the army.

If we may predicate our judgment by subsequent events Magoffin proved himself a very astute and convincing emissary. On the 8th of August General Armijo had published and sent into all parts of the territory his proclamation,[143] couched in bombastic terms, calling his people to arms to meet the invader, and still, though the response to this call was very flattering, Armijo, when the crucial moment arrived, deserted his post at Apache Pass and fled to Mexico.

MAGOFFIN'S MISSION IS SUCCESSFUL

---

[143] Prior to the arrival of Cooke and Magoffin, Armijo had been most active in his endeavors to rouse the people. He was much concerned personally, and lost no effort to bring to bear every pressure possible in the raising of a force sufficient to repel the American advance. His proclamation of August 8th was found in the *Vigil Papers,* New Mexico Historical Society Col., Santa Fé, and is as follows:

"The Governor and Commanding General of New Mexico to its Inhabitants:

"Fellow Countrymen:—At last the moment has arrived when our country requires of her children a decision without limit, a sacrifice without reserve, under circumstances which demand everything for our salvation.

"Questions with the United States of America which have been treated in a dignified and decorous manner by the Supreme Government remain undecided, being the unquestionable rights of Mexico over the usurped Territory of Texas, and on this account it has not been possible to maintain diplomatic relations with the Anglo-American government, whose minister extraordinary has not been received. The forces of that government are advancing through this department; they have crossed the northern frontier and are now near the Colorado river.

"Hear, then fellow citizens and countrymen, the signal of alarm which summons us to battle!

"The eagle which made us equal under our national standard, making us all one family, calls upon you to-day, in the name of the Supreme Government and under the chief of this department, to defend the strongest and most sacred of all causes. By your noble efforts and heroic patriotism, you well know how without foreign help, to maintain your national independence. But thanks be to the Almighty, it will not come to pass. The Mexicans of to-day are the same as those of 1810, who, though divided and without a country, subdued the power and lowered the pride of a foreign nation!

"With the army and people united in the defense of our threatened independence, in support of outraged national honor and the rights of our villified country, they form an invincible union.

"Fellow countrymen, aiding the regular army you will strengthen the sentiment of loyalty among the defenders of the nation. Now to the call! Comrades in arms, honestly united, victory shall be ours!

"Remember that the Author and Conserver of society inscribed in the golden book the following truthful words: 'A country divided within itself

The fact that the government at Washington, even to this day, refuses to disclose the contents of the papers filed by Don Santiago Magoffin, in which it is believed that Magoffin "itemized" his expenditures, lends color to the general belief that the same means which had theretofore purchased favors for the Santa Fé traders enabled Magoffin to convince General Armijo that it was best for him that he abandon the idea of making any defense at the Apache Pass, a point on the route to Santa Fé which might have been held by a very few men of spirit and bravery. One hundred men, fairly well armed, behind the entrenchments which Armijo had prepared, with the cannon which he had, could have successfully commanded the pass and compelled the American army to take another course in its march to Santa Fé.

It was not so easy a matter, however, to compromise and conciliate some of the officers of the army, but in this the customary Hibernian wit, coupled with his known plausibility, enabled Magoffin to arrange matters with Archuleta, the second in command. He called this officer's attention to the proclamation of General Kearny in which the general only claimed the territory *east of the Rio Grande*, and suggested to him that by proclamation he might secure for himself all of western New Mexico. By thus appealing to Archuleta's am-

---

shall be destroyed.' Do not permit these words to escape you! Do not permit your personal interests to separate you from the common cause, and, with union, spirit and true patriotism, you may be assured the Mexican Republic will command the respect of its enemies and will demonstrate to the civilized world that she is entitled to be numbered among the free and enlightened nations of the earth!

"We are fortunate in having at the head of the supreme government an illustrious, honorable and patriotic general, who in the past has sustained with dignity and energy the sacred rights of our country; one who will lead us to victory. Let us prepare ourselves for the coming conflict which has been forced upon us. Let us not belittle the power of the enemy nor the character of the obstacles we must surmount!

"The god of war is also the protector of the justice of nations and, with his powerful help, we will add another brilliant page to the history of Mexico, and demonstrate to the world, if possible, for impossibilities are not to be expected, that our beloved country is entitled to be known as a free and independent republic. So far as concerns the defenses of this department on account of this invasion, your governor depends entirely upon your own pecuniary resources, your determination and your convictions, all founded upon reason, justice, equity and public convenience.

"Be assured that your governor is willing and ready to sacrifice his life and all his interests in the defense of his country. This you will see demonstrated by your chief, and friend, my fellow-countrymen.

"MANUEL ARMIJO (Rubric)
"Santa Fé, Saturday, the 8th day of August, 1846."

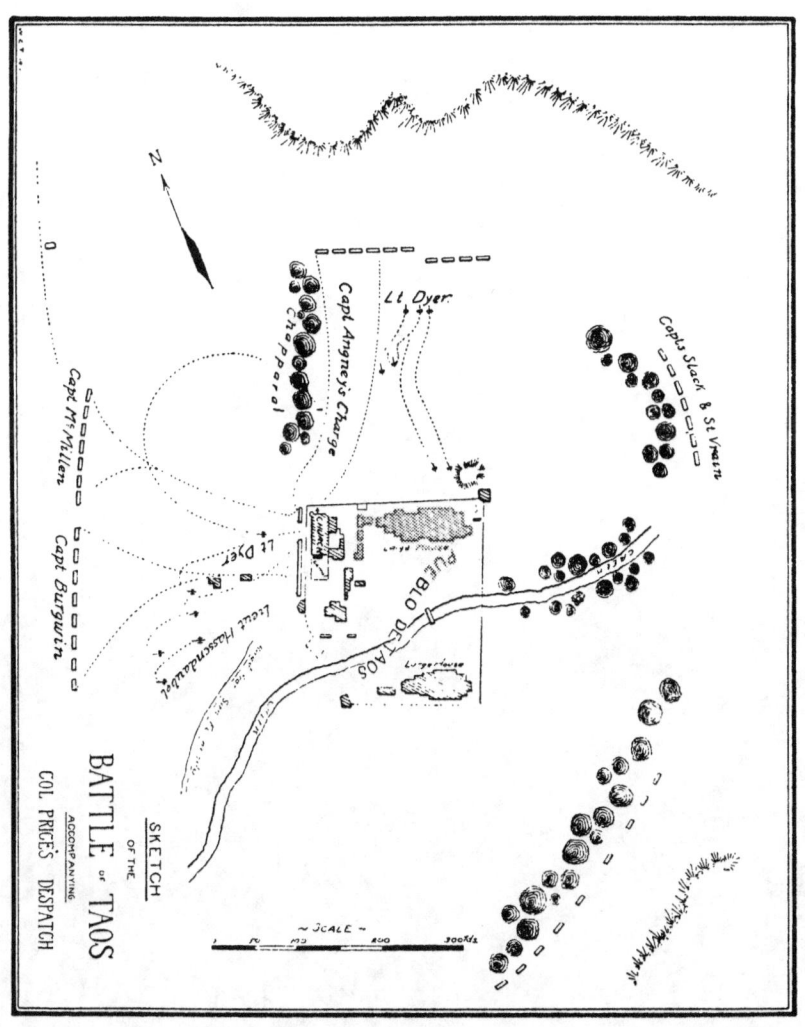

bition, the American "ambassador" succeeded in securing an open road to Santa Fé.[144]

On the 13th of August the army had arrived at the Sapello river, where Kearny was advised that the Mexican forces were assembling at Apache canyon, about fifteen miles from the city of Santa Fé; that the pass was strongly fortified and that Kearny had best go around it by way of Ojo de Vaca and Galisteo. The day following the American general received word from Armijo that he would meet him on the plains near Las Vegas, the message being delivered by an officer of lancers, accompanied by a sergeant and two privates. At this point the army was joined by Major Swords, Lieutenant Gilmer, and Captain Weightman, who brought with him and presented to Kearny his commission as brigadier-general. These officers had heard that a battle was to be fought the following day near Las Vegas and had ridden sixty miles in order to participate in the engagement.

On the morning of the 15th of August, 1846, precisely at eight o'clock, General Kearny and staff galloped into the plaza of Las Vegas, where he was met by the alcalde, Don Juan de Dios Maes, and a concourse of people. Pointing to the top of an adobe building, one story in height, and located on the north side of the plaza, General Kearny suggested to the alcalde that if he would go to the top of the building, he and his staff would follow,

GENERAL KEARNY ENTERS LAS VEGAS AND DELIVERS PROCLAMATION

---

[144] Bancroft, H. H., *History of Arizona and New Mexico*, p. 414: "Unfortunately we have no definite information from New Mexican sources respecting Armijo's preparations, real or pretended, for defense; and the fragmentary rumors that found their way into current narratives are meagre, contradictory and of no value. The governor understood perfectly his inability to make any effective resistance; and all that he did in that direction was with a view merely to 'save his responsibility' as a Mexican officer, even if he did not, as is probable, definitely resolve and promise not to fight. The people were called upon, as usual in such cases, to rise and repel the invader; and a considerable force of the militia was organized and joined the two or three hundred soldiers of the army. These auxiliaries were, however, but half in earnest and most inadequately armed. If any considerable portion of them or their officers ever thought seriously of fighting the Americans, their patriotic zeal rapidly disappeared as the numbers and armament of the invaders became clearly known from returning scouts, who, in many instances, were captured and released by Kearny. With perhaps two thousand men — though American reports double the number — Armijo seems to have marched out to Apache canyon with the avowed purpose of meeting the enemy; but on the last day, in consequence of differences of opinion between the general and his

and from that point, where all could see and hear, he would speak to them, which he did as follows:

"Mr. Alcalde and People of New Mexico: I have come amongst you by the orders of my government, to take possession of your country and extend over it the laws of the United States. We consider it, and have done so for some time, a part of the territory of the United States. We come amongst you as friends, not as enemies; as protectors, not as conquerors. We come among you for your benefit, not for your injury.

"Henceforth I absolve you from all allegiance to the Mexican government, and from all obedience to General Armijo. He is no longer your governor [great sensation in the plaza]; I am your governor. I shall not expect you to take up arms and follow me to fight your own people who may oppose me; but I now tell you, that those who remain peaceably at home, attending to their crops, and their herds, shall be protected by me in their property, their persons and their religion; and not a pepper, not an onion shall be disturbed or taken by my troops without pay, or by the consent of the owner. But listen! He who promises to be quiet and is found in arms against me, I will hang!

"From the Mexican government, you have never received protection. The Apaches and the Navajós come down from the mountains and carry off your sheep, and even your women, whenever they please. My government will correct all this. It will keep off the Indians, protect you in your persons and property; and I repeat, will protect you in your religion. I know you are all great Catholics; that some of your priests have told you all sorts of stories; that we would illtreat your women and brand them on the cheek, as you do your mules on the hip. It is all false. My government respects your religion as much as the Protestant religion and allows each man to worship his Creator as his heart tells him is best. Its laws protect the Catholic as well as the Protestant; the weak as well as the strong, the poor as well as the rich. I am not a Catholic myself; I was not brought up in that faith, but at least one-third of my army are Catholics and I respect a good Catholic as much as a good Protestant.

"There goes my army! You see but a small portion of it; there are many more behind; resistance is useless.

"Mr. Alcalde, and you two captains of militia! The laws of my

officers, the former dismissed the auxiliaries to their homes, and with his presidial troops retreated to the south by way of Galisteo, near which point he left his cannon. Armijo was blamed by the many who were hostile to the invaders and who were ashamed to see their country thus surrendered without a struggle. Doubtless the governor, had he desired it, might have waged a guerilla warfare that would have given the foe much trouble; and there is much cause to believe that his reason for not doing so was not a praiseworthy desire to prevent the useless shedding of his subjects' blood."

country require that all men who hold office under it shall take the oath of allegiance. I do not wish for the present, until affairs become more settled, to disturb your form of government. If you are prepared to take oaths of allegiance, I shall continue you in office and support your authority.''

The captains did not protest but looked with downcast eyes upon the earthen roof upon which they were standing. Noticing his attitude, General Kearny said to one of them, in the hearing of all the people: "Captain, look me in the face, while you repeat the oath of office!" The oath was administered through the interpreter, Robidoux, and the general and his staff descended, mounted, and galloped away to the head of the column.

The sun was shining brightly; for the first time since leaving the Missouri river, the guidons and colors of each squadron, battalion, and regiment were unfurled. The trumpeters sounded "to horse" with spirit and the rocky hills to the west multiplied and re-echoed the call.

Leaving Las Vegas, it was expected that the troops would meet with some opposition at a point a few miles distant, but nothing occurred and the command moved on toward Tecolote where Captain Cooke and Dr. Connelly were met. Here and at the next town, San Miguel del Bado, the general made the same character of address as had been made at Las Vegas.

At every step reports came to the general that Armijo had collected a formidable force and would oppose his passage at Apache canyon. When the command reached the ancient town of Pecos, Kearny was notified by a Mexican coming from the direction of Glorieta that Armijo [145] and his army had ingloriously fled.

---

[145] General Manuel Armijo was not unlike others of his nation and time. He was not to the purple born and was of low extraction. As we have seen he finally managed to obtain foothold in the official circles at Santa Fé and was made collector of customs. Later he became governor, and again, after the assassination of Governor Perez was made governor of the territory. He was essentially a cruel man, not only to foreigners but to his own people. He undoubtedly entertained the same ideas of the American occupation and the causes for the war with Mexico as other state executives and military commanders of the Mexican republic. At the city of Mexico, and in all the newspapers of the republic, great attempts had been made to exasperate the minds of the people against the Americans. The war was represented to be one for national existence and that it was the wish of the United States to destroy the Mexican nation. It was declared to be a war of rapine and plunder, many generals in their proclamations to the people and to the soldiery, declaring that the United States intended to oppress them, to rob their churches, and desecrate

On the morning of the 18th of August Kearny had reached a point twenty-nine miles from Santa Fé. Not a hostile arrow or rifle was now between the Army of the West and the ancient capital of New Mexico. The general determined to make the march in one day and raise the American colors over the ancient palace before sundown. Fifteen miles from Santa Fé the column reached the point deserted by Armijo. It is a gateway, which, in the hands of a competent engineer and one hundred resolute men would have proved a second Thermopylae. As has been said, had the position been defended with spirit and ability, General Kearny would have

---

their altars. General Arimjo knew the falsity of these accusations and the injustice and absurdity of such imputations; nevertheless he used every available means of disseminating these statements throughout New Mexico where they found many believers.

Ruxton, an Englishman, traveling in Mexico the year following the flight of Armijo, on his way from the city of Mexico north, met General Armijo near Durango. In his book, *Adventures in Mexico*, p. 118, Ruxton says: "I stopped and had a long chat with Armijo, who, a mountain of fat, rolled out of his American 'dearborn' and inquired the price of cotton goods in Durango, he having some seven wagon-loads with him, and also what they said in Mexico of the doings in Santa Fé, alluding to its capture by the Americans without any resistance. I told him there was but one opinion respecting it expressed all over the country — that General Armijo and the New Mexicans were a pack of arrant cowards; to which he answered, "Adios, they don't know I had but seventy-five men to fight three thousand. What could I do?"

On the 13th of December, 1853, while the legislative assembly was in session at Santa Fé, Dr. Henry Connelly, a member of the council, who had been a friend of General Armijo for many years prior to the Mexican war, offered the following resolution, which was unanimously adopted, viz: "Resolved, That this Council has heard with profound regret of the death of our distinguished citizen, General Armijo, who expired on the 9th day of this month. Resolved, That this Council offer the most sincere condolence to the family and friends of General Armijo and to the Territory for the loss of one of its greatest benefactors. Resolved, That in respect to the memory and distinguished services of General Armijo this Council now adjourn until 10 o'clock tomorrow." James H. Quinn was the president and Elias T. Clark the secretary of the council at this time.

Bustamante, in *Nuevo Bernal Diaz*, ii., 103-5, gives an account of the flight of Armijo and the causes. It is replete with mis-statements and of no value historically whatever.

The records of the war department fail to reveal any regular report of the occupation of Santa Fé made by General Kearny. A brief statement is found in his letter of August 24th on page 59-60 of Cutts's *The Conquest of California and New Mexico by the Forces of the United States in the years 1846 and 1847*, James Madison Cutts, Phil., 1847. This work gives a résumé of the entire conquest, the earliest published, and contains many original documents which are not found elsewhere. The most complete record of the march to Santa Fé is to be found pp. 15 to 32 of Emory's *Notes of a Military Recconnoisance from Fort Leavenworth in Missouri to San Diego in California*, U. S. Gov. Doc. 30th cong., 1st sess. H. Ex. Doc. 41, Sen. Ex. Doc., 7. This is a diary day by day down to and including Kearny's march to California. The

Gen. "Kit" Carson and Friends, 1865

Standing—Col. E. H. Bergman, Col. C. P. Cleaver, Gen. N. H. Davis, Col. H. M. Enos, Dr. Basil K. Norris, Col. J. C. McFerran. Sitting—Gen. D. H. Rucker, Gen. Christopher Carson, Gen. James H. Carleton

been compelled to turn it by taking the road by way of Ojo de Vaca and Galisteo. On the way to Santa Fé Kearny was met by the acting secretary who brought a letter from Vigil, the lieutenant governor, which informed the general officially of the flight of Armijo and of his readiness to receive him in Santa Fé with the hospitalities of the city.

The advance of the American column arrived in sight of the city of Santa Fé at three o'clock in the afternoon of the 18th of August, 1846; by six o'clock the entire army was at the confines of the capital. The general and his staff, and some other officers of the army, were received at the old palace by Lieutenant-governor Vigil, assisted by about thirty representative citizens of the city. Refreshments were served by Governor Vigil and as the sun sank behind the far-distant Jemez and Valles mountains, painting the clouds which overhung the lofty ranges with a glorious combination of saffron, opal, purple, and golden color, the American flag was hoisted over the ancient palace and a salute of thirteen guns from cannon planted on the eminence, afterwards known as Fort Marcy, declared the conquest of New Mexico complete.

THE AMERICAN ARMY ENTERS SANTA FÉ

On the morning following General Kearny addressed nearly the entire population of Santa Fé, assembled in the plaza for the purpose of hearing him.[146]

---

work by Captain Philip St. George Cooke, *Conquest of New Mexico and California*, p. 34 *et seq.*, gives the march of the Army of the West. In this Cooke says: "I commanded the advance guard and held to the main road, not receiving orders to take the obscure route, known to the general, which turned the position at the canyon. As I passed it, I concluded that important information had been received in the night. So it proved, and I found at the rocky gorge only a rude breastwork of large trees felled across it. It had evidently proved impossible to give coherence to the wretched mass of our opponents who were now for the first time assembled together. They became panic stricken at once on the approach of such an imposing array of horsemen of a superior race, and it appeared, over estimated our numbers, which the reports of ignorance and fear had vastly magnified."

Doniphan's Expedition, by Colonel John T. Hughes, Cincinnati, 1847, is the standard authority as to the events occurring during the conquest of New Mexico. There is a reprint of this work contained in Connelley's *War with Mexico, 1846-1847 — Doniphan's Expedition and the Conquest of New Mexico and California*, Bryant and Douglas, Kansas City, Mo., 1907. See also *The Military Occupation of New Mexico, 1846-1851*, R. E. Twitchell, Denver, 1909, which contains many valuable biographies of persons prominent during that period.

[146] General Kearny's address was as follows:

"New Mexicans: We have come amongst you to take possession of New

Immediately after Kearny had concluded his address, a response was made by Don Juan Bautista Vigil y Alarid, which is fairly expressive of the opinions entertained by a large number of the representative citizens of the territory. Mr. Vigil said:

"General: The address which you have just delivered, in which you announce that you have taken possession of this great country in the name of the United States of America, gives us some idea of the wonderful future that awaits us. It is not for us to determine the boundaries of nations. The cabinets of Mexico and Washington will arrange these differences. It is for us to obey and respect the established authorities, no matter what may be our private opinions. The inhabitants of this department humbly and honorably present their loyalty and allegiance to the government of North America. No one in this world can successfully resist the power of him who is stronger.

"Do not find it strange if there has been no manifestation of joy and enthusiasm in seeing this city occupied by your military forces. To us the power of the Mexican republic is dead. No matter what her condition, she was our mother. What child will not shed abundant tears at the tomb of his parents? I might indicate some of the causes for her misfortunes, but domestic troubles should not be made public. It is sufficient to say that civil war is the cursed source of

---

Mexico, which we do in the name of the government of the United States. We have come with peaceable intentions and kind feelings toward you all. We come as friends, to better your condition and make you a part of the republic of the United States. We mean not to murder you or rob you of your property. Your families shall be free from molestation; your women secure from violence. My soldiers shall take nothing from you but what they pay for. In taking possession of New Mexico, we do not mean to take away from you your religion. Religion and government have no connection in our country. There, all religions are equal; one has no preference over the other; the Catholic and the Protestant are esteemed alike. Every man has a right to serve God according to his heart. When a man dies he must render to God an account of his acts here on earth, whether they be good or bad. In our government, all men are equal. We esteem the most peaceable man, the best man. I advise you to attend to your domestic pursuits, cultivate industry, be peaceable and obedient to the laws. Do not resort to violent means to correct abuses. I do hereby proclaim that being in possession of Santa Fé, I am therefore virtually in possession of all New Mexico. Armijo is no longer your governor. His power is departed; but he will return and be as one of you. When he shall return you are not to molest him. You are no longer Mexican subjects; you are now become American citizens, subject only to the laws of the United States. A change of government has taken place in New Mexico and you no longer owe allegiance to the Mexican government. I do hereby proclaim my intention to establish in this department a civil government, on a republican basis, similar to those of our own states. It is my intention, also, to continue in office those by whom you have been governed, except the governor, and such other persons as I shall appoint to office by virtue of the authority vested in me. I am your governor — henceforth look to me for protection."

THE WAR WITH MEXICO 211

that deadly poison which has spread over one of the grandest and greatest countries that has ever been created. To-day we belong to a great and powerful nation. Its flag, with its stars and stripes, covers the horizon of New Mexico, and its brilliant light shall grow like good seed well cultivated. We are cognizant of your kindness, of your courtesy and that of your accommodating officers and of the strict discipline of your troops; we know that we belong to the republic that owes its origin to the immortal Washington, whom all civilized nations admire and respect. How different would be our situation had we been invaded by European nations! We are aware of the unfortunate condition of the Poles.

"In the name then, of the entire Department, I swear obedience to the Northern Republic and I render my respect to its laws and authority.

"JUAN BAUTISTA VIGIL y ALARID (Rubric)
" Governor.
"Santa Fé, August 19, 1846." [147]

Three days after the conclusion of these ceremonies General Kearny published an official proclamation which is given in the notes.[148]

---

[147] *Vigil Papers*, Ms. New Mexico Historical Society, Santa Fé.

[148] *Ibid.*, New Mexico Historical Society: ''Proclamation! As by the act of the Republic of Mexico, a state of war exists between that government and the United States; and as the undersigned, at the head of his troops, on the 18th instant, took possession of Santa Fé, the capital of the department of New Mexico, he now announces his intention to hold the department, with its original boundaries (on both sides of the Del Norte) as a part of the United States, under the name of the Territory of New Mexico.

''The undersigned has come to New Mexico with a strong military force, and an equally strong one is following him in the rear. He has more troops than is necessary to put down any opposition that can possibly be brought against him, and therefore it would be but folly or madness for any dissatisfied or discontented persons to think of resisting him.

''The undersigned has instructions from his government to respect the religious institutions of New Mexico, to protect the property of the Church, to cause the worship of those belonging to it to be undisturbed, and their religious rights in the amplest manner preserved to them; also to protect the persons and property of all quiet and peaceable inhabitants within its boundaries against their enemies the Eutaws, the Navajós and others; and when he assures all that it will be his pleasure, as well as his duty, to comply with those instructions, he calls upon them to exert themselves in preserving order, in promoting concord, and in maintaining the authority and efficacy of the laws. And he requires of those who have left their homes and taken up arms against the troops of the United States, to return forthwith to them, or else they will be considered as enemies and traitors, subjecting their persons to punishment and their property to seizure and confiscation for the benefit of the public treasury.

''It is the wish and the intention of the United States to provide for New Mexico a free government, with the least possible delay, similar to those in the United States; and the people of New Mexico will then be called on to

Meanwhile Kearny had been visited by the chiefs of several Pueblo tribes, who gave in their submission and expressed great satisfaction over the arrival of the American forces. At the interview they stated that it had been a tradition with them that the white man would come from the far east and release them from the bonds and shackles which had been imposed upon them by the Spaniards.[149] The same night a message was received from General Armijo, asking on what terms he would be received, but this proved to be only a ruse on his part to gain time in his flight to Chihuahua. A flagstaff was erected in the plaza. A site for a fort was selected, plans drawn up by Captain Emory, and in a short time work was begun on Fort Marcy, which was built of adobe and was constructed by the volunteer soldiery. On the 24th General Kearny reported to Washington that the "people of the Territory are now perfectly tranquil

---

exercise the rights of freemen in electing their own representatives to the territorial legislature. But, until this can be done, the laws hitherto in force will be continued until changed or modified by competent authority; and those persons holding office will continue in the same for the present, providing they will consider themselves good citizens and are willing to take the oath of allegiance to the United States.

"The United States hereby absolves all persons residing within the boundaries of New Mexico from any further allegiance to the Republic of Mexico, and hereby proclaims them citizens of the United States. Those who remain quiet and peaceable will be considered good citizens and receive protection — those who are found in arms, or instigating others against the United States, will be considered traitors and treated accordingly.

"Don Manuel Armijo, the late governor of this department, has fled from it; the undersigned has taken possession of it without firing a gun, or spilling a single drop of blood, in which he most truly rejoices, and for the present will be considered as governor of the Territory.

"Given at Santa Fé, the capital of the Territory of New Mexico, this 22nd day of August, 1846, and in the 71st year of the independence of the United States.

"S. W. KEARNY,
"By the Governor: "Brig. Gen. U. S. A.
"JUAN BAUTISTA VIGIL y ALARID."

[149] Emory, W. H., *Notes of a Military Reconnoissance*, etc., p. 6: "For several days representatives of the Indians of other pueblos, as well as chiefs from the Utes, Navajós and Apaches came to Santa Fé to see General Kearny. Many of the lower classes of the Mexican population, who had been led to believe that the terrible 'Americanos' intended to rob, pillage and murder, and a large number of the higher class who had left the city of Santa Fé, fearing the insults of a lawless soldiery, now returned to their farms and homes. General Kearny's speech and the proclamation seems to have allayed the fears of the people and restored confidence in all except a few malcontents and revolutionists who considered that they had been deceived into surrendering on the pretext that Kearny only proposed to claim and take possession of that part of New Mexico lying *east of the Rio Grande.*"

and can easily be kept so. The intelligent portion know the advantages they are to derive from the change of government and express their satisfaction at it." On the 27th General Kearny gave a grand ball to the officers [150] and citizens. Rumors of the approach of a hostile force from Chihuahua determined Kearny to march down the valley of the Rio Grande, which he did with nearly half his force, going as far as Tomé, but no opposition was encountered of any kind and on the 7th of September Kearny returned to Santa Fé, reporting that the "inhabitants of the country were found to be highly satisfied and contented with the change of government, and apparently

---

[150] There were five companies of the 1st U. S. dragoons, whose officers were Captains Edwin V. Sumner (acting major), Philip St. George Cooke, Thomas Swords (Asst. Q. M.), Benj. D. Moore, John H. K. Burgwin, Henry S. Turner (Adj. Gen.), Abraham R. Johnston, and Philip R. Thompson. The lieutenants were Patrick Noble, Thomas C. Hammond, Rufus Ingalls, John W. Davidson, Joseph McElvain, C. J. L. Wilson, and Oliver P. H. Taylor.

Colonel Alexander W. Doniphan was in command of the 1st Missouri volunteers; lieutenant-colonel, C. F. Ruff; William Gilpin, major; the captains were Waldo, Walton, Moss, Reid, Stephenson, Parsons, Jackson, and Rodgers; sutler, C. A. Perry; adjutant, G. M. Butler; surgeon, Geo. Penn; assistant surgeons, T. M. Morton and I. Vaughn.

In *Doniphan's Expedition*, by W. E. Connelley, is found a complete roster of this regiment and other troops serving in New Mexico at this period.

A battalion of light artillery, under Major Clark, consisted of two companies from St. Louis, under captains Weightman and Fischer, about 250 men. A battalion of infantry had 145 men in two companies, commanded by Captains Angney and Murphy. There was also a troop of volunteer cavalry from St. Louis called the "Laclede Rangers," 107 strong, under Captain Hudson; this troop was attached to the U. S. Dragoons.

Lieut. W. H. Emory, Lieut. W. H. Warner, Lieut. J. W. Abert and Lieut. W. B. Peck of the U. S. topographical engineer corps were with the expedition.

Connelley, in his *Doniphan's Expedition*, gives the following as officers in addition to those above mentioned: L. C. Garnier and C. Kribbin, lieutenants, Captain Fischer's company of artillery; Captain Weightman's company, Lieutenants Andrew J. Dorn, Edmond F. Chouteau, John O. Simpson, and John R. Gratiot; Captain Murphy's company, Lieutenants Geo. R. Gibson and Jno. W. Gibbons; Captain Angney's company, Lieutenants L. J. Eastin and Charles R. Moller; Captain Hudson's company (Laclede Rangers), Lieutenants R. S. Elliott, L. T. Lebaurne, Henry D. Evans; Captain Rodgers's company, Lieutenants John B. Duncan, Crockett Harrison, and Benj. F. Murray; Captain Hughes's company, Lieutenants John Hinton and Nicolas B. Wright. Congreve Jackson was also captain of this company, which was 'G' and came from Howard county, Missouri. Captain Stephenson's company, Lieutenants F. G. McDonald, Scott Richardson, and John Campbell; Captain Reid's company, Lieutenants, C. I. Miller, F. A. Boush, and W. P. Hicklin; Captain Moss's company, Lieutenants L. B. Sublette, J. H. Moss, and Henry T. Ogden; Captain Walton's company, Lieutenants James Lea, R. I. Barnett, D. B. Graves; Captain Waldo's company, Lieutenants John Reid, D. I. Clayton, H. I. Chiles.

vied with each other to see who could show us the greatest hospitality and kindness. There can no longer be apprehended any organized resistance in this Territory to our troops."

Upon his return from the South General Kearny sent a detachment of troops under Major Gilpin and Lieutenant-Colonel Congreve Jackson, now the successor of Lieutenant-Colonel Ruff,[151] elected by the volunteers, who was afterward given a commission in the regular army, to Abiquiú and Cebolleta on the Navajó frontier.[152] Meanwhile a plan of civil government had been arranged and was announced on the 22d of September whereby Charles Bent was appointed governor, Donaciano Vigil, secretary, Richard Dallam, marshal, Francis P. Blair Jr., United States attorney, Charles Blumner, treasurer, Eugene Leitensdorfer, auditor, and Joab Houghton, Antonio José Otero, and Charles Beaubien, judges of the superior court. A code of laws was promulgated.[153] On the 24th, general orders were issued designating the force to accompany Kearny to California, three hundred men of the U. S. 1st dragoons, Major Sumner, and the Mormon Battalion,[154] five hundred in number, under Captain Cooke.

KEARNY NAMES OFFICERS FOR CIVIL GOVERNMENT, PROMULGATES CODE OF LAWS, AND LEAVES FOR CALIFORNIA

---

[151] Colonel Ruff was very much disliked by the volunteers, owing to his being a strict disciplinarian. Hughes says of him: "Colonel Ruff, though ill qualified to govern volunteer troops, has some experience in military affairs, is well acquainted with tactics, and neither to 'extenuate nor aught set down in malice,' is certainly a brave man and a good soldier." Colonel Ruff distinguished himself under General Winfield S. Scott, later on, in Mexico.

[152] For a full account of this expedition see *Doniphan's Expedition*, by W. E. Connelley, p. 268.

[153] Relative to the *Kearny Code*, in his letter to Adjutant General Jones, General Kearny says: "I take great pleasure in stating that I am entirely indebted for these laws to Colonel A. W. Doniphan, of the 1st Regiment of Missouri mounted volunteers, who received much assistance from private Willard P. Hall of his regiment. These laws are taken, part from the laws of Mexico, retained as in the original — a part with such modifications as our laws and constitution made necessary; a part are from the laws of Missouri Territory; a part from the laws of Texas and Coahuila; a part from the statutes of Missouri; and the remainder from the Livingston Code; the organic law is taken from the organic law of Missouri Territory."

[154] The Mormon Battalion consisted of about 500 Mormons, who entered the service as a means of reaching California, where, according to the terms of their enlistment, they were to be discharged. For a full history of this organization, see Tyler's *Mormon Battalion*.

THE WAR WITH MEXICO 215

On the 25th Kearny [155] left Santa Fé, reached Alburquerque on the 29th, thence down the Rio Grande, across the *Jornada del Muerto*, thence by the Mimbres valley, across the range to the Gila, and westward to the Pacific Coast, reaching San Diego in December. Kearny left orders that Doniphan's regiment, on the arrival of the 2d Missouri volunteers, Colonel Sterling Price, should march south to join General Wool at Chihuahua.

On the 5th of October Kearny met an express sent by Commodore Stockton and Lieutenant-Colonel Fremont, who reported that they

---

[155] On the 24th, Kearny wrote the adjutant general of the army as follows:
"Head. Qr. Army of the West, Santa Fé, New Mexico, Sept. 24, '46.

"Sir: Having finished all my public business in this place, having organized a civil government for the Tery. by appointing the officers & causing a set of laws to be prepared & published for it, & having made the necessary Military arrangements for maintaining the perfect order, peace & quiet, now so happily existing, I intend in compliance with the instructions from the War Dept to leave here tomorrow with Major Sumner & his 300 Dragoons for Upper California, as I informed you in my letter of the 16th Inst — I leave orders for Capt Allen & his (Infy) command of Mormons to follow our trail, as soon as they reach here, & they will be accompanied from here by about 80 Mounted Vols. under Captain Hudson — I send to you copies of all orders which have been issued by my directions, which may explain some subjects omitted in my letters — On the 20th Inst I received a letter from Col Price dated the 10th & 12 miles west of the crossing of the Arkansas — He had with him 4 cos of his Regt 2 had proceeded up the Arkansas towards Bent's Fort, & the remaining 2 were several days march in his Rear. This is the only information Public or Private received by his express to me, and I was indebted for this to his being in want of provisions, for which he asked, & which I ordered forthwith to be returned to him from a train coming from Bents Fort. We are very much behind the times in the way of information which causes some inconvenience here & may give more to others & to your office in Washington. We have not even received the promotions and Appointments made in July, & know not who are the Field officers of the 1st or 2nd Dragoons — I leave directions for Col Price to remain in command of the Troops in this Tery. He will have his own Regt of Mounted Vols. — a Batallion of 2 Cos. of Infy. under Captain Angney, & a Battn. of 2 Cos. of Horse Arty. & a part of Captain Hudson's Co. of Laclede Rangers under Major Clarke.— These will be more than sufficient to preserve quiet thro-out the Tery. & to protect the inhabitants from the Navajo, Eutaw and Apache Indians, who have hitherto caused them so much trouble by killing their people & stealing their flocks & cattle — Deputations from the last two Nations have at my request been in to see me & promise good conduct in future — I hope to see in a few days a deputation from the Navajoes — In my letter to you of the 1st Inst, I stated my intention of raising an Infy. Compy. from the Mexican population — The plan has been abandoned as unnecessary at this time — It may answer a good purpose next year — On the arrival of Col. Price's Regt. here, Col Doniphan with his Regt will proceed to Chihuahua & report to Brig. Genl. Wool (as will other troops if any more should come here from Missouri) as I informed you in my letter of the 24th ulto — Finding that horses cannot be of service in this country & that they could not possibly travel to California, I have directed the Qr. Mr. to Mount the 1st Dragoons on Mules & send the Dragoon horses back to Fort Leav-h, where they can be

were already in possession of the Californias and that the war was ended in that quarter. Having received this intelligence he directed Major Sumner to return with two hundred of the dragoons, reserving the remainder as an escort for himself.

The fruits of this great expedition, coupled with the great successes of the naval and military forces of the United States operating simultaneously on the coast of California, time has shown to have been of inestimable value to our country. New Mexico and California, conquered but afterward ceded by Mexico to the United States, an area of territory embracing nearly ten degrees of latitude, lying adjacent to Oregon and extending from the Pacific Coast to the Rio Bravo, gave an empire to the United States, and its acquisition was second only in importance to the purchase from Napoleon, of Louisiana, in 1803. Gold had not been discovered in

---

rendered servicable — We will all use our exertions to reach Monterey as early as possible, from whence I hope to report to you by the 10th Dec. or before — I hope to hear from you at that place.

"Brig Genl. U. S. A.   Very Resp-y Yr. ob Servt.
"Adjt Genl. U. S. A.   S. W. KEARNY
"W—n.   Brig. Genl U. S. A.

"Francisco Sarracino (Pajarito) is hereby appointed prefect of the district of the southwest in place of Francisco Armijo y Ortiz, this day removed. Miguel Romero is hereby appointed alcalde at the Placeres, in place of Julian Tenorio, this day removed.

"S. W. KEARNY,
"Brig. Gen. U. S. A.

"Santa Fé, N. M., Sept. 22, 1846.

"Order of General Kearny Regulating Licenses for Stores, Duties on wagons, etc.

"The following sums will be collected in place of those established April 11, 1844:—

License for dry goods store, per month,	$2.00
Do grocery store	$4.00
do taverns	$5.00
do Public billiard tables	$3.00
do Monte table, chuza or game of chance, per night,	$1.50
do ball, where money is charged for attending	$2.00

"Licenses for above must be obtained and paid for in advance; if not, then five times the foregoing sums to be charged and the individuals confined until the amount is paid. Wagons from the Arkansas or Chihuahua, with goods belonging to individuals and not public ones, each — $4.00. Pleasure carriages from the above places, each — $2.00. Wagons or carriages belonging to individuals, entering the public plaza — $.25. The above sums will be collected by the collector of Santa Fé, and turned over to the treasurer of the city for the benefit thereof; the treasurer and collector keeping correct account of all sums received, and for which they will be held strictly responsible. The collector of Galisteo will collect the same amount for each wagon or carriage as above; both to take effect from the 22nd, the day of New Mexico becoming a part of the U. S."

Missionary Bishops of the Protestant Episcopal Church
1. Rt. Rev. William F. Adams. 2. Rt. Rev. James C. Talbott. 3. Rt. Rev. George K. Dunlop. 4. Rt. Rev. John Mills Kendrick

THE WAR WITH MEXICO

California; the great copper mines of Arizona and New Mexico had not been dreamed of by men of Anglo-American blood, and the immense agricultural and horticultural resources of the golden state, not to mention those of New Mexico and Arizona, had not been given the slightest thought by the statesmen of that day. The possession of the ports of San Diego, Monterey, and San Francisco immediately enabled the United States to command the commerce of the Pacific Coast, and at that time, in the whaling business alone, the capital invested exceeded forty millions of dollars. Today the assessed valuation of property in some of the cities in California exceeds by many millions of dollars the entire cost of the war with Mexico; a single copper mine in Arizona has produced copper bullion of greater value in dollars than the total amount of the national debt of our country after our war with Mexico had been concluded, and the value of the coal and coke already produced in New Mexico and Colorado exceeds the cost of all that portion of the United States embraced within the Louisiana purchase and the territory acquired by the annexation of the republic of Texas, as well as that secured under the terms of the treaty of Guadalupe Hidalgo.

Colonel Sterling Price with his regiment of Missouri volunteers arrived at Santa Fé about ten days after the departure of Kearny.

COLONEL STERLING PRICE ARRIVES AT SANTA FÉ

On the 9th and 12th of October, in two divisions, came the Mormon Battalion, which later moved on to California.

While on the march to the south Kearny sent back orders to Santa Fé to Colonel Doniphan to undertake a campaign against the Navajós before proceeding to Chihuahua. Doniphan and his regiment left Santa Fé on the 26th of October, and from Alburquerque he sent a portion of his troops down the valley as far as Valverde for the protection of a caravan of traders. With a small party he then went to Cubero, to which place Colonel Jackson had moved his force from Cebolleta. Here he received a despatch from Major Gilpin, at that time on the San Juan river in the Navajó country, to whom he sent word to assemble all the Navajós possible at the Bear Spring—Ojo del Oso. Doniphan and Jackson now left Cebolleta and marched to the headwaters of the Rio Puerco, thence northwestward and joined Gilpin on October 21st. Here they met the chiefs of the Navajós, who professed friendship and admiration for the Americans, but giving expression to their detestation for the Mexicans and their inability to understand why the Americans were opposed to their carrying on the usual warfare against them. A treaty was finally signed on the 22d of November by Doniphan, Jackson, and Gilpin and fourteen Navajó chiefs. Doniphan returned by way of the pueblo of Zuñi and joined his command at Valverde about the 12th of December.[156]

Colonel Doniphan now ordered the march to Chihuahua. The advance of the army was under Major Gilpin who with his command moved down the left bank of the Rio Grande. Lieutenant-Colonel Congreve Jackson followed on the 16th, with another detachment.[157]

COLONEL DONIPHAN MARCHES TO CHIHUAHUA

During the time when Doniphan was in the Navajó country, Colonel Price, commanding at Santa Fé, had dispatched Lieutenant-

---

[156] For a full account of this treaty see *Doniphan's Expedition* by W. E. Connelley, p. 286.

Bancroft, H. H., *History of Arizona and New Mexico*, p. 421: "In September, Lieutenant-Colonel Jackson with three companies had been sent to Cebolleta on the frontier; and from this point apparently before Kearny's last orders were known, Captain John W. Reid, with thirty volunteers and a chief called Sandoval as guide, starting the 20th of October, had in twenty days made a somewhat remarkable entry far to the west and north into the heart of the Navajó country." For a full account of this march by Reid, see *The Military Occupation of New Mexico, 1846-1851*; by R. E. Twitchell, pp. 98-99.

[157] Ruxton, Geo. F., *Adventures in Mexico*, p. 177. Mr. Ruxton, an Englishman, traveling through the country at the time the American army and the caravan of traders were camped at Valverde, says: "Among the trees and open spaces were drawn up the wagons, formed into a corral or square, and close together, so that the whole made a most formidable fort, and, when filled with some hundred rifles, could defy the attacks of Indians or Mexicans. Scattered about were tents and shanties of logs and branches of every conceivable form, round which lounged wild-looking Missourians, some cooking at the camp-fires, some cleaning their rifles or firing at targets — blazes cut in the trees, with a bull's eye made from wet powder on the white bark. From morning till night the camp resounded with the popping rifles, firing at marks for prizes of tobacco, or at any living creature which presented itself. The oxen, horses, and mules were sent out at daylight to pasture on the grass of the prairie, and at sunset made their appearance, driven in by the Mexican herders, and were secured for the night in the corrals. My own animals roamed at will, but at every evening came to the river to drink, and made their way to my camp, where they would frequently stay round the fire all night. . . . Colonel Doniphan, who commanded, had just returned from an expedition into the Navajó country for the purpose of making a treaty with the chiefs of that nation, who have hitherto been bitter enemies of the New Mexicans. From appearances no one would have imagined this to be a military camp. The tents were in line, but there all uniformity ceased. There were no regulations in force with regard to cleanliness. The camp was strewn with the bones and offal of the cattle slaughtered for its supply, and not the slightest attention

Colonel Mitchell, with an escort of ninety-five men, selected from his regiment and from the battalion of Missouri volunteer artillery, under Major Clark, to open a communication with General Wool, who was supposed to have already reached Chihuahua. The detachment left Santa Fé on the 1st of December and came up with Colonel Doniphan at Valverde on the 17th. On the following day they proceeded in company with him, and the remainder of the 1st Missouri, upon the route already taken by Gilpin and Jackson. Before leaving Valverde, Colonel Doniphan was informed that the Mexicans were collecting a force at Paso del Norte, to intercept his march, and an order was therefore sent to Major Clarke, of the artillery battalion at Santa Fé, to join him at the earliest moment with one hundred men and a battery of four six-pounders and two twelve-pounder howitzers. These howitzers had been constructed expressly for field service.

A few miles south of Fray Cristobal, the road to Chihuahua, instead of following the windings of the Rio Grande, pursues a direct course over a dry plain, the *Jornada del Muerto*, completely destitute of water at that time. In its progress from the Missouri river the army had passed over some similar tracts but none so extensive, and though the command was poorly provided with food or clothing for this journey, every privation and hardship was endured without a murmur.

The army having crossed the desert followed down the valley of the Rio Grande to the neighborhood of the present town of Doña Ana where intelligence was received that
THE BATTLE OF BRAZITO seven hundred Mexican troops and six pieces of artillery had arrived at El Paso. The column moved forward presenting a very picturesque appearance;

was paid to keeping it clear from other accumulations of filth. The men, unwashed and unshaven, were ragged and dirty, without uniforms and dressed as and how they pleased. They wandered about, listless and sickly looking, or were sitting in groups playing at cards, and swearing and cursing even at the officers if they interfered to stop it (as I witnessed). The greatest irregularities constantly took place. Sentries, or a guard, although in an enemy's country, were voted unnecessary; and one fine day, during the time I was there, three Navajó Indians ran off with a flock of 800 sheep belonging to the camp, and killing the two volunteers in charge of them, and reaching the mountains in safety with their booty. Their mules and horses were straying over the country; in fact, the most total want of discipline was apparent in everything. These very men, however, were as full of fight as game-cocks, and shortly after defeated four times their number of Mexicans at Sacramento, near Chihuahua.''

the soldiers armed and mounted, and the white wagon sheets of the traders' wagons gleaming brightly in the sunlight.

About three o'clock in the afternoon of Christmas day, Colonel Doniphan had halted, with the advance of five hundred men, on an arm of the Rio Grande, known as the Brazito, for the purpose of making camp; the horses were unsaddled and sent some distance from the camp to graze, and the men were busily engaged in bringing wood and water. While thus employed a heavy cloud of dust was suddenly discovered rolling up from the south, and in a moment after, the advance guard descried the enemy approaching in force. Lieutenant-Colonel Jackson was several miles in the rear at Doña Ana, with the remainder of the troops. The rally was instantly sounded, the men being formed in open order on foot as skirmishers, throwing the extreme points of the two wings towards the river to protect the flanks and the baggage. The enemy halted within half a mile and formed in line of battle, the Vera Cruz lancers on the right, the Chihuahua battalion on the left, and the infantry and El Paso militia, with a two-pounder howitzer, in the center. The Mexican cavalry were gayly decorated with bright scarlet coats and white belts, with shining brass helmets and dark waving plumes, and their polished sabres and escopetas, and their long lances, ornamented with pennons of red and green, glistened in the rays of the evening sun. Just as the Americans were forming, a Mexican officer, bearing a black flag, rode up to their line, and demanded that the commander should accompany him to confer with the officer in command of the enemy. Notwithstanding his declaration, that the penalty of a non-compliance with the demand would be a charge, without quarter, he received a peremptory refusal, and returned to those who sent him.[158]

Upon his return the enemy advanced to the charge, opening a simultaneous fire from his entire line. When within rifle-shot the Mexicans attempted to file to the right and left, and pass the flanks

---

[158] Connelley, W. E., *Doniphan's Expedition*, p. 375, note 93: "The black flag carried by the Mexicans was afterward picked up on the battle-field of Sacramento. It came into the possession of Major Merriwether Lewis Clark, of the artillery, and was by him brought back to St. Louis. It now belongs to his nephew, Major William Clark Kennerly, who has lent it to the Missouri Historical Society, St. Louis, in the library of which institution it is carefully preserved. It is a small black flag, on one side of which, in white, are painted two skulls, with cross-bones below each. On the other side is the following inscription: *Libertad ó Muerto.*"

of the opposing force. Doniphan's men had so far reserved their fire, but they now opened upon the enemy from right to left, with such spirit and effect that they were immediately thrown into confusion. Captain Reid had succeeded in mounting about twenty men, and as the lancers were rallied to the charge on the American left, he fell furiously upon them with his small force, and after a desperate contest, lasting about twenty minutes, succeeded in putting them to flight. As the enemy's infantry gave way, Lieutenant Wright charged upon them with his company, and captured the howitzer. This completed the overthrow of the enemy who fled in all directions toward the south.[159]

By this defeat the Mexican army was completely disorganized and dispersed. The American loss was none killed and eight wounded.

DONIPHAN LEAVES FOR EL PASO — THE BATTLE OF SACRAMENTO

It was the only battle fought by Doniphan's command on what is today American soil.

On the 28th of December Doniphan occupied El Paso, which surrendered without a struggle. Here he remained about six weeks awaiting the arrival of the artillery from Santa Fé under Major Clark and Captain Weightman. These arrived on the 1st of February, 1847, and consisted of 117 men and six pieces of cannon. On the 8th the army began its advance upon the city of Chihuahua. The capture of this city had been deemed of the greatest importance, so much so that General Wool with

---

[159] Connelley, W. E., *Doniphan's Expedition*, pp. 374-375: "The Chihuahua infantry and cavalry were posted on their left, and consequently operated against our right wing. They advanced within gun-shot, and took shelter in the chapparal, discharging three full rounds upon our line before we returned the fire. At this crisis, Colonel Doniphan ordered the men to '*lie down on their faces, and reserve their fire until the Mexicans came within sixty paces.*' This was done. The Mexicans supposing they had wrought fearful execution in our ranks, as some were falling down, while others stood up, began now to advance, and exultingly cry out '*bueno, bueno,*' whereupon our whole right wing, suddenly rising up, let fly such a galling volley of yager balls in their ranks, that they wheeled about and fled in the utmost confusion. By this time the Howard company, and others occupying the center, had repulsed the enemy with considerable loss, and taken possession of one piece of his artillery, and corresponding ammunition. This was a brass six-pound howitzer. Sergeant Calloway, and a few others of that company, first gained possession of this piece of cannon, cut the dead mules loose from it, and were preparing to turn it upon the enemy, when Lt. Kribben, with a file of artillery-men, was ordered to man it.

"The consternation now became general among the ranks of the Mexicans, and they commenced a precipitate retreat along the base of the mountains. Many of them took refuge in the craggy fastnesses. They were pursued by the Americans about one mile; Captain Reid, and Captain Walton, who by this

3,500 men and a heavy park of artillery had been directed thither for its subjugation. On the 28th, near the city of Chihuahua, the American army came in sight of the enemy at a place called Sacramento. All day long an immense eagle, sometimes soaring aloft and again sweeping down amongst the fluttering banners, followed the line of march and seemed to herald the news of victory. Like the Romans of old, the soldiers regarded the omen as good.

The approach of the American troops had been for a long time anticipated by the authorities of Chihuahua and preparations were made to obstruct their advance by Governor Angel Trias and General José Heredia, the general commanding the district.[160]

---

time had mounted a few of his men, followed them still further. All now returned to camp, and congratulated one another on the achievement. The Mexican loss was 71 killed, 5 prisoners, and not less than 150 wounded, among whom was their commanding officer, General Ponce de Leon. Also a considerable quantity of ammunition, baggage, wine, provisions, blankets, and a great number of lances, some guns, and several stands of colors, were among the spoils.''

See report of Colonel Doniphan, from Chihuahua, March 4, 1847, which gives full details of the battle of Brazito. See also *The Military Occupation of New Mexico*, R. E. Twitchell, pp. 102-104. Biographies of Doniphan and others of his officers are found in the same work, pp. 325, 329, 337-339, 346-347.

[160] According to Heredia's official report, dated March 2, 1847, he had but 1,575 men and ten pieces of artillery. In this estimate he could not have included all the militia and rancheros who were present at the battle of Sacramento, and the Americans certainly captured more than that number of guns including the culverins. Colonel Doniphan, in his report, dated March 4th, says that ''the force of the enemy was 1.200 cavalry from Durango and Chihuahua, with the Vera Cruz dragoons, 1,200 infantry from Chihuahua, 300 artillerymen, and 1,420 rancheros, badly armed with lassoes, lances and machetes, or corn knives.''

A complete plan of the Mexican fortifications was given to Colonel Doniphan by Captain Santiago Kirker and some of the Delaware Indians who were with Kirker. In his *Doniphan's Expedition*, note 99, pp. 388-9, Connelley says: ''Meredith T. Moore says that at the south end of the *Jornada*, above Brazito, a man appeared on the west bank of the Rio Grande and called over to the army. He was questioned by the officers, who finally ordered him to cross the river to the encampment, which he did, bringing with him some half dozen Delaware Indians. He proved to be James Kirker. He was dressed as a frontiersman of his day — fringed buck-skin hunting shirt and breeches, heavy, broad Mexican hat, and huge spurs, all embellished and ornamented with Mexican finery. He was mounted on a fine horse, which he regarded with great affection and to which he gave most careful attention. In addition to a Hawkins rifle, elegantly mounted and ornamented with silver inlaid on the stock, he was armed with a choice assortment of pistols and Mexican daggers. He said he had been living some years in Mexico in the service of the governor, who contracted to pay him so much each for Apache scalps he might take. In hunting down these Indians, he had employed a force of thirty or forty Delawares. Some time before the war was declared between the United States and Mexico

At a meeting of the departmental assembly of Chihuahua, Trias presiding, it had been decided that when Doniphan's men had been captured, they were to be stripped of their money and arms, and sent on foot to the city of Mexico; and a quantity of cord was cut in suitable lengths for tying the prisoners, which was afterwards captured at the battle. General Heredia, with Generals Justiniani, Garcia Conde, and Ugarte and Governor Trias, who acted as brigadier general, advanced to the pass of Sacramento about the middle of February, with near four thousand troops, regulars and militia, ten pieces of field artillery and six culverins, or rampart pieces. The position was skilfully and strongly fortified, under the direction of General Code, who was afterward detached with 800 cavalry to observe the American force, and on the approach of Doniphan fell back to the main body of the Mexican army. The road to the rancho of Sacramento, in front of which the enemy had fortified themselves, followed the course of an open level valley, bounded on either side by ranges of sterile mountains. The Mexican position

---

the governor of Chihuahua owed him $30,000 for Indian scalps, he said; and instead of paying him, had repudiated his claim and threatened to arrest him and his Delawares and throw them into prison. Most of the Indians had returned to their own country, but he, with those he could find had set out for the American army. Some of the Delawares went home by way of Santa Fé; others remained with the army and went home by way of New Orleans. James Peacock says the Delawares came with Kirker. Some of them had seen the fortifications at Sacramento, and one of them in conversation with Peacock drew in the sand with a stick a plan of all the works and a map of the locality in which they were situated. He told Peacock that the Mexicans reminded him of his first efforts to trap birds when he was a little boy; that they had constructed their fortifications on the theory that the Americans would walk into a trap set in plain view, when by deploying to the right the trap might be avoided; that the Mexicans expected the Americans would march along the road in the ravine upon which all their artillery was trained. Peacock took the Indian to Doniphan, for whom he drew designs of the Mexican fortifications, and gave a description of all the surrounding country. And the American army did at Sacramento exactly what the Delaware suggested to Peacock that it would do — turn to the right and avoid the Mexican artillery. The fact that it was the Delaware who had a knowledge of the Mexican fortifications would indicate that Kirker had not recently been at Chihuahua or Sacramento. Moore says Kirker was absolutely fearless; that he was a fine rider, well accomplished in the daring horsemanship affected by the old trappers and plainsmen of the time, such as leaning over from the saddle so far that his long hair would sweep the ground with a horse at full speed. He knew all the trails of northern Mexico, and where water could be found along them. He spoke the Spanish language well, also a number of Indian languages; he proved a valuable acquisition to the army.''

Thomas Forsythe, another celebrated frontiersman, was with the American army. It is supposed that Forsythe is the man who shot General Ponce de Leon at the battle of Brazito.

was upon an elevated plain, in the center of a sort of peninsula formed by two large arroyos, branches of the Rio Sacramento.[161]

In the march from El Paso south the caravan of wagons, owned by traders with goods intended for the Chihuahua market, was placed in command of Major Owens. These wagons were arranged in four parallel lines, with intervals of fifty feet. The artillery marched in the interval of the center; and the remainder of the troops, except two hundred cavalry proper, who were in the advance, marched in the intervals on the right and left. By this means the strength of the force was concealed and its position masked. Another object for this arrangement of the caravan was to have the wagons serve as a breastwork in case of attack.

Arriving within three miles of the enemy's fortifications, a reconnoissance was made by Major Clark, who discovered that the Mexican infantry occupied the batteries and redoubts and that the cavalry was drawn up in front. The column now continued its course along the road about a mile and a half, and the cavalry

---

[161] These arroyos were called the Seco and the Sacramento. The Arroyo Seco on the north inclines to the south when it reaches the eastern range of mountains, and, uniting with the Arroyo Sacramento, they together form the main river. The road to Chihuahua crosses the peninsula from north to south; on its left the plain rises abruptly in a bench, fifty feet high, sloping upward from every side towards the northeast corner, where it culminates in a rocky knoll, called the Cerro Frijoles, one hundred and fifty feet above the plain; but on the right it is smooth and unbroken, descending gradually from the hilly bench along the base of which the road passes. On the southern bank of the Arroyo Sacramento there is a range of mountains, separated by deep gullies and forming right angles with the course of the stream. The easternmost ridge is the Cerro Sacramento, which rises on the right of the road, just in the rear of the rancho Sacramento. Below the Cerro Sacramento on the east is the valley of the Rio Sacramento, about one mile in width, through which passes the road to Chihuahua.

Upon the Cerro Frijoles, was a redoubt and battery, with a stone wall, and abattis in its rear, extending across the bed of the Arroyo Seco to the mountains on the opposite bank. Seven hundred yards west of the Cerro Frijoles there was another redoubt. There was a redoubt also at the northwest corner, and one at the southwest corner of the bench on the left of the road, with three other redoubts at intervals between them. Near the ford of the Arroyo Sacramento was a stone corral or enclosure, surrounding a spring. The corral and the redoubts were all connected, with the exception of short intervals, by breastworks of stone and trenches for the protection of infantry, thus forming an unbroken line of fortifications, overlooking and commanding the gorge of the Arroyo Seco, and the road across the peninsula throughout its whole extent. On the Cerro Sacramento there was a strong battery, which commanded the road as it approached the ford below it. About two miles west of the ford, on the Arroyo Sacramento, was the hacienda of Torreon, from which another road led through a canyon in the mountains to the main route to Chihuahua.

Representative New Mexicans of the Nineteenth Century
1. Don Salvador Armijo. 2. Don José Leandro Perea. 3. Don Pedro Y. Jaramillo. 4. Don Juan Santistevan. 5. Don Pedro Sanchez.
6. Don Tomas C. de Baca

still further, when they suddenly diverged to the right for the purpose of gaining the level portion of the plain fronting the position of the enemy on the west. This movement was soon perceived by the enemy and General Conde advanced with a body of cavalry, masking four pieces of artillery, to prevent the Americans from gaining the elevation. The manœuvre was executed too rapidly to render that possible, and Colonel Doniphan formed his men, and the advance column of the caravan of wagons was corralled before the enemy came within reach of his guns.

The Americans were all dismounted, except three companies, under Captains Reid, Parsons, and Hudson. Major Clark occupied the center with his artillery; the first battalion on the right was commanded by Lieutenant-Colonels Mitchell and Jackson, and the second battalion, on the left, by Major Gilpin. The action was commenced about three o'clock in the afternoon by a brisk fire from the American battery, which was returned by the enemy. At the third discharge the Mexican lancers gave way and retired behind the redoubts with their artillery, having lost several men killed and a number wounded. Anxious to improve the advantage gained, Colonel Doniphan ordered a charge upon the enemy's line of intrenchments and batteries. At the word, his men sprang forward with cheers and shouts. Captain Weightman advanced with the howitzers at full speed, upon the redoubts at the southwest corner of the bench, supported by the cavalry under Captains Reid, Parsons, and Hudson; Major Clark followed the movement as fast as practicable a little further to the left; and the remainder of the troops dashed rapidly forward on foot. While they were advancing, the enemy's cavalry were twice rallied for a charge upon the left flank of the wagons following in the rear of the American line, but they were easily dispersed by the fire of Major Clark's guns. Captain Weightman unlimbered his pieces within fifty yards of the redoubts, and the cavalry and infantry rushing boldly up to the breastworks, drove the enemy before them with their sabres and rifles.

As the Americans entered the line of intrenchments east of the road, a warmer and more effective fire was opened from the battery on the height of Cerro Sacramento, which had been constantly playing upon them, and where a large body of Mexicans had now rallied. Major Clark promptly placed his pieces in position, in the redoubt at the southwest corner of the bench, twelve hundred yards distant, and in a short time silenced the enemy's guns. Meanwhile Lieutenant-Colonels Mitchell and Jackson, with the first battalion remounted, and Captain Weightman's howitzers, had bravely charged up the hill, followed by Major Gilpin with the second battalion on foot. Before they reached the battery the enemy had abandoned it, and his entire force was scattered in flight. The cavalry and the howitzers immediately pushed forward in hot pursuit. The road was strewn with the arms and accoutrements which the Mexicans soldiers had thrown down as they hurried towards Chihuahua. Governor Trias was among the first to reach the city, and the seat of government was instantly ordered to be removed to Parral. Night put an end to the carnage. The enemy lost all his artillery, ten wagons, and large quantities of provisions; three hundred were killed, about the same number wounded, and forty were taken prisoners.[162] Several national and regimental standards were also cap-

---

[162] Hughes, J. T., *Doniphan's Expedition* (Connelley), note, p. 413: "One of the lieutenants of the Mexican artillery stood to his guns, until he was wounded and captured. Colonel Doniphan asked him if he did not know, before the action came on, that the Mexicans would be defeated. The lieutenant replied: '*I did not; and if they had stood to their posts, as I encouraged them to do, you never would have driven us from our strong position. I am now your prisoner; but I do not regret fighting for the liberty and honor of my country. I will encourage my people still to resist foreign invasion.*' Colonel Doniphan was so well pleased with the patriotic devotion of the young officer, that he immediately gave him his liberty."

Edwards, Frank S., *A Campaign in New Mexico with Colonel Doniphan*, London, 1848, says, in describing the battle of Sacramento: "As we form, the enemy's artillery opens upon us, and at that instant Weightman's clear voice is heard: 'Form battery, action front, load and fire at will,' and our pieces ring out the death knell of the enemy. Now comes the friendly struggle between our gunners, who shall pour in the deadliest and quickest fire, and beautifully are those pieces served, mowing lane after lane through the solid columns of the Mexicans. In the center of the battery, their horses bounding at every discharge, stand Clark and his officers; as the balls fly through the opposite ranks and the shells tear their columns, shout after shout is heard from our men.

"Further to our right sits Colonel Doniphan on his beautiful chestnut charger, with his leg crossed over the saddle, steadily whittling a piece of wood, but with his eye glancing proudly over the ranks of his little band. As the cannonading becomes hotter, he quietly says: 'Well! they're giving us ―― now, boys!' and passes coolly to the left of our position, untouched by the copper hail that pours around him.

"And here we are (at a distance too great for anything but cannon), sitting on our horses dodging Mexican balls as they come humming through our ranks, first striking the ground about midway, and so becoming visible. It was surprising the skill which we soon obtained in this employment. After a few shots, we could tell to a foot where the copper messengers would alight.

tured, and among the colors was the black flag exhibited at the battle of Brazito. Colonel Doniphan had but one man killed and eight wounded, some of them mortally. Major Owens, of Independence, Missouri, lost his life in this battle. He accompanied Captain Reid in his charge and was killed in storming the enemy's redoubts.

The way was now opened to Chihuahua, and on the 1st of March Colonel Doniphan took formal possession of the city and department in the name of the American government. Here, in the en-

---

Although, a few minutes before, joke after joke was passing among us, the silence was now almost unbroken, for nothing acts so well, by way of safety valve to a man's courage, as having to sit on horseback half an hour and dodge cannon balls. As yet we knew of no injuries amongst us; but suddenly a German close by blurts out, 'I'se kilt!' and, tumbling off his horse, rolls up his trousers, showing a severe contusion on his leg, caused by a stone thrown up by the ricochet of a cannon ball; around the limb goes a handkerchief, and up mounts the man again. At that moment a groan bursts from the line to my left, and a man is borne dying from the ranks, while off goes the head of Lieutenant Dorn's horse. Hot work on all sides!

"So confident are the Mexicans, that some of the richest citizens of Chihuahua have come out as spectators; but now, judging wisely, off they fly at full speed to the city, giving notice of the probable result but are so little believed that, like true prophets before them, they are actually stoned in the streets.

"A shell explodes directly in the ranks of the enemy — they draw back behind their entrenchments, and we immediately advance until within four hundred yards; again the deadly shower opens from our ranks, fiercely returned. The order to charge rings through our lines — Colonel Mitchell, on his favorite white charger, Roderic, waves his saber as he leads us on; rumbling and crashing behind us comes Weightman with his howitzers, leaving the rest of the battery in position to cover our advance. Dashing past us goes Major Owens, waving his hand in an exulting manner, and shouting out, 'Give it to them boys! They can't withstand us!' and away he goes, falling in two minutes a corpse, struck in the forehead by a grape-shot while storming the redoubts, and being so close to the gun that the fire actually burned his clothes. Rapidly is our charge made; but just fairly underway, it is about to be ruined! A countermanding order, as if from Doniphan, is given by a drunken officer whose rank (alone) requires respect. In surprise we suddenly halt within a few yards of the redoubts, and are fully exposed to the whole enemy's fire. 'For God's sake, advance!' roars out sutler Pomeroy, who was fighting in the ranks. Our hesitation vanishes and away we instantly dash forward, gallantly led by Mitchell and Gilpin, while Weightman fires his howitzers, loaded with canister, with great effect, and again advancing, wheels them to the right and left, throwing in another charge of grape and canister, and raking the whole line of the enemy's position. To our left is a battalion of brave cavalry from Durango, who have arrived on the field only half an hour before — 'tis their last fight — they are terribly cut to pieces, and are forced to retreat. A piece of their artillery being dismounted, they attempt to 'snake' by fastening their lassoes to it, and drag it along the ground, but they are overtaken and made prisoners and the gun is ours. Our men, pouring over the embankments, actually pushed the Mexicans out. Now comes the rout; the Mexicans give way; and *sauve qui peut* is their only object. We are in possession of their main position. The rest of our battery comes galloping up to occupy it. A

joyment of the luxuries and hospitalities which almost caused them to forget the hardships they had endured, they remained for several weeks, without the occurrence of any incident of extraordinary moment. Doniphan and his army evacuated the city on the 25th of April, 1847. In the tattered uniforms which they had worn from St. Louis and Fort Leavenworth, Colonel Doniphan and his men presented themselves before General Zachary Taylor at Walnut Springs on the 26th of May, having marched over plain and desert from the capital of the Internal Provinces. They were desirous of seeing more service under the command of Taylor, but he was unable to gratify their wishes. Here they left the artillery which had been brought from Santa Fé, and taking with them the captured guns, they marched to the Rio Brazos, where they embarked for New Orleans. Here they were mustered out of service and returned to Missouri, having traveled, during their absence, more than six thousand miles; nearly two thousand miles more than the famous march of Xenophon and the Greeks in their retreat from Asia. The retreat of Xenophon and the expedition of Cyrus against his brother Artaxerxes form the only parallel to Doniphan's expedition recorded in the history of the world.[163]

Colonel Sterling Price of the 2d Missouri volunteers, who remain-

---

body of their lancers reforms and prepares to renew the attack — but — they are soon sent after their flying companions. We are about congratulating ourselves on a victory, when — bang goes a cannon, and a ball bounds amongst us, knocking the saddle blanket off the mule of one of our company, from which he has this instant dismounted. A cloud of white smoke curls gracefully upward from a hitherto masked battery to the right upon yon high mountain, as shot after shot falls among us. Two of our six-pounders are at once placed in one of the deserted entrenchments and commence a well-directed fire, which soon dismounts one of the enemy's pieces. Up charges Mitchell at the head of his company, and takes the position; yet down, with headlong speed, dashes an officer, waving a Mexican flag — one of our gunners points his cannon at him — a moment and he would have been no more, but his horse is recognized, 'tis Colonel Mitchell's Roderic while the colonel himself is the standard bearer.

"Numerous skirmishes occur as pursuit takes the place of resistance. Weightman dashes on with the cavalry toward the city. Looking over his shoulder, he sees his howitzers halted on the hillside instead of following him, and galloping back, he shouts 'On with that battery! If I knew who had halted you I'd cut him down.' The officer who had done so said not a word.

"But the battle is won. And gradually we assemble on the battlefield. The enemy are fast disappearing in the distance, baffling pursuit."

[163] Connelley, W. E., *Doniphan's Expedition*, at pages 427, 428, 429, 430, 431, 432 and 433 gives the full report of this battle as made by Doniphan, March 4, from the City of Chihuahua.

ed in command of the troops at Santa Fé after the departure of Kearny and Doniphan, was not a strict disciplinarian. He was a good officer, however, and displayed both ability and energy in the field. Relaxation and excesses were frequently witnessed among the troops under his command and subordination and good order were not much in evidence. The wholesome restraints imposed by General Kearny were gradually disregarded.[164] During the fall of 1846, and the ensuing winter, the soldiers [165] were employed in the construction of the fort on the hill commanding the town, known as Fort Marcy, in honor of the head of the war department. There was a great deal

DISAFFECTION AMONG THE INHABITANTS OF NEW MEXICO

---

[164] Colonel Price was appointed a brigadier-general of volunteers, July 20, 1847. He was a descendant of Lord Baltimore and was born in Prince Edward county, Virginia, September 14, 1809. Very little is known of his early life. He was a graduate of Hampden-Sidney college and came to Missouri in 1830, settling in Chariton county. He was a man of fine character. He was elected to the legislature and in 1842 was speaker of the house of representatives. He was elected to congress in 1844 and resigned his seat to accept a commission as colonel of the 2d Missouri volunteers, which regiment was raised by him for the war with Mexico. After the treaty of Guadalupe Hidalgo he returned to Missouri, and in 1852 was elected governor of the state, which office he held for four years. He rose to the rank of major-general in the Confederate army and led the Confederate forces with great skill at the battles of Wilson's Creek and Pea Ridge. On the 20th day of September, 1862, he fought the battle of Iuka, and later on was in the battle of Corinth. In Missouri he was familiarly known as 'Old Pap Price' and was beloved by all his men. After the Civil War he went to Mexico where he sought service with the emperor Maximilian. He returned to Missouri and died September 29, 1867, at St. Louis.

[165] Ruxton, G. F., *Adventures in Mexico*, refers to the Americans and soldiers in Santa Fé at this time as ''the dirtiest, rowdiest crew I have ever seen collected together. Crowds of drunken volunteers,'' says he, ''filled the streets, brawling and boasting, but never fighting. Mexicans, wrapped in serapes scowled upon them as they passed. . . . Under the portales were numerous monte-tables, surrounded by Mexicans and Americans. Every other house was a grocery, as they call a gin or whiskey shop, continually disgorging reeling, drunken men, and everywhere filth and dirt reigned triumphant.''

Bancroft, H. H., *History of Arizona and New Mexico*, p. 439, says: ''For a time indeed, a greater degree of vigilance and discipline was observed; but the former with its accompaniments of severe punishments, habitual distrust and oppressive regulations, rapidly destroyed the confidence and friendliness before shown by large portions of the native population; while the latter soon became relaxed, and the soldiers more turbulent and unmanageable than ever. The New Mexicans were regarded as at heart deadly foes, and were treated accordingly.''

Ruxton, G. F., *Adventures in Mexico*, p. 197, writing of his experience in passing the night with the family of a Taos Indian, says: ''The patrona of the family seemed rather shy of me at first, until, in the course of conversation, she discovered that I was an Englishman. '*Gracias á Dios*,' she exclaimed, 'a Christian will sleep with us tonight and not an American.''

of time, however, neither wisely nor profitably spent and many of the soldiers fell victims to disease. Price had a number of enemies in the army and at home in Missouri and these were constantly writing letters to the Missouri newspapers relating the conditions [166] as they existed in New Mexico according to their standpoint. In it all there was a great deal of petty politics. There was a great deal of sickness, supplies were obtained with difficulty and the Indians of the plains were constantly attacking the caravans. The Navajós, notwithstanding their treaty of peace with Colonel Doniphan, still continued their raids. The situation was still further complicated by disagreements between the military and civil authorities and by serious troubles between the officers themselves; in fine, there was much dissatisfaction with the administration of affairs in the military department.

The proclamations issued by General Kearny ignored the claim that eastern New Mexico belonged to Texas, and his published intention of retaining all of the country as a permanent possession of the United States came as a great disappointment to those leading Mexicans who had been led by Magoffin to believe that west of the Rio Grande some one of them "might set up a government of his own." The position of the national administration, when it had been advised of General Kearny's acts,[167] was declared in a message from President Polk who said that Kearney's acts, so far as they purported to establish a permanent territorial government and to give the in-

[166] Ruxton, *Adventures in Mexico*, p. 197, says: "I found all over New Mexico that the most bitter feeling and most determined hostility existed against the Americans, who certainly in Santa Fé and elsewhere have not been very anxious to conciliate the people, but by their bullying and overbearing demeanor toward them, have in a great measure been the cause of this hatred which shortly after broke out in an organized rising of the northern part of the province, and occasioned great loss of life to both parties."

In a letter from Santa Fé published in *Niles' Register*, lxxii, 252, it was declared that the soldiers were a degenerated military mob, open violators of law and order and that they daily heaped injury and insult upon the people; that one-half of the captains did not know how many men were in their commands nor where they were to be found, and that the officers themselves were seen nightly at fandangos and even less reputable places of dissipation. It was claimed that the soldiers were never drilled and that nothing but confusion and misrule existed. It was declared that at least one-fifth of the entire command had died from the effects of dissipation and that Price's lack of military education and his apparent inability to control either officers or men had produced among the New Mexicans the strongest feelings of disgust and hatred and that a desire to rebel existed among the inhabitants.

[167] *Letter* to General Kearny from the secretary of war. *Ex. Doc.* 60, p. 179.

habitants political rights as citizens, under the constitution of the United States, had not been recognized, nor approved; otherwise everything that he had done, and the instructions upon which they were based, "were but the amelioration of martial law, which modern civilization requires, and were due, as well as the security of the conquest, to the inhabitants of the conquered territory." The president further stated that "it will be apparent that if any excess of power has been exercised, the departure has been the offspring of a patriotic desire to give to the inhabitants the privileges and immunities so cherished by the people of our own country, and which they believed calculated to improve their condition and promote their prosperity. Any such excess has resulted in no practical injury, but can and will be early corrected in a manner to alienate as little as possible the good feelings of the inhabitants of the conquered territory."

Kearny and Doniphan had no sooner left the territory than rumors of intended revolt among the natives were constantly being circulated. These could be traced to no authoritative source. It was also believed that Mexico intended sending a substantial force from Chihuahua for the purpose of regaining the territory. This belief was entirely shattered when news came of the battle of Brazito. General Price had nearly two thousand men with whom he felt fully able to keep the territory in subjection, although many of these were on the sick-list. The main force was stationed at Santa Fé. Small detachments were stationed at other towns, notably Alburquerque, on the Mora and another at Cebolleta, on the Navajó frontier. But with all their belief in their ability to handle the situation, Santa Fé came near proving a Capua to the American soldiers. Frequent altercations occurred between the Mexican inhabitants and the soldiers; the natives, naturally, were jealous of foreign interference; many of the disbanded militia which Armijo had called out lingered in the vicinity of Santa Fé, ready to be employed, if opportunity presented itself; the civil officers who had been displaced viewed Governor Bent, Secretary Vigil, and the other appointees under the newly established government, with emotions of hatred and ill-will. The Pueblos were violently hostile and some of the most prominent and influential citizens in the territory, led on by the clergy, as is well known, labored to foment the disaffection which was rapidly gaining ground. News that an insurrectionary movement was on foot and apt to be launched at any moment came to General Price through Secretary Vigil. Don Diego Archuleta, who considered that he had been cheated, owing to the representations made to him by Santiago Magoffin, was a leader in the movement. He was ably assisted by Don Tomas Ortiz and others. When Price was notified he immediately caused the arrest of those supposed to be implicated and an investigation was had, in the course of which it appeared that a plan had been formed for a general uprising on Christmas eve. The principal leaders, Ortiz and Archuleta, escaped in the direction of Chihuahua, the project was further frustrated by the arrests which had been made and in a few days the alarm entirely subsided.[168]

---

[168] These men considered themselves to be patriots, unwilling to see their country lost without a single effective blow. They were Tomas Ortiz, who had been chief alcalde of Santa Fé, Juan Felipe Ortiz, the vicario, Diego Archuleta, Domingo C. de Baca, Miguel E. Pino, Nicolas Pino, Manuel Chaves, Santiago Armijo, Agustin Duran, Pablo Dominguez, José Maria Sanchez, Antonio Maria Trujillo, Santiago Martinez, Pascual Martinez, Vicente Martinez, Antonio Ortiz (of Arroyo Seco), Facundo Pino, Rev. Antonio José Martinez, Fr. Leyva of San Miguel. Not one of these had favored the abandonment of Apache Pass by Armijo, and all were related either by blood or marriage.

The plan as formed by these men was that on the appointed day those engaged in the conspiracy in Santa Fé were to gather in the parochial church and remain concealed. Meanwhile friends from the surrounding country under the lead of Archuleta were to be brought into the city and distributed in various houses where they would be unobserved. At midnight the church bell was to sound and then the men within the church were to sally forth and all were to rendezvous immediately in the plaza, seize the cannon there, and aim them so as to command the leading points, while detachments under special orders were to attack the palace and the quarters of General Price, and make them prisoners. The people throughout the whole north had been secretly notified and were only awaiting news of the rising at Santa Fé in order to join in the revolt and make it a success.

A full account of the manner of escape of Don Tomas Ortiz is to be found in *The Military Occupation of New Mexico, 1846-1851*, R. E. Twitchell, Denver, 1909.

The only definite and literally preserved testimony of the facts in this affair is that of Don José Maria Sanchez, who says that on December 15th he was summoned by Don Miguel Pino to a meeting at the house of Tomas Ortiz. He found there Tomas Ortiz, Diego Archuleta, Nicolas and Miguel Pino, Santiago Armijo, Manuel Chavez, Domingo C. de Baca, Pablo Dominguez, Juan Lopez, Tomas Vaca, Blas Ortega, and Fr. Leyba. Agustin Duran, it appears, was not at this meeting, but he also confessed. Sanchez stated that Diego Archuleta was the leader at the meetings and made the motion for the nomination of a governor and a commanding general. He named Don Tomas Ortiz for the first office and himself for the second. The motion carried and the proceedings were signed by every one present. This paper was hid in the house of the mother of the Pinos. The writing has never been recovered. At the meeting the date set for the assault was fixed at the 19th of December;

Representative New Mexicans of the Nineteenth Century
1. Don Trinidad Alarid. 2. Col. Max Frost. 3. Major Harry R. Whiting.
4. Don Antonio Ortiz y Salazar. 5. Col. Albert J. Fountain. 6. Don Francisco Antonio Chavez. 7. Don Benito Baca. 8. John H. Knaebel. 9. Don Felix Martinez

THE WAR WITH MEXICO

The leaders of this revolution were men of restless and unsatisfied ambition. Their inactivity lasted but a brief period. A second and still more dangerous uprising was plotted. The experience gained in the failure of the first attempt prompted the most absolute secrecy in the formation of the plans for the second. Everywhere in the northern counties the people secretly began to arm and equip themselves; this was not known to the military authorities, and on the 19th of January, 1847, the rebellion broke out in several parts of New Mexico. On the 14th of January, Governor Bent had left Santa Fé to visit Taos; five days later he was foully assassinated in his own residence in that village.[169] Early on the morning of the 19th of January, the insur-

THE ASSASSINATION OF GOVERNOR BENT AT TAOS

---

afterward, owing to the fact that a sufficient number of those outside of the city had not been notified, the day for the uprising was postponed until Christmas eve.

General Price in his report of February 15, 1847, says: "An officer, formerly in the Mexican service, was seized, and on his person was found a list of all the disbanded Mexican soldiers in the vicinity of Santa Fé. Many other persons supposed to be implicated were arrested and a full investigation proved that many of the most influential citizens in the northern part of the territory were engaged in the rebellion."

Doña Tules Barcelo, a woman of shady reputation, was the person who notified Donaciano Vigil of the intended uprising and gave him the names of the ones most prominent in the affair.

[169] Governor Bent knew of the discontent prevailing, but was in no wise alarmed for his personal safety; but he misjudged those whom he had always assisted and underestimated the influence of the treacherous men who had professed for him the warmest friendship and whom he had personally known for more than twenty years. A few days prior to his departure for Taos he issued the following proclamation: "You are now governed by new statutory laws and you also have the free government promised to you. Do not abuse the great liberty which is vouchsafed you by it, so you may gather the abundant fruits which await you in the future. Those who are blindly opposed, as well as those whose vices have made them notorious, and the ambitious persons who aspire to the best offices, also those persons who dream that mankind should bow to their whims, having become satisfied that they cannot find employment in the offices which are usually given to men of probity and honesty, exasperated [Tomas Ortiz and the old revolutionist, Diego Archuleta] have come forth as leaders of a revolution against the present government. They held a meeting in this Capital about the middle of last month, which was attended by some foolish and imprudent men who were urged to follow the standard of rebellion. Their treason was discovered in time and smothered at its birth. Now they are wandering about and hiding from people, but their doctrines are scattered broadcast among the people, thereby causing uneasiness, and they still hold to their ruinous plans. . . There is still another pretext with which they want to alarm you and that is the falsehood that troops are coming from the interior in order to re-conquer the country. What help could the department of Chihuahua, which is torn by factions and reduced to insignificance afford you? Certainly none. . . I urge you to turn a deaf ear to

rectionists, led by Pablo Montoya and a Taos Indian, known as Tomasito, entered the city, joined the resident members of the revolutionary movement and began the attack. The houses of the resident Americans were destroyed. The Indians, under the leadership of Tomasito, visited the house of Governor Bent, and firing through the door, wounded him in the chin and stomach; the door was next broken down and his body pierced with arrows. Amidst the fiendish yells of the Indians he was scalped.[170] His daughters give graphic

---

such false doctrines and to remain quiet, attending to your domestic affairs, so that you may enjoy under the law, all the blessings of peace, and by rallying around the government, call attention to the improvements which you deem material to the advancement of the country and that by so doing you may enjoy all the prosperity which your best friend wishes you."

The persons killed at Taos were Louis Lee, acting sheriff of Taos, Cornelio Vigil, prefect, J. W. Leal, district attorney, Pablo Jaramillo, a brother of Mrs. Bent, and Narcisco Beaubien, a son of Don Carlos Beaubien, circuit judge, and Governor Bent.

[170] Charles Bent was a native of Virginia, having been born in Charlestown, in 1797. His father was of English ancestry; his mother was part French. He was a very highly educated man and graduated from the United States Military Academy at West Point. He resigned from the army and engaged in mercantile pursuits at St. Louis, Missouri. In 1828 he left for the far west over the Santa Fé Trail, looking for a location for the establishment of business, and, with his brother William, built the post known as Bent's Fort on the Arkansas. He went to Santa Fé in 1832, where the Bent brothers established a general merchandizing business. He was afterward a business partner of Colonel Céran St. Vrain and so continued until the date of his death. In 1829 Bent was the captain of the big caravan from Franklin, Missouri, to Santa Fé, which was escorted by Major Riley. Bent had six brothers. The firm of Bent and St. Vrain was one of the most important engaged in the fur trade. It ranked next to the American Fur Company. They also had a fort on the South Platte. Governor Bent was married to Maria Ignacia Jaramillo, a daughter of Don Francisco and Apolonia (Vigil) Jaramillo, who died at Taos, April 13, 1883. Mrs. Bent's sister, Josefa Jaramillo, was the wife of Colonel Kit Carson. His remains are buried in the National cemetery at Santa Fé.

Prince, L. Bradford, *Address* at ceremonies attending the unveiling of the painting of Governor Bent which hangs in the capitol at Santa Fé, said: "The leaders in the north stirred up the Indians of the pueblo of Taos, and were only waiting for the proper time to strike a decisive blow. It was evident that the people were much excited, and their animosity was directed not only against the Americans among them, but also against those of their own people who had accepted office under the new government. During the day Governor Bent was advised to leave town for his own safety, but he had no thought of personal danger. All through the night of January 18th the village of Taos was in an uproar. Nearly all the Indians from the pueblo were in town and the saloons and public halls were filled with people. Demagogues were haranguing the populace and inflaming their passions. Whisky and wine were flowing without stint and the excitement and increased with the passing hours. Under the incendiary persuasion of Pablo Montoya, 'The Santa Ana of the North' and Tomasito Romero, an influential Pueblo Indian, the Mexicans and Indians were aroused to a condition of frenzy."

Mrs. Teresina Scheurich, daughter of Governor Bent, gave a statement of

accounts as to the details of the massacre. The portrait of Governor Bent in the capitol at Santa Fé was painted from one which hangs on the wall in the residence of his daughter at Taos, for which Governor Bent sat on his last visit to St. Louis, in 1844. The unveiling of the portrait occurred at Santa Fé, March 1, 1910, under the auspices of the Daughters of the American Revolution.

---

the facts surrounding the murder of her father, to Governor Prince, as follows: "I was only five years old at the time, but I well remember every circumstance as if it was but yesterday. It was early in the morning and we were all in bed. We were awakened by the noise of many people, crowding into the placita. My father was at home from Santa Fé on a short visit and had refused a military escort. The night before he was warned of danger and urged to fly, but though there were several horses in the corrals, he declined. He had always treated everybody fairly and honestly and he felt that all were friends and he would not believe that they would turn against him. Hearing the noise he went to the door and tried to pacify the crowd yelling outside. In the adjoining room, my mother, Mrs. Carson, and Mrs. Boggs, who were with us, and we children, were trembling with fear, all except my brother Alfredo. He was only ten years old, but had been reared on the frontier, and he took down the shotgun and going to my father's side, said, 'Papa, let us fight them.'

"While my father was parleying with the mob, Mrs. Carson and Mrs. Boggs, aided by an Indian woman who was a slave (*peon*), dug a hole through the adobe wall which separated our house from the next. They did it with only a poker and an old iron spoon; I have still the poker that they used. We children were first pushed through the hole and then the women crawled through after us. My mother kept calling to my father to come also, but for quite a while he would not. When he did try to escape he was already wounded and had been scalped alive. He crawled through the hole, holding his hand on the top of his bleeding head. But it was too late. Some of the men came after him through the hole and others came over the roof of the house and down into the yard. They broke down the doors and rushed upon my father. He was shot many times and fell dead at our feet. The pleading and tears of my mother and the sobbing of us children had no power to soften the hearts of the enraged Indians and Mexicans.

"At first they were going to take the rest of us away as prisoners, but finally decided to leave us where we were. They ordered that no one should feed us, and then left us alone with our great sorrow. We were without food and had no covering but our night-clothing, all that day and the next night. The body of our father remained on the floor in a pool of blood. We were naturally frightened, as we did not know how soon the miscreants might return to do us violence. At about three o'clock the next morning, some of our Mexican friends stole up to the house and gave us food and clothing. That day, also, they took my father to bury him. A few days later we were allowed to go to their house. Mrs. Carson and Mrs. Boggs were sheltered by a friendly old Mexican, who took them to his home, disguising them as squaws, and set them to grinding corn on metates in his kitchen."

Colonel Kit Carson was in California with General Kearny at the time of the murder of Bent. Boggs was on the plains, en route with the United States mail, a contract to carry which had been given him by the government. It was believed that if Carson and Boggs had been at Taos, Bent would not have been murdered, as Carson had great influence with the Mexicans and Indians. They stood in great fear of him.

Intelligence of the murders committed at Taos and elsewhere reached Santa Fé on January 20, and circulars written by the revolutionists, calling upon the people of the Rio Abajo for aid, were also intercepted. The lower order of Mexicans of the Taos valley and of the small towns in the vicinity rose en masse and joined with the Pueblo Indians in the work of pillage and murder. They organized themselves into a revolutionary army, appointed leaders, and sent circulars to different parts of the territory inciting the people to rebellion. All the towns in the northern part of the territory except Tecolote and Las Vegas declared in favor of the insurrection. At the last named place an attempt to incite the population was defeated by the timely presence of Captain Hendley, of Lieutenant-Colonel Willock's battalion, with a portion of his grazing detachment. At Arroyo Hondo, some twelve miles from Taos, at Turley's mill, eight men were attacked and seven killed on the same day as the massacre of Governor Bent.[171]

NEWS OF THE UPRISING REACHES SANTA FÉ—GENERAL PRICE'S CAMPAIGN

---

[171] Ruxton, G. F., *Travels in Mexico*, pp. 227-229: "There were in the house at the time of the attack, eight white men, including Americans, French-Canadians, and one or two Englishmen, with plenty of arms and ammunition. Turley had been warned of the intended insurrection, but had treated the report with indifference and neglect, until one morning a man named Otterbees, in the employ of Turley, and who had been despatched to Santa Fé with several mule-loads of whiskey a few days before, made his appearance at the gate on horseback, and, hastily informing the inmates of the mill that the New Mexicans had risen and massacred Governor Bent and other Americans, galloped off. Even then Turley felt assured that he would not be molested, but, at the solicitations of his men agreed to close the gate of the yard round which were the buildings of the mill and distillery, and make preparations for defense.

"A few hours after a large crowd of Mexicans and Pueblo Indians made their appearance, all armed with guns and bows and arrows, and, advancing with a white flag, summoned Turley to surrender his house and the Americans in it, guarantying that his own life should be saved, but that every other American in the valley of Taos had to be destroyed; that the governor and all the Americans at Fernandez and the Rancho had been killed, and that not one was to be left alive in all New Mexico. To this summons Turley answered that he would never surrender his house nor his men, and that, if they wanted it or them, 'they must take them.'

"The enemy then drew off and after a short consultation commenced the attack. The first day they numbered about five hundred, but the crowd was hourly augmented by the arrival of parties of Indians from more distant pueblos, and of New Mexicans from Fernandez, La Cañada, and other places.

"The building lay at the foot of a gradual slope in the sierra, which was covered with cedar-bushes. In front ran the stream of Arroyo Hondo, about twenty yards from one side of the square, and on the other side was broken

The circulars that had been intercepted conveyed the intelligence to General Price that it was the intention of the revolutionists to advance upon Santa Fé, as soon as they had concentrated their forces, which were coming together as fast as possible. The garrison at Santa Fé was considerably reduced, in consequence of a number of the mounted men having been sent off in different directions to graze their horses, but Price immediately despatched orders to Major Edmondson, at Alburquerque, to return to headquarters with

ground, which rose abruptly and formed the bank of the ravine. In the rear, and behind the still-house, was some garden ground inclosed by a small fence, and into which a small wicket gate opened from the corral. As soon as the attack was determined upon, the assailants broke, and, scattering, concealed themselves under the cover of the rocks and bushes which surrounded the house. From these they kept up an incessant fire upon every exposed portion of the building where they saw the Americans preparing for defense. They, on their part, were not idle; not a man but what was an old mountaineer, and each had his trusty rifle, with good store of ammunition. Wherever one of the assailants exposed a hand-breadth of his person, there whistled a ball from an unerring barrel. The windows had been blockaded, loop-holes being left to fire through, and through these a lively fire was maintained. Already several of the enemy had bitten the dust, and parties were constantly seen bearing off the wounded up the banks of the Cañada. Darkness came on, and during the night a continued fire was kept up on the mill, while its defenders, reserving their ammunition, kept their posts with stern and silent determination. The night was spent in running balls, cutting patches, and completing the defenses of the building. In the morning the fight was renewed, and it was found that the Mexicans had effected a lodgment in a part of the stables, which were separated from the other portions of the building, and between which was an open space of a few feet. The assailants, during the night, had sought to break down the wall and thus enter the main building, but the strength of the adobes and logs of which it was composed resisted effectually all their attempts.

"Those in the stable seemed anxious to regain the outside, for their position was unavailable as a means of annoyance to the besieged, and several had darted across the narrow space which divided it from the other part of the building, and which slightly projected, and behind which they were out of the line of fire. As soon, however, as the attention of the defenders was called to this spot, the first man who attempted to cross, and who happened to be a Pueblo chief, was dropped on the instant, and fell dead in the center of the intervening space. It appeared an object to recover the body, for an Indian immediately dashed out to the fallen chief, and attempted to drag him within the cover of the walls. The rifle which covered the spot again poured forth its deadly contents, and the Indian, springing into the air, fell over the body of his chief, struck to the heart. Another and another met with a similar fate, and at last three rushed at once to the spot, and, seizing the body by the legs and head, had already lifted it from the ground, when three puffs of smoke blew from the barricaded window, followed by the sharp cracks of as many rifles, and three daring Indians added their number to the pile of corpses which now covered the body of the dead chief.

"As yet the besieged had met with no casualties; but after the fall of the seventh Indian, in the manner above described, the whole body of assailants with a shout of rage, poured in a rattling volley, and two of the defenders of the mill fell mortally wounded. One, shot through the loins, suffered great

the detachment of the 2d Missouri under his command, and to Captain Burgwin, commanding a squadron of the 1st dragoons, stationed at the same place, to join him with one troop, and to leave the other at Santa Fé. Having made these preparations for securing the post and leaving Lieutenant-Colonel Willock, of the separate battalion of Missouri mounted volunteers, in charge, Price marched to the north to suppress the revolt, on the morning of the 23d of January, at the head of five companies of the 2d Missouri, Captain Angney's battalion of infantry and a company of Santa Fé volunteers, accompanied

agony, and was removed to the still-house, where he was laid upon a large pile of grain, as being the softest bed to be found.

"In the middle of the day the assailants renewed the attack more fiercely than before, their baffled attempts adding to their furious rage. The little garrison bravely stood to the defense of the mill, never throwing away a shot but firing coolly and only when a fair mark was presented for their unerring aim. Their ammunition, however, was fast failing and, to add to the danger of the situation, the enemy set fire to the mill, which blazed fiercely, and threatened destruction to the whole building. Twice they succeeded in overcoming the flames, and, taking advantage of their being thus occupied, the Mexicans and Indians charged into the corral, which was full of hogs and sheep, and vented their cowardly rage upon the animals, spearing and shooting all that came in their way. No sooner, however, were the flames extinguished in one place, than they broke out more fiercely in another; and as a successful defense was perfectly hopeless, and the number of the assailants increased every moment, a council of war was held by the survivors of the little garrison, when it was determined, as soon as night approached, that every one should attempt to escape as best he might, and in the meantime the defense of the mill was to be continued.

"Just at dusk, Albert and another man ran to the wicket gate which opened into a kind of enclosed space, and in which was a number of armed Mexicans. They both rushed out at the same moment, discharging their rifles full in the faces of the crowd. Albert, in the confusion, threw himself under the fence, whence he saw his companion shot down immediately, and heard his cries for mercy, mingled with shrieks of pain and anguish, as the cowards pierced him with knives and lances. Lying without motion under the fence, as soon as it was quite dark he crept over the logs and ran up the mountain, traveled day and night, and, scarcely stopping or resting, reached the Greenhorn, almost dead with hunger and fatigue. Turley himself succeeded in escaping from the mill and in reaching the mountains unseen. Here he met a Mexican, mounted on a horse, who had been a most intimate friend of the unfortunate man for many years. To this man Turley offered his watch (which was treble its worth) for the use of his horse, but was refused. The inhuman wretch, however, affected pity and commiseration for the fugitive, and advised him to go to a certain place, where he would bring him or send him assistance; but on reaching the mill, which was now a mass of fire, he immediately informed the Mexicans of his place of concealment, whither a large party instantly proceeded and shot him to death.

"Two others escaped and reached Santa Fé in safety. The mill and Turley's house were sacked and gutted, and all his hard-earned savings, which were considerable and concealed in gold about the house, were discovered, and, of course, seized upon by the victorious Mexicans."

by Captain St. Vrain, a partner of Governor Bent in the merchandising business. Among others in St. Vrain's company were Manuel Chaves and Nicolas Pino, two prominent Mexicans who had been arrested as conspirators a month before. The entire force consisted of 353 men, together with four twelve-pounder mountain howitzers, under Lieutenant Dyer of the ordnance.

The company of Santa Fé volunteers, composed of men with large experience on the frontier, who alone were mounted, moved in the advance. Nearly every man in the company had been a warm personal friend of Governor Bent. Early in the afternoon of the 24th the enemy was discovered, about 1,500 strong, occupying an advantageous position upon the heights east of the plaza of La Cañada de Santa Cruz, which commanded the road to that village. They were also in possession of three houses at the base of the hills, from which a warm fire was kept up. Colonel Price immediately formed his line of battle. The artillery was thrown forward on the left flank and beyond the creek, the dismounted men occupying a position where they would be in some degree protected by the high bluff bank of the Santa Cruz from the fire of the enemy until the wagon train could be brought up; the artillery opened on the houses occupied by the enemy and on the more distant heights on which alone the guns could be brought to bear. The enemy discovering the wagons to be more than a mile in the rear sent a large party to cut them off, and it became necessary to detach Captain St. Vrain's company for their protection. This service was rendered in a most satisfactory manner. As soon as the wagon train had been brought up, Captain Angney was ordered to charge with his battalion of infantry and dislodge the enemy from the houses opposite the right flank, from which a warm fire was being poured upon the Americans, which was accomplished in a most gallant manner. A charge was now ordered upon the enemy at all points where he was seen in force. Captain Angney with his command, supported by Lieutenant White's company, charged up one hill, while St. Vrain's company turned the same in order to cut off the enemy while in retreat. The artillery, supported by Captains McMillan, Barber, and Slack, with their companies, at the same time took possession of some houses enclosed by a strong corral densely wooded with fruit trees, from which a brisk fire was kept up by the enemy, and of the heights beyond. In a few moments the enemy was dislodged and flying in all directions. The nature of the ground rendered pursuit hopeless and Colonel Price with the troops took up quarters in the town. In the morning the enemy again showed himself on the distant heights, but retreated so hastily that he could not be overtaken. The American loss in this battle was two killed and six wounded; that of the enemy, was thirty-six killed and forty-five wounded.[172]

On the 27th Colonel Price advanced up the Rio Grande as far as Los Luceros, where, early on the 28th, he was joined by Captain Burgwin, commanding a company of the 1st dragoons and a company of the 2d regiment of Missouri mounted volunteers, under Lieutenant Boone. At the same time Lieutenant Wilson, 1st dragoons, who had volunteered his services, came up with a six-pounder which had been sent from La Cañada. On the 29th, his entire force now consisting of 479, rank and file, Colonel Price marched to La Joya where it was learned that a party of the enemy, sixty or eighty strong, had posted themselves on the slopes of the mountains which rise on each side of the Rio Grande at Embudo. The road by Embudo was impracticable for artillery or wagons and Captain Burgwin with his company and the companies under St. Vrain and Lieutenant White, 180 strong, were sent in that direction. Pushing forward Captain Burgwin discovered six or seven hundred of the enemy posted on the sides of the canyon. The rapid slopes of the mountains rendered the position of the enemy very strong and its strength was increased by the dense masses of cedar, piñon, and large boulders which everywhere offered shelter. The action was commenced by Captain St. Vrain, who, dismounting his men, ascended the mountain to the left, doing much execution. Flanking parties were thrown out on either side and, ascending the hills rapidly, soon put the enemy to flight. The American loss in this engagement was one man killed and one severely wounded, both belonging to Captain St. Vrain's company.[173] The enemy's loss was twenty killed and sixty wounded.

FIGHT AT EMBUDO

On January 30th Captain Burgwin marched to Las Trampas,

---

[172] Sterling W. Price, *Report*, Sen. Doc. No. 442, 56th cong., 1st sess., pp. 9-10. The killed were Graham of Company B of the infantry battalion and G. Messersmith, a teamster who volunteered for the occasion. The wounded were Lieutenant Irvine of Company A of the infantry battalion, and privates John Pace, Caspers, of the mounted artillery, Lieutenant Dyer's detachment, and privates Aulmon, Murphy and Mezer, all of the artillery.

[173] The man killed was named Papin, a resident of Santa Fé. The person wounded was a negro named Dick, a slave who had belonged to Governor Bent.

Delegates in Congress
1. W. S. Meservy. 2. J. M. Gallegos. 3. Miguel A. Otero. 4. J. Francisco Chaves. 5. R. H. Weightman. 6. Francisco Perea. 7. Stephen B. Elkins. 8. Trinidad Romero. 9. Francisco A. Manzanares

where he waited the arrival of the wagons and artillery which had been compelled to seek a more southerly route.

The main body of the army having arrived at Las Trampas, Colonel Price proceeded with his entire command for Taos. Crossing the mountains, through roads filled with new-fallen snow, two feet in depth, the soldiers, marching in front of the artillery and wagons, with unwearied patience and constancy, in order to break the way, many of them frost-bitten, entered San Fernandez de Taos on the 3d of February. Here it was learned that about seven hundred of the enemy were posted at the pueblo of Taos. The place was strongly fortified. Here were the two pueblos, each capable of sheltering five or six hundred men. In addition there were a number of smaller buildings and in the northwestern angle stood the church, with a narrow passage between it and the outer wall. The buildings and the exterior walls were pierced for rifles.

<small>THE BATTLE OF TAOS</small>

A reconnoissance was made, and Lieutenant Dyer took position with the artillery on the western side of the village. A warm fire was kept up till sunset, when, as the ammunition wagon had not arrived, and the troops were suffering from the inclemency of the weather, they returned to San Fernandez. The following day the attack was renewed. On approaching the town, Captain Burgwin was stationed within two hundred and sixty yards of the western flank of the church, with his company and two howitzers, in command of Lieutenant Hassendaubel of Major Clark's artillery battalion. Lieutenant Dyer was ordered to take position with the six-pounder and the remaining two howitzers, about three hundred yards from the northern wall, so as to obtain a cross-fire upon the church, the most feasible point of attack. The mounted men, under Captains St. Vrain and Slack, moved around to the eastern side of the town, to intercept any fugitives who might attempt to escape in that direction, and the remainder of the troops were directed to support Lieutenant Dyer. Promptly at nine o'clock the batteries opened, and in two hours no breach had been effected in the walls of the church. Orders were therefore given to storm the building. Captain Burgwin advanced on the western side with the dragoons and one company of the 2d Missouri, while Captain Angney approached the northern wall with his battalion and two companies of the 2d Missouri.

The enemy held out manfully, and poured a terrible fire upon the assailants, who succeeded in gaining the cover of the wall on the western side of the church. As soon as the Americans had established themselves, they commenced plying their axes in an attempt to effect a breach. A temporary ladder was also constructed, by the aid of which the roof was fired. Captain Burgwin, and a small party, penetrated into the corral in front and endeavored to force the door of the church. They found the attempt fruitless, and, being exposed on all sides to the fire of the enemy, the party was compelled to retire to their former position, carrying with them their daring leader, mortally wounded. In the meantime several holes had been cut in the western wall, through which shells were thrown by hand, doing good execution. Lieutenant Wilson now came with the six-pounder, and poured a heavy fire of grape into the town. Between three and four o'clock in the afternoon the gun was run up, and opened on the church at sixty yards, the enemy still continuing their deadly volleys. After firing several rounds one of the holes, cut with the axes, was widened into a considerable breach. The six-pounder was further advanced within ten yards — a shell and three rounds of grape were thrown into the opening, and before the echoes had died away, a party of stormers, headed by Lieutenant Dyer, of the ordnance, and Lieutenants Wilson and Taylor, of the 1st dragoons, sprang through the smoke and falling ruins into the center of the church. The enemy fled before them, and shortly after abandoned the whole western part of the town. Some took refuge in the houses on the east, and others attempted to escape to the neighboring hills, but were mercilessly cut down by the mounted men under Captains St. Vrain and Slack.

The American troops were quietly quartered in the houses on the western side of the village; during the night of the 4th of February and early the following morning the old men and women of the enemy appeared before Colonel Price as supplicants, bearing their children, their images and crosses, and humbly sued for peace. Their request was granted on condition that Tomas, the Pueblo Indian, should be delivered up to him. This was done and Colonel Price then returned to San Fernandez with his command. In this engagement the Americans had seven killed and forty-five wounded, many of them mortally. One hundred and fifty of the enemy were killed and the number of his wounded was still greater. The prompt action of Colonel Price put an end to the insurrection. All of the leaders except Cortés were dead, and, although the American forces remained for several days at San Fernandez, no other indications of disaffection were discovered, and the command therefore returned to Santa Fé.[174]

On the day following the murder of Governor Bent some traders, on their way to the Missouri river, were captured just as they were

[174] Of the leaders openly engaged in this revolution Tafoya was killed at La Cañada; Chavez fell at Taos. Tomasito was shot in an altercation with a soldier named Fitzpatrick in the guard-room at San Fernandez, and Montoya was hanged at San Fernandez on the 7th of February. It will be remembered that General Kearny assumed to transfer the allegiance of the inhabitants of New Mexico from their own government to that of the United States. If this could have been done, which it could not under the laws of nations, the revolutionists were all guilty of treason, and the execution of Montoya would therefore have been justified. Colonel Price seems to have regarded the matter in this light; but a few weeks later he was advised that the government of the United States had disapproved a part of the official acts of General Kearny — transferring the allegiance of the Mexican citizens.

Captain Burgwin died on the morning of the 7th of February. In reporting the fact to the adjutant general of the army, Colonel Wharton of the 1st Dragoons says: "Having known long and intimately the late captain, I cannot forbear observing that for personal worth and professional excellence in his particular arm of the service the deceased has left no superior behind him. The announcement of his death — this morning learned — has cast a gloom over the hearts of all at this post who ever knew him professionally or personally." This report was made from Fort Leavenworth, April 1, 1847.

In the month of June, 1847, among other Indians raiding, infesting, and marauding on the Santa Fé Trail were the Comanche and Kiowa Indians; also some of the Delawares from the Missouri frontier. One Delaware, who made his escape from Taos, after the battle at that place, had been known to have spent the spring and a part of the summer amongst the Comanches. At Taos he fought desperately against the Americans and is supposed to have killed the gallant Captain Burgwin and three or four of the regulars who were shot down in the assault on the church. After the defeat of the insurgents, he made his escape from that country, came out to the Arkansas river, where he found the Cheyennes, told them what had happened at Taos, and that in the battle he killed five Americans. He used every effort in his power to induce the Cheyennes to join him in a war against the whites, representing them as a bad people and the ruin of all Indians. This argument having failed, he remained but one night and started the next morning for the Comanches. This Delaware who was well known in this country by the name of "Big Nigger," left the west and went to Westport, Missouri, in the summer of 1847, where he displayed a rifle known to have belonged to a man by the name of Sharp, who was killed in June on Walnut creek on the Arkansas river.

For a full and complete account with all the official reports concerning this insurrection, see *Insurrection against the Military Government in New Mexico and California, 1847 and 1848*, Sen. Doc. No. 442, 56th congress, 1st session.

entering the town of Mora. The insurrectionary force was under the command of Manuel Cortés. All of these men were taken out and shot. The most prominent among them was Lawrence L. Waldo, of Westport, Missouri, father of Henry L. Waldo, of Las Vegas. Mr. Waldo had been engaged in the Santa Fé trade for many years. Like Governor Bent, he was respected and liked by the masses of the Mexican people and by the Indians. On the 15th of February, 1847, an official proclamation, issued from the government printing office at Santa Fé, recites the events occurring at this time at Mora and the steps which were taken to suppress the insurrection at that place. In this publication, a copy of which is on file in the records of the war department at Washington, it is said:

THE MURDER OF CULVER, WALDO, AND OTHERS AT MORA

"On the 25th ultimo Captain Hendley (of Colonel Willock's battalion) who was in command of the grazing parties on the Rio Mora, marched with 80 men to the town of Mora to suppress the insurrection there and arrest the murderers of Messrs. Culver, Waldo, Noyes and others, who were massacred at that place.

"He found a body of Mexicans, under arms, prepared to defend the town, and while forming his men into line for attack, a small party of the insurgents was seen running from the hills. A detachment was ordered to cut them off, which was attacked by the main body of the enemy. A general engagement immediately ensued, the Mexicans retreating to the town and firing from the windows and loop-holes in their houses. Captain Hendley and his men closely pursued, rushing into their houses with them, shooting some, and running others through with their bayonets.

"A large body of the insurgents had taken possession of an old fort and commenced a fire from the loop-holes. Captain Hendley, with a small party, had taken possession of an apartment in the fort and, while preparing to fire it, was shot by a ball from an adjoining room. He fell and died in a few moments. Our men, having no artillery, and the fort being impregnable without it, retired to Las Vegas. The enemy had twenty-five killed and seventeen taken prisoners. The American loss was one killed and three wounded.

"On the 1st instant, Captain Morin, who had been ordered from Santa Fé by Colonel Willock to succeed Captain Hendley in the command, proceeded with a body of men and one piece of cannon to Mora and razed the towns (Upper and Lower Mora) to the ground, the insurgents having fled to the mountains. Several Mexicans were captured, supposed to be concerned in the murder of Messrs. Culver, Waldo and others, and, after many threats, were forced to show where the bodies were buried. Seven of them were found and carried to Las Vegas for interment."[175]

Subsequent to the battle at the Taos pueblo there does not appear to have been much activity among the revolutionists except in localities east of the mountains. In the month of May a grazing party and a wagon train were attacked and two or three men killed and a large number of horses and mules driven off. They were pursued by Major Edmonson, who overtook them in force in a deep canyon in Red river, where a severe engagement ensued, the details of which are given in a note.[176]

---

[175] In his report from Las Vegas to General Price, dated January 25, 1847, Captain W. S. Murphy, 1st Missouri volunteers, says: "Romulus Culver of Chariton; Ludlow Waldo, of Jackson; Mr. Prewitt [Benjamin] of Santa Fé; Lewis Cabanne, of Missouri, and four or five others in company were taken prisoners, robbed and shot at Mora-town on or about the 20th of the month. The leader of the forces at that place is a man by the name of Cortéz."

The only towns or communities on the east side of the mountains not taking part in the uprising were Las Vegas and Tecolote, in San Miguel county, as appears from Captain Hendley's last report to Colonel Price, in which he says: "On the evening of the 20th inst. myself and Lieut. N. J. Williams happened at this place (Las Vegas) just as the town had assembled in general council to hear the same circular read that has been forwarded to you from Taos. The alcalde of this place (Juan de Dios Maes) declared against the insurrection, and stopped the express and forwarded the letter to you. Early the next day I took possession of this place with a part of my command and have ordered the balance to join me to-day."

Mr. Waldo was a brother of Captain Waldo of Doniphan's regiment. In a letter written to Captain Waldo by him, six days prior to his death at Mora, he said: "It seems that a general mistake has been made by all that were acquainted with the *gente* of this Territory in regard to their willingness to be subjected to the rule of the United States. It is satisfactorily ascertained that not one in ten is *á gusto*, and, as far as I can judge, and I am well acquainted with the eastern side of the mountains, not one in one hundred is content."

The bodies of those killed at Mora, when brought to Las Vegas, were buried on the hill to the west of the town (old town) but the exact location is not known.

[176] *Insurrection against the Military Government in New Mexico and California*, 1847 and 1848, *Senate Doc.* No. 442, 56th cong., 1st sess., *Report* of D. B. Edmondson, major commanding, pp. 21-24: "Upon my arrival at San Miguel I was informed that a large party of Cheyenne and Apache Indians had gone to the mouth of the Mora on Red river to join a marauding party of Mexicans and others, numbering 300 to 400, and commanded by the outlaw, Cortéz, and that small detachments were being sent into the settlements to commit depredations on the property of the citizens and American soldiers. On my arrival at Las Vegas, May 20, being informed that a party of about 50 Indians were in the mountains thirty miles north, having with them about 200 stolen animals, I despatched Company F, Captain Morin, in pursuit. On the same day Company B, Captain Dent, was sent to disperse a marauding party said to be about forty miles south of this place. On the evening of the same day I received information of the surprise of our grazing party under Captain

In the month of June, 1847, there was trouble at Las Vegas. Lieutenant Brown and three men, pursuing horse-thieves, were killed. Property and equipment which had belonged to Brown were found in the possession of some of the inhabitants of the town. Major Edmondson attacked the town, killed ten or twelve men, found indications of a new revolt, captured the town and sent about fifty

DEATH OF LIEUTENANT BROWN —
FIGHT AT LAS VEGAS

Roberson near Wagon Mound by a party of Indians and Mexicans, in which we lost one man killed and two wounded, and about 250 horses. Being destitute of mounted men in consequence of the departure of the commands of Captains Morin and Dent, on the morning previous, I immediately ordered in the grazing parties from the Ocaté. I was thus enabled by the use of some government animals to mount between 75 and 80 men, with which command I reached Captain Roberson's camp on the evening of the 24th. I there found Captain Brown (with 12 wagons laden with goods belonging to our sutlers, Messrs. Rich and Pomeroy) who had been attacked the previous day at Santa Clara Springs (eight miles distant) by the Indians, who made a desperate effort to get possession of the wagons. Failing in that attempt, they drove his oxen out of reach of gun-shot and deliberately killed them to the number of between 60 and 70. The killing of the cattle was doubtless intended to detain the wagons and thus afford an opportunity to surprise and get possession of them. On the following morning, 25th, leaving about 30 men for the protection of the sutler's wagons, I organized two scouting parties, one under charge of Captain Holloway, and the other in charge of Lieutenant Elliot, with directions to rendezvous at Santa Clara Springs the following night. We that day discovered where the enemy had corralled their animals a few days previous in the mountains, about 15 miles south of Santa Clara Springs, but had left in the direction of Red river. On the following morning, after forming an advance or spy party, under command of Captain Holloway, company E, the remainder were formed into three platoons; number one, commanded by Captain Roberson; number 2, by Lieutenant Elliot and number three by Lieutenant Brown, company F. Thus organized I proceeded to follow the trail discovered on the day previous to the canyon of Red river. I entered it with Captain Roberson's command, leaving the commands of Lieutenants Elliot and Brown behind, the company of spies going some fifty minutes in advance in order to prevent surprise. Descending into the canyon with great difficulty through the rocks, leading our horses and following the meanderings of the Indian trail about half a mile, I discovered three Indians secreted behind the rocks about 200 yards from our trail. Supposing that a large number might be there secreted, and having myself the advantage of the ground, I ordered a halt until the rear of the command should arrive. Whereupon the three Indians, who had no doubt been placed there as sentinels, made a rush for their horses, they being close at hand and ready-saddled. They were immediately fired upon, killing one of them and unhorsing another; the two remaining Indians mounted one horse and thus made their escape for the time. We then continued to descend to the bottom of the canyon, and with some difficulty effected a crossing of the river. Pursuing the tracks up the bank of the river, we passed the two Indians above spoken of, who immediately made a desperate attempt to reach the main body of the enemy, who were then in our rear, but were immediately pursued and both slain before they could reach their party. The hills around us were by this time literally covered with Indians and Mexicans, who witnessed the tragedy

prisoners to Santa Fé, also burning the mill of the alcalde, Juan de Dios Maes, who was charged with complicity.

In the month of July a detachment of thirty-one soldiers was attacked at La Cienega, near Taos, Lieutenant Larkin and five men being killed. On the approach of reënforcements, however, the enemy fled. Subsequent to this time there does not seem to have been any important engagement other than the fight with Cortéz, near Anton Chico or La Cuesta, in which more than four hundred

---

and opened fire upon us from every point occupied by them. The bottom of the canyon was so narrow as to expose our men to the fire of the enemy from the hills on either side, which were very rocky and so nearly perpendicular as to render a charge impossible. I determined to re-cross the river in view of occupying some high points on the opposite side which would at all times command the outlet from the canyon, but the enemy, understanding the order, or anticipating it, got possession of the ford before the men could be rallied, who were somewhat scattered in pursuit of the two Indians spoken of. I then returned up the river some half mile and took possession of a point of rocks which was out of gun-shot reach from the hills on the opposite side of the river, but being too far from the river to command access to water, I determined to occupy a point more favorably situated, in passing to which Lieutenants Elliot, Miller and Searcy, who were in the rear, discovered a large party of Mexicans rapidly descending the hill (who had escaped my notice), rallied about 20 men and kept them in check until the main body got possession of the point last designated. The men were immediately ordered to dismount, conceal their horses as far as possible, and take advantage of the rocks until the enemy should approach sufficiently near to enable us to make a charge, sending at the same time a detachment to the bank of the river to secure the water and prevent the enemy passing up the canyon in our rear. Our troops being thus disposed of, the fight commenced at the three several points and continued without intermission about four hours, the enemy alternately advancing and retreating as new recruits arrived. About sunset, having driven beyond our reach the Indians and Mexicans, finding a large portion of the troops out of ammunition, many of our men having ceased firing for want of it, and knowing that we would necessarily have to fight our way out of the canyon, as the enemy occupied the passes, I determined to reach the open ground at the top of the canyon before dark, which was effected in good order, except in fording the river, where the enemy, anticipating our movement, were concealed in considerable numbers, opened a hot fire, wounding two of our men and killing several horses. After crossing the river we returned the fire of the Indians and drove them back with the loss of five killed and several wounded. We then proceeded to the top of the hill in good order, reaching it at dark, whereupon our troops were immediately formed for action; but no enemy appearing, we marched to water and encamped for the night, in view of returning to the canyon the following morning. Our number in the engagement was seventy-seven; the number of the enemy could not be correctly ascertained, but have been variously estimated at from 400 to 600. Our loss was one man killed and 3 slightly wounded, while the enemy's loss was reported at 41 killed. The number of their wounded could not be ascertained, as they were moved off the field as fast as they fell. On consulting with the officers the next day, 27th, and finding that that portion of our troops furnished by the grazing parties (composing much the largest portion of the command) were entirely out of ammunition, we were reluctantly compelled to suspend operations until a further

revolutionists took part. A number was slain and about fifty prisoners taken, the others fleeing to the mountains.

The bodies of Governor Bent and Captain Burgwin were brought to Santa Fé by Colonel Price and on the 16th of February were buried in the cemetery at the capital; the remains of Captain Burgwin were afterwards disinterred and taken to Fort Leavenworth.

AFFAIRS AT SANTA FÉ — ACTING GOVERNOR VIGIL

Immediately following the news of the death of Governor Bent, Donaciano Vigil, secretary of the territory, acting as governor, issued a proclamation to the people of the territory as follows: [177]

"TRIUMPH OF PRINCIPLES OVER TURPITUDE.

"The Provisional Governor of the Territory to its Inhabitants:

"FELLOW CITIZENS:— The gang of Pablo Montoya and Cortéz, in Taos, infatuated in consequence of having sacrificed to their caprice his excellency, the governor, and other peaceable citizens, and commencing their great work of plunder by sacking the houses of their victims, according to principles proclaimed by them, for the

---

supply could be obtained. Upon re-entering the canyon we found that the enemy had left on the night after the battle in great haste, leaving horses, cattle, camp equipage, etc., not taking time to scalp or strip our man lost in the action, as is their custom. We pursued them with all possible dispatch to their first camping ground in their retreat, where, from appearances, they had made a division of their property and forces. We continued to follow their traces many miles on the plains, until, getting among large herds of mustangs or wild horses, it became impossible to track them further."

[177] At the same time that this proclamation was issued, still another was distributed throughout the territory, in which Acting Governor Vigil says: "*Fellow Citizens*: Your regularly appointed governor had occasion to go on private business as far as the town of Taos. A popular insurrection, headed by Pablo Montoya and Manuel Cortéz, who raised the cry of revolution, resulted in the barbarous assassination of his excellency, the governor, of the greater part of the Government officials, and some private citizens. Pablo Montoya, whom you already know, notorious for his insubordination and restlessness, headed a similar insurrection in September, 1837. Destitute of any sense of shame, he brought his followers to this capital, entered into an arrangement, deserted, as a reward for their fidelity, the unfortunate Montoyas, Esquibel and Chopon, whose fate you know, and retired himself well-paid for his exploits to his den at Taos. The whole population let the weight of their execration fall on others and this brigand they left living on his wits — for he has no home or known property, and is engaged in no occupation. Of what kind of people is his gang composed? Of the insurgent Indian population of Taos, and of others as abandoned and desperate as their rebellious chief. Discreet and respectable men are anxiously awaiting the forces of the Government in order to be relieved from the anarchy in which disorder has placed them and this relief will speedily be afforded them. In the year 1837 this mischievous fool took, as a motto for his perversity, the word 'Canton,' and now it is 'the

Cheyenne Prisoners Captured by General Custer, March, 1869
Raiders on Santa Fé Trail

purpose of making proselytes, yesterday encountered in the vicinity of La Cañada the forces of the government, restorative of order and peace, and in that place, unfortunately for them, their triumph ended; for they were routed with the loss of many killed and 44 prisoners, upon whom the judgment of the law will fall.

"Their hosts were composed of scoundrels and desperadoes, so that it may be said that the war was one of the rabble against honest and discreet men; not one of the latter has as yet been found among this crew of vagabonds, unless, perhaps, some one actuated by the fear of losing his life while in their power or of being robbed of his property. The Government has the information and congratulates itself that within ten days the inquietude caused you by the cry of alarm raised in Taos will cease, and peace, the precursor of the felicity of the country, will return to take her seat on the altar of concord and reciprocal confidence.

"The ringleaders of the conspiracy, if they should be apprehended, will receive the reward due to their signal crimes, and the Government, which for the present has been compelled to act with energy in order to crush the head of the revolutionary hydra which began to show itself in Taos, will afterwards adopt lenient measures, in order to consolidate the union of all the inhabitants of this beautiful country, under the aegis of law and reason.

---

re-union of Taos!' Behold the works of the champion who guides the revolution! And can there be a single man of sense who would voluntarily join his ranks? I should think not.

"Another of his pretended objects is to wage war against the foreign government. Why, if he is so full of patriotism, did he not exert himself and lead troops to prevent the entry of American forces in the month of August, instead of glutting his insane passions and showing his martial valor by the brutal sacrifice of defenseless victims, and this at the very time when an arrangement between the two governments, with regard to boundaries, was expected? Whether this country has to belong to the government of the United States or return to its native Mexico, is it not a gross absurdity to foment rancorous feelings toward people with whom we are either to compose one family, or to continue our commercial relations? Unquestionably it is.

"To-day or to-morrow a respectable body of troops will commence their march for the purpose of quelling these disorders of Pablo Montoya, in Taos. The government is determined to pursue energetic measures toward all the refractory until they are reduced to order, as well as to take care of and protect honest and discreet men; and I pray you that, harkening to the voice of reason, for the sake of the common happiness and your own preservation, you will keep yourselves quiet and engaged in your private affairs.

"The term of my administration is purely transitory. Neither my qualification nor the ad interim character, according to the organic law in which I take the reins of government, encourage me to continue in so difficult and thorny a post, the duties of which are intended for individuals of greater enterprise and talents; but I protest to you, in the utmost fervor of my heart that I will devote myself exclusively to endeavouring to secure you all the prosperity so much desired by your fellow-citizen and friend.

"January 22, 1847. DONACIANO VIGIL."

"I hope, therefore, that, your minds being now relieved of past fears, you will think only of the security and protection of the law; and, uniting with your Government, will afford it the aid of your intelligence, in order that it may secure to you the prosperity desired by your fellow-citizen and friend.

"DONACIANO VIGIL.
"Santa Fé January 25, 1847."

These proclamations and a circular entitled "Supreme Government of the Territory," in which Governor Vigil calls attention to the events transpiring during the preceding ten years and the character of the men who were leaders in the conspiracy, had a good effect in the restoration of peace and order and in preventing any outbreaks in other portions of the territory, other than the activities of Cortéz and his band on the eastern side of the mountains. This Circular,[178] commenting upon the causes of the revolution of 1837 and also as to the conduct of the people of Taos toward the foreign residents of Taos during the Texas troubles of 1843, declared that the vicious element in that portion of New Mexico,

"in the year 1843 rose and sacked the tithe granaries situated at various points in the valley of Taos and the government, shrinking from the duty of punishment of this excess and castigating, at least, the principal culprits, approved, or for the same reason, so completely overlooked it, that no notice was taken of the affair. Encouraged by the impunity which attended this crime, in the beginning of July, in the same year, they re-assembled with criminal views of a more enlarged nature; for they proposed to themselves and attempted, in the first place, to kill the few Americans and French who had married and settled among them; and although they did not consummate this, owing as well to want of unanimity among themselves as to their failing to effect a surprise, they sated their rapacity by plundering the stores and houses of the wealthiest foreigners. The local authorities, with the view of quieting the complaints of the injured individuals, commenced some proceedings which, from the mode in which they were carried on, necessarily led to no result. On this application was made to the government, but with the same result; and finally, after much expense and trouble, through the indifference and connivance of the said authorities and of the government, the injured parties were ruined, and the miscreants who perpetrated the crime were left to enjoy, in absolute impunity, the fruit of their plunder.

---

[178] The two proclamations and the circular letter are to be found in full in *Insurrection against the Military Government in New Mexico and California in 1847 and 1848*, Sen. Doc. 442, 56th cong., 1st sess.

"The apathetic and criminal conduct of the previous administrations with respect to popular commotions gave so much encouragement to the perpetrators of these crimes that those who originated the plan of the revolution which has just been quelled found no difficulty whatever among the people of Taos, already adepts in such proceedings.

"According to statements made by the Indians of the town of Taos, who have appealed to the clemency of the commander of the forces employed in the restoration of order, the same Diego Archuleta who, in the middle of December, last year, planned a revolution in this city, which, being discovered in time by the government, was quelled before it burst forth, is the individual who, before flying from the country, aided by the so-called generals Pablo Montoya, Manuel Cortéz, Jesus Tafoya, and Pablo Chavez, instigated them to the insurrection and proceedings which they carried into execution, and persuaded them that they might enter Santa Fé without resistance, and might subsequently, with little trouble, destroy or drive out of the country all the forces of the government.

"The individuals mentioned are, so far as now known, the chiefs of this band of murderers and thieves. Diego Archuleta fled in a cowardly manner from the Territory before the commencement of the revolution which he himself planned and counselled; Chavez and Tafoya fell in action; Montoya was executed at Taos, and the assassin, Cortéz, is wandering a fugitive in the mountains. There are besides at the disposal of the tribunals various individuals arraigned as accomplices, upon whom, if guilty, the judgment of the law will fall.

"The government troops triumphed over the rebels successively at La Cañada, Embudo and Taos where the victory was decisive. There were killed in the field and town of Taos about two hundred rebels; the remainder begged for their lives and a pardon, which was granted them; and they were left at liberty to pursue their occupations in the security and peace which they themselves had disturbed."

The facts as outlined in the proclamations and the logical arguments of Governor Vigil easily had a salubrious effect upon the people of the territory. At the same time, during the month of March, at Santa Fé, the vigorous prosecution of the individuals who had been taken "in arms" against the American authority by the district attorney, Frank P. Blair, was productive of good results. A large number of persons who had been arrested or captured were discharged for want of testimony sufficient to indict them for "treason" against a government of which they were not citizens! Prior to the conflict at Taos and the murder of Governor Bent and others, a circular letter was distributed among the people. A copy of this letter was brought to Santa Fé and delivered to the vicario, Juan Felipe Ortiz, who, although he had been prominently identified with the conspiracy of December, 1846, saw fit to place this letter in the hands of Colonel Price. It was used against several of the individuals who were indicted and tried at Santa Fé, among others, Don Antonio Maria Trujillo. This letter bore date January 20, 1847, was sent out by General Jesus Tafolla and was countersigned by Antonio Maria Trujillo.[179] The letter was addressed to several native military officers and was accompanied by certain orders in relation to the revolution and its conduct.

All of the indictments [180] in the cases before the March term,

---

[179] The letter and the orders are as follows:

"To the Defenders of their Country: With the end to shake off the yoke bound on us by a foreign government, and as you are military inspector general, appointed by the legitimate commander for the supreme government of Mexico, which we proclaim in favor of; the moment you receive this communication, you will place in readiness all the companies under your command, keeping them ready for the 22d day of this month, so that the forces may be, on the day mentioned, at that point. Take the precaution to observe, if the forces of the enemy advance any toward these points, and if it should so happen, appoint a courier and despatch him immediately, so that exertions may be doubled, understanding that there must not be resistance or delay in giving the answer to the bearer of this official document.

"By the order of the Inspector of Arms, Don Antonio Maria Trujillo, I herewith send you this despatch (or order) that the moment this comes to hand, you will raise all the forces, together with all the inhabitants that are able to bear arms, connecting them also with persons in San Juan de los Caballeros, by tomorrow, counting from the 22d day of the present month, and not later than eight o'clock in the morning.

"We have declared war with the American and it is now time that we shall all take our arms in our hands in defense of our abandoned country. You are held responsible for the execution of the above order.

"Juan Antonio Garcia.
"Sor. So. Dn. Pedro Vigil."

[180] The records in the office of the clerk of the District Court at Santa Fé contain the record of this trial and all papers used in connection therewith. The indictment and Judge Houghton's sentence were as follows:

"UNITED STATES OF AMERICA } ss
  "Territory of New Mexico }

    "In the United States District Court, at the March Term, 1847.

"The Grand Jurors for the district of New Mexico, on the part of the United States of America, on their oaths present that Antonio Maria Trujillo, of the county of Taos, in the Territory of New Mexico, being a citizen of the United States of America, but disregarding the duty of his allegiance to the government of the United States aforesaid, and wholly withdrawing the allegiance, duty and obedience which every true and faithful citizen of the said government and of right ought to bear toward the citizens of the United States, on the 20th day of January, in the year 1847, and on divers others days

THE WAR WITH MEXICO 253

1847, of the United States district court, territory of New Mexico, were prepared by Francis P. Blair, Jr., who also conducted the trials which were had before Chief Justice Houghton. There were a great many convicted in addition to the chief conspirator, Trujillo, in passing sentence upon whom, Judge Houghton was very impressive. The age and family connections of the prisoner produced much sympathy for the convicted man, and Governor Vigil, although firm in his belief that the most vigorous punishment should be meted out to the persons responsible for the murder of Governor Bent, asked the president [181] of the United States to pardon Trujillo.

---

as well before as after, with force and arms, at the county aforesaid and Territory aforesaid, together with divers other false traitors, to the jurors aforesaid unknown, did then and there maliciously, wickedly and traitorously levy war against the government of the United States of America and did, then and there, maliciously and traitorously endeavour and attempt to subvert the laws and constitution of the government, to the evil example of all others in like cases offending and against the peace and dignity of the government of the United States."

The sentence of the court: "Antonio Maria Trujillo: A jury of twelve citizens, after a patient and careful investigation, pending which all the safeguards of the law, managed by able and indefatigable counsel, have been offered you, have found you guilty of the high crime of treason. What have you to say why the sentence of death should not be pronounced against you?

"Your age and gray hairs have excited the sympathy of both the court and the jury, yet while each and all were not only willing but anxious that you should have every advantage placed at your disposal that their highly responsible duty under the laws to their country would permit, you have been found guilty of the crime alleged to your charge. It would appear that old age has not brought you wisdom nor purity nor honesty of heart. While holding out the hand of friendship to those whom circumstances have brought to rule over you you have nourished bitterness and hatred in your heart. You have been found seconding the acts of a band of the most traitorous murderers that ever blackened with a recital of their deeds the annals of history. Not content with the peace and security in which you have lived under the present government, secure in all your personal rights as a citizen, in property, in person and in your religion, you gave your name and influence to measures intended to effect universal murder and pillage, the overthrow of the government and one wide-spread scene of bloodshed in the land. For such foul crimes an enlightened and liberal jury have been compelled, from the evidence brought before them, and by a sense of their stern but unmistakable duty to find you guilty of treason against the government under which you are a citizen. And there only remains to the court the painful duty of passing upon you the sentence of the law, which is that you be taken from hence to prison, and there remain until Friday, the 16th day of April next, and that at 2 o'clock in the afternoon of that day, you be taken thence to the place of execution and there be hanged by the neck till you are dead, dead, dead. And may the Almighty God have mercy on your soul."

[181] Immediately after the conclusion of the trial of Trujillo, Governor Vigil addressed a letter to the secretary of state, James Buchanan, in which he says: "A petition was immediately laid before me, signed by the presiding justice, one of the associate justices, United States district attorney, the

The president declined but requested Governor Vigil to do so, which was accordingly done.

After the adjournment of the session of court at Santa Fé, under military escort, Chief Justice Houghton and Associate Justice Beaubien proceeded to Taos, where a term of court was held and at which a number of persons were tried for murder and treason. Several were convicted and hung during the month of April. Present at the trial, which was conducted in a court room surrounded and guarded by armed soldiers, were the daughters of the murdered governor, his brothers William [182] and George Bent, Lucien B. Maxwell, and a large number of prominent citizens of the territory. Judges

counsel for the defense, most of the members of the jury, before whom the accused was tried and many of the most respectable citizens praying that the execution of the sentence of the court be suspended until a petition could be laid before the President of the United States for the pardon of the prisoner on the ground of his age and infirmity.

"Though feeling assured that the accused had had a fair trial and had been justly sentenced and legally convicted I still feel justified in granting the prayer of the petition, signed as it is by the court and the jury before whom he was tried and convicted.

"I am informed that a petition will be immediately forwarded to the President praying for the pardon of Trujillo on the grounds above stated. I trust the President will give the matter careful consideration. The prisoner is about seventy-five years of age, necessarily infirm and evidently near the end of his days; and although as the head of an influential family much was done in his name to excite and forward the late rebellion, still on account of his years and the near termination of his career I cannot but consider him a proper subject for the mercy of the government.

"The United States district court is still in session at this capital having under trial three indictments for treason against three prominent persons in the late rebellion. Twenty-four prisoners have been discharged for want of testimony to indict them for treason, and also on the ground that they have been under the influence and deceived by the representations of men who had always exercised tyrannical control over them.

"I am informed that there are upward of forty prisoners confined in the northern district awaiting their trial at the coming term of the United States district court for that district. I can not do less than commend the diligence and at the same time the justice with which the tribunals of the Territory discharge their duties. With the highest sentiments of esteem, truly your most obedient servant,

"DONACIANO VIGIL."

[182] William Bent appears to have been the first of the Bent brothers to go to the Rocky Mountain country, but his brother Charles, the governor, must have soon joined him there, and these two, with Céran St. Vrain, established the early trading post on the Arkansas about where the city of Pueblo now stands. Here some frontiersmen, with Mexican or Indian wives, had attempted to do some farming; the settlement is mentioned by Colonel Fremont, who visited it several years later. After occupying this post for a few years they moved down to the post afterwards known as Bent's Fort. George and Robert Bent, other brothers, did not come out to the fort until after it was completed —

Houghton and Beaubien also presided at this trial. An eye-witness has preserved to us an account of the proceedings. He says:

"Court assembled at nine o'clock. On entering the room, Judges Beaubien and Houghton were occupying their official stations. After many dry preliminaries, six prisoners were brought in — ill-favored, half-scared, sullen fellows; and the jury of Mexicans and Americans — Chadwick, foreman — being empaneled, the trial commenced, F. P. Blair, jr., prosecuting attorney, assisted by —— Wharton, a

---

perhaps not until it had been in operation for some time. Benito Vasquez was at one time a partner in the company.

In his testimony before the joint commission which inquired into Indian affairs on the plains, in 1865, William Bent stated that he had first come to the Arkansas and settled near the present site of the city of Pueblo in 1824. When it was determined to construct the adobe fort on the Arkansas, the Bents employed a number of Mexican laborers who made the adobes. Only a short time after work was commenced the smallpox broke out in a very severe form. William Bent, Céran St. Vrain, and Kit Carson, and some other frontiersmen who were there, all caught the disease and, though none died, they were so badly marked by it that some of the Indians who had known them well did not recognize them when they again met. During the prevalence of the epidemic Bent sent one of his Mexican herders north to warn the Cheyennes not to come to the post. This Mexican's name was Francisco and on his way to the Black Hills he met a large war-party of Cheyennes then on their way to the fort. He told them what had happened and not to come near until they were sent for. The Indians obeyed and it was not until some time later, when all of the infected material at the post had been burned, that Bent and St. Vrain set out for the Black Hills to find the Indians and invite them to return to the post and trade. This was about 1830. Some time before his death Kit Carson said that at one time more than 150 laborers (Mexicans) were employed in building the post. Besides this fort, Bent and St. Vrain owned St. Vrain's Fort on the South Platte and Adobe Fort on the Canadian. These posts were built for trade with the northern Indians, the Sioux and the Cheyennes, who seldom came as far south as the Arkansas. The Adobe Fort on the Canadian was built by request of the Kiowa chiefs, Little Mountain (To-hau-sen) and Eagle Tail Feathers, and Shaved Head, a Comanche, and Poor Bear, a big chief of the Jicarilla Apaches. Shaved Head was a great chief and very friendly to the white people; he wore the left side of his head shaved, while the hair on the right side was very long, hanging below his waist; his left ear was perforated with many holes, made with a blunt awl, heated red hot; through these suspended many little brass rings. Before peace was made between the allied Cheyenne, Arapaho, the Kiowa, and the Apache, in the year 1840, the last three named tribes were afraid to visit Fort Bent, and for this reason they asked Colonel Bent to build Fort Adobe. Although William Bent had a Cheyenne wife he managed to keep on good terms with the enemies of the Cheyenne tribe.

In the business at the fort William Bent took care of matters while his brother Charles took care of affairs with the Mexican settlers and the trade to Taos and to Santa Fé. It is uncertain when St. Vrain, Lee, and Vasquez became partners, or how long they remained as such. George and Robert Bent, who came out from St. Louis, may have been partners, but there is nothing of documentary proof to show it. Robert died in 1847. George Bent was married to a Mexican lady by whom he had two children who went to St. Louis, Missouri, to school. George died in 1848, at the fort, and F. P. Blair, Jr., was

great blowhard. The counsel for the defense, whose name I have forgotten, was, as well as Wharton, a volunteer private, on furlough for the occasion. They had no doubt joined the ranks in hopes of political preferment on their return home, and the forests of Missouri may yet re-echo with Wharton's stentorian voice, proclaiming to his hero-worshiping constituents how he 'fought, bled, and died' for his country's liberties. . . Mr. St. Vrain was interpreter. When the witnesses (Mexican) touched their lips to the bible, on taking the oath, it was with such a combination of reverential awe for the book, and fear of *Los Americanos*, that I could not repress a smile. The poor things were as much frightened as the prisoners at the bar. It certainly did appear to be a great assumption on the part of the Americans to conquer a country, and then arraign the revolting inhabitants for treason. American judges sat on the bench, New Mexicans and Americans filled the jury-box and American soldiery guarded the halls. Verily, a strange mixture of violence and justice — a strange middle-ground between the martial and common law.

"After an absence of a few minutes, the jury returned with a verdict of 'guilty in the first degree' — five for murder, one for

---

guardian for his children. He was buried near his brother, Robert, in the graveyard which lay a short distance northeast of the northeast bastion of the fort.

About 1835 William Bent married Owl Woman, the daughter of White Thunder, an important man among the Cheyennes, and at that time the keeper of the medicine arrows. There were four children of this marriage, Mary, born about 1836, Robert in 1839, George in 1843, and Julia in 1847. Owl Woman died in 1847 in giving birth to Julia and Colonel Bent afterwards married Yellow Woman, a sister of Owl Woman. Charles Bent was a child of this second marriage. Colonel Bent understood the Sioux language thoroughly, having learned it while in the employ of the American Fur Company as early as 1816.

About seventy miles above Bent's Fort and immediately on the Arkansas river, there was a small settlement, the principal part of which was composed of old trappers and hunters; the male part were mostly Americans, Missouri-French, Canadians, and Mexicans. They had a tolerable supply of cattle, horses, mules, etc.; they raised a good crop of beans, corn, pumpkins, and other vegetables. They numbered about 150 souls, and of this number about sixty were men, nearly all having wives and some having two. These wives were of various Indian tribes, as follows: Blackfoot, Assiniboine, Aricaras, Sioux, Arapaho, Cheyenne, Pawnee, Snake, Sinpach (from west of the Great Lakes) Chinook, (from the mouth of the Columbia) Mexicans, and Americans. The American women were Mormons; a party of Mormons wintered there and on their departure for California, left behind two families. These people lived in two separate establishments near each other; one called "Pueblo" and the other "Hardscrabble." Both villages were fortified by a wall twelve feet high composed of adobe. These places became the resort of idlers and loafers. They were also the depots for the smugglers of liquor from New Mexico; and it was recommended by American army officers that the places be carefully watched.— *Appendix to the Report of the Commissioner of Indian Affairs*, Ex. Doc. 1, 1847.

Pueblo Indian Governors who visited Washington, D. C., in 1862, to whom President Lincoln gave Canes, now used by all the Pueblo Governors as Badges of Authority

treason. Treason, indeed! But so it was; and as the jail was overstocked with others awaiting trial, it was deemed expedient to hasten the execution, and the culprits were sentenced to be hung on the following Friday — hangman's day. When the concluding words — 'muerto, muerto, muerto — dead, dead, dead' — were pronounced by Judge Beaubien, in his solemn and impressive manner, the painful stillness that reigned in the court-room, and the subdued grief manifested by a few by-standers, were noticed not without an inward sympathy. The poor wretches sat with unmovable features; but, I fancied that, under the assumed looks of apathetic indifference, could be read the deepest anguish. When remanded to jail till the day of execution, they drew their *serapes* more closely around them and accompanied the armed guard.[183]

[183] Garrard, Lewis H., *Wah-to-Yah and The Taos Trail.* Hua-to-ya — Ute word meaning ''The Twins;'' Dr. E. L. Hewett ascertained this from the Utes on the southern Ute Reservation. Mr. Garrard, who was present at the trial of the murderers of Governor Bent, gives a different account of the killing than that given by Mrs. Scheurich. He says: ''With Hatcher I visited the house in which Governor Bent was murdered; who, with the district attorney, J. W. Leal, came from Santa Fé to issue a proclamation. While here in Fernandez, with his family, he was, one morning early, roused from sleep by the populace; who, with the aid of the Pueblos de Taos, were collected in front of his dwelling, striving to gain admittance. While they were effecting an entrance, he, with an axe, cut through an adobe wall into another house. The wife of the occupant, a clever though thriftless Canadian, heard him; and with all her strength, rendered him assistance, though she was a Mexican. He retreated to a room, but seeing no way of escaping from the infuriated assailants who fired upon him through a window, he spoke to his weeping wife and trembling children, clinging to him with all the tenacity of love and despair; and taking paper from his pocket, endeavoured to write; but fast losing strength, he commended them to God and his brothers, and fell pierced by a Pueblo's ball. Rushing in and tearing off the gray-haired scalp, the Indians bore it away in triumph.''

Mr. Garrard gives the facts, as given to him, of the killing of the other Americans and the son of Judge Beaubien, as follows: ''The district attorney, Leal, was scalped alive and dragged through the streets, his relentless persecutors pricking him with lances. After hours of acute suffering he was thrown to one side in the inclement weather. He entreated, implored them earnestly to kill him — to end his misery. A compassionate Mexican at last closed the tragic scene by shooting him. Stephen Lee, brother to the General, was killed on his own housetop.

''Narciso Beaubien, son of the presiding judge of this district — the same young man in our company last fall — with his Indian slave, hid in an outhouse at the commencement of the massacre under a straw-covered trough. The insurgents on the search, thinking they had escaped, were leaving, but a woman-servant to the family — going to the housetop called them with the words — 'Kill the young ones and they will never be men to trouble us.' They swarmed back and cruelly put him to death and scalping him and his slave, thus adding two more to the unfortunate victims of unbounded passion and long-cherished revenge.

''Narciso had been to Cape Girardeau college below St. Louis for five years; and when he left was proficient in the French, Spanish and English languages, as well as versed in usual college studies. During the route he often

"Court was in daily session; five more Indians and four Mexicans were sentenced to be hung on the 30th of April. A remarkable circumstance was that whenever Chadwick [184] was on the jury as foreman, the prisoners were returned 'guilty in the first degree.'

"In the courtroom . . . were Señora Bent, the late governor's wife, and Señora Boggs, giving in their evidence in regard to the massacre, of which they were eye-witnesses. Señora Bent was quite handsome; a few years since, she must have been a beautiful woman — good figure for her age; luxuriant raven hair, unexcep-

---

dwelt with delight on his return home and of the different duties and pleasures to be performed and enjoyed. When we parted at Bent's Fort — he for the valley of Taos, I for the village — his last words were a warm and pressing invitation to pay him a lengthy visit; but two short months had scarcely passed ere he was numbered among the slain. His being a native — his mother a Mexican — and the advantages he possessed over his fellow-citizens by a liberal education would have given scope for his undoubted talents to be exerted in his own land and for its material benefit."

[184] The character of men who composed these juries is best understood when we read an anecdote by Garrard, who says: One little Frenchman, Baptiste, by name, with not two ideas above eating and drinking, was duly empanneled as a juror, to try the first six subsequently sentenced. On going into the consulting room, Baptiste went to Chad, and asked — "Monsieur Chad-*week!* vot sall I say?" "Keep still, man, until we talk awhile to the rest about it," rejoined Chad, "do not be in such a hurry."

"Oui! oui! oui! eh bien! c'est bon; tres bien! mais Monsieur, vot sall ve do avec sacre prisonniers — sacre enfants —"

"Baptiste! man, keep still; why, hang them, of course; what did you come in here for?" angrily replied he, much annoyed. "Wait till I am done with these Mexicans (part of the jury) and I will tell you what to do."

Chadwick and Baptiste were chosen as jurors to try nine others of the persons charged and as soon as the jury-room door was closed, he sung out — "Hang 'em, sacre enfants des garces, dey dam grand rascale," now getting excited, and pacing the room, "porque dey kill Monsieur Charles [Governor Bent], dey take son top-knot, vot you call 'im-sculp; dis enfant, he go ondare too, mais, he make beeware — run, you 'Merican say-pour le montaigne — wagh! A-ah! oui, Monsieur Chad-week, you no tink so! — hang 'em, hang 'em-s-a-c-r-e-e!"

Garrard was a close observer and gives a good description of the costumes of the times. He says: "The women do not wear bonnets, using instead the *reboso* or mantilla — a scarf of cotton and silk, five to six feet in length, by two or more in width — which serves as covering for the head and body. So dexterous are they in its management, that in cooking or walking it is retained, forming a graceful and pleasing contrast to the bonneted and hooded civilized lady. A skirt is worn a trifle shorter than the present States fashion, so that it can hardly be called a dress; the figure above the waist, is invested with a chemise, with short arms; but, so sparing were they of material, or so bound to follow unrelenting fashion, or through desire to show their fair shoulders, etc., the chemises were too low-necked. The Cheyenne maidens, on the contrary, wore their buckskin sacques, fitting closely to the throat.

"The men, generally speaking, wear pantaloons open on the outside seam of the leg, and lined with buttons, to fasten at pleasure; while underneath, a pair of white drawers is disclosed to view — a fancy colored shirt and vest, and an oblong blanket, with a hole in the center for the head."

tionable teeth, and brilliant dark eyes, the effect of which was heightened by a clear brunette complexion. The other lady, though not so agreeable in appearance, was much younger. The wife of the renowned mountaineer, Kit Carson, was also in attendance. Her style of beauty was of the haughty, heart-breaking kind — such as would lead a man with a glance of the eye to risk his life for one smile. I could not but desire her acquaintance. The dress and manners of the three ladies bespoke a greater degree of refinement than usual.

"The courtroom was a small, oblong apartment, dimly lighted by two narrow windows; a thin railing kept the by-standers from contact with the functionaries. The prisoners faced the judges and the three witnesses (Señoras Bent, Boggs and Carson) were close to them on a bench by the wall. When Mrs. Bent gave in her testimony, the eyes of the culprits were fixed sternly upon her; on pointing out the Indian who killed the governor, not a muscle of the chief's face twitched, or betrayed agitation, though he was aware her evidence unmistakably sealed his death warrant — he sat with lips gently closed, eyes earnestly centered on her, without a show of malice or hatred — an almost sublime spectacle of Indian fortitude, and of the severe mastery to which the emotions can be subjected. Truly, it was a noble example of Indian stoicism!

"On the day fixed by the court for the execution of the condemned revolutionists, before nine o'clock in the morning, active preparations were made for the last act in the tragedy. The soldiery were mustered. The reverend padres, on the solemn mission of administering the sacrament and offering spiritual consolation, in long black gowns, with meek countenances, passed the sentinels. Lieutenant-Colonel Willock, in command, ordered every American in Taos under arms. On the tops of the houses women and children craned their necks trying to catch a glimpse of the prisoners and soldiers. The prison was at the edge of the town; no houses intervened between it and the fields to the north. One hundred and fifty yards distant had been erected a scaffold — two upright posts and a cross-beam. At last, the word was passed that the prisoners were coming. Eighteen soldiers received them at the gate, with their muskets at port arms — the six abreast, with the sheriff of the county (Metcalfe) on the right — nine soldiers on each side. A number of 'mountaineers,' all armed with Hawkins rifles and 'Green river' knives, formed in line behind the prisoners, each with his rifle at rest in the hollow of his arm, the right hand resting on the stock, ready to fight on his own initiative, at the least intimation of an attempted rescue.

EXECUTION OF THE REVOLUTIONISTS AT TAOS

"The miserable victims marched slowly, with down-cast eyes, arms tied behind, their heads bare, with the exception of white cotton caps, fastened on behind, to be pulled over the face at the last ceremony.

"The *azoteas* in the vicinity were black with women and children, determined to witness the first execution by hanging, in the valley of Taos, save that of Pablo Montoya, the leader of the revolutionists, who had been hung the day after the battle, convicted by a drum-head court martial. No men were near; a few, afar off, stood moodily looking on. On the flat jail-roof was placed the six-pound howitzer which had been used during the battle of Taos, ready loaded and ranging the gallows. Near was a complement of soldiers to serve the gun, one holding in his hand a lighted match.

"The entire command, except those serving as guards, was paraded before the jail and in sight of the gibbet, Colonel Willock, on a handsome charger, from his position commanding a view of the whole. When within a few yards of the gallows, the side-guard, filing off to the right and left, formed, at regular distances from each other, three sides of a hollow square, the mountaineers and personal friends of the late governor and others who had been slain forming the fourth and front side, in full view of the trembling prisoners, who marched up to the scaffold, under which was a government wagon, with two mules attached. The driver and the sheriff assisted the doomed men in, ranging them on a board, placed across the hinder end, which maintained its balance, as they were six, an even number, two on each extremity, and two in the middle. The gallows was so narrow they touched. The ropes,[185] by reason of size and stiffness, despite the soaping given them, were adjusted with difficulty, but, through the indefatigable efforts of the sheriff and a lieutenant of

---

[185] Garrard, L. H., *Wah-to-yah or the Taos Trail*, p. 220: "The sheriff (Metcalfe, formerly a mountaineer, son-in-law of Estes) was in want of the wherewith to hang the criminals, so he borrowed our rawhide lariats, and two or three hempen picket cords of a teamster. In a room adjoining the bar, we put the hangman's noose on one end, tugging away quite heartily. A while after we had been talking of the propriety etc., of taking the Mexicans' lives, said Hatcher: 'This hos has feelin's hyar,' slapping his breast, 'for poor human natur in most any fix, but for these palous (*pelados*) he doesn't care a cuss.'

" 'Yes,' replied I 'they scalped Leal alive, and butchered innocent persons.'

" 'This coon,' remarked Hatcher, 'has made Injuns "go under," somewagh! — but he's never sculped 'em 'live; this child's no niggur, an' he says its onhuman — agin natur — an' they ought to choke. Hello! Met, these riatas mity stiff — won't fit; eh, old feller?'

" 'I've got something to make 'em fit-good 'intment-don't ermit very sweet parfume; but good 'nough; freeze into it, boys,' said Metcalfe, producing a real's worth of Mexican soft soap, 'this'ill make 'em slip easy — a long ways too easy for them, I 'spect.'

"We rubbed in the 'intment,' until the nooses could have 'warranted' to serve the intended purpose, without hitching; on the teamster's hard ropes we used an unusual quantity. One item in Met's bill of expenses, was: 'To soft soap for greasing nooses — 12½.' "

Missouri volunteers, all preliminaries were arranged. The latter, officiating as deputy sheriff for the occasion, seemed to enjoy the position — but the blue uniform looked sadly out of place on a hangman. With rifles grounded, the consummation of the fearful tragedy was awaited. No crowd was around to disturb; a death-like stillness reigned. The spectators on the azoteas seemed scarcely to move — their eyes directed to the painful sight of the doomed wretches, with harsh halters now circling their necks. The sheriff and his assistant sat down; and, succeeding a few moments of intense expectation, the heart-wrung victims said a few words to their people.

"Only one said he had committed murder and deserved death. In their brief but earnest appeals, the words '*madre*' and '*padre*' could be distinguished. The one who had been convicted of *treason* showed a spirit of martyrdom worthy of the cause for which he died — the liberty of his country; and, instead of the cringing, contemptible recantation of the others, his speech was a firm asseveration of his innocence, the unjustness of his trial and the arbitrary conduct of his murderers. With a scowl, as the cap was pulled over his face, the last words he uttered between his gritting teeth were '*Carajos, los Americanos!*' We can now see the atrocity of hanging that man for treason; with the execution of those charged with murder no fault could be found.

"Bidding each other '*adios*' with a hope of meeting in heaven, at a word from the sheriff, the mules started, and the wagon drawn from under the gallows. No fall was given, and their feet remained on the board till the ropes drew taut. The bodies swayed back and forth, and, coming in contact with each other, convulsive shudders shook their frames; the muscles, contracting, would relax, and again contract, and the bodies writhed horribly. While thus swinging the hands of two came together, which they held with a firm grasp till the muscles loosened in death. After forty minutes suspension, Colonel Willock ordered the command to quarters and the howitzer was taken from its place on the prison roof. The soldiers were called off; the women, children and population soon collected, while the sheriff delivered the dead bodies to the weeping relatives. The murder of Governor Bent had been avenged!"[186]

The prisoners brought to Santa Fé by Colonel Price and those taken by Major Edmonson at Las Vegas, in all some twenty-five or thirty, were tried by court-martial, sentenced to death, and executed. The last of those to be hanged were executed on the 3d of August, 1847. Many others are said to have been flogged and set at liberty.

COURTS-MARTIAL AND EXECUTIONS AT SANTA FÉ

---

[186] Garrard, L. H., *Wah-to-yah or the Taos Trail*, pp. 226-227.

Indians other than those of the pueblo of Taos were aiding the insurgent Mexicans in their guerilla warfare east of the mountains and the Apaches also joined the band under Manuel Cortéz. On the plains, incited, as it is believed, by the Mexicans, the Comanches, Pawnees, and Arapahos became very troublesome. There was hardly a party of traders over the Santa Fé trail that escaped attack and many were killed and large numbers of cattle and mules were lost. Lieutenant Love with a company of dragoons escorting government funds had five men killed and lost all of his animals in June. Later on comparative security was restored by stationing troops at different points. These troops, however, were not of the best, being volunteers, and apparently their officers had small control over them.[187] In the west, the Navajós were again raiding the valley of the Rio Grande, murdering and stealing, and paying no attention to the treaty which had been made in October the year previous with Colonel Doniphan.

Shortly after the executions of August 3d, Price left Santa Fé for the states, leaving Lieutenant-Colonel E. W. R. Newby in command. Meanwhile two regiments of volunteers, one of infantry and the other of cavalry, an infantry battalion, and later another battalion of cavalry and artillery, under Lieutenant-Colonel Gilpin, known as the Indian Battalion, which had been stationed on the plains guarding the traders from attacks of the Indians, came to New Mexico. In the month of December Price came back with a commission as brigadier-general and resumed the command of the department. There were now about three thousand men in the ninth military department and

---

[187] Garrard, L. H., *Wah-to-yah or the Taos Trail*, p. 285, gives us some idea of volunteer discipline. While on the plains he met a company of volunteers doing guard duty. He says: "Volunteer-like, they were in the rear, at the side, and in advance of their commander; they, disregarding military deference, he military control. For a mile and a half, others were strung along the trail, in irregular squads, riding, sauntering carelessly, some without arms, and a few with muskets, beating the sage bushes for hares. On passing the three baggage wagons, the first lieutenant — the same who helped the sheriff at the Taos execution — poked his head under the wagon-sheet. He was in his shirtsleeves, his hair uncombed, and altogether he was a rare specimen of that peculiar genus, known as a Missouri volunteer officer. He shouted as I passed — 'How are ye — would ye like to hang any more Mexicans? Now wasn't that a tall time down to Touse!'"

with a part of these General Price marched south and in March, 1848, fought the last battle of the war at Santa Cruz de Rosalia, near Chihuahua.

Upon the return of Price from Chihuahua and the announcement of peace, the volunteers, except two companies, returned to their homes, leaving New Mexico in August and September, 1848. The force of regular troops was now increased and in 1849 the entire number of troops in the department was 885, including a garrison at El Paso. In the spring of 1849, a force of volunteers was called into service and a company of Mexicans and Pueblo Indians served in a campaign against the Navajós, led by Colonel John M. Washington. During the absence of Price in the south the command had devolved upon Colonel Newby in 1847 and in 1848 it was held by Major Benjamin L. Beall. In September, 1848, Colonel John M. Washington assumed command and in October, 1849, he was relieved by Lieutenant-Colonel John Munroe.

In 1848 Colonel Newby made a campaign against the Navajós and secured a treaty with that tribe. In 1849 Colonel Washington also led an expedition to the Navajó country, starting from the pueblo of Jemez on the 22d of August with 350 men and accompanied by the United States Indian agent, James S. Calhoun. On the 30th of the month, at Tunicha, several hundred Navajós were met and negotiations for a treaty were begun. While this was going on, a dispute arose about a horse, and when Colonel Washington ordered its seizure, the Indians ran away and were fired upon, losing several men, among them their noted chief, Narbona. On the 6th of September the army reached Canyon de Chelly, where on the 9th, a treaty was signed. The return march was by way of Zuñi, Laguna, and Alburquerque. This treaty was made only to be broken, for it is said that the Indians reached the settlements before the soldiers and stole mules almost in sight of the flag-staff in the plaza at Santa Fé.[188]

CAMPAIGN AGAINST THE NAVAJÓS

Donaciano Vigil, after the death of Governor Bent, was acting governor of New Mexico; he did not desire to hold the office and strongly recommended the appointment of Colonel Céran St. Vrain,

[188] Washington's reports, iii-15, including the treaty. Calhoun's reports, 202-10. Also *Indian Affairs Report*, 1858, p. 188.

but the authorities at Washington did not care to act in the matter and, in December, 1847, General Price appointed him governor of the territory. In the same month a legislative assembly met at Santa Fé. To this assembly Governor Vigil delivered an able address, its character and sentiment demonstrating that he was a man of marked ability and fully alive to the changed condition of affairs.[189] This assembly was organized by the election of Don Antonio Sandoval as president of the legislative council and Captain W. Z. Angney as speaker of the house of representatives. Ten acts were passed, among which was one establishing a university and providing for funds for its support; an act in relation to replevin, one regulating ejectments and one calling for a convention of delegates to meet in the city of Santa Fé, in the month of February, 1848. These acts were all approved by Governor Vigil and were also approved by General Price, by special orders.[190]

GOVERNOR DONACIANO VIGIL

---

[189] Donaciano Vigil was a native New Mexican and was born September 6, 1802. He occupied a number of public positions under the Mexican régime, both civil and military, and enjoyed the confidence of the people. He was active in the expeditions against the Navajós in 1823, 1833, 1836, and 1838. He was taken prisoner during the revolution of 1837 at La Cañada. Later he was military secretary under Governor Armijo and was twice a member of the departmental assembly. He was an officer under Armijo at the time of the coming of General Kearny. Governor Vigil issued the first proclamation for an election in New Mexico under American authority. The first American deliberative body in the territory was elected at this election. Governor Vigil after his term of office as governor expired held many positions of honor and trust under the government. He was chosen repeatedly to the territorial legislature, his last term being in 1864-5. He was a staunch Union man during the Civil War. He died at Santa Fé, at the residence of his son, Epifanio, on the 11th day of August, 1877. There are no two opinions as to his high character, his patriotism, and his sagacity. His remains lay in state, draped with the flag of his adopted country, in the old palace, just where he had been almost uninterruptedly for half a century, intimately and honorably associated with the affairs of New Mexico. The history of the career of Donaciano Vigil, the firm friend of liberty and humanity, belongs to the people of New Mexico. His is a record of which the people may be proud; a record which all lovers of free government will the more delight to honor as time elapses and his distinguished merits are best understood. It is a record which the native son of New Mexico should ever try to emulate.

For complete biography of Governor Vigil, see *The Military Occupation of New Mexico, 1846-1851*, pp. 207-228.

[190] *Session Laws*, 1847 (pamphlet) copy in library of Frank Springer, Esq., Las Vegas, New Mexico.

The approval of General Price appears in this pamphlet as follows:
"Headquarters, 9th Military Department, Santa Fé, N. M.,
"February 5, 1848.
"The foregoing Legislative enactments of the Territory of New Mexico,

Prominent Officers during the Civil War Period
1. Col. Richard Hudson. 2. Dr. McKee. 3. Col. W. L. Rynerson
4. Capt. Donaciano Montoya

THE WAR WITH MEXICO   265

The treaty of Guadalupe Hidalgo was ratified on May 30, 1848, and was proclaimed at Santa Fé in August. Under this treaty New
Mexico became a part of the
TREATY OF GUADALUPE HIDALGO — United States, the boundary on
COLONELS WASHINGTON AND MUNROE the south being the Rio
Grande, the Upper Gila, and a
line uniting these rivers just above the latitude of El Paso. Choice of citizenship was given to the residents of New Mexico. In the matter of government the new conditions involved some perplexing questions and the administration at Washington took the position that the "termination of the war left an existing government, a government de facto, in full operation; and this will continue, with the

having been duly reviewed by the Commanding General of the Territory, they are hereby approved, and will be duly observed.
"By order of the Brigadier General,
"W. E. Prince,   STERLING PRICE."
"A. D. C. & A. A. A. Gen."

On the same day General Price abolished the offices of territorial secretary, U. S. attorney and U. S. marshal, by special order.— *Order No. 10*, Gen. Price, *Rec. War Dept.*, Wash., *Reports* of General Sterling Price, 1848.

Licensed gambling houses were also established by this order, the license being fixed at two thousand dollars per annum.

Ritch, W. G. in *Legislative Blue-Book of the Territory of New Mexico*, pp. 98-9, Santa Fé, 1887, gives a list of the members of this assembly and its officers, as follows: Council — Antonio Sandoval, president; Henry Henrie, clerk; James Hubbell, door-keeper. Members, central district, José Francisco Vaca, J. A. Sandoval, Juan Tulley; northern district, Nicolas Lucero, Pascual Martinez; southern district, Antonio Sandoval, Juan Otero; House; William Z. Angney, speaker; clerk, James Giddings; door-keeper, E. J. Vaughn; members, Santa Fé county, Manuel Alvarez, W. Z. Angney, Antonio M. Ortiz; Santa Ana county Tomas Baca, Jesus Sandoval; San Miguel county, Miguel Sanchez, Antonio Sais, Levi J. Keithley; Rio Arriba county, José R. Vigil, José Antonio Martinez, Mariano Lucero; Taos county, José Martin, George Gold, Antonio José Ortiz; Bernalillo county, Juan Perea, Rafael Armijo; Valencia county, William Skinner, Juan Cruz Vaca, Juan C. Chavez, Rafael Luna, Juan Sanchez.

In his address to this assembly Governor Vigil said in part: "If your government here is to be republican, if it is to be based upon democratic-republican principles, and if the will of the majority is to be one day the law of the land and the government of the people, it is evident for this will to be properly exercised, the people must be enlightened and instructed. It is particularly important in a country where the right of suffrage is accorded and secured to all that all should be instructed and that every man should be able to read to inform himself of the passing events of the day and of the matters interesting to his country and government. This is the age of improvement, both in government and in society and it more particularly becomes us when commencing as it were a new order of things, to profit by and promote such improvements, and they can only be encouraged and promoted by diffusing knowledge and instruction among the people. . . All that the legislature can do in the cause of education for the people is most earnestly pressed upon them and will meet with my hearty approval and co-operation."

presumed consent of the people, until congress shall provide for them a territorial government." In accordance with this position of the American government, Vigil continued in office until October 11, 1848. He was succeeded by Colonel Washington,[191] who exercised the functions of a military and civil governor combined.

---

[191] Among other things, General Price gave the members of the convention some advice, the tone of which is very significant. He said: "You can now secure the protection of a government which imposes no bonds upon the conscience, which will protect you in the unmolested enjoyment of your personal, political and religious rights, under the regulation of equal laws. In short, you have it in your power to secure for New Mexico all the rights and privileges of citizens under the freest government in the world. . . And I express the hope that, in view of your serious and important duties, the deliberations of the convention will be conducted with the strictest propriety and decorum; and though the *right freely and properly to express opinions should not be restricted, yet I desire all to understand that seditious and indecorous language against the constituted military or civil authorities, calculated to inflame or excite the people against the government, my desire for the peace and welfare of the Territory will induce me immediately to notice. The utterers of such language will be held responsible and called to a strict account.*"

Colonel Washington entertained Colonel John C. Fremont at the time the latter was in Santa Fé, subsequent to the disastrous experiences of the "Pathfinder" in the mountains at the head of the Rio del Norte. In a letter to Senator Thomas H. Benton, written at Socorro, New Mexico, Fremont says: "Letters which I have forwarded by Mr. St. Vrain, will inform you that we were overtaken, and surrounded by deep and impracticable snows in the Rocky Mountains at the head of the Del Norte. We lost all our animals and ten men, the mules frozen, and the men starved to death, Proue only excepted. He was frozen. The miscarriage of an express party under Mr. King was a secondary cause of our greatest calamity in the loss of our men. In six days after leaving my camp in the mountains, I overtook this party, they having been out twenty-two days, and King having been starved to death. In four days afterward I reached the settlements, in time to save many, but too late to rescue all the men. Relief was immediately sent back, but did not meet them in time to save all. . . The officers of the army stationed in the country have been uniformly prompt and liberal in their attentions to me, offering me all the assistance in their power. Among those whom I ought particularly to mention is Major Beale who is in command of the Northern District, Capt. Judd, Lt. Thomas, Dr. Webb, and Captain Buford. Colonel Washington desired me to call on him without reserve for anything at his command. He invited me to dine with him, one out of the two days I spent at Santa Fé, and dined with me at the officers' quarters on the other. Major Weightman (of Washington, son-in-law of Mr. Cox) was very friendly in his attentions to me, and Captain Brent of the Quartermaster's department, gave me some effective aid in my equipment. Among the citizens who have treated me with some attention, I make it a duty to recommend to your attention, when you may meet him, our fellow citizen of St. Louis, Mr. F. X. Aubrey. You will remember him as having lately made an extraordinary ride from Santa Fé to Independence. We have been traveling together from Santa Fé to this place. Among other acts of kindness, I received from him a loan of $1,000, to purchase animals for my journey to California."

Colonel Fremont attributed many of his misfortunes at the head of the Rio del Norte to his guide, who was a celebrated "mountaineer." He says: "At

In the month of February, 1848, General Price published an address to the members of the convention which had been called for by resolution of the convention or session of the legislature held in the previous year. This convention did not meet until the following October, nearly four months after the signing of the treaty of Guadalupe Hidalgo. The session continued four days and accomplished little other than the framing of a memorial to congress asking for the "speedy organization by law of a territorial civil government," and at the same time protesting against the claims made by the state of Texas, and against the introduction of slavery.[192]

CONVENTION OF 1848

---

the Pueblo, I had engaged as a guide an old trapper well known as 'Bill Williams,' and who had spent some twenty-five years of his life in trapping various parts of the Rocky Mountains. The error of our journey was committed in engaging this man. He proved never to have in the least known, or entirely to have forgotten, the whole region of country through which we were to pass. We occupied more than half a month in making the journey of a few days, blundering a tortuous way through deep snow which already began to choke up the passes, for which we were obliged to waste time in searching.''

Fremont's fourth expedition was undertaken, mainly, at his own expense. Those who assisted him were Colonel Robert Campbell and Thornton Grimsley of St. Louis; Dr. George Engleman, also of St. Louis, a man of scientific attainments and great zeal, also assisted in many ways. The expedition left for the west October 19, 1848, and arrived at Bent's Fort November 16. The disasters of the expedition are detailed in a letter to his wife, written from Taos, N. M., where Colonel Fremont was stopping at the home of Colonel Kit Carson. See *Life, Explorations and Public Services of John Charles Fremont*, Boston, Ticknor and Fields, 1856.

[192] The memorial to congress is as follows: "We the people of New Mexico respectfully petition congress for the speedy organization of a territorial civil government. We respectfully petition congress to establish a government purely civil in its character. We respectfully represent that the organic and statute law promulgated under military orders of September 22nd, 1846, with some alterations would be acceptable. We desire that the following offices be filled by appointment of the president, by and with the advice and consent of the senate, the governor, secretary of state, judges, United States attorney and United States marshal. We desire to have all the usual rights of appeal from the courts of the Territory to the supreme court of the United States. We respectfully but firmly protest against the dismemberment of our territory in favor of Texas or from any cause. We do not desire to have domestic slavery within our borders; and until the time shall arrive for admission into the union of states, we desire to be protected by congress against the introduction of slaves into the Territory. We desire a local legislature, such as is prescribed by the laws of New Mexico September 22nd, 1846, subject to the usual veto of congress. We desire that our interests be represented by a delegate admitted to a seat in congress. Considering that New Mexico has a population of from seventy-five thousand to one hundred thousand, we believe our requests to be reasonable and we confidently rely upon congress

Trouble arose over the enforcement of the order of General Price providing for revenue for the payment of the expenses of the government. Meetings were held protesting against this order, and in October the government at Washington ordered a refund of all duties collected on goods brought into the territory from the United States, which had been collected subsequent to the 30th day of May. On this account the salaries of all officials named pursuant to the provisions of the laws, as promulgated by General Kearny, remained for the most part unpaid at the time New Mexico was finally made a territory.[193]

---

to provide New Mexico with laws as liberal as those enjoyed by any of the territories.

"Signed: Antonio J. Martinez   Santiago Archuleta
           Elias P. West   James Quinn
           Donaciano Vigil   Manuel A. Otero
           Francisco Sarracino   Gregorio Vigil
           Juan Perea   Ramon Luna
           Antonio Sais   Charles Beaubien
                                      José Pley

"Santa Fé, October 14, 1848."

The memorial was sent to Senators Thomas H. Benton and John M. Clayton. Senator Clayton had been a strong friend of New Mexico; he had advised the people "to meet in convention, provide for a cheap and simple government, and take care of yourselves until congress can provide for you." When the memorial was received by the senate it evoked some comment, particularly from the senators representing southern states, who were astounded at the "insolence" of the people of New Mexico. The records of congressional debate, the messages of the president of the United States show an almost endless discussion at this time of the true status of New Mexico.

[193] When the old régime came to an end there was a deficit of $31,562. See *Sen. Ex. Doc.* 71, 32d cong., 1st sess. In this document is found 'a tabulated list of all persons holding office under the code of laws as announced by General Kearny and is our only authority as to the personnel of officials during that period. The persons so holding office are:

Name	Office	Date
Charles Bent	Governor	September 22, 1846
Donaciano Vigil	Governor, Acting	January 19, 1847
John M. Washington	Governor	October 11, 1848
John Munroe	Governor	October 23, 1849
Joab Houghton	Judge Supreme Court	September 22, 1846
Antonio José Otero	Judge Supreme Court	September 22, 1846
Charles Beaubien	Judge Supreme Court	September 22, 1846
Donaciano Vigil	Secretary of Territory	September 22, 1846
E. Leitensdorfer	Auditor	September 22, 1846
Joseph Naugle	Auditor	June 1, 1849
Richard Owens	Auditor	July 20, 1850
Charles Blumner	Treasurer	September 22, 1846
Hugh N. Smith	Attorney General	October 1, 1846
Murray F. Tuley	Attorney General	June 25, 1849

In the month of September, 1849, another convention was held at Santa Fé, attended by nineteen delegates.[194] This body elected Hugh N. Smith as a delegate to congress, adopted a plan of government which he was instructed to place before congress and secure its adoption. Colonel Washington declined to officially recognize the acts of this convention. Mr. Smith proceeded to Washington, but congress,

CONVENTION OF 1849

Name	Office	Date
Merrill Ashurst	Attorney General	October 2, 1850
James H. Quinn	Attorney Southern District	October 19, 1846
Elias P. West	Attorney Southern District	August 21, 1849
Murray F. Tuley	Attorney Southern District	November 29, 1849
Merrill Ashurst	Attorney Southern District	October 2, 1850
James W. Leal	Attorney Northern District	December 10, 1846
Theodore D. Wheaton	Attorney Northern District	March 29, 1847
Francis P. Blair, Jr.	United States Attorney	September 22, 1846
Richard Dallam	United States Marshal	September 22, 1846
Lucien F. Thurston	Prefect Santa Fé County	August 18, 1846
Franco. Ortiz Y Delgado	Prefect Santa Fé County	February 18, 1848
Francisco Sandoval	Prefect Santa Ana County	December 1, 1846
Miguel Montoya	Prefect Santa Ana County	September 22, 1848
Manuel A. Baca	Prefect San Miguel County	December 1, 1846
Herman Grolman	Prefect San Miguel County	September 22, 1848
Salvador Lucero	Prefect Rio Arriba County	December 1 1846
José Pablo Gallegos	Prefect Rio Arriba County	September 22, 1848
José A. Manzanares	Prefect Rio Arriba County	April 29, 1849
Salvador Lucero	Prefect Rio Arriba County	August 12, 1850
Cornelio Vigil	Prefect Taos County	December 1, 1846
Vicente Martin	Prefect Taos County	February 10, 1847
José M. Valdez	Prefect Taos County	September 22, 1848
James H. Quinn	Prefect Taos County	April 10, 1849
Robert Carey	Prefect Taos County	June 19, 1849
José M. Valdez	Prefect Taos County	February 15, 1850
José M. Sanchez	Prefect Valencia County	July 16, 1847
James L. Hubbell	Prefect Valencia County	September 22, 1848
Manuel A. Otero	Prefect Valencia County	June 15, 1849
Ramon Luna	Prefect Valencia County	April 15, 1850
Franco. Sarracino	Prefect Bernalillo County	September 22, 1846

[194] These meetings only lasted two days — Sept. 24-26. The members were: Bernalillo county, Manuel Armijo, Ambrosio Armijo; Rio Arriba county, Joseph Naugle, Salvador Lucero; San Miguel, Gregorio Vigil, Manuel A. Vaca; Santa Ana, Miguel Montoya, Francisco T. Vaca; Santa Fé, Manuel Alvarez, E. V. Deroin, W. Z. Angney; Taos, Céran St. Vrain, Antonio J. Martinez, Antoine Leroux; Valencia, Juan J. Sanchez, William C. Skinner, Mariano Silva, Antonio J. Otero, Manuel A. Otero. Rev. A. J. Martinez was president and James H. Quinn secretary.

The committee to report a plan, etc., was composed of W. Z. Angney, Joseph Naugle, Wm. C. Skinner, F. T. Vaca, A. J. Otero. Colonel Washington, Judge Houghton, and Donaciano Vigil accepted seats in the convention. There was a majority report by Mr. Skinner and a minority report by Mr. Naugle, both of which appear in *H. Ex. Doc. 17*, 31st cong., 1st sess., pp. 93-

in July, 1850, by a vote of 92 to 86 declined to admit him as a delegate. While Mr. Smith was endeavoring to secure a seat in congress, efforts were being made in New Mexico to form a state government, inasmuch as it was believed that the administration at Washington desired the admission of New Mexico at the earliest day possible.

"About this time," says Davis, "two opposite parties sprang up, one in favor of a state, and the other of a territorial form of government, which engendered a great deal of excitement and ill feeling.

EFFORTS FOR STATE GOVERNMENT

Several large public meetings were held by the respective parties at Santa Fé. The agitation of a state government originated with the national administration. In the spring of 1849, James S. Calhoun went to New Mexico as Indian agent, but, upon his arrival, declared that he had secret instructions from the government at Washington to induce the people to form a state government." The matter continued to be one of open discussion without much effect in favor of a state government until the arrival of Colonel George A. McCall, who came from the east to join his regiment then in New Mexico.[195]

---

104. Francisco Sarracino, who had been governor of New Mexico under Mexican rule, was named as a "substitute" delegate to congress. At the same session of congress admission was refused to a delegate elected from Utah-Deseret.

Calhoun, J. S., Indian Agent, Santa Fé, New Mexico, October 16, 1849, *Report*:

"Sir: I forward to you, for the information of whom it may concern, the printed *Journal of the Convention of the Territory of New Mexico*. It is stated that the election for delegates was held 'in conformity with the proclamation of Lieutenant Colonel Beall, civil and military commandant' etc. etc., I have not been able to procure a copy of the proclamation, therefore one is not enclosed to you. Before the Honorable Hugh N. Smith left for Washington, he informed me that Governor Washington had refused to approve, or rather to recognize officially, the actions and doings of this convention. All of which I submit to you without any additional remark. I am with great respect, your obedient servant, J. S. Calhoun.

"Hon. T. Ewing,

"Secretary of the Interior, Washington, D. C."

[195] The position of the national administration is well defined in a letter from Secretary of War Crawford to Colonel McCall, *Cal. and N. Mex. Mess.*, 1850, pp. 280-1: "Since their annexation these territories, in respect to their civil government, have in a great measure depended on the officers of the army there in command; a duty it is considered as falling beyond their appropriate spheres of action. This condition has arisen from the omission of congress to provide suitable governments, and in regard to the future there is reason to believe that the difficulties of the past are still to be encountered. . . It is not doubted that the people of New Mexico desire and want a government organized. . . The question readily occurs, how that government can be

Colonel McCall found the people of New Mexico divided into two parties, as has been stated, the state party led by Calhoun, Alvarez, and Pillans, and the territorial by Colonel Céran St. Vrain, Judges Houghton, Beaubien, and others. He informed the people that there was no likelihood that a territorial form of government would be granted by congress and that President Zachary Taylor was determined that a state government should be formed so that the question of slavery and the boundary with Texas should be settled.

It will be seen that affairs were in a very muddled condition. Naturally the people paid close attention to the advice given by Colonel McCall. They were anxious to be rid of the military rule which had now existed for nearly four years. The people who had come from the states of the union did not take kindly to the rule of a military commander in time of peace. To them a government of this sort was intolerable and the only question for determination for them was the securing of a strictly civil form of government at the earliest possible moment. The situation was aggravated by the apparent subserviency of the so-called judicial branch of the government to the orders, wills, whims, and caprices of the military commander and his subordinates. Colonel McCall's representation of the position of the government at Washington had its effect and the "territorial" party at last yielded their preference and joined in the advocacy of a state government. At a public meeting held in the city of Santa Fé, on the 20th of April, 1850, resolutions were passed, among others declarations requesting the military and civil governor, Colonel John Munroe, to issue a proclamation calling upon

CONVENTION OF 1850

---

supplied. I have already adverted to past and still existing difficulties that have retarded and may continue to retard the action of the United States in respect to this necessary and first want. To remove it may, in some degree, be the part of the duty of officers of the army on whom, under the necessities of the case, has been devolved a partial participation in their civil affairs. It is therefore deemed proper that I should say that it is not believed that the people of New Mexico are required to await the movements of the Federal government in relation to a plan of government for the regulation of their own internal concerns. The constitution of the United States and the late treaty with Mexico guarantee their admission in the union of our states, subject only to the judgment of congress. Should the people of New Mexico wish to take any steps toward this object . . . it will be your duty and the duty of others with whom you are associated not to thwart but to advance their wishes. It is their right to appear before congress and ask for admission into the union."

the people of the territory to elect delegates to a convention to be held at Santa Fé on the 15th day of May following.[196]

Colonel Munroe issued the proclamation and the convention assembled at Santa Fé on the 15th day of May, 1850, James H. Quinn being elected president, and after sessions lasting ten days framed a constitution for the state of New Mexico, the work of Joab Houghton[197] and Murray F. Tuley.

---

[196] *Sen. Ex. Doc.* 60, 31st cong., 1st sess.

[197] Joab Houghton was chief justice of the superior court by appointment of General Kearny; his associates were Carlos Beaubien and Antonio José Otero.

He was born in the year 1811, in the state of New York, where he received a common-school as well as a collegiate education. He was a civil engineer by profession. When thirty-three years of age he came to New Mexico and in the year 1845 was appointed United States consul at Santa Fé. About the same time he engaged in merchandising with Eugene Leitensdorfer, and, from 1846 to 1848, theirs was one of the leading mercantile houses west of the Missouri river. The firm had its store on the corner of what was known as the Galisteo road and San Francisco street in Santa Fé. After his appointment by General Kearny, Judge Houghton held his first term of court for Santa Fé county in December, 1846, and continued to hold court regularly at the appointed terms up to his retirement from the bench in 1852. Judge Houghton presided at Taos in the trials of the men accused of the murder of Governor Bent. He was not educated to the bar and the records of his court, from 1846 to 1850, fairly demonstrate, from the crude manner in which the entries are made and from the decidedly peculiar and irregular method of entering orders, judgments, and decrees, that his experience in dispensing justice in those turbulent and troublous times was anything but satisfactory either to himself or to litigants.

During the Civil War he was a stanch Union man, asserting his sentiments when it required nerve to maintain his patriotism. In 1862 Judge Houghton was an acting U. S. district attorney and as such drew several indictments against prominent citizens. In the year 1865, when Judge Houghton was again appointed to the bench, he was assigned to the 3d judicial district and while officiating as judge had before him various suits brought under the act of congress of March 3d, 1863, authorizing the confiscation of property in certain cases. By his rulings in these cases he laid himself open to the severest criticism, much of which was brought about through his lack of legal knowledge. The *New Mexican* of December 15, 1865, says: "It is now clear that Judge Houghton is wanting in all the essentials necessary to a speedy and satisfactory administration of justice, and his appointment to the bench is but another evidence that those not bred in the law should not be entrusted with its administration." His court was called a "prize court;" and so great was the indignation in certain quarters against the judge, the United States attorney, and the marshal, that on December 5, 1865, they were denounced to their faces as unmitigated scoundrels. It is impossible now to realize how overwhelming was the excitement and prejudice of those days. The exercise of calm judgment seems to have been almost an impossibility. In his two official terms he appears to have filed but one written opinion; that was in the case of *Archibeque vs. Miera*, in 1869, in which year he was succeeded by Judge Bergen, appointed by President Grant.

After his retirement from the bench Judge Houghton practised law and

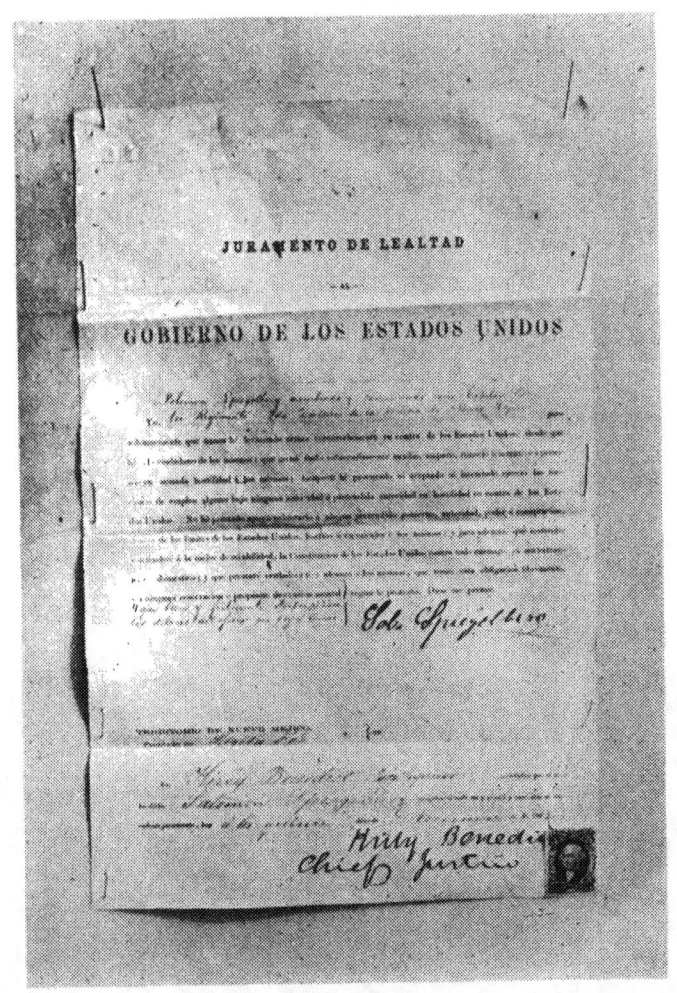

Fac-simile of Oath of Allegiance Administered to Captain Solomon Spiegelberg by Chief Justice Kirby Benedict during the Civil War

The constitution, as framed, shows that it was modeled after the constitutions of the newer states of the Union, and, among other things, contained a clause prohibiting slavery, in order to meet the views of the native New Mexicans who were pronouncedly opposed

lived in Santa Fé until February, 1876. He drew the original plans of the capitol which was commenced by the general government before the Civil War and which twenty-five years afterward was completed as the "Federal building" at Santa Fé. In 1876 he married a daughter of Captain Shoemaker, military store keeper and ordnance officer at Fort Union, N. M.

The legislative assembly of the territory passed a memorial to congress asking for his removal in 1868. Many incidents in Judge Houghton's career are narrated in *The Military Occupation of New Mexico, 1846-1851*, pp. 171-180, R. E. Twitchell, Denver, 1909. Judge Houghton died at Las Vegas, N. M., in 1877.

Charles Hipolyte Trotier, Sieur de Beaubien, was the son of Paul Trotier, Sieur de Beaubien, and Louise Adelaide Durocher, and was born in Canada, at Three Rivers. Several members of his ancestry became prominent in the affairs of the Dominion and in the United States. The first representative of the name in Canada was Jules Trotier, who was born in France, at St. Malod-'lye au Perche, in 1590, where he was married to Catherine Loyseau. His son, Antoine, Sieur des Ruisseaux, married Catherine Lefebone, of which marriage there was a son, Michael, Sieur de Beaubien, the first of the family to be called Beaubien, Seigneur de la Riviere du Loup. The latter married Agnes Godfroy de Linctot, and, after her death, he married Therese Mouet de Moras. Louis Trotier, Sieur de Beaubien, son of the second marriage, married Marie Louise Robida Manseaux. Of this marriage Charles Hipolyte Trotier, Sieur de Beaubien, was born. He left Canada for the United States during the war of 1812, and came to New Mexico in 1823, in company with a number of French Canadians who were making investigations in the province. Beaubien went directly to Taos, at which place, in 1827, he married Paula Lobato, daughter of one of the most prominent citizens of New Mexico. Of this marriage there were born Narciso, who was murdered during the revolution at Taos, in 1847; Luz, who married Lucien B. Maxwell; Leonor, who married V. Trujillo; Juanita, who married L. D. J. Clouthier; Teodora, who married Frederick Muller; Petrita, who married Jesus G. Abreu; and Pablo, who married Rebecca Abreu.

Prior to the American occupation of New Mexico, a prominent citizen of New Mexico, who was collector of customs for the government, on its northern frontier, the Arkansas river, Don Guadalupe Miranda, had asked for a grant of land from his government, and this grant was made to Beaubien and Miranda, who had previously agreed to the partnership. After the grant had been made, Miranda sold his interest to Beaubien, who by the purchase, became possessed of over a million acres of land, the value of which today with its cities, villages, coal mines, and coking plants approximates fifty million dollars. The grant comprised a tract of land larger than three states the size of Rhode Island. It was made by Manuel Armijo, at that time governor of New Mexico, with whom Miranda was a great favorite, and who was also well disposed toward Beaubien. He was a man of fine character and held his judicial position up to the time of the creation of the territory of New Mexico. He died February 10, 1864.

Antonio José Otero, the third member of the "Kearny Court," was a native of Valencia county, New Mexico, having been born at the town of Valencia on the 13th day of March, 1809. His father's name was Vicente Otero, and his mother was Gertrudes Chaves. His grandfather was Pedro

to slavery in any form. The constitution was adopted on the 20th of June, with little if any opposition, and at the same time state officers were elected. The legislature assembled on the first of July of the same year at Santa Fé,[198] where they elected two senators in congress,

---

Otero, who came to Santa Fé about the year 1776. He afterwards moved to Valencia. Judge Otero lived at Peralta, when the Americans took possession of New Mexico, and was thirty-five years of age when Kearny made him judge.

He presided over the third district court, which at that time comprised everything south of Santa Fé and all of what is today the territory of Arizona. He was a man of large views and commanding influence, and was held in high esteem by those who knew him personally. He received a portion of his education at Laguna, N. M., where he was taught by Father Peñol, a Franciscan friar. He also studied with the eminent Rev. Antonio José Martinez, of Taos. He was endowed by nature with fine intellectual powers, all of which were developed and strengthened by a discipline which enabled him to comprehend readily and accurately the important questions demanding his attention in after years. On the whole, viewed from any standpoint, he seems to have given far greater satisfaction than did Judge Houghton. He was an excellent man and a just and impartial judge. He died in 1871, about sixty-one years of age, honored and respected by all. Though the population of New Mexico is so largely Spanish, Judge Otero is the only man of Spanish origin who ever held a place in the supreme court of the territory. He was a very cautious man, rarely giving expression to an opinion until, upon reflection, the matter under consideration was clearly and definitely fixed in his mind. It is a matter of more than passing notice that Judge Otero, born and reared under the Spanish and Mexican governments, whose laws and customs were so different from those of the United States, growing to manhood in a portion of the world, at that time far removed from all the influences of modern thought and civilization, residing in a locality whose inhabitants were engaged six months in every year in wars with hostile Indians, could so well fill his place upon the bench. He delivered the only opinion from the superior court which has been preserved — the case of *Joab Houghton, admr., vs. Manuel Armijo*.

[198] This legislative assembly memorialized congress in no uncertain language, portraying the conditions existing in New Mexico at that period as follows: "The inhabitants of New Mexico, since February 2, 1848, have groaned under a harsh law, forced upon them in time of war, when they were thought undeserving of confidence.

"The military is independent of and superior to the civil power.

"The inhabitants have no voice or influence in making the laws by which they are governed.

"Some power other than the congress of the United States, has made judges dependent on its will alone for the tenure of their offices, and the amount and payment of their salaries.

"Some power other than the congress of the United States has subjected us to a jurisdiction foreign to the constitution and unacknowledged by our laws.

"We are taxed without our consent and taxes when collected are not applied to the public benefit, but embezzled by officers irresponsible to the people.

"No public officer in New Mexico is responsible to the people. Judges unlearned in law, decide upon life, liberty and property. Prefects and alcaldes impose fines and incarcerate without the intervention of a jury.

"Alcaldes assail the rights of the people freely who exercise their religion

Francis A. Cunningham and Richard H. Weightman. At the state election Henry Connelly was elected governor and Manuel Alvarez lieutenant-governor. Dr. Connelly, being absent in the states, Alvarez was acting governor for the time being, who, supported by Major Weightman and the legislature then in session, as well as by all of the newly elected officials, attempted at once to put the state government into full operation without waiting for any action by congress. This action caused a very lengthy and acrimonious correspondence between Governor Alvarez and Colonel Munroe, who forbade any assumption of civil power by the officials who had been chosen by the people.[199] The position taken by Colonel Munroe brought forth a vigorous protest [200] from the legislature as appears

---

without restriction and dictate to congregations what priest shall administer the sacraments of the church.

"The full extent of the power to control and injure which this unrestrained and organized band of office-holders wielded can only be entirely understood when it is known that the military commander held to no accountability civil officers charged with assaults upon the religion of the country and embezzlement of the public funds.

"The influence of the quartermaster's department in the elections was by no means an inconsiderable one. With its army of employes, with its contracts to let, with its agencies to purchase the entire surplus of the corn and forage of the country, and with its easy means of communication by express, at government expense, it proved itself very formidable; and this influence with some honorable exceptions was thrown against the state party.

"This web of influence extending to the frontiers of New Mexico was, like the other, organized and, like it, also easily managed from the center; and the managers of both webs were acting in concert and, as has already been told, against the state party.

"At this time there was available only one printing-press in the entire territory, and it belonged to the government. This press was sold and fell into the hands of the territorial party. It was used solely for the advancement of the interests of that faction and, being owned by an army sutler and contractor, and edited by Judge Houghton and the chief clerk of the quartermaster, all communications of the state party were excluded from the columns of the paper. That party could not secure the printing of its ballots and upwards of twenty thousand tickets, issued by the state party, were written out by hand.

"With the press against the state party, the office holders against it, and the moneyed interests of the government against it, it cannot be said that the state movement was born of or grew to manhood by executive influence. It appears clearly that the voice of the people, as expressed by their ballots, made itself heard under very difficult circumstances." — *Letter* of R. H. Weightman, 32d congress, 1st session, p. 325.

[199] The position taken by Colonel Munroe and by Mr. Alvarez is well outlined in an official communication from Alvarez to Colonel Munroe, of July 13, 1850. See *The Military Occupation of New Mexico, 1846-1851*, R. E. Twitchell, Denver, 1909, where this letter is given in full.

[200] Twitchell, R. E., *The Military Occupation of New Mexico, 1846-1851*, pp. 191-2, gives the text of this resolution as follows: "*Whereas*, a letter

from a resolution adopted by that body. Among other things the legislature provided for the election of county officers, which acting Governor Alvarez attempted to carry into effect by issuing writs of election, which Colonel Munroe also forbade by proclamation to the people, in which he declared all such elections null and void. In consequence of this opposition on the part of the commander of the department, the elections were not held and matters moved on for some months the same as before the state organization was effected.[201]

In the meantime Richard H. Weightman, one of the senators-elect,

---

signed by John Munroe, styling himself civil and military governor of New Mexico, and directed to Lieutenant-governor Manuel Alvarez, has just been communicated to the legislature in which said Munroe expresses a determination to maintain the civil authorities hitherto administering the government of New Mexico, and also threatens to use all the forces at his disposal to resist the effective operation of the state government now in complete organization, with an evident intention to overawe the people, legislature and different departments of the government, and to annul by means of military power the peaceable desires of the people; and, *Whereas,* seven-eights of the entire population of New Mexico are clearly in favor of putting in immediate operation the civil state government lately adopted by them by an unheard of unanimity and to be relieved from the sinking, ineffective and abhorent system which they have peacefully respected for nearly four years; *Resolved;*

"1. That it is the indisputable right of the people in the absence of congressional legislation on the subject to organize a civil government and put it in immediate operation.

"2. That the right of exercising any civil function by the commander of the ninth military department (if it ever existed) was superceded by the organization of the state government.

"3. That we heartily approve the communication despatched by vice-governor Alvarez to Colonel Munroe, dated July 13, 1850.

"4. That we heartily approve the intention of Governor Alvarez to establish and maintain in operation the government just organized.

"5. That the people have a clear and sacred right to take any steps to put in operation the state government and that this right was superior to and entirely independent of the military government hitherto existing in this Territory.

"6. That Colonel J. Munroe has no legal or other right to restrict the peaceful action of the people in organizing a government; nor had he authority either in law or from the general government, to subject the action of the late convention to any conditions or limitations whatever.

"7. That the commander has assumed a power not delegated to the President of the United States and directly in opposition to the expressed principles of President Taylor in his reply to the investigations made by the congress of the United States.

"8. That the secretary of state be required to furnish copies of the above preamble and resolutions to Colonel J. Munroe, Governor Alvarez and to the senators and representatives to congress."

[201] After Colonel Munroe had been served with a copy of the resolutions passed by the legislature, he communicated (by swift express across the plains) with Washington as to the correctness of the position which had been taken by

Fac-simile of Passport given to Lehman Spiegelberg by Gen. H. H. Sibley

went to Washington to present the constitution of New Mexico, ask
for her admittance to the
NEW MEXICO IS MADE A TERRITORY — Union, and claim his seat. Up-
COMPROMISE BILL OF 1850 on his arrival he found that
the compromise bill of September 9, 1850, in which was included the act organizing a territorial government for New Mexico, had just passed congress, which at once took precedence of the state organization. The new territorial government went into operation on March 3, 1851, James S. Calhoun having been appointed and sworn in as governor. The "state" government of New Mexico "so soon was done for that it wondered what it was begun for."

---

him. In response he received a letter from C. M. Conrad, secretary of war, as follows:

"The President has learned with regret that any misunderstanding should exist between a portion of the people of New Mexico and yourself in relation to the government of that country, and hastens to relieve you from the embarrassment in which that misunderstanding has placed you.

"I have now the pleasure to inform you that congress has at length passed a law providing for the establishment of a territorial government in New Mexico. The President will proceed with the least possible delay to organize the government; and as soon as it goes into operation, all controversy as to what is the proper government of New Mexico must be at an end, and the anomalous state of things which now exists there will be determined. You will perceive, however, that the same act (a duly authenticated copy of which accompanies this communication) also fixes the boundary between New Mexico and Texas, and that its operation is suspended until the assent of Texas shall have been given to the boundary established by the act.

"Although there is little doubt that such assent will be given, yet as some time must elapse before it can be obtained, it is proper that some instructions should be given for your guidance in the interval.

"It is at all times desirable that the civil and military departments of the government should be kept entirely distinct. Although circumstances may occasionally arise which require a temporary departure from this principle, that departure should cease with the necessity which occasioned it. No necessity seems to exist at present for departing from it in regard to New Mexico. The country is represented to be tranquil; and, although the inhabitants have undertaken to establish a government for themselves without authority of a previous act of congress, nevertheless there is no reason to believe that in so doing they intended to throw off their allegiance to the United States; and as the government they seek to establish is entirely consistent with the lawful authority and dominion of the United States in and over the Territory and its inhabitants, the President does not consider himself bound to suppress it by military force. Unless, therefore, it should become necessary to suppress rebellion, or resist actual hostilities against the United States (an event hardly to be apprehended), or unless the inhabitants or a portion of them should demand from you that protection which is guaranteed to them by the ninth article of the treaty of Guadalupe Hidalgo, you are directed to abstain from all further interference in civil or political affairs of that country." — *New Mexico Correspondence*, etc., 1850, *Sen. Ex. Doc.*, 1, pp. 92-109.

There had been no substantial reason for the denial to the people of New Mexico of a territorial form of government for so long a period as had intervened since the treaty with Mexico. In the first petition for admission the people of New Mexico had declared that they were opposed to slavery. The fact that the domestic institutions of some of the states were distasteful to New Mexicans was not a sufficient reason for withholding some sort of government other than the strange mixture of civil and military which continued after the treaty of Guadalupe Hidalgo. Had New Mexico been admitted to the Union in 1850, her constitution would have prohibited slavery. There were not a thousand residents in the territory at that time who had been born in the United States and the Mexican population was over sixty-five thousand, nearly all of the latter being opposed to slavery, but the factious temper of the times was such that the slightest pretext for argument gave rise to angry conflict and in the light of events transpiring during that period and until the actual breaking out of hostilities in the war between the states, there was no chance for the admission of New Mexico into the Union.

The true sentiment of New Mexicans was reflected ten years later by their contribution in men for the Federal armies, in the great conflict for the preservation of the Union and the suppression and eradication of an institution which, at the first opportunity, in convention assembled, the people had declared to be obnoxious to all liberty loving citizens.

COLONEL DONIPHAN'S ARMY MARCHING THROUGH THE JORNADA DEL MUERTO, THE "JOURNEY OF DEATH"
Reproduced from the work of William H. Richardson.

BIBLIOGRAPHY

Archives	Court Records, Santa Fé, N. M.
Bancroft, Hubert H.	*History of Arizona and New Mexico*, San Francisco, 1889.
Bustamante, Carlos M.	*Nuevo Bernal Diaz*, Mexico, 1847, 2 vols.
Chittenden, H. M.	*History of the American Fur Trade*, New York, 1902.
Cooke, Philip St. George	*Conquest of New Mexico*, New York, 1878.
Connelley, W. E.	*Doniphan's Expedition*, Kansas City, Mo., 1907.
Calhoun, J. S.	*Reports.* Indian Affairs Reports, Washington, 1858.
Davis, W. W. H.	*El Gringo*, New York, 1856.
Emory, W. H.	*Notes of a Military Reconnoisance*, etc., Gov. Doc., 30th cong., 1st sess., Sen. Ex. Doc. 7.
Edwards, F. S.	*Campaign in New Mexico*, London, 1848.
Garrard, L. H.	*Wah-to-yah*, Cincinnati, 1849.
Hughes, John T.	*Doniphan's Expedition*, Cincinnati, 1847.
Kendall, George W.	*Texas-Santa Fé Expedition*, New York, 1844.
Kearny, Stephen W.	Letters from Secretary of War, Ex. Doc. 60.
Meline, J. F.	*Two Thousand Miles on Horseback*, New York, 1867.
Niles' Register	Baltimore, 1811-1849, 76 vols.
New Mexico	*Session Laws*, 1847. Copy in possession of Frank Springer, Esq., Las Vegas, N. M.
	Correspondence, 1850, Sen. Doc. I.
Owen, Charles H.	*Journal of American History*, vol. ii.
	Historical Sketches, etc., New York, 1883.
Prince, L. B.	*Address* at Santa Fé at unveiling of portrait of Governor Bent.
Price, Sterling W.	*Report of*, Sen. Doc. 442, 56th cong., 1st sess.
Richardson, James D.	*Messages and Papers of the Presidents*, Washington, 1897.
Ruxton, George F.	*Adventures in Mexico*, New York, 1848.
Ritch, W. G.	*Legislative Blue Book*, Santa Fé, 1887.
Santa Fé Archives	Smithsonian, Washington, D. C.
Smith, Ashbel	*Reminiscences of the Texas Republic.*
Senate Ex. Doc. 60	31st cong., 1st sess.
Taylor, Zachary	*Letter*, Ex. Doc.
Twitchell, R. E.	*Military Occupation of New Mexico, 1846-1851*, Denver, 1910.
Vigil Papers	New Mexico Historical Society, Santa Fé, N. M.
Washington, Col. J. M.	*Reports* to Secretary of War, Washington.

CHAPTER VII

TERRITORY OF NEW MEXICO — THE ORGANIC ACT — CIVIL AND MILI-
TARY AUTHORITIES — COL. E. V. SUMNER — LEGISLATIVE AS-
SEMBLIES — DELEGATES TO CONGRESS — INDIAN CAM-
PAIGNS — COUNTIES — POPULATION — AGRICULTURE
AND STOCK-RAISING — GADSDEN PURCHASE —
DISPUTED BOUNDARIES — THE MESILLA
VALLEY — EXPLORATIONS

THE organic law of the territory of New Mexico — the act of September 9, 1850 — was similar to the acts of congress by which other territories had been created and organized. This act determined the northern and western boundaries of the state of Texas and provided for a relinquishment to the United States [202] of

---

[202] During the period of American occupation, the military authorities at Santa Fé paid no attention to the claims of Texas and would not recognize the attempt of that state to extend the jurisdiction of its courts over the disputed territory. In 1850, Texas sent a special commissioner to Santa Fé, with full power and instructions to extend the civil jurisdiction of the state over what the legislature of Texas had seen fit to designate as the "unorganized counties of El Paso, Worth, Presidio and Santa Fé." Upon his arrival at Santa Fé, the Texan commissioner, Robert S. Neighbors, met with opposition from the military authorities and from the people generally. This occurred in the spring of 1850. Public meetings were held and Neighbors and Texas were loudly denounced. — Davis, W. W. H., *El Gringo*, pp. 110-111. The military governor at Santa Fé had received instructions from Washington not to come into conflict with the Texan commissioner, but Colonel Munroe secretly favored the "territorial" party, while the "state" party favored the Texan scheme and he did all that he could to thwart the commissioner's plans. Neighbors issued a proclamation for an election, but nobody went to the polls and the entire proposition fell through.

Thrall, H. S., *History of Texas*, p. 360, says: "Colonel Munroe paid no attention to the Texas judge (S. M. Baird), and proceeded to order an election of a territorial delegate to the U. S. congress. Governor Wood requested the legislature to put the whole military power of the state under his control, that he might enforce the claim; but in a correspondence with the state depart-

Union and Confederate Soldiers in New Mexico, 1861-1866

1. Capt. A. Mennet. 2. Major Irving W. Stanton. 3. Col. Cyrus H. De Forrest. 4. Major D. L. Huntington. 5. Col. J. F. Bennett. 6. Major Eugene Van Patten. 7. Col. J. A. La Rue. 8. Col. E. B. Willis. 9. Major José D. Sena

all territory exterior to the same. The state of Texas was paid ten million dollars. The territory, as thus organized in 1850, included the New Mexico and Arizona of today with a small portion of Colorado. Texas was never justified in making the claims which she did as to her western boundary being the Rio Grande, but if the Texans really had no faith in the claim when first made, they asserted their ownership so frequently and with such vigor that they finally came to the conclusion that it was just. At any rate Texas was strong enough to compel a payment of ten million dollars by the general government, whether the claim was just or not. The demands of the creditors of the state of Texas had much to do with the acceptance of the act of congress.[203] By the compromise measures determined upon by congress after debates lasting more than six months, the

ment at Washington he was notified that if Texas attempted a forcible possession of Santa Fé, the Texans would be treated as intruders. In the heat of the controversy some of our writers contended that if the delegate from New Mexico was admitted to his seat in congress, the Texas delegates should withdraw, and the state resume her separate nationality.''— Secretary of War — *Letter* — to Colonel Munroe — *Cal. and N. M. Mess.*, 1850, p. 272.

[203] The governor of Texas was notified by the president of the United States that New Mexico was a territory of the United States, with the same extent and the same boundaries which belonged to it while in the actual possession of Mexico before the treaty of Guadalupe Hidalgo. ''The executive government of the United States,'' said Zachary Taylor, ''has no power or authority to determine what was the true line of boundary between Mexico and the United States before the treaty of Guadalupe Hidalgo, nor has it any such power now, since the question has become a question between the State of Texas and the United States. So far as the boundary is doubtful, that doubt can only be removed by some act of congress, to which the assent of the state of Texas may be necessary, or by some appropriate mode of legal adjudication; but, in the meantime, if disturbances or collisions arise or should be threatened, it is absolutely incumbent on the executive government, however painful the duty, to take care that the laws be faithfully maintained; and he can regard only the actual state of things as it existed at the date of the treaty, and is bound to protect all the inhabitants who were then established and who now remain north and east of the line of demarcation, in the full enjoyment of their liberty and property, according to the provisions of the ninth article of the treaty. In other words, all must be now regarded as New Mexico which was possessed and occupied as New Mexico, by citizens of Mexico at the date of the treaty, until a definite line of boundary shall be established by competent authority.''

The importance of immediate action by the congress of the United States in the settlement of this boundary question, was most apparent. All considerations of justice, general expediency, and domestic tranquility demanded it. It was seen that no government could be established for New Mexico, either state or territorial, until it was ascertained just what New Mexico was, and what were her rightful limits and boundaries, and the president recommended to congress that the general government ''*would be justified in allowing an indemnity to Texas not unreasonable or extravagant but fair and liberal, and awarded in a just spirit of accommodation.*''

"irrepressible conflict" between the north and south was postponed a decade. Through the outcome of the struggle the south gained a more satisfactory fugitive slave law and the north secured the prohibition of the slave trade in the District of Columbia. California was admitted as a free state. New Mexico [204] and Utah became territories without provisions prohibiting slavery. The main point was won by the southern representatives in defeating the provision prohibiting slavery in the territories, but the north gained a free state and made no further concessions to the slave-holding interests.

James S. Calhoun was the first governor of New Mexico subsequent to the military occupation period. He had been in New Mexico since July, 1849, holding the position of Indian agent for the territory, which office he filled with great credit to himself; during his incumbency he furnished the government with a great deal of very valuable

ADMINISTRATION OF GOVERNOR JAMES S. CALHOUN

---

[204] The boundaries as defined were as follows: "Beginning at a point in the Colorado river where the boundary line with the Republic of Mexico crosses the same; thence eastwardly with the said boundary line to the Rio Grande thence following the main channel of said river to the parallel of the 32° north latitude; thence east with said degree, to its intersection with the 103° longitude west of Greenwich; thence north with said degree of longitude to the parallel of 38° north latitude; thence west with said parallel to the summit of the Sierra Madre; thence south with the crest of said mountains to the 37° north latitude; thence west with said parallel to its intersection with the boundary line of the state of California; thence with said boundary line to the place of beginning." That part lying west of longitude 109° was detached in 1863 to form Arizona; and that part above latitude 37° in 1867 was attached to Colorado. There was also a large addition in 1854 by the Gadsden Purchase, most of which was detached with Arizona. Utah was organized in 1850 and included the later Nevada, Utah, and those parts of Colorado and Wyoming which lie south of latitude 42° and west of the mountains. There was a little strip of the territory acquired from Mexico lying between latitude 38°, the mountains, and the Arkansas river, that does not seem to have been provided for in the final settlement of 1850.

Bancroft, H. H., *History of Arizona and New Mexico*, p. 456, writing of the position taken by Texas as to its claim of territory as far west as the Rio Grande, says: "In congress, while Texan representatives never lost an opportunity of declaiming on the unquestionable validity of their claim, there was much difference of opinion, even among southern members, on its original merits; but in this, as in every phase of the whole matter, all was merged in the slavery issue. Texas was a slave state, and eastern New Mexico, if decided to be a part of Texas, would be an immense territory gained at once for the south, whatever might be the result farther west. This was the only real strength of the Texas claim in congress beyond the zealous efforts of the Texans themselves... This phase of the slavery question also caused northern members to favor a territorial government in New Mexico, as a choice of evils, even if slavery could not be prohibited."

Chief Justice Kirby Benedict

information [205] relative to the Indians in the territory. Other officials appointed at the same time were Hugh N. Smith, as secretary, who was not confirmed, his confirmation having been prevented by R. H. Weightman, the delegate in congress, who desired to secure the position for Manuel Alvarez, who was not a citizen of the United States. William S. Allen was appointed secretary, and Grafton Baker, chief justice, with John S. Watts and Horace Mower as associate justices; Elias P. West, United States attorney and John G. Jones, U. S. marshal. Governor Calhoun was inaugurated on the 3d day of March, 1851, and so far as the records show the new government was launched in a very quiet manner. Shortly after his inauguration the governor issued a proclamation calling for an election and in June of that year the first territorial assembly met at Santa Fé in rooms in the old palace. From a financial standpoint affairs were in a deplorable condition, inasmuch as from its very beginning the expenses of the territorial government were paid solely by the issue of warrants upon a treasury in

---

[205] The *Reports* of J. S. Calhoun while Indian agent are to be found in *H. Ex. Doc.* 17, pp. 191-228, 31st cong., 1st sess., *Sen. Ex. Doc.* 1, pp. 125-143, 31st cong., 2nd sess., and *H. Ex. Doc.* 2, pp. 448-467, 32d cong., 1st sess. In his report of October 4, 1849, Calhoun gives the population of the Pueblo Indians as 6,524, above five years of age, not including the Moquis. He says that Bent's Fort on the Arkansas had been burned by William Bent; declares that the Indians are very troublesome; advises the construction of military roads and the building of army posts. He thought that the Indians should be placed on reservations and made to realize the power of the United States. He recommended the establishment of agencies at Taos, to include the Utes, at Zuñi for the Navajós, and at Socorro for the Apaches and Comanches; thought there should be a sub-agent at every pueblo for a year, at least. In the spring of 1851 the Indians were worse than ever. The losses of live stock in the counties of Santa Ana and Bernalillo during the years 1846-1850, not including government animals, were 150,231 sheep, 893 horses, 761 mules and burros, and 1,234 cows.

Depredations by Indians during the American occupation period — 1846-1850 — are given in a table prepared from estimates taken by assistant U. S. Marshals as follows. — Bartlett, J. R., *Personal Narrative*, vol. ii, note p. 386:

Counties	Sheep	Mules	Horses	Horned Cattle
Santa Fé	16,260	570	267	894
Taos	17,080	1,032	1,764	5,600
Rio Arriba	43,580	1,960	658	2,382
San Miguel	50,000	7,000	3,000	21,000
Santa Ana and Bernalillo	154,915	749	987	1,302
Valencia	171,558	376	372	1,463
Total	453, 293	12,887	7,050	31,581

which there were no funds. Governor Calhoun was overwhelmed with complaints from citizens whose property was constantly being stolen by the marauding savages, and, having been in office only six months, he wrote to his superiors at Washington — "without a dollar in our territorial treasury, without munitions of war, without authority to call out our militia, without the coöperation of the military authorities of this territory, and with numberless complaints and calls for protection, do you not perceive I must be sadly embarrassed and disquieted?" In addition to the duties of the office of governor, Calhoun was by virtue of his office in charge of Indian affairs as superintendent, and at this time the savages were causing a great deal of distress. The governor had not been in office three months before he began having trouble with Colonel Sumner, the commander of the military department. The latter was inclined to regard the depredations of the Indians as of slight importance and the report of Governor Calhoun of 1851 shows the grievous antagonism between the military and civil authorities [206]

---

[206] *Journal of American History*, vol. iii, p. 546, Letter from John Greiner, Oct. 1, 1851, from Santa Fé, describes conditions as they were at this time. He says: "Between the savage Indians, the treacherous Mexicans and the outlawed Americans, a man has to run the gauntlet in this country. Three governors within twelve years have lost their heads and there are men here at present who talk as flippantly of taking Governor Calhoun's head as though it were of no consequence whatever. Everybody and everything in this . . . country appears at cross purposes. In the first place the civil and military authorities are at war. Colonel Sumner refuses to acknowledge the right of the Governor to send Indian agents with him to the Indian country — and will not afford the proper facilities for them to go — and the governor refuses to send them. The governor and secretary of the Territory can not hitch horses. The American residents are at war with the governor, while the Mexican population sides with him. Even the missionaries are at logger-heads. The Baptist preacher, Reed, is at war with the Methodist, Nicholson, and 'wice-wersa.' While the Presbyterian, Kephart, has turned editor and is raising the . . . in general through the columns of the *Santa Fé Gazette*. The American troops are at war with the Indians, and if they could only catch them (the Navajós), would give them fits, but Colonel Sumner is on his way back from their country without even seeing one of them. Since his expedition started, the Indians have come into this country within twenty miles of Santa Fé, and have robbed the citizens and run off their stock. Two Americans have been murdered lately here by Mexicans, owing I think to their own impudence, and the governor is charged with aiding and abetting the deed, although seventy miles distant from the scene of operations — and they make no bones of saying they will avenge the deaths upon him. Yet I have never known him to give any cause for such hostilities; cool, calm and deliberate, he is not easily thrown off his guard, and you may depend upon it, if he does fall, it will be with his face to the sky and his feet to the foe. And there will be men who will die with him. I have been residing at Taos lately, among the Eutahs and Apaches, who get

Merchants and Freighters on the Santa Fé Trail—the Spiegelberg Brothers
Willi, Lehman, Jacob S., Levi, and Emanuel

brought about by conflicting instructions and lack of policy on the part of the general government.

Colonel E. V. Sumner, 2d dragoons, assumed command of the ninth military department in July, 1851, having marched from Fort Leavenworth with a considerable force. It was under his instructions that government farms were cultivated by soldiers; an enterprise which did not meet with much success. Colonel Sumner also brought with him, in addition to large quantities of agricultural implements, numbers of fine cattle and horses. His instructions were to select new sites for military posts, to act in concert with the superintendent of Indian affairs, to inflict severe punishment upon the hostile Indians and, as far as possible, effect a reduction in the expenses of the department. In the fall after the arrival of Colonel Sumner the Apaches [207] in the south became very hostile. Governor Calhoun advised the giving of arms to the Mexican people with which they could fight the Indians, but Colonel Sumner refused to do so. At this time the total number of soldiers in New Mexico was less than one thousand and the efforts of the several military commanders to subdue the Apaches, as described [208] by an official in the Indian

---

drunk whenever they get a chance and boast of how many whites they have killed, and talk very glibly of the scalps they intend to take. There is a great and deep gulf between the American and Mexican yet, and the love they bear each other has by no means waxed warm. There is hardly an American here that stirs abroad without being armed to the teeth, and under his pillow pistols and bowie knives may always be found. None go to bed without this precaution.''

[207] It was believed that the Apaches in the south intended forming an alliance with the Indians in the northern part of New Mexico — the Jicarillas and Utes — and Governor Calhoun sent representatives to the northern Indians to prevent such an amalgamation of interests — from an Indian standpoint.

[208] *Journal of American History*, p. 550, *Letter* from John Greiner, March 31, 1852: ''Our troops are of no earthly account. They cannot catch a single Indian. A dragoon mounted will weigh 225 pounds. Their horses are all as poor as carrion. The Indians have nothing but their bows and arrows and their ponies are as fleet as deer. Heavy dragoons on poor horses, who know nothing of the country, sent after Indians who are at home anywhere, and who always have some hours of start, how long will it take to catch them? So far, although several expeditions have started after them, not a single Indian has been caught! The southern Apaches are at war, they run off all the stock they care for and laugh at their pursuers. The Governor applied to the commandant to give the Mexicans arms to defend themselves. He complied, the other day, by giving an order for 100 stand, and when the arms were looked after they were found to be unfit for use. The military disbursements made here kept the people alive and everything was done on the most extravagant plan. Now Colonel Sumner has stopped all this. Money is getting very scarce. Many of the Americans are leaving here. Others have nothing to do and they think if a change be made by making a 'row' they are ready for it. They have nothing

department at Santa Fé at the time, give us some idea of the difficulties under which the colonel commanding the department labored, and possibly throw some light upon the very pessimistic reports made by him to the secretary of war and his reasons for making them. His picture of conditions existing in New Mexico, from his standpoint, is anything but flattering.[209] In the latter part of the

---

to lose and everything to gain. The Governor goes into the States in a few weeks, if able to travel. The Secretary goes in to see his family by the mail tomorrow. The governor appoints Alvarez governor and myself superintendent of Indian affairs. Quere? Has he the power to appoint a successor? The Secretary appoints his successor, the governor his. This right is also disputed. The Attorney-general resigns to-day. The Prefect has just come here stating that he would have to let the prisoners out of jail because there is nothing to feed them on. The Chief Justice of the Territory, Baker, has been absent all winter at Washington and although he 'steams it high' sometimes, he is by far the best of the Judges on the bench. Although the Associates are steady, sober, moral men, but nothing else, no one has any confidence in their decisions. Even the missionary, Mr. Nicholson, shakes the dust off his shoes in a few days for the States, satisfied that this is not even missionary ground. If, traveling on the road, you meet an American, you put your hand on your pistol for fear of accidents.''

[209] *Report*, of Col. E. V. Sumner to the secretary of war, May 27, 1852, *Sen. Doc. No. 1*, 32d cong., 2d sess.: ''Believing that at some leisure moment you would like to see an exact picture of New Mexico, I have drawn up the enclosed paper. The facts cannot be controverted; some of the inferences may be questioned, but I think every one of them can be maintained.'' This report is one of the most drastic ever written concerning the people of New Mexico.

Col. E. V. Sumner was an eminent officer. He was born in Boston, Mass., in 1796. He received his education in his native city and at the neighboring academy of Milton. He did not attend the West Point Academy. He entered the service of the United States March 3, 1818, with the appointment of 2d Lt. of Infantry. He served in this regiment in the Black Hawk War, and in various duties, with credit and efficiency, till, in 1833, he was transferred to the 2d dragoons, with the rank of captain. This brought him into active service, on the western frontier, among the Indian tribes. In 1846 he had attained the rank of major in his regiment. The breaking out of the Mexican War provided a new field of duty. He was with General Scott from the landing of the army at Vera Cruz to its arrival at the capital of Mexico, and was distinguished at every point where opportunity for action presented itself. He was wounded shortly after the landing at Vera Cruz and was brevetted lieutenant-colonel for bravery. At Molino del Rey where he was constantly under fire, he maintained his position and held in check a Mexican division of five thousand men, thus contributing materially to the success of the American arms. For this he was brevetted colonel. In July, 1848, he was commissioned lieutenant-colonel of the 1st dragoons. In 1851, and for the two following years he was in command of the 9th Military Department, New Mexico, and for a part of the time acted as civil governor. In 1855 he was promoted to the colonelcy of his regiment. He conducted an expedition against the Cheyennes, in Kansas, in 1857. The following year he was placed in command of the Western Department and rendered great service during the border troubles of the period.

During the war of the rebellion, on the defection of General Twiggs, he was commissioned Brigadier General and was sent to the Department of the Pacific,

TERRITORY OF NEW MEXICO 287

year 1852 the country was reported at peace, that the Indians, generally, were friendly, that the Navajós and Apaches were quiet and "for the past five months have scarcely committed a depredation." This state of comparative peace lasted a little more than a year. Governor Calhoun left New Mexico for the states in May, 1852, and died en route, in the month of June. At this time the governor, secretary, chief justice, attorney general, district judge, and two Indian agents were all absent from New Mexico. The only civil official remaining was an Indian agent,[210] who was later appointed secretary of the territory. Even though Colonel Sumner reported that the Indians were quiet, still he saw nothing in New Mexico worth keeping, his views of the country and its people and prospects being very unfavorable. He was of the opinion that it was impos-

whence, in 1862, he was called into active service in the Army of the Potomac. He took part in the battles of Seven Pines and Fair Oaks, Virginia. He was greatly distinguished by his gallant conduct in the Seven Days Battles which succeeded the engagement at Fair Oaks and was slightly wounded. He was made major-general of volunteers and brevet major-general in the regular army and commanded the 2d army corps in McClelland's campaign in Maryland, in September, 1862. He was wounded at the battle of Antietam. He was with General Burnside, in command of the second and ninth corps, forming the right grand division at the battle of Fredericksburg. His division was the first to cross the Rappahannock. In the disastrous results of the day it received the heaviest losses. He was now appointed to the command of the Department of the Missouri, but on the day of the publication of the order, died suddenly, on the 21st day of March, at Syracuse, New York, where he was sojourning for a brief period. His integrity and patriotism, through forty-four years of public service, entitle him to a high place among the defenders of his country.

[210] *Letter* of John Greiner, acting superintendent of Indian affairs, July 31, 1852: "Left in charge of the superintendency of Indian affairs by Governor Calhoun, without a dollar to pay expenses, without any means provided to meet any of the Indians, with only one Indian agent in the Territory and he in the Navajó country, with a rumor that the Comanches are forming a league with the other wild tribes to pounce down upon New Mexico and Texas, with suspicions that some devilment is afoot among the Pueblos, with rumors of revolutions among the Mexicans, with Governor, Chief Justice and Secretary absent in the States, you can judge of my condition. . . Colonel Sumner is here claiming to be acting Governor and the Military are ambitious of governing the Territory. As soon as the Secretary takes his post, Sumner says he will remove the troops from here, for no other reason than to embarrass the civil authority and to make it apparent that the civil authorities cannot govern the Mexicans. The prisoners who are in jail will have to be turned loose because Sumner will refuse to furnish rations at present and this will breed confusion and disorder. The merchants will be appealed to through the interest they have in supplying the troops and odium will be attempted to be thrown upon the civil authority to accomplish this purpose. A thousand vexed and intricate questions will have to be settled without any rule to guide or law to govern, and what will be the result nobody knows."

sible to maintain a civil government in New Mexico without the aid of the army, making it virtually a military government, costly and burdensome, without helping the natives, who would only become the more worthless as more government money was expended in the country. "Withdraw all the troops and the civil officers," was his advice, "and let the people elect their own civil officers and conduct their government in their own way under the general supervision of our government. It would probably assume a similar form to the one found here in 1846; viz: a civil government, but under the entire control of the governor. This change would be highly gratifying to the people. There would be a *pronunciamento* every month or two, but these would be of no consequence, as they are very harmless when confined to Mexicans alone." Major R. H. Weightman,[211] however, who was delegate in congress, successfully defended the people of New Mexico, and by convincing argument succeeded in securing the indefinite postponement of any consideration of the recommendations of the secretary of war, who favored the purchase of all the property in New Mexico, held in private ownership, and abandoning the country to the wild tribes.

The treaty made with the Navajós by Colonel Washington, in 1849, having been broken by the Indians, and also another treaty made by Governor Calhoun and himself at Jemez, Colonel Sumner led an expedition with his dragoons into the Navajó country, penetrating as far as eight or ten miles into the Canyon de Chelly, but he was compelled to retire without accomplishing anything.

MILITARY POSTS ESTABLISHED

Fort Defiance, in the heart of the Navajó country, was built about this time. Its location was one of the most eligible in the Navajó region, being at the mouth of Canyoncito Bonito, a favorite spot with the Indians and near fertile valleys and good water. Colonel Sumner also built Fort Union, in Mora county, where he established headquarters of the department.[212]

---

[211] *Speech* of R. H. Weightman, *Congressional Globe*, 1852-53, p. 103 *et seq.*

[212] Fort Defiance was a very important post; it was built by Major Backus and was garrisoned with three companies, one of light artillery and two of infantry. The quarters of the officers and men were built around a large parade, some three hundred by two hundred yards. Some of the buildings were of adobe and others of pine logs. The officers' quarters were upon the north side and fronted upon the parade. Besides a battery of six-pounders, there were also six mountain howitzers.

Fort Union, built by Colonel Sumner, was a hundred and ten miles from

Merchants and Freighters of the Santa Fé Trail Period

1. Louis Robidoux. 2. A. Staab. 3. Don Juan Cristobal Armijo. 4. Bernard Seligman. 5. Don Nestor Armijo. 6. Charles Ilfeld. 7. James L. Johnson. 8. Herman Ilfeld 9. Solomon Spiegelberg. 10. W. Elsberg

TERRITORY OF NEW MEXICO

The survey of the boundary line between the United States and Mexico was begun prior to 1850. John B. Weller was the first commissioner, and the survey began in the west in June, 1849. John C. Fremont was named as the successor of Weller, but he resigned, and John R. Bartlett was appointed in June, 1850. Bartlett arrived at El Paso in November, 1850, having crossed the state of Texas from the coast. The Mexican commissioner was General Pedro Garcia Conde. Active operations in the field began in 1851, the headquarters of the American party being at the Santa Rita copper mines for several months. In less than a year nearly all of the boundary, so far as the southern line of New Mexico is concerned, had been surveyed.[213] After the arrival of Mr. Bartlett at the cop-

THE BOUNDARY SURVEY

Santa Fé, in the Mora Valley. It was an open post, without either stockades or breastworks, and had somewhat the appearance of a frontier village. It was laid out with broad, straight streets crossing each other at right angles. The houses were built of logs, and the quarters of officers and men were good.

Other posts built during the American occupation period and by Colonel Sumner while he was commanding the department, and by his successors, were: Fort Conrad, later called Fort Craig; Fort Fillmore, below Las Cruces; Rayado, in the present Colfax county, forty miles from Taos; Abiquiu, on the Chama river; at Los Lunas; and Fort Massachusetts, near where Fort Garland was afterward built; Cantonment Burgwin, near Taos; Fort Marcy — Santa Fé, and Alburquerque; Fort Wingate, old Fort Wingate; Fort Fauntleroy; Fort Stanton, Fort Sumner, on the Pecos, at Bosque Redondo; Fort Bliss, near El Paso; Fort West, at Pinos Altos; Fort Webster, near the copper mines at Santa Rita. Fort Cummings, Fort Thorne, and Fort Bascom were other posts. There was also a garrison at Socorro at one period, and at Cebolleta.

[213] Bancroft, H. H., *History of Arizona and New Mexico*, pp. 469-470, says: By the terms of the treaty of Guadalupe Hidalgo of 1848, the line was to follow the Rio Grande up "to the point where it strikes the southern boundary of New Mexico; thence westward along the whole southern boundary of New Mexico (which runs north of the town called Paso) to its western termination; thence northward along the western line of New Mexico until it intersects the first branch of the river Gila (or if it should not intersect any branch of that river, then to the point on the said line nearest to such branch, and thence in a direct line to the same); thence down the middle of said branch and said river until it empties into the Rio Colorado." The southern boundary of New Mexico had indeed been somewhat indefinitely fixed at one point as just above El Paso, leaving that town in Chihuahua; but I have found no evidence that any western boundary had ever been fixed at all or even thought of. There may have been, however, a kind of tacit agreement, as being a matter of no practical importance, that the line between Chihuahua and Sonora, that is, a line between Janos and Fronteras in about longitude 108° 30' extended northward indefinitely. In no other sense had New Mexico a western boundary, and in equity had the treaty gone no further, this should have been the line adopted. But the treaty contained an additional provision that "the southern and western

per mines he was visited by Mangas Coloradas, or Red Sleeve, chief of the Apaches, accompanied by twelve or fifteen of his tribe. Mangas Coloradas claimed that he was a friend of the Americans and that his people desired peace. He remembered having met General Kearny and Colonel Cooke several years before. He seemed to understand the causes for the war with Mexico and its results.[214]

Under the provisions of the treaty of Guadalupe Hidalgo the residents of New Mexico were privileged to leave the territory or remain either as citizens of one country or the other, but all those who failed to make known their choice within one year were to become citizens of the United States. The Mexican government made an appropriation to aid those of New Mexico who preferred to retain their Mexican nationality. All told probably one thousand five hundred or two thousand New Mexicans, during the years 1848-50, withdrew with their slaves and possessions to Chihuahua. Padre Ramon Ortiz and Manuel Armendaris came from Chihuahua, representing the Mexican government, and endeavored in every way possible to persuade the people to leave New Mexico and retain their nationality.[215] In the spring of 1849, Colonel Washington, civil and military governor,

CHANGE OF CITIZENSHIP
BY NEW MEXICANS

limits of New Mexico mentioned in this article, are those laid down in Disturnell's map of Mexico, edition of New York, 1847.''

See Bartlett, J. R., *Personal Narrative*, etc.; *U. S. and Mex. Boundary Survey* (1854-1855), *Report* of Wm. H. Emory, Wash., 1857; *Report* of the secretary of the interior, July, 1852, *U. S. Gov. Doc.*, 32d congress, 1st sess., *Sen. Ex. Doc.* 119; also *Sen. Ex. Doc.* 121, 32d cong., 1st sess. This contains Graham's *Report on Boundary Line between the United States and Mexico.*

There was a quarrel between all of those connected with this survey, growing out of jealousies between the military, civil, and scientific branches of the commission.

[214] Bartlett, J. R., *Personal Narrative*, p. 301, vol. i, says: ''Our protection of the Mexicans he did not seem to relish; and could not comprehend why we should aid them in any way after we had conquered them, or what business it was to the Americans if the Apaches chose to steal their mules, as they had always done, or to make wives of their Mexican women, or prisoners of their children. I told them the Americans were bound to do so and could not break their word; and if they (the Apaches) committed any farther depredations on Mexico, we should not shield them from the consequences.''

[215] Bancroft, H. H., *History of Arizona and New Mexico*, pp. 472-473, says: ''Ortiz claimed that in the first county visited, that of San Miguel del Vado, 900 out of 1,000 families eagerly agreed to go, and that the whole number of emigrants was likely to reach 80,000; but that the territorial authorities, frightened at the prospect, threw obstacles in the way. For this reason, or because of financial difficulties, or because the people, on reflection, became less desirous of quitting the land of their birth — to say nothing of the possibility

issued a proclamation calling upon all those who desired to make their election, as provided for in the treaty, to do so in the manner therein pointed out. They were directed to appear before the prefects of their respective counties on or before the first day of the month of June following and make their election in writing in order to retain the rights of Mexican citizenship or lose the privilege. The clerk of the prefecture was required to attach a certificate to the record in which the names were enrolled and to send the same to the secretary of the territory, who was directed to have them published and to send a copy to each county. The law was substantially complied with in these particulars, a large number availing themselves of this privilege.[216]

THE LEGISLATURE OF 1851

The first New Mexico legislature convened at Santa Fé, June 2, 1851. Seven of the members-elect were priests. Rev. Antonio José Martinez was elected president of the council at the first session, and at the second session, which met in December following, Rev. J. Felipe Ortiz, vicario of the diocese, was chosen to fill that position. In his message to the assembly, Governor Calhoun fa-

that the honest presbitero greatly exaggerated the original enthusiasm — very little was accomplished.''

Mexico. Col. Leyes y Decretos, 1848, p. 309. The governor of New Mexico compelled Padre Ortiz to suspend his personal visits to the different counties, alleging that there was danger of revolt. He consented at first to the appointment of sub-agents, but this privilege was also suspended as soon as it became evident that the desire to emigrate was so general among the people. Ortiz also claimed that unfair advantage had been taken of the inhabitants preventing them from making the declaration required by the treaty.

[216] Davis W. W. H., El Gringo, pp. 331-332, says: ''At the fall elections in 1853, many whose names were found on this record as having elected to retain the rights of Mexican citizens, offered to vote, and upon being challenged, swore that they were citizens of the United States. Several of those who voted under these circumstances were afterward indicted for false swearing, and upon the trial of the first case called, out of some forty in all, these questions came up. The record was offered in evidence to prove that the defendant was a Mexican citizen, and that in swearing at the polls that he was a citizen of the United States he had perjured himself, and became liable to the pains and penalties in such cases. The court, after listening to lengthy arguments upon both sides, overruled the offer, declared the book not a legal record and of course, not evidence — that the proceedings on the part of Colonel Washington were illegal and without authority, and that those who had made an election in this manner had not parted with their rights as citizens of the United States. This decision disposed of all the indictments pending, all of which were nol. pros'd.''

In the printed transcript of testimony in the election contest of Otero versus Gallegos are found many names of prominent men who declared their Mexican citizenship, among others, Don Miguel Pino.

vored the establishment of a penitentiary, a system of public schools, laws providing for the organization of the militia and informed the representatives of the people of his acts in making a treaty of peace with the Navajós. In the matter of treating with the Indians there was but one opinion, so far as the legislature was concerned, and that was voiced by a resolution offered by Theodore Wheaton, speaker of the house of representatives, in which it was declared that "any peace made with the Navajó Indians without an entire restitution of all Mexicans held by them in a state of slavery and also of all property taken by them from the citizens of the territory within the last five years, or its equivalent, together with at least fifty hostages of the principal Indians of the nation, as guarantees for the observance of the treaty, would be not only futile and impolitic, but contrary to the principles of humanity and the best interests of the territory." Governor Calhoun had been notified by General Pino of serious depredations by Indians in the south and during the session in December, Robert T. Brent, a member of the legislature from Santa Fé, while crossing the *Jornada del Muerto* was cruelly murdered and scalped by the Apaches. This news brought out a vigorous resolution from the house of representatives wherein it was declared that "since the entrance of the American army under General Kearny this Territory has been a continual scene of outrage, robbery and violence carried on by the savage nations by which it is surrounded; that citizens daily are massacred, stock stolen, our wives and daughters violated and our children carried into captivity." The delegate in congress was asked to secure the passage of an act requiring the organization of at least two regiments of volunteers, to be armed, equipped, subsisted and paid by the general government. The legislature also desired the building of arsenals and presidios at various points on the frontier. At this very time Colonel Sumner, the military commander of the department, was reporting that the Indians were quiet.[217] The body of Brent was brought to Santa Fé

[217] It is impossible to understand the radical differences in opinion as expressed by various authorities on this subject. Mr. Bartlett, who was at the copper mines of Santa Rita about this time, says that "no one could venture alone, with safety, three miles from the settlements" on account of the Indians. That "two of the largest and most widely spread tribes, the Comanches and the Apaches, are as actively hostile to the Americans and the Mexicans as they were before the country occupied by them became a part of the Union. At no period have the incursions been more frequent, or attended with greater atrocities, than at the present time" [1852].

at the expense of the territory. Governor Calhoun in a message to the legislature stated that he had made arrangements to meet certain Navajó chiefs at Santa Fé; that the Indians were told that it was the intention of the governor to have them murdered, and on this account only two came to see him, the others remaining beyond the pueblo of Jemez. The governor was of the opinion that had it not been for this false statement made to the Indians by interested parties, every captive would have been released, and that it was his intention to lay the matter before the court, so that the parties, whose names he had, might be prosecuted for treason!

At the December session of the legislature the territory was divided into nine counties — Taos, Rio Arriba, Santa Fé, San Miguel, Santa Ana, Bernalillo, Valencia, Socorro, and Doña Ana — with names and boundaries substantially as in earlier times. The county seat of Valencia was located at Tomé, that of Rio Arriba at Chamita, and Santa Ana at Peña Blanca. Justices' courts were established.

When Governor Calhoun left the territory for the east, John Greiner, afterwards appointed secretary, was placed in charge of civil and Indian affairs by Governor Calhoun. As we have seen, the governor died while on his journey and Greiner remained at the head of affairs until the arrival of Governor William Carr Lane.[218] Very shortly after his arrival a controversy arose over the southern boundary line in regard to which a proclamation was issued by Governor Lane who claimed that New Mexico had jurisdiction over the Mesilla valley.[219] There was much popular

ADMINISTRATION OF
WILLIAM CARR LANE

[218] Governor Lane was a native of Fayette county, Pennsylvania, having been born December 1, 1789. He was of English ancestry. He received his education at Jefferson and Dickinson colleges. In 1813 he visited the northwest territory. He was a surgeon in the army of the United States. In 1818 he was married to Miss Mary Ewing, daughter of Nathaniel Ewing, of Vincennes, Indiana; about this time he resigned his commission in the army, and came to the city of St. Louis. He was the first quartermaster-general of the state of Missouri and the first mayor of the city of St. Louis. He served in the state legislature and was a member of the faculty of Kemper college. He was appointed governor of New Mexico by President Millard Fillmore.

[219] Bancroft. H. H., *History of Arizona and New Mexico*, says, p. 652: "The United States and Mexican commissioners agreed upon an initial point on the Rio Grande, which gave the Mesilla Valley to Mexico. Before this agreement, it appears that a few settlers from Doña Ana, a little farther north, had entered the valley; and after it a Chihuahua colony under Rafael Ruelas had colonized the district in 1849-1850 as Mexican soil. While I find no evidence, as

feeling upon the subject in New Mexico, the citizens seeming determined not to give up the district in question.

I have before stated, that any other line was ever agreed upon down to the date of the Gadsden treaty, which settled the whole matter in 1853-54, yet there was a senate report against the Bartlett line, and the appropriation bill forbade the expending of money on the survey until it should appear that the line was not farther north of El Paso than it was laid down on Disturnell's map, the president accordingly declining to authorize the expenditure. . . The only troublesome point left in later years was respecting the validity of the Mexican colony grants made after 1848, and therefore not protected by the treaty of Guadalupe Hidalgo.''

Relative to this matter, Governor Lane, in a letter written at Washington, D. C., January 23, 1854 — *Gov. Doc.*, 33d cong., 1st sess., H. of R. No. 81 — says: ''When I went to New Mexico in the summer of '52, I was urged by the delegate from that Territory to claim jurisdiction over the Mesilla district and take possession of it by force. For reasons that will be apparent to you, I declined to adopt this course, but as soon as I was informed that the government of the United States had repudiated Bartlett's line (which was in February) after consulting the attorney-general of the Territory, I issued a proclamation and claimed jurisdiction of the country until the boundary line should be established by the two governments. The claim of jurisdiction was resisted by military force by the authorities of the state of Chihuahua, in which resistance I have reason to believe the authorities of Chihuahua were encouraged by certain officers of the United States army. Under this state of things, I deemed it to be advisable to attempt to take the country by force of arms by means of N. Mex. and Texan volunteers, who were importunate in their demands that I should take the country and restore our citizens to their rights of person and property in this district. The invasion of these rights under the authorities of the state of Chihuahua had been undisguised and scandalous, according to the reports which I received. I deemed it advisable to lay the whole subject before the President of the United States as soon as possible, and forwarded my communication to the President from where I then was (some 300 miles south of Santa Fé) whence the packet was taken by Hon. Grafton Baker, at my solicitation, to this city.''

Bartlett, J. R., *Personal Narrative*, pp. 212-214, says: ''Immediately preceding, and after the war with Mexico, the Mexican population occupying the eastern bank of the Rio Grande in Texas and New Mexico were greatly annoyed by the encroachments of the Americans, and by their determined efforts to despoil them of their landed property. This was done by the latter either settling among them, or in some instances forcibly occupying their dwellings and cultivated spots. In most cases, however, it was done by putting 'Texas head-rights' on their property. These 'head-rights' were grants issued by the state of Texas, generally embracing 640 acres, or a mile square, though they sometimes covered very large tracts. They were issued to persons who had served in her wars, like our military land-warrants, and also to original settlers.

''With these land certificates, or 'head-rights,' many Americans flocked to the valley of the Rio Grande, and in repeated instances, located them on property which for a century had been in the quiet possession of the old Spanish colonists and their descendants. The latter, to avoid litigation, and, sometimes in fear of their lives, abandoned their homes, and sought a refuge on the Mexican side of the river. Doña Ana, a modern town on the eastern bank of the Rio Grande, being a desirable place, and moreover selected by the United States for one of its military posts became an attractive point for speculators,

Shortly after his arrival Governor Lane, in his capacity of superintendent of Indian affairs, evolved a policy of keeping the Indians quiet by giving them rations, believing that this was a better method than fighting. He made treaties with the Apaches in the southwest and northeast, in which he agreed to give them rations for five years, and also additional aid provided they would work. A large number of the Jicarillas in the north were induced to settle on farms west of the Rio Grande on the Rio Puerco. Governor Lane expended about twenty thousand dollars in the execution of this policy, and when, his treaties not being approved, the food supply was cut off, the Apaches became worse than ever, and went on the war-path.

TREATIES WITH INDIANS BY GOVERNOR LANE

Governor Lane was a man of superior ability. He was nominated for delegate to congress, his opponent being José Manuel Gallegos. On the returns Gallegos received 4,971 and Lane 4,526; Lane contested the election but was unsuccessful.

Governor Lane, after the election for delegate, left New Mexico, the secretary, William S. Messervy,[220] acting as governor until the

and was in consequence pounced upon by them, and covered by the Texan land-warrants. Whether the Mexican occupants of the town and lands adjacent were the lawful owners or not it is needless to investigate; it is sufficient to say they were the first settlers, and had long been in undisturbed possession. They now became alarmed. Litigations commenced; some applying to the authorities of New Mexico, Texas, or the United States, for protection. Failing to obtain it, several hundred abandoned their property and homes in despair, and sought an asylum in Mexican territory, preferring the very uncertain protection they could obtain there to remaining as citizens of the United States.

''With this resolution, a spot was selected on the opposite or western side of the river, six or eight miles below Doña Ana, which, it was believed, would be within the limits of Mexico. On the 1st of March, 1850, sixty Mexicans, with Don Rafael Ruelas at their head, most of whom had been domiciled at Doña Ana, abandoned their homes on account of their many grievances, and moved to the lands known as the Mesilla, where they established themselves. . . More than half the population of Doña Ana removed to Mesilla within a year. When the boundary line was established in April, 1851, and it became certain that La Mesilla was south of the boundary line, according to the treaty map, their fears were removed, and a day was set apart for public rejoicing. For the whole population had determined to abandon the place if the boundary line had run south of the village, and thus placed them under the jurisdiction of New Mexico.''

[220] W. S. Messervy was a native of the state of Massachusetts. He came to Mexico long before the Mexican war; was engaged in business at Santa Fé for several years, where he built up a large fortune. He was a man of fine talents and enjoyed the confidence of the people. He and A. W. Raynolds were candidates for delegate against R. H. Weightman in 1851.

arrival of David Merriwether [221] in 1853, who held the office until 1857. Governor Merriwether was no stranger to New Mexico. He had been an Indian trader prior to 1820, and in 1819 accompanied a party of Pawnees as far as the Spanish frontier on the north, where

ADMINISTRATION OF GOVERNOR DAVID MERRIWETHER

---

[221] David Merriwether was a Virginian by birth, but, with his father's family, removed to Kentucky in 1805. He was appointed governor of New Mexico by Franklin Pierce in 1853 and entered upon the discharge of his duties in the month of August of that year. Filled with a desire for adventure, so common to Kentuckians of his time, he entered the employ of the American Fur Company in 1818 and in their employ spent three years in hunting and trapping upon the plains and waters of the far west. His life was a continued scene of adventure and hardship, in which practical school he finished his education and graduated for the pursuits of life. In the year 1819 he was sent with a party of Pawnees for the purpose of opening trade with New Mexico, in order to exchange their furs and other goods for bullion and to obtain permission to hunt and trap upon the streams of New Mexico. They had advanced as far west as the Canadian Fork when they were attacked by a party of Spanish troops, most of the Indians killed, and himself and a negro boy made prisoners. They were conducted to Santa Fé, about a hundred and twenty miles distant, and brought before Melgares, the governor of New Mexico, by whom he was accused of being a spy of the United States, and was thrown into prison. He was repeatedly brought before the governor and closely questioned as to his motives in coming into the country, with the design, as it appeared, of entrapping him into some hostile admission, in the absence of any evidence against him. The only medium of communication was a priest who spoke French, which language Merriwether partly understood. He was confined in the prison adjoining the palace for about a month when he was released.

When arrested he and his servants were both well armed and mounted upon fine horses but their captors had stripped them of everything but the clothes upon their bodies. Merriwether sought an interview with the governor, and represented to him their condition; that to be driven into the mountains without any arms to kill game was certain death, and he had better kill them at once and shorten their misery. This appeal had some effect; and although their own property was not restored to them, he gave each one a mule, an old gun, and a few charges of powder and lead. They were not permitted to leave the country by the same route they had entered it, but were sent by the way of Taos in charge of a corporal and two men. The escort accompanied them some little distance above that place when they suddenly left them and returned to Santa Fé. The weather was cold and the mountains covered with snow, and they found themselves turned adrift in an unknown country. They had many hundred miles of inhospitable plains and mountains to traverse and had two almost useless guns and a small supply of ammunition to kill game and defend themselves from hostile Indians. But there was no time to be lost in contemplation; the situation was unfortunate; before taken prisoner, Merriwether had appointed a place of rendezvous, where such of the Indians as might be able to make their escape were directed to go and await his coming. Merriwether now took a direction for that point, as well as he was able to do without a guide or a knowledge of the country, being guided by the sun during the day and the stars at night — killing game as they went at the risk of bringing hostiles upon them at the report of their guns. After traveling several

Maxwell's Mansion on the Cimarron

they encountered a Spanish force by which the Pawnees were utterly defeated, Merriwether taken prisoner, carried to Santa Fé and placed in confinement in the military *carcel*. When he arrived at Santa Fé to assume duties of executive of the territory, the roof of the room in which he had been confined many years before fell in. This the people interpreted as a favorable omen.

days across the mountains that lie on the eastern confines of New Mexico, in constant fear of being attacked, and suffering from the cold, they reached the place of rendezvous, and found three Pawnee Indians waiting for them. The meeting was pleasant to all parties, and they remained there a few days making the necessary preparations for the continuance of their journey. They resolved to seek some good location upon the headwaters of the Arkansas where they could remain until spring and then return to the settlements.

They took up the line of march from the rendezvous and after traveling in a northerly direction for several days they came to a cave upon the headwaters of the Arkansas that promised to answer their purpose of a winter residence. It was a large cavern in the side of a hill and the rocks from above projected over somewhat in the shape of a portico. They set to work and made the place as comfortable as possible. Their greatest fear was in being discovered by hostiles and they took constant precautions to prevent their whereabouts being known. Time hung heavily upon their hands, as they were afraid to venture from the mouth of the cave unless they were compelled to do so in search of food. Among other expedients to kill time Merriwether amused himself in fashioning a stone to represent a man's face and upon which he stretched a piece of skin. When the skin was dried he took it off, cut holes for the eyes, nose and mouth and thus had a respectable looking mask. When finished he laid it away in the cave, without imagining the valuable service it would be able to render him before the winter was passed. One day nine strange Indians came to the cave, whom they suspected very strongly of some hostile intention, and were therefore uneasy while they remained. They were anxious to look at everything in and about the premises and after having seen everything there was in the outer apartment, one of them desired to know what was behind the curtain. It was desirable to preserve the inner part of the cave from the eyes of the strangers, and, as they were not able to do so by force, they had to resort to strategem. Merriwether now thought of his mask and feeling certain that he would be able to make it serve him a good purpose in the emergency, replied to the inquiry of the Indians that they kept their *Great Medicine* behind the curtain. This excited the curiosity of the visitors the more and they demanded to see him right away, as they wanted to know whether he looked like their medicine-man. He endeavored to satisfy their curiosity in various ways but nothing would do but a sight of him. Finally he told the Indians that he would go in and consult with the *Great Medicine*, and if he should be willing to see strangers he would return and admit them. Once behind the screen he arranged his plans to give the Indians a good fright. He fixed the skin-mask upon the point of a rock, and putting a lighted candle within it, returned to the outer apartment. He told them that if they should see fire and smoke coming out of his eyes, nose and mouth it was a sure sign that the *Great Medicine* was very angry and they must look out for themselves. They were to be admitted one at a time. The skin screen was carefully drawn aside to let one in, who entered; but seeing the fire and smoke streaming out of the holes in the mask, he took it for granted that the Great Spirit was in a towering rage, and was about to devour the whole of them, and therefore took

Governor Merriwether, immediately after his arrival in the country, began a regular series of visits to all of the more important towns and settlements of the territory, usually accompanying the court parties in "riding the circuit." He found that the Indians of the country were for the most part hostile. However, he succeeded in negotiating several treaties with different tribes, but these were not approved by the government. During the rule of Merriwether Kit Carson was made Indian agent at Taos, his skill in handling the savages having been considered remarkable.

Governor Merriwether was a firm believer in controlling the Indian by force of arms [222] and recommended in his message to the New

---

to his heels, yelling like a demon, followed by all of his companions. Thus they rid themselves of these ugly visitors, and probably this little stroke of ingenuity was the means of saving their lives. They were afraid, however, that the Indians might return with others to see the white man's medicine, to whom the harmless mask might not appear so terrific, and therefore resolved to break camp and seek a more secure location. They took up their march that evening through deep snow, with their packs upon their backs, and traveled all night and the next day before they camped. Before they laid down to sleep, the mask with the candle inside, was placed on the point of a high rock so that in case the strange Indians should follow their trail, they would first be saluted by the *Great Medicine* they so much feared. Thence they continued their journey and reached a trading post in safety, at which they spent the remainder of the winter. Later Merriwether had a duel with an Indian chief, in which the governor received a lance wound in his thigh and the Indian was brained with a hatchet by the negro servant, for which act he was freed after they had returned to the settlements.

[222] When Merriwether was on his way to New Mexico, two young Mexican girls made their escape from the Kiowa Indians and joined the train with which he was traveling. He afterwards forwarded them to their homes in Chihuahua, whence they had been stolen nearly two years before. They made their escape in the following manner: One day they were sent out by the Indians to herd the animals, when, on ascending a hill, they espied the wagon-train coming across the prairies just west of the Arkansas. Mounting their horses they started for the wagons. They reported themselves to the wagon-master, a man named McCarthy, from whom they received the kindest treatment. The following day some thirty or forty Indians overtook the train and demanded the girls, but McCarthy denied all knowledge of them, having previously concealed them in the wagons, so they could not be found. The Indians were determined and made an attempt to search the wagons, when the teamsters took down their arms and showed fight. One old squaw, whose slave one of the girls had been, was in the act of getting into a wagon, when McCarthy laid her sprawling with the butt end of his whip. The following day a government train, with which was General Garland, was overtaken and the rescued captives were delivered to the governor.

These girls told the governor of an American woman with a small child whom they had seen in captivity and who was obliged to submit to the most brutal and inhuman treatment. They said that one day, while traveling, one of the Indians seized the child, threw it up in the air and caught it upon the point of his lance as it came down. The rest of the band amused themselves

Mexico legislative assembly that it memorialize congress to remove the Indians to places remote from the frontier. He also desired the organization of a strong volunteer force to be equipped and paid by the general government. He was fully alive to the spirit of progress of the west and called the attention of the people to the efforts making by other states and territories to secure the construction of the Pacific railroad and advised the organization of an exploring party to ascertain a feasible route through New Mexico.

Prior to the coming of Merriwether, the Indians had become so dangerous and active in their raids that acting Governor Messervy called out the militia of Rio Arriba and San Miguel counties for the purpose of assisting in the protection of the frontier, but for want of ammunition and equipment they were of little service. Indeed, most of Merriwether's rule was taken up in handling Indian troubles. At this time the total amount of cash receipts for the territorial treasury was $3,886.36 and the total expenditures in cash and unpaid warrants amounted to $6,520.07, the total outstanding indebtedness of the territory being $9,680.59. With no financial aid from the general government, the civil authorities had small resources with which to protect the inhabitants from the hostile tribes which surrounded them on all sides. When it became necessary for Merriwether to notify the Jicarilla Apaches that he could no longer make them presents or furnish them with rations they, together with the Utes, went on the war-path. Finally, after an active campaign by the military, led by Lieutenants Bell and Davidson, in one battle in which over twenty dragoons were killed, the Jicarillas were conquered and made a treaty of peace in July, 1854.[223] The Utes were

in the same manner, and thus they passed the child around among them upon their lance-heads until the dead body was pierced like a sieve.

During Governor Merriwether's administration two Mexican boys, Domingo Benavides and Pedro Miguel Gonzales, captured by the Cheyennes, near Anton Chico, were returned to their families through the efforts of the governor.

[223] Bancroft, H. H., *History of Arizona and New Mexico*, p. 667: "From this time these tribes were friendly, though committing occasional thefts, or even worse depredations, and sometimes accused of other offenses of which they probably were not guilty. The frequent raids of other tribes from the west and east made it difficult in many cases to identify the real culprits."

Reports on the condition of these Indians and their prospects were very conflicting. For full information relative to the subject see *Report* of Governor Merriwether of September, 1854, in *Ind. Aff. Rept.*; also Colonel Fauntleroy's reports in 1855, in *U. S. Gov. Doc.*, 34th cong., 1st sess., *H. Ex. Doc.* 1, pt. ii, pp. 56-72. Lieutenant Maxwell, Joseph E., of the 3d infantry, was killed near Ft. Union on June 30, 1854. The legislative assembly, during

finally defeated in a decisive campaign by Colonel Fauntleroy, ending in May, 1855. The northern part of New Mexico, outside of the Navajó country was overrun with the Utes and Jicarillas. The Jicarilla country was properly east of the Rio Grande, and the Mohuache Utes also claimed this section as their home, the agency for both tribes being at Taos, and later at Cimarron, on the ranch of Lucien B. Maxwell. The Ute country was west of the river, stretching northwestward into Colorado and Utah, where most of the tribe lived, and the agency for those Utes who roamed in northwestern New Mexico was situated at Abiquíu. The Utes and Jicarillas were in a way related by marriage and were naturally averse to restraint of any kind. The Utes were brave, war-like, better armed than the other tribes, and were skilful hunters; bold in the assertion of their rights to the broad tract over which they ranged, wholly opposed to farming or reservation life, they were willing to be friendly and abstain from depredations if liberally supplied with food. Their ideal was to retain their hunting grounds, periodically visiting an agency to receive their gifts, which must not be less than other tribes received — and having free access to the settlements, where whiskey could be procured. The Jicarillas were equally fond of whiskey, somewhat more treacherous and cruel, less brave and energetic as warriors and hunters, making pottery, and farming sometimes on a small scale, and regarding theft as a natural means of supporting themselves, if no easier way could be found. A large reservation near the settlements, where they could lead an easy, vagabond, drunken life would have pleased them well enough.[224]

Merriwether's administration, memorialized congress asking that the Jicarillas be put on a reservation.

The Indian agents serving during this period, in addition to the superintendent — the governor — were in 1851: R. H. Weightman, who was elected to congress in that year; John Greiner, who was stationed at Taos for a time; Abraham R. Wooley and E. H. Wingfield, who was dismissed in 1853. In 1852 Michael Steck and S. M. Baird were appointed and in the following year, Kit Carson, H. L. Dodge, J. M. Smith and E. A. Graves were appointed. In 1854-1856 Lorenzo Labadie and S. H. Montgomery were named. Agents at later periods, prior to the Civil War, were A. G. Mayers, W. R. Harley, S. F. Kendrick, Diego Archuleta, S. M. Yost, R. S. Cowart, and J. Walker. Also John T. Russell, J. A. Manzanares, and Fernando Maxwell.

[224] *U. S. Gov. Doc.*, 35th cong., 1st sess. *H. Ex. Doc.* xi, p. 82. The New Mexico legislature was continually memorializing congress and it was always pointed out that the Indians were worse and the people less protected than when the Americans came, and that this occurred although there was a large ex-

During nearly all of Governor Merriwether's administration the Apaches were giving trouble in the southern and southeastern portions of the territory. The bands causing most of the trouble were the Mescaleros on the east, between the Pecos and the Rio Grande, and the Mimbres and Mogollones, sometimes called the Gila Apaches, and the Navajós on the west. Altogether there were four or five thousand of these marauding savages. There were very few years in which these tribes were not committing ravages of some sort. In these years battles, actions, engagements, and skirmishes with these Indians were numerous and give some idea of the condition of affairs existing at that time in southern New Mexico. In addition to the list given in the note there were many other engagements fought within the boundary of Texas and in the present limits of the territory of Arizona.[225]

THE APACHES IN NEW MEXICO

---

penditure of money in the maintenance of the military establishment. Just how much truth there may have been in these reports we can not say — but the situation was bad enough. The constant cry for regiments of volunteers, however, seems to be accounted for by a desire on the part of large numbers of New Mexicans to secure easy and profitable employment with the government as paymasters.

[225] 1850, fight on the *Jornada del Muerto*, detachment of Troop H, 1st dragoons, February 2d. 1852, January 24-February 19th, near Laguna on the *Jornada del Muerto*, Troops D, E and K, 2d dragoons; February 6th, near Ft. Webster, N. M., K Company, 3d infantry. 1855, White mountains, Troop H, 1st dragoons, January 15th; Peñasco river, near White mountains, January 19th, Troop B, 1st dragoons; March 19th, Cochotope Pass, Chowatch valley, N. M., Troops D and F, 1st dragoons and D company, 2d artillery; May 1-2, Chowatch valley, N. M., Troop D, 1st dragoons and D company, 2d artillery; June 13th, on Pecos river, Company I, 5th infantry. 1856, March 20th, Almagre mountains, N. M., Companies B and I, 3d infantry; March 29th, Mimbres mountains, Companies B and I, 3d infantry; November 30th, Sacramento mountains, N. M., detachment of Company C mounted riflemen and G company, 1st dragoons. 1857, March 9, Mimbres mountains, Detachment Company G mounted riflemen; March 11th, Ojo del Muerto, detachment Company B mounted riflemen; May 24th, Mogollon mountains, Companies C, D, and I, mounted riflemen; Company B and detachment of Company E, 3d infantry. June 27th, Gila river, Companies B and G, 1st dragoons; B, G, and K, mounted riflemen; Company C and detachments F and K, 3d infantry; Companies B, H, and I, 8th infantry; December 7th, Ladrones mountains, detachment Company F, mounted riflemen; December 13th, Dragoon Springs, detachment Company F, mounted riflemen. 1858, March 11, Huachuca mountains, detachment Company G, 1st dragoons; May 30, near Ft. Defiance, detachment Company I, mounted riflemen; Companies B and G, 3d infantry; August 29th, Bear Springs, detachment Company I, mounted riflemen. September 9th to 15th, Laguna Chusca and vicinity, Companies A, F, H, and I, mounted riflemen; Companies B and C, 3d infantry. November 9th, Carrizozo, Company F, 3d infantry. 1859, January 25, Whetstone Springs, detachment Company D, 1st dragoons; February 8th, Dog Canyon, Sacramento mountains, detachment Company D,

In 1852-1853 there was a considerable number of the Gila Apaches near Ft. Webster and, under the care of Agent Wingfield, they were induced to make a treaty under a promise of rations for five years, that being Governor Lane's policy. This treaty, however, was not confirmed and when their rations were cut off the Indians began their marauding expeditions. In 1854, the Mescaleros began giving much trouble and campaigns were made against them by Lieutenant Sturgis and Captain Ewell, with such success that in March, 1855, they were suing for peace, and in June a treaty was made by Governor Merriwether, by which a reservation was designated near Fort Stanton, and a new post established at this time and named for a captain killed in the campaign. This officer was Captain Henry W. Stanton, 1st dragoons, who was killed in an engagement on the 19th of January, 1855, with the Mescalero Apaches, in the Sacramento mountains. The treaty was not approved, but an agency was from this time maintained at the fort and the Mescaleros, or at least a part of them, kept the peace, received their goods and in some seasons did some small farming.

Governor Merriwether also made a treaty with the Mimbres [226] Apaches in 1855, who behaved very well for a time thereafter.

The Mogollon Apaches gave much more trouble and, on account of the campaign made by Colonel Bonneville in 1857, these and the

---

mounted riflemen. April 27th, Near Ft. Fillmore, Company D, 1st dragoons; November 12-26, various fights with the Pinal Apaches, Company D and detachment Company G, 1st dragoons; Company A and detachments Companies C and H, mounted riflemen; November 14, Tunica, detachments Companies B, C, E, and G, 3d infantry; December 3d, Santa Teresa, detachment Company A, mounted riflemen; December 18th, detachment Company A, mounted riflemen, at Santa Teresa.

[226] Mr. J. R. Bartlett, while at the copper mines, became very well acquainted with this tribe and the chiefs, particularly Mangas Coloradas. Bartlett caused the tailor of his expedition to make a fine suit of clothes for Red Sleeve. It was made of blue broadcloth. Mangas was very pleased with his suit, which consisted of a frock coat lined with scarlet and ornamented with gilt buttons. His pantaloons, at his request, were opened from the knee downward, after the fashion of the Mexicans, with a row of small fancy buttons on one side and a broad strip of scarlet cloth on the outer side from the hip downward. A white shirt and a red silk sash completed his dress. While the tailor had the suit in hand Red Sleeve visited him daily to watch its progress and a child might have envied him his delight. But in putting them on his Indian character was most strikingly displayed. He insisted on wearing his shirt outside his pantaloons, and all of Bartlett's efforts to reverse the arrangement were without effect. Bartlett also had Mangas Coloradas dine with him and he says ''on these occasions his conduct was marked with as much decorum as though he had been used to civilized society all his life.''

Mimbres went on the war-path and continued hostile for more than a year. H. L. Dodge, agent of the Indians, was killed by the Mogollones in 1857.[227]

The first tribe of Indians with which the Americans established treaty relations was the Navajó. At the time of the American occupation they numbered about ten thousand, and THE NAVAJÓ INDIANS occupied the northwestern part of New Mexico. They caused the military more trouble between 1850 and 1860 than all the other New Mexico Indians combined. They made treaty after treaty only to break them whenever fancy suited. They are a pastoral people, also cultivate the soil and manufacture blankets. As Mr. Bancroft says, "conscious of their strength, they paid little heed to the rights of other tribes by all of whom they were hated. For many years plundering raids on the Mexican flocks and herds had been their leading though not their only industry. In this warfare they had lost more captives — to become slaves of the New Mexicans — than they had taken, but in the taking of live-stock the advantage had been largely in their favor. On the merits of the long struggle, except that it had originated in the predatory instincts of the Indians, each party was about equally to blame, instances of treachery and outrage being frequent on both sides for a century past. To the Americans, on their taking possession of the territory, the Navajós professed friendship but could hardly understand how that should interfere with their warfare on the Mexicans; and presently they came to class the Americans with their old foes, and to regard chronic war with the United States as their normal occupation for the future. Having no realization of their new enemy's power they deemed the conditions of the struggle about equal. Regarding the proffer of peace as an indication of weakness or fear, they were willing, when hard-pressed at any point, to make a treaty, which they broke just as soon as their interests seemed to require it. Treaty-making was simply an incidental feature of their business, like treaty-breaking; and had plausible pretext been deemed essential, the New Mexicans, continuing like the Indians their raids as of old, rarely failed to furnish them.[228]

---

[227] For reports of military operations of 1854-1855, see *U. S. Gov. Doc.*, 34th cong., 1st sess., *H. Ex. Doc.* i., pt. ii., 56 *et seq*. For reports of Bonneville's campaign see 35th cong., 1st sess., *H. Ex. Doc* ii., pt. ii., 135-141; *H. Ex. Doc.* No. 2, 35th cong., 2d sess., p. 20 *et seq*.

[228] At the town of Cebolleta on the Navajó frontier during the years 1850

Another complicating circumstance was the fact that the Navajós were much less completely than other tribes under the control of their chiefs, so that one portion of the nation often made war when the rest deemed it not wrong but unwise. No tribe was more in need of or likely to be so much benefited by a sound whipping."

As we have seen, the Navajós had broken their treaties with Doniphan, with Washington, and with Sumner, the last named having made two treaties with them. In 1855, Governor Merriwether negotiated and concluded a treaty with this tribe which was not approved by the general government. Comparative peace lasted, however, during his administration, although the tribe was not thoroughly subdued until eight years later.

Major R. H. Weightman was the first delegate in congress, in which position he proved himself a most capable representative of the people.[229]

DELEGATES IN CONGRESS

Weightman came to New Mexico in 1846 with the Army of the West, under General Kearny, and was present at the occupation of Santa Fé. He was present in the battle of Sacramento, Chihuahua, where he fought with great gallantry.

---

to 1860 there was a band or company of Mexicans known as ''Cebolleteños,'' whose principal occupation was stealing of Navajó girls and boys for purposes of sale to the Mexicans. It was a custom, whenever a wealthy Mexican had arranged for the marriage of a son or daughter, to give these ''Cebolleteños'' an order for one or two Navajó boys or girls to be given to the newly wedded pair as a bridal gift.

[229] Richard Hanson Weightman was born in the District of Columbia, was educated at the United States Military Academy at West Point, and, at the beginning of the war with Mexico, lived in St. Louis, Missouri. He married a Miss Cox of Washington, D. C. When the call was made by the governor of Missouri for troops, intended to become a part of the Army of the West, under command of General Kearny, the county of St. Louis, which then included the city of St. Louis, was asked to furnish the artillery for the expedition, while the northern river counties were asked to furnish the riflemen. Major Merriwether Lewis Clark, of St. Louis, a graduate of West Point and a veteran of the War of 1812 and the Black Hawk War, undertook to raise the two batteries required. A meeting was held May 28, 1846, in the office of a justice of the peace, over a blacksmith shop on Third street between Pine and Olive. Here was organized Battery A, Missouri light artillery. Weightman was unanimously elected captain. The other officers chosen were: Andrew J. Dorn, and Edmund F. Chouteau, first lieutenants, and John O. Simpson, second lieutenant. The sergeants were John R. Gratiot, afterwards elected a second lieutenant while marching across the plains, Davis Moore and A. V. Wilson; William H. Thorpe, William Clark Kennerly, Clay Taylor, John R. White, and George W. Winston, corporals.

In the Civil War Weightman was in Price's army at the battle of Wilson's Creek, in which engagement he was slain. He was a very capable officer. In his report of the battle and the death of Weightman, General Price said:

The Government Distributing Rations to the Indians

After the war he returned to New Mexico and took part in the stormy times subsequent to the treaty of Guadalupe Hidalgo ending in the formation of the territory by the act of 1850. He was elected delegate and in that capacity made many strenuous defenses of the people of New Mexico upon the floor of congress. When his term expired he returned to Santa Fé where he practised law with some success, later on returning to Missouri, where upon the breaking out of the Civil War he cast his fortunes with the confederacy and was killed in action at the battle of Wilson's Creek. Weightman was very active in the politics of New Mexico. Together with Captain W. Z. Angney, a lawyer from Missouri, who had served with him during the Mexican War, he inaugurated a campaign against Hugh N. Smith, who had been sent to Washington to look after the interests of the people, and through the efforts of Weightman congress refused to seat him.

On the 18th of August, 1854, occurred the fatal rencontre between Major Weightman and Francis X. Aubrey, resulting in the death of the latter. The facts in this affair, THE KILLING OF F. X. AUBREY as they were given by the witnesses at the preliminary hearing and afterward at the trial in the district court in Santa Fé, show clearly that Weightman acted in self-defense. The committing magistrate was Justice Davenport and the trial judge was Kirby Benedict. W. W. H. Davis represented the territory in the prosecution and Major Weightman was defended by John S. Watts and S. M. Baird. It was shown that Aubrey returned from California [230] to Santa Fé

"Among those who fell mortally wounded upon the field of battle, none deserves a dearer place in the memory of Missourians than Richard Hanson Weightman, Colonel commanding the first brigade of the second division of the army. Taking up arms at the very beginning of this unhappy contest, he had already done distinguished services at the battle of Rock Creek, where he commanded the state forces after the death of the lamented Holloway; and at Carthage, where he won unfading laurels by the display of extraordinary coolness, courage and skill. He fell at the head of his brigade, wounded in three places and died just as the victorious shouts of our army began to rise upon the air."

[230] *Missouri Republican*, September 26, 1854: "We publish to-day the traveling notes of Mr. Aubrey, taken during his late trip from San José to Santa Fé. They contain much valuable information in regard to the nature and resources of the country through which he passed, and they possess a melancholy interest as a record of the last journey which the daring adventurer made. A good many letters were received yesterday from Santa Fé, all of which make mention in sorrowful terms, of the death of Aubrey. It was an

on the 18th of August, about two o'clock in the afternoon, and stopped at the store of Mercure brothers, situate midway of the block on the south side of the plaza. At the time, Major Weightman was sitting in the southeast corner of the plaza, and seeing Mr. Aubrey ride up, remarked that Aubrey had come and that he must go to see him. Weightman then went to the store, and as he entered, Aubrey was in the act of drinking; they shook hands in a friendly manner, Aubrey asking Weightman to drink with him, which he declined to do and took a seat on the counter. A general conversation then took place between all present relative to the journey of Aubrey to California and return which lasted a minute or two, when Aubrey began to talk about the newspaper called *Amigo del Pais*, which Weightman had formerly edited in Alburquerque. He asked Weightman what had become of his paper, the reply being that the paper had died for want of subscribers. Aubrey then said that any such lying paper ought to die. Weightman asked him what he referred to, when Aubrey said, "Last fall you asked me for information about my trip which I gave you, and you afterwards abused me." Weightman replied that it was not so; whereupon Aubrey brought his fist down upon the counter with considerable force, and repeated: "I say it is so." Weightman then got off the counter and took in his right hand a tumbler about one third full of liquor and water and pitched the contents into Aubrey's face. Weightman then put the tumbler on the counter, stepped back a pace or two and placed his hand upon his belt. When Aubrey received the contents of the glass in his face he immediately drew a five-

occurrence universally regretted, and the regret seems to have been heightened by the achievement which he had just accomplished of making the trip from San José to Peralta in twenty-nine days — not unaccompanied, as has been supposed, but with a company of sixty men, and bringing with them to Peralta a wagon which had been driven the whole distance. We have seen a letter from Dr. Connelly which states this fact and it furnishes irrefutable evidence that a railroad from Alburquerque to San Francisco is practicable, and that, as mules and wagons can be driven between San José and Alburquerque, or Peralta, in twenty-nine days, it is by all odds the best route which has yet been discovered for a railroad to the Pacific. Now take the southwestern branch of the Pacific Railroad of Missouri, extend it to the Missouri border, as it has been determined to do, push it to Alburquerque and thence to the Pacific, and we shall be able to make St. Louis the great central route for the trade of California and the Indies.''

In the issue of the *Republican* containing the above is also found copied from the *Santa Fé Gazette* the account of the killing of Aubrey from which the text is written.

shooter from his left side, and, as he brought it up in front, one barrel was prematurely discharged before it was on a level with Weightman's person and the bullet went into the ceiling. When Weightman saw Aubrey draw his pistol, he drew a bowie knife from his belt; they clinched, and before Aubrey had time to bring his pistol down and fire a second time, Weightman stabbed him in the abdomen. About the time that the parties came together, two of the by-standers seized hold of them, but it was too late to prevent the mischief. Aubrey was caught in the arms of Henry CunIffe and died in about ten minutes. Weightman went to his quarters where he was arrested by the United States marshal. The following day the case was heard before Judge Davenport, sitting as a committing magistrate, who bound him over in the sum of two thousand dollars. Aubrey was buried in the parochial church, his remains having been followed to the grave by a great concourse of friends.[231] Major Weightman was indicted [232] at the term of court in Sep-

[231] *Santa Fé Gazette*, 1854. The attorney appearing for the territory before Judge Davenport says: ''This affair caused much excitement, and as is always the case, the friends of the respective parties disagree; those of Major Weightman contending that the stabbing was done in self-defense, while Aubrey's friends take the contrary side. As we were the prosecuting officer before the examining court, we have no opinion of our own to express in reference to the matter; but will state in addition to what we have already written, that there was no evidence given upon the examination that Major Weightman drew or attempted to draw his knife before Mr. Aubrey drew his pistol. Whether the homicide was justifiable in self-defense or not, we deplore it as being a melancholy and unfortunate affair, and no one regrets its occurrence more than we do. We had never seen Mr. Aubrey, but always heard him spoken of as a pleasant and agreeable man. Major Weightman we have known nearly a year, and in our personal intercourse he has always treated us in a gentlemanly manner. Mr. Aubrey was buried Saturday afternoon in the Parroquial church.''

[232] The record of this trial is as follows: ''Territory of New Mexico vs. Richard Hanson Weightman. Murder. This case was called up for trial, Thursday, the 21st of September, and a jury sworn and empanelled without a challenge being made, either on the part of the Territory or the accused. The case was opened by W. W. H. Davis, esq., acting Attorney General, for the territory, when the following witnesses were sworn and examined: Henry Mercure, being duly sworn says: That he knew Francis X. Aubrey; that he is now dead; he arrived from California on the 18th of August, and stopped at our house; several of his friends came to see him, amongst whom was Major Weightman; he shook hands with them and asked them to drink with him, which they declined; several remarks were made about the trip. Aubrey said to Weightman he thought he had gone to the States; Weightman replied that circumstances had kept him here; Aubrey asked what had become of the paper called *Amigo del Pais* — if it were dead; to which Weightman replied, it was; Aubrey said such lying papers ought not to live; Weightman asked how that was; Aubrey said, last fall when he came from California, Weightman asked

tember, 1854. The testimony having all been taken, Judge Benedict charged the jury as follows:

"The court instructs the jury that if they believe, beyond any reasonable doubt, from the evidence given in this case, that Aubrey drew a five-barreled loaded Colt's pistol, with intent to shoot at and greatly injure the person of Weightman; and that Aubrey was in the act of preparing the pistol and placing it in the position and manner with which to shoot the defendant, Weightman; and that by reason of such acts of Aubrey, the life or person of Weightman was put in immediate and great danger, and that he had no reasonable and safe means in his power to avoid or escape the danger in which he was placed, without taking the life of Aubrey, to secure his (Weightman's) own life, and that under such circumstances he instantly drew his knife and wounded Aubrey so that he quickly died of the wound, then, upon so believing, they (the jury) will find the defendant not guilty in manner and form as the defendant, Weightman, is charged in the indictment."

The jury, after deliberating about one hour, brought in a verdict of not guilty.[233]

---

him for a report of the route, which he gave him, and that he had published the contrary, which made it a perfect lie. Maj. Weightman told him it was not so; Aubrey said it was so; Weightman got up from where he was sitting and took a glass of liquor that was on the counter and threw the liquor in Aubrey's face; the glass was nearly half full; then Weightman stepped back; while Aubrey was taking his pistol from his belt, a shot went off in the ceiling; Weightman walked up to him; they seized hold of one another; I jumped over the counter and took hold of Maj. Weightman, and my brother took hold of Aubrey; then I saw a knife in Weightman's hand covered with blood; I told him to let go and he said that Aubrey was hurt; we parted them; Aubrey fell in Henry CunIffe's arms; Weightman went off; Aubrey died a short time afterward. Aubrey was struck in the belly below the navel; I saw the wound while Dr. Leon was dressing it; that looks like the knife I saw in Weightman's hand; Aubrey died in my store about ten minutes after he was cut."

On cross-examination the witness said: "Weightman was sitting on the counter; he took the glass of liquor in his right hand; I found the glass afterwards on the counter; after the pistol was drawn out it went off; it was a five-shooter; I don't know what Aubrey said while he was drawing out the pistol; I did not hear him say anything; my brother, CunIffe, Richardson and Conklin were present; and others might have been; the store has two doors fronting on the street; a good many were there when Aubrey fell; it was some two or three minutes, more or less, after I got hold of them they were scuffling; the difficulty was near the east door; Aubrey was near the east door when it commenced; the space outside of the counter is, in some places, six, some eight and in some ten feet wide, there being a good many things piled up there; they met friendly; some four or five minutes elapsed before the difficulty occurred."

The other witnesses, Joseph Mercure, Richardson and Henry CunIffe gave about the same testimony as the above; there was no material difference.

[233] The finding of the jury (translation) was as follows: "We, the jury, having considered with sufficient care, after having heard the evidence exhibited before the Honorable Court in the cause confided to us, have unani-

As we have seen, Major Weightman was succeeded as delegate to congress by José Manuel Gallegos, who defeated William Carr Lane for the office. The struggle was largely one between the two factions of the Catholic church, one headed by Rt. Rev. J. B. Lamy and the new clergy brought by him to the country, and the other by the Mexican priests, who were very unfavorably disposed toward the new representative of church authority. The grounds of contest on the part of Lane were that votes of Pueblo Indians cast for him had been illegally rejected. There were also charges of fraud in voting and counting; the congressional committee paid very little attention to these. The vote for Gallegos, however, was cut down to 2,806 and 2,227 for Lane. The congressional committee decided, for all practical purposes, at least, that the Pueblo Indians were not entitled to the elective franchise. In 1855, Gallegos was again elected, according to the governor's certificate, but, in a contest, his seat was given to Don Miguel A. Otero,[234] who held the office for three successive

mously agreed and are of the opinion that the defendant is not guilty, because he committed such an act in defense of his person.
"Vincente Garcia,
"Foreman of the jury."
Aubrey's Journal from California to New Mexico may be found at pp. 84-96 of *The Western Journal and Civilian*, vol. xi, no. 2, Nov., 1853; vol. xi, old style; vol. v, new style.

[234] *U. S. Gov. Doc.*, 34th cong., 1st sess., *H. Miscl. Doc.* 5, 15, 114; *House Repts.* 90. This report contains all of the testimony taken in the contest. The vote was 6,914 to 6,815, making Gallegos's majority 99. The congressional committee gave Otero 290 majority. There were about 1,400 disputed Mexican votes. The chief ground of this contest was the voting by men who, after the treaty of Guadalupe Hidalgo, had chosen — not in legal form as was claimed — to remain citizens of Mexico, but had changed their minds. Congress was not disposed to recognize these as citizens of the United States. Otero alleged, among many other frauds, that in one precinct the priest of San Juan received and read all the votes, rejecting those which were not for Gallegos. Bishop Lamy and his friends in the priesthood worked for Otero.

Miguel A. Otero was born in the plaza of Valencia, Valencia county, New Mexico, June 21, 1829, his parents being Don Vicente and Doña Gertrudis (Aragon) de Otero, natives of Spain and descended from distinguished families. Don Vicente held many positions of honor and trust under the Spanish and Mexican governments, having been judge and alcalde in his home county. Miguel Antonio Otero received his education at St. Louis University, Missouri. His parents desired to have him study for the priesthood, but after leaving the university Mr. Otero went to Fishkill on the Hudson, in a college at which place for some time he held a position as a member of the faculty. Later he returned to Missouri where he studied law and was admitted to the bar. Later he returned to New Mexico where he became prominently identified with the public affairs and politics of the territory. He was elected to the legislature from Valencia county and in 1855 was elected delegate in congress over José Manuel Gallegos. This office he filled with credit to himself and fidelity to the

terms, defeating S. M. Baird in 1857 and José M. Gallegos in 1859. In the election of 1859, John S. Watts, who was later elected delegate over Don Diego Archuleta, in a speech at Mesilla, made some remarks relative to the Otero family which resulted in a bloodless duel between the two. It does not appear that congress took much interest in the affairs of New Mexico during this period other than the conduct of military affairs and the Indian question, which was always under discussion, involving as it did the property rights of citizens of states, whose representatives in congress were entitled to vote. Congress, however, did as much for New Mexico as it did for any other territory.[235]

---

people. In 1861 he was appointed secretary of New Mexico by Abraham Lincoln. It is said that prior to the breaking out of hostilities between the north and south Mr. Otero, while in Washington, gave expression to very pronounced pro-slavery sentiments. He was one of the organizers of the great mercantile firm of Otero, Sellar and Company, later Gross, Blackwell and Company, and now Gross, Kelly and Company. He was one of the organizers of the San Miguel National Bank of Las Vegas, and was its first president, holding the position until the date of his death, May 30, 1882. In politics, Mr. Otero was a democrat. He was a man of fine address, animated by the most generous impulses and of more than ordinary literary and professional attainments. He was very prominent in his efforts to secure the building of the Atchison, Topeka & Santa Fé railroad into New Mexico and gave the promoters and builders of that great company much valuable assistance. In 1857 Mr. Otero was married to Mary Josephine Blackwood, a native of Charleston, South Carolina, of which marriage there were four children, three of whom are still living, Page B., a resident of Santa Fé, Miguel A., governor of New Mexico under McKinley and Roosevelt, now a resident of Santa Fé, and Marie J., now a resident of Paris, France. Mr. Otero had many warm friends attracted by his sterling qualities and the numerous public services he rendered the people of his native territory.

[235] *Acts of Congress* in relation to New Mexico, appropriations, etc., during the decade 1850-1860 are the organic act and appropriation of $20,000 for public buildings and $5,000 for a library; 1851, appropriation of $34,700 for territorial government, $18,000 for the Navajó Indians and $135,530 for payment of the volunteers of 1849; 1852, $31,122 for the government of the territory; 1853, appropriation of $32,555 for government expenses and $10,000 for Indian service; authorizing legislature to hold extra session of 90 days; authorizing employment of translator and clerks, sessions of 60 days instead of 40 days, payment of code commissioners; 1854, appropriation for government $31,620, $50,000 for public buildings, roads $32,000, and Indian service $45,000; appointing surveyor general and donating lands to settlers; increasing salary of governor to $3,000, and judges to $2,500; attaching Gadsden Purchase to New Mexico; authorizing payment of civil salaries for 1846-1851 under the Kearny code; and establishing a collection district; 1855, appropriation for government $35,500 including $2,000 for archive vaults, Indian service $52,500, surveys $30,000, Texas boundary $10,000, raising governor's salary to $3,000; 1858, appropriation for government, $33,000; Indian service, $85,000; road, $150,000; creating a land district; confirming Pueblo land grants; 1859, appropriation for government, $17,000, Indian service, $75,000; 1860 appropriation for government, $23,500, Indians, $50,000, capitol, $50,000, confirming

A treaty was concluded between the United States and Mexico by James Gadsden, in 1853.[236] Under this treaty the boundary line, fixed by the treaty of 1848, was moved

THE GADSDEN PURCHASE southward so as to give to the United States, for a consideration of ten million dollars, all of the territory in the Arizona of today, at that time a part of New Mexico, south of the Gila river. The boundary, as finally fixed by this treaty, December 30, 1853, was the Rio Grande up to latitude 31° 47', due west one hundred miles; south to latitude 31° 20'; west on that parallel to longitude 111°; thence in a straight line to a point in the Colorado river twenty miles below the junction of the Gila; up the middle of the Colorado to the intersection of the former line, *i. e.*, to the mouth of the Gila; and thence on the former line to the Pacific ocean. Besides the addition in territory the United States secured a release from the responsibility, provided for under the treaty of 1848, for outrages by Indians living in the United States committed in Mexican territory. At this time claims on account of ravages by Apaches, Comanches, and Lipan Indians had been presented by Mexico amounting to millions of dollars.[237]

---

private and town land grants; 1861, appropriation for government, $20,500, Indians, $50,000, roads, $50,000; act attaching all north of latitude 37° to Colorado.

[236] *U. S. Govt. Doc.*, 33d cong., 1st sess., *House Ex. Doc.* 109, 47th cong., 2d sess., *House Miscl. Doc.* 45.

New Mexico Compiled Laws, 1897, contains text of this treaty.

James Gadsden was a South Carolinian, a soldier and a diplomat. He graduated at Yale in 1806 and soon afterward entered the United States army. He served with marked distinction in the War of 1812, was appointed aide-de-camp to General Jackson in 1818, took part in the Seminole War; was military inspector of the southern division in 1820 and conducted the removal of the Seminole Indians to the southern part of Florida. After his retirement from the army, he became a planter in Florida and was a member of the legislature of that territory. Later he became president of a South Carolina railroad company. After the treaty with Mexico, he retired to private life.

[237] Bartlett, J. R., *Personal Narrative*, vol. ii, pp. 384-385, says: "The Apaches had been more bold than usual during the spring and summer of 1852; and the whole frontier had suffered from their inroads. Many men had been killed within a few miles of El Paso; and at the astronomical observatory, at Frontera eight miles distant, a man was pierced with arrows while herding the animals within a few rods of the house. Mr. Magoffin's corral had been several times entered, and his mules stolen; and many other citizens there had been sufferers. On two occasions, while I remained at Magoffinsville, the Indians made attempts to run off the animals of the Commission, but were frustrated, by being discovered in time to prevent the stampede. No one could venture alone with safety, three miles from the settlement, and when I went to take a ride, if it was extended as far as three miles, I felt it necessary to be ac-

The United States was much the gainer by the terms of this treaty. The settlement of the boundary dispute was satisfactory; a route for a railroad to the Pacific was obtained and whether the United States ever intended to pay the claims for Indian depredations or not, still the international complications apt to arise were adjusted to the satisfaction of all concerned.[238] The government of

---

companied by several friends. Such was the state of the Mexican frontier in 1852.

"As the question has been repeatedly asked, what is to be done with the large tribes of Indians on the Mexican frontier? And as there is still a diversity of opinion on the subject, I shall take the present occasion to make a few suggestions, based upon what I have learned from personal observation, and my intercourse with the Indians. It is known that we already have along this frontier, but chiefly in the state of Texas and the territory of New Mexico, a large military force, embracing full two-thirds of the army, which is supported at an enormous expense. Military posts have been established at various points on the Rio Grande and in the very heart of the Indian country in Texas and in New Mexico. Yet two of the largest and most widely spread tribes, the Comanches and Apaches, are as actively hostile to the Americans and the Mexicans as they were before the country occupied by them became a part of the Union. At no period have the incursions been more frequent, or attended with greater atrocities, than at the present time. The Comanches pass across the Rio Grande into Mexico, in bands of three hundred or four hundred, and penetrate the very heart of Chihuahua; they have passed into Durango and Zacatecas, and have traversed Coahuila and Nuevo Leon. The extent of the depredations and murders committed would be appalling, if summed up. Yet the system flourishes in full vigor, notwithstanding the efforts made to suppress it on the part of the United States, in compliance with the solemn stipulations of the treaty with Mexico."

[238] *Congressional Globe*, 1853, 1854, contains the *Debates* on the subject of this treaty.

General Santa Anna declared that he had never for a moment expected the United States would keep the agreement by paying for damages done by the Indians. In the United States the necessity for keeping this article of the treaty was fully understood and to secure its abrogation was recognized as an immense gain, which indeed was true.

Bancroft, H. H., *History of Arizona and New Mexico*, pp. 492-93: "Under the treaty of 1848, the commissioners . . . had agreed on latitude 32° 22' as the southern boundary of New Mexico, but the United States surveyor had not agreed to this line, had perhaps surveyed another in 31° 54', and the New Mexicans claimed the Mesilla valley between the two lines as part of their territory. The United States were, to some extent, bound by the acts of their commissioner; but Mexico, besides being wrong on the original proposition, was not in condition to quarrel about so unimportant a matter. On the other hand, the northern republic could afford to pay for a railroad route through a country said to be rich in mines; and Mexico, though national pride was strongly opposed to a sacrifice of territory, was sadly in need of money and sold a region that was practically of no value to her. In both countries there was much bitter criticism of the measure, and a disposition to impute hidden motives to the respective administrations.

"It is a remarkable circumstance that in Mexico, both by the supporters and foes of the measure, it was treated as a cession of the Mesilla valley in settle-

the United States had acquired a great deal of very valuable information by explorations, surveys and reconnoissances [239] made by American army officers during the occupation period both prior and subsequent to the treaty of 1848, and this was greatly complemented by the information gained in the work of the boundary survey.[240]

ment of the boundary dispute, though that valley was, in reality, but a very small and unimportant portion of the territory ceded.''

The Gadsden treaty was not ratified and published until 1854, when commissioners were sent from both governments to establish the boundary. An important road was opened in 1858, over which ran for two years Arizona's first stage, the Butterfield overland line from Marshall, Texas, to San Diego, carrying the mails and passengers twice a week, until service was stopped by Indian depredations. In 1856 the U. S. government took military possession of the Gadsden Purchase, and Forts Buchanan, Mohave, and Breckinridge were established. Owing to the mining operations, the population increased considerably from 1855 to 1860 and Tucson and Tubac prospered somewhat. At the latter town the first newspaper in Arizona was published, from 1858 to 1860, the *Weekly Arizonian*. Congress added southern Arizona or the Gadsden Purchase to New Mexico, in which country the territory north of the Gila was included. The territory of New Mexico, on January 18, 1855, attached the Gadsden Purchase to Doña Ana county, but it was felt that Arizona should be a distinct territory, and many efforts were made to obtain from congress a territorial government. A constitutional convention was held by the people of Arizona, and officers for the proposed territory were elected and laws were adopted. Nothing came from this attempt to organize the territory, and although New Mexico was in favor of a division, it was only on February 24, 1863, that Arizona was admitted as a territory of the United States. The name ''Arizona,'' so it is claimed, comes from the former Papago locality of ''Arizonac'' or ''Arizonaca,'' probably meaning ''place of small springs,'' a few miles from the present Nogales, where some celebrated nuggets of silver were discovered in 1736-1741.

[239] *Notes of a Military Reconnoissance*, etc., W. H. Emory, Wash., 1848, with plates, scientific appendix, and tables; also Abert's notes of the journey as far as Bent's Fort, and a brief note by Colonel P. St. George Cooke.

Journal of Captain Abraham R. Johnston, *Ex. Doc.* No. 41, 30th cong., 1st sess.

Colonel Cooke described the march to Santa Fé and the later one to California.

Report of Lieutenant J. W. Abert of his examination of New Mexico in the years 1846-1847.

General Kearny gave instructions for a survey of the country. This was made by Abert and Peck.

In 1849, Lieutenant J. H. Simpson made an exploring tour from Ft. Smith, Arkansas, westward to Santa Fé, and Captain Marcy, coming from Ft. Smith by the same route, went down the river to the Mesilla valley.

Lieutenant Simpson's record of the expedition to the Navajó country and the Canyon de Chelly under Colonel J. M. Washington, is one of the most interesting and valuable of all the records of explorations made during that period. His report is found in *U. S. Govt. Doc.*, 31st cong., 1st sess., *Sen. Ex. Doc.* No. 64, with a map.

For explorations of this time see also *U. S. Govt. Doc.*, 31st cong., 1st sess., *Sen. Ex. Doc.* 12, *H. Ex Doc.* 45, with maps.

[240] United States and Mexican Boundary Survey, *Report* of William H.

314   LEADING FACTS OF NEW MEXICAN HISTORY

W. W. H. Davis, who had been United States attorney for New Mexico in 1853-54, was secretary of the territory in 1857 and acted as governor for eleven months until the arrival of the successor to Governor Merriwether, Abraham Rencher, who served as executive until the close of 1861. Governor Rencher was a lawyer, had been a member of congress, and also served as minister to Portugal. Secretary Davis was a man of very firm character. He was an author of considerable merit, and wrote several books dealing with the history of the territory of New Mexico.[241] The ad-

ADMINISTRATION OF ABRAHAM RENCHER

Emory, major 1st cavalry and U. S. commissioner, Wash., 1857. The narratives of Emory and Michler with other matter directly connected with the geographic survey, filled 252 pages of volume i, the remainder of the work being devoted to the geology, botany, and zoology of the expedition. Along the line as surveyed, monuments of stone or iron were erected at frequent stations, from each of which careful sketches of the topography in different directions were made, in order that the sites of the monuments, if destroyed by Indians — as they often were — might be easily found without repetition of the complicated observations and calculations. The Mexicans were eager to complete the work, because $3,000,000 of the purchase money was payable only on such completion.

Bancroft, H. H., *History of Arizona and New Mexico*, pp. 494-495: "In 1857, Edward F. Beale opened a wagon road on the 35th parallel, following nearly the route of Whipple and Sitgreaves. He left Zuñi in August, and reached the Colorado in January, 1858. Another important exploration was that of Lieutenant J. C. Ives. In November, 1857, he arrived at the head of the gulf on a schooner from San Francisco, which also brought an iron sternwheel steamer fifty feet long, built for the trip in Philadelphia, and named the *Explorer*. On this craft, launched the 30th of December, Ives left Ft. Yuma on Jan. 11th 1858, and on March 12th had passed through the Black Canyon of the Colorado and reached the mouth of Virgin river. Returning to the Mohave villages from this point, he sent the boat down to the fort and with part of his scientific corps, being joined also by Lieut. Tipton, with an escort of 20 men, he started eastward by land. He reached Ft. Defiance in May and thereafter made a most elaborate report of his explorations."— *U. S. Gov. Doc.*, 36th cong., 1st sess., *H. Ex. Doc.* 90.

[241] W. W. H. Davis was born in the state of Massachusetts in the year 1820. He was a lawyer by profession and a politician of the old school. He was an officer of volunteers in the war with Mexico, holding a commission as 1st lieutenant in the 1st Massachusetts infantry. He distinguished himself by very gallant conduct in several engagements. He was a member of the Historical Society of Pennsylvania; wrote *El Gringo, or New Mexico and her People*, *The Spanish Conquest of New Mexico*, *History of the 104th Pennsylvania Regiment*, was a journalist of considerable ability, and died at Doylestown, Pennsylvania, in 1910. The *Ledger*, Philadelphia, says of him: "Though he had lived to be 90 years old it was not his age that distinguished him; he had commanded attention when he served with Caleb Cushing in the Mexican War; he made his mark when he came home and settled at Doylestown, and his territorial service in New Mexico in Pierce's administration increased his distinction; home again at Doylestown, he made the *Democrat* a model of the old fashioned Pennsylvania political newspaper, and when he went out once more to battle no one

ministration of Governor Rencher was a very stormy one, growing out of the many raids and outbreaks of the Navajós and other hostile tribes. A treaty with the Navajós had been broken by them. In 1858 a negro servant was killed at Fort Defiance, the Navajó who killed him giving as an excuse for the outrage that he had had trouble with his wife and Navajó custom required that some one must die on this account. The military authorities determined to compel a surrender of the Indian murderer and, in August, 1858, the commander of the post, Colonel D. S. Miles, commenced a campaign, in which there were several engagements; about fifty Indians and seven or eight soldiers were slain. Captain McLain was seriously wounded. The Indians lost a great deal of live-stock and in December began to sue for peace. Captain Blas Lucero, in command of a company of spies, all New Mexican volunteers, did good service in this campaign, and, along with Captain Elliott, Captain Hatch, Captain Lindsay, and Major Brooks, is mentioned in the official reports of the campaign. Governor Rencher [242] did not approve of

could look on the swarthy soldier who rode at the head of the 10th Pennsylvania without instinctively saluting him. He was, in fact, one of the most forceful of the many brilliant field officers who gave glory to our state volunteers, and after his final return from war he carried on the civic battles of his party with the gallantry and devotion of a soldier, as honest as he was brave. We have not many such individual figures in politics now. Bucks county owes him much and Pennsylvania should hold his memory in honor.''

[242] The report of Governor Rencher is found in *U. S. Gov. Doc.*, 36th cong., 2d sess., *H. Ex. Doc.* vi., no. 24.

J. P. Dunn, *Massacres of the Mountains*, New York, 1886, gives an excellent account of this war with the Navajós.

In *Indian Affairs Report*, Joint Special Committee, 1867, at pages 330-34 is found testimony of witnesses on the subject of the campaign. One of the witnesses before the committee, Kenyon, says that the killing of the negro by the Navajó chief was nothing but a pretext on the part of General Garland for yielding to the pressure brought on him by the native citizens of New Mexico for a war of plunder and for the securing of captives.

The first engagement was on the 29th day of August, 1858, near the Ojo del Oso, in which a detachment of Company I of mounted riflemen defeated the Indians. From the 9th to the 15th of September there was a number of fights in which the military were successful. Other engagements occurred between September 19th and 24th in the Canyon de Chelly; on the 25th at Laguna Negra, and three days later in the Chusca valley and mountains. On October 1st a fierce battle was fought at the Ojo del Oso in which Companies A, F, H, and I of the mounted riflemen, and Company B, 3d infantry, and Company K, 8th infantry, participated. During the months of October and November, battles were fought at Laguna Chusca, near Fort Defiance, San Juan river, Rio Puerco of the West, Ojo del Oso, Canyon Bonito, Juan Chú mountains. From the 19th of October until November 18th the campaign was very active, two columns of troops moving rapidly in all directions through the Navajó country.

this campaign nor of the armistice and treaty of peace, involving indemnification in live-stock for the depredations which had been committed by the Indians, the liberation of all captives who might desire it, and the fixing of bounds which the Indians were not to pass. This treaty [243] was made by Colonel Bonneville, the successor of General Garland in command of the department.

At the session of the legislative assembly in 1859 a resolution was passed calling upon Governor Rencher for information as to the treaty which had been made by Colonel Bonneville, and asking particularly whether or not the Navajós had complied with its terms. A demand was also made for the establishment of another military post in the Navajó country and the organization and equipment of a regiment of volunteer troops was urged.

CAMPAIGNS AGAINST THE NAVAJÓS

Matters were brought to a crisis in the spring of 1860 when the Navajós boldly attacked Fort Defiance in the night-time, but were driven off without serious loss. This is the only instance where any hostile Indians in New Mexico, since the American occupation, ever attacked a strongly garrisoned post.[244]

---

[243] The Indian agents and the people of New Mexico regarded the treaty as a sad mistake and their views seem to have been well taken. As was the Navajó custom the treaty was made only to be broken and in the following year an expedition was made, under Major Simonson, in which it was hoped to force compliance with the treaty, but he failed and the Indian depredations continued. One fight was had, near Jemez, on the 16th of October, in which the troops engaged were mounted riflemen; other fights occurred in November and December.

An expedition against the Pinal Apaches was also made in 1859, and in November 12-26, there were several engagements, the force of soldiers consisting of detachments of the 1st dragoons and mounted riflemen.

[244] *Report* of Captain Shepherd, 3d U. S. Inf. *Sen. Doc.*, 2d sess., 36th cong., vol. ii, 1860-1861. In his report of this attack the commanding officer says: "The Navajó Indians made an attack upon the post on the 30th of April. The attack was begun shortly after the moon went down and about four o'clock in the morning, fully half an hour before the break of day, and was executed with considerable sagacity and skill, being on three sides. The enemy got possession of the hill on the east side of the post, which rises like a wall overlooking the post and is within short firing distance. They also took possession of the ravine on the southwest corner of the garrison where are the corrals and magazines; and the third and most important point of attack was the west side and northwest corner of the post, where they took possession of the garden fences and the wood-piles, and the rear of the sutler's store. In all three of these points of attack, the enemy were enabled to approach in the night undiscovered, and the peculiar and extraordinary location of the post offers these facilities. Notwithstanding this, it was never deemed probable that they would ever have the hardihood to attack the post, although such has been threatened by them ever since the post has been established. The

The authorities at Washington, at last recognizing the gravity of the situation, ordered an active campaign, which was made by Colonel Canby during the following winter, 1860-1861.

attack was begun by their firing at the sentinel, No. 2, over the corrals and near the ravine; immediately afterwards war-whoops and yells of a thousand savages resounded on all sides; upon this the sentinel retreated, with the other two men belonging to that post, who were acting as pickets. These three men, on reaching the end of the commissary store-house, forty yards distant, commenced firing in return, raking the gate-way of the corrals, and, by doing so, prevented the enemy from taking possession of the corrals. The three companies composing the garrison turned out promptly and took their positions for defense as indicated in the post orders, No. 17, Feb. 7th, without confusion, although the enemy's fire appeared to be pouring in from all directions. As soon as formed, Lieut. Hildt, with part of Co. C, third infantry, attempted to get into the garden on the west side of the post, but was driven back to the corners of the company bake-house and laundress' quarters by the heavy fire of the enemy, who were screened behind the fences and wood-piles. From the corners of the buildings the fire was returned to the enemy. On my arrival here, where there appeared to be the heaviest fire, I, without knowing of the presence of Lieut. Hildt, took ten men of this company and proceeded with despatch to station them at the sutler's store. The enemy were found in force at the northwest corners of the sutler's store and outhouses, and had actually entered through the window and were robbing the sleeping apartment in the rear, first having driven out one of the clerks and attempting to cut into one of the store-rooms. About four of the party were sent through the front door into the back-yard of the store, and the remainder of the party, six in number, were directed to fire from the north corner at the enemy. Immediately after discharging their pieces at the enemy so heavy a fire was poured into the party that three of them were wounded, viz: Private Sylvanus Johnson, mortally, and Corporal McComb and Private Gibson, slightly. The party then stepped inside the ante-room of the store to re-load. Johnson, on being wounded, said, 'I am shot,' and stepped into the room along with the others, but never spoke again, being wounded by an arrow through the heart. He died in about three minutes. As soon as the party had re-loaded, they sallied forth, and by the assistance of the others, who had been ordered hither, the premises were cleared as far as observable in the darkness. At this moment, seeing Lieut. Hildt, who had come to the point of fire, he was ordered to occupy, with a part of the company, the log house, twenty yards off, used as Co. E bakery, and from which the enemy had killed and wounded our men. This was promptly executed, seeing which, I hastened, on a run, to the southwest corner of the post, where was kept up a brisk fire by Co. E under Lieut. Whipple, and finding that he had secured the magazine, the corrals and stables containing the animals, and was with the company inside the hay corrals, discharging the enemy from the ravine, I next proceeded to the east side of the post, and found Company B in place between the post and the front of the abrupt hill on the east. Lieut. Dickinson was directed, in command of the company, to maintain his position, but not to scale the hill till further orders, fearing their being shot by our own men on being seen as must necessarily happen in a line of sight against the sky. Thence hastening back to the position of Co. C, it was found that the enemy were in retreat up the mountainside, leaving one nearly dead behind. The day commencing to dawn, Lieut. Hildt was ordered to pursue with Co. C. On ascending the mountain the men with him were fired upon by the men in the garrison; whereupon he halted and orders were countermanded. Soon after, there being a little light, the

In this campaign the regular troops were aided by a large force of volunteers, including many Pueblo and Ute Indians. The raising and employment of the volunteers caused a great deal of confusion. Governor Rencher called upon Colonel Fauntleroy for arms with which to equip the volunteer troops, which had been organized pursuant to an act of the legislative assembly for the purpose of waging war upon the Navajós. This Colonel Fauntleroy refused to do. Later on troops having come from Utah and the expedition having been organized, the people, in a meeting at Santa Fé, called on the governor to raise a regiment of volunteers. He refused, and at an-

---

enemy were seen in force on the hills on the north and near the post. Company C was ordered to be formed for the purpose of attacking them. As soon as formed it was fired at from the crest of the hill on the east side. This caused Lieut. Hildt to deploy the company immediately. Both Captain Johns and Lieut. Hildt were then ordered to clear the heights to the north. Lieut. Dickinson was thereafter immediately ordered with Co. B to scale the rocky hill on the east side; and after a short but brisk fire the enemy were dispersed from their position, whence they had hitherto fired with impunity, owing to the protection afforded by the rocks. On ascending the crest of the hill on the east side I observed a cloud of dust rising from a hollow behind the hills to the north, and in which direction Captain Johns and Lieut. Hildt had been sent with Company C; therefore about twenty men, with 1st Sergeant Sheels, of Co. B, were ordered to join Captain Johns. Not being quite light enough yet to see well, some of Captain Johns command began to fire at those directly on the right and under Lieut. Hildt; consequently this command had to halt. This unavoidable delay enabled the enemy to get away with their horses much better than they otherwise could have done. A few minutes after, judging it to be sufficiently light, Captain Johns's command, thus strengthened and numbering about 100 men, was ordered to advance, and in a little while, the enemy got within fire, which caused them all in that direction to flee in confusion, leaving one of their number, a chief, dead on the ground, with his pony standing at his side. This command pursued the enemy nearly a mile further and they returned bringing to the post the dead chief, but the pony had to be killed on account of his wildness and the difficulty of securing him. On the return of this party, Company B was withdrawn from its position on the east side. Lieut. Whipple, with Co. C, could have pursued the enemy after dawn as they retreated west up the mountains south of the canyon, but he wisely refrained, considering that it would leave the post too much exposed. The conflict from the beginning at four o'clock until the return of the pursuing parties, continued about two hours. Our loss proved to be only those before stated. Although there was a brisk fire with fire-arms by the enemy, yet it is somewhat singular that all the injury was done by arrows. The enemy succeeded in robbing the sleeping apartments of everything which both clerks, Mr. Kennon and Mr. McBride, had, their loss being about $100 in clothing each. The dead chief is known to have lived about the great canyon de Chelly, had several wives and was a large property holder of both horses and sheep. The Indian left dying on the ground behind the sutler's store was young and robust looking, and, although shot through the neck, with part of the spine torn away, lived for some minutes. One Indian, either dead or badly wounded, must have been dragged up the mountain under cover of darkness, as the marks of his draggling feet were readily traced. One Indian was

other meeting it was resolved to take the matter in their own hands, although Governor Rencher, in a proclamation, issued in August, warned the people against such action. The action of the people was very annoying to Governor Rencher and he placed the blame upon Don Miguel A. Otero, delegate in congress, who had declared, in a speech in congress, that the people of New Mexico were fully capable of taking care of themselves in Indian matters.

During the years 1859 and 1860, according to the report of the Indian agent for New Mexico, nearly three hundred citizens had been killed by the Indians; in one locality alone, on the Rio San Juan

---

shot and seen to be carried away as Co. B scaled the crest of the rocks on the east side of the garrison. Blood was discoverable in several places, not in the same line, about Co. C wood-pile, and which was traceable up the side of the mountain. Blood was also discoverable on the crest of the rocks on the east side of the post; and there is reason to believe that the pursuing party under Captain Johns wounded one or more in the pursuit, besides killing the chief. The loss of the enemy must have been very heavy, judging from the fact of their leaving two of their number on the ground which is well known is never done if it can possibly be avoided; what injury that portion of the attacking force suffered who began the attack and were stationed in the ravine through which flows the rivulet of the post, could not be ascertained. It was evident, however, that a large force was there and were driven away by Lieut. Whipple. In fact the attacking force on all sides, could not be reckoned at less than a thousand warriors, consisting probably of the whole available force of the tribe, and may, therefore, have been two thousand. A captive Navajó woman brought here to-day by a party of Mexicans reports that the Indian dragged up the mountain-side, before spoken of, was killed, and that he was a nephew of Sarcilla Largo; that besides the two left dead on the ground here, six have already died and that more were so badly wounded as to be unable to survive. It should be borne in mind that all the attacks have been from the beginning growing bolder, better planned and executed, and this too, in the face of the command being on the alert and prepared. The Navajós are perfectly aware that this garrison is now not more than half as strong as when the war began on the 17th of January last. Sixty-three men have been discharged, and died since that date; and Company G, 3rd infantry, withdrawn to the Ojo del Oso; and every mail wagon takes down about twenty-five more discharged men. The men, while in the service, are cheerful and prompt in their courage, but appear glad to get away when their terms expire. The duty is harassing, and danger is imminent, and both are every day increasing. There has not been the slightest exaggerated coloring in my reports of the condition of things here with the Indians, in fact, they might possibly be accused of being understated. I shall not fail at all times to have a better system of defense than was thought necessary before this attack; but, anyone who has ever been here would know how deficient the place is for defense, except by considerable force. The post ought never to be abandoned until a lasting peace is beaten into these Indians, who already believe that we are afraid of them, judging doubtless, of our inaction in not assuming the offensive. At each return of planting and green-corn season, they appear peaceable, but their peace will end unless they be well chastised. It has been my opinion all along and was so expressed in my report of the 23rd of January last that if two more infantry companies had been sent here

and the Rio Las Animas, the mines had been abandoned and forty Americans and fifteen Mexicans had been murdered. Colonel Canby did not accomplish much other than the destruction of large numbers of cattle and sheep belonging to the Indians, which caused the hostiles to sue for peace and an armistice of twelve months was agreed upon.

In the month of July, 1861, all of the troops were withdrawn from the Navajó country, excepting two companies of mounted riflemen at Fort Fauntleroy. The Indians, however, continued their depredations, although one band, under chief Sandoval, kept the terms of the armistice. The wealthier Indians seemed desirous of maintaining peace, but the younger element, under some of the chiefs, could not be controlled. The hostility of the Indians was increased by an outrage committed at Fort Fauntleroy, owing to a dispute over a horse race. The Indians were fired upon by the troops and a large number were killed and wounded. Lieutenant-Colonel Manuel Chavez [245] was in command at the time and gave the order to fire

in February last, an area of 150 miles in diameter, the post being the center, could have been freed from Indians, and most probably marauding parties could have thus been kept away from the settlements. At all events the enemy could have been met darefully. This report is made long in order that the Colonel commanding may form some idea of the attack and the manner of its repulse.''

In the month of August, 1860, two companies of the 2d dragoons, the 5th and 7th infantry and three companies of the 10th infantry, arrived in the department of New Mexico. See *Report* of Colonel Fauntleroy to General Scott, from Santa Fé, August 5, 1860, *Sen. Doc.*, 2d sess., 36th cong., vol. ii, 1860-1861.

The Navajós at this time were still on the war-path and were very active in their depredations upon the border settlements. On July 30, 1860, a band of these Indians murdered some citizens and seized stock within ten miles of Santa Fé and were attacked on the 1st of August by some Mexican citizens at a point about forty-five miles from Santa Fé. Ten of the attacking party were killed and wounded. They reported an Indian loss of about twenty. Lieutenants Pegram and Wagner, with the only troops at hand (12 men of the rifles), serving as guard for the public stores, were sent immediately to the scene of the affair. They reported that there were about twenty-five or thirty Indians in the band; that they were Navajós; they crossed the Rio Grande, exultant over their success. The Navajós were raiding in the vicinity of Alburquerque and Manzano and two companies of infantry were sent in pursuit. The arrival of the troops from Utah gave the colonel commanding (Fauntleroy) hopes of being able to handle successfully the situation. Captain Duncan of the mounted rifles was ordered with his command, Company E, to Alburquerque to coöperate with Captain Sykes who was scouting on both sides of the river with only poor success.

[245] Reference has been made to the organization of volunteer troops and the meeting of citizens at Santa Fé. This meeting was held in August, 1859. It was resolved that an expedition be formed to wage war on the Navajós and

Union and Confederate Officers, New Mexico, 1862
1. Gen W. H. Loring, C. S. A. 2. Gen. E. R. S. Canby, U. S. A. 3. Gen. H. H. Sibley, C. S. A. 4. Gen. John R. Baylor, C. S. A.

with the artillery. Some women and children were killed with the bayonet.

Education during this period, so far as concerned the masses of the people, made no headway. Nowhere in the United States were educational affairs in so lamentable a condition. Owing to the continued depredations of hostile Indians it was impossible to maintain schools of any sort whatever in the outlying districts or settlements. Even in the larger towns there were practically no public schools. The clergy were opposed to any public school system, even though there were no funds by which they could establish and maintain Catholic institutions. There were plenty of prominent citizens and officials, sent from the states by the several presidents, who realized the importance of educating the people. But there were also a great many influential men of Spanish and Mexican birth who did not believe in educating the common people. At the legislative session of 1854-1855 an act was passed providing for a tax for the support of and establishing a system of public schools. The proposition was referred to the people with the astonishing result that 5,016 votes were cast against and 37 votes for the tax,[246] in

EDUCATIONAL AND OTHER MATTERS DURING THE DECADE

Don Miguel E. Pino was elected colonel and Manuel Chavez, lieutenant-colonel. Under the authority of the meeting a company of 150 men was raised, the men furnishing their own mounts and equipment. Afterward the force was increased to four hundred men, who invaded the Navajó country, punished the Indians severely, and drove off great numbers of their stock, killing a great many cattle and sheep for subsistence. Their ammunition finally gave out and they were compelled to return to the settlements.

After the affair at Fort Fauntleroy, Governor Rencher issued a call on the militia of the territory but there was a feeble response. See his *Message*, 1862, *Records*, secretary's office, Santa Fé.

Bancroft, H. H., *History of Arizona and New Mexico*, p. 678: "There was no change in 1862, except that the Navajós became somewhat bolder in their raids, which extended to all parts of the country. There were no campaigns by regular troops, though the establishment of Ft. Wingate moved the Indians in December to send in one of their petitions for peace. Some raids were made by New Mexican companies, but all efforts to organize a general movement by the militia were unsuccessful. General Carleton took command in September, but his attention for the rest of the year was devoted mainly to the Apaches."

During 1861, on July 25th, near Mesilla, a battle was fought with the Apaches, the regulars engaged being Companies B and F, mounted riflemen, and Companies A, B, D, E, G, I, and K, of the 7th infantry. On the 27th there was a surrender by the Indians at San Augustin Springs. On September 26 occurred a very spirited engagement at Fort Thorn, in which Troops C, G, and K, 3d cavalry, defeated a large band of hostiles.

[246] Davis, W. W. H., in a note, p. 195, of *El Gringo*, says: "The election

four counties, whose citizens were allowed to vote upon the acceptance or rejection, although exempted from the general operation of the law.

There were private schools,[247] four colleges, and one or two academies, all under the control of the church, and the reports of 1860 show that these were attended by six hundred pupils, taught by thirty-three teachers. In 1859-1860 the legislature provided for a school in each settlement, supported by a tax of one-half a dollar for each child, the justice of the peace having in charge the employment of teachers and the probate judge acting as county superintendent. Attendance was required from November to April. This system continued for many years. Today it is difficult to understand how such a condition was permitted to exist, but the opposition of the wealthier classes was pronounced and effective. The system of peonage, then in vogue, had much to do with the public sentiment among the more powerful members of society and they did not believe it the part of good citizenship to provide, by taxing themselves, the means for educating the "peon" classes. This sentiment prevailed for

---

was ordered by the proclamation of the governor, and was held on the 31st day of March, 1856, with the following result, viz:

Counties	For the Law	Against the Law
Taos	8	2150
Rio Arriba	19	1928
Santa Ana	8	456
Socorro	2	482
	37	5016

"The returns show that, in a popular vote of 5,053, there were only 37 men to be found in favor of public schools, a fact which exhibits an opposition to the cause of education truly wonderful. This great enmity to schools and intelligence can only be accounted for as follows; that the people are so far sunk in ignorance that they are not really capable of judging of the advantages of education. From this result the cause of education has but little hope from the popular will, and the verdict shows that the people love darkness rather than light."

[247] Davis, W. W. H., *El Gringo*, p. 194, says: "The education of the females has, if anything, been more neglected than that of the males, and the number of them who can not read and write is greater. Gregg, who wrote ten years ago, in speaking of female education in New Mexico, says: 'Indeed, until very recently, to be able to read and write on the part of a woman was considered an indication of very extraordinary talent; and the fair damsel who could pen a billet-doux to her lover was looked upon as almost a prodigy.' This picture is a little overdrawn, but, at the same time, except among the few wealthy families, it is a rare thing to see a woman who possesses these useful accomplishments."

many years and was not thoroughly eradicated until the coming of the transcontinental railways and the immigration from the states.

With the coming of Rt. Rev. John B. Lamy, and the establishment of day and boarding schools by him at Santa Fé, during this period, a great advance was made, but the work of this distinguished prelate can not be given here, and will be found in a separate chapter. The American missionaries who came to New Mexico at this time endeavored to establish schools, and, in some instances, were able to gather together a few pupils, but the opposition of the Catholic clergy to the children being educated in Protestant institutions was so great that very little was accomplished.

In the year 1853, the president of the United States recommended the appointment of a surveyor-general for New Mexico, and congress by an act of July 22, 1854, provided PUBLIC LANDS AND LAND TITLES for the appointment of such an official, extended the operation of the land laws over the territory, and gave to every citizen residing in New Mexico before 1853, or settling in the territory prior to 1858, a donation of one hundred and sixty acres, to be patented after an occupation of four years. The usual grant of two sections in each township, 16 and 36, for schools, and two townships for a university was made. William Pelham was named as surveyor-general and arrived in Santa Fé in December, 1854, and, in the month of April, 1855, established an initial point for base and meridian lines at a hill on the west bank of the Rio Grande, in latitude 30° 19'.

Surveys were gradually made under the direction of this official, but the appropriations being small, little was accomplished, the authorities at Washington believing that surveys should not be too rapidly made until private and Indian land claims were settled. The full discussion of Spanish and Mexican land grants [248] in New Mexico is reserved for a subsequent chapter. A land

---

[248] Bancroft, H. H., *History of Arizona and New Mexico*, p. 647: "New Mexico being an old province, settled for two centuries and a half by an agricultural community, the best portions of the territory along the rivers and susceptible of irrigation had naturally long been reduced to private ownership under Spanish and Mexican grants, protected in theory by the treaty of 1848. In a general way, these New Mexican private claims, and the problems arising in connection with them, were the same as in California . . . but, on the other hand, there was no influx of settlers and speculators to foment controversy and fraud, and to create an active demand for the segregation of the public lands."

office was opened at Santa Fé in 1858, but there were no sales of public lands until after 1863. A few donation claims were filed and some were patented. The total area surveyed was 2,293,142 acres, the area of the territory being 77,568,640 acres or 121,201 square miles.[249]

The dangers from hostile Indians served to prevent any large degree of development of the mineral resources of New Mexico during this period. Some prospecting was done and some discoveries were made in different sections. In the late fifties some work was done in the southern part of the territory. The census reports of 1860 mention only one silver and three copper mines, all of which were in Doña Ana county. The governor, in his message of 1861-1862, alludes to the gold mines of Pinos Altos, rich placers near Fort Stanton, and the work in the Santa Fé county placers near Golden; also the copper mines at Santa Rita and Hanover. Very little was known of the mineral resources of the country owing to the constant hostility of the wild tribes.

MINES AND MINING

The peonage system had long been in force in New Mexico. Peonage consisted in the acceptance by an individual voluntarily of servitude for the payment of debt; it involved no loss of civil rights, no sale or transfer of service and no legal obligation on the part of the children of peons.[250] There was also a system of enslavement of Indian captives, which was, of course, based upon no law. These

THE PEONAGE SYSTEM

---

[249] *U. S. Land Com. Reports*, 1855-1863. These contain the annual reports of the surveyor-general during this period.

[250] Davis, W. W. H., *El Gringo*, pp. 231, 232, writing of the peonage system says: "Another peculiar feature of New Mexico is the system of domestic servitude called peonism, that has existed, and still exists, in all Spanish-American colonies. It seems to have been an institution of the civil law, and in New Mexico is yet recognized by statute. The only practical difference between it and negro slavery is, that the peons are not bought and sold in the market as chattels; but in other respects I believe the difference is in favor of the negro. The average of intelligence among the peons is lower than that among the slaves of the Southern States; they are not so well cared for, nor do they enjoy so many of the blessings and comforts of domestic life. In truth, peonism is but a more charming name for a species of slavery as abject and oppressive as any found upon the American continent.

"The statutory law recognizing its existence in the Territory is dignified with the title of 'Law regulating contracts between masters and servants.' This is all well enough on paper, as far as it goes, but the statute is found to be all on the side of the master. The wage paid is the nominal sum of five dollars per month, out of which the peon has to support himself and family.

Prominent Officers and Soldiers Civil War Period
1. Gen. John P. Slough. 2. Col. J. M. Chivington. 3. Capt. Smith H. Simpson.
4. Don Candelaria Garcia

captives were bought and sold, in some families many being held in this sort of bondage. There were few military or civil officials who did not possess these Indian captives. The peonage system was not affected by the emancipation proclamation, inasmuch as it was not regarded as involuntary servitude, but was finally abolished by act of congress in 1867.[251]

The Protestant Christian missionaries came to New Mexico shortly after the conquest in 1846, but found the field anything but inviting. They had great difficulty in securing any sort of foot-hold and became greatly discouraged. A Baptist missionary, who came as early as 1849, began a mission school at Santa Fé and erected the first Protestant church in the territory. The Methodists also

PROTESTANT MISSIONS

The act provides among other things, that if the servant does not wish to continue in the service of the master, he may leave him upon paying all that he owes him; this the poor peon is unable to do, and the consequence is that he and his family remain in servitude all their lives. Among the proprietors in the country, the master generally keeps a store, where the servant is obliged to purchase every article he wants, and thus it is an easy matter to keep him always in debt. The master is required to furnish the peon with goods at the market value, and may advance him two-thirds the amount of his monthly wages. But these provisions, made for the benefit of the peon, are in most instances disregarded, and he is obliged to pay an enormous price for everything he buys, and is allowed to run in debt beyond the amount of his wages, in order to prevent him leaving his master. When parents are, as the statute terms it, 'driven into a state of slavery,' they have the right to bind their children out as peons, and with this beginning they become slaves for life. When a servant runs away from his master, the latter goes before a justice of the peace, or some other civil magistrate, and takes out a 'warrant of the debt,' which authorizes the arrest of the peon in any part of the Territory. One of the most objectionable features in the system is, that the master is not obliged to maintain the peon in sickness or old age. When he becomes too old to work any longer, like an old horse who is turned out to die, he can be cast adrift to provide for himself. These are the leading features of peonism, and, in spite of the new name it bears, the impartial reader will not be able to make anything else out of it than slavery."

[251] *Indian Affairs Report, Joint Special Com.*, 1867, p. 326; Judge Kirby Benedict, chief justice of the supreme court of New Mexico at one period, testifying on this subject, said that, in addition to the Indian captives, orphans and children of the destitute were often sold into slavery by their relatives. He said that a sound, healthy, intelligent girl of eight years was worth four hundred dollars, or more. The children of peons were not regarded as saleable property but were treated as citizens. He estimated the number of these servants at from 1,500 to 3,000. Under the laws these Indians were entitled to their freedom, there having been several court decisions in their favor; but the Indians did not seek the aid of the courts. He stated that those who held them were exceedingly sensitive of their supposed interest in them, and were easily alarmed at any movements in the courts which might be construed as an attempt to dispossess them of what they considered to be their property rights.

It was the opinion of Governor Connelly that congress should pay for the

maintained a missionary at Santa Fé in 1850, but he remained only two years. The Baptist mission and church property were purchased by the Presbyterians shortly after the close of the Civil War. The first Episcopal service ever held in New Mexico was in 1863. The old adobe church erected by the Baptists was demolished in the early eighties and the present brick edifice was built upon its site by the Presbyterians.

In the year 1850, according to the United States census, the population of the territory, exclusive of Indians was 61,547, and in 1860 the number had increased to 80,567. The burden of taxation during the decade was not heavy. The salaries of all territorial officials and members of the legislative assembly were paid by the general government. The total property valuation in 1850 was $5,174,471 and in 1860 it had increased over four-fold, the census showing that in the latter year the valuation was $20,838,780. The total taxation in 1860 was $29,790, or $9,255 for the territory, $12,485 for the counties, $3,550 for towns, and $4,500 miscellaneous. The territorial debt in 1860 was $3,673, which was constantly diminished, until, in 1863, there was a surplus of $3,080 in the territorial treasury.[252]

POPULATION AND TAXABLE PROPERTY

At the first session of the legislature the capital was fixed at Santa Fé. Congress appropriated, in 1850, for the erection of public buildings, $20,000 with which the construction of the first capitol was commenced, this sum being used in the building of the foundation walls. In 1854, congress made an additional appropriation of $50,000, which was expended in raising the structure one story and a half. In 1860, another appropriation of $60,000 was secured but it was off-set by the direct war-tax of 1862. The breaking out of the rebellion stopped all further construction and nothing was done towards the completion of the edifice until the late eighties, when the delegate in congress secured an appropriation for the completion of the building. It has since been known as the federal building but has never been used for capitol purposes. The original plans for this structure were drawn by chief justice Joab Houghton.

---

freedom of these captive Indians, the number of whom he estimated at six hundred.

The act of congress abolishing peonage was passed March 2, 1867. See *Congressional Globe*, 1866-7, appendix, 238.

[252] *U. S. Census reports*, 7th and 8th census.

BIBLIOGRAPHY

Aubrey, F. X.	Journal of, *Western Journal and Civilian*, vol. xi, No. 2, Nov., 1853.
Bancroft, Hubert H.	*History of Arizona and New Mexico*, San Fran., 1889.
Bartlett, J. R.	*Personal Narrative*, New York, 1854.
Bonneville, Col.	*Campaigns in New Mexico*, H. Ex. Doc., 35th cong., 1st sess.
Cal. and New Mexico Messages	Letter to Col. John Munroe, 1850.
Congressional Globe	Speech of R. H. Weightman on New Mexico.
Calhoun, J. S.	*Reports of*, H. Ex. Doc. 17, 31st cong., 1st sess.
Davis, W. W. H.	*El Gringo*, New York, 1856.
Dunn, J. P.	*Massacres of the Mountains*, New York, 1886.
Emory, W. H.	*Notes of a Reconnoisance*, etc., Washington, 1848.
House Ex. Doc. xi, 35th cong., 1st Session.	
Journal of American History	*Letter* of John Greiner, New York.
Johnston, A. R.	Journal of, *Ex. Doc.* 41, 30th cong., 1st sess.
Lane, Wiliam Carr	Letter of, *Gov. Doc.*, 33d cong., 1st sess.
Missouri Republican	Files of, St. Louis, Mo., 1854.
Santa Fé Gazette	Files of, San Francisco, California.
Sumner, E. V.	*Report* of, Sen. Doc. 1, 32d cong., 2d sess.
Senate Ex. Doc. 121, 32d cong., 1st sess.	
Thrall, H. S.	*History of Texas*, St. Louis, Mo., 1879.
U. S. Land Com. Reports	Reports of Surveyor General, 1855-1863.
U. S. Census Reports	Seventh and Eighth census.

CHAPTER VIII

THE CATHOLIC CHURCH IN NEW MEXICO — CAREER OF MOST REV. JOHN B. LAMY AND HIS SUCCESSORS, 1851 TO 1911 — THE PROTESTANT CHURCHES — THEIR WORK SINCE THE AMERICAN OCCUPATION

AT the time of the Mexican war the Archbishop of Baltimore was the only metropolitan in the United States. The provincial councils of the Church were attended by the bishops of sees which had been created within the limits of the old diocese of New Orleans. The diocese of St. Louis had no fixed limits in the west and was regarded by the American church authorities as extending to the Pacific coast. Missionaries were sent to the Rocky Mountain region and into the northwest.[253] About two months after the conquest of New Mexico by General Kearny, St. Louis was made a metropolitan see.[254] New Mexico had not yet become a territory of the United States. Subsequent, however, to the execution and signing of the treaty of Guadalupe Hidalgo, the Rt. Rev. Joseph Anthony Laureano de Zubiría, a man of great piety, energy, and zeal, bishop of Durango, who had twice before, as we have seen, visited New Mexico, made a third visitation in the month of October, 1850.

The fact that New Mexico was in the control of the Americans, although not yet erected into a territory, did not cause any lack of religious ardor on the part of Bishop Zubiría. Believing that the time had come when their faith was exposed to many dangers, the good bishop urged the Catholics to restore their dilapidated churches,

---

[253] Father De Smet traveled in company with a large number of Indians from the Missouri and Yellowstone rivers to Fort Laramie, in 1851, where a great council was held in that year to form treaties with the several tribes. In 1840 Father De Smet established missions among the Nez Perces and Flathead Indians.

[254] Shea, John Gilmary, *History of the Catholic Church in the United States*, p. 36.

Rev. Donato M. Gasparri, S. J.

and maintain in proper Catholic manner the true worship of God, to uphold, as he said "our most holy Catholic and only true religion, amid those who professed heterodox creeds, who by the liberal system of the existing government, had now full power to enter and reside in that part of his diocese." [255]

Always alive to the interests of the church, the American hierarchy, recognizing this addition to the territory of the United States, and the presence within the newly acquired areas of a vast number of Catholics, made urgent request upon the Holy See for action in church matters in New Mexico. Bishop Zubiría was not advised, nor were the church authorities at Santa Fé, of the appeal which was thus made by the American hierarchy. The Holy See at once erected New Mexico into a vicariate apostolic and named Rev. John B. Lamy, a priest of the diocese of Cincinnati, to take charge and reorganize religious affairs in the territory.[256] On his arrival he quickly ascertained that the New Mexican clergy felt unwilling to recognize his authority. Bishop Zubiría, at the time of his visit the year previous, had given no intimation that the Holy See had in mind a canonical subdivision of the diocese of Durango, nor had, in fact, so far as they knew, New Mexico been formally detached from it, and on this account they felt in duty bound to still regard Bishop Zubiría as their superior. Here the wisdom of Bishop Lamy demonstrated itself. Having in mind only the welfare of the people he proposed to the Very Rev. Juan Felipe Ortiz, vicario, that a journey be made to Durango for the purpose of a personal interview with Bishop Zubiría, so that all objection to his authority might be immediately removed. With a guide, Bishop Lamy, on horseback,

[255] Act of Visitation, Santa Fé, October 22, 1850.
[256] Shea, John Gilmary, *History of the Catholic Church in the United States*, p. 307: "He was born at Lempdes, France, October 11, 1814, of a family fruitful in vocations. Educated at Clermont and the Seminary of Montferrand, he was ordained in December, 1838, by Mgr. Ferron, Bishop of Clermont. While assistant priest at Chapre, in 1839, he volunteered to join Bishop Purcell for the Ohio mission. Stationed at Wooster, and subsequently at Covington, he showed zeal, piety, devotedness, and an endurance which shrank from no toil. Large and scattered bodies were carefully attended to keep the faith alive and enable all to fulfill their duties to God. From these labors he was called by the word of Pope Pius IX. Submitting to the yoke imposed, he was consecrated at Cincinnati, on the 24th of November, 1850, and immediately set out for his vicariate by way of New Orleans and Texas. While taking this long and unusual route he met with an accident and was laid up for months at San Antonio, so that he did not reach Santa Fé till the summer of 1851."

traveling over miles of desert infested with savage Apaches, made this journey. He was well received by Bishop Zubiría, who, in view of the facts as presented, resigned all jurisdiction to the American portion of his diocese, leaving to his worthy successor the arduous work of accomplishing the great reforms which were required.[257]

The imperative necessity for a change in the matter of administration of church affairs in New Mexico had been well known for many years. Reports of a scandalous nature touching the conduct of the priesthood in New Mexico had been carried to the states by traders and travelers over the Santa Fé trail. A great many of these reports were false, but some, and these concerned the morals of members of the priesthood, were only too true. During the last years of Spanish and the twenty-five years of Mexican rule the power of the clergy in secular affairs was overwhelming. Together with the military they governed the country. Far removed from the seat of the diocese, Durango, safely intrenched, some of the priests in outlying districts were a reproach to the religion they taught.[258] A man

---

[257] When Bishop Lamy came to Santa Fé, he was accompanied by Rev. Joseph P. Machebeuf, who had been a pioneer priest in Ohio. When they arrived at Santa Fé, and prior to Bishop Lamy's departure for Durango, a most unusual incident occurred, and one which reflects no credit upon the then chief justice of the supreme court of New Mexico, Hon. Grafton Baker. Bishop Lamy's first work was to obtain possession of the churches and all ecclesiastical property. The civil authorities were in possession of the military chapel, having used it for secular purposes since the occupation; there was no question as to the right of the church to this property, but Judge Baker did not care to give up possession or recognize the claims of the church. Judge Baker, having indulged too liberally, and while laboring under the effects of his indiscretion, publicly announced that he would not give up the church to Bishop Lamy but would have them both (Bishop Lamy and Father Machebuef) hanged from the same gibbet. Judge Baker evidently did not understand the temper of his auditors. The following morning his impolitic remarks were told throughout the city and indignation was great. A petition was circulated and signed by more than a thousand people, Catholics and Protestants alike, civilians and soldiers, asking for justice and a return of the church property to the bishop. In the meantime an excited mob had gathered at Baker's residence. He called upon the military authorities for protection, but this was declined by Colonel Sumner. For two hours Father Machebeuf and an officer from the post stood between this mob and Judge Baker, who begged for mercy and promised to do justice. In the evening he went to the residence of Bishop Lamy, apologized for his words and conduct and on the day following in open court, held in the church itself, in the presence of the governor and all of the civil and military authorities, solemnly turned the property over to the bishop.

[258] Howlett, Rev. W. J., *Life of Rt. Rev. Joseph P. Machebeuf, D. D.*, pp. 179, 180: "The scarcity of priests was so great that Bishop Lamy and Father Machebeuf were obliged to become real missionaries again. . . Where the Mexican priests could be reanimated with zeal they were assisted and en-

of noble and lofty character, of heroic spirit, capable and just in all his dealings, Bishop Lamy was indeed the good surgeon who knew how and where to apply the knife to the cancer. Returning without delay, having traveled nearly two thousand miles, the good bishop visited all the churches and missions of his vicariate. He found great abuses existing, and by kind and patient advice endeavored to recall the clergy to a true ecclesiastical spirit, but very few responded. Very Rev. Juan Felipe Ortiz, [259] who had for many years been virtually independent in the rule of the church in New Mexico, was the center of opposition. Another who defied the bishop was Rev. J. M. Gallegos,[260] pastor of the important church at Alburquerque.

couraged, but where nothing could be done with them in this way they were relieved from duty and permitted to go away, or they were suspended from all exercise of their ministry. . . A few exemplary and zealous priests were found by Bishop Lamy during the first few months of his administration, who were willing to devote themselves to the care of extensive districts until more help would come, and thus the faith was at least kept alive.''

The neglect which the people suffered and endured is shown by a letter written by Father Machebeuf, shortly after his coming to New Mexico, in which he says: ''The lack of instruction and other helps has left religion in a deplorable condition in New Mexico. Its practice is almost entirely lost, and there remains little but the exterior shell. With such ignorance the consequent corruption can easily be imagined, and all the immorality that must flow from it. . . . In spite of their ignorance and immorality, they hunger for instruction, and they have a great devotion to the Blessed Virgin. It is a blind devotion, and is sometimes mixed with fanaticism and superstition, but it gives us hope that, explained and properly directed, it will lead to good results.''— *Letter of Rev. J. P. Machebeuf, Peña Blanca, N. M., May 31, 1852.*

[259] Shea, John Gilmary, *History of the Catholic Church in the United States*, p. 661: ''The condition of Bishop Lamy as Vicar Apostolic was one of difficulty; his powers were limited, the diocese of Durango had not been canonically divided. He saw many evils to redress, but did not act harshly. On some points he insisted; one was that mass should be said every Sunday and holiday in the parish church or one of the authorized chapels, so as to afford the faithful an opportunity of fulfilling their duty. The other point was that the excessive fees demanded for marriage, baptisms, and burials, should be reduced, as they were far in excess of even the amounts allowed by the old arancels. The Mexican priests assembled and threatened to lay their grievances before the Bishop of Durango, and even to appeal to Rome. One of the suspended priests, José Manuel Gallegos, contrived to have himself returned as delegate to congress, but Mr. Otero was declared the legal delegate. *Freeman's Journal*, Nov. 23, 1853; *Detroit Catholic Vindicator*, July 29, 1856. Before it was decided, Gallegos attacked Bishop Lamy in a speech to the House. The leader in the opposition was Very Rev. Juan Felipe Ortiz, who, as Vicar-General, had been almost absolute. When Bishop Lamy proposed to divide the parish of Santa Fé, and erect new churches for the convenience of the faithful, Ortiz claimed to be *parochus proprius*, and set out for Durango.''

[260] Howlett, Rev. W. J., *Life of Rt. Rev. Joseph P. Machebeuf, D. D.*, p. 191 *et seq*: ''Among those who refused to listen to the kindly counsels of the Bishop was a certain Padre Gallegos, pastor of the important church of Albur-

Padre Gallegos was a very influential and popular man, powerful in his parish and elsewhere. His conduct was such that he seemed to court the wrath of his superior in ecclesiastical authority. Bishop Lamy was equal to the emergency, however, and withdrew all privileges and faculties from the recalcitrant priest. Rev. Machebeuf was sent to Alburquerque to take charge of the parish. The experiences of Father Machebeuf in carrying out this order of Bishop Lamy are well told by the reverend father himself, who says:

"My position was sufficiently delicate and difficult, for he was very popular in his set. I took advantage of his temporary absence in Old Mexico to take possession of the church and to announce from the pulpit the sentence of the Bishop, suspending him from the exercise of any priestly function. Some time later, when I was visiting some Indian parishes in the mountains, about seventy-five miles from Alburquerque, I heard that the Padre had returned and was going to dispute the possession of the church with me the next Sunday. This did not alarm me, but I thought it best to be prepared, so I sent a messenger in haste to the Bishop to get a confirmation in writing of the sentence pronounced upon the Padre, and my authorization in clear terms to administer the affairs of the parish. I returned to Alburquerque on Saturday night, and on Sunday morning I went to the church an hour earlier than usual in order to be on the ground and ready for anything that might happen. What was my astonishment upon arriving here to find the Padre in the pulpit and the church filled with people whom I knew to be his particular friends. These he had quietly gathered together, and now he was inciting them to revolt, or at least to resistance. I tried to enter the church through the sacristy, but this communicated with the presbytery, which he still occupied, and I found the doors locked. Going then to the main door of the church I entered, and assuming an air of boldness I commanded the crowd to stand aside and make room for me to pass. Then, as one having authority, I forced my way

---

querque. We have no hesitancy in naming him, as the whole affair was public, and his previous and subsequent career was well known. Alburquerque was the second city of importance in the Territory, and was headquarters for a large number of American troops. The Padre was very popular with certain classes in the parish, and these were the rich, the politicians and business men, few of whom had any practical religion. With these he drank, gambled and danced, and was generally a good fellow. He was a man of more than ordinary talent, and on that account he received considerable respect and deference. His conduct, however, gave scandal to the good within the fold, and also to those without the fold, for it furnished them an occasion for reviling the church. Failing to effect any good by exhortations and warnings, Bishop Lamy was obliged to withdraw all privileges and faculties from the recalcitrant priest, and Father Machebeuf was sent to take charge of Alburquerque and conciliate the people."

through the crowd and passed up by the pulpit just as the Padre pronounced the Bishop's name and mine in connection with the most atrocious accusations and insulting reflections. I went on until I reached the highest step of the sanctuary, and then turning I stood listening quietly till he had finished. Then all the people turned to me as if expecting an answer. I replied, and in the clearest manner refuted all his accusations, and I showed, moreover, that he was guilty of the scandals which had brought on his punishment. I then took from my pocket the letter which my courier had brought me from the bishop, and I read it in a loud voice. To finish, I called upon him to justify himself, or at least to answer, if he had any reply to make. But, not a word; he went out as crestfallen as a trapped fox and left me in peaceful possession of the church. I sang the high mass as usual, and preached on the Gospel of the day without making the least allusion to the scene which had just taken place. A few days later, to repair his humiliating defeat, he went to the neighboring villages and used every means to arouse the people, and he succeeded in getting together twenty-five or thirty of the most influential and the richest, with some of his intimate friends from Santa Fé. These, profiting by the absence of the Prefect, who was an intimate friend of mine, came to me in a body, and, with an air of insolence and bravado, ordered me to leave the parish, adding that they did not want any of my administration, and if I did not go they would have recourse to other measures. At that moment the good God must have given me patience and strength that were more than natural, for I answered them with firmness that I had come to take possession of the parish by order of the highest ecclesiastical authority, and that I would receive no orders except from that same authority. I told them that they might take such measures as they saw fit, but, like the sentinel on guard, I would not quit my post, and as the shepherd of the flock I was ready to die for my sheep rather than abandon them.

"This short and forcible answer disconcerted them; they did not have a word to say in reply, but returned to the Padre to apprise him of the little success of their mission. They did not know that I was an Auvergnat. *Latsin pas.* Never give up!

"Hardly had they left me when the Prefect, whom some one had notified of the affair, came up in a fury. He had already given orders for their arrest and appearance in court, but I reasoned with him and finally persuaded him to drop the matter, for I was sure that such a course would be the best in the end. This, in effect, was the case, for a re-action took place in my favor and several deputations waited upon me to offer their services and protect me if necessary. I thanked all of them for their good will, but I declined any protection, as I did not fear any trouble. This scene took place on Saturday, and on Sunday morning I went to the church unattended by anyone except by the sacristan, and the only change I noticed was that everyone I met saluted me with apparently greater respect than ever. There were only three men from Alburquerque who took part in the rebellion; all the rest were from the Ranchos, or villages on the lands of the rich proprietors.

"From that moment the Padre lost all hope of driving me away, and, abandoning the Church, he went into politics. There was no doubt about his talents, and he used them to good effect in his new field, for through them he worked every kind of scheme until he succeeded in getting himself elected to the Congress of the United States as Delegate from the Territory of New Mexico."

The great wisdom and ability of Bishop Lamy were now apparent. Twelve times in the interest of the people of his diocese he crossed the plains from Santa Fé to Kansas City and St. Louis. In 1852, he brought back a small colony of the sisters of Loretto, one of whom perished on the journey through the wilderness. The convent and academy of our Lady of Light in Santa Fé, and five other convents and schools have been the fruit of his planting "amid the tears, afflictions, poverty and exile of this noble sisterhood."[261] The ar-

---

[261] The mother-house of the first-born sisterhood of the west — the Lorentines of Kentucky, an order founded in 1812, furnished the first Sisters for New Mexico. Six were chosen, but only four ever reached Santa Fé. Sickness forced one to return to Loretto and another died en route; her mortal remains were laid away on the border line of western civilization.

No less than twelve other establishments trace their origin either directly or indirectly to the coming of these Sisters. Bishop Lamy and the four who survived the trip reached Santa Fé towards the end of September, 1852.

Bishop Lamy had left Santa Fé in the spring of 1852, to assist at the first plenary council of Baltimore. This was his first crossing of the so-called "American Desert." It was at this council that a petition was made by the fathers to the Holy See to have him appointed titular bishop of Santa Fé. The bulls were not delayed and the bishop of Agathon became bishop of Santa Fé.

"On Sunday," says Mother Magdalena, in her *Annals of Our Lady of Light,* "June 27, 1852, after mass, the Sisters destined for Mexico, left the Mother house of Loretto; Mother Mathilda Mills and Sisters Catherine, Mary Magdalen, Monica, Hilaria and Roberta. The same day they arrived at Bardstown, and on Thursday morning, July 1st, they reached St. Louis, and were kindly received by Archbishop Kendrick. In the meantime they visited the Convent of St. Ferdinand at Florissant, and spent a few days with their own Sisters. As soon as they heard of the Bishop's return from New Orleans, they joined him at St. Louis, and on the 10th of July left by the steamer 'Kansas' which was to convey them as far as Independence. With them traveled a family and some other persons belonging to the Bishop's suite.

"The Sisters had accepted the mission in a true spirit of self-abnegation; yet they little dreamed, as the spires of the city receded from view, how soon Providence was going to put their virtue to a test. There had already been some cases of cholera on board, when, on Friday, the 16th, at two A. M., Mother Mathilda was attacked; her sufferings lasted till about two o'clock in the

rival in Santa Fé of the four Sisters of Loretto marked an era in the history of the church in New Mexico. Having stopped at the bishop's ranch, near the present station of Lamy, on the 26th of September, the party left the ranch and started for Santa Fé. The people of the capital, led by Very Rev. Juan Felipe Ortiz and other Mexican priests, met them on the highway several miles from the city. As they entered the ancient city, the crowd increased to such an extent that the carriages could scarcely pass through the narrow streets of the ancient capital. Triumphal arches had been erected, and the bells of the several churches were pealing. They were received at the door of the cathedral, presented with holy water, and led to the foot of the altar. The *Te Deum* was sung, accompanied by the music of the period, violins, guitars, etc., and the ceremonies terminated with the episcopal blessing.[262]

afternoon of the same day, when she gave her soul into the hands of her Maker, after having received the sacraments of penance and Extreme Unction at the hands of the Bishop. Two hours later the steamer landed at Todd's warehouse, six miles from Independence. In the meantime Sister Monica had also contracted the disease, and the landing was truly affecting, the Sisters following the couch of their dying Sister and the coffin of their dead Mother. The inhabitants stood in such dread of the cholera that the Sisters were not allowed to enter their houses, and were therefore obliged to remain in the warehouse.''

Mother Mathilda was buried in the graveyard at Independence, Mo.

After enduring the usual hardships of the journey across the plains, on the 18th of September, 1852, the party reached Las Vegas. The next morning mass was said at a private dwelling not far from the town. Father Machebeuf and the sisters were sent to what was known as the Bishop's ranch, near the station on the line of the A., T. & S. F. Ry., known as Lamy, where they remained until the following Sunday, when they proceeded to Santa Fé.

[262] The Sisters did not open the school immediately, as they needed time in which to acquire a proper knowledge of the Spanish language. After these Sisters had been in Santa Fé a short period, others came from Kentucky, solicited by Bishop Lamy, who had gone to Rome. The property now occupied by them was acquired a little later. At the time of its purchase there was built upon it a structure known as La Casa Americana, because it had a shingled roof. An orchard and grounds were laid out and the new home was occupied in September, 1855. Since that period the Sisters of Loretto have prospered and accomplished a great work in New Mexico. The convent of the Annunciation, in Mora, was established in 1854, when Archbishop Salpointe was the parish priest. In 1853 the convent of St. Joseph was established in Taos, under the care of the Rev. Gabriel Ussel, the parish priest. The convent of Our Lady of Guadalupe was first established in Alburquerque in 1866, but was discontinued in 1869. In the same year was established the convent of the Immaculate Conception, in Las Vegas. In 1870 the Visitation Academy was established at Las Cruces, through the generosity of Rt. Rev. J. B. Salpointe, at that time vicar apostolic of Arizona, in whose diocese Las Cruces was included. The convent of Our Lady of the Sacred Heart was established in 1875 in Bernalillo. Later, in 1879, the convent of Mount Carmel was established in Socorro.

In the year 1853, leaving Rev. Machebeuf in charge at Santa Fé, Bishop Lamy went to France and thence to Rome, where he was most kindly received by Pope Pius IX. He made a personal appeal to the Pope for laborers, and a company of zealous French priests [263] and ministerial students returned to America with the bishop, arriving at Santa Fé, November 15, 1854. Churches in all parts of New Mexico were revived or established by their efforts. The Rev. Peter Eguillon, afterwards vicar-general and parish priest of the cathedral, was one of this party. Rev. Eguillon himself was sent to France in 1859, for teachers, and in October of that year arrived with four brothers of the Order of San Miguel, and nine priests and ecclesiastics. Then was begun St. Michael's college at Santa Fé. The first building was erected in 1879.

Another grand welcome met Bishop Lamy upon his return. The

---

[263] Most Rev. J. B. Salpointe, *Soldiers of the Cross*, pp. 207, 208: "The first one who responded to the call of the young bishop of Santa Fé was the Rev. Peter Eguillon, then the first assistant priest of one of the principal churches of the city (Clermont). This priest was kept about a year in Santa Fé to teach theology to some seminarians, and to prepare them for their ordination. In October, 1855, he was sent as parish priest to Socorro, where he remained until November 4th, 1858, when he was appointed parish priest of the Cathedral and Vicar General of the diocese. Father Eguillon died on the 21st of July, 1892, in the seventy fourth year of his age, after thirty years of meritorious and fruitful work in the missions of New Mexico. The second one was Rev. Anthony Juillard, a zealous priest, who remained only a few years in the diocese owing to bad health, and returned to France, where he died in 1888. The third was Rev. Stephen Avel, who, on the 3rd of August, 1858, died as parish priest of Mora. These three priests came from the diocese of Clermont. With them also came the Revs. Damaso Taladrid and C. Martin, whom the Bishop had met in Rome. Of the same party were three seminarians, viz: the Revs. John Guerin, a deacon, who was ordained priest on the 22rd of December, 1854, and who died as parish priest of Mora, June 10th, 1885; Eugene Paulet, a sub-deacon, ordained priest December 22nd, 1855, who died in France in 1887, having been the parish priest of Belen for over thirty years, and Xavier Vauré, a deacon who died on the day of his arrival at Santa Fé of a disease he had contracted on the plains."

With the caravan across the plains were also the Rev. Eulogio Ortiz, a priest from New Mexico, who had accompanied the Bishop to Europe; Jesus M. Ortiz and Florencio Gonzales, who had been sent previously to France for a course in the seminary of Clermont; an Irish family named Covington, and a gentleman named McCarthy, a personal friend of the bishop.

Priests who came later, at the solicitation of the Very Rev. Machebeuf, who had been sent to France for that purpose, were the Revs. Gabriel Ussel, Joseph M. Coudert, Agustin Truchard, John B. Ralliere, John B. Fayet, and Joseph Fialon.

The Rev. Fayet was sent to San Miguel as assistant priest, and later became parish priest; he established schools at San Miguel.

There were, in 1859, eighteen parishes or heads of missions in the diocese of Santa Fé.

Celebrated Apache Chiefs
1. Victorio. 2. Mangas Coloradas. 3. Natchez. 4. Geronimo

CATHOLIC CHURCH IN NEW MEXICO

entire population met him, triumphal arches were erected over the streets of the capital, a body of U. S. cavalry escorted him, and salvos of artillery hailed him. The same day occurred the death of Xavier Vauré, a young man of great talent, who had come with the bishop from France.

The new priests were not long in mastering every detail of the great work before them, and, under the united efforts of a numerous and zealous clergy, religious conditions improved rapidly. The people were instructed in doctrine and made to see its practical obligations, and the moral tone of every community was proportionately elevated.

After the establishment of the college of St. Michael a subscription from the clergy and citizens of five thousand dollars was the beginning of the buildings now to be seen at Santa Fé belonging to this most worthy institution. In the year 1883 it was incorporated as a college.

Bishop Lamy enlisted the Sisters of Charity in Cincinnati in their work of founding a hospital and sanitorium, which with its extensive buildings has become famous in Santa Fé. The work of these Sisters has been almost immeasurable, ministering to the sick and afflicted, and to the orphans, many hundreds of whom have been nurtured and educated by them.

One of the most important parishes in New Mexico outside of Santa Fé, was that of Taos. Its pastor, from 1826, was Rev. Antonio José Martinez. In his younger days this priest was married and had one child, a girl, but death early robbed him of both his wife and daughter. He then began his preparation for the priesthood in a seminary in Mexico. After his ordination he entered the Concursus for the parish of Taos, recently vacated by the Franciscans, and received the appointment. Father Martinez was a man of great learning and was not long at Taos before his zeal led him to open a school in which he became the principal teacher.[264]

FATHER ANTONIO JOSÉ MARTINEZ
EXCOMMUNICATED BY BISHOP LAMY

---

[264] Rev. Antonio José Martinez, who was regarded by many as one of the principals in the revolution of 1847, was one of the most remarkable men ever identified with the history of New Mexico. He was born in the county of Rio Arriba in 1793 and was a grandson of General Martinez, who came from Chihuahua in the early part of the seventeenth century. His opposition to Americans and their institutions was made manifest in many ways. He realized

In 1856, Father Martinez, who had already been elected a member of two legislative assemblies of the territory, since the American occupation, was a great politician; he had some words with Bishop Lamy, who criticised him for his political activities, the worthy bishop being of the opinion that members of the clergy should not take part in the politics of the country. Father Martinez never had been well disposed towards the bishop, having been identified in every way with the Rev. Juan Felipe Ortiz, the vicario, the leader of the opposition to the bishop when he first came as vicar apostolic. Father Martinez tendered his resignation of the parish of Taos to Bishop Lamy, giving as his reasons old age and infirmity. The resignation was accepted and Father Damaso Taladrid, a Spaniard whom Bishop Lamy had met in Rome, was appointed in his place. Unfortunately Father Taladrid entertained the notion that, being a Castillian, he occupied in every way a somewhat higher position than that held by any of his Mexican brethren. This assumption of superiority annoyed Father Martinez greatly and it was not long before friction developed between them, the pride of both admitting of no mutual concessions. After his resignation and retirement

---

that the coming of the American was a death blow to his power and prestige in the country and he is said to have done everything he possibly could to create a sentiment of suspicion and distrust against the American people. He was acknowledged to have been one of the most brilliant men of his time. No one, except those actually engaged as principals in the insurrection of 1846-1847, knew positively just what part he took in the uprising. He was a very crafty man and the American authorities never could affirmatively fix upon him any active participation, although in later years there were many native citizens, who had been identified with the movement, who did not hesitate to declare that they had been guided by his counsel and advice. He established a printing office, the first in New Mexico, in which he printed his own school books, catechisms, and some few books of church ritual and service. For a short time also, he published a small newspaper, *El Crepusculo*, the first newspaper published in the territory. His private residence was used for his quasi college and many of the priests of New Mexico during the years of Mexican rule studied under him. He died at Taos, July 27, 1867, and his remains are buried in the cemetery at that place.

Rev. W. J. Howlett, in his *Life of Bishop Machebeuf*, says of him: "It was said that he had much to do with the uprising of the Indians and Mexicans at Taos, when Governor Bent and about fifteen Americans and their Mexican sympathizers were massacred on Jan. 19, 1847. He at least shared with the Indians and Mexicans in hatred for the Americans, and, in their ignorance of events and conditions outside of their little valley, they imagined that they were but beginning a patriotic war which would result in freeing their country from the foreigner, who was supposed to be an enemy to their race and to their religion. The suspicion is probably well founded, although the U. S. Government did not find Father Martinez guilty of direct complicity in the unfortunate insurrection."

Father Martinez said mass, and occasionally officiated solemnly at the parish church, and the difficulty arose over the marriage ceremony between some of the relatives of Father Martinez. Instead of referring their differences to the bishop for settlement, they spread their troubles among their friends, finally coming to an open rupture, and Father Martinez set up an independent church. Bishop Lamy hearing of this, went twice to Taos to confer with the two priests, but Father Martinez had fallen into the hands of bad advisers and refused to submit. No alternative was left to Bishop Lamy, after all sorts of fatherly advice and admonitions had been unheeded, but to suspend Father Martinez from the exercise of every priestly function. This did not end the trouble, for Father Martinez continued in his rebellion, and was followed into schism by a large number of those who had always known and respected him, and who could not now imagine that he could be in the wrong. Besides, his relatives were powerful in Taos and had the pride of wealth and position, which would permit neither him nor them to accept what they considered a humiliation.

In addition to this case there was a priest, Mariano de Jesus Lucero, at Arroyo Hondo, twelve miles north of Taos, whom Bishop Lamy had been obliged to suspend for irregularities and schismatical tendencies, and who had been a pupil and great friend of Father Martinez. These two now joined their forces and continued their opposition to Bishop Lamy, until he was obliged to go to the extreme in punishment and to pronounce upon them the sentence of excommunication.[265]

---

[265] Howlett, Rev. W. J., *Life of Bishop Machebeuf*, pp. 230-232: "Many of these simple people knew nothing of the discipline of the Church, and they looked upon this as a persecution against their old pastor. They were willing to stand by him even in opposition to the Bishop, and the relatives of the priests and their more influential friends were cunning enough to take advantage of their ignorance and friendship in order to arouse still more this spirit of opposition, and to intimidate the Bishop if possible. The old idea of a foreign tyranny was also injected into the controversy, and when it became known that Father Machebeuf was coming to publish the sentence of excommunication threats of personal violence were openly made."

De Fouri, Rev. J. H., *Catholic Church in New Mexico*, p. 125: "As he had been many years parish priest of Taos, and his family being one of the most noted in that district he drew to himself a party, either in Taos or in the missions that were attached to Taos. Thus remained affairs to the death of Father Martinez, July 28th, 1867, who gave no sign of submitting to the Bishop, and demanded before dying, to be buried in his own chapel, and Father Lucero buried him, acting as pastor of the schismatics."

The vicario, Father Machebeuf, was chosen by Bishop Lamy to publish the sentence of excommunication. There were living in Taos at this time three of the most prominent citizens of New Mexico, Colonel Christopher Carson, Judge Carlos Beaubien, and Colonel Céran St. Vrain, all of whom were Catholics, friendly to Bishop Lamy and to his representative, the vicario. These men, together with a large number of other prominent members of the church, both American and Mexican, sent word to those of the Martinez faction that no repetition of the events of January 19, 1847, would be permitted; that if any indignities were offered to Father Machebeuf, serious trouble would ensue.[266]

Three successive Sundays the warnings from ecclesiastical headquarters were pronounced; calls were made for the submission and repentance of the recalcitrant priests, but no response came. On the appointed Sunday the big church at Taos was crowded with people; the friends of Father Martinez were well represented. Mass was sung by the vicario, and in his sermon he explained the nature and effects of excommunication. The dreadful sentence was then pronounced amidst the most intense silence; the people dispersed and no hostile movement was made by the friends of the misguided priest. The followers of the rebellious priest kept up the opposition and the opposition church until after the death of Martinez, who died and was buried by Lucero in schism. A mission given by the Jesuits, in 1869, brought back the Martinez family, and the return of the others was easily accomplished.

In 1859, Arizona, the lower part of which had become a part of the United States in 1854, by virtue of the Gadsden Treaty, was annexed, by decree of the Holy See, to the diocese of Santa Fé. To ascertain whether or not missions could be established there the

---

[266] Howlett, Rev. W. J., *Life of Bishop Machebeuf*, pp. 231, 232: "Beaubien had lost a son in the massacre of 1847, and he had no love for Martinez, who he said 'has always been treacherous, and is now afflicted with the bighead. Let him look out!'

"Let it be said here that Carson, Beaubien and St. Vrain were thoroughly prepared and had their men advantageously posted to watch every movement of the enemy, and any attempt at creating a disturbance would have been vigorously met. 'We shall not let them do as they did in 1847,' said Kit Carson, 'when they murdered and pillaged. I am a man of peace, and my motto is: Good will to all; I hate disturbances among the people, but I can fight a little yet, and I know of no better cause to fight for than my family, my Church and my friend Señor Vicario.'"

Very Rev. Machebeuf [267] was sent to visit that locality, from which, after meritorious labor, he was recalled by Bishop Lamy, reaching Santa Fé in November, 1859. He was later sent to Colorado, which had now been annexed to the Santa Fé diocese. In 1868 he was appointed vicar apostolic of the vicariate apostolic of Colorado and Utah, and, in the month of August of the same year, in St. Peter's cathedral, Cincinnati, Ohio, was consecrated bishop of Denver by Archbishop Purcell.

In 1863, Bishop Lamy, in company with one of his priests, Rev. J. M. Coudert, visited the principal settlements of Arizona. Leaving Alburquerque, he proceeded by way of Cebolleta, the pueblo of Zuñi, and other important points in western New Mexico, reaching Prescott in the month of December. Thence, by way of Mohave, he went to Los Angeles, returning to New Mexico, in company with a body of U. S. troops under command of Captain Johnson, in April, 1864.[268] Two years later Most Rev. J. B. Salpointe, at the time officiating as priest of the parish at Mora, in company with three priests, left New Mexico for Arizona. The party, at the request of Bishop Lamy, was furnished with an escort of U. S. troops by order of General J. H. Carleton, at that time commanding the department.[269] In 1868, the territory of Arizona was made a vicariate

---

[267] Right Rev. Joseph P. Machebeuf, first Catholic bishop of Denver, was born at Riom, France, August 11, 1812. He was ordained in 1836. Three years later he came to America, offered his services to Bishop Purcell, of Cincinnati, and performed misionary work in Ohio until 1850. In 1851 he came to New Mexico with Bishop Lamy and was created vicar-general of the diocese. In New Mexico and Arizona he aided the bishop in his great work of rejuvenation. He was the "*alter ego*" of his superior. It is said that upon the occasion of his first appearance at Santa Fé in his clerical capacity, not having been too warmly introduced by the Rev. Lujan, at that time one of the priests at the capital, having sung mass and made a short address to the people in his native tongue, not a word of which was understood by the great majority of his hearers, a controversy arose as to what religion the stranger might belong. "He must be a Jew or a Protestant," said some, "because he does not speak as Christians do." "Quien sabe?" replied others. "Still he said mass in Latin, like a priest who knows how, and in truth he sings better than our priests."' A devout woman of the parish, hearing the conversation stopped the controversy by exclaiming: "He is a good Catholic! Did you notice how he made the sign of the Cross before giving his sermon?"

Bishop Machebeuf built the first Catholic church in Colorado. He died August 10, 1889, leaving his works for his monument.

[268] De Fouri, Rev. J. H., *Catholic Church in New Mexico*, pp. 80-101. Father DeFouri gives a very graphic account of this journey of three thousand miles on horseback.

[269] Salpointe, Rev. J. B., *Soldiers of the Cross*, pp. 242, 249.

apostolic, of which Most Rev. Salpointe was elected bishop. He received his episcopal consecration in Europe.

In 1865 Bishop Lamy [270] was able to make report to the Propaganda that on reaching New Mexico he found ten priests, neglectful and extortionate, churches in ruins, and no schools; that now he had thirty-seven priests, and six ecclesiastics in minor orders soon to be ordained, had built forty-five churches and chapels, holding from three hundred to a thousand persons; that he had repaired eighteen or twenty; that he had four houses of Sisters of Loretto, three of Brothers of the Christian Doctrine, all in a prosperous and flourishing condition. He estimated the Catholics in New Mexico at one hundred thousand, nine thousand being Pueblo Indians; in Colorado, three thousand; in Arizona, five thousand.

In the month of February, 1875, by decree of Pope Pius IX, Santa Fé was erected into a metropolitan see, and Bishop Lamy made its archbishop, with the vicars apostolic of Colorado and of Arizona as suffragans. The pallium was brought to New York by his excellence, Monsignor Roncetti, delegated by the Pope to carry the insignia to Archbishop McCloskey of New York, afterward elevated to the cardinalate.[271] The cere-

SANTA FÉ MADE AN ARCHDIOCESE

---

[270] Bishop Lamy to Cardinal Prefect Barnabo, March 12, 1865.

Bishop Lamy attended the second plenary council of Baltimore. He was so highly appreciated for his great work that he received the singular honor of being intrusted alone to bring the acts of the council to the Holy See for its approbation. He was equally at home whether in the hut of the Indian, the cabin of the miner, or in the Vatican at the feet of the Pontiff.

[271] Salpointe, Most Rev. J. B., *Soldiers of the Cross*, pp. 264, 265: ''The ceremony took place on the 16th of June, 1875, in the house of the Christian Brothers, St. Michael's College, where better accommodation for the people could be found than in the old St. Francis Cathedral. During mass, which was celebrated by Bishop Machebeuf, two short addresses were given, one by the Vicar General, Very Rev. Peter Eguillon in Spanish, and one by the Vicar Apostolic of Denver in English. Both were explanatory of the ceremony of the day, and were listened to with great satisfaction by the large congregation. When the time came, according to the rubrics, for the imposition of the Pallium, the Archbishop, kneeling before the altar, had it placed on his shoulders, while the proper formula was read by the Vicar Apostolic of Arizona, delegated for the purpose.''

This was a day never to be forgotten in the history of the church in New Mexico. Bishop Salpointe, standing, placed the pallium on the shoulders of the new archbishop, saying: ''For the honor of Almighty God and the Blessed Mary, ever Virgin, of the holy apostles, Saints Peter and Paul, of our Lord Pope Pius IX of the Holy Roman Church, and of the Church of Santa Fé confided to your care, we deliver you the pallium taken from the tomb of Saint Peter, which signifies the plenitudes of the episcopal power, with the title and

mony for the investiture of the pallium was had on the 16th of June, 1875, Mgr. Salpointe, then vicar apostolic of Arizona, having been delegated by the Roman prelate, Roncetti, and charged with the delivery of this insignia of church authority.

On the 15th of August, 1867, the order of the Jesuits was introduced into Bishop Lamy's diocese. Their efforts resulted in a great revival of zeal and devotion throughout the territory. They founded a school at Alburquerque, and a college at Las Vegas in 1877. They also instituted the printing of a religious newspaper, the *Revista Catolica*, the first number of which was issued January 2, 1875. On the 18th of January, 1878, an act to incorporate the society of the Jesuit Fathers of New Mexico was passed by the territorial assembly by a two-thirds vote over the veto of Samuel B. Axtell, at that time governor of New Mexico. The act was annulled by the congress of the United States. The act as passed gave unlimited power to acquire, hold, and transfer all kinds of property, both real and personal, and the exemption from taxation of all the effects and property of the corporation. Governor Axtell, in his veto message, was very bitter in his denunciation of the bill and used very strong language, hardly temperate in character for an executive, not only against the society but against its leader, Father Gasparri. The act was clearly unconstitutional and should never have been introduced for the consideration of the assembly.

THE JESUITS IN NEW MEXICO

An enduring monument to the sacrifices of Archbishop Lamy and of his priests and the Catholic people of New Mexico, is the beautiful

---

name of Archbishop, which you shall use within your church on certain days, as is determined in the privileges granted by the Apostolic See.''

Following this investiture, Archbishop Lamy rose and turning to the immense throng, spoke with words coming from his heart; expressions of gratitude to the Holy Father, of confusion for himself thus raised without merit of his own, of thanks to the clergy and the people, who by their presence signified their interest in the great honor which had been conferred upon him. After the benediction had been pronounced, the multitude, with bands playing, banners flying and loud huzzahs for His Grace, proceeded to the plaza. In the evening the city was beautifully illuminated. In front of the cathedral were transparent portraits of Pope Pius IX, Archbishop Lamy, and Bishops Machebeuf and Salpointe. In the plaza music was discoursed by the U. S. government band. Seats were reserved for the prelates and the clergy; an address was made by Colonel William Breeden, in English, and another by Major José D. Sena in the Spanish language. The military, the territorial and other civil authorities, Protestant and Catholic, all participated in doing honor to the best loved man in all New Mexico.

and massive cathedral at Santa Fé. Its corner stone was laid July 14, 1869. The main building with two imposing towers has been erected at a cost of approximately one hundred and fifty thousand dollars. It is still incompleted. The part of the building completed to the arms of the cross is one hundred and twenty feet long, and sixty feet broad, while the height of the middle nave is fifty-five feet. The ceiling is arched in Roman style. The walls are of native stone. The ceilings have this peculiarity; they are made of red volcanic tufa, very light; this substance was obtained from the summit of the Cerro Mogino, about twelve miles from Santa Fé. The towers are of cut stone, now eighty-five feet in height, and the spires which will crown them eventually will reach an elevation of one hundred and sixty feet.[272] A magnificent chapel built entirely through the efforts of the Sisters of Loretto adorns the grounds of the order in Santa Fé. This structure was commenced in 1873, is built of stone, with veins and arches of the purest Gothic style. It was through the efforts of Archbishop Lamy that the Sisters of Charity and the Sisters of Mercy also established themselves in the territory.

THE CATHEDRAL OF ST. FRANCIS DE ASSIZI

On the 19th of February, 1885, the Rt. Rev. J. B. Salpointe came to Santa Fé as coadjutor to the Most Rev. Archbishop Lamy. He was promoted to the archepiscopal see of Anazarba on October 11th

---

[272] The construction of the cathedral was begun by an American architect; he was not qualified for the work and the contract was rescinded and given to two French architects, Antoine Mouly and his son, Projectus. The ceremonies attending the laying of the corner stone on July 14, 1869, were very impressive. The stone contained the names of the president of the United States, General U. S. Grant, the governor of New Mexico and other territorial officials who were present. Coins of gold, silver, and copper, documents, and newspapers were also used. Three days afterward some miscreant stole the corner stone, with its contents, and nothing was ever heard of it afterward. Skilled workmen on this building, at various times, were Michael Machebeuf, Vincente Digneo, Cayetano Palladino. The building as now (1911) used was completed by two contractors, Messrs. Monier and Machebeuf. A portion of the old cathedral was demolished and the adobes and stone used for grading some of the streets of the capital. This work was done under the direction of Charles M. Conklin and other volunteers who performed the service without cost to the church authorities.

The window over the door is filled by a beautiful stained etching representing Christ among the doctors in the temple, expounding the scriptural law. This was placed in honor of the city of Santa Fé, the city of the Holy Faith. The remaining windows are the gifts of various individuals, the names of the donors showing on the cathedral glass of which they are made. They were manufactured by Felix Gaudin, of Clermont-Farrand, France.

Prominent New Mexicans and Mescalero Apache Chiefs at Fort Stanton — Mescalero Apache Reservation, 1875
Standing, Left to Right, Major L. G. Murphy, Capt. Chambers McKibben, Col. Emil Fritz. Sitting, Center Row, Left to Right, Domingo, Cadette, Head Chief, Peso

of the same year, by the resignation of his predecessor.²⁷³ After his resignation Archbishop Lamy retired to a small country place in the mountains surrounding the headwaters of the Tesuque river. This place was called "Villa Pintoresca;" here the venerable prelate built a small house and chapel, and when he felt the weight of years, it was to this beautiful place he was accustomed to go for rest and quiet.

RT. REV. J. B. SALPOINTE NAMED COADJUTOR

Early in the month of January, 1888, while at his country residence, Archbishop Lamy, in retirement, with the title of Archbishop of Cizicus, was taken ill. He was brought to the city of

---

²⁷³ On the first Sunday of September, 1885, the following circular was read in all the parochial churches of the archdiocese:

"For some years past we had asked of the Holy See a coadjutor in order to be relieved of the great responsibility that rested on our shoulders since the year 1850, when the supreme authority of the Church saw fit to establish a new diocese in New Mexico, and in spite of our limited capacity we were appointed its first Bishop. Now our petition has been heard and our resignation accepted. We are glad, then, to have as a successor the illustrious Archbishop Mon. Salpointe, who is well known in this bisphoric and worthy of administering it, for the good of the souls and the greatest glory of God.

"What has prompted this determination is our advanced age, that often deprives us of the necessary strength in the fullfillment of our sacred ministry, though our health may apparently look robust. We shall profit by the days left us to prepare ourselves the better to appear before the tribunal of God, in tranquility and solitude.

"We commend ourselves to the prayers of all, and particularly those of our priests who, together with us, have borne and still bear the burden of the day, which is the great responsibility of directing souls in the road of salvation. Let the latter remember that, in order that their holy ministry be of any benefit their example must accompany their instructions. It is with pleasure that we congratulate the most of the clergy of this diocese for their zeal and labors; and we desire that those who might have failed in their sacred duties may give henceforth, better proofs of being the worthy ministers of God.

"We also commend ourselves to the prayers of the faithful, whose lively faith has edified us on many an occasion. We exhort them to persevere in this same faith, in their obedience to the Church, in their faithfulness to their daily obligations, in the religious frequence of the Sacraments, and in the devotion to the Blessed Virgin Mary, which is one of the most efficacious means of sanctification.

"Finally, we hope that the few religious communities that we have had the happiness to establish in this new diocese will offer some memento in their prayers for our spiritual benefit.

"We ask of all to forgive us the faults we may have committed in the exercise of our sacred ministry, and, on our part, we will not forget to offer to God our humble prayers for all the souls that the Lord has intrusted us for so many years.

"J. B. Lamy, Archbishop.

"Given at Santa Fé, N. M., on the 26th day of August, 1885."— *Translation from the Spanish.*

Santa Fé, where, on the 14th of February, he very unexpectedly passed away. His remains were deposited, on the 16th of February, in a vault which is now covered by the main altar of the cathedral. His successor in the archepiscopal see has said that "the life of the Most Rev. John B. Lamy in New Mexico was that of an apostle. Bishop Lamy was pious, humble and charitable. Anybody, poor or rich, found him always accessible and ready as far as was in his power, to help the needy." He was in truth the pioneer bishop of the southwest. He did the work of a pioneer; he put his religion on a firm basis; he gave it form and foundation, and to him more than any other is due the praise of New Mexicans for the great stability and progress of the faith in the new southwest.

DEATH OF ARCHBISHOP LAMY

In the month of August, 1891, the Rev. Placidus L. Chapelle, D. D., rector of St. Matthew's church in the city of Washington, was appointed Bishop of Arabissus and coadjutor to Archbishop Salpointe. He was consecrated the same year by His Eminence, Cardinal Gibbons, in the cathedral of Baltimore. Bishop Chapelle was an able assistant to the venerable archbishop. He went abroad in 1893 in search of missionaries, visited the Pope and, on the 10th of May of that year, had conferred upon him the title of the archepiscopal see of Sebaste. On the 9th of January, 1894, he became the archbishop of Santa Fé by the resignation of Archbishop Salpointe. The pallium was conferred upon him at Santa Fé, October 17, 1895, by His Eminence, Cardinal Gibbons.[274]

ARCHBISHOP PLACIDUS L. CHAPELLE

---

[274] Salpointe, Most. Rev. J. B., *Soldiers of the Cross*, pp. 279, 280: "The occasion was made the most remarkable of all solemnities, either civil or religious, ever witnessed in Santa Fé. His Eminence, Cardinal Gibbons, Archbishop of Baltimore, who was to preside at the festival, arrived at Santa Fé by a special train, Tuesday, October 15. The entire population of the city was at the depot to welcome the first Cardinal of the Holy Roman Church, who came to honor New Mexico with a visit. All the school children, the sodalities and associations of the city, the National Guard, after His Eminence had been received with the most enthusiastic hurrahs, formed in line and proceeded through the principal streets, which were profusely illuminated, to the residence of the Archbishop. On the 17th, at ten o'clock, an imposing procession of prelates and priests formed at the residence of the Archbishop and escorted Cardinal Gibbons to the Cathedral. The prelates were Archbishop Kain of St. Louis, Bishop Donahue of Wheeling, Bishop Hennessy of Wichita, Bishop

On February 28, 1896, His Eminence, Cardinal Satolli, delegate apostolic to the United States, arrived at Santa Fé, where, for a few days, he was the guest of Archbishop Chapelle. The cardinal celebrated pontifical mass in the cathedral March 1, 1896.

CARDINAL SATOLLI VISITS NEW MEXICO

Archbishop Chapelle visited all parts of the diocese, administered confirmation to 28,000 candidates, and brought from Europe twenty-two missionaries, almost all of whom are today acting as parish priests.

On December 1, 1897, Archbishop Chapelle was appointed to the see of New Orleans as successor to Archbishop Janssens. He was appointed apostolic delegate extraordinary for Cuba and Porto Rico. After the Spanish-American war he was sent to Havana. Later, he returned to New Orleans where, in giving aid to the people of his diocese who were stricken with yellow fever, he contracted the dread disease and died on the 9th day of August, 1905. Truly, "the blood of the martyrs is the seed of the church."

Archbishop Chapelle was succeeded by the Most Rev. Peter Bourgade, D. D., who was consecrated in the cathedral of Santa Fé by Archbishop Lamy May 1, 1885, as titular bishop of Thamaucum and vicar apostolic of Arizona. On the 8th of May, 1897, he was made bishop of Tucson and was transferred to Santa Fé January 7, 1899. He received the sacred pallium from

ARCHBISHOP PETER BOURGADE

Montgomery of Los Angeles, Bishop Dunn of Dallas, Bishop Gabriels of Ogdenburg, Bishop Beaven of Springfield, Bishop Bourgade of Tuscon, and the Archbishops Chapelle and Salpointe of Santa Fé, also Monsieur Stephan of Washington. This beautiful line was headed by seventy-five priests from different dioceses and almost all those of New Mexico, all wearing cassock and surplice. After the gospel of the Pontifical Mass, Archbishop Kain of St. Louis delivered an eloquent sermon on the history and meaning of the pallium. Bishop Bourgade of Tucson, at the end of the mass, read a very interesting paper, written in Spanish by the Most Rev. Archbishop Salpointe, on the history of the Church in the province of Santa Fé. Then the Cardinal arose, and after paying an eloquent tribute to the first Bishop of Santa Fé, the late Archbishop Lamy, and to the newly retired Archbishop Salpointe, he, at last, addressed himself, with evident high personal regard, to Archbishop Chapelle before placing on his shoulders the Pallium, as required to complete the dress of a new Archbishop.

"Archbishop Chapelle returned his thanks to the Cardinal in English and then spoke briefly in Spanish, explaining to the throng gathered in the church the meaning of the brilliant ceremonies of the day."

Bishop Matz of Denver, Colorado, October 4, 1899. He died at Mercy hospital, Chicago, Illinois; his remains are buried in the cathedral of Santa Fé by the side of those of Archbishop Lamy, by whom he was ordained to the priesthood and consecrated as bishop. Archbishop Bourgade was a native of Clermont-Ferrand, France, and came to New Mexico in 1869 with Revs. Anthony Jouvenceau, Agustin Morin, Agustin Bernard John Chaucot, and Andrew Escallier.

Archbishop Bourgade was succeeded by the Most Rev. J. B. Pitaval, who had been pastor of Aspen, in the diocese of Denver, Colorado. He was consecrated bishop of Sora and appointed auxiliary bishop by the Most Rev. Peter Bourgade, D. D., in the cathedral of Santa Fé, July 25, 1902; was promoted to the see of Santa Fé January 3, 1909, confirmed by pontifical bulls February 1, 1909, and was invested with the sacred pallium by the Rt. Rev. N. Matz, bishop of Denver, Colorado, in the cathedral of Santa Fé, August 18, 1909.

ARCHBISHOP J. B. PITAVAL

In the fall of 1851 when Archbishop Lamy came to New Mexico as vicar apostolic, he found only ten priests in the entire territory now embraced within the confines of New Mexico and Arizona.[275]

---

[275] Salpointe, Mt. Rev. J. B., *Soldiers of the Cross*, pp. 282, 283: "These priests were the Rev. Frs. José Manuel Gallegos, José de Jesus Leiva, Mariano Lucero; José de Jesus Lujan; Antonio José Martinez; Vincente Montaño; Fernando Ortiz; Ramon Salazar and Juan Trujillo.

"To these were added successively the Rev. Frs. Accorsini, Joseph; Aelterman, Gillan; Avel, Etienne; Bernal, Pedro; Bernard, Bonito; Birmingham, Patrick; Boucard, Francisco; Bourdier, N.; Brun, Carlos; Brun, J. B.; Cabello, N.; Carpentier, N.; Chavez, Manuel; Cooney, J. V.; Coudert, José Maria; Courbon, Juan B.; Defouri, James H.; Deroches, Jules; Docher, Antonio; Eguillon, Pedro; Faure, J. B.; Fayet, J. B.; Fialon, Joseph; Fleurant, Miguel; Fourchegu, Antonio; Francolon, J. B.; Garcia, Samuel; Garnier, J. M.; Gatignol, Francisco; Gilberton, Paul; Gonrey, Joseph; Gourbeyre, Alex; Grevelowski, Alex; Grom, Ignacio Maria; Guerin, J. B.; Hayes, Thomas Ambrosio; Jouvenceau, Antonio; Jouvenceau, Francisco X.; Jouvet, N.; Juillard, George; Lassaigne, Pedro; Lamy, Antonio; Latour, Juan; Lestra, Francisco; Machebeuf, Joseph; Mariller, J. B.; Martin, Pedro; Martinez, Philberto; Mathonet, N.; Medina, Ramon; Merle, N.; Monacum, Pedro; Nayrolles, H.; O'Keefe, Timothy; Ortiz, Eulogio; Parisis, Etienne; Paulet, Eugenio; Picard, Juan; Pinard, Francisco; Peyron, Clemente; Pouget, Henrico; Ralliere, J. B.; Ribera, Manuel; Ribera, R.; Rednon, Agustin; Remuson, Luciano; Rodriguez, N.; Rogiers, Donato; Rolli, Miguel; Rousset, L. E.; Salpointe, J. B.; Seux, Camilo; Splinters, J. G.; Tafoya, Sembrano; Taladrid, Damaso; Thorwartz, N.; Truchard, Agustin; Ussel, Gabriel; Valezy, Joseph; Vassal, Agustin; Vermar, Antonio; and Vigil, José Miguel; a total of 83 brought during the administration of Archbishop Lamy.

"During the administration of Archbishop Chapelle, the following priests

He found the affairs of the church in a woeful condition. The total number of inhabitants was about ninety thousand of which more than sixty thousand were whites. There were only ten priests, a tremendous disproportion between priest and people. Archbishop Lamy brought a renewal of life and vigor when New Mexico became a part of the United States. To him and to his successors and their assistants is due, more than to any other agency, the great progress, prosperity, and improvement of the people. Year by year the numbers of the faithful have increased; churches have everywhere been erected; hatred and prejudice, once spread broadcast against the faithful in New Mexico, are gradually disappearing; the Catholic faith, at first despised by many who came to New Mexico after the American occupation period, now receives honor from its enemies; colleges and seminaries have been built where young men and women find opportunity for education in the arts and sciences; homes for orphans, hospitals carried on by religious women, and schools where the poor of both sexes are educated, have come, and all because of the activities and Christian example displayed by Archbishop Lamy, his followers and successors. In New Mexico, since 1851, it may safely be said that the personality of the chief representatives of the church has been the strongest moral power in the uplift of the native people. The Catholic population of New Mexico in 1910, as shown by the national census, was one hundred twenty-one thousand, five hundred fifty-eight. Complete information as to results accomplished by the church since 1851 is found in the table at the conclusion of this chapter.

The missionaries of the Protestant denominations who came to New Mexico at the time of the American
PROTESTANT MISSIONS occupation found it almost impossible to
AND CHURCHES make any progress. Labor as they would, it was not until the early sixties that any substantial results were obtained.

---

were brought to New Mexico: Alverhne, S., Balland, C., Barrau, C., Cazales, A., Cellier, A., Deshores, F., Dumarest, N., Gauthier, J., Girma, F., Haelterman, Alph., Lammert, C., Le Guillon, F., Martin, A., Mayeux, M., Mombour, F., Moog, T., Olier M., Paulhan, Edw., Pelzer, T., Rabeyrolles, A., and Roux, T., a total of 22.

"Since the time of Archbishop Chapelle the following have been added: Revs. J. Pugens, C. Pobst, A. Besset, J. Hartman, A. Casanié, T. Plautard, J. Pajot, L. Cellier, E. Bertrom, J. Collin, L. DeLavelle, G. Charrié, J. Krayer and J. Molinié.''

The Baptist missionaries were the first to come to New Mexico. In July, 1849, Rev. Henry W. Read, a Baptist missionary, arrived at Santa Fé. He soon opened a school where the English language was taught. In 1852, Rev. Samuel Gorman came to New Mexico as a missionary to the Pueblo Indians. He established himself at the pueblo of Laguna where he taught and preached until 1860. The Baptists were the first to erect a Protestant church in New Mexico. This was erected at Santa Fé and was dedicated on the 15th day of January, 1854. During the Civil War interest in the work declined and the property was sold to the Presbyterians. Before the close of the Civil War period missions were carried on at Laguna, Ft. Defiance, Alburquerque, and Socorro.

THE BAPTISTS

Rev. E. G. Nicholson was the first missionary of the Methodist church to come to New Mexico. He came to Santa Fé in 1850, held services for about two years, and abandoned the work. From time to time thereafter various efforts were made to establish missions, but without permanent success until the advent of Rev. Thomas Harwood, in 1871. This able man established himself at Watrous, where a mission school was opened. Although he met with many obstacles he has ever since continued in the work in New Mexico. Later on mission schools were opened at other points in the territory.[276]

THE METHODISTS

The building of the railroads into New Mexico, bringing a great increase of population, was of great assistance to the Protestant churches, and nearly every city and village of any consequence today has its church, and the outcome of the efforts of its ministers and missionaries has been most gratifying. In 1880, Rev. Thomas Har-

---

[276] Schools were established at Tiptonville, La Joya, Escondido, Cerro, Alburquerque, Las Vegas, Peralta, Socorro, Ranchito, Old Alburquerque, Dulce, Las Cruces, Martinez, Frampton, Wagon Mound, and other places.

On the 14th of September, 1875, a clergyman of the Methodist church, Rev. F. J. Tolby, was murdered on the road east of Elizabethtown, in Colfax county. It was charged, at the time, that the murder was a political one, as Mr. Tolby had been very outspoken in his criticism of some of the men and leaders of political affairs of the territory at that time. There was a great deal of excitement at Cimarron and it was only through the prompt leaving of the county by one or two prominent men, who fled to Santa Fé, that summary vengeance was not taken upon them. The church authorities and leading politicians of New Mexico did everything possible to have an investigation made. Nothing was ever discovered, however, determining who were the guilty parties.

wood established at Santa Fé the *New Mexico Christian Advocate*. This became the official paper of the Methodists in the territory and aided materially in the missionary work. It was printed in both the English and Spanish languages.

The Protestant Episcopal Church held its first service at Santa Fé in the summer of 1863. The services were conducted by the Rt. Rev. J. C. Talbot, at the time missionary bishop and afterward bishop of Indiana. Assisting him were Revs. M. A. Rich and A. H. DeMora, a Spanish clergyman, who preached in the Spanish language. In 1868, New Mexico was visited by Bishop Randall of Colorado, the territory having been placed under his jurisdiction.

THE EPISCOPALIANS

No church organization was effected, however, until the year 1874, when the general convention of the church created a missionary jurisdiction of New Mexico and Arizona and elected William Forbes Adams, D. D., of New Orleans, as the first bishop. The new bishop arrived at Santa Fé in February, 1875, and the first service was held on the seventh day of that month. Bishop Adams resigned in 1877. For several years after the departure of Bishop Adams, Rev. Henry Forrester was the only Episcopal clergyman in New Mexico. He remained in charge of the church at Santa Fé until 1879, when he moved to Las Vegas, afterwards going to Alburquerque where he remained until 1892, when he was appointed by the presiding bishop as superintendent of mission work in the republic of Mexico. The first Episcopal church in New Mexico was built at Las Vegas, and was consecrated by Bishop Spalding of Colorado. The structure was of adobe bricks and is still standing.

In 1880 the church was regularly organized by the holding of the primary convocation of the missionary jurisdiction of New Mexico and Arizona, in St. John's church, at Alburquerque. Bishop Spalding presided. L. Bradford Prince and William W. Griffin [277] of

---

[277] William W. Griffin was born in Clarksburg, West Virginia, in April, 1830. He came to New Mexico, in 1860, by way of Little Rock to Galveston, Texas, thence to New Mexico, walking the greater part of the distance. He was a clerk in the office of the United States quartermaster at Santa Fé; he held the position of deputy collector of internal revenue. He was a civil engineer and was in the employ of the government as a surveyor for many years. For many years he was identified with the First National Bank of Santa Fé. Lucien B. Maxwell became its first president and later on Mr. Griffin became its cashier and president, holding the latter position until his death in December, 1889. Mr. Griffin was a very enterprising and influential man. He was chairman of the

Santa Fé were elected respectively chancellor and treasurer of the jurisdiction.

At the general convention held in New York in 1880, the Rev. George K. Dunlop was elected bishop and was consecrated in St. Louis, Missouri, November 21, 1880. It was during the administration of Bishop Dunlop that the edifice at Santa Fé, known as the Church of the Holy Faith, was constructed. Through his efforts the handsome church structure in Las Vegas was partially built. Bishop Dunlop died March 12, 1888. His successor was Rev. J. Mills Kendrick, of Ohio, who was consecrated January 18, 1889. In 1892 New Mexico was separated from Arizona and became a missionary district by itself. Bishop Kendrick is still in charge of the jurisdiction. A summary of the work of the Episcopalian church is found in the note.

In the year 1851 the Presbyterian Missionary Union sent Rev. W. T. Kephardt to New Mexico. He was more of a politician than a missionary. He soon identified himself with newspaper work, became the editor of the *Santa Fé Gazette*, and espoused the anti-slavery cause. The work of the missionaries during the first ten years of their labors was unsatisfactory, and little was really accomplished until the Civil War period, confronted as they were by the same conditions and influences as were met by the other denominations. During these early days of Protestant missionary work, it must be remembered that other than the native New Mexicans and Indians, the population of New Mexico was very limited. The "American"—so called—was a type unto himself. Some of the best and some of the worst representatives of the American people were to be found in New Mexico. The "American" was found principally at or in the vicinity of the numerous army posts in the territory. At any rate, outside of the army, the actual residents of American birth were, in point of numbers, a very insignificant element of the total population.

THE PRESBYTERIANS

---

republican committee for several years. He was a Mason, and one of the organizers of Montesuma lodge, No. 1, Santa Fé, and was its Master for several years. He was the first Grand Master of the Grand Lodge of the territory. In 1866 he was married to Miss Jennie M. Miller, a native of the state of Missouri, of which union there were six children. Two of these, William E. and Arthur, served with distinction in Roosevelt's regiment of Rough Riders during the Spanish American War.

William F. Bonney—"Billy the Kid"

In 1866 the Presbyterians purchased from the Baptists the church edifice of the latter at Santa Fé. In 1867 a school was established at Santa Fé under the Presbyterian Board of Home Missions, followed, in 1872,[278] by another at Taos, which was in charge of Rev. J. M. Roberts. In 1876, early in the year, the Rev. John Menaul established a school at the pueblo of Laguna, which was continued for upwards of twenty years. Rev. Menaul obtained a printing press and with his own hands printed tracts and other documents in the Spanish language, distributing them throughout all parts of the territory.

In this year was commenced the publication of a newspaper called the *Revista Evangelica*, which, however, went out of existence in 1879. In the fall of 1876 a mission school was established among the Zuñi. In 1877, the secretary of the Board of Home Missions visited all of the church missions in New Mexico and in the following year Dr. Menaul [279] began the publication of a newspaper called

---

[278] Stewart, Robert Laird, D. D., *Life of Sheldon Jackson*, New York, 1908. Rev. Sheldon Jackson visited New Mexico in 1870, at which time the territory of New Mexico was almost as distinctively Mexican in its language, customs, civilization, and methods of accomplishment in every field of labor, as when it became a part of the United States a quarter of a century before. He found the 'field itself, throughout its vast extent, was distinctively foreign missionary ground, its population being alien in faith, language, customs, education and sympathies. It was also included within the bounds and under the care of a newly organized presbytery and synod, every rood of which was recognized as home mission territory. It was in a word, the meeting-place of both branches and departments of the missionary work of the Church.''

''As the advance agent of the Home Board, and of the synod, Sheldon Jackson was concerned mainly with the magnitude of the work before him and the most direct methods of accomplishing it. His first trip to New Mexico included Santa Fé, the ancient capital of the Territory. . . At Santa Fé, he found congenial associates and a cordial welcome at the home of the Rev. D. F. McFarland, who opened the first mission in the Territory, under commission of the Board of Domestic Missions (O. S.), November 22, 1886. In October, 1871, the Presbytery of Santa Fé, which covered the entire Territory, reported only two ministers and five churches. One of this number was a chaplain in the army, two were pastors of home mission churches, and two were missionaries to the Navajó Indians. Beside these, there were six ministers belonging to other connections or denominations, making in all a missionary force of eleven representatives of the Protestant Church.''

[279] In 1870 Rev. John Menaul had been sent by the Foreign Board of the Presbyterian Church to the Navajó Mission, where he remained until the spring of 1875. The experience which he had among the Navajós, and later, for a few months among the Apaches, was a valuable preparation for his work at the pueblo of Laguna. In 1852, Rev. Samuel Gorman, a Baptist missionary, had found his way to the pueblo of Laguna. For almost a year he met with only poor success. Through the efforts of Captain H. L. Dodge of the army, he succeeded in making some headway, and finally, the Indians adopted him and

La Solona. When Dr. Menaul went to Laguna for the purpose of establishing the mission which had ceased to exist since the death of Rev. Gorman, he was accompanied by Rev. Sheldon Jackson, B. M. Thomas, Indian agent, and the Rev. George Smith of Santa Fé. The mission was reëstablished on the day following their arrival. The church and school at Laguna were supported for several years by a church society of Albany, New York, when they were finally turned over to the Woman's Executive Committee of the Presbyterian Church.

During the early years of service on the part of the Presbyterian missionaries, they, like all the others, encountered much opposition. The work was necessarily slow; but its progress has been rapid and most encouraging in results. Many schools were established and successfully maintained. In 1895 the work had so progressed that every town of importance in New Mexico had its Presbyterian church. In 1908, the synod of New Mexico, which now covers the field once held by the presbytery of Santa Fé, reported to the assembly of that year five presbyteries, having under their care ninety-one churches. At that time the working force of the synod consisted of sixty-nine ministers, five licentiates, sixteen local evangelists, seven Indian assistants, and eighty-seven missionary teachers.

The Congregational church was organized in New Mexico in the year 1880. In the fall of that year a delegation of clergymen direct from the national council of that THE CONGREGATIONALISTS church, visited New Mexico. Shortly afterward the First Congregational Church at Alburquerque was incorporated and commenced its work under the charge of Rev. J. M. Ashley. Later a church was built at Santa Fé. During the past three decades a large number of congregations have been organized in different parts of the territory, all of which have been very successful.

The first Jewish temple was erected at Las Vegas in the year 1885.

---

his family as members of the pueblo. Notwithstanding this action on the part of the Indians, however, he was unable to get the children to come to a school which he opened. He finally left and became pastor of the church at Santa Fé. When he left, the mission was given into his charge. He died in July, 1861, and at the time of his death was governor of the pueblo.

PROTESTANT CHURCHES IN NEW MEXICO 355

HEBREWS
Another was built some years later at Alburquerque. There are now three congregations in the territory having a membership of one hundred and twenty heads of families.

Many other Protestant denominations are in a flourishing condition in the territory at the present time, statistics as to which may be found in the note which follows.[280]

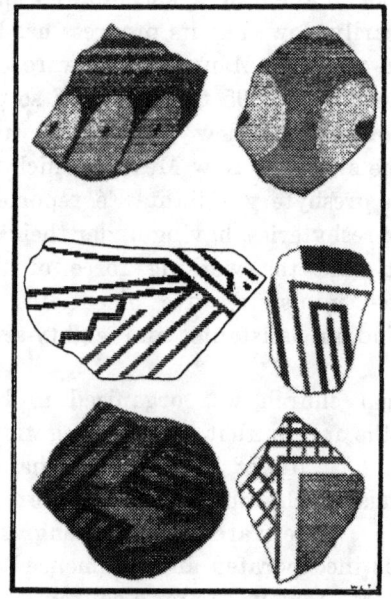

PRE-SPANISH POTTERY SHARDS,
GILA BASIN

---

[280] According to the latest available tables showing church organizations, members, places of worship, value of property, parsonages, and Sunday schools, there are in New Mexico today religious bodies as follows:

BIBLIOGRAPHY

Church Records	Santa Fé, New Mexico.
Catholic Vindicator	Detroit, July 29, 1856.
DeFouri, Rev. J. H.	*Catholic Church in New Mexico,* San Fran., 1887.
Freeman's Journal	November 23, 1853.
Howlett, Rev. W. J.	*Life of Rt. Rev. J. P. Machebeuf,* Pueblo, Colo., 1908.
New Mexican	Newspaper, Santa Fé, N. M.
Revista Catolica	Periodical, Las Vegas, N. M.
Shea, John Gilmary	*History of the Catholic Church in the United States,* New York, 1892.
Salpointe, Mt. Rev. J. B.	*Soldiers of the Cross,* Banning, Calif., 1898.
Stewart, Robert Laird	*Life of Sheldon Jackson,* New York, 1908.

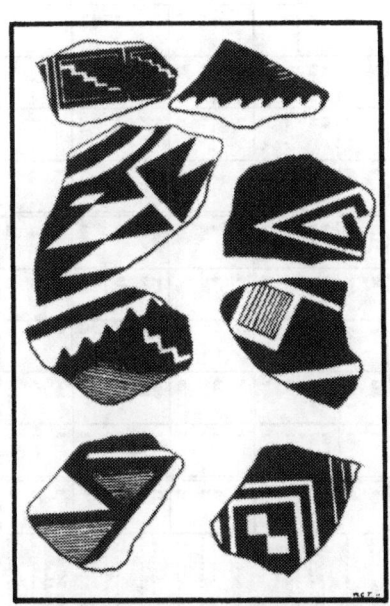

PRE-SPANISH POTTERY SHARDS,
GILA BASIN

Note 280 — Concluded.

ORGANIZATIONS, COMMUNICANTS OR MEMBERS, PLACES OF WORSHIP, VALUE OF CHURCH PROPERTY, DEBT ON CHURCH PROPERTY, PARSONAGES, AND SUNDAY SCHOOLS, BY DENOMINATIONS

DENOMINATION	Total number of organizations	COMMUNICANTS OR MEMBERS			SEX		PLACES OF WORSHIP							VALUE OF CHURCH PROPERTY		DEBT ON CHURCH PROPERTY		PARSONAGES		SUNDAY SCHOOLS CONDUCTED BY CHURCH ORGANIZATIONS			
		Num. of organizations reporting	Total number reported	Num'r of organizations reporting	Male	Female	Number of organizations reporting			Num'r of church edifices reported	Num'r of organizations reporting	Seating capacity of church edifices reported	Num'r of organizations reporting	Value reported	Num'r of organizations reporting	Amount of debt reported	Num'r of organizations reporting	Value of parsonages reported	Num'r of organizations reporting	Num'r of Sunday schools reported	Num'r of officers and teachers	Num'r of scholars
							Church edifices	Halls, etc.															
Advent bodies	6	6	218	6	88	130	2	3	2	2	2	500	4	$2,500					6	6	8	223
Seventh-day Adventist Denomination	6	6	218	6	88	130	2	3	2	2	2	500	4	2,500					6	6	38	223
Baptist bodies	69	69	2,405	54	892	1,134	28	30	29	29	27	6,175	31	67,350	13	$6,039	9	$9,350	57	40	246	2,145
Baptists:																						
Northern Baptist Convention	69	69	2,406	54	902	1,134	29		29	29	27	6,175	31	67,350	13	6,039	9	9,350	57	40	246	2,145
Southern Baptist Convention	57	40	2,381	40	716	1,088	27		28	28	26	6,075	30	66,550	13	6,039	9	9,350	36	39	246	2,136
National Baptist Convention (Colored)	4	4	61	4	52	7	1		1	1	1	100	1	800								
Brethren (Plymouth)	1	1	11	1	2	9		1											1		2	9
Brethren (Plymouth)—I	1	1	6	1	2	4		1											1	1	4	35
Christadelphians	1	1	10	1	4	6																
Congregationalists	5	5	270	5	101	169	4		4	4	4	240	5	20,150	2	1,000			4	6	29	235
Disciples or Christians	16	16	1,092	16	427	665	5		5	5	5	1,725	8	49,900	2	2,500	2	1,200	8	6	65	654
Disciples of Christ	11	11	953	11	377	528	5	1	5	5	5	1,725	8	49,900	2	2,500	2	1,200	8	8	65	624
Churches of Christ	5	5	139	5	50	70		4												1	3	30
Independent churches	3	3	20	1	10		1		1	1	1	150	1	4,000					2	2	4	45
Jewish congregations	3	3	130	1			1		1	1	1	155	1	5,000								
Latter-day Saints	6	6	738	6	345	393	4		4	4	4	1,910	4	7,065	1	1,150			6	7	116	467
Church of Jesus Christ of Latter-day Saints	5	5	684	5	328	356	4		4	4	4	1,910	4	7,065	1	1,150			5	6	113	450
Reorganized Church of Jesus Christ of Latter-day Saints	1	1	54	1	17	37													1	1	3	17
Lutheran bodies	3	3	100	3	32	68	2		2	2	2	350	2	4,000	1	1,000	1	1,500	3	3	16	129
General Synod of the Evangelical Lutheran Church in the United States of America	2	2	59	2	15	44	2		2	2	2	350	2	4,000	1	1,000	1	1,500	2	2	13	99
Evangelical Lutheran Joint Synod of Ohio and Other States	1	1	41	1	17	24													1	1	3	30
Methodist bodies	115	114	6,560	105	2,858	3,805	80	9	81	78	75	15,896	84	205,485	15	8,685	46	55,365	97	92	694	5,834
Methodist Episcopal Church	69	61	3,518	54	1,286	1,907	50	8	51	45	43	10,484	50	125,735	10	5,735	30	29,050	51	55	248	2,759
African Methodist Episcopal Church	2	2	83	2	20	63			2	2	2	450	2	5,000	1	300	1	1,500	1	1	12	50
Methodist Episcopal Church, South	43	43	2,892	46	1,024	1,584	25	6	25	28	28	4,720	29	70,830	6	2,510	17	22,515	31	31	247	2,989
Colored Methodist Episcopal Church	3	3	68	3	27	41	5		3	3	2	263	3	3,750	2	140	1	300	3	4	17	54
Presbyterian bodies	54	54	2,085	53	1,097	1,028	45		45	44	44	8,500	45	112,585	5	5,000	15	26,700	50	54	294	2,729
Presbyterian Church in the United States of America	53	53	2,064	52	1,038	1,021	44		44	43	43	8,350	44	109,085	5	5,000	14	21,200	49	53	286	2,719
Presbyterian Church in the United States	1	1	71	1	24	47	1		1	1	1	150	1	3,500			1	2,500	1	1	8	70
Protestant Episcopal Church	18	18	659	15	237	405	13		14	13	13	3,175	16	66,750	1	240	8	19,800	15	15	73	539
Reformed bodies	2	2	70	2	34	36	1		1	1	1	150	1	600	1	100	1	400	3	3	6	250
Christian Reformed Church	2	2	70	2	34	36	1		1	1	1	150	1	600	1	100	1	400	1	1	6	250
Roman Catholic Church	330	330	121,558	296	51,507	51,676	284	15	280	275	273	91,899	293	406,900	12	91,913	43	77,455	100	129	191	7,932
Salvationists	9	9	30	9	19	11	1		1	1	1	450	2	10,150	2	3,500			9	9	8	50
Salvation Army	9	9	30	9	19	11	1		1	1	1	450	2	10,150	2	3,500						

CHAPTER IX

NEW MEXICO DURING THE CIVIL WAR — COLONEL W. W. LORING — GENERAL H. H. SIBLEY — CONFEDERATE INVASION — COLONEL JOHN R. BAYLOR — FALL OF FORT FILLMORE — MAJOR E. LYNDE —. NEW MEXICANS NOT SECESSIONISTS — HATRED OF THE TEXANS — BATTLE OF VALVERDE — CONFEDERATE OCCUPATION OF ALBURQUERQUE AND SANTA FÉ — ENGAGEMENTS AT APACHE CANYON AND GLORIETA — FIGHT AT PERALTA — CONFEDERATE RETREAT — COLORADO VOLUNTEERS — ARRIVAL OF THE CALIFORNIA COLUMN — GENERAL J. H. CARLETON — GOVERNOR HENRY CONNELLY — DELEGATES IN CONGRESS — GOVERNORS MITCHELL, PILE, GIDDINGS, ARNY, AXTELL, AND WALLACE — BENCH AND BAR — LINCOLN COUNTY WAR — ADVENT OF RAILROADS — POPULATION — STATISTICS — 1861-1880

IT has been stated by some historians that the New Mexicans, so far as they had any knowledge of the great questions which brought about the war of secession, were southern sympathizers. This is not true. There were a very few of the more prominent families whose tendencies were in that direction.[281] The masses of

---

[281] Bancroft, H. H., *History of Arizona and New Mexico*, p. 681: "Their commercial relations in early times had been chiefly with southern men; the army officers with whom they had come in contact later had been largely from the south; and the territorial officials appointed for the territory had been in most cases politicians of strong southern sympathies. Therefore most of the popular leaders, with the masses controlled politically by them, fancied themselves democrats, and felt no admiration for republicans and abolitionists. Yet only a few exhibited any enthusiasm in national politics, apathy being the leading characteristic, with a slight leaning on general principles to southern views."

Greeley, Horace, *American Conflict*, vol. ii, p. 21: "Her Delegate in Congress, Miguel A. Otero, had issued (Feb. 15, 1861) and circulated an address to her people, intended to disaffect them toward the Union, and incite them to favor the Rebellion; but her democratic governor, Abraham Rencher, though a North Carolinian, upon receiving news of Lynde's surrender, issued a procla-

the people, however, were Union men.[282] The feelings entertained by some of the most prominent were quickly changed when the first invasion of New Mexico came from the state of Texas. The New Mexicans had not lost their hatred for the people of that state. While this fact undoubtedly had great influence in fixing a sentiment of loyalty to the Union among the native citizens [283] of the

mation calling out the entire militia force of the Territory, to act as a home guard; which call, though it added inconsiderably to the effective force of her defenders, was calculated to exert a wholesome influence upon public opinion, and keep restless spirits out of mischief.''

Greeley, Horace, *Ibid*, p. 20: ''Her Mexican population, ignorant, timid, and superstitious, had been attached to the Union by conquest, scarcely fifteen years before, and had, meantime, been mainly under the training of Democratic officials of strong pro-slavery sympathies, who had induced her Territorial legislature, some two years before, to pass an act recognizing slavery as legally existing among them, and providing stringent safeguards for its protection and security — an act which was still unrepealed.''

[282] Bancroft, H. H., *History of Arizona and New Mexico*, p. 684: ''When the test came, even in the height of apparent confederate success, they did nothing of the kind, the masses favoring the union cause, and furnishing five or six thousand troops, volunteers and militia, to resist the invasion. A few prominent natives, including some branches of the Armijo family and even the delegate in congress, used their influence and money against the union, but without avail, most of the wealthy and influential families being pronounced union men.''

See also Lossing's *Pictorial History of the Civil War*, vol. ii, pp. 185-188, where it is declared that Hon. Miguel A. Otero, delegate in congress, published an address in February, 1861, inciting the people of the territory to rebel against the Union. Prominent in their support of the Union cause were Facundo Pino, José M. Gallegos, José A. Martinez, Donaciano Vigil, Trinidad Romero, Pedro Sanchez, F. P. Abreu, Miguel E. Pino, J. Francisco Chavez, Francisco Perea, Manuel Chaves, Rafael Chacon, José D. Sena and Manuel D. Pino.

Governor Lew Wallace, in a *message* to the legislature, says: ''I have yet to hear of one native born of a Mexican mother who refused to support the old flag.'' See also lists of New Mexicans serving as volunteers and militia in *U. S. Gov. Doc.*, 37th cong., 2d sess., *H. Ex. Doc.* 58.

[283] Bancroft, H. H., *Ibid*, pp. 685-686: ''It was hoped that California, or at least southern California, would be brought by inclination and intrigue into the confederacy. It was thought that the strong southern element would be able to control Colorado. Some reliance was probably placed in the hostility of the Mormons to the government, so far as Utah was concerned. Arizona was known to be controlled by secessionists. The native New Mexicans were confidently expected to espouse the southern cause as soon as there might be a show of success. And the Apaches and Navajós were looked upon, not exactly as partizans of the south, but as a potent factor in the defeat of the union forces. Troops in the territory were barely sufficient for defensive warfare against the Indians, and New Mexico was a long way from Washington, even if there had not been a need of all available forces nearer the national capital. Moreover, there were military stores in the New Mexican forts worth capturing, to say nothing of the opportunity for a display of exuberant Texan patriotism, even if the Californians and Coloradoans, by failing to perform their part of the contract, should render it impossible to carry out the scheme in

territory, still it cannot truthfully be said that this hatred of the Texans was the strongest popular feeling among the natives, far outweighing their devotion either to the north or to the south.[284]

The Confederates intended to occupy all of the country which had

its grander phases and extend the confederacy to the Pacific shores. The project was a grand, and from a southern point of view, a legitimate one, with good apparent prospects of success. It failed, not only because the confederate forces in general were as fully occupied in the east as were the federals, so that the enterprise had to be intrusted to the Texans alone, whose resources were limited, but because New Mexican sympathy for the south and animosity for the national government proved less potent than their union proclivities, prejudice against African slavery, and hatred of Texas; because California not only remained true to the union, but sent a column of volunteer troops to drive the rebels out of Arizona; and above all, because Colorado under energetic union management, not only was able to control the strong secession element within her borders, but to send a regiment which struck the decisive blow in ridding her southern neighbor of invaders.

[284] The conditions prevailing in the Mesilla valley at this time are well outlined in a letter to Judge John S. Watts from W. W. Mills, a loyal citizen of El Paso, wherein he says: ''I assure you that I find matters here in a most deplorable condition. A disunion flag is now flying from the house in which I write, and this country is now as much in the possession of the enemy as Charleston is. All the officers at Fort Fillmore, except two, are avowedly with the South, and are only holding on to their commissions in order to embarrass our Government, and at the proper time turn over everything to the South, after the manner of General Twiggs. The Mesilla *Times* is bitterly disunion, and threatens with death any one who refuses to acknowledge this usurpation. There is, however, a latent Union sentiment here, *especially among the Mexicans*, but they are effectually overawed. Give them something to rally to, and let them know that they have a government worthy of their support and they will teach their would be masters a lessson. The soldiers, also, in defiance of the teachings of their officers and the offer of gold from Hart, are yet faithful, and if a second lieutenant were to ask them to follow him, they would tear down his flag and throw the *Times* office into the river in one hour. Fifty of them could now go to Ft. Bliss and bring up all the government stores from that place, but instead of this a few thieves came up from El Paso a few days ago and stole 40 of the horses belonging to the mounted company at Fillmore. No effort was made to retake these horses, although the soldiers plead with their officers to allow them to follow the thieves. If Colonel Roberts, from Stanton, or any other faithful officer, would come here and take command, all would be right in three days. About 300 Texas troops are expected at Ft. Bliss in about two weeks from this time, and if something is not done before that time Fort Fillmore will be surrendered. I have yet faith that this will be prevented. The only reason why I do not go immediately to Santa Fé is that I think I can be of service to you here when you come to hold your court, and I claim it as my right to take part in the fight here, if fight it must be. I go to El Paso tomorrow, but will return in a few days to await coming events.''

Colonel Baylor, on October 25, 1861, writing to General Sibley, bears witness to the fact that the sentiment among the Mexican population was for the Union. He says: ''The Mexican population are decidedly Northern in sentiment, and will avail themselves of the first opportunity to rob us or join the enemy. Nothing but a strong force will keep them quiet. I would again urge that re-enforcements cannot be too soon sent up.'' — *War of the Rebellion*, series 1, vol. iv, p. 133.

become a part of the United States by reason of the war with Mexico and the Gadsden Purchase. Early in 1860, the secretary of war, Floyd, sent Colonel W. W. Loring, of North Carolina, to command the department of New Mexico, while George B. Crittenden, who had been sent out for the same purpose as Colonel Loring, was placed by the latter in command of an expedition against the Apaches, which was to start from Fort Stanton in the early part of 1861. It was the business of these men to attempt the corruption of the patriotism of the officers under them and to induce them to lead their men into Texas and give them to the service of the rebellion. One of these officers, Lieutenant-Colonel B. S. Roberts of Vermont, who had joined Crittenden at Fort Stanton, perceiving the intentions of his commander, refused to obey any orders that savored of a treasonable purpose, and, procuring a furlough, he hastened to Santa Fé, and denounced Crittenden to Colonel Loring. He was astonished when, instead of thanks for his patriotic service, he received reproof for meddling in other people's business, and discovered that Loring was also a traitor. Roberts was ordered back to Fort Stanton, but found an opportunity to warn Captain Hatch, the commander at Alburquerque, and Captain Morris, who held Fort Craig, both on the Rio Grande, as well as other loyal officers, of the treachery of their superiors. The iniquity of Loring and Crittenden soon became known to the army in New Mexico and they found it necessary to leave suddenly and unattended. Of the 1200 regular troops in New Mexico, only a very few proved treacherous to their country. Loring and Crittenden made their way to Fort Fillmore, just below Las Cruces, thence to Texas, afterwards serving with distinction in the armies of the Confederacy. After the war was over General Loring offered his services to the Khedive of Egypt and was known as Loring Pasha.[285]

Colonel E. R. S. Canby succeeded Loring in the command of the department. Among other officers who espoused the southern cause

---

[285] Lossing, B. J., *Pictorial History of the Civil War*, vol. ii, pp. 185-188.
General Loring rose to the rank of major-general in the service of the Confederacy. Prior to his departure he endeavored to induce Colonel Manuel Chaves and other prominent New Mexican Indian fighters to join him, offering them commissions in the Confederate service; not one accepted his offer. Loring, after his return to the United States from his service in Egypt, wrote a book, *A Confederate Soldier in Egypt*. He was also known as Fereek Pacha. He held the rank of general in the army of the Khedive.

Patrick F. Garrett

and left New Mexico, was Major H. H. Sibley. At this time the territorial secretary, Alexander M. Jackson, resigned and went south with Loring and Sibley, the last named being later commissioned a brigadier-general and ordered to organize an expedition for the invasion of New Mexico. Jackson became his adjutant-general. The brigade was organized during the summer of 1861 and in November began its advance from San Antonio, Texas. The plans for this expedition were the boldest and most comprehensive of any of the treacherous schemes of the leaders of the rebellion. Sibley's brigade consisted of two and one-half regiments, indifferently equipped. Smallpox and pneumonia proved fatal in many instances and there was a great scarcity of necessary supplies.

Prior to the arrival of General Sibley,[286] the confederates had already begun their operations. Lieutenant-Colonel John R. Baylor, second mounted rifles, C. S. A., occupied Fort Bliss in the month of July and later in the same month took possession of the plaza of La Mesilla. Fort Fillmore, at this time, was commanded by Major Isaac Lynde, a native of the state of Vermont. This officer professed to be loyal. While leading a portion of his com-

---

[286] The treachery of Sibley is manifest in a letter written by him to Colonel Loring, from Hart's Mill, El Paso, Texas, June 12, 1861. In that letter he says: "We are at last under the glorious banner of the Confederate States of America. It was indeed a glorious sensation of protection, hope, and pride. Though its folds were modest and unpretending, the emblem was still there. The very Southern verdure and familiar foliage, as we progressed on our journey, filled us with enthusiasm and home feeling. . . I regret now more than ever the sickly sentimentality (I can call it by no other name) by which I was overruled in my desire to bring my whole command with me. I am satisfied now of the disaffection of the best of the rank and file in New Mexico, and that we are regarded as having betrayed and deserted them. I wish I had my part to play over again; no such peace scruples should deter me from doing what I considered a bounden duty to my friends and my cause. I do not advocate the meeting of duplicity and dishonesty by the like weapons, but if I capture the treasury buildings, I shall certainly not send back to my enemy the golden bricks.''

In the month of March, 1861, a convention was held at Mesilla, purporting to be a "Convention of the People of Arizona," acting separately from the government of the territory of New Mexico, repudiating the United States and attaching themselves to the Confederate states. This convention adopted resolutions, one of which was "That we will not recognize the present Black Republican administration, and that we will resist any officers appointed to this Territory by said administration with whatever means in our power." Don Lorenzo Labadie, at the time United States Indian agent, was served with a copy of this resolution by the editor of the Mesilla *Times* and was threatened with tar and feathers in the event he attempted to exercise the duties of his office.

mand towards the plaza of Mesilla [287] he fell in with a few of Colonel Baylor's men, and, after a short skirmish, retreated to the fort. He gave orders on the 27th of July for the evacuation of the post and started with his command for Fort Stanton. He was pursued by Colonel Baylor and overtaken near the San Agustin Springs. The major portion of his troops was willing to fight, but Lynde ignominiously surrendered his entire command. On the 1st of August Colonel Baylor issued a proclamation as governor,[288] estab-

---

[287] Captain C. H. McNally, 3d U. S. cavalry, says of this fight: "This was 9 a. m. on the 25th. At the same time positive word was brought back that the Texans were in the town of Mesilla. After that we laid quietly in garrison until 4 a. m. when he moved the whole forward, putting McNally, with 22 men, in front, with the order to go on and feel his way. He had four 12-pounder mountain howitzers. He first fired two shells at long range. Ordered McNally to form and go ahead. McNally kept ahead until he got within 60 or 70 yards of the Texans. Halted, and reported in person that they were there in the jacals and corn fields. First McNally knew they fired one shot that cut away his saber; the second struck him. Then fired a volley of about 80 shots. They had no artillery. McNally dismounted and fired at random. They fired another volley. Remounted, not being supported. Sent to Major Lynde, who could not be found, and not being supported by infantry or artillery, ordered his men to retreat. In this fire one sergeant and one corporal were wounded and one man killed. In retreating, the Seventh infantry fired into us. I retreated behind the battery, and found the infantry still in the rear. There McNally fainted from loss of blood and was carried from the field. The last he heard was an order from Major Lynde to retreat."

[288] This proclamation was given at Mesilla on the 1st day of August, 1861, and was as follows:

"Proclamation
To the People of the Territory of Arizona:

"The social and political condition of Arizona being little short of general anarchy, and the people being literally destitute of law, order, and protection, the said Territory, from the date hereof, is hereby declared temporarily organized as a military government until such time as Congress may otherwise provide.

"I, John R. Baylor, lieutenant-colonel, commanding the Confederate Army in the Territory of Arizona, hereby take possession of the said Territory in the name and behalf of the Confederate States of America.

"For all the purposes herein specified, and until otherwise decreed or provided, the Territory of Arizona shall comprize all that portion of New Mexico lying south of the thirty-fourth parallel of north latitude.

"All offices both civil and military, heretofore existing in this Territory, either under the laws of the late United States or the Territory of New Mexico, are hereby declared vacant, and from the date hereof shall forever cease to exist.

"That the people of this Territory may enjoy the full benefits of law, order, and protection, and, as far as possible, the blessings and advantages of a free government, it is hereby decreed that the laws and enactments existing in this Territory prior to the date of this proclamation, and consistent with the Constitution and laws of the Confederate States of America and the

lished the territory of Arizona, and took possession in the name of the Confederacy. At the time of the surrender Lynde's commissary, Captain A. H. Plummer, who held $17,000 in government

provisions of this decree, shall continue in force and effect, without interruption, until such time as the Confederate Congress may otherwise provide.

"The said Territory of Arizona from the date hereof is hereby temporarily organized under military government until such time as Congress may otherwise provide. The said government shall be divided into two separate and distinct departments, to wit: The executive and judicial. The executive authority of this Territory shall be vested in the commandant of the Confederate Army in Arizona. The judicial power of this Territory shall be vested in a supreme court, two district courts, two probate courts, and a justice of the peace, together with such municipal and other inferior courts as the wants of the people may from time to time require. The two district judges shall constitute the supreme court, each of whom shall determine all appeals, exceptions and writs of error removed from the district court wherein the other presides. One of the said judges shall be designated as the chief justice of the supreme court. There shall be but one session in each year, which shall be holden at the seat of government. The district judges shall hold two terms of court every year in their respective judicial districts. They may likewise hold special terms whenever in their opinion the ends of public justice require it.

"The judicial districts of this Territory shall be divided as follows; The first judicial district shall comprise all the portion of Arizona lying east of the Apache Pass, the district and probate courts whereof shall be holden at La Mesilla. The second judicial district shall comprize the remainder of the Territory. The district and probate courts shall be holden at Tucson. The governor shall likewise appoint one probate judge and sheriff and the necessary justices of the peace in and for each judicial district. The constables shall be appointed by the respective justices of the peace. Each district judge shall appoint his own clerk, who shall be *ex-officio* clerk of the probate court within such districts. The district and probate courts of the two districts shall be holden at such times as heretofore provided by the legislature of New Mexico for the counties of Doña Ana and Arizona.

"All suits and other business now pending in any of the late courts of New Mexico within this Territory shall be immediately transferred to the corresponding courts of this Territory, as herein established. The style of all process shall be the Territory of Arizona, and all prosecutions shall be carried on in the name of the Territory of Arizona.

"There shall likewise be appointed by the governor an attorney-general, secretary of the Territory, treasurer, and marshal, whose duty and compensation shall be the same as heretofore under the laws of New Mexico.

"The city of Mesilla is hereby designated as the seat of government of this Territory.

"All Territorial officers shall hold their respective terms of office until otherwise provided by congress, unless sooner removed by the power appointing them.

"The salaries, fees, and compensation of all Territorial officers shall remain the same as heretofore in the Territory of New Mexico.

"The treasurer, marshal, sheriffs, and constables, before acting as such, shall execute to the Territory a bond, with good and sufficient securities, conditioned for the faithful discharge of their official duties, in the same manner as heretofore provided under the laws of New Mexico.

"All territorial officers, before entering upon their official duties, shall take an oath or affirmation to support the Constitution and laws of the Confederate

drafts, which he might have saved, handed them over to Colonel Baylor. For this cowardice or treachery, Lynde was dismissed from the army, and Plummer was reprimanded.[289] The troops

States and of this Territory and faithfully to discharge all duties incumbent upon them.

"The bill of rights of the Territory of New Mexico, so far as consistent with the Constitution and laws of the Confederate States and the provisions of this decree, is hereby declared in full force and effect in the Territory of Arizona.

"Given under my hand at Mesilla this 1st day of August, 1861.

"J. R. Baylor,
"Gov. and Lieut. Col., Comdg. Mounted Rifles, C. S. Army."

[289] Greeley, Horace, *American Conflict*, vol. ii, p. 19-20; says: "Nearly all of the army officers who were disloyal, headed by Loring and Crittenden, made their escape and rendezvoused at Ft. Fillmore, commanded by Major Lynde. Here they renewed their intrigues, finding a large portion of the officers equally traitorous with themselves. But Major Lynde appeared to hold out against their solicitations. His forces, however, were so demoralized that soon afterward when he led 480 of them, out of 700, to the village of Mesilla, he fell into an ambuscade of 200 badly armed Texans, and, after a skirmish, wherein his conduct can only be vindicated from the imputation of cowardice by the presumption of treason, he ordered a retreat to the fort, which his men were next day engaged in fortifying, when surprised, at 10-30 A. M. by an order to evacuate that night. The commissary was ordered to roll out the whiskey, from which the men were allowed to fill their canteens and drink at discretion. No water was furnished for the weary march before them, over a hot and thirsty desert. They started as ordered; but, before they had advanced ten miles men were dropping out of the ranks and falling to the earth exhausted or dead drunk."

It is quite interesting to know the disposition of the "Federal drafts" which were taken (?) from Plummer. In the Confederate correspondence we find that these drafts were all paid except one for $1,000. Reporting from Mesilla, on December 14, 1861, Colonel Baylor stated to Judah P. Benjamin, secretary of war, C. S. A., that the "Federal drafts captured at the surrender of Fort Fillmore, amounting in all to $9,500, $5,500 of which were on the assistant treasurer of New York; the other $4,000 were drawn on the assistant treasurer at Saint Louis, Mo. I sent the drafts by Mr. William McGrorty to New York for collection, which resulted as follows; $4,500 were paid by the assistant treasurer, New York; the other $1,000 draft was not paid. Mr. Cisco, the assistant treasurer, stating that the drawer had no funds in the treasury to his credit. The $4,000 draft on assistant treasurer Saint Louis was left by Mr. McGrorty in New York for collection. Saint Louis being under martial law, Mr. McGrorty felt it unsafe to go in person. I have since received no information if the drafts have been collected or not. I have paid out of the above amount the following sums, viz: $500 was claimed by Lieutenant Plummer, acting assistant quartermaster, U. S. Army, as private funds, which I refunded him. Four hundred and eleven dollars paid Samuel J. Jones, sutler at Fort Fillmore, for corn delivered the quartermaster, U. S. Army, and not paid for by the United States. The corn was in store at Fort Fillmore when the post was abandoned, and Lieutenant Plummer, acting assistant quartermaster, certified to Mr. Jones' claim after the capture of the Federal troops at San Agustin Springs. Three hundred dollars I have paid Mr. McGrorty for part of his expenses to New York in prosecuting the collection of said drafts. The balance $3,289. I send you herewith the quarter-

Henry L. Waldo, Chief Justice 1876-1878; Attorney-General
1878-1880
Solicitor for New Mexico, A., T. and S. F. Ry. Co., 1882-1912

surrendered in this despicable manner were, officers and men, 410. Colonel Baylor, in his official report, gave as his reasons for releasing them on parole that he could not "with less than 300 men, guard

---

master's receipts for that amount. The drafts on Saint Louis, left in New York for collection, I will duly account for when informed of the payment thereof."

William McGrorty, was an older brother of Col. J. P. McGrorty, in 1885 appointed collector of internal revenue for Arizona and New Mexico by President Cleveland.

Report of Major I. Lynde, *War of the Rebellion*, series I, vol. iv, pp. 5-6: "Fort Craig, N. Mex. August 7, 1861. Sir: On the 26th of July I had the honor to report the fact of an unsuccessful attempt to dislodge the Texan troops from the town of Mesilla, since which events of the greatest consequence to my command have occurred. They are now prisoners of war. On that day I had reliable information that the enemy would in the course of the night receive a battery of artillery, and if I moved to intercept it with a sufficient force for the purpose they were ready to attack the fort in my absence, and, as I have previously reported, the fort is indefensible against artillery, being perfectly commanded by sand-hills for at least half the circle, and the only supply of water at the distance of one and a half miles. Other officers, with myself, became convinced that we must eventually be compelled to surrender if we remained in the fort, and that our only hope of saving the command from capture was in reaching some other military post. I therefore ordered the fort to be evacuated, and such public property as could not be transported with the limited means at the post to be destroyed as far as time would allow, and at 1 o'clock A. M. on the 27th of July I took up the line of march for Fort Stanton, which was believed to be the most practicable point to reach, and was reported to be threatened by the enemy. I had no personal knowledge of the road, but it was reported to me that the first day's march would be 20 miles to San Agustin Springs, where there would be abundance of water for all the command. Until daylight the command advanced without difficulty, but when the sun arose the day became intensely hot, and soon after the men and teams began to show signs of fatigue, and I found that the distance was greater than had been represented. About 6 miles before reaching the Springs commences a short ascent to a pass in the Organ Mountains, and here the men and teams suffered severely with the intense heat and want of water, many men falling and unable to proceed. Up to this time there was no indication of pursuit. I now determined to push forward with the mounted force to the Springs, and return with water for the suffering men in the rear. When I had nearly reached the Springs word was brought me that a mounted force was approaching in our rear; but it was believed to be Captain Gibbs, R. M. R., with his command, and soon after that supposition was confirmed by another express. On reaching the Springs I found the supply of water so small as to be insufficient for my command. After procuring all the water that could be transported by the men with me I started back to the main body. After riding some distance I became so much exhausted that I could not sit upon my horse, and the command proceeded without me, under the command of Lieutenant Cressey, R. M. R., and I returned to the Springs. Soon after it was reported to me that a part of the teams had given out and could not be brought up, and that large numbers of the infantry had become totally overpowered with the intense heat. At this time an express from Captain Gibbs reported that eight companies of mounted men, supported by artillery, and a large force of infantry, were approaching our rear guard. I had the 'Call to arms' sounded, and found that I could not bring more than 100 men of the infantry

over 600 and meet another force of 240 of the enemy that is looked for daily." The captured troops were marched to Las Cruces and there paroled. At this point Colonel Baylor was joined by Brigadier-General Albert Sidney Johnston, with a party of officers of the U. S. army, who had resigned and were *en route* for Richmond, Virginia. Colonel Baylor tendered to General Johnston the command of his forces, which was accepted by this distinguished officer, who remained in command until there was no further necessity for his services.[290]

During all this period Colonel Canby, in command of the department, was very active. He proceeded with the organization of the

---

battalion on parade. Captain Gibbs, with a mounted force, now rode into camp, and stated to me that eight companies of mounted Texans (supported by a regiment of infantry, more or less) were approaching; that they had driven in or captured our rear guard (composed of three companies of infantry) and the men that had given out in the rear. Three of the four mountain howitzers that we had with us were with the wagons in the rear and were captured. They were guarded by one company of infantry acting as artillery. Captain Gibbs also reported that his company, men and horses, had been without water for twenty-four hours. Under these circumstances, I considered our case hopeless; that it was worse than useless to resist; that honor did not demand the sacrifice of blood after the terrible suffering that our troops had already undergone, and when that sacrifice would be totally useless. A body of mounted Texans followed Captain Gibbs to the vicinity of the camp, when a parley was held, and I surrendered my command to Lieutenant-Colonel Baylor, of the C. S. Army."

Captain Alfred Gibbs, 3d cavalry, says of this affair: "I heard Major Lynde say 'I agree to these terms,' and I called to some of the officers to come up. When we came up, all the officers being present, I think, Major Lynde said: 'Colonel Baylor, to avoid bloodshed, I conditionally surrender this whole force to you, on condition that officers and their families shall be protected from insult and private property be respected.' Nearly every officer protested earnestly, and even violently, against this base surrender; but Major Lynde said: 'I am the commander of these forces, and I take upon my shoulders the responsibility of my action in the matter.' The altercation by Major Lynde's subordinates became so violent that Colonel Baylor asked who was commander of that force and responsible for their action, when Major Lynde again repeated as above." — *War of the Rebellion*, ser. I, vol. iv, p. 11.

Assistant Surgeon J. Cooper McKee, U. S. A., *Ibid*, p. 11, says: "I am unable to express to you [Surgeon General U. S. A.] the deep grief, mortification, and pain I, with the other officers, have endured from this cowardly surrender of a brave, true command to an inferior force of the enemy, without having one word to say or firing a single shot. I, among other officers, entered my solemn protest against the surrender, but we were peremptorily told by Major Lynde that he was the commanding officer. To see old soldiers and strong men weep like children, men who had faced the battle's storm in the Mexican war, is a sight that I hope I may never again be present at. A braver or truer command could not be found than that which has in this case been made a victim of cowardice and imbecility."

[290] Baylor, John R., Lieutenant Colonel, *Report of, War of the Rebellion*, ser. i, vol. iv, pp. 18-20.

militia and volunteers for the inevitable contest, crippled throughout by the want of money, munitions and supplies of all kinds. Even directions and orders, so plentifully bestowed on most subordinates, were not vouchsafed him from Washington, where the absorption of all energies in the more immediate and momentous struggle on the Potomac and the Missouri, denied him even an answer to his frequent and importunate requisitions and representations.

As late as November 18, 1861, Colonel Canby advised the military authorities at Washington that the operations in his department had been greatly embarrassed and almost paralyzed for want of funds in the pay department. Many of the regular troops had not been paid for more than twelve months and the volunteers had not been paid at all. This fact occasioned a great deal of dissatisfaction in both classes of troops, and almost effectually put an end to the raising of additional volunteers. This condition of affairs had been reported by Canby several times but no heed was paid to his requests. In this desperate situation Canby made an unsuccessful attempt to borrow money for the government; later, in order to secure the funds he agreed, together with the chief commissary and the chief quartermaster, that all arrearages should be repaid in treasury notes, bearing interest. He requested that the government take proper steps to redeem this promise, as many of the leading merchants and capitalists of the territory had pledged their credit for the repayment of the loan. This arrangement was made by Major Donaldson, chief quartermaster, and without the confidence reposed in him by the people of New Mexico the loan never could have been negotiated. He communicated with William Gilpin,[291] governor of the territory

---

[291] William Gilpin was the youngest son of Joshua Gilpin, a direct descendant of the De Guylpyns who invaded Great Britain with William the Conqueror. His ancestor in America was Joseph Gilpin, a Quaker, who came in 1696 and settled on the Brandywine, in Delaware County, Pennsylvania, where William Gilpin was born, October 4, 1822. A brother was attorney general of the United States, appointed by Andrew Jackson. William Gilpin was educated in England. He had as tutor Nathaniel Hawthorne. He entered the United States Military Academy where he was taught by Montgomery Blair and George G. Meade. He received a commission as lieutenant in the 2d dragoons and served in the Seminole War. He asked the government for permission to lead an exploring expedition to the head-waters of the Columbia river; his application was denied; he then resigned from the army, moved to St. Louis, edited a newspaper, and espoused the cause of Senator Thomas H. Benton, who was his life-long friend. He joined the expedition under Colonel John C. Fremont, in 1843. He made a report of the expedition which was made a senate document. When the war with Mexico was declared Gilpin enlisted in the 1st regiment

of Colorado, asking his aid in the furnishing of volunteers. Governor Gilpin, intensely loyal, immediately began the organization of companies of volunteers, which were destined thereafter to render great service in the saving of New Mexico and the southwest from Confederate domination.[292]

Immediately after the surrender of Lynde, Fort Stanton was

---

[292] Missouri volunteers, commanded by Colonel A. W. Doniphan; he was elected major of the regiment and acquitted himself with great credit. After the war was over, he was asked by Governor Edwards of Missouri to raise a regiment of volunteers to guard the Santa Fé trail; this was done and the command was known as Gilpin's Battalion, Missouri mounted volunteers. With this command he crossed the Raton mountains, March 10, 1848, descended the Canadian through the Apache and Comanche country, fought many battles with the Kiowas and was mustered out of service after peace was declared with Mexico. His command during its period of service marched over three thousand miles. It is said that Gilpin was the only man, in 1860, in Jackson county, Missouri, who voted for Abraham Lincoln. At the inauguration of President Lincoln, along with General James H. Lane of Kansas and Cassius M. Clay of Kentucky, he helped guard the White House, sleeping in that edifice each night. Lincoln appointed him governor of Colorado, in which position he served two years, 1861-1863. He was a great student and wrote several valuable books. He predicted the founding of a great city where Kansas City now stands. In an address, speaking of the future of the great west, delivered in Cole county, Missouri, in 1847, among other things he said: "During the Revolution, little armies, issuing from the Alleghenies, passed over Kentucky, the Northwest Territory and Tennessee. These new countries had been reconnoitred and admired. With hardy frames, confirmed health, and recruited year by year of peace, these soldiers returned to occupy the choice spots which had been their bivouac and camping grounds. From the campaigns of war grew settlements of peace, and populous states displaced the wilderness. Another war came, with another generation; armies penetrated Michigan, upper Illinois and into Mississippi. The great Mississippi, crossed at many points, ceased to be a barrier, and the steamboat appeared, plowing its yellow flow. Five great states and 2,000,000 of people emblazon its western bank. And now again have come another generation and another war. Your little armies have scaled the eternal barriers of the mother mountain of the New World and buried for a time in the mazes of its manifold peaks and ridges, have debouched at many points upon the briny beach of the Pacific. Passing round by the great oceans, a military marine simultaneously strikes the shore and lends them aid. Thus is the wilderness reconnoitred in war, its geography illustrated and its conquerers disciplined. Your soldiers, resting for a time at home, will sally forth again, and wielding the weapons of husbandry, give to you new roads that will nurture commerce and a sisterhood of maritime states on the new-found ocean."

[292] Governor Gilpin in his response to the request made by Colonel Canby, August 14, 1861, reported the organization of two volunteer companies of infantry — Company A, Captain J. P. Slough, 101, Company B, Captain Samuel F. Tappan, 101, which had been ordered to report for muster into the service of the United States at Fort Garland. Gilpin states that "the election just concluded exhibits an overwhelming popular majority in favor of the administration. It also reveals a strong malignant element essential to be controlled. The dependence exclusively of this industrial population upon supplies imported from the states over a line of communication of 800 miles, liable to be

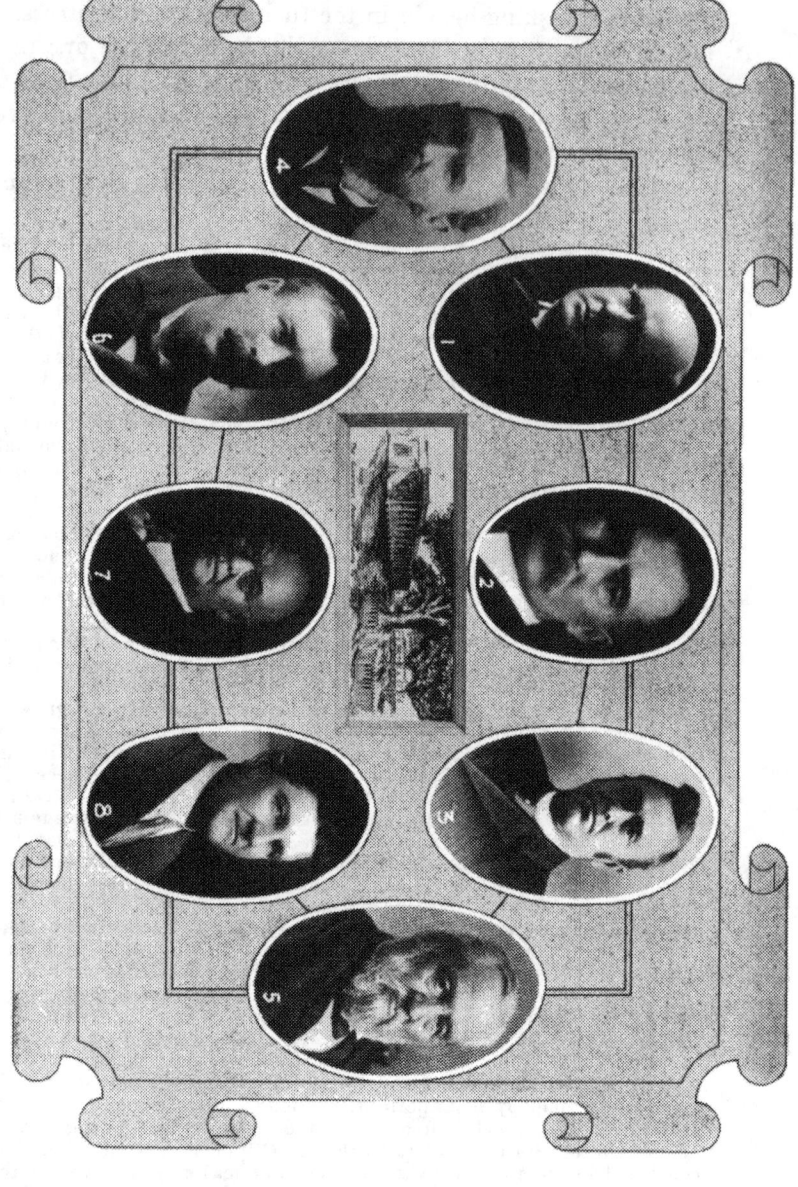

Justices of the Supreme Court of New Mexico

1. Needham C. Collier, 1893. 2. Albert B. Fall, 1893. 3. Napoleon B. Laughlin, 1894. 4. Humphrey B. Hamilton, 1895. 5. William D. Lee, 1889. 6. Jonathan W. Crumpacker, 1898. 7. Benjamin S. Baker, 1902. 8. Edward A. Mann, 1904

abandoned, orders were given for the destruction of all supplies at
cut off by Indians as well as other hostile attacks, makes a complete home organization peremptory for self-defense.''

Governor Gilpin on October 26, 1861, wrote Colonel Canby that ''the strong and malignant element within this Territory [Colorado], added to the destitution of arms and ammunition of any kind up to this time, has rendered absolutely necessary the delay to furnish a garrison for Fort Wise. The population of the Arkansas River is not numerous enough to furnish one company, and to send them from the mining region has been impossible, from want of arms, ammunition, food, clothing, transportation or money to procure any of these essentials. I am incessantly occupied to comply with your requisitions at the earliest moment. The malignant secession element of this Territory has numbered 7,500. It has been ably and secretly organized from November last, and requires extreme and extraordinary measures to meet and control its onslaught. The core of its strength has at present withdrawn to gather strength from Texas, Utah, Arkansas, and from the country of the Confederate Cherokee, Creek and other Indians. They contemplate to return with overwhelming strength and precipitate the neighboring Indians upon us. To prepare for what may be accomplished by them is my duty. This country open everywhere to the East, can only be defended by a sufficient force to meet the enemy in the field. It also enters into their plans to capture Forts Wise and Garland; to surround New Mexico and invade it from the north. The Indian populations west of Arkansas have united with the rebel war to the amount of 64,500, capable of furnishing an efficient army for operations upon these Territories, familiar with this country, and allied to the Georgians who sympathize with secession, and form a large proportion of our mining population.''

Colonel Canby was not overly enthusiastic as to the loyalty and courage of the volunteer troops which were ordered mustered into service in New Mexico. There was pronounced disloyalty among the New Mexicans living in the Mesilla valley at this time, and over 200 had enlisted under the banner of the Confederacy. In the neighborhood of Alburquerque, in the *Rio Abajo*, prominent men — *ricos* — discouraged the native citizens from responding to the call for volunteers. On the 16th of August, 1861, Colonel Canby reported to the adjutant general of the army, St. Louis, Missouri, advising him of the fact that of the thirty-two companies authorized to be organized only nineteen had been completed, and that these ''were below the minimum organizations prescribed by General Orders, No. 15, May 4, 1861.'' He said that ''The people of the Territory, with few exceptions, I believe are loyal, but they are apathetic in disposition, and will adopt any measures that may be necessary for the defense of the Territory with great tardiness, looking with greater concern to their private, and often petty interests, and delaying or defeating the objects of the Government by their personal or political quarrels. I question very much whether a sufficient force for the defense of the Territory can be raised within its limits, and I place no reliance upon any volunteer force that can be raised, unless strongly supported by regular troops. The most that can be hoped from them will be the occupation of two or three important points, which may be fortified and held by them until the policy of the Government with regard to this Territory has been settled and expressed.''

There was much concern manifest by certain leading officers and citizens as to the effect of the order to withdraw the regular troops from New Mexico for the purpose of sending them south to assist in putting down the rebellion. In a letter to General Fremont, commanding at St. Louis, Captain W. R. Shoemaker, of the ordnance, at Fort Union, said: ''We trust that these statements in regard to the late events and present state of affairs in this Territory will reach you in time to arrest the operation of the order for the with-

that post, and the command ordered to proceed to Alburquerque.[293]

drawal of the regular troops from here at this time [August, 1861], as the whole aspect of affairs throughout New Mexico has completely changed since there has been time to make any representation to the authorities at Washington. I know that you are well acquainted with the character of this population, and need only to inform you that the volunteers recently raised here are not composed of the rancheros, or even of the better class of Mexicans, but, on the contrary, for you to see how entirely defenseless the Territory will be if the U. S. Army is withdrawn."

In a communication to Colonel Canby, concurred in and signed by Colonel Céran St. Vrain, 1st regular New Mexico volunteers, and by Lieutenant-Colonel Christopher Carson, of the same regiment, Captain Shoemaker declared that "the property belonging to the United States in his charge at Fort Union, by the inventory taken on June 30th, amounted to $271,147.55 eastern cost, exclusive of the post store houses, outworks, etc., and embraces all the fixtures for a new arsenal for the Territory of an expensive character;" that "a residence of twelve years among the people enables me to know and it is the opinion of every well informed, candid person resident among them, that without the support and protection of the Regular Army of the United States they are entirely unable to protect the public property in the Territory, or the lives of such officers, civil and military, as may be left among them after the withdrawal of the regular forces now under your command, no matter how many there may be or how well armed the New Mexican volunteers are. A view of the present invasion by the Texan troops on the south, the threatened invasion on the east from Arkansas and Upper Texas, and the almost certain capture of all the posts and public property in the Territory, if left unguarded by the regular troops under your command, induces me to make this representation, with the hope that you will at least delay the movement now contemplated until after the present state of affairs in New Mexico is made known to the authorities in Washington and they shall have been heard from on the subject."

[293] *War of the Rebellion*, ser. I, vol. iv, p. 22, *Report* of Lieutenant-Colonel B. S. Roberts.

After Colonel Roberts had ordered the abandonment and destruction of Fort Stanton, the post was occupied by Captain Walker's company of Colonel Baylor's command. In his report to General Van Dorn, Colonel Baylor states that "by express from Fort Stanton I learn that upon the receipt of the news that Major Lynde had surrendered, Colonel Roberts, in command of that post, fled in haste, leaving the post on fire, which was extinguished by a storm of rain. Most of the commissary and quartermaster's supplies were saved and a battery." Colonel Baylor also reported the capture of Captain Hubbell and nine men in a skirmish near Fort Craig. These were New Mexican volunteers. At this time, August, 1861, Fort Craig was garrisoned by 350 regular and 180 volunteer troops.

In the month of August, 1861, a detachment of Baylor's command had a number of fights with Indians in the neighborhood of Fort Stanton and Fort Bliss, in which a number of his soldiers were slain. These fights with Indians induced him to urge upon General Van Dorn the sending of more men to him for the reason that he found it impossible to hold the troops of the United States in check and at the same time be continually operating against hostile Indians. *Report* of Colonel Baylor, *War of the Rebellion*, ser. i, vol. iv, p. 26.

On June 20, 1861, Canby called upon Governor Rencher for three companies of volunteers "to aid in the protection of the eastern frontier of this Territory and guarding the trains on the routes from the Arkansas to this department." These companies were to form a part of one of the regiments later to be organized under Order No. 15, May 4, 1861. These companies were raised in San

The post was shortly occupied by the Confederates but a timely rain quenched the fire and most of the commissary and quartermaster's supplies were saved to the invaders.

In a skirmish at Cañada Alamosa, September 25, 1861, south of Fort Craig, Captain John H. Mink, of the New Mexico mounted volunteers, surrendered to Captain Coopwood, commanding a force of about 115 men. The enlisted men who were captured [294] were released on parole but Captain Minks and Lieutenant Medina were held as prisoners. Later the victorious Texans were defeated by a detachment of regular troops from Fort Craig.

Miguel county and were armed and equipped at Fort Union. He also, two days later, called upon the governor for four companies of foot volunteers, to rendezvous at Alburquerque and one company of foot and one of mounted volunteers to rendezvous at Fort Craig and a like number at Fort Stanton.

Colonel Canby took prompt action in the matter of strengthening all of the southern posts. Robert H. Stapleton, who lived near Fort Craig, was authorized by the governor to raise the mounted company. Colonel M. E. Pino, who had been appointed by President Lincoln to the command of the 2d regiment of New Mexican volunteers, was also active and designated the companies that assembled at Alburquerque.

The military authorities at Washington were kept well advised of the condition of affairs in New Mexico and the necessity for the organization of mounted troops. In a communication to Hon. Simon Cameron, secretary of war, July 3, 1861, Judge Perry E. Brocchus, then at the nation's capital, said: ''The President informed me last evening that you had completed your report, and advised me to call upon you in reference to the troops about to be raised in New Mexico. Advices from Governor Stanton and Judge Watts urge the importance of having three regiments, two of them to be mounted, and, in view of threatened aggressions in the northern as well as the southern portion of the Territory by the domestic foe, immediate action in the premises is deemed absolutely necessary. . . . If you would most effectually strengthen the government of the United States, physically and morally, in that recently conquered and imperfectly loyalized region of our country; if you would plant most deeply in the soil of New Mexico and in the hearts of her people the staff from which floats the 'flag of the free,' you must show the good faith of giving them ample protection, alike against the marauding savage and the rebellious domestic foe.''

[294] *War of the Rebellion*, ser. i., vol. iv, p. 31, *Report* of Captain Bethel Coopwood. The known intention of the Confederates to invade New Mexico from the south, together with a suspected invasion from the north and east, were not the least of the troubles confronting Colonel Canby. In a letter to the headquarters of the army at St. Louis, he gives in detail the great embarrassment under which he was laboring on account of depredations by the Indians. The Navajós were constant in their daring raids. The Mescalero Apaches were committing depredations, and incursions had been made by the Kiowas and Comanches, ostensibly in pursuit of the Utes, but their depredations were not confined to them. The troubles with the Navajós, Colonel Canby declared, were greatly aggravated by the illegal acts of a portion of the Mexican people, who made war upon the Indians for booty and captives. These raids upon the Navajós were upheld by the moral sense of the community and he believed that so long as the Mexican raiders could find a ready sale for their plunder and their captives, it was impossible to prevent retaliation by the Indians.

It had been the purpose of General Sibley to invade New Mexico early in the fall of 1861, but he was still at Fort Bliss [295] on January 1, 1862. Shortly afterward he moved forward at the head of 2,300 men, many of them veterans of the Mexican War, and a large majority experienced Indian fighters. For Colonel Canby's regulars they entertained a wholesome respect, but the Mexican militia and volunteers, as usual, only excited the Texan derision of a foe whom they had been bred to despise. General Sibley was very confident of success, having issued a proclamation to the people of the territory,[296] and, advancing by way of Fort Thorn, found the Union forces under Canby in force at Fort Craig, on the Rio Grande. The

---

[295] *War of the Rebellion*, ser. i, vol. iv, p. 89. Colonel Canby received a report from El Paso (Old Mexico), dated January 17, 1862, to the effect that General Sibley and staff arrived in El Paso about a month previous; that his staff officers were A. M. Jackson, I. Ochiltree, Captain Dwyer, and Judge Crosby, assistant quartermaster and "receiver of property to be confiscated in New Mexico." The report further states that the "first and second regiments are now between Robledo and Santa Barbara and are now fortifying themselves. They have taken only four additional pieces of artillery besides those belonging to Colonel Baylor's command (32-pounders). General Sibley and staff were to leave Mesilla for Fort Thorn on yesterday, the 16th instant. The second regiment is expected next week. The troops are badly provisioned and armed; have had about 200 horses stolen since they passed here. Their only hope is to march into New Mexico in quick time, or engage in a war with Mexico (El Paso) to procure provisions. They have no money, and their paper is only taken by the merchants, not by the Mexicans. The Mexican population (El Paso, Mexico) are much opposed to them, also at Mesilla and Doña Ana. Yrrisarri and Armijo goods at Mesilla have been confiscated, and that is the order of the day. S. Hart has done more to aid and assist them than the balance of the capitalists have, and has gone so far as to give a list of the principal capitalists in New Mexico, to confiscate their property, and that is their aim."

[296] *War of the Rebellion*, ser. I, vol. iv, pp. 88-90. This proclamation was well calculated at that particular time to exercise a pernicious influence upon the least intelligent of the New Mexican people. Colonel Canby says that there is no doubt that it was prepared by ex-Secretary A. M. Jackson and was a part of a plan arranged before he left the country. Several packages, containing the proclamation, addressed to persons of influence in the territory were intercepted, Jackson believing that they still were southern sympathizers. Canby immediately took steps to counteract its effect by communicating with the most influential people of the territory.

The proclamation was as follows: "An army under my command enters New Mexico, to take possession of it in the name and for the benefit of the Confederate States. By geographical position, by similarity of institutions, by commercial interests, and by future destinies New Mexico pertains to the Confederacy.

"Upon the peaceful people of New Mexico the Confederate States wage no war. To them we come as friends, to re-establish a governmental connection agreeable and advantageous both to them and to us; to liberate them from the yoke of a military despotism erected by usurpers upon the ruins of the former free institutions of the United States; to relieve them from the iniquitous taxes

territorial legislature had authorized Governor Connelly, who had succeeded Governor Rencher, to call into service the whole force of the territory to resist invasion; in a message the governor congratulated the people upon their patriotism and declared that the Federal [297] force was sufficient to resist the invader from Texas.

and exactions imposed upon them by that usurpation; to insure and to revere their religion, and to restore their civil and political liberties.

"The existing war is one most wickedly waged by the United States upon the Confederate States for the subjugation and oppression of the latter by force of arms. It has already failed. Victory has crowned the arms of the Confederate States wherever an encounter worthy of being called a battle has been joined. Witness the battles of Bull Run, Manassas, of Springfield, of Lexington, of Leesburg, of Columbus, and the capture in the Mesilla valley of the whole force of the enemy by scarcely half their number.

"The army under my command is ample to seize and to maintain possession of New Mexico against any force which the enemy now has or is able to place within its limits. It is my purpose to accomplish this object without injury to the peaceful people of the country. Follow, then, quietly your peaceful avocations, and from my forces you have nothing to fear. Your persons, your families, and your property shall be secure and safe. Such forage and supplies as my army shall require will be purchased in open market and paid for at fair prices. If destroyed or removed to prevent me from availing myself of them, those who so co-operate with our enemies will be treated accordingly, and must prepare to share their fate.

"It is well known to me that many among you have already been forced by intimidation or inveigled by fraud into the ranks of our foes. The day will soon arrive when you can safely abjure their service. When it comes, throw down your arms and disperse to your homes, and you are safe. But persist in the service and you are lost.

"When the authority of the Confederate States shall be established in New Mexico, a government of your best men, to be conducted upon principles with which you are familiar and to which you are attached, will be inaugurated. Your religious, civil, and political rights and liberties will be re-established and maintained sacred and intact. In the meantime, by virtue of the powers vested in me by the President and Government of the Confederate States I abrogate and abolish the law of the United States levying taxes upon the people of New Mexico.

"To my old comrades in arms, still in the ranks of the usurpers of their Government and liberties, I appeal in the name of former friendship. Drop at once the arms which degrade you into tools of tyrants, renounce their service, and array yourselves under the colors of justice and freedom! I am empowered to receive you into the service of the Confederate States; the officers upon their commissions, the men upon their enlistments. By every principle of law and morality you are exonerated from service in the ranks of our enemies. You never engaged in the service of one portion of the old Union to fight against another portion, who, so far from being your enemies, have ever been your best friends. In the sight of God and man, you are justified in renouncing a service iniquitous in itself and in which you never engaged.

"Done at headquarters of the Army of New Mexico by me this 20th day of December, A. D. 1861. H. H. Sibley,
"Brigadier-General, Army C. S."

[297] *War of the Rebellion*, ser. I, vol. iv, p. 81. Colonel Canby's entire

On the 18th of February, 1862, General Sibley appeared before Fort Craig and a cavalry force was sent out by Colonel Canby for the purpose of defeating the apparent intention of the Confederates to pass to the west of the fort. This was only a manœuver on the part of the Confederates for the purpose of protecting their crossing of the Rio Grande some miles below the fort. Colonel Canby, after the crossing of the river had been accomplished by the enemy, threw detachments of the 5th, 7th,[298] and 10th regular infantry, and Car-

BATTLE OF VALVERDE

---

force in New Mexico at the time of Governor Connelly's message was as follows, according to the "field return" of the department of New Mexico:

GARRISONS, ETC.	PRESENT				Aggregate Present and Absent
	OFFICERS		MEN		
	For Duty	Total	For Duty	Total	
Fort Marcy...................	12	14	288	352	396
Fort Garland.................	3	3	102	125	130
Fort Union...................	39	40	721	869	1140
Alburquerque.................	28	29	502	624	720
Fort Craig and Vicinity.......	62	68	1803	2065	2266
Cubero	11	14	225	297	312
Abo Pass.....................	9	9	141	151	216
Hatch's Ranch................	5	5	25	39	191
Camp Connelly................	6	6	83	107	144
En Route to Santa Fé.........	1	1	39	53	59
En Route to Fort Wise........	1	1	70	70	72
Total	177	190	3999	4755	5646

In the month of January, prior to the departure of General Sibley from El Paso, the Federal commander was uncertain whether the invasion would be made by way of the Pecos river or up the Rio Grande, across the Jornada to Fort Craig. At this time the garrison at Fort Craig consisted of seventeen companies, among which six were regulars and nine volunteers; a force sufficient in the judgment of Colonel Canby to hold the post against any force that the Confederates could bring against it. It was believed that the country could not be invaded with more than 2,000 men in one body. If the invasion came by way of Pecos, Canby felt that Fort Craig could sustain itself until the invasion could be disposed of. If the demonstration came by way of Fort Craig, all the available force in the department was to be turned in that direction at once. Governor Connelly was requested to hold the militia in readiness for any service required of them; this service was the replacement of regulars and volunteers ordered withdrawn from posts not immediately threatened.

[298] Hayes, A. A., *An Unwritten Episode of the Late War*, pp. 166-167.

Colonel Canby, according to Hayes, gave his entire force as 3,810 and Sibley's as 2,600. In reality there were about 3,000 men in Sibley's command when it left Fort Fillmore. Colonel Canby's command was composed of eleven companies of the 5th, 7th and 10th U. S. infantry; seven troops of the 1st and 3d U. S. cavalry; McRae's battery, served by two companies of the 2d and 3d cavalry; Captain Dodd's company B, 2d Colorado volunteers; Lieutenant-Colonel Christopher Carson's 1st regiment New Mexico volunteers; 17 com-

son's and Pino's volunteers, across the river to prevent the occupation by the Confederates of the neighboring mesa which commanded the fort. The following afternoon the cavalry under Major Duncan and a light battery commanded by Captain McRae were also sent across and the Texans at once opened a heavy fire of artillery upon them. According to an account in a Santa Fé paper the volunteers in Pino's regiment behaved badly, in spite of the efforts of their officers to control them. Carson's regiment behaved well. The conduct [299] of the volunteers influenced Canby in returning that night

panies of 2d, 3d, 4th, and 5th New Mexico volunteers; a spy company and 1,000 militia. General Sibley's force consisted of Reily's and Green's regiments; five companies of Steele's regiment; five companies of Colonel Baylor's regiment; also Teel's and Riley's batteries. According to Hollister, in his *1st Regiment of Colorado Volunteers*, Captain Dodd's company had been in New Mexico, sent by Governor Gilpin, some months prior to the engagement at Valverde.

Hayes, A. A., in his *An Unwritten Episode of the Late War*, pp. 165, 166, says: "The number of regulars of all arms in the spring of 1862 was put by General Roberts at nine hundred. There were two regiments of New Mexico volunteers, the first having notable officers. The nominal colonel was Céran St. Vrain, the courtly French pioneer, frontiersman, and trader, whose name has been familiar for half a century on the border, in the nomenclature of the mountain region, and in books of travel and romances. The lieutenant-colonel, and acting commander, was Kit Carson; the major, J. F. Chaves; and one of the captains, Albert H. Pfeiffer, a very paladin of the frontier — a mild-mannered, blue-eyed, kindly man, and, in the estimation of his fellows, probably the most desperately courageous and successful Indian fighter in the West. The colonel of the second was Miguel Pino."

A number of the officers of minor grades in the regular army desired to accept commissions in the volunteers. Colonel Canby declined to permit this to be done, and as one of his reasons for this action, said: "The prejudice of the Mexican population towards the Americans is so great that if the field officers are taken altogether from the latter class, it is to be apprehended that it will delay, if it does not defeat, the organization of these regiments. This is not, perhaps, a good military reason, but it is a necessity, from the character of the people we have to deal with. I have also instructed two or three of the most efficient volunteer officers now in the service that, if they would induce the men of their regiments to enter the service for three years, I would recommend them for commissions as field officers. Colonel Gallegos and Lieutenant-Colonel Valdez are among them, and until I can learn what these men are going to do, I could give no definite answer to your question, even if there were no other obstacles to a favorable answer." — *Letter* of Colonel Canby to Col. G. R. Paul, Fort Union, New Mexico, January 15, 1862.

[299] Colonel Canby, like every other commander of the regular army who had preceded him since the American occupation and the revolution of 1847, had a very erroneous idea of the Mexican character. These ideas were undoubtedly formed from statements made to him by leading "Americans" then living in the territory. In January, 1862, in a report to the adjutant general of the army, he said, in commenting upon the fact that no funds had been received for the payment of the volunteer troops: "It is greatly to be apprehended that the volunteer forces already organized will melt away by desertion, and the people of New Mexico will be rendered still more apathetic than they now

to the fort. The Texans had been without water for an entire day, and that night they lost 200 mules, which were captured by the guards at Fort Craig while the animals were wandering about in search of water.

About eight o'clock, on the morning of the 21st, Canby ordered Colonel Roberts to proceed seven miles up the river, on the west bank, and keep the enemy from reaching the water at the only point where the sloping banks would permit. The action was begun with two hundred and twenty regular cavalry, together with McRae's battery, planted at the ford, and supported by two companies of regulars and two companies of Carson's regiment. A galling fire was opened upon the enemy. At half past eleven the remainder of the infantry came up, were thrown across the river and formed in line of battle. The Texans made a gallant charge, but were repulsed. Colonel Roberts now sent McRae's battery over, together with two twenty-four pounders under Lieutenant Hall. The fire of the artillery continued until after three o'clock, when Colonel Canby, with Pino's regiment of volunteers, came on the field. He was about to order a general advance, when a demonstration on the part of a portion of the Confederate right drew off a part of the infantry supporting McRae's battery. Immediately it was charged by a thousand Texans [300] under Steele, who had been drawn up in a thick wood

---

are, even if the disaffected of both classes are not stimulated into active opposition to the government. The Mexican people have no affection for the institutions of the United States; they have a strong, but hitherto restrained hatred for the Americans as a race, and there are not wanting persons who, from the commencement of their troubles, have secretly but industriously endeavoured to keep alive all the elements of discontent and fan them into flames. The long-deferred payment of the volunteers has given so much plausibility and coloring to their representation as to have produced a marked and pernicious influence upon these ignorant and impulsive people.'' — *War of the Rebellion*, ser. i, vol. iv, pp. 84-85.

[300] Greeley, Horace, *American Conflict*, vol. ii, p. 22, says: ''When his (Sibley's) advance, 250 strong, under Major Pyron, reached Valverde, a point, at 8 A. M., where the river bottom was accessible, fully seven miles from the fort, they found themselves confronted by a portion of our regular cavalry, Lt.-Col. Roberts, with two efficient batteries, Capt. McRae and Lieut. Hall, supported by a large force of regular and volunteer infantry. Our batteries opening upon him, Pyron greatly outnumbered, recoiled, with some loss, and our troops exultingly crossed the river to the east bank, where a thick wood covered a concentration of the enemy's entire force. The day wore on, until nearly 2 P. M., when Sibley, who had risen from a sick bed that morning, was compelled to dismount and quit the field, turning the command-in-chief over to Col. Thomas Green, of the 5th Texas, whose regiment had meantime been ordered to the front. The battle was continued, mainly with artillery, wherein

Gross, Blackwell & Company, and Employes, 1881

and behind some sand-hills. This was a most desperate charge, the men relying principally upon their revolvers and bowie-knives, and being maddened by thirst. Volley after volley of grape and cannister was poured into the courageous enemy as they made a desper-

---

the Federal superiority, both in guns and service, was decided, so that the Texans were losing the most men in spite of their comparatively sheltered position. To protract the fight in this manner was to expose his men to constant decimation without a chance of success. Canby, who had reached the field at 1 P. M., considered the day his own and was about to order a general advance, when he found himself anticipated by Green, at whose command his men, armed mainly with revolvers, burst from the wooded cover and leaped over the line of low sand-hills behind which they had lain and made a desperate rush upon McRae's battery confronting them. . . . Our supporting infantry, twice or thrice the Texans in number, and including more than man for man of regulars, shamefully withstood every entreaty to charge. They lay grovelling in the sand in the rear of the battery until the Texans came so near as to make their revolvers dangerous, when the whole herd ran madly down to and across the river, save those who were overtaken by a cowardly death on the way.

"Simultaneously with this charge in front, Maj. Raguet, commanding the Texas left, charged our right at the head of his cavalry, but the disparity of numbers was so great that he was easily repulsed."

Mr. A. Mennet, of Las Vegas, New Mexico, who was in the fight at Valverde, on the Confederate side, stated to the writer that "on the morning of February 21, 1862, General Sibley, commanding the Confederate army, remained in his ambulance near the battle field; mention was made by a number of men in the command that he was so much under the influence of liquor that Colonel Tom Green was obliged to assume command. The Federals crossed over to our side of the river with a battery of two guns under Lieutenant McRae. In the afternoon Major Lockridge called for 500 volunteers to charge the battery which soon fell into our hands, notwithstanding its being supported by a large force of volunteers and some regulars. Our loss was comparatively light compared with that of the enemy. We suffered the loss of our brave commander, Major Lockridge, who fell while leading the charge. Lieutenant McRae, commanding the battery, fought and died like a hero, defending his guns."

Captain A. Mennet is a native of Switzerland, having been born in Switzerland in the year 1840. He came to the United States while yet a youth and located in St. Louis in 1859, which city he shortly left for New Mexico. He joined Col. John R. Baylor's command at El Paso, prior to the fall of Fort Fillmore. He took part in the battle of Valverde and assisted in the capture of McRae's battery; with Sibley's army he marched as far north as Alburquerque, and in the retreat of that general, after the battle of Glorieta, accompanied the last division of his troops. General Sibley's command was reorganized at San Antonio, Texas, and in the reorganization Captain Mennet was commissioned a second lieutenant of Alderete's company and was later transferred to the "Brigand Company," which was composed of New Mexicans and Arizonans. He shortly received his promotion to a first lieutenancy and in 1863 was made a captain in Colonel Medicine's regiment of cavalry. After the war he served as an interpreter under Colonel Dupin, of the French army, in Nuevo Leon and Tamaulipas, Mexico, in the days of the Emperor Maximilian. In 1866 he returned to the United States by way of Vera Cruz, Havana, and New Orleans. Two years later he entered the employ of Otero, Sellar & Company, Hays City, Kansas, continuing with that company until 1881, when he joined the organization of the Browne & Manzanares Company, with whom he has since that time been continuously associated.

ate rush upon McRae's battery. They were a thousand when they started; in a few minutes a hundred had been slain and wounded. But all in vain. Captain McRae, disdaining surrender, was killed upon one of his guns. Lieutenant Michler also fell and Lieutenant Bell was twice wounded. The supporting troops acted very badly; the guns were lost and Canby's army, driven across the river, retired in great disorder to the fort, leaving the route up the valley of the Rio Grande free to the victorious enemy. No part of the Federal army stopped until safely within the walls of Fort Craig. The guns of McRae's battery were lost and many small arms were taken by the enemy. The losses of men were about equal,[301] 60 killed and 140 wounded on either side. Among the Confederate dead or severely wounded in the decisive charge were Lieutenant-Colonel Sutton,

---

[301] Bancroft, H. H., *History of Arizona and New Mexico*, p. 696, says: "This fight of Valverde, as it is known, reflected little credit on the federal arms. Many individuals and a few companies fought bravely, but such is the discrepancy of testimony that I make no attempt to point out cases of bravery or cowardice, blunders or wise management. The Texans, though victorious, lost probably more than the Federals, whose loss was about 90 killed and mortally wounded and 100 wounded."

Hollister, *1st Regiment of Colorado Volunteers*, says that the Federal loss was 64 killed, 26 mortally wounded, 100 wounded; Texans, 200 killed, 200 wounded. Lossing, *Pictorial History of the War*, says the Federals lost 62 killed and 142 wounded; the Texans about the same.

Reports of Colonel Ed. R. S. Canby, February 22 and March 1, 1862: "Orders were accordingly sent to Captain Selden to fall back slowly and cover the retreat, and to the other commanders to recross the river. The movement of Selden's column, four companies of the 5th infantry, in the immediate presence and under the fire of the enemy, was admirably executed, the command moving with deliberation, halting occasionally to allow the wounded to keep up with it, and many of the men picking up and carrying with them, the arms of their dead comrades. The other columns, under the personal superintendence of Colonel Roberts, crossed over without disorder, confusion or loss.

"On the west bank of the river, the troops that had escaped from the battle were found to be much scattered, but the regular troops were easily collected and sent forward in the direction of the fort. Pino's regiment — of which only one company (Sena's) and part of another, could be induced to cross the river — was in the wildest confusion, and no efforts of their own officers, or of my staff, could restore any kind of order. More than one hundred men from this regiment deserted from the field.

"The battle was fought almost entirely by the regular troops (trebled in number by the Confederates), with no assistance from the militia, and but little from the volunteers, who would not obey orders, or obeyed them too late to be of any service. The immediate cause of the disaster at Valverde was the refusal of one of the volunteer regiments to cross the river and support the left wing of the army. The contemporary operations of the right wing were eminently successful, but the confusion produced by the loss of the battery could not be remedied in season to retrieve the fortunes of the day. The retreat was effected in good order, and without further loss."

Major Lockridge, Captains Lang and Heurel, and several lieutenants. Colonel W. L. Robards and Major Raguet were also wounded. Captain N. B. Rossel, of the regulars, was captured while crossing the river.

General Sibley decided that there was no danger in leaving Canby's army in his rear and, leaving his wounded at Socorro, advanced to Alburquerque and Santa Fé which fell without resistance. A very few of the prominent native citizens cast their lot with the Confederacy, including one of the wealthy Armijo families at Alburquerque, but the great mass of the people not only adhered to the Union, but, with a vivid memory of the past, hated the Texans with an honest hatred.[302]

At Cubero, sixty miles west of Alburquerque, there was stationed a small command of New Mexican volunteers, having charge of some commissary and ordnance stores. Through the efforts of some Confederate sympathizers this post surrendered and some sixty muskets and three thousand rounds of ammunition fell into the hands of General Sibley.

At Alburquerque there was a large supply of stores in charge of Captain Herbert M. Enos, assistant quartermaster. On the 1st of March he learned that the Confederates, numbering four hundred cavalry, had reached the town of Belen. Immediately he ordered the ammunition wagons to be taken to Santa Fé, and in the evening ordered the burning of the balance of the stores. The provisions and supplies were rescued by the inhabitants and some of the wagons were captured near the Sandia mountains. The most valuable supplies were located at Santa Fé and Major Pyron was ordered to the capital with a force sufficient to capture the city. The Federal of-

[302] Hayes, A. A., in his *Unwritten Episode of the Late War*, p. 168, says that the conduct of the native New Mexicans, after the battle of Valverde, in adhering to the Union "must have been sadly disappointing and infinitely annoying to Sibley and his adjutant, the same Jackson who was Davis' partisan in 1851, and late Secretary of the Territory . . . it should be made known that they brought money, mules and provisions, and placed them at the disposal of the National troops, greatly no doubt, to the gallant but deluded ex-secretary's surprise. Still, Sibley doubtless reasoned that this was a small matter, and that all would be well when he should be safely in possession of the booty at the Fort Union arsenal; and he knew well the road thither through Apache Canon — just as the Persian Hydarnes, in B. C. 480, doubtless knew well the road to some Grecian Fort Union through the Pass of Thermopylae. The only obstacle was a few of those brave men who in every age and country are in the best sense Spartans."

ficers, however, had anticipated this movement and, on the 4th of March, sent forward to Fort Union a train of one hundred and twenty wagons, escorted by the entire Federal force at the post.

The Confederate commander determined to concentrate his entire force at Santa Fé and in due time proceed against Fort Union, hoping to repeat the successes of his army at Valverde, but he was doomed to disappointment.

The reports of Canby's defeat and the Confederate advance soon reached the territory of Colorado, of which as we have seen William Gilpin was at the time the governor.

BATTLES OF APACHE CANYON AND PIGEON'S RANCH He had been active in the organization of troops and when the news came of Sibley's success he had already moved, as far as the Raton pass, an efficient body of loyal, frontier fighting men. The Colorado volunteers marched from Denver on February 22d, the day after the engagement at Valverde, through snow nearly a foot deep, and reached the foot of the Raton mountains on March 7th. After crossing the mountains, marching sixty-seven miles in a single day, the force reached Fort Union on the 11th, where they were thoroughly armed and equipped by Major Paul, U. S. A. A portion of the command setting out in advance for the purpose of recapturing Santa Fé from the small Confederate force which was reported to be there, unexpectedly met Major Pyron with his Texan troops at Apache canyon. A fierce engagement ensued later. The Colorado volunteers had marched along the Santa Fé trail in the direction of Glorieta, when at midnight the presence of the Confederate pickets was discovered. The following morning, March 27th, these were surprised and captured, together with two Confederate lieutenants.[303] Major J. M. Chivington was in command of the Colorado troops, consisting of two hundred and ten cavalry and one hun-

---

[303] *Letter from a Confederate Soldier*, war relic room, State House, Denver, Colorado.

The impression which the Confederates under Pyron received of the gallantry and fighting qualities of the Colorado troops is well stated in a letter from a Confederate soldier who was in this engagement. "If it had not been for those devils from Pike's Peak, this country would have been ours . . . Instead of Mexicans and Regulars, they were regular demons, that iron and lead had no effect upon, in the shape of Pike's Peakers. Up the canyon we went for four miles, when we met the enemy coming down at double quick, but the grape and shell soon stopped them. But before we could form in line of battle their infantry was upon the hills on both sides of us, shooting us down like sheep. . . . They had no sooner got within shooting distance of us than

dred and eighty infantry. The command moved forward to the head of the canyon when a battery of two guns, occupying the main road, opened upon them with grape and shell. Finding himself under a destructive fire Chivington deployed two companies of sixty men as skirmishers on the mountain side to the left of the road and one company was also advanced to higher ground on the right. The mountain sides were covered with a growth of pine, piñon and dwarf cedar. For more than an hour the opposing infantry kept up a stubborn firing, when Captain Jacob Downing,[304] commanding the Union forces on the right, succeeded in partly flanking the enemy's position.

The Texans now showed signs of retreat, when the cavalry under Captain Cook charged them gallantly, running the Texans down

---

up came a company of cavalry at full charge, with swords and revolvers drawn, looking like so many flying devils. On they came, to what I supposed certain destruction, but nothing like lead or iron seemed to stop them, for we poured both into them from every side like hail in a storm. In a moment these devils had run the gauntlet for half a mile and were fighting hand to hand with our men in the road. The houses that I spoke of before were 700 or 800 yards to the right of the road, with a wide ditch between it and them. Here we felt safe, but again were mistaken. No sooner did they see us than some of them jumped the ditch, and like demons, came charging on us. It looked as if their horses' feet never touched the ground until they were among us.''

[304] *Journal* of Major Downing. Major Downing gives the following account of the events leading up to the coming of the Colorado troops and the battle at Apache canyon or Glorieta: "We went into camp at Weld (Colorado) and the regiment was drilled there and spent the winter of 1861 in quarters. We then got news of Canby that the battle of Valverde had been fought; that he had been whipped and had applied for assistance. The question was about marching, but the Colonel did not show any disposition to move, so I wrote an article signed 'Union,' urging that the regiment be sent to the front to help Canby. After the publication of this article I was placed under arrest. But after a time the regiment got so mutinous about being detained here that Colonel Slough had it announced that he had received orders from General Hunter to go to the assistance of Canby. Then he gave the orders to march. I was released and headed my company — D. We marched six miles that afternoon in six inches of snow. The men were poorly clad, didn't have enough to keep them warm. The guns were of mixed variety and not all of the same caliber. The next morning we started and marched about forty miles, there being about three feet of snow on the Divide. We kept it up until we reached the point called Red River, and there the Colonel thought the men couldn't stand the continued forced march, but I made up my mind to march that night, and the companies fell in. The Colonel joined us about midnight; and we continued to Maxwell's ranch, on the Cimarron. Next morning we started for Fort Union, and arrived about eight o'clock in the evening, and went into camp outside the fort. We were armed, clothed and furnished with plenty of commissary and quartermaster's stores — arms and ammunition. Then we started to meet the Texans, approaching from Santa Fé, sending four companies as an advance. We met the enemy about eleven o'clock in Apache canyon, and had a battle with their advance, whipped them and drove them back, killing

under their horses' feet. At the same time they were pressed by Downing's men and driven up a side canyon where they were received with volleys from the men under Captains Anthony and Wyncoop,[305] resulting in the surrender of about seventy of the Texans. It was now near sunset and fearing reënforcements would overtake them in the darkness, and there being no water in the canyon, the Union forces fell back to Pigeon's ranch, where they encamped. The Union loss in this engagement was five killed and fourteen wounded. The Confederates suffered heavily, losing seventy-one prisoners, thirty-five killed, and forty-three wounded.

"This seems to have been a drawn battle," says Hayes. "The great fight was on the 28th, when the Texans had come up in force, and Colonel Slough [306] had arrived with the rest of his regiment, two

---

quite a number, and taking about one hundred and fifty prisoners. Our bugler came in sounding the alarm and we marched to the point of rocks where we could see them. They had two batteries in position. Company D, of which I was captain, crossed the front of the batteries and got into the timber on the right. Companies A and E, Captains Scott Anthony and Wyncoop, went in on the left. When Company D got almost to the rear and on the flank it opened fire, and I gave the signal to Major Chivington that we were opening the fight and charged down upon the batteries. Company K was ordered then to charge, being mounted. Riding down the canyon on a narrow road, a ravine on one side and a mountain on the other, it gallantly charged the enemy. The Texans made two further stands, but we drove them back, and that closed the battle for the first day, after gathering up the prisoners. The whole time covered was probably between four and five hours. Then we fell back to Pigeon's Ranch because there was water there and we could not get it anywhere else in the canyon, and waited for the approach of the main column.''

Hayes, A. A., *Unwritten Episode of the Late War*: "Zat Chivington," said the excellent M. Valle to the writer, "he poot 'is 'ead down, and foight loike mahd bull!"

[305] Major Wyncoop, a prominent citizen of Colorado after the war, moved to New Mexico in the eighties and lived at Santa Fé where he died. He was at one time warden of the New Mexico penitentiary. He was a gallant soldier and a good citizen.

[306] John P. Slough was the descendant of an English family which came to America before the Revolution. Matthias Slough, his ancestor, was the first colonel named by General Washington after the latter had been chosen as commander-in-chief of the colonial troops. His father, General John P. Slough, was a native of Ohio. In 1856, Colonel Slough came to Denver where he was engaged in the practice of the law when the Civil War began. Under direction of Governor Gilpin he raised the 1st Colorado volunteers and became its colonel. After the battles at Apache canyon and Glorieta he was summoned to Washington by President Lincoln; he was soon named military governor of Alexandria, Virginia; here he had command of the reserve forces detailed for the protection of the national capital. General Slough was one of the military pall-bearers at the funeral obsequies of President Lincoln. He was appointed chief justice of the supreme court of New Mexico by President Johnson. At the session of the supreme court in 1867 he wrote one of the three opinions

howitzer batteries under Captains Ritter and Claflin, and some regular infantry, prominent among the officers of whom were Captains W. H. Lewis, 5th regiment, and A. B. Carey, 13th regiment. At an early hour in the morning was conceived and put into execution a strategical movement of great merit. A brave New Mexican, Manuel Chaves,[307] led a detachment of about four hundred men, commanded by Chivington, and comprising two battalions of regulars and volunteers under Lewis and Carey, up a steep ascent and along a terribly difficult path toward the rear of the Texans, where were their wagons and supplies of all kinds under a guard.''

that were rendered and during that year announced an important decision in which the Pueblo Indians were declared to be citizens of the United States.

On Sunday, December 15, 1867, Chief Justice Slough was shot and killed in the office of the Fonda (Old Exchange Hotel) at the corner of the plaza in Santa Fé, by Captain W. L. Rynerson, at that time a member of the territorial legislature from the county of Doña Ana.

[307] Colonel Manuel Chaves was a lineal descendant of General Fernando Duran de Chaves, one of the officers with the re-conquistador, Don Diego de Vargas. The family dates back to the twelfth century. Don Bernardino Duran de Chaves, son of Don Fernando, had a child, Diego Antonio de Chaves, whose son, Pedro de Chaves, married Doña Catalina Baca, of Tomé, Valencia county, New Mexico. A sister of Doña Catalina was the indirect cause of the massacre of nearly all the inhabitants of the town of Tomé by Comanche Indians. Don Pedro de Chaves had a number of children, among whom was Don Julian Chaves, the father of Don Manuel, whose full name was Manuel Antonio Chaves. Don Manuel was born in the town of Atrisco, opposite the city of Alburquerque on the 18th day of October, 1818. His mother was Doña Maria de la Luz Garcia de Noriega, a daughter of Captain Francisco Garcia de Noriega. In 1844 he was married to Doña Vincenta Labadie, a great grand-daughter of the famous Spanish captain, Don Sebastian Martin. He died at his home, at San Mateo, Valencia county, New Mexico, in 1889, leaving a family of eight children, one of whom, Don Amado, was the first superintendent of public instruction of New Mexico, and who has held many offices of trust in New Mexico. Another son, Don Ireneo, was an official translator of the court of private land claims and also clerk of the court. Colonel Manuel Chaves was an Indian fighter and took part in a bitter campaign against the Navajós when only sixteen years of age. He was a resident of Santa Fé when General Kearny took possession of the city. He held a commission under General Manuel Armijo and was one of the officers under that general who was in favor of holding the Apache pass against Kearny and his troops. He was accused of being one of the conspirators for the uprising of December, 1846. He was placed in prison by order of General Sterling Price, was tried by court martial, defended by Captain Angney, one of Price's officers, and acquitted. When the revolution broke out at Taos in January, 1847, Colonel Chaves enlisted as a private soldier under Colonel Céran St. Vrain and fought with the American troops in all the battles ending with the engagement at Taos. In 1855 he was in command of troops in a campaign against the Utes and Jicarilla Apaches. In a fight with these savages, a young Apache chief, lance in hand, charged upon Chaves, who killed him with a shot from his rifle. During this campaign he participated in engagements with the Indians at Cochotopa pass, Nepesta, Cerro Blanco and El Rito, in all of which his troops were victorious. In 1859 he took part in the campaign against the

The remainder of Slough's command,[308] seven or eight hundred strong, met the Confederates half a mile beyond Pigeon's ranch. The Unionists were outnumbered and acted on the defensive, and after a fight lasting about five hours were forced back to a new position half a mile farther east and finally to Kozlosky's ranch and stage station. The Union loss in this battle is given at from twenty

---

Apaches under Mangas Coloradas. When the Civil War broke out he was offered a commission in the Confederate army by Colonel W. W. Loring, then in command of the department at Santa Fé. He declined with thanks and later became lieutenant-colonel of the 2d regiment, New Mexico volunteers, taking part in the battles of Valverde and Apache canyon. Colonel Chaves was a man of small stature, but his powers of endurance were remarkable. In fights with Indians he was pierced with arrows many times. Indeed, these old wounds were the ultimate causes of his death.

Asa B. Carey, brigadier-general, U. S. A. retired, was born in the state of Connecticut; appointed to West Point Military Academy from that state, July 1, 1854; breveted second lieutenant, 6th U. S. Inf., July 1, 1858; appointed second lieutenant, 7th U. S. Inf., October 22, 1858; first lieutenant, 13th U. S. Inf., October 24, 1861; appointed major and paymaster, October 5, 1867; lieutenant colonel, department paymaster general, March 27, 1895; colonel, assistant paymaster general, June 10, 1898; brigadier-general, paymaster-general, January 30, 1899; retired, July 12, 1899.

In 1860 this officer marched with his regiment from Utah to New Mexico. From April, 1860, to September, 1861, with his company participated in campaign against the Navajós, under command of Colonel Canby. During 1861-1862, after return from Navajó campaign, he served as depot quartermaster at Alburquerque and at Fort Union. Took prominent part in battle of Glorieta, helping capture and destroy the Confederate wagon train. Upon the creation of eastern district of New Mexico commanded troops in that district — comprising all of New Mexico east of the Pecos river, with headquarters at Fort Union. In the campaign of 1863 against the Navajós assigned to duty as chief quartermaster under the command of Colonel Christopher Carson, and was with Carson's force until May, 1864. After close of the Navajó campaign served as chief quartermaster of the department of New Mexico. In 1865 served as mustering officer and mustered all the volunteer troops in New Mexico out of service. General Carey was stationed at Santa Fé as chief paymaster from 1868 to 1874 and thereafter served in the office of the paymaster-general at Washington. He was considered a very able officer and served his country with distinction in New Mexico.

[308] Hayes, A. A., *Unwritten Episode of the War*, p. 169: "There is no doubt that the Texans surprised the force left under Slough to fight them in front. Sibley was not in command — a fact which, after the fiercest recrimination among his informants, the author only ascertained beyond a doubt by an interview with the barber who shaved him that very morning, twenty miles away from the scene of action. He seems to have been supplied (perhaps for medical purposes!) with whiskey. The actual commander was Colonel W. R. Scurry, who was not killed, but lived to fight again (a fact which the author commends to the thoughtful consideration of the friends in Santa Fé who proposed to show him the grave where Scurry was buried in the town cemetery).

"M. Valle, or Pigeon, says, 'Gooverment manns vas at my ranch, and fill 'is cahnteen viz my whiskey (and Gooverment nevaire pay me for zat viskey); and Texas mahns coom oop, and soorprize zem, and zey foight six hour by my vatch, and *my vatch vas slow!*' "

Builders and Operators of the Atchison, Topeka & Santa Fé Railroad

1. William B. Strong, President. 2. A. A. Robinson, Chief Engineer and General Manager. 3. George B. Lake, Assistant Engineer. 4. W. R. Morley, Assistant Engineer. 5. Avery Turner, the conductor of the first railroad train operated in New Mexico

to fifty killed, forty to eighty wounded, and fifteen to twenty prisoners; that of the Confederates, thirty-six to one hundred and fifty killed, sixty to two hundred wounded, and one hundred prisoners.

When Colonel Chivington and his command, led by Colonel Manuel Chaves, reached the Confederate rear, they drove off the enemy's guard, spiked the cannon, bayonetted eleven hundred mules, burned sixty-four wagons, and destroyed all of the Confederate supplies, thus rendering it impossible for the Confederates to continue their offensive operations. "This," says Bancroft, "virtually ended the campaign; the 'Pike's Peakers' had proved more than a match for the 'Texan Rangers,' saving New Mexico for the Union; and Chivington, presiding elder of the Methodist church in Colorado, had made himself the hero of the war."

Colonel Scurry, having received word of the disaster in his rear, sent in a flag of truce, asking an armistice for the purpose of burying his dead, and caring for his wounded. This was granted by Slough. The Confederates, however, retreated to Santa Fé, which place was shortly abandoned and the retreat continued down the valley of the Rio Grande.

Colonel Canby now sent orders to Slough to protect Fort Union, and, much against the wishes of his troops, the army fell back to the fort, arriving on April 2d. Slough now resigned his commission,[309] and new orders having been received, under command of Colonel Paul, the army marched southward. Galisteo was reached on the 10th where a staff officer from Canby met the command.

Colonel Canby,[310] leaving Fort Craig garrisoned by volunteers

---

[309] Col. Slough resigned because of his disgust at not being permitted to pursue the Confederates. On the 9th, according to Hayes, Colonel Paul marched from Bernal Spring toward Santa Fé, meeting on the way Major Jackson and party, with a flag of truce, and soon learned that Santa Fé had been evacuated. On the 12th he wrote from Galisteo that the Union troops had been cheered on entering the capital.

[310] Hayes, A. A., *Unwritten Episode of the War*, p. 170: "One cannot write the history of this remarkable campaign without mentioning the strong opinion of some of Carson's fiery fighters, and even at least one officer of distinction and experience, that victory was within their grasp at Valverde, and lost by mismanagement; but no suggestion of what 'might have been' can be allowed to weigh against the splendid reputation of Canby. Nor can one entertain any animadversions against him for not capturing the whole rebel force after Peralta, inasmuch as it is perfectly well known that he had no desire to take prisoners whom he could not feed; and, inasmuch, also, as his judgment in this regard was more than borne out by the subsequent reduction of his own men to quarter rations."

Colonel Canby was massacred by the Modoc Indians, a victim to the results

under Colonel Kit Carson, on April 1st, had marched northward with eight hundred and sixty regulars and three hundred and fifty volunteers.

In the retreat a portion of Sibley's disorganized force had reached Alburquerque, and here, on the 8th of April, a portion of the Union forces made a demonstration; nothing effective was accomplished, however, and these troops proceeded to Tijeras canyon on the 13th, where they joined the main body of Union troops under Colonel Paul. The following day, Major Chivington having succeeded to the colonelcy of the Colorado regiment, the regulars and volunteers proceeded to Peralta, where the Confederates were posted. Colonel Chivington was extremely anxious to assault the Confederate position [311] but Canby would give no orders to that effect. The Confederate forces belonged to the commands of Pyron, Steele, Scurry, and Greene. The Texans [312] took advantage of a stormy night,

---

of the villainous treatment of Indians by white civilians. This occurred at Lava Beds, California, April 11, 1873. His rank at the time was brigadier-general, U. S. A.

"Away in the West," says Hayes, "these brave officers and men fought like heroes for their country (from what they saved her let the reader form his own conclusions), and what was their reward? Practically nothing; . . . That these events were not known, and have not since been known in the East, is hardly surprising, in view of the fact that other matters of transcendant importance, far nearer home, were contemporaneous with them. Fort Henry was taken on February 6th, Roanoke Island on February 8th, and Fort Donelson on February 16th. The battle of Pea Ridge ended on March 8th, the *Monitor* fought the *Merrimac* on March 9th, and the great engagement at Shiloh occurred on April 6th and 7th. Probably not one in ten thousand suspected that such a threatening movement was making in the rear of our armies; and it would have been equally surprising and terrible to have heard suddenly that a junction had been effected with the Mormons, and that mischief had already been done which could be repaired, if at all, only at the cost of hundreds of lives and millions of money. Instead of this, the bright days of May saw Sibley, disheartened and demoralized, resting at the same Fort Bliss from which he had marched with fell purpose four months before. The valley of the Rio Grande would know him no more, and he doubtless sought his accustomed consolation in the flowing bowl."

[311] Bancroft, H. H., *History of Arizona and New Mexico*, p. 698: "On the 15th a belated Texan train coming in sight from Alburquerque was captured by thirty mounted Coloradoans, who lost one man and killed four, taking one gun, a dozen prisoners, seventy mules, and fifteen horses. Presently the Confederates opened fire with their artillery, which was answered, the firing being continued to some extent all day, with but slight and unrecorded effect. The Colorado troops retired to the river, and planned an attack under cover of the banks, but Canby forbade the movement. He is accused of an unwillingness to kill his old comrades, of jealousy toward the volunteers, and even of cowardice."

[312] Colonel Chivington says: "They disputed our crossing for four days and nights whenever we attempted to cross; and we tried to get sufficiently far in advance to cross without being subjected to their artillery fire. On the

forded the river and escaped. In order to escape an engagement with Canby, Sibley determined to take advantage of a great bend of the Rio Grande to the west, and having abandoned a part of his wagon train,[313] to cross the mountainous country through the canyons, thereby cutting off many miles of heavy marching. Seven days' rations were packed on mules, the wagons abandoned, and all

---

fourth night they burned their transportation, and abandoned everything except some light vehicles, packed their provisions, and took to the mountains.''

Hayes, A. A., *Unwritten Episode of the War*, p. 170, says, relative to the demonstration at Alburquerque, that "April 15th, the troops fell on Sibley's rear, capturing a large train and a number of prisoners, and killing many of the escort. The next day the town (Peralta) was bombarded, and during the following night Sibley escaped across the river under cover of the darkness, and in a sand-storm of long duration. His rear was again attacked, and more damage done.''

Hayes also says of the ''demonstration'' at Alburquerque, that Major Duncan, 3d cavalry, was seriously wounded. Chivington says that "they fought all day at long range, and at night Canby took a side route and attempted to form a junction with us, and Sibley escaped down the Rio Grande with his force.''

[313] After a close pursuit of one hundred and fifty miles, says Colonel B. S. Roberts, "he was obliged to break up his force into small parties, having left all along the line of his retreat his ambulances, and the private and public stores of his entire command.''

Colonel Canby officially reported him as having left behind "in dead and wounded, and in sick and prisoners, one half of his original force.''

During the Confederate occupation of Alburquerque eight mountain howitzers which had belonged to the government of the United States and had been captured by Sibley were buried in a field nearly opposite the present home of Major H. R. Whiting. Many years afterward their location was described to Major Whiting, who found them under about eighteen inches of earth, though the Confederate officer (Major Teel) informed him that they had been buried several feet deep. Two of these guns (Napoleons) are now in the custody of the Grand Army of the Republic post at Alburquerque. It is worthy of note that at the time of the breaking out of hostilities General Longstreet, distinguished in the Civil War, was serving as major and paymaster at Alburquerque.

Bancroft, H. H., *Ibid*, pp. 698-699, writing of the retreat by Sibley says: "On the 16th and 17th the armies advanced slowly southward in sight of each other on opposite sides of the river, the Texans burning some of their baggage on the way to La Joya; but on the 18th the confederates had disappeared, to be seen no more, leaving, however, some of their sick and disabled, with a few wagons which were found by Captain Grayden on a trip to the western side.''

Canby in his official report quotes a prisoner as having told him "that out of the 3,800 men and 327 wagons that were with us when we left Fort Fillmore, only 1,200 men and 13 wagons remained together when they were obliged to flee to the mountains.''

One of the prisoners taken by Canby, at the time of the retreat, was ex-Surveyor General William Pelham.

Horace Greeley, in his *American Conflict*, states that "Sibley, in his weakened condition, evidently did not like this proximity. 'In order,' as he says in his report, 'to avoid the contingency of another action in our then crippled condition,' he set his forces silently in motion soon after nightfall, not down the river, but over the trackless mountains, through a desolate, waterless waste,

heavy baggage destroyed. The route was a most difficult one, there being no water or roads, but Sibley was equal to this emergency. In ten days, on seven days' rations, he reached a point on the lower Rio Grande where supplies had been ordered sent to him. The troops were quartered at every village along the Rio Grande from Doña Ana to Fort Bliss.

General Sibley having made good his escape, the Union forces under Colonels Paul, Chivington, and Captain Morris, crossed the Rio Grande near Socorro and there learned definitely of the direction taken by Sibley in his flight for the lower country. Following down the river the troops passed over the battle field of Valverde, the volunteers camping on the spot, and the regular troops proceeding to Fort Craig. Colonel Canby [314] declined to further pursue the re-

---

abandoning most of his wagons, but packing seven days' provisions on mules, and thus giving his adversary the slip. Dragging his cannon by hand up and down the sides of most rugged mountains. . . . He naively reports that 'sufficient funds in Confederate paper was provided them to meet every want, if it be negotiated;' and honors the brothers Rafael and Manuel Armijo — wealthy native merchants — who, on his arrival at Alburquerque, had boldly avowed their sympathy with the Confederate cause, and placed stores containing $200,000 worth of goods at his disposal. He states that, when he evacuated Alburquerque, they abandoned luxurious homes to identify their future fortunes with those of the Southern Confederacy, and considerately adds, 'I trust they will not be forgotten in the final settlement.' In closing, General Sibley expresses the unflattering conviction that 'except for its political geographical position, the Territory of New Mexico is not worth a quarter of the blood expended in its conquest;' and intimates that his soldiers would decidedly object to returning to that inhospitable, undesirable country. These and kindred considerations had induced his return to Fort Bliss, Texas, and now impelled him to meditate a movement without orders still further down the country.''

[314] In 1865 Colonel Christopher Carson was promoted to brigadier-general of volunteers for his gallantry at Valverde and other services.

In his report of the battle of Valverde Colonel Canby mentions the fact that Sena's company of volunteers was one of two that did not refuse to cross the river. It may be well here to state that the Sena referred to by Canby was Major José D. Sena. Major Sena was a native of Santa Fé, having been born at the capital in 1837. His father was Don Juan Sena, a native of Mexico, who came to the territory of New Mexico and engaged in mercantile pursuits. At the outbreak of the Civil War Major Sena, together with Colonel Francisco Perea, raised a company which became a part of Pino's regiment of volunteers. He was made captain and for meritorious services during the Confederate invasion was promoted to major. At the battle of Valverde, leading his men across the river, while in mid-stream he found himself in a shower of bullets fired by both friend and foe. At the close of the war, and while General Carleton was in command of the department, Major Sena had charge of the rebuilding of Fort Marcy (Santa Fé). Resigning his commission, Major Sena became sheriff of Santa Fé county, which office he held for twelve years. He occupied many offices of honor and trust and for many years was an interpreter in the courts of New Mexico, in which profession he had few if

treating foe and shortly returned to Santa Fé, leaving the southern district in command of Colonel Chivington. On the 7th of August the "California Column," under command of General James H. Carleton, reached the Rio Grande, and on the 21st day of September of that year he assumed command of the department. The "California Column" originally consisted of the 1st California infantry, ten companies, under the command of Colonel James H. Carleton; 1st California cavalry, five companies, under command of Lieutenant-Colonel E. E. Eyre, Lieutenant-Colonel Davis having resigned and gone east, was killed at Beverly Ford, Virginia, June 9, 1863; Light Battery A, U. S. artillery, under command of Lieutenant John B. Shinn, and Company B, 2d California cavalry, under the command of Captain John C. Cremony. This command contained 1,500 men, well drilled, well disciplined, and all eager to show their soldierly qualities. Before leaving California there was added to the troops above mentioned, the 5th California infantry, under command of Colonel George W. Bowie, which brought the strength of the "Column" to about 2,350 men, rank and file. The first news of the coming of the "Column" conveyed to Colonel Canby came from John Jones, an express rider, sent forward by Carleton, along with Sergeant William Wheeling, Company F, 1st infantry, and a Mexican named Chaves. The last two were killed by the Apaches, and horribly mutilated. Jones succeeded in making his escape and reached the Rio Grande, at Picacho, about five miles above Mesilla. Here he was taken prisoner by the Confederates and brought before Colonel Steele, who examined him, threw him into jail, relieved him of his despatches, which contained the information of Carleton's coming. He managed, however, while in jail to communicate with Unionists on the outside and sent word to Colonel Canby of the approach of the command under Carleton.

any superiors. He read law at Alexandria, Virginia, was admitted to the bar and became a most successful advocate, particularly in criminal cases. He held the office of register of the U. S. land office. In politics he was an uncompromising republican. He married Isabella C. de Baca, a descendant of one of the most noted families of the territory. Of this marriage there were eighteen children, eleven of whom grew to maturity. A son, Colonel José D. Sena, Jr., has been active in the affairs of New Mexico, having been mayor of the city of Santa Fé and clerk of the supreme court, both of which positions he has filled most acceptably. The death of Major Sena occurred at Santa Fé.

The National Guard escorted his remains to their last resting place and Governor Prince delivered a most eloquent eulogy on the life and deeds of this loyal American citizen.

On the 15th day of August, 1862, Mesilla was made the headquarters of the district of Arizona, and had as a garrison Companies B, C, D, and K, 1st infantry, and Company A, 5th infantry, Shinn's Light Battery A, 3d U. S. artillery, Companies A and E, 1st infantry, B, 5th infantry, and the regimental bands of the 1st and 2d cavalry, were sent as a garrison to Fort Fillmore. Company A, 1st infantry, was sent to El Paso, then known as Franklin, to guard a flour mill belonging to Judge Simeon Hart, a notorious Confederate, and very influential and wealthy man, and for the purpose of apprehending the "mail carrier" of the Confederates, Captain Skillman, who afterwards was killed by Captain Albert H. French, at Spencer's ranch, near Presidio del Norte, April 15, 1864, while attempting to carry the Confederate mail into Texas. All of the regular troops were soon relieved and sent north to Fort Craig, while some of the Californians proceeded to Forts Quitman, Bliss, and Davis, in Texas, and raised the flag of the Union.

In this manner the Overland mail route was opened and all of the United States military posts in Arizona, southern New Mexico, and northwestern Texas were re-occupied by troops composing the "California Column."

Before the end of the year the Colorado volunteers, some of whom had been engaged in expeditions against the marauding Indians, had all returned to their native state, their places being taken in the several garrisons by the troops which had accompanied Carleton from California.[315]

---

[315] Carleton, James H., *Report to A. A. Gen. Drum, Department of California,* September 20, 1862: "It was no fault of the troops from California that the Confederate forces fled before them. It is but just to say that their having thus fled is mainly attributed to the gallantry of the troops under General Canby's command. That they were hurried in their flight, by the timely arrival of the advance guard of the 'California Column' under Lieutenant-Colonel Eyre there cannot be a doubt. The march from the Pacific to the Rio Grande by the 'California Column' was not accomplished without immense toil and great hardships, or without many privations and much suffering from heat and want of water. . . . The march of the 'Column from California,' in the summer months, across the great desert in the driest season that has been known for thirty years, is a military achievement creditable to the soldiers of the American army; but it would not be just to attribute the success of this march to any ability on my part. That success was gained only by the high physical and moral energies of that peculiar class of officers and men who composed the 'California Column.' With any other troops, I am sure I should have failed."

On the 18th of September, 1862, General Carleton assumed the command of the department of New Mexico, General Canby having been ordered east by the war department. The "Column" was soon distributed throughout the depart-

It has been noted that Henry Connelly [316] and Miguel A. Otero succeeded Abraham Rencher and A. M. Jackson in the offices of governor and secretary, respectively, having been appointed to these positions by Abraham Lincoln. These appointments were made entirely upon the solicitation and rec-

CIVIL AFFAIRS DURING THE WAR PERIOD

ment, and active operations commenced against the hostile Indians — the Apaches and the Navajós. Treason was at a discount in New Mexico, and no treasonable utterances were allowed; when anything of this kind was attempted, it resulted in the person being immediately arrested, confined in the guardhouse, and tried by a military commission. The most incorrigible of this class of persons was Samuel J. Jones, the well known pro-slavery sheriff at Lecompton, Kansas, in 1857 and 1858. Upon the advent of Colonel Baylor's forces in 1861, he was the post sutler at Fort Fillmore, owning a fine estate at Mesilla, and during the Confederate occupation of the territory, he was constantly in hot water with the Confederates, but not on account political matters, however, as he was an unadulterated fire-eater. After the ''Column'' arrived in the district of New Mexico, Jones was brought up in the guard-house about once a month.

[316] Henry Connelly was of Irish descent, his forefathers having been citizens of the county of Armagh, Ireland. About the year 1769 the Connellys came to America and settled where now is built the city of Charleston, South Carolina. His ancestors in America were heroes of the Revolution, fighting in the patriot armies of Washington, Greene, Morgan, Gates, Lincoln, and Pinckney. After the Revolution some of the Connellys moved west into Kentucky, Dr. Henry Connelly's father settling in Nelson county of that state about the year 1789. Henry Connelly was educated in the county schools. Afterwards he attended the medical school of the Transylvania University at Lexington, Kentucky, being among the first to graduate from that institution. He graduated in 1828 and soon left Kentucky for Missouri and settled in Liberty, Clay county, of that state. In the same year he left the state for Chihuahua, Mexico. Here he was employed as a clerk and later on purchased the establishment; he was in business in the city of Chihuahua for many years and had for a partner, Edward J. Glasgow who had been in business at Mazatlan. He was married in Mexico in the town of Jesus Maria in the year 1838. There were three children born of this marriage, one of whom, Peter, is now living in Kansas City, Missouri. Prior to the breaking out of the war with Mexico, Dr. Connelly brought his children to Missouri and returned to Chihuahua. His wife died a few years afterward. Dr. Connelly was in Santa Fé at the time that General Kearny reached Bent's Fort on the Arkansas, and acted as agent for Governor Armijo at the time when Captain Cooke arrived in the capital. Prior to Doniphan's capture of the city of Chihuahua, about the time of the battle of Brazito, Dr. Connelly was arrested by the Mexican authorities and taken to Chihuahua and confined, but was subsequently released. He remained in Chihuahua until the close of the war, leaving that city for Santa Fé some time in 1848, in which place he resided up to the time of his death. He also had a home at Peralta, Valencia county, where he married Dolores Perea, widow of Mariano Chaves, the father of Colonel J. Francisco Chaves, from whom the author received most of the above information. He was engaged in merchandising in New Mexico from the time that he came from Chihuahua and had houses in several plazas in the territory. He was twice appointed governor of the territory by President Lincoln. He was an intensely loyal man during the Civil War, and it was

ommendation of John S. Watts,[317] in whose integrity and loyalty President Lincoln had great confidence. Judge Watts persuaded the president that notwithstanding the pro-slavery tendencies of Otero and the position which he had taken just prior to the breaking out of hostilities, under all the conditions then existing in New Mexico, he was the man of New Mexican birth best fitted to carry out the policies of the administration in this jurisdiction. Otero had been the delegate in congress since 1855 and Watts was his successor, having been elected with practically no opposition over Diego Archuleta. Otero held the office of secretary during the year 1861 when he was succeeded by James H. Holmes, who also served but one year. He, in turn, was replaced by W. F. M. Arny, who held the office until 1867 and again in 1872. Owing to the illness of Governor Connelly the duties of executive, during Arny's incumbency of the secretaryship, were largely performed by the latter.

The civil officials of the war period coöperated in every way possible with the commanding general of the military department of New Mexico. At the time of the Confederate occupation of the capital there were several prominent citizens and merchants, not of native birth, who were distinctly disloyal and openly greeted the coming of the army under General Sibley with expressions of congratulation. There were, however, among the native population,

---

largely through his influence that the leading citizens of New Mexico refused to ally themselves with the invading Confederates under General Sibley. Socially he was a man of great refinement and intelligence. His services to the territory deserve a monument. He died at Santa Fé, in the month of July, 1866.

[317] John S. Watts was a native of the state of Indiana, where he studied law and was admitted to the bar. He was a prominent figure in New Mexican affairs for many years. He was named one of the associate justices of the supreme court of New Mexico by Millard Fillmore at the time New Mexico was made a territory and was assigned to the second judicial district with headquarters at Alburquerque. He held office until 1854 when he was succeeded by Perry E. Brocchus, appointed by Franklin Pierce. Judge Watts removed to the capital where he began the practice of law. In 1861 he was elected delegate to congress, with practically no opposition. He enjoyed the confidence of Abraham Lincoln. His career as delegate was marked by great industry in behalf of the people of New Mexico. He was not a candidate for reëlection and was appointed chief justice, in 1868, after the death of Judge Slough. He was succeeded in this position by Judge Palen, who was appointed by President Grant. Thereafter he resumed the active practice of the law and was a very important factor in the affairs of the territory until he returned to his native state, where he died in 1876. Judge Watts was a great student and fond of historical research. During his incumbency he wrote seven opinions which appear in the New Mexico supreme court reports.

Prominent Men of Affairs in New Mexico last half of the Nineteenth Century
1. Wilson Waddingham. 2. Lawrence P. Browne. 3. Marcus Brunswick.
4. John P. Sellar. 5. Don Lorenzo Lopez. 6. William H. Chick

men of great influence and power, who stood loyally by their Union sentiments. Prominent among these were Don Facundo Pino, Don Miguel E. Pino, Colonel J. Francisco Chaves, Colonel Francisco Perea, Don José Manuel Gallegos, Don Diego Archuleta, Don Anastasio Sandoval, Don Trinidad Romero, and the leading citizens of every county of the *Rio Arriba* or upper portion of the territory. There was also a number of prominent men and officials, then living at Santa Fé, whose pro-Union sentiments and activity did much toward discouraging any inclination toward the south or its representatives and sympathizers. A leader among these was the chief justice of the territory, Kirby Benedict.[318]

Judge Benedict was easily the leader of the bench of New Mexico during what may be called the second judicial period, the first being that of the court established by General Kearny. His associates upon the bench were Chief Justice J. J. Davenport, John S. Watts, Perry E. Brocchus, William F. Boone, William G. Blackwood, Sidney A. Hubbell, Joseph G. Knapp, and Joab Houghton. The second

[318] Kirby Benedict was a native of the state of Connecticut. He was born in 1811. He was appointed associate justice of the supreme court of New Mexico, in 1853, by Franklin Pierce. Soon after attaining his majority he removed to the state of Illinois, where he was a distinguished member of the bar and a personal friend of Abraham Lincoln and Stephen A. Douglas. He was a man of great ability whose honesty and integrity were never questioned. Historical research and literary pursuits had a special charm for him. This characteristic is found in the wording of all the opinions delivered by him while a member of the supreme court, of which there were twenty-two. When he first came to New Mexico he was assigned to the old third district, comprising the counties of Taos and Rio Arriba, with headquarters at Taos. He continued in this office for a period of five years, when he was appointed chief justice and removed to Santa Fé, presiding over the first district. In 1860 the counties of Taos and Rio Arriba were added to the first district. In 1866 he was succeeded by John P. Slough. Judge Benedict had been a candidate for re-appointment and his failure to retain the office which he had held for thirteen years caused him to become very irritable and morose. He began the practice of the law, but his personal habits were such that he had many difficulties with the presiding judges and was finally suspended from practice. This was done at a session of the supreme court held in 1871. He made several demands for reinstatement, unaccompanied by any apology for his previous conduct, and finally, finding that course unavailing, he tendered an apology and asked to be restored to his position as a member of the bar of the court. His application was referred to a committee, consisting of Justices Hubbell and Houghton and William Breeden, "to report whether the habits and character of Kirby Benedict are such as to make him a fit person to practice in this court." The action of the court came as a great surprise to Benedict, and greatly humiliated, he withdrew his application and soon thereafter died.

While presiding judge, with headquarters at Taos, Judge Benedict delivered the famous sentence of death, pronounced upon José Maria Martin. This

period may be said to have extended from the date of the organiza-

"judicial gem" was repeated to the writer, as hereafter follows, by Colonel William Breeden, whose fund of stories of the bench and bar of the second period, was almost inexhaustible. José Martin had been convicted of murder in the district court held at Taos, and the crime was shown to have been of a very aggravated nature and without provocation. Judge Benedict evidently concurred in the finding of the jury. When the time for sentence had arrived the prisoner was brought before the judge, who addressed him as follows:

"José Maria Martin, stand up! José Maria Martin, you have been indicted, tried and convicted by a jury of your countrymen of the crime of murder, and the court is now about to pass upon you the dread sentence of the law. As a usual thing, José Maria Martin, it is a painful duty for the judge of a court of justice to pronounce upon a human being the sentence of death. There is something horrible about it, and the mind of the court naturally revolts from the performance of such a duty. Happily, however, your case is relieved of all such unpleasant features and the Court takes positive delight in sentencing you to death!

"You are a young man, José Maria Martin; apparently of good physical condition and robust health. Ordinarily you might have looked forward to many years of life, and the Court has no doubt you have, and have expected to die at a ripe old age; but you are about to be cut off in consequence of your own act. José Maria Martin, it is now the spring-time, in a little while the grass will be springing up green in these beautiful valleys, and on these broad mesas and mountain sides flowers will be blooming; birds will be singing their sweet carols, and nature will be putting on her most gorgeous and her most attractive robes, and life will be pleasant and men will want to stay, but none of this for you, José Maria Martin; the flowers will not bloom for you, José Maria Martin; the birds will not carol for you, José Maria Martin; when these things come to gladden the senses of men, you will be occupying a space about six by two beneath the sod, and the green grass and those beautiful flowers will be growing above your lowly head.

"The sentence of the Court is that you be taken from this place to the county jail; that you be there kept safely and securely confined, in the custody of the sheriff until the day appointed for your execution. (Be very careful, Mr. Sheriff, that he have no opportunity to escape and that you have him at the appointed place at the appointed time.) That you be so kept, José Maria Martin, until — (Mr. Clerk, on what day of the month does Friday, about two weeks from this time come? March twenty-second, your Honor). Very well,— until Friday, the twenty second day of March, when you will be taken by the sheriff from your place of confinement to some safe and convenient spot within the county (that is in your discretion, Mr. Sheriff, you are only confined to the limits of this county), and that you be there hanged by the neck until you are dead, and the Court was about to add, José Maria Martin, 'May God have mercy on your soul,' but the Court will not assume the responsibility of asking an Allwise Providence to do that which a jury of your peers has refused to do. The Lord could not have mercy on your soul! However, if you affect any religious belief, or are connected with any religious organization, it might be well for you to send for your priest or your minister and get from him, — well, — such consolation as you can; but the Court advises you to place no reliance upon anything of that kind! Mr. Sheriff, remove the prisoner."

It may be added that the court records of Taos county fail to reveal anything as to the final outcome of this case. It is known, however, that José Maria Martin was never hanged but made good his escape and was never heard of.

tion of New Mexico into a territory, in 1851, down to the great influx of "Americans" caused by the construction and advent of the railroads in New Mexico. Chief Justice Davenport compiled the laws of the territory. He was a man of strong opinions and splendid moral character and adorned the bench during his incumbency. The second period covered a term exceeding thirty years. During this time the people of New Mexico were practically isolated from the outside world; there was no telegraph or railroad, nothing but the stage coach, and thirty days were required for letters to reach the eastern portions of the United States. The judges, all conditions considered, worked laboriously. To be sure, they were a law unto themselves in their districts.[319] There were few law books even at the capital, and on the circuit text books and reports were unheard of. A copy of the compiled laws and an occasional *Chitty's Pleadings* was the working library of the New Mexico judge and lawyer during the early days. The districts as established by General Kearny continued until late in the sixties, when a new distribution [320] oc-

---

[319] From 1846 until 1860 the territory was divided into three judicial districts. The chief justice always resided at Santa Fé. The first district comprised the counties of Santa Fé, San Miguel, and Santa Ana; court held at Santa Fé. The second district, the counties of Bernalillo and Valencia, and after their organization, the counties of Socorro, Doña Ana, and Arizona; court was held at Alburquerque, and sometimes, by special order, at Socorro. The third district comprised the counties of Taos and Rio Arriba, the headquarters being at Fernandez de Taos.

[320] The districts in 1860 were arranged so that the first district comprised the counties of Santa Fé, Santa Ana, San Miguel, Mora, Taos, and Rio Arriba. The second district comprised the counties of Bernalillo, Valencia, and Socorro. The third district comprised the counties of Doña Ana, Grant, and Lincoln.

From the date of the organization of the Kearny court down to the advent of the railways, in 1879, a period of thirty-three years, all of the opinions rendered by the supreme court of New Mexico number eighty-four, volume 1 of the New Mexico *Reports* containing eighty-one reported cases. In 1852, two cases are reported; in 1853, ten; in 1854, three; in 1855, two; in 1856, none; in the years 1875 and 1876 only two, and in the years 1877 and 1878 none at all, and in 1879 there are three.

The chief justices from 1846 until 1879 were Joab Houghton (Kearny court), 1846; 1851, Grafton Baker; 1853, J. J. Davenport; 1858, Kirby Benedict; 1866, John P. Slough; 1868, John S. Watts; 1869, Joseph G. Palen; 1876, Henry L. Waldo; 1878, Charles McCandless; 1879, L. Bradford Prince. These also presided over the court of the first district.

The judges of the second district during the period were, in 1846 (Kearny court), Antonio José Otero; 1851, John S. Watts; 1854, Perry E. Brocchus; 1859, W. F. Boone; 1861, Sidney A. Hubbell; 1867, Perry E. Brocchus; 1870, Hezekiah S. Johnson; 1876, John I. Reddick; 1877, Samuel B. McLin; 1878, Samuel C. Parks.

The judges of the third district were (district in the north, court at Taos),

curred, the southern portion of the territory requiring it on account of the great increase in population, and litigation of serious importance. By this arrangement the major portion of the business of the courts was thrown into the first district, which covered the entire northern half of the territory, embracing seven counties [321] until the county of Santa Ana was abolished, when there were six.

1846, Charles Beaubien (Kearny court); 1851, Horace Mower; 1853, Kirby Benedict; 1858, W. G. Blackwood. (District in the south, Doña Ana, Lincoln and Grant), 1861, Joseph G. Knapp; 1865, Joab Houghton; 1869, Abraham Bergen; 1870, Benjamin J. Waters; 1871, Daniel B. Johnson; 1872, Warren Bristol.

Perry E. Brocchus, associate justice of the supreme court, in 1857-1859 and again in 1867-1869, was a native of Baltimore, Maryland. He was appointed the first time by President Buchanan. Before coming to New Mexico, he had been associate justice of the supreme court of Utah, appointed by President Fillmore. He was also appointed in 1861, but, owing to his inability to cross the plains, did not qualify. He was removed from office by President Grant in 1869. He was a man of great force of character and personal courage. Colonel William Breeden, a warm personal friend of Judge Brocchus, relates the following story: "On one occasion, while holding court in Socorro, he had some trouble with Kirby Benedict. Brocchus was somewhat hard of hearing and was very sensitive over the deficiency. Benedict was presenting a motion to the court, and in the argument, spoke in a very loud voice and with violence of gesture. Justice Brocchus quietly stopped him, saying, 'Judge Benedict, it is not necessary for you to speak so loudly. The court hears you without difficulty, and your loud tones and gesticulations are exceedingly unpleasant to the court.' Benedict apologized, resumed his argument, and speedily was as loud and vehement as ever. Once more the court stopped him and said, 'Judge Benedict, your tone of voice and your violence are offensive to the court, and you must be more moderate or suspend your remarks.' Again Judge Benedict apologized and remarked, in extenuation of his conduct, that in the heat of argument he had forgotten the court's instructions. Brocchus then said: 'Judge Benedict, you may proceed, but hereafter do not be so forgetful of the court's wishes.' Benedict again resumed and presently was sawing the air with his hands and lifting his voice like the Bull of Bashan. Brocchus stood the very patent indignity for a few minutes, then rapping on the bench, said: 'Mr. Sheriff, the court takes a recess for five minutes.' He then climbed down from the bench, took the distinguished Benedict by the lapel of his coat, and said: 'You impudent old scoundrel, you howl at this court and the court will thrash you all over the room.' Benedict was profuse in his apologies and Brocchus released him, resumed his seat, and informed Judge Benedict that he might proceed, which was done with great moderation."

[321] The first session of the legislative assembly — June-July, 1851 — defined the judicial districts of the territory and at the session held in December-January, 1851-1852, divided New Mexico into nine counties, with the former boundaries, except a change between Socorro and Doña Ana, changing the county seat of Valencia to Tomé, Rio Arriba to San Pedro de Chama, and Santa Ana to Peña Blanca. Later, in 1852-1853, the county seat of Doña Ana was changed to Las Cruces; in 1853-1854, the county seat of Bernalillo county was changed from Ranchos to Alburquerque, and that of Socorro to the town of Socorro; in 1855-1856 the town of Mesilla was again made the county seat of Doña Ana, and in 1856-1857 the county seat of Socorro was changed to Limitar. In the years 1859-1860 the assembly created the county of Arizona

The courts were arranged so that sessions were held in succession, thereby forming a regular circuit, in this manner adjusting matters so that the court officers and lawyers could leave Santa Fé and proceed in turn to San Miguel, Mora, Colfax, crossing the mountains to Taos, thence to Rio Arriba and finally returning to Santa Fé, the entire circuit occupying about three months. The other districts and the several courts held therein were so arranged that no session conflicted with the terms of the court in the first district. The influence of the Santa Fé bar was paramount in the early days and nothing was done in the way of holding courts which could possibly interfere with the business interests of the lawyers living at the seat of government.

Chief Justice Joseph G. Palen, who succeeded to the position in 1869, was a man of strong character. Although of unyielding prejudices, his instincts were lofty and uncompromising in matters of wrong or right. Possessed of great dignity he exacted a proper respect for his high office from litigants and lawyers alike. His private character was unblemished. He was as fearless as he was incorruptible and in profundity of legal knowledge has had no superior upon the bench in New Mexico.[322] At the time of the Civil

out of the territory acquired by the Gadsden Purchase, fixing the county seat at Tubac; also created the county of Mora, with seat at Santa Gertrudis de Mora, changed the county seat of Rio Arriba to Plaza Alcalde, and that of San Miguel to the lower plaza of Las Vegas. The tenth assembly changed the county seat of Arizona county to Tucson, and created a county of San Juan, in the extreme northwestern portion of the territory with seat at Baker City; the ensuing session, 1861-1862, repealed the act creating San Juan county and added the remaining parts of Arizona county to the county of Doña Ana; changed the county seat of San Miguel back to the plaza of San Miguel. In 1876 the county of Santa Ana was merged into Bernalillo county. Out of the original nine county sub-divisions other counties have been formed, until, together with the original nine, the territory, in 1911, was divided into twenty-six counties, the name and date of formation of which are as follows: Bernalillo, January 6, 1852; Chaves, February 25, 1887; Colfax, January 25, 1869; Curry, February 15, 1909; Doña Ana, January 6, 1852; Eddy, February 25, 1887 Grant, January 30, 1868; Guadalupe, February 23, 1905; Lincoln, February 13, 1880; Luna, March 16, 1901; McKinley, February 23, 1899; Mora, January 6, 1859; Otero, January 30, 1899; Quay, February 28, 1903; Rio Arriba, January 6, 1852; Roosevelt, February 28, 1903; Sandoval, March 10, 1903; San Juan, February 24, 1887; San Miguel, January 6, 1852; Santa Fé, January 6, 1852; Sierra, April 3, 1884; Socorro, January 6, 1852; Taos, January 6, 1852; Torrance, March 16, 1903; Union, February 28, 1895, and Valencia, January 6, 1852.

[322] Joseph G. Palen was born in the year 1812, in Palenville, Greene county, New York. He received his education in the local schools and at Harvard and Amherst colleges. He read law with the celebrated Ambrose L.

War the most active members [323] of the bar were Judges Houghton and Watts, Messrs. Ashurst, Tompkins, Wheaton, Clever, Baird, Henrie, Hubbell, Johnson, Jackson, and Greiner. At the close of the war many prosecutions were instituted for the confiscation of property, the defendants being those who had aided and encouraged the rebellion by rendering assistance to the Confederate army during its invasion of the territory. The court in which most of the prosecutions were begun was presided over by Judge Joab Houghton, who, in 1865, had for the second time received an appointment to the bench.[324]

Jordan, and for many years practiced in Hudson, New York. He was appointed postmaster of that city in 1861 and continued in the office until appointed chief justice of New Mexico by President Grant, April 15, 1869. He was re-appointed March 20, 1873, and held the position until the day of his death, which occurred at Santa Fé, December 21, 1875. Judge Palen counted among his closest friends Messrs. Elkins, Catron, Breeden, and Waldo, members of the bar of his court. His apparent personal regard for these men excited great animosity in the breasts of other and older members of the Santa Fé bar whose personal habits and looseness of character did not appeal to Judge Palen's sense of morals.

[323] The members of the bar during what may be termed the first generation were Hugh N. Smith, Elias P. West, Henry C. Johnson, Merrill Ashurst, James H. Quinn, Theodore D. Wheaton, Richard H. Tompkins, R. H. Weightman, John E. Garey, William Z. Angney, Palmer J. Pillan, S. M. Baird, W. W. H. Davis, and W. H. Henrie. Some rare anecdotes are told of the habits and manners of some of these earlier members of the bar. The Civil War came on, bringing with it tense situations and sharp divisions. Its close brought many new men, some from the east and some from the Pacific coast, arriving with the celebrated "California Column," who shortly became prominent at the bar and in other walks of life.

The attorneys-general for the period were, 1846, Hugh N. Smith; 1848, E. P. West; 1852, Henry C. Johnson; 1852, Merrill Ashurst; 1854, Theodore D. Wheaton; 1858, Richard H. Tompkins; 1859, Hugh N. Smith; 1860, S. M. Baird; 1860, 1861, R. H. Tompkins; 1862, Charles P. Clever; 1862, Stephen B. Elkins; 1863, Charles P. Clever (resigned); 1867, Merrill Ashurst; 1869, Thomas B. Catron.

The United States attorneys were, 1846, Frank P. Blair, Jr.; 1847, Hugh N. Smith; 1851, Elias P. West; 1853, W. W. H. Davis; 1855, W. C. Jones; 1858, R. H. Tompkins; 1860, Theodore D. Wheaton; 1861, Merrill Ashurst; 1867, S. B. Elkins.

The clerks of the supreme court were, 1847, James M. Giddings; 1854, L. D. Sheets; 1856, Augustin de Marle; 1859, Samuel Ellison; 1866, William M. Gwynne; 1867, Peter Connelly; 1868, Samuel Ellison; 1869, William Breeden.

[324] During the war of the rebellion he was a stanch Union man, asserting his sentiments when it required nerve to maintain his patriotism. In 1862, Judge Houghton was an acting United States district attorney, and as such drew several indictments for treason against prominent citizens. In the year 1865, when he was again appointed to the bench, he was assigned to the third judicial district, and, while officiating as judge, had before him various suits brought under the act of congress of March 3, 1863, authorizing the confiscation of property in certain cases. By his rulings in these cases, Judge

It does not appear that the delegates in congress from New Mexico accomplished very much for their constituents during this period. In 1863 Colonel Francisco Perea [325] was elected over J. M. Gallegos by a vote of 7,231 to 6,425. In 1865, Colonel J. Fran-

DELEGATES IN CONGRESS

Houghton laid himself open to the severest criticism, much of which was brought about through his lack of legal knowledge. The *New Mexican* of December 15, 1865, says: "It is now clear that Judge Houghton is wanting in all the essentials necessary to a speedy and satisfactory administration of justice, and his appointment to the bench is but another evidence that those not bred in the law should not be entrusted with its administration."
This court was called a "prize court;" and so great was the indignation in certain quarters against the judge, the United States attorney, and the marshal, that on December 5, 1865, they were denounced to their faces as unmitigated scoundrels. It is impossible now to realize how overwhelming was the excitement and prejudice of those days. The exercise of calm judgment seems to have been almost an impossibility. In his two official terms Judge Houghton appears to have filed but one written opinion. In the year 1869, he was succeeded by Judge Bergen, appointed by President Grant.
In 1849, Judge Houghton fought a bloodless duel with Major R. H. Weightman. The parties met in an arroyo, near the city of Santa Fé; when the command "fire" was given, only one shot was heard — that from Weightman's pistol, the ball from which passed close to Houghton's ear. Houghton who was slightly deaf, insisted that he had not heard the word of command. Weightman then lifted both of his hands in the air and told Houghton to shoot; the seconds interposed, however, and the party left the grounds, Weightman still insisting that what he had said concerning Judge Houghton was the truth. Weightman had made some very objectionable statements concerning Judge Houghton in a public address delivered at Socorro.
[325] Francisco Perea was born at Padillas, Bernalillo county, New Mexico, January 9, 1830. He was the third child of Juan Perea who married Josefa Chaves. Juan Perea, the father, was born at Corrales, Sandoval county, New Mexico, in the year 1802 and was the son of Pedro Jose Perea and Barbarita Romero de Perea. His great-grandfather Don Pedro Ascencion Perea came to New Mexico from the City of Mexico about the year 1780. The maternal grandfather of Francisco Perea was Francisco Javier Chaves, governor of New Mexico, two of whose sons, Mariano and José, held the same office.
At the outbreak of the Civil War Colonel Perea, after consultation with his grandfather and with his uncle, Jose Leandro Perea, became active in his efforts for the Union, visiting many localities in the Territory and urging the people to remain steadfast for the government. At his own expense he recruited a battalion and was commissioned lieutenant-colonel of the regiment. He was in command of the post at Alburquerque during the winter of 1861-62 from which place he directed several campaigns against the Navajó. He participated in the battle of Apache Canyon. He served several times as a member of the legislative assembly. In 1863 he was elected delegate in congress, in which position he acquitted himself with great honor and credit. He was a personal friend of President Lincoln and was seated very close to the President at the time he was assassinated. Colonel Perea was twice married, his first wife, Dolores Otero, being a daughter of Judge Antonio José Otero and his second, Gabriela Montoya. Of each marriage eighteen children were born; of the first only one is now living, Mrs. Amelia Parenti; of the second ten survive. Colonel Perea received his education in a Jesuit college in St. Louis and also had as instructor, in a school in New York, the celebrated

cisco Chaves [326] was chosen over Colonel Perea by a vote of 8,511 to 6,180, and in 1867, Charles P. Clever over Chaves, 8,891 to 8,794. The election of Clever was certified by the governor, and pro forma by the secretary, and the delegate took his seat. Secretary Heath, however, made a separate certificate stating that the election was fraudulent; this action of the secretary was endorsed by the legislative assembly, and after a long and bitter contest, Colonel Chaves was seated. In 1869 Colonel Chaves was again elected, his opponent being Don Vicente Romero, but in the following election, owing to the independent candidacy of Major José D. Sena, Colonel Chaves was defeated by J. M. Gallegos. During this campaign, which was a very bitter one, a riot occurred in the streets of Mesilla, resulting in the killing and wounding of a number of people. A meeting had been held on the 27th of August, 1871. After the meeting was over the democrats and republicans formed in two processions and marched around the town of Mesilla; coming from opposite directions the two processions met in front of the store of Reynolds and Griggs. I. N. Kelley, a democrat, and John Lemon, a republican, engaged in angry political discussion as the processions came together. In the excitement Apolonio Barela, a prominent citizen, intentionally or otherwise fired his pistol in the air. Immediately

Spanish scholar and patriot Mariano Velasquez. Colonel Perea is a resident of the city of Alburquerque. — From Ms. *Sketch of Life of Francisco Perea*, W. H. H. Allison, Alburquerque, N. M.

[326] J. Francisco Chaves was born in Los Padillas, Bernalillo county, New Mexico, June 27, 1833. In 1841 he entered St. Louis University. His education was finished with a two years' course in the College of Physicians and Surgeons in New York City, and in 1852 he returned to the territory. His grandfather, Don Francisco Xavier Chaves, was governor of New Mexico under the republic of Mexico. His father, Don Mariano Chaves, was born December 31, 1799, and was married to Dolores Perea, the daughter of Pedro Jose Perea, a descendant of one of the early settlers of New Mexico. Don Mariano Chaves was chief of staff under Governor Manuel Armijo in the revolution of 1837. He was inspector general of all the military forces of New Mexico. Subsequently, in 1840, Don Mariano was made political chief. When Colonel Chaves' father sent him to St. Louis to receive his education, he said to him: "The heretics are going to over-run all this country. Go and learn their language and come back prepared to defend your people." In 1852 and 1853 Colonel Chaves made overland trips to the state of California. He served as a soldier in campaigns against the Navajós prior to the Civil War. In 1861 he was commissioned major of the 1st New Mexico infantry, by President Lincoln, and was afterward promoted to a lieutenant-colonelcy for gallant and meritorious services. In 1862 he took part in the battle of Valverde, and later on helped to establish Fort Wingate, of which post he was in command for a long period. He was honorably mustered out of the service of the United States in 1865. Returning home he began the study of the law and in due

Governors of New Mexico under the Act of March 3, 1851
1. Lionel A. Sheldon, 1851-5. 2. Edmund G. Ross, 1885-9. 3. William T. Thornton, 1893-7. 4. Miguel A. Otero, 1897-1906. 5. L. Bradford Prince, 1889-93. 6. Herbert J. Hagerman, 1906-7. 7. George Curry, 1907-10

NEW MEXICO DURING THE CIVIL WAR   401

Kelley, who carried a heavy pick-handle, struck Lemon a fierce blow upon the head, felling him to the ground. The next instant Felicitas Arroyas y Lueras shot Kelley, inflicting a mortal wound. The fighting now became general. Nine men were killed and forty or fifty wounded in this fight. Judge Hezekiah S. Johnson, of the 2d district, was sent for, there being no judge in the district. He came from Alburquerque, stayed three days and returned without taking any action. No indictments were ever returned and no one was punished.

In 1873 and again in 1875 Stephen B. Elkins [327] was elected, de-

---

course was admitted to the bar. During the later seventies he held the position of district attorney for the 2d judicial district. In politics he was a stanch republican and in 1858, while absent campaigning against the Navajós, was elected a member of the house of representatives of the territorial legislative assembly, taking his seat in 1860. In 1865 he was elected delegate in congress from New Mexico and served in the 39th and 40th congresses. In 1875 he was elected a member of the legislative council from Valencia county and was reëlected to every succeeding legislature. He was appointed superintendent of public instruction by Governor Otero in March, 1901; re-appointed in 1903 and was filling the position at the time of his death. He was assassinated at seven o'clock on the evening of Saturday, November 26, 1904, at Pinos Wells, New Mexico.

Colonel Chaves was married in 1857 to Mary Bowie, who died in 1874, leaving two children, Lola and Francesca. The former married Mariano Armijo, descendant of a prominent family of Bernalillo county, New Mexico. The latter died in 1895. Colonel Chaves was a man of firm convictions, fearless, and a justly acknowledged leader of his party, in the councils of which he was always a potent factor.

[327] Stephen Benton Elkins, lawyer, financier, secretary of war in the cabinet of President Harrison, and for many years a member of the United States senate from West Virginia, was born in Perry county, Ohio, September 26, 1841. His father, who had come from the Rappahannock river, in Virginia, with his parents in 1827 and settled in Perry county, Ohio, was a farmer. A few years after the birth of Stephen, his parents moved to Missouri where he received a good public school education. Later he entered the state university of Missouri, from which he was graduated in 1860. He was a very ambitious young man and applied himself to whatever he undertook with great diligence. After his graduation he took up the study of the law without a preceptor and in 1863 was admitted to the bar. He performed some military service during the war of the rebellion on the side of the Union. In the last years of the war he determined to go to the far west. He came to New Mexico and established himself in the Mesilla valley, locating at Mesilla, the county seat of Doña Ana county. Realizing the necessity of acquiring the Spanish language, he soon became very proficient in that tongue. Stalwart and capable, he soon attracted important clients and with his practice his popularity grew. In 1866 he was elected a member of the house of representatives of the legislative assembly and won such unusual distinction that in the following year he was made attorney general of the territory. In 1868 President Johnson appointed him United States attorney for the territory, and he was one of the few officials of that administration whom President Grant did not remove from office. In his capacity as U. S. attorney he enforced the act of congress relative to peonage

feating Gallegos in the first and Don Pedro Valdez in the second contest. From 1861 many efforts were made to secure the admission of New Mexico [328] into the Union. During Elkins's incumbency he

in the territories. In 1869 Mr. Elkins was elected president of the First National Bank of Santa Fé, which position he held for thirteen years. His income from his law practice and other sources was large and, being very economical in his expenditures, at an early date he was able to associate himself with Jerome B. Chaffee and others of the state of Colorado, in mining enterprises which proved very profitable. In 1873 he was elected delegate to congress from the territory and in 1875, while traveling in Europe, was reelected by a large majority notwithstanding the fact that he had positively declared that he would not accept another term. Having been elected, however, he responded to the call of duty, and during his second term won national reputation by his brilliant and determined efforts to secure the admission of New Mexico as a state.

His first wife, Sallie Jacobs, whom he had married in Lexington, Missouri, in 1866, having died in Santa Fé, leaving him two daughters, Mr. Elkins, while in congress, married a daughter of Henry Gassaway Davis, at the time a senator from West Virginia. After the expiration of his term in congress Mr. Elkins moved to New York. He became interested in extensive tracts of coal lands in West Virginia to which state he removed, where he became largely interested in the development of the railroads and natural resources of that state. He continued to take an important part in national politics and served for several years as a member of the national republican committee. In 1884 he was elected chairman of the executive committee; he was mainly instrumental in bringing about the nomination of James G. Blaine in 1884, of Harrison in 1888 and 1892. In 1891 he was appointed secretary of war in the Harrison cabinet and served until February, 1894, when he was elected United States senator. He took his seat the following year and was reëlected in 1901 and again in 1907. Among the achievements standing to the credit of Senator Elkins is the Elkins anti-rebate bill, soon after he entered the senate; legislation providing for many important improvements of the Ohio, Kanawha, and Big Sandy rivers; innumerable material amendments to the railroad bills of 1907 and 1910, and many modifications of the tariff. He was first to suggest the use of army engineers in the construction of the Panama canal.

During the late sixties and until after the expiration of his second term in congress Mr. Elkins was the senior member of the law firm of Catron and Elkins, of Santa Fé, New Mexico. He formed many warm friendships with the leaders among the native people in New Mexico, and during all the years subsequent to his departure from the territory, was always found ready and willing to assist the people of the territory. He died January 4, 1911. Resolutions prepared by a committee of the bar of the supreme court of the territory, respecting the life and labors of this distinguished citizen, were presented at the January term, 1911, of the court, and ordered incorporated in the records of the court.

[328] Efforts of 1861. *U. S. Gov. Doc.*, 36th cong., 2d sess., *Sen. Misc. Doc.* II; *House Journal*, 534, 560. In 1866, by legislative enactment the governor was authorized to call a convention, to be elected the first Monday in March, to meet at Santa Fé the fifth Monday in April, and the constitution to be voted on the fourth Monday in June. *Laws*, 1865-6; *H. Mis. Doc.* 57, 39th cong., 1st sess., with proclamation. In 1869-71 efforts were made to secure admission as the state of Lincoln. *Laws*, 1869-70, p. 190-5, appendix. 4. *Idem*, 1871-2, p. 54-6; bills in congress referred and reported. *U. S. Acts*, 41st cong., 2d and 3d sess.; *Congressional Globe*, 1869-71, as per index, including a *Speech*

NEW MEXICO DURING THE CIVIL WAR 403

labored incessantly in behalf of his constituents and had it not been for an unfortunate circumstance, under his guidance a bill for the admission of New Mexico into the Union would have become law. At a crucial time, an inflammatory speech made in congress by Julius Caesar Burrows, on what was known as the "force bill," greatly antagonized the entire southern delegation. When the speaker had finished the southern representatives were highly incensed. Elkins came in a few moments prior to the conclusion of the speech and was among the first to congratulate the speaker. This act was noticed by the southern members, some of whom, in a vote taken later on, helped pass the measure so far as Colorado was concerned but registered their votes in the negative as to New Mexico.[329] This

---

made by Colonel J. Francisco Chaves in favor of the measure, in the *Globe* of 1870-1, appendix 244; *Sen. Journal*, 41st cong., 3d sess., 500. *Idem*, 42d cong., 1st sess., 203, *House Journal*, 237. Meanwhile a convention was held at Santa Fé and a constitution was formed. This was approved by the governor February 1st, and an act of the legislature ordered an election for the first Monday in June, state officers to be elected, if the constitution was adopted, on the first Monday in September. See *New Mex. Journal*, 1871-2, appendix. The vote was not received in time to be legally counted before the period expired and the movement came to naught. *N. Mex. Mess. of Governor*, 1873, pp. 17-18. The house bill on the state of Lincoln was tabled in the senate, *Cong. Globe*, 1871-2, p. 2950; and presently a bill to extend the time of voting was referred in the house. The legislative assembly of 1873-4 sent another memorial to congress and a bill was passed by the house but referred by the senate. *Cong. Globe*, 1873-4; *H. Rept.* 561, 43d cong., 1st sess. In 1875 the house bill was passed by the senate with amendments, another resolution having been received from the New Mexico assembly, 44th cong., 1st sess. *Senate Report* 69; *H. Mis. Doc.* 63. In 1876 there was another memorial and another bill, which passed the senate after much discussion, but did not go beyond reference to a committee in the house. 43d cong., 1st sess.; *H. Mis. Doc.* 190; *Globe*, 1875-6, per index; 43d cong., 2d sess. *H. Journal*, 577, 645; 44th cong., 1st sess.; *House Report*, 503.

See Bancroft, H. H., *History of Arizona and New Mexico*, pp. 720, 721. and note.

[329] Patterson, Thomas M., *Thoughtless Act defeated Statehood*, Rocky Mountain News, Denver. Thomas M. Patterson, ex-United States Senator from the state of Colorado, tells the story of how New Mexico failed and Colorado won in the fight for statehood, as follows: "The first session of the 43rd congress commenced on the first Monday in December, 1873. Very shortly after it convened Jerome B. Chaffee and Stephen B. Elkins, who had been elected from the Territory of New Mexico to the 43rd congress, determined to make a united effort for the admission of both Colorado and New Mexico into the Union. They were both men of great social and political influence in Washington, particularly Mr. Chaffee, who was not only considerably older than Mr. Elkins, but was also a much wealthier man, with a wider and more influential political acquaintance. They were both republicans and determined to make the admission of the two territories a party measure, the reason being that the republicans were in a decided majority in the senate and house, and they knew it would require party pressure to induce the many eastern members and senators

action on the part of the democrats in the house proved a fatal political blunder for, at the national election in 1876, the electoral

to vote for the admission of any new states. They were certain that, could it be made a caucus measure, there were republicans enough, and to spare, in both branches to give the territories statehood. Whether the republicans did make their admission a caucus measure, I never learned positively, but it was understood at the time the bills were introduced that the republicans of both houses would, with practical unanimity, support the measure. The bills were introduced in the house at the same time, and were referred to the committee on territories. They were both reported back to the house with favorable recommendation at the same time, and the house passed both bills at the same time, and with practically the same vote. After their passage by the house, both went over to the senate at the same time, and were referred to the committee on territories. This all occurred at the first session of the 43d congress, in the early part of the year 1874, and though that session held well into the summer of that year, the bills were allowed to slumber in the committee without action. Not that the friends of the measure in the senate did not urge action, but a majority of the committee were in no hurry then, as they have never been since, to accelerate the admission of new states into the sisterhood. That was the situation when I was elected delegate in the summer of 1874. The second session of the 43rd congress would convene in December, 1874, and since the session must end on the fourth of March, 1875, and all measures uncompleted at that time must totally fail, I made up my mind to go to Washington immediately after the new year of 1875, to add whatever influence I could bring to bear in behalf of the measures. When I reached Washington the bills were yet with the senate committee on territories, but Chaffee and Elkins succeeded in having them favorably reported back by the committee shortly afterward. The measures went to the senate calendar, there to remain fixtures until that body could be moved to take action upon them. . . The senate passed both bills, but before doing so amended them in four or five minor particulars. Not one of the amendments was important, but it was necessary to amend them to carry out the plans of the senatorial cabal that was opposed to the admission of new states. Upon their passage by the senate the friends of the two ambitious territories went into consultation. They knew the dangers that beset them, should the regular course be adopted — that of referring them to the house committee on territories — so a desperate remedy was resorted to as the alternative. The friends agreed that, instead of referring them to the committee, they would have them laid, in parliamentary language, 'upon the speaker's table.' The enemies of statehood were quite willing that they should be given that chute, for it would require a two-thirds vote of the house to take them from the table to ratify the senate amendments and pass the bills as then amended. But on sending them to the speaker's table the shoals and quicksands of the committee, and the deadly perils of a filibuster in the very last days of the session, were all avoided. . . .

"About a week before the close of the session, however, we were able to count the necessary two-thirds, and the friends of the measure were ready for action. But right then there occurred an unlooked for and very disquieting event. It put the plans of statehood up in the air very badly, and it lost statehood for New Mexico and took some of the votes from Colorado it would otherwise have had. What was called a 'force bill' had passed the senate and was before the house. Sam Randall was leading the democrats in a filibustering struggle to defeat it. The feeling upon both sides was bitter in the extreme. Fiery speeches had been made; the southern democrats drew the line of personal friendship along the debate. They believed they were fighting to preserve their states and homes from negro domination, and those familiar

vote of the Centennial state was cast for Rutherford B. Hayes for the presidency, thereby defeating Samuel J. Tilden, the nominee of

with the feeling of the south, where carpet-bag rule and negro domination were in the balance, can judge of the bitterness of that feeling. There was a young republican congressman in the house from Michigan. He was then unknown to fame, except that a rumor from the wilds of Michigan set him down as a Columbian orator of prodigious carrying power. His name was Julius Caesar Burrows . . . who made a speech on the 'force bill;' he grilled the southerners from head to foot, and tortured them in the fires of his oratory. It was a bitter, exasperating speech, and the southerners listened with gleaming eyes and gritting teeth. Burrows closed with a flood of invective that brought republicans and democrats to their feet, and as he sat down, the republican side and the galleries burst out with hand-clapping and applause. Mr. Elkins came into the chamber about five miuntes before Mr. Burrows closed his speech. He entered it through a door very close to the desk from which Mr. Burrows was speaking. He was immediately attracted by the orator and stood, as if spell-bound, listening to him. He was manifestly carried away by the fervor and swelling voice and earnest manner of Burrows, and when Burrows closed he rushed up to him, and was the very first to shake him by the hand and congratulate him upon the mastery of his effort. Scores of other members gathered about Burrows' seat and shook his hand, but Elkins was the very first. Fatal enthusiasm! The fervor of Columbian oratory would not move the experienced and self-poised Elkins to-day to so foolish an act — foolish, I mean, having in mind the admission of a state or any other matter of half the importance. The democrats — particularly the southern ones, those who had been won over to Colorado and New Mexico statehood — witnessed Elkins rush for Burrows and his congratulations with set teeth and ominous mutterings. That evening it was known that a number of them who had been counted friends of statehood would vote against New Mexico, at least, and Colorado might possibly be included in their wrath. We all set about fixing up the dislodged fences, but how well the work was done could not be told until the votes were actually recorded. I had been a witness of it all — had seen Mr. Elkins when he entered the chamber, saw him stand as if rooted to the floor, saw him rush up the very first to congratulate Burrows, and felt intuitively that the delegate from New Mexico had committed a fatal blunder. I was not mistaken. I will never forget the event of that final vote on the bills for the admission of Colorado and New Mexico. It was two o'clock in the morning of the last day of the session — March 4th. James G. Blaine was speaker of the house. He was not in the chair in the early part of the night, nor until after midnight. He had been an honored guest at some important function. He entered the chamber between twelve and one o'clock, clothed in full evening dress, just as he had left the fashionable dinner function. It then became a mere question as to when the votes might be taken. Some matters of perhaps greater importance even than statehood had to be gotten out of the way. At length Speaker Blaine was ready for the test. He was the friend of statehood, and he was to determine the most propitious moment for the effort. He gave the signal to the member who was to make the necessary motion, and he arose in response to the call. 'Mr. Speaker,' he said, and Blaine recognized him. It was understood that the test should come on Colorado first. 'I move,' said the recognized member, in a loud clear voice, 'that the bill for the admission of Colorado, with the amendments of the senate, be taken from the speaker's table, that the amendments of the senate be concurred in, and that the bill as amended do pass.'

"Immediately there was a loud demand by the democrats for the ayes and noes, and the speaker, ruling that the demand was seconded by a sufficient

the democratic party. Had New Mexico been admitted at the time the chances for democratic success were far greater than they were in Colorado.[330]

In the campaign of 1877 Don Trinidad Romero [331] was elected

---

number, ordered the clerk to proceed with the calling of the roll. Would Colorado receive the requisite two-thirds vote? That question, and the uncertainty of the answer, caused several hearts in that great chamber almost to cease beating. The whole house was still as the roll call proceeded, for interest in the matter had grown to be intense — the friends and opponents of statehood hoped for and expected the victory. It was not until after the roll call of nearly 350 members had been completed that those who followed the count knew that Colorado had won the day, or rather, the night.

"As was usually the case on roll call, a number had not voted when their names were called, and after the call had been completed, those, each in his turn stood by his seat to be recognized by the speaker and when his name was called by the clerk, he announced his vote and had it recorded. It was only then, after a proceeding that required more than thirty-five minutes, that the friends of Colorado statehood knew that its future was assured. . .

"But what of New Mexico? Immediately on the announcement of the Colorado vote by Speaker Blaine — it was the necessary two-thirds, with five or six to spare — the member who had moved in the Colorado bill made the same motion as to the New Mexico measure. A roll call was demanded and ordered, and the roll was called. As it was being proceeded with it was noted that now and then a democrat who had voted for Colorado voted against New Mexico. Would there be enough to change the Colorado outcome? There was! Those who followed the call knew that enough such votes had been cast to defeat New Mexico, and even before those not voting and who asked to have their votes recorded had been accommodated, it was known that New Mexico was not yet to become a state. It failed to obtain the necessary two-thirds by less than Colorado had received above it."

[330] Elkins was nominated for his second term in congress without his consent; in fact he notified the leaders of the republican party that he would not be a candidate for reëlection. He was in Holland at the time of his nomination and was not in New Mexico when the election was held. While he received a majority of the votes cast in the election as shown by the official returns and received the certificate of election from the secretary, still he did not receive a majority of the votes cast. He was counted in by the leaders of the republican party. This fact was never known by Elkins. This information was imparted to the writer by the leading republican of the territory at the time of the election, who also acted as one of his principal campaign managers.

[331] Trinidad Romero was born in Santa Fé county, June 14, 1835. His great-grandfather, Cristoval Romero, was a native of Spain, his grandfather, José G. Romero, was born in the city of Mexico and his father, Miguel Romero, was born in Santa Fé county, New Mexico, in 1798. His father took an active part in the public affairs of New Mexico prior to the American occupation period; was present at Apache Pass at the time of the retreat of Governor Armijo, and was appointed an alcalde by General Kearny prior to that officer's departure for California. He married Miss Delgado, a descendant of a noted Spanish family, whose immediate ancestor, Manuel Delgado, was an officer in the army of Spain, and was located at Santa Fé in the last quarter of the eighteenth century. Don Trinidad was one of a family of ten children. In 1855 he married Valeria Lopez, a descendant of one of the noted New Mexican families. He served as probate judge of San Miguel county for a number of

over Pedro Valdes, and in 1879 Don Mariano S. Otero [332] was successful in the contest in which Don Benito Baca was his opponent. A résumé of congressional action in behalf of New Mexico from 1864 to 1880 is found in a note.[333]

---
years, was a member of the territorial legislature, delegate to the fifty-fifth congress, and was appointed United States marshal for New Mexico by Benjamin Harrison. He is now a resident of Mora county, New Mexico.

[332] Mariano Sabino Otero was born at Peralta, New Mexico, August 28, 1844. He was a descendant of one of the noted families of New Mexico, his father, Juan Otero, and his three uncles Miguel Antonio, Manuel Antonio and Antonio José Otero having been prominent in New Mexican affairs during Mexican and American rule. Mr. Otero received his education at St. Louis University. He held several important county offices, was a member of the legislative assembly and delegate in congress in 1878, which office he filled with credit. He wielded great influence during his career, was shrewd in business affairs, of progressive ideas and in every sense a representative New Mexican. He married Filomena, a daughter of José Leandro Perea. He died at Alburquerque, February 1, 1904.

[333] Other than the usual appropriation bills, actions on contested election cases, and matters referred to in the text and in other notes, the acts of congress relative to New Mexico during the period 1864-1880 were as follows:

1864-65: Joint resolution to facilitate communication with New Mexico. Joint communication of delegates of the territories approving the constitutional amendment abolishing slavery. Act to establish post roads.

1865-66: Bill to confirm land claim of J. S. Ramirez, passed by the senate.

1866-67: Bill to abolish peonage passed congress; also, after much discussion, a bill to prohibit restriction of suffrage on account of race or color. Bill to provide for biennial sessions of the legislature passed the house.

1867: An act legalizing the acts of the legislature at its session of 1866-7. Bill to settle private land claims referred to committee, as also were many other bills earlier and later on this subject; and also bills on war and Indian claims.

1867-68: Resolution for the relief of Navajó captives held as peons, passed both houses. Several bills on lands, railroads, claims, and other subjects introduced by Delegate Clever, but not finally acted on; bill for the relief and reservation of Navajós at Bosque Redondo passed by the house and amended by the senate.

1868-69: Act on the Vigil and St. Vrain land grants for the benefit of settlers. Act providing for biennial sessions of the legislature; also amending the organic act on the passing of bills over the governor's veto by a two-thirds vote; also making the governor the superintendent of public buildings at a salary of one thousand dollars; also making the salary of the secretary two thousand dollars from 1867.

1869: Act repealing the acts of the legislature to impose a capitation tax on bovine cattle introduced from other states and territories.

1869-70: Bill to annul part of a New Mexico law on executions and mortgages; also bill to authorize a state constitution, referred to a committee; act increasing the salary of justices to three thousand dollars.

1870-71: Bill to authorize a state constitution under the name of Lincoln, reported by the senate committee, but again referred to the senate committee.

1871: Bill to pay volunteers' claims, tabled in the house. Bill to confirm Rio Grande land claim, passed both houses apparently, but referred to the house committee in 1871.

1871: Act to authorize the legislature to meet on the first Monday in December, and authorizing an election.

Attempts to organize a territorial government for that portion of New Mexico now included within the limits of Arizona were made in congress as early as 1857. Mr. Gwyn, of California, introduced a bill in the senate to organize the territory of Arizona; but there were jealousies on the railroad question, which resulted in the defeat of the bill. Mr. Green, of Missouri, in 1860, introduced a bill to provide "temporary government for the Territory of Arizuma," which also failed. Various other attempts were made, none of which was successful. During the year last named, a movement began at Mesilla, New Mexico, to make a separate territory. Under it Sylvester Mowry, well known as an army officer and owner of the Mowry mine, in the Patagonia mountains, was chosen delegate, though he was never admitted to a seat in congress. A convention was held at Tucson, in which several well known citizens of the place were concerned. J. Ross Browne,[334] in his valuable work, *Adven-*

TERRITORY OF ARIZONA

1871-72: Bill to enable land claimants to test the validity of their claims, referred to senate committee. Act to pay the salary of the secretary as superintendent of public buildings to June 1872, but repealing the act of 1868 which gave that salary. Act granting right-of-way to the New Mexico Gulf Railroad.

1872-73: Act for completing the military road from Santa Fé to Taos. Bill to survey private land grants at government expense referred to the house committee. Bill to donate ten sections of land for finding water in the desert, tabled. Bills to extend the time of voting on the state constitution and to create a new land district referred to a committee.

1873-74: Bill for a state constitution passed by the house and referred by the senate. Act creating a new land district.

1874-75: Bill for a state constitution passed by the senate with amendments.

1876: Bill for a state, passed by the senate, and referred by the house.

1876-77: House bill to pay Indian depredation claims, tabled.

1877: Bill to attach Grant county to Arizona, referred to house committee.

1877-78: Bill to annul the act of the legislature incorporating the Society of Jesuits, passed by the senate, and referred by the house. Bill for the relief of mounted volunteers, passed by the senate, and referred by the house.

1878: Act providing that the legislature shall not exceed twelve councilmen and twenty-four representatives, at $4 a day, the president and speaker, each, to receive $6.

1878-79: Act annulling the act of the legislature incorporating the Society of Jesuits.

[334] Browne, J. Ross, *Adventures in the Apache Country*: "The rebellion broke out in April, 1861. The Butterfield Overland Mail line was stopped at the same time, in view of the dangers that threatened it; and an act of congress was passed changing the route. During the month of July the only federal troops in the Territory shamefully and without cause abandoned it, and marched from Fort Breckindidge and Fort Buchanan to Cook's Springs, when they heard the Texan rebels were coming. Without waiting to ascertain the number or prepare for any defense, they burned all their wagons, spiked their cannon,

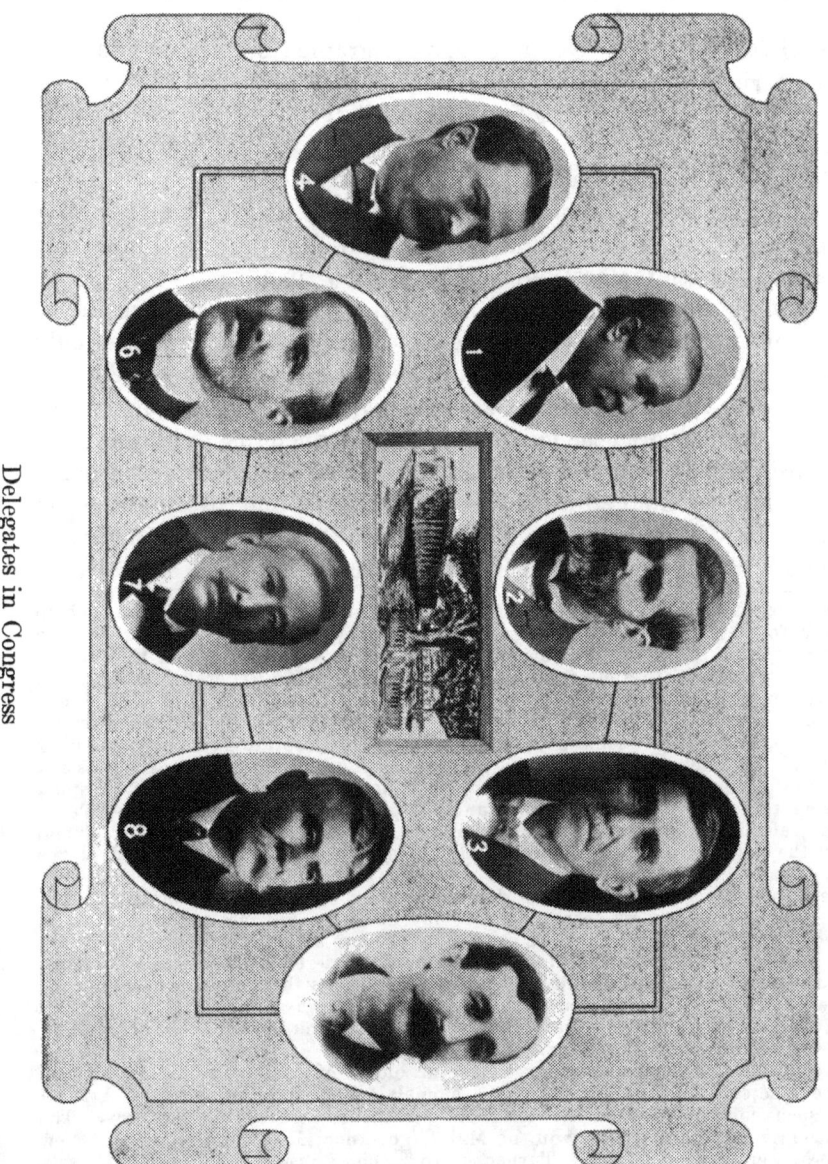

Delegates in Congress

1. Thomas B. Catron. 2. Don Antonio Joseph. 3. Harvey B. Fergusson. 4. Don Mariano S. Otero. 5. Don Tranquilino Luna. 6. Bernard S. Rodey. 7. Don Pedro Perea. 8. William H Andrews

tures in the Apache Country, gives a graphic picture of affairs at this period.

Nothing remained of Union rule until 1863, when it was reëstablished. A few American miners held on to their locations in the Cerbat and Hualapai mountains. In the Salt river valley there was a ranch or two; elsewhere, except at Tucson and Yuma, there was nothing of life to be found except a few natives, the Pimas and Papagoes, with the hostile Apaches at every turn.

At last congress was forced by military necessity to turn its attention to this region — in which the Gila valley formed the only open roadway from the southwest to the Pacific. On the 24th of February, 1863, the organic act was passed.[335] The people of New Mexico had favored the measure since 1858 when the territorial legislature passed resolutions in regard to it and recommended a north and south boundary line on the meridian 109 and also the removal of all New Mexican Indians to northern Arizona. In 1862, while John S. Watts was delegate in congress from New Mexico, he strong-

and packed their provisions on mules over the mountains to Fort Craig. There were four companies, numbering altogether, 450 men. They had heard of the surrender of Fort Fillmore toward which they were marching, and this caused them to take a different route. At Fort Fillmore 500 federal troops of the regular army surrendered to about 250 renegade Texans, ragged, undisciplined, poorly armed and badly equipped. A scattering company of these roving bandits, under the command of the guerilla chief, Captain Hunter, numbering about 100, reached Tucson on the 27th of February, 1862, and took possession of the place. Most of the inhabitants had fled to Sonora for safety, or stood ready to join the rebels. Hunter and his party held possession of the Territory, advancing as far as the Pima villages, and even threatening Fort Yuma, till the advance of the California Column in May, when they retreated to the Rio Grande. The few citizens and traders, who remained loyal to the government, and the managers and workmen employed at the mines, being thus left at the mercy of lawless desperadoes, roving bands of Apaches and Sonoranians, fled from the country as fast as they could procure the means of escape. Many of them were imprisoned, and some were murdered. The hostile Indians, ignorant of our domestic disturbances, believed they had at length stampeded the entire white population. On the public highways they fell upon small parties and slaughtered them. It was their boast and is still their belief, that they had conquered the American nation.''

[335] Colonel J. Francisco Chaves, then an officer of volunteers in New Mexico, was ordered to act as escort for the officials for the new territory of Arizona to such point as they might designate for the capital of the territory. The officers were John N. Goodwin, of Maine, governor; R. C. McCormick, of New York, secretary; William F. Turner, of Iowa, chief justice; William T. Howell, of Michigan, associate justice; Joseph A. Allyn, of Connecticut, associate justice; Almon Gage, of New York, district attorney; Levi Bashford, of Wisconsin, surveyor-general; Milton P. Duffield, of California, marshal; and Charles D. Poston, of Kentucky, superintendent of Indian affairs. When the party reached the Navajó Springs they concluded they were in Arizona, and

ly favored the separation and was one of the chief advocates of a bill to that effect then pending in the house.

W. F. M. Arny, secretary of the territory, had been performing the duties of governor of New Mexico during the years 1865-1866, when General Robert B. Mitchell [336] was appointed governor by President Johnson. He had not been long in office before he became involved in a controversy with the legislative assembly, which passed resolu-

ADMINISTRATION OF GOVERNOR ROBERT B. MITCHELL

---

there on the 31st of December, they celebrated the organization of the territory of Arizona. On the journey they had several encounters with the Indians and some of the escort were killed, but they succeeded in driving off the savages with some loss among them. When they reached Granite, now called Prescott, the governor decided to make that the capital and Colonel Chaves was permitted to return with his troops to New Mexico, making the return trip over a new route.

The convention which was held at Tucson continued from the 2d to the 5th of April, 1860. James A. Lucas was president. The places represented were Mesilla, Santa Rita del Cobre, Las Cruces, Doña Ana, La Mesa, Santo Tomas, Picacho, Amoles, Tucson, Arivaca, Tubac, Sonoita, Gila City, and Calabazas. A territory was organized with the following counties: 1. Doña Ana, all east of the Rio Grande; 2. Mesilla, from the river west to the Chiricahua mountains. 3. Ewell, from the mountains west of a line crossing the Little Desert, near the center; and 4. Castle Dome, all west of Ewell county. The Ewell for which the county was named was Captain R. S. Ewell, U. S. A., afterward a major general in the Confederate army.

[336] Robert Byington Mitchell was born in Richland county, Ohio, April 4, 1823, and died in Washington, D. C., January 26, 1882. He received his collegiate education at Washington College, Washington, Pennsylvania, and afterward studied law, practising his profession at Mansfield, Ohio, 1844 to 1846, when he enlisted with the Ohio volunteers for the Mexican War and served as first lieutenant of the 2d infantry from September 4, 1847, to July 26, 1848, on which date he was honorably mustered out. He returned to Ohio and resumed the practice of law and in 1856 moved to Kansas, settling at Paris, Linn county, in 1857. He was an active participant in the free state cause and served the territory in many ways; first as a member of the territorial house of representatives, 1857 and 1858, later as a delegate to the Leavenworth constitutional convention, being elected March 25, 1858. At the time of the Marias des Cygnes massacre, May 19, 1858, Mitchell organized a posse of men (among them James Montgomery) to follow the notorious Hamilton and his party into Missouri; unfortunately these outlaws escaped the pursuing party.

Mitchell was a member of the Free State convention at Topeka, April 28-29, 1858, and a candidate for congress in the democratic convention at Lawrence, October 25, 1859. He was appointed treasurer of Kansas territory February 11, 1859, serving until February, 1861, and was the first adjutant general of the state, holding that office from May 2 to June 30, 1861. He likewise served as president of the territorial relief convention, meeting at Lawrence November 14, 1860.

On June 20, 1861, he was mustered into the U. S. service as colonel of the 2d Kansas volunteer infantry; in 1862 this organization was merged into the 9th Kansas with Colonel Mitchell as commanding officer, March 15th, of the same year the name of the regiment was changed to 2d Kansas volunteers and

tions calling for his removal. He was charged with having absented himself during a session of that body, with the removal of certain officials appointed by Secretary Heath, and refusing to sanction a memorial passed in his absence. He took it upon himself to name a delegate in congress. The legislature determined to send all its enactments not approved by him to congress for confirmation, at the same time asking that the absolute veto power of the governor be abrogated, which was granted by an amendment to the organic act, passed in 1868. During his administration the Moreno mines were discovered, peonage was abolished, the governor issuing a proclamation on the subject. The supreme court of the territory rendered a decision declaring the Pueblo Indians to be citizens. The county of Grant was created, the first daily mail from the east was established, and the Navajó Indians were returned from Bosque Redondo to their old home in the northwest. Attorneys-general were Charles P. Clever, S. B. Elkins, and Merrill Ashurst.[337] The military tele-

again on March 27th to 2d Kansas cavalry. April 8, 1862, Colonel Mitchell was promoted to brigadier-general and commanded the 9th division, 3d army corps, Army of the Ohio, in the battle of Perryville, and the cavalry corps of the Army of the Cumberland in the battle of Chickamauga. While colonel of the 2d Kansas he was severely wounded at the battle of Wilson's Creek; he made the charge at the side of General Lyon, who was commanding, and they fell together, General Lyon to his death.

On December 14, 1866 he was appointed governor of New Mexico, continuing in that office until 1869. He then returned to Kansas, and was at Paola, Miami county, for a time, being a delegate to the Liberal Republican convention held at Topeka in 1872, where he received the nomination of that body to congress. He shortly moved to Washington, D. C., where he died.

[337] Charles P. Clever, was born in Cologne, Prussia, in 1827. He came to the United States in 1848 and settled at Santa Fé, New Mexico, in 1850. He was engaged in merchandising from 1855 to 1862, being a member of the firm of Seligman and Clever. In 1857 he held the position of United States marshal for the territory. At this time he began the study of the law; admitted to the bar in 1861, he at once entered upon the active practice of the profession. Appointed adjutant general by Governor Connelly in 1861, he served as adjutant on the staff of Colonel Canby at the battle of Valverde. In 1867 was candidate for delegate to congress, received the certificate, but in a contest, his opponent, Colonel J. Francisco Chaves, was given the seat. In 1864 was made commissioner to codify the laws. He was a man of great strength of character; had many friends and many enemies. He died in 1874.

Merrill Ashurst, who filled the office of the attorney general from 1852 to 1854, and again from 1867 to 1869, was born in Alabama; came to New Mexico in September, 1851, and began the practice of his profession at Santa Fé. He was a man of unusual ability, a convincing orator and very successful as a prosecutor. He died in 1869, while serving his second term as attorney general.

Theodore Wheaton came to New Mexico with General Kearny, and belonged to the 1st Missouri volunteers under Colonel A. W. Doniphan. After the war

graph was put into operation and Fort Sumner was abandoned. During the administration of Governor Mitchell occurred the fatal encounter between Chief Justice John P. Slough and Colonel William L. Rynerson. Judge Slough had made some very bitter and slurring remarks concerning Rynerson, who, at the time, was a member of the legislative assembly from Doña Ana county. These were reported to Rynerson who immediately proceeded to the Fonda, or Exchange hotel, called upon Judge Slough, demanding a retraction. Instead of giving him any satisfaction Slough endeavored to draw a derringer which he carried. At the same moment Colonel Rynerson drew his own weapon, firing and killing Slough instantly. This affair occurred December 15, 1867. A coroner's jury, after a full investigation, fully exonerated Rynerson, who was also afterward tried in the district court and acquitted.[338] During the administration of Governor Mitchell, Brigadier-General Christopher Carson passed away. He died at Fort Lyon, Colorado, May 23, 1868.[339]

he practiced his profession in the courts of the territory; he assisted in the prosecution of the murderers of Governor Charles Bent. He served as a member of the legislature from Taos county, in 1852, and was speaker of the house of representatives of the 2d and 3d sessions of the legislature. From 1861 to 1866 he was United States attorney. He died at Ocaté, New Mexico, in 1875.

[338] William Logan Rynerson was born in Hardin county, Kentucky, a few miles from the birthplace of Abraham Lincoln, in 1836. He went to California late in the fifties, walking across the plains over a portion of the Oregon trail. He engaged in mining in California and also read some law. When the 1st California volunteer infantry was organized at San Francisco, he enlisted and was made first sergeant of Company C of the regiment, January 1, 1862. He was promoted to second lieutenant February 5, 1862. In April of the same year he was promoted to a first lieutenancy of Company B, the same regiment. He served as adjutant of the regiment until August 9, 1864, when he was appointed captain. Early in 1865 he was transferred to the staff as captain and assistant quartermaster of volunteers and served until he was mustered out in 1866. He then settled in Mesilla, Doña Ana county, later moving to Las Cruces. He was admitted to the bar and practised his profession in the third district until the time of his death. He served as a member of the house of representatives and was later elected a member of the legislative council of the New Mexico assembly. He was the nominee of a faction of the republican party for the delegateship in congress but was defeated. He received the appointment of district attorney for his district several times and was a member of the constitutional convention of 1889. He died at Las Cruces, July 4, 1893.

[339] Christopher (Kit) Carson was born in the state of Kentucky in the year 1809. Later his parents moved to the state of Missouri, where, at fourteen years of age, he was apprenticed to David Workman. He ran away from Workman and joined a caravan bound for Santa Fé, in the year 1826, the party being in charge of Colonel Céran St. Vrain. The caravan reached Santa Fé in the fall of that year and during the following two years Carson traveled over New Mexico, going as far south as Chihuahua and west to the Gila river. He worked at the Santa Rita mines. Carson's first Indian fight was while under the leadership of Ewing

NEW MEXICO DURING THE CIVIL WAR 413

Mitchell's administration was far from harmonious. He was succeeded in 1869 by William A. Pile, afterward minister to Venezuela.

ADMINISTRATION OF WILLIAM A. PILE

The feature of Governor Pile's administration was his alleged sale of a large portion of the *Santa Fé Archives* as waste paper. His action in this regard raised a stormy protest at the time. In truth he did dispose of a great many of these ancient documents, but it is not generally believed that they were actually used

---

Young. A party of American trappers and traders had been driven into the settlements, with the loss of most of their property. Young organized an expedition for the purpose of punishing the Indians and trading and trapping in the northwest. On this expedition fifteen Indians were killed, the whites losing none of their own number. During this trip Carson distinguished himself in many ways. The party returned to Santa Fé in 1830. For the following four years he led the life of a mountaineer and trapper and there were few parts of the entire Rocky Mountains from Montana to New Mexico that were not visited by Carson. From 1834 to 1842 Carson was ''hunter'' for the Bents. He was expected to supply the fort on the Arkansas, which had a force of forty men, with fresh meat by his rifle. He had no trouble in so doing, for he was a dead shot and game was plenty. During this time he married an Indian girl, who died within a year after the marriage, leaving him a baby daughter. In 1842 he returned to Missouri, visiting St. Louis, where he met Colonel John C. Fremont, who engaged him as guide for his first expedition. In 1843 Fremont again sent for Carson. This time he was required to lead the expedition to the Pacific coast. They reached Salt Lake in August, turning thence to the northwest, making their way across the arid regions to Oregon, and thence southward through the Sierras to the valley of the Sacramento. The passage of these mountains was made in the depth of winter; the men were compelled to eat their saddles and the mules were eating each other's tails before the valley was reached. The mountains were as new to Carson as they were to Fremont, but the former's skill was invaluable in many emergencies. He saved Fremont's life. The party reached Sutter's mill March 6, 1844. Carson had known Sutter years before in Santa Fé. Under their very feet were the golden sands which five years later made California famous. The expedition returned and reached Fort Bent in July, 1844. Carson now determined to establish a ranch, but had barely begun when Fremont again sent for him to guide another expedition to California by a more direct route. He accepted and in 1846 participated in the taking of California from the Mexicans. Carson had been sent east with despatches; coming across by the southern route he met General Kearny and command; Kearny ordered him to return to California, sending the despatches on by another express by way of Santa Fé. Having reached California and the vicinity of Los Angeles and San Diego, Kearny met the Mexicans in force. Kearny ordered an attack upon the Mexican advance, the command being under Captain Johnson, with Carson as second officer. Johnson's party of fifteen was reënforced by Captain Moore with twenty-five men. Moore ordered an attack upon the enemy's center, hoping to create a division and create confusion in the ranks of the enemy. The American loss in this engagement was thirty killed and wounded. The Americans were compelled to retreat. The following morning the march toward San Diego was resumed. Towards nightfall the Mexican attack was renewed. The Americans retired to a hill a short distance away. The situation was desperate and a council was held as to the best course to pursue. Carson took part in the council and volunteered to try and pass through the lines of the

for waste paper purposes. Many of them have since come to light. The counties of Colfax and Lincoln were created at this time. There was considerable advance in the mining industry during this administration.[340]

---

enemy and reach Commodore Stockton at San Diego. Lieutenant Beale, U. S. N., volunteered to accompany him. These brave men left the camp as soon as it was dark. They removed their shoes, in order to insure silence while passing the triple line of sentries around the foot of the hill. Several times, as they crept cautiously along, these sentinels could have touched them with their rifles. Their advance was very slow, but finally they cleared the Mexican lines. For a distance of more than two miles they had crawled upon the ground, sometimes each hearing the other's heart beat, so deathly was the stillness. Through the thorny bushes and cactus they trod with shoeless feet. All that night and the day following and into the night they continued their journey. At last the challenge of the sentinel at San Diego was heard. They were taken into the presence of Commodore Stockton, their story was told and at once a force of 200 men was sent by forced marches to relieve Kearny and his men. Carson was detained in San Diego, as without proper care there was danger of losing both of his feet, so severely had they been lacerated. Lieutenant Beale was partially deranged by the hardship of the journey, and did not fully recover his health for more than two years. Returning to the east, by way of Santa Fé, bearing despatches, Carson was entertained at St. Louis, Missouri, by Thomas H. Benton. Reaching Washington, Mrs. J. C. Fremont met him at the station, declaring that her husband's description of him made an introduction unnecessary, and conducted him to her own and her father's house. Carson was lionized while in Washington. From 1849 to 1854 Carson had many adventures with the Indians, some of which are marvelous in the relation. After the peace with Mexico, Carson built a home on the Rayado, where he lived with his wife and his niece, Teresina Bent, afterward the wife of Aloys Scheurich, who was with him when he died. In the year 1854, Carson was appointed Indian agent for the Ute, Apache and Pueblo tribes. This position he held until 1861. In the preceding year, on a trip to the San Juan country, in northwestern New Mexico, Carson fell from his horse and received injuries which were indirectly the cause of his death eight years later. When the Civil War broke out Carson immediately began the organization of a regiment of volunteers, which became the 1st New Mexico cavalry, of which Colonel Céran St. Vrain was made colonel. This regiment was mustered at Fort Union. St. Vrain soon resigned and Carson became the commander. The regiment fought at Valverde and acquitted itself with credit.

In 1863, Carson led an expedition against the Navajós. A portion of his command was mustered out at Alburquerque in 1865, the remainder of the regiment later garrisoning Fort Garland, Colorado. These were mustered out of service at Santa Fé in 1867. During the last years of his life Carson lived with Thomas Boggs near the mouth of the Purgatoire river in Colorado. His wife died on the 27th day of April, 1867, and Carson passed away on the 23d day of May the year following, at Fort Lyon. A monument to his memory stands in front of the Federal building at Santa Fé, erected by the G. A. R. A statue of Carson caps the frontiersman's monument in Denver. Carson was physically a man of small stature; his forehead was large and his eyes expressive. He was fearless and a man of great intelligence although uneducated, and often had the officers of his command read to him, thus storing away in a retentive mind a wealth of knowledge that few of his time could equal.

[340] According to the census of 1860, the population of the territory, exclusive of Indians was 80,567. The census of 1870 showed an increase to

In 1871 Marsh Giddings was appointed governor by President Grant. This period marked the first investment of foreign capital in lands in New Mexico. Lucien B. Max-
ADMINISTRATION OF well,[341] son-in-law of Carlos Beaubien,
GOVERNOR MARSH GIDDINGS one of the original grantees of the famous Beaubien and Miranda land grant, at this time known as the "Maxwell Ranch," sold the property to Jerome B. Chaffee, David H. Moffatt, and Wilson Waddingham, who six

---

90,573, of which 82,193 were natives of the territory; 2,760 born in other parts of the United States; 3,903 Mexicans, and 1,717 other foreigners. The assessed valuation of property in 1870 was $18,000,000, less than in 1860, when it was $20,000,000; the decrease was brought about mainly through the cutting off of Arizona and the lower portion of the state of Colorado. The Moreno mines were still being successfully worked and yielded in 1869, $200,000 while in 1870 the production showed a marked increase. Many rich silver lodes were discovered in Grant county. Silver and copper were found in Socorro county and anthracite coal was being mined in Santa Fé county, near the placer workings. On July 8, 1869, telegraphic communication was opened to the east. In this year was published the first newspaper in Colfax county, the *Lantern*, issued at Elizabethtown, then a thriving mining community. The Sisters of Loretto established a school at Las Vegas.

There were no public buildings in New Mexico during this period with the exception of the old palace which was used for all public purposes. On this structure, in 1866-67, repairs were made at government expense in the sum of five thousand dollars. The condition of this building was made the subject of many reports by many governors. In 1868-69 the secretary of the territory was made ex-officio superintendent of public buildings, with a salary additional of $1,000; the salary clause was repealed in 1872. See 42d cong., 2d sess., *H. Ex. Doc.* 128. There were estimates as to repairs made by various governors and secretaries, but little was ever done.

The finances of the territory from 1864 to 1871 seem to have been fairly good. In the first named year, there was surplus in the treasury of $5,416. Three years later this surplus only amounted to $15 and in the following year had increased to $17,029. In 1871 the debt amounted to $70,000.

The revenue act of 1869-70 imposed a tax of twenty cents on the $100 for territorial and five cents for county purposes. Property to the value of $500 was exempted from taxation; also certain implements and certain live stock.

Lincoln county was created January 16, and Colfax county January 25, 1869.

[341] Lucien Benjamin Maxwell was a native of Kaskaskia, Illinois, and became one of the most striking figures of the early mountain frontier. Every trader and plainsman in the Rocky Mountain region knew Maxwell. Beaubien, the father-in-law of Maxwell, and Guadalupe Miranda received from the Mexican government, during the administration of governor Manuel Armijo, the grant of land which later became famous as the Maxwell land grant. Beaubien finally purchased Miranda's interest in the property. Beaubien died in 1864 and Maxwell purchased the grant from the heirs, becoming its sole proprietor. He made large sums of money thereafter in various ways and finally built for himself a great house at Cimarron, where he entertained lavishly. This house, at the time, was as much of a palace as the times and the country could afford. Many men famous in those days were his guests. His table service was for the most part of sterling silver. Covers were laid daily for more than two dozen

months later, disposed of the property to an English company for $1,350,000. It is said that Maxwell received $750,000 for the property.

During the administration of Governor Giddings, Captain John Martin [342] succeeded in finding water upon the noted *Jornada del Muerto*, the terror of all travelers theretofore upon this portion of the old Santa Fé-Chihuahua trail. It was proposed in congress to

---

persons. Maxwell invariably kept a large amount of money — gold and silver coin — on hand. This money was the proceeds of the sale of his sheep, cattle, and grain, principally to the United States government, at enormous figures.

Maxwell founded the First National Bank of Santa Fé. The original stock certificates of this institution were unique, bearing a vignette of Maxwell with a cigar in his mouth. Maxwell was a man of unbounded generosity and possessed unlimited confidence in those whom he trusted. He was very charitable. He was eccentric, improvident, liberal, the last named characteristic being remarked even in those days. His friends found in him an object of undying affection. His love for the mountains and plains was unconquerable. Though rough in manner, there was nothing of the desperado about him. In the spring of 1871, Stephen B. Elkins, at the time a rising figure in the political history of New Mexico, with Thomas B. Catron and others determined upon establishing another bank at the capital. Maxwell, having tired of his banking experience, sold out to these men. Maxwell invested over a quarter of a million dollars in bonds of a corporation formed for the construction of the Texas Pacific Railroad. This investment proved a complete loss. Maxwell's wife was Luz Beaubien. Three of their nine children still survive. The last years of his life were spent at Fort Sumner, where he died in comparative poverty, July 25, 1875.

[342] John Martin, soldier and pioneer, was a native of Caledonia, New York, where he was born in 1829. He enlisted for the war with Mexico with General Winfield Scott, was present at the storming of Chapultepec, and after the war shipped on a sailing vessel bound for San Francisco, rounding the Horn, and arriving at the Golden Gate in 1849. He remained a citizen of California until the breaking out of the Civil War when, at the call for volunteers, he enlisted and was elected first lieutenant of Company D, 1st California infantry, of which J. H. Carleton was colonel. He marched with his regiment from the coast to the Rio Grande. He took part in many campaigns against the hostile Apaches and for several years was in command of the military escort accompanying the United States mail north from Las Cruces. In 1867 he went to the place called by him "Aleman," where he began sinking a well in the hope of striking water. He was successful, finding the precious fluid at a depth of eighty-six feet. He sunk the well one hundred sixty-four feet, the dimensions being six by four feet. Here he established a ranch and stage station, the place thereafter being known as Jack Martin's well. He also conducted a government forage agency. He continued living here until 1875, engaged in the business of stock raising. In the latter part of 1875 he moved to Santa Fé where he conducted the famous Fonda or Exchange hotel, continuing in this business until the date of his death in 1877. He was survived by his wife and four children, two of whom have been prominent in the political and official history of the territory, William E. and John A., the former several times a member of the legislative assembly, official court interpreter, clerk of the district court, deputy superintendent of the penitentiary, and prominent public speaker and politician, the latter register of the U. S. land office at Las Cruces.

Chief Justice and Associate Justices of the Supreme Court of New Mexico,
Appointed by President Cleveland in 1885
E. V. Long, C. J.   William H. Brinker, A. J.   W. F. Henderson, A. J.   Reuben A. Reeves, A. J.

grant to him ten sections of land as a reward for his efforts, but the bill was defeated.

In 1871 a state constitution was formed by a convention held at Santa Fé for that purpose. The governor approved the constitution on the 1st of February, and by an act of the legislative assembly, an election was ordered for the first Monday in June, state officers to be elected on the first Monday in September should the constitution be adopted. Unfortunately the vote was received too late to be legally counted and the movement failed. The legislative assembly of 1872 passed an act providing for a school board in each county and in the year following the Jesuit college, one of the most prominent educational institutions in the territory for many years, was established at Alburquerque. In 1874 by congressional enactment a land office was established at La Mesilla; during this period, the demand for lands having constantly increased, the work of surveying the public domain was carried on as rapidly as possible, the congress making large increase each year in the appropriations for that purpose. In 1873 the public road from Santa Fé to Taos was completed, congress having appropriated twenty-five thousand dollars for that work.

On the 3d day of June, 1875, Governor Giddings died in office and was succeeded by William G. Ritch,[343] who had been secretary since

[343] William G. Ritch was born in Ulster county, New York, in 1830, and died at Engle, New Mexico, September 14, 1904. In 1855 he removed to Hudson, Michigan, and later to Oshkosh, Wisconsin, where he held several civil offices. At the breaking out of the Civil War he enlisted in the 46th Wisconsin infantry, serving as a first lieutenant and adjutant of the regiment. After the war was over, he was elected member of the state senate of Wisconsin and later a presidential elector, voting for President Grant. He became editor and proprietor of a newspaper in Wisconsin but his health failing he came to New Mexico, seeking a change of climate. He was appointed secretary by President Grant in 1873, which position he filled with honor and credit for three consecutive terms. He was the first president of the New Mexico Historical Society which was reorganized in 1880, having been originally incorporated in 1859-60. He was president of the bureau of immigration and was the first individual of importance in the official life of New Mexico to take steps looking toward the bringing of settlers to New Mexico from the states. He was public spirited and gave much thought to the betterment of conditions in New Mexico. He was the author of *Aztlan* or *Illustrated New Mexico*, which reached many annual editions. His *Legislative Blue Book* is an authority often cited and quoted. To Mr. Ritch may be given much of the credit for ''lifting the 'Kingdom and Province of New Mexico' out of its centuries of abeyance and suspension, to its present position in the great southwest, loyal and ready to contribute its full measure of the elements of empire and general prosperity in the race for place among the states of the Union.''

1873, as acting governor, the duties of the governor being performed by him until the appointment of Samuel B. Axtell, who was inaugurated July 30 of the same year.[344]

ADMINISTRATION OF GOVERNOR SAMUEL B. AXTELL

Samuel B. Axtell was inaugurated governor of New Mexico on the 30th day of July, 1875. During his administration the United States military telegraph was completed south to La Mesilla. At this period in the history of New Mexico the territory was the asylum eagerly sought by nearly all of the desperate men on the southwestern frontier. Colfax county on the north, particularly the Elizabethtown mining district, and Lincoln county in the southeast, were the catch-basins for the reckless and criminal element.[345] In the last named county a feud was begun which, in the annals of New Mexico, is known as the "Lincoln County War." The cause of this trouble and era of crime may be traced to the rivalry existing between prominent cat-

[344] During the administration of Governor Giddings, February 12, 1875, the arch-diocese of Santa Fé, with the vicariates apostolic of Arizona and Denver as suffragans, was created by papal bull of Pius IX, and the bishop of Santa Fé, Rt. Rev. J. B. Lamy, was made metropolitan of the province. On June 16th, while Secretary Ritch was acting as governor, Bishop Lamy received the pallium, and was consecrated to this arch-episcopal see in the presence of an assemblage of distinguished divines and civil and military officials from all parts of New Mexico.

[345] Hough, Emerson, says: "There was no one part of the remoter west which could claim any monopoly in the product of hard citizens, but there can be small challenge to the assertion that southeastern New Mexico, for twenty years after the Civil War, was without doubt, as dangerous a country as ever lay out of doors. The Pecos valley caught the first of the great west-bound Texas cattle herds at a time when the maverick industry was at its height. Old John Chisum had perhaps sixty to eighty thousand head of cattle. It was easier to steal these cattle than to raise cows for one's self. As for refuge, there lay the central mountains of New Mexico. As for a market, there was the military post of Fort Stanton, with the beef contracts for supplying the Mescalero Indian reservation. Between the market and the Pecos cow herds ran the winding valley of the Bonito, like a cleat on a vast sluiceway. It caught bad men naturally. Thus the Lincoln County war of 1879 to 1880 was a matter of topography rather than of geography. It was foregone that there should be factional fighting in that country sooner or later. Some of the Chisum cow-punchers turned out as thieves and gradually from these and other complications became evolved the famous Murphy and McSwain factions, who engaged in fighting so bitter that the government of the United States took a hand, deposed Governor Axtell of New Mexico, and sent out General Lew Wallace with extraordinary powers, and others to stop the killing. There were perhaps two hundred men killed in southeastern New Mexico from 1875 to 1881."

Mr. Hough is mistaken in the number of men killed during the troubles in Lincoln county and the Pecos valley during the period mentioned.

tlemen at the time living in Lincoln and the Pecos valley, respectively. Both were furnishing cattle for the Mescalero Indian agency and each accused the other of stealing from their respective herds. This was the basis for the war, although the acts and depredations in which the sympathizers of these two principals were involved may have brought on the crisis. Others believe, and not without reason, that the turbulence that terrorized the entire community, was the result of the outlawry established by such desperadoes as Billy the Kid.

During Governor Axtell's [346] administration the prefect system of county government was abolished and the present system of boards

---

[346] Samuel Beach Axtell was born in Franklin county, Ohio, October 14, 1819. An ancestor was an officer in the Revolutionary army and his grandfather was colonel of a New Jersey regiment during the war of 1812. His father was a farmer. Governor Axtell was a graduate of the Western Reserve college at Oberlin and was admitted to the bar in Ohio. In 1851 he went to California and engaged in gold mining and upon the organization of the counties of the state was elected district attorney of Amador county, holding this office three terms. He removed to San Francisco in 1860, was elected to congress in 1866 and 1868 as a democrat. He changed his political faith at this time and allied himself with the republican party of which he was a stanch supporter to the time of his death. In 1874 he was appointed governor of Utah by President Grant and in the following year was transferred to New Mexico, being inaugurated governor July 30, 1875. He was superseded in this position by General Lew Wallace, appointed by President Hayes in 1878. In 1882 he was appointed chief justice of the supreme court of New Mexico, assuming the duties of the office in August of that year. In 1885, Grover Cleveland having been elected president, he resigned the office in May of that year. He was a man of high principles, absolutely without fear. On the bench he endeavored at all times to secure what he saw fit to designate as "sustantial justice" for all litigants and judicial precedents which interfered with the main object of trials in his court, or with equity from his standpoint, were ruthlessly cast aside. In 1890 he was elected chairman of the territorial republican committee. He died August 7, 1891, at Morristown, New Jersey.

Conditions, methods, and practices obtaining in the courts of New Mexico during Judge Axtell's incumbency, and the fearless character of this jurist are well exemplified in the relation of incidents occurring in one or two cases tried before him. In a celebrated criminal trial at Las Vegas, although Judge Axtell had been warned that his life would be forfeited if he dared to sit in the case, promptly on time he opened court. On this occasion he compelled the sheriff to search all of the court attendants and the spectators before he allowed the case to proceed. As a result forty-two revolvers were piled on the table, some having been taken from the attorneys in the case. Each man carrying a weapon into the court room was fined ten dollars for contempt of court, and no show of resistance was made when the fine was collected.

In another case before him the defendant, a poor young man, whose farm was in jeopardy, had no attorney. Seeing that the case was going against the man unless he could obtain legal counsel, Judge Axtell descended from the bench and began conducting the cross-examination with the remark: "It takes thirteen men to steal a poor boy's farm in New Mexico." Upon the conclusion of the submission of evidence, he instructed the jury to find a verdict

of county commissioners was established. On January 10, 1876, Henry L. Waldo was appointed chief justice of the supreme court by President Grant, his associates upon the bench being Warren Bristol,[347] of the third district, and, in the second, in the year 1876 John I. Reddick, in 1877 Samuel B. McLin, and in 1878 Samuel C. Parks.

A large number of notable occurrences [348] took place during the administration of Governor Axtell. Although devoid of all railroad connection with the outside world the territory and its few industries

in behalf of the defendant. When the foreman announced a disagreement, the judge discharged the jury, announced a verdict in behalf of the defendant, and told the sheriff never to allow any one of the discharged jurymen to serve again in San Miguel county.

It is related that during the term of William Breeden, as attorney general, when Judge Axtell, whose habits were exemplary, had made some very caustic remarks to some of the attorneys who had been addressing him, the former rose and, looking Judge Axtell in the eye, remarked: "Don't be too hard on the lawyers, your honor; you might be a lawyer yourself some time you know."

[347] Warren Bristol was born at Stafford, New York, March 19, 1823. He received his education in the schools and academies of that state and was admitted to the bar in Lockport. He removed to Minnesota and located in Hennepin county, where is now built the city of Minneapolis. In 1855 he presided over the first republican state convention held in Minnesota and was a delegate to the Baltimore convention of 1864 which nominated Abraham Lincoln. In 1872 he was appointed associate justice of the supreme court of New Mexico by President Grant, which office he held for thirteen years, filling the position with great honor and credit. He resigned in 1885, Grover Cleveland, democrat, having been elected president. He presided at the trial of William H. Bonney, a desperado known as "Billy the Kid." In 1889 he was delegate to the constitutional convention. He died at Deming, New Mexico, January 12, 1890.

[348] On September 14, 1875, Rev. F. J. Tolby, a clergyman of the Methodist Episcopal church, was murdered on the highway east of Elizabethtown. In 1876, a Presbyterian Mission school was established at the pueblo of Laguna by Rev. John Menaul. On April 15th of this year Louis Clark, a prominent citizen of Rio Arriba county, was assassinated in his residence at Plaza Alcalde. In the month of May the Denver & Rio Grande Railroad was completed to Fort Garland and to Trinidad. In October, 1876, Presbyterian Mission schools were established at Zuñi. In 1877 telegraphic communication was extended to San Diego, California, and to El Paso, Mexico. The Grand Lodge of Free and Accepted Masons of New Mexico was organized. On August 11 of this year occurred the death of Donaciano Vigil. He died at Santa Fé; his remains were removed to the legislative chambers where they remained in state until buried, on the 13th, with civic honors, in the Rosario cemetery. On January 11, 1878, an act incorporating the Jesuit Fathers of New Mexico, containing general powers in the matter of the establishing of educational institutions and the right to own an indefinite amount of property, all forever exempt from taxation, was passed over the veto of Governor Axtell. The act was annulled by unanimous vote of congress February 4, 1879. On February 2, the general incorporation act for railroad and telegraph lines was passed. St. Michael's college at Santa Fé was erected during this year. In the month of August the territory was visited by General William Tecumseh Sherman and a great reception, attended by the civil and military authorities, was given at Santa Fé in his honor.

Prominent New Mexicans of the Nineteenth Century
1. Don Gaspar Ortiz. 2. Don Francisco Lopez. 3. Don Jesus G. Abreu
4. Don Miguel Romero

continued to progress. Mining was successfully carried on in several localities; stock raising, always a prime industry of the country, flourished and the inhabitants looked forward to an era of great prosperity owing to the rapid advance of the railroad which, in 1876, had been constructed to Trinidad, Colorado.

Governor Axtell was superseded as executive by the appointment of General Lew Wallace, appointed by President Hayes, with in-

ADMINISTRATION OF
GOVERNOR LEW WALLACE

structions to leave no stone unturned in the restoration of peace and tranquility in the territory at the earliest possible moment. He was inaugurated October 1, 1878. Within a week thereafter a proclamation from the president of the United States relative to the use of United States troops in aid of the civil authorities was published. Governor Wallace very soon espoused the cause of the McSwain faction in the Lincoln county disturbances. His predecessor had been charged with upholding the opposition which had centered in the firm of Dolan and Riley. Chief Justice Waldo had resigned his position on the bench and had received the appointment of attorney general from Governor Axtell, succeeding William Breeden [349] in that position. The chief justiceship was filled by the appointment of Charles McCandless.[350] Governor Wallace, in his efforts to restore peace and tranquility, favored the prosecution of the commander at Fort Stanton for an unwarranted use of troops in the disturbances in Lin-

---

[349] William Breeden was born in the state of Kentucky. He came to New Mexico after the Civil War and held a position with the government revenue service; he was clerk of the supreme court and of the court of the first judicial district in 1869, when he began the practice of the law. In 1872 he was appointed attorney general and held the office until near the close of Governor Axtell's administration when he resigned. He was again appointed to this position by Governor Sheldon in 1881 and held the office until it was abolished in 1889. Colonel Breeden was regarded by a great many as the shrewdest politician and most capable lawyer of his time in New Mexico. He was a delegate to the national republican convention which nominated R. B. Hayes for president in 1876. For many years he was the chairman of the republican organization in New Mexico. He was an excellent lawyer, an able prosecutor, and a natural leader of men. His health failed him in 1888. He is now living near Boston, Massachusetts.

[350] Charles McCandless was appointed chief justice by President Hayes early in 1878. He presided at one term of court in Santa Fé county in that year and then returned to the east. He was a man of considerable ability. He tendered his resignation to the president shortly after his return to his native state of Pennsylvania. He was a man of too fastidious tastes for conditions in New Mexico existing at that time.

coln. This course the attorney general declined to pursue. In fact before the court of inquiry, asked for by the accused officer, Colonel N. A. M. Dudley, Judge Waldo appeared as counsel for the defense. Later on the governor attempted to appoint Eugene A. Fiske attorney general. In this he was not sustained by the supreme court of New Mexico and a vacancy existed in the office from February 14, 1880, to June 22, 1881, when William Breeden was named for the position by Governor Sheldon.

The beginning of the so-called Lincoln county war occurred when John H. Tunstel was killed by a sheriff's posse seeking to levy an attachment upon property belonging to Tunstel. The latter had as friend and employe, William H. Bonney, later famous as "Billy the Kid." The resulting fights [351] and legal contests cannot be properly dignified by the name of "war" inas-

THE LINCOLN COUNTY WAR

[351] On April 1, 1878, a party of five, "Billy the Kid," Fred Wait, Henry Brown, Jim French and one other, adherents of the McSwain faction, while secreted in a corral behind Tunstel and McSwain's store, shot and killed Major William Brady, the sheriff of the county, who was opposed to the McSwain faction, and George Hineman, who was with Brady at the time. This added fury to the feud and terrorized the law-abiding citizens of the county. George W. Peppin was appointed sheriff by Governor Axtell. Peppin was friendly to the side which opposed McSwain which was led by J. J. Dolan and John H. Riley. A party of McSwain men, armed with a warrant, issued by a justice of the peace, set out for Tularosa to get a man reported to have stolen some of their horses. Among this party of twelve or fourteen were "Billy the Kid," George W. Coe, Fred Wait, and Henry Brown, the remainder being natives. They stopped on the way and the four Americans went up a hill to get a drink at a spring. While kneeling they heard shooting in the direction of the remainder of the party, and soon perceived that the Mexicans were engaged in a fight with a party of five, belonging to the Dolan and Riley faction. One of the latter named Bernstein was killed, and the remaining four started up the hill and came upon "Billy the Kid" and his comrades. A hot fight ensued, but no one was killed save Bernstein. For his death "Billy the Kid," Coe, Brown and Wait were indicted. While returning from Tularosa the McSwain party had another encounter with their enemies near the Mescalero agency. It was April 5, and while they were taking dinner at Dr. Blazer's house, one mile from the agency, and Coe and John Middleton were standing guard, a man known as "Buckshot" Roberts, heavily armed, rode up on a mule. McSwain's men determined to arrest him. Dick Brewer called for volunteers to help, and "Billy the Kid," Charles Bowder, and George W. Coe responded. Bowder ordered Roberts to throw up his hands, but Roberts, who had his cocked Winchester on his lap, responded "Not much, Mary Ann." Both men fired almost simultaneously. Roberts was shot through the stomach, while the bullet from his gun took effect in George Coe's hand, tearing it almost to pieces. The ball first struck the gun barrel, thus deflecting it from Coe's breast. Roberts continued shooting, one shot scraping Coe's breast, Middleton was hit in the chest, and Bowder's cartridge belt was shot off. After driving his foes to retreat, Roberts went into the house and taking a feather-bed, placed himself upon it in

much as personal enmity and a general spirit of lawlessness which at the time pervaded the section of New Mexico wherein the events transpired were the real elements of dispute. The events which followed the killing of Tunstel were in reality the culmination of the hatred provoked by many larcenies of range cattle, intensified by the alliance with opposing sides of many persons who had individual scores for adjustment according to the formula of the cowboy period. After the killing of Tunstel his sympathizers organized themselves into a party known as the McSwain faction and a sort of guerilla warfare continued for the following eighteen months until finally broken up by the civil authorities with the aid of the military. The battle that ended the war was fought at Lincoln in July, 1878. Sheriff Peppin had called upon the United States forces as a posse comitatus. The troops consisted of a company of infantry, a troop of cavalry, some artillery — a gatling gun and a twelve pounder. The troops were drawn up before McSwain's front door, where the latter and some fifteen men were stationed, and demanded the arrest of the entire party. McSwain refused and read the order of President Hayes stating that the military had no authority to interfere or assist the civil authorities. While the attention of the McSwain force was attracted to the parleying in front, some of the opposing faction going to the rear of the house and, as is said, pouring oil on the roof and window sills, set fire to the building. For a long num-

---

front of the door. Dick Brewer, going below the house to an old saw mill, from which he could see into the door, began firing at Roberts from behind a log. Several shots were exchanged and Roberts succeeded in killing Brewer with a ball through the head. About this time a detachment of soldiers from the agency came up and put a stop to the fight by driving off the McSwain men. Roberts died of his wound four hours later.

The next fight of importance took place at the Fritz ranch, four miles below Lincoln, one afternoon about sundown. Some thirty men of the Dolan and Riley faction, while unsaddling their horses and making camp at the spring in the grove of walnuts beside the public road, discovered Frank McNabb, Frank Coe, and Abe Sanders riding down the road towards them. Sanders was a non-partisan, but the other two were McSwain men. A general firing began from the camp. Sanders was shot from his horse immediately. McNabb's horse was disabled and he took to the hills, but was pursued and surrounded and killed while making a last stand behind a tree. Meanwhile Coe had put his horse to a gallop down the road, but was followed by a shower of bullets. When he had reached a point in the road fully twelve hundred yards below the camp, a ball from a buffalo hunter's rifle struck his horse, passing through its head and coming out at the eye. The horse turned a summersault in falling, while Coe escaped to the hills. He was there surrounded and taken prisoner and brought to Lincoln. The next day, while a fight was going on between the two factions, he escaped and joined his friends.

ber of hours those in the house had to fight both fire and bullets, but when night came they one by one made a run between volleys to the river, and thence made good their escape to the hills. "Billy the Kid" [352] and McSwain stayed to the last, and when only they

---

[352] William H. Bonney — "Billy the Kid" — a fighter and desperado belonging to the McSwain faction, or at least fighting and killing with those sympathizing with that side in the Lincoln county troubles, was killed by Pat Garrett, sheriff of Lincoln county. The "Kid" was guilty of the murder of nine men. At the time of the death of the "Kid," John W. Poe, now a resident of Roswell, New Mexico, was a deputy sheriff under Garrett. The "Kid" had been sought for by the officers ever since the close of the Lincoln county war. He had been arrested, but had escaped from jail, killing his jailers. Poe lived at White Oaks, where lived an old man named George Gwynne, who came to him one day with the information that the "Kid" was at Fort Sumner. Poe replied that there must be some mistake; but Gwynne insisted that he was right; and his evident sincerity determined Poe to make an investigation. He reported to Garrett in Lincoln, to whom he told what had been said by Gwynne. Garrett did not put any faith in the story but finally determined to go to Fort Sumner. They went by way of Roswell, accompanied by Deputy Sheriff McKinney, and on July 12 started for Fort Sumner, riding all night. The next day they lay concealed among the hills and on the morning of the 14th arrived in the vicinity of the town where the desperado was said to be in hiding. As Poe was not acquainted in Fort Sumner, it was decided that he should go into the town and reconnoiter while the others remained in the sand-hills until they could hear from him. If he could not obtain the desired information in Fort Sumner he was to ride seven miles to Sunnyside to see a man named Rudolph, carrying a note to him from Garrett. He reached Sumner about noon on the 14th of July but could hear nothing of the whereabouts of the "Kid." In his interview with Rudolph the latter became excited and denied that the "Kid" was anywhere in the vicinity of Fort Sumner and said that he believed about it as Garrett did. Poe was convinced that he was on the right track and leaving Rudolph rode at night to the place where Garrett and McKinney were stationed — at an avenue of cottonwood trees about four miles from the fort. Garrett finally consented to go to the house of a certain woman where they believed the "Kid" would be found if in that neighborhood. They rode to within a quarter of a mile of the fort and secreted themselves in a peach orchard within twenty steps of the back door of the house. There they remained from nine until eleven o'clock but saw or heard nothing. Garrett proposed returning home without letting the people know that they had been in the vicinity but Poe insisted upon going to the home of Pete Maxwell and asking him if the "Kid" had been seen in the neighborhood. They went to Maxwell's home, the sheriff proposed to go in, saying, "I am well acquainted with Maxwell and know where his bed room is." Garrett made his way toward the house while Poe and McKinney sat on the steps outside. It was a long adobe dwelling with a gallery extending from end to end and a picket fence flush with the east end of the house which was on the street. Maxwell's room was in the east end. Garrett had been inside only a few minutes when Poe saw a man coming along the fence, barefooted, bare-headed, and in his shirt-sleeves. The fence concealed them and Poe supposed it was Maxwell or some of his friends. The man came within four feet before he saw them. As soon as he did so he jumped on the gallery, pulled his pistol and cried, "*Quien es?*" Poe answered, "Don't be afraid; there is no one here to hurt you." The "Kid" stepped over the threshold, then putting his head outside, again asked, "*Quien es?*" Poe moved to-

Presidents of the New Mexico Bar Association
1. William B. Childers. 2. A. A. Jones. 3. William A. Vincent. 4. Neill B. Field. 5. James G. Fitch

were left their opponents made a rush and endeavored to enter the house. They were checked, however, and one of their number, Robert Beckwith, was killed. The "Kid" then made his escape and McSwain, who knew nothing about the use of firearms, was shot before he could get out of the house. Thus closed the "war," three months before the arrival of Governor Wallace in New Mexico. During his incumbency, in his executive capacity, he did nothing in the way of bringing about a termination of hostilities or a cessation of the existing troubles. The principal attorneys at Santa Fé and in the territory were retained by the Dolan and Riley faction. These men had been friends and connected with the administration of Governor Axtell. Their dislike for Wallace and his methods was apparent. In his efforts to carry out some of his policies in the matter of prosecutions the governor sought to influence the presiding judge of the third district, Warren Bristol, by intimating that he could "bend the law" to meet certain legal objections which were proving an obstacle to the success of his measures. If the fame of Governor Wallace rested upon any of his official acts in New Mexico it would be far from secure. However, while executive, he wrote a portion of *Ben Hur* when occupying the old palace as his official residence.

The principal event occurring during the administration of Governor Wallace was the building into New Mexico of the Atchison, Topeka and Santa Fé Railroad. Under a charter issued by the territory to the New Mexico and Southern Pacific Railroad Company the line crossed the Raton mountains November 30, 1878, and in February, 1879, the first passenger train, carrying members of the Colorado legislature, was run to Otero station, Colfax county. The line

---

ward him a second time and the "Kid" ran up to Maxwell's bed. The room was dark and he did not see the sheriff. He leaned over the bed and asked Maxwell who it was on the outside. Maxwell felt that something was going to happen and jumped out of bed. About this time the "Kid" noticed the sheriff and covered him with his pistol and began backing off, saying, "*Quien es? Quien es?*" It was probably so dark that he could not distinguish Garrett. At all events he did not shoot but Garrett did, the ball passing through the heart of the "Kid." Garrett fired a second shot, not being able to see the effect of the first, and, after waiting a few moments, rushed for the door. They could not tell the effect of the shots and fearing to enter the room in the darkness, lest they might meet the fate of so many others at the hands of the desperado, they placed a light on the window-sill so that it would shine into the room, and there they saw that the bullet had done its work — that he who had so often taken life had at last given up his own to the officers of the law.

reached Las Vegas, July 1, 1879, and was formally opened to passengers and traffic on July 7th. The line was extended to Santa Fé, February 9, 1880; to Alburquerque, April 22, at both of which places great demonstrations were made by the people. Following down the Rio Grande valley it was completed to Deming, March 10, 1881, where a connection with the Southern Pacific Railroad was made, thus forming the first all-rail route across New Mexico to San Francisco. In June, 1879, the territory was visited by Lieutenant-General Philip H. Sheridan; public receptions and balls were held at Santa Fé in his honor; later the commanding general of the department, Major-General John Pope, also visited Santa Fé where a reception was tendered him by the citizens of the capital.

The entrance of the railroad marked a new era in the annals of the territory. In advance of and accompanying its construction and completion came an army of energetic American citizens who immediately began the building of towns, the purchase and stocking of immense cattle ranches, the prospecting and development of mines, and the establishment of many industrial enterprises an account of which appears in another chapter devoted to the growth and progress of the country from the advent of the railways to the present time. The population, according to the tenth census, was 109,793, exclusive of Indians. Of this number 91,271 were natives of New Mexico, 9,471 born in other parts of the United States, 5,173 Mexicans, and 2,873 other foreigners.

Santa Rita Copper Mine, 1850

BIBLIOGRAPHY

Bancroft, H. H.	*History of Arizona and New Mexico*, San Fran., 1888.
Browne, J. Ross	*Adventures in the Apache Country*, New York, 1871.
Canby, Col. E. R. S.	Official Reports, *War of the Rebellion*, ser. i, vol. iv.
Greeley, Horace	*American Conflict*, Hartford, 1866.
Hayes, A. A.	*Unwritten Episode of the Late War*, London, 1881.
Hollister, O. G.	*1st Reg. Col. Volunteers*, Denver, 1863.
Lossing, B. J.	*Pictorial History of the Civil War*, Hartford, 1868.
Patterson, Thomas M.	*Rocky Mountain News*, Denver.
Read, B. M.	*Illustrated History of New Mexico*, Santa Fé, 1911.
War of the Rebellion	Ser. i, vol. iv, Washington.

Navajó Chief

CHAPTER X

INDIAN CAMPAIGNS — ARMY POSTS — MILITARY COMMANDERS — THE APACHE AND NAVAJÓ INDIANS — BOSQUE REDONDO — COMANCHES, APACHES, UTES, AND PUEBLOS — THE RESERVATIONS — VICTORIO'S RAIDS — GERONIMO — HIS RAIDS AND CAPTURE — GENERAL NELSON A. MILES — 1864-1887

THE Confederate invasion under General Sibley made the withdrawal of all regular troops from the Indian country imperatively necessary and the New Mexican settlements were left exposed to the unrestrained depredations of the Apaches and Navajós. In the south, in the neighborhood of Fort Stanton, the ranches were entirely abandoned. Many natives were killed, their ranches destroyed, and the stock driven off by the murderous savage. The miners in the country were forced from the mining camps and many were slain.

As we have seen, Brigadier-General James H. Carleton [353] re-

---

[353] Brevet Major-General James H. Carleton was appointed second lieutenant, 1st U. S. dragoons, October 18, 1839; promoted to first lieutenant, March 17, 1845; captain, February 16, 1847; breveted major, February 23, 1847, for gallant and meritorious conduct at Buena Vista, Mexico; major 6th U. S. cavalry, September 7, 1861; commissioned colonel 1st California volunteer infantry and recognized as of that grade from August 7, 1861. He was appointed brigadier-general of the U. S. volunteers April 28, 1862; breveted lieutenant-colonel and colonel U. S. A., March 13, 1865, for meritorious services in New Mexico; breveted brigadier-general U. S. A., on same day for gallant services in the northwest and also breveted major-general U. S. volunteers for meritorious services during the war. Mustered out of volunteer service, April 30, 1866; lieutenant-colonel 4th U. S. cavalry July 31, 1866. Until September 12, 1865, he was in command of the department of New Mexico; thence to April 30, 1866, in command of the district of New Mexico. He was born in Eastport, Maine, and died January 7, 1873. General Carleton served in New Mexico prior to the Civil War as a captain, with his regiment, during the years 1855, 1856, and 1857. His record is one of the best of the "old army" and ante-bellum days.

The officers commanding the department, or the district, of New Mexico, succeeding General Carleton were General George Sykes, 1867; General George W. Getty, 1867-71; General Gordon Granger, 1871-3 and 1875-6; General J. I.

lieved Colonel Canby of the command of the department September 18, 1862, and during the ensuing four years conducted military operations in New Mexico and Arizona.

Carleton's first movement was against the Mescalero Apaches, against whom he sent Colonel Christopher Carson with five companies of New Mexican volunteers. His orders were to slay the men without parleying and bring in the women and children as prisoners. "For the first time," says Bancroft, "a definite policy was adopted. Carleton's idea, and a very sensible one, was to chastise the savages thoroughly, and show them that there was to be no more trifling. No treaties were to be made, and no terms accepted except unconditional surrender as prisoners of war." Carson's first conflict was with a band of Mescaleros. Two of their principal chiefs, José Largo and Manuelito, were killed, beside a number of warriors. The Indians soon discovered that a vigorous war was in store for them and their chieftains went to Santa Fé with their agent, to sue for peace. The terms required of them were accepted. They were removed to Fort Sumner and the Bosque Redondo, on the Pecos river, while a constant warfare was kept up upon the hostiles who refused to come in. By the spring of 1863 about four hundred Mescaleros had submitted, and were living in peace at the Bosque, while the other bands had been forced to suspend their raids, Fort West, at Pinos Altos, having been garrisoned.[354]

Gregg, 1873-4; General Thomas C. Devin, 1874-5; Colonel James F. Wade, 1876; General Edward Hatch, 1876-81; General Luther P. Bradley, 1881; General R. S. Mackensie, 1881-3; General Stanley, 1883-4; General Bradley, 1884-6; General Swayne, 1885; General Grierson, 1886-8; General Eugene A. Carr, 1888-90; Colonel Pearson, 1890-94.

[354] Fort Craig, below San Marcial, on the Jornada del Muerto was strengthened in the beginning of 1863. An expedition was sent against the Gila Apaches, who were fiercely raiding the ranches and ruining settlements at the head of the Mimbres river and the Pinos Altos. Mangas Coloradas, a notorious Indian, was captured and brought into Fort McLeod. The next day, while attempting to escape, he was killed by the guard. Two engagements at the Pinos Altos mines resulted in the loss of forty-seven Indians, sixteen of whom, including the wife of Mangas, were wounded. The 1st cavalry, California volunteers, who were the troops chiefly engaged in the Gila country, soon after, following a trail of Apache warriors for seventy-five miles, discovered their camp. About sixty men dismounted and surrounded the camp, while the rest of the men made a charge upon it. The Apaches were completely routed, some horses were captured which had been run off from Fort West, and twenty-five warriors were killed. On their return from this engagement, they were attacked by the Indians in a canyon, and again the soldiers turned the tide against the savages, even climbing, one over the other, the

In this same year, Colonel Carson was sent into the northwest against the Navajós; the plan of removing all the Indians to Fort Sumner on the Pecos was developed. July 20th was fixed as the date after which every Navajó was to be treated as hostile, and orders were repeatedly issued to kill every male Indian capable of bearing arms.[355] While there were no great fights or victories, from a military point of view, and while there was but

CAMPAIGN AGAINST NAVAJÓS

perpendicular walls of the canyon, to dislodge their assailants, who hurled upon them showers of arrows, but were again defeated, with a loss of twenty-eight killed, while only one of the troops of the government was slain. By the end of February the Mescaleros were completely subjugated in New Mexico. A hundred fled to Mexico or to join the hostile Gila Apaches; but these were vigorous fighters and afterward returned to commit depredations in the neighborhood of Fort Stanton.

[355] Meline, James F., *Two Thousand Miles on Horseback*, pp. 284-285: "The Navajós had their Talleyrands and their Metternichs as well as their betters. How profoundly they regretted what had occurred — how ardently they desired the resumption of these amicable relations, etc. Mutual respect, profound consideration, etc., and all the other verbose stock in trade of diplomacy — they could set forth as handsomely and as hypocritically as Prussian protocol. 'Some bad young men of the tribe had committed this robbery, or that murder, and their heads' — to-wit, the heads of the ambassadors — 'were bowed down with grief. Other treaties had been broken, but this treaty — ah, this treaty — should be kept sincerely. You shall see.' Well, we did see. Finally, General Carleton, an officer of superior military and administrative talents, broke up the time consecrated farce of treaty. Soon after he assumed command in New Mexico, an eminently respectable deputation of eighteen Navajó chiefs with keen perspective of indefinite presents, called upon him to know if he would not make a treaty. The general is from the state of New Hampshire and characteristically answered their question with another question: 'What do you want of a treaty?' 'That we may hereafter have peace.' 'Well, then,' was the unexpected reply, 'Go home, stay there, attend to your own affairs, commit no more robberies or murders upon this people, and you have peace at once, without the trouble of a treaty.' Treaties, the general informed them, appeared to confuse matters and involved the double labor to the Navajós of making and breaking them. They, the Navajós, well knew that they never kept them, and he, the general, was not a child to be beguiled by them. 'Now,' he continued, 'Go; and if you rob or murder any of this people, so surely as the sun rises, you shall have a war you may not soon forget.' Navajó discomfited, said he had never been treated that way before. Refused a treaty! Was such a thing ever heard of? They were good Indians though. They would return to their country, and try to persuade their young men to behave. The result was, that in a few weeks, the robbery and murder of Mexicans began again. Then came a Navajó message that a large portion of them were peaceably disposed. This was in the spring of 1863. General Carleton sent them word that, as they all lived together, he could not distinguish friends from foes; that those who claimed to be friendly should come out from among the others and go to the Bosque Redondo, a large and beautiful tract of land forty miles square, with six thousand acres of arable land, on the Pecos river, where they should be cared for and allowed to want for nothing. Indian reply was not polite, but it was perfectly intelligible. Not a Navajó would come. Another message from the

slight diminution in the frequency and extent of depredations, yet by continuous and active operations in all parts of the country, and by prompt refusal to entertain any proposition of peace or the old time treaties, a very great progress was made in the essential task of showing the Indian that their foe was at last in earnest, and that they must yield or be exterminated. A beginning was also made at the Bosque Redondo, where over two hundred Navajó prisoners were gathered, or were at least en route at the end of the year. At the beginning of 1864 Carson and his forces marched to the Canyon de Chelly, and while the direct result of the campaign was only twenty-three killed, thirty-four captured, and two hundred surrendered, and while there were continued hostilities in other regions, yet from this time the Indians began to surrender in large numbers, and before the end of the year, the Navajó wars were practically at an end and over seven thousand of the tribe were living at Bosque Redondo.[356]

general that they had better consider the matter more maturely. They might have until the 20th of July with the door of peace left wide open. Once closed it should never be opened again. But the Navajós said they had heard 'Big Talk' before that meant nothing; had listened years to the cry of 'Wolf' that came not. And they scouted the soldier's warning. True to his promise the war opened on the very day set by General Carleton, July 20, 1863. A regiment of New Mexicans, with more than a century of accumulated wrong and oppression to avenge, were at once placed under the command of a man who understood his Indian well — Kit Carson. These troops knew neither summer rest nor winter quarters, but pursued the Indian foe relentlessly month after month, night and day, over mesas and deserts and rivers, under broiling suns and the rough winter snows, killing and capturing them in their most chosen retreats, until finally, broken and dispirited under a chastisement, the like of which they had never dreamed of, small bands began to come in voluntarily; then larger ones, and finally groups of fifties and hundreds, nearly comprising the strength of the tribe. The prisoners as fast as received were despatched to the Bosque Redondo and those who remained in arms sent out white flags in vain. Throughout 1864 and 1865 and the present year, the war went on under these conditions, and the result is that some eight thousand Navajós, including a few Apaches, are now living peaceably at the Bosque, engaged in agriculture and manufactures, 400 miles from their old homes and 90 miles east of the Rio Grande settlements.''

[356] During the year 1863 the number of Indians killed under the vigorous military operations of General Carleton was 301; 87 were wounded and 703 captured. Their depredations in only five counties of New Mexico caused the loss as stated in the official records, of sixteen citizens killed, 224 horses, 4,178 cattle, 55,040 sheep, and 5,901 goats; in other counties the losses were equally severe and the estimate for several previous years was not less. In January, 1864, the citizens of Colorado and the Ute Indians were pressing the Navajó from the north on account of their robberies of stock in that direction. The troops were pushing hard upon the scattered bands, taking advantage of the snows and severe cold of the season to increase their distress and thus more rapidly to accomplish their subjugation. The purpose of

The Kiowa Apaches, Comanches, and some other tribes of the eastern plains, roaming in the northeastern part of New Mexico, became very troublesome in 1864-6.

KIOWA-COMANCHE CAMPAIGN   Colonel Carson and other officers, with regulars and New Mexican volunteers, were sent against them, operating from Fort Bascom. The campaign conducted by Carson reflected small credit upon him and the troops under his command. In fact had it not been for the artillery his entire command would have been destroyed.[357]

the Navajós to resist so powerful an enemy was broken. On the last day of February General Carleton reported that 3,000 Navajós had been captured, or surrendered for removal to Bosque Redondo. For the first time in 180 years these brutal and fierce savages were acknowledging their defeat. As quickly as possible they were transferred to the reservation, but their sufferings on the journey were very great. Many died from their exposures to the cold, while others who were driving their flocks across the mountain ranges were greatly hindered by the deep snows.

[357] *Reports*, 17th B. A. E. (1896), p. 1: "The Kiowa Apache, with a part of the Comanche, made their winter camp on the South Canadian, at 'Red-Bluff' on the north side, between Adobe Walls and Mustang Creek in the Panhandle. While here early in the winter they were attacked by the famous scout, Kit Carson, with a detachment of troops, assisted by a number of the Ute and Jicarilla Apaches. According to the Indian account five persons of the allied tribes, including two women, were killed; the others, after a brave resistance, finally abandoned their camp, which was burned by the enemy. . . The engagement is thus mentioned in the testimony of an army officer a few months later. 'I understand Kit Carson last winter destroyed an Indian village. He had about four hundred men with him, but the Indians attacked him as bravely as any men in the world, charging up to his lines and he withdrew his command. They had a regular bugler who sounded the calls as well as those sounded for troops. Carson said if it had not been for his howitzers few would have been left to tell the tale. This I learned from an officer who was in the fight. The engagement is described in detail by Lieut. Geo. H. Pettis, who had charge of the two howitzers during the fight. The expedition which consisted of 335 volunteer soldiers and 72 Ute and Jicarilla Apache Indians, was under command of Col. Christopher Carson, the noted scout and Indian fighter, then holding a commission in the 1st N. M. Inf. . . Starting from Ft. Bascom, N. M., they proceeded down the Canadian, the intention being to disable the Indians by taking them by surprise in their winter camp as Custer did on the Washita four years later. The first village, a Kiowa camp, consisted of 176 *tipis*, was discovered on the Canadian at the entrance of a small stream, since known as "Kit Carson" creek, in what is now Hutchinson County, Texas, a short distance above Adobe Walls. The attack was made at daybreak of November 25th, 1864. After some resistance the Kiowa retreated a few miles down the river where there were other camps of the allied Kiowa, Apache and Comanche. Reënforced from these they returned and made a desperate attack upon the invaders so that Carson was glad to retire after burning the upper village, although the other camp against which the expedition was directed was in plain sight below. The battle lasted all day, the Indians disputing every foot of his advance and following up his retreat so closely that only the howitzers saved the troops from destruction. In the early part of the engagement, the soldiers corralled their horses in an

Frank Springer, President New Mexico Bar Association—
Paleontologist

The Bosque Redondo reservation, as a means of civilizing the Indians, was a complete failure. As a military measure, for the purpose of demonstrating to the warlike Navajós the power of the American government, Carleton's policy of removal was wise. The Navajós were but poor farmers and from lack of skill, ravages of the corn worm, and various other causes, the crops failed year after year. They lost their flocks and herds. The

BOSQUE REDONDO A FAILURE

---

old abandoned adobe building. This Pettis called the Adobe Walls, but which was probably the ruins of the trading post built by Bent twenty years before. The adobe walls where Quanah led his celebrated fight were not built until 1873 or 1874 and were some distance down the river. Several white captives, women and children, were in the hands of the Indians at the time of the attack, but none of these were rescued. The Kiowa also saved all their horses, although most of their winter provisions and several hundred dressed buffalo skins in the first village, together with the *tipis*, were destroyed by the troops. Quite a number of the enemy as skirmishers, being dismounted and hid in the tall grass in front, made it hot for most of us by their excellent markmanship, while quite the largest part of them, mounted and covered with their war-dresses, charged continually across our front from left to right and vice versa, about two hundred yards from our line of skirmishers, yelling like demons and firing from the necks of their horses at intervals. About two hundred yards in rear of their line all through the fighting at Adobe Walls was stationed one of the enemy who had a cavalry bugle and during the entire day he would blow the opposite call that was used by the officer in our line of skirmishers; for instance, when our bugler sounded the advance, he would blow retreat and when ours sounded retreat, he would blow advance. Ours would signal "halt," he would follow suit, so he kept it up all day, blowing as shrill and clear as our very best bugler. Carson insisted it was a white man, but I have never received any information to corroborate this opinion. It was most probably a Kiowa, possibly Satanta himself, who was famous for a bugle, which instrument he blew on state occasions. Deeming it unsafe to remain longer after destroying the first village, Carson formed the troops in marching order, with skirmishers in front and on the flanks, and the howitzers bringing up the rear, and began the return march. The enemy was not disposed to allow us to return without molestation and in a very few minutes was attacking us on every side by setting fire to the high grass of the river bottom, they drove us to the foot-hills and, by riding in rear of the fire, as it came burning toward us, they would occasionally get within a few yards of the column. Being enveloped in smoke, they would deliver the fire of their rifles and get out of harm's way before they could be discovered by us. On the side of the troops Pettis reports two soldiers killed and twenty-one wounded, several mortally, together with one Ute killed and four wounded. He puts the Indian loss at nearly one hundred killed and between one hundred and one hundred and fifty wounded. The official report which he quotes makes the number of tipis in the village destroyed about 150 and the Indian loss in killed and wounded together only sixty. Among these were four crippled or decrepit old Indians who were killed in the *tipis* by a couple of Ute squaws searching for plunder. . . A single instance of Indian bravery is noticed by Pettis. At one of the discharges a shell passed directly through the body of a horse on which was a Comanche riding at full run and went some two hundred or three hundred feet farther on before it exploded. The horse on being struck went headforemost to earth, throwing his rider as it

grazing was insufficient. There was the greatest difficulty in keeping them from starvation. They were attacked by the Comanches and other Indians of the plains. They quarreled with the Mescaleros, who ran away in 1866, after their agent had been driven off on a charge of irregular dealings in cattle. Under the new conditions the health of the Indians was impaired, and the ravages of disease became alarming. The indomitable spirit of the Navajós was broken.

In 1867, during the administration of General Grant, and by authority of congress, an Indian peace commission was organized to consider the causes of war, and to present some plan for the civilization of the Indians. The ability and experience of this commission could not be questioned. It was composed of Generals W. T. Sherman, Harney, Terry, and Augur; Colonels W. F. Tappan, John B. Sanborn; Senators J. B. Henderson and N. G. Taylor. In 1868 this commission reported that during fifty years, to the beginning of 1867, the United States government spent $500,000,000 and 20,000 lives in Indian warfare. Our wars, they said, with Indians had been almost constant, and they unhesitatingly affirmed that the government had been uniformly unjust toward the Indian. According to the records of the Indian department, Vincent Collyer, another United States commissioner, declared, "that the Apache Indians were the friends of the Americans when they first knew them and they have always desired peace with them. When placed upon reservations, in 1858 and 1859, they were industrious, intelligent and made rapid progress in the arts of civilization. The relations of the Apaches with the Americans were peaceable until the latter adopted the Mexican theory of extermination and by acts of inhuman treachery and cruelty made them our implacable foes; and this policy resulted in a war that in ten years from 1861 to 1870 cost forty million dollars and one thousand lives." In one year the Apaches killed 363 citi-

---

seemed 20 feet into the air, with his hands and feet sprawling in all directions, and as he struck the earth apparently senseless, two other Indians, who were near by, proceeded to him, one on each side, and throwing themselves over on the sides of their horses, seized each an arm and dragged him from the field between them amid a shower of rifle balls from our skirmishers. . . . More than a score of times we were eye-witnesses to this feat.' "

zens and soldiers of the United States, wounded one hundred and forty, and devastated the country for many miles.

On the first of June General Sherman and Colonel Tappan, of the peace commissioners appointed by President Grant, signed a treaty with the Navajós by which they should be returned to their country, schools should be established, and school houses built for every thirty children between the ages of six and sixteen years among them, their education made compulsory, the heads of families given one hundred and sixty acres of land for individual ownership, seeds and agricultural implements, flocks and cattle, and one hundred dollars the first year, twenty-five dollars the second and third years, with clothing and other articles needed to encourage and aid them in beginning and living a civilized and industrious life. But few of the provisions of this treaty by the government were ever carried out, particularly those which pertained to education and civilization. The Navajós returned with joy to the country of their ancestors and resumed their pastoral and nomadic life.[358]

[358] *Report* of W. T. Shelton, Indian superintendent. On account of the extensive area of the Navajó reservation, and owing to the fact that a majority of these Indians frequently change their location in order to find desirable grazing for their herds of sheep and goats, it is impossible to take an accurate census. The total population is estimated to be about 7,000. Of this number there cannot be less than 2,000 children of school age. The Indians living east of the Arizona line are by their own efforts making rapid strides toward progress. Those living along the river (San Juan) are taking out ditches and utilizing the land available for farming purposes.

Stock-raising, blanket-weaving and silver-smithing are the principal industries of the Navajó Indian. It is a poor family that does not possess from 100 to 1,000 head of sheep and goats. Their revenue from these sources exceeds $500,000 per annum. The Navajós are employed at all places in this country where labor is desired. They receive employment in the beet fields, at various mines and on the railroads, and are generally given the preference over other Indians and Mexicans.

In 1868 Virgil Mastin, a prominent merchant of Pinos Altos, was killed by the Navajós on the road near that mining camp. A fortnight later Captain Richard Hudson, commander of a company of citizen soldiery organized pursuant to orders from Governor R. B. Mitchell, was shot through both arms near this camp. Colonel Hudson, now a resident of Deming, N. M., is one of the most widely known of the early pioneers. He is an Englishman by birth, and in early childhood came to the United States. In 1852 when only thirteen years of age, he went to San Francisco. In 1861 he helped organize the 1st California regiment, but the regiment never saw active service. He later joined company I, 5th California infantry, was made sergeant, and later promoted to a lieutenancy. He came to New Mexico with the command under General J. H. Carleton. He remained in the service until the close of the war, being mustered out at Fort Union, in 1866. He was the first sheriff of Grant county and served two years. He was at one time the owner of Hudson's Hot Springs, at the same time being engaged in the cattle business.

The Mescalero Apaches numbered between six and eight hundred in 1866, at which time about four hundred were gathered at Bosque Redondo, but, owing to trouble with the Navajós, they left the reservation and raided all southern New Mexico. In their raids they were often joined by bands of the Chiricahuas.

APACHES, MESCALEROS, CHIRICAHUAS, VICTORIO, MANGAS, NANÉ, AND LARGO

In 1871 John Bullard, a prominent citizen of Silver City, New Mexico, was killed by the Apaches, while leading a force of volunteers against them; the tragedy occurred near the present site of Clifton, Arizona. He had brought his command to a point near this place when a band of Apaches was seen. He divided his command and, after detailing a guard for the pack-train, gave the command to move forward and strike the enemy from the north and from the south. Captain Bullard and a companion suddenly ran upon an outlying Indian, who was running in evident effort to reach and give the alarm to his friends. Bullard's companion fired, wounding the Indian in the thigh; Bullard also fired, his bullet piercing the body of the Indian, who sank slowly to the ground. The two rushed forward, when the dying Indian, in his last agony, raised a revolver with both hands, aimed at Bullard, whom he evidently recognized as the leader. Bullard saw his danger; he had failed to throw a fresh charge into his rifle and called to his companion to shoot. Two shots were fired almost simultaneously. The Indian fell with the entire top of his head blown away, while Bullard reeled and fell into a half recumbent position. He tore open his shirt, gazed a moment at the bleeding wound, and without a word or groan, fell back dead. The ball had pierced his heart. Speedy vengeance followed. Within a few minutes fourteen other Apaches lay dead upon the ground, while the remainder of the hostiles scattered among the huge boulders, many badly wounded as was afterwards learned from the Fort Grant reservation, where the Indians took refuge. The attacking party suffered no further loss, and an Apache boy was captured and brought to Silver City. He was taken in charge by "General" Wardwell, who afterwards surrendered him to his tribe. The remains of Captain Bullard were brought to Silver City, and the interment took place in the cemetery which then occupied the slope to the south and west of Professor Light's present residence. Major Kelly brought over a company of troops from Fort Bayard, and military honors were accorded the dead. The remains were afterwards removed to the cemetery east of town and to the southward of the Fort Bayard road, where they now rest. The loss of John Bullard was deeply felt. He had been a recognized leader; one of the principal streets of the town bore his name, and to this day a shade of regret colors the old timer's mention of the man's name. A public meeting was held, and resolutions were adopted expressive of the general grief. It was by a remarkable coincidence that Major Kelly and his command had just returned to Fort Bayard from a raid among the hostiles, in which they also succeeded in killing fourteen braves. The effect of the two blows was most salutary. For years afterward Silver City enjoyed comparative peace, in so far as the immediate surroundings of the town were concerned. Almost coincident with these tragic events, others of the Warm Spring Apaches made their presence felt near the Mexican border. Kearl and Miller's train was moving northward laden with freight for Fort Bayard. Charles Kearl and his wife, accompanied by six men, had ridden out several miles in advance of the train. They were attacked and but two escaped, one of these badly wounded and dying a day or two later. The bodies were horribly mutilated, especially that of Mrs. Kearl, then but recently a bride. Beside the Kearls, the dead were Gus Hepner, Charles DeLard, and three men named Sutherland, Bellhouse, and Burnham.

The early settlers of Silver City never forgave the Apaches for the untimely death of John Bullard, and shortly after the tragedy a measure was introduced in congress providing for an appropriation of $30,000 to defray the expenses of gathering their enemies upon permanent reservations. The people of Silver City thereupon held a mass meeting, at which Richard Yeomans presided and William H. Eckles acted as secretary. With I. J. Stevens, James Bullard, and E. M. Pearce, they formed a committee of resolutions, who, after calling the attention of congress to the fact that the proposed action was a misappropriation of public moneys, concluded with the following, which was unanimously and enthusiastically adopted: "Resolved: That by the expenditure of $30,000 among volunteers, the Indians can be gathered upon reservations where they will stay forever."

In 1873-4 a reservation was made for the Mescaleros near Fort Stanton and they were kept under control and some progress was made in agriculture and in education, although they were constantly engaged in feuds with miners, prospectors, stock-raisers, and settlers. At the time of the Victorio raids a large number of the Mescaleros joined in his marauding expeditions. Since the expatriation of Geronimo there has been very little trouble with these Indians, their population at this time being about five hundred. Of all the many tribes of Apaches, only remnants of the Mescaleros and Jicarillas now remain in New Mexico and these are all under perfect control.

In 1868, when the reservation at Bosque Redondo was abandoned, the Chiricahua Apaches were removed to the Ojo Caliente reservation in Grant county, New Mexico. These Indians remained here until 1877. Victorio, one of the greatest Apache chiefs and remarkable characters in southwestern Indian history, was their leader. Through the influence of settlers and over the remonstrance of the principal officers of the army, the government determined to remove these Indians to the San Carlos reservation in Arizona. The removal took place under military guard. Victorio fled from this reservation twice, only to be driven back by the military. In April, 1879, Victorio took the war-path, having resolved never to give up. In company with less than thirty warriors he left the Mescalero reservation, near Fort Stanton, where he had found refuge for some months. In the fight at the Ojo Caliente reservation he surprised and killed the guards and captured forty-five horses belonging to the 9th cavalry. He was immediately joined by about one hundred and fifty Indians from the reservation and at once commenced the most devastating Indian war of the southwest. The conflict ended with the capture of the successor of Victorio,[359] Geronimo, in 1887. This war resulted in

---

[359] According to Pope's *Report* there were no very serious troubles until the fall of 1879, although there were a great many depredations and isolated murders. After the fight at the Ojo Caliente reservation, Colonel Edward Hatch took command, killing about 100 Indians and driving Victorio into Mexico. Victorio crossed the frontier twice and was finally killed in Mexico.

Victorio's raid actually began on the ranch of Patrick Coghlan, at the time in Doña Ana county, New Mexico.

A remnant of Victorio's band of Apaches, thirty-seven in number, in 1903, was living in the Republic of Mexico, occupying a narrow canyon in the Guadalupe mountains, about twenty miles east of Zaragosa, a station on the Mexican Central Railroad. These Indians are leading a miserable existence and have made overtures several times to be permitted to return to the United States.

When Victorio first left the reservation, in the fight at Ojo Caliente, he

the murder of one hundred and forty citizens in the counties of Grant, Sierra, and Socorro alone. Victorio was a man past fifty years of age when he began this struggle. He was assisted in the leadership by two great chiefs, Loco and Nané, the latter his son-in-law. Everywhere pursued by the government mounted forces, still he was able to elude them, meanwhile murdering the settlers and pillaging the ranches of the country. His entire force never exceeded 300 men. Victorio was an intrepid warrior. He attacked, even while pursued by the government troops, wagon trains, ranches, mining camps, and American and Mexican troops. Entirely reckless of the outcome he terrorized large mining camps and successfully eluding

killed six of Captain Hooker's men. Joe Yankie and Nicolas Galles gathered a company and fought the renegades at the place now known as Lake Valley — McEvers' ranch. The command under Galles lost fourteen men, the loss being much greater by the Indians, the latter being armed with government carbines, while the volunteers had only light Winchester rifles.

In December, 1879, J. B. McPhearson and a party of five, who made their homes in Sierra county, learned that Victorio was on the war-path and started out to meet the Apaches who were headed towards the settlements in that locality. They succeeded in killing one Indian, wounding another, and capturing all the horses of the marauding party without loss to themselves. On August 21, 1881, a troop of forty soldiers, accompanied by an equal number of citizens under the leadership of McPhearson, met a body of about ninety Apaches in Gavalan canyon, where a desperate fight occurred. Lieutenant Smith, George W. Daly, manager of the Lake Valley Mining Company, and five of the soldiers were killed, and four others died later of their wounds. The battle continued during the day. The Indians captured all the horses and equipment of the attacking party and probably would have exterminated the whites had not a fresh body of troops come to their relief about nightfall.

An incident which created intense excitement throughout the western part of New Mexico in the spring of 1880 was the murder of James C. Cooney and a number of other miners by a band of Apaches under Victorio. Cooney had been quartermaster sergeant in the 8th U. S. cavalry, and while performing scouting duties in the Mogollon mountains in western Socorro county discovered silver. After his discharge from the army he organized the Cooney mining district and began development of extensive properties in Socorro county. His brother, Captain Michael Cooney, hewed from the solid rock, near the scene of the murder, a sepulcher for the body. The door is sealed with cement and ores from the mine, and in these ores has been wrought the design of a cross. His friends among the miners also hewed a cross of porphyry which was placed upon the summit of the rock tomb.

In January, 1881, a band of Apaches under chief Nané suddenly descended upon the little town of Chloride, killed two men named McDaniels and Overton, seriously wounded another named Patrick, stole many horses and cattle and fled before a show of defense could be made.

United States Indian agents for these southern Apaches were, at Santa Fé, 1868-9, John Ayres; at Fort McRae, 1869-70, Charles E. Drew; at Fort Craig, 1870-1, A. G. Hennisee; O. F. Piper, 1871-3; John Ayres, in 1872; B. M. Thomas, 1873-4; John M. Shaw, 1874-6, and James Davis, 1876-77.

In all of his raids Victorio was assisted by large numbers of the Mescalero Apaches.

his soldier pursuers, he would suddenly appear in some unexpected quarter. He outwitted two generals of the American army and one in command of the Mexican [360] forces. He captured from the governor of Chihuahua, in one campaign, over five hundred horses. He and his warriors killed over two hundred New Mexicans, more than one hundred soldiers and two hundred citizens of the Mexican republic. At one time the armies of both countries combined to destroy him, but he made his escape. On another occasion Colonel Buel, with one thousand cavalry and three hundred Indian scouts, pressing him on the north, Colonel Carr with six hundred cavalry on the west and General Grierson with the 10th cavalry on the east, were only able by the most severe fighting to drive him into Mexico at a time when he proposed to again invade the territory. In 1883 the American forces which had been coöperating with the Mexican separated, and while the troops of our sister republic were returning through Chihuahua they discovered the Apaches under Victorio encamped near a lake located in the vicinity of the Tres Castillos. Victorio had with him about a hundred warriors, four hundred women and children, and many horses and other animals and much booty. The Mexicans soon surrounded the Indians, who sought shelter in the rocks of the canyons. The battle began in the evening and continued during the entire night. At early dawn Victorio was seen on the summit of one of the crags of the Tres Castillos, basaltic hills which rose directly from the plain. For an hour after day-break the firing continued when suddenly the Indians ceased. Their ammunition was exhausted. The Mexicans now charged them with great bravery, the Indians falling beneath a pitiless fire. Victorio, several times wounded, finally fell, shot through the heart. The remainder of his band now surrendered. In addition to the warriors who fell in this battle, eighteen women and children shared the same fate. This war was the result of the greed of the settler and the corrupt policy of the government in the management of Indian affairs in the southwest. If Victorio had been permitted to remain at the Ojo Caliente reservation it is more than likely that the terrible devastation following his removal to San Carlos would never have occurred.

[360] On July 29th, 1882, a treaty was effected with the Republic of Mexico by virtue of the provisions of which the Apaches might be pursued across our southeren boundary and vice versa, by American and Mexican troops respectively.

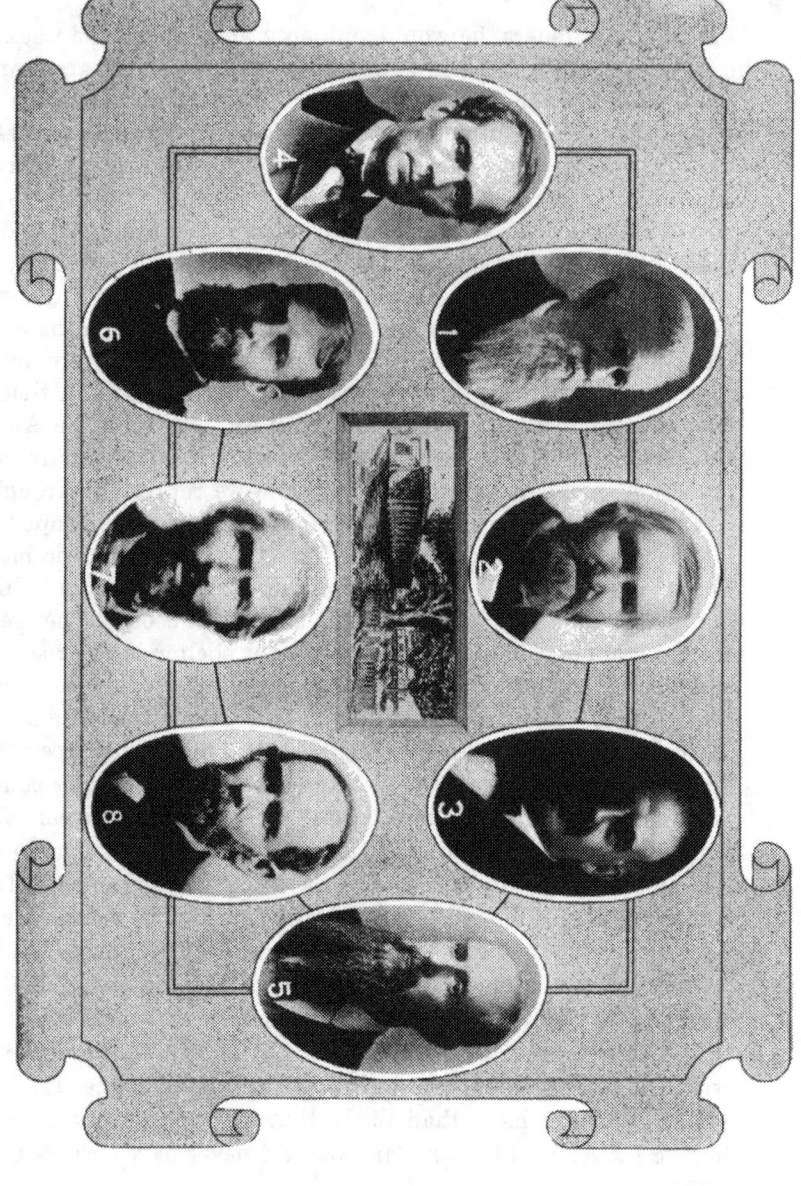

Justices of the Supreme Court of New Mexico
1. Alfred A. Freeman, 1890. 2. Samuel C. Parks, 1878. 3. Edward P. Seeds, 1890. 4. Joseph G. Palen, 1869. 5. James O'Brien, 1893. 6. Thomas Smith, 1893. 7. Hezekiah S. Johnson, 1870. 8. Warren Bristol, 1872

Victorio had been killed, his band had been decimated; and yet the southern portions of the territory were again raided by the murderous Apaches in the spring of 1883. General George Crook, who ten years before had subjugated the Apaches, was recalled to the command of the government forces in Arizona. The Chiricahuas, disturbed on account of the occupation of the country by mining men and cattle raisers, left the reservation and went on the war-path, killing the chief of the Indian police before leaving. Seven hundred and ten members of the tribe thus made their escape. They were pursued to the Mexican boundary, but they left a trail of murder and death behind them, killing every settler, miner, and ranchman whom they met en route. The presence of these hostile Indians in Chihuahua and Sonora [361] was a menace to the lives and property of the inhabitants of southern New Mexico, whose only protection was a small body of troops commanded by Captain Emmet Crawford, aided by a body of 150 Apache scouts. The troops and scouts patrolled over two hundred miles of the Mexican frontier.

CONQUEST OF THE CHIRICAHUAS — GENERAL GEORGE CROOK

In the month of March, 1883, twenty-six Chiricahuas, led by a celebrated chief, Chato, broke through the American patrol and swept over that portion of Grant county in the vicinity of Silver City. On the main road to Silver City, this band met Judge H. C. McComas, wife, and child, a boy, six years of age. The parents were murdered and horribly mutilated and the boy carried into captivity. The fate of Judge McComas roused the inhabitants of the southern counties of the territory. Chato and his band of warriors had passed by the Mexican troops and the American patrol, had ridden eight hundred miles into American territory, and were now murdering and pillaging almost within sight of the principal city in Grant county. In a few days twenty-five Americans and Mexicans had

---

[361] In the state of Sonora these hostiles were attacked by Mexican troops who killed eighty-five and captured thirty of the Indians; of those captured there were only fifteen warriors. About 650 Chiricahuas, 150 of whom were warriors, reached the Sierra Madre fastnesses. From secure strongholds in the mountains they raided the ranches of the Mexicans, attacked the small settlements, making captives, and driving to the mountains great numbers of horses and other live stock.

The bodies of Judge McComas and wife were found by John A. Moore. McComas was a native of Virginia and came to Silver City in 1880. His wife was a sister of Eugene Ware, deceased, the Kansas poet, known under the nom de plume of "Ironquill."

been slain and the hostiles made good their return to the mountains of Mexico. On May 1, 1883, arrangements having been made by which American troops were again permitted to pass over into Mexico while in pursuit of the Apaches, General Crook began his campaign, his forces consisting of 150 officers and men, together with about 100 Apache scouts. On May 11th, 150 Apache scouts, commanded by Captain Crawford and Lieutenants Gatewood and Mackey, left the main command and started ahead with four days' rations, keeping one day in advance of the regular troops. On the 15th the scouts reported from Captain Crawford that the Apaches were near at hand and in less than an hour word was received that fighting had commenced. At dark the command under Crawford came to the main camp, reporting that they had fallen upon the bands of the chiefs Chato and Bonito, killing nine, and capturing two boys, two girls, and one young woman, a daughter of Bonito. The presence of the American troops seems to have produced a great sensation among the Indians; presently they began to ask for terms of surrender, which were granted and all of the hostiles were returned to the reservation in Arizona. Geronimo was the last chief to surrender.[362]

On the 17th of May, 1885, Geronimo, Chihuahua, Natchez, and Mangas, with forty-two men and ninety-six women and children, again took the war-path and began raiding through the western portion of the territory. They were pursued into the Mogollon mountains, where they were defeated by a small command of government troops. The Indians, however, scattered into small bands and ravaged the areas lying in Grant, Sierra, and Socorro counties. Geronimo and his band were driven into Mexico, the remainder of the Indians following this chief into that country a little later in the year. Geronimo sought to induce the Mescalero Apaches

GERONIMO'S RAID OF 1885

[362] General Crook started on May 24th, with 237 captives, Chiricahuas, including three chiefs, Chato, Chihuahua, Kawterme, Loco, Bonito, Mangas, Zele, and Nané. On the 29th Geronimo joined the troops, increasing the number of captives to 384. Crook, in this campaign, did not lose a single man. Five Mexican women, captives, were restored to their people. The fate of the son of Judge McComas was never ascertained. When the first attack was made by Crawford's men upon Chato's band, he was said by the Indian women to have fled into the thicket and was never seen afterward. Crook did not disarm the captive Indians. They had great confidence in this general. Crook was severely criticized for his conduct of this campaign, notwithstanding his success.

to join him in this raid, but the movement failed owing to the vigilance of General Crook. In the summer an expedition was organized for the purpose of pursuing these Indians but nothing was done other than the establishment of a patrol along the Mexican border.[363]

On April 1, 1886, General Crook asked to be relieved, and, on the following day, General Nelson A. Miles was by President Cleveland assigned to the command, with instructions to carry on ceaselessly the most vigorous operations, having in view the destruction or capture of all of the hostile Apaches in Arizona or New Mexico. The department embraced a territory of about 300,000 square miles, in which all told there were 47,000 In-

CAMPAIGNS OF GENERAL NELSON A. MILES

---

[363] During this raid a boy, Santiago McKim, on the 11th day of September, 1885, while herding stock accompanied by his brother, fifteen years of age, on the Mimbres river, Grant county, fifteen miles from San Lorenzo, was captured by the Indians. He was playing around some rocks when he heard a rifle shot and saw six Indians rushing toward the place where his brother had been sitting. He attempted to run away, but was overtaken by the Apaches, who inquired of him how many men were in the ranch house some distance away. Learning that there were none, the Indians rounded up all the stock, took the boy with them, and left his brother shot through the shoulder and his head crushed with a stone. This boy was with the Apaches seven months and was restored to his friends at the time of the surrender of Geronimo and other Apache chiefs to General Miles.

Geronimo extended his raid to within three miles of Silver City, killing twenty-six persons and wounding many others. Those known to have been killed were: James Montgomery, on the Little Blue; Robert Benton, on the Big Blue; Nat Luse, Peter Anderson and Robert Smith, at Alma; ——— Smith, on the Little Blue; two brothers Lutton on the Middle Blue; Calvin Orwig, A. W. Lyons, at Alma; John Madden and ——— Bunting, ——— Green, and a young man named Prather. Soldiers and citizens took up the pursuit, and a few days later Captain (afterwards General) H. W. Lawton and his command engaged in a fight in Guadalupe canyon, in which several soldiers were killed. In September following Brady Pollock, a stock-raiser, was killed by the Apaches seven miles from Lake Valley. About the same time George Horn and a son of John McKim were added to the victims. Others who lost their lives were: September 29, A. L. Sabourne, merchant of Cooney; November, Charles Moore and William McKay, near Lake Valley; November, John T. Shy and family, and Andrew J. Yeager and wife, near Cold Springs; George C. Hay and Jacob Halling, at Lake Valley; December, George Kinney, a freighter, at Cactus Flat on the Mogollon road; also Charles Clarke; ——— Lilly, ——— Prior, and Ethel Harris, near Alma; in the same vicinity, Surgeon T. D. Maddox, U. S. A., and four privates. Names of others slain were William Waldo, a brother of Judge H. L. Waldo, Williams, May, Wright, Papinaw, Grudgings, and Polland. On December 23d President Cleveland was asked by wire by citizens of Socorro for sufficient protection and on January 6th, 1886, the stock men and other citizens met at Socorro and offered a reward of $250 for each Indian scalp. On the following March 25th Geronimo's band was captured and two days later surrendered to General Crook. On March 29th he escaped with twenty-five bucks and sought refuge in Old Mexico.

dians of all tribes. Yet, of all these, there were at the time comparatively few who could be considered as hostiles.[364]

His arrangements having all been completed, General Miles selected Captain H. W. Lawton, 4th cavalry, to command a force designated for the pursuit of the hostiles south of the Mexican border. "Lawton," says General Miles, "as a young officer had rendered distinguished services in the Civil War and most excellent services in Indian campaigns on the frontier in Texas, Arizona, and New Mexico — a resolute, brave officer, active and ambitious. He was a giant in stature and a man of great energy and endurance. He was afterward the most distinguished general in Cuba and the Philippines, where he was killed. At that time he was the ideal leader of a body of brave, active men."

Lieutenants Johnston, Finley, Benson, Brown, Walsh, and Smith, efficient officers, were ordered to report to Lawton. For Lawton's command, General Miles selected one hundred of the best soldiers that could be found in the department, all expert riflemen, and a small number of scouts and guides. Assistant Surgeon Leonard Wood, a young athlete from Harvard, was directed to accompany the command.

The commands having been organized, General Miles awaited developments on the part of the hostiles, not knowing at that time in what district they were located. The Indian position was soon disclosed by their making a raid from Mexico into southwestern

---

[364] Miles, Gen. Nelson A., *On the Trail of Geronimo*: "The Indian wars in New Mexico and Arizona had been for years attracting public attention. The history of the conflict between the Indians and the white race in that remote country would carry us back through the centuries to the first occupation of that region by the Spaniards, fifty years before the pilgrims landed at Plymouth Rock. The Apaches believed themselves to be the first and superior man. They excelled in activity, cunning, endurance and cruelty. They recognized no force or authority superior to their own. Led by Magnus-Colorado, Cochise, Victorio, and later by Geronimo, Natchez, Chato, and Magnus, they kept that whole country in a state of terror. General Crook had been for years trying to subjugate them and bring them under control, and finally, on April 1st, 1886, he asked to be relieved from command of that department. On April 2nd, I was, by President Cleveland, assigned to the command. It seemed a very undesirable duty and a most difficult undertaking. Under a military rule at that time, I had just been deprived of my personal staff officers and was obliged to go to Arizona alone. I knew but few of the officers or troops serving in that department and less of the topography of the country. I had, however, followed the history of those hostilities and traced the movements of the Indians on the military maps. On arriving at Ft. Bowie, Arizona, I assumed the command of the department and divided the country up into districts of observation, making the post commanders responsible for keeping their districts clear of hostile Indians."

Arizona. They were pursued by troops under Captain Lebo, Lieutenants P. H. Clarke, H. C. Benson, Captain Hatfield, and Lieutenants Brown, Walsh, and Brett. In their encounters with the Indians the latter were always defeated but made good their escape. The troops, however, kept constantly upon their trail and the pursuit was carried on into New Mexico and Mexico.

Captain Lawton followed them into Mexico, to the Yaqui country, two hundred miles south of the boundary. This pursuit was kept up for five months by the several commands until finally the Indians were worn out and in condition for surrender. A wounded warrior brought word to General Miles of the great distress in which the hostiles found themselves. This Indian, in charge of Lieutenant Gatewood, was sent by General Miles to the hostile camp with a demand for surrender. In the meantime Lawton was also in communication with Geronimo, who sent word to Lawton that he would surrender to the highest authority. This was finally accomplished.[365]

---

[365] Miles, General Nelson A., *On the Trail of Geronimo*, in *Cosmopolitan*, 1911: "This was communicated to me and I answered that if he sent assurance that he was acting in good faith I would go down to meet him near the Mexican border. He sent his brother to Fort Bowie, Arizona, as an earnest of his honest intentions, and for eleven days his camp marched north near the troops of Captain Lawton. I went down to Skeleton Canyon, near the Mexican line, and there met Captain Lawton's command with the Indians camped a short distance away. Geronimo came to me to ask what disposition would be made of him in case he surrendered. He said that if they were all to be killed, he might just as well die fighting. He prayed only that we would spare his life and those of his people. He was told that he must surrender as a prisoner of war and accept what disposition the government deemed best to make of him and his followers; that we did not kill our prisoners; that their future would depend upon the orders of the president at Washington. He was informed that I had directed Colonel Wade to move all the Indians at the Apache agency in northern Arizona out of the Territory; that he and his people would be removed; that Indian depredations and atrocities must end forever in that country. He was in no position to dictate terms. I explained to him the folly of contending against the military with all its advantages of communication and transportation. While watching a corporal use the heliograph and flash a message in a few seconds by the sun's rays, a day's journey for his horse, he was struck with awe and amazement. He sent an Indian runner to Natchez, who remained out in the mountains, to tell him that he was in the presence of a power he could not understand, and that Natchez was to come in and come quick. He afterward stated that he had seen these flashes on the mountain peaks, but thought they were spirits and not men. They then formally surrendered and placed themselves under our control. The day following I took Geronimo and Natchez and four others of the principal men, with the escort of a troop of cavalry, and made a march of sixty-five miles to Ft. Bowie, Captain Lawton following three days later with the rest of the Indians. A small band, under Magnus, that remained out, was pursued for weeks by Lieutenant C. E. Johnston, and finally captured by troops under Captain Charles L. Cooper. Thus the country was cleared from the devastating and terrifying presence of the Apaches. . . Their final re-

General Miles was tendered a banquet and reception at Santa Fé. The people of New Mexico and Arizona presented him with a handsome sword. The Damascus blade, grip, and large India star sapphire were the only parts of the sword and scabbard not made of gold. The presentation occurred at Tucson, Arizona, at a banquet given in honor of General Miles in 1887.

In this effective manner the Chiricahuas, the worst of all the Apache tribes, were not only subdued but removed from the country. This policy of removal, so strongly urged by General Miles, was, as usual, condemned by the friends of the Indians in the east. The people of New Mexico, however, whose friends and property had been ruthlessly destroyed by these savage marauders, demanded that Geronimo, Natchez, Chato, and other chiefs be delivered to the civil authorities, for trial and punishment on charges of murder. The policy of expatriation, however, recommended and carried out by General Miles, was confirmed, and peace restored to the people of New Mexico and Arizona.[366]

In the year 1870 the Jicarilla Apaches, from 750 to 950 in number, and three bands of Utes, numbering from 1,500 to 1,800, lived on what is known as the Maxwell grant in the northern part of New Mexico, with agencies at Cimarron, east of the Rio Grande, and at Abiquiú, or finally at Tierra Amarilla, in the west. The sale of the grant necessitated their removal. In 1872 and again in 1878 an attempt was made to remove them south to Fort

JICARILLA APACHES AND UTES

---

moval to the Indian Territory, where they were placed under charge of Colonel Scott, one of the best officers in the service, changed them from wild savages to peaceful citizens.''

[366] Credit for the final capture of Geronimo has been given to various officers, including Generals Miles and Lawton. The credit actually belongs to Lieutenant Gatewood of the 6th cavalry, who, with a small detachment, overtook Geronimo and brought him into camp. Gatewood later retired from the army and made his home in Denver, Colo. Even in the army proper recognition has seldom been accorded to him for his success in bringing this old scoundrel in. From the day of his surrender to that of his death at Fort Sill he was a prisoner. Always, until his expiring moments, he hoped to be returned to his native mountains in Arizona. At one time, while at Fort Sill, pointing to the west, this Apache chief declared, ''The sun rises and shines for a time, and then it goes down, sinks, and is lost. So it will be with the Indian. When a boy my father told me that the Indians were as many as the leaves on the trees, and that in the north they had many horses and furs. I never saw them, but I know that if they were once there they have gone. The white man has taken all they had. It will be only a few years when the Indians will be heard of only in the books which the white man writes.''

Stanton, but most of them were permitted to go to the Tierra Amarilla, on the northern confines of the territory, on a reservation of 900 square miles, set aside in 1874. Their annuities being suspended in 1878, on account of their refusal to move southward in accordance with an act of congress of that year, they resorted to thieving. In 1880 the act of 1878 was repealed and a new reservation was set aside on the Rio Navajó, to which they were removed. Here they remained until 1883, when they were transferred to Fort Stanton, but in 1887 were again returned to the reservation set aside for them in the Tierra Amarilla region, by executive order of February 11th of that year, where they have since resided.[367]

In the historical period the various tribes of Pueblo Indians have been confined to the area extending from northeastern Arizona to the Pecos river in New Mexico, and from Taos in the north to a few miles below El Paso, Texas.

THE PUEBLO INDIANS

The Pueblos remain the same peaceable, inoffensive, industrious, credulous, and superstitious people that they have always been. There has been but small change in their character and primitive manner of living. With the exception of the uprising of 1847, these Indians have given the government

---

[367] The Utes at Abiquiú pretended at times a willingness to settle on a reservation in the San Juan valley, but this was not acceptable to the government, though often recommended by agents. It was deemed desirable to move them to a reservation of their tribe in southern Colorado; and in 1868 a treaty was made to that effect; but the Utes refused to go, alleging that the treaty had been fraudulent, and dissatisfied because an agency site had not been chosen on the Los Pinos as promised. By several acts of congress, of 1877-8, and by abolishing the southern agency, they were finally removed to the Colorado reservation in April to July, 1878; and New Mexico was thus rid of them.

During the period the following were agents for these Indians in New Mexico: Jicarillas and Mohuache Utes, Levi J. Keithley, 1864-65 (Ferd. Maxwell was special agent in 1864); Lorenzo Labadie, 1865-66, Manuel S. Salazar, 1866, E. B. Dennison, 1866-70, W. P. Wilson, 1870, Charles F. Roedel, 1870-72. The agency was now abolished, but the Indians remained and were in charge of R. H. Longwell, 1872-73, Thomas A. Dolan, 1873-74, Longwill, 1874, Alex G. Irvine, 1874-75, John E. Pyle, 1875-76, and B. M. Thomas (Pueblo agent) in 1876 to 1883, when the Indians were finally removed.

The agents at Abiquiú and Tierra Amarilla (Capote and Payuche Utes, also some Jicarillas at times) were Head or Pfeiffer in 1864-65; Diego Archuleta, 1865-67 (Manuel Garcia, special agent); W. F. M. Arny, 1867-68; James C. French, 1868-69; John Ayres, 1869; J. B. Hanson, 1869-71 (Captain A. S. B. Keyes also named in 1869); John S. Armstrong in 1871-72 (the agency was transferred from Abiquiú to Tierra Amarilla); W. S. De Frees, 1872-73; W. D. Crothers, 1873-74 (C. Robbins and F. Salazar also named as being in charge in 1874); Sam A. Russell, 1874-78. The Utes were removed and the agency abolished in 1878, but the remaining Jicarillas were in charge of B. M. Thomas, the Pueblo agent, in 1878-1883.

448 LEADING FACTS OF NEW MEXICAN HISTORY

small trouble. In matters of education they have made considerable advances. Their lands have all been confirmed and patented to them and these are exempt from taxation. Although citizens of the United States they do not care to exercise the functions pertaining thereto. The general government has aided them materially in the construction of irrigation canals and reservoirs. A table relative to these Indians prepared by the bureau of ethnology appears in the note.[368]

PRE-SPANISH POTTERY SHARDS,
GILA BASIN

---

[368] Bureau of American Ethnology, *Bulletin 30*, pt. 2.

Prominent New Mexicans of the Nineteenth Century
1. Don Roman A. Baca. 2. Dr. E. C. Henriques. 3. Dr. R. H. Longwill.
4. Horace F. Stephenson.

POPULATION OF THE VARIOUS PUEBLOS FROM 1630

PUEBLO	Language	1630	1680	1760	1788	1790-3	1797-8	1805	1809	1850	1856	1860	1864	1871	1874	1889	1901-5
Abiquiu	[Genizaros, mixed]			166	1,181	216	176	134	126		"Mexicanized"						
Abo	Piro		800	Abandoned about 1675													
Alameda	Tigua		300														
Acoma	Keres	2,000	1,500	1,052		820	757	731	816	350	1,200	523	491	436	500	582	759
Alamillo	Tigua		300														
Belen	[Genizaros, mixed]			(a)				107	"Mexicanized"								
Chilili	Tigua		500	Abandoned about 1675													
Cochiti	Keres		300	450		720	505	656	697	254	800	172	229	243	400	300	300
Cuyamunque	Tewa		(b)			Abandoned between 1760 and 1805											
Galisteo	Tano		c 800	(d)													
Hano l.	Tewa				375(?)											161	
Isleta (N. M.)	Tigua		2,000	e 304	e 2,103	410	e 603	419	487	751	600	250	786	768	1,200	1,037	988
Jemez	Jemez	3,000	5,000	373		485	272	264	297	365	800	440	346	344	800	474	450
Laguna	Keres			600	1,368	668	802	940	1,022	749	450	650	988	927	900	970	1,884
Nambe	Tewa			204		155	178	143	155	111	800	927	161	78	100	81	100
Pecos	Jemez	2,000	f 600	g 599		152	189	104			500	103	94				
Picuris	Tigua		2,000	328	212	254	251	250	313	222	800	Moved to Jemez in 1888	122	127	150	120	125
Pojoaque	Tewa		3,000	99	368	53	79	100		48	500	143	29	32	20	18	(h)
Puaray	Tigua		200			Abandoned about 1675						57					
Quarai	Tigua		600			Abandoned about 1696											
San Cristobal	Tano		(i)														
Sandia	Tigua		3,000	291	596	304	116	314	364	241	500	217	197	186	225	150	74
San Felipe	Keres		j 600	458	452	532	282	289	405	800	800	360	427	482	400	501	475
San Ildefonso	Tewa		800	484	k 1,076	240	251	175	283	500	500	154	161	156	570	186	250
San Juan	Tewa		300	316	k 1,566	260	202	194	208	568	500	341	385	426	350	573	425
San Marcos	Tano		600	Abandoned in 1680													
Santa Ana	Keres			404	452	356	634	450	550	399	500	316	298	373	500	264	226
Santa Clara	Tewa		300	257	134	134	193	186	220	279	600	179	144	189	50	187	325(?)
Santa Cruz	Tewa			316	k 1,076	Abandoned and re-established				"Mexicanized"							
Santo Domingo	Keres		150	424	608	650	1,483	533	720	666	800	261	604	735	1,000	930	1,000
Sia	Keres			568	1,055	275	262	254	286	124	450	117	103	121	125	113	125
Socorro (N. M.)	Piro		600		Abandoned in 1680; moved to Texas												
Tajique	Tigua		300		Abandoned in 1675												
Taos	Tigua	2,500	2,000	505	578	518	531	508	527	361	800	363	361	397	575	324	425
Tesuque	Tewa		200	232		138	155	131	160	119	700	97	101	98	125	94	100
Zuni	Zuni	10,000	2,500	664	1,617	1,935	2,716	1,470						1,550	1,500	1,547	1,514

a See Isleta. b See Nambe. c Probably includes San Cristobal. d See Pecos. e Includes Tome and Belen. f Probably includes Cuyamunque and Jacona. g Includes Galisteo. h "Mexicanized." i See Galisteo. j Includes Santa Ana. k Includes Spaniards. l Established about 1700.

BIBLIOGRAPHY

Archives	*New Mexican*. In secretary's office, capitol, Santa Fé, N. M. Socorro, Grant, and Doña Ana counties. Office of probate clerk, Socorro, Silver City, and Las Cruces, N. M.
Bancroft, H. H.	*History of Arizona and New Mexico*, San Francisco, 1888.
Bureau of Ethnology	*17th Ann. Report*, 1896; *Bulletin 30, Pt. 2; Handbook of American Indians*, Washington, 1911.
Carleton, Gen. J. H.	*Reports* of 1863, 1864, 1865, 1866, War Department, Washington, D. C.
Crook, Gen. George	*Reports* of, War Department, Washington, D. C., 1885, 1886.
Enterprise	Newspaper, files of, Silver City, N. M., 1883, 1884, 1885, 1886, 1887.
Hayes, A. A.	*New Mexico Campaign*, Magazine of Am. Hist., Feb., 1886.
Indian Affairs	*Reports*, U. S. Gov. Doc., 41st cong., 2d sess., Sen. Miscl. Doc., 97, Washington, D. C.
Meline, J. F.	*Two Thousand Miles on Horseback*, New York, 1867.
Miles, Gen. Nelson A.	*On the Trail of Geronimo*, Cosmopolitan Magazine, vol. li, 1911.
New Mexican	Newspaper, Santa Fé, N. M., files of, 1867-1887.
New Mexico	*Reports* and *Messages* of Governors, 1866-1888. *Session Laws* and *Council* and *House Journals*, 1867-1887, Santa Fé, N. M., office of Secretary of State.
Pope, Gen. John	*Reports* of, War Department, Washington, D. C., 1877, 1878.
Shelton, W. T.	*Report* of, Indian Affairs Reps., Washington, D. C.

CHAPTER XI

Spanish and Mexican Land Grants — Act of Congress Creating Office of Surveyor General — Private Land Claims — George W. Julian — Efforts for Congressional action — Establishment of Court of Private Land Claims — The Court and Its Work — The Barony of Arizona — Peralta-Reavis

GENERAL STEPHEN W. KEARNY, commanding the Army of the West, invading New Mexican territory, was the first officer of the United States to declare to the people of New Mexico that their rights of person and property would be held inviolable. In making this statement he was carrying out the instructions given to him by the president of the United States. General Zachary Taylor had the same instructions and published and distributed a proclamation among the inhabitants south of the Rio Grande to the same effect. For nearly half a century the people of New Mexico endeavored, by petition, memorial, and through their delegates in congress, to compel the American congress to listen to the demands of justice respecting their rights of property.

At the close of hostilities with Mexico, two years after General Kearny had planted the American flag in the plaza at Santa Fé, the two governments entered into a treaty [369] by the provisions of which it was most solemnly guaranteed that the people of New

---

[369] *Compiled Laws of New Mexico*, 1897. Articles viii and ix of the treaty of Guadalupe Hidalgo provided: "Art. viii. In the said Territories, property of every kind, now belonging to Mexicans not established there, shall be inviolably respected. The present owners, the heirs of these, and all Mexicans who may hereafter acquire said property by contract, shall enjoy with respect to it, guarantees equally ample, as if the same belonged to citizens of the United States. Art. ix. The Mexicans who, in the Territories aforesaid, shall not preserve the character of citizens of the Mexican Republic, conformably with what is stipulated in the preceding article, shall be incorporated into the union of the United States, . . and in the meantime shall be maintained and protected in the free enjoyment of their liberty and property."

Mexico should be maintained and protected in the free enjoyment of their liberty and property. The treaty of Guadalupe Hidalgo, as originally formulated by the commissioners of the two republics, contained an article recognizing the grants made by Mexico, coupled with a provision allowing the claimants under contracts for the colonization of lands which had not been fulfilled or executed, further time within which to carry out the provisions of the contracts made with Mexico, and to receive their grants of land pursuant thereto. This provision was so objectionable that the entire tenth article of the treaty was eliminated, after protracted debate in the United States senate, when the American government sent other commissioners to present the amended treaty to the Mexican government for ratification.[370] This commission carried a letter from the secretary of state in the cabinet of the president [371] of the United States to the Mexican minister of foreign affairs, explaining the objections to the suppressed articles of the treaty, and stating that "the treaty provides amply and specifically, in its 8th and 9th articles, for the security of property of every kind belonging to Mexicans, whether held under Mexican grants or otherwise, in the

[370] *Treaty* between The United States and Mexico. *Executive Doc.* No. 52 (Senate), 30th cong., 1st sess.

[371] James Buchanan, afterward president of the United States, in this letter said: " . . . To resuscitate such grants, and to allow the grantees the same period after the exchange of the ratifications of this treaty, to which they were originally entitled, for the purpose of performing the conditions on which these grants had been made, even if this could be accomplished by the power of the government of the United States, would work manifold injustice.

"These Mexican grants, it is understood, cover nearly the whole sea-coast and a large portion of the interior of Texas. They embrace thriving villages and a great number of cultivated farms, the proprietors of which have acquired them honestly by purchase from the state of Texas. These proprietors are now dwelling in peace and security. To revive dead titles, and suffer the inhabitants of Texas to be ejected under them, from their possessions, would be an act of flagrant injustice, if not wanton cruelty. Fortunately this government possesses no power to adopt such a proceeding.

"The same observations equally apply to such grantees in New Mexico and Upper California. The present treaty provides amply and specifically in its 8th and 9th articles for the security of property of every kind belonging to Mexicans, whether held under Mexican grants or otherwise, in the acquired territory. . .

"And here it may be worthy of observation, that if no stipulations whatever were contained in the treaty to secure to the Mexican inhabitants, and all others, protection in the free enjoyment of their liberty, property, and the religion which they profess, these would be amply guaranteed by the constitution and laws of the United States. These invaluable blessings, under our forms of government, do not result from treaty stipulations, but from the very nature and character of our institutions."

acquired territory." For the express purpose of influencing the Mexican government to accept the treaty as proposed, these commissioners were authorized to make explanations respecting the amendments as suggested by the United States senate.

"The suppression of the 10th article of the treaty," says a distinguished New Mexican lawyer [372] and authority, "as originally negotiated, naturally aroused the suspicions of the Mexican government, and notwithstanding its desperate situation, exhausted by the war, with a hostile flag flying over its capital, and notwithstanding the solemn assurances of the American Secretary of State, that the 8th and 9th articles contained the most ample guarantees, that gov-

---

[372] Frank Springer. *Address* of when president of the New Mexico Bar Association, January 7, 1890.

Frank Springer, the son of Francis and Nancy R. Springer, was born at Wapello, Iowa, June 17, 1848. He received his education in the public schools and at the State University of Iowa. He was admitted to the bar in Iowa in 1869 and came to New Mexico in 1873, settling at Cimarron, where, on October 10, 1876, he was married to Josephine M. Bishop. He immediately took foremost rank in his chosen profession and has since been recognized as one of the leaders of the New Mexico bar. In 1890 he was elected president of the New Mexico Bar Association, in which capacity he delivered an address dealing entirely with the urgent necessity for the immediate settlement by the congress of the United States, through a proper tribunal, of titles under Spanish and Mexican land grants. The bill which finally became law was drafted principally by him. The bar association attached so much importance to this address that it was printed in full and distributed among members of congress and filed with the land department at Washington. The subject matter of the address produced a profound impression at Washington with the president of the United States and members of congress alike. A direct result was the passage of the act establishing the court of private land claims. As attorney for the trustees of the Maxwell Land Grant Company Mr. Springer achieved his greatest professional success. In the trial of many causes in the courts of New Mexico in which that company was a party, and in the final determination of the title of the company to the lands embraced within the limits of the grant, as confirmed by congress, decided in favor of the company in *United States v. The Maxwell Land Grant Company*, his preparation, argument, and management were masterly, calling forth encomiums of praise from members of the supreme court of the United States. He is the president of the board of trustees of the Maxwell Land Grant Company, whose business affairs under his management and direction have been phenomenally successful. He retired from the active practice of his profession in 1906, since which time he has given much attention to scientific study and research. He was twice a member of the legislative council of New Mexico, in which position he rendered the territory great service. As a paleontologist he takes first rank among scientists in America. He is the author of *Revision of the Palaeocrinoidea*, 1879-86 (Phila. Acad. Natural Science); *North American Crinoidea Camerata*, 1897; *Uintacrinus, Its Structure and Relations*, 1901; also numerous papers in scientific periodicals. He is a member of the Archæological Institute of America, and a patron of the school of American Archæology at Santa Fé, New Mexico. Through the magnificent generosity of Mr. Springer the restorations, in part, and many of the mural decorations in the Old Palace have been accomplished under the direction of Dr. Edgar L. Hewett, director of the school.

ernment, at the last moment, before it would exchange ratifications of the treaty, insisted upon a formal representation on the subject by the American commissioners. The result of this was the execution, on May 26th, 1848, of a supplemental document, which to all intents and purposes became a part of the treaty. It was called a protocol,[373] in which were recorded the explanations which their excellencies, the commissioners of the United States of America, gave in the name of their government, in regard to the amendments made by the senate."

---

[373] James K. Polk, president of the United States, *Message* from, to the House of Representatives, February 8, 1849: "The protocol asserts that 'the American government, by suppressing the tenth article of the treaty of Guadalupe Hidalgo, did not in any way intend to annul the grants of lands made by Mexico in the ceded territories;' that 'these grants, notwithstanding the suppression of the article of the treaty, preserve the legal value which they may possess; and the grantees may cause their legitimate titles to be acknowledged before the American tribunals;' and then proceeds to state that, 'conformably to the law of the United States, legitimate titles to every description of property, personal and real, existing in the ceded territories, are those which were legitimate titles under the Mexican law in California and New Mexico up to the thirteenth of May, 1846, and in Texas up to the second of March, 1836.' The former was the date of the declaration of war with Mexico, and the latter that of the declaration of independence by Texas.

"The objection to the tenth article of the original treaty was not that it protected legitimate titles, which our laws would have equally protected without it; but that it most unjustly attempted to resuscitate grants which had become a mere nullity, by allowing the grantees the same period after the exchange of the ratifications of the treaty to which they had been originally entitled after the date of their grants, for the purpose of performing the conditions on which they had been made. In submitting the treaty to the Senate, I had recommended the rejection of this article. That portion of it in regard to lands in Texas did not receive a single vote in the Senate. This information was communicated by the letter of the Secretary of State to the minister for foreign affairs of Mexico, and was in possession of the Mexican government during the whole period the treaty was before the Mexican congress, and the article itself was reprobated in that letter in the strongest terms. Besides, our commissioners to Mexico had been instructed that neither the President, nor the Senate of the United States, can ever consent to ratify any treaty containing the tenth article of the treaty of Guadalupe Hidalgo in favor of grantees of land in Texas or elsewhere.' And again: 'Should the Mexican government persist in retaining this article, then all prospects of immediate peace is ended; and of this you may give them an absolute assurance.'

"On this point the language of the protocol is free from ambiguity; but, if it were otherwise, is there any individual American or Mexican who would place such a construction upon it as to convert it into a vain attempt to revive this article which had been so often and so solemnly condemned? Surely no person could for one moment suppose that either the commissioners of the United States or the Mexican minister for foreign affairs ever entertained the purpose of thus setting at naught the deliberate decision of the President and Senate, which had been communicated to the Mexican government with the assurance that their abandonment of this obnoxious article was essential to the restoration of peace."

The meaning of this protocol was plain. Rationaly interpreted it declared that the nullification of the 10th article of the treaty was not intended to destroy valid, legitimate titles to land which existed, and were in full force independently of the provisions and without the aid of the article in question. Notwithstanding the fact that the 10th article had been expunged from the treaty, these grants were to "preserve the legal value which they may possess." The refusal to revive grants which had become extinct was not to invalidate those which were in full force and vigor. That such was the clear understanding of the United States senate, and this in perfect accordance with the protocol, is manifest from the fact that, whilst they struck from the treaty this unjust article, they at the same time sanctioned and ratified the last paragraph of the eighth article of the treaty, which declares that, "in the said territories, property of every kind, now belonging to Mexicans not established there, shall be inviolably respected. The present owners, the heirs of these, and all Mexicans, who may hereafter acquire said property by contract, shall enjoy, with respect to it, guarantees equally ample as if the same belonged to citizens of the United States."[374]

Without any stipulation in the treaty to this effect all such valid titles, under the Mexican government, were entitled to protection under the constitution and laws of the American government.

At any rate the statements made by the American commissioners, Sevier and Clifford, as embodied in the protocol, were accepted by the Mexican minister, and the Mexican government[375] ratified the treaty as modified by the senate and government of the United States.

On May 30, 1848, the ratifications of the treaty were exchanged. After the lapse of a few years, owing to the great tide of immigration to the state of California and the consequent acquisition of lands by the American homeseeker, prospector, miner, and stockraiser, the courts had before them questions involving the validity of titles to lands in that state. These questions finally came before

[374] *Ex. Doc.* No. 50, H. of R., 30th cong., 2d sess.
[375] Twelve days after the ratification of the treaty by Mexico, the American flag was taken down from the national palace in the City of Mexico and the colors of the Mexican republic were hoisted.
The provisional president of the Mexican republic, Don Manuel de la Peña y Peña, signed the ratification of the treaty, at Querétaro, May 30, 1848.

the supreme court of the United States for determination and a long line of decisions emanated from that tribunal, declaring the right of the holders of Mexican titles to protection and recognition by the government. These early decisions are interesting and deserve mention in the history of the time.[376]

---

[376] U. S. Supreme Court *Reports*, 19 Howard, 364, *United States v. Sutherland*. This case was decided in 1856. In its opinion the court declared: "In construeing grants of land in California, made under the Spanish and Mexican authorities, we must take into view the state of the country and the policy of the government. The population of California, before its transfer to the United States, was very sparse, consisting chiefly of a few military posts and some inconsiderable villages. The millions of acres of land around them, with the exception of a mission or a rancho on some favored spot, were uninhabited and uncultivated. It was the interest and policy of the king of Spain, and afterward of the Mexican government, to make liberal grants of these lands to those who would engage to colonize or settle upon them. Since this country has become a part of the United States, these extensive rancho grants, which then had little value, have now become very large and very valuable estates. They have been denounced as 'enormous monopolies, princedoms,' etc., and this court have been urged to deny to the grantees what is assumed the former governments have too liberally and lavishly granted. This rhetoric might have a just influence when urged to those who have a right to give or refuse, but the United States have bound themselves by a treaty to acknowledge and protect all bona fide titles granted by the previous government, and this court have no discretion to enlarge or curtail such grants to suit our own sense of propriety, or defeat just claims, however extensive, by stringent rules of construction, to which they were not originally subjected."

In U. S. Supreme Court *Reports*, Wallace, 404, *United States v. Moreno*, decided in 1863, the court announced that "These two sovereignties [Spain and Mexico] are the spring heads of all the land titles in California, existing at the time of the cession of that country to the United States by the treaty of Guadalupe Hidalgo. That cession did not impair the rights of private property. They were consecrated by the law of nations, and protected by the treaty. A right of any validity before the cession was equally valid afterward, and while it is the duty of the court in the cases which may come before it, to guard carefully against claims originating in fraud, it is equally their duty to see that no rightful claim is rejected. No nation can have any higher interest than the right administration of justice." In the same volume of reports at page 368, *United States v. Auguisola*, it is said that "The United States have never sought by their legislation to evade the obligation devolved upon them by the treaty of Guadalupe Hidalgo to protect the rights of property of the inhabitants of the ceded territory, or to discharge it in a narrow or illiberal manner. They have directed their tribunals, in passing upon the rights of the inhabitants, to be governed by the stipulations of the treaty, the law of nations, the laws, usages, and customs of the former government, the principles of equity, and the decisions of the supreme court so far as they are applicable. They have not desired the tribunals to conduct their investigations as if the rights of the inhabitants to the property which they claim depended upon the nicest observance of every legal formality. They have desired to act as a great nation, not seeking, in extending their authority over the ceded country, to enforce forfeitures, but to afford protection and security to all just rights which could have been claimed from the government they superseded."

Thirteen years after the decision of the above case, the supreme court of

Representative Delegates to the Thirteenth National Irrigation Congress, El Paso, Texas, November, 1904

From the Republic of Mexico, the State of Texas, and the Territory of New Mexico, who prepared Resolution leading to the final determination of water rights in the Rio Grande by the Governments of the United States and Mexico

California was admitted to the Union. The representatives [377] in the senate, of that state, were influential enough to induce the president of the United States, in 1850-51, in a message to congress, to urge action upon the claims in that state arising under the terms of the treaty of Guadalupe Hidalgo, and, pursuant to the provisions contained in the eighth article of the treaty, congress passed an act, approved March 3, 1851, entitled "An Act to settle the private land claims in the State of California." This act made provision for the appointment of a commission composed of three commissioners, to continue for three years, with a secretary qualified to act as interpreter, and necessary clerks, and an attorney to represent the United States. Numerous subsequent acts extended and continued this commission in force.

New Mexico, however, with a voteless delegate in congress, could secure no such tribunal as was given to the state of California. The congress, on July 22, 1854, passed an act creating the office of surveyor general, by the terms of the eighth section of which it was made the duty of this officer, under instructions to be given by the secretary of the interior, to ascertain the origin, nature, character,

---

the United States, in the *Tameling Case*, 93 U. S. Reps., in enunciating its views upon Mexican land titles, declared that "We have repeatedly held that individual rights of property in the territory acquired by the United States from Mexico, were not affected by the change of sovereignty and jurisdiction. They were entitled to protection, whether the party had the full and absolute ownership of the land, or merely an equitable interest therein, which required some further act of the government to vest in him a perfect title."

[377] The Californians left no stone unturned in securing an early adjudication of the titles to lands arising under the Spanish and Mexican grants. The surveyor general for that state, Samuel D. King, as early as September 30, 1851, in a *Report* to the secretary of the interior, said: "It must be remembered that until within a very few years, and as long as the country remained under the Spanish and Mexican jurisdiction, the lands in this extreme and very sparsely settled portion of their territory were considered as being of very little, if any, value, except as open ranges for numerous large herds of horses, or for cattle raised solely upon account of their hides and tallow, and their almost only articles of export.

"Hence the lands were freely granted away to those desirous of establishing ranches for this purpose, and in large sized tracts. But very few, indeed, if any, of these grants were ever actually surveyed under the former government. The grants generally, after specifying the length and breadth of the tract, or its area, as being at a particularly designated place, describe it by some general and vague reference to other grants, water-courses, or mountain ranges, or refer to a rough figurative plat or sketch accompanying the application or grant as defining the boundaries."

Under the various acts of congress the United States has confirmed in California 538 claims, having a total acreage of 8,332,431.24, the smallest being for 1,770 and the largest 133,440.78 acres.

and extent of all claims to land under the laws, usages, and customs of Spain and Mexico. He was authorized to issue notices, summon witnesses, administer oaths, etc., and required to make full reports to the secretary of the interior, to be laid before congress for final action, "with a view to confirm *bona fide* grants," on all claims originating before the cession by the treaty of Guadalupe Hidalgo, denoting the various grades of title, with his decision as to their validity or invalidity; also to report as to all pueblos, the extent, locality, number of inhabitants, and nature of title of each; and, until final action by congress on such claims, all lands covered thereby to be reserved from sale or other disposal by the government, and not subject to the donation clause in the act. William Pelham was appointed surveyor general and on August 25, 1854, John Wilson, commissioner of the general land office, issued an order containing a most elaborate set of instructions,[378] which order

---

[378] The honorable, the secretary of the interior must have had a high appreciation of the attainments of the presidential appointee, William Pelham, for among the "necessary acts" contemplated by the act of congress and required of him, as set out in the "instructions," he was ordered, among other duties, to acquaint himself "with the land system of Spain as applied to her ultra marine possessions, the general features of which are found — modified, of course by local requirements and usages — in the former provinces and dependencies of that monarchy on this continent. For this purpose you must examine the laws of Spain, the royal ordinances, decrees, and regulations as collected in White's *Recopilacion*, 2 vols." He was referred to the decisions of the supreme court of the United States, reported in Peters's and Howard's *Reports* and required "to examine them carefully in connection with the Spanish law, and the legislation of congress on the subject, in order that you may understand and be able to apply the principles of the Spanish system as understood and expounded by the authorities of our government."

Upon his arrival at Santa Fé he was required "to make application to the governor of the Territory for such of the archives as relate to grants of land by the former authorities of the country." He was instructed to "see that they [the archives] are kept in a place of security from fire, or other accidents, and that access is allowed only to land owners who may find it necessary to refer to their title records, and such references must be made under your eye, or that of a sworn employe of the government." He was ordered "to proceed at once to arrange and classify the papers in the order of date, and have them properly and substantially bound; . . you will then have schedules," he was instructed, "Marked 1, of them made out in duplicate, and will prepare abstracts (No. 2), also in duplicate, of all the grants found in the records, showing the names of grantees, date, area, locality, by whom conceded, and under what authority."

He was ordered "to prepare in duplicate, from the archives or authoritative sources, a document (marked No. 3), exhibiting the names of all the officers of the Territory who held the power of distributing lands from the earliest settlements of the Territory until the change of government, indicating the several periods of their incumbency, the nature and extent of their powers, concerning lands; whether, and to what extent, and under what condi-

was approved on the same day by the secretary of the interior, R. McClelland.

It is not recorded whether Surveyor-General Pelham was able to carry out to the letter the instructions given him by the secretary of the interior. It is known that he made application to the governor of the territory, David Merriwether,[379] for such of the archives as related to land grants, which he declined to deliver, giving as his reason that their selection from the large amount of papers composing the public archives of the territory would involve an immense amount of labor and a heavy expenditure, which he was not authorized to incur. Governor Merriwether permitted the surveyor-general to remove the archives to the office of the latter, where they were examined and separated. On the 18th of January, 1855, Surveyor-General Pelham issued a notice to "The Inhabitants of New Mexico" relative to the filing of claims for lands to be passed upon by him under the provisions of the act of 1854. Many of the owners of grants were averse to responding to this notice and declined to file any papers [380] relative to their titles to lands in the territory.

---

tions and limitations, authority existed in the governors or political chiefs to distribute (repartir) the public domain; whether in any class of cases they had the power to make an absolute grant; and if so, for what maximum in area; or whether subject to the affirmance of the department or supreme government; whether the Spanish surveying system was in operation, and since what period in the country, and under what organization; also with verified copies in the original, and translations of the laws and decrees of the Mexican republic, and regulations which may have been adopted by the general government of that republic for the disposal of the public lands in New Mexico.''

[379] William Pelham, surveyor-general, *Report*, September 30, 1855: "He, however, allowed me to remove the packages containing such papers as related to the grants of land in the country from their deposit, and examine them in my own office; whereupon, I immediately assigned two of my clerks to separate them. On the last day of July this difficult duty was accomplished, and from one hundred and sixty-eight packages, averaging one hundred and sixty-eight thousand papers, of every nature and description imaginable, one thousand seven hundred and fifteen grants, conveyances of land, and other documents referring to claims to lands, have been selected, and are now being arranged and classified in a systematical form in this office. It will, however, be impossible to have them properly and substantially bound, as required by your instructions on account of the different shapes and forms in which they are found — some existing on large sheets of foolscap paper, while others are to be found on half sheets, and others again on scraps of paper, which can never be bound in any convenient form."

[380] The commissioner of the general land office in his *Report* for 1856, says: "The selection from the archives of the Spanish and Mexican governments, which were turned over to the surveyor general's office by the governor of

The act of July 22, 1854, reserved to congress the province of finally passing upon all private land claims by direct legislative enactment. No provision was made for adversary proceedings, nor for surveying the boundaries of the tracts reported by the surveyor-general, so that intelligent action might be taken upon cases as they came before congress. Notwithstanding this difficulty, however, congress proceeded to confirm the greater part of the claims. This action was had in 1860, congress acting upon a report of the house committee on private land claims.[381]

New Mexico, resulted in a collection of 1,014 grants and documents relating to land titles, of which 197 are private grants. These have all been classified, alphabetically arranged, and constitute permanent official records.

"From the advices received at this office from the surveyor general of New Mexico and other sources, it is evident individuals claiming lands under former governments before the treaty of Guadalupe Hidalgo of 1848, are very averse to respond to the call made on them by the surveyor general's notice of January 18, 1855, to produce the evidence of their claims to his office at Santa Fé; some from fear of losing the evidence of their titles, inspired, it is supposed, by designing individuals. In many instances the Pueblo Indians have been deterred from filing their title papers with the surveyor general, in the apprehension they would never again get possession of them. Others conscious of an indisputable possessory right of landed estates, feel perfect security on the subject, and do not care to exhibit, much less file, their title papers, for the purpose of enabling the surveyor general to report upon the claims to congress for confirmation under the act of July 22nd, 1854.''

Surveyor-General Pelham reported, September 30, 1855, that fifteen claims had been filed for examination and adjudication, and in commenting upon the small number said: "The difficulties and expense to which parties filing claims in this office are subjected will account for the limited number which have been filed; and I respectfully recommend further legislation on the subject, as the present law has utterly failed to secure the object for which it was intended.''

[381] The act of June 21, 1860, confirmed the private land claims recommended for confirmation by the surveyor-general in his letter to the commissioner of the general land office, January 12, 1858, Nos. 1, 3, 4, 6, 8, 9, 10, 12, 14, 15, 16, 17, and 18, and the claim of E. W. Eaton, with the proviso that the claim of John Scolly and others (No. 9) was not confirmed for more than five square leagues, and the claim of Vigil and St. Vrain (No. 17) for not more than eleven square leagues to each.

The same act declared that the heirs of Luis Maria Baca, who claimed the land confirmed to the Town of Las Vegas (No. 20) might select and locate, in five parcels, the same quantity of vacant, non-mineral land, the confirmations by said act only to be construed as relinquishments on the part of the United States, and not to affect adverse rights.

At the time of the passage of the act of June 21, 1860, the committee on private land claims of the house of representatives had reported, among other matters: "It is now ten years since the Territory of New Mexico was acquired, and nearly four years since the surveyor general of the Territory was authorized to examine and report to us, the private land claims of its people; and although protected, as is supposed, by treaty, in the enjoyment of their property, no man in that Territory, without some action of Congress, can say that his title, however acquired, would hold against any claimant, who might

SPANISH AND MEXICAN LAND GRANTS 461

In the instructions to the surveyor-general special attention was given to the lands belonging to the Pueblo Indians and, with its usual promptness in dealing with matters affecting the rights of Indians, congress, on December 22, 1858, confirmed seventeen Pueblo Indian grants. In 1861 there had been surveyed twenty-five claims of town and private land claims, covering an area of 2,070,094 acres. In 1862-3 there had been examined of all classes forty-eight claims, and approved by congress thirty-eight. The surveyor-general constantly protested his inability to do justice to the work, urging the appointment of some kind of a commission, and congressional committees fully realized the impossibility of founding correct decisions on the meagre data furnished, predicting much more serious difficulties in the future; but no change was made in the system, and matters were allowed to drift.[382] The whole number [383] of private land claims filed in the office of the surveyor-gen-

---

purchase his lands from the government. . . But as Congress may not create such a board, and as it is due to the parties interested that the titles by which their lands are held should not be passed over to be settled by another generation, your committee have authorized me to report favorably (with one or two modifications) upon all the claims recommended for confirmation by the surveyor general; with the understanding that, should the action of Congress conform to the views of the committee as to this board, the claims may be finally determined under the new law. . .

"But for the gross injustice to the people of New Mexico of delaying for an indefinite period action upon their claims, and the certainty that under existing arrangements Congress can never consider them under more favorable circumstances than at this time, your committee would not have been willing to report upon any individual claims, for the reason first stated — want of time to examine fully, and the unknown quantity of land claimed by most of the parties.

"This last difficulty can not be obviated, without a survey of the lands, and that, it is presumed, will not be ordered by Congress, in advance of recognition of title."

[382] The honorable, the secretary of the interior, in his *Report*, in 1880, said: "After the lapse of nearly thirty years, more than 1,000 claims have been filed with the surveyors general, of which less than 150 have been reported to Congress, and, of the number so reported, Congress has finally acted upon only 71. The construction of railroads through New Mexico and Arizona, and the consequent influx of population in those Territories, render it imperatively necessary that these claims should be finally settled with the least possible delay. I have, therefore, the honor to recommend that the attention of Congress be called especially to this subject, with a view to securing action upon the claims pending before it, and upon the pending bill providing for the settlement of the remaining claims."

[383] *U. S. Land Office Reports*, 1864 *et seq*. Bearing upon land grants in New Mexico, congressional action appears in *U. S. Gov. Doc.*, 39th cong., 1st sess.; 40th cong., 2d sess., *H. Rep.* 71; 3d sess., *Senate Report*, 198. *Reports* on various claims 41st cong., 3d sess., *H. Ex. Doc.* 106; 42d cong., 2d sess., *H. Ex. Doc.* 296; *H. Miscl. Doc.* 181; 42d cong., 2d sess, *Senate Journal*, 344,

eral down to 1886, exclusive of the earlier Pueblo Indian claims, was 205. Of these thirteen were originally rejected and 141 approved, leaving fifty-one not acted upon.

President Cleveland, shortly after his inauguration in 1885, appointed George W. Julian surveyor-general for New Mexico and William Andrew Jackson Sparks, commissioner of the general land office. These men, steeped in prejudice against New Mexico, its people, and their property rights, sought to establish in the public mind that, by the acts of former officials charged with the administration of public land affairs in New Mexico, the government had been despoiled of millions of acres of land, instituted and prosecuted a policy of investigation relative to the former disposition of the public domain which, in the final outcome, proved a complete failure, owing to its virulence and partisan political character. By instructions from Commissioner Sparks, July 23, 1885, the surveyor-general reëxamined thirty-five of the claims originally approved by his predecessors, disapproving twenty-three of them. Not content with officially passing upon the matters coming regularly before him, this official, for strictly partisan political purposes, saw fit to use his name and office in a vain attempt [384] to destroy the titles to

---

562; *H. Mis. Doc.* 181; 3d sess, *H. Ex. Doc.* 68; *Sen. Doc.* 37, 40, 45, 50. *Reports* and *Doc.*, 42d cong., 3d sess., *H. Ex. Doc.* 37, 40, 128; 43d cong., 1st sess. *H. Ex. Doc.* 148-9, 206, 213, 258, 280; *Sen. Doc.* 3, 35, 58. 43d cong., 1st sess., *H. Ex. Doc.* 239; *Sen. Doc.* 43, 56; 2d sess, *H. Ex. Doc.* 62; *Sen. Doc.* 2, 335, 38. 44th cong., 1st sess., *H. Rept.* 50; *Sen. Doc.* 31. Discussion; *Cong. Globe*, 1873-6, per index. *Id.*, 1876-7, 44th cong., 2d sess., *H. Repts.* 110-111. 45th cong., 2d sess., *H. Repts.* 149, 222, 463. 45th cong., 3d sess, *H. Rep.* 59.

[384] Frank Springer, president New Mexico Bar Association, *Address* of, 1890:
"One of these persons, a man who has been on all sides of almost every question he has touched, came out here, according to his own confession, to inaugurate a raid on New Mexico land titles. The amazing spectable was then presented, of a United Stater surveyor general, holding office under an act of congress, having for its object the settlement of titles, deliberately and professedly undertaking to overturn a large part of what his predecessors had done; setting himself up as a court of review upon their acts; taking up cases passed upon years before, and without notice to the parties in interest, or an opportunity for them to be heard, declaring their titles fraudulent and void. These performances were without jurisdiction, and in legal effect absolutely null; yet they derived importance in the public mind from the fact that they were given out to the press and published as official decisions, were printed by the General Land Office as such, and scattered broadcast over the land. Titles that have been confirmed by congress and patented, and even decided by the highest courts of the country to be good and valid, and free from fraud, were not safe from the venomous tongue of this official scandal monger. Not content with the mischief he could do by his mendacious fictions in the form of official reports, this modern Thersites sought, and to the

land grants in New Mexico by contributing articles to influential periodicals in which he endeavored to besmirch the character of prominent citizens of the territory and to impeach the integrity of every official who had held office in New Mexico during the thirty years preceding his incumbency. The pernicious influence of this political mountebank was far reaching in the eastern states of the Union; but it awakened the people of New Mexico to a fuller sense of the necessity for a speedy determination of the titles to Spanish and Mexican land grants by congressional action. In his annual address to the members of the New Mexican Bar Association, in 1890, the retiring president of the association outlined a policy and course of procedure which, in part at least, was embodied in the act of congress establishing the court of private land claims.

Differences in opinion between the senate and house of representatives as to methods of procedure in the disposition of the private land claims in New Mexico, Arizona, and Colorado, prevented the adoption of any practical system. The people of New Mexico, although pronounced in their beliefs as to the best manner of disposing of these matters, were willing to adopt almost any system, provided it would afford relief.

In his annual message, December 1, 1889, President Benjamin Harrison called the attention of congress to the matter, saying: "The unsettled state of the title to large bodies of land in the Territories of New Mexico and Arizona, has greatly retarded the development of these Territories. Provision should be made by law for the prompt trial and final adjustment, before a judicial tribunal or commission, of all claims based upon Mexican grants. It is not just to an intelligent and enterprising people that their peace should

lasting discredit of the managers of that journal obtained, space in the *North American Review*, for the utterance of a paper, which for wilful distortion of facts, and wholesale villification of public officers in all departments of the government, has rarely had a parallel. He writes it as surveyor general of New Mexico, and claims belief upon that ground. It is entitled, 'Land Stealing in New Mexico.' He states that he 'overhauled the work of his office for the past thirty years,' and declared it to be for the most part 'legalized spoliation and robbery.' He asserts, in effect, that the 'governors, judges, district attorneys, legislatures, surveyors general and their deputies, marshals, treasurers, and county commissioners' have all been the tools of the land thieves; that the surveyor general's office has been a mere bureau in the service of the grant claimants. He charges that congress, in confirming forty-seven of these Mexican titles, 'has criminally surrendered the monopolists not less than 5,000,000 acres of land.' In short, official honesty was an unknown quantity until the advent of George W. Julian.''

be disturbed and their prosperity retarded by these old contentions. I express the hope that the differences of opinion as to the methods may yield to the urgency of the case."

At this session of congress, the delegate from New Mexico, Antonio Joseph,[385] introduced a bill providing for the establishment of a land court. Other bills [386] for the same purpose were introduced by representatives from the states. Public meetings were held in various localities in New Mexico and a committee of prominent citizens, of which L. Bradford Prince, at the time governor of New Mexico, was chairman, was sent to Washington for the purpose of procuring the passage of legislation looking to the establishment of a court or commission with power to dispose of the question of land titles in New Mexico.[387] On April 28, 1890, Mr. Wickham, from the committee on private land claims of the house, as a result of the deliberations of

[385] Antonio Joseph was born in Taos, N. M., August 25, 1846. He received his early education in the private schools of New Mexico, at Taos and at Santa Fé. Later he attended Webster College, St. Louis, Missouri. March 11, 1881, he married Elizabeth M. Foree, of Clark county, Missouri. Mr. Joseph held several county offices, was a member of the territorial assembly and was elected delegate from New Mexico to the 49th, 50th, 51st, 52d and 53d congresses, which position he filled with great credit. His political record was most honorable. For many years he lived at Ojo Caliente, of the hot springs at which place he was the proprietor. He died at Ojo Caliente, Taos county, in 1910. His remains are buried at Santa Fé.

[386] James B. McCreary, of Kentucky, H. R. 376, Dec. 18, 1889; Charles P. Wickham, of Ohio, H. R. 4613, January 13, 1890, in the house; Senator Ransom, December 10, 1889, S. 1042, and Senator Wolcott, Dec. 16, 1889, S. 1321, in the senate.

[387] On March 6, 1890, the territorial bureau of immigration unanimously passed a resolution looking to the sending to Washington of a delegation of prominent citizens to urge action on this subject. Pursuant to this resolution, a commission of fifty leading citizens, appointed by Governor Prince, was named, twenty-five of whom accompanied Governor Prince to Washington. The governor was elected chairman of this committee and Ira M. Bond and George H. Cross were chosen as secretaries. This delegation called upon the president, every member of the cabinet, the assistant secretary of the treasury, the commissioner and deputy commissioner of the general land office, and the Mexican minister, and had specially satisfactory interviews in relation to land grant titles with the president, secretary John W. Noble and secretary James G. Blaine. They were also accorded hearings by the senate committees on territories, private land claims, and public lands, and by the house committees on territories, education, private land claims, and irrigation. Everywhere the suggestions of the delegation were well received; and their request to President Harrison that he should still further aid in securing the passage of a bill was so effective that, on the 1st of July, the president sent to congress a special message on the subject. (*Messages*, etc., Richardson, vol. ix, p. 75). This was accompanied by a copy of the correspondence between the department of state and the Mexican government, and a report from the secretary of the interior. The latter embodied a list of the New Mexican land grants reported by the surveyor general but not acted upon by congress, 111 in num-

El Paso, Texas, November, 18, 1904.

The undersigned Mexican Delegates to the Irrigation Congress have had no time to make a comparison of the two projects to store the waters of the Rio Grande. The International Dam project and the Elephant Butte Dam project, but assumes, for actual purposes, that the Data given by Mr. Hall in his report read yesterday at Convention Hall, in regard to flow, sediment, evaporation, distances to bed rock, etc, are correct, and that it is thoroughly practicable to bring to the site of the Old Mexican Dam, above El Paso, the water necessary for the areas that were previously irrigated, and that said quantity of water will be given to Mexico, without cost, at that point. Surveys to be made by the Engineers of the United States Reclamation Service to determine the number of acres upon the Mexican side of the Rio Grande, which can be so irrigated, said surveys to be subject to the approval of the Mexican Government.

Under those considerations, the Mexican Delegation endorses the Elephant Butte Dam project, as explained by Mr. Hall, said endorsement to be subjected to the approval of the Mexican Government, as the Delegates have no instructions whatever as stated yesterday at Convention Hall by the Delegate from Tlaxcala, Sr. Carranza.

We, the undersigned committe, representing the American side of the Rio Grande Valley, heartily and unanimously endorse the above statement and presentation, made by the Honorable Delegation, representing the Mexican Republic, and through them, the Mexican side of the said Rio Grande Valley, subject to the approval of the United States Government.

Fac-simile of Resolution approving the Construction of the Elephant Butte Reclamation Project

Adopted by Delegates from Mexico, Texas, and New Mexico at the Thirteenth National Irrigation Congress, El Paso, Texas, November, 1904

SPANISH AND MEXICAN LAND GRANTS

that committee, reported a bill entitled, "A Bill to establish a United States Land Court and to Provide for a judicial investigation and settlement of private land claims in the Territories of Arizona, Utah, Wyoming and New Mexico, and in the states of Colorado and Nevada," and on the same day Senator Ransom, chairman of a similar committee of the senate, reported the bill introduced by himself and amended by the committee, entitled, "A Bill to establish a United States Land Court and to Provide for the Settlement of private land claims in certain states and territories." While these bills differed in details, and also in some important particulars, still they agreed in the general principles involved. All recognized, however, the danger which lay in the difficulty of obtaining consideration of the bills in time to secure the passage of some measure by both houses before the close of the session. President Harrison sent a special message to congress on the subject and on the 3d day of March, 1891, a bill entitled "An act to Establish a Court of Private Land Claims in certain States and Territories" having passed both houses of congress, received the executive approval.

COURT OF PRIVATE LAND CLAIMS

The official existence of this tribunal was begun by its formal organization at Denver, Colorado, July 1, 1891, and ceased, by operation of law, June 30, 1904.[388] The court was strictly non-partisan in its composition. Three of the five justices were from the republican and two from the democratic party. One of the republican members was from a southern and one of the

---

ber, and containing 6,643,938 acres, which were withdrawn from entry until final decision as to their title was rendered; this report set forth the existing situation and the need of speedy relief. "What is most needed," said the secretary of the interior in his report, "is legislation that will put in motion machinery which, within a reasonable time, would settle finally public and private rights growing out of said claims." The message of the president urged immediate action on the part of congress, and concluded as follows: "The entire community where these large claims exist, and all of our people are interested in an early and final settlement of them. No greater incubus can rest upon the energies of a people or the development of a new country than that resulting from unsettled land titles. The necessity for legislation is so evident and so urgent that I venture to express the hope that relief will be given at the present session of congress." The message of the president had great weight, and the differences between the proposed measures pending in the house and senate were reconciled and the amended bill passed just at the close of the congressional year, receiving the executive approval on the 3d of March, 1891.

[388] The chief and associate justices of this court were Joseph R. Reed, chief justice, from Iowa; associate justices, Thomas C. Fuller, North Carolina; Wil-

democrats was from a northern state. Four had served as officers in the war between the states, three on the federal and one on the confederate side, and the fifth member had held the office of assistant United States attorney during the war. In ability and judicial experience the members were fully qualified for the duties of this unique tribunal.[389]

The purpose and sole jurisdiction of the court were the consideration and adjudication of the titles to all the lands claimed to have been derived by grants from Spain and Mexico situate within the area ceded by Mexico to the United States under the treaty of Guadalupe Hidalgo, and the treaty of 1853, known as the Gadsden Purchase, all situate within the present states of Colorado, New Mexico, Arizona, California, Nevada, Utah, and Wyoming.[390]

---

bur F. Stone, Colorado; William W. Murray, Tennessee; Henry C. Sluss, Kansas; and later to fill vacancy caused by the death of Justice Fuller, F. I. Osborne of North Carolina. Other officers of the court were Matt G. Reynolds, United States attorney, Missouri; James H. Reeder, clerk, Kansas; T. B. Baldwin, deputy, for Colorado; Ireneo Chaves, deputy for New Mexico; Eusebio Chacon, interpreter; Luman F. Parker, stenographer; and Edward L. Hall, marshal.

[389] Wilbur F. Stone, *The Only Court of its Kind in the World*, in *Report of M. A. Otero*, governor of New Mexico, to the secretary of the interior, 1903: "It was gratifying that there was created a real court, not a hybrid cross between a board of arbitration and a coroner's inquest, like the old crude 'commission' of California, but a court commensurate with the importance of its object and purpose, fully equipped and clothed with all the powers — within the scope of its jurisdiction — of the circuit and district courts of the United States. . .

"In consideration of the purpose of the court, and the importance and peculiar character of the subject matter of its jurisdiction, it was conceded by the members of the joint committee of the senate and house which agreed upon the bill for final passage by congress, that the court ought to be essentially non-partisan in its make-up, and should be constituted so as to preclude the least taint or suspicion of party or political imputation, in order to inspire confidence in its integrity of decision when dealing with the vast property rights which had been the subject of good faith by treaty between two sister republics. To this end and it was suggested in committee whether it would not be wise to incorporate in the act a provision requiring that the persons to be chosen as justices of the court should not all be of the same political party. But Senator Edmunds, the chairman of the joint committee, remarked that such a provision would better be omitted, as it might suggest the very thing to be avoided, and that he would himself represent the view of the committee to the President touching this point. This he did the next day after the passage of the bill, and the selection of the members of the court by President Harrison was considered in keeping with that view."

[390] California, although included in the treaty session, was not included within the territorial jurisdiction of the court. Soon after the admission of that state, with its senators and congressmen, it was found easy to provide for a tribunal to settle these grants within the limits of that state; the tribunal provided by acts of congress was a "commission," with appeals and re-

The establishment of this tribunal created great satisfaction in the several jurisdictions mentioned. For more than forty years the country had been practically without relief, although as we have seen, under the treaty of Guadalupe Hidalgo, special stipulations had been entered into protecting titles.

Although many private acts had been passed by congress confirming land grants, the system was very unsatisfactory, not being judicial, always ex parte and sometimes unjust, congress acting more through political influences, confirming some grants which never should have been acted upon favorably and declining to confirm others where affirmative action should have been taken. Indeed, no claimant could secure congressional confirmation of his title unless provided with funds for a long sojourn at Washington, the organization of a lobby, and the buying of the army of official and nonofficial cormorants which has always infested the capital of the nation.

With the gradual disappearance of the hostile Indian from the great plains, with the constant increase in land values in Colorado and northern New Mexico, owing to the large development of the stock-raising and mining industry, the claimants and possessors of lands, the title to which had come through Spanish and Mexican grantees, and in many cases even where these titles had been confirmed by congress, were constantly being harassed and annoyed by the refusal of the immigrant to recognize their claims. The ordinary American knew nothing of "grants" and deemed it the inalienable right of American citizenship to "take up" and "hold down" mines, farms, ranches, and water rights whenever he found any not actually covered with habitations or cultivated fields. To him the claim that any one man or syndicate could be the rightful owner of a million acres of land was preposterous. With the coming of the railroads the situation became more serious. Demagogues and anti-land grant agitators thrived. The lives of rightful owners were threatened; judges were intimidated, and, through enterprising newspaper correspondents, the eastern press was flooded with stories of the "robber land barons of New Mexico." Fifty

---

views by the United States district court for California and the supreme court of the United States. Titles of this nature in California were settled between the years 1850 and 1865.

years passed slowly by before this fallacy of the squatter's reasoning became apparent to all right minded men.[391]

The court of private land claims was unique in character, and its establishment and work mark an interesting epoch in the history of New Mexico and of the general government as well. In its purpose, jurisdiction, and functions it was unlike any other ever established in the United States. Its function being, primarily, to determine the validity of title as between the United States and the grantee claiming under a foreign nation, it involved:

First, a legal interpretation of the terms of the treaties between the two governments.

Second, a consideration of international law, the civil law of Spain, founded upon the Roman civil law; the edicts, ordinances, and decrees of the Spanish crown, reaching back two or three centuries, relating to the crown possessions of the Indies.

Third, the laws and statutes, federal, departmental, and state, of Mexico subsequent to the independence of that government in 1820.

---

[391] *Report of the Governor of New Mexico*, 1903, p. 378: "Even the local land offices of the government did much to encourage these abuses. Not through ignorance, for every grant was notoriously well known, but from disregard of grant rights and lust for fees of the office, entries were allowed to be made upon grant lands the same as upon public domain, notably in southern Colorado and New Mexico, and of course squatters would pre-empt the best portions — those which were irrigable. This practice was made all the more aggravating when, afterwards, congress, in confirming these grants which the United States never owned and had by solemn treaty stipulated to protect, provided that all such squatter entries, although illegal when made, should be excepted from the confirmation, and the grantee should be graciously allowed to select a like area where he could find it on some part of the public domain, it might be in widely separated parcels miles away from his granted tract and of little value for any purpose; or, he could, as provided in the act creating the Court of Private Land Claims, accept pay from the United States at the price of $1.25 per acre for such excepted area, the latter in many cases being at the time of such adjudication worth from twenty-five to fifty dollars per acre. It is proper to note that these outrageously unjust provisions were the result of legislation at the instance of the majority of eastern members of congress who knew no more of the geography, topography, climatic and physical conditions or the necessity for irrigation in the farther west than they knew of the moon, and seemed to care as little, presuming, if they cared to indulge in any presumption whatever, that all these lands in the far western territories were the same as those in the rainy, well-watered, and timbered regions east of the Mississippi river. Members from the few states in the country west of the Mississippi, and the voteless delegates of Territories, were helpless and could only beg but not demand from that class which Governor Gilpin was wont to characterize as '——— salt water tyrants of the Atlantic Coast.'"

See also *Reports of the Governor of New Mexico*, 1895, pp. 1-14; 1896, pp. 3-10.

Fourth, the restrictive provisions of the act of congress creating the court.

Fifth, the decisions of the federal courts of the United States in the review of cases involving similar questions arising in California and under the Florida and Louisiana purchases, and also involving somewhat of the customs, definitions, interpretations, and traditionary usages touching the estate and tenure of Spanish and Mexican grant titles; and lastly, such of the law of evidence,[392] realty, descent, alienation, and equitable rights as are applicable under rules of judicial procedure in courts of the United States.

"An interesting feature of the business of the court" says one of its able justices,[393] "is the historic romance attaching to the settlement and holding of these lands. The documentary evidence in many cases had to be supplemented by the oral testimony of witnesses, relating to occupation, abandonment by Indian hostilities, heredity, and family pedigree of claimant, dating back to a time when witnesses from seventy-five to one hundred years old testified to what, when children, they had heard told by their aged grandfathers. Here were brought out the stories of the marches northward into the frontier provinces across arid deserts, over drifted sands, through prickly cactus, thorny mesquite-chapparal, and under burning suns reflecting the blinding light from wastes of snow-white alkali, on and on to the welcome, pine-clad mountains, with their cool streams and fertile valleys. Then the settlements, the building of the rude adobe and *jacal* dwellings, the little mission church with its venerated cross, the forts for defense, the pastoral life, with flocks of sheep and cattle, and the oft contention over watering places — the life over again of the patriarchal age of Abraham and Lot. Then the hostile raids of the Indians, the massacres, captivities, flights, years of wars and persistent returns.

"In these stories one could look back in fancy over the long trails these settlers followed and see the marches of the first Spanish invaders, the old conquistadores who, like the Crusaders of the middle ages, clad in all the panoply of Spanish cavaliers, resplendent in the glamour of the conquest of a New World, rode forth from the Halls of the Montezumas, on that long stretch of mountain plateau from

---

[392] All the muniments of title which constituted the written or documentary evidence in the cases before the court were in the Spanish language, the oldest being known as "archive" documents or records. The translation of these required the services of experts who had years of experience as translators and custodians of the archives and were familiar with the script, nomenclature, and formula of these ancient legal documents and their forms of authentication and peculiar rubrics. These archives were on parchment or royal sealed paper and the more ancient were full of abbreviations, like middle-age Latin.

[393] Wilbur F. Stone.

the City of Mexico to El Paso del Norte, and thence up the Rio Grande to its mountain sources — a journey of nearly three thousand miles — bearing the flag of Spain and the banner of the Cross, the mailed warriors going before and the black-robed priests following behind, and with glittering pomp and holy zeal bayoneting, baptizing and benevolently assimilating the natives '*de las Indias.*'

"The old world has scoffed at the lack of interesting history in America. The history of the Atlantic colonies and Mississippi states has been immortalized by the novelist and poets, like Cooper and Campbell, in tragic and bloody song and story, but the greater romance in the drama of American history, touched upon by the pens of Prescott and the Spanish chroniclers, is spread over the sunlands of the trans-Missouri and Pacific half of the continent, now the graveyard of the mystic Toltec, the golden templed Aztec, the peaceful Pueblos, and the fierce Apaches — the Bedouins of the American Desert."

The reflections of the able jurist, seemingly digressive, are most germane to the real genesis of the subject matter presented to and adjusted by the court of private land claims.

The territorial jurisdiction of this court was the largest of any trial court ever established by man. The area comprised was larger than the republic of France or the German empire.

During the existence of the court the total area of land for which suits were brought and service had on the United States amounted to 35,491,020 acres. The claims confirmed by decrees of the court, which were satisfied by the approval of the surveys made in execution of the decrees, amounted to 2,051,526 acres of land, and the amount rejected by the court was 33,439,493 acres. On the 30th of June, 1904, all of the business pending before the court was concluded.[394]

[394] *Report* of the attorney-general, 1904, p. 96. In his *Report* to the attorney-general of the United States, Matt. G. Reynolds, United States attorney for the court of private land claims, says: "Annual reports were submitted each year of the business transacted. In many instances, in the decrees of confirmation, the exact area was not specified for lack of official survey, but the estimated area covered thereby was approximately stated in the reports from this office. . . You are also advised that all records, files, and documents that have been in the possession of the United States attorney or assistants and employees from time to time, obtained from other offices and departments, as well as private individuals, have been returned, and not one has been lost or mislaid. The clerk of the court, Mr. Ireneo L. Chaves, advises me that all papers, files, and records in the possession of the court belonging to any other public office of the United States have been returned, and not one has been lost or mislaid, and that all papers, files, and records in the possession of or appertaining to said court have been delivered to the surveyor-general of the Territory of New Mexico and receipts taken therefor. . . It would be

It was ascertained by the court, in passing upon the many cases before the tribunal that quite a large number of grants had been made by officials who had not possessed the legal authority they had sought to exercise, and notwithstanding the fact that these grants had been made in good faith, the lack of authority in the granting officials brought about their rejection by the court. This error arose chiefly from the frequent changes in the constitution and legislation of the government and the great distance of the frontier provinces from the seat of the central government at the City of Mexico; so that a provincial governor would continue exercising his functions for months or a year before he could learn of a change in his authority. This was especially true under Spanish rule, when the ordinances and decrees of the crown, made beyond the seas, could not be promulgated and made known to the viceroys in Mexico until after the lapse of a year or more.

Under these conditions many grants, made perhaps a century before the court was established, had existed with titles undisputed by the people and by the government under which they were granted, and in strict equity were justly entitled to be held good, but a rejection was imperative because of the limiting provisions of the act of congress creating the court, which required proof of strict legal authority in the granting powers, and a rigid compliance with law in the form and manner of its execution. The marked ability and efficiency displayed by the representatives of the government, attorneys, experts,[395] translators, and other employes had much to

a great misfortune if these papers, files, and records should be removed from the Territory where the land is situated. . . The accurate amount of land which has been confirmed, and the surveys approved by the court within the Territory of New Mexico, is 1,934,986 acres, less than 6 per cent. of the area claimed. In Arizona the area claimed was not so large, excepting the fraudulent claim of J. A. Peralta Reavis and wife for 'La Baronia de Arizonaca,' for 12,467,556 acres. . . The areas were reduced from 837,679 acres claimed to 116,539 acres confirmed, and surveys approved by the court.''

A complete schedule or list of the grants decided by the court of private land claims in New Mexico, lists of those appealed and decided by the supreme court of the United States, together with much valuable information will be found in the *Report* of the attorney-general of the United States at pages 96-109 inclusive. This was a final report of the United States attorney for the court.

[395] *Report* of the attorney-general, 1904, pp. 98-9: ''It is but proper that mention should be made,'' says Mr. Reynolds, ''of those who have been associated with me on behalf of the Government, and upon whom I have relied and trusted at all times, and none of whom have I ever found unworthy or neglectful of the trust and confidence reposed in them, and to each should be accorded full measure of credit for such success as the government and the

do with the rejection of grants which otherwise would have been confirmed.

The area of land claimed by the famous James Addison Peralta-Reavis and wife amounted to 12,467,456 acres, covering all of the best portion of Arizona and a fair part of New Mexico. This claim was found to be entirely fictitious and fraudulent. The history of this case in itself would fill a large volume, full of romance, which can only be briefly epitomized here. This fraud attempted against the government was the most stupendous in the history of the world. Reavis was a native of

THE PERALTA-REAVIS FRAUD

---

people may in the years to come deem the settlement of land titles in the territory acquired from Mexico in 1848 and 1853. In 1894, Mr. Summers Burkhart, of Alburquerque, New Mexico, was appointed special assistant to the Attorney-general and assigned to the office as assistant at my request, and continued in that capacity for two years. His fidelity in the discharge of duty to the office and Government merit the good will and respect of Government and the people. Upon his resignation, in March, 1896, Mr. William H. Pope, of Santa Fé, N. Mex., was appointed to succeed him and continued with the office until the litigation was substantially concluded, when he resigned to accept appointment under the Philippine Commission as judge of the first instance. To Mr. Pope is due much of the credit for the painstaking and careful preparation and trial of some of the most important cases tried. . . His fidelity and ability in the discharge of the many and burdensome duties and the magnificent success accompanying the same deserve special commendation by those associated with him, the Government, and the people; no official connected with this entire litigation rendered better and more lasting service for good than Mr. Pope, and his public service since on the bench in the Philippine Islands and on the supreme bench of New Mexico is but a continuation of that high and honorable standard fixed and attained by him in the Court of Private Land Claims.

"Mr. Will M. Tipton was appointed special agent and expert by the Attorney-General at my urgent solicitation in 1892, and remained for nine years the confidential and trusted associate of the United States attorney. No one rendered more valuable assistance than he. His accurate knowledge of Spanish, expert study of handwriting, thorough familiarity with land titles in the Southwest, and his acquaintance with the details of public survey, combined to make him conspicuously qualified for the work to which he was called; and when to these qualities, indicative of the widest versatility, were added his thoroughness and untiring industry, it is not overestimating him to say that he was simply invaluable to the government.

"Mr. Henry O. Flipper was employed as special agent and Spanish expert in 1893, having reference to private land claims lying within the Gadsden Purchase. During the seven years Mr. Flipper was connected with this office his fidelity, integrity, and magnificent ability were subjected to tests which few men ever encounter in life. How well they were met can be attested by the records of the Court of Private Land Claims and the Supreme Court of the United States. To Mr. Tipton and to Mr. Flipper is due the credit of all of the expert work upon Spanish and Mexican archives and the translation of the laws and decrees applicable to land grants situate in the ceded territory.

"There were employed in the office from time to time a number of special agents either for general or special work, and among the latter deserving of

The Court of Private Land Claims—Chief Justice and Associates
Standing: Wilbur F. Stone, Henry C. Shluss
Sitting: Thomas C. Fuller, Joseph R. Reed, Chief Justice, W. M. Murray

Henry county, Missouri. He served in the Confederate army during the Civil War. After the war he became a resident of St. Louis, where he first became identified with the attempt to defraud the government, having there come into the possession of certain papers, as he claimed, purporting to be a grant made by the king of Spain to Don Miguel de Peralta de la Cordoba, made in the year 1748, conferring title to a tract of land of about 1,300,000 acres.

Prior to the establishment of the court of private land claims, Reavis enlisted the assistance of many persons of wealth and influence in the promotion of his alleged claim. In all of his efforts before the land offices, the surveyor-general of Arizona, and at Washington before congress, he failed.

Shortly after the organization of the court at Santa Fé he filed his claim, not the original claim which he had been promoting for many years, but an entirely new one in which he alleged that his wife, Doña Sofia Loreto Micaela de Peralta Reavis, neé Maso, y Silva de Peralta de la Cordoba, was the great-granddaughter of Don Miguel Nemecio Silva de Peralta de la Cordoba y Garcia de Carrillo de la Falces, a Spanish gentleman of noble birth and distinction, holding under the royal authority of Spain the titles of grandee of Spain, Sir Knight of the Redlands, Baron of Arizonaca, gentleman of the king's chamber with privileged entrance, captain of dragoons, aide-de-camp and ensign of the royal house, Sir Knight of the military orders of the Golden Fleece of St. Mary of Montesa, and of the royal and distinguished orders of Carlos III, and of the insignia and fellowship of the royal college of Our Lady of Guadalupe — and other titles too numerous to mention.

His petition set forth that Don Miguel, being in the confidence of the king of Spain, Philip V, in the year 1742, was made a royal inspector and business agent of the city of Cadiz, and as such was sent to the interior provinces of the viceroyalty of New Spain, with secret instructions for the investigation of cer-

---

special mention being Mr. Levi A. Hughes, of Santa Fé, N. Mex., employed on the Peralta Reavis claim. Mr. Hughes' services in that connection in California were most excellently performed and proved of inestimable value in defeating the claim and in securing the conviction of Peralta Reavis.''

Other experts, translators and employes mentioned by Mr. Reynolds in his report are Messrs. Sherrard Coleman, Clayton G. Coleman, Page B. Otero, Clarence Key, Epifanio Vigil, L. F. Parker, Jr., William J. McPherson, Vernon Beggs, and Francisco Delgado. The last named compiled all of the data for the report made by Mr. Reynolds.

tain grievances relative to the revenues of the crown; that on account of his services in this matter the king "declared his purpose to have selected and located to him" the barony of Arizona, or some other land or property. The petition further set forth that not only did Philip V, in 1744, confer this grant upon the "Baron of Arizonaca" but Ferdinand VI, in 1748, affirmed the same grant; that actual possession was delivered to Don Miguel and in 1778 all of these proceedings were confirmed by Carlos III.[396]

It was alleged that the first Don Miguel had a son, Don Jesus Miguel, who became the second baron of Arizona, who married and was survived by a daughter, Doña Sofia Laura Micaela Silva de Peralta de la Cordoba de Sanchez y Ybarra de Escobeda; that she married Don José Ramon Carmen Maso y Castillo, of Cadiz, Spain, in 1860, and that, on March 4, 1862, there were born to them twins, a girl and a boy, the girl later becoming the wife of Reavis. That these children were born while the Masos were en route to San Francisco from southern California.[397]

---

[396] It was also alleged that the grant was to contain 300 square Spanish leagues of land situate in the northern part of the vice-royalty of New Spain and to be of such form as not to interfere with previous concessions; that it was to include all of the lands, waters, and currents, and all of the minerals, and everything appertaining to the land; that the originals of the confirmatory decrees have always been in the proper archives of Spain and Mexico; that the action of the Inquisition of Mexico on October 10, 1757, specifically designated the proposed location of the grant; that on January 3, 1758, the viceroy of Mexico ordered possession to be given to the newly created baron; that an act of juridical possession of May 13, 1758, recited that said act corresponded with the map etched upon a monumental rock in the center of the west boundary line of the grant, lying at the eastern base of Maricopa mountain, and of the nobility, primogeniture, state, and emoluments of said baron, and of the legitimacy, nobility, and primogeniture of his son, Jesus Miguel Silva de Peralta de la Cordoba y Sanchez de Bonilla — the second baron of Arizona — by his wife, Doña Sofia Ave Maria Sanches de Bonilla y Amaya; that by a codicil to his will, dated January 13, 1788, the first baron devised to his son, Jesus Miguel, all the property known as the barony of Arizona; that on February 1, 1824, the first baron died in Guadalajara, leaving his wife and son, Jesus Miguel, the latter being his only heir, and that his will and codicil were admitted to probate in the city of Guadalajara, after which the executors administered the estate, including the barony of Arizona.

[397] It was alleged that the birth of this female descendant of the first Baron of Arizona occurred on a ranch at Agua Mansa, near San Bernardino, California, while Don José, known as José Maso, with his wife and mother and father-in-law, and an American friend, named John A. Treadway, were en route to San Francisco. It was declared that these children were baptized at the old church of San Salvador, the god-parents being the maternal grandfather and paternal grandmother, and Louis Robidoux and his wife, Flavia Castillo, and that the mother and the boy twin died a few days later. The

About two years after the arrival of the Masos in California, a man named Treadway, who had been of the party, and who had been acting as guardian for the alleged infant heiress, went to Sacramento, where it was said that he died. About 1867 the girl's grandmother also died. A year later the nurse, Tomasa, died, leaving the child in the custody of A. E. Sherwood, in whose house she had lived since 1862. In 1869, Sherwood, being unable to provide for her education, gave her to John W. Snowball of Knight's Landing, who raised and educated her. From 1876 to the year of her alleged marriage by contract with Reavis, she resided with various persons, being a member of the household of John D. Stevens, of Woodland, in 1882, the year in which, according to the story of Reavis, her association with Reavis was begun.

These facts constitute an epitome of the claim presented by Reavis and his wife. In proof of his allegations he had a mass of evidence which had every appearance of being genuine and conclusive. There were copies, duly certified, of the contents of books of record, alleged to have been found in the Guadalajara archives, all of which referred to the allegations concerning the events transpiring between 1742 and 1778. The genealogy of the mythical baron of Arizona was traced back for centuries in Spain, and it appeared that he was the possessor of all the titles which were enumerated in the petition. All that was necessary was to prove that the wife of Reavis was the great-granddaughter of Don Miguel, the first baron of Arizonaca. So trifling a matter of proof as this did not worry this cunning swindler. During the same year that he filed his petition he secured depositions in California which appeared to establish the identity of his wife. Many lawyers of high standing were of the opinion that the government would not be able to with-

records of this church contain what purport to be entries of the baptism and burial. The remainder of the party continued on to San Francisco, where they remained some time, there forming the acquaintance of a number of people who testified to facts showing that they had been in that city. In July, 1862, Doña Carmelita Maso, the mother of Don José Maso, and a nurse named Tomasa, accompanied Treadway to the Sherwood valley in Mendocino county, California. Maso shortly afterward visited Spain for the purpose of obtaining from the Spanish government a sum of money which it was alleged was due him and his father-in-law. Later on his father-in-law also went to Spain, but before he departed it was claimed that he made a will in San Francisco, to which he added a codicil after his arrival in Spain, leaving all of his property to his infant granddaughter. Both men died in Spain a few years later.

stand the contention made by Reavis. The interest in the two territories was great, for upon the outcome depended the title to a tract of land with an area of nearly 20,000 square miles. Its western boundary was a line west of Phoenix, Arizona, and its eastern boundary reached Silver City, New Mexico.

The government, however, was equal to the situation. Largely through the efforts of Levi A. Hughes and Will M. Tipton, who secured most of the evidence to support the government's claim of fraud, the claim failed. Assisting the United States attorney was Severo Mallet-Prevost, of New York, afterwards secretary of the Venzuela boundary commission. Summers Burkhart, of Alburquerque, also represented the government.

No sooner had the claim been filed than the government began sending agents to every point where it was believed evidence could be found. Mallet-Prevost and one of the judges went to Spain. Levi A. Hughes went to California.

In Spain it was ascertained that the will of the second baron of Arizona, in the records in Madrid, was a forgery; that no such person as Don Miguel Nemecio Silva de Peralta had ever been a member of the orders of the Golden Fleece, Charles III, and Montesa; that while Reavis was in Spain, in 1886, he had been detected in the act of attempting to introduce into the archives in Seville forged papers relating to the grant and had fled from Spain before he could be apprehended. An examination of the archives at Guadalajara by Mr. Tipton showed that the language used in some of the decrees was not good Spanish, and that some of the statements made were not historically consistent. In a decree of 1758 a reference to the *judicio de conciliacion*, a proceeding unknown in Spanish court procedure until after the adoption of the constitution of 1812, was found.

Mr. Tipton, in an account of this case and its preparation for trial on the part of the government, says:

"The *cedula* of 1742, appointing the Baron of Arizona a royal inspector, was found in a manuscript book of *cedulas* of over 500 pages, which had been arranged and bound in 1766. The *cedula* in question was upon two leaves, on the second of which three words bore evidence of having been written over other words which had been erased. These words were *visitador*, inspector, *Baron*, baron, and *Arizonaca*, Arizona. The first leaf was in a single handwriting and contained no such changes. Much study was given to this document, and the results were these: The first leaf was a forgery throughout, having been skillfully interpolated for a genuine leaf which had been as skillfully removed. The second leaf was genuine, excepting the three changed words. The problem was to decipher the words originally written under these. After a prolonged study, this was accomplished. The word *virrey*, viceroy, had originally been written in place of *visitador*, inspector; *conde*, count, had been written under *Baron*, baron; while Fuenclara, the same in English, had occupied the space covered by *Arizonaca*, Arizona. The riddle was solved. The *cedula* claimed by Reavis to show the appointment of the Baron of Arizona as inspector of New Spain, had been in its original form a *cedula* advising the city of Guadalajara of the fact that the King had appointed the Count of Fuenclara as Viceroy of New Spain.

"The study of the other three books gave similar results. The book showing the genealogy of the first Baron of Arizona consisted of thirty-eight leaves, the first and two last being genuine, except where an attempt had been made on the latter to change, in the notary's certificate, the words stating the number of leaves of which the instrument was composed. Between leaves 1 and 37, thirty-five leaves of solidly forged matter, showing the noble descent and purity of blood of Mrs. Reavis' great-grandfather had been interpolated. In the notarial certificate on the last page a pen stroke had been drawn across several words, and the words *treinta y ocho*, thirty-eight (the number of leaves in the book), had been changed from their original form. When deciphered they were found to have been *ciento sesenta y nueve*, one hundred and sixty-nine. So this genuine certificate had originally been attached to some genuine document containing that number of leaves, and it had been altered by the forger to make it agree with the number contained in the spurious document to which he attached it.

"The book of proceedings relating to the probate of the will of the first Baron was at first sight somewhat puzzling, because much of it was genuine; but it took but a few days to separate the genuine from the forged portions. There was no mention of the Baron of Arizona, either by name or by any one of his numerous titles, in any genuine part of it. This was also true with regard to every other document in the archives purporting to relate to the grant.

"The last book was one of parchment containing copies of various *cedulas* and depending for its authenticity on the signature appearing on the last page, of Urbano Antonio Ballesteros, a royal notary. The genuine signatures of this officer were numerous in the archives, and the scientific comparison of the signature in question with these, quickly demonstrated that it was a bungling forgery."

The results of the investigation made by Levi A. Hughes were equally startling. He discovered that the manuscript records of the ancient church of San Salvador had been mutilated by the removal of entire leaves and the substitution of others containing forged entries regarding the baptism of the Maso twins and the death of the mother and the infant son. From Louis Robidoux [398] and his wife he obtained a denial of all knowledge of the occurrence. He likewise ascertained that all of the depositions on which Reavis depended to establish the identity of his wife were false. He ascertained that Reavis's wife was the daughter of John A. Treadway by an Indian woman with whom he had lived in the Sherwood valley. He found the man who had buried Treadway on November 21, 1861, more than six months before the time when it was alleged that he had brought the infant daughter of Maso to Sherwood valley.

The claim was heard by the court in June, 1895. The court found that the grant was utterly fictitious and fraudulent and that the documents offered by the claimants had been forged and surreptitiously introduced into the Spanish archives at Madrid, Seville, and Guadalajara; that the records of the parish of San Bernandino and San Salvador were forgeries; that no such person as Miguel Nemecio Silva de Peralta de la Cordoba had ever existed and that the petitioners were in no manner related to or connected with the imaginary and mythical baron of Arizona.

A more cunning, accomplished, and resourceful swindler than Reavis was never born. In poverty and in obscurity he was the author of and executed, without confederates, a crime requiring marvelous

---

[398] Louis Robidoux was the son of Joseph Robidoux, a native of Montreal, Canada. Joseph, the elder, came from the western part of France about the middle of the eighteenth century. Joseph Robidoux came to St. Louis, Missouri, late in the eighteenth century and was engaged in the fur trade. He had nine sons and daughters. Joseph laid out the present city of St. Joseph, Missouri, naming the principal streets of the city for his children. Antoine Robidoux, the fourth son of Joseph, was born in St. Louis in 1791. He and his brother Louis were early identified with the Santa Fé trade; both lived at Taos and at Santa Fé. Antoine married the adopted daughter of Governor Armijo. He lost his eyesight at the age of fifty-six years. He acted as guide and interpreter for General Kearny at the time of the American occupation and interpreted the proclamations of that commander at Las Vegas and at Santa Fé. Antoine died at St. Joseph, Missouri, August 29, 1860. His wife, during the later years of her life, lived at the Sisters convent in Durango, Colorado, where she died at a very old age. Antoine Robidoux was a man of commanding figure, courageous, and was the hero of many exploits with the Indians of the Plains. It is said that he was the master of five languages and spoke nearly every Indian idiom in the plains and mountain country.

ingenuity and magnificent audacity. In the early years of his promotion of this gigantic fraud he was successful in securing the influence and abundant financial aid of some of the most prominent and wealthy men in the country. With funds received from them he rose to affluence, became the intimate of millionaires and prominent government officials, had a country house on Staten Island and a magnificent home on the Pacific coast; took his wife to Spain where she was introduced to the Spanish court as the fourth baroness in the line of an illustrious ancestry and the heiress of an estate as large as the kingdom of Spain.

When the time came for the hearing he had exhausted all of his financial resources and, with the assistance of a briefless attorney, his former counsel, now cognizant of the gigantic swindle, having deserted him, tried his own case. After the decree rejecting his claim, he was indicted in the district court of the first judicial district, at Santa Fé, tried, convicted, and sentenced to the penitentary.

The make-believe baroness, the half-breed Indian woman, never was a knowing party to the attempted fraud. When Reavis was sent to the penitentiary, she was entirely without means, was deserted by her former friends, and compelled to perform menial service for the support of herself and twin boys.

In magnitude and in romance of crime no case ever paralleled this in the civil jurisprudence of the world. The documents of title in Spanish, with the translations, illustrated with maps, plats, royal seals, rubrics, genealogical trees, and photographs of ancient personages of the mythical Peralta family, together with the transcript of the oral testimony taken at the hearing of the claim, fill two large printed volumes, now in the records of office of the surveyor-general for New Mexico. Mr. Tipton says, "This monstrous edifice of forgery, perjury and subornation was the work of one man. No plan was ever more ingeniously devised; none ever carried out with greater patience, industry, skill and effrontery."

Reavis remained in the penitentiary at Santa Fé from July 18, 1896, to April, 1898. Upon the expiration of his term he left New Mexico and went to California.

BIBLIOGRAPHY

Archives — Surveyor-General's office, Santa Fé, N. M.
Buchanan, James — *Letter* of; *Sen. Ex. Doc.* 60.
Bureau of Immigration — New Mexico, *Report of*, March 6, 1890.
Congress of U. S. — *Acts* of, 1860, confirming private land claims.
Emory, W. H. — *U. S. and Mex. Boundary Survey*, 1854-5, Washington, 1857, 3 vols.
Guadalupe Hidalgo — *Treaty of, Compiled Laws of New Mexico*, 1884, 1897, *Sen. Ex. Doc.* 52; 30th cong., 1st sess.
Gadsden Purchase — *Treaty* of Mesilla, 1853; *Compiled Laws of N. M.*, 1897.
Julian, George W. — "Land Stealing in New Mexico," *North American Review*, 1890.
King, Samuel D. — Surveyor-General of California, *Report* of, Sept. 30, 1851.
McCreary, James B. — *Bill* prepared by, H. R. 1889.
New Mexico — Session Laws, *Memorials*, 1853-1887.
Otero, Miguel A. — *Report* of; Governor of New Mexico, 1903.
Peralta-Reavis, J. Addison — Hearing of his Claim; *Report* of; office of Surveyor-General, New Mexico, Santa Fé, N. M.
Polk, James K. — *Message* of, February 8, 1849, *Ex. Doc.* 50, H. of R., 30th cong., 2d sess.
Pelham, William — Surveyor-General, New Mexico; *Instructions to*, August 25, 1854; *Report of*, September 30, 1855.
Richardson, James D. — *Messages of the Presidents*, vol. ix, Washington, D. C.
Reynolds, Matt. G. — *Report* of Attorney-General, 1904.
Stone, Wilbur F. — *The Only Court of its Kind in the World*; Report of M. A. Otero, Governor of New Mexico, 1903.
Springer, Frank — *Address* of; *Report* of N. M. Bar Association, 1890.
Secretary of Interior — *Report* of, 1880.
Tipton, Will M. — *Extracts* from *Article* by, *Sunshine Magazine*, Los Angeles, California, February and March, 1898.
United State Supreme Court — *Reports* of; 19 *Howard*; 1 *Wallace*; *Peters*.
United States Land Office — *Reports* of, 1864, *U. S. Gov. Docs.* 39th cong., 1st sess., 40th cong., 2d sess; *House Rep.* 71, 3d sess, *Sen. Rep.* 198; *Reports* of Various Claims, 41st cong., 3d sess.; *H. Ex. Doc.* 106, 42d cong., 2d sess; *H. Ex. Doc.* 296; *H. Miscl. Doc.* 181; 42d cong., 2d sess., *Sen. Jr.* 344, 562; *H. Miscl. Doc.* 181; 3rd sess., *H. Ex. Doc.* 68, *Sen. Doc.* 37, 40, 45, 50; *Reports* and *Doc.* 42d cong., 3d sess., *H. Ex. Doc.* 37, 40, 128; 43d cong., 1st sess., *H. Ex. Doc.* 148-9, 206, 213, 258, 280, *Sen. Doc.* 3, 35, 58; 43d cong., 1st sess., *H. Ex. Doc.* 239, *Sen. Doc.* 43, 56; 2d sess, *H. Ex. Doc.* 62;

BIBLIOGRAPHY 481

	Sen. Doc. 2, 335, 38; 44th cong., 1st sess, *H. Rep.* 50; *Sen. Doc.* 31; Discussions in *Congressional Globe*, 1873-1876, per Index, *Id.*, 1876-7; 44th cong., 2d sess, *H. Reps.* 110, 111; 45th cong., 2d sess., *H. Reps.* 149, 222, 463; 45th cong., 3d sess, *H. Rep.* 59.
Wickham, Chas. P.	*Bill* prepared by, H. R. 4613, January 13, 1890.
Wolcott, Edward	*Bill* prepared by, S. 1321, Dec. 16, 1889.
Wilson, John	Com. G. L. O. *Instructions* from, to W. Pelham, Aug. 25, 1854.
White's	*Recopilacion.*
Zabriskie, J. C.	*Public Land Laws of U. S.*, San Francisco, 1870; *Supplement*, 1877.

BENT'S FORT ON THE ARKANSAS RIVER

CHAPTER XII

ADVENT OF THE RAILWAYS — GOVERNORS AND THEIR ADMINISTRATIONS — LEGISLATIVE ENACTMENTS — DELEGATES IN CONGRESS — NATIONAL LEGISLATION — INDUSTRIAL PROGRESS — MINES AND MINING — CITIES AND TOWNS — EDUCATION — THE FERGUSSON ACT — RECLAMATION ACT — NATIONAL AID IN IRRIGATION — POLITICAL AFFAIRS — CRIMES AND CRIMINALS — LABOR STRIKES AND TROUBLES — EFFORTS FOR STATEHOOD — SPANISH-AMERICAN WAR — ROOSEVELT'S ROUGH RIDERS — CONGRESSIONAL INVESTIGATING COMMITTEES — SENATOR ALBERT J. BEVERIDGE — THE ENABLING ACT — CONSTITUTIONAL CONVENTION — STATE ELECTION — 1880-1912

THE advent of the railroads in New Mexico was the beginning of an era of permanent prosperity for the people of the territory. The wonderful rapidity with which the great transcontinental transportation lines were constructed was not less marvelous than the astonishing awakening of the people to the fact that at last New Mexico was really in touch with the enlightened progress and modern methods of the people of the eastern states.[392]

---

[392] *Session Laws of New Mexico*, 1880. The legislature of New Mexico, in session at the time the line was constructed into the capital, passed a resolution demonstrating how appreciative of changed conditions the people were. The resolution follows:

"Resolved, that the legislature of New Mexico observes with pleasure and satisfaction the completion of a line of railroad to the City of Santa Fé, the capital of the Territory, and the rapid extension of the same southward through the great valley of the Rio Grande.

"That this event may well be regarded as the most important in the history of the Territory, as the beginning of a new era in which, through the development of its resources and the improvements which are certain to follow the establishment of means of rapid communication with other parts of the country, New Mexico may be expected soon to take her position in the American Union to which she is by nature justly entitled.

"That in the celebration of the advent of the road to the capital, which

Attorney for Court of Private Land Claims and Assistants
1. Matt G. Reynolds. 2. Levi A. Hughes. 3. William M. Tipton.
4. Summers Burkhart

The first passenger train [393] into New Mexico brought the members of the legislature of the state of Colorado to Otero, on the line of the Atchison, Topeka and Santa Fé Railroad, in Colfax county, February 13, 1879. One year later the line had been constructed southward through the counties of Mora, San Miguel, and Santa Fé, over the Glorieta Pass, and southward to the valley of the Rio Grande. In five years more there had been constructed by three great railway corporations one thousand two hundred and fifty-five miles of railway in New Mexico. These were the New Mexico and Southern Pacific Railroad Company, the Rio Grande, Mexico and Pacific Railroad Company, and the New Mexican [394] Railroad Com-

took place on the 9th day of February, 1880, participated in by the representatives not only of the City of Santa Fé but of the Territory, this assembly recognizes an evidence of the good will and progressive tendency of the whole people with regard to the important improvements and changes which are now at hand.''

[393] If it had not been for the panic of 1873, the building of the line of the Atchison, Topeka and Santa Fé Railroad would have been accomplished five years sooner. Prior to 1873, Henry Strong, then president of the railroad company mentioned, together with Dutch associates interested in the Maxwell land grant, had made all arrangements for the construction of the line from its then terminus, near Granada, Colorado, to Cimarron, in Colfax county, New Mexico. The panic of 1873, the failure of J. Cooke and Company, and other disasters of that period compelled an abandonment of plans which would have made Cimarron the center of the industrial development which afterward came to Pueblo and Trinidad, in the state of Colorado.

[394] The original incorporators of the railroad companies controlled by the Atchison, Topeka and Santa Fé Railroad Company were William B. Strong, Miguel A. Otero, Frederick W. Pitkin, Henry C. Nutt, Albert A. Robinson, Jefferson Raynolds, James L. Johnson, Henry M. Atkinson, William W. Griffin, José Placido Romero, William Breeden, Edward Hatch, and Henry L. Waldo.

William B. Strong was born in Brownington, Vermont, and was educated in the Pangborn school at Burlington in that state. While a young man he removed to Wisconsin. His first railroad work was done on a line which is now a part of the Chicago and Northwestern system. He began as a station worker, then became an operator and station agent. He was promoted by various stages until he became successively general superintendent of the Michigan Central Railroad, and general superintendent of the Chicago, Burlington and Quincy Railroad. On December 17, 1877, he came to the Atchison, Topeka and Santa Fé as vice-president and general manager. On July 12, 1881, he was elected president of the company, which position he held until September 6, 1889. When Mr. Strong began his work with the ''Santa Fé'' the line extended from Topeka across Kansas into Colorado. He immediately pushed the work of extending the system. He brought about the lease of the Denver and Rio Grande lines and the purchase of the stock of that company. Protracted litigation followed this purchase as well as an actual physical contest of great vigor in which considerable bloodshed and destruction of property took place — the Denver and Rio Grande Company using physical force in its efforts to recover the property it had leased to the Santa Fé Company. After the Santa Fé had won all of the fights, both in the field and in the courts, an offer to refund to the Santa Fé all the cash it had expended in the purchase

pany, subsidiary corporations of the Atchison, Topeka and Santa Fé Railroad Company; the Atlantic and Pacific Railroad Company, the Southern Pacific Railroad Company, and the Denver and Rio Grande Railroad Company.

It has often been remarked that the main transcontinental line of the Atchison, Topeka and Santa Fé Railroad should have been constructed through the city from which the present railway system takes its name.[395] Such was the first intention of the projectors and

and the contest proved tempting to the board of directors in Boston and a settlement was made on that basis. Mr. Strong pushed the line to Santa Fé by 1880, and to El Paso and Deming in a little more than a year later. Next came heavy construction in Kansas and the Indian Territory. Kansas City was reached from Topeka by acquisition of three lines between the two towns. The Leavenworth, Lawrence and Galveston road became the Southern Kansas Railway, owned by the Santa Fé. In 1886, the Gulf, Colorado and Santa Fé had been acquired in Texas, and lines begun from Chicago and St. Louis to Kansas City. The Chicago line was completed under the name of the Chicago, Santa Fé and California. The St. Louis line was built only to Union, Mo. This property was sold after the re-organization of the Santa Fé. The Atlantic and Pacific was built from Isleta, N. M., to the Needles, Calif., by the Atlantic and Pacific Railroad Company, owned one-half by the St. Louis and San Francisco and one-half by the Santa Fé. The Southern California line was purchased, as also the Sonora Railway, in Mexico. Thus at the time of Mr. Strong's retirement from the system he had been the prime mover in the work of expanding the system from a line through Kansas to a system with about 2,500 miles of track in Kansas and about 5,000 miles outside of Kansas, the extremities of the system being Chicago, St. Louis, Superior, Neb., Pueblo, Colo., San Diego, Calif., Guaymas, Mexico, El Paso and Galveston, Texas.

Mr. Strong was a powerful man physically and mentally. He worked like a whirlwind. No speed was too great and no hours were too long when he had a task in hand. He was, however, a most kindly and patient man, with the utmost concern for the good will of his employes and the patrons of the system. He insisted on a thorough commissary method, and the Harvey system of hotels and dining halls is the result. He always paid great attention to the forming of a correct public opinion as the best foundation for satisfactory relations between the company and the public. Under his management the company was never accused of any disrespect for or disregard of either technical law or the rules of good conduct. The sudden construction of a vast competitive mileage affecting all branches of the company's business, both through and local, together with the bad business conditions generally, caused a temporary halt in the development of the business of the system and a default which led to a receivership and re-organization.

Mr. Strong's was the master railroad mind of his time. He has lived to see all his theories about the property fully vindicated. At this time (January, 1912) he is living in Los Angeles, California, an invalid from the effects of partial paralysis.

[395] Henry L. Waldo, at the time of the building of the Santa Fé in New Mexico a resident of the capital city, was the confidential personal and legal adviser of Mr. Strong in all matters affecting the interests and policies of the railroad company in New Mexico. His advice and counsel were also sought and followed in matters arising in other jurisdictions.

He is the son of Lawrence Ludlow Waldo and Mary Elizabeth (Cantrell) Waldo. He was born in Jackson County, Mo., January 16, 1844. His father

Early Bankers of New Mexico
1. William W. Griffin. 2. Jefferson Raynolds. 3. Joshua S. Raynolds.
4. Rufus J. Palen. 5. John W. Poe. 6. E. A. Cahoon

builders of the railroad, but physical conditions, as developed by a large number of surveys, demonstrated to the 'officials of the company that a route through the capital city of the territory was not

---

was engaged in merchandizing over the old Santa Fé and Chihuahua trails as early as 1829, continuing in this business until January 19, 1847, when, returning from Santa Fé to Westport, Mo., he was captured by the Mexicans, under Manuel Cortez, near Mora. New Mexico. Cortez was a leader of the revolutionists, at that time in rebellion against the authority of the Americans, who had taken possession of the country. The elder Waldo, with five companions, by the order of Cortez, was taken across the river Mora, near where the town of that name now stands, and mercilessly shot. By those who knew him he is said to have been a man of courtly manners and distinguished personality.

Henry L. Waldo received a very limited education in the common schools of his native county; he attended the University of Missouri a part of one year. In 1862, with the caravan of George Bryant, he crossed the great plains to Santa Fé. Returning to Westport, the following year he removed to California, where he read law and was admitted to the bar of that state. In 1870, he was married to Lucy Maria Mills, daughter of Dr. Augustus and Eliza (Buckner) Mills, of Kentucky. Of this union five children were born, three of whom, Mamie, Thomas A., and Helen (Waldo) Rogers, survive. A son, Henry L., Jr., died January 26, 1892, from injuries received while practicing in the gymnasium of an eastern college which he was attending at the time.

Removing to Santa Fé, from California, in 1873, Judge Waldo entered upon the practice of his profession and took charge of the interests of Stephen B. Elkins, in the firm of Catron and Elkins, who was at that period the delegate in congress from New Mexico. On January 10, 1876, he was appointed chief justice of the Supreme Court of New Mexico by President Grant, holding the office for two years, when he resigned. His career upon the bench proved highly satisfactory to the bar and litigants alike. At this period in the history of New Mexico it was the custom for attorneys to address juries in the Spanish language. Judge Waldo put an end to this custom and compelled the use of interpreters. Resuming the practice of his profession he formed a partnership with William Breeden, a distinguished member of the bar of New Mexico. Shortly after his resignation as chief justice he was appointed attorney general by Samuel B. Axtell, governor of New Mexico. This office he held until 1880, when his partner, William Breeden, was appointed to the office by Lionel A. Sheldon, at that time governor. When he was appointed chief justice, as well as when named attorney general, Judge Waldo was a prominent member of the democratic party. This fact, however, seems not to have weighed heavily with the appointing power, which was of opposing political faith. While holding the office of attorney general, in representing the territory in the courts, the records disclose the fact that he was uniformly successful. In 1883, when the law department of the Santa Fé Railroad Company was systematized, he was appointed its solicitor for New Mexico, a position which he has held until the present (January, 1912). Having in charge all of the business of the railroad company in New Mexico, he gave up his private practice, dissolving his partnership with William Breeden in 1883. Since that time upon him have devolved the duties of counsellor for the company in all its business relations in New Mexico. Although never a member of the legislative assembly of the territory, no man in its entire history has been the author of so many of its legislative enactments resulting in benefit to the people; at the same time it may be said that through his influence much proposed legislation, vicious and harmful in its tendency, failed of enactment. Charged with the responsibility of guarding great interests, in other jurisdictions the prey of politicians and demagogues, his great dignity,

feasible. So anxious were the officers and directors of the company to place the ancient city upon the main line that an engineer, not in the employ of the company when the several surveys for routes had been made, was detailed to make surveys and check over all of those which had been reported by the regular locating engineers. His report was of such a character as to preclude any idea of ever constructing the main line to the capital.[396]

integrity of purpose, and unimpeachable character enabled him to deal with political officials and bosses of whatever party, without fear or favor.

Judge Waldo is a man of great practical wisdom. In all his professional undertakings and engagements his striking personality has always been in evidence. Averse to any semblance of notoriety, he was never known to evade responsibility in order to escape possible criticism. For many years the trusted representative of great corporate interests, he never advocated nor permitted his influence or name to be used in support of any measure inimical to the people. He is a plain, straightforward, unassuming gentleman, a profound thinker, an able lawyer, and a fearless advocate of what he believes to be for the best. Possessed of intense convictions he has always been aggressive and fearless in defending his opinions. He has worked out his own standards of character and conduct. Apparently austere in demeanor, he is possessed of those qualities of character and temperament which discover great sympathetic impulses where long friendships have ripened into affection. Reaching manhood when the Missouri river was the western border of civilization, Judge Waldo is essentially a product of that rugged honesty, consistent conservatism, and marked ability so characteristic of his day and generation.

[396] Many persons living in Santa Fé have always believed that the main line was not built through the city solely because of demands made by certain citizens of that place and refusals on their part to coöperate along lines suggested by the officers of the railway company. This is untrue. It was reported to Mr. Strong and to the largest stockholders in the New England states, among them Mr. Nickerson, Mr. Cheney, and Mr. Speare, that personal reasons governed the locating engineer, Mr. W. R. Morley, in recommending the present route from Glorieta to Lamy and thence to the valley of the Rio Grande; that the opposition of himself and his friends, notably Frank Springer and J. M. Cunningham, to Thomas B. Catron and R. H. Longwill, who lived at Santa Fé, was such that his report was biased and entirely unfair; that his survey was not worthy of consideration and that a feasible route, on proper grades, could be ascertained by impartial effort. All of these statements from the people of Santa Fé were considered by Mr. Strong and his board of directors. It was determined to engage the services of one of the most competent engineers familiar with railroad construction in the Rocky Mountains, have surveys made by him and all of those made by Mr. Morley and Mr. George B. Lake checked. Such an engineer was employed. He made several surveys, one from Las Vegas directly through the mountains west to Santa Fé; he made others and checked all the work that had been done by the regular engineers of the company. His report sustained the recommendations of the regular engineers and the line from Glorieta via Lamy was adopted and constructed. When the people of Santa Fé and the county of that name ascertained that the main line was to be constructed in this manner, for the purpose of securing a line to the capital they held an election and voted, in aid of the construction of the line from Lamy to Santa Fé, bonds of the county in the sum of $150,000. Otherwise the city of Santa Fé would have no connection with the main line what-

1880 TO 1912

The men who invested their capital in the construction [397] of railroads in New Mexico never believed that at the time of construction there was traffic sufficient to support such gigantic enterprises, but they were persuaded that the roads would soon create a profitable business for themselves. The construction of the line of the Atchison, Topeka and Santa Fé Railroad not only quickened the entire territory into new life, attracting immigration from all portions of the United States and abroad, but actually created the traffic which now makes its operation profitable.

On March 10, 1881, all-rail connection across the continent, [398] via New Mexico and Arizona, was established by the junction at Deming

---

ever. The courts afterward held these bonds to be illegal, but the congress of the United States validated the issue.

The locating and constructing engineers of the company were A. A. Robinson, afterward the general manager of the Santa Fé and later the president of the Mexican Central Railway Company, W. R. Morley, who lost his life in Mexico by the accidental discharge of a rifle, and George B. Lake, now deceased.

In 1878, Mr. Morley filled the position of engineer in charge of construction of the Atchison, Topeka & Santa Fé Railroad, under Mr. A. A. Robinson, Chief Engineer. He was prominently identified with, and took an active part in what is known as the "Grand Canyon War," the early struggle between the A. T. & S. F. R. R. Co. and the Denver and Rio Grande R. R. Co. for control of the Grand Canyon of the Arkansas River. A braver man than Morley never located a railroad line; he was full of the fire that burns in the breast of the truly heroic. No knight ever battled for his king with a more loyal heart or with less fear than Morley fought for the A. T. & S. F. Ry. D. & R. G. Ry. Co. vs. Canyon City & San Juan R. R. Co., *99 United States*, 463. He was accidentally shot and killed in the Republic of Mexico. His remains are buried in the cemetery at Las Vegas, New Mexico. A magnificent shaft, erected by his friends, marks his last resting place.

[397] The constructed and operated mileage of these companies on January 1, 1885, was as follows: N. M. & S. P. Rd., Raton Pass (Colorado state line) to San Marcial, 353; R. G. M. & P. Rd., San Marcial to Deming and El Paso, 205; Santa Fé branch, 18; New Mexican Rd., branch lines to Las Vegas Hot Springs, to Blosburg, Carthage, Lake Valley, and Magdalena, and the S. C. D. & P. Rd., Deming to Silver City, 104; the Atlantic and Pacific, Alburquerque to Arizona line and siding spur at Gallup to coal mines, 179; the Southern Pacific, El Paso to the Arizona line, 182; Lordsburg and Clifton branch, 50; the Denver and Rio Grande Rd., Antonito to Española, 79; and Antonito to Amargo, 85 miles.

[398] Other railroad lines which have been constructed in New Mexico since the pioneer period of railroad building are the Colorado and Southern, which crosses the northeastern corner of New Mexico, its mileage being entirely in Union county; the Chicago, Rock Island and Pacific Railroad, built in 1898; the El Paso and Southwestern, completed in 1903; the Lordsburg and Hachita, built by the Arizona Copper Company; the Arizona and New Mexico, from Lordsburg to Clifton; the Santa Fé Central Railway, completed August 13, 1903; the St. Louis, Rocky Mountain and Pacific, from Raton to Cimarron, and from Raton to Des Moines, in Union county; the Pecos Valley and Northeastern, now owned by the Atchison, Topeka & Santa Fé Railway Company, entering the territory from the south on the Texas line thence to Roswell, Clovis, and Texico;

of the two divisions of the Southern Pacific Railroad. Deming was also the point of junction of this road with the Santa Fé from the north, and the completion of these two roads placed New Mexico in communication by the shortest routes with the Pacific Coast, the Gulf and the northern cities of the United States.

Almost simultaneously with the Atchison, Topeka and Santa Fé the Denver and Rio Grande Railway was built into New Mexico from the north, near Antonito.

Formerly engaged in overland freighting across the plains to the mountains and the southwest were a number of enterprising men, who, keeping pace with the advance of railway construction, finally located their permanent places of business in New Mexico, contributing in great measure to the industrial and commercial progress and importance of the territory.[399]

---

the Eastern Railway Company of New Mexico, which line extends from Rio Puerco, on the main line of the Santa Fé, west of Isleta, to Texico, on the eastern line of New Mexico, known as the "Belen Cut-off," now owned by and a part of the Santa Fé system.

[399] The companies most prominently engaged in this business were Chick, Browne and Company, later Browne and Manzanares; and Otero, Sellar and Company, later Gross, Blackwell and Company, today Gross, Kelly and Company.

Lawrence P. Browne was born in Lancaster county, Pa., December 7, 1830. When quite young his parents removed to Peru, Ill., where he received a common school education. Afterward he attended Jones's commercial college at St. Louis, Mo., in which city he began his business career. In 1852 he went to Kansas City, entering the employ of Joel Walker, at the time engaged in merchandizing and trade with the Indians. In 1857, on the death of Walker, he associated himself with W. H. Chick, with headquarters at Kansas City and with a branch at Leavenworth, Kas. Their place of business in Kansas City was located on the "Levee" at the foot of Delaware street. In 1866 the place was destroyed by fire and the firm moved to Junction City, Kansas, thence following the line of construction of the Union Pacific, with stores at Ellsworth, Sheridan, and Kit Carson, from which latter place the entire business was removed by wagons to Granada, Colorado, on the line of the Atchison, Topeka and Santa Fé Railroad; thence following the construction of the railroad they moved west and south until the business was finally established at Las Vegas, N. M. In a business way L. P. Browne was known to the people of half the continent. He was a man of honest impulse and honorable action. He died in Kansas City, Mo., December 5, 1893. In his business career he established thirty-five houses and gained a most distinguished position in the commercial world. His high sense of honor felt the slightest discredit as poignantly as a wound, and at the close of a long and useful life there were none to cast reflection upon a single action of his career.

Francisco A. Manzanares was born at Abiquiú, Rio Arriba county, N. M., Jan. 25, 1843. His ancestors were from Spain and were among the early settlers in New Mexico. His grandfather, Anselmo Manzanares, was a very prominent man. His son, José Antonio Manzanares, father of Francisco, was born at Nacimiento, Rio Arriba county, where he married Maria Manuela Valdez, also a descendant of the early Spanish settlers. José A. Manzanares was a Union

Last Supreme Court of the Territory of New Mexico
Standing, Left to Right—Associate Justices Clarence J. Roberts, Ira A. Abbott, Ed. R. Wright, Merritt C. Mechem. Sitting, Left to Right—Associate Justice John R. McFie, Chief Justice William H. Pope, Associate Justice Francis W. Parker

The concluding year of Governor Wallace's administration had witnessed these great advances in the industrial prosperity of the territory. He retired from office at the expiration of his term and was succeeded by Lionel A. Sheldon. Many occurrences of importance are recorded during this eventful year, the legislative assembly being particularly active in the consideration and passage of laws beneficial to the people of the territory.[400]

---

man during the Civil War, and was of great prominence and influence. He served in both branches of the legislative assembly and held the office of Indian Agent for the Utes and Apaches. He was a man of marked intellectual power and business capacity. Francisco A. Manzanares received his education under Fr. Antonio José Martinez, later attending school in St. Louis and New York. His business career was begun in Kansas City, where he entered the employ of the firm of Chick, Browne and Company, afterward becoming a partner in the firm. In 1871, he married Antonia Baca, a member of the noted family of that name.

Politically Mr. Manzanares was always a stanch democrat. He was elected delegate from New Mexico to the 48th congress, his opponent being Tranquilino Luna, of Valencia county. Luna was given the certificate of election but the seat was contested by Manzanares in which he was successful. He declined to accept the nomination of his party for a second term, owing to the demands of his business associates. He was a distinctive political figure in the history of the territory, being the acknowledged leader of his party. He died at Las Vegas, September 16, 1904.

Miguel A. Otero was the senior member of the firm of Otero, Sellar and Company. He was a man of distinguished attainments, strong individuality, and a fine appreciation of the higher ethics of life. His was a conspicuous part in the development of the territory. He was the organizer of the firm of Otero, Sellar and Co., of which partnership the firm of Gross, Blackwell and Co. was the direct successor. He died May 30, 1882. The firm of Otero, Sellar and Company was organized in 1867. During the construction of the A., T. & S. F. Railroad the main house was located at Las Vegas, N. M. Jacob Gross and Harry W. Kelly at that time became connected with the firm. A. M. Blackwell was connected with the old firm of Chick, Browne and Company. In 1881 these three organized the firm of Gross, Blackwell and Company and purchased the business of Otero, Sellar and Company.

Jacob Gross was born in Baltimore, Md., but his entire business life was spent in the west. He is now a resident of St. Louis, Mo. A. M. Blackwell was a native of Carrollton, Mo. He retired from the firm in 1901, when the firm of Gross, Kelly and Company was organized. He died suddenly at St. Louis, Mo., February 14, 1912. H. W. Kelly was born in Leavenworth, Kas., in 1858 and began his business career at the age of fifteen. In 1879 he came to Las Vegas and has ever since been identified with its growth and development. In the business life of New Mexico he stands among the foremost. He was a member of the constitutional convention of 1910.

[400] *Session Laws of New Mexico*, 1880: Feb. 10, 1880; county of San Juan attached to Rio Arriba county, and Tierra Amarilla made county seat. Feb. 11; general incorporation law authorizing local corporations to hold property for churches, parishes, and educational, literary, scientific, and benevolent associations. General Incorporation Act for cities enacted. Feb. 12; act admitting foreign corporations upon equal terms with those organized under the laws of New Mexico. Feb. 15; act to establish the bureau of immigration. The bureau was organized, April 15, with principal office at Santa Fé.

On June 4, 1881, a personal friend of President Garfield, Lionel A. Sheldon,[401] of Ohio, was inaugurated governor at Santa Fé. New

On February 15, celebration of advent of the line of railroad into Santa Fé by an excursion to the Missouri river, in Pullman coaches, given by the railroad company to the territorial officials, members of the legislature, and business men of New Mexico.

On April 9, the Santa Fé Gas Company was organized and gas delivered through mains for the first time in the history of New Mexico on December 5 following.

On May 14, the first street railway company in New Mexico was organized, the line being built at Alburquerque, connecting the new and the old towns.

On July 7-15, General Ulysses S. Grant, Mrs. Grant, and Mrs. Fred. Grant visited New Mexico and were publicly received at Santa Fé and Las Vegas.

On October 15, Chief Victorio, driven from New Mexico into Old Mexico, was overtaken at Los Castillos, in the state of Chihuahua, and given battle by Mexican troops; in the conflict 75 Indians were killed, and 68 women and children taken prisoners.

On October 28, Rutherford B. Hayes, President of the United States, Mrs. Hayes, Secretary of War Ramsey, General William Tecumseh Sherman, and others of the presidential party, returning from the Pacific Coast through New Mexico, visited Santa Fé and were received with great public and military demonstrations.

On December 10, the Texas, Santa Fé and Northern Railroad Company, a line afterward built from Española to Santa Fé, was incorporated.

In 1880, according to the census returns, the number of schools (public) in New Mexico was 162, but there were only 46 school buildings, and the average attendance was 3,150. Sixty per cent of the inhabitants of the territory over ten years of age were unable to read.

In this year a reasonably fair educational bill, providing for the support of public schools by tax, was defeated; a similar effort in 1876 and 1878 had also failed. It was not until the following session of 1882 that the legislative assembly authorized the organization of school districts and the support of schools by public revenues.

[401] Lionel A. Sheldon is of Norman descent, his ancestors having settled in Yorkshire, England, about the time of the Conquest, one of whom was afterward appointed lord mayor of London, another bishop of Canterbury, and a third a lieutenant general. In 1646, three brothers of this family came to America, and from one of them Governor Sheldon is descended. He was born in Worcester, New York, August 30, 1831. He read law and was admitted to the bar, taking active part in political and military affairs of the time. In 1858 he was appointed brigadier general of militia, and at the outbreak of the Civil War joined the Union army, commanding a troop of volunteer cavalry. He was soon promoted to a colonelcy and brevetted brigadier general, taking part in a number of engagements. In 1868, 1870, and 1872 he was elected to congress from a New Orleans district; he later became attorney for the government in the Alabama claims. In 1880 he was a member of the Chicago convention which nominated James A. Garfield for the presidency and several days after his inauguration was his guest at the White House. Sheldon had been in Garfield's regiment during the war, was his warm personal friend, and, relying upon his influence with the administration, when he assumed the executive chair in New Mexico, he antagonized several leaders of his party in New Mexico, thereby injuring his influence with the legislatures and ultimately causing dissensions which disrupted the party and made possible the election of a democrat as delegate to congress for ten years. Governor Sheldon devoted much attention to the militia of New Mexico. Colonel Max Frost was his adjutant general,

ADMINISTRATION OF
GOVERNOR L. A. SHELDON

Mexico was then enjoying a great period of prosperity. The live stock, mining, and other industries were making tremendous strides. Investments and speculation in land grant holdings, town and city lots in all the cities [402] and towns along the new railway lines, and in other collateral enterprises, marked the prosperity of the period. All-rail connection across the continent had just been established and an immense immigration to the new southwest was anticipated by all. In July of this year the Atlantic and Pacific Railroad from Alburquerque west to the Arizona line had been completed.[403]

The legislative assembly of 1882 passed a school law, which was an improvement on any the territory had ever had, although by no means in keeping with the American idea of public educational enactments.[404]

1881-1883, and Col. E. L. Bartlett in 1883-1884. In 1884 he called out the national guard to aid in putting down an Apache outbreak of that year under Geronimo. It was largely through his efforts that New Mexico changed its policy of sending its convicted criminals to the penitentiary at Ft. Leavenworth and constructed its own penal institution at Santa Fé. After his retirement as governor in 1885, he was appointed one of the receivers of the Texas Pacific Railway Company by Judge Pardee. He is now living in California.

[402] In 1880 there were no towns of any importance in the territory except Santa Fé.

[403] Lewis Kingman was the chief engineer of the Atlantic and Pacific Railroad.

[404] *Report* of Governor Sheldon, 1884: "The advantages of the new school law are that it creates a tangible system, and it is simpler and more efficient. It imposes greater restraints upon improper expenditure of the school funds, and severer penalties for abuses and neglect of duty on the part of school officers, and it should be added that duties are more specifically and clearly defined. There is also an increase of tax to the extent of one-half mill on the dollar for school purposes. I estimate that the school fund of the Territory, on the basis of the present assessments, will be nearly $100,000, including the sum derived from the poll tax. . . Surely no field in the United States offers a richer opportunity for improvement in educational affairs than New Mexico."

This law provided for a tax of three mills on the dollar for school purposes.

Other acts passed by the assembly of 1882 were: Act regulating the territorial library; protecting coal mines and miners; regulating railroad fares and rates; defining a system of revenue; taxing cattle owned in other states and territories; authorizing the ransom of Apache captives; appropriating $3,000 in aid of the Sisters of Charity of Santa Fé; changing the county seat of Colfax county, the boundary between Colfax and Mora, between Mora and San Miguel, Santa Fé and San Miguel, and San Miguel and Valencia, and fixing the county seat of Doña Ana county at Las Cruces.

Memorials of this assembly were: for the settlement of private land claims; for the cession of the old palace to the Historical Society; opening a part of the Mescalero Apache reservation for settlement, and for a repeal of the United States law of 1878 forbidding the use of troops as a posse comitatus.

The territorial librarian's *Report* of 1883 contains a catalogue of 1,810

Until the month of August, 1882, succeeding Charles J. McCandless in 1879, L. Bradford Prince occupied the position of chief justice of New Mexico. His term of office covered all the transition period between the old condition of affairs and the new era of progress and development. The criminal business incident to the advent of the railroads was phenomenal, and the sudden increase in values and changes in business methods resulted in a flood of civil suits. The volume of court business increased steadily, and although the first judicial district, presided over by Judge Prince, covered over one-half of the entire territory, with characteristic energy the accumulated business of years was cleared away. During his incumbency 1,184 civil and 1,483 criminal cases, by prompt and vigorous trials, were disposed of. During this period he also found time to make a compilation of the general laws of New Mexico.

The greater part of the summer of 1883 was given over to the Tertio-Millennial Celebration, the most interesting and comprehensive historical commemoration ever undertaken in the country, the program of pageants extending over a period of thirty-three days. During the summer, the city of Santa Fé was filled with visitors from all parts of the east; many excursions of chartered Pullman cars brought the people from points in New England. Every tribe of Indians in New Mexico, with large delegations, took part in the various ceremonies. Many very distinguished visitors attended. The expenditures were far in excess of the receipts, but in every other respect the entertainment was a pronounced success.

TERTIO-MILLENNIAL CELEBRATION AT SANTA FÉ

In 1881 Tranquilino Luna,[405] of Valencia county, was elected dele-

---

volumes. He makes mention of having in his possession 144 pasteboard boxes containing the classified archives. The alleged sale of some of these archives for wrapping paper, in the time of Governor Pile, has been elsewhere mentioned. Governor Marsh Giddings boxed up about five cords of such remnants as could be rescued, to protect them from the weather and further loss. — New Mexico *Official Reports*, 1882-3, pp. 31-35. Samuel Ellison was the territorial librarian in 1882-3.

[405] Tranquilino Luna was a native of Los Lunas, New Mexico, having been born June 29, 1847. He was the son of Antonio José Luna, descended from Don Domingo de Luna, who came to New Mexico shortly after the Spanish reconquest and settled at Los Lunas upon a large tract of land known as the San Clemente grant. His son, Don Enrique de Luna, a prominent man of his day, was the father of twelve children. Don Enrique lived to the age of ninety-one years. His son, Don Antonio José Luna, father of Tranquilino Luna, was born

gate to the 47th congress, but was defeated for re-election by Francisco A. Manzanares, of San Miguel county, after a contest initiated by the latter, resulting in his favor, although Luna had been given the certificate on the face of the returns.

DELEGATES IN CONGRESS

The twenty-sixth legislative assembly convened at Santa Fé in February, 1884. Trouble ensued over the organization of the council. The members of the upper house from the counties of Bernalillo and Santa Fé were refused their seats on allegations of fraudulent election, and the contestants without certificates were sworn in by the secretary of the territory, on a vote of the other members that they were entitled, prima facie, to their seats. A rival council, under the leadership of J. Francisco Chavez, of Valencia county, was organized, but nothing, other than dissensions extending over a period of years, was the result of this attempt, in reality, to defeat the purposes of the leading politicians at Santa Fé to retain control of the affairs of the territory. Realizing that the construction of the railways, the building of new towns and cities, the growth incident to the new status of the territory, would sooner or later jeopardize the continued location of the capital at Santa Fé, Thomas B. Catron,[406] member of the

ERECTION OF THE CAPITOL AT SANTA FÉ

at Los Lunas in 1808. He was a man of affairs, wealthy, and the owner of immense flocks of sheep, for which, prior to the American occupation and afterward, he found a market by driving large numbers to California. He stood high in the estimation of his fellow men, was a man of marked intellectual power, sound judgment, and inflexible integrity of character. He married Isabella Baca, daughter of Don Juan Cruz Baca, of Belen, N. M. Of this marriage there were nine children, the eldest, Don Jesus M., attaining the age of fifty-two years. Don Tranquilino Luna was a man of signal ability, and held many offices of public trust and confidence. He died in November, 1892, leaving one son, Maximiliano Luna, in the Spanish-American war an officer in Roosevelt's Rough Rider Regiment, who lost his life while serving in the army of the United States in the Philippine Islands.

[406] In Bernalillo county, under the leadership of Charles Montaldo, of Alburquerque, a fraudulent registration was consummated and hundreds of illegal votes were cast or counted in the new town where he lived.

The legislature was organized in the interests of the city of Santa Fé and its political leaders of the republican party faith. The "rump" council, under the leadership of Colonel Chavez, had among its members some who were regularly elected. The passage of the bill providing for the erection of the capitol brought out many charges of corruption of members. These charges, in part, were true. Don Diego Archuleta, a member from Rio Arriba county, was taken to the house of representatives while suffering from a severe attack of pneumonia. His vote was necessary in order to pass the bill. The exposure

council from Santa Fé, assisted by the business men of the city and the church authorities, determined to enact a law whereby a capitol building commensurate with the dignity and demands of the growing territory should be erected at Santa Fé. Strong opposition to this movement came from various portions of the territory, notably from Alburquerque. Charges of corruption were freely made, but the bill was passed and the capitol and the penitentiary buildings were constructed.[407] This assembly also provided for the compilation of the laws of New Mexico, general and local, and a commission was appointed for that purpose.[408]

The troubles with the Apaches in the southern part of the territory were so severe that Governor Sheldon decided to call out the companies of the National Guard, located at several of the smaller towns in the south. Notable in the command of these troops, whose principal duty was the guarding of watering places frequented by the hostiles during their raids, was Colonel Albert J. Fountain, of

incident to this performance brought about his death a few days later. This building was constructed, as was also the penitentiary, and from that time until the incumbency of Governor Otero, the location of the capital was a source of constant agitation in the several assemblies meeting during the period named. On May 12, 1892, the capitol, with many valuable records and public documents, was destroyed by fire, supposed to have been of incendiary origin. José Armijo y Vigil, of Socorro county, was the president of the legislative council; Benjamin M. Read, of Santa Fé, clerk; Amado Chaves, of Valencia, was speaker of the house; David Martinez, Rio Arriba, clerk.

[407] Other enactments by the 26th legislative assembly were: An act relative to habeas corpus, mandamus and prohibition; 14 separate acts in relation to practice in the courts; relating to the office of attorney general and creating the office of assistant; relating to the supplying of water to cities and towns; establishing public schools; several acts in relation to crimes and offenses; several acts in relation to mines and mining. In all there were 114 general, special, and local acts. Among others was an act providing for the preservation and exhibition of historical antiquities and making an appropriation to that end. This appropriation enactment specially provides that all "articles purchased with funds of the Territory shall be registered as being purchased with the money of the Territory, and shall never be disposed of by said society (the Historical Society of New Mexico) in any way, and in case said society shall at any time be dissolved or become extinct such articles shall become the property of the Territory or State of New Mexico." The act providing for the building of the penitentiary authorized an issue of bonds in the sum of one hundred and fifty thousand dollars for the purpose. The bond issue authorized for the erection of the capitol amounted to two hundred thousand dollars. The members of the original capitol building commission were: Governor Sheldon, Mariano S. Otero, Narciso Valdes, W. L. Rynerson, José Montaño, Antonio Abeytia y Armijo, Roman A. Baca, Vicente Mares, John C. Joseph, Cristobal Mares, Lorenzo Lopez, Rafael Romero, and A. S. Potter.

[408] The members of the commission appointed by the governor, under this act were: Edward L. Bartlett, Charles W. Greene, and Santiago Valdez. Irineo L. Chaves was the secretary of the commission.

La Mesilla. The troops under Colonel Fountain rendered signal service in these campaigns, and also gave aid to the local peace officers in ridding the grazing localities in Grant, Sierra, and Socorro counties of bands of cattle thieves, or "rustlers," who infested the southern part of New Mexico at this time. Lawlessness was rife in southwestern New Mexico and the governor was compelled to evoke the aid of the militia to protect the lives and property of settlers. Colonel Fountain [409] was given authority to break up these bands of

---

[409] Albert J. Fountain was born on Staten Island, New York, October 23, 1838. He was of French Huguenot descent. His was a wonderful career. After receiving his education in the public schools and at Columbia college he made a tour of the world; the relation of his experiences would fill volumes. Returning to America from Canton, where he had been a prisoner, he went to Sacramento, and soon left for Nicaragua as correspondent for a California newspaper. While acting as representative of the paper he was arrested by Walker, of the Walker Filibustering Expedition, and was sentenced to be shot for having communicated to his paper the true object of the expedition, which had been organized in the slave-holding interests. In disguise as a woman he made his escape and finally reached San Francisco. Here he began the study of the law and had just been admitted to the bar when the Civil War broke out; in August, 1861, he enlisted in the 1st California Vol. Infantry, and was commissioned a lieutenant. He marched across the desert under General Carleton, his company being in the advance. At Apache Pass the command was attacked by Cochise and his band of Apaches, numbering about 1,200. Fountain had 110 men; a battle lasting two days resulted in the defeat of the Indians. In 1863, General Carleton sent Fountain to Ft. McRae to open the road, which was then beset with hostiles. The work was accomplished and Fountain was mustered out of the service in August, 1864. Early in 1865, having been commissioned a captain of volunteer cavalry by General Carleton, he had a desperate encounter, with his troops, with the Apaches, in which he was wounded and left on the field. He was brought off during the night and sent to El Paso. Later he was appointed custom-house officer at El Paso, but left the service to join the forces under General Juarez in Mexico. He was commissioned a colonel in his army. After the taking of Chihuahua he returned to El Paso. He received an appointment from General Sheridan as a judge of election under the reconstruction act and was subsequently made assessor and collector of internal revenue for the western district of Texas. In 1868, he was elected to the senate of that state, representing thirty-two counties in the western part of the state. Upon the election of Flannigan to the senate of the United States, Colonel Fountain became president of the senate. He was appointed brigadier general of the state guards by Governor Davis. In 1875, he returned to New Mexico. He participated in the first campaign against the Apache chief, Victorio; he organized the 1st Battalion of N. M. Cavalry, was commissioned major, and was in the field during the entire campaign in command of these troops. In 1885, as colonel of the 1st N. M. Cavalry, he took part in the campaign against the Apache chief, Geronimo. He was appointed special counsel for the government by President Cleveland, aiding the U. S. attorney, Thomas Smith, in the prosecution of persons charged with land frauds, holding the position four years. In 1888, he was a member and speaker of the New Mexican house of representatives. In 1889, he was named as assistant U. S. attorney by President Benjamin Harrison. Later on he was the special counsel, aiding in the prosecution of cattle thieves, of the New Mexico Stock Asso-

"rustlers," and through his efforts a number were killed in open conflict and many others arrested and sent to the penitentiary at Ft. Leavenworth, Kansas, where the prisoners from New Mexico were incarcerated.

It was known among some of the leading politicians of New Mexico, personal friends of Stephen B. Elkins and other intimate political associates of James G. Blaine, early in the spring of 1884, that Blaine and Logan would most likely be the republican candidates for the presidency and vice-presidency that year. With Mr. Blaine as president and General Logan president of the senate, the principal republican politicians of the territory had convinced themselves that the admission of New Mexico into the Union would not be long deferred. The defeat of the republican ticket in the election came as a great shock to those who believed that New Mexico would soon be able to take her proper place in the sisterhood of states. The full force of the disappointment was not materially lessened by the appointments made by President Cleveland for New Mexico. Edmund G. Ross,[410] a resi-

ADMINISTRATION OF GOVERNOR EDMUND G. ROSS

---

ciation, and had much to do with driving "rustlers" out of the territory or sending them to the penitentiary. Colonel Fountain was a prominent figure in the military, political, and professional life of New Mexico. On October 27, 1862, he was married at La Mesilla, N. M., to Mariana Perez de Ovante, a member of a prominent Mexican family. Of this marriage there were twelve children. Colonel Fountain and his youngest son, Henry, were foully assassinated by cattle rustlers, on his way from Tularosa to Las Cruces, N. M., on April 1, 1896. His murderers are unknown, and no one has ever been punished for the infamous crime.

[410] Edmund G. Ross was born in Ashland, Huron county, Ohio, December 7, 1826. He was a printer by trade. In 1847, following his trade he traveled through several of the western states, and, in 1848, returned to Ohio, where he was married to Fannie M. Lathrop. Seven children were born of this marriage. In 1856, in Wisconsin, he organized a party of "Free-Staters" to travel overland to Kansas, reaching Topeka early in August of that year. Here, with a brother who had preceded him, he organized and published a paper known as the *Tribune*. He took part in the "Border Wars" of the period. In 1859, he was elected and served as a member in the Wyandotte Constitutional Convention which framed the constitution under which Kansas was admitted to the Union. When the Civil War broke out, he raised a company of volunteers and was chosen captain. This company was "E" 11th Kansas Infantry. In 1864, he was promoted to the rank of major. In the several engagements with the Confederate army under General Sterling Price he served with his regiment, notably at the battles resulting in Price's retreat from Missouri. In one engagement three horses were shot from under him and his shoulder straps were shot away. In July, 1865, following the suicide of Senator James H. Lane, Governor Crawford appointed him to fill the senatorial vacancy, and upon the convening of the legislature, in January, 1867, he was elected to the office for the term

Col. Theodore Roosevelt, 1st Vol. Cav., U. S. A.

Theodore Roosevelt

dent of Alburquerque, N. M., who had been a prominent figure in
the early history of the state of Kansas and a United States senator
from that state, was commissioned as governor, George W. Julian,
surveyor general, George W. Lane, secretary, Romulo Martinez,
marshal, and William A. Vincent,[411], W. H. Brinker,[412] W. F. Henderson,[413] justices of the supreme court. Very shortly after his
appointment as chief justice, Vincent was removed from office by the
president, charged with too much intimacy with Stephen W. Dorsey,
a prominent citizen of the territory, whom the government had
selected for prosecution charged with land frauds, and which prosecution would have been heard before Judge Vincent. The vacancy
caused by the removal of Vincent was filled by the appointment of
E. V. Long,[414] of Indiana. This court was in all probability the

expiring in March, 1871. On account of the vote cast by him in the senate in
the Andrew Johnson impeachment case, he was politically and socially ostracized in the state of Kansas. His vote saved President Johnson from impeachment. Senator Ross was always satisfied that he had voted in a proper
manner and afterward said, that "Mr. Lincoln, had he lived, would have pursued much the same policy of reconstruction as indicated by the established
fact that he had determined to adopt precisely the initial measures thereto
which Mr. Johnson did inaugurate and carry out." History shows that Governor Ross was justified in the vote he cast.

After the expiration of his term of office as governor of New Mexico he
went to work at his trade, being employed in the office of the *New Mexican* at
Santa Fé. From Santa Fé he went to Deming, where he edited the *Headlight*
until 1893. When Mr. Cleveland was elected to the presidency the second
time Governor Ross was urged for re-appointment, but it was believed that the
office required a younger man and another was appointed. Governor Ross died
at Alburquerque, May 9, 1907.

[411] W. A. Vincent is a native of the state of Illinois. He left New Mexico
and has since practiced his profession in Chicago. The charges made against
him were without foundation; the president acknowledged that he had acted
too hastily and tendered him the appointment of chief justice of one of the
northern territories, but it was declined. He was the first president of the New
Mexico Bar Association. He is now a resident of Chicago, Illinois.

[412] W. H. Brinker was a native of the state of Missouri. He was prominent
in his profession in that state before his appointment to the bench in New
Mexico. In 1889, he removed to the territory of Washington and was named
United States attorney for Washington by President Cleveland during the
second administration of the latter.

[413] W. F. Henderson was a native of the state of Arkansas. He had been in
the Confederate army. He held many offices in his native state, the principal
being attorney general. He returned to Arkansas in 1889, where he died some
years later.

[414] Elisha Van Buren Long was born in Wayne county, Indiana, March 7,
1836. He received his education in the public schools of his native county and
at Fort Wayne college. He studied law and was admitted to the bar. In 1872,
he was appointed circuit judge of the fourth judicial district of Indiana; later
he was elected to the position and held the office for thirteen years. He was a
delegate to the national democratic conventions of 1860, 1876, and 1884. In

strongest, intellectually, ever sitting on the bench in New Mexico. Later, when the fourth judicial district was created, Reuben A. Reeves was named associate justice and assigned to the first district with headquarters at Santa Fé. The chief justice removed to Las Vegas, where he presided over the fourth district court.

With the advent of the officials named by President Cleveland for the offices of United States attorney, surveyor general, and registers of the two land offices, an assault upon the titles to LAND FRAUDS lands in New Mexico was inaugurated which for virulence of action and incapacity of management has never found a parallel in the history of the United States. Prominent men from every section of the country were indicted, but in every instance these prosecutions failed, either for lack of proof or the unwillingness of juries to convict. Charges of bribery of minor officials of the government charged with the investigations in connection with the prosecutions which were initiated were frequent. The principal men whom the government sought to convict in the northern portion of the territory were Colonel Max Frost,[415] register of the land office at Santa Fé, and Don Pedro San-

---

1892, after coming to New Mexico, he was a delegate to the national convention of that year. He held the office of chief justice of New Mexico for six years. When the board of trustees of the town of Las Vegas grant was organized he was named by the court one of the trustees under the law providing therefor. In 1873, he was married to Alice R. Walton. Judge Long has always been a consistent member of his party, standing high in its councils.

[415] Maximilian Frost was born January 1, 1852, at New Orleans, La. His father lost his life in battle during the Civil War; his mother died at the age of 48, leaving him an orphan in early boyhood. There were three brothers and three sisters.

The year 1876 found Colonel Frost in Santa Fé as chief clerk in the signal service, U. S. A., having in charge the construction of the military telegraph line in New Mexico. Shortly after his arrival he became a correspondent of the Santa Fé *New Mexican*, and in seven years became its editor and later the owner of the newspaper. He was attached to the office of the surveyor general of New Mexico, holding an important clerical position; later he became deputy U. S. surveyor. William G. Ritch, acting governor, appointed him to the office of adjutant general. He was re-appointed by Governor Lew Wallace, and personally conducted an expedition into the San Juan country for the suppression of outlaws and renegade Navajos and Utes who were stealing cattle and committing other depredations in that portion of New Mexico. He was again appointed adjutant general by Governor L. A. Sheldon. In 1881, he was appointed register of the U. S. land office at Santa Fé by President Garfield. He was re-appointed by President Chester A. Arthur. During the first Cleveland administration every effort possible on the part of the government was evoked for the purpose of convicting him of complicity in land frauds in the territory. The government failed. Frost was tried and convicted before E. V. Long, chief justice, but, on motion for a new trial heard by Long and his successor in the

chez,[416] a prominent and wealthy citizen of Taos county. In its efforts to connect these men with thefts of the public domain the government signally failed. Growing out of the charges of land frauds and these prosecutions, however, came a determined effort on the part of the people of New Mexico to secure affirmative action on the part of the congress of the United States looking to an adjudication of these titles, which finally resulted, during the administration of President Harrison, in the passage of an act creating the Court of Private Land Claims, the labors of which tribunal are discussed in another chapter.

The election of 1884 resulted in the choice of the democratic nominee for delegate. Dissensions in the republican party, confined largely to the leaders, accomplished the defeat of the regular republican nominee, L. Bradford Prince.[417] William L. Rynerson

---

first district, Reuben A. Reeves, a jurist of great probity and strength of character, Frost was given a new trial and acquitted.

Colonel Frost held a commission as colonel in the national guard from 1883 to 1886. For twelve years he was secretary of the Bureau of Immigration; was the author of many books and pamphlets relative to the resources of New Mexico. He was a member of the republican central committee for twenty-five years; was its secretary for twelve years, and very prominent in the politics of the territory.

He became the owner of the *New Mexican* in 1883. He was a Mason of great prominence, having been grand master in 1885. He was twice married; his first wife, Lydia Hood, died in 1887, leaving one son, Graehme. His second wife was Maud Pain, who is still living at Santa Fé.

As managing editor of the *New Mexican* Colonel Frost achieved his greatest success. Through the columns of that newspaper he was able to mold public opinion in a manner unsurpassed by any journalist in the west. In the ranks of the party press of republican faith there has appeared no successor to Colonel Frost. He exercised great power and influence in the councils of his party, and through the columns of his newspaper did more than any other in the upbuilding of the territory. He died at Santa Fé in October, 1909.

[416] Pedro Sanchez was born in Valencia county, N. M., February 22, 1831. He was the son of Don Cristobal Sanchez, who, with his family, moved to Taos county, locating at Cordoba, near the present village of Taos, in 1837. At the age of sixteen, Pedro was thrown entirely upon his own resources. He became a farmer in 1862, locating upon the place in Taos county which thereafter was his home. At the breaking out of the Civil War he enlisted in the third regiment of mounted volunteers and served under General E. R. S. Canby for eight months. He held the rank of major. With his regiment he took part in the battle of Valverde. The ability and worth of Mr. Sanchez frequently called him to public office. He served in many sessions of the legislative assembly, and was once president of the council. He was United States Indian agent for the Pueblos in 1880-84. He was supervisor of the census of 1890. Politically Mr. Sanchez was a republican, very strong as a public speaker and wielding great influence among his people. He was an author of considerable ability, and wrote the *Life of Fr. Antonio José Martinez*. He died at his home in Taos county in 1904.

was the candidate of a faction of the party which bolted the regular convention at Santa Fé. Antonio Joseph, of Taos county, was elected, and was, thereafter, reëlected for four consecutive terms. During his ten years in congress Mr. Joseph labored unceasingly for the passage of a bill admitting the territory to the Union. His efforts, owing to the antagonism of eastern members of congress of both political parties to the admission of any additional western states, invariably resulted in failure. He rendered valuable service in securing the passage of the bill creating the court of private land claims, and was successful in securing the many annual appropriations for his constituency.

DELEGATE IN CONGRESS ANTONIO JOSEPH

From the very beginning of his administration Governor Ross had a tempestuous time. Arriving at Santa Fé early one morning, with the rising sun, he took the oath of office and was hailed as Montezuma. Governor Sheldon was unceremoniously aroused from his quarters in the palace of the governors, and the new executive assumed charge. He was never popular with the republicans. The twenty-seventh legislative assembly,[418] which convened in December, 1886, was overwhelmingly republican, and led by Colonel J. Francisco Chaves in the council and by minor leaders in the house, the path of the executive was thorny. Policies advocated by the governor were ignored, and it was with the greatest difficulty that he was able to secure any legislation which would redound to the credit either of himself or his party. A number of acts were passed, but nearly all had been introduced by prominent members of the republican opposition.

LEGISLATIVE ASSEMBLIES

The twenty-eighth legislative assembly, in its policy of antagonism to the administration, was more strenuous than its immediate predecessor. In order to override the executive veto, the republican ma-

---

[417] Joseph received 12,271, Prince 9,930, and Rynerson 5,192 votes.

[418] The stockmen of New Mexico were particularly active at this session and procured the passage of a number of laws affecting the live stock industry. The first law providing for the incorporation of irrigation companies was passed at this session. Other acts were: Providing for the incorporation of building and loan associations; creating the county of San Juan; for the protection of wives and families; defining the crime of murder; establishing a school for the deaf and dumb; relating to the Historical Society of New Mexico; providing for service of process upon railroad companies, and for the organization of savings banks.

jority saw fit to unseat a sufficient number of democratic members to enable the republicans at any time to command a two-thirds vote of either house of the assembly. The leader in the upper house, a parliamentarian with few equals and no superiors, Col. Chaves, and the leader of the house of representatives, Col. Albert J. Fountain, controlled matters, guided by the republican caucus, in a manner never before paralleled in a New Mexican legislature. One hundred and forty-five laws were passed, nearly every one of which was first passed upon and recommended by a committee of the New Mexico Bar Association, of which Edward L. Bartlett and Frank W. Clancy were members. Governor Ross used his veto power on nearly every measure, but in each instance the power of the republican leaders was brought into play and the vetoes were not sustained. Benjamin Harrison had been elected president of the United States, and the republican party was soon to dominate in the affairs of the territory. To prevent the governor from keeping his appointees in power for a period of two years after his own successor had been named by a republican president, this assembly saw fit to abolish the office of attorney general and create that of solicitor general,[419] the appointment to which should not be made by the governor until the first of October following the adjournment of the assembly, by which time it was known that a change in the executive would have been accomplished. Another act made it a felony for any one to impersonate this official. Several laws of this kind, purely political in their nature, were the outcome of partizan efforts by the republican leaders of the territory to embarrass and circumvent the governor and the leaders of his party. The most important act passed by this assembly was one entitled "An act relating to the Finances of the Territory of New Mexico," [420] under the provisions of which the finances were placed upon a cash basis. Prior to this time there had been

---

[419] *Session Laws of New Mexico*, 1889, ch. 144, p. 351.

[420] *Session Laws of 1889*, ch. 32, p. 65 *et seq*. This act was introduced by Pedro Perea, member of the council from Bernalillo county. The act created ten different funds and provided in what manner they should be used. For the purpose of defraying the expenses of the territory until the revenues provided for by the act should come into the treasury, a bond issue in the sum of two hundred thousand dollars was authorized, known as Provisional Indebtedness Bonds, and the money derived from the sale of these was distributed in the several funds in sums provided for by the act. Fiscal years were established and levies for these years were provided for. This act was drawn by Henry L. Waldo, the solicitor for New Mexico of the Atchison, Topeka and Santa Fé Railroad Company.

much scandal growing out of speculation in territorial warrants, as it was generally believed that a few individuals living at Santa Fé were in position to secure advantage in time of payment of debts of this character. This enactment forever closed the door to this sort of speculation.[421] Governor Ross's administration was also hampered by the raids of the hostile Apaches, and it was during the closing years of his incumbency that the pestilential Apache was silenced forever.

Benjamin Harrison commissioned L. Bradford Prince [422] governor

---

[421] Another enactment of vital importance in the growth and standing of the territory was the act of February 28, 1889, by which was "created and established within and for the Territory of New Mexico an institution of learning, to be known as 'The University of New Mexico.'" This institution was located near Alburquerque. The School of Mines located at Socorro, was established by the same act, as was also the New Mexico College of Agriculture and Mechanic Arts, at Mesilla Park. The New Mexico Normal University, at Las Vegas, was established by an act of 1893. The New Mexico Military Institute, at Roswell, was established by an act passed February 23, 1893. The Normal School at Silver City was established in 1893.

Several important *Memorials* to the President of the United States were passed, one of which related to the contemplated removal of the Apache chief, Geronimo, and his band, from their place of confinement in Florida, to the Mescalero reservation in southern New Mexico. The assembly was strongly opposed to this reported intention of the government, saying that "such removal would be a standing menace to the peace and well-being of the territory;" that "in the year 1885, Geronimo and his band of hostile Apaches fled from their reservation at San Carlos, in the Territory of Arizona, and made a predatory raid into southern New Mexico, which was attended with all the atrocities of savage warfare; without any provocation from the people of New Mexico, they invaded our territory, destroyed isolated settlements, slaughtered our peaceful citizens without regard to age or sex, interrupted travel, captured our mails, paralyzed business, and imposed upon the executive of this Territory the necessity of calling the territorial militia into service for the protection of the lives and property of our citizens, at an expense of fifty-four ($54,000) thousand dollars;" that "for months this hostile band of savages set at defiance the powers of the general government and of this Territory, and were not captured until many lives had been lost and vast sums of money expended in the effort."

In another *Memorial* relative to an executive order withdrawing certain territory in the county of San Juan from settlement, the legislature characterized the order as "productive of very great and grievous wrong to a large number of honest and law abiding American citizens, and in its scope and tendency is oppressive, tyrannical and subversive of the principles of republican government."

[422] L. Bradford Prince was born in Flushing, New York, July 3, 1840. He is a lineal descendant, on the maternal side, of Governor William Bradford, of Plymouth, who came to this country on the Mayflower. His great-grandfather was Governor Bradford, of Rhode Island, and his grandfather, Governor Collins, of the same state. His paternal ancestors were the founders of the well known Prince family of Long Island. He is a graduate of Columbia Law School. Very early in life Governor Prince developed an aptitude for political matters. He was a delegate to all the state conventions in New York from 1866 to 1878, was elected a delegate to the national republican convention which nominated

of New Mexico in the spring of 1889, very shortly after his inauguration as president. There was great opposition to this action of the president among the leaders of the republican party in New Mexico, but Governor Prince, backed by the great financial interests of the east, and by the president of every great railroad company in the west, as well

ADMINISTRATION OF GOVERNOR
L. BRADFORD PRINCE

General Grant, and the following year became a member of the New York state republican committee. In 1870, '71, '73, and '74 he was a member of the New York assembly, and in 1875 was elected to the state senate by an overwhelming majority. His legislative career was highly honorable and useful. He was selected as one of the judges to conduct the impeachment trial of two noted judges of his state; he was also selected for the purpose of formally impeaching Judge Barnard at the bar of the senate, charged with high crimes and misdemeanors. Governor Prince is an author of repute, having written, among other works, *Historical Sketches of New Mexico*. He was appointed chief justice of the supreme court of New Mexico by President Hayes in 1878, which office he resigned, in May, 1882, to engage in other matters. The impartiality of his administration as chief justice was approved by the business interests of the territory. Ever since his coming to New Mexico Governor Prince has at all times been foremost in the ranks of her citizens, doing his utmost, at home and abroad, for the welfare and prosperity of the people. He framed the act under which the bureau of immigration was organized. In 1881, he prepared a compilation of the laws of New Mexico. In 1883, he became president of the Historical Society of New Mexico. In procuring statehood for New Mexico, Governor Prince did as much as any other citizen. His administration of the affairs of the territory, while governor, was characterized by its progressive spirit, always having in view the industrial advancement of the territory. Socially no occupant of the old Palace, before or since, so elaborately entertained the people of all classes. For many years he has been identified as member and officer of the Trans-Mississippi and National Irrigation congresses, where he accomplished much for the best interests of the west. Governor Prince was married on the first of December, 1879, to Hattie E. Childs, who died within three months thereafter. On the 17th of November, 1881, he was united in marriage with Mary C. Beardsley, of Oswego, New York, a descendant of one of the most prominent families of the state, and a lady of charming individuality. Since his retirement from the office of governor, he has practiced his profession in the courts of New Mexico, devoting much time to horticultural pursuits, maintaining his residence in the county of Rio Arriba, near Chamita, from which county he was a member of the legislative council in the 38th legislative assembly.

Benjamin Morris Thomas was born in Warren county, Indiana, on the 25th of July, 1843. His parents were Horatio and Rebecca (Day) Thomas, both natives of Philadelphia, who removed to Indiana about 1836. His early life was spent on his father's farm, performing the usual duties of a farmer's son and acquiring such education as the district schools afforded. He entered Wabash college, graduating in 1864, with the degree of A. M. He studied dentistry and practiced that profession in Valparaiso, Indiana, until 1870, when, on account of loss of health, he came to New Mexico. In 1871, he entered the United States Indian service and held office continuously under the Indian bureau until 1883, having had charge during that time of Victorio's band of southern Apaches, all of the Pueblos of New Mexico, as well as the Cimarron and Tierra Amarilla agencies of Utes and Jicarilla Apaches. He was also

as by a great majority of the representative business men of New Mexico, was appointed and confirmed, holding the office for four years. Benjamin Morris Thomas was secretary during this administration.

The twenty-eighth legislative assembly passed an act providing for the holding of a constitutional convention. A feeling of keen disappointment, almost of indignation, was experienced in New Mexico when the territories of the northwest were made states of the Union and New Mexico and Arizona omitted from the list. The political reason, well known in Washington, for this action on the part of congress, was that New Mexico and Arizona were both represented in congress by men of democratic political faith. The injustice of the action of congress was too obvious to require characterization. The people of New Mexico, in the face of this apparent disregard of their rights as stipulated in the treaty of Guadalupe Hidalgo, proceeded in a dignified manner to perfect every preliminary that could possibly be required as a requisite to admission, and to prepare themselves for the position in the union of states corresponding with their history, their character, and their real importance, whenever the time should arrive, leaving to congress the responsibility for their deprivation of the rights of self-government. The congress, whether of republican or democratic complexion, for nearly a quarter of a century thereafter, never saw

THE CONSTITUTIONAL CONVENTION OF 1889

---

assigned to special duty in connection with all of the agencies in New Mexico. He was with Agent Miller of the Navajós, when the latter was killed by them in 1872 and himself received an arrow shot through a blanket he was wearing at the time. He was the center of many turbulent and stirring incidents while agent for the southern Apaches. He might appropriately be called "The Father of Education" for the Pueblos, for he inaugurated the present system of day-schools among them and established at Alburquerque the first boarding and industrial school; also he secured the first contingent of pupils, twenty in number, for the training school at Carlisle, Pa. In 1883 he was appointed register of the land office at Tucson, Arizona, and served four and one-half years in that capacity. It was during his incumbency of that office that the forfeited railroad lands which included a part of the celebrated Peralta-Reavis grant and the Salt River Valley were thrown open to settlement. In 1889, he was appointed by President Harrison secretary of New Mexico, the duties of which office he discharged most acceptably until his death. Dr. Thomas was a man of forceful character and high ideals; he was possessed of some administrative ability, with a conscience that never permitted him to swerve from what he deemed right. In religion he was a Presbyterian and gave valuable aid to the cause of Presbyterianism in New Mexico. His death occurred on the 2d of October, 1892.

Battle of Las Guasimas

fit to shirk this responsibility and, session after session, continued in its opposition to the demands of the people of New Mexico.

The delegates chosen under the provisions of the act providing for the convention met at Santa Fé, September 3, 1889, and continued in session until the 23d of that month. The convention was composed of men of the highest character and ability, who patiently devoted their time and talents to the great work intrusted to them, receiving no pecuniary compensation whatever. The result of their labors was worthy and reflected honor upon the territory at large, the constitution as prepared being without doubt the best at that time formulated in the United States. Copies of it were laid before congress, but no action was taken. The constitution as drafted, with some minor amendments, added at a session beginning August 18, 1890, and continuing for three days, was submitted to the people on October 7, 1890, for ratification. The leaders of the democratic party, prior to the election for delegates to this convention, had declined to take part in framing the constitution, the position taken by them having been caused by differences of opinion between the leaders of the two great parties as to the representation which should be accorded the democratic party in the convention. There was only one democrat in the convention, L. S. Trimble, of Alburquerque. Owing to this opposition and influences brought to bear upon the population of native birth, the constitution failed of adoption, the vote in favor being 7,493 and against, 16,180.

The members of the supreme court, United States attorney, and marshal, appointed by President Harrison, were James O'Brien, chief justice, John R. McFie, William D. Lee, A. A. Freeman, and Edward P. Seeds, associate justices, Trinidad Romero, marshal, and Eugene A. Fiske, United States attorney.[423]

[423] James O'Brien was born May 15, 1837, in Wicklow, Ireland, and came to America at the age of twelve, settling in Ohio, in Clark county, in the common schools of which he received his early training. He graduated from Notre Dame University in 1858. He held the chair of ancient languages at his alma mater until 1863, when he accepted a similar position at Sinsinawa Mound college in the state of Wisconsin. In 1864, he married Catheryn Lyons, of Galena, Ill. Later he studied law, was admitted to practice in March, 1868, and began the practice at Lansing, Iowa. In the summer of 1870, he removed to Caledonia, Minn., where he died November 5, 1909. He held the office of county attorney in Minnesota for several years; was state senator four years, and was appointed chief justice of the supreme court of New Mexico by Benjamin Harrison and served from 1889 to 1893. Judge O'Brien ranked with the best lawyers of his state. His command of language was marvelous. As a teacher he was

The twenty-ninth legislative assembly was notable inasmuch as it enacted the first public school law worthy of the name. At the open-

thorough and energetic; as a writer, fluent and forcible; as a speaker, pleasing beyond the majority of really good speakers; as a lawyer and judge he was able, painstaking, honorable, and upright. He was a man of very firm convictions. He left five children, two sons and three daughters, the former residents of Minnesota, and the last named being the wives of Jerry Leahy, David J. Leahy, and John Joerns, respectively, all residents of New Mexico.

John R. McFie was born in Randolph county, Ill., October 9, 1848, and is the son of John and Elizabeth (Borland) McFie, natives of Scotland. His parents emigrated to America in 1845. He received his education in the public schools of Sparta, in his native state, and read law in the office of J. Blackburn Jones, Esq. He practiced his profession in Illinois until 1884; he was elected twice a member of the legislature of that state. In 1884, he came to New Mexico with a commission from President Arthur as register of the U. S. land office at Las Cruces, which position he filled until December 17, 1885. In January, 1886, he formed a law partnership with S. B. Newcomb, which connection continued until his elevation to the bench by President Harrison, in 1889, a position he occupied for four years. In 1898, he was again appointed an associate justice of the supreme court by President McKinley and occupied the position until the organization of the state government, having been reappointed by Presidents Roosevelt and Taft. On the 9th of October, 1876, Judge McFie married Mary Steel, of Missouri, a daughter of Matthew Steel, an early pioneer of St. Louis. Five children have been born of this marriage, one of whom, Ralph E., served in Roosevelt's Rough Riders in Cuba, and since the Spanish-American War has lived in the Philippine Islands, where he has served the government in the military and civil service. A reading of the *Reports* of the supreme court of New Mexico containing opinions written by Judge McFie demonstrates his great ability as a jurist.

William D. Lee was born in Indiana, November 8, 1830. He was a member of the distinguished Lee family in Virginia. His grandmother belonged to the Baldwin family of the Old Dominion. On both sides of the family his immediate ancestors were active in public affairs and were participants in the Revolution. He was educated at De Pauw university and in the law department of the University of Indiana, graduating at the last named institution in 1852. He practiced law in Indiana until the outbreak of the Civil War when he was made captain of "E" company, 135th Indiana Vols., and served in the Army of the Cumberland; took part in the battle of Nashville and was with Sherman in his march to the sea. After the war he returned to Lafayette, Indiana, where he resumed the practice of his profession. He came to New Mexico in 1876, settling at Las Vegas. In 1889, he was appointed associate justice of the supreme court by President Harrison and presided over the second judicial district court for four years. Upon his retirement from the bench, with the incoming of the second Cleveland administration, Judge Lee began the practice of his profession in Alburquerque. In 1865, he was married to Naomi A. Reese. Of this union there are five sons and two daughters. Judge Lee was one of the organizers of the republican party. He died in Los Angeles, California, in 1909.

Trinidad Romero is the descendant of one of the oldest New Mexican families. His father was Don Miguel Romero y Baca, who was born in Santa Fé county in 1798. Don Trinidad was born in that county in 1835. In 1855, he married Valeria Lopez, of which union eight sons and daughters were born. For many years he was active in the politics of New Mexico. He held several offices of trust and confidence in San Miguel county, where he now resides. He was chosen delegate to the 45th congress of the United States, a position which he

ing of the session in December, 1890, Governor Prince, in his message, called special attention to the necessity for a modern comprehensive public school system as being the most
THE PUBLIC SCHOOL important matter for the consideration of the
LAW OF 1891 legislature. On February 12, 1891, a bill,[424] framed by L. R. E. Paullin, a member of the house of representatives, was passed which marked a new era in the

filled with honor and credit. In 1889, he was appointed U. S. marshal, succeeding Romulo Martinez, of Santa Fé county.

Eugene A. Fiske was born in the state of New Hampshire, and was the son of Allen Fiske and Mercy Rogers Parmenter. He received his education in the common schools of his native state and in Massachusetts. At the age of sixteen he enlisted for the war of the rebellion, was wounded, and mustered out of service as a lieutenant in the 8th U. S. Veteran Volunteers. After leaving the army he graduated from the law department of Columbian university at Washington, D. C., and thereafter served in various department offices in the capital. He came to Santa Fé in 1876, where he began the practice of his profession. In 1889, he was appointed United States attorney and held the office for four years. He died at Santa Fé in 1910.

Edward Paxon Seeds was born August 1, 1855, in Wilmington, Delaware. His parents removed to the state of Iowa in 1856, locating in Dubuque and later in Manchester. Judge Seeds received his education in the common schools and at the State University of Iowa, from which institution he was graduated in 1887, with the degree of LL.B. Beginning the practice of the law in Manchester, he soon became identified with the politics of his state. He held the office of state senator in 1888 and 1890, and at the request of Senator Allison and David B. Henderson, at that time speaker of the house of representatives, he was named as associate justice of the supreme court of New Mexico. Judge Seeds performed the duties incumbent upon him in a manner highly creditable. Many political questions, of great consequence and importance, came before him for determination, most of these arising out of the political and other notable disturbances occurring in the county of Santa Fé at that time. At the expiration of his term, Judge Seeds returned to Iowa, expecting to return to New Mexico, where he intended to practice his profession. The unexpected death of his father prevented this. After his return to Iowa he held a professorship in the law department of the University of Iowa, and for the past eleven years has occupied the position of deputy auditor for the war department at Washington, D. C., where he is now living.

A. A. Freeman came to New Mexico, commissioned an associate justice of the supreme court by President Harrison, from Tennessee, in which state he had been prominent as a lawyer and politician. He held the office of associate justice four years, retiring at the expiration of his term. He practiced law, after leaving the bench, in Socorro, where he presided as judge. He afterward located in Carlsbad, Eddy county, where he also practiced his profession. He left New Mexico in 1908, and is now living in the state of Washington.

[424] *Session Laws*, 1891, ch. xxv, pp. 45-60. The act provided for a territorial board of education, consisting of the governor, superintendent of public instruction, and the presidents of the University at Alburquerque, the Agricultural College at Mesilla Park, and St. Michael's College at Santa Fé. The superintendent was named by the governor. The board selected books every four years. Examination of teachers was provided for, and also the construction of schoolhouses, bonding of school districts, in fact, almost everything required for a modern public school system.

educational history of New Mexico. Amado Chaves [425] was the first superintendent of public instruction and performed the duties of the office with great credit. Under his supervision there was great improvement, schools were established, buildings erected and, in all portions of New Mexico, educational matters received an impetus which has never been retarded. Under the system as established, with the several amendments which have been made to the original act, the schools have quietly but steadily moved on toward the accomplishment of their purpose, endeavoring to be thorough in the essentials, liberal in general culture and earnest in the effort to strengthen character and train for good citizenship and practical life.[426] No opposition has ever been encountered in any part of the

---

[425] Amado Chaves, the first superintendent of public instruction of New Mexico, was born at Santa Fé, April 16, 1851. He is a direct lineal descendant of Gen. Bernardino Duran de Chaves, who came to New Mexico with Don Diego de Vargas, in 1692. The line of descent is Diego Antonio Duran de Chaves, Pedro Antonio Chaves, Julian Chaves, and Manuel Antonio Chaves, the father of Don Amado. All of his immediate ancestors were prominent in the military and civil affairs of New Mexico covering a period of two centuries. His father was a colonel in the Mexican army, and during the Civil War held a commission as lieutenant-colonel, 2nd Reg. N. Mex. Vol. He was one of the greatest Indian fighters of his day. Colonel Manuel Antonio Chaves married Vicenta Labadie, and Don Amado is the second son of that union. He received his education at St. Michael's college, Santa Fé, and in Washington, D. C., where he attended a business college conducted by Bryant and Stratton; he also attended Georgetown University, and, taking up the law as a profession, received instruction at the National University Law School, from which institution he was graduated in 1876, receiving his diploma from the hands of General Grant, who was ex-officio president of the institution. While living in the capital he filled a position in the Interior Department for several years. Returning to New Mexico, in 1882, he was elected a member of the house of the legislative assembly and was chosen speaker of that body. His position as superintendent of public instruction was in the beginning very arduous, but he performed his duties in excellent manner. There was a great prejudice in some quarters against the public school system, but Mr. Chaves was successful in establishing the system upon a firm and lasting basis.

On October 4, 1893, Mr. Chaves was united in marriage with Kate N. Foster, nee Nichols. Mr. Chaves is of brilliant intellect, social in manners, and highly respected in the professional and business circles of the state. He held the position of superintendent a second time in 1904-5.

[426] Hiram Hadley succeeded Mr. Chaves in the office, holding the same for two years, 1905-7. Of the six persons who have held the position, Professor Hadley stands without a superior in ability as a trained educator, capable of performing the duties of the position. He was born in Clinton county, Ohio, in 1833, received a common school education, attended Haverford college, Penn., and Earham college, Indiana, receiving, in 1885, from the latter the honorary degree of master of arts. He began teaching in 1850 and has been almost constantly engaged in educational work since that time. In 1890, when the Agricultural College was founded, he was elected its first president. In 1894, he occupied the position of acting president of the University at Alburquerque. In 1895, he accepted the position of professor of history and philosophy in the

Capt. Maximiliano Luna, First U. S. Vol. Cavalry

territory in the matter of employment of English-speaking teachers in districts where, prior to the enactment of the law of 1891, only Spanish had been taught. In truth, the Spanish-speaking people have evinced an almost universal desire and purpose to have competent teachers, well-versed in the English language, employed and assigned to teach in isolated districts where, in times past, the only schools existing were those in which the Spanish language alone was used.[427]

On the night of February 5, 1891, while the legislature was in session, a most dastardly outrage was perpetrated in the city of Santa Fé in the attempted assassination of J. A. Ancheta [428] and other members of the twenty-ninth legislative assembly. The following day a joint resolution authorizing the governor to offer a reward of twenty thousand dol-

ATTEMPTED ASSASSINATION OF ANCHETA AND CATRON

Agricultural College, which he filled until appointed superintendent of public instruction by Governor Otero. He is the author of *Language Lessons*. He is a resident (January, 1912) of Mesilla Park, New Mexico.

[427] In three years after the passage of the act of 1891, great progress had been made, as is shown by the following table of statistics for 1894:

COUNTY	No. of Districts	TEACHERS			ENROLLMENT			AVERAGE DAILY ATTENDANCE		
		Males	Females	Total	Males	Females	Total	Males	Females	Total
Bernalillo	52	34	41	75	1,758	1,359	3,117	1,116	949	2,065
Colfax	30	20	22	42	798	722	1,520	538	490	1,028
Doña Ana	31	10	21	21	699	562	1,261	......	......	......
Eddy	12	9	9	18	594	398	892	341	332	673
Grant	37	11	31	42	824	647	1,471	1,507	1,278	2,785
Guadalupe	18	10	4	14	298	188	486	258	150	408
Lincoln	42	14	10	24	......	......	......	950	865	1,835
Mora	47	18	5	23	527	398	925	388	202	620
Rio Arriba	30	26	4	30	966	464	1,430	497	149	646
San Juan	22	12	7	19	317	192	509	315	139	454
San Miguel	93	49	36	85	2,234	1,516	3,750	1,643	1,137	2,780
Santa Fé	25	23	4	27	542	285	827	431	212	643
Sierra	15	10	6	16	357	279	636	189	142	331
Socorro	49	34	15	49	1,288	899	2,187	756	563	1,319
Taos	32	23	6	29	789	360	1,149	510	220	789
Valencia	37	21	1	22	754	277	1,031	555	165	720
Union	17	......	......	......	......	......	......	......	......	......
	589	324	222	546	12,945	8,526	21,471	9,994	6,993	16,987

Chaves county—no report.

[428] Joseph A. Ancheta was born at Mesilla, N. M., July 21, 1865. He was the son of Don Nepomuceno Ancheta, a refugee from Old Mexico during the revolution of 1856. He received his education at St. Michael's College, Santa Fé, and graduated in 1882. He spent four years at Notre Dame University, near South Bend, Indiana, graduating in 1886. The same year he was admitted

lars for the capture and conviction of the guilty persons was unanimously passed. Although every effort was made for the apprehension of the persons who perpetrated this outrage, it was never known, until after the statute of limitations had run, who were the guilty individuals.

Control of the county and city of Santa Fé had been lost to the leaders of the republican party for several years. The success of the opposition was directly traceable to the popularity and influence of two prominent men, Romulo Martinez and Francisco Chavez. In 1885, Martinez was the sheriff of Santa Fé county. The national administration now being democratic, Martinez was appointed United States marshal; Chavez, who had been chief deputy, was made sheriff of the county. Thereafter Chavez was the most powerful political personality in the county. Among others of his strong political adherents and friends were Sylvestre Gallegos and Francisco Gonzales y Borrego. In the election of 1890 the last named had been chosen as coroner, who was also ex-officio chief of police of the city of Santa Fé. By virtue of the incorporating of the city of Santa Fé, which occurred about this time, the office of coroner became of no value, as the duties of chief of police were now performed

---

to the bar by the supreme court of Indiana, and in the following December was admitted in New Mexico. Returning to New Mexico, he settled at Silver City. He was appointed district attorney, in 1889, by the president of the legislative council, pursuant to an act of that year. He was elected to the legislative council of the twenty-ninth and thirtieth legislative assemblies in 1890 and 1892. About half past eight o'clock in the evening of February 5, 1891, while attending a meeting of one of the committees of the council, held in the office of T. B. Catron, at that time in the Griffin building on the corner of Palace and Washington avenues, Mr. Ancheta was shot in the neck and left shoulder with a charge of buck-shot fired from the street through a window, against which he was leaning. The persons who fired the shots were mounted and made good their escape in the darkness. A shot from a rifle was also fired through the window, passing close to the head of one of the members of the committee standing in the middle of the room. Thomas B. Catron was standing facing a desk, almost immediately in front of Mr. Ancheta and the window. Upon the desk was piled a large stack of legal papers; two of the buck-shot struck these papers and Mr. Catron escaped injury. No motive for the shooting of Ancheta could ever be discovered. It was believed at the time that it was the intention to assassinate Mr. Catron. Large sums of money were expended in employing detectives in a fruitless endeavor to apprehend the would-be assassins. Mr. Ancheta recovered from his wounds. Several years afterward, from a statement under oath, made by José Amado Martinez, at the time of the attempted murder friendly to and a confidant of the conspirators, it was definitely ascertained that the design was to murder Mr. Catron and not Mr. Ancheta. The peace officers of Santa Fé county made no effort whatever, at the time, to capture the scoundrels. Mr. Ancheta died at Silver City, N. M., in 1898.

by an appointee of the mayor of the city. Gonzales y Borrego, considering himself imposed upon and not being able to obtain another office from his party friends, sent his resignation to the board of county commissioners. The board declined to accept it and the matter was held in abeyance for some time. Meanwhile, still much dissatisfied, he appealed to Thomas B. Catron for advice and openly declared himself to be republican in his politics. Mr. Catron advised him not to resign his position as coroner. He thereupon asked to withdraw his resignation, but the county board forthwith accepted it and named Sylvestre Gallegos in his place. Bitter personal and political differences resulted. At a public dance, given at a hall on San Francisco street, in the capital, shortly afterward, hot words were had between these two men. Gallegos invited Borrego into the street to fight the matter out. The challenge was accepted, a large crowd following the principals. In the fight which ensued Gallegos was killed. This unfortunate affair was the beginning of the most deplorable series of murders, assassinations and tragedies ever registered in the annals of the territory of New Mexico.[429] The principal

---

[429] Immediately after the killing of Gallegos, Gonzales y Borrego was taken to the county jail where he was put in irons. About midnight, Sheriff Chavez, who had been out of the city at the time of the killing, came to the jail and assaulted Gonzales y Borrego in a brutal manner. At the hearing before the justice of the peace he was released upon bail. Among other witnesses relied upon by Borrego, in his plea of self-defense, was Faustin Ortiz. Some time afterward Ortiz mysteriously disappeared, and after a lapse of considerable time his body, covered with wounds, was uncovered in the sands of the arroyo Mascareños, near the point where the arroyo is crossed by the track of the Denver and Rio Grande railroad in the city of Santa Fé. It was charged and believed by many that Ortiz had been murdered on account of his having championed the cause of Borrego; that he was induced to visit the office of the justice of the peace, in the county jail building, on the pretext of examining some furniture with a view of purchasing; that while there he was set upon by Juan Ortiz, the justice of the peace, Eustaquio Padilla and others, all deputy sheriffs, and murdered; that subsequently his body was removed in the night-time and buried in the sands of the arroyo. These facts were testified to by José Amado Martinez in a trial before Chief Justice Thomas Smith in which Eustaquio Padilla was charged with the murder of Ortiz. Padilla was acquitted. At the first term of the district court held in Santa Fé county, after the murder of Ortiz, the grand jury returned indictments against a number of very prominent persons, including Sheriff Chavez, charging them with the murder of Ortiz and as accessories thereto. These indictments were all quashed for the reason that the jury returning them was summoned under the jury act of 1889, it being held that the jury was not a jury of the vicinage. *Laws of 1889*, ch. 96, sec. 4, p. 227. Thereafter, although brought before the grand jury summoned under the act of the subsequent legislature, no indictments were returned for the murder of Ortiz. The mother of Ortiz was insistent in her demands that the murderers of her son be punished; finally an indictment against Juan Ortiz was returned; he was tried and acquitted. On the 29th of May, 1892, while going from the

tragedy resulting from the killing of Sylvestre Gallegos was the assassination of Francisco Chavez, ex-sheriff of Santa Fé county, one of the most prominent men in the community, and the hanging

city to his residence across the Rio Santa Fé, at a point on the Denver and Rio Grande railway bridge, almost in front of the Guadalupe church, Francisco Chavez, who had resigned his office of sheriff, was brutally assassinated. Later on, in front of the residence of the archbishop, Juan Pablo Gallegos, who had been a deputy under Sheriff Chavez, was shot and killed by Francisco Gonzales y Borrego, while in company with Laureano Alarid, Antonio Gonzales y Borrego, and another. Gallegos was lying in wait for Gonzales y Borrego; at the time of his death he was endeavoring to fire his own pistol; a knife and a sling-shot or "billy" were found on his person. Gonzales y Borrego was tried for this killing and acquitted. After the murder of Sheriff Chavez, the mother of Faustin Ortiz no longer insisted that the murderers of her son should be punished. Prior to that time her demands upon the governor and the prosecuting officers had been most vigorous, but no evidence was available which would justify an indictment, and the trial of any one would have resulted in an acquittal. The murder of Sheriff Chavez created a great sensation in Santa Fé and throughout the entire territory; by reason of his personal presence, his generous disposition, and other commendable traits of character, Chavez had many friends and followers. His prominence and the cowardly character of his murder aroused intense public feeling and indignation. Investigation, during the administration of Governor Thornton, who succeeded L. Bradford Prince in the office, led to the arrest of Francisco Gonzales y Borrego, his brother, Antonio Gonzales y Borrego, Laureano Alarid, Hypolito Vigil, and Patricio Valencia. At the time of the arrests, Vigil was killed while resisting the officers. At the June term, 1894, of the district court, Santa Fé county, they were indicted for the murder of Chavez. At the March term, 1895, a special term was called by N. B. Laughlin, associate justice; Judge Laughlin deemed himself disqualified to sit and asked Associate Justice H. B. Hamilton, of the 5th district, to preside. The trial began April 28, 1895, and the defendants were each found guilty. A motion for a new trial was overruled. An appeal was taken to the supreme court, but the judgment was affirmed. Other proceedings were had in the supreme court of the United States, but without result favorable to the defendants. Efforts were made with the president of the United States to secure a commutation of the sentence. They were unavailing. The principal counsel for the accused was Thomas B. Catron, who, on account of the vigorous manner in which he had conducted the defense, the money which necessarily had been expended, and the malicious statements and insinuations of political rivals and enemies, was charged with having more than a professional interest in the outcome of the case. The defendants were finally hanged. Prior to their execution they confessed their guilt, but denied that Mr. Catron or any other outside of those who had been formally charged with the crime had been connected with the murder in any capacity whatever. Revenge was the controlling motive in this great crime. The mother of Faustin Ortiz, at whose residence these men were accustomed to meet at times, exerted an influence over them on account of the murder of her son. Hipolito Vigil became a party to the conspiracy owing to his intimacy with a woman with whom Chavez was also on friendly terms. Laureano Alarid was a relative by marriage of the Borregos. A desire for political supremacy may possibly have been a motive, but at the time Chavez was assassinated he had ceased to be a political power in the county; the effort on the part of designing persons to connect prominent republican politicians with this infamous crime was born of malice and a selfish desire to discredit and effectually silence the really powerful men at that time in control of the republican party.

Courtesy of Henry D. Macdona
Battle of San Juan Hill

of the men who were guilty of the crime. Charges that the crime was a political assassination, involving men of great prominence, were made not only in Santa Fé but elsewhere throughout the territory. It was made an issue in two political campaigns, but the guilty persons remained unpunished until the succeeding administration. Other acts of lawlessness were committed in various portions of the territory at this time, notably the fence cutting, assaults, and murders committed by the "White Cap" organizations in San Miguel and other counties in the northern part of New Mexico.

INDUSTRIAL CONDITIONS — POPULATION — STATISTICS

The total assessed valuation of the property in the territory in 1887 was $45,462,459; in 1888, it was $45,690,723, and in 1899, $46,041,010. The total amount of territorial indebtedness,[430] in 1889, was $870,960.94. Owing to the beneficial effects of the act of 1889, before referred to, the financial condition of the territory, in 1890, as reported by the auditor,[431] was exceptionally good. Up to and including the year 1890 there had been constructed, since 1879, one thousand, three hundred and sixty-four miles of railway in the territory. The most important railroad enterprise of the year 1890 was the commencement of construction of the line of railway from Pecos City, in Texas, up the Pecos valley. Twenty-three companies organized for the purpose of reclamation of lands by means of irrigation filed their articles of incorporation in the years 1889 and 1890. The live stock industry, in which there had been a serious depression in 1888, revived during the two succeeding years and sales were very large. No industry in

---

[430] This indebtedness was divided as follows: Outstanding warrants, $150,960; capitol building bonds, $200,000; penitentiary building bonds, $120,000; capitol contingent bonds, $50,000; current expense bonds, $150,000; and provisional indebtedness bonds, $200,000.

The total expenses of the territory for the year ending March 3, 1890, were $149,430.39. The territorial auditor reported a surplus of $40,000.00 in the treasury, which, under the law, was applied to the liquidation of outstanding warrants. During the year $30,000 of penitentiary building bonds were redeemed and cancelled. These bonds bore 7% interest, had a number of years to run, and the territory was required to pay 117 for those thus cancelled and retired.

[431] Trinidad Alarid, of Santa Fé county, was the territorial auditor at this time. He is a native of Santa Fé county, the descendant of a noted family of New Mexico. He was first appointed in 1872 by Governor Marsh Giddings, and held the office until 1891, when he was succeeded by Demetrio Perez, appointed by Governor Thornton. Since 1891, Mr. Alarid has held several important county offices and is now living at Santa Fé.

New Mexico was more prosperous at this time than that of sheep raising. Favorable legislation by congress had so enhanced the price of wool [432] that gratifying profits were reported in every quarter.

The prospects of the mining industry at this period in the history of New Mexico were never brighter. The action of congress in placing a tariff on imported galena ores was of great benefit to the low grade galena-silver producing mines of the country. The total output of the territory for the year 1889 and previous years is given in a note.[433]

The national census for 1890, so far as the enumeration in New Mexico was concerned, was very unsatisfactory, the total population being given at 153,076, a number far below the actual number of people at that time living in the territory. The supervisor of the census and the superintendent in charge in New Mexico were accused of carelessness and inefficiency. It was believed that a fair enumera-

[432] *Report* of L. Bradford Prince, governor, 1890: "The spring wool clip was in round numbers 6,000,000 pounds and, with the fall clip, the production reached 10,000,000 pounds. 300,000 wethers were sold during the year at an average price of $1.50 to $2.00."

[433] The following table is made up from the reports of the express companies and other reliable sources:

YEAR	GOLD	SILVER	TOTAL
1846-1881	$10,350,000	$3,622,000	$13,972,000
1882	691,000	1,985,000	2,676,000
1883	700,000	3,376,000	4,076,000
1884	709,000	3,700,000	4,409,000
1885	911,000	4,381,000	5,292,000
1886	797,000	5,671,000	6,468,000
1887	617,000	4,275,000	4,892,000
1888	863,000	4,285,000	5,148,000
Total	$15,638,000	$31,295,000	$46,933,000

It was at this time that the country was being much agitated over the "Crime of 1873." The legislative assembly, on January 16, 1891, memorialized the senate and congress of the United States that "the present financial policy of this Government in maintaining gold as the single money metal, resulting in the hoarding of the nation's wealth in the financial centers, is rapidly paralyzing the industries of this Territory, causing stagnation in all business enterprises, and can not but result disastrously to our every interest, be it mining, manufacturing, agricultural or commercial. Hence we most respectfully request that by proper legislation providing for free and unlimited coinage of silver, this money metal be at once restored to its natural position upon an equality with gold, and the injustice done by the Acts of 1873 in some measure atoned for by the establishment of a bi-metallic standard in 1891, and your memorialists will ever pray." This resolution or memorial was drafted by Governor Prince, at that time a strong advocate of the free and unlimited coinage of silver.

tion would have shown a population of not less than 185,000 people.[434]

On the 12th of May, 1892, the capitol building was destroyed by fire and many public documents were lost. The collection of ancient papers known as the *Santa Fé Archives* was saved. The fire was supposed to have been of incendiary origin. There was no insurance upon the building.

The return to power of the democratic party, as a result of the national election of 1892, was hailed with delight by the political leaders of that faith in New Mexico. New Mexicans were demanding a restoration of peace and good order and an end of the era of lawlessness which had reigned in several of the counties. The need of younger men for the places at the disposal of the administration was urged upon the president, and particularly that these should be chosen from the citizens of New Mexico, who were cognizant of the conditions and public and political requirements. The

ADMINISTRATION OF
GOVERNOR WILLIAM T. THORNTON

---

[434] *Report* of L. Bradford Prince, governor, 1890: "The peculiar condition in New Mexico as to nationality and language; some communities speaking English and some Spanish, and some being divided in language, presents an unusual difficulty. . . It cannot be denied that in a considerable number of districts the enumerators were careless and did not seem to appreciate the importance of obtaining a full record, if that required much trouble. . . The result was seen in returns manifestly imperfect in many respects, and in an enumeration far from complete. . . We may safely say that New Mexico has a population which should appear by the census of not less than 180,000."

The population by counties, according to the census, is as follows for 1880 and 1890 (exclusive of tribal Indians):

COUNTY	1880	1890	COUNTY	1880	1890
Bernalillo	17,225	20,388	San Miguel	20,638	24,167
Colfax	3,398	7,961	Santa Fé	10,867	13,392
Doña Ana	7,612	9,157	Sierra		3,635
Grant	4,539	9,659	Socorro	7,785	9,575
Lincoln	2,513	7,003	Taos	11,029	9,863
Mora	9,751	10,552	Valencia	13,095	14,332
Rio Arriba	11,023	11,502			
San Juan		1,890	Total	119,475	153,076

The population of the principal towns, so far as they can be separated from surrounding precincts was:

Santa Fé	6,038	Socorro and San Antonio	2,591
Alburquerque (new town)	3,794	Raton and Buena Vista	2,196
Alburquerque (old), Griegos and Candelarias	2,265	Fernandez de Taos	1,712
East Las Vegas	2,310	Mesilla and Bosque Seco	1,642
Las Vegas (North and South)	2,383	Gallup	1,204
Las Cruces	2,518	Deming	1,181
Silver City	2,279	Pinos Altos	1,012

demands of the local leaders met with approval at Washington. William T. Thornton,[435] a former law partner of Thomas B. Catron,

[435] William T. Thornton was born in Calhoun, Henry county, Mo., February 9, 1843. His father was Dr. W. Thornton and his mother, Caroline V. Taylor. Governor Thornton received his education in a private school near Sedalia, Mo., and afterward graduated from the law department of the University of Kentucky. In 1861, he enlisted in the Confederate army as a private, serving with the army of General Sterling Price for two years. He was captured by Union forces during the retreat of the Confederates from Springfield, Mo., in February, 1862, and sent to Alton, Ill., where he was kept in confinement for nearly a year, when he was exchanged and served until the close of the war. In 1876, he was elected a member of the legislature of his native state. His health partially failing, he came to Santa Fé in 1877. In 1880, he was elected a member of the legislative assembly, and, in 1891, was chosen mayor of Santa Fé, the nominee of both political parties. In April, 1893, he was appointed governor of New Mexico and served his full term of four years. Shortly after the nomination of his successor by President McKinley, he left the territory and took up his residence in Mexico, where he engaged in mining. He is at the present time (January, 1912) a resident of the city of Santa Fé.

Thomas Smith is a native of the state of Virginia, having been born in Culpeper county, July 26, 1838. His father, Governor William Smith, was a descendant of two of the most prominent and notable families of the Old Dominion, the Donaphins and the Smiths. He received his education in Virginia and graduated from William and Mary college. He studied law in the University of Virginia. At the outbreak of the Civil War he joined the Kanawha Rifles, but was soon commissioned major of the 36th Virginia, C. S. A. He was in command of his regiment at the battle of Fort Donelson and captured a battery from the Union forces. He successfully withdrew his troops from the fort during the negotiations for a surrender and was afterward promoted to the rank of colonel. He was promoted to the rank of brigadier-general shortly before the evacuation of Richmond. After the war he resumed the practice of his profession and held a number of political offices in his native state. In 1885, he was appointed United States attorney for New Mexico, holding the office four years, during which time he conducted the prosecution of many New Mexicans for alleged land frauds. After the election of Benjamin Harrison as president, he returned to Virginia, and in 1893 was appointed chief justice by President Cleveland. On the 10th of October, 1894, he was married to Elizabeth Fairfax Gaines, a daughter of Judge William Gaines, of Virginia. This office he held four years, when he again returned to Virginia, where he is now living.

Albert Bacon Fall was born at Frankfort, Kentucky, November 26, 1861. His ancestors were Scotch and came to America in 1812, locating in Trigg county, Ky. His great-grandfather served under the Duke of Wellington, having been lieutenant-colonel of the Scotch Grays of the English army. Judge Fall was privately educated. He read law at Frankfort, Ky., in the office of Judge Lindsley, afterward a member of the senate of the United States. Prior to his coming to New Mexico, in 1888, Judge Fall had lived in Texas, where he was engaged in the real estate business. Shortly after his arrival in New Mexico he began his career in the political affairs of Doña Ana county, and was elected to the legislative assembly twice as a democrat. He was appointed associate justice of the supreme court in 1893, but resigned in 1895. While a member of the legislature he materially assisted in the passage of the "Paullin" public school law. He was commissioned a captain in the 1st Territorial Regiment during the Spanish-American War but saw no active service. Returning to New Mexico, after the mustering out of his regiment, he resumed the

Major W. H. H. Llewellyn, First U. S. Vol. Cavalry

was appointed governor, and Thomas Smith, who had been United States attorney during the former Cleveland administration, was named as chief justice of the supreme court; Albert B. Fall, N. B. Laughlin, Needham C. Collier, and Humphrey B. Hamilton were appointed associate justices. Edward L. Hall was named as United States marshal, and J. B. H. Hemingway, United States attorney. Lorion Miller, who had been clerk of the district court under Judge

practice of the law. In 1897, he was appointed attorney general of New Mexico, which office he again held in 1907. After the Spanish-American War, in 1903, he was elected a member of the legislative council of the 35th legislative assembly. Since that time Judge Fall has affiliated with the republican party, in which he has been as prominent and as powerful in council as was his position with the democratic party. He was a member of the constitutional convention in 1910, representing Otero county. He is now a resident of Three Rivers, New Mexico. At the session of the first state legislature in March, 1912, he was chosen United States senator.

Napoleon B. Laughlin is a native of Illinois, having been born at Grand Tower, Jackson county, July 24, 1844. His ancestors fought in the Revolution. He is a graduate of the University of Missouri. After his graduation he removed to the state of Texas, where he engaged in the practice of the law. He came to New Mexico in 1879. The following year he was elected to the lower house of the legislative assembly. In 1886, he was elected a member of the legislative assembly, on this occasion representing the county of Santa Fé in the council. In July, 1894, he was appointed associate justice of the supreme court and presided over the first judicial district, serving the full term of four years. In 1883, he married Kate Kimbrough, of Dallas, Texas, of which union there are two daughters. Subsequent to his retirement from the bench Judge Laughlin has practiced his profession at Santa Fé, where he is now living.

Needham C. Collier is a native of Georgia, the son of Bryan W. Collier and Martha Bryan. He served as a soldier in the Confederate army. In 1866, Judge Collier entered Georgetown University, Washington, D. C., from which institution he was graduated in 1868. He came to New Mexico in 1885, locating at Alburquerque. In 1891, he formed a law partnership with O. N. Marron, an active young lawyer of that city. He was appointed associate justice of the supreme court in 1893, succeeding William D. Lee, and presided over the second judicial district. In 1882, he was married to Annie Collins, a native of Savannah, Georgia. After the expiration of his term of office, Judge Collier removed to St. Louis, Mo., where he is now living, practicing his profession.

Humphrey B. Hamilton was born in Perry county, Illinois, October 26, 1850. He was of Scotch-Irish descent, his forebears having emigrated from Scotland prior to the Revolution. They were prominent in the military and civil affairs of the colonies. His paternal grandfather was one of the early pioneers of the state of Missouri. Judge Hamilton received his education in the common schools of Illinois, read law and was admitted to the practice in 1871. He began the practice of his profession at Jefferson City, Mo., where he remained until 1885, when he came to New Mexico, locating at Socorro. In 1895, he was appointed associate justice of the supreme court of New Mexico, a position which he filled with marked impartiality and ability. Upon the expiration of his term Judge Hamilton resumed the practice and died in the year 1900.

Lorion Miller was born in the state of Maryland, April 4. 1857. He was the son of John Miller and Sarah E. Gray. His father was killed during the Civil War, by Kansas "Jayhawkers," under command of "Bill" Ewing. He received his education in the common schools of Missouri, to which state his

W. H. Brinker during his term as judge of the second district, was appointed secretary of the territory.

Thoroughly committed to a policy of reform in the administration of the affairs of the territory, the governor's well-known activity in matters of public interest found immediate opportunity for achievement in the discovery and punishment of the murderers of Francisco Chavez. Although the unhappy condition of the financial affairs of the country at that time prevented his employing himself along customary lines beneficial to the people, still he found abundant occasion for a display of his unique talents. Bringing to bear every resource within the grasp of the executive, removing the prosecuting and peace officers of Santa Fé county from office, believing them to be either indifferent or incompetent in the prosecution of the persons believed by many of the people of the territory to be guilty of the assassination of Chavez, he bended his entire energy to the conviction and punishment of these men. Satisfied of the guilt of the Borregos and committed to a policy of enforcement of the laws of New Mexico at whatever cost, particularly the punishment of the men who had murdered Chavez, counseled by men of note but with biased judgment, he sacrificed the friendship and good opinion of men with whom his personal relations for more than twenty years had been of the most intimate character, by permitting it to appear that his administration endorsed the policies and politics involved in several collateral court proceedings growing out of the conduct of the defense of the Borregos.[436]

---

father had moved in 1858. He also graduated at the Agricultural college of that state. He came to New Mexico in 1881. In 1885, he was appointed clerk of the district court of the second judicial district by Judge W. H. Brinker, which position he held until 1888. Upon the accession of Grover Cleveland to the presidency, Mr. Miller received the appointment of secretary of the territory, serving his full term of four years. August 3, 1886, he married Wrenneta Bostick, of Fort Smith, Arkansas. After his retirement from the office of secretary he devoted himself to business pursuits at Alburquerque and later at El Paso, Texas, where he died in 1909.

[436] At the session of the supreme court of New Mexico, in August, 1895, Jacob H. Crist, district attorney, appointed by Governor Thornton, who conducted the prosecution of the Borregos, filed a number of affidavits charging Thomas B. Catron and Charles A. Spiess, attorneys for the Borregos, with unprofessional conduct during the trial. He also filed a petition calling the attention of the court to these affidavits, asking the court to act in the matter. These attorneys were charged with having endeavored to procure false affidavits from witnesses in the trial and in other ways to have acted with impropriety in the matter of the giving of testimony in the case. The court deemed the charges of sufficient gravity to call for an investigation, and appointed John P. Victory,

The great strike of employes of the Atchison, Topeka and Santa Fé Railroad Company, identified with the American Railway Union, wherein upward of one thousand employes of the company, at the time in the hands of receivers, lost their positions, occurred during the administration of Governor Thornton. As an executive he took no part in the suppression of the troubles growing out of this strike. It was handled entirely through the courts of the first and fourth judicial districts and by the department of justice at Washington, under direction of President Cleveland.

The election held in November, 1894, resulted in the choice of Thomas B. Catron [437] as delegate to the 54th congress. Other than

---

a brother-in-law of the governor, at that time holding the office of solicitor general, William B. Childers, A. A. Jones, S. B. Newcomb, and Bernard S. Rodey, the first three being prominent political partisans, opposed to Messrs. Catron and Spiess, the two remaining members of the committee being of the same party faith as the accused men; all were prominent members of the bar. The committee was ordered to prepare and file such charges as might be deemed proper in its judgment. Under this order the committee prepared and filed five separate and distinct specifications, charging five unprofessional acts. The court, composed of Chief Justice Thómas Smith, Associate Justices Laughlin, Collier, Hamilton, and Fall after hearing the testimony, dismissed the proceedings, saying: "Prominent citizens of this community, officials in high standing, prominent members of the bar, reputable business men in large number, have come upon the stand and have testified, without qualification, that they would not believe these witnesses under oath, in consequence of their character, their reputation, and their standing in the community." Each member of the court filed a separate opinion, the one by Justice Laughlin dissented, being, as is stated in the opinion, "irresistibly driven to the conclusion, however unpleasant it may be, that the legal evidence contained in the record sufficiently sustains the charge of unprofessional conduct on the part of the respondent during the progress of the trial of said Borrego case and I so find."

[437] Thomas B. Catron is of German stock, his ancestors having emigrated from Germany to the state of Virginia in the year 1765. His grandfather was Christopher Catron, of Wythe county, in the western part of the state of Virginia. His father was John Catron, third son of Christopher, who was born in White county, Tennessee. to which state Christopher Catron had removed from Virginia. The mother of Thomas B. Catron was Mary Fletcher, of Montgomery county, Virginia. In the year 1815, John Catron, with his father's family, removed to Missouri and located at Old Franklin, the eastern terminus of the old Santa Fé Trail; thence the family removed to Lafayette county, Missouri, in 1817, where Thomas B. Catron was born, October 6, 1840.

Receiving his early education in the common schools of the county and in the Masonic college at Lexington, Missouri, he graduated at the University of Missouri in the class of 1860, with the degree of B. A., later having conferred upon him by the University the degree of Master of Arts.

At the outbreak of the Civil War, he enlisted in Hiram Bledsoe's battery in the army of General Sterling W. Price, C. S. A., took part in the battles of Carthage, Wilson Creek, Dry Fork, Lexington, and Pea Ridge. After the battle of Pea Ridge, with his battery he accompanied the army under General Van Dorn to Mississippi and was in the siege of Vicksburg. Later he took part in the battles of Corinth, Iuka, Farmington, Lookout Mountain, Missionary Ridge,

laboring for the passage of an enabling act for New Mexico, the securing of the usual appropriations, DELEGATES IN CONGRESS and the routine work of a territorial representative in congress very little was accomplished by the delegates.

In 1896, he was defeated for reëlection by Harvey B. Fergusson, of Alburquerque, owing to a disaffection in the republican party in Bernalillo county and the attacks made upon him in all portions of the territory embodying the charges made in the disbarment proceedings referred to in a note.

The career of Delegate Fergusson [438] in the congress of the United

---

and with the troops in the department of the Gulf, and was in all the engagements around Mobile Bay in 1864. He was surrendered at Meriden, Mississippi, with the entire command under Lieutenant-General Richard Taylor, being in command of the Third Missouri Battery, at the time of the surrender.

After the war, having returned to his native state, he began the study of the law. In 1866, he came to Santa Fé, arriving on July 27, of that year. He had not yet been admitted to the practice, but shortly after his arrival was appointed district attorney for the third judicial district, at that time composed of the county of Doña Ana only. Settling in La Mesilla, he was admitted to the bar, June 15, 1867. In 1887, he married Julia A. Walz, of Mankato, Minnesota, of which union there were born five children, four of whom survive, John W., Charles Christopher, Thomas B., and Fletcher A.

In 1872, he was appointed United States attorney by President Grant, his law partner, Stephen B. Elkins, being delegate in congress from New Mexico. Prior to this time, from 1869, he had been attorney general of New Mexico. He served as a member of the legislative council from Santa Fé county in the 26th, 29th, 33rd, and 36th legislative assemblies; was mayor of Santa Fé, president of the board of education of that city, and has been identified with the social, political, professional, and commercial life of the territory for nearly half a century. In 1895, he was elected president of the New Mexico Bar Association. Until the year 1896 he was recognized as the leader of the republican party, framed its policies, wrote its platforms, controlled its conventions, represented the party in national conventions, and was a member of the republican national committee. With the administration of Governor Miguel A. Otero, aided by the executive, a powerful party machine was erected and Mr. Catron was compelled to divide the leadership with younger men ambitious for political preferment and recognition in the party councils. He was a member of the constitutional convention of 1910, elected from Santa Fé county, where he has always maintained his leadership. At the first session of the state legislature in March, 1912, he was chosen United States senator.

Mr. Catron is possessed of great strength of character and has as many enemies as he has friends. Easily leader of the bar of New Mexico, for many years he has enjoyed a practice in keeping with his ability.

[438] Harvey B. Fergusson is a native of the state of Alabama, born in 1848. He received his education in the academic department of Washington and Lee University, of Virginia, receiving the degree of Master of Arts in 1873. He was a teacher of languages and mathematics during this period. After the completion of his classical course he entered the law department of his alma mater, receiving the degree of LL.B. the following year. In 1876, he began the practice of his profession at Wheeling, West Virginia, where he became a part-

Prominent New Mexicans of the Nineteenth Century
1. Col. Kit Carson. 2. Carlos Beaubien. 3. Aloys Scheurich.
4. James Conklin

States, as a delegate from New Mexico, was signalized by his success in securing the passage of the act of June 21, 1898, known as the Fergusson act. This enactment was one of the most important laws ever passed by the congress of the United States affecting the interests of citizens and residents of the territory. Pursuant to its provisions all sections of school lands numbered 16 and 36 in every township of the territory, New Mexico was given the right to lease such lands, consisting of about four million acres, for the support of its public schools. Fifty sections were granted for the erection of public buildings at the capital at Santa Fé when New Mexico became a state in the Union; two townships were reserved for the establishment of a university of New Mexico, and sixty-five thousand acres, together with all saline lands, were granted for the use of the university. One hundred thousand acres were set aside for the use of the agricultural college.[439]

---

ner in the firm of Jacob, Cracraft and Fergusson. As a member of this firm he came to New Mexico, in 1882, as attorney for the North Homestake Mining Company, at that time having important litigation in the courts of New Mexico. During this period he determined to remain permanently in the territory, and located at Alburquerque, where he has since practiced his profession with success. In 1894, he served as special attorney of the government in the prosecution of the officers of the Alburquerque National Bank, which had closed its doors during the panic of 1893.

He was chosen delegate to the fifty-fifth congress, serving his constituents with great ability by securing the passage of the act which bears his name, although both senate and house of representatives were in majority of opposing political faith. Mr. Fergusson has always occupied a high place in the councils of his party. He is easily accorded a position among the leaders of the New Mexico bar. He was chosen one of the delegates to the constitutional convention of 1910 from Bernalillo county, being the only representative of his party from that county, his election, however, resulting from a disaffection in the ranks and leadership of the republicans. At the state election, in November, 1911, he was elected a member of the sixty-second congress.

[439] Mr. Fergusson has stated to the writer that it would have been impossible for him to have secured the passage of this act had it not been for the friendly interest of the speaker of the house of representatives, at that time, Thomas B. Reed, who, by special appointment with Mr. Fergusson, accorded him, at his residence, at the capital, an opportunity to explain succinctly the provisions of his proposed measure. After hearing Mr. Fergusson's explanation and argument, the speaker became convinced of the merit of the measure and thereafter made it possible for the delegate to bring his bill before the house and secure its passage.

By virtue of its provisions the proceeds arising from the sale of all lands covered by the act were ordered set aside as permanent funds for university and agricultural college purposes. Five per cent of the proceeds of the sales of public lands sold by the United States subsequent to the passage of the act was set aside as a permanent fund for the support of the common schools. Further grants of non-mineral and unappropriated lands were also made, being for the establishment of permanent water reservoirs for irrigation purposes,

Under the provisions of this law the territorial legislature, by an act approved March 16, 1899, established a board of public lands, consisting of the governor, solicitor-general, and commissioner of public lands, for the leasing, sale, and general management of all public lands or public funds granted to the territory. The office of land commissioner was created, and Alpheus A. Keen, a life-long friend of governor Miguel A. Otero, was named by the executive for this position.[440]

---

five hundred thousand acres; for the improvement of the Rio Grande in New Mexico and the increasing of the surface flow of the water in that stream, one hundred thousand acres; for the establishment and maintenance of an asylum for the insane, fifty thousand acres; for the establishment and maintenance of a school of mines, fifty thousand acres; a school for the deaf and dumb, fifty thousand acres; for a reform school, fifty thousand acres; for an institution for the blind, fifty thousand acres; for normal schools, one hundred thousand acres; for a hospital for disabled miners, fifty thousand acres; for a military institute, fifty thousand acres; for the enlargement and maintenance of the territorial penitentiary, fifty thousand acres. The palace of the governors and all the lands and appurtenances connected therewith were also granted to the territory by this law.

[440] The following statement shows the total acreage of school lands to which New Mexico became entitled by virtue of the Fergusson act; the total estimated losses from the grant by reason of land grants, military and Indian reservations, forest reserves, patented lands, etc., and the status in 1910 of the lands selected by the territory in lieu of the above losses:

Total estimated area of sections 16 and 36, granted to
New Mexico by the act of June 21, 1898.......... 4,244,480

Deductions:
Indian Reservations............................220,216.87
Forest Reserves...............................184,405.18
Land Grants, etc..............................501,091.40
Military Reservations.......................... 8,724.32
Mining Claims, etc............................ 3,152.04
Patented Lands................................ 22,090.23
Timber Reservations........................... 1,920.00
                                                         941,600.04

Total Area of Sections 16 and 36, title to which is absolutely
vested in New Mexico......................................3,302,879.96
Lands selected by the territory and approved by the department of
the interior in lieu of deductions on account of Indian reservations, etc... 307,082.00

Lands to which the territory has absolute title.................3,609,961.96
Lands selected by the territory and awaiting approval of the department of the interior.................................... 397,870.59

Lands to be selected:
In lieu of selections rejected by land offices........ 27,000.00
In lieu of deductions for mining claims, etc........ 3,152.04
In lieu of deductions for patented lands........... 22,090.23
In lieu of deductions for forest reserves.........184,405.18
                                                         236,647.45

The free silver heresy of 1896 found few supporters in New Mexico, although the territory was surrounded by states on the east and north and the territory of Arizona on the west where the political adherents of William J. Bryan were to be found in great number. Early in 1896, Mr. Bryan visited New Mexico, made a number of addresses at the principal cities and towns, was entertained by Governor Thornton at Santa Fé, and, in the democratic national convention of that year, succeeded in securing the support of the New Mexican delegation. There were a few converts from the republican party but this loss was fully offset by the refusal of many old line democrats to support the democratic platform. However, Thomas B. Catron, renominated by the republican party for delegate to congress, was defeated by Harvey B. Fergusson. The causes leading up to this result are not chargeable to any change of political front on the part of the people of New Mexico at that period. In 1894, his plurality over Anthony Joseph, democrat, was 2,762. In 1896, he was defeated by 1,930 votes. The democratic party elected a majority of the members of the council, while the republicans controlled the lower house, William H. H. Llewellyn, of Doña Ana, being the speaker of the latter, and Antonio Joseph, the president of the upper branch of the assembly. Thereafter, during the entire territorial period, the republican party secured and maintained control of both branches of the legislative assembly.

ADMINISTRATION OF
GOVERNOR MIGUEL A. OTERO

William McKinley had no sooner been inaugurated president than the leading politicians of New Mexico, solicitous for their own futures in the territorial political arena, laid siege to the presidential citadel in the matter of appointments in New Mexico. The applicants most strongly urged for the position of governor were Pedro Perea, William H. H. Llewellyn, and George H. Wallace, later named as secretary. Mr. Perea failed because of the neglect of Senator Elkins to keep an appointment with the president and the secretary of the interior. Major Llewellyn was successfully opposed

---

Grand total of lands to which the territory has absolute title, lands to which it has no absolute title but which have been segregated from the public domain and are awaiting approval by the department of the interior, and lands not yet selected....4,244,480.00
  In 1910, 71,080.95 acres of these lands had been sold at an average price of $3.22 per acre.

by one of the great corporations of the country. Mr. Wallace was not deemed sufficiently representative for the position of executive. Confronted by this situation, the president, having renewed an acquaintance with Miguel A. Otero,[441] made when Benjamin Harrison was nominated for the presidency at Minneapolis, who was in Washington pressing his claims for appointment to the office of United States marshal, highly impressed by his charming personality, tendered to him the governorship of the territory. He was soon confirmed by the senate and upon his return to New Mexico was re-

---

[441] Miguel Antonio Otero 2nd, son of Miguel Antonio Otero, formerly delegate in congress from New Mexico, and, in 1861, secretary of the territory, and Mary Josephine Blackwood, was born in St. Louis, Missouri, October 17, 1859. With his parents, returning to New Mexico, he crossed the Great Plains at the early age of two years. He received his education at Notre Dame University, South Bend, Indiana, and after his graduation filled the position of bookkeeper in the great frontier forwarding and merchandizing firm of Otero, Sellar and Company, of which his father was the senior member. Later he became cashier of the San Miguel National Bank, of Las Vegas. In 1886, he was elected probate clerk of San Miguel county, and during the incumbency of Chief Justice James O'Brien, was clerk of the fourth judicial district court. He married Miss Caroline Emmett, December 19, 1888, of which union one son, Miguel Antonio Otero 3rd, was born. He represented New Mexico in the republican national convention in 1888 and served upon the committee which notified Benjamin Harrison of his nomination for the presidency. It was on this occasion that he met William McKinley, a member of the same committee, and who, upon his own election to the presidency eight years later, named him governor of New Mexico. This position he filled with great credit for nine years, retiring in 1906. During his incumbency, under his leadership and with the patronage of his office, the republican party organized a political machine so powerful that even the appointment of notary public was considered in some localities a great favor and mark of political recognition. Induced to ally themselves with a political party so well organized, through the favor of the executive in the matter of political appointments, many prominent men, formerly occupying exalted positions in the councils of the democratic party, flocked to the standard of republicanism set up by a leader who acknowledged no equal and brooked no rivalry in his leadership. Under his domination and at his instance the republican territorial convention of 1904, a majority of whose delegates had been instructed to cast their votes for the renomination of Bernard S. Rodey, who had been chosen delegate to congress in 1900 and 1902, the last time by a majority of nearly ten thousand votes, repudiated their instructions and voted for the nomination of William H. Andrews, one of the delegates to the convention and himself instructed to cast his vote for Mr. Rodey. So potent was his leadership while executive, that he was enabled to remove from office and utterly destroy politically the leaders in some counties offering any opposition, among them the chairman of the republican territorial central committee. When George Curry became governor of New Mexico, in 1909, he appointed Mr. Otero treasurer of the territory, a position which he continued to hold until the fall of 1911, when he resigned in order to accept the nomination by the progressive republicans of Santa Fé county for state senator, for which office he was defeated by B. F. Pankey, the regular republican nominee. Mr. Otero is today (1912) a resident of Santa Fé.

ceived and feted at all the principal cities en route to the capital, where he was inaugurated in the summer of 1897, the ceremonies attendant being the most elaborate and impressive until that time ever seen in the ancient capital. Other appointments made during the year for New Mexico were John R. McFie, J. W. Crumpacker, Frank W. Parker,[442] Charles A. Leland, and William J. Mills, justices of the supreme court, George H. Wallace, secretary, William B. Childers,[443] United States attorney, and Creighton M. Foraker, United States marshal, each one of whom, with the exception of the last named, was induced to believe that he owed his appointment to the efforts and endorsement of the executive of the territory. This belief was heightened and strengthened by the fact that New Mexico's representative in congress, Harvey B. Fergusson, was of political faith opposed to that of the national administration. To this may be added the well known personal relations existing between the president and Governor Otero, which were of the most friendly and intimate character. Governor Otero's power and influence at the White House continued during the two terms of President Roosevelt's incumbency and was occasioned largely through the assistance

[442] Frank Wilson Parker was born in Sturgis, Michigan, October 16, 1860, the son of James Wilson and Marie Antoinette Parker. He received his education in the public schools of his native city, and later was graduated from the University of Michigan with the degree of LL. B. He came to New Mexico in 1881, located at Socorro, at that time believed by many to be the coming metropolis of the territory. Removing to Mesilla, he later changed his residence to Kingston, in Sierra county, then a thriving mining community. In 1883, he removed to Hillsboro, where he practiced his profession until elevated to the bench, January 10, 1898, by President McKinley, a position held by him during the remaining years of the territorial period. He was elected a member of the constitutional convention of 1910 from Doña Ana county and at the first state election, November 7, 1911, was elected a justice of the supreme court of the state of New Mexico.

[443] William Burr Childers was born at Pulaski, Tennessee, March 20, 1854. He received his education in the common schools of his native state, later attended Washington and Lee University, graduating from the academic department in 1873 and the law department in 1874. Following his graduation he remained in Pulaski until 1875 when he removed to St. Louis, Mo., remaining in that city until December, 1879. He came to New Mexico on the first day of the following year and located at Alburquerque, where he practiced his profession until a short time prior to his death, which occurred in 1909. He occupied many positions of honor and trust during his career. He was United States attorney for nine years, from June, 1896, until March, 1905. Mr. Childers was a lawyer of great ability and in the practice was always accorded a most liberal clientele. Politically, until the campaign of 1896, he was a leader of the democratic party and was chairman of its territorial central committee for several years. In 1896, he supported the nominees of the ''gold'' wing of his party, and thereafter identified himself with the republican administrations and policies.

rendered by the governor in the organization of the New Mexican troops which became a part of Colonel Roosevelt's Rough Rider regiment during the Spanish-American war, and the unsought endorsement of his administration of New Mexican affairs by ex-officers of that famous regiment, many of whom the governor saw fit to appoint to more or less lucrative or honorary offices within the patronage of the executive.

Safely installed in office, occupying quarters in the old Palace of the Governors, the executive immediately began the institution of reforms in the finances of the territory and its several counties. Educated to business methods, a financier of no mean ability, his efforts within a brief period were crowned with pronounced success. Alive to the efforts of certain speculators and owners of great landed interests on both sides of the Rio Grande in the vicinity of El Paso, Texas, to commit the general government to the construction of an international dam and reservoir in the valley of the Rio Grande, a short distance above the city of El Paso, in the state of Texas, Governor Otero addressed a communication [444] to the Honorable John

---

[444] In a protest to the secretary of state, accompanying a copy of the opinion rendered by Gideon D. Bantz, judge of the third judicial district court, in the suit of the *United States of America v. The Rio Grande Dam and Irrigation Company*, in which Judge Bantz held that the Rio Grande was not a navigable stream as contended by the government, above El Paso, and that the waters thereof are local waters under local control by authority of congress, and that their interruption and diversion are not in violation of any law of the United States or any treaty, Governor Otero said: "As governor of the Territory of New Mexico, and in defense of what I believe to be the highest rights of her people, I desire to enter an earnest protest against the execution of the Treaty between the United States and the Republic of Mexico, whereby the Republic of Mexico asserts, and seeks to obtain, joint control of the waters of the Rio Grande and other rivers flowing through the Territory of New Mexico, and to prevent the construction of systems of storage and irrigation along said streams in said Territory. A draft of such treaty, as I have been reliably informed, has been prepared by the representative of the Mexican government and is now pending for consideration by your department. In support of this protest I beg leave to submit the following facts and reasons why such treaty should not be entered into by the government of the United States.

"1. The Rio Grande enters the Territory of New Mexico at a point near the town of Antonito, in the state of Colorado, flows through the central portion of the Territory a distance of about five hundred miles, emerging therefrom near the City of El Paso, in the state of Texas, and is the most important river of said Territory.

"2. The Rio Grande is really a small stream of water. It flows rapidly through the mountains of northern New Mexico, through the valleys of the central and southern portions of the Territory. It passes through many fertile valleys in the northern part of the Territory, and from the central part to the southern boundary, it flows practically through one continuous broad and fertile valley.

Sherman, secretary of state, protesting against the execution of a treaty between the American and Mexican governments at that time pending or proposed by the Republic of Mexico. The protest made

"3. The most thickly settled portion of the Territory of New Mexico is the Rio Grande valley. For many years almost the entire population of the Territory was congregated along this stream, and the wealth of the Territory, as represented by its agriculture, horticulture, and mining industry, is found in this valley and tributary to it, with this exception that the Pecos and Gila valleys within the last few years have been developed very rapidly and are fast becoming rivals of the Rio Grande.

"4. The Rio Grande is not a navigable stream in any part of the Territory of New Mexico, and never has been, nor has it ever been used for any beneficial purpose other than for agriculture, horticulture, mining, and stock raising. From a residence in the Territory of New Mexico of more than eighteen years, I am very familiar with this stream, and from this knowledge I can say that it is absurd to claim that the Rio Grande is, or ever has been, a navigable stream. Indeed, the nature of this river in the central and southern portions of the Territory makes it impossible that it shall ever be a navigable stream. In those portions of the Territory the banks are almost entirely sand, the banks being constantly cut away until the stream has become so wide that it has a depth of but a few inches. Large sand bars form every few miles in the stream, rising near and sometimes above the surface of the water, so that, unless during the flood time in the spring, even logs could not be floated upon its waters, and so far as I am aware no such attempt has been made. This river goes perfectly dry during the cropping season, and I have known it to be entirely without water for a distance of 230 miles from the southern line of the Territory. Within the last ten years the Rio Grande has been dry for a distance of 150 miles above the city of El Paso, one-half of the time during the cropping season, and during those years said river has been entirely dry from the city of El Paso, Tex., to the Concho, a distance of 200 miles below. There is a time during the spring of each year, usually during the months of May and June, when a large quantity of flood water passes down this stream from the rains and melting snows in the mountains of Colorado and New Mexico, and during this period there is sufficient water for all of the lands now under cultivation along said river in said Territory, and indeed much more than is necessary for such purpose; but after the flood waters have ceased to flow it is an exceptional year when there is sufficient water for the lands now under cultivation.

"5. The people of New Mexico have been using the waters of the Rio Grande for many years for the purposes of irrigation, and have constructed systems of irrigation suitable to the necessities of the different valleys along the banks of that stream. Large areas of fertile lands now under cultivation, and great quantities of grain, fruits, and forage are raised by the people of the Territory by means of irrigation from this stream; and, indeed, it is impossible to raise crops in the Territory of New Mexico, especially in the Rio Grande Valley, without artificial irrigation. Water rights have been obtained in the ditches constructed by the people at great expense, and to prevent the use of the waters of the Rio Grande for the purpose of irrigation would practically destroy New Mexico and make it what it once was — a portion of the Great American Desert, ruining thousands of people settled along this stream, and destroying vast amounts of valuable property.

"6. A system of storage reservoirs along the Rio Grande is, in my judgment, absolutely essential to the growth and prosperity of the people and the Territory, for the reason that there are large quantities of the most fertile lands lying in their arid condition even along the banks of said river, because they can not be irrigated from the present supply of water and the ditches now existing;

by New Mexico's executive had great force and in a large measure prevented the construction of the dam at that point, resulting afterward, in the adoption of the Elephant Butte project by the govern-

and yet, during the time the flood waters are passing and during the winter months sufficient water passes by unused to irrigate every foot of irrigable land in the valleys along said stream. If these waters could be stored in reservoirs, sufficient water could be obtained to guarantee a permanent supply of water during the cropping season of each year and every year, and thus furnish homes and fields for cultivation of crops for a largely increased population. To concede the claim of the Republic of Mexico to the use of the waters of the Rio Grande within the Territory of New Mexico would be destructive of the rights of the people of the Territory, for the reason that it would prevent the storage of water, which is essential to the further development and prosperity of that Territory, in that it would prevent the erection of dams and reservoirs for the storage of waters for irrigation and other purposes, not only as to the waters of the Rio Grande, but also as to the waters of the Pecos, and I submit that when the United States obtained the lands embraced in said Territory under and by virtue of the treaty of Guadalupe Hidalgo and the Gadsden purchase it obtained also the waters of the streams within the limits of said Territory, for the use and benefit of the people settling upon said lands now embraced in the Territory of New Mexico, and that there is nothing in the treaties ceding said lands to the United States that gives the Republic of Mexico any claim or right whatever in the waters of the Rio Grande flowing within the limits of the Territory of New Mexico.

"I believe it to be a fact susceptible of abundant proof that the Rio Grande River is not a navigable stream for a distance of 1,000 miles below the city of El Paso; that the waters of the Rio Grande flowing through the Territory of New Mexico never reach any navigable portion of said stream during the cropping season. On the contrary, I believe it to be a fact that said waters cease to exist between the city of El Paso and the mouth of the Concho River, about 200 miles below, almost every year during the summer season, and I submit the navigable portion of said river, which, I understand, exists near the mouth of said stream, is not affected in any way by the waters flowing through the Territory of New Mexico.

"I desire to call your attention to the lack of good faith of those who are setting up the rights of the Mexican Government to demand that the waters of the Rio Grande shall be allowed to flow through the Territory of New Mexico to the boundary line between Mexico and the United States, and from thence on to the sea, on the ground that the use of these waters for irrigation in New Mexico is depleting the navigable extent of this river, especially in view of the fact that the citizens of Mexico themselves have, I am reliably informed, diverted, and are now using nearly all the water of the Concho River, which flows northward through the northern States of Mexico and empties into the Rio Grande, and which, it has long been understood in this country, is the largest confluent of the Rio Grande and contributes most to its navigable character. It is a fact well known in this country that the irrigation plants and systems of the citizens of Mexico on the Concho River have been very greatly increased within the last few years and subsequent to the time when the large canal systems had been built on the Rio Grande in New Mexico and Colorado. This is also true, I am informed, of every other stream which lies within the Republic of Mexico and which is confluent of the Rio Grande.

"I am of the opinion that the desire for this treaty originated in the interest of, or has become part of, a movement for the erection of what is to be known as an 'international dam,' to be located near the city of El Paso, Tex., and from information I have received I am impressed with the thought that this

SAGAMORE HILL. Nov 12th 1911

My dear Col. Twitchell,

Half the officers and men of my regiment came from New Mexico; and no Colonel ever commanded a finer fighting regiment. Moreover they were just as good on the march and in camp as in battle; these men of the plains and mountains, bold riders and skilled riflemen, who faced danger unflinchingly and endured hardship uncomplainingly. I regard the fact that I was one of them as well-nigh the most precious heritage I can leave my children.

Sincerely yours
Theodore Roosevelt
Sometime Colonel 1st U.S.V. Cavalry

Fac-simile of Letter from Col. Theodore Roosevelt relative to Personnel of Roosevelt's Rough Riders

ment reclamation service, and the delivery of a limited amount of water from the Rio Grande to lands lying within the valley of the Rio Grande, in the vicinity of Ciudad Juarez, in the state of Chihuahua. The determination on the part of the United States Reclamation Service to construct the Elephant Butte project, and the determination of the issues involved in the suit of the government against a private corporation seeking to build a dam and reservoir at the same point, entailed a great loss upon private foreign capital enlisted in the enterprise and for which the general government has failed to make any reparation whatever. In the course of two years following his appointment, Governor Otero, ably assisted by the attorney general of the territory,[445] and aided by several legislative

movement is mainly promoted by individuals residing in the city of El Paso, and Ciudad Juarez, on the opposite bank of the river, who own and control large bodies of land sought to be irrigated by this international dam, hence it is intended to prevent the storage of the waters of the Rio Grande in New Mexico, in order that they may flow unobstructed to this international dam. Now, it is certain that the construction of this international dam will not benefit a single citizen of the entire Territory of New Mexico. The dam, if constructed, being below the southern boundary of said Territory, the waters impounded by said international dam would flow back upon and submerge some of the cultivated land of New Mexico. Therefore, the construction of the international dam can not in any way benefit the people of the Territory of New Mexico, but on the contrary it would be decidedly injurious. It is a fact, however, that during the winter months of each year large quantities of water flow unused to any great extent by the people along this river, and I am fully satisfied that sufficient water flows down the Rio Grande during the winter months and the flood waters of the stream, to fill many large reservoirs in New Mexico, as well as the international dam, if constructed, at El Paso, consequently there appears to be no good reason why people of the Territory of New Mexico should not be allowed to provide for their own prosperity by the construction of reservoirs in the Rio Grande Valley, notwithstanding the erection of the international dam, but I must earnestly protest against the execution of a treaty which shall deprive the people of New Mexico of the right of impounding the waters which belong to them alone, but at the same time award the right of impounding the water by others, and especially citizens of a foreign country."—*Letter* of Governor M. A. Otero, September 27, 1897, to John Sherman, secretary of state.

[445] Edward Leland Bartlett was a native of the state of Maine. He received his education in the common schools and at Bowdoin college in that state. His parents removed to the state of Kansas when General Bartlett was quite young. He studied law and was admitted to the practice in Kansas where he became quite a prominent figure in the social, professional, and business circles of the state. He removed to New Mexico shortly after the advent of the railways, and with his wife made Santa Fé his home. He filled the office of adjutant general of New Mexico for several years; held many offices of honor and trust; was solicitor general under Governor L. Bradford Prince, and attorney general under Governor Otero. Few men of recent years living in New Mexico enjoyed the social popularity accorded to General and Mrs. Bartlett. The latter founded the Woman's Board of Trade of Santa Fé, was a

enactments, reported the refunding of large amounts of territorial bonded indebtedness at lower rates of interest. The same wise policy was pursued in adjusting the bonded indebtedness of a number of the counties of the territory, particularly those which had defaulted in the payment of interest. In this manner the credit of the territory was made stable and that of the counties restored.

The principal event of territorial, not to say national, importance occurring during the administration of Governor Otero was the organization of New Mexico's quota of THE SPANISH-AMERICAN WAR volunteers for the war with Spain. President McKinley, on April 23, 1898, issued his proclamation calling for 125,000 troops to serve two years. On the same day the adjutant general of New Mexico, Col. H. B. Hersey, received notice from Washington that the territory would be called upon for cavalry for service in Cuba. Two days later Governor Otero received word from the secretary of war asking what New Mexico could do in the matter of recruits for a regiment of western cowboys for special service, and announcing that Captain Leonard Wood, U. S. A., would be the commander of such troops, with Theodore Roosevelt as lieutenant-colonel.[446] Governor Otero

---

leader in all social affairs at the capital during the most brilliant period of army life at Ft. Marcy, the headquarters of the military district, and made her influence and prestige the agency by which much was accomplished in the civic uplift of the capital city. General Bartlett's was a most charming personality; a gifted after-dinner speaker; a story teller of rare accomplishments, he was always a welcome guest at every entertainment. He was the founder of the New Mexico Bar Association and served as its secretary from its beginning until his death, which occurred at Santa Fé in 1904.

[446] The names of the men from New Mexico in Roosevelt's Rough Riders, as obtained from the muster-out roll, are as follows:

FIELD AND STAFF.—Major, Henry B. Hersey, Santa Fé; first lieutenant and quartermaster, Sherrard Coleman, Santa Fé; first lieutenant and adjutant, Thomas W. Hall, Lake Valley, who, on account of disability tendered his resignation, which took effect Aug. 1, 1898.

HOSPITAL CORPS.—First lieutenant, James A. Massie, Santa Fé; steward, James B. Brady, Santa Fé; steward, Herbert J. Rankin, Las Vegas.

Troop A.—Corporal, George L. Bugbee, Lordsburg; Troopers: Fred W. Bugbee, Lordsburg, wounded in head in battle of San Juan, July 1, 1898; William Bulzing, Santa Fé; Lawrence E. Huffman, Las Cruces; Harry B. Pierce, Central City.

Troop B.—Troopers: James A. Butler, Albuquerque; Robert Day, Santa Fé; John C. Peck, Santa Fé; George C. Whittaker, Silver City; Wallace W. Wilkerson, Santa Fé.

Troop D.—Troopers: Charles H. Green, Albuquerque; Emmett Laird. Albuquerque; Eugene Schupp, Santa Fé; Theodore Folk, Oklahoma City, N. M. (?), transferred to Troop K, U. S. V. C., May 11, 1898.

Troop E.—Captain, Frederick Muller, Santa Fé; first lieutenant, Wm. E.

immediately replied that New Mexico's quota, which was limited to 340 men, would be ready for service and offered an additional number of cavalry and a battalion of mounted riflemen. He also ten-

Griffin, Santa Fé; first sergeant, John S. Langston, Cerrillos; quartermaster sergeant, Royal A. Prentice, Las Vegas; sergeant, Hugh B. Wright, Las Vegas; sergeant, Albert M. Jones, Santa Fé; sergeant, Timothy Breen, Santa Fé, wounded in arm and sent to hospital July 1, 1898; sergeant, Berry F. Taylor, Las Vegas; sergeant, Thomas P. Ledgwidge, Santa Fé; corporal, Harmon H. Wyncoop, Santa Fé, wounded in line of duty and sent to hospital July 2, 1898; returned to duty Sept. 4, 1898; corporal, James M. Dean, Santa Fé, wounded in left thigh, in line of duty, and sent to hospital June 24, 1898; returned to duty Aug. 31, 1898; corporal, Richard C. Connor, Santa Fé; corporal, Ralph E. McFie, Las Cruces; trumpeter, Arthur J. Griffin, Santa Fé; trumpeter, Edward S. Lewis, Las Vegas; blacksmith, Robert J. Parrish Clayton; farrier, Grant Hill, Santa Fé; saddler, Joe T. Sandoval, Santa Fé; wagoner, Guilford B. Chapin, Santa Fé. Troopers: Roll Almack, Santa Fé; John M. Brennan, Santa Fé; José M. Baca, Las Vegas; George W. Dettamore, Clayton, wounded in line of duty and sent to hospital July 1, 1898; Freeman M. Donovan, Santa Fé; William T. Easley, Clayton; Frank D. Fries, Santa Fé; Joseph Gisler, Santa Fé; James P. Gibbs, Santa Fé; William R. Gibbie, Las Vegas; John D. Harding, Socorro; Daniel D. Harkness, Las Vegas; William M. Hutchinson, Santa Fé; William H. Hogle, Santa Fé; Arthur J. Hudson, Santa Fé; John Hulskotter, Santa Fé; William S. E. Howell, Cerrillos; Thomas L. Hixon, Las Vegas; Thomas B. Jones, Santa Fé; Charles W. Jacobus, Santa Fé; Charles E. Kingsley, Las Vegas; Frank Lowe, Santa Fé; Dan Ludy, Las Vegas; Hyman S. Lowitski, Santa Fé; James E. Merchant, Cerrillos; William J. Moran, Cerrillos; Samuel McKinnon, Madrid; Charles E. McKinley, Cerrillos, wounded in the head in line of duty, July 1, 1898; Charles F. McKay, Santa Fé; Frederick A. McCabe, Santa Fé; John C. McDowell, Santa Fé; Amaziah B. Morrison, Las Vegas; Lloyd L. Mahan, Cerrillos; Henry D. Martin, Cerrillos; Otto F. Menger, Clayton, wounded in left thigh, July 1, 1898; William C. Munger, Santa Fé; Adolph F. Nettleblade, Cerrillos; Thomas Roberts, Golden; John E. Ryan, Santa Fé, wounded July 1, 1898; Ben F. Seaders, Las Vegas; Arthur V. Skinner, Santa Fé; William C. Schnepple, Santa Fé; Edward Scanlon, Cerrillos; William W. Wagner, Bland; George Wright, Madrid; Charles W. Wyncoop, Santa Fé; George W. Warren, Santa Fé; first sergeant, William E. Dame, Cerrillos, discharged per O. reg. Comds. Aug. 10, 1898; sergeant, Frederick C. Wesley, Santa Fé, wounded July 1, 2 or 3, 1898, and discharged on account disability August 26, 1898.

Troop F.—Captain, Maximiliano Luna; first lieutenant, Horace W. Weakley; second lieutenant, William E. Dame, transferred from Troop E to F; First sergeant, Horace E. Sherman; sergeants: Garfield Hughes, Thomas D. Hennesy, William L. Mattocks, James Doyle, George W. Armijo, wounded in action June 24, 1898; Eugene Bohlinger, Herbert W. King; corporals: Edward Donnelly, John Cullen, Edward Hale, Arthur P. Spencer, John Boehnke, Albert Powers, wounded in action July 1, 1898; Wentworth S. Conduit. Farriers: Ray V. Clark, wounded July 1, 2 or 3, 1898; Charles R. Gee; wagoner, Jefferson Hill; bugle, Arthur L. Perry, wounded July 1, 2 or 3, all from Albuquerque. Troopers: H. L. Albers, wounded in action June 24, 1898; Ed. J. Albertson, wounded in action June 24, 1898; James Alexander, Charles G. Abbott, James F. Alexander, James S. Black, Robert Z. Bailey, wounded in action June 24, 1898; Jeremiah Brennan, Walter C. Burris, John H. Bell, William O. Cochran, Calvin G. Cleland, Edward C. Conley, Willard M. Cochran, Charles C. Cherry, Louis Dougherty, John C. De Bohun, William Farley, Will Freeman, wounded July 1, 1898; Henry M. Gibbs, wounded July 1, 1898; William D. Gallagher;

dered his own services, if needed. When it was known that such a regiment was to be organized, Governor Otero was deluged from all parts of New Mexico with applications to join. Four troops was

Samuel Goldberg, wounded July 1, 1898; Otis Glessner, John D. Green, Albert C. Hartle, wounded June 24, 1898; Charles O. Hopping, George Hammer, Stephen A. Kennedy, Charles E. Leffert, Guy M. Lusk, John M. Leach, Thomas Martin, John B. Mills, Herbert P. McGregor, wounded July 1, 1898; William E. Nickell, Otto W. Nesbitt, George W. Newitt, John W. Neal, Charles A. Parmelee, Frank T. Quier, Millard L. Raymond, Harry B. Reed, Clifford L. Reed, wounded June 24, 1898; Charles L. Renner, Edwin L. Reynolds, Arthur L. Russell, Adolph T. Reyer, Albert Rogers, Lee C. Rice, Lewis E. Staub, William G. Shields, Arthur H. Stockbridge, George H. Sharland, John G. Skipwith, James B. Sinnett, Edward Tangen, Norman O. Trump, George E. Vinnedge, Louis C. Wardwell, Paul Warren, Charles E. Watrous, Beauregard Webber, John Walsh, Thomas J. Wells, all from Albuquerque. Private, James Douglass, Albuquerque, discharged on account of disability. Second lieutenant, Maxwell Keyes, Albuquerque, promoted to adjutant, August 1, 1898. Privates transferred from Troop F to I, May 12, 1898: Joseph F. Flynn, Hedrick Ben Goodrich, Walter Hickey, Michael Hogan, Harry Bruce King, George M. Kearney, Lewis Larson, John McCoy, Charles A. Nehmer, Leo G. Rogers, Hyman Rafalowitz, Edwards John Spencer, Carl J. Schearnharst, Jr., Frank Temple, Joseph L. Bawcom.

Troop G.—Captain, William H. H. Llewellyn, Las Cruces; first lieutenant, John Wesley Green, Gallup; second lieutenant, David J. Leahy, Raton, on sick list from July 1 to Sept. 3, from wound received in San Juan battle; first sergeant, Columbus H. McCaa, Gallup; quartermaster sergeant, Jacob S. Mohler, Gallup; sergeants: Rolla A. Fullenweiden, Raton; Matthew T. McGehee, Raton; James Brown, Gallup; corporals: Henry Kirah, Gallup; James D. Ritchie, Gallup; Luther L. Stewart, Raton, wounded in battle June 24; John McSparron, Gallup, wounded July 1; Frank Briggs, Raton; Edward C. Armstrong, Albuquerque; William S. Reid, Raton; Hiram E. Williams, Raton; farrier, George V. Haefner, Gallup; saddler, Frank A. Hill, Raton; wagoner, Thomas O'Neal, Springer; trumpeters, Willis E. Somers, Raton; Edward G. Piper, Silver City.

Troopers: Alvin C. Ash, Raton, absent from July 1 to Sept. 7, on account of wound received in battle; Arthur T. Anderson, Albuquerque; Robert Brown, Gallup; John J. Beissel, Gallup; Cloid Camp, Raton; Marion Camp, Raton; Thomas F. Cavanaugh, Raton, wounded June 24; Michael H. Coyle, Raton; wounded June 24; Frederick Fornoff, Albuquerque; Wm. C. Gibson, Gallup; John Goodwin, Gallup; John Henderson, Gallup, absent July 1 to Sept. 2 on account of wounds; Albert John Johnson, Raton; John S. Kline, San Marcial; Bert T. Keeley, Lamy; Elias M. Littleton, Springer; Fred P. Meyers, Gallup. reduced from first sergeant to trooper on account of absence caused by wound received in battle July 1; Daniel Moran, Gallup; John Noish, Raton; T. W. Phipps, Bland; Archibald Petty, Gallup; George H. Quigg, Gallup; Walter D. Quinn, San Marcial; Wm. Radcliff Gallup; Richard Richards, Albuquerque; Robert W. Reid, Raton, absent from June 24 to Sept. 8 on account of wounds; George Roland, Deming, wounded June 24; Charles M. Simmons, Raton; Charles W. Shannon, Raton; Neal Thomas, Aztec; Grant Travis, Aztec; Richard Whittington, Gallup; Lyman E. Whited, Raton; William D. Wood, Bland; Clarence Wright, Springer. George D. Swan, Gallup, and Frank M. Thompson, Aztec, discharged on account of disability. Samuel T. McCulloch, Springer, deserted from camp at Tampa, Fla., Aug. 4, 1898. Eugene A. Lutz, Raton, died in yellow fever hospital, Aug. 15, 1898. Henry J. Haefner, Gallup, killed in battle June 24. Transferred to Troop I May 12: Sergeant, Henry J. Arendt,

Officers, Roosevelt's Rough Riders

New Mexico's quota and these were mustered at Santa Fé within eight days after the presidential proclamation had been issued.

The major portion of the regiment, which was mobilized at San Antonio, Texas, was composed of men from Arizona, New Mexico,

Gallup; troopers, Henry C. Bailie, Gallup; Wm. J. Love, Raton; Evan Evans, Gallup; Oscar W. Groves, Raton; Wm. H. Jones, Raton; John H. Tait, Raton; Harry Peabody, Raton; Alexander McGowan, Gallup; John Brown, Gallup; Joseph B. Crockett, Raton.

Troop H.—Captain, George Curry, Tularosa; first lieutenant, William H. Kelly, Las Vegas; second lieutenant, Charles L. Ballard, Roswell; sergeants, Nevin P. Gutilius, Tularosa; Oscar de Montell, Roswell; Michael C. Rose, Silver City; Nova A. Johnson, Roswell; corporals, Marton M. Morgan, Silver City; Arthur E. Williams, Las Cruces; Frank Murray, Roswell; Morgan O. Llewellyn, Las Cruces; James C. Hamilton, Roswell; Charles P. Cochran, Eddy; trumpeter, Gaston R. Dehumy, Santa Fé; farrier, Robert L. Martin, Santa Fé; wagoner, Taylor B. Lewis, Las Cruces.

Tropers: Albert B. Amonette, Roswell; Columbus L. Black, Las Cruces; John B. Bryan, Las Cruces; Frank Bogardus, Las Cruces; Thomas F. Corbett, Roswell; John S. Cone, Tularosa; Abel B. Duran, Silver City; Jose L. Duran, Santa Fé; Lewis Dorsey, Silver City; George B. Doty, Santa Fé; Frederick W. Dunkle, Las Vegas; Arthur L. Douglas, Eddy; Frank A. Eaton, Silver City; Augustus C. Fletcher, Silver City; James B. Grisby, Deming; James M. Hamilton, Deming; Leary O. Herring, Silver City; Robert C. Houston, Hillsboro; Amandus Kehn, Silver City; Frank H. Lawson, Las Cruces; John Lannon, Hillsboro; Thomas A. Mooney, Silver City; George F. Murray, Deming; Charles H. Ott, Silver City; Lory H. Powell, Roswell; Norman W. Pronger, Silver City; John F. Pollock, Tularosa; Alexander M. Thompson, Deming; Daniel G. Waggoner, Roswell; Curtis C. Waggoner, Roswell; Patrick A. Wickham, Socorro. Sergeant, William L. Rynerson, Las Cruces, discharged by reason of special order U. S. army. Transferred to Troop I May 12, 1898: Sergeant, John V. Morrison, Santa Fé; privates, Robert E. Lee, Donahue; C. Darwin Casad, Las Cruces; Numa C. Frenger, Las Cruces; George Schafer, Pinos Altos; Morris J. Storms, Roswell. Edwin Eugene Casey, Las Cruces, died in hospital at Camp Wyckoff, N. Y., Sept. 1, 1898. Samuel Miller, Roswell, deserted from Tampa, Fla., June 28, 1898.

Troop I.—First lieutenant, Frederick W. Wientge, Santa Fé; first sergeant, John B. Wylie, Fort Bayard; sergeant, William H. Waffensmith, Raton; corporals: Numa C. Frenger, Las Cruces; William J. Sullivan, Silver City; William J. Nehmer, Silver City; Hiram T. Brown, Alburquerque; trumpeter, Robert E. Lea, Doña Ana.

Troopers: Horton A. Bennett, Tularosa; Frank C. Brito, Pinos Altos; Charles D. Casad, Mesilla; George M. Coe, Albuquerque; Henry C. Davis, Santa Fé; Thomas P. Dolan, Pinos Altos; Robert W. Denny, Raton; Evan Evans, Gallup; Joseph F. Flynn, Albuquerque; John R. Gooch, Santa Fé; Oscar W. Groves, Raton; Hedrick Ben Goodrich, Santa Fé; Ernest H. Hermeyer, Roswell; William H. Jones, Raton; Cal Jopling, La Luz; Harry B. King, Raton; Alexander McGowan, Gallup; Ben F. T. Morris, Raton; Roscoe E. Moore, Raton; Harry Peabody, Raton; John P. Roberts, Clayton; Louis Larsen, Santa Fé; Carl J. Schearnhorst, Jr., Santa Fé; George Schafer, Pinos Altos; John H. Tait, Santa Fé; John L. Twyman, Raton; Harry B. Wiley, Santa Fé; Roy O. Wisenberg, Raton.

Troop K.—First sergeant, Frederick K. Lee, Organ. Troopers: William C. Bernard, Las Vegas; Stephen Easton, Santa Fé, transferred to Troop H, July 15, 1898. Private, Joseph L. Duran, Santa Fé.

Oklahoma, and the Indian Territory. The others came from universities, aristocratic social clubs, and other eastern and New England sources. This regiment was a perfect exemplification of the adaptability of the average American citizen. Its service in Cuba demonstrated its equality with veteran troops and few trained men in the regular service showed more soldier-like qualities. The regiment had a reputation for bravery, based upon the supposition that every man was a cowboy direct from the short-grass country, and that reputation had to be sustained. The fact remains, however, that Roosevelt's Rough Riders were clerks, stenographers, college men, coal diggers, bar tenders, printers, railroad men, mechanics, hack drivers, miners, prospectors, and a respectable contingent of "punchers" of the true southwestern plains variety. That they were rough riders or very shortly became such no doubt exists. That they were good soldiers every one admits. It may seem disappointing to dispel the romance built around a regiment of which New Mexico and the whole nation is so proud, but it is only justice to the average young American to state the truth. It made no difference to the man who hurried to Santa Fé to enlist in this noted regiment what had been his calling. He responded to the call of the president of the nation in time of need; he performed his duty and whether cow puncher, coal digger, college graduate, or millionaire, he became a soldier, by his action under fire, commanding the admiration of the world.

On May 29, 1898, the regiment broke camp at San Antonio, Texas, and proceeded by rail to Tampa, Florida, the trip consuming four days. On the morning of June 14th, the troops boarded the transport Yucatan bound for Cuba. One troop, Captain George Curry's, was left behind. It was announced by Colonel Wood that only three troops from New Mexico would be permitted to take part in the campaign in Cuba, Muller's, Llewellyn's, and Curry's or Luna's. To settle the matter Captains Luna and Curry flipped coins to determine whose command should be the third troop. Captain Luna won. For nearly a week prior to the departure of the Rough Riders transports loaded with troops steamed to the southwestward escorted by battleships, cruisers, and torpedo boats. On the morning of June 22, the troops began disembarking at Daiquiri, a small port near Santiago de Cuba, after this and other nearby points had been

1880 TO 1912

shelled for the purpose of dislodging the enemy if found in that locality.

Before leaving the United States the regiment had been brigaded with the First and Tenth Regular Cavalry under Brigadier General Young, as the Second Brigade, BATTLE OF LAS GUASIMAS which, with the First Brigade, formed a division of cavalry commanded by Major General Joseph Wheeler, a Confederate veteran of the Civil War. On the afternoon following the landing, the troops were ordered forward through a narrow trail, arriving after midnight at Siboney.

On the 24th, the order to advance was given. All unexpectedly the enemy opened fire. During the advance Henry J. Haefner, of Troop G, fell, mortally wounded. His comrades dragged him behind a tree where he was propped up and, asking for his canteen and rifle, which were handed to him by Colonel Roosevelt in person, he began loading and firing, which he kept up until the line moved forward. He died during the engagement.

The enemy was soon driven from his position when a temporary lull followed on the American right. The firing was soon resumed. A perfect hail of bullets swept high over the advancing line. A rapid charge by the American forces and the enemy abandoned his position in the skirmish line. The loss to the Rough Riders was eight killed [447] and thirty-four wounded; the 10th cavalry lost one killed and ten wounded. This engagement, the first on Cuban soil, is known officially as the battle of Las Guasimas.

The day following the engagement at Las Guasimas saw the regiment moving forward a distance of about two miles. During this period General Young was stricken with the fever and Colonel Wood succeeded to the command of the brigade, leaving Colonel Roosevelt in command of the regiment. On June 30th, orders were received for the march against the city of Santiago, but it was not until the middle of the afternoon that the regiment took its position in the marching columns.

About six o'clock, on the following morning, July 1, the fighting

---

[447] The officers and men in the New Mexican troops killed and wounded at Las Guasimas were, killed: Haefner, Troop G; wounded: Corporal James M. Dean, Troop E; Sergeant George W. Armijo, Troop F; H. L. Albers, Troop F; Ed. J. Albertson, Troop F; Robt. Z. Bailey, Troop F; Albert C. Hartle, Troop F; Clifford L. Reed, Troop F; Luther L. Stewart, Troop G; Michael H. Coyle, Troop G; Robert W. Reed, Troop G; George Roland, Troop G.

began at El Caney. Throughout the entire campaign the enemy used smokeless powder, which rendered detection of his location well nigh impossible. Soon after the beginning of the artillery engagement, Colonel Roosevelt was ordered to march his command to the right and connect with General Lawton — an order impossible to obey. The heat was intense and many of the men began to show signs of fatigue early in the day; the Mauser bullets drove in sheets through the trees and chapparal; the bulk of the enemy's fire appeared to be practically unaimed, but his zone of fire covered the entire battlefield. Although the troopers were scattered far apart, taking advantage of every scrap of cover, man after man fell dead or wounded. Soon the order came to move forward and support the regulars in the assault on the hills in front. Waving his hat aloft, Colonel Roosevelt shouted the command to charge the hill on the right front. At about the same moment the other officers gave similar orders, and the exciting rush at "Kettle Hill" began. The first guidons planted on the summit of the hill, according to Roosevelt's account,[448] were those of Troops G, E, and F of his regiment, under their captains, Llewellyn, Luna, and Muller. Says Edward Marshall:[449]

"The situation was, perhaps, the most exasperating that troops can be called upon to endure. Several regiments were ahead of the Rough Riders, among them the Ninth regular cavalry. This regiment was made up of colored men. I counted its lieutenant-colonel, Hamilton, among my dearest friends, and was with his regiment more than I was with any other during the days preceding our departure from Tampa. I know those negro troopers to be brave men, and indeed they proved themselves to be among the best soldiers in the United States army, later that same day. Colonel Hamilton was

[448] *Story of the Rough Riders*, Edward Marshall, New York, 1899: "Perhaps it is not quite accurate for me to call this part of the battle 'The Charge up San Juan Hill,' for this hill was not properly a part of San Juan Hill. It was a little preceding hill, and between it and San Juan Hill proper was a slight depression containing a shallow pond of water. At the top of this first hill were some large sugar kettles, so that the regiment named it 'Kettle Hill,' so that in speaking of it, they could differentiate between it and San Juan Hill. Here the Rough Riders put in what was by all odds the hardest part of their fighting, and lost far more men than they did after they began to ascend the eminence after which the battle is named. The bullets flew like bees around those kettles and like bees they were very busy. But they were not gathering honey. They were spilling blood. Not less than a dozen of the Rough Riders went down here and several were killed outright."

[449] *Story of the Rough Riders*, p. 185.

Officers First Territorial U. S. Volunteer Infantry

killed in the charge up San Juan Hill, and his men lost very heavily. They were black heroes every one of them. But they lay ahead of the Rough Riders and did not attempt to go beyond their orders which were to lie there and wait for some one to tell them, from General Shafter, to go ahead. That Colonel Hamilton was as brave a man as Colonel Roosevelt and as brave a man as any man ever was I do not doubt for a moment, but his regular army training did not stand him in good stead that day. He had been a soldier all his life and he did what a soldier is supposed to do — he did what he was told to do. He had been told to wait. Colonel Roosevelt understood the necessity of obeying orders as well as Hamilton did, but Colonel Roosevelt had not been turned into a fighting machine by years of discipline, and he thought for himself when his superior officers failed to think for him. Colonel Hamilton did not. So Colonel Roosevelt was the hero of San Juan Hill, although the opportunity for heroism had been before Colonel Hamilton just as long as it had been before Colonel Roosevelt. Hamilton doubtless saw the necessity for the charge as soon as Roosevelt did, but he waited for some superior to see it too. Roosevelt waited a reasonable time for his superiors to see it, and then he went ahead on his own hook.

"There was great confusion at this time," says Colonel Roosevelt, "the different regiments being completely intermingled — white regulars, colored regulars, and Rough Riders. We were still under a heavy fire and I got together a mixed lot of men and pushed on from the trenches and ranch houses which we had just taken, driving the Spaniards through a line of palm trees and over the crest of a chain of hills. When we reached these crests we found ourselves overlooking Santiago."

Here Colonel Roosevelt was ordered to advance no further, but to hold the hill at all hazards. With his own command were all the fragments of the other five cavalry regiments at the extreme right. The Spaniards had fallen back upon their supports, and our troops were still under a very heavy fire from rifles and artillery. Our artillery made one or two efforts to come into action on the infantry firing line, but their black powder rendered each attempt fruitless. In the course of the afternoon the Spaniards made an unsuccessful attempt to retake the hill. A few seconds of firing stopped their advance and drove them into cover of the trenches. The troops slept that night on the hill-top, being attacked but once before daybreak — about 3 A. M. — and then for a short time only.[450] At dawn

---

[450] In the attack on San Juan Hills the American forces numbered about 6,600; the Spanish, about 4,500. The American total loss in killed and wounded was 1,071. The fighting continued July 2, but most of the Spanish firing

the attack was renewed in earnest. The Spaniards fought more stubbornly than at Las Guasimas, but their ranks broke when the Americans charged.

The firing was energetically resumed on the morning of the 3rd, but during the day the only loss to the Rough Riders was one man wounded.[451] At noon the order to stop firing was given, and a flag of truce was sent in to demand the surrender of the city. For a week following, peace negotiations dragged along. Failing of success, fighting was resumed shortly after noon on the 10th, but it soon became evident that the Spaniards did not have much heart in their work. About the only Rough Riders who had any chance for active work were the men with the Colt automatic guns and twenty picked sharp-shooters who were on the watch for guerillas. At noon on the 11th, the Rough Riders, with one of the Gatlings, were sent over to the right to guard the road to El Caney; but no fighting was necessary, for the last straggling shot had been fired by the time they arrived.

On the 17th, the city of Santiago formally surrendered; two days later the entire division was marched back to the foot hills west of El Caney where it went into camp with the artillery. Here many of the officers and men became ill, and as a rule less than fifty present were fit for any kind of work. All clothing was in rags; even the officers had neither socks nor underwear. The authorities

---

proved harmless. During the day the American force in the trenches was increased to about 11,000, and the Spaniards in Santiago to upwards of 9,000. As the day wore on, the fight, though raging fitfully at intervals, gradually died away. The Spanish guerillas caused the Americans much trouble, however. They were located, usually, in the tops of trees, and as they used smokeless powder, it was almost impossible to locate and dislodge them. These guerillas showed not only courage but great cruelty and barbarity. They seemed to prefer for their victims the unarmed attendants, the surgeons, the chaplains and hospital stewards; they fired at the men who were bearing off the wounded in litters, at the doctors who came to the front, and at the chaplains who held burial services.

[451] The officers and men of the New Mexican troops or New Mexicans in other troops in the regiment killed or wounded in the three days' fighting were: Fred. W. Bugbee, Troop A; Timothy Breen, Troop E; Harmon Wynkoop, Troop E; George W. Dettamore, Troop E; Charles E. McKinley, Troop E; Otto Menger, Troop E; John E. Ryan, Troop E; Frederick Wesley, Troop E; killed in action, H. C. Green, Troop E; John F. Robinson, Troop E; wounded, Albert (Perry) Powers, Troop F; Ray V. Clark, Troop F; Will Freeman, Troop F; Henry M. Gibbs, Troop F; Samuel Goldberg, Troop F; Herbert P. McGregor, Troop F; Arthur L. Perry, Troop F; Lieut. David J. Leahy, Troop G; John McSparren, Troop G; Alvin C. Ash, Troop G; John Henderson, Troop G; Fred. P. Myers, Troop G; Geo. Roland, Troop G.

at Washington, misled by reports received from some of their military and medical advisers at the front, became panic stricken and hesitated to bring the army home, lest it might import yellow fever into the United States. The real foe, however, was not yellow fever but malarial fever. The awful conditions surrounding the army finally led to the writing of the historic "Round Robin," in which the leading officers in Cuba showed that to keep the army in Santiago meant its complete and objectless ruin. The result was immediate. Within three days orders came to put the army in readiness to sail for home. The order came on the 6th of August. The next morning the Rough Riders sailed on board the Miami, which reached Montauk point, the east end of Long Island, New York, on the afternoon of the 14th. The following day the troops disembarked and camped at Camp Wyckoff. The regiment remained here until September 15th, when its members received their discharges and returned to civil life.[452]

[452] There was not a single member of this regiment from New Mexico, officer or enlisted man, who went to the war with any idea of "freeing Cuba" from Spanish domination. The one idea was "Remember the Maine." The contempt which the New Mexican had for the Cubans and the Cuban soldiers was not changed after experiences had with them on the island. Captain Dame, promoted for bravery in action, says of the Cubans: "The Cubans are but little better than the buzzards that hover over the army. They have done no fighting that I know of but never miss an opportunity to rob the soldiers' packs which have been thrown aside by the sick and by the soldiers just before going into battle. They are to be found in the rear and around the commissary but not in the front. In fact they are human buzzards and I would not trust them any more than I would a coyote."

H. B. Hersey was born at Williamstown, Vermont, July 28, 1861. He received his education at the state normal school and at Norwich University. Immediately following his graduation Major Hersey entered the weather service of the United States government. He came to Santa Fé, New Mexico, in 1891, where he filled the position of weather observer and section director of the territorial weather service. In June, 1897, he was commissioned adjutant-general of New Mexico by Governor Otero. He assisted materially in the organization of the New Mexican contingent of the first U. S. Volunteer Cavalry, and, resigning his commission as adjutant-general, was commissioned major in the famous regiment. He did not accompany the regiment to Cuba, but was left in command of the Rough Rider troops which remained at Tampa. After the war he resumed his position in the U. S. Weather Bureau, and has devoted much time to aviation, representing the government in several important experimental flights.

James A. Massie, M. D., is a native of Guelph, Canada, where he was born in 1870. He received his professional education at the University of Toronto, where he studied six years, afterward serving in the hospitals in Toronto, Glasgow, Edinburg, London, Dublin, and Birmingham. He filled the position of chief surgeon for the Anchor line of steamships plying between Glasgow, Bombay, and Calcutta for several years. In 1897, he visited the United States and decided to

Under the second call for volunteers in the war with Spain a regiment popularly known as the "Big Four," was organized from Arizona, New Mexico, Oklahoma, and Indian Territory, and became

become a citizen, filing his first papers shortly after his arrival in the last named year. On May 2, 1898, he was appointed surgeon of the First U. S. V. Cav., with the rank of major, by Governor Otero. Returning from the war, he renewed the practice of his profession at Santa Fé, N. M., where he is now living.

Frederick Muller, captain of Troop E, First U. S. Vol. Cav., was born in Wurtemberg, Germany, in 1862, and received his education in the best technical schools of the German empire. In 1879, he came to America, locating in New York. He enlisted, in 1882, in the 6th U. S. Cavalry, with which regiment he served five years. He was with Troop D under General Crook and General Miles in the campaigns against the Apache chief, Geronimo. Securing his discharge from the army, he traveled extensively and finally located at Santa Fé, in 1888, where he was engaged in the general merchandizing business. Prior to the war with Spain he filled several county and district offices with credit. He held a commission as major in the New Mexico National Guard, and resigned to accept the captaincy of Troop E of the Rough Rider regiment. Returning from the war, where he served with great gallantry, he was appointed receiver of the United States land office at Santa Fé, a position he has held under three national administrations. He is now a resident of Santa Fé, N. M.

William Elkins Griffin was born in Santa Fé, N. M., in 1867. He is the son of William W. Griffin, deceased, for many years president of the First National Bank of Santa Fé. He received his education in the public schools of Santa Fé and at Swarthmore college; also at Pierce business college in Philadelphia. At the breaking out of the war with Spain he was an officer in the New Mexico National Guard, resigning to accept a commission as first lieutenant of Troop E, 1st U. S. Vol. Cav. He was quartermaster of the regiment and served in Cuba during the campaign. Returning from the war, he entered the banking business and is now cashier of the United States Bank and Trust Company, Santa Fé, N. M.

Sherrard Coleman, second lieutenant of Troop E, 1st U. S. Vol. Cav., is a native of Virginia, having been born at Jardone Castle, Louisa county, in August, 1864. He received his education in the public schools of his native state. He was in the service of the Chesapeake and Ohio Railway Company for a period, and in 1887 came to Santa Fé, where he took a position with the government as special agent of the Interior Department and was assigned to the Court of Private Land Claims. In his native state he was an active member of the national guard, and was an officer in the New Mexico National Guard at the breaking out of the war. He was commissioned second lieutenant of Troop E, April 25, 1898. After the war he served in the Philippine Islands.

Maximiliano Luna was born in Los Lunas, New Mexico, June 16, 1870, and received his education at the Jesuit college in Las Vegas and at Georgetown college, District of Columbia. In the 29th legislative assembly he filled the position of chief clerk of the council. In 1893-4 he was probate clerk of his native county; at the election in the last named year he was elected sheriff and held the office two years. In 1896, he was elected a member of the house of representatives of the 33d legislative assembly of New Mexico and was chosen speaker of that body. In 1897, he was commissioned captain of Troop F, New Mexico National Guard, which command he resigned to accept the commission of captain of Troop F, 1st U. S. Vol. Cav. He commanded his troop in Cuba, where he served with gallantry. Returning from the war, he remained a short time in New Mexico, when he received a commission as lieutenant in the regular army; was sent to the Philippine Islands, and was drowned while crossing a river, at the time serving on the staff of Major-General H. W. Lawton. Captain

Prominent New Mexican Educators
1. Dr. W. E. Garrison. 2. Hiram Hadley. 3. Dr. F. H. H. Roberts. 4. Dr. C. M. Light. 5. Brother Botulf. 6. Dr. E. McQueen Gray. 7. Col. James W. Willson.

a part of the First Army Corps, commanded by Major-General James H. Wilson, and the Third Brigade, commanded by Brigadier-General John N. Andrews. The New Mexico battalion went to Whipple Barracks, where it was joined by the Arizona contingent, and two months later proceeded to Camp Hamilton, Lexington,

Luna was a young man of great promise. The 34th legislative assembly passed appropriate resolutions covering his career and death. The territory placed a memorial in bronze and a bust of this lamented young man in the capitol. He was the son of Tranquilino Luna, delegate to the 47th congress, and a distinguished son of the Luna family.

H. W. Weakley was born in Shelbyville, Indiana, in 1868. He received his education in the public schools of his native city. Coming to the west, he was a citizen of Colorado, where he joined the 2d regiment of national guards of that state, belonging to the Chaffee Light Artillery. He was a druggist by profession. He received a commission as first lieutenant in the 1st U. S. Vol. Cav. from Governor Otero, and served with Troop F in Cuba. He was a gallant soldier.

Lieutenant Maxwell Keyes, of Troop F, was a grandson of Lucien B. Maxwell. His father was Major Keyes, of the U. S. army. Lieutenant Keyes was born at Ft. Sill, Indian Territory, in 1873. He received his education at the college of the Christian Brothers, St. Louis, Mo. His father was a major in the 3d U. S. Cavalry, and his residence followed that of his father, who was stationed at a number of army posts throughout the west and northwest. He was second lieutenant of Troop F, commissioned by Governor Otero. After the end of the Cuban campaign, where he served with his regiment, he continued in the service of the United States, and served in the Philippine Islands. He was regimental adjutant, 1st U. S. Vol. Cavalry.

William Henry Harrison Llewellyn, captain of Troop G, was born in Monroe, Green county, Wisconsin, September 9, 1851. The family is of Welsh origin, and was founded in America by Dr. Joseph Llewellyn, the great-grandfather of Major Llewellyn, who emigrated to the United States from Wales and settled in Westmoreland county, Virginia. His son served in the War of 1812, as did also his son, who was a lieutenant and fought at Sackett's Harbor. Joseph Llewellyn also served as an officer of the 2d Kansas Cavalry in the Civil War. After the war he removed to Iowa. His son, William H. H. Lewellyn, was educated in the common schools of Iowa, and at Tabor college in that state. In 1866, when fifteen years of age, he went to Montana and engaged in gold mining at Trinity Gulch. In the spring of 1881, Major Llewellyn came to New Mexico as agent for the Mescalero Apache Indians. The following year he was made agent for the Jicarilla tribe of Apaches and, in 1883, removed them to the Mescalero reservation. He held this position five years and was signally successful as the government's representative in this arduous service. In 1885 he formed a partnership with Rynerson and Wade, prominent attorneys in southern New Mexico, and began the practice of the law. Later he served as live stock agent for the Atchison, Topeka and Santa Fé Railroad Company, a position held by him for eight years. He was a delegate to the republican national convention of 1884, in 1900, and in 1904. In 1896, he was elected a member of the 32d legislative assembly and was chosen speaker of the house of representatives. He received his commission as captain of Troop G from Governor Otero, and served with great gallantry and distinction at Las Guasimas and San Juan Hill. He has also enjoyed the confidence and personal friendship of Colonel Roosevelt, who, when president, appointed him United States attorney for New Mexico, a position he held until 1907. He served as a member of the lower house from Doña Ana county in the 35th legislative assembly, and was appointed district

Kentucky, where the regiment was completed by the arrival of the volunteers from Oklahoma and the Indian Territory. Thence they were ordered to Camp Churchman, Albany, Georgia, where the fortunes of war caused them to remain, until finally mustered out in 1899. The regiment was made up entirely of western men, from every trade and profession. Each company enlisted up to 140 and 150 men, and by selection, was brought down to the required number.[453]

The officers and enlisted men of these regiments, returning to their homes in New Mexico, soon became identified with the political and

attorney for the eighth district by Governors Otero and Mills. At the first state election, November, 1911, Major Llewellyn was chosen a member of the first legislature of the state, representing the fifteenth legislative district — Doña Ana county, New Mexico.

John Wesley Green was born in Newark, Ohio, in 1861. At the age of seventeen he was attached to the signal corps of the regular army, serving under Captain Allen in New Mexico. At the age of nineteen he was a sergeant in the 15th U. S. Inf., in which regiment he served five years in the campaigns against the Apaches in Arizona, New Mexico, and western Texas. In later years he held several offices of honor and trust in Bernalillo county and was marshal of the town of Gallup. He received his commission as first lieutenant of Troop G from Governor Otero. After his return from the war he lived in New Mexico for several years, and was superintendent of the territorial penitentiary, appointed by Governor George Curry.

David J. Leahy was born in La Salle county, Ill., in 1867. He was educated in the northern Indiana normal school at Valparaiso. He came to New Mexico in 1891, and became principal of the schools at Springer, and later was chosen school superintendent of Colfax county. When the call came for volunteers he organized the contingent from Raton, thirty-two in number, and was commissioned a second lieutenant of Troop G by Governor Otero. He received a gunshot wound on July 1, 1898, in the charge up San Juan Hill. Returning from the war, he was appointed clerk of the district court of the sixth judicial district, with headquarters at Alamogordo, when that district was created and Justice E. A. Mann chosen as presiding judge. This position he held until appointed United States attorney by President Roosevelt, on the retirement of Major W. H. H. Llewellyn, in 1907. Captain Leahy was a delegate to the republican national convention in 1904. At the first state election, in 1911, he was elected judge of the fourth judicial district.

[453] Company E of this regiment was mustered in Alburquerque, July 8, 1898, its officers being: Captain, John Borrodaile; first lieutenant, L. H. Chamberlin; second lieutenant, L. A. McCrea; first sergeant, A. H. Norton; Q. M. S., John Munn.

Company F was mustered in Las Vegas. Officers: Captain, W. C. Reid; first lieutenant, W. O. Morrison; second lieutenant, A. Luntzel; first sergeant, E. Sporleder; Q. M. S., G. C. Palmer.

Company G was mustered at Santa Fé, July 13, 1898. Officers: Captain, William Strover; first lieutenant, Page B. Otero; second lieutenant, J. P. S. Mennet; first sergeant, B. Pearce; Q. M. S., T. F. Kyle.

Company H was mustered at Las Cruces, July 17, 1898. Officers: Captain, A. B. Fall; first lieutenant, J. W. Catron; second lieutenant, N. E. Bailey; first sergeant, John G. Bagley; Q. M. S., Llewellyn A. Herring.

business life of the territory. Several of them received commissions from the president of the United States and served their country most loyally and acceptably in the Philippine Islands.

The nominee of the republican party for delegates at the election held in 1898 was Don Pedro Perea of Bernalillo county, son of Don José Leandro Perea, a noted citizen of the territory during the last half of the nineteenth century. Mr. Perea was elected over Harvey B. Fergusson, receiving 18,722 votes to 16,659 for his opponent. Very little was accomplished in congress by Mr. Perea, and in the year 1900, Bernard S. Rodey, republican, was elected over Octaviano A. Larrazolo, democrat, receiving 21,557 votes while Mr. Larrazolo, who was not heartily supported in some of the counties where his party was in heavy majority, received only 17,857.

DELEGATES IN CONGRESS

In 1902, Mr. Rodey [454] was again elected delegate to congress, on this occasion defeating the leader of the democratic party, Harvey B. Fergusson, by 9,696 votes, the largest majority ever given a candidate for delegate in the history of New Mexico. He was a candidate for a third term as delegate, responding to what was believed to be an almost overwhelming sentiment among the people. Through the power of Miguel A. Otero, governor, and the connivance of sev-

[454] Bernard Shandon Rodey was born in the County Mayo, Ireland, in 1856. In 1862, he was brought to Canada by his parents, and subsequently resided with them in the state of Vermont, close to the Canada line; his parents were farmers. At an early age he left the farm and located in Boston, where he took employment as a clerk and stenographer. In the spring of 1881, he came to Alburquerque as private secretary and stenographer in the office of the general manager of the Atlantic and Pacific Railroad Company. Later he was appointed official court reporter in the second judicial district under Judge Joseph Bell. He now finished his reading of the law, was admitted, and began a general practice, in which he was very successful for a number of years. He was a member of the council from Bernalillo county in the twenty-eighth legislative assembly, and had much to do with the framing and passage of the educational bills under which the Agricultural college was established. He was chosen delegate to the fifty-seventh and fifty-eighth congresses. Defeated for the nomination for delegate to the fifty-ninth congress by William H. Andrews, he ran independent and received 3,419 votes out of a total of 43,011 cast at the election, Mr. Andrews being chosen, receiving 22,305 to 17,125 for George P. Money, democrat. In 1906, although the leaders of the republican party in New Mexico regarded him as a bolter, President Roosevelt appointed him judge of the district court of Porto Rico. This was the first time in the history of the United States that a citizen of a territory was nominated by the president for a position upon the federal bench. Mr. Rodey held this position until the close of the Roosevelt administration, when he was appointed United States attorney for one of the districts in the territory of Alaska, a position which he now holds.

eral prominent leaders of the republican "machine," he was defeated in convention.[455] Practically all of Mr. Rodey's efforts while delegate were given over to an earnest endeavor to procure statehood for New Mexico. Rather than see New Mexico fail in being admitted he consented to the enactment of a law by the fifty-ninth congress, originating in the house of representatives, which provided for the admission of Oklahoma and Indian Territory as one state under the name of Oklahoma, and of New Mexico and Arizona as one state under the name of Arizona. The congressional committee which reported this bill, itself controlled and dominated by influences in the New England and Eastern states at heart opposed to the admission of any western territories, with Albert J. Beveridge, the representative of a clique of eastern senators, a senator from the state of Indiana, well aware that the territories of New Mexico and Arizona would never consent to a union which had been happily dissolved in the early "sixties," believed that this bill would be a solution of the "Statehood for the Territories" promise contained in the republican national platforms. There was no possible excuse for keeping Oklahoma out of the Union, and every member of congress, with the possible exception of Mr. Rodey, knew that when the referendum to the people of New Mexico and Arizona was had, either one or both of the territories would decline to come into the

---

[455] There appeared to be no opposition to the re-nomination of Mr. Rodey; there was none among the people; he was bitterly opposed, however, by Governor Otero and his office-holding cabinet; Rodey had never been popular with the leaders of the party; he was entirely too popular, as the results of two elections had demonstrated, with the people; he also claimed as friend Frank A. Hubbell, at that time chairman of the republican territorial committee and a political rival of Governor Otero. The fight was directed as much against Mr. Hubbell as it was against Mr. Rodey; in fact, if Mr. Rodey would have given his consent to the naming of a chairman of the territorial committee, to be named by Governor Otero, he would have received the nomination. This he declined to do, believing that Mr. Hubbell was in great measure responsible for the success which had been his at the polls. On the Saturday evening prior to the territorial convention, which was held at Alburquerque, September 12, 1904, every newspaper of consequence in New Mexico was of opinion that the nomination of Mr. Rodey was assured. A proposition was made to Mr. Rodey looking to the elimination of Mr. Hubbell as a factor in territorial politics. It was steadfastly declined. The convention met with Col. J. Francisco Chaves as chairman. When the time arrived for the nomination of candidates, Major W. H. H. Llewellyn, United States attorney, who had asked of Mr. Rodey the privilege of placing his name before the convention, arose and nominated William H. Andrews. Delegations which had been instructed for Mr. Rodey voted for Mr. Andrews, who received the nomination, and at the election which followed the latter was elected, after a contest which in many ways was as spectacular as it was scandalous.

Pens used by President William Howard Taft in Signing the Enabling Act of 1910

Union under the conditions imposed by the bill.[456] At the general election of 1906, New Mexico voted for and Arizona against the proposition, the vote in Arizona being 16,265 against and 3,141 for this hypocritical and iniquitous measure.

Mr. Andrews, possessed of great political acumen and experience, having been prominent and active in the politics of the state of Pennsylvania before his coming to New Mexico, enjoying the confidence of and assisted by the support of the entire congressional delegation of the state of Pennsylvania, not to mention the personal friendship and sympathy of Senator Matthew S. Quay, proceeded immediately to outline a plan for his own political career in New Mexico. Laboring day and night for his constituents, Mr. Andrews, in his capacity as delegate, has had no superior in the congress of the United States. Again chosen as the standard bearer of his party in 1906, he defeated Octaviano A. Larrazolo [457] by a vote of 22,915 to 22,649, William P. Metcalf, socialist, receiving 211 votes. In

[456] The vote on the question of joint statehood with Arizona was:

COUNTIES	YES	NO	MAJORITY YES	MAJORITY NO
Bernalillo	2,623	1,087	1,536	
Chaves	1,279	308	971	
Colfax	12,177	793	1,384	
Doña Ana	1,512	290	1,222	
Eddy	871	278	593	
Grant	980	696	284	
Guadalupe	611	608	3	
Lincoln	519	500	19	
Luna	207	170	37	
McKinley	259	89	170	
Mora	1,606	394	1,212	
Otero	795	351	444	
Quay	572	267	305	
Rio Arriba	676	2,028		1,362
Roosevelt	1,020	91	929	
Sandoval	518	438	80	
San Juan	763	122	641	
San Miguel	2,503	1,688	815	
Santa Fé	697	1,447		750
Sierra	307	418		111
Socorro	2,040	455	1,595	
Taos	822	1,070		257
Torrance	551	275	276	
Union	705	731		26
Valencia	1,582	122	1,460	
Total vote	26,195	14,735	13,966	2,506

Majority for joint statehood, 11,460.
Arizona defeated the measure by its adverse vote, the total majority against the proposition being: 1,664.

[457] The election of 1906 was contested by Mr. Larrazolo, but was decided adversely to him by the congress of the United States. Gross frauds and irregularities were charged against the republican party managers in the conduct of the election in the counties of Colfax, Valencia, Socorro, and Torrance.

1908, again opposed by Mr. Larrazolo, he was successful in the contest, receiving 27,605 votes to 27,217 for Mr. Larrazolo, and 1,056 for Mr. Metcalf, socialist. This was the largest vote until that time ever polled in New Mexico.

The statehood question, ever paramount in the public mind in New Mexico, was advocated at Washington by Mr. Andrews and the bills for the admission of the territory, introduced by him, were handled so adroitly that finally, after more than sixty years of effort, an enabling act for New Mexico and Arizona, admitting them into the Union as separate states, became law. In the securing of appropriations for public buildings and other matters of vital importance to the people, he easily surpassed any delegate in congress from New Mexico. His energy, activities, and unusual performances in this regard awakened in the hearts of some of the leaders, who had made it possible for him to defeat Mr. Rodey, the same hostility and, for the same reasons, coupled with charges against him concerning matters with which the people of New Mexico had had no part or concern, prior to the election of 1908, made him the target for as much political abuse as was ever hurled upon a political adversary of opposing faith or principles. Notwithstanding this pre-convention villification from republican leaders and some of the newspapers of that faith, Mr. Andrews secured the nomination and was successful in the election which followed.[458]

The political policies and methods advocated and pursued by Governor Otero are susceptible of adverse criticism. This can not be said of his administration so far as the business interests of New Mexico were involved. Calling to his aid in the conduct of his office the business methods with which he was familiar and in which he had received a thorough education, he accomplished much for the welfare of New Mexico. To him may be attributed the estab-

---

[458] William H. Andrews, delegate to congress from New Mexico in the fifty-ninth, sixtieth, and sixty-first congresses, was born in Youngsville Pennsylvania, January 14, 1842. He was educated in the common schools of his state. During the years of his residence in Pennsylvania he was an influential factor in the politics of the state, having been chairman of the republican state committee in 1889 and 1890; he was a state senator, 1895-98, and again in 1901-02. He came to New Mexico in the last named year and became interested in mining enterprises in Sierra county. He promoted and secured the necessary capital for the construction of the Santa Fé Central Railway. He was chosen a member of the legislative council of the 35th legislative assembly, representing the counties of Socorro and Sierra. He is now (1912) a resident of the city of Alburquerque.

lishment of the office of traveling auditor, an official, whose duties well performed by Governor Otero's first appointee, have been responsible for the excellent condition of the finances of New Mexico and the official conduct of the revenue collecting officers. The passage of the law creating the office of insurance commissioner is attributable to him. During his administration, the growth and prosperity of New Mexico were almost phenomenal. The building of railroads was re-commenced and capital not only sought but made extensive investments. The passage of the Reclamation Act by congress and the commencement of construction of the great governmental irrigation enterprises in the southwest occurred during his administration. The several legislative assemblies, dominated by the party of his faith, reposing confidence in his recommendations as voiced in his several bi-ennial messages, passed many laws beneficial to the people. Influenced by memorials and urged in reports to the secretary of the interior, the congress of the United States created additional judicial districts. New counties were formed; an asylum for the blind located at Alamogordo was provided; a miners' hospital was established at Raton, and other institutions in which the people were interested were either created or enlarged through liberal legislative appropriations.

During his term of office the territory was visited by two presidents of the United States. The visit of President Roosevelt, in May, 1903, on his way to the Pacific coast, was a matter of great pride and satisfaction to the citizens of the territory. At Santa Fé and Alburquerque, where the presidential party made stops of several hours, elaborate receptions were tendered and the warm enthusiasm with which the chief executive of the nation was greeted, as well as the memorable words he spoke at both places, made the occasion historic.

At the time of his retirement from the governorship, New Mexico was never in a more prosperous condition. In all lines of industry there was great activity. The territorial finances were in most excellent condition. From the first year of his incumbency, Governor Otero labored for a reduction of the bonded debt of the territory. In this he was very successful.[459] The end of each fiscal year during

---

[459] J. H. Vaughn, territorial treasurer, *Report* for 1905: "In my report covering the year ending June 1, 1904, the statement showing the Territorial

his administration found a balance of respectable proportions in the treasury of New Mexico.[460]

Governor Otero was not an applicant for re-appointment. He

bonded debt to be $1,163,900 included an issue of casual deficit bonds to the amount of $101,800, for the redemption of which bonds funds were then on deposit with the National Bank of Commerce in New York, but the bonds at that time had not been paid and returned to this office for proper cancellation. Since the date of that report these bonds have been paid and regularly canceled.

In the past year the bonded debt has been decreased by the following payments: Casual deficit bonds, $101,800; capitol building bonds, $196,000; provisional indebtedness bonds, $13,000; certificate of indebtedness, $100; total, $310,900, leaving the outstanding bonded indebtedness on June 1, 1905, $853,-000, and on this same date there were balances in bond sinking funds available to redeem outstanding bonds aggregating the sum of $60,164.94, making the net Territorial debt $792,835.06.

The revenues have been ample to meet all current expenses provided for under the appropriations, and the general financial condition and credit of the Territory is most gratifying.''

[460] *Ibid.*, 1906, p. 75: Balance, June 1, 1904, $439,493.86; Receipts during year 1904 to June 1, 1905, $641,924.60; Total to be accounted for, $1,081,418.46; Payments during year, $900,503.36; Balance, June 1, 1905, $180,915.10. Receipts during 1906, $749,854.41; Payments during year, $620,769.51; Balance June 1, 1906, $310,150.60.

The total assessed valuation of property for purposes of taxation for the year 1903 was $39,596,951.79; for 1904, $39,297,239.53; for 1905, $40,085,405.93.

A uniform system of accounting was put into force by the traveling auditor in all of the county treasurers's offices. In 1905, the receipts of all the counties in taxes from all sources and the disbursements were:

COUNTY	BALANCE JANUARY 1, 1905	RECEIPTS FOR YEAR	DISBURSEMENTS FOR YEAR	BALANCE JANUARY 1, 1906
Bernalillo	$ 28,382.50	$222,806.94	$205,935.15	$45,254.29
Chaves	16,657.67	142,151.25	97,794.97	61,013.95
Colfax	43,675.27	125,923.31	127,878.92	41,719.66
Doña Ana	30,751.26	61,086.87	74,990.39	16,847.74
Eddy	36,275.88	103,499.24	98,112.79	41,662.33
Grant	48,837.62	105,119.23	105,422.03	48,534.82
Guadalupe	14,989.38	32,017.66	30,568.34	16,438.70
Lincoln	19,434.35	44,195.49	43,208.45	20,421.39
Luna	17,083.30	61,954.76	55,888.80	23,149.26
McKinley	19,450.81	45,418.62	41,612.45	23,256.98
Mora	17,048.41	38,690.87	37,602.89	18,165.15
Otero	19,717.00	78,490.30	87,345.70	10,861.60
Quay	9,116.56	26,329.99	25,941.58	9,504.97
Rio Arriba	15,639.25	36,758.46	35,769.57	16,628.14
Roosevelt	3,154.81	39,918.58	24,115.50	18,957.89
Sandoval	7,060.09	22,261.64	13,591.58	15,730.15
San Juan	5,290.07	33,680.50	28,163.60	10,806.97
San Miguel	39,277.91	154,252.62	152,772.75	40,757.78
Santa Fé	15,176.70	76,573.89	69,756.24	21,994.35
Socorro	23,197.87	86,159.59	77,173.99	32,183.47
Sierra	15,693.97	39,377.81	41,095.10	13,976.68
Taos	16,583.68	24,568.26	27,445.37	13,706.57
Torrance		10,728.66	3,734.77	6,993.89
Union	37,959 25	62,192.31	62,545.48	37,606.08
Valencia	42,380.74	57,803.70	53,200.14	46,984.30
Total	$542,834.35	$1,731,969.31	$1,621,665.55	$653,157.11

William J. Mills, last Governor of the Territory of New Mexico

had filled the executive chair a greater continuous period than any
other governor, Mexican or American, with the exception of Manuel
Armijo. Early in the year 1906, Herbert J. Hagerman [461] was appointed to succeed him. When nominated, the new governor was scarcely known to the people of New Mexico. It was generally believed that he had been chosen for the express purpose of assisting in uncovering frauds in the sale and disposal of lands acquired by the territory under the Fergusson Act of June 21, 1898. Influences at Washington, investigations by special agents, and reports from disinterested but prominent citizens had convinced the secretary of the interior, Ethan Allen Hitchcock, that great frauds in the location and disposal of coal lands to corporations and special interests, to some of which the territorial officials and their friends were parties, had been committed. The correction of these abuses was determined upon by the Washington authorities. It was generally believed, and afterward claimed by Governor Hagerman, that the policies inaugurated by him in New Mexico, were outlined by President Roosevelt himself.

ADMINISTRATION OF GOVERNOR HERBERT J. HAGERMAN

Governor Hagerman, utterly unfamiliar with the methods in vogue in New Mexican politics, except by hearsay, was not qualified by experience with the talent necessary for the carrying out of the policies which were initiated by him immediately after his inauguration. A man of lofty ideals, sincere in his efforts and looking to the correction of the abuses which he believed existed in the public affairs of the territory, he lacked tact in carrying his plans into effect Shortly after assuming the duties of executive, several in-

---

[461] Herbert J. Hagerman was born in Milwaukee, Wisconsin, December 15, 1871. His father, J. J. Hagerman, was the leading factor in the modern development of the agricultural resources of the Pecos valley in southeastern New Mexico. Governor Hagerman received his early education in the public schools and graduated from Cornell University. After graduation he entered the diplomatic service of the United States and served as assistant secretary under two American ambassadors to Russia, Ethan Allen Hitchcock and Charlemagne Tower. Resigning this position, he was appointed governor of New Mexico early in 1906, and served until 1907, when he resigned. Since that time he has lived at Roswell, New Mexico, where he has been active in the social, business, and political life of the community. In 1911, he was largely instrumental in the organization of the progressive republican forces of the territory, and, in great measure, contributed to the defeat of Holm O. Bursum, republican candidate for governor, and other candidates on the regular republican state ticket.

cumbents of territorial and district offices remained filled by appointees of Governor Otero, every one of whom had received his appointment by recommendation of the republican machine, of which Holm O. Bursum was the chief, being at the time the chairman of the republican territorial central committee. Governor Hagerman also made the serious mistake of consenting to the retention in office of James Wallace Raynolds,[462] secretary of New Mexico, and also the secretary of the committee of which Mr. Bursum was the chairman. Mr. Raynolds was the business partner of Governor Otero, and the office of secretary of the territory was the most lucrative of any in New Mexico, whether filled by presidential or gubernatorial selection. He was possessed of more than ordinary ability and his counsel was generally followed by the leaders of the republican party. In education and general knowledge he was superior to any of the prominent politicians with whom he was associated and whose confidence he enjoyed. What Governor Hagerman needed was a man in the position held by Mr. Raynolds in whom he could repose entire political confidence. This opportunity came to him, but he ignored the chance, which, if it had been taken advantage of, would have made his career successful and would have so firmly established him in the good graces of the president that the charges which the leading politicians subsequently brought against him either would never have been made, or, if urged, would have had no force at the White House.[463]

[462] James Wallace Raynolds was born in Pueblo, Colorado, in 1873. He was the son of Jefferson and Martha (Cowan) Raynolds, his father being one of the most prominent of the early bankers of New Mexico. In 1891, he entered the Massachusetts Institute of Technology, graduating in the mining engineering course in 1896. Returning to New Mexico, he was appointed assistant secretary of the territory, under George H. Wallace. Upon the death of the latter, in 1901, he was appointed secretary by President McKinley. In December of the same year, he was re-appointed by President Roosevelt, and again in 1905, he was named for the position. The biennial report and legislative *Manual* of 1905, prepared by him, is one of the most comprehensive official publications ever issued in the history of the territory. He was appointed superintendent of the penitentiary, April 23, 1909. He was the secretary of the territorial republican central committee and demonstrated his shrewdness as a politician and a leader. His health failing him, he was compelled to resign the position of superintendent of the penitentiary, and, while being taken to Excelsior Springs, Mo., for treatment, died on the train, near Tucumcari, New Mexico, March 10, 1910.

[463] Governor Hagerman received a letter from the president, Theodore Roosevelt, intimating that he would be much gratified if Governor Hagerman could find a suitable position in his power to give to Captain George Curry, who

The chairman of the republican central committee at the time of Governor Hagerman's induction into office was Holm O. Bursum, who occupied the position of superintendent of the territorial penitentiary. Together with Solomon Luna,[464] national committeeman, and Secretary Raynolds he was without doubt the most potent factor in the republican organization. One of the first acts of the new

was at the time in the Philippine Islands in the service of the government, but desirous of returning to New Mexico. Captain Curry had been an officer in the Rough Rider regiment; had served with great distinction in military as well as civil positions in the Philippines and was a personal friend of the president. Governor Hagerman consulted with none of his intimates relative to this request from Colonel Roosevelt, and, in reply, wrote the president that he knew of nothing within the governor's patronage which he could offer Captain Curry unless possibly it might be the position of game warden. Educated in diplomatic circles, it is almost inconceivable that Governor Hagerman could have failed to recognize the force of this "presidential desire." It is small wonder, in the light of political events occurring just at that time — the republican national convention of 1908 was in sight — that President Roosevelt gave ear to the charges that would enable him to replace Governor Hagerman with a man who at least knew the rudiments of the American game of politics. No one in New Mexico, familiar with the political situation at the time and cognizant of the trend of territorial affairs, but knows that had Governor Hagerman intimated to the president that the secretaryship of New Mexico was a fitting reward for Captain Curry's services to his country, Mr. Raynolds would have been succeeded by Captain Curry, Governor Hagerman would have had the benefit of counsel from one of the most astute politicians in New Mexico, and the political history of the territory and the first state campaign would not be written as found in this volume.

[464] Solomon Luna was born at Los Lunas, New Mexico, October 18, 1858. He is the son of Don Antonio José Luna and Isabella (Baca) Luna, whose ancestors came to New Mexico early in the eighteenth century. Mr. Luna received his education from private tutors and graduated from St. Louis University. Having reached his majority, he followed in the line of his distinguished ancestors and became prominently interested in the sheep raising industry, a business which he has since continued to follow. In point of numbers and invested capital Mr. Luna is the most heavily interested of any sheep owner in New Mexico. In 1881, was consummated his marriage to Miss Adelaida Otero, daughter of Don Manuel Rito Otero, a representative of the old and distinguished family of that name. She is the granddaughter of Judge Antonio José Otero, whom General Kearny elevated to the bench of New Mexico at the time of the American occupation of the territory. Mr. Luna has been called to public office many times by the people of his native county of Valencia; in 1885, he was elected probate clerk; in 1892, he held the office of sheriff, and in 1894, he was chosen treasurer and collector of the county, a position which he has held ever since. In 1896, he was chosen the member of the national republican committee from New Mexico, a position he still holds. Mr. Luna has been a great power in the republican politics of New Mexico. In business life, he is considered to be one of the ablest and shrewdest. He is vice-president of the First National Bank of Alburquerque and is heavily interested in the business life of that city. Mr. Luna, more than any other, is responsible for the nomination of H. O. Bursum as the republican candidate for governor at the election in November, 1911, which resulted in his defeat. The great majority of his party believed that Mr. Luna should have been the candidate for governor and, with Mr. Luna's

executive was the removal of Mr. Bursum [465] as superintendent of the penitentiary and the appointment of Arthur Trelford, an expert prison manager who had been employed in some capacity at the Federal prison near Fort Leavenworth, Kansas, to the position.

This action on the part of the governor resulted in arraying against him and his administration whatever influence could be exerted by the friends of Mr. Bursum and the active machine politicians of the territory. The appointment of a non-resident to the superintendency of the penitentiary was unwise and impolitic; but the governor had ideas of prison management and proposed to introduce them in New Mexico. From a business standpoint and as an experiment in criminology and prison discipline it is possible that the appointment was made with some wisdom; the fact remained, however, that New Mexico and her people as a whole were not interested in such experiments. There were plenty of men in New Mexico capable of filling the position. It failed signally in making a good impression upon the politicians, who regarded the prison superintendency as a political office. The governor, having investigated the accounts of Mr. Bursum as superintendent, charged him with

---

consent, he would have been the unanimous choice of the first republican state convention, but Mr. Luna had espoused the cause of Mr. Bursum, had given his word to support him, and it was not possible, as Mr. Luna believed and declared, for him to become the gubernatorial candidate.

[465] Holm O. Bursum was born in Fort Dodge, Iowa, in 1867. His parents were Frank O. and Maria (Hilton) Bursum, who came to the United States from Norway in 1865. Until nine years of age, Mr. Bursum lived on a farm; during two years he attended the public schools of Fort Dodge and, at the age of eleven, began to earn his own living. When thirteen he came to New Mexico and located at Raton, just as the Santa Fé railroad was being constructed through New Mexico. He removed to San Antonio, New Mexico, and later to Ft. Wingate, where he was employed in freighting and contracting. Shortly afterward, he became interested in mining, sheep raising, and other enterprises. In 1894, he was elected sheriff of the county of Socorro. In 1898, he served in the upper house of the legislative assembly, where he established a reputation as a legislator of marked ability. In 1899, he was appointed superintendent of the penitentiary by Governor Otero and held the position until removed by Governor Hagerman. In 1904, he was chosen chairman of the republican central committee, a position which he filled with great credit, leading his party to victory in every campaign down to and including the election of delegates to the constitutional convention of 1910. As a delegate to the republican national convention of 1908, he was largely responsible for the incorporation into the republican national platform of that year of the definite statehood plank, upon which the statehood movement so largely depended for its final outcome in congress. The position taken by Mr. Bursum and the manner in which he handled the situation at the Chicago convention of 1908 is an episode of historic importance. Mr. Bursum was the republican candidate for the position of governor of the state at the election in November, 1911, and was defeated.

Members of the Constitutional Convention of 1910
1. H. M. Dougherty. 2. Nestor Montoya. 3. Charles Springer. 4. Francis E. Wood. 5. Charles A. Spiess. 6. Granville A. Richardson. 7. J. M. Cunningham

having converted to his own use large sums belonging to the penitentiary earnings fund. This shortage was strenuously denied by Mr. Bursum, who, under protest, paid over large sums of money to the territory, and afterward, by means of an act of the legislature permitting suits to be brought against the territory in certain cases, secured a judgment acquitting him of the charges made. The fact still remained, however, that the financial conduct of the affairs of the penitentiary had not been of a character which appealed with any force to the business men of the territory, and although the judgment was in Mr. Bursum's favor, there were a great many who did not hesitate to condemn his management and held him to blame on that account. This belief became very apparent at the election of 1911, when Mr. Bursum was defeated for the governorship, being compelled to make a defensive campaign, owing to the charges which were made against his management of the penitentiary. This belief, whether warranted by the facts or not, was the principal factor in accomplishing his defeat at the polls.[466]

---

[466] Frederick H. Pierce, chairman of the board of penitentiary commissioners at the time of this investigation, says:

"After Mr. Hagerman became governor, he wished to have some changes made in the methods of managing prisoners, of which Mr. Bursum did not approve; and differences arose between them growing out of this. Then the governor, without consulting the board of commissioners, who, under the law, were responsible for the administration of the penitentiary, brought an accountant from Colorado to examine the accounts and make a report to him. No complaint had been made by the governor to the board of anything wrong in the accounts or the management; nor did the Colorado accountant call upon the board for any assistance or explanation. He made a report to the governor, claiming that there was a shortage in the accounts, and that Mr. Bursum owed the territory for money received and not paid over. Thinking there might be some error or oversight in his books, Mr. Bursum immediately deposited in the territorial treasury the first amounts claimed, until the matter could be looked up. Then further amounts were claimed, amounting to several thousand dollars. This Governor Hagerman demanded that Mr. Bursum should immediately pay over. Mr. Bursum insisted that the report was not correct; that his accounts were not short, and asked for time to have them examined by some other expert, in order that he might answer the charges and show the real facts. This was refused, and the governor notified him that if the amount claimed was not paid into the treasury at once, he would cause suit to be brought for it against his bondsmen. Mr. Bursum was at the time chairman of the republican central committee in the midst of a campaign. Realizing the injury to his party that would be caused by the bringing of such a suit, however unfounded, which could not possibly be decided before the election, Mr. Bursum, while insisting that he did not owe the territory anything, paid over the amount that was claimed by the attorney general, amounting, with that already paid, to upward of four thousand dollars. He paid this under protest that he did not owe it. He was then removed from office by Governor Hagerman.

"There was no way under the law at that time by which the territory could

At the session of the assembly in 1907, Governor Hagerman had a stormy experience. The friends of Mr. Bursum and the republican machine were in power in the lower house and were able to pass an act through the legislature by which it was possible to have a judicial determination of the differences between the governor and Mr. Bursum in the matter of the financial management of penitentiary affairs. Governor Hagerman was charged by his enemies with procuring votes in the upper house in the matter of confirmations of his appointees by promises of appointments made to several of the members of that body. If this was so he was only pursuing a course which had become a custom in New Mexico, practiced for many years, whether under republican or democratic administrations.

As has been stated, it was the general belief that Governor Hagerman had been appointed with the purpose of correcting abuses in the matter of the disposal of the public lands. The interior department and the department of justice were particularly active in their efforts in uncovering frauds and meting out punishment to wrongdoers in this regard. Grand juries in several of the judicial districts made investigations on charges preferred by the United States attorney and a number of indictments of influential and prominent men were returned. The territory was flooded with special agents and one or two assistant attorneys general made investigations.

Prior to the appointment of Governor Hagerman a contract or agreement had been made with the officers of the territory for the purchase of certain public lands, in which a corporation known as the Pennsylvania Development Company had become interested. The payment of the purchase price for these lands and the execution

---

be sued, or by which a person paying money to the territory, even though under protest, could have the matter investigated in court; but afterward a law was passed during Mr. Hagerman's administration, and without objection from him, allowing suit to be brought by any one under such circumstances. Mr. Bursum brought such a suit. The case was publicly tried in court, with the result that, after hearing all the testimony that any one had to offer, the court found that instead of Mr. Bursum owing the territory the money he had paid, the territory owed him at the time over a hundred dollars. Judgment was given ordering the money he had paid to be refunded. During the trial the court appointed the territorial traveling auditor to make a report on the facts, which he did after a thorough investigation of the original entries, invoices and vouchers, books of the penitentiary and territorial treasury, and sworn testimony of witnesses. He was the official charged by law with the examination of the accounts of county officers and private banks, and had been himself appointed by Governor Hagerman.''

and delivery of the deeds therefor had not been consummated. Governor Hagerman, convinced that the agreement was lawful, completed the transaction by delivering the deeds and accepting the money from the representative of the company, Willard S. Hopewell. There is no doubt that Governor Hagerman was actuated only by the best of motives in thus handling the matter, but, in the condition of affairs political then existing, there was no good political reason for his not declining to assume any responsibility and to have referred the claimants to the courts for such remedy as the law provided. His action gave his political enemies the opportunity they sought, and, coloring his acts as much as possible with charges of looked for support from democratic sources, it was no difficult matter to make out a case which would convince the average political reformer, sent out from Washington for purposes of investigation, that the act of the executive was contrary to all precedent and blameworthy in the extreme.[467] In the month of April, 1907, like a

---

[467] Alvord W. Cooley, an assistant attorney general, made the report or furnished the president with the information which culminated in a request for Governor Hagerman's resignation. Immediately after it was made known to Governor Hagerman that his resignation was desired, a great many messages were sent from New Mexico urging the president to reconsider his action. Others were sent protesting against any such action on the part of the president. In a letter to Governor Hagerman, relative to these telegrams and the reasons which had been potent in bringing about the request for his resignation, President Roosevelt said:

"The White House, Washington, D. C.
"May 1, 1907.

"My Dear Mr. Hagerman:
"Mr. Gifford Pinchot has presented me your telegram to him in which you ask that it be brought to my personal attention, stating that hundreds of people have sent telegrams to the president protesting against my accepting your resignation, and stating furthermore that if my action in requesting your resignation is not revoked it will be a calamity to the territory, and that if I will reconsider this action you are positive I will see the injustice and unwisdom of it from every point of view.

"This renders it necessary for me to write you very plainly. You made, as I am informed, a good secretary of legation at the court of St. Petersburg. All that I have heard of your private life is to your credit. Furthermore, I believe you have done certain excellent things while you were governor, and of course, I will permit nothing good you have done to be undone. But I must add that on the whole I think you have been an unsatisfactory governor and that your removal from the position is imperatively demanded. If it were not for my knowledge of your previous career and of your standing in private life, and my consequent reluctance to believe that your motives were as improper as certain of your acts would indicate, I should have removed you instead of requesting your resignation. I have not thought it necessary to go into any matters as to which there was any chance of controversy, and the department of justice has been as anxious as I have to show you all consideration and to

bolt from the blue, at least to the friends of the governor, came a request from the president of the United States for the governor's resignation. A large number of the loyal friends of the executive

resolve every doubt in your favor. Assistant Attorney General Cooley in his report purposely omitted, as he informed me, the inference which he believes ought legitimately to be drawn from the facts, that in the land grant transaction, wherein I believe your conduct was blameworthy, you were actuated in your improper and presumably unlawful action, by your desire to secure the aid of certain democratic politicians in a faction fight. I decided that in this matter I would give you the benefit of the doubt. Also as to your action in appointing six members of the legislative council to lucrative positions, although there seems to be no doubt that it amounted to the bartering of offices by you in return for legislative support. As for the hundreds of people who have telegraphed me on your account I cannot say that I have seen all the telegrams, but I have seen a great many of them. I have received an even larger number from persons in New Mexico who protested against your retention in office, and have also received numerous statements that neither set of telegrams is really spontaneous. There has been no single instance in which the appointment of Mr. Curry as your successor has not received hearty commendation.

"I have found that it was unnecessary to consider anything save Assistant Attorney General Cooley's letter from the department of justice. This sets forth the state of facts which your personal explanation when before me in no way relieved, and which makes it impossible in my judgment to retain you in office unless I am content to abandon all idea of holding public officers in New Mexico, or indeed elsewhere, to any proper standard of official conduct. This report of the department of justice related to your delivery of certain deeds to the Pennsylvania Development Company. It appears that the grant of land was agreed to before you became governor, was on its face grossly fraudulent and that the transaction could not be completed save by your action, made with full knowledge of its fraudulent character. An investigation into the matter of these New Mexico land grants had been made by the secretary of the interior and submitted to congress. Chairman of the Committee of Public Lands of the House of Representatives, Hon. John F. Lacey, on May 17, 1906, wrote to the secretary of the interior that the proposed grant would be a violation of law, the particular grant being, as the secretary of the interior officially stated, in all essential respects the same as the grant you consummated. You state that this document was never officially called to your attention, but it appears that you certainly had knowledge of it when you acted, and it further appears that the commissioner of public lands, in view of the report, expressed his unwillingness to deliver the deeds to the representative of the Pennsylvania Development Company, Mr. Hopewell. It was his business and not yours, and you could only act in his absence, though of course, you could have removed him if you had been willing to remove him, for refusing to take the improper and fraudulent action, which in his absence, you took in his behalf. You, however, obtained an opinion from the attorney general (the same gentleman whom the newspapers report as now organizing meetings to ask for your retention in office), which opinion, Mr. Cooley rightly stigmatizes as 'an absurdity,' for as Mr. Cooley says, it is only explicable on the ground either that the attorney general thought there was no absolute evidence of a violation of the law, (a conclusion which it is inconceivable he could have reached or that you could have reached) or else that as there were difficulties attendant upon the enforcement of the law you should go out of your way to violate it. You took advantage of the absence of the commissioner of public lands on official business, to go yourself with the attorney general, Mr. Reid, to his office and yourself to complete the transaction. It was here suggested to you by a clerk in the land office that

made earnest effort to induce President Roosevelt to reconsider his action and decline to accept the resignation which had been forwarded to Washington. They were unsuccessful and Captain George Curry, the personal friend of the president, in whose interest he had written the governor suggesting his appointment to some position in New Mexico, was named in his stead.

At the time of his appointment Captain Curry was still in the

---

the matter should be delayed until the commissioner could be communicated with as, if you wired him, it would be possible to get him back to Santa Fé inside of two days. You refused to permit the delay although there was absolutely no reason for such refusal on your part; you directed the clerk to compute the amount due as payment of principal and interest, to which he replied that he had no power to do so, and that the seal had not been affixed to twenty-three of the deeds. You then directed him to bring all the papers to your office, together with the seal of the board of public lands, and in the presence of the clerk and Mr. Hopewell, the beneficiary of your grossly improper and probably unlawful conduct, you affixed the seal to the twenty-three deeds and handing them to Mr. Hopewell asked if he considered that a delivery. Hopewell replied that he did and handed them back to you with the request that they be recorded on the deed records of the commissioner of public lands. You handed them to the clerk with instructions to have them recorded and these instructions were carried out. The deeds were returned to you and you handed them to the attorney for the Pennsylvania Development Company. You accepted from Mr. Hopewell his personal check for $11,143.74, which you subsequently deposited in the office of the commissioner of public lands.

"The department of justice reports that 'it seems entirely clear that Governor Hagerman's action was both illegal and improper. The act of congress of June 21, 1898, supra and section I, chapter 74, laws of New Mexico, of 1899, supra, clearly made the contract illegal at the time Governor Hagerman alleges it was entered into. The delivery of the deeds could not have been enforced by the grantees or by the Pennsylvania Development Company which was not a party to the contract. The governor had every reason to believe, owing to his correspondence with the secretary of the interior, that the transaction was of very doubtful legality in spite of the opinion of his attorney general. It was clearly his duty, in my judgment, to withhold the delivery of the deeds and let the matter be tested in the courts, if the grantees named in the deeds saw fit to mandamus the commissioner of public lands. His action in usurping the duties of the commissioner in his absence was both illegal and unjustifiable.

"'It was entirely competent for him to enforce the carrying out of his wishes by administrative methods in removing a public official and appointing some one in sympathy with his policies but it was neither legal nor justifiable to adopt the course he did.'

"With the above statement I entirely agree. If I permit such an act by the highest officer in the territory to go unpunished, I cannot hold to account any subordinate official for any infraction of his duty. It is a grave question in my mind, whether I ought to remove you instead of requesting your resignation. I resolved the doubt in your favor and requested your resignation. Under no circumstances would I reconsider this action.

"Very truly yours,
"THEODORE ROOSEVELT.

"Hon. H. J. Hagerman,
"Santa Fé, N. Mex."

Philippine Islands and during the period intervening between the time of the acceptance of the resignation of Governor Hagerman and his return to the United States, James Wallace Raynolds, the secretary of the territory, performed the duties of the office of governor. The bitterness of spirit and the feelings entertained by Governor Hagerman growing out of his retirement from office are reflected in a letter afterward written by him to the president.[468]

---

[468] "Alburquerque, N. M., May 15, 1907.
"To the President: Washington, D. C.
"Mr. President: I have to acknowledge receipt of your letter of May 1. I have been previously informed that the matter of my removal, through the form of resignation, from the governorship of New Mexico, was by you considered as a 'closed incident,' and could not admit of any further discussion or consideration whatever. Your letter appears inconsistent with this view. It is at once a challenge and an invitation which it would be both discourteous and cowardly to decline, though it offers the unpleasant alternative of a controversy with you, or submission to the impeachment of my integrity at your hands without an effort to defend myself.

"As a preface to what I must say, it should be stated that I regret that my telegram to Mr. Pinchot, when shown to you, did not convey the idea which I hoped to convey. I did not intend myself to express the opinion that my removal would be a calamity, as you seem to think I did. It should also be stated that I do not expect any revision or change by you in your action in demanding and accepting my resignation. As far as I am concerned all question of the governorship is a thing of the past. I cannot rest quietly and unprotesting under the stigma which you would put upon me. You would not do so if you were in my place. I have the right, however, to expect and ask of you, as a matter of common fairness and justice that you make public acknowledgement of the fact, when convinced of it — and that you will be convinced I must not doubt if you take the time to give the matter as I present it, a calm and careful examination — that I have been unjustly treated, and that my action as to the Pennsylvania Development Company deeds for which I was removed by you, was commendable and not blameworthy.

"Due regard to your exalted station forbids that I should reply to your letter in language which would be justifiable under the provocation it offers, if you were not President of the United States, but I am not permitted by my sense of propriety to forget what is due to your great office as well as to myself. I hope, however, that my reply will not be considered the less forceful because of the absence of harsh language.

"At least four newspapers in the Territory controlled by Mr. Bursum, whose removal by me as superintendent of the penitentiary you also approved, from the time of my removal persistently asserted that I was removed because of my refusal to be subservient to Mr. Bursum and his political machine, and that the Pennsylvania Development Company transaction was merely a convenient pretext. You have minimized, if you have not utterly destroyed, a growing public sentiment in the Territory in favor of an honest administration of public affairs. In the opinion of many of the best men of New Mexico public affairs in the Territory have reached such a crisis that its material prosperity is seriously threatened, and therefore, at some sacrifice of personal inclination and pride, I appeal to you to leave out of consideration my personality and any mistakes you may think I have made, and to give grave and careful consideration to political conditions in New Mexico from the standpoint of these people who have loyally supported me in my efforts for the realization of their (and

His closest adviser and counsel during his administration was William C. Reid whom the governor had called to the attorney generalship in the first days of his incumbency. Mr. Reid's well known integrity, ability as a lawyer, and reputation as a citizen are a sufficient answer to the charges made by the assistant attorney general, afterward associate justice, Alvord W. Cooley, that the opinion given by him to Governor Hagerman deserved to be characterized as an "absurdity." [469] Only a reference to this report and quotations used by President Roosevelt have been available but the language quoted is alone sufficient to condemn it and arouse suspicion, in the light of subsequent events, that some motive not disclosed was a controlling cause in the selection of the language employed in passing judgment upon the conclusions of a fellow member of the profession. Mr. Cooley was shortly afterward appointed an associate justice of the supreme court of New Mexico, to fill the vacancy caused by the expiration of the term of office of Associate Justice Edward

---

my own) ideals of good government. As a republican, I cannot but feel that the future of my party in what is to be a great state of this Union, is at stake, and that I would fail of party loyalty as well as in the duties of good citizenship, unless I did everything possible to impress upon you these conditions.

"I have the honor to be your obedient servant,

"H. J. HAGERMAN."

[469] William C. Reid was born in the state of Indiana, December 16, 1868. He received his early education in the schools of his native state. He read law and was admitted to the bar, in Ohio, in 1894. The following year he came to New Mexico, and, locating in Las Vegas, was employed as business manager of the *Optic*, a newspaper in that city. After a service of one year with this newspaper he entered upon the practice of law. In 1896-7 he served as chief clerk of the house of representatives of the 33rd legislative assembly. In 1901 he was appointed assistant United States attorney, which position he resigned in September, 1904. Prior to tendering his resignation he had taken up his residence in Roswell, and became a partner in the firm of Richardson, Reid and Hervey. The large practice enjoyed by this firm made it necessary for him to sever his connection with the office of the United States attorney. This firm was retained by the elder Hagerman in all his business in the Pecos Valley and through this connection Mr. Reid became acquainted with Governor Hagerman.

In June, 1898, responding to the call of his country, he organized a company in Las Vegas, which afterward became Company F of the 1st Ter. Inf., which was mustered for the Spanish-American war, but never saw active service. He was commissioned captain of this company by Governor Otero.

In June, 1906, he was appointed attorney general of the territory by Governor H. J. Hagerman, a position which he filled with credit and ability. He retired with the Hagerman administration and resumed the practice of law, being now senior member of the firm of Reid and Hervey. He is an assistant attorney for the Atchison, Topeka and Santa Fé Railway Company in New Mexico, having charge of the trial of causes in the courts of southeastern New Mexico.

A. Mann,[470] who had presided over the sixth judicial district court.

Ormsby McHarg, another assistant attorney general, was active in New Mexico at this period, and, during the administration of Governor Curry, had charge of land fraud prosecutions in the courts of the territory. As has been stated, several indictments of prominent men were secured, all of which, during the administration of Governor Curry and for reasons best known in Washington and not disclosed at the department of justice, were suddenly dropped or later disposed of on demurrer in the courts where they had been returned. The entire change of front on the part of the administration at Washington in its policy of land fraud prosecutions in New Mexico has never been fully understood by the people of the state.

Edward P. Holcombe, another agent or attorney from Washington, made two visits to New Mexico, the first as a special land agent of the interior department, and later as a special emissary from President Roosevelt, as Holcombe declared. Upon his arrival at Santa Fé, on the second visit, he frankly stated that his mission was to secure evidence upon which to base criminal prosecutions. After a complete investigation of matters, however, he was unable to find anything wrong in the affairs of the governor's office, nor in the office of the commissioner of public lands, and later stated that the action of the governor, insofar as the public lands were concerned, was not only right but the best course that could have been taken.

The money paid as final settlement for the lands purchased for the Pennsylvania Development Company by Willard S. Hopewell, was,

---

[470] Edward A. Mann was born at Beatrice, Nebraska, in 1867. He received his education in the public schools of the states of Nebraska, Kansas, and Texas, and for two years attended the college at Belle Plain, Texas. He read law and was admitted to the practice in 1891. The first three years of his professional life were spent in Norton, Kansas, whence he removed to Cripple Creek, Colorado. Leaving Colorado he removed to Gehring, Nebraska, where he followed the practice until 1903. In the last named year he became a citizen of New Mexico, locating in Las Cruces. In June, 1903, he was appointed associate justice of the supreme court of New Mexico by President Roosevelt and was assigned to the newly created sixth judicial district. He was re-appointed in December, 1903, and served his full term of four years. Upon the expiration of his term of office he removed to Alburquerque where he shortly formed a partnership with John Venable, who had been clerk of the district court of the second judicial district under Justice Ira A. Abbott. Here he soon became identified with the business and political life of the community. He was appointed district attorney by Governor William J. Mills, but the supreme court of New Mexico, in a suit to try his title to the office, held that the governor was without power to remove his predecessor, George S. Klock, who had been displaced for political reasons.

Opening Session of the Constitutional Convention of 1910

under the instructions of the attorney general, deposited as a special fund by the commissioner of public lands and was not distributed, as it would have been ordinarily, so that in the event the general government later decided that the deeds should not have been delivered, the territory would be in position to refund the money and take back title to the lands. It is evident to the legal mind that if there was no authority to convey title to the lands, or to deliver the deeds, the lands could be recovered in a proper proceeding. Edward P. Holcombe, the so-called special emissary of the president, approved of the action of Governor Hagerman in delivering the deeds, as he ordered this fund distributed, thus placing it beyond the power of the territory to recover the lands without an act of the legislative assembly appropriating money for purposes of tender to the holders of the deeds. Just what authority Mr. Holcombe had by which he assumed to order the commissioner of public lands to distribute any funds in his charge has never been satisfactorily explained but this "order" was in keeping with every official act of this special agent while in New Mexico, who did not hesitate to impress an associate justice of the supreme court of New Mexico with the power of his position and threaten him with dismissal by telegraphic order from President Roosevelt, if he did not comply with the demands of himself and Mr. Ormsby McHarg.

The period covered by the administration of Governor Hagerman was one of the most prosperous ever enjoyed by the people. The sheep industry was particularly fortunate. The great timber areas of New Mexico, hitherto unexploited successfully by capital, began to attract attention and the lumber industry made great progress. The cities and towns made rapid growth, great areas of public lands in the eastern portions of the territory were taken up and put in cultivation, hundreds of miles of railroad were constructed, all of which brought about great changes in conditions and served to begin the development of the great resources of the country.

Through the national reclamation service and private enterprise many new irrigation projects were commenced and several finished. The financial condition of the territory was most favorable.[471] Dur-

---

[471] Herbert J. Hagerman, *Message* of, to 37th legislative assembly, Jan. 21, 1907:

"On December 1, 1904, the commencement of the 56th fiscal year, there were balances in the various funds to the amount of $249,147.95.

"Receipts from taxes and other sources from December 1, 1904, to Novem-

ing a series of years, beginning with the administration of Governor Otero, the bonded debt was gradually reduced, without hardship to the tax-payers. In this regard the financial management of territorial affairs under two administrations was most remarkable, for in seven years the bonded debt was reduced $406,600.00, resulting in a reduction of annual interest charges from $73,200.00 in 1899 to $45,800.00 annual interest charge on the total bonded debt as it then existed. Never in the history of any western territory has so remarkable a showing in the management of its finances been recorded.

ADMINISTRATION OF GOVERNOR GEORGE CURRY

The return of Captain George Curry to New Mexico, carrying a commission as governor from his comrade in arms, through the fortunes of war, fate, and the voice of the people, chief magistrate of the nation, was a source of marked gratification to his old friends. By the politicians of republican faith his appointment was hailed with pleasure, believing that with his aid the warring elements of the party would soon be harmonized. Prior to the Spanish-American war Captain Curry had been one of the most prominent of the leaders in the democratic party, but now declared his allegiance to the principles of the party in power at Washington. Mustered out with his regiment he was soon the recipient of another commission in the army and left the United States for the Philippine Islands where he served with great credit and distinction.[472] His abandonment of the party of his

---

ber 30, 1906, were $1,442,615.65 making a total of $1,691.763.60 to be accounted for.

"Payments for the corresponding period amounted to $1,331,762.70, leaving a balance in the treasury at the close of business on November 30, 1906, of $360,000.90.

"All claims within the appropriations made were paid, and in addition thereto the bonded debt has been reduced from $949,300.00 to $843,000.00, a reduction of $106,300.00, as follows: Capitol building bonds, due March 1, 1905, redeemed, $96,000. Current expense bonds due May 2. 1907, redeemed, $10,000.00; casual deficit bonds, due May 1, 1923, redeemed, $300.00.

"While the territorial bonded debt is now $843,000.00 there are balances in sinking funds available to redeem outstanding bonds aggregating $103,302.82, making the net territorial debt, $739,697.18.

"On May 2, 1907, $40,000.00 six per cent current expense bonds will become due, for which there are funds on hand to pay, and on November 1, 1907, an additional $50,000.00 current expense bonds mature and payment will be promptly met. The remaining $50,000.00 current expense bonds, due May 1, 1908, will be paid, and after that no bonds will mature until May 1, 1919.''

[472] George Curry was born in Bayou Sara, Louisiana, in 1862. He is the

youth was caused by the discovery, while in the Philippines, fighting the battles of his country, upon the bodies of natives slain in combat, copies of letters from William J. Bryan, the democratic standard-bearer, which served as an encouragement to the natives in their insurrectionary struggle against the government of the United States.

When Governor Curry assumed the reins of government in New Mexico there were misgivings, not only in the territory but at the nation's capital. Space can not be given to a recital of the dissensions which rent the territory at the time; the furious resentment of the people at the indignities which had been heaped upon them by special agents and self-seeking special assistant attorneys general, was everywhere apparent. To many it appeared that the republican party was broken up, and to those acquainted with the situation it seemed absurd to send a democrat who, notwithstanding his success in suppressing revolts among the Moros, would be an easy mark for the political intriguers of New Mexico. Captain Curry had been absent nearly a decade, and was inaugurated the day after

---

son of George and Clara Curry. His mother was a native of Ireland, and his father was born in Kentucky. His father was killed after the Civil War. When less than twelve years of age he removed with his mother to Dodge City, Kansas; here his mother died in 1879. After the death of his mother, Captain Curry came to New Mexico, locating at Ft. Stanton, where he secured employment on a stock ranch. Later he filled a position as clerk in the store of J. C. Delaney, post-trader, which employment continued until 1884. In that year he located in the town of Lincoln, where he was given charge of the mercantile establishment of James J. Dolan, and also appointed deputy county treasurer, his employer, at the time, serving as treasurer of Lincoln county. Captain Curry at this period entered upon his political career. In 1888, he was elected probate clerk of Lincoln county; in 1890, county assessor; in 1892, sheriff, and in 1894 he was chosen to represent the counties of Lincoln, Chaves, Eddy, Doña Ana, and Grant in the legislative council. His course in the assembly reflected credit upon himself and the democratic party then in control of the governorship and both houses of the assembly. At the outbreak of the war with Spain he received a commission as captain of Troop H in Roosevelt's Rough Rider regiment, 1st U. S. Vol. Cavalry, but did not serve in Cuba, his troop remaining at Tampa, Florida. His lieutenants were W. H. Kelly and Charles L. Ballard, both capable officers. Mustered out with his regiment, he received a commission in the army and served in the Philippine Islands; took prominent part in the military service; was chief of police of the city of Manilla and governor of Samar. Called to the United States by President Roosevelt, he returned to New Mexico with a commission as governor and was inaugurated August 8, 1907. He held the office three years and resigned, his successor being William J. Mills, who was inaugurated March 1, 1910. Governor Curry now engaged in business pursuits but still took an active part in the struggle for statehood. In 1911, he was nominated by the republican party for congress and received the highest number of votes cast of any of the four candidates for that position.

his arrival in the capital. Those who listened to the addresses at the inaugural ceremonies believed that they could hear the roar of the breakers which would wreck the ship of state. The address of Albert B. Fall, attorney general, was particularly pointed and acrimonious. But Governor Curry put on the velvet glove. He was conciliatory and made it plain to all that he was a republican, not only in form and by word, but was convinced of the righteousness of the principles of that party. He immediately engaged in the work of building for the territory's future, and made politics and politicians a matter of secondary importance.

He appointed James M. Hervey attorney general, interested himself in the work of law revision [473] and the building up of the national guard. During the previous year the total acreage taken up by homesteaders was somewhat larger, so that there were made during the fiscal years prior to June 30, 1908, more than 30,000 original entries, homestead and desert land, covering a total of more than 5,000,000 acres. More people came to New Mexico during his administration than during any two decades preceding. The bonds of the territory commanded a higher premium than ever in its his-

---

[473] During the Hagerman administration a commission to revise the laws had been provided for by legislative enactment. Governor Curry made changes in the personnel of this commission. Of the members doing most of the consistent work in this revision were James M. Hervey, Julius Staab and Benjamin M. Read.

Benjamin M. Read is the son of Benjamin Franklin and Ignacia (Cano) Read, and was born at Las Cruces, New Mexico, in 1853. His father was a native of Baltimore, and came to New Mexico in 1846. Mr. Read received his education at St. Michael's College, Santa Fé. He was private secretary of Governor Marsh Giddings, in 1871. He was a teacher at St. Michael's college in 1875, and had charge of the schools of Santa Fé until 1880. He was private secretary to Governor Lionel A. Sheldon, and while filling this position read law and was admitted to the practice in 1885. He was elected to the house of representatives from Santa Fé county in 1900 and was chosen speaker, a position which he filled with credit. He was appointed a member of the commission to revise the laws in 1907. He is the author of *Guerra Mexico-Americana*, Santa Fé, 1910, and *Historia Ilustrada de Nuevo Mexico*, Santa Fé, 1911. The latter work has been translated into the English language.

Curry, George, Governor, *Report of*, to secretary of the interior; *Archives*, office of secretary, Santa Fé, N. M.: "New lines of railroad are being built into undeveloped coal fields, rich mining districts and timber regions, and through farming sections, bringing in thousands of settlers and hastening the development of the Territory in general.

"Mercantile and banking pursuits have kept pace with the growth in all other branches of business. Seventeen new banks. nine national and eight territorial, have been established during the past year.

"The development of the coal-mining industry has increased correspondingly. It is estimated that during the past year the coal mines of New Mexico have

Prominent New Mexicans of the Nineteenth Century
1. A. A. Grant.   2. John Chisholm.   3. J. J. Hagerman.   4. J. C. Lea

tory, and the territorial [474] and county finances were never in better condition. The territory began the construction of good roads; it began the inauguration of projects under the Carey Act, and progress was universal in every line of material activity. Late in the fall of 1909, Governor Curry became convinced that his own financial

---

produced 2,530,000 tons of coal at an average selling price at the mine on board cars of $1.60 per ton, and 225,000 tons of coke at an average selling price of $4.00 per ton.

"The lumber mills in New Mexico have during the past year produced an average of 300,000 feet per day.

"It is conservatively estimated that the wealth of the Territory has during the year increased not less than $25,000,000.00.

"Entries made at the several land offices were:

LAND OFFICE	ORIGINAL HOMESTEAD ENTRIES		DESERT ENTRIES	
	Number	Acres	Number	Acres
Clayton	8,291	1,257,074.76	246	37,908
Roswell	3,260	509,715.83	284	50,879
Santa Fé	2,872	443,209.72	203	32,631
Las Cruces	539	78,704.00	237	41,012
Total	14,962	2,288,704.31	970	162,430

[474] Charles V. Safford, Traveling Auditor, *Report* of, Aug. 27, 1910:

"All appropriations have been promptly paid.

"During the past year the territorial rate of taxation has been materially reduced, having been lowered to 11 mills from 14.45 the year previous—nearly a 24 per cent reduction.

"All territorial institutions, penal, educational, charitable, and others, have lived within their incomes as fixed by legislative acts.

"The territorial bonded debt has been decreased, interest payments promptly met, and the credit of the territory generally improved.

"Bonds issued by the territory, counties, and municipalities, bearing low rates of interest, when offered for sale, have been eagerly sought for by the bond buyer.

"Substantial cash balances, adequate for all purposes, have been maintained. Such cash balances have been kept on deposit with approved banks, named as depositories of public funds, and amply protected by good and sufficient bonds, upon which interest is derived on daily balance, at the rate of 3 per cent per annum.

"Property returns for taxation purposes are made on a basis of not to exceed 20 per cent of actual value. If returns were made on basis of full valuation, the tax rate would only amount to 2.2 of 1 per cent.

"No deficiencies have occurred in any of the departments.

"As shown by the statement immediately following, on June 1, 1909, there was to the credit of the various territorial funds, $527,198.16. During the year there was collected from sources other than taxation $353,891.23, and from taxation $679,023.40; making the total collections and receipts by the treasurer $1,032,914.63, and the total to be accounted for by the treasurer $1,560,112.79. There was expended for all purposes $1,074,963.65, leaving aggregate balances of $485,149.14 on hand June 1, 1910."

interests demanded that he resign the position of governor, which he did, and William J. Mills, who had served as chief justice of the supreme court of New Mexico for twelve years, was asked, on November 24th, while holding a term of court in Union county, by the secretary of the interior whether he would accept the governorship if tendered him, also requesting an immediate answer. The answer was in the affirmative, and on December 20, 1909, his name having been sent to the senate by the president, he was duly confirmed.

Tendering his resignation to the president, Governor Curry asked that it be accepted as of March 1, 1910. This was done. On March 1, with simple ceremonies, the last governor [475] of New Mexico under the Act of March 3, 1851, took the oath of office in front of the capitol, in the presence of a large concourse of people. Chief Justice William Hayes Pope,[476] who had been named as the successor of the retiring chief justice, administered the oath of office.

ADMINISTRATION OF GOVERNOR
WILLIAM JOSEPH MILLS

[475] William Joseph Mills was born in Yazoo City, Mississippi, January 11, 1849. His father was William Mills, of Virginia, and his mother Harriet Beale, of Philadelphia, Pa. His father having died when the governor was yet a child his mother moved to Connecticut, where she was married to William H. Law. Governor Mills attended private schools and was graduated from the Norwich Free Academy. He attended the law school of Yale University and graduated in 1877. He was married January 14, 1885, to Alice Waddingham, daughter of Wilson Waddingham, for many years heavily interested in New Mexico, at West Haven, Conn. After his graduation he practiced law in New Mexico and Connecticut until his appointment to the chief justiceship of the territory by President William McKinley, January 31, 1898, succeeding Thomas Smith, of Virginia. He was twice re-appointed by President Roosevelt. While living in Connecticut he served in both houses of the legislative assembly of that state, at that time being affiliated with the democratic party. When named chief justice by President McKinley, it was considered that he was what was then termed a "gold" democrat. He shortly renounced all allegiance to the democratic party and has since been identified with the republican party. Governor Mills is a man of fine literary attainments. His inaugural address was a forcible declaration as well as a polished literary production.

[476] William Hayes Pope is the son of Major Joseph J. Pope, and was born in Beaufort, South Carolina, June 13, 1870. He is of Scotch-Irish ancestry. His forebears in America were identified with the patriots of the Revolution, fighting for freedom in the Colonial armies. His father was a Confederate soldier, and died in 1873. William Hayes Pope received his early education in Georgia, graduating in the high school of Atlanta in 1886. He matriculated at the Georgia state university, where he graduated in 1889 with the degree of Master of Arts. In 1890, he was graduated from the law department of the university with the degree of LL.B. After his graduation he entered the law firm of Hoke and Burton Smith, the former being secretary of the interior during the second administration of Grover Cleveland. His health becoming somewhat impaired, Judge Pope came to New Mexico in 1894 and located at

1880 TO 1912   567

The outgoing governor, the justices of the supreme court, all of the territorial officials, and the secretary, Nathan Jaffa,[477] were present. Governor Curry made a short address, dealing with the salient features of his administration, and Governor Mills, in an elaborate discourse, outlined the policies which would mark his conduct of public affairs.[478]

Santa Fé where he became associate editor of the *New Mexican*. In 1895, he resumed the practice of his profession. He held the office of assistant to the attorney for the court of private land claims where he added materially to his reputation at the bar. He later held the office of attorney for the Pueblo Indians. After the Spanish-American war, he was appointed a judge of the first instance in the Philippines, where his labors came under the personal notice of President Taft, then governor-general of the Islands. Returning from the Philippines, in 1903, he was appointed associate justice of the supreme court of New Mexico and was re-appointed in 1907. Some of the most scholarly opinions of the court, delivered by Judge Pope, are found in the reports. He was a member of the board which had charge of the rebuilding of the capitol. He was appointed chief justice of the supreme court by President Taft in 1910 and established his headquarters at Roswell, where he had presided over the district court for that district. He was nominated for the position of judge of the district court for the district of New Mexico by President Taft, January 22, 1912, his nomination being later confirmed by the Senate of the United States.

[477] Nathan Jaffa, the last territorial secretary, is one of the most successful and prominent business men of the southwest. The personal friend of Governor Curry, he received the appointment through the latter's recommendation to the president. He is a native of Germany and was born, December 28, 1863. He came to America at the age of fourteen, locating at Trinidad, Colorado. After a period of four years in that city, where he was engaged in various employments, he came to Las Vegas, New Mexico, where he took charge of the mercantile establishment of Jaffa Brothers. Later he established the firm of Jaffa-Prager Company, located at Roswell, where a great mercantile business was established. He married Essie Strauss, of Trinidad, Colorado. During his term Mr. Jaffa made great improvement in the business methods of his office. Prior to the state convention of 1911 he was prominently considered by many of the members of his party in connection with the nomination for governor of the state, but declined to allow his name to go before the convention. He occupies a high position in the social and business life of New Mexico and his standing is owing to his own efforts. He is a type of the self-made American citizen.

[478] The personnel of the last supreme court of the territory of New Mexico was chief justice, William H. Pope; associate justices, John R. McFie, Frank W. Parker, Ira A. Abbott, Merritt C. Mechem, Clarence J. Roberts, and Edward R. Wright.

Ira A. Abbott was appointed an associate justice of the supreme court of New Mexico by President Roosevelt in December, 1904, succeeding Benjamin S. Baker, one of the ablest jurists ever on the New Mexico bench. Judge Abbott was born in Barnard, Vermont, in 1845. He was a soldier during the last year of the Civil War, in the 9th Vermont Volunteer Infantry, and participated in the closing events of the great struggle around Richmond, Virginia. His command was among the first to enter the capital of the Confederacy after the surrender. After the war, Judge Abbott entered Dartmouth college and graduated in 1870. He read law and also filled the chair of mathematics in Phillips Academy, Andover, Mass. He practiced law in Massachu-

The last territorial administration saw the same prevailing spirit of progress, increase in land values, improved educational facilities, and general prosperity which had characterized the four years preceding. The census for 1910 showed an increase of 67.6 per cent in population over 1900, the entire population amounting to 327,396.

The territory of New Mexico, at the time of its admission to the Union, was possessed of a great deal of property consisting of public buildings, all of which had been paid for in funds derived from

---

setts until 1898 when he became judge of the district court of Essex county, at Haverhill. With the admission of New Mexico into the Union, Judge Abbott returned to the state of Massachusetts. Prior to his departure a banquet and reception were tendered him at Alburquerque where many addresses laudatory of his career were made by the members of the bar and representative men of the second judicial district over which he had presided.

Merritt C. Mechem is a native of Ottawa, Kansas. He was born October 10, 1870. He came to New Mexico March 23, 1903, and located at Tucumcari, where he began the practice of law. He had received his education at Ottawa Baptist University, at Ottawa, Kansas, and at the Kansas State University at Lawrence. He was admitted to the bar at Fort Smith, Arkansas, in 1895. March 16, 1905, he was appointed district attorney for Quay and Guadalupe counties. In 1909, he was elected a member of the territorial council for the fifth district, composed of the counties of Quay, Guadalupe, and San Miguel. In the same year he was appointed associate justice of the supreme court by President Taft and assigned to the seventh district, with headquarters at Socorro. At the election of 1911, he was elected judge of the seventh district without opposition.

Edward R. Wright was born at Skaneateles, New York, June 23, 1877. He attended the public schools of his native county. He is a graduate of Hamilton college, Clinton, New York. Judge Wright came to New Mexico in September, 1901, and in December of that year took up his residence at Santa Rosa, where he lived until appointed to the bench. He was admitted to the practice in New Mexico in 1902; was district attorney for the counties of Guadalupe and Quay in 1907. In July, 1910, he was appointed associate justice of the supreme court of New Mexico, succeeding Alvord W. Cooley, resigned. He was assigned to the sixth district with headquarters at Alamogordo. He was nominated for justice of the supreme court of New Mexico by the republican party at the first state election and was defeated by R. H. Hanna, progressive republican.

Clarence J. Roberts was born in Jefferson county, Indiana, in 1873. He received his primary education in the common schools. He taught school for several years, paying the expenses incident to his collegiate education. At the age of 19, he began reading law and two years later was admitted to the bar of his native state. He was elected county attorney for Jefferson county, Indiana, and held that office until he removed to the state of Colorado in 1905. Here, at Trinidad, he formed a partnership with Jesse G. Northcutt. In 1907 he removed to Raton. He was elected a member of the legislative assembly of New Mexico in 1909. A year later he was chosen a member of the constitutional convention where he rendered valuable service. The same year he received the appointment of associate justice of the supreme court of New Mexico and presided over the fourth judicial district court. In 1911, he was elected to the state supreme court and upon the organization of the court, in January, 1912, was chosen chief justice.

Venceslao Jaramillo
M. L. Stern
Candelario Vigil
Francis E. Wood
Harry W Kelly
Eufracio F Gallegos
Solomon Luna
Anesotos O Abeytia
W. C. Murray
Stephen B Davis
Squire Hartt Jr
Benj. F Pankey
Norman W Bartlett
Thomas H. O'Brien
Onesimo L. Martinez
George A. Brown
José D Sena
Margarito Romero
Victor Ortega
N. Segura
T. B. Catron

Jno. J Hinkle
H M Compton
Frank H Winston
W D Murray
Silvestre Mirabal
Salome Martinez
H M Dougherty
C. R. Brice
Luciano Mass
Samuel Eldodt
Francisco Gauna
E. M Lucero
Arthur H Harllee
Albert Fall
Eugenio Romero
Alejandro Sandoval
J. Frank Romero
Tranquilino Labadie
William B Walton
J W Childers
John Becker
John E. Kruse
Ed F Saxon

Fac-simile of Signatures of the Framers of the Constitution of 1910

the sale of bonds and from direct legislative appropriations raised in the annual levies for taxation.[479]

The construction of good roads continued during the administra-

The last officials of the Territory of New Mexico were:

Office.	Name.	Residence
Governor	William J. Mills	Las Vegas
Secretary	Nathan Jaffa	Roswell
Assistant secretary	Edwin F. Coard	Santa Fé
Attorney general	Frank W. Clancy	Alburquerque
Assistant attorney general	Harry S. Clancy	Santa Fé
Auditor	Wm. G. Sargent	El Rito
Traveling auditor and bank examiner	Charles V. Safford	Aztec
Asst. traveling auditor and bank examiner	Robert C. Rankin	Las Vegas
Treasurer	Rufus J. Palen	Santa Fé
Commissioner of public lands	Robert P. Ervien	Clayton
Asst. commissioner of public lands	Mateo Lujan	Bueyeros
Territorial engineer	Charles D. Miller	Las Cruces
Superintendent of insurance	Jacobo Chavez	Los Lunas
Superintendent of public instruction	James E. Clark	Alburquerque
Asst. superintendent of public instruction	Acasio Gallegos	Tajique
Librarian	Lola C. Armijo, (Mrs.)	Santa Fé
Adjutant general	A. S. Brookes	Santa Fé
Superintendent of penitentiary	Cleofes Romero	Las Vegas
Captain of mounted police	Fred Fornoff	Santa Fé
Parole officer	Henry S. Allison	Raton
Game and fish warden	Thomas P. Gable	Santa Fé
Oil inspector	Malaquias Martinez	Taos

[479] William J. Mills, *Report* to Secretary of the Interior, 1911:

INSTITUTION	Furniture Fixtures Equipment	Personal Property	Real Estate	Buildings	Total
Agricultural College	$134,613.88	$ 4,675.60	$ 37,350.00	$ 93,825.00	$ 270,464.48
Blind Asylum	3,150.00		8,000.00	26,000.00	37,100.00
Deaf and Dumb Asylum	1,850.00	350.00	4,500.00	24,000.00	30,700.00
Insane Asylum	43,076.99	10,070.19	21,504.30	197,344.67	271,996.15
Miner's Hospital	3,700.00	50.00	2,000.00	45,700.00	51,450.00
New Mexico Military Institute	20,000.00	14,400.00	50,000.00	153,184.49	237,584.49
Normal School, Silver City	15,000.00	18,000.00	10,000.00	65,000.00	108,000.00
Normal University, Las Vegas	13,713.30		20,000.00	75,300.00	109,013.30
New Mexico Penitentiary	67,592.91	5,991.50	7,558.00	97,005.00	178,167.41
School of Mines, Socorro	15,200.00		2,000.00	70,000.00	87,200.00
University, Alburquerque	25,000.00	6,500.00	2,000.00	85,050.00	118,550.00
Spanish-American Normal	2,000.00		250.00	25,000.00	27,250.00
Reform School, Springer	2,031.55	2,457.20	4,700.00	10,000.00	19,188.75
Armories					
Alburquerque			4,750.00	20,586.00	25,336.00
Las Cruces			1,500.00	14,406.00	15,906.00
Las Vegas			2,500.00	15,003.00	17,503.00
Silver City			500 00	14,406.00	14,906.00
Santa Fé			500.00	14,169.00	14,669.00
Roswell			1,000.00	14,406.00	15,406.00
Capitol Building and Extension	15,000.00		20,000.00	275,000.00	310,000.00
Executive Mansion	9,000.00		12,000.00	25,000.00	46,000.00
	$370,878.63	$362,494.49	$212,862.30	$1,369,405 16	$2,006,640.58

tion of Governor Mills, and from the time of the creation of the commission, consisting of the governor, territorial engineer, and the commissioner of public lands, in 1909, there were examined over one thousand miles of highway, and more than five hundred miles additional were surveyed and platted. In the main, the construction of these roads was good, the principal roads being the Picacho Hill road from Roswell to Lincoln, the La Bajada Hill, on the road from Santa Fé to Alburquerque, the road between Silver City and the mining camps in the Mogollon Mountains, and the Camino Real, north of Las Vegas, extending in the direction of Raton, and over the Raton Pass to the Colorado state line. The total receipts and expenditures of the commission from the date of its establishment to July 1, 1911, were $134,538.44. Convict labor was used in 'the construction of these highways.

The total disbursements in the maintenance of the public institutions for the year ending June 30, 1911, were $580,488.19 and there were balances in the several institution funds on June 30, 1911, amounting to $104,655.46.

In the construction of the public roads the several counties made liberal appropriations, many localities contributing more than the amount derived from the general territorial fund devoted to road purposes.

On the first day of June, 1910, there was to the credit of the various territorial funds $485,149.14. During the year there was collected from sources other than taxation the sum of $363,986.62, and from taxation $653,703.99, making a total of collections and receipts by the treasurer of $1,017,690.61 and a total to be accounted for of $1,502,839.75. The expenses for all purposes during the fiscal year

The Territory was possessed of large bodies of land, as follows:
Granted by the Fergusson Act.............................. 5,589,252.72
Less acreage sold... 71,080.95

                                                                         5,518,171.77
Granted by Enabling Act of 1910........................... 6,569,520.00
Grounds occupied by Palace of Governors................... 2.60

Grand total... 12,087,694.37
The total receipts of the commissioner of public lands, including balances from 1910, were $168,129.52 and the total expenditures for the fiscal year ending June 30, 1911, for schools, institutions, etc., was $137,747.22; with certain withdrawals and the Carey Act, $8,724.81, leaving a balance June 30, 1911, of $21,657.49.

were $977,564.63, leaving aggregate balances in the hands of the treasurer on June 1, 1911, of $525,275.12. The financial condition of the territory was never better. The total bonded indebtedness was $975,000.00. The total assessed valuation of property in New Mexico for 1911 amounted to $60,448,880.75. The total county and school district bonded indebtedness was, for the counties, $3,400,909.42, and for school districts, $708,631.13. The income and cost of county governments is given in a note.[480] In 1911, the banking interests [481] of New Mexico were in a most prosperous condition.

In public education there had been marked progress and advancement. The census of 1910 showed 99,308 persons of school age. The school enrollment in June, 1911, was approximately 58,000. More than 1,600 teachers were employed in about 1,200 elementary schools

---

[480] County receipts:—

Balances, June 30, 1910........................		$1,423,417.00
Taxes collected...............................	$2,458,654.33	
Licenses	135,671.77	
Poll taxes....................................	39,379.97	
Fines	13,363.71	
From the Territory for the benefit of the public schools	66,252.23	
From sale of county and school bonds..........	127,930.41	
County proportion of Forest Reserve funds received from Territorial Treasurer.............	21,915.81	
All other receipts.............................	98,595.81	
		$4,395,181.29

County expenditures:—

Cost of county governments paid from general county funds...............................	319,542.11
Boarding prisoners............................	14,850.69
Cost of holding courts........................	203,369.66
Interest on bonded debt.......................	173,405.78
Wild animal bounties..........................	32,515.38
Roads and bridges.............................	189,716.14
Public buildings...............................	215,395.86
Territorial taxes..............................	604,888.38
Treasurers' and assessors' commissions..........	171,460.70
Municipal taxes...............................	209,273.12
Public schools.................................	838,085.79
Bonds redeemed...............................	61,789.90
All other expenses.............................	83,677.45
Aggregate balances on hand, July 1, 1911.......	1,277,210.33
	$4,395,181.29

[481] There were 87 banking institutions, 42 national and 45 territorial, with a capitalization of $3,343,490.00, and total resources and liabilities of $26,417,853.72. There were 13 building and loan associations with assets of $1,331,293.64.

and in 30 high schools. In 1911, 1,600 teachers were enrolled in the various institutes and summer schools. Expenditures for the support of the public schools were $949,448.60, of which $541,440.56 were for wages and $288,705.64 for new buildings, grounds, and repairs. The total amount invested in school property was $1,288,672.75.[482]

---

[482] Nathan Jaffa, *Legislative Manual*, 1911, pp. 31-2: "The school system is thoroughly adequate and is a model, from the smallest district school to the state university, school of mines, agricultural college and normal schools. The system is complete, is under the direction of competent men and women and is abundantly and enthusiastically supported by the people. The education of every child may be completed in New Mexico at the lowest possible expense. The common schools have already an endowment of about four million acres of land, under grants by congress and by the terms of the enabling act, will receive four million acres more.

"At its minimum value of $3 an acre, this land will give the public school system a magnificent endowment which will support it at the lowest possible cost to the tax payer. Vast bodies of this land are now valued at $10 an acre. It is, in fact, the policy of the land department to sell none of this land at any price less than $10 an acre.

"*Territorial Board of Education.*—The Territorial Board of Education consists of nine members: the governor, superintendent of public instruction, and seven members appointed by the governor; five of said seven from the heads of territorial educational institutions, the president of St. Michael's College of Santa Fé and the superintendents of schools in the four cities of the territory, ranking highest in population at the time the appointment is to be made; two of said seven to be citizens interested in education who are not professional teachers— one of whom shall be a county superintendent. The board apportions the territorial school fund to the various counties, specifies duties of county superintendents, prepares examinations for applicants for teachers' certificates, selects the text-books for public schools, and has full control of county institutes. The governor is ex-officio president of the board and the superintendent of public instruction ex-officio secretary.

"*Chief Territorial Officer.*—The superintendent of public instruction is appointed by the governor, by and with consent of the council, for a term of two years. He visits various counties in the interest of education; holds teachers' institutes; prepares courses of study for county teachers' institutes and for the common schools of the territory, and keeps a record of the proceedings of the territorial board of education. The salary allowed is three thousand dollars per annum.

"*Chief County Officer.*—A superintendent of schools for each county is elected at each general election and holds office for two years. He apportions the general county school fund among the several districts in the county, and has charge of the common school interests of the county, being required to visit the various schools of the county and to enforce compliance with the provision of the school law. His salary is based on the number of school rooms in session for at least three months of each year and upon the amount collected from the three mill territorial levy for school purposes. The maximum salary is fifteen hundred dollars per annum.

"*School Directors.*—Three directors for each district in the county are elected, one each year, for a term of three years. They have general care and keeping of the school property of the district; provide for school sites, and pay teachers' wages and interest on school bonds. They receive no salary and are

There was a great increase in the number of final and commuted homestead entries during the last years of territorial government, indicating that a very considerable portion of the settlement of dry-farming areas is permanent, substantial, and successful.

One of the most important enactments of the New Mexico legislature was the act of 1909, whereby the Museum of New Mexico was established and located at the capital. This institution is under the control and management of a board of directors or regents, appointed by the governor.[483] A chronological list of the principal events occur-

SCHOOL OF AMERICAN ARCHAEOLOGY AT SANTA FÉ

---

prohibited from being interested in any contract for expenditure of the school funds.

"*City and Town Boards of Education.*—A board of education is elected in each organized city and town, consisting of two members from each ward, who hold office for four years. This board organizes and maintains a system of graded schools; exercises control over school property, and levies a special tax for the support of the city and town schools.

"*School Age and Compulsory Education.*—The school age is from five to twenty-one years. Children between the ages of seven and fourteen, who are not in attendance at some private school or not under physical disability, may be compelled by the school authorities to attend the public school each year for the entire term of school in their respective districts.

"*Educational Institutions.*—The school system of New Mexico includes the territorial institutions which are supported by general territorial funds. These are the University of New Mexico, New Mexico College of Agriculture and Mechanic Arts, New Mexico Normal School, New Mexico Spanish-American Normal School, New Mexico Normal University, New Mexico School of Mines, New Mexico Military Institute, Institute for Deaf and Dumb, and Institute for the Blind. There are about twelve hundred public schools in the territory supported by the regular school taxes with an enrollment of fifty-six thousand pupils, twenty thousand of whom are Spanish-American and one hundred are negroes.

"There are nearly seventy sectarian schools with an enrollment of five thousand pupils and about twenty private schools with an enrollment of three hundred pupils. In addition there are twenty-five Indian schools under direct Federal supervision with a total enrollment of over two thousand pupils.

"The United States has two especially large Indian schools in the territory, one at Santa Fé and the other at Alburquerque. The Santa Fé institution alone is a community in itself, consisting of about twenty substantial brick buildings of varying sizes, the larger ones being two stories in height. In addition to the Indian schools of the Federal government, Santa Fé has another similar institution under the Sisters of the Blessed Sacrament, whose guiding spirit is Mother M. Katherine and in private life was Miss Catherine Drexel of the famous Drexel family of multi-millionaires in Philadephia. The Presbyterian Mission has two large institutions in Santa Fé for the education of the native children, and another similar school in Alburquerque."

[483] William J. Mills, *Report* of, 1911:

"The most important work of the museum during the past year has been that of putting in repair the Old Palace of the Governors. which, under the stipulations of the legislative act, has been made the home of the museum and

ring during the last decade of territorial government is given in a note.[484]

of the School of American Archæology. The funds for the repair of the building have been furnished largely by public-spirited citizens of New Mexico. The work of repair has consisted in the removal of modern woodwork from the doors, windows, and fireplaces, and the restoration of these interesting architectural features to their original form as nearly as can be determined. The modern plastering and papering of the walls have been replaced by cement work of the most durable character, simulating as nearly as possible the original finish of the rooms. The modern cloth and wall-paper ceilings have been removed, laying bare the ancient *vigas* and hand-chopped slabs of centuries ago.

"The rooms, thus repaired, present much of the appearance which they had before the modernizing of the past half century was done. All of the building, which has been turned over for the use of the Museum of New Mexico, has been thus put in repair, and now affords office facilities for the school and museum, a number of excellent exhibition rooms, and a large room, formerly occupied by the United States post office, for the purpose of library and lecture hall.

"The museum has during the past year been visited by a large number of travelers. Almost without exception, artists, scientists, historians, and travelers have spoken in highest approval of the spirit in which all the alterations of the building have been made and the plan upon which the museum is being developed. The museum is kept open every day in the year, and the number of visitors is constantly increasing.

"The relations between the museum and the School of American Archæology have been all that was contemplated by the act of the legislature. There is perfect unity of purpose and harmony of action. The collections of the museum have accumulated rapidly, and at present rate it can be but a matter of a little time until the capacity of the building is overtaxed to accommodate the collections on hand.

"It is the purpose of the regents and director to make this museum display the history of the Southwest for the past thousand years. No other part of the United States is so rich in archæological remains, and the history of the Southwest is full of dramatic interest. It will be the function of this museum to preserve all that is best in New Mexico's historic past, and especially it is the intention to preserve the Old Palace of the Governors as a monument to the Spanish founders of the civilization of the Southwest, as provided in the organic act."

[484] 1900. Population of New Mexico, 195,310, according to the census.
June 4. New capitol building completed and dedicated.
1901. April 13. George H. Wallace, secretary of New Mexico, died.
1902. August 29. Disastrous floods along Mimbres river in Grant county. Three hundred inhabitants rendered homeless. Governor issued proclamation calling for contributions of food, clothing and financial aid.
1903. February 13. Bills providing for asylum for deaf and dumb, at Santa Fé; reform school, at El Rito; an institute for the blind, at Alamogordo; and a hospital for disabled miners at Raton, became law, and boards were appointed by the governor.
February 28. Roosevelt county created from portions of Chaves and Guadalupe counties. Governor appointed county officers for Roosevelt county on March 31.
February 28. Quay county created from portions of Guadalupe and Union counties. Governor appointed county officers for Quay county on March 31.
March 12. Bill providing for erection of armories for the national guard at Las Vegas and Alburquerque became a law, and armory boards of control were appointed by the governor.

For sixty long years the people of New Mexico pleaded, agitated, and fought for admission as a state.[485] Again and again they were on the point of being admitted when the cup was dashed from their lips. The credit for the passage of the enabling act of 1910 must be given to the arduous labors and indefatigable energy of New Mexico's last delegate in congress, William H. Andrews. To

ENABLING ACT FOR NEW MEXICO

March 16. Leonard Wood county created from portions of Guadalupe and Valencia counties, and governor appointed county officers on April 25,
September 25. Roswell incorporated as a city.
1904. September 17. Wm. G. Ritch, secretary of New Mexico for thirteen years, died.
September and October. The most disastrous floods in the history of New Mexico occurred during these months. From the latter part of September until the 18th of October it rained almost continuously. Millions of dollars worth of property were destroyed and hundreds of families rendered homeless. Railroad traffic completely demoralized for two months.
November 26. Col. J. Francisco Chaves, soldier, statesman and citizen, assassinated.
1905. February 4. Law enacted creating "New Mexico Mounted Police."
February 4. "Flood Sufferers Relief" bill appropriating $50,000 passed both houses. Congress later invalidated this measure.
1906. January 23. Miguel A. Otero retired as governor of New Mexico. Herbert J. Hagerman inaugurated as governor.
September 4. Apportionment of house and council districts changed by proclamation of the governor.
1907. Leasburg diversion dam completed and dedicated; first unit of Elephant Butte irrigation project of the U. S. Reclamation Service.
March 21. Act approved authorizing the erection of an annex to the capitol building and an executive mansion.
August 8. George Curry inaugurated as governor.
December 18. First passenger train was operated on the "Belen cut-off" of the Eastern railway, a part of the A. T. & S. F. system.
1908. January 1. Anti-gambling law passed by 37th legislative assembly and approved March 21, 1907, became operative, prohibiting gambling in New Mexico.
July 1. Bureau of forestry reorganized and New Mexico placed in Division No. 3 together with Arizona, Oklahoma, Arkansas and Porto Rico, headquarters for this division established at Alburquerque, N. M., December 1st, with large corps of officials and assistants.
1909. February. Curry county created.
March. New Mexico Museum established at Santa Fé in old palace.
New Mexico Spanish-American normal school established at El Rito. Clovis incorporated as a city.
1910. March. Wm. J. Mills inaugurated governor.
October 3. Constitutional convention met to frame constitution for proposed state of New Mexico; adjourned November 21.
1911. January 21. Constitution for new state, New Mexico, ratified by large majority at special election.

[485] The most dastardly performance by a committee of congress ever witnessed in the history of the American people was that of the famous "Beveridge Committee" of the senate of the United States, appointed pursuant to Senate Resolution No. 282. This committee was composed of Senators Beveridge (chair-

be sure, many of the leading citizens of New Mexico assisted in the accomplishment of the people's "one great idea," but Delegate Andrews succeeded where other delegates for more than half a century had failed. His immediate predecessor, Bernard S. Rodey, had devoted almost his entire service in futile attempts to secure the rights of complete citizenship for his constituents.[486]

---

man), Dillingham, Burnham, and Heitfield, a sub-committee of the senate committee on territories. Never before in the history of the American people were the qualifications and fitness of the people of a territory subjected to and passed upon by a committee of either branch of the American congress. The very presence of the committee, in the light of its acts and report, was an insult to the people of the four remaining territories. This committee held sessions in this territory at Las Vegas, Santa Fé, Alburquerque, Las Cruces, and Carlsbad, commencing on Wednesday, November 12, and ending November 21, 1902. This investigation was not in the form usual in hearings before committees in Washington, where voluntary statements are received from those in attendance, but was rather in the form of a legal proceeding in which witnesses were called and sworn and then testified in answer to questions from the members of the committee. A large number of witnesses were thus examined on particular points as to which the committee desired to obtain information, and the witnesses themselves were selected and summoned by the committee, with the exception of a very few, who were produced at the request of Delegate Bernard S. Rodey.

This committee arrived in New Mexico without notice; its method of procedure — closed doors, one witness at a time; the fact that the committee was provided with lists in advance; that it heard some and would not hear others; that it avoided calling the best classes before it; that the investigation was not as to the resources of the country or its financial ability to maintain a state government; and that the greater portion of the line of inquiry was as to the speaking of Spanish, its use in the schools and courts, in the houses and on the streets; all these things aroused a very bitter feeling against Senator Beveridge, thoroughly merited, and was not lessened when the committee made its report. When the report appeared the indignation of the people was most pronounced. There is no doubt that Senator Beveridge was either greatly prejudiced against the admission of New Mexico, or he was the tool of the cabal of New England senators who did not desire the admission of any western territories no matter what their fitness or qualifications. The report was carefully drawn, with an evident desire to appear fair, but it approached the subject from a thoroughly eastern point of view and was one-sided, misleading. and intended so to be, for the purpose of still further prejudicing the people of the eastern states against the people of the southwest.

[486] L. Bradford Prince, *Struggle for Statehood*, Santa Fé, N. M., 1910, page 118:

"To say that he was devoted to the cause of statehood is to state the case mildly. He was enthusiastically devoted to it. He set before himself as the one great object to be attained during his congressional service, the passage of an enabling act for New Mexico. Everything else was subordinated to it, in order that this particular matter could have undivided attention.

"In Washington and New Mexico, in hotels and on railroad trains, in public speech and in conversation, in season and out of season, this was his one great theme; and nothing could weary him so long as there was an argument to answer or an auditor to convince.

"At the very outset of his congressional work, at the opening of the 57th congress, he endeavored to arrange with the speaker so that the New Mexico

Fac-simile of Signatures of the Framers of the Constitution of 1910

Delegate Andrews [487] took up the work where it had been left by Delegate Rodey. Mr. Andrews's methods were entirely different from those of Mr. Rodey. From long and intelligent acquaintance with affairs political, Mr. Andrews knew the full value of quiet, convincing conversation. He also understood the value of personal friendships brought about through favors rendered to those who were full-fledged members of congress and which, being a delegate

statehood bill should be the first introduced in that session, and actually succeeded in having it recorded as House Bill No. 2. The bill, as usual, went to the committee on territories.

"Unfortunately there was great activity relative to the territories at this session. While but three of the regularly organized territories still existed, each was making heroic efforts to be admitted to the Union and each was selfishly anxious to be the first to receive consideration. Among the statehood bills then in the committee on territories were No. 2, the New Mexico bill just named; No. 152, an Enabling Act for Oklahoma; No. 2015, a similar bill for Arizona; No. 4570, authorizing single statehood for Oklahoma and Indian Territory; No. 9675, providing for the union of Oklahoma and Indian Territory; No. 11992, another bill for Arizona singly; No. 11995, a similar bill for New Mexico; and No. 12543, 'to enable the people of Oklahoma, Arizona, and New Mexico to form constitutions and state governments, and be admitted into the Union on an equal footing with the original states.'

"On April 1, 1902, the committee, through Mr. Knox, reported in favor of the latter measure, thus uniting all the territories in one omnibus bill. (Report No. 1309). In this shape it passed the house on May 9th and was received by the senate on May 12th.

"It was at this stage of the long struggle, that Senator Quay of Pennsylvania became such an ardent champion of New Mexico, that the grateful people through their legislature named one of their counties for him.

"The question of forming one state by uniting New Mexico and Arizona, became prominent at this time, the bill which elicited most debate being H. R. 14749, which was an enabling act for Oklahoma and the Indian Territory as one state, and for New Mexico and Arizona as one state. On this, Senator Beveridge made a notable speech, entitled 'Arizona the Great,' in closing the discussion on February 6, 1905, in which he pictures the glory of the combined state in these eloquent words: 'Not Arizona the little, but Arizona the great; not Arizona the provincial, but Arizona the national; not Arizona the creature of a politician's device, but Arizona the child of the Nation's wisdom.'"

[487] L. Bradford Prince, *Ibid.*, pp. 121-2: "On December 13th, 1905, Mr. Andrews introduced H. R. 7042, an enabling act with the usual title, which took the customary course of reference to the committee on territories. Soon afterwards, on January 20, 1906, Mr. Hamilton, chairman of the committee, presented a bill quite similar to the one discussed during the preceding session, to enable Oklahoma and the Indian Territory to become one state, and New Mexico and Arizona another; and this passed the house almost immediately, on January 25th. At the opening of the second session of this congress (the 59th) Senator Teller introduced a bill for separate statehood for New Mexico (Senate 7079); the jointure project having been rejected by the vote of Arizona in November; and as there was no chance for action at that time, he reintroduced the same bill at the beginning of the next congress on December 4, 1907 (Senate 515, 60th Congress).

"Two days before, on December 2nd, the first day of the session, Delegate Andrews introduced a single statehood bill for New Mexico, in the usual form

without a vote, it was easy for him to undertake. When any member of congress had some pet measure Mr. Andrews would go out of his way to secure for that member the aid of his powerful friends in congress from the state of Pennsylvania. In this way the delegate brought to his assistance and ardent support, when the time came for him to ask for reciprocity, many members who helped "just because Andrews asked them." His close connection with Senators Quay and Penrose supplied him with an influential standing that was valuable in the extreme. He was known as the "Third Senator from Pennsylvania." From December, 1905, until December, 1909, when the 61st congress met, during which time Mr. Andrews had been elected from New Mexico on the statehood issue, he labored in season and out for the passage of a statehood bill. On January 17, 1910, the so-called Hamilton Bill — H. R. 18166 — was passed by the house of representatives without opposition. It was received in the senate the following day and referred to the committee on territories, of which Senator Beveridge was the chairman,[488] a pronounced foe of New Mexico, whose plotting and in-

(House Bill No. 4). At his request, Senator Penrose presented the same bill in the senate on December 9th (Senate 1484). It was on this house bill that the hearing was held on January 29, 1908, referred to elsewhere. Practically the same bill was re-introduced at the beginning of the short session of that congress, December 8, 1908; as that was the time when action had been promised a year before by certain officials in Washington; but, as usual, that promise turned out to be only a subterfuge for delay.

"On February 3, 1909, Hon. E. L. Hamilton, of Michigan, chairman of the house committee, who deserves a warm spot in the heart of every New Mexican on account of his constant friendliness to the territory, introduced House Bill No. 27607 of the 60th congress, being an enabling act for New Mexico and one for Arizona, combined in one bill, but entirely separate in their operations. This was the conclusion of the house committee on the subject of statehood for the territories, after various hearings and full consideration during the greater part of two sessions."

[488] Prince, L. Bradford, *Struggle for Statehood*, Santa Fé, N. M., 1910, page 122: "It was well known that Senator Beveridge had in mind a number of provisions varying from those in the Hamilton bill, and his ideas took official shape in a bill introduced in the senate on January 31, by Senator Dillingham (for Mr. Beveridge) who was absent from Washington. This bill, known as Senate 5916, had exactly the same title as that of the Hamilton bill, and was immediately referred to the same committee.

"Thanks to strong influences outside of congress, pre-eminent among which was that of President Taft, who insisted that the pledge contained in the republican national platform should be fulfilled by the admission of the territories, there was now little outspoken opposition to statehood for either New Mexico or Arizona; and the senate committee, having both bills before it, was in a position to settle all details. Various hearings were held, including that of February 18th, referred to in another chapter, and the committee gave careful

triguing finally availed him nothing, for he was outgeneraled by the delegate from New Mexico. Senator Aldrich, at the time the greatest force in the senate, at heart was opposed to New Mexico and Arizona and did not propose to let any bill pass which would admit either of the two remaining territories to statehood. He, too, was no match for Delegate Andrews in political maneuvering.

"For three months," says L. Bradford Prince,[489] "the statehood bill remained on the calendar of the senate, and until June 15th there was always a doubt as to the final result. As time passed congress became restless at the length of the session, and the members expressed great anxiety for an adjournment not later than Saturday, June 18th. Several times the consideration of the statehood bill had been postponed in order to allow other measures of national importance to be taken up, and the last of these was what was known as the conservation bill. While the action of the committee on territories appeared to be in good faith, yet there were still many who were suspicious of its real desire for the passage of the bill.

"At length, on June 15th, at half past five in the afternoon, the conservation bill was passed; the statehood bill was immediately announced, and as the hour was late, by general agreement it was made 'unfinished business,' which would bring it up at two p. m. on every day until finally disposed of; and the senate then adjourned.

"On the succeeding day at exactly two o'clock Vice-President Sherman laid the statehood bill before the senate as the subject then in order. Senator Beveridge as chairman of the committee on territories, explained the proposed amendments embodied in the senate bill. The most important was that which required the statehood elections in Arizona to be held under the territorial law as it existed before the disfranchising statute of the last legislature; others related to the donations of public lands, to the payment of territorial and local debts, etc.

"He was followed by Senators Frazier, Nelson, Hughes, and Smoot. All were in favor of statehood, but the democratic senators preferred the Hamilton or House Bill. Senator Frazier, speaking

attention to the subject until March 14th, when Mr. Beveridge made a report, using the Hamilton bill (H. R. 18166) as its basis, but striking out all of that bill and substituting the Beveridge bill with a few slight amendments.

"This report put the bill on the calendar as No. 388, and brought the matter squarely before the senate."

[489] L. Bradford Prince, *Struggle for Statehood*, Santa Fé, N. M., 1910, pp. 124-5. "It is well known that Senator Aldrich and his friends were of the confirmed opinion that the house would not concur. The distinguished gentleman from Rhode Island would never have permitted the bill to proceed thus far had he not been assured that the house would not follow the senate. Delegate Andrews outwitted him."

for the democrats on the committee, opposed the senate substitute because it sought to fix the qualifications of voters in Arizona. Senator Hughes also advocated the house bill because it did not place so many restrictions on the new states as were contained in the senate bill. Senator Smoot insisted on immediate admission and said that even if both new states were to be democratic he would favor their admission as a right.

"The only division was as to preference for the senate or the house bill. The vote on this question was by strict party lines, the republicans voting for the senate bill and the democrats for the house bill, the result being 42 to 19 in favor of the former. On the final vote on the passage of the bill, the vote was unanimous!

"While this result was extremely gratifying, there was still much apprehension felt as to the result in case the house declined to concur in the senate amendments and insisted on a conference. The latter was the usual course of procedure, and it was freely asserted that the two houses would never agree. In fact, it was intimated that the action of the senate would not have been so harmonious but for the general belief that the house would non-concur.

"Here again the president did good service to New Mexico. He held conferences with several influential members of the house, including Chairman Hamilton, and urged that the senate amendments should be concurred in without conference. His influence was very effective, and many who preferred the house bill agreed to sink their personal desires in order to avoid any risk as to the final passage of the bill. The president was also anxious to have early action in order that the bill might be signed before his contemplated journey to the Yale commencement on Monday, the 20th. Another factor that contributed to this action was the desire for an early adjournment of congress, and the certainty that a conference, followed by a disagreement, would bring about a long debate that would greatly retard the close of the session.

"Mr. Andrews, upon whose judgment many relied, concluded that now that success was actually within its grasp, it was better for the territory to accept the senate amendments and end the matter forever, than to run any risk of failure through a disagreement of the house. Governor Mills, who was in Washington at the time, concurred in this view and telegraphed on the 17th that the house would probably accept the action of the senate. On that day the bill still lay on the table of the speaker, not yet announced.

"Shortly after two o'clock on the afternoon of Saturday, June 18th, Speaker Cannon laid the bill as amended in the senate before the house. There was a moment of suppressed excitement, and then Mr. Lloyd of Missouri, the senior democratic member of the committee, rose and said that while he was not entirely satisfied with the senate bill, yet in order to insure immediate statehood for the territories he would not oppose it. Instantly, Mr. Hamilton, the committee chairman, moved to concur in the senate amendments. Shouts of 'vote, vote,' arose from all sides of the house. The question was put, viva voce, there being no demand for a roll call, and the house concurred by a unanimous vote!

"The deed was done! The long conflict of sixty years was over! Members crowded around Delegate Andrews to offer congratulations. All knew that the passage of this bill had been the object of his labors for years and that this was the happiest moment of his life.

"The good news was flashed to Santa Fé, and in a moment by direction of acting Governor Jaffa, the national flag was unfurled on the tall staff at the corner of the historic Palace, and following the lead of the *New Mexican*, where the news was first received, all the buildings on the Plaza were quickly covered with red, white and blue.

"That was on Saturday.

"The president had signified his desire to affix the signature which would give legal vitality to the bill and transform it into a law, before leaving Washington on Monday; so, all the preceding formalities were hastened.

"On Monday morning, notwithstanding its length, the statehood bill was properly enrolled and ready for the official signatures. As soon as the house assembled it was signed by Speaker Cannon; then it was hurried to the senate chamber, where the vice-president affixed his autograph at exactly half past twelve.

"From the capitol it was quickly conveyed to the White House, where the president was ready to act. Here were assembled several of those who had been most active in achieving its success, with such representatives of the two territories as were in the national capital. The house committee was represented by Chairman Hamilton, whose self-abnegation in allowing the senate bill to be substituted for his own should not soon be forgotten, and by Representatives Guernsey and Cole. The senate committee was appropriately represented by its chairman, Senator Beveridge. Postmaster General Hitchcock, who had rendered efficient aid, represented the cabinet. Delegate Andrews from New Mexico, and Delegate Cameron from Arizona, the actual representatives of the newly enfranchised commonwealths, were prominent, and beside them were Thomas B. Catron, of Santa Fé, H. I. Latham, of Phoenix, and J. T. Williams, of Tucson, with Ira M. Bond, the well known New Mexican correspondent, and others interested.

"The president said a few words of congratulation, and then proposed to affix his official signature. The postmaster general presented a gold pen, with the request that it should be used, and Delegate Andrews produced the unique gold-banded quill taken from the great American eagle captured in Taos, and furnished for the occasion, in its beautiful case, as a patriotic service by George B. Paxton, when he had no thought that death would forbid his presence at the ceremony. The president wrote half of the signature with the former and the remainder with the latter; returning the pens to the donors as mementos of this great historic occasion.

"The White House clock stood at 1:40 p. m.

"That signature ended the drama of the 'Struggle for Statehood.' There had been more than fifty statehood bills in the sixty years of effort. Those few penstrokes transformed a statehood bill into a statehood law."

It was difficult for the people of New Mexico to believe that the long-looked for moment had arrived. In every city and town there were demonstrations and speech-making. Upon his return to the territory, Delegate Andrews was greeted by great crowds of his constituents. Receptions were held in his honor where the gratitude of the masses found expression in the speeches of the political leaders and prominent citizens.

In accordance with the provisions of the Act of June 20, 1910, nine days later the governor issued his proclamation for the election of delegates to a constitutional convention, fixing September 6, 1910, as the day on which the election should be held.[490]

---

[490] Under the requirements of the enabling act, the governor, chief justice, and secretary of the territory, June 28, 1910, apportioned the delegates to be elected to the constitutional convention, in accordance with the voting population as shown by the vote cast at the election for delegate in congress in the year 1908, the apportionment being as follows:

Bernalillo	8	Luna	1	San Miguel	9
Chaves	4	McKinley	1	Santa Fé	5
Colfax	6	Mora	5	Sierra	2
Curry	2	Otero	3	Socorro	5
Doña Ana	4	Quay	5	Taos	4
Eddy	2	Rio Arriba	6	Torrance	3
Grant	4	Roosevelt	3	Union	4
Guadalupe	4	Sandoval	2	Valencia	3
Lincoln	3	San Juan	2		

Under the provisions of the act of congress the greater portion of the actual work incident to statehood devolved upon the secretary of the territory, and practically all of this was done during the fiscal year ended June 30, 1911.

One hundred thousand dollars were appropriated by congress to defray the necessary expenses of holding the convention and the elections prescribed by the enabling act, to be locally expended by the secretary of the territory under the direction and in the discretion of the secretary of the interior. The disbursing and accounting of this money involved a vast amount of detail, especially in the preparation and certification of vouchers, and naturally the work of

In July, following the issue of the governor's proclamation, meetings of the republican and democratic central committees were held at Alburquerque. An effort was made to hold a non-partisan convention. The chairman of the republican committee favored this proposition, but the majority of the republican committee were opposed to any arrangement with the opposition, and, with the exception of two or three counties, notably Otero, Socorro, and Rio Arriba, the two last mentioned considered safely republican, partisan tickets were nominated. The election was duly held at which the republican party elected more than two-thirds of the delegates to the convention.[491]

---

checking and paying the various claims took up considerable time, although every effort was made to settle all accounts as promptly as possible.

Of the one hundred thousand dollars appropriated there remained unexpended sixteen thousand two hundred and seventy-six dollars and ninety-eight cents.

[491] The members of the constitutional convention, with their political affiliation marked with the letter "R" for republican and "D" for Democrat, from the several counties, were: Bernalillo county—Herbert F. Raynolds, R; A. A. Sedillo, R; M. L. Stern, R; Anastacio Gutierrez, R; Nestor Montoya, R; Francis E. Wood, R; E. S. Stover, R; H. B. Fergusson, D. Chaves county—John I. Hinkle, D; G. A. Richardson, D; Emmet Patton, D; Green B. Patterson, D. Colfax county—Francisco Gauna, R; Thomas H. O'Brien, R; Charles Springer, R; Norman W. Bartlett, R; Clarence J. Roberts, R; George S. Brown, R. Curry county—John W. Childers, D; Thomas J. Mabry, D. Doña Ana county—Frank W. Parker, R; Isidoro Armijo, R; Charles E. Miller, R; Winfred E. Garrison, R. Eddy county—M. P. Skeen, D; C. R. Brice, D. Grant county—A. H. Harllee, D; J. B. Gilchrist, D; W. D. Murray, R. Guadalupe county—Salome Martinez, R; John G. Clancy, R; Tranquilino Labadie, R; Reymondo Harrison, D. Lincoln county—Andrew H. Hudspeth, D; Jacobo Aragon, R; John H. Canning, R. Luna county—James N. Upton, D. McKinley county—Gregory Page, R. Mora county—E. M. Lucero, R; Daniel Cassidy, Sr., R; Anastacio Medina, R; Juan Navarro, R; Fred S. Brown, R. Otero county—Albert B. Fall, R; George E. Moffett, D; J. Lee Lawson, D. Quay county—C. C. Davidson, D; Charles H. Kohn, R; Ed. F. Saxon, D; John L. House, D; Reed Holloman, R. Rio Arriba county—Venceslado Jaramillo, R; T. D. Burns, R; Perfecto Esquibel, R; Jose A. Lucero, R; Samuel Eldodt, D; J. H. Crist, D. Roosevelt county—James A. Hall, D; C. M. Compton, D; W. E. Lindsay, R. Sandoval county—Alejandro Sandoval, R; E. A. Miera, R. San Juan county—R. W. Heflin, D; M. D. Taylor, D. San Miguel county—Margarito Romero, R; Atanacio Roibal, R; J. M. Cunningham, R; S. B. Davis, Jr., R; Luciano Maes, R; Harry W. Kelly, R; Eugenio Romero, R; Nepomuceno Segura, R; Charles A. Spiess, R. Santa Fé county—B. F. Pankey, R; José D. Sena, R; Victor Ortega, R; George W. Pritchard, R; Thomas B. Catron, R. Sierra county—Edward D. Tittman, D; Frank H. Winston, R. Socorro county—H. M. Dougherty, D; James G. Fitch, D; H. O. Bursum, R; A. C. Abeytia, R; J. Frank Romero, R. Taos county—Malaquias Martinez, R; Onesimo Martinez, R; Squire Hartt, Jr., R; William McKean, R. Torrance county—William McIntosh, R; A. B. McDonald, R; Acasio Gallegos, R. Union county—Eufracio Gallegos, R; Candelario Vigil, R; George W. Baker, R; F. C. Field, R. Valencia county—Solomon Luna, R; John Becker, R; Sylvestre Miraval, R.

In the presence of the largest assemblage ever gathered in the hall of the house of representatives, in the capitol, at 2 o'clock, October 3, 1910, the constitutional convention began its task of formulating the organic law of the new state. Thomas B. Catron, of Santa Fé county, called the convention to order. Rev. Jules Deraches, as the personal representative of the Archbishop of Santa Fé, delivered the invocation. A roll call showed that all of the delegates elected were present, except W. D. Murray, of Grant county, and A. B. McDonald, of Torrance county. The oath was administered by Associate Justice John R. McFie. The convention was composed of 71 republicans and 29 democrats. In accordance with caucus selections, Charles A. Spiess,[492] of San Miguel county, was nominated and elected president of the convention. His opponent was Harvey B. Fergusson, of Bernalillo. George W. Armijo[493] was elected chief clerk and Harry R. Whiting,[494] sergeant at arms.

CONSTITUTIONAL CONVENTION OF 1910

---

[492] Charles A. Spiess is of German-Swiss ancestry. He was born at Warrensburg, Missouri, March 19, 1867. He was raised on a farm and received his education in the public schools and at the state normal school at Warrensburg. He came to New Mexico in 1888 and, in 1890, located at Santa Fé, where he entered the law office of Thomas B. Catron and was admitted to the bar in 1891. He formed a partnership with Mr. Catron which continued for several years. In 1898, he was appointed district attorney for the counties of Santa Fé, Taos, Rio Arriba, and San Juan. He afterward filled a similar position in the fourth judicial district, holding the office until 1903. He represented Santa Fé county in the council of the legislative assembly in 1896. After his removal to Las Vegas, he was three times elected to the same body. In all of the positions his record may be called brilliant. In his capacity of legislator he framed many progressive and beneficial statutes. In the 37th and 38th assemblies he was the presiding officer of the council, filling the position with marked ability. He has long held a place among the leaders of the New Mexico bar.

[493] George W. Armijo was born in Peralta, Valencia county, March 16, 1877. He is the son of Mariano Armijo and Lola Chaves Armijo, and a grandson of Col. J. Francisco Chaves. He was educated at the college of the Christian Brothers, St. Louis, Mo. After his return to New Mexico, he filled a number of minor city and county offices. In 1898, he was one of the first to offer his services to his country and enlisted forthwith in Troop F, Roosevelt's Rough Riders; was wounded in the fight at Las Guasimas. After the war, he returned to Santa Fé; was elected probate clerk of Santa Fé county. In 1911, he was the republican nominee for member of the corporation commission and was defeated. He is now secretary of that commission.

[494] H. R. Whiting was born at Detroit, December 2, 1837. He is of English ancestry, his forebears having come to America before the Revolution, settling in New York. His great-grandfather was a soldier in the Revolutionary war and his grandfather was an officer in the war of 1812. He received his education in the common schools and at Dartmouth college. At the outbreak of the

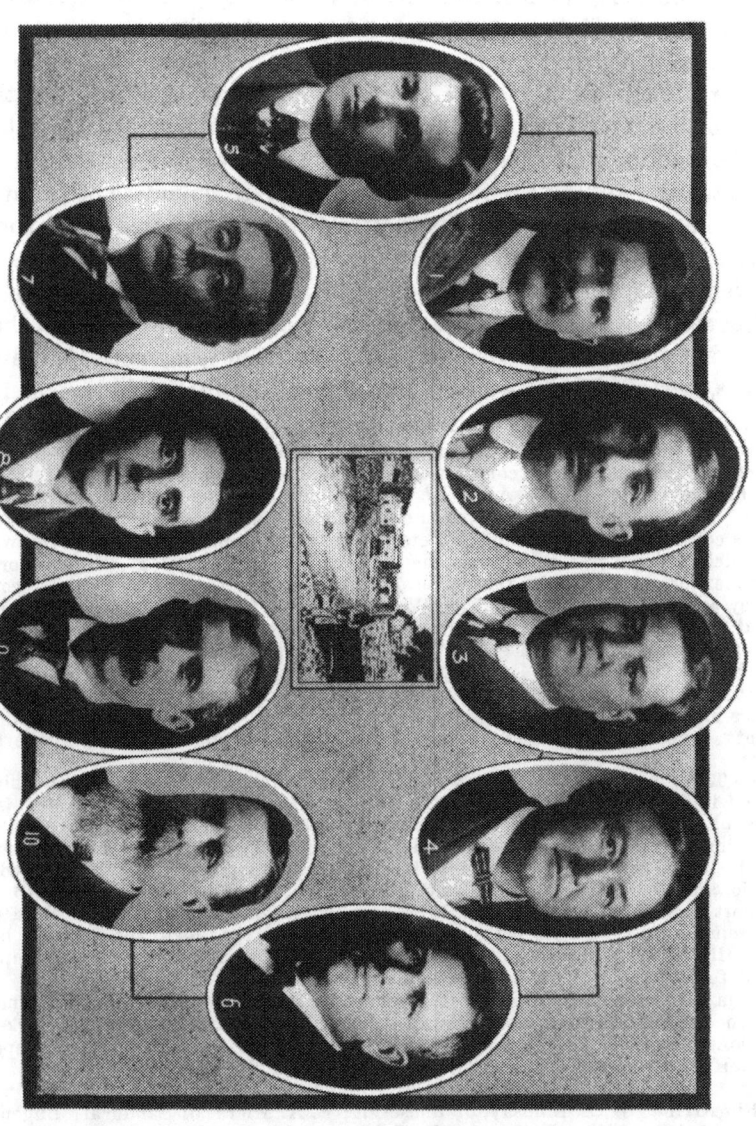

Members of the Constitutional Convention of 1910

1. W. E. Lindsay. 2. W. D. Murray. 3. Antonio A. Sedillo. 4. B. F. Pankey. 5. John I. Hinkle. 6. H. O. Bursum. 7. Thomas D. Burns. 8. Venceslado Jaramillo. 9. Samuel Eldodt. 10. Eugenio Romero

The candidacy of Mr. Spiess was warmly opposed by a leading newspaper at Alburquerque; he was charged with being the representative of "special interests," but this opposition availed little in the republican caucus as he received more than two-thirds of the votes of the republican members. The republican majority, directed by the leaders of the party, however, determined to keep control of the situation and by resolution provided for a committee of twenty-one members which had for its chairman, Solomon Luna. This committee was charged with the duty of selecting all committees of the convention, a duty ordinarily incumbent upon the president of a deliberative body of this dignity and character. It may be said that this committee had for its members [495] the men who, more than any others, performed the work of the convention, dictated the policies

Civil War he served on the staff of General McKinstry, with the rank of captain of volunteers. In 1862, he aided in raising the 24th Michigan Infantry, in which regiment he held a commission as second lieutenant; participated in all the battles fought by the Army of the Potomac and was captured at Gettysburg. Was confined in Libby prison eight months; was exchanged and returned to his command, then in front of Petersburg; served until the close of the war at which time he was serving on the staff of Major General S. W. Crawford. For meritorious service at the battle of Petersburg he was promoted to a captaincy and after the battle of Five Forks was brevetted major. He was wounded at Fredericksburg. After the war, Major Whiting came to New Mexico as a member of the staff of the New York *Herald*, spending a year in writing letters about New Mexico. In 1868, he was appointed clerk of the United States court at Alburquerque, a position which he held for ten years. He held the offices of probate clerk, assessor, and county school superintendent of Bernalillo county, respectively. He has been a United States commissioner twenty-seven years.

[495] This committee was a sort of "steering" affair. The newspaper which voiced its opposition to Mr. Spiess's candidacy was the *Alburquerque Morning Journal*, a powerful factor in the business and political life of New Mexico. This journal, itself owned by individuals in sympathy with every interest with which, in its utterances editorially, it charged Mr. Spiess with too close connection, for several years the leading newspaper of New Mexico, declined to support the republican ticket in 1911, and to its condemnation of the head of the republican ticket. its espousal of the cause of the dominant faction, numerically, of the republican party in Bernalillo county, may be chiefly attributed the defeat of some of the party's candidates.

This "Committee on Committees" was composed of the following: Francis E. Wood, of Bernalillo county; Charles Springer, of Colfax; Frank W. Parker, of Doña Ana; W. D. Murray, of Grant; Tranquilino Labadie, of Guadalupe; John H. Canning, of Lincoln; Gregory Page, of McKinley; Fred S. Brown, of Mora; Albert B. Fall, of Otero; Reed Holloman, of Quay; Perfecto Esquibel, of Rio Arriba; W. E. Lindsay, of Roosevelt; E. A. Miera, of Sandoval; Eugenio Romero, of San Miguel; Thomas B. Catron, of Santa Fé; Frank H. Winston, of Sierra; Holm O. Bursum, of Socorro; Malaquias Martinez, of Taos; Acasio Gallegos, of Torrance; Eufracio Gallegos, of Union, and Solomon Luna, of Valencia. Every member was a political leader and power in the county which was represented by him in the convention.

of the republican majority, and without the support of whom, no article of the constitution could have been adopted.

The adoption of the resolution by which the committee of twenty-one was practically the arbiter of all measures advocated by members of the convention was the beginning of caucus control of the convention. A very respectable number of the members-elect of the constitutional convention were chosen upon a platform calling for the adoption of the initiative and an effective referendum and other "progressive" ideas of government, but the republican caucus, controlled by leaders opposed to these "progressive principles," once it secured the presence of the members who had advocated their adoption, bound them hand and foot, in this manner eliminating all independence of action or individuality, except as declared in the caucus, on the part of members thus compelled to vote for measures and articles in which they did not concur and which became a part of the constitution notwithstanding their opposition.

The convention completed its labors on November 21, 1910, and it may be said that the constitution as framed by the convention was a model of conservatism, when compared with present day progressive ideals. The democratic minority, through its leaders, was consistent in its opposition to many of the principal articles, but several so-called "conservative" democrats, men of great influence, declared that, in the election soon to be called, they would support the constitution, which they did.[496]

There were a great many of the democratic leaders, however, who did not approve of the constitution. The objections urged by them are voiced in a manifesto signed by the member of the national democratic committee from New Mexico, Andreius A. Jones, which was published and found wide circulation prior to the election when the constitution was submitted to the people for ratification or rejection.[497]

---

[496] The following democratic members of the convention voted for the constitution as framed: C. C. Davidson, Reymundo Harrison, G. A. Richardson, Samuel Eldodt, T. J. Mabry, C. R. Brice, C. M. Compton, and H. M. Dougherty. The following voted against it, the majority because of the party pledges: J. W. Childers, H. B. Fergusson, James G. Fitch, J. B. Gilchrist, A. H. Harllee, R. W. Heflin, James E. Hall, John I. Hinkle, J. L. House, A. H. Hudspeth, J. L. Lawson, George E. Moffet, Green B. Patterson, E. F. Saxon M. P. Skeen, M. D. Taylor, Edward D. Tittman, James N. Upton, and William B. Walton. All but seven of these later signed the document.

[497] This statement of objections was issued from Santa Fé, December 17,

The constitution as framed was of a kind which appealed to the judgment of the people in almost every particular. The extremists in government were disappointed, but that was to be expected. Some of these, because women were not given full suffrage; others because prohibition was not provided for directly; others because the Spanish-speaking citizen was so thoroughly protected in his rights;

1910, and was framed by a convention made up of prominent members of the democratic party. It was as follows:

"We democrats from a large majority of the counties of New Mexico, in convention assembled, do declare that we condemn the constitution framed by the convention recently in session, and now before the people for their consideration, for the following reasons, to wit:

"1. That said constitution is made very difficult of amendment by its provisions.

"2. That the provisions for the establishment of the judiciary system is inexcusably extravagant and imposes needless burdens of expense on the people, in that it creates more judicial districts than are necessary and imposes salaries that are higher than the labors and responsibilities of the judicial office require; and further, that it invests the legislature with power to create an additional number of judicial offices in any district, without any constitutional limitations; and further, that said provision does not provide for a non-partisan judiciary, nominated at a general direct primary of the people, regardless of party and to be elected at elections to be held at other times than at the general elections.

"3. That the terms of office of the judges provided for, are too long for the best interests of the people in that it restricts the power of control over the office.

"4. That the legislative provision is needlessly extravagant, in that it doubles the number of members of both houses of the legislature, and increases the per diem compensation over that in effect and amply sufficient under our territorial government.

"5. That the compensation provided for the state officials is higher than the duties of the respective offices require, or the tax-payers can afford.

"6. That the salaries provided for the members of the state corporation commission are higher than are warranted by reason of the fact that their duties are merely clerical under the provision creating the commission.

"7. In general, the expense of the government necessitated by the proposed constitution will greatly increase the burden of taxation which already rests heavily on the people.

"8. That the board of equalization provided by the constitution will consist wholly of elective officers who have campaign debts to pay.

"9. That the districting of the proposed state, both for judicial and legislative purposes, is plainly inequitable and in some instances imposes a great hardship on the people.

"10. That the constitution does not provide a limit on taxation for county, district and municipal purposes.

"11. That the constitution does not provide any reservation of power in the people for direct legislation by means of the initiative, a practical referendum, for a direct primary or an advisory selection of United States senators by popular vote.

"12. That the constitution does not make provision for an effective and honest election law or for a corrupt practices act.

"13. That it is provided in section II of the enabling act, passed by congress, that all lands granted in quantity or as an indemnity shall be selected

but, in the main, although a quarter of a century earlier it would have been considered radical in its many innovations, the convention submitted an instrument under which intelligent legislatures may formulate laws for the progress of the people and the advancement of the state.

The election for the ratification or rejection of the constitution as framed was held January 21, 1911, at which a total of 45,141 votes were cast, 31,742 in favor of and 13,399 against ratification, a total

---

under the direction and subject to the approval of the secretary of the interior from the non-mineral public land of the United States by a commission composed of the governor and attorney general of the state and the surveyor general, an officer of the United States.

"Section 2, article XII, of the proposed constitution, provides that the commissioner of lands shall select and locate all public lands. Section 4, article IX, provides that one million acres of land granted to the state by congress for the payment of railroad bonds of Grant and Santa Fé counties, shall be selected and located by the proper officers of the state. The proposed constitution is therefore in direct conflict with the enabling act notwithstanding the general provision contained in section IX of article XXI of the proposed constitution and no lawful method is provided for the selection of all institutional lands and the lands with which it was expected to pay the railroad indebtedness of Santa Fé and Grant counties. If the constitution is adopted the state will necessarily issue its bonds for the payment of the railroad indebtedness of Santa Fé and Grant counties to more than one million dollars and the state be obligated to that extent and neither of said counties relieved of such indebtedness. The institutions will be deprived of all rentals from the lands intended for them and it will be impossible to amend the constitution in this respect earlier than four years after the institution of the state government. As the selection of such lands involves a decision as to their being mineral or non-mineral in character, it is unreasonable to suppose that congress, even by special legislation, would confer upon the commissioner of lands of the state the sole power to make such selection.

"Wherefore this convention, having the subject under the most earnest and thoughtful consideration, both before and during its deliberation, does declare its judgment to a candid world that the rejection of the submitted constitution will be for the highest and best interests of the people of New Mexico as a body of American citizens under a government of, for and by the people. We earnestly urge all good citizens throughout the Territory to act accordingly in the pending campaign; but the party fealty of democrats shall not be called in question for their vote on the constitution whether it be for or against.

"We therefore appeal to the patriotic spirit of all citizens of the Territory to disapprove the proposed constitution for the reasons above set forth and for the further reason that the way is provided and the method easy, under the enabling act, for them to secure a better constitution and one in accord with their sentiments, expressed through the ballot box on January 21st, 1911, inasmuch as that act is mandatory on the governor to call members of the constitutional convention together again twenty days after the election if the constitution submitted is disapproved by the people.

"We submit, in conclusion, that this question transcends partisan politics — is in no sense a party one — and appeals to patriotism and for the untrammeled exercise of the conscience of the individual voter.

"Willis Brown, Secretary.   A. A. JONES, Chairman."

Members of the Constitutional Convention of 1910

1. Gregory Page. 2. W. B. Walton. 3. Margarito Romero. 4. Malaquias Martinez. 5. Alexander Read. 6. Reed Holloman. 7. Herbert F. Raynolds. 8. Stephen B. Davis, Jr. 9. José D. Sena. 10. Solomon Luna.

majority for the constitution as presented of 18,343. Only four of the twenty-six counties voted against its adoption.[498]

The pronounced majority by which the constitution was adopted was not a perfect index of popular judgment as to the merits of the instrument. There was an overwhelming desire for statehood at any price. Many of the radical element were well aware of the substantial opposition to statehood which existed in the populous states of the Atlantic seaboard. They realized, if the constitution was rejected, that affirmative legislation by congress was necessary in order to hold another session. The vast majority believed that this was the only chance. They considered that the constitution as presented was a sort of compromise measure and its rejection at the time would be an experiment which might result in great misfortune. There was an apparent determination on the part of the people to make the majority as large as possible so that the world would come to know what were the sentiments of New Mexicans on the subject of statehood rather than on the merits of the constitution submitted for their approval or rejection.

In due course a certified copy of the constitution, as ratified, was submitted to the president of the United States and to congress for approval in conformity with the enabling act. On February 24, 1911, the president, in a message to the senate and house of representatives, recommended the approval of the same by congress.[499]

---

[498] These counties were Lincoln, Roosevelt, San Juan, and Sierra. Prior to the election of January 21, 1911, under a resolution passed by the constitutional convention, the secretary of the territory caused to be printed and mailed to every registered voter in New Mexico, a copy of the constitution, printed in the language he best understood.

[499] William Howard Taft, *Message* to the senate and house of representatives: "To the Senate and House of Representatives: The act to enable the people of New Mexico to form a constitution and state government and to be admitted to the union on an equal footing with the original states, as passed June 20, 1910, provides that when the constitution, for the adoption of which provision is made in the act, shall have been duly ratified by the people of New Mexico in the manner provided by the statute, a certified copy of the same shall be submitted to the president of the United States and to congress for approval, and if congress and the president approve of such constitution, or if the president approves of the same and congress fails to disapprove the same, during the next regular session thereof, then that the president shall certify said fact to the governor of New Mexico, who shall proceed to issue his proclamation for the election of state and county officers etc.

"The constitution, prepared in accordance with the act of congress, has been duly ratified by the people of New Mexico, and a certified copy of the same has

Four days after receiving the message from the president, the committee on territories of the house of representatives approved the constitution submitted by the people of New Mexico, and, on March 1, the house gave its formal approval to the document. Three days later, Senator Dillingham, of the senate committee on territories, reported House Joint Resolution Number 295. Senator Owen, of Oklahoma, objected to the passage of the resolution unless the approval of the Arizona constitution was made a part of the resolution. Senator Owen fully expected that the resolution would carry, but Senator Bailey, with several other democrats, voted against the Arizona rider, as did all the regular republicans, and it was voted down by a vote of 45 to 39, thus ending the statehood matter in the sixty-first congress.

The elections of 1910 resulted in a change of control of the house of representatives; the republican party was no longer in power in the senate, several of the so-called "progressive" republican senators voting with the democrats whenever any question involving their ideas of government was at stake. This condition of affairs gave the democratic leaders of New Mexico hope that by careful manipulation congress might be induced, in its action upon the approval of the New Mexico constitution, to include some amendment which would either defeat the constitution altogether or compel the advocates of statehood to accept the terms offered. A meeting of prominent democrats was held at Alburquerque, where, what was afterwards known as House Joint Resolution No. 14, providing for the so-called "blue ballot" was born, Andreius A. Jones being its acknowledged parent. At this meeting a committee was sent to Washington having in view the passage of this amendment, which afterward became known as the Flood resolution. The fate of the constitution submitted by the people of New Mexico, during the summer of 1911, hung in the balance. A reference chronologically to events occurring during the discussion of the Flood resolution

---

been submitted to me and also to congress, for approval in conformity with the provisions of the act.

"Inasmuch as the enabling act requires affirmative action by the president, I transmit herewith a copy of the constitution, which I am advised has been separately submitted to congress, according to the provisions of the act, by the authorities of New Mexico, and to which I have given my formal approval.

"I recommend the approval of the same by congress.
"WHITE HOUSE, February 24, 1911.   WILLIAM H. TAFT."

and other proposed amendments is given in a note.[500] On the 8th of August, H. J. R. Number 14, the Flood resolution, requiring Arizona to vote again on the article in its constitution providing for the recall of the judiciary, and a re-submission of the New Mexico amendment clause passed the senate by a vote of 53 to 18.

On the 15th of August, President Taft, in a special message to the

[500] On March 4, Delegate Andrews's resolution, amended to include Arizona, was defeated by a vote of 45 to 39. Senator Owen conducted a single-handed filibuster for more than eleven hours. In his speech he contended that "Arizona had a progressive constitution with the initiative and referendum. New Mexico, on the other hand, has not. Arizona is democratic and progressive. New Mexico is republican and retrogressive." He announced his determination to hold the floor until time to adjourn, thus keeping the senate from approving the reports on appropriation bills, unless the two territories were admitted together. Finally, he was assured that there would be an extra session, called immediately after the close of the 61st, Vice-president Sherman bringing him this word from the president. Senator Owen then consented to yield the floor if a vote were taken immediately on the amended resolution. He knew that if it passed both territories would come in; if it did not, both would be kept out until the extra session. The result was the defeat of the resolution.

On April 4, at the extra session, Congressman Flood introduced a joint resolution admitting the states of Arizona and New Mexico on an equal footing with the other states. Delegate Andrews introduced a resolution admitting New Mexico, and Delegate Cameron, of Arizona, introduced a similar resolution affecting Arizona.

April 13, 18, 21, 22, 25, 26, 27, 28, and 29 were devoted to hearings before the house committee on territories, during which members of the committee became convinced that New Mexicans should vote on a substitute for Article XIX, the amending article, and the people of Arizona should vote on the recall of the judiciary, both territories to become states regardless of the outcome of the election.

May 12, the Flood resolution was reported to the house with the amendment regarding elections in the two territories above described.

May 23, the Flood resolution, as amended, passed the house without division, after motion of the minority leader, Mann, to recommit the resolution to committee had been lost, 54 to 214.

May 25, the Flood resolution was received by the senate and referred to the committee on territories.

June 16, 17, and 23, hearings were held by the senate committee on territories.

June 24, the Flood resolution, with minor amendments, was voted on by the senate committee on territories, and the chairman of the committee was authorized to make favorable report to the senate.

July 11, the Flood resolution was reported favorably to the senate.

July 13, an amendment by Senator Nelson, of Minnesota, in the nature of a substitute for the Flood resolution, was presented. This amendment would adopt the New Mexico constitution without change and required Arizona to cut out the recall of the judiciary before becoming a state.

July 14, an agreement was reached by which a vote was to be taken on the statehood matter on August 7th.

August 8th, the Nelson substitute was defeated in the senate by a vote of 43 to 26. The Flood resolution, requiring Arizona to again vote on the recall of the judiciary and re-submission of New Mexico amendment clause, was passed by a vote of 53 to 18.

house of representatives, vetoed the Flood resolution providing for the admission of the new states. His reasons for exercising the executive power of veto were based upon his thorough disapproval of the recall-of-the-judiciary feature in the Arizona constitution. The fact that the fate of the New Mexico constitution was bound up with that of Arizona made no difference to the president in formulating his opinion upon the question of admission. President Taft spared no words in his condemnation of the recall feature of the Arizona constitution, which he declared would compel judges to make their decisions under "legalized terrorism." "The provision of the Arizona constitution," he said, "in its application to county and state judges, seems to me so pernicious in its effect, so destructive of independence in the judiciary, so likely to subject the rights of the individual to the possible tyranny of popular majority, and therefore to be so injurious to the cause of free government, that I must disapprove a constitution containing it."

Much of the message was devoted to a discussion of the functions of the courts under the constitution. The president dwelt at length on the necessity of freeing the judiciary as much as possible from politics or popular influence, and referring to the recall provision asked, "Could there be a system more ingeniously devised to subject judges to momentary gusts of popular passion than this?"

On the afternoon of August 18, the senate passed a resolution presented by Senator William Alden Smith by a vote of 53 to 8. It was stated that this resolution was acceptable to the president. In the debate over the resolution, the house of representatives was charged with evading a vote on the presidential veto, and the president was likewise charged with endeavoring to coerce the people of Arizona on the proposed recall of the judiciary. On the final vote Senators Bailey and Heyburn were the only two senators opposing it, who had also voted against the passage of the original Flood resolution.[501]

On the 19th, the Smith-Flood resolution, which had passed the senate the day before, was passed by the house of representatives by a viva voce vote.

---

[501] Twenty-two republicans, twenty-seven democrats, and four "progressive" or "insurgent" senators voted in favor of the Smith-Flood resolution. Two democrats, two republicans, and four insurgents voted against it.

Prominent New Mexicans of the Nineteenth Century
1. Numa Reymond. 2. John H. Riley. 3. S. M. Ashenfelter.
4. Dr. L. G. Kennon

"Well, gentlemen, it's done," said President Taft, in the executive office in the White House at eight minutes after three o'clock in the afternoon of August twenty-first, nineteen hundred eleven, as he finished affixing his seal of approval upon the resolution admitting New Mexico and Arizona as states in the Union.

The executive office was crowded [502] with persons interested in the signing of the resolution, and deep silence prevailed as with four different pens the president completed his signature and the date, and the deed was accomplished.

The enthusiasm which prevailed in New Mexico on receipt of the news was rampant all over the state. Bonfires blazed in every town from Folsom to Columbus, and from Farmington to Carlsbad. Many meetings were held in all parts and the joyous citizens let out all of the pent-up enthusiasm for six months accumulating during the statehood struggle now so gloriously ended.

The signing of the resolution ended the fight for statehood, the struggle having continued for fifty-eight years, a contest unparalleled in the history of the United States. The records of human achievement fail to record a more remarkable struggle for self-government than the prolonged, determined, and patriotic campaign of the people of New Mexico. For more than half a century the fight was carried to the enemy; in the face of discouragements, setbacks which would utterly discourage a less vigorous and virile people; in the face of years of contumely, ridicule, slander and villification, indifference and misrepresentation, New Mexico finally won her

---

[502] There were present Delegate Andrews and Delegate Cameron; Congressman Flood, Senator Penrose; Congressman Connell, Weydeman Draper, Hoval Smith, of Arizona, and some newspaper representatives. The word had passed that the resolution would be signed at three o'clock, and at about that hour the visitors began to arrive at the executive office. A few minutes after three all were shown to the president's room, where he sat at a desk. The clerk laid the resolution before the president. "Has anyone gone over this," said he, looking around as though he wanted to be sure he was not signing the original Flood resolution. Senator Penrose assured the president it was all right, but the nation's executive proceeded to read it himself. He then picked up a pen and wrote the word "Approved." He was given another pen and wrote "William Howard Taft." With a third pen he wrote "August 21," and with a fourth, the year, "1911."

After the signature had been affixed some of those present grouped themselves on one side of the room, with the president in the foreground, and a photograph was taken. No formal program had been arranged, and those present were ushered out, while the president proceeded to work on his veto message on the cotton bill.

right to a star in the flag. Many factors combined to bring about the successful culmination of the struggle. From 1900 to 1910 the growth of the country was remarkable; its rapidity and tremendous scope have never been equaled in the west. Thousands of sturdy, progressive Americans, the class which has built up every frontier state, poured into her borders. The vast natural resources of the great southwest were only beginning to be realized at home and abroad; great enterprises for the reclamation of the arid lands and the building up of the country were inaugurated. Millions of dollars came into the country and out of an historic, romantic, and picturesque past sprung up a marvelous present and looms a gigantic future. The people of the new state are well qualified to administer government without the aid of the bureaus at Washington. Let us hope that wisdom and progressive moderation will characterize the efforts of the people so that there may be a full appreciation of the benefits conferred by self-government as well as of the duties which are imposed in the exercise of that great American function.

Pursuant to the provisions contained in the enabling act, the governor of New Mexico, William J. Mills, was notified by the president of the United States of the passage of the resolution, whereupon the governor issued his proclamation calling an election of state and county officers, the members of the legislature, and two representatives in congress. In addition, pursuant to the Smith-Flood resolution, the voters in New Mexico were called upon to decide whether or not the constitution should be made easier of amendment. For this purpose a special "blue ballot" [503] was provided for, bearing

---

[503] The proposed amendment, as specified in the Smith-Flood resolution, was as follows:

"*Article XIX — Amendment*

"Section 1. Any amendment or amendments to this constitution may be proposed in either house of the legislature at any regular session thereof; and if a majority of all members elected to each of the two houses, voting separately, shall vote in favor thereof, such proposed amendment or amendments shall be entered on their respective journals, with the yeas and nays thereon.

"The secretary of state shall cause any such amendment or amendments to be published in at least one newspaper in every county of the state, where a newspaper is published once each week, for four consecutive weeks, in English and Spanish, when newspapers in both of said languages are published in such counties, the last publication to be not more than two weeks prior to the election at which time said amendment or amendments shall be submitted to the electors of the state for their approval or rejection; and the said amendment or amendments shall be voted upon at the next regular election held in said state, after the adjournment of the legislature proposing such amendment or amendments,

upon it the proposed amendment to Article XIX of the constitution, such ballot to be delivered to the individual by the election officers whether requested or not.

The election day was fixed for November 7. Immediately the two great political parties, through their regular machinery, issued calls for delegate conventions, the republican party naming Las Vegas, September 28th, and the democratic party, Santa Fé, October 2nd.

---

or at such special election to be held not less than six months after the adjournment of said legislature, at such time as said legislature may by law provide. If the same be ratified by a majority of the electors voting thereon, such amendment or amendments shall become part of this constitution. If two or more amendments are proposed, they shall be so submitted as to enable the electors to vote on each of them separately; provided, that no amendment shall apply to or affect the provisions of Sections 1 and 3 of Article 7 hereof, on elective franchise, and Sections 8 and 10 of Article 12 hereof, on education, unless it be proposed by vote of three-fourths of the members elected to each house and be ratified by a vote of the people of this state in an election at which at least three-fourths of the electors voting in the whole state and at least two-thirds of those voting in each county in the state shall vote for such amendment.

"Sec. 2. Whenever, during the first twenty-five years after the adoption of this constitution, the legislature, by a three-fourths vote of the members elected to each house, or, after the expiration of said period of twenty-five years, by a two-thirds vote of the members elected to each house, shall deem it necessary to call a convention to revise or amend this constitution, they shall submit the question of calling such convention to the electors at the next general election, and if a majority of all the electors voting on such question at said election in the state shall vote in favor of calling a convention the legislature shall, at the next session, provide by law for calling the same. Such convention shall consist of at least as many delegates as there are members of the house of representatives. The constitution adopted by such convention shall have no validity until it has been submitted to and ratified by the people.

"Sec. 3. If this constitution be in any way so amended as to allow laws to be enacted by direct vote of the electors, the laws which may be so enacted shall be only such as might be enacted by the legislature under the provisions of this constitution.

"Sec. 4. When the United States shall consent thereto, the legislature, by a majority vote of the members in each house, may submit to the people the question of amending any provision of Article 12 of this constitution on compact with the United States, to the extent allowed by the act of congress permitting the same, and if a majority of the qualified electors who vote upon any such amendment shall vote in favor thereof the said article shall be thereby amended accordingly.

"Sec. 5. The provisions of Section 1 of this article shall not be changed, altered, or abrogated in any manner except through a general convention called to revise this constitution as herein provided.

"Sec. 4. That the probate clerks of the several counties of New Mexico shall provide separate ballots for the use of the electors at said first state election for the purpose of voting upon said amendment. Said separate ballots shall be printed on paper of a blue tint, so that they may be readily distinguished from the white ballots provided for the election of county and state officers. Said separate ballots shall be delivered only to the election officers authorized by law to receive and have the custody of the ballot boxes for use at said election, and shall be delivered by them only to the individual voter and

At this time the republican party was in control in a large majority of the counties of New Mexico; every federal official was of that faith, and every officer, district or territorial, held his office by virtue of the governor's appointment. The chances for republican success at the polls were brilliant; the situation was well understood by the democratic leaders, who hoped that this condition would prove a disadvantage to their opponents in selecting candidates for their state ticket. The democratic hope was realized. Prior to the

---

only one ballot to each elector at the time he offers to vote at the said general election, and shall have the initials of two election officers, of opposite political parties written by them upon the back thereof. Said separate ballot shall not be marked either for or against the said amendment at the time it is handed to the elector by the election officer, and if the elector desires to vote on said amendment, the ballot must be marked by the voter, unless he shall request one of the election officers to mark the same for him, in which case such election officer so called upon shall mark said ballot as such voter shall request. Any elector receiving such ballot shall return same before leaving the polls to one of the election judges, who shall immediately deposit same in the ballot box, whether such ballot be marked or not. No ballots on said amendment except those handed to said electors and so initialed shall be deposited in the ballot box or counted or canvassed. Said separate ballots shall have printed thereon the proposed amendment in both the English and the Spanish languages. There shall be placed on said ballots two blank squares with dimensions of one-half inch and opposite one of said squares shall be printed in both the English and the Spanish languages the words, 'For constitutional amendment,' and opposite the other blank square shall be printed in both the English and Spanish languages the words, 'Against constitutional amendment.'

"Any elector desiring to vote for said amendment shall mark his ballot with a cross in the blank opposite the words 'For constitutional amendment,' or cause the same to be so marked by an election officer as aforesaid, and any elector desiring to vote against said amendment shall mark his ballot with a cross in the blank square opposite the words 'Against constitutional amendment,' or cause the same to be so marked by an election officer as aforesaid.

"Sec. 5. That said ballots shall be counted and canvassed by said election officers, and the returns of said election upon this amendment shall be made by said election officers direct to the secretary of the Territory of New Mexico at Santa Fé, who, with the governor and chief justice of said territory, shall constitute a canvassing board; and they, or any two of them, shall meet at said city of Santa Fé on the third Monday after said election and shall canvass the same. If a majority of the legal votes cast at said election upon said amendment shall be in favor thereof, the said canvassing board shall forthwith certify said result to the governor of the territory, together with the statement of votes cast upon the question of the ratification or rejection of said amendment; whereupon the governor of said territory shall by proclamation declare the said amendment a part of the constitution of the proposed state of New Mexico, and thereupon the same shall become and be a part of said constitution; but if the same shall fail of such majority, then Article XIX of the constitution of New Mexico as adopted on January twenty-first, nineteen hundred and eleven, shall remain a part of said constitution.

"Except as herein otherwise provided, said election upon this amendment shall be in all respects subject to the election laws of New Mexico now in force."

President Taft Signing the Proclamation Admitting New Mexico into the Union

assembling of the convention, at a meeting of the republican territorial central committee, the question of the right to seats in the convention by two contesting delegations from Bernalillo county, known as the "Hubbell" and "Gillenwater" delegations, was determined in favor of the "Hubbell" delegation, although the delegation led by Mr. Gillenwater offered to compromise the difficulty by agreeing to accept one-half a vote each in the convention, and leave the question of party regularity to a county convention afterward to be called for the nomination of county officers. This offer was declined and the "Hubbell" delegation was declared regular and given seats in the convention.

On the 28th of September, the convention met and was organized in the interest and by the friends of the candidacy of Holm O. Bursum for the governorship. Strong influences were brought to bear upon the party leaders having in charge Mr. Bursum's interests, to dissuade them from jeopardizing the success of the party at the polls by placing his name at the head of the ticket. To no avail, however, and, on the 28th of September, he was nominated by a vote of 228 to 75 for Secundino Romero, of San Miguel county. The remainder of the ticket was dictated by the friends of Mr. Bursum. It was believed by those who were responsible for the ticket that the great republican majority could not be overcome, and the opposition to the nomination of Mr. Bursum was overestimated.[504] The leaders

---

[504] The Alburquerque *Morning Journal*, the most influential newspaper in New Mexico, commenting upon the methods which obtained at the Las Vegas convention, on the morning of the nomination of Mr. Bursum, said: "The state machine forgets that the announcement of its present brazen program has already had the effect of driving hundreds of disgusted republicans into the democratic party.

"It forgets that there is a limit beyond which the loyalty of true republicans will not go.

"It forgets that the progress of education and enlightenment and development in New Mexico has enabled a good many citizens to see through the party label to the man underneath; and that there are many people who are in favor of a political pure food law, making mis-branding a crime.

"The machine forgets that the old regime of terrorism is passing rapidly with the increase in the number of un-muzzled newspapers, the increase in railroads and automobile lines and other means of communication and the resulting vast increase in publicity that has come in the past five years.

"The machine forgets in short that the people of New Mexico are not having as much of their thinking done by proxy as in former years.

"The fatal defect in the whole program, now as heretofore, is in the fact that neither Mr. Bursum nor his henchmen have awakened to the realization of New Mexico's progress; and utterly fail to take the hardheaded voter into account."

did not fear a defensive campaign, believing that the people of New Mexico could not be led to accept the charges which were certain to be made against Mr. Bursum by his opponents as true. With one or two exceptions the remainder of the ticket nominated at the Las Vegas convention was representative of the party strength and could not have been improved upon.[505] A feature of the convention was the speech of Octaviano A. Larrazolo,[506] a delegate from San Miguel county, placing in nomination for the governorship the name of Secundino Romero. Mr. Larrazolo, only a few weeks before, in an open letter to William C. McDonald, chairman of the democratic committee, had renounced his allegiance to the democratic party

[505] The ticket nominated by the republican state convention was as follows: For governor, Holm O. Bursum; lieutenant-governor, Malaquias Martinez; secretary of state, Secundino Romero; auditor, William G. Sargent; treasurer, Sylvestre Miraval; attorney general, Frank W. Clancy; superintendent of public instruction, A. B. Stroup; commissioner of public lands, Robert P. Ervien; justices of the supreme court, Frank W. Parker, Clarence J. Roberts, and Edward R. Wright; corporation commissioners, George W. Armijo, Hugh H. Williams, and M. S. Groves; members of congress, George Curry and Elfego Baca.

[506] Octaviano Ambrosio Larrazolo, the son of Dn. Octaviano Larrazolo and Da. Donaciana Corral de Larrazolo, was born at Allende, state of Chihuahua, Mexico, December 7, 1859. He came to the United States in 1870, in company with the Mt. Rev. J. B. Salpointe, then vicar apostolic of Arizona, and subsequently Archbishop of Santa Fé. Mr. Larrazolo received his education at St. Michael's college, Santa Fé, finishing his education in 1876. The following year he taught school at Tucson, Arizona. In 1878, he removed to Texas, settling at San Elezario, in El Paso county, where he was principal of the public school from 1878 until 1884. In 1885, he was appointed chief deputy district and county clerk of El Paso county, holding the position one year. During this period he also filled the position of clerk of the United States district and circuit courts for the El Paso branch in the western district of Texas, which position he resigned, in 1886, in order to accept the nomination, on a nonpartisan ticket, for the office of clerk of the 34th judicial district of Texas, to which office he was elected and reëlected in 1888, the last time the candidate of the democratic party. In 1888, he was admitted to the bar at El Paso, and two years later was elected district attorney for the 34th judicial district. He was reëlected in 1892 without opposition and served until the expiration of his term, in 1894.

In 1895, Mr. Larrazolo removed to Las Vegas, New Mexico, where he has since made his residence, practicing his profession.

In 1900, and again in 1906 and 1908, he received the democratic nomination for delegate in congress, but was defeated. No nominee of his party in recent years in New Mexico received so many votes as were cast for him. He contested the election of 1908, but failed in substantiating the charges of fraud which were made, and William H. Andrews retained the seat, the certificate to which had been given him upon the face of the returns.

Mr. Larrazolo enjoys the reputation of being the most gifted orator among the Spanish-American people of New Mexico, and is an acknowledged leader of his race.

and declared his intention henceforth to affiliate with the republicans "because the democratic party of the territory, or at least a very considerable portion of it, had manifested a decidedly unfriendly feeling and disposition toward the Spanish-American element in New Mexico to which he belonged." The impassioned remarks of this gifted orator and representative of the Spanish-American people, appealing to the convention for recognition for the native New Mexican, was an index of the sentiments of many of the delegates present.

The democratic convention met at Santa Fé on the 2d day of October, and, after two days' deliberation, placed in nomination a ticket,[507] which, with the exception of two or three candidates, its best friends confessed was weak. Great political sagacity, however, was displayed in the nomination of William C. McDonald for governor. A business man of sound conservative judgment, his candidacy at once appealed to the business interests of the new state. The chief criticism urged against his opponent was a laxity of business methods in the conduct of public affairs when in charge of the territorial penitentiary as superintendent. There were many capable business men, non-partisans, heavy tax-payers, who had always regarded the question of statehood as one of doubtful benefit to the whole people. This class of citizens, anxious to witness the success of state government, believed that the affairs of the state were safer in the hands of Mr. McDonald than in the control of Mr. Bursum and cast their votes for the former.

Herbert J. Hagerman, with the assistance of friends in all parts of New Mexico, supported the candidacy of the democratic nominee. The prohibitionists, who considered that they had been badly treated by the republican majority in the constitutional convention, did everything possible to encompass the defeat of the republican candi-

---

[507] The nominees of the Santa Fé convention were: Governor, William C. McDonald; lieutenant-governor, E. C. de Baca; secretary of state, Antonio Lucero; auditor, Francisco A. Manzanares; treasurer, O. N. Marron; attorney general, W. D. McGill; superintendent of public instruction, A. N. White; commissioner of public lands, J. L. Emerson; justices of the supreme court, R. H. Hanna (progressive republican), Summers Burkhart, and W. A. Dunn; corporation commissioners, George H. Van Stone (progressive republican), O. L. Owen, and Seferino Martinez; members of congress, Harvey B. Fergusson and Paz Valverde. Mr. Manzanares, the candidate for auditor, subsequently withdrew from the ticket, and Francisco Delgado was substituted by the democratic committee.

date. The Las Vegas convention had advised the voters to defeat the "blue ballot" amendment. The Santa Fé convention declared in its favor. Thousands of republicans and democrats who had voted for the adoption of the constitution, who had been willing to sacrifice almost anything in order that statehood might be attained, now that it was assured, voted for the "blue ballot" amendment, and many republicans, influenced by the stand taken by the democratic party in its platform on this subject, voted for Mr. McDonald [508] and other candidates on that ticket as well.

For the first time in a decade, the democratic party conducted an effective campaign along educational lines. The leadership of the chairman, Andreius A. Jones,[509] was effective. The result was not a

[508] William C. McDonald is one of the pioneers of the town of White Oaks, Lincoln county, having been identified with the business interests of that county for thirty years. He came to New Mexico in the spring of 1880 and found a largely undeveloped region. Mr. McDonald was born in Herkimer county, New York, on the 25th of July, 1858, and spent the days of his youth in the usual manner of farmer lads. His elementary education, acquired in the common schools, was supplemented by a course in Casenovia seminary. He made his home at the place of his birth and taught school for three years after the completion of his own education. At the same time he took up the study of law, it being his desire to enter the legal profession. In the spring of 1880, he came to New Mexico, and located at White Oaks. His capital was very limited, but he had a knowledge of surveying and civil engineering which came into good play in this region, which was just being opened to civilization. He carried on business as an engineer for ten years, when, in 1890, he accepted a position as manager of the Carrizozo Cattle Company, an English syndicate owning a very large ranch southwest of White Oaks. He has since continued in this capacity and his grandfather was an officer in the war of 1812. He received his duca- and the confidence and trust reposed in him. Although he has never engaged in the practice of law, his knowledge of it has proved beneficial in the protection of the interests in his charge. He was elected a member of the house of representatives of the 29th legislative assembly from Lincoln county. He was assessor of the county in 1886, and in 1905 and 1906 was chairman of the board of county commissioners. In 1910, he was made chairman of the democratic central committee.

[509] Andreius A. Jones, the son of James H. W. and Hester A. A. (May) Jones, was born near Union City, Tennessee, May 16, 1862. He received his education in the public and private schools of Union City, and graduated from Bethel college, McKensie, Tennessee; also attended the University at Valparaiso, Indiana, where he received the degrees of B. S. and A. B. He came to New Mexico, September 13, 1885, where, at Las Vegas, he taught school until January, 1888. He was admitted to the bar in the last named year and to the bar of the supreme court of the United States in 1894. He was elected mayor of Las Vegas in 1893; was appointed district attorney by Governor Edmund G. Ross in 1889, but did not qualify because of a change in the law by a republican legislature. He was appointed district attorney by Governor William T. Thornton, served less than a year and resigned. At the national democratic convention held in Chicago in 1896, he was a member of the committee on platform and resolutions. In 1906, he was elected chairman of the democratic

William C. McDonald, first Governor of the State of New Mexico

triumph for the principles of democracy. It was a rebuke to machine methods and boss rule, particularly in the counties of Bernalillo and Sandoval. It was not so much a reflection upon Mr. Bursum as a man as it was a condemnation of the methods which had characterized his administration of the public business when superintendent of the penitentiary and consequent lack of confidence in his capacity as an executive. It was discovered to the skeptic, as to the fitness of New Mexico for statehood, that there actually existed in our midst a public conscience that could be awakened and which would assert itself when opportunity arose. Strength was also given to the democratic ticket by placing thereon two active representatives of the progressive or insurgent wing of the republican party.[510] In the counties of Bernalillo and Sandoval, normally and without factional strife or dissension returning republican majorities of more than two thousand votes, democratic majorities were returned to themselves sufficient to elect the democratic candidate for governor.

In accordance with the provisions of the act of congress the canvassing board, consisting of the governor, secretary, and chief justice, met in the council chamber of the capitol and canvassed the returns of the election held on November 7. The board was engaged almost five weeks in the performance of this duty. During the progress of the canvass the two political parties were represented by counsel who rendered some assistance to the board in arriving at a determination of some of the important questions raised during the progress of the count. The republican candidates were represented by Thomas B. Catron and Albert B. Fall, the democratic candidates, by Neill B. Field and the progressive republicans by C. D. Cleveland. The contentions made by the representatives of the democratic party were nearly all sustained by the canvassing board. On December 30, 1911, the certificates were prepared and signed ready to be forwarded to Washington.[511]

---

territorial central committee, and in 1908 was chosen national committeeman. He was president of the New Mexico Bar Association in 1893. He has long occupied a foremost position among the leaders of his profession and is recognized as one of the most capable counselors and leaders of his party. He is a resident of Las Vegas and is interested in live stock raising and irrigation enterprises.

[510] R. H. Hanna, elected justice of the supreme court, and George H. Van Stone, candidate for corporation commissioner. In a contest instituted by O. L. Owen, democrat, against Van Stone, Owen was declared entitled to the office.

[511] Neill B. Field is a native of Louisville, Kentucky, where he was born,

The total vote cast at the election was 60,842, of which the socialists polled from 1,787 for governor to 2,026 for secretary of state, the republicans and democrats dividing the remainder, only three tickets having been in the field, two progressive republican candidates, both of whom were elected, running on the democratic ticket.

The constitutional amendment to make the constitution more

February 6, 1854. He received his education in the public schools of that city and at Forrest Academy, a celebrated preparatory school of the south. At the early age of fifteen, at the close of his preparatory course, he was offered and accepted employment in the office of the clerk of the Jefferson Circuit Court at Louisville, since which time he has been directly connected with the administration of justice in some capacity. He read law in the office and under the direction of Henry J. Stites, a nisi prius judge of great reputation, and was admitted to the bar before he arrived at his majority. Mr. Field came to New Mexico in 1882, settling at Socorro, where he practiced his profession in connection with Judge Albert Hagan, formerly of Salt Lake City. In 1884, he removed to Alburquerque, where he has since practiced with great success, being recognized as the leader of the local bar and among the foremost lawyers of the Southwest. He was president of the New Mexico Bar Association in 1882. Mr. Field, although occupying a leading position in the councils of the democratic party, has never held any political elective office in New Mexico, except in 1893, when he was chosen mayor of the City of Alburquerque.

The official count, as certified to Washington, was as follows, on the state and congressional ticket:

Governor: W. C. McDonald, democrat, 31,016; H. O. Bursum, republican, 28,019; McDonald's plurality, 2,997.

Congressmen: George Curry, republican, 30,162; H. B. Fergusson, democrat, 29,999; Elfego Baca, republican, 28,836; Paz Valverde, democrat, 28,353; Curry's plurality, 1,809; Fergusson's plurality, 1,163.

Lieutenant-governor: Malaquias Martinez, republican, 28,906; E. C. de Baca, democrat, 29,642; de Baca's plurality, 1,736.

Secretary of state: Secundino Romero, republican, 28,392; Antonio Lucero, democrat, 29,692; Lucero's plurality, 1,300.

State auditor: William G. Sargent, republican, 29,574; Francisco Delgado, democrat, 29,133; Sargent's plurality, 441.

State treasurer: Silvestre Miraval, republican, 28,977; O. N. Marron, democrat, 29,867; Marron's plurality, 890.

Attorney general: Frank W. Clancy, republican, 30,162; W. D. McGill, democrat, 28,721; Clancy's plurality, 1,441.

Superintendent of public instruction: A. B. Stroup, republican, 29,411; A. N. White, democrat, 29,522; White's plurality, 111.

Commissioner of public lands: R. P. Ervien, republican, 29,706; J. L. Emerson, democrat, 29,242; Ervien's plurality, 464.

Justices of the supreme court: Frank W. Parker, republican, 29,583; C. J. Roberts, republican, 29,681; E. R. Wright, republican, 29,541; R. H. Hanna, progressive republican, 29,674; Summers Burkhart, democrat, 29,453; W. A. Dunn, democrat, 29,423; Parker's plurality, 130; Roberts's plurality, 258; Hanna's plurality, 133.

Corporation commissioners: George W. Armijo, republican, 29,108; H. H. Williams, republican, 29,835; M. S. Groves, republican, 29,783; George H. Van Stone, progressive republican, 29,451; O. L. Owen, democrat, 28,509; Seferino Martinez, democrat, 28,577. Through a mistake in printing, 1,032 votes were cast for Sol Owen and could not be counted for O. L. Owen. Williams's plu-

easily amended carried by 12,066 majority, the total vote for the amendment being 34,897, and against it, 22,831.[512]

The certificates of the canvassing board were sent to Washington, arriving at the capitol during the first week in January, 1912, and, on the 6th day of January, the president signed the proclamation [513] admitting New Mexico into the union of states.

rality, 1,326; Groves's plurality, 1,206; Van Stone's plurality, 343. In a proceeding in the district court of the first judicial district, Owen was later declared entitled to the office.

[512] Only seven of the 26 counties voted against the amendment, and in one county only was the majority overwhelmingly against it — Valencia; the southeastern counties, the prohibition strongholds, gave the heaviest majority for it, it being the claim of the prohibitionists that their first efforts after the organization of the legislature will be the offering and submission of an amendment providing for state-wide prohibition.

The following were elected to the senate and house of representatives of the first state legislature:

Senate: John S. Clark, East Las Vegas, R; Juan Navarro, Mora, R; L. C. Ilfeld, Las Vegas, R; Thomas D. Burns, Tierra Amarilla, R; J. F. Sulzer, Alburquerque, Progressive; E. A. Miera, Cuba, R; Isaac Barth, Alburquerque, D; Edwin C. Crampton, Raton, R; Eugenio B. Gallegos, Gallegos, R; Benjamin F. Pankey, Lamy, R; Squire Hartt, Jr., Taos, R; Boleslo Romero, Los Lunas, R; Charles J. Laughren, Deming, R; Abelino Romero, San Marcial, Progressive; William M. McCoy, Mountainair, R; Herbert B. Holt, Las Cruces, R; Gregory Page, Gallup, R; John M. Bowman, Alamogordo, R; James F. Hinkle, Roswell, D; Fred. F. Diepp, Carlsbad, D; A. J. Evans, Portales, D; C. H. Aldredge, Tucumcari, D; Thomas J. Mabry, Clovis, D; William B. Walton, Silver City, D.

House of Representatives: Zacharias Padilla, Los Lunas, R; Miguel Baca, Los Lunas, R; Conrad N. Hilton, San Antonio, R; Thomas Cooney, Mogollon, R; John B. Burg, Alburquerque, R; Thomas A. Gurule, Alburquerque, R; Rafael Garcia, Alburquerque, R; Roman L. Baca, Santa Fé, R; Charles C. Catron, Santa Fé, R; Julian Trujillo, Chimayo, R; José P. Lucero, Lumberton, R; George W. Tripp, East Las Vegas, R; José Lobato, Tecolote, R; Francisco Quintana, Las Vegas. R; Blas Sanchez, Wagon Mound, R; Remigio Lopez, Roy, D; J. H. Skidmore, Raton, R; M. C. Martinez, Raton, D; Manuel Cordova, Taos, R; Luis R. Montoya, Taos, R; Marcos C. de Baca, Bernalillo, Progressive; O. T. Toombs, Clayton, R; Juan D. Casados, Clapham, D; James W. Chaves, Willard, R; J. G. Clancy, Puerto de Luna, R; John A. Young, Gallup, R; Duncan McGillivray, Gallup, R; W. H. H. Llewellyn, Las Cruces, R; Preciliano Moreno, Las Cruces, R; James V. Tully, Glencoe, R; Charles P. Downs, Alamogordo, R; James W. Mullens, Roswell, D; John T. Evans, Roswell, D; W. E. Rogers, Roswell, D; Hugh M. Gage, Carlsbad, D; Florence Love, Loving, D; P. E. Carter, Portales, D; S. J. Smith, Deming, D; A. S. Goodell, Silver City, D; Robert H. Boulware, Silver City, D; George H. Tucker, Hillsboro, D; W. H. Chrisman, Aztec, R; J. W. Campbell, Tucumcari, D; J. L. House, House, D; W. W. Nichols, Clovis. D; Antonio D. Vargas, Ojo Caliente, R; Tranquilino Labadie. Santa Rosa, R; Manuel P. Manzanaes, Fort Sumner, R; W. E. Blanchard, Arabela, R.

[513] The proclamation was signed by President Taft at 1:35 p. m. The New Mexicans present were Congressmen George Curry and Harvey B. Fergusson, William H. Andrews, A. C. Ringland, A. B. McGaffey and Mrs. McGaffey, Charles Curry, and John W. Roberts. A photograph was taken. President Taft said: "Well, it is all over, I am glad to give you life." Then he smiled

William C. McDonald, first governor of the state of New Mexico, was formally inducted into office shortly after 12 o'clock, January 15, 1912. The inauguration ceremonies were conducted at the main entrance to the state capitol, in the presence of seven or eight thousand people. A more beautiful day was impossible. The ceremonies were impressive, and, save for the frequent outbursts of applause, the people stood hushed with interest. There was some slight delay in the opening of the formal program, although the arrangements had been made with the greatest care. It was close to 12 o'clock when the first governor of the Sunshine State, accompanied by William J. Mills, the last territorial governor, entered an open carriage, at the Palace Hotel and, accompanied by the first battalion of the First New Mexico Infantry, and a retinue of citizens, started for the capitol. Adjutant General A. S. Brookes, master of ceremonies, and Major Frederick Muller, grand marshal, had full charge of the parade. The line was led by the police force of the city of Santa Fé and the New Mexico Mounted Police on horseback. Next came the First Regiment band and the Santa Fé battalion of the national guard regiment, in command of Colonel E. C. Abbott. The carriage containing Governor McDonald and Governor Mills followed, escorted by Adjutant General Brookes and aides. The people had been gathering about the main entrance to the capitol for two hours and when the head of the inaugural parade came in sight the banked thousands broke into rounds of mighty cheers. The guardsmen formed in double line along the sidewalks with the regimental band stationed beneath the platform, which had been raised on the main stairway.

Upon the platform were seated Mrs. McDonald, Miss McDonald, Mrs. William J. Mills, Judge N. B. Laughlin, and Attorney-General Frank W. Clancy, while immediately in the rear sat Archbishop

---

and added: "I hope you will be healthy." Governor Curry, on behalf of the people of New Mexico, thanked the president. Ex-Delegate Andrews and Congressman Fergusson also made brief acknowledgement of thanks. The proclamation was signed in duplicate, the pen being furnished by Delegate Andrews. The duplicate copy and the pen have been filed with the Historical Society of New Mexico.

In all portions of New Mexico there was great rejoicing when the telegraph announced that the work, hopes, and prayers of more than sixty years had come

J. B. Pitaval, Vicar-General Fourchegu, and other members of the clergy. Around the platform, crowding the stairway and portico and the approaches to the capitol, the leading citizens of New Mexico were gathered.

Chief Justice Clarence J. Roberts, of the state supreme court, arose and presented Governor Mills.[514] The retiring governor spoke for thirty minutes. The chief justice then arose and, facing Governor McDonald, administered the oath of office. The chief justice spoke the solemn words of the oath so that every intonation could be heard at the outer edge of the assemblage. The responses of Governor McDonald were ringing and intense. The oath of office was administered at exactly 12:29 p. m. The chief justice then called upon Archbishop Pitaval, who delivered a brief but impressive invocation for the welfare of the new state.

The inaugural address was an able exposition of governmental ideas and was impressively delivered. In the peroration, Governor McDonald said:

"Laws and rules can help direct, but cannot make good people — happy and prosperous — but right-thinking, honest citizens can, under our form, make good government. You are entitled to be served by a mind unbiased by inordinate party zeal, which may be unjust to those who differ, but are equally sincere and honest; by will unhampered by careless or questionable promises that might compromise the best efforts for a free government of the expressed will of the people; and by a heart free from malice or hatred toward

to full fruition. The transformation from a mere territory to full statehood meant much to the people. New Mexico had proved its worthiness again and again; for many years, the question had not been one of fitness; it was expediency and politics that kept the people from the privilege guaranteed under the provisions of the treaty of Guadalupe Hidalgo.

[514] In his address, Governor Mills devoted the greater part of his time to a review of his administration; recalling the program outlined by him at his inauguration and calling attention to the manner in which his policies had been carried out. He referred to the increased surplus in the state treasury, to the decrease in the state debt, and to the decrease of more than four mills in the tax rate for territorial purposes during that period. He alluded to the development of the public school system, of irrigation projects and agriculture, and to the good roads program so well begun. Having reviewed his administration and expressed his thanks to the officials who had served with and under him, he turned to the incoming governor and spoke briefly of the arduous duties about to be undertaken by him, of the grave responsibility and of the opportunities open to the first governor for the development, advancement, and welfare of the new commonwealth. There was great applause as Governor Mills assured Governor McDonald that in every effort for the advancement of the state and the welfare of the people, in every movement for better conditions, he would have the continued support of all good citizens, regardless of party affiliations.

any, and which beats in sympathy with the great cause of humanity.

"Awed by the solemnity, and yet sustained by the enthusiasm of the occasion, fully impressed with the importance of the responsibilities that are placed upon me, I have taken the oath that binds me to your service. And now, trusting the Power that controls the destinies of men and nations, and the encouragement and inspiration that comes through the confidence of a generous people, I shall take up the work that with the blessing of the Almighty, I trust may redound to the benefit of our new state and to the good of the whole people."

As Governor McDonald concluded his address, and as the applause subsided, a mixed chorus, dressed and formed into a living flag, sang the inauguration ode. The evening ceremonies opened with the illumination of the plaza, the welcome arch, the dome of the capitol, and the palace of the governors, along the portal of which ancient structure blazed the names of the heroes of early Mexican history. The general reception in the palace of the governors, from eight to ten o'clock, and the inaugural ball in the armory closed the festivities of the greatest day in its history and completed the formal ushering into office of the first governor of the state of New Mexico.

Military Post near El Paso, 1851

BIBLIOGRAPHY

Archives	Office of Surveyor General, Santa Fé.
Alburquerque *Morning Journal*	Newspaper, Files of, Alburquerque, N. M.
Enabling Act	*Records*, Office of Secretary of State, Santa Fé.
Hagerman, Herbert J.	*Message* of, Office of Secretary of State, Santa Fé.
Jaffa, Nathan	*Legislative Manual*, Office of Secretary of State, Santa Fé.
Larrazolo, Octaviano A.	*Election Contest; Congressional Record*, 60th Cong. Washington, D. C.
Memorials	*Session Laws* of New Mexico, 1880-1909. State Library, Santa Fé.
Marshall, Edward	*Story of the Rough Riders*, New York, 1899.
Mills, William J.	*Reports* of, Office of Secretary of State, Santa Fé.
New Mexican	Newspaper, Files of, Santa Fé.
Otero, Miguel Antonio	*Reports* of, 1897-1906. Office of Secretary of State, Santa Fé.
Optic	Newspaper, Files of, Las Vegas.
Prince, L. Bradford	*Reports* of, Office of Secretary of State, Santa Fé; *Historical Sketches*, New York, 1882; *Struggle for Statehood*, Santa Fé, 1910.
Ritch, W. G.	*Legislative Blue Book*, Office of Secretary of State, Santa Fé.
Reports	Territorial Librarian, 1883, State Library, Santa Fé; *Official Reports*, 1882-1883, Secretary of State, Santa Fé; Superintendent of Public Instruction, Santa Fé.
Records, Military	Adjutant General's Office, Santa Fé.
Read, Benjamin M.	*Guerra Mexico-Americana*, Santa Fé, 1909. *Historia Ilustrada de Nuevo Mexico*, Santa Fé, 1910.
Roosevelt, Theodore	*The Rough Riders*, New York, 1910.
Session Laws of New Mexico, 1880-1909	State Library, Santa Fé.
Sheldon, Lionel A.	*Report* of, 1884, Office of Secretary of State, Santa Fé.
Safford, Charles V.	*Reports* of, Files of State Auditor, Santa Fé.
Vaughn, John H.	*Reports* of, Office of State Treasurer, Santa Fé.

INDEX

INDEX

ABBOTT, IRA A., associate justice, 567; biog. note 478
Abert, Col. J. W., report of, 15, note 13; 87, note 60; cited 313, note 239
Abiquiu, 166; 214; Indian agency, 447, note 367
Abreu, Dn Mariano, death of, 62
Abreu, Dn Ramon, alcalde, Taos, 60; death of, 62
Abreu, Dn Santiago, mentioned, 56; death of, 62
Acequia, 176, note 118
Acts of Congress, relative New Mexico, 1864-1880, 407, note 333; July 22, 1854, 460; June 21, 1860, 460, note 381; confirming grants, 460, note 381
Adams, Rt. Rev. William Forbes, 351
Adobe Walls, battle, 432, note 357
Advertiser, Boone's Lick, 135, note 92
Agriculture, 176
Agriculturists, Mexicans not, 175, 176
Alamo, mentioned, 61
Alaria, Dn Jesus Maria, death of, 62, note 46
Alarid, Trinidad, 513, biog. note 431
Alburquerque, City of, 1861, captured by Sibley, 379
Alcaldes, 9; mayores, 9, 15
Alencaster, Governor, 195
Alvarez, Dn Manuel, trader, 126; stations, 137, 138, 283; 275; controversy with Col. Munroe, 275, note 199
Alvino, Fr., mentioned, 55
Allen, W. S., Secretary, 283
Allison, W. W. H., cited, quoted, 399, note 325
American Archaeology, School of, 573, note 483
American Conflict, Cited, 357, note 281; 364, note 289
American Fur Company, 99
American Fur Trade, Cited, 93, note 63; 95, note 65

Amigo del Pais, newspaper, 307, note 232
Amusements, Games, 159
Ancheta, J. A., 509, biog. note 428
Andrews, W. H., 544, note 455; 545, 546, biog. note 458; 577, notes 486, 487, 488; 579, 580, 581, 582
Angney, Capt. W. Z., Speaker House of Reps., 1st Assembly, 264, note 190
Annals of Congress, Cited, 98, note 69
Anton Chico, 247
Apache Canyon, battle of, 380, note 303; 381, note 304; 383, 384, notes 306, 308
Apache Pass, 204, 205, note 145
Apaches, Campaigns, 31, 34, 35, 36; hostility of, 40, 44; depredations, 47, note 38; Jicarillas, massacre Dr. White, 124, 125; troubles, 1850-59, 301, 302, 311; Mogollon, 302; Mescaleros, leave Bosque Redondo, raids, 436; Chiricahuas, 436, 438, 439; Jicarillas, 1870, no. of, 446; removed to Ft. Stanton, 447
Appropriations, New Mexico, 1850-1860, 310, note 235
Arapaho, Indians, habitat, 2, note 21
Archives, Santa Fé, 492, note 404
Archuleta, Col. Juan Andrés, maltreated by Utes, 48
Archuleta, Gen. Diego, mentioned, 9; 232, note 168; 251; defeated delegate in congress, 310, 493, note 406
Aricara, Indians, mentioned, 93
Arizona, Part of diocese of Santa Fé, 340; vicariate apostolic, 341; Territory of, proclaimed by Col. Baylor, 362, note 288; Mesilla, capitol, 288; district of, 389; Territory of U. S., 408, note 324; Col. J. F. Chaves, escorts officials, note 335; convention of 1860, 409, note 335
Arizonaca, Baronia de, Fraudulent claim, 472, 473, notes 396, 397; investigations by Court of Private Land Claims, 476, 477, 478

Arkansas, river, Ford of, 115, note 83; 127; boundary, 17; Indians on, 21; 93, 114, 115, 127, 197

Armijo, General Manuel, Indians' ears, 48; opposition to decree of Santa Anna, 57, 58; asamblea general, 63; recognizes Gonzales as governor, 64; Alburquerque, 64; revolution, 64; Santa Fé, Palace, declares himself governor, 64; La Cañada, 65; character of, 65, 66, 67, note 49; Texas-Santa Fé expedition, 74, note 52; Cooke's surrender, 78; Snively, 85; McLeod, 80, note 55; proclamation, Aug. 8, 1846, 203, note 143; 207, note 145; resolutions, death of, 208; note 145; Ruxton, 208, note 145; Apache Pass, 204, 205, note 145; 549

Armijo, George W., 584, biog. note 493

Armijo, Rafael and Manuel, Confederate sympathizers, 387, note 313

Army of the West, Officers, 200, Santa Fé, 209, 213, note 150

Arny, W. F. M., Secretary, act'g gov., 392, 410

Arrow Rock, 103, note 74

Arroyas de Lueras, Apolonio, 401

Arroyo Hondo, 236, note 171

Asamblea Departmental, 12, note 9; minutes missing, note 9; last sesssession, 13, note 9; decree 1844, 15, note 13

Asamblea General, established, 63; meeting of, 63, 64; resolutions of, 63, 64

Ashley, Rev. J. M., 354

Ashurst, Merrill, attorney general, 411, note 337

Assembly Legislative, 264; session laws, 1847, note 190; members of, 265, note 190; 274, note 198

Astor, John Jacob, 99

Attorneys General, list of, 1846-1869, 398, note 323

Aubrey, F. X., 305; death of, note 230; Journal of, 309, note 232

Augur, General, 434

Axtell, Samuel B., Governor, 417, 418, 419, biog. note 346; chief justice, 183, note 125

Ayuntamientos, 5, 9, note 9; 15

BACA, Captain Bartolome, governor, 25; Navajós and Apaches, 26; 42, 43, 118

Baca, Jesus Maria, printer, death of, 184, 185

Baca, Luis Maria, heirs of, Las Vegas, grant, 460, note 381

Baca, Roman A., 594, note 407

Bailes, 160, 161

Baird, James, 98, notes 68, 69; 102, 114

Baird, S. M., defended Weightman, 305

Baker, Benjamin S., Associate Justice, 567, note 468

Baker, Grafton, Justice, dispute with clergy, 330, note 257; 283

Baltimore, Archbishop of, 328

Bancroft, H. H., cited, 66, note 49; 73, note 51; 80, note 55; 85, note 59; 89, note 62; 179, note 120; quoted, 202, note 142; 205, note 144; 220, note 165; 282, note 204; 289, note 213; 293, note 219; 299, note 223; Gadsden treaty, 312, note 238; 314, note 240; 321, note 244; land grants, 1850-60, 323, note 248; 357, notes 281, 282, 283; confederate retreat, 387, note 313; statehood, 1861-76, 403, note 328.

Banks, 571, note 481; see Statistics

Bantz, G. D., Associate Justice, 526, note 444

Baptists, 350

Bar Association, action of, 462, note 384; early members, 397, 398, note 323

Barcelo, Tules, 233, note 168

Bardstown, 94

Barela, Apolonio, 400

Barlow and Sanderson, stage line, 141

Baronia de Arizonaca, Fraudulent claim, 472, 473, notes 396, 397; investigations by Court of P. L. C., 476, 477, 478

Barreiro, cited, 9; *Ojeada*, cited, 13, note 11

Bartlett, E. L., 494, note 408; 501, 529, biog. note 445

Bartlett, John R., 289, 290, notes 213, 214; 302, note 226 quoted, 311, note 237

Baston de Justicia, 9

Baylor, Col. J. R., letter, 359, note 284; occupies Ft. Bliss, 361; Mesilla, 361, note 286; skirmish, 362; proclamation, 362, note 388; 366

Beale, Edward F., wagon road, 35th parallel, 314, note 240

Beall, Major Benj. L., 263

INDEX

Beaubien, Don Carlos, 87, note 60; 214; biog., 273, note 197
Beaubien & Miranda, land grant, sold, 415
Beaubien, Narciso, 234, note 169; 257, note 183
Becknell, Capt. William, Santa Fé Trail, 103, note 74; 2nd expedition, 104, 105, note 76
Bedstead, Pike, 156
Belen, 166
Bell, Lieut., Indian campaign, 1853, 299, note 223
Benavides, Domingo, captive, 299, note 222
Benedict, Kirby, Justice, 305; Weightman trial, 306; instructions, 308, note 233; peonage, 325, note 251; 392, biog. note 318; associates, 393; sentence, José Maria Martin, note 318
Ben Hur, 148, written, note 99
Bent, Charles, Governor, 87, note 60; death of, 233, note 169; 234; biog., note 170; portrait, 235, 248
Bent Family, 120, note 87
Bent, William, 120, note 87; 254; biog., 255, note 182
Benton, Thomas H., senator, 108, note 78; 197, note 135; memorial, 268, note 192
Bent's Fort, 115, 119, 120, note 87; 200, 201, note 139
Beveridge, Albert J., 544, 575, note 485; 578, 579
Big Copper Mine, 182, note 124; contempt proceedings, 183, note 125
Big Four, regiment, 540, 541; officers of 542, note 453
Big Nigger, 243, note 174
Billy the Kid, 418, 420, 422; Lincoln county war, 422, note 351; biog., 423, note 352. See *W. F. Bonney*
Black Flag, 220, note 158
Blackwell, A. M., 489, note 399
Blackwood, W. G., justice, 393
Blair, Frank P., Jr., 200; biog., note 140; 214, 251
Blue Ballot, 594, note 503; 602
Blumner, Charles, 214
Board of Home Missions, Presbyterian, 353, note 278
Bocanegra, minister, Mexico, 88, note 61
Boggs, Mrs. Thomas, 234, note 170
Bond, Ira M., 464, note 387; 581
Bonito, Apache chief, 442

Bonneville, Col., 105, note 76; Apache campaign, 302; Navajós, 1858, 316, note 243
Bonney, W. F. See *Billy the Kid*
Bosque Redondo, Navajós return from, 410; Apaches removed to, 429, 430, 431, notes 355, 356; failure of policy, 433; Apaches, 436; abandoned, 438
Boundary survey, 289, note 213
Bourgade, Mt. Rev. Peter, 347; death of, 348
Bradley, Gen. Luther P., 429, note 353
Brady, William, sheriff, killed, 422, note 351
Breeden, William, attorney general, 421; biog., note 349; 483, note 394; 485, note 395
Brenham, Dr. R. F., 73
Brent, Robert T., killed by Apaches, 292
Bridger, James, 113, note 81
Brocchus, Perry E., justice, letter to Simon Cameron, 1861, 371, note 293; biog., 393, note 320
Brooks, Major, Navajó campaign, 1858, 315
Brown, J. C., surveyor, 1825-7, 115, 116
Brown, Russell and Co., 126
Browne, J. Ross, quoted, 408, note 334
Browne, L. P., 488, note 399
Brinker, Wm. H., 497; biog., note 412; 518
Bristol, Warren, justice, 419; biog., note 347
Bryan, W. J., 523, 563
Bryant, Col., trader, 127
Buchanan, James, president, message, treaty Guadalupe, 452, note 371
Buell, Col., Apache compaign, 440
Bullard, Captain John, killed by Apaches, 436
Burgwin, Captain, 238, 241; wounded, 242, 243, note 174; 248
Burials, 164, note 110
Burkhart, Summers, ass't attorney, court of P. L. C., 471, 395
Bursum, H. O., 549, note 461; 550, 552, biog., note 465; penitentiary matters, 553, note 466; 554, 597, note 504; 598, note 505
Bustamente, Carlos M., quoted, 54, note 40; 67, note 49; cited, 74, note 52; *Apuntes*, 88, note 61

CACHES, 114

614   LEADING FACTS OF NEW MEXICAN HISTORY

Calhoun, James S., Indian agent, 270, note 194; governor, 277, 282, 283, note 205; proclamation, 283; leaves N. M., 287, note 210; message as to Indians, 293

California Column, arrival of, 388; officers, 388, 389; Mesilla, 389

California, titles, 1848, 455, 457, notes 377, 389

California, trails to, 142, 143, note 96

Campbell, Richard, 143, note 96

Cañada Alamosa, skirmish, 371

Canadian river, 118, 127

Canby, Gen. E. R. S., Navajó campaign, 1860-1, 317, 319; commander, 1861, 366, 367, 369, note 292; volunteers, 370, note 293; Sibley, El Paso, 372, notes 295, 296; Ft. Craig, 372; entire force, 374, note 297; Valverde, 374, note 298; Col. Paul, note 298; volunteers, 299, 376, 377; report, Valverde, 378, 301; reputation, 385; death, 385, 310; leaves Ft. Craig, 385; marches up Rio Grande, report of battle of Valverde, 388. note 314; pursuit of confederates, 388; relieved, 429

Canyon de Chelly, 263

Capitol, building of, 493, note 406; 494; burning of, 515

Capitol, first plans, 326

Caravan, Santa Fé Trail, 1843, Warfield, 88; 1844, wagons, value merchandize, 89, 92; organization, 109, note 79; 123; list of 1825-1834, 133, 134, note 92

Carey, Gen. Asa B., 383; Apache canyon, note 306; biog., note 307

Carleton, Gen. James H., escort, archbishop Salpointe, 341; command in New Mexico, 428; biog., note 353; Mescalero campaign, 429; policy, 429; Carson, 429; Navajó campaign, note 355; 1863, Indians killed, wounded and captured, 431, note 356; Kiowa, 432, note 357; reports, note 357

Carr, Gen. Eugene A., 429, note 353; Apache campaigns, 440

Carretas, 175, note 117

Carson, Gen. Christopher, with Fremont, 87, note 60; McKnight, 103, 113, note 81; 125, 235, note 170; Indian agent, 298; Valverde, 375, 376, 377, notes 300, 301, 302; Ft. Craig, 1861, 386; brigadier general, 388, note 314; biography, 412, 413, note 339; Mescalero campaign, 429; Navajó, 430, note 355; Canyon de Chelly, 431; 1864-1866, Kiowa, 432, note 357; Comanche, 432, note 357

Castro, Fr., 55

Cathedral, of St. Francis, corner stone, 344, note 272

Catholic church, 328; population, 1910, 349

Catron, Thomas B., 493, 510, note 428; 512, note 429; 518, note 436; elected delegate, 519; biog., note 437

Cavallero, Captain, pronunciamento, 64

Cebolleteños, 304, note 228

Census, 7th and 8th, cited, 326, note 252. See *Population*

Central system, government, Mexico, 53, 54, note 41

Cevolleta, 214, 217, 303, note 228

Chaffee, Jerome B., Maxwell grant, 415

Chambers, Samuel, 98, note 68, note 69; 102, 114

Change of citizenship, 290, 291, notes 215, 216

Chapelle, Placidus, L. Mt. Rev., 346, 347, note 274; pallium, 364, 347, note 274; archbishop, New Orleans, apostolic delegate, death of, 347

Chato, Apache chief, 441; kills Judge McComas, 441, 442

Chaves, Amado, 494, note 406; 508, biog., note 425

Chaves, Ireneo L., clerk court of P. L. C., 470, note 394; 494, note 408

Chaves, Col. J. Francisco, delegate congress, 399; biog., note 326; 493, note 406; 500

Chavez, scout, killed, 1862, 389

Chavez, Dn Antonio José, murder of, 83

Chavez, Dn Francisco Javier, 25; biog., note 24

Chavez, Francisco, 510, 512, killing of, 512, note 429; 518

Chavez, Dn José Antonio, 9 C., 470, note 394; 494, note 408

Chavez, Gen. Jesus Maria, 9

Chavez, Col. Manuel Antonio, 67, note 49; commander Ft. Fauntleroy, 320, note 244; Apache canyon, 382; biog., note 307

Chavez, Dn Mariano, 86, note 59

Cheney, B. P., 486, note 396

INDEX 615

Cheyenne, Indians, captives taken from, 299, note 222
Chick, Joseph S., Santa Fé Trail, location, 105-107, note 77
Chick, W. H., 488, note 399
Chihuahua, 13; traders imprisoned, 96 102; 43, 47; troops sent from, 1838, 64
Chihuahua, Apache chief, 442, note 362
Childers, W. B., 525, biog., note 443
Chiricahuas, raids by, 436; conquest, 441
Chittenden, H. M., 93, note 63; 95, note 65; 96, note 66; 97, note 67; quoted, 102, 103, 104, note 75; Kit Carson, 113, note 81; 117, note 85; quoted, 118, 123; list of caravans, 133, note 92; quoted, 136, 198, note 136
Chivington, Col. J. M., Pigeon's ranch, 380, note 303; Apache Canyon, 383, 384, note 308; Col. 1st Col. Reg., 386, note 311; pursuit of Sibley, 388; commander southern district, N. M., 1862, 388
Chloride, Apache raid, Nane, 439, note 359
Chopon, Gen., revolutionist, 65
Chouteau, Auguste P., expedition, 98; biog., 99, 100, 101, note 70; 104, 116, note 84
Chouteau Island, 17, note 14; 115, 116, note 84
Christopher Carson, Mrs, 235, note 170
Chronology, 1875-1879, 420, note 348; 574, note 484
Church of Holy Faith, 352
Churchman, Camp, 542
Cimarron desert, 121, 122, note 88
Cimarron, Indian agency, 446, 300
Cimarron river, 104, 105
Cities, population, 1890, 515, note 434. See *Population*
Ciudad Juarez, 529
Civil affairs, 1861-1865, 381
Civil War, 357-380, notes 281-313. See Canby, Sibley
Claims, Indian, 1853, amount of, 311
Clancy, Frank W., 501
Clark, William, governor, 100
Clarke, Elias T., 208, note 145; killed, 420, note 348
Clarke, Major M. L., 219, 224
Cleveland, Grover, president, 462, 498
Clever, Charles P., delegate in congress, 399, 400; biog., 411, note 337
Cochise, Apache chief, 444, note 364
Cochiti, pueblo of, massacre of Navajós, 42
Coghlan, Patrick, ranch, 438, note 359
Cold Spring, 85
Coleman, Sherrard, 540; biog., note 452
Colfax, county, created, 414
Collier, Needham C., associate justice, 517, note 435
Collins, James L., quoted, 125, 126
Collyer, Vincent, quoted, 434
Colonization law, Iturbide, 5, 8, note 7
Colorado, state of, admitted, 403, 404, 405, note 329
Colorado Volunteers, leave Denver, 380; Ft. Union, 380; Pigeon's ranch, 380, note 303; Pike's Peakers, note 303, note 304; leave New Mexico, 390, note 315
Cook, Capt. Pigeon's ranch, 381, note 304
Cooke, Gen. P. St. George, 17, note 15; 18, 19, note 18; 23, 24, note 22; 25, note 23; disarms Col. Snively, 88, note 61; 88, note 61; quoted, 202, note 141; 214, 315, note 239
Cooke, William G., Texas comr., 73; surrender, 78
Cooley, Alvord W., associate justice, 555, note 467; 559
Comanche, Indians, campaigns, 1864-6, 432, note 357; 21, 22; Pattie's fight, 28, 29, note 26; campaigns, 31; Mexican fear, 32, 33, 34, 35; attack trains, 127, 128, 311
Commissioners, American, to Mexico, 455, note 375
Commissioners, county system, established, 419
Compilation of laws, commission, 494, note 408
Confederates, 1861, operations, 361; Mesilla, note 286; El Paso, 372, note 295; note 296; Ft. Craig, 372; Valverde, 374, note 298; battle of Valverde, 375, 376, note 300; north, 378; Socorro, Alburquerque, Santa Fé, 378, 379; Pigeon's ranch, Apache Canyon, 383, 384; retreat, 386, note 311; 387, note 313
Confirmation, land grants, 1860, 460, note 381; 461, notes 382, 383
Congregationalists, 354
Congress, Mexican, members of, 9

Congressional Globe, cited, debates, Gadsden treaty, 312, note 228
Conklin, James, 102; biog., note 71
Constitution, Mexican, 1814, 7; 1836, 8; 1824, 8; 1835, 53; American, 1871, 416; 1850, 274
Connelly, Henry, Governor, route, Chihuahua, 119, 120, 203; governor, 275; 1861, militia, 373, note 297; 390, note 316; biog., note 316
Connelley, W. E., *Doniphan's Expedition*, cited, 213, note 150; 214, note 152; 221, note 159; 228, note 163
Constituent Congress, Mexican, 4, 8
Constitution, of 1910, 586, 587, 588, 589; ratification, 589, note 498; approval by president, note 499; 590; congressional action, 591, note 500; 592, note 501; final approval, 593; blue ballot, 594, note 503
Constitutional convention, of 1889, 504, 505; of 1910, election, apportionment, 582, note 490; 583; delegates, note 491; meeting of, 584; steering committee, 585, note 495; adjournment, 586, note 496; objections to constitution, 586, note 497; 587; election, 588, 589
Convention, 1848, message of Gen. Price, 266, 267, note 191; memorial, 267, note 192; members, 268, note 192; 1849, 269, note 194; members, note 194; 1850, 271, 272
Cooney, J. C., killed, Apaches, 439, note 359
Cooper, Col. Benj., 103, note 75
Cooper, Braxton, 103, note 75
Cooper county, history, 103, note 75
Cooper, Stephen, 103, note 75
Coopwood, Capt. Bethel, 371; report of, note 294
Copper bells, 179, note 120
Cordova, Treaty of, 36
Cortez, Manuel, 243, 244, 247; Indians with, 262
Coudert, Rev. J. M., 341
Council Grove, 109, note 79; 111
Counties. list of, established, seats, 396, note 321
Counties, population, 1890, 515, note 434
Courting customs, 162, 163
Courts martial, Santa Fé, 261
Crawford, Capt. Emmet, 441
Creoles, 23
Crepusculo, 184
Crespi, Bishop, visit of, 164, note 110

Crime of 1873, 514, note 433
Crist, J. H., 518, note 436
Crittenden, George B., 1861, 360
Croix, Gen. Teodoro de la, 7, note 4
Crook, Gen. George, Apache campaigns, 441, note 361; 442, note 362; relieved, 443
Cross, George H., 464, note 387
Crumpacker, J. W., associate justice, 525
Cubero, surrender, 1861, 379
Cuisine Mexican, 156, 157
Culver, Romulus, killed at Mora, 244
Cunningham, Francis A., senator, 275
Curry, Capt. George, 534, 555; biog., note 472; 564, note 473
Curumpaw, creek, 127
Custom house, duties, 132, note 91
Cutts, J. Madison, cited, 208, note 145
Cuyamungue, 65

DALLAM, RICHARD, 214
Daly, George W., killed, Apaches, 439, note 359
Daughters, American Revolution, 235
Davenport, J. J., chief justice, 305; compiles laws, 394
Davidson, Lieut., Indian campaign, 299, note 223
Davis, W. W. H., *El Gringo*, cowardice of natives, 29, note 26; 54, note 41; 67, note 49; quoted, 164, note 110; 171, note 115; cited, 175, note 117; 280, 202; Weightman, 305; biog., 314, note 221; education, 1854-55, 321, note 246; peonage, 324, 325, note 250
De Courcey, Lt., Taos, 202
Decree, April 17, 1837, opposition, 56, 57, note 42; March 31, 1844, opening ports, 89, note 62
De Fouri, Rev. J. H., 152, quoted, 339, note 265; cited, 341, note 268
Delaware Indians, with Kirker, 222, note 160; Taos, 243, note 174
Delegates in congress, 1863-1870, 399
Del Valle, Franco. Marin, governor, 151, note 102
De Mora, Rev. A. H., 351
De Mun, Julius, expedition of, 98, 99, 101, note 70
De Neve, Dn Felipe, 7, note 4
Departmental council, 53
Departments, established, 53; New Mexico, 53; council, 53
De Smet, Fr., missionary, 328, note 253

INDEX 617

De Vargas, Dn Diego, Santa Cruz, 168, note 113
Devin, Gen. Thomas C., 429, note 353
Diario del Gobierno, mentioned, 67, note 49
Diego, Juan, 154, note 104
Diplomacy, Mexican, 194
Diputados, New Mexico, names, 10, note 9
Discipline, 1848, Gen. Price, 262, note 187
Dodge City, 115, note 83
Dodge, H. L., Indian agent, Apaches, 304, note 227
Dolan, James J., 422, note 351; 424
Doña Ana, 219
Donaldson, Major, quartermaster, negotiates loan, confederate invasion, 367
Doniphan, Col. A. W., campaign, Navajós, 217; treaty, 218, note 156; Chihuahua, 218; Brazito, 219, 220, 221, notes 158, 159; Sacramento, battle of, 221, 222, 223, note 160; enters Chihuahua, 227, 228; Gen. Taylor, Walnut creek, 228; reaches New Orleans, mustered out, 228
Doniphan's expedition, 209, note 145; 221, note 159; 228
Dorsey and Kroeber, cited, 22, note 21
Downing, Major Jacob, journal of, cited, 381, note 304; Pigeon's ranch, 382
Dry Cimarron, 124
Dry farming, 564, note 473
Dunne, J. P., 315, note 242
Duncan, Major, Valverde, 375; wounded, 386, note 312
Dunlop, Rt. Rev. George K., 352
Durango, state of, 13, 166
Dwellings, New Mexican, 155

EDMONDSON, MAJOR, 237; Red river, 245, note 176; Las Vegas, 246
Education, 1850-1860, 321, 322, notes 246, 247; American missionaries, 323; public school, 1891, 507, note 424; 571, 572, note 482
Educational Institutions, 184
Edwards, Frank S., quoted, 226, note 162
Eguillon, Rev. P., 336, note 263
Elephant Butte, 527, 528
El Caney, 536, 538, 539, note 452
Election, 1911, 595, 596; republican ticket, 598, note 505; democratic ticket, 599, note 507; majorities, 602, note 511
Elias, Gen. J. M., 79, 80, note 55
Elkins, Stephen B., delegate, 401; biog., note 327; statehood, 402, 403; the fatal handshake, 403, 404, notes 329, 330, 496, 523
Elliott, Capt., Navajó campaign, 1858, 315
Ellison, killed, 127
Ellison, Samuel, 492, note 454
El Paso, city of, Doniphan arrives, 221, 526, note 444
Emory, Col. W. H., 208, note 145; 212, note 149; 313, note 239; 314, note 240
Empresarios, 5
Enabling act, of 1910, 575, note 485; 576, note 486, 487
Enos, Col. Herbert M., Alburquerque, 1861, 379
Enquirer, St. Louis, 102
Episcopalians, 351, 352; 1st church, 351
Escoto, soldier, death of, 62
Escudero, Dn Manuel, 118
Esquivel, Juan José, 63; death of, 65
Ewell, Capt., 302
Expedition, Texas-Santa Fé, leaves Austin, 73, 74; surrender of, 78; sent to Mexico, 79, note 55; released, 80

FALCONER, THOMAS, 81, note 55
Fall, Albert B., associate justice, 517; biog., note 435; attorney general, 564
Fandangos, 160, 161
Fauntleroy, Col., reports of, 1855, 299, note 223; campaign, 1855, 300; refuses arms to Gov. Rencher, 318, 319; report of, 320, note 244
Federal law, October, 1835, 11, note 9; March 20, 1837, 12, note 9
Ferdinand VII, 3
Fergusson Act, June 21, 1898, 521, 522, notes 439, 440; 549, 570, note 479
Fergusson, H. B., delegate, 520; biog., note 438; 521, note 439; 523, 525, 543, 584
Fernandez de Taos. See *Taos*
Fewkes, J. Walter, 179, 121
Field, Neill B., 601; biog., note 511
Finances, 1864-71, 415, note 340; act of 1889, 501, notes 419, 420; 543

First Ter. Vol. Inf., 540, 541; officers, 542, note 453
Fiske, Eugene A., 421, 505, 507, note 423
Fitzgerald, Texas-Santa Fé expedition, 75
Flagellantes, 170, note 114
Flipper, H. O., court of P. L. C., 427, note 395
Flood Resolution, 590, 592, note 501; 594, note 503
Floyd, secretary of war, 360
Fonda, 138
Foraker, C. M., 525
Forrester, Rev. Henry, 351
Forsyth, Thomas, 223, note 160
Fort Bascom, 432, note 357
Fort Bayard, 437
Fort Bliss, 390
Fort Craig, 372, Canby, 374; forces, 374, note 298; retreat to, 376, 377, notes 300, 301; Carson commands, 429, note 354
Fort Davis, 390
Fort Defiance, 228, note 212; Indians, 315, note 242; Navajós, 1860, 316, 317, note 244
Fort Fauntleroy, Indians, 320, command of, Col. M. A. Chaves, 320
Fort Fillmore, 361, 362; evacuated, garrisoned, 389
Fort Grant, 436
Fort Leavenworth, 25
Fort Marcy, 209
Fort McLeod, 429, note 354
Fort Osage, 115, 116, note 84
Fort Quitman, 390
Fort Stanton, evacuated, 369; Indian reservation, 438
Fort Sumner, Apaches moved to, 429, note 430; abandoned, 411
Fort Thorn, 372
Fort Union, supplies at, 370, note 292; 379
Fort West, 1863, garrison, 429
Fountain, Albert J., 494, 495; biog., note 409; 501
Fountain creek, 87, note 60
Fowler, Jacob, 102
Franciscans, list of, 1540-1822, 188, 189, 190, 191, note 131
Franklin, Mo., 103, 104, 106, 107, 108
Franklin, town of, 389
Fray Cristoval, 219
Fremont, Gen. John C., 87, note 60; entertained, Taos, Santa Fé, 266, 267, note 191; boundary commissioner, 289
French, Capt. A. H., 389
French traders, 93
Freeman, A. A., 505, 507, note 423
Frost, Col. Max., 498; biog., note 415
Fueros, 13

GABINETE MEXICANO, Texas-Santa Fé expedition, 80, note 55
Gadsden, James, biog., 311, note 236
Gadsden Treaty, 1853, 311, note 236; boundaries, 311, note 238; debates, 312, note 238
Galisteo, river, 205
Gallegos, Rev. José Manuel, delegate, 295, 309, note 234; religious troubles, 331, note 260; 332
Gallegos, Sylvestre, 510, 511; killing of, note 429; 512
Galles, Nicolas, Apache fight, 439, note 359
Gallinas, Rio, 130
Gambling, 158, note 106
Garcia, Conde, General, 223, 225, 289
Garita, Santa Fé, excursions, 65
Garrard, L. H., 255, 256, 257, note 183
Garrett, Patrick, sheriff, 424, note 352
Garza, General, 6, note 3
Gasparri, Rev. D. M., 343
Gatewood, Lieut., Apache campaign, 442; Geronimo, 446, note 366
Gazette, Santa Fé, 307, note 231
Geronimo, Apache chief, 438; raid, 1885, 442, notes 362, 363; persons killed, 443, note 363; surrender, 445, 446
Getty, Gen. Geo. W., 428, note 353
Gibbons, Cardinal, Santa Fé, 346, note 274
Gibbs, Capt. Alfred, 366, note 389
Giddings, Gov. Marsh, 415, death of, 417, note 344
Gila, Apaches, 301; fights, note 225; 302
Gillenwater, W. H., 597, note 504
Gilmer, Lieut., 205
Gilpin, Gov. William, 217, 224, 225; communicates with Canby, 367; biog., 376, note 291; 368, note 292
Glenn, Hugh, trader, 102
Gobernadores, 9; list, 25, note 24
Gonzales, José, revolutionary governor, 63, note 47; death of, 65
Gonzales, Pedro Miguel, 299, note 22
Gonzales y Borrego, Francisco, 510,

INDEX 619

511, note 429; trial of, 512, note 429; 518, note 436
Gorman, Rev. Samuel, 350
Granger, Gen. Gordon, 428, note 353
Grant, U. S., 490, note 399
Grants, list, confirmed, rejected, court of P. L. C., 471, note 394
Greeley, Horace, 357, note 281; cited, 289; Valverde, 376, note 300; retreat of confederates, 387, note 313
Green, Col. Thomas, Valverde, 5th Tex., 376, note 300
Green, J. W., 542; biog., note 452
Greene, Chas. W., 494, note 408
Gregg, Dr. Josiah, *Commerce of the Prairies*, cited, note 9; 14, note 12; quoted, 18, note 17; cited, 42, note 34; quoted, 43, 44; cited, 54, note 41; 62, 63, notes 46, 47; quoted, 83, 85, 86, note 59; cited, 87, note 60; 88, note 61; 89, note 62; mistake as to Becknell, 105, note 76; quoted, 107; cited, 108, note 78; 109, note 79; 114, 118; quoted, 131; note 91; summary of trade, 134, 150, note 101; 154, note 104; 158, notes 106, 108; quoted, 159, 160, 165, note 111; 177, note 119; 180, note 122; quoted, 181; bishop of Durango, 187, note 130
Gregg, Gen. J. I., 428, note 353
Greiner, John, Indian agent, 124, 284, note 206; 285, note 207; letter, 287, note 210
Grierson, Gen., 429, note 353
Griffin, W. E., 540; biog., note 452
Griffin, William W., 351; biog., note 277
Grito de Dolores, 3
Gross, Jacob, 489, note 399
Guadalupe, chapel of, 152, 165, note 111
Guadalupe Hidalgo, treaty of, 265; boundaries, 265, 267, 328, 369, 370, 451, 452, 453, 455, note 375; 457, 377
Guasimas, Las, battle of, 535, 539, note 452

HADLEY, HIRAM, 508; biog., note 426
Haefner, H. J., death of, 535, note 447
Hagerman, Herbert J., administration, 549; biog., note 461; 550, note 463; 551, 554, 555, note 467; letter to Roosevelt, 558, note 468; 559, 560; message, 560, note 471

Hall, Edward L., 517
Hall, Lieut., 376, note 300
Hall, Willard P., 214, note 152
Hamilton Bill, 578, note 487
Hamilton, Camp, 541
Hamilton, Colonel, 536
Hamilton, E. L., 578, note 487; 581
Hamilton, Humphrey B., associate justice, 517, note 435
Hanna, R. H., associate justice, 601, note 510
Harney, General, 434
Harrison, Benjamin, president, message, land grants, 465, 524
Hart, Simeon, 389, 372, note 295
Harwood, Rev. Thomas, 350; *New Mexico Christian Advocate*, 351
Hassandaubel, Lt., 241
Hatch, Capt., Navajó campaign, 1858, 315; Civil War, 360
Hatch, General Edward, 429, note 353; Apache campaigns, 1879, Victorio, 438, note 359
Hayes, A. A., cited, confederate and federal armies, 374, note 298; native volunteers, Valverde, 398, note 300, 301; reputation of Canby, note 310; 382, 384, note 308
Hayes, Rutherford B., president, proclamation as to troops, 401, 490, note 399
Heath, John, expedition, 104
Hemingway, J. B. H., 517
Henderson, John B., senator, peace commission, 434
Henderson, W. F., associate justice, 497; biog., note 413
Hendley, Captain, 236; death of, Mora, 236
Hennepin, Fr., 115, note 82
Heredia, General José, 222, note 160; 223
Hersey, H. B., 530, note 446; 539; biog., 452
Hervey, J. M., attorney general, 564
Heurel, Capt., Valverde, 378
Hidalgo, 3, 7
Hierarchy, American, 329
Hinojos, Capt. Blas, 42, note 33; death of, 44; anecdote, 45, note 36
Historical Society of Missouri, 101, note 70
Historical Society of New Mexico, appropriations, 494, note 407; 500, note 418
Hitchcock, Ethan Allen, 549
Holcombe, E. P., 560

620 LEADING FACTS OF NEW MEXICAN HISTORY

Holmes, James H., secretary, 392
Hombres Buenos, 13
Hopewell, W. S., 555, 560
Hough, Emerson, quoted, 418, note 345
Houghton, Joab, justice, 214; constitution 1850, 270; biog., 272, note 197; plans 1st capitol, 326; biog., 398, 399, note 324
Houston, General Samuel, letter, Santa Anna, 70, 71, 72; Texas-Santa Fé prisoners, 80, 81
Howard county, Missouri, history, 103, note 75
Howard, member Texas-Santa Fé expedition, 75
Howitzers, Alburquerque, 1862, 387, note 313
Howland, Samuel, 75, note 53
Howlett, Rev. W. J., *Life of Bishop Machebeuf*, quoted, 330, 331, notes 258, 260
Hubbell, Captain, captured, 1861, 370, note 293
Hubbell, F. A., 544, note 455
Hubbell, Sidney A., judge, 393
Hudson, Captain, 225
Hudson, Col. Richard, Apaches, 1868, 435, note 358; biog., note 358
Hughes, Col. John T., 209, note 145
Hughes, Levi A., Court of Private Land Claims, special assistant, 472, note 395; Peralta-Reavis claim, 476, 477
Hurtado, Lieut., death of, 62
Hutchinson, Kansas, 112

IGUALA, plan of, 3, 5, 6
Independence, Mo., 108, 127, 139, note 94
Indian Agents, list, 300, note 223; Apache, 439, note 359; 447; list of, 1864-87, 447, note 367
Indians, Calhoun's Reports, 283, note 205; depredations, 283, note 205; 284, note 206; 285, note 207; 287, note 210; Brent killed, 292, note 217; 293; treaties, 298, 299, note 223; captives, 298, note 222; reports, 299, note 223; Jicarillas, 299; battles, list, 301, note 225; 302, note 226; 311, note 237; depredations, 1859-60, 319; campaigns, 1864-1887, 428-450, notes 353-366; expense of campaigns, 434, 440, 441, 442, notes 360, 361, 362; General Crook, 440, 442, 443; General Miles, 443-446, note 366; number of murders, 1819, 1867, 434
Indian Outrages, Santa Fé Trail, 18, note 17; 20, 21, 22, 43
Industrial Conditions, 1890, 513, note 430; 548, note 460; 565, note 474
Infantry, 6th U. S., 17; dine with Col. Viscarra, 23, 24
Inman, Henry, 113
Instituent Council, 4
Insurrection, 1846-7, 229, 230, 231, note 166, note 167; leaders of, 232, note 168; news of, Santa Fé, 236
Intelligencer, Missouri, cited, 95, note 65; 103, note 72; 104, note 75; 127
International Dam, 526, note 444
Iturbide, Emperor Agustin de, 3, 4; coronation of, notes 1, 4, 5; banishment, 5, note 2; abdication, 5, 6; death of, 6, note 3; medallions, 51
Ives, Lt. J. C., 314, note 241

JACOBA, Mexican girl, 30, note 27
Jackson, A. M., ex-secretary, 1861, 372, note 295
Jackson, Lt. Col. Congreve, 214, 217
Jaffa, Nathan, 567, biog., note 477; 572, note 482
Jaramillo, Pablo, killed, Taos, 234, note 169
Jefes Politicos, 8, 16; list, 25, note 24
Jews, 354
Jicarilla, Apaches. 43; enmity for Americans, 50; location, 300
Johnson, Andrew, president, 410
Johnson, Captain James, Apaches, 45, 46
Johnson, Capt., escort Bishop Lamy, 341
Johnson, Hezekiah S., justice, 401
Johnston, Capt. A. R., journal of, 313, note 239
Johnston, Gen. Albert Sidney, command, Mesilla, 366, note 290
Joint Statehood, 544; vote on, note 456
Jones, A. A., 586; manifesto, note 497; Flood resolution, 590; biog., note 509
Jones, J. G., U. S. marshal, 283
Jones, Samuel J., 390, note 315
Jornada del Muerto, 35; 47, note 38
José Largo, Mescalero. Apache, 429
Joseph, Dn Antonio. delegate, grants, 464; biog., note 385; 500, note 417; 523
Juan José, Apache, killing of, 45, 46
Judicial districts, 394, notes 319, 320;

INDEX 621

judges, note 320; 396, note 321; 1853-299, note 223
Judicial Tribunals, 9, 198, note 136
Jueces de Letras, 13
Julian, George W., surveyor general, 462; character, acts, 462, note 384; 497
Junction City, Kas., 141
Junta Departamental, 9, note 9
Juntas, established, 53; government of, 53
Justice, administration of, 198, note 136
Justices, Court of Private Land Claims, 465, note 388
Justices, list, 393, note 320
Justiniani, General, 223

KANSAS CITY, Mo., 108; 488, note 399
Kaskaskia, Ill., 93
Kearl, Charles, killed, Apaches, 437; companions, 437
Kearny Code, 214, note 153
Kearny, Gen. S. W., 17, 43; commands Army of the West, 200; biog., note 141; Las Vegas, 206; Apache Pass, 208; address, 209, 210, note 146; proclamation, 211, 212, note 147; 213; names civil officers, 214; leaves for California, 215, note 155; 451
Keen, A. A., 522
Kelley, I. N., 400; killed, 401
Kelly, H. W., 489, note 399
Kelly, Major, 437
Kemp, Capt. Charles, 46, note 37
Kendall, George W., *Texas-Santa Fé Expedition*, cited, 66, note 49; 69, note 50; quoted, 74; cited, 75, note 53; quoted, Salazar, 76, 77, 78, note 55; cited, 197, note 134
Kendrick, Rt. Rev. J. Mills, 352
Kephart, Rev. W. T., 352
Kettle Hill, 536, note 448
Keyes, Maxwell, 541, biog., note 452
Kingman, Lewis, 491, note 403
Kiowa, Indians, habitat, 19, note 19; campaign 1864-66, 432, note 357
Kirker, James, 33, note 30; meets Doniphan, 222, note 160
Knapp, Joseph G., justice, 393

LA CAÑADA, battle of, 239, notes 172, 173
La Castrenza, 150; inscription, 151, note 102
La Cienega, 247

La Cuesta, 75
Laguna, 263
Lake, Geo. B., 486, note 396
La Lande, Baptiste, 93; biog. 94, note 63
Lamar, Gen. Mirabeau B., president, Texas, expedition to Santa Fé, 69, 70
Lamy, Mt. Rev. John B., 152, note 103; education, 323; vicar apostolic, 329, biog. 329, note 356; journey, Durango, 331; crosses plains, 334; bishop Santa Fé, note 261; Rome, 1853, 336, note 263; Pope Pius IX, 336; reception, Santa Fé, 336, 377; journey, California, 1863, 341, note 268; report to Propaganda, 342; Santa Fé, metropolitan see, 342, note 270, 271; archbishop of Santa Fé, 342, note 271; retirement, 345, note 273; death of, 346
Land Frauds, 498
Land Grants, 197; Spanish and Mexican, 451-481
Lane, G. W., 497
Lane, William Carr, governor, 125; 107, note 115; administration, biog., 293, note 218; Mesilla Valley, 294, note 219; treaties, 220; candidate for delegate, 295
Lang, Captain, Valverde, 378
Largo, Apache chief, 436
Larkin, Lt., fight at La Cienega, 247
Larrazolo, O. A., 543, 545, note 457; 546, 598; biog., note 506
Las Trampas, 241
Las Vegas, 130, 202; fight at, 246; town of, land grant, 460, note 381
Laughlin, N. B., associate justice, 517, note 435
La Verdad, 184
Lawton, Gen. H. W., Apache campaign, 444; death, 444, 445; surrender of Geronimo, note 365
Leahy, D. J., 506, note 423; 542, biog., note 452
Leal, J. W., killed at Taos, 234, note 169
Lee, Louis, killed at Taos, 234, note 169
Lee, William D., associate justice, 505, 506, note 423
Legislatures, 1851, 291; acts of, 482, note 392; 489, note 400; 491, note 404; 500, note 418; 501, note 419; 420, 502, note 421; 506, 507, note

424, note 427; 514, note 433. See *Assemblies*
Le Grand, A., trader, 107
Leitensdorfer, Eugene, 214
Leiva, Fr., 55
Leland, C. A., associate justice, 525
Lemon, John, 400, 401; killed, Mesilla, 401
Lewis, Captain, Texas-Santa Fé expedition, 75
Licenses, Order of Kearny, 216, note 155; gambling, 265, note 190
Lincoln county, established, 214
Lincoln County War, 418, note 345; 422, note 351; 423
Lindsay, Capt., Navajó campaign, 1858, 215
Lipan, Indians, 311
Little Arkansas, 84
Live stock, 500, note 418
Llewellyn, W. H. H., 523, 536, 541, biog., note 452
Lobato, Capt. Ventura, defeat of, 85
Lockridge, Major, Valverde, death of, 377, note 300
Loco, Apache chief, 439
Long, Elisha V., 497, note 414
Long, Major S. H., 128
Longwill, R. H., 486, note 396
Lopez, Damasio, Gachupin, 180, 181
Lopez, Lorenzo, 494, note 407
Loring, Gen. W. H., 360, note 285
Los Cerillos, 62
Lossing, B. J., 360, note 385
Louisiana, 93, 185
Lucero, Captain Blas, Navajó campaign, 1858, 315
Lucero, Rev. Mariano de Jesus, 339, note 265
Luna, Capt. Max., 534, 536, 540, biog., note 452
Luna, Solomon, 551, biog., note 464
Luna, Tranquilino, 492, biog., note 405
Lynde, Major Isaac, Ft. Fillmore, 361, 362; Mesilla, note 287; surrender of, 362; dismissed, 363; report of, 365, note 289

MACHEBEUF, RT. REV., J. P., 330, note 257; letter, note 258; quoted, 332, 333, 334, 341; biog., note 267
McCall, Col. Geo. A., 270, note 195; 271
McCandless, Charles, justice, 421, note 350, 492
McClanahan, 98

McComas, Judge H. C., killed by Apaches, 441, note 361
McCoy, J. C., address by, 139, note 94
McCreary, J. B., senator, land grants, 464, note 386
McDaniel, David, hung, 84
McDaniel, John, 83; hung, 84
McDonald, W. C., 598; governor, 599, note 507; biog. 600, note 508; 601, note 511; 604, 605, 606, 607
McFie, J. R., associate justice, 505, 506, note 423; 525
McGrorty, William, 365, note 389
McHarg, Ormsby, 560, 561
McKee, J. Cooper, 366, note 289
McKim, Santiago, captive, 443, note 363
McKinley, William, 523, 530
McKnight, Robert, crossed plains, 98, notes 68, 69; 102; imprisoned, 98, 103
McLeod, Gen. Hugh, Texas-Santa Fé expedition, 73
McLin, Samuel B., justice, 419
McNally, Charles H., Mesilla skirmish, 362, note 387
McNees' Creek, 127
McNees, trader, death of, 127
McPhearson, J. C., Apaches, 439, note 359
McRae, Captain, battery, Valverde, 375, 376, note 300; death of, 377
McSwayne, faction of, Lincoln County War, 422, 423, note 351; death of, 424
Mackensie, Gen. R. S., 429, note 353
Mackey, Lt., Apache campaign, 442
Madariaga, Fr., 66, note 49
Maes, Dn Juan de Dios, 202, 206, 207; mills burned, 247
Magoffin, James, 202, note 142; mission, 203
Majors, Alexander, trader, anecdote, 112, note 80
Mallet Brothers, expedition, Santa Fé Trail, 92
Mangas Coloradas, Apache chief, 290, note 214; 302, note 226; captured, 429, note 354; 436, 442
Mann, Edward A., associate justice, 559, biog., note 470
Manuelito, Mescalero, 429
Manzanares, F. A., 488, biog. 399; 493
Marcy, Capt. R. B., Apaches, quoted, 50, 51
Marmaduke, Col., 107
Marriage, 162, 163, note 109

INDEX

Marshall, Edward, 536, note 448
Martin, Captain John, water on Jornaada del Muerto, 416, biog. 416, note 342
Martin, José Maria, sentence of, 393, note 218
Martinez, David, 494, note 406
Martinez de Lejanza, goveror, division of N. M. into districts, 15, note 13
Martinez, Dn Salvador, 62
Martinez, Juan Antonio, alcalde, Taos, 43
Martinez, Rev. Antonio José, 63; president convention 1849, 269, note 194; 1851, 291; excommunicated, 337, 338; biog., note 264; 339, note 265; 340, note 266; death of, 340
Martinez, Romulo, 497, 510
Massie, J. A., 539, note 452
Mastin, Virgil, killed, Apaches, 435, note 358
Mather, Thomas, 116
Matz, Rt. Rev. N., 348
Maxwell, Jos. E., Lieut., killed, 1854, 299, note 223
Maxwell, Lucien B., 87, note 60; Indian agency, 300; sells grant, 416; biog., note 341
Means, John, death of, 127
Mechem, M. C., associate justice, 568, biog., note 478
Medina, Lieut., surrender, 371
Melgares, Dn Facundo, 7, 16; expedition of, 97, note 67
Meline, J. F., Santa Fé trade, 137, 194, note 132; quoted, 429, note 335
Memorials, legislative, 502, note 421
Menaul, Rev. J., 353, note 279
Merchants, American, Santa Fé, 1838, 63
Merriwether, David, governor, Indian trader, 102; administration, 296; biog., anecdote, note 221; Pawnees, 1819, 297, note 221; 298; recovers captives, 299, note 222; Apaches, 301, note 225; treaty, 304, 459
Mescaleros, Apaches, 301; fights, note 225, 302; Geronimo intrigues, 436
Mesilla, 361; convention, 1861, 361, note 286; skirmish, 362, note 287; Baylor's proclamation, 362, 363, 364, note 288; A. S. Johnston, 366; native population, 372, note 296; Gen. Carleton, 389; headquarters, district of Arizona, 389; riot, John Lemon killed, 400, 401; land office, 416

Messages of Presidents, 199, note 137
Messervy, W. S., secretary, biog., 295, note 220; act'g gov., 295, 296; calls out militia, 299
Metcalf, W. P., 545, 546
Methodists, 350
Mexicans, treatment of Indians, 33, note 30; 34, 35, 36
Mexican War, 194, 199, note 137; justification for, 199, note 137; English officers, 199, note 137; last battle, 262
Mexico, City of, 3, 4
Mexico, Republic, 5, 17; rebellion, 1837-8, 64, 65; treaty as to Apaches, 440, note 360; 527, note 444
Mex. Mem. Guerra, cited, 80, note 55
Miles, Col. D. S., campaign, Navajos, 313, note 242
Miles, Gen. Nelson A., Apache campaigns, 443, 444, note 364; officers under, 444, 445, note 365; Geronimo, surrender, 445, note 365; sword presentation, 440
Military authorities, claims of Texas, 280, note 202; build posts, 288, 212
Military commanders, list, 428, note 353
Military establishment, Mexican, 41, 42
Military posts, 288
Miller, Capt. Fritz, 534, 536, 540, biog., note, 452
Miller, David J., 67, note 49
Miller, Lorion, secretary, 5, 7, note 435
Mills, W. J., chief justice, 525; gov. 566; biog., note 475; report, 569, note 479; 573, note 483; proclamation, 594; address, 605, note 514
Mills, W. W., letter from, 359, note 284
Mimbres, Apaches, 303, note 227
Mines and Mining, 177, note 119; 178, 179, note 121; 180, note 122; 182, 183, 1850-1860, 324; 1860-1870, 414, note 340
Mink, Capt. John H., surrender, 371
Mirage, 122, note 88
Missionaries, American, 323, 328, note 253
Mississippi, river, 93
Missouri Fur Company, 99
Missouri Republican, quoted, Aubrey, 305, note 230
Mitchell, Lt. Colonel, 219
Mitchell, Robert Byington, governor, 410; biog. note 336

Moffat, David H., buys Maxwell grant, 415
Mogollon, Apaches, 302, note 227
Mogollon Mountains, 442
Monroe, Col. John, 263, 271; issues proc. for delegate convention, 1850, 272, note 196; controversy with Manuel Alvarez, 275, note 199; letter from secretary of war, Conrad, 276, note 201
Montaldo, Chas, 493, note 406
Monterde, Gen. J. M., 82, 89, note 62
Montoya, Dn Antonio Abad, revolutionist, death of, 65
Montoya, Dn Desiderio, revolutionist, death of, 65
Montoya, Pablo, revolutionist, 1846-7, 234
Mooney, James, cited, 19, 20, notes 19, 21, 22
Mora, Americans shot, 245, note 175; Capt. Hendley, 244, note 175
Mora, river, 130
Morelos, 7
Moreno Mines, 410
Morley, W. R., 486, note 396
Mormon Batallion, 214, note 154; arrival of, 217
Morning Journal, Alburquerque, 597, note 504
Morris, Capt., 388
Morrison, William, 93; biog., 94, note 63
Mother Matilda, death of, 335, note 261
Mount Vernon, Mo., 107
Mower, Horace, justice, 283
Mowry, Sylvester, 408
Mungo-Merri-Paike, General Z. M. Pike, 195, note 133
Muniments of title, land grants, 469, note 392
Munos, Captain, Vera Cruz dragoons, conduct, 66
Munroe, death of, 127

NAFERE, 56
Nane, Apache chief, 436
Napoleon, 195
Narbona, Dn Antonio, governor, 43
Narbona, Navajó chief, killed, 263
Natchez, Apache chief, 442, note 362
National council, 5
Navajó, Indians, campaigns, murdered, Cochiti, 42, 43; Perez campaign, 44; Doniphan's campaign, 217; treaty, 218; Washington's campaign, 263; Narbona, 263; population, 1846, 303; raids, 303; treaties, 1850-53, 315, note 242; campaign, 315, 316, 317; attack at Ft. Defiance, 316, note 244; Pueblos and Utes, 318; San Juan river, 319, 320, note 244; 321: Bosque Redondo, 433, 434; return to reservation, 435, note 358; population, statistics, note 358
Navarro, José Antonio, 73, 80
Negro troops, 536, note 448
Newby, Col., 262
New Mexicans, overland trade, 118; manners, 157; gambling, 158, note 106; 160, 161, 162, note 108; native dress, 172, 173, note 116; 174, mechanic arts, 174, 175, note 117; southern sympathizers, 357, 358, notes 281, 282, 283, 284; Yrrisari and Armijo, 372, note 295; conduct at Valverde, notes 299, 300, 301
New Mexico, 6, 7; Mexican territory, 7, note 4; 8; department, 8, note 5; 13; 1st executive, 16; principal settlements, 146; act of March 3, 1851, 277; organic act, 280, note 202; boundaries, 282, note 204; survey, 289, note 213; counties, 293; justices' courts, 293; county seats, 1851, 293; finances, 1853, 299; appropriations by congress, 1850-1860, 310, note 235; population, property, 1850-60, 326, note 252
New Orleans, 93
New Spain, 5
Nicholson, Rev. E. G., 350
Nickerson, Thos., 486, note 396
Niles Register, cited, 73, note 51; 84, note 58; 87, note 60; 116, note 64

OCATÉ, 129
O'Brien, James, chief justice, 505; biog., note 523
O'Donoju, Dn Juan, 3
Officials, list, military occupation period, 1846-1850, 268, 269, note 193; last territorial, list, 569, note 478
O'Gorman, Rev. Thomas, quoted, 186, 187, note 129
Ojo Caliente, Indian reservation, 438, note 359
Ojo del Oso, 217
Ojo de Vaca, 205
Ortega, soldier, death of, 62
Ortiz, Captain Tomas, 232, note 168
Ortiz, Padre Ramon, 291, note 215
Ortiz, Very Rev. Juan Felipe, 185,

187, 252; president council, 1851, 291; center opposition Bishop Lamy, 331
Osage, Indians, 104
Otero, Antonio José, judge, 214; biog., 273, note 197
Otero, Dn Mariano S., delegate, 406; biog., note 332; 494, note 407
Otero, Dn Miguel A. 1st, delegate, 1855, 309, note 234; biog., note 234; defeated S. M. Baird, 1857; Gallegos, 1859, 310; Rencher-Fauntleroy controversy, 319; southern sympathizer, 357, note 281; secretary, 391; 489, note 399
Otero, Dn Miguel A., 2nd, governor, report of, 1903, quoted, 466, note 389; 468, note 391; 522, 524; biog., note 441; 525; protest, international dam, 526, note 444; 530, note 446; 531, 532, 533, 543, 546, 547, 548
Otero-Gallegos, election contest, 291, note 216; 309, note 234
Our Lady of Light, convent, 334, notes 261, 262
Overland mail route, 1862, 390, 408, note 324

PALACE OF THE GOVERNORS, 147, 148, 149, note 101; restoration, 573, note 483
Palen, Joseph G., justice, biog., 397, 398, note 322
Pankey, B. F., 524, note 441
Parker, Frank W., associate justice, 525; biog., note 442
Parks, Samuel C., justice, 419
Parishes, established, 166
Parroquia, 151, 152, note 103; described, 166, note 112
Parsons, Captain, 225
Passenger train, first, 425
Paso del Norte, 89, note 62; custom house, 89, note 62; 177
Patterson, Thomas M., senator, *Thoughtless Act*, quoted, 403, 404, note 329
Pattie, James O., *Personal Narrative*, quoted, 26, 27, 28, 29; cited, 36, notes 31, 32; Santa Rita, 37, 38, 39, 40, 178, note 120
Paul, Col. E. R., 1861, Ft. Union, 380; pursues confederates, 388
Pawnee, Indians, Merriwether, 298
Pawnee Rock, 112, 113
Pawnee villages, 93

Peace commission, 434; treaty, 435
Pearson, Gen., 429, note 353
Pecos, river, 29
Pelham, William, surveyor general, 323; captured, 1861, 387, note 313; 458, 459
Peña, Dn Manuel de la, provisional president, Mexico, 455, note 375
Penitentes, 168, note 114
Pennsylvania Development Co., 554, 560
Penrose, Boies, 578
Peonage, system, 324, 325, notes 250, 251
Peppin, sheriff, Lincoln county, 423, note 351
Peralta-Reavis, James Addison, fraudulent claim of, 472, 475; trial, sentence, 479
Perea, Col. Francisco, delegate, 392, 399; biog., note 325
Perea, José Leandro, 543
Perea, Pedro, 523, 543
Perez, Col. Albino, governor, comandante principal, 44, notes 35, 36; governor, 55; fight La Cañada, 61; flight and death of, 61, 62
Phillebert, trapper, 99, 100
Philippine Islands, 563
Pierce, F. H., 553, note 466
Pigeon, M. Valle, quoted, 381, note 304, note 308
Pigeon's ranch, battle, 381, note 304; 382
Pike, Gen. Zebulon M., 7, 92, 94, note 64; 96; copper mines, 179, note 121; 195
Pile, William A., governor, 413; sells archives, 413
Pino, Dn Facundo, 392
Pino, Dn Juan Estevan, 56
Pino, Gen. Miguel E., 292, 321, note 245; 391, note 216; Valverde, 375; troops under, conduct of, 375
Pino, Dn Nicolas, 232, note 168
Pino, Dn Pedro Bautista, 9, 101, 186, note 129
Pinos Altos, 1863, Indian fights, note 354
Pitaval, Mt. Rev. J. B., 348; archbishop of Santa Fé, 348
Placers, old and new, 180, note 122; 181, note 123
Plaza, Santa Fé, 154
Plummer, Capt. A. H., 363
Poe, John W., 424, note 352
Poinsett, Joel R., 171, note 115

626 LEADING FACTS OF NEW MEXICAN HISTORY

Point of Rocks, 128
Pojoaque, 61
Polk, James K., president, Guadalupe Hidalgo, 454, note 373
Pope, Gen. John, 32, note 28; 426
Pope Pius IX, receives Archbishop Lamy, 336
Pope, William H., court of private land claims, special assistant, 472, note 395; chief justice, 566; biog., note 476
Population, 1860-1870, 414, note 340; 10th census, 426; 1844, 15, 16, note 13; 1890, 514, 515, note 434; 1900, 574, note 484; 1900, 574, note 484
Pratt, killed, 128
Prefects, system abolished, 419
Presbyterians, 352; purchase Baptist church, Santa Fé, 353
President, United States, claims of Texas, 231, note 203
Presidio del Norte, custom house, 89, note 62
Price, General Sterling, arrives, Santa Fé, 217; biog., 229, note 164; troops, 231; Taos insurrection, 237, 238, 239, 240, 242; official reports, 244, 245, note 175; goes to "States," 262; Vigil governor, 263, 264, 267, note 192
Priests, secular provided, 166; parishes established, 166; list of, 189, 190, note 131; power, morals, 330, note 258; 331, 348, note 275
Prince, L. Bradford, chief justice, 492, 500, note 417; biog., 502, note 422; quoted, 756, note 486; 487, 488, governor, land grants, 464, note 387; execution of Gov. Gonzales, 65, note 48; quoted, "Old Palace," 147, 148; copper mines, 179, note 121; Taos insurrection, 234, note 190
Printing press, 184
Private land claims, court of, established, 465, note 388; jurisdiction, 446-449, note 389, note 391; areas confirmed or rejected, 470, note 394; names of attorneys, employes, agents and assistants, 473, note 395
Protestant missions, 325, 349, 350; schools, 350, note 276
Protocol, Guadalupe Hidalgo, meaning of, 455, note 374
Provincial deputations, 8, 9, note 9
Provincias Internas, 7
Public buildings, 1860-70-80, 414, note 340

Public lands, 1854, 323, notes 248, 249
Pueblo, city of, site, mentioned by Fremont, 87, note 60; first trading post, 93
Pueblo Indians, opposition to taxes, 60, notes 43, 44; hatred for Mexicans, 60, note 44; list, revolution, 1837, 61; proclamation, 61; with Captain Lovato, 86, 87; rebellion of, 1680, 43
Punishments, character, 14, note 12
Purcell, James, 94, 95, note 64, note 65
Pursley. See Purcell
Pyron, Major, 376; Valverde, note 300; Santa Fé, 379

Quay, M. S., 545
Quinn, James H., 208, note 145; secretary, convention, 1849, 269, note 194; president, convention, 1850, 272

Raguet, Major, Valverde, 378
Raids, Texans, 82
Railroads, advent of, 482, note 392; 483, note 393; incorporators, note 393; 484, note 394, note 396; 487, notes 397, 398; 488, 490, note 400; 491, 513; strike, 1894, 519
Randall, Rt. Rev., 351
Rascon, Dn Juan, 185
Raynolds, J. W., 550; biog., note 462; 558
Read, Benj. M., 494, note 406; 564; biog., 473
Read, Rev. H. W., 350
Reclamation service, 529
Reddick, John I., justice, 419
Red river, 128
Reeves, R. A., 498
Refugees, Spanish, 23
Regular army, protests against withdrawal, 1861, 370, note 292; 374, note 297; Valverde, 377, 378, note 301
Reid, Capt. John W., 218, note 156; Brazito, 221, 225
Reid, W. C., 559; biog., note 469
Religion, conditions, 1846, 185, 186, notes 128, 129
Religious customs, 152; ceremonies, processions, 164, 165; instruction, 169, 170, 171
Rencher, Abraham, governor, 314, 315; Navajó, 315; report of, note 242; Navajós, 1858, 316

Reredos, 151, note 102
Revista Catolica, established, 343
Revolution, 1837-8, 53; causes of, 54, 55, 56, note 41
Revolutionists, prosecutions, 251; indictments, 252, notes 179, 180; convictions, Taos, 255, 256, 257, note 183; executions, 258, 259, 260, 261, notes 185, 186
Reynolds & Griggs, store, 400
Reynolds, Matt. G., U. S. attorney, court of P. L. C., report of, 470, note 394, 395
Rich, Rev. M. A., 351
Riley, John H., 422, note 351; 424
Riley, Major Bennett, 17, note 16; 109
Rio Abajo, 23, 61, 146, 147, 177
Rio Arriba, 146, 147
Rio Colorado, 128
Rio Grande, 7; hostilities on, 197
Rio Grande, 526, note 444
Rio Puerco, 217
Rio Sacramento, 224, note 161
Ritch, William G., secretary, 1875, 417; biog., note 343
Roads, 570
Robards, Col. W. L., Valverde, 378
Roberts, Clarence J., associate justice, 568; biog., note 478
Roberts, Lt. Col., 360; Valverde, 376, note 300
Roberts, Rev. J. M., 353
Robidoux, Dn Antonio, trader, 126, 207
Robinson, A. A., 483, note 394; 486, note 396
Rock creek, 124
Rocky Mountain Fur Co., 123
Rodey, Bernard S., 543; biog., note 454; 544, note 455; 577
Romero, Dn Trinidad, 392; delegate, 406; biog., note 331; 505, 506, note 423
Romero, Dn Vicente, 400
Romero, Rafael, 494, note 407
Romero, Secundino, 597
Ronquillo, José Maria, inspector, 64
Roosevelt, Theodore, 525, 526, 530, note 446; 531, 537, 535, note 447; 536, notes 448, 449; 537, note 450; 538, note 451; 539, note 452; visits New Mexico, 547; letter to Hagerman, 555, note 467; 557, 560, 561
Rosario, chapel of, 62, note 45
Ross, E. G., 496; biog., note 410; 500, 501, 502
Rossell, Major N. B., Valverde, 378

Rough Riders, 526; list of, 530, note 446; 531, 532, 533, 534, 535, note 447; 536, note 448; note 449; 537, note 450; 538, note 451; 539, note 452
Round Mound, 128
Round Robin, 539
Ruff, Lt. Col., 214, note 151
Ruxton, Geo. F., Apaches, 33, note 30; Armijo, 208, note 145; 218, note 157; 229, note 165; 236, 237, note 171
Rynerson, Col. W. L., 400; biog., 412, note 338; 494, note 407; 500

SAFFORD, CHAS. V., 565, note 474
Saint Louis, diocese of, 328; metropolitan see, 328, note 254; 100, 101
St. Charles, Mo., 118
Saint Michael's college, established, 337
St. Vrain, Ceran, 120, note 87; letter from, 136, note 93; Taos, 239, 240, 241, 242; declines governorship, 263
Salazar, Capt. Damasio, 74; capture of Texans, 75, 76; conduct of, 76, 77, 78, 79; character of, 78, 79, 80, note 50
Salpointe, Mt. Rev. J. B., 165, note 111; 166, note 112; penitentes, 168, 169, note 114; quoted, 171, 188, note 131; 341, note 269; 342, note 271; 345, note 273; 346, note 274
San Antonio, 534
San Bernardino, 144
Sanborn, Col. J. B., 434
San Carlos, Indian reservation, 438
Sanchez, Dn Pedro, 156, note 105; 498, note 416
Sandoval, Anastacio, 392
Sandoval, Dn Antonio, president council, 1st assembly, 264, note 190
Sandoval, Navajó chief, 320
San Elizario, 36
San Juan, mission, 166
San Juan Hill, 536, note 448; 539, note 452
San Miguel, 104, 105, 130, note 90
San Miguel, order of, 336
San Miguel del Bado, mission, 166
Santa Anna, General, revolt of, 4, 5, 55, 70, 71, 72; closes ports, 88, 89, note 62
Santa Clara, springs, 129
Santa Cruz, de la Cañada, 9, 60; fight at, 61, 62, 67, note 49
Santa Fé Archives, Libro del Ordenes,

Armijo, 1843, 87, note 60; 195, note 133; proclamation of Governor Perez, education, 57, 58, note 42; 67, note 49
Santa Fé-Chihuahua trade, 82
Santa Fé, city of, 7, 9, 15, note 13; 25; captured, 1837, 63; army leaves, 65; old Fonda, 138, 146, 192; population, 146, note 98; buildings, 147, 205; capitol, 326; appropriations, 1850, 1854, 1860, 326; war tax, 1862, 326; 1861, supplies, 379; metropolitan see, 342; cathedral, 344, note 272; railroad enters, 486, note 396
Santa Fé Gazette, 352
Santa Fé Trail, troops, 17, 21, 91, 144; first caravans, 92, 93; second, 93; Indians, 108; stations, 112, 123, 128, 137, 138; route, 115, note 84; appropriation of 1825, 116, 119, note 86; winter travel, 125, 126; fight, Wagon Mound, 129, 130; Santa Fé, 131, 133, note 92; 137
Santa Rita, copper mines, Pattie, treaty with Apaches, 37, 38, 39, 40, 289
Santiago de Cuba, 534, 538
Santo Domingo, Pueblo, 62
Sarracino, Dn Francisco, 1849, 270, note 194
Satolli, Cardinal, 347
Scheurich, Mrs. Teresina, 234, note 170
Scurry, Col. W. R., Pigeon's ranch, Apache Canyon, 383, note 308; retreat, 385
Seeds, E. P., 505, 507, note 423
Selden, Major, Valverde, 378, note 301
Sena, Major José D., Valverde, 378, note 301; 388; report of Canby, biog., note 314; defeated for delegate, 400
Sena, Mrs. José D., anecdote, 172, note 116
Senators, United States, 1850, 275
Shawnee, Indians, 48
Shea, John Gilmary, 328, note 254; 331, note 259; 185, 186, notes 127, 128
Sheldon, L. A., 489, 490, note 401; 491, note 404; 494
Shelton, W. S., Indian agent, report, 435, note 358
Sheperd, Capt., Ft. Defiance, report of, 1860, 316, note 244
Sheridan, Gen. P. H., visits N. M., 425

Sherman, Gen. W. T., 434, 490, note 399
Sherman, John, 526, note 444
Shoemaker, Captain, supplies, Ft. Union, 370, note 292
Sibley, Gen. H. H., treason of, 361, note 286; 372, note 295; El Paso, 372, note 295; proclamation, 372, note 296; Valverde, 374, note 298; 376, note 300; 378; retreat of, 385, 386, notes 310, 311; 387, note 315
Sibley, Geo. C., 116
Silver City, 436, 437
Simpson, Gen. J. H., 313, note 239
Sioux, Indians, 35
Sisters of Charity, 337
Sisters of Loretto, 334, 335, notes 261, 262
Skillman, Captain, 389
Slack, Captain, 242
Slaves, Mexicans, captured, 36
Slough, Col. J. P., 382; biog., note 306; 384, note 308; resigns, 385, note 309
Smith, 98
Smith, Ashbel, 199, note 137
Smith, Hugh N., delegate, 1849, 269, note 194; secretary, not confirmed, 283
Smith, Jedediah S., murdered by Comanches, 123, 124, note 89
Smith, Thomas, chief justice, 517; biog., note 435
Smith, Wm. Alden, 592
Snively, Colonel, expedition, 84, 85, note 59; defeated Mexicans, 85, 197
Society of Jesus, introduced, 343; controversy, legislature, 343
Socorro, 36; Indian fight at, 47, 48
Sonora, 43
Sovereignty, change of, 198
Spain, laws of, 6, 13
Spaniards, exclusion of, 54, 55
Spanish-American War, 526, 530, note 446; 531, 532, 533, 534, 535, note 447; 536, notes 448, 449; 537, note 450; 538, note 451; 539, note 452
Spanish cortes, 9
Sparks, W. A. J., Comr. G. L. O., 462
Speare, Alden, 486, note 396
Spencer's ranch, 389
Speyer, M., 126
Spiess, Charles A., 418, note 436; 518, note 436; 584; biog., note 492; 585
Springer, Frank, 453, 454; biog., note 372; address, 462, note 384; 486, note 396

INDEX 629

Stages, overland, 139, 140, 141, note 95
Stanley, Gen. D. S., 429, note 353
Stanton, Capt. H. W., killed, Apaches, 302
State government, efforts for, 1849, 1850, 270, 272, note 196; 274, note 198; 1861-1876, 402, note 328; 578, 579, 580, 581, notes 487, 488; 582, 590, 591, 592, notes 500, 501, 502; finally attained, 593
Statistics, 1890. 513, 514, 515, notes 430, 432, 433; 1904, 548; valuations, note 460; 1905, note 460; 561, note 471; 564, notes 473, 474; 568, 570, 571, notes 479, 480, 481; population, 1900, 574, note 484
Steele, Col., Valverde, 376, note 300
Stewart, Robert Laird, DD., 353, note 278
Stoddard, Amos, 93
Stone, Wilbur F., justice, P. L. C., 466, note 389, note 469
Storrs, Augustus, U. S. consul, 107, 115, note 84; 116
Strong, W. B., 483, note 394
Sturgis, Lieut., 302
Sumner, Col. E. V., 126, 127, 214, 216; controversy with Calhoun, 284, note 206; 285, notes 207, 208; report of, 286, note 209; biog., note 209; Navajó expedition, 288; military posts, 288, note 212
Supreme court, clerks of, 1846-1869, 398, note 323; United States, 456, note 376; last territorial, 567, note 478
Sutherland case, 456, note 376
Sutter, John A., 144
Sutton, Capt., 78
Sutton, Lt. Col., Valverde, 378
Swayne, General, 429, note 353
Swords, Major, 205
Sykes, Gen. George, 428, note 353

TAFT, WM. H., 589, note 499; 591, 593, note 502; signs act of admission, 604, note 513
Talbot, Rt. Rev. J. C., 351
Tampa, 534
Taos, 9, 87, note 60; custom house. 89, note 62; 115; mission, 166; battle of, 241, 242; killed and wounded, 242, 243, note 174; Indians, 42, 50; military road, 417
Tappan, Col. W. F., 434
Taylor, Gen. Zachary, state government, 1849, 1850, 271, note 195; 451
Taylor, N. G., senator, 434
Telegraph, military, operation of, 411
Terrazas, Rev. Juan Tomas, 166
Territorial deputations, 8, 9, note 9
Terry, General, 434
Tertio-Millenial, 492
Texans, raids by, 196
Texas, republic, boundary claims, 69, 70; independence of, 196, 197, 281, note 203; 282, note 204
Third Order of St. Francis, 165, 166, note 112; last chapel, 167, note 112; establishment of, 167, note 113
Thomas, Benjamin M., Indian agent, 354, 504, note 422
Thompson, Waddy, 80, note 55; biog., 89, note 62
Thornton, Wm. T., 516; biog., note 435; 523
Thrall, H. S., 280, note 202
Tierra Amarilla, Jicarilla agency, 446, 447
Tipton, William M., special ass't, court of P. L. C., 472, 395; Peralta-Reavis, 476, 477
Tolby, Rev. F. J., 350, note 276; 420
Tomasito, Taos Indian, 236, 242
Trappers, costumes, 30, note 27
Treason, prosecutions, 251; indictments, 252, notes 179, 180; convictions, trials, at Taos, 255, 256, 257, note 183; executions, 258, 259, 260, 261, notes 185, 186
Treaty, of 1819, 17
Trelford, Arthur, 552
Tres Castillos, Victorio's last stand, 440
Trias, Angel, governor, 222, 223
Trimble, L. S., 505
Trujillo, Gen. Antonio Ma., trial, 252, 253, notes 179, 180, 181
Tunicha, 263
Tunstel, John H., killing of, 421, 422, 423
Turley's Mill, battle, 236, note 171

UNITED STATES, boundary of, 17; Santa Fé trail, 17; survey of, 1825, 116; attorneys of, list, 1846-1869, 398, note 323
Upper Cimarron Springs, 122, 123, 127
Utah, territory, 282
Ute, Indians, habitat, 48, trouble with. 49, 185, 300; character, 300; agency, 300, 447, note 367

VALDEZ, NARCISCO, 494, note 407
Valdez, Santiago, 494, note 408
Valverde, battle of, 374, 375, 376; notes 298, 299, 300, 301; report of, 378, note 301; killed and wounded, 378, note 301; 388, 220
Van Ness, Texas-Santa Fé expedition, 75
Vaughn, J. H., 547, note 459
Vera Cruz, 55
Victorio, Apache chief, 436; raids, 437, note 359; raids of, 1879, 438, note 359; 439, 440; Tres Castillos, death of, 440
Victory, Jno. P., 518, note 436
Vigil, Dn Antonio, execution of, 65
Vigil, Dn Cornelio, killed at Taos, 234, note 169
Vigil, Dn Donaciano, governor, 44; sergeant, secretary, Asamblea, Governor Gonzales, 64, 214; act'g governor, 248; issues proclamation, 248, 249, note 177; 250, 251, note 178; 254, 255, governor, 263, 269; biog., 264, note 189; 266
Vigil, Dn Gregorio, 130, note 90
Vigil, Juan Bautista, 209; address, 210, 211
Vigil papers, 211, note 147
Vincent, Wm. A., 497; biog., note 411
Vineyards, 177
Viscarra, Col. Antonio, 16, 17, 18; Mexican escort under, 21, 22, 23; dinner by, 23; description, 23, 24, 25, 26, 42, 102

WADDINGHAM, WILSON, buys Maxwell grant, 415
Wade, General James F., 429, note 353
Wagon Mound, 129; Indian attacks, 129, 130
Wah-to-yah, 128
Waldo, Dr. David, Taos, 118; magnitude Santa Fé trade, 133
Waldo, Henry L., 101, note 70; chief justice, 419; attorney general, 421; counsel for Gen. Dudley, 421, 484; biog., note 395; 501, note 420
Waldo, Lawrence L., shot, Mora, 244, 245, note 175
Waldo, McCoy and Co., 126
Waldo, William, 101, note 70
Walker, Capt. Joseph, 103, note 75
Wallace, George H., 523, 524, 525
Wallace, Lewis, governor, 148, note 99; 420; advent of railroads, 425, 489
Walnut creek, 127
Warfield, Col., 83; Mora, 85; retreat, 85, 88, 197
War of the Rebellion, cited, quoted, 365, note 289; 370, note 293; notes 294, 295, 296, 297; pay of troops, 299, 377, note 301
Washington, 194, 197, 204
Washington, Col. J. M., command, Santa Fé, 263, note 188; Navajó campaign, 263; killing of Narbona, 263; address, 266, note 191; Fremont, note 191; 269
Watts, John S., justice, 283; Weightman, 305; speech, Mesilla, 1859, 310; delegate in congress, 310, 359, note 284; 391; biog., note 317
Watrous, 350
Weakley, H. W., 541; biog., note 542
Weightman, R. H., 205, 221, note 159; senator, 275, 276; delegate, 283, 288, note 211; biog., 304, 305, note 229; killing of Aubrey, 305, note 230; trial, 307, notes 231, 232; instructions of Benedict, 308; acquittal, 308, note 233
Weights and measures, 132, note 91
Weller, John B., 289
West, Elias P., 283
Westport, Mo., 139, note 94
Wheaton, Theodore, speaker, 292, 411; biog., note 337
Wheeler, Gen. Joseph, 535
Wheeling, William, killed, 389
Whipple, and Sitgreaves, 314, note 240
Whiting, H. R., howitzers, 387, note 313; 584; biog., note 494
Wilson, B. D., observations of, 83, note 57
Wilson, John, Comr. G. L. O., 1854, 458, 459; report of, note 380
Wilkinson, General James, 96, note 65
Willard, Dr., 118
Williams, Ezekiel, 104, note 75
Willock, Lt. Col., 236
Wingfield, E. H., Indian agent, 302
Wislizenus, Dr. A., 122, note 88; 130; cited as to copper mines, 78, note 120; visits placers, 181, note 123; 182
Wood, Gen. Leonard, Apache campaign, 444, 530
Wool, Gen., 197, note 135
Wootton, Dick, 121, note 87

Workman-Rowland, party of, 144
Wright, E. R., associate justice, 568; biog., note 478
Wyckoff, Camp, 539
Wyncoop, Major, 382, note 305

YOACUM, HENRY, *History of Texas*, cited, 86, note 59
Young, Ewing, 143, notes 96, 97
Young, Gen. S. M. B., 535

ZACATECAS, 12; troops from, 1838, 64, 65
Zubiriá, Dn José Antonio, bishop of Durango, visit of, 1833, 167, note 112; 187, note 130; 188; visit of 1850, 328, 329, note 255
Zuñi, visited by Col. Doniphan, 263

www.ingramcontent.com/pod-product-compliance
Lightning Source LLC
Chambersburg PA
CBHW071426300426
44114CB00013B/1334